My Dear Sister

Edited by
Richard Neitzel Holzapfel
and David M. Whitchurch

My Dear Sister

LETTERS BETWEEN **JOSEPH F. SMITH** AND HIS SISTER **MARTHA ANN SMITH HARRIS**

Edited by Richard Neitzel Holzapfel and David M. Whitchurch

RSC BYU

DESERET BOOK

Published by the Religious Studies Center, Brigham Young University, Provo, UT,
in cooperation with Deseret Book Company, Salt Lake City.
http://rsc.byu.edu

Printed in the United States of America by Sheridan Books, Inc.

DESERET BOOK is a registered trademark of Deseret Book Company.
Visit us at DeseretBook.com.

Cover and interior design and layout by Kelly Nield of Hales Creative. Visit halescreative.com

Cover photo of Joseph F. Smith and Martha Ann Smith Harris, ca. 1868. Courtesy of Carole Call King.

ISBN 978-0-8425-2848-1

Library of Congress Cataloging-in-Publication Data

Names: Holzapfel, Richard Neitzel, 1954- editor of compilation. | Whitchurch, David M., editor of compilation.
Title: My dear sister : letters between Joseph F. Smith and his sister Martha Ann Smith Harris / edited by Richard Neitzel Holzapfel and David M. Whitchurch.
Description: Provo, Utah : Religious Studies Center, Brigham Young University; Salt Lake City : Deseret Book Company, [2018]. | Includes bibliographical references and index.
Identifiers: LCCN 2013036710 | ISBN 978-0-8425-2848-1 (hard cover : alk. paper)
Subjects: LCSH: Smith, Joseph F. (Joseph Fielding), 1838-1918--Correspondence. | Harris, Martha Ann Smith, 1841-1923--Correspondence. | Church of Jesus Christ of Latter-day Saints--Presidents--Correspondence.
Classification: LCC BX8609 .M9 2018 | DDC 289.3092/2 [B] --dc23
LC record available at https://lccn.loc.gov/2013036710

Contents

Mrs. Martha Ann Harris,

Provo.

My Dear Sister Martha:- I feel impressed to write you this morning, not that I have any thing outlin in my mind to say, nor because I have nothing else to do; for I have no time to be idle, and none to spar indeed my time is not sufficient for the duties requir

I feel interested in the welfare of your family, fo their welfare is yours. You cannot feel prosperou nor happy unless they are prospered and are movin in the line of duty, and faithful to their callings an true to their principles, to their religion and to God and man. Neither can they be happy and success ful unless they are walking in these paths.

First and foremost we owe allegiance to Hi who is the giver of life, and all other good things. N Latterday Saint can enjoy the Spirit of God withou sincerely acknowledging Him, remembering <u>him</u>, honoring him in their lives and in the first fruit of all their increase. Merely living, or living on for the present life, to make money, to accumulate ric

Acknowledgments

We are indebted to and grateful for the many individuals who have made this book possible. Particularly, we express our deepest appreciation for the generosity and patience of Carole Call King, descendant of William Jasper Harris and Martha Ann Smith Harris (daughter of Hyrum and Mary Fielding Smith). This project started with her discovery of and willingness to share her family heritage of letters written by Joseph F. Smith to his sister Martha Ann Smith Harris, Carole King's great-grandmother. Additional Harris family members helped us along the way, including David S. and Ruth Mae Harris, Leland Harris, Carol Hafen Jones, Carol MacFarlene, and Mary Corbett Taylor. Joseph Fielding McConkie and Mark L. McConkie, great-grandsons of Joseph F. Smith, also provided important primary sources for this book, including an original black-and-white silent film featuring Joseph F. and two original letterpress copybooks that contained additional letters written to Martha Ann by Joseph F.

We are also indebted to the Office of the President of The Church of Jesus Christ of Latter-day Saints for providing copies from its collection of Martha Ann's letters to her brother Joseph F. These additional letters, written over many decades, provided a more complete picture of the written conversation between two devoted, loyal, and loving siblings.

The authorization to reproduce the letters and images found in this book comes from L. Tom Perry Special Collections, Harold B. Lee Library, Brigham Young University; from the Intellectual Property Office, the Church History Library, and the Church History Museum of The Church of Jesus Christ of Latter-day Saints; from the International Society Daughters of Utah Pioneers; and from various Smith and Harris family members who are cited in the captions. We have digitally enhanced a few of the historical photographs to remove modern notations from them.

We are grateful to the staff, including former staff members, at the Church History Library and the Church History Museum for their assistance with photographic and other research requests. In particular, we thank Christi Adams, Zackary Baker, Chad Barker, Madeline Bethke, Anya Bybee, Brittany A. Chapman, Christine Cox, W. Randall Dixon, Keith A. Ereckson, Carly Farley, Marlin Hamblin, Alan Johnson, Melanie Nef, Elise Reynolds, Glenn N. Rowe, William W. Slaughter, Ardis Kay Smith, Tyler Thorsted, Brittany Volquardsen, and Trevor Wylie.

Staff members at the L. Tom Perry Special Collections in the Harold B. Lee Library at Brigham Young University provided invaluable help. We are especially grateful to Cindy Brightenburg, Gordon Daines, and Tom Wells for their assistance.

We also give thanks to the many Brigham Young University students who assisted on this long project: Austin Ballard, Andrew Bateman, Zanna H. Beckstead, Melissa W. Bennett, Emily Broadbent Benz, Kim Matheson Berkey, Kevin Brandvoldt, Devin Butler, Michael Q. Cannon,

Rebekah Ellsworth, Jacob Frandsen, Jasmin Gimenez, Jef L. Huntington, McKenna Johnson, Phillip V. LeCheminant, Rachel Christensen Nelson, Mallory Hales Perry, Jennifer Price, Jessica Coleman Radmall, Nyssa L. Silvester, Katie M. Skovran, Stanley J. Thane, Ben Tingey, Emily Wright, and Joseph Hyrum Wright. Their research, attention to detail, and editing have made this a far better book.

Susan Glenn, an accredited genealogist, turned over every stone to identify a few people mentioned in the letters whom we were unable to identify.

We appreciate Stephen C. Taysom and Nathaniel R. Ricks for reviewing the penultimate draft and providing important and thoughtful suggestions. We also express gratitude to several blind peer reviewers who worked with the Religious Studies Center publication office at Brigham Young University. These unknown scholars provided feedback, raised important questions, identified additional sources to consider, and helped us avoid making some mistakes of fact and interpretation. Their help has proved invaluable.

W. Paul Reeve, a colleague in the Department of History at the University of Utah, and Kenneth L. Alford, Alexander L. Baugh, J. B. Haws, and Andrew H. Hedges, colleagues in the Department of Church History and Doctrine at Brigham Young University, read parts of the manuscript and provided helpful comments.

We are grateful for Thomas A. Wayment, former director of the RSC publication office, and Scott C. Esplin, the recently appointed director of that office, as well as Joany O. Pinegar, R. Devan Jensen, Don L. Brugger, Brent R. Nordgren, Emily V. Strong, Ashlin Awerkamp, Emily Cook, Megan Judd, and Michael Ray Morris Jr. at the RSC for their help in bringing this book to print. We thank Kelly Nield and his staff at Hales Creative for designing and typesetting this book and its cover.

Financial assistance from the Department of Church History and Doctrine, the Department of Ancient Scripture, and the Religious Studies Center at Brigham Young University, which provided funds to pay for student research, was important in our efforts to complete this project.

Additionally, several individuals, including Clair and Mary Ann Anderson, M. Russell and Barbara Ballard, Douglas Heiner, Steven and Kalleen Lund, Ron and Jody Malouf, Von and Glenda Memory, the Fred and Jolene Rockwood Family Foundation, and Blake and Nancy Roney, made donations to a BYU gift account between 2013 and 2018. Their generosity and encouragement allowed us to complete the final stretch of our long journey and publish this book in color so we could highlight some of the visually interesting photographs, envelopes, letters, letterpress copybooks, and journals.

Finally, we express our deepest appreciation and love to our families for their patience, support, and constant encouragement.

Abbreviations

BYU .... L. Tom Perry Special Collections, Harold B. Lee Library, Brigham Young University, Provo, UT

CHL......... Church History Library, The Church of Jesus Christ of Latter-day Saints, Salt Lake City, UT

CHM .... Church History Museum, The Church of Jesus Christ of Latter-day Saints, Salt Lake City, UT

USHS........ Utah State Historical Society, Salt Lake City, UT

UU .... Annie Clark Tanner Western Americana Collection, Special Collections Department, J. Willard Marriott Library, University of Utah, Salt Lake City, UT

To my Darling Rachel from
Her loving Papa and Brother

Joseph F. Smith and his son and biographer, Joseph Fielding Smith, ca. 1915. Courtesy of CHL.

Introduction and Historiography

It has been eighty years since *The Life of Joseph F. Smith: Sixth President of The Church of Jesus Christ of Latter-day Saints* was published in 1938.[1] Written by his son Joseph Fielding Smith (1876–1972), this biography became an instant classic and contained source material unavailable to the public. Not only did Joseph Fielding know his father as an intimate family member, but he also worked closely with him before and after his mission as a young man (1899–1901) and then observed his father in another small circle as he served for nine years in the Quorum of the Twelve Apostles during the time his father was President of the Church. Finally, Joseph Fielding Smith had complete access to a rich collection of Joseph F. Smith papers, including diaries, letters, sermons, reminiscences, and other related Church material preserved in the archives at Church headquarters, as he prepared his father's biography.

In the past several decades, historians have made significant advances in reconstructing the story of the Church and the lives of its leaders, including the life of Joseph F.[2] Using primary source material at various institutions, especially at the Church History Library, these historians have helped Latter-day Saints appreciate, understand, and expand their understanding of the remarkable story of God's people, human and fallible, trying to do the will of a perfect God—sometimes failing and sometimes succeeding in their efforts.

Some of Joseph F.'s sources became available in 2003 with the creation of *Selected Collections from the Archives of the Church of Jesus Christ of Latter-day Saints*.[3] Since then, the Church History Library has continued to digitize and preserve electronically additional sources. (Note that because all primary sources cited in the footnotes herein reside in the Church History Library unless otherwise noted, for space reasons the source citations dispense with listing that repository.)

1. Joseph Fielding Smith, *The Life of Joseph F. Smith: Sixth President of The Church of Jesus Christ of Latter-day Saints* (Salt Lake City, UT: Deseret Book, 1938).
2. In contexts herein treating Joseph F. Smith's younger years, he is referred to as "Joseph F.," the name used affectionately by his sister Martha Ann and others who were close to him. In contexts dealing with his official capacity as President of the Church, he is referred to as "President Smith" or by his full name.
3. Richard E. Turley Jr., ed., *Selected Collections from the Archives of the Church of Jesus Christ of Latter-day Saints*, 2 vols. (Provo, UT: Brigham Young University Press, 2003).

Joseph F. has been the subject of these recent efforts. For example, Hyrum M. Smith III and Scott G. Kenney published in 1981 a collection of letters written by Joseph F. to his missionary sons.[4] Kenney followed up with an interpretive essay on the trials of the young Joseph F.[5] Ten years later, Nathaniel R. Ricks edited and published some of Joseph F. Smith's first mission journals (1856–57).[6] In 2012 David M. Whitchurch and Mallory Hales Perry published a study highlighting a letter from Joseph F. to Susa Young Gates.[7]

A symposium focused on Joseph F. Smith's life and ministry was sponsored by the BYU Department of Church History and Doctrine, BYU Religious Studies Center, and the Church History Library in 2012. The proceedings, *Joseph F. Smith: Reflections on the Man and His Times*, were published the following year.[8]

Recently, historian Stephen C. Taysom has contributed to the subject by publishing important interpretive essays on Joseph F.'s life as he prepares a comprehensive biography of Joseph F., tentatively titled *"Like a Fiery Meteor": The Life of Joseph F. Smith*. This work will become the definitive biography for years to come.

However, even with the primary sources now available and the excellent interpretive essays and books being written about Joseph F., we will never really be able to say we are in a position to reconstruct Joseph F.'s life in a way that would allow us to know him as those who lived with him knew him. As Taysom has observed, "Very early in my research it became clear to me that I was never going to get the 'real' JFS. I was never going to find the guy who lived and walked and ate and rolled his eyes. Most of the things that made him the fluid human being who completely inhabited every second of his 80 years on earth are gone. What I am dealing with is the version of JFS that is left behind in the archival traces of his life."[9] To underscore this point, Taysom adds, "Imagine if you suddenly died tomorrow and a stranger had to reconstruct your life only from things you had written or things that others had written about you. And not everything that was ever written, just those things that survived the ravages of time and nature and that people happened to save. Those sources would reveal a lot about you, but they would be of limited assistance in getting at you as a living, vital personality."[10]

Nevertheless, collecting the fragmentary sources and carefully examining them in context, to "see through a glass darkly," is still worthy of effort.[11] Joseph F.'s life belongs to the Latter-day Saints, not just his descendants, because Joseph F. dedicated his life and ministry to his people.

4. Hyrum M. Smith III and Scott G. Kenney, comp., *From Prophet to Son: Advice of Joseph F. Smith to His Missionary Sons* (Salt Lake City, UT: Deseret Book, 1981). See also Joseph Fielding McConkie, ed., *Truth and Courage: The Joseph F. Smith Letters* (n.p., 1988).
5. Scott G. Kenney, "Before the Beard: Trials of the Young Joseph F. Smith," *Sunstone* 120 (November 2001): 20–42.
6. Nathaniel R. Ricks, ed., *"My Candid Opinion": The Sandwich Islands Diaries of Joseph F. Smith, 1856–1857* (Salt Lake City, UT: Signature Books, 2011).
7. David M. Whitchurch and Mallory Hales Perry, "Friends and Enemies in Washington: Joseph F. Smith's Letter to Susa Young Gates, March 21, 1889," *Mormon Historical Studies* 13, nos. 1–2 (Spring/Fall 2012): 210–29.
8. See Craig K. Manscill et al., eds., *Joseph F. Smith: Reflections on the Man and His Times* (Provo, UT: Religious Studies Center, Brigham Young University; Salt Lake City, UT: Deseret Book, 2013).
9. Matt Bowman, "Scholarly Inquiry: A Conversation with Stephen C. Taysom," *Juvenile Instructor*, 25 May 2016, https://juvenileinstructor.org/scholarly-inquiry-a-conversation-with-stephen-c-taysom/.
10. Bowman, "Scholarly Inquiry."
11. See 1 Corinthians 13:12.

LETTERS AS SOURCES

When reconstructing a life or preparing a historical study, historians utilize many types of primary resources, including letters, diaries, and autobiographical reminiscences. Each type is a personal window into past lives and provides historians with particular opportunities and challenges. An autobiographical reminiscence is easily discerned as being distinct and different from a diary or letter because generally a long period of reflection has occurred before it was created. This long period provides nuanced interpretations of the past by the author, sometimes reconstructing the past in a way that does not always match the contemporary record of events.

Although diaries and letters are often contemporary accounts of one's life, they are more different from each other than one might recognize at first. For example, diaries are a more recent form, while letters are a much older form (think of the Apostle Paul's letters in the New Testament). Further, they each had their own purpose; letters were meant to be part of a dialogue between two or more people, while diaries were written to oneself and form a kind of self-dialogue or self-reflection.

Historians have discovered a treasure trove of information in Joseph F.'s diaries, some thirty-six volumes housed in the Church History Library.[12] Joseph F. presumably began keeping a diary at the beginning of his first mission—a mission to Hawai'i in 1854. Unfortunately, two volumes beginning with his arrival in September 1854 to the end of 1855 were destroyed in a fire at the mission headquarters in June 1856. Those covering 1856–57 survived and were published in 2011.[13]

THE NATURE OF LETTERS

There were well-established conventions regarding nineteenth-century letters, including how they should be written, what they should and should not contain, how they were to be read, and how they were to be sent. Scholars often classify letters into distinctive categories such as administrative, business, diplomatic, personal, and travel. Joseph F.'s letters to his sister may bridge several categories but are decidedly personal for the most part.

Nineteenth-century grammar, spelling, usage, and vocabulary are in many ways much different from today's literary conventions. People often spelled a word, particularly proper nouns, the way they heard them, and they often spelled words differently in the same letter.[14] Written American English was still fluid in the second half of the nineteenth century.

LETTER COLLECTIONS

Many important letter collections have been published in the recent past. For example, the annotated letters of John Adams, second president of the United States, are published in nine volumes.[15] Latter-day Saints were introduced to letters by Brigham Young (1801–77) to some of his sons in an important collection entitled *My Dear Son: Letters of Brigham Young to His Sons*.[16] The letters between Ellen Spencer Clawson of Salt Lake City and Ellen Pratt McGary of San Bernardino in the 1850s concern two women who had been childhood friends in Nauvoo, Illinois, and crossed the

12. See Joseph F. Smith papers, 1854–1918, MS 1325. Some of Joseph F.'s journals, letters, and other items in this collection are currently closed to research. All primary sources cited in this book are found in the CHL unless otherwise noted.
13. See Ricks, *"My Candid Opinion."*
14. See, for example, Martha Ann to Joseph F., 3 May 1857, herein.
15. L. H. Butterfield et. al, *Adams Family Correspondences* (Cambridge: Harvard University Press, 1963–2007).
16. Dean C. Jessee, ed., *My Dear Son: Letters of Brigham Young to His Sons* (Salt Lake City, UT: Deseret Book, 1971).

plains together to Utah in the 1840s. This fascinating correspondence was published in *Dear Ellen: Two Mormon Women and Their Letters*.[17]

As already noted, in 1981 Hyrum M. Smith III and Scott G. Kenney, two of Joseph F.'s descendants, published a selection of letters written to his sons while they served full-time missions.[18] Two other collections, *Post-Manifesto Polygamy: The 1899–1904 Correspondence of Helen, Owen, and Avery Woodruff* and *In the Whirlpool: The Pre-Manifesto Letters of President Wilford Woodruff to the William Atkin Family, 1885–1890*, remind us of the importance of letters as primary sources in providing additional depth and breadth to the Latter-day Saint story.[19]

JOSEPH F. AND MARTHA ANN SMITH HARRIS LETTER COLLECTION

Carole Call King did not realize the treasure she inherited when her father, Anson B. Call Jr. (1900–1993), passed away.[20] Busy with the funeral and other family demands, she overlooked the contents of one box. Left unnoticed on a closet shelf for some time, it caught her attention one day as she was putting away the vacuum. In the bottom of the box, underneath her mother's chiffon wedding dress, she found three small, long, narrow boxes neatly wrapped in tissue paper. On them her grandmother Sarah Lovina Harris Passey (1883–1961) had written in her own hand the words "Letters to mother."[21]

King opened the box and discovered inside nearly a hundred original letters written by Joseph F. Smith, the sixth President of The Church of Jesus Christ of Latter-day Saints. Joseph F., "for by that name he was affectionately called," had addressed and sent them to his younger sister Martha Ann Smith Harris (1841–1923), King's great-grandmother.[22]

Richard Neitzel Holzapfel, a professor from Brigham Young University, contacted King after hearing about an 1854 letter that she had found in one of the boxes that included a lock of Joseph F.'s hair in the envelope. In the course of their conversation, Holzapfel learned about the other letters and arranged to visit with her the following day at her home in Mountain Green, Morgan County, Utah. King graciously showed him the collection of handwritten letters, many of which were inside their original envelopes. During their conversation, King gave Professor Holzapfel permission to

---

17. S. George Ellsworth, *Dear Ellen: Two Mormon Women and Their Letters* (Salt Lake City, UT: Tanner Trust Fund, University of Utah Library, 1974).
18. See Smith and Kenney, *From Prophet to Son*. One of these letters, Joseph F. to Joseph Fielding Smith, 20 June 1899, was reprinted in Larry E. Morris, *A Treasury of Latter-day Saint Letters* (Salt Lake City, UT: Eagle Gate, 2001), 40–42.
19. See Lu Ann Faylor Snyder and Phillip A. Snyder, eds., *Post-Manifesto Polygamy: The 1899–1904 Correspondence of Helen, Owen, and Avery Woodruff* (Logan, UT: Utah State University Press, 2009); and Reid L. Neilson, ed., *In the Whirlpool: The Pre-Manifesto Letters of President Wilford Woodruff to the William Atkin Family, 1885–1890* (Norman, OK: Arthur H. Clark Company, 2011).
20. An earlier report of the discovery of the letters was published in 2004. See David M. Whitchurch, "'My Dear Sister': Letters between Joseph F. Smith and His Sister, Martha Ann Smith Harris (1854–1916)," *Mormon Historical Studies* 5, no. 1 (Spring 2004): 195–202.
21. Carole Call King noted, "I received all the family history material when my parents died. I really don't think my darling mother knew about the treasured letters her mother left her. There were so many boxes of papers, photographs, letters, etc., she probably never went through all the things she had. My grandmother, Sarah Lovina Harris Passey, youngest child of Martha Ann Smith Harris, saved the letters received from her mother." Carole Call King to Richard Neitzel Holzapfel, 14 October 2014, in editors' possession.
22. See Charles W. Nibley, "Reminiscences of President Joseph F. Smith," *Improvement Era* 22, no. 3 (January 1919): 191–98; see also Joseph F. Smith, *Gospel Doctrine: Selections from the Sermons and Writings of Joseph F. Smith*, comp. John A. Widtsoe, 5th ed. (Salt Lake City, UT: Deseret Book, 1939), 656.

Sarah Lovina Harris Passey, ca 1906–7. Sarah was the youngest daughter of Martha Ann and the one who had preserved her mother's letters, including those sent to Martha Ann by Joseph F. Courtesy of Carole Call King.

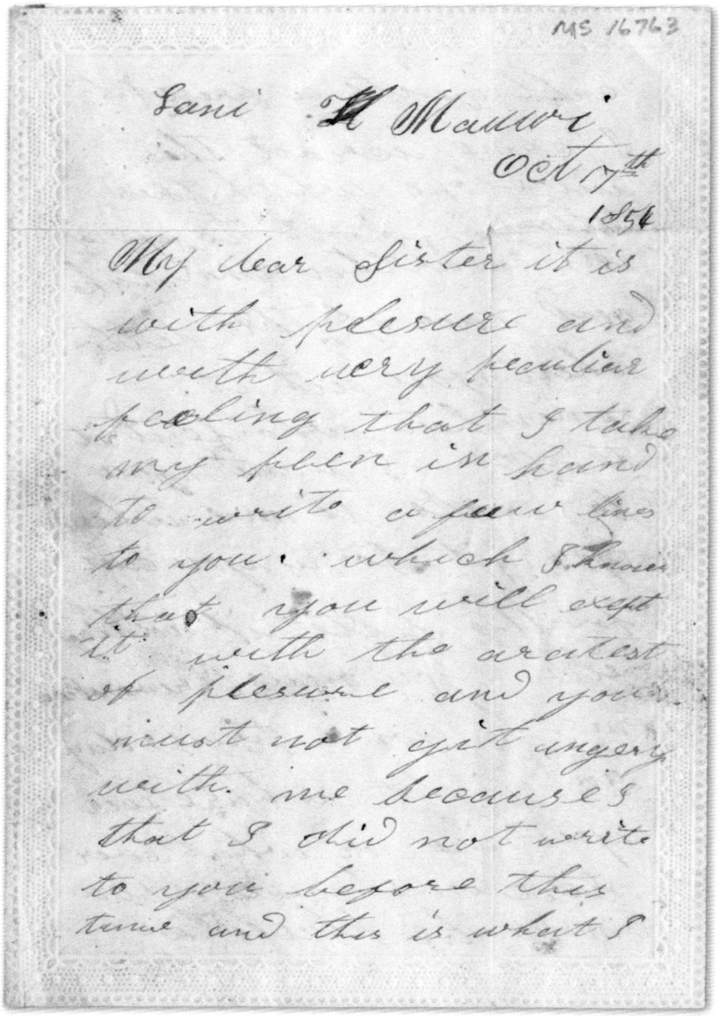

MS 16763

Lani H Mauwi
Oct 17th
1854

My dear Sister it is with plesure and with very peculiar feeling that I take my pen in hand to write a few lines to you which I know that you will exept it with the greatest of plesure and you must not git angery with me becouse that I did not write to you before this time and this is what I

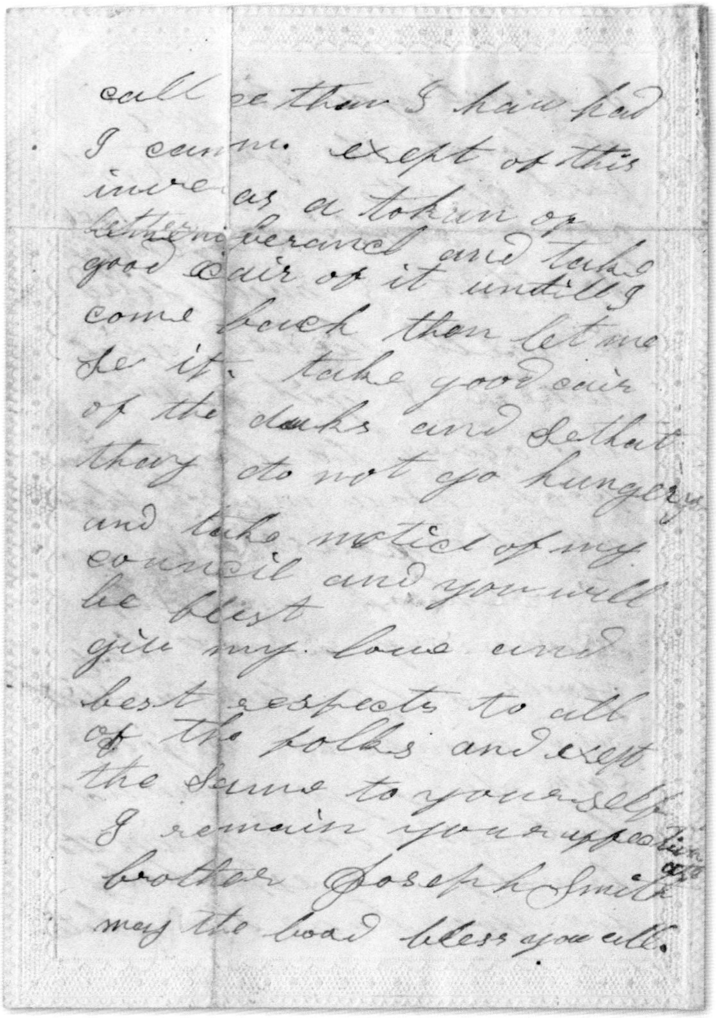

call rather than I have had I cannot exept of this inver as a token of remembrance and take good care of it untill I come back then let me se it, take good care of the ducks and se that they do not go hungery and take notice of my council and you will be blest give my love and best respects to all of the folks and exept the same to yourself I remain your affectionate brother Joseph F Smith
may the lord bless you all.

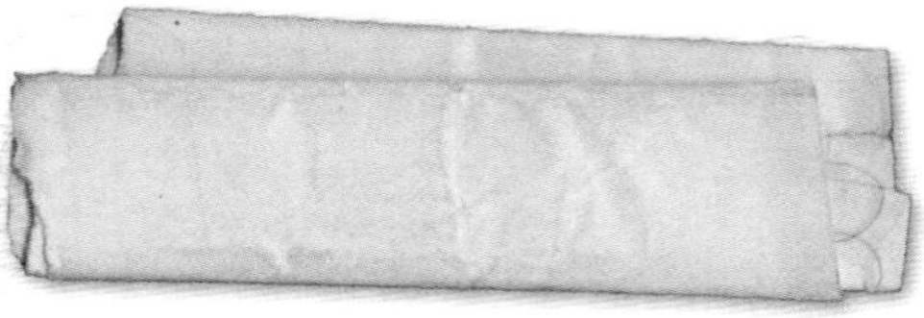

Martha ann Smith
Great Salt Lake
City U T teritory

Letter from Joseph F. to Martha Ann, 17 October 1854 (pp. 1 and 4), with envelope and lock of hair. This the first known extant letter in the collection written to Martha Ann from Hawai'i. This letter was in possession of Carole Call King, along with the other letters her grandmother had preserved. King eventually donated the collection to the CHL. Courtesy of CHL.

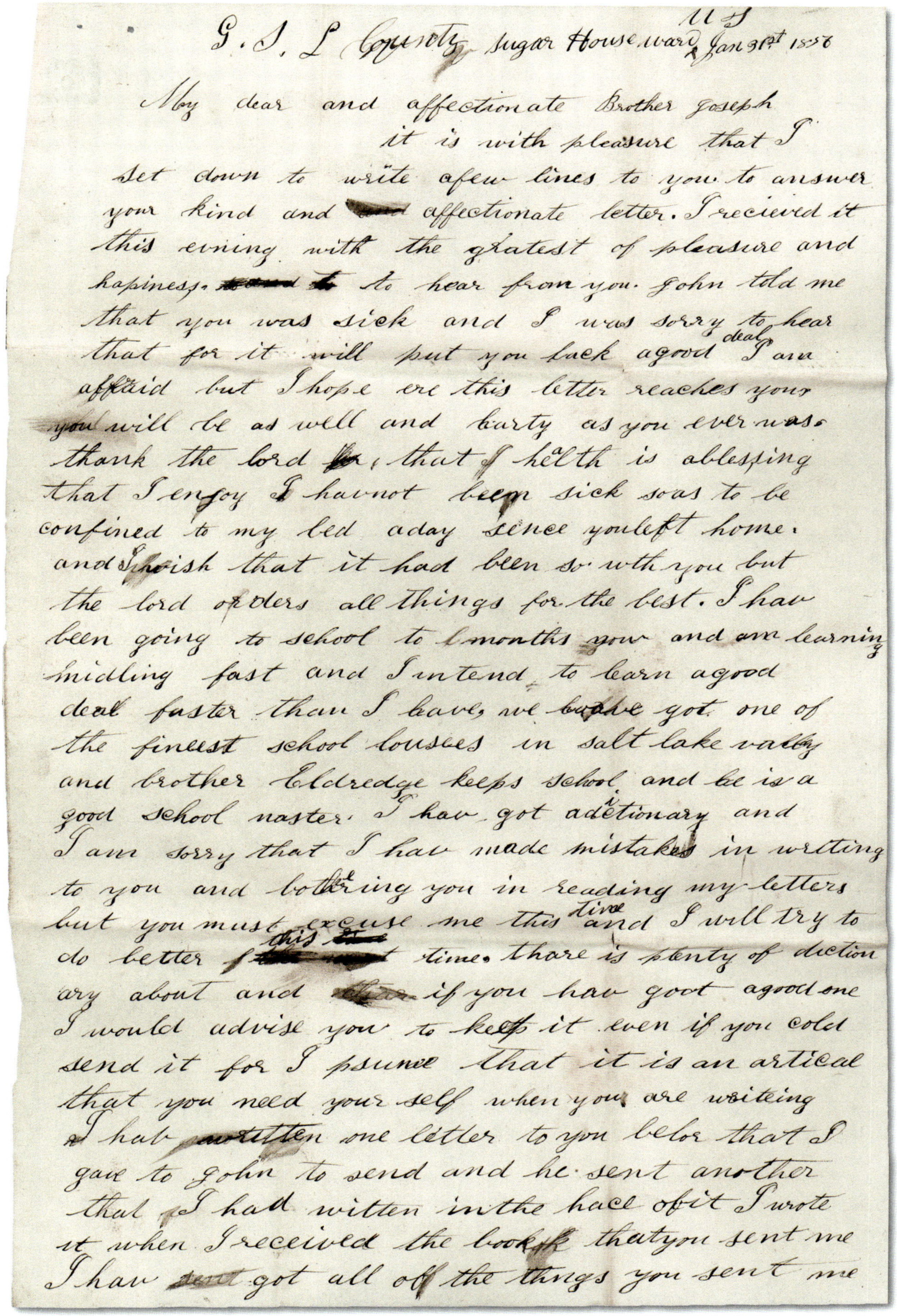

G. S. L. County Sugar House ward U S Jan 31st 1856

My dear and affectionate Brother Joseph
it is with pleasure that I
set down to write afew lines to you to answer
your kind and affectionate letter. I recieved it
this evining with the gratest of pleasure and
hapiness. to hear from you. John told me
that you was sick and I was sorry to hear
that for it will put you back agood deal I am
affraid but I hope ere this letter reaches your
you will be as well and harty as you ever was.
thank the lord; that of helth is ablessing
that I enjoy I havnot been sick soas to be
confined to my bed aday sence youleft home.
and I wish that it had been so with you but
the lord orders all things for the best. I hav
been going to school to 6 months now and am learning
midling fast and I intend to larn agood
deal faster than I have, we have got one of
the finest school houses in salt lake valley
and brother Eldredge keeps school and he is a
good school master. I hav got adictionary and
I am sorry that I hav made mistakes in writing
to you and bothering you in reading my letters
but you must excuse me this time and I will try to
do better this time. thare is plenty of diction
ary about and if you hav goot agood one
I would advise you to keep it even if you cold
send it for I psume that it is an artical
that you need your self when you are writeing
I hab one letter to you befor that I
gave to John to send and he sent another
that I had witten in the hace of it I wrote
it when I received the books that you sent me
I hav got all of the things you sent me

Letter from Martha Ann to Joseph F., 31 January 1856 (p. 1). This is Martha Ann's first known surviving letter to her brother. Courtesy of CHL.

copy, transcribe, and publish this important collection of personal letters between Joseph F. and Martha Ann.

In the months that followed, Holzapfel invited a colleague, BYU professor David M. Whitchurch, to join the project. Whitchurch oversaw the challenging transcription effort, producing summaries of each letter along with a biographical register. At the same time, Holzapfel began searching in several institutional repositories for additional letters, researching material for historical summaries for each decade represented in the letter collection, and gathering information to be used to annotate each letter to help readers contextualize the documents.

Another important development occurred when Carole Call King donated the collection of letters and envelopes to the Church History Library in Salt Lake City.[23] In response to Carole Call King's generosity, the Church provided Holzapfel and Whitchurch copies of Martha Ann's letters to Joseph F. housed in their collection, which had previously been closed to researchers. Additional letters were donated to the Church History Library by other Harris family members.[24]

Holzapfel and Whitchurch searched the Church History Library and the libraries at Brigham Young University, the University of Utah, and the Utah State Historical Society looking for additional letters. Eventually, they discovered nineteen of Joseph F.'s letterpress copybooks at the Church History Library, two in private possession, and one at the University of Utah.[25]

Copies of sixty-nine letters are preserved only in Joseph F.'s letterpress copybooks, the originals not having survived.[26] Additionally, one incomplete original Joseph F. letter was handed down in the family. Fortunately, a complete copy of that letter is found in one of the copybooks.[27]

The letterpress copybooks offer clues to help date letters when questions arise about the exact date of composition. In cases where original letters are damaged by tears or holes, copies from the letterpress copybooks have made it possible to produce more complete and accurate transcriptions.

LETTERPRESS COPYBOOKS

Historians Barbara Rhodes and William Wells Streeter observe, "Letterpress copybooks are an early type of document copying process. They were commonly used in office environments throughout the 19th century."[28] Rhodes and Streeter continue:

> The historic copy press process involved the transfer of ink on a freshly written document to a moistened sheet of copying paper through the use of direct contact and pressure. The books were manufactured specifically for this purpose and would have been purchased blank. The user would have written a letter on a regular sheet of writing paper but with

23. Carole Call King donated her collection of letters to the CHL on 6 July 2001; see MS 16763, Carole C. King Collection, 1854–1916.
24. Shirlee Passey Williams, Verna Passey Call's sister, donated several letters, including letters from Joseph F. to Martha Ann, to the CHL. Barry K. Williams provided Carole Call King with additional letters on 19 July 2000.
25. The fact that Joseph F. kept copies of his letters may suggest that he was concerned about the future interpretation of his life and wanted to preserve his own viewpoint. Another possibility is that he kept copies of his letters so he could reference them as needed. We appreciate Nathaniel R. Ricks for sharing this insight.
26. When the transcription of a nonextant letter is based on a copy found in the letterpress copybook, we have noted this in the first footnote.
27. Joseph F. to Martha Ann, 22 May 1890, herein.
28. Barbara Rhodes and William Wells Streeter, *Before Photocopying: The Art and History of Mechanical Copying* (New Castle, DE: Oak Knoll Press & Herald Bindery, 1999), 113.

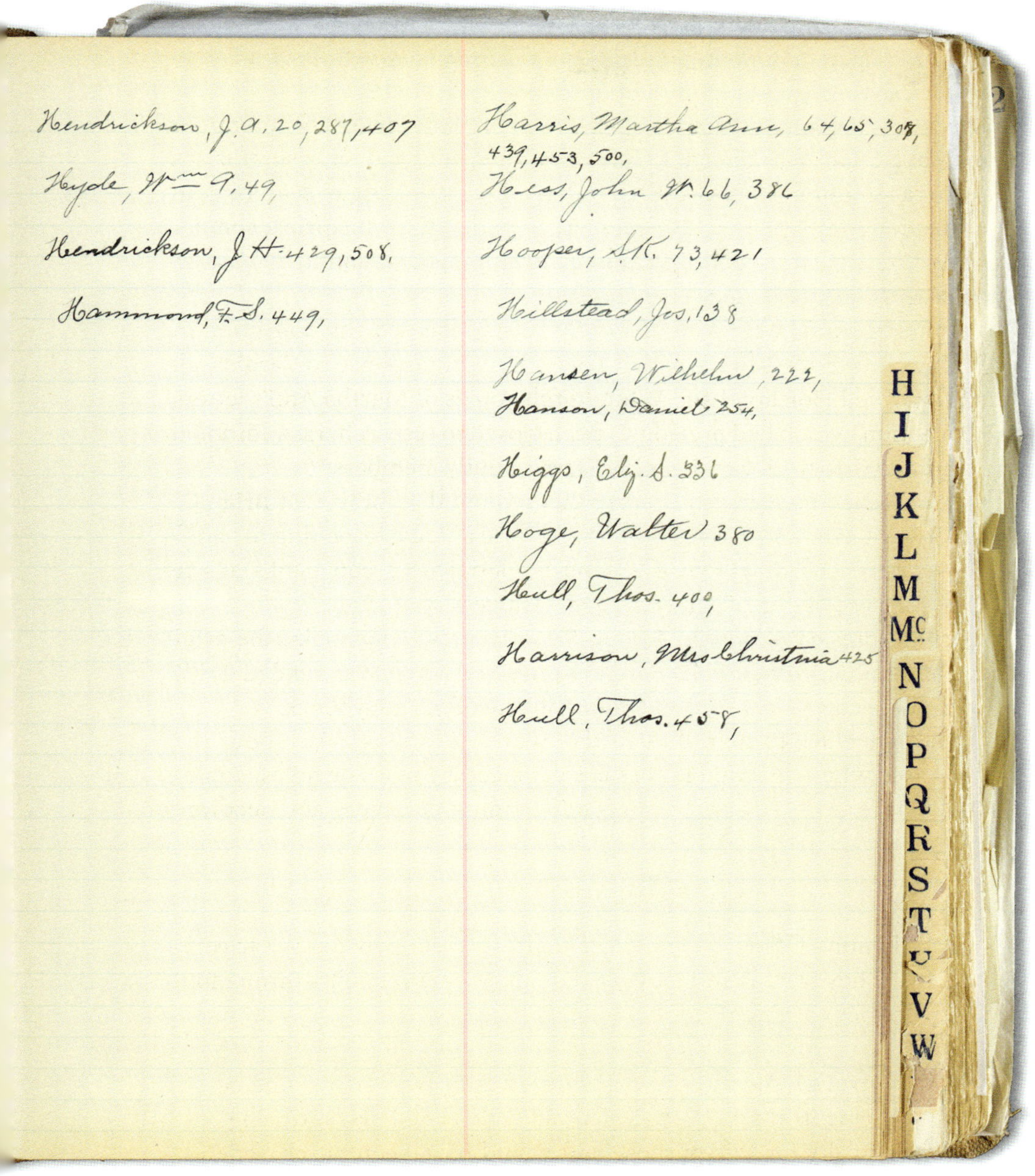

Hendrickson, J. A. 20, 287, 407
Hyde, Wm 9, 49,
Hendrickson, J H. 429, 508,
Hammond, F. S. 449,

Harris, Martha Ann, 64, 65, 308, 439, 453, 500,
Hess, John W. 66, 386
Hooper, S.K. 73, 421
Hillstead, Jos. 138
Hansen, Wilhelm, 222,
Hanson, Daniel 254,
Higgs, Elij. S. 336
Hoge, Walter 380
Hull, Thos. 400,
Harrison, Mrs Christina 425
Hull, Thos. 458,

H I J K L M Mc N O P Q R S T U V W

Joseph F. Smith letterpress copybook, 23 November 1899 through 3 February 1902. It is open to the index section highlighting the letter *H*. A clerk identified six letters written to Martha Ann in this copybook. Courtesy of CHL.

specially formulated copying ink. A sheet of copying paper would have been dampened and the original document laid onto the damp sheet. The book would be closed and put into a copy press, transferring the ink onto the copying book page. Because the soluble copying ink was transferred directly, it left a mirror image print to be read from the verso of the thin paper.[29]

Professor JoAnne Yates of MIT's Sloan School of Management adds: "These letter presses were used by some individuals and businessmen in the first half of the nineteenth century, but they only came into general use in the second half of the century. A letter press reduced the labor cost, both by decreasing copying time and by allowing an office boy to do the copying once performed by a

29. Rhodes and Streeter, *Before Photocopying*, 9.

more expensive clerk. At the same time, it eliminated the danger of miscopying. Copies were now facsimiles of the letter sent, down to the signature."[30]

Generally, letterpress copybooks begin with an index, allowing the letters to be located rather quickly. However, owners or clerks sometimes missed letters during the indexing process, and as a result a page-by-page search was required for this project in order to find all of Joseph F.'s letters to Martha Ann that had been copied into the letterpress copybooks.

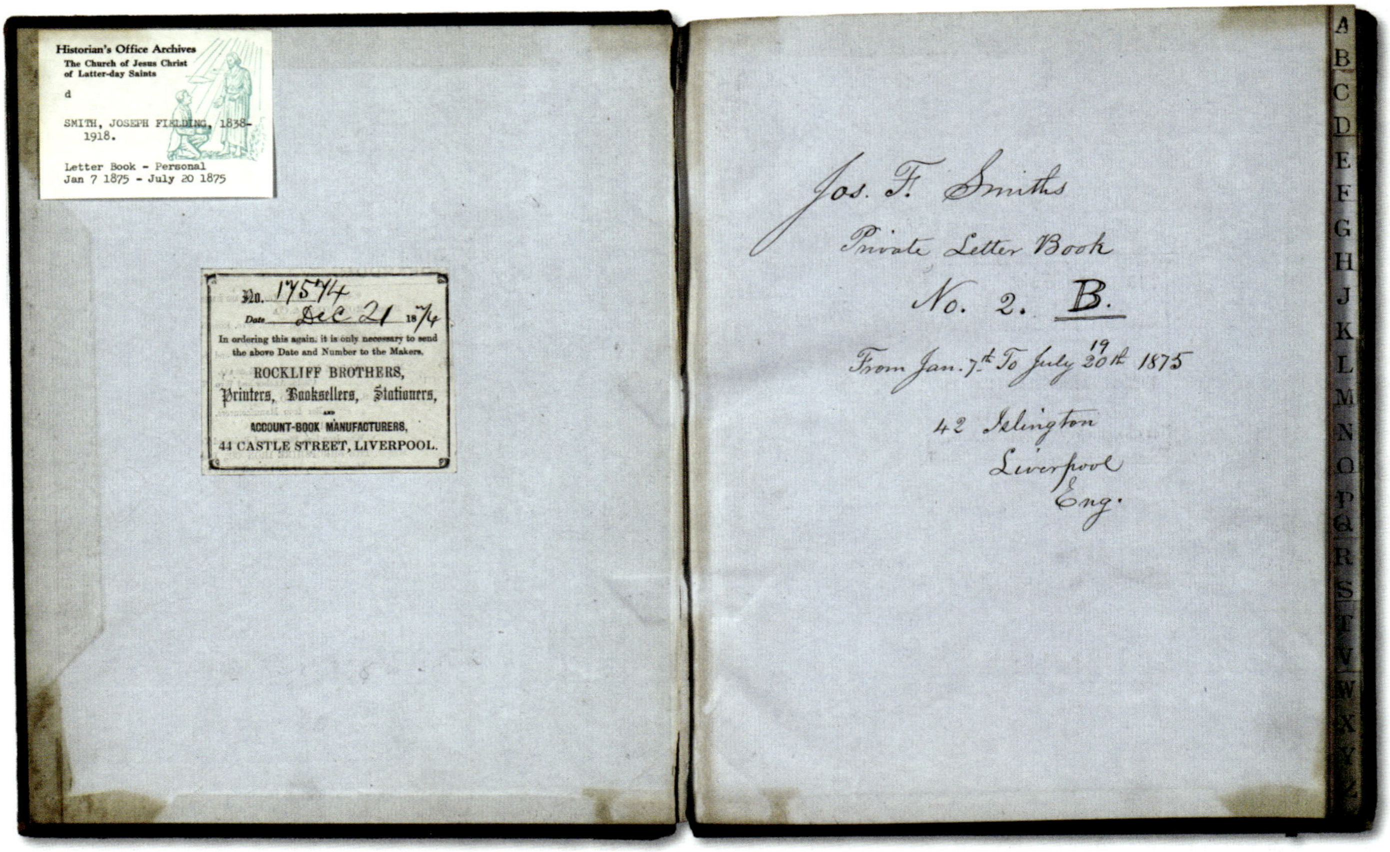

Inside cover of Joseph F.'s second letterpress copybook, covering the period of 7 January through 20 July 1875. Courtesy of CHL.

Apparently, Joseph F. purchased his first letterpress copybook in Liverpool, England, while he served as president of the European Mission.[31] A photocopy of this letterpress copybook is preserved in the Annie Clark Tanner Western Americana Collection, Special Collections Department, J. Willard Marriott Library, University of Utah, Salt Lake City. Joseph F. wrote on the page facing the inside cover, "Joseph F. Smiths Letter Book No. 1-A From July 17, 1874 to December 31, 1876."[32]

30. JoAnne Yates, *Control through Communication: The Rise of System in American Management* (Baltimore: Johns Hopkins University Press, 1989), 26–28.

31. Inside the letterpress copybook is a sticker that reads "W. Pitt & Co. Wholesale Stationers, and Account-book Manufacturers, 2, Strand Street, Liverpool." Joseph F. Smith Family papers, Annie Clark Tanner Western Americana Collection, Special Collections Department, J. Willard Marriott Library, University of Utah, Salt Lake City.

32. Joseph F. Smith letterpress copybook, 17 July 1874 through 31 December 1876.

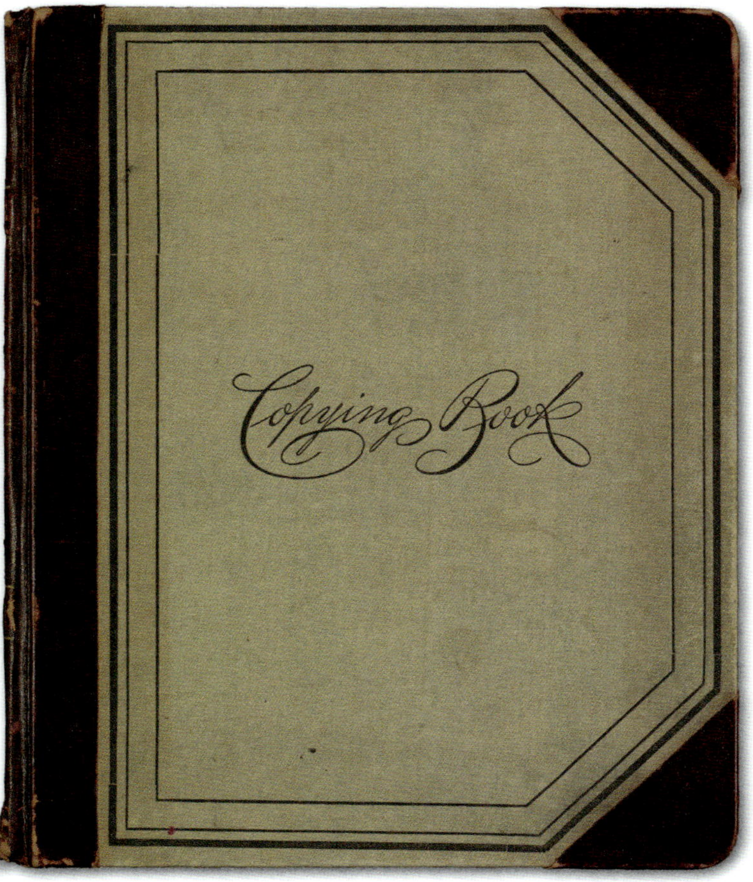

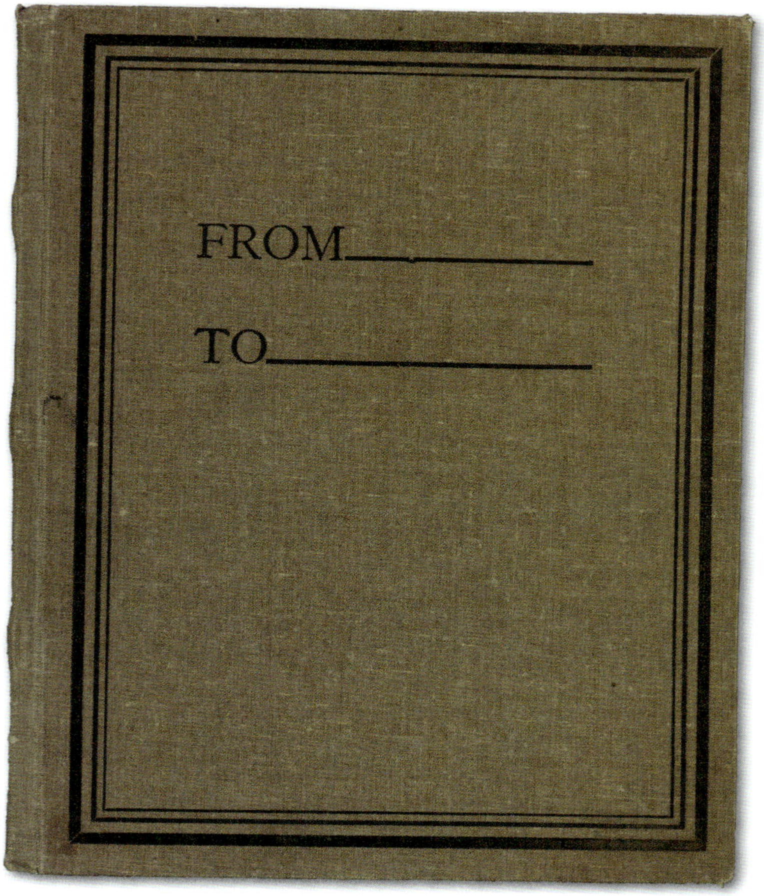

Letterpress copybooks, 16 March 1895–4 September 1896 (left) and 2 March 1888–29 August 1888 (right). Courtesy of Mark L. and Mary Ann McConkie.

Joseph F.'s nineteen letterpress copybooks that are preserved in the Church History Library cover various time frames from 7 January 1875 through 27 March 1917 with some major gaps.[33]

As noted earlier, the letterpress copybooks preserve copies of original letters now lost as well as copies of many extant original letters written after 1875.[34] When combined with the original letters of Martha Ann to Joseph F. that were preserved in the CHL, we have additional sources that provide important and interesting information. Many of the original letters are preserved with their accompanying envelopes. The additional information gleaned from the envelopes themselves, including postage marks and Joseph F.'s handwritten comments on the front or back, are invaluable.

33. These letterpress copybooks are located in the CHL. They cover 7 January–20 July 1875; 19 July 1875–7 September 1879; 6 June–10 December 1877; 9 September 1879–12 September 1883; 18 May–16 June 1880; 19 September 1881–15 January 1884; 14 September 1883–14 March 1890; 18 January 1884–3 May 1889; 12 November 1885–4 March 1886; 17 March 1890–1 May 1891; 1 May 1891–25 November 1882; 26 November 1892–19 March 1895; 4 September 1896–1 April 1898; 5 April 1898–20 November 1899; 23 November 1899–3 February 1902; 2 February 1902–4 April 1905; 2 April 1905–1 May 1907; 4 May 1907–19 September 1909; 20 September 1909–26 February 1912; 9 March 1912–7 November 1914; and 7 November 1914–27 March 1917.

34. The first example of an extant original letter that has a copy preserved in a letterpress copybook is Joseph F. to Martha Ann, 31 March 1875, herein.

Additionally, some of Joseph F.'s original letters were often written on preprinted letterhead, providing even more information about the context of the letters. None of this kind of information is preserved in the letterpress copybooks.

We have included a representative sampling of the images of the letters and envelopes for each decade. Many more images of the original letters, envelopes, and copies from the letterpress copybooks exist. The decision to limit the number of images used herein is based on the desire to provide more historical context with introductory essays, photographs of the people and places mentioned in the letters, introductions for each decade, extensive annotation for each letter, and a biographical register.

RESEARCH CONTINUED

Whitchurch took charge of the entire project and worked tirelessly to provide additional annotations, finish the historical summaries for each chapter, and complete a penultimate draft while Holzapfel was on academic leave from BYU between 2010 and 2013 while he served as a mission president. On his return to BYU during the summer of 2013, Holzapfel reengaged in the project and continued research and writing. In 2014 Holzapfel and Whitchurch learned of two additional letterpress copybooks in private possession covering the periods March 1888 through August 1888, March 1895, and September 1896. Mark L. McConkie, a great-grandson of Joseph F. Smith, had obtained them from his father and mother, Bruce R. and Amelia Smith McConkie. Amelia was Joseph Fielding Smith's daughter and Joseph F.'s granddaughter. Holzapfel flew to Colorado to examine them and found they contained additional letters addressed to Martha Ann.[35]

Under the date 29 August 1888, Joseph F. provided important information about some of his missing letters: "The following correspondence is continued from my coppy book opened in Washington D. C. Feb. 1888. This book was laid aside Aug. 29th 1884. Four years ago today when I left Salt lake City on a mission with Elders Erastus Snow and John Morgan to Colorado, Arizona and New Mexico, and S. Eastern Utah. from which date until now I have been in Exile on account of persecutions and prosecutions under the Edmunds and Edmunds-Tucker Laws. On Sept. 15th I copied one letter in this book. Most of my letters since 1884 have not been copied in any book."[36]

The letters from Joseph F. to Martha Ann that were discovered in one of these letterpress copybooks added to the growing collection of letters and filled an important gap in the correspondence. McConkie allowed Holzapfel to take the letterpress copybooks to Salt Lake City to be digitized. Copies were donated to the Church History Library and the originals returned. Additionally, McConkie graciously gave permission to include the letters in this book.

THE FINISH LINE

Holzapfel and Whitchurch continued preparing the manuscript for publication during the next two years, providing additional annotations to the letters, expanding the historical summaries, and adding additional images from the Smith and Harris families and institutional repositories. The search for additional letters and efforts to complete the research ended in 2018.

This book contains all the known surviving letters—241—between Joseph F. and his sister Martha Ann.

35. See Joseph F. to Martha Ann, 6 August 1895; 27 September 1895; [1 November] 1895; 28 March 1896; and 21 April 1896, herein.

36. Joseph F. Smith letterpress copybook, 29 August 1888, 139, in private possession. Courtesy of Mark L. and Mary Ann McConkie.

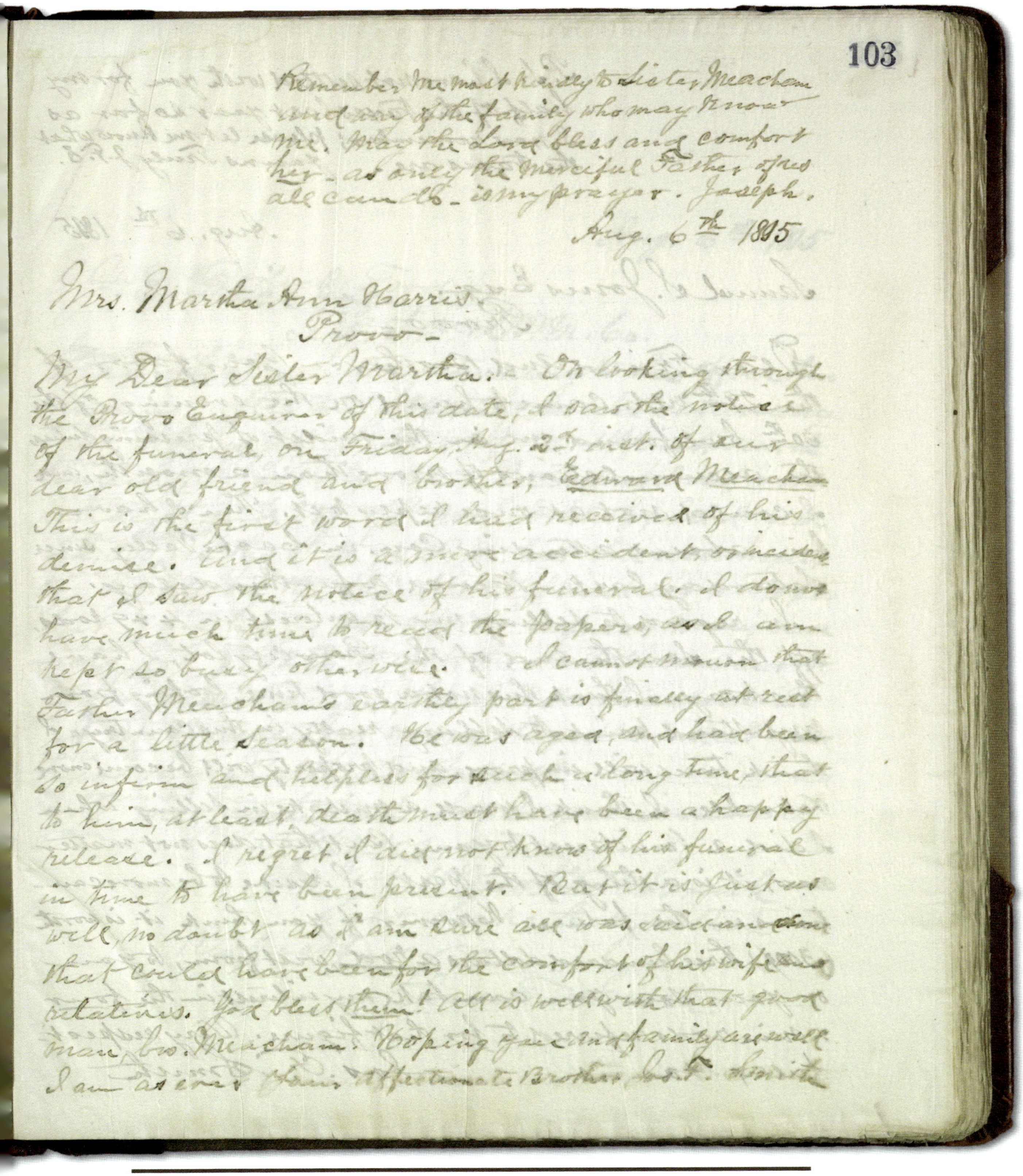
103

Remember me most kindly to Sister Meacham and any of the family who may know me. May the Lord bless and comfort her—as only the Merciful Father of us all can do—is my prayer. Joseph.

Aug. 6th 1895

Mrs. Martha Ann Harris.
Provo—

My Dear Sister Martha: On looking through the Provo Enquirer of this date, I saw the notice of the funeral, on Friday, Aug. 2d inst. of our dear old friend and brother, Edward Meacham. This is the first word I had received of his demise. And it is a mere accident or incident that I saw the notice of his funeral. I dont have much time to read the papers, as I am kept so busy otherwise. I cannot mourn that Father Meacham's earthly part is finally at rest for a little season. He was aged, and had been so infirm and helpless for such a long time, that to him, at least, death must have been a happy release. I regret I did not know of his funeral in time to have been present. But it is just as well, no doubt as I am sure all was done and done that could have been for the comfort of his wife and relatives. God bless them! All is well with that good man bro. Meacham. Hoping you and family are well I am as ever Your Affectionate Brother Jos. F. Smith

Letter from Joseph F. to Martha Ann, 6 August 1895, copy found in Joseph F.'s letterpress copybooks under that date. Courtesy of Mark L. and Mary Ann McConkie.

JOSEPH F. AND MARTHA ANN LETTERS

The first letter in the collection is dated 17 October 1854 and was handwritten on plain paper by Joseph F. when he was a fifteen-year-old inexperienced and undereducated young missionary living on the island of Maui in the Kingdom of Hawai'i, identified as the Sandwich Islands in the letters.[37] Martha Ann's first letter in the collection, dated 31 January 1856, was written when she was fourteen and living in Salt Lake City in Utah Territory.

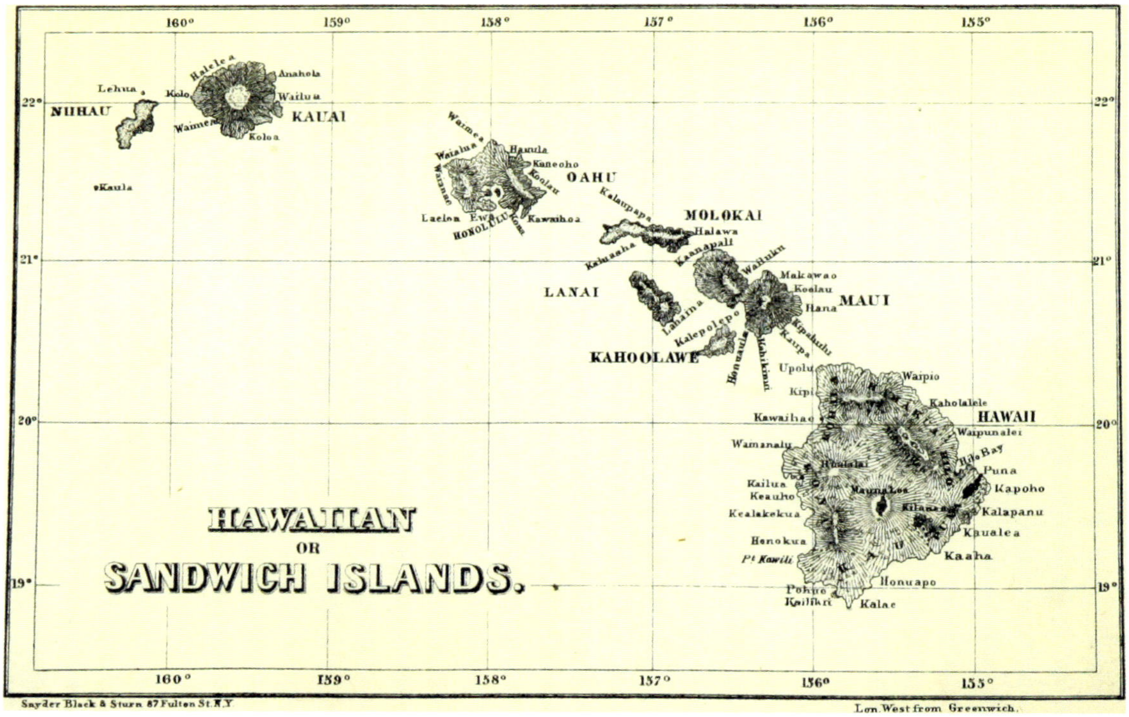

Hawaiian or Sandwich Islands, in Edward T. Perkins, *Na Motu: or, Reef-Rovings in the South Seas* (New York: Pudney & Russell, 1854).

The last two letters in the collection are dated 13 December and 19 December 1916. The earlier letter was written by Martha Ann, on high-quality paper without lines. At this time she was a much-beloved seventy-five-year-old mother, grandmother, and great-grandmother living in Provo, Utah, a city that had come of age since she moved there in the 1860s.

The final letter in the collection was typed by Joseph F. on official Church stationery. He was a much-beloved seventy-eight-year-old President of the Church living in Salt Lake City, the largest city in Utah—the state capital and the world headquarters of The Church of Jesus Christ of Latter-day Saints.

Much had changed in the Church, Utah, America, and the world from the time when the first letter was handwritten in 1854 to when the last letter was typed in 1916. For example, the

37. Joseph F. crossed oceans many times in his life, beginning in 1854. Martha Ann had no such opportunity. In 1914 Joseph F. arranged for his seventy-three-year-old sister to see the Pacific Ocean; see Joseph F. to Martha Ann, 24 June 1914, and Martha Ann to Joseph F., 7 July 1914, herein. This was not the last time Joseph F. arranged for her to spend time in Southern California.

Kingdom of Hawai'i no longer existed; it had been absorbed into the United States as a territory.[38] Additionally, Utah was a territory when Martha Ann received the first letter from Hawai'i, but it had already been a state for more than twenty years when she and Joseph F. exchanged letters in December 1916.[39]

Of course, other changes had swept across the landscape in Utah, the nation, and the world during the more than sixty years that separated the first letter from the last letter. For example, when Martha Ann said goodbye to her brother in 1854, neither she nor Joseph F. could have imagined a

Group portraits of Joseph F.'s younger children, December 1896, photograph by C. R. Savage, Salt Lake City, Utah. The portrait of eight daughters was taken on 12 December 1896 and the portrait of eight sons on 19 December 1896. Courtesy of CHL.

38. An independent kingdom between 1810 and 1893, Hawai'i became an independent republic briefly from 1894 through 1898, when it was annexed by the United States as a territory.
39. Utah was organized as an incorporated territory of the United States on 9 September 1850 by the Organic Act of Congress in 1850 and became the forty-fifth state on 4 January 1896.

William Jasper and Martha Ann Smith Harris family reunion, 11 April 1912, photograph by George Edward Anderson, Springville, Utah. This is one of four photographs taken on this occasion by the well-known photographer George Edward Anderson. In this view, the entire family was positioned outside the main entrance of the Provo Sixth Ward building with Martha Ann prominently placed in the center holding two grandchildren. Courtesy of Carole Call King.

day when women voted and ran for public office.[40] Joseph F. had supported women leaders such as Emmeline B. Wells in their effort to achieve woman's suffrage in Utah in 1896.[41]

Another change was in their individual familial relationships. Martha Ann and Joseph F. were unmarried orphaned children in 1854, but by 1916 Martha was a widowed mother of a large

40. Women voted in Utah between 1870 and 1887 but were disenfranchised by the United States government during the battle over plural marriage.
41. See Carol Cornwall Madsen, *An Advocate for Women: The Public Life of Emmeline B. Wells, 1870–1920* (Provo, UT: Brigham Young University Press; Salt Lake City, UT: Deseret Book, 2006), 250–51, 303.

multigenerational family and Joseph F. was the husband to four living wives with an even larger multigenerational family.[42]

Martha Ann and Joseph F.'s correspondence collection does not contain all the letters they wrote to each other; they both mention letters they received that are not extant.[43] For example, in May 1880 Joseph F. noted, "It has been a long time since I wrote to you, and I have received several letters for which I am indebted to you."[44] We did not find any letters written by Martha Ann in 1880, so we assume these letters have been lost to the ravages of time and nature. Also, a fire in Hawai'i during Joseph F.'s first mission in 1856 destroyed his trunk and the contents inside, including the letters Martha had sent to him previously.[45] When Martha Ann found out about the fire, she asked Joseph F. if her letters had been destroyed: " <did> you gitt your letters all burnt up or did you save enny of them. pleas tell me about it in the next letter you write to me."[46] In his follow-up letter Joseph F. noted, "Well, now for your letter; you asked me if all my letters ware burnt, or if any were remaining. all those I recieved before the misfortune ware burned,[47] but no axident has yet happened to those I've recieved since."[48]

Some of Joseph F.'s letters written before he began the practice of keeping copies through a letterpress copybook have been lost. For example, he noted in his journal: "Tuesday April 29th 1862. I wrote to President Kimball, and also, a letter of 12 pages to Uncle J. Fielding, Aunt Hannah Fielding, Aunt Thompson, Mary Jane Taylor, and Martha Ann Harris."[49] Since no letter to Martha Ann dated 29 April has been found, we assume it may have not survived.

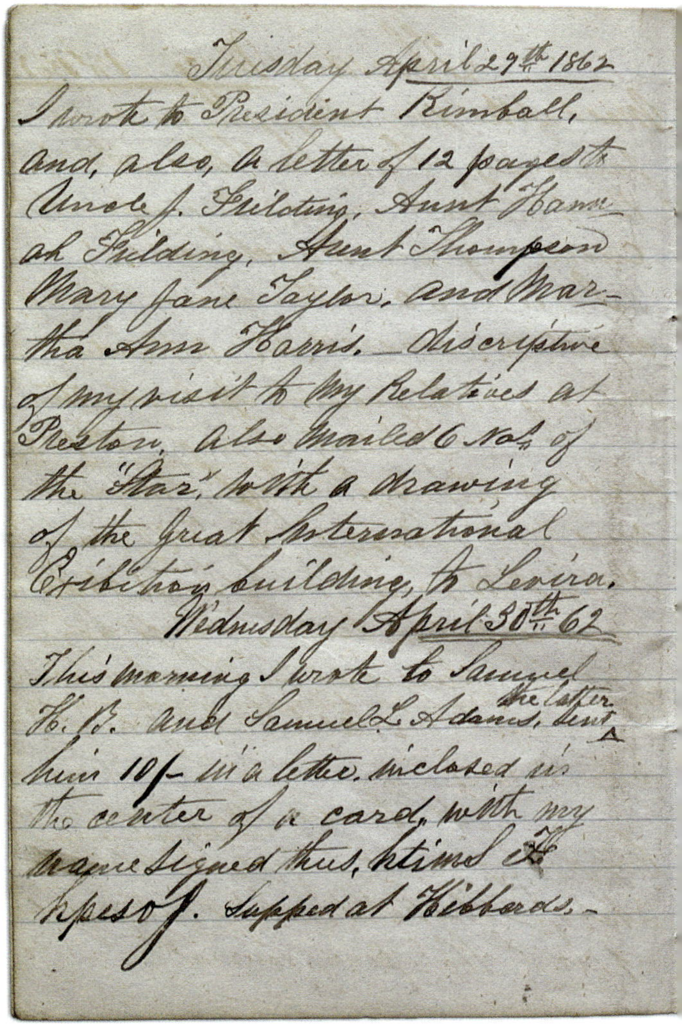
Tuesday April 29th 1862
I wrote to President Kimball,
and, also, a letter of 12 pages to
Uncle J. Fielding, Aunt Hannah Fielding, Aunt Thompson
Mary Jane Taylor, and Martha Ann Harris. Discriptive
of my visit to my Relatives at
Preston, also Mailed 6 No's of
the "Star" with a drawing
of the Great International
Exibition building, to Levira.
Wednesday April 30th 62
This morning I wrote to Samuel
H. B. and Samuel L. Adams, sent the latter
him 10/- in a letter, inclosed in
the center of a card, with my
name signed thus, htims E.
kpeso J. Supped at Hibbards.

Joseph F.'s journal for 29 April 1862. Courtesy of CHL.

42. See Lisa Olsen Tait, "'A Modern Patriarchal Family': The Wives of Joseph F. Smith in the *Relief Society Magazine*, 1915–19," in Manscill et al., *Joseph F. Smith: Reflections on the Man and His Times*, 74–95; and Edith E. Smith Patrick, comp., *Brief Histories of the Family of President Joseph F. Smith and Julina L. Smith* (n.p., n.d.). See appendix A (Joseph F.'s wives and children) and appendix B (Martha Ann's husband and children).
43. Joseph F. mentions receiving more than eighty letters from Martha Ann that are no longer extant. The one he mentions was written in 1855: "Your kind and affectionate letter of March 31st [1855]." See Joseph F. to Martha Ann, 9 June 1855, herein. The last letter mentioned by him was in 1916: "Your Card of gratulation in remembrance of myself and Nov. 13th and that of Artie's, reached me this morning." See Joseph F. to Martha Ann, 14 November 1916, herein.
44. See Joseph F. to Martha Ann, 21 May 1880, herein.
45. See Joseph F. to Martha Ann, 17 April 1857, herein; see also Joseph F., journal, 26 June 1856.
46. Martha Ann to Joseph F., 17 December 1856, herein.
47. See Joseph F., journal, 26 June 1856; and Martha Ann to Joseph F., 17 December 1856, herein.
48. Joseph F. to Martha Ann, 17 April 1857, herein.
49. Joseph F., journal, 29 April 1862.

Like other nineteenth- and early twentieth-century letters, Joseph F. and Martha Ann's letters are records containing cultural, historical, linguistic, and social information. Not surprisingly, the letters are interwoven throughout with observations about family matters, including rather mundane concerns and incidents. Additionally, the letters are full of shared life experiences, including births, marriages, sicknesses, and deaths of immediate and extended family members and friends.

Maintaining good health without antibiotics and other advances in medicine during this period was a great concern. In a letter to his first cousin once removed, John L. Smith (1823–93), Joseph F. noted, "We have had the measles, colds, coughs, canker, and one thing and then another ever since last Dec. and are not thro' with it yet. Tho' we are getting somewhat accustomed to it. And are much better. I am fearful however that one of our little ones has the whopping cough and if so we have 6 more liable to take it. What the end may be no man knoweth!"[50]

As to be expected, there are also references to historically significant events—for example, the Utah War in 1857; the Church's actions to counteract the move by Walter M. Gibson (1822–88) to create an independent Latter-day Saint rogue colony in Hawai'i beginning in 1861; the visits of Alexander Smith (1838–1909) and David Smith (1844–1904), Joseph Smith and Emma Hale Smith's sons and Joseph F. and Martha Ann's cousins, to Salt Lake City in the 1860s when Alexander and David arrived as missionaries for the Reorganized Church of Jesus Christ of Latter Day Saints; the US government's legal campaign to end plural marriage in the 1880s; and the political situation in Utah following statehood in 1896.

S. George Ellsworth, a much-respected western, Utah, and Latter-day Saint historian and university professor, emphasizes the value of letters.

> Personal letters have a way of being quickly lost, misplaced, or purposely destroyed. Rare indeed are collections of significant family letters. Their preservation can be attributed to familial piety, a historic sense, sentimentality, accident, or just plain squirrel tendencies. Yet there is no more valuable record of personal reflections of events, institutions, and contemporary attitudes than the letter written from the heart and intended only for the eye of the receiver. The author of a journal, by the very act of maintaining entries, implies interest in the preservation of his life events for himself or posterity. Not so with letters. Hurriedly written, full of apologies for spelling or penmanship with promises to do better next time, the personal letter provides the only record of intimate conversation though taking place at a distance. Through letters one is permitted to glimpse into the heart of another's life and age.[51]

This is true of this remarkable family letter collection preserved by Martha Ann and her descendants and fellow Church members, to whom Martha Ann and Joseph F. were dedicated all their lives.

The letters of the last two decades, from about 1900 through 1916, become noticeably more sporadic, with much shorter content. Additionally, there are no extant letters from the last two years of Joseph F.'s life (1917–18). This is likely due to a combination of factors, including advances in communication. For example, in a letter written in June 1899, Joseph F. asked Martha Ann to respond by telegraph: "Want to do Temple-work next week for the Fieldings. Expect Rachel Burton

50. Joseph F. to John L. Smith, 21 May 1883.
51. Ellsworth, *Dear Ellen*, x.

down next Monday. Can you come? Let me know by Deseret wire.[52] All well here."[53] In another letter to Martha Ann written in 1911, Joseph F. noted that he sometimes used the telephone to relay information: "We will keep you posted by letter or phone as to his condition."[54]

Additionally, improved travel between Salt Lake City, where Joseph F. lived, and Provo, where Martha Ann lived, a relatively short distance of forty-five miles, made visits much easier during the last several decades of their lives. Also, Joseph F., as President of the Church, was no longer assigned to foreign missions that separated him from family in Utah for long periods of time, making it less critical to write letters to them.

Joseph F. Smith and party, ca. 1902–3. Courtesy of Anne Alice Smith Nebeker.

He often saw Martha Ann or members of her family during his frequent visits to Provo and visits by family to Salt Lake City. These visits would naturally allow Joseph F. to obtain information about Martha Ann's health and family concerns. Martha Ann, later in life, also traveled to Salt Lake City to attend general conference twice each year and generally stayed with Joseph F.

52. The Deseret Telegraph Company was formed in 1867 and connected Latter-day Saint settlements along the Wasatch Front, both north and south.
53. See Joseph F. to Martha Ann, 16 June 1899, herein.
54. See Joseph F. to Martha Ann, 6 November 1911, herein.

They both used their connections with other family members to keep in contact and expected that letters written to other family members would be shared among them. For example, Joseph F. noted in a letter to Martha Ann, dated 25 July 1857, "I wrote a long letter to Aunt Thompson yesterday-evening—gave her a short history of my travels for the last three or four months, it may b be interresting to you, if you have an oppertunity of hearing it."[55] In 1881 he asked his nephew William J. Harris Jr. to provide information to Martha Ann: "I did not write to your mother when our last baby was born, but you could tell her, what the baby was like as you saw it."[56] On another occasion, Julina Smith mentioned, "I am going to write a little to Martha Ann and send her the babies photograph."[57]

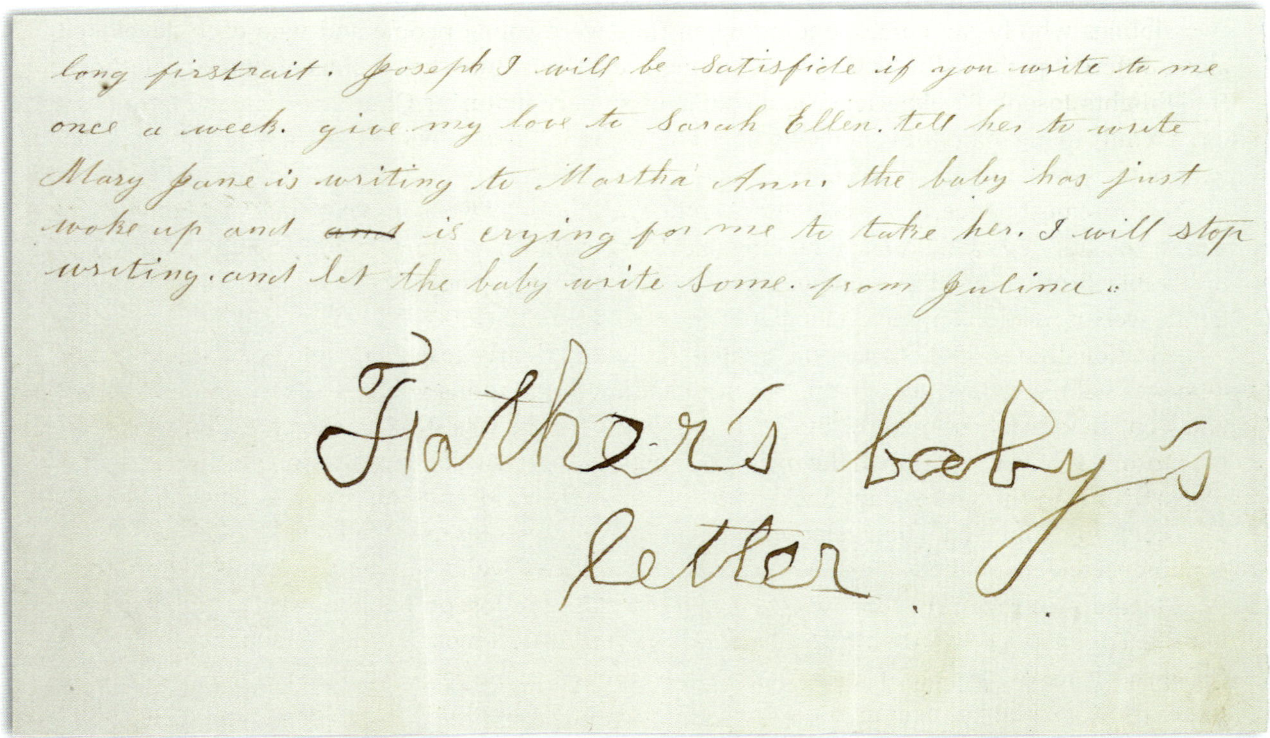
long firstrait. Joseph I will be Satisfide if you write to me
once a week. give my love to Sarah Ellen. tell her to write
Mary Jane is writing to Martha Ann. the baby has just
woke up and ~~and~~ is crying for me to take her. I will stop
writing. and let the baby write some. from Juline.

Father's baby's
letter.

Letter from Julina Smith to Joseph F., 23 April 1868 (reverse side). Julina mentions that their young daughter "Mary Jane is writing to Martha Ann." Apparently Mary Jane finishes the letter to Joseph F. Courtesy of CHL.

In a letter written to one of his sons, George Carlos Smith (1881–1931), Joseph F. asked him to contact Martha Ann's husband, William Jasper Harris (1836–1909), to request the use of his horse and buggy: "I intend to visit Provo tomorrow morning by Oregon Short Line. Meet us at the Station with Uncle William's buggy."[58]

During the fall of 1898, one of Joseph F.'s daughters was attending Brigham Young Academy. In his letters to her, he often made reference to his sister. In one letter Joseph F. thanked her for taking time to visit his sister and her family: "I am glad you go down to see Aunt Martha occasionally, and

55. Joseph F. to Martha Ann, 25 July 1857, herein.
56. Joseph F. to William J. Harris Jr., 9 September 1881.
57. Julina Smith to Joseph F., 17 May 1868.
58. Joseph F. to George C. Smith, 23 November 1898.

we all want to be remembered to her and to all the children."[59] Nearly three months later, he asked her to pass along his greetings to the family from whom she received room and board in Provo and to his sister: "With kind love to Bro. and Sister Boyden, to Aunt Martha and her family."[60]

In the later years of life Joseph F. and his sister had large families that naturally took more of their time, so it is not surprising that fewer letters between them were being written. Joseph F. observed in September 1895 the shifting nature of their letter writing: "Your favor of the 22nd inst. Came to hand on the 23rd inst. I did not expect an answer to my letter, therefore to hear from you was an unexpected surprise. In former years we corresponded once in a while, but of late this practice seems to have gone into disuse."[61]

The Joseph F. and Martha Ann letter collection provides insights into the relationship between two siblings who began corresponding when they were young people and who each developed along different paths in life as they were prematurely thrust into the responsibilities of adulthood. It highlights Joseph F.'s experience as a young missionary, maturing Church leader, and father of a large family living in multiple households.[62] The collection also provides insight into Martha Ann's experiences growing up in Salt Lake City and aging in Provo, where daily toil and survival were often of foremost concern. We also learn about Martha Ann's work in her family and community, where she fulfilled many roles, including provider, caregiver, supporter, and friend. Martha Ann, unlike her brother, lived in a monogamous household. Nevertheless, she was part of a complex family web of relationships as a member of the Hyrum Smith (1800–1844) family.

Additionally, the letter collection demonstrates very clearly Joseph F.'s role as an older brother who was willing to provide personal counsel and direction to his younger sister, and later to her children, on a variety of matters. Surprisingly, even when he was still a teenager, the letters reveal that Joseph F. had also assumed the role of Martha Ann's parents, both father and mother. This may be partly due to the siblings' unique position as the only children of Hyrum and Mary Fielding.[63] This certainly influenced their relationship in positive ways—Joseph F. felt deeply responsible and genuinely concerned about Martha's temporal and spiritual welfare and her personal happiness.

Martha Ann regularly acknowledged her gratitude for Joseph F.'s attention to the details of her life. For example, in 1874 Martha Ann wrote, "to my truest most faithfull friend that I have had sence the death of my dear Mother you have never forsaken me you have been more than a brother to me you have filled as near as could bee the plase of a Father I do feel greatfull to you for all you have done and may the God we try to sirve reward you for I never can more than bee greatfull."[64]

As in most family relationships, Martha Ann and Joseph F. did not always understand each other. Complex family relationships naturally complicated their own relationship from time to time. Joseph F. mentioned one such situation in 1898: "I was very sorry you left us so abruptly on the morning you went away. It was so unnecessary—but of course we are all <u>free agents</u>, and will

59. Joseph F. to Alice Smith, 24 September 1898.

60. Joseph F. to Alice Smith, 12 December 1898.

61. Joseph F. to Martha Ann, 27 September 1895, herein.

62. Joseph F. and Martha Ann's many letters to other people have also survived. For letters by Martha Ann, see Carole Call King, "History of Martha Ann Smith Harris, 1841–1923" (unpublished manuscript in editors' possession), 97–100, 141–44, 294–95, 302–3.

63. Hyrum's older children, Joseph F. and Martha Ann's half siblings, also took interest in their welfare. However, Joseph F. never fully trusted his older half brother John's ability to handle finances and manage his life; see letters from Joseph F. to John Smith in the CHL (MS 2861). Additionally, Mercy Fielding Thompson also served as a surrogate mother to her niece and nephew.

64. Martha Ann to Joseph F., 31 May 1874, herein.

only be held for our voluntery acts. I did not follow you to the Depot—for the reason you made <it> unwise if not impossible for me to do so. You had a full half hour, I should think, to wait at the station before the train started. We were all sorry to have you leave us feeling as you did. I hope your feelings may change when you know us better."[65]

However, their lifelong commitment and loyalty to one another allowed them to soothe any tension they may have had at specific times. Throughout the letters, Joseph F. is acutely aware that his life had often provided him opportunities that his sister did not enjoy. In 1869 he wrote, "I feel condemned sometimes when I see the comfortable situation of my family and know that my own sister does not enjoy as much."[66] In 1877 he also noted, "I wish you were as strong and healthy as I am, and as well or better clad."[67] As they grew older, his feelings became even more tender as he considered Martha Ann's deteriorating health and seemingly never-ending financial challenges.

Despite Joseph F.'s own pressing financial concerns as his own family grew in size, he was nevertheless mindful of Martha Ann's situation.[68] Highlighting Joseph F.'s efforts to assist Martha Ann, the letters mention gifts he sent from time to time, including for weddings and births, and especially during the holidays.[69] Additionally, through the letters we discover that at some point Joseph F. provided Martha Ann a monthly allowance, which increased over time to help her make ends meet.[70] In the end Joseph F., despite his distinct advantages in life, admired his sister for her tenacity and endurance. For example, he noted in his diary a letter he had received in 1862 from his Aunt Zina Huntington, who praised Martha Ann: "Martha Ann was up last evening to see us. Looks stately and fine as ever, one of God's noble women. If you could see those noble boys of her, it would do your soul very good. Men in miniature."[71]

For Martha Ann, these letters provide insight into the day-to-day struggles of survival on the pioneer frontier. She is very much self-aware. For example, she wrote Joseph F. in 1863, "I am not a very good writer which you are well aware off but what I write ill composed as it is comes from my heart and I mean it I may not not have the languege of some nor the talent for writing that this will ed<i>fye a preson say ferinstence <that> Levira[72] has but my life has been far differenty spent to what hrs has been I have had to earn my bred by hard labor ever sence my m<o>thr died[73] I have ben obliged to work hard and it does not have a tendencey to refine any ones mind to such things."[74]

Her letters also provide a woman's view of life's rhythms—marriage, childbearing, sickness, family financial concerns, and death.[75] She does not provide counsel or direction to her older brother; she clearly sees her role as one who receives counsel, direction, and help. The nineteenth- and early

65. Joseph F. to Martha Ann, 13 October 1898, herein.
66. Joseph F. to Martha Ann, 24 December 1869, herein.
67. Joseph F. to Martha Ann, 25 August 1877, herein.
68. For example, Joseph F. borrowed five hundred dollars to pay taxes in 1895 and sold some property at a loss the following year to again pay taxes; see Smith and Kenney, *From Prophet to Son*, 30. Nevertheless, he purchased train tickets for Martha Ann and William during this economically challenging period; see Joseph F. to Martha Ann, 16 November 1896, herein.
69. See other examples: Joseph F. to Martha Ann, 1 February 1906, 24 December 1910, and 19 December 1916, herein.
70. See Joseph F. to Martha Ann, 8 March 1907, herein.
71. See Joseph F., journal, 9 April 1862.
72. Levira Annette Clark Smith.
73. Mary Fielding Smith, Joseph F. and Martha Ann's mother, died on 21 September 1852.
74. Martha Ann to Joseph F., 3 April 1863, herein.
75. Her letters may provide additional perspectives into the male-female dynamics within the broader Latter-day Saint marriage structure.

twentieth-century context reveals much about the multifaceted relationship Joseph F. and Martha Ann experienced over a long period.

Pen and paper served to strengthen the bond between Joseph F. and Martha Ann throughout their lives. That they preserved some of their letters is not surprising since for many people of that era letters often became a representative keepsake of a loved one who was far away. A special letter was often carried with a person or tucked under a pillow as a means of embracing a cherished personal connection.

Because Martha Ann remained in Utah, many of Joseph F.'s letters were preserved. Since he was on the road, traveling from continent to continent during the 1850s, 1860s, and 1870s, some of her letters to him did not survive. This was also true for the difficult years of the second half of the 1880s when Joseph F. was on the move and in hiding to avoid prosecution for plural marriage.

As noted above, the letter collections range in date over nearly six decades, from 1854, when Joseph F. first arrived in the Sandwich Islands, to 1916, just two years before his death. The nearly lifelong personal correspondence between Joseph F. and Martha Ann demonstrates a brother and sister who cared deeply for each other—a brother who was concerned for the well-being of his younger sister and a sister who adored her older brother.

Envelope for letter from Martha Ann to Joseph F., 29 July 1856, with a postmark of 5 August 1856. Courtesy of CHL.

Another important aspect of the collection is that many of the original envelopes from Joseph F.'s letters were preserved by Martha Ann and subsequently by her family. At first, letters were folded and sealed with wax so they could be sent without a cover (envelope). Eventually, innovation produced machines that made envelopes relatively inexpensive. Advances in making postal stamps, coupled with postal reforms in the United States, allowed an increasing number of Americans to communicate with family, friends, and others. Joseph F. and Martha Ann took advantage of these advances, as demonstrated by the letters, envelopes, and postal services they used to communicate with each other.

This publication includes all known letters written between Joseph F. and Martha Ann from 1854 to 1916. During that time, there are just nine years of correspondence for which no known record of their communication exists (1859, 1865–67, 1882, 1889, 1903–4, and 1908). The historical overview and introduction to the letters for each decade, along with the footnotes included with each letter, provide illuminating context. The following chart summarizes the locations from which the letters were sent and the approximate years in which they were written.

LETTERS FROM JOSEPH F. SMITH TO MARTHA ANN SMITH HARRIS

Place of origin	*Number of letters*
Sandwich Islands [Hawaiian Islands] (1854–58)	13
Salt Lake City, Utah, USA (1858)	1
British Isles [Great Britain] (1860–63)	8
Sandwich Islands [Hawaiian Islands] (1864)	2
Salt Lake City, Utah, USA (1868–74)	33
British Isles [Great Britain] (1874–75)	10
Salt Lake City, Utah, USA (1875–76)	3
British Isles [Great Britain] (1877)	1
Salt Lake City, Utah, USA (1877–84)	16
No address provided (1877–84)	7
Sacramento, California, USA (1885)	1
Sandwich Islands [Hawaiian Islands] (1885)	4
No address provided (1887)	1
Salt Lake City, Utah, USA (1890–1916)	40
No address provided (1890–1916)	53
Total	**193**[76]

LETTERS FROM MARTHA ANN SMITH HARRIS TO JOSEPH F. SMITH

Place of origin	*Number of letters*
Salt Lake City, Utah, USA (1854–67)	23
No address provided (1854–67)	3
Provo, Utah, USA (1868–1916)	20
No address provided (1868–1916)	2
Total	**48**

Total Letters between Joseph F. and Martha Ann **241**

76. An incomplete letter found in the CHL (Carole C. King Collection, 1854–1916, MS 16763, fragment 4) consists of four pages of a larger letter. These pages represent pages two, three, four, and five as indicated by the last page being marked as "Page 5." This letter is in Joseph F.'s handwriting. These pages are undated and do not contain a general greeting or salutation. Internal evidence suggests that this was written while Joseph F. was serving his first mission in England (1860–63), because it mentions his wife Levira and compares the weather of England and America. There are twelve lines before Joseph F. begins a new paragraph, "Dear William." This is followed by ninety-three lines apparently addressed to William Jasper Harris. This may be a letter within a letter and, if so, could be to Martha Ann. But because of the uncertainty, we have not included this fragment as part of the collection, and it is not represented in the numbers above.

WRITING SKILLS AND IMPROVEMENT

It is clear that both Joseph F. and Martha Ann lacked the benefits of long-term formal educational opportunities, as the letters are full of spelling, grammar, syntax, and mechanical errors. Joseph F. estimated the extent of his formal education to have been just a little over three years.[77]

For example, in an early letter to Martha Ann, Joseph F. counseled her to improve her writing even as he was trying to improve himself: "I hope that the school will soon start again that you can keepe going as much as posible. I want to see you improve in writing, and every thing els, when you write take pains and make the letters all plain and destinct, and be shure to spell all of the words right that you can; . . . now I will worant that if you will go to school with a prayerful heart, and your mind on your studies, insted of being upon play and folly, that you will learn faster than ever you did in your life before. the thing of it is be prayerful, pray morning and night."[78]

Later in life, when he became more proficient, Joseph F. still noted that he was not a good speller but offered advice about writing so that his children would be better than he was: "I do not attempt to counsel your spelling because I am a good speller myself, but only because I would like you to spell and write better than I."[79]

A brief review of the original 1850s letters demonstrates that Joseph F. and Martha Ann began with about the same command of English and writing skills. Their spelling, grammar, usage, mechanics, and calligraphy clearly reveal a lack of formal and informal education. Given their life experiences from their births to 1854, this is not surprising. They lived in several frontier communities that were brand-new or recently established; they both worked to assist the family with chores and responsibilities that were sometimes only expected of older children and adults; they were unable to follow a daily schedule, which included attending school, on a regular basis; they did not live in a house for significant periods of time; and finally, they experienced many tragic events, including the murder of their father and the early death of their mother.

Scholars have observed that immigration and migration impacted nineteenth-century frontier culture.[80] Generally accepted social niceties and cultural refinements were either forgotten entirely or so weakened that children struggled to completely assimilate them. It was the nineteenth century after all, and pioneering only added to the challenge of creating a refined society with all of the opportunities that a more stable community could afford children.

Joseph F. improved dramatically in his language ability and calligraphy. His mission diaries from the 1850s reveal important themes that are also highlighted in his letters to Martha Ann. Joseph F. became a voracious reader of books, newspapers, and other items that came into his hands. He also practiced his writing by keeping a daily journal and maintaining a remarkable correspondence with numerous people, and he used a dictionary and other sources to increase his vocabulary.[81] Lists of new words are found on envelopes and in notebooks and journals. His letters and journals show that he used these new words often and that they became familiar to him. By 1916, when the last letters in this collection were prepared, Joseph F. had become a skilled orator and writer with a rich vocabulary. He was able to draw from a wide variety of published materials, including poems, hymns, biographies, and other reading material. In the end, Joseph F. was indefatigable in

77. See Kenney, "Before the Beard," 26.
78. Joseph F. to Martha Ann, 18 October 1855, herein.
79. Joseph F. to Hyrum M. Smith, 17 December 1896; see Smith and Kenney, *From Prophet to Son*, 52.
80. See Stanley B. Kimball, *Historic Sites and Markers along the Mormon and Other Great Western Trails* (Urbana: University of Illinois Press, 1988).
81. See Ricks, *"My Candid Opinion,"* xiv–xvi.

his effort to improve and learn. Taysom notes, "I am dazzled by his intellect and his unbreakable will."[82] Reading this collection of letters will most likely confirm Taysom's assessment.

Martha Ann, on the other hand, remained at about the same skill level and may have lost some of her calligraphy skills, as one might expect, in the last decades of her life. Limited in life opportunities of traveling and exposure to a wide variety of print culture, she instead spent most of her time raising a family, including grandchildren and great-grandchildren. Martha Ann's daily work was often of a different kind than that of her brother. Working with her hands to sew in limited lighting made it more challenging to pick up a book, keep a journal, or write many letters. That she wrote letters to a variety of people is not surprising given she was a member of an important Latter-day Saint family. However, buying a new pen or paper was sometimes impossible—choosing bread over writing supplies was not a hard decision.[83] To help defray these extra expenses in later life, Joseph F. sent her self-addressed stamped envelopes. He added a handwritten postscript in a typed letter to Martha Ann in 1896: "Please find herewith a stamped Envelope."[84] Given her struggles and limited opportunities, we are fortunate that she chose to write even when she was reluctant to do so.

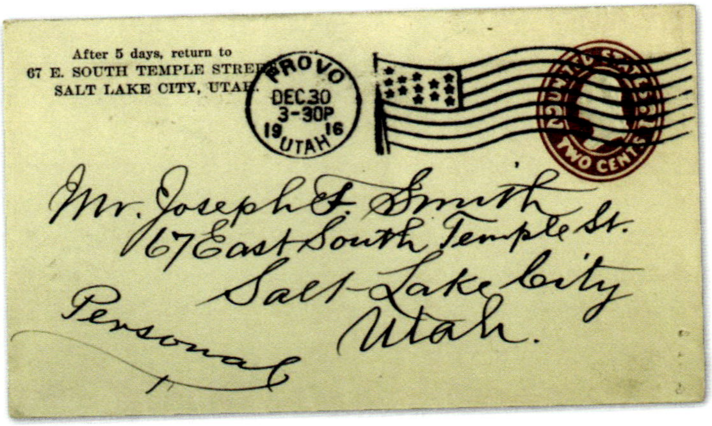

A prestamped, self-addressed envelope in Joseph F.'s hand. Postmarked 20 December 1916, it was sent to Martha Ann so she could write Joseph F. without incurring expense. Courtesy of CHL.

The collection also reveals much about a period of great transition in Latter-day Saint history. Joseph F. and Martha Ann not only witnessed but also participated in the events that brought the exiled Latter-day Saints to the Great Basin seeking refuge from persecution. Their lives also spanned the early decades of the twentieth century, when the Church was becoming a somewhat respected American religious institution.

Most telling throughout their six decades of correspondence are Joseph F.'s reflections and personal counsel to his sister about his mission and Church experiences, his perspectives on education and local and national political events, his thoughts on proclaiming the gospel of Jesus Christ, his profound grief after the death of a child, his devotion to his family and the Church, and the gratitude and love he and his sister shared for each other. Additional insights can be gained from a careful analysis of these letters. Certainly, future studies on a variety of topics will benefit from this remarkably rich collection of personal letters.[85]

82. Bowman, "Scholarly Inquiry."

83. For Willie, Martha Ann's son, Joseph F. supplied pens, paper, envelopes, and stamps to help defray the cost of writing letters to him. See Joseph F. to Martha Ann, 18 January 1870; and Martha Ann to Joseph F., 13 December 1916, herein. Martha Ann was also running a household and often had little spare time for self-improvement.

84. Joseph F. to Martha Ann, 21 April 1896, herein.

85. See, for example, David M. Whitchurch, "The Pedagogy of a Church Leader: Lessons Learned from Joseph F. Smith's 1854–1916 Letters to His Sister, Martha Ann Smith Harris," *Religious Educator* 2, no. 2 (2001): 83–107.

JOSEPH F.'S LETTERS

The letters between Joseph F. and Martha Ann are part of a much larger collection of correspondence written and received by him. Many of these letters are preserved in public and private repositories, primarily the Church History Library. A brief review of these various collections reveals that Joseph F. was a prolific letter writer, as noted above. For example, between 1895 and 1914, Joseph F. wrote hundreds of letters to twelve missionary sons. Some 334 copies of these letters alone are preserved in the Church History Library, with additional original letters in the private possession of descendants.[86]

A comparison between the letters written to his missionary sons and those sent to his sister reveals Joseph F.'s effort to encourage improvement and offer suggestions and corrections regarding grammar and spelling. As their father, he was going to provide encouragement to each of them to improve their communication skills.

Another interesting facet of Joseph F.'s correspondence collection is a number of letters partly or fully written in Hawaiian. These are written to or received from Church members in Hawai'i, a missionary son, and those living in the Hawaiian settlement of Iosepa in Skull Valley, Tooele County, Utah.[87]

Interestingly, a selection of his letters was published in Joseph F.'s lifetime.[88] During the nineteenth century, it was a common practice in the Church to publish letters from missions, emigrating companies (both land and ocean), and Church leaders.[89]

Of special note, Joseph F. dictated two letters on 24 May 1918 into a recording machine, preserving his voice for future generations to hear. One letter was addressed to President Joseph Eckersley (1866–1960), a stake president living in Loa, Wayne County, Utah.[90] The other was addressed to his son Calvin Schwartz (1890–1966), who was an army chaplain stationed at Camp Lewis, a US military installation located about nine miles south-southwest of Tacoma, Pierce County, Washington. Extracts from both letters were published in 1972 after the recording was discovered in Salt Lake City.[91]

The letter to Calvin shows how Joseph F. handled the numerous letters that flooded to him: "I have received this morning your most welcome favor and have read its contents with a great deal of interest. Your mother was here this morning while the letter was being read to me and was extremely pleased to hear from you."[92] Although this letter had been read to him (implying secretarial assistance), for much of Joseph F.'s life most of his letter writing had been done without a secretary or stenographer. For example, Joseph F. responded to a son's request to obtain more help in 1905: "In your letter of July 21st answering mine of June 30, you give me a good lecture on taking

86. See Smith and Kenney, *From Prophet to Son,* 89.

87. Located about seventy-five miles southwest of Salt Lake City in Skull Valley, Iosepa (the Hawaiian equivalent for *Joseph*) was a Latter-day Saint Polynesian settlement established primarily for Hawaiian members who had immigrated to Utah beginning in 1889. More than two hundred people lived in the community before it was abandoned following the plans to build a temple at Lā'ie, O'ahu, Hawai'i, in 1917. See Matthew Kester, *Remembering Iosepa: History, Place, and Religion in the American West* (New York: Oxford University Press, 2013).

88. See, for example, "Extracts from Letters of Elder Joseph F. Smith to His Family," *Woman's Exponent* 6, no. 9 (1 October 1877), 67.

89. See, for example, Reid L. Neilson and Nathan N. Waite, eds., *Settling the Valley, Proclaiming the Gospel: The General Epistles of the Mormon First Presidency* (New York: Oxford University Press), 2017.

90. An excerpt is available via YouTube: http://www.youtube.com/watch?v=BZcMP6flPuc.

91. The location of the original recording cylinder is unknown at this time.

92. "Record Transcription," *New Era*, January 1972, 66.

care of myself and of having a stenographer to assist me in writing my letters, &c. All of which I accept in the loveliest kindness. But my son, I never yet put upon another any burden I was not willing to carry myself."[93] This insight makes his large body of correspondence all the more remarkable.

To keep up with a large amount of correspondence, Joseph F. asked the Salt Lake City postmaster, Arthur L. Thomas (1851–1924), to "arrange for three deliveries of mail daily to the Church office at about 9 and 11:30 a.m., and 4 p.m. and for collecting daily, the last, about 6:30 p.m."[94]

In several letters, Joseph F. talks about the challenges he faced in keeping up with his correspondence. Later in life, as a counselor to Church Presidents, Joseph F. naturally placed their requests above other considerations. For example, he wrote to son David Asael Smith (1879–1952) a letter but was required to end it early: "Bro. [Lorenzo] Snow has called for me, so I will have to conclude this letter."[95]

In many letters, Joseph F. mentions his habit in later life to write to family members late in the evening: "I have been very busy today . . . but have not had time. It's now after 8 p.m. and I have not had my dinner."[96] Having received a letter on 13 December 1898 from his daughter Edna Melissa Smith (1879–1958), who was attending Brigham Young Academy in Provo, Utah, he responded on 16 December: "I have been so busy I could not get a moment during office hours to write you. It is now just 8 p.m. All are gone from the office long ago except the guard and myself."[97]

In a letter dated 12 July 1899, Joseph F. wrote Louise Emily Shurtliff Smith (1876–1908), his daughter-in-law, a short letter that provides insight into his efforts to communicate with family members. At the time, his son Joseph Fielding Smith (1876–1972) was serving a full-time mission in the British Isles. Joseph F. wrote, "I have concluded to put an end, at least temporarily, to the admonition of my consciences and the prompting of my desire to writ you a few words. I have been O so busy—all the time and have so many 'irons in the fire', that I have neglected to write, and have keenly felt condemned for it. We are all usually well. I am alone in the office, and it is 8 pm."[98]

In 1908 he noted in a letter to his son E. Wesley Smith (1886–1970), who was serving a mission in Hawai'i at the time, "I am devoting a portion of this sabbath day to the task of answering letters. My time is so much occupied during working hours from day to day that I have but little time, and that generally after I should be a rest in bed for correspondence, I am availing myself today of the services of your brother Joseph F. to assist me in replying to communications from mission fields and elsewhere to which I feel bound to reply."[99]

As we began this project, we examined a number of entries in Joseph F.'s diaries along with the corresponding letters written at the same time. In some instances, Joseph F.'s letters provide more details than his diaries; this is especially true of the latter period of his life. In one specific case, the letters are the only record written by his own hand of his activities that have been preserved.[100]

Of course, in many other cases, Joseph F.'s journals record daily experiences over multiple days, weeks, and months and therefore present a much more comprehensive word picture of his daily life and concerns. The letters between him and another person cannot provide such a picture because large gaps of time exist between each letter. However, because Joseph F. kept a remarkable

93. Joseph F. to Alvin F. Smith, 10 August 1905; and Smith and Kenney, *From Prophet to Son*, 89.
94. Joseph F. to Arthur L. Thomas, 30 September 1898.
95. Joseph F. to David A. Smith, 12 December 1898.
96. Joseph F. to George C. Smith, 8 November 1898.
97. Joseph F. to Edna M. Smith, 16 December 1898.
98. Joseph F. to Louise S. Smith, 12 July 1899.
99. Joseph F. to E. Wesley Smith, 17 May 1908.
100. As noted above, his diaries for the period from his arrival in Hawai'i in September 1854 to the end of 1855 were lost in a fire in June 1856, so his letters from that period are important to help reconstruct his personal history.

Joseph F. Smith at a writing desk, ca. 1916. Courtesy of CHL.

correspondence schedule, a study of his incoming and outgoing letters provides a remarkable and fuller view of his world, concerns, and insights. In many of his letters, he goes well beyond most of his journal entries on specific subjects.

MARTHA ANN'S LETTERS

Although not as voluminous as Joseph F.'s letter collection,[101] Martha Ann's collection is remarkable because it spans the time from when she was a teenager in the 1850s to when she approached the end of her life in the early 1920s.[102] The hundreds of extant letters provide a window into her life and experiences as a member of a complex, multigenerational family network throughout her life.

An examination of the letters she received and retained reveals Martha Ann's participation in extended conversations with family, friends, and associates.[103] For example, in early 1923 E. Wesley Smith (1886–1970), who was serving as president of the Hawaiian Mission, wrote:

> Our Beloved Aunt Martha: How happy and extremely delighted we were to received your excellent letter, so full of good cheer and encouragement. We highly appreciate this letter, coming from you, in your own handwriting, an own sister to our beloved father. . . . Your big generous heart is manifest in this letter. Oh, what a wonderful spirit you have; always thinking about other people, sympathizing with them; praying for them and wishing blessings upon their heads, always desiring to be helpful and striving to aid. All these expressions of love from you have more than repaid us for any little thing we may have done in your behalf in the past.[104]

Unfortunately, most of the letters Martha Ann wrote were not retained or did not survive. As already mentioned, we know of at least eighty letters she wrote to Joseph F. that are not extant.

Toward the end of her life, Martha Ann wrote what would become her last surviving letter. At the time, Martha Ann's grandson John Clifford Harris (1900–49) was serving in the Southern States Mission. In a ten-page letter addressed to John's friend Francis Joanna Sherrell Spears (1880–1956) of Cookeville, Tennessee, she shared her testimony of the restored gospel, her reminiscences of the Prophet Joseph Smith and her father, Patriarch Hyrum Smith, and thanked Joanna for showing kindness to her grandson.[105]

Given the realities of nineteenth-century pioneer life, Martha Ann's reluctance to write (owing to her poor penmanship and spelling),[106] the loss of her earliest letters to fire, and the vagaries of preserving family letters through succeeding generations, it is remarkable that we have as many of her letters as we do—more than seventy in all and as many as three hundred letters she received from friends and family members, including her brother Joseph F.[107]

101. Like Joseph F.'s letter collection, Martha Ann's letters are mostly found in the Church History Library, with a few others scattered among family members.
102. See Martha Ann to Joseph F., 31 January 1856, herein; and Martha Ann to Joanna Spears, [Fall] 1920.
103. Martha Ann also engaged in a lifetime correspondence with many of her extended family members, in particular her sisters-in-law, the wives of Joseph F. See, for example, Martha Ann to Julina Smith, 21 December 1889.
104. E. Wesley Smith to Martha Ann, 27 January 1923; original spelling preserved.
105. Martha Ann to Joanna Spears, 1920.
106. See, for example, Martha Ann to Joseph F., 2 March 1856, herein; and Joseph F. to Martha Ann, 12 November 1883, herein.
107. In Martha Ann's letter collection are a number of letters written to her that mention additional letters she had written that are not extant. As noted, Joseph F. mentioned as many as eighty letters he had received from Martha Ann that have not survived.

Editorial Method

We had several audiences in mind as we prepared this volume. First there are the descendants of Joseph F. and Martha Ann. Another audience is those who are interested in the Latter-day Saint past but who are not trained historians. We have also kept in mind our academic colleagues. For family members and armchair historians, we have provided a general overview and historical introductions for the six decades. Our university colleagues will not find much new in these general overviews. However, we have provided accurate transcriptions of the letters and annotations for professional historians who may want to draw on this important letter collection to produce interpretive works.[1]

All letters between Joseph F. and his sister Martha Ann were carefully transcribed following a systematized process to ensure reliability and accuracy of transcription. The letters retain the original spelling, superscripts, underlines, and strike-throughs. Some punctuation has been added for clarity. In most cases, when an individual is first mentioned in the letter collection, the reader is provided with a short summary of the person and his or her connection to Joseph F. and Martha Ann. For additional information, the reader is referred to the biographical register, appendix D. Wherever necessary, footnotes have been added to clarify potentially confusing references to individuals mentioned in the letters. This is especially true when only a first or last name is mentioned in a letter that could refer to more than one person. For example, twenty-one people mentioned in the letters have the first name of John. Whenever this happens, a footnote clarifies which John is referred to, if known. In most instances, to save space in the footnotes, biographical details including birth dates, marriage dates, and death dates are found in appendix D. Entries in the biographical register are organized by surname given at the time of birth. Women are listed by maiden name as given in the footnotes.

1. Reid L. Neilson, ed., *In the Whirlpool: The Pre-Manifesto Letters of President Wilford Woodruff to the William Atkin Family, 1885–1890* (Norman, OK: Arthur H. Clark Company, 2011), 21–22.

TOP MARGINS

The salutation, date, and other information appear in various positions in the original letters. In the transcription, all introductory information has been placed flush left at the top of the page. All line endings above the greetings have been honored. One such example can be seen in Joseph F.'s letter dated 22 June 1864:

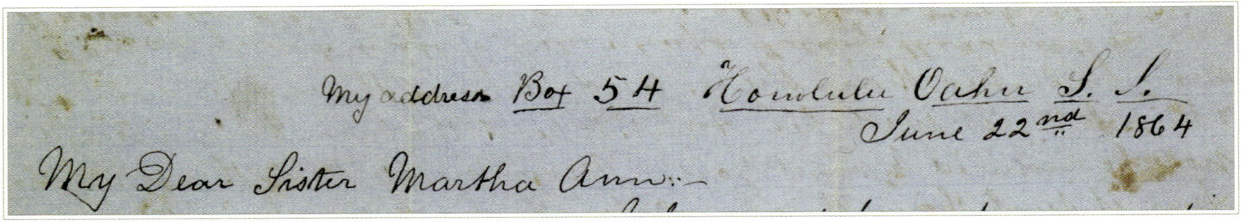

My address Box 54 Honolulu Oahu S.I.
June 22nd 1864

My Dear Sister Martha Ann:—
I have not heard from you since I left, only that Hyrum was sick, but mending. And that William

SIGNATURES

Signatures in the original letters are found in different positions: centered, adjusted right, along the margin, and so on. In the transcribed letters, the signatures have most often been placed flush left. Exceptions were made for letters in which Joseph F. signed his name on the final line of the body of the letter. For example, in his 9 June 1855 letter, Joseph F.'s signature appears below the paragraph, as seen in the first example below. The second example comes from a letter dated 21 June 1869, in which Joseph F. signed his name on the same line as his concluding sentence.

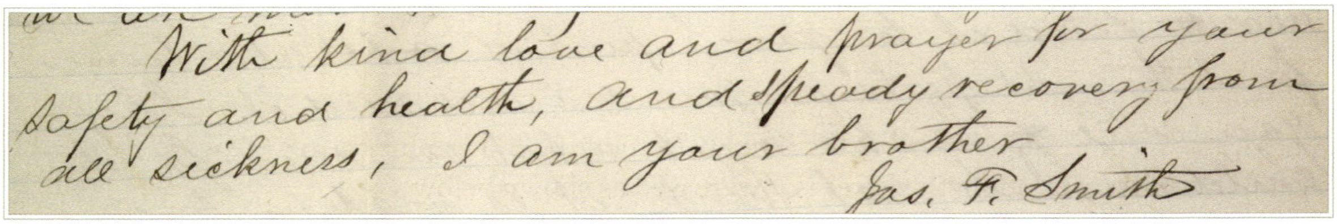

With kind love and prayer for your safety and health, and speady recovery from all sickness. I am your brother
Jos. F. Smith

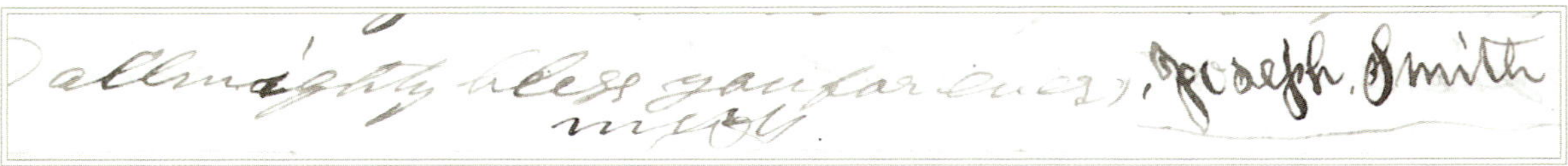

allmighty bless you for everr. Joseph Smith

PERIODS AND COMMAS

It is often difficult to distinguish between commas and periods in the original letters. In cases where it was impossible to clearly distinguish the two (a frequent occurrence throughout Joseph F.'s letters) and either form of punctuation would be appropriate, the transcribers have made a decision based on modern grammatical rules in keeping with the context of the letter. Two examples are listed below using the letters dated 14 July 1856 and 1 November 1854, respectively.

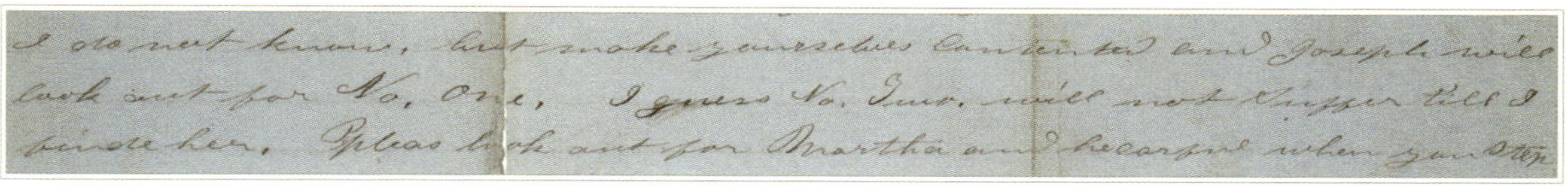

I do not know, but make yourselves contented and Joseph will look out for No. One. I guess No. Two, will not suffer till I finde her. <P>please look out for Martha and be carful when you step

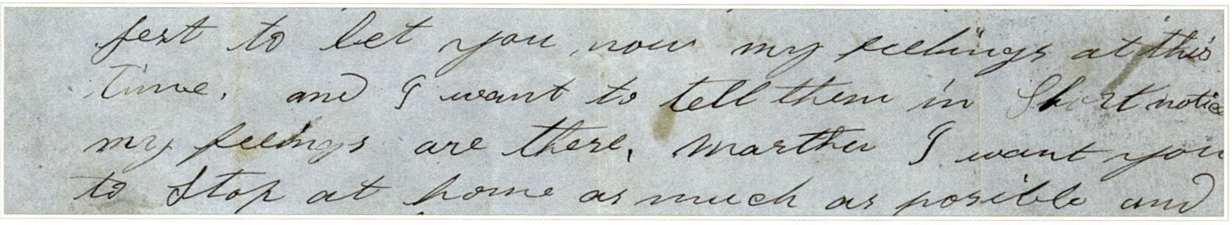

jest to let you now my feelings at this time, and I want to tell them in short notice my feelings are there. Martha I want you to stop at home as much as possible and

CAPITALIZATION

Both Joseph F. and particularly Martha Ann used upper- and lowercase letters arbitrarily throughout their letters, with no clear pattern or rule in mind. In order to minimize reader distraction, capital letters within a sentence have been transcribed as lowercase. Martha Ann inconsistently used the capital letters *D*, *F*, *J*, *L*, *M*, and *S*, while Joseph F. inconsistently used the capital letters *A*, *J*, *L*, *M*, and *S*. For example, in his letter dated 18 October 1855, Joseph F. writes the word *sharp* with a capital *S*. In transcription, the letter is lowercased as shown below.

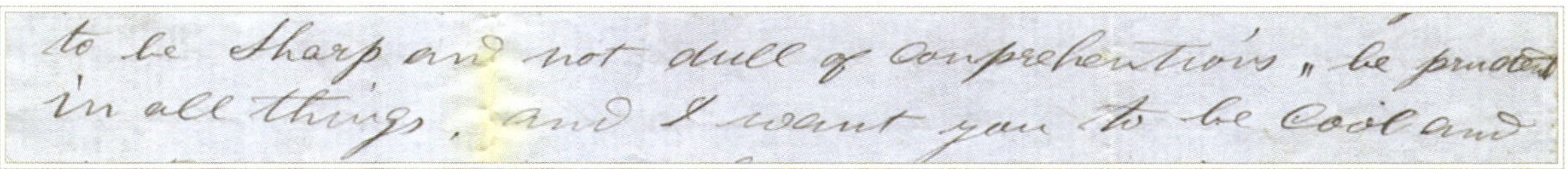

to be sharp and not dull of comprehentions, be prudent in all things, and I want you to be cool and

PAGINATION

A standard format of [**p. x**] is used to distinguish new pages of the letter (where *x* represents the page number at the top of a new page). The page number is placed within the transcribed text precisely where the page break occurs in the letter. For example, in the letter of 21 June 1869, the page ends after the word *closed*.

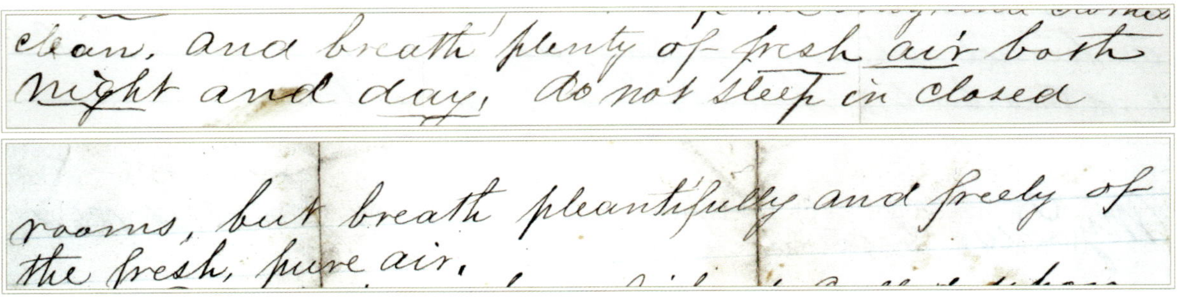
clean, and breath plenty of fresh air both night and day, do not sleep in closed
rooms, but breath pleantifully and freely of the fresh, pure air.

clean. and breath plenty of fresh air both night and day, do not sleep in closed [**p. 2**] rooms, but breath pleantifully and freely of the fresh, pure air.

It was not uncommon, however, for Joseph F. and Martha Ann to end a page midword, as demonstrated in the 25 July 1857 letter, in which the word *remember* is split between two pages. In such cases, the page number has been inserted midword.

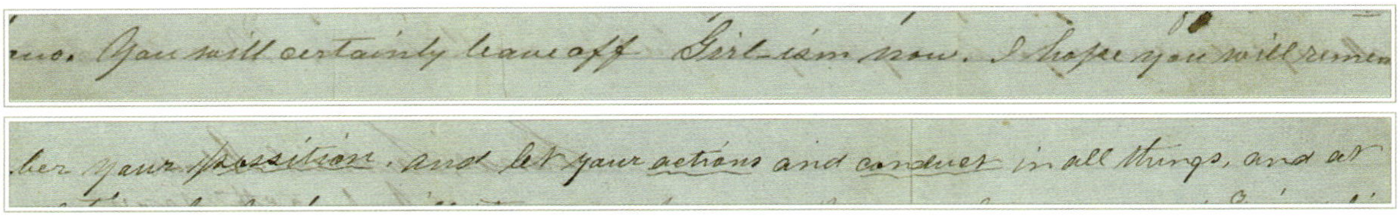
ous. You will certainly leave off Girl-ism now. I hope you will remem
ber your possition, and let your actions and conduct in all things, and at

ous. You will certainly leave off Girl-ism now. I hope you will remem[**p. 2**]ber your possition, and let your actions and conduct in all things, and at

LINE ENDINGS AND PARAGRAPHS

Broken words that begin on one line and finish on the next, or words that end a line with a portion of the word written above or below it, have been joined to read as a single word. For example, in the letter of 25 July 1857, a portion of the word *posible* ends on one line and continues on the next, as shown below.

recieved no answers— just emulate her hand write, Martha— as neer as pos
ible— she writes first rate. devote as much time as posible in learning to write.

recieved no answers—just emulate her hand write, Martha—as neer as posible—she writes first rate. devote as much time as posible in learning to write.

Paragraphs in the original manuscript have been indented in the transcription for clarity, regardless of the page justification on the original letter. Actual line endings are not included in the transcribed letters.

DASH

Joseph F. used dashes abundantly, often in place of a comma or a period. To simplify the transcription process and to avoid trying to determine whether his dashes represent commas or periods, the transcribers used modern grammar conventions to distinguish actual dashes from the other use. A dash followed by a space represents a comma or a period, while a dash with no space represents an actual dash. Three examples are provided below. In the first, the dash seems to function more like a period, and in the second, the dash seems to function more like a comma. The third example shows a dash that appears to function more like an actual dash. The following examples are respectively taken from the 7 December 1870, 1 March 1862, and 17 August 1869 letters.

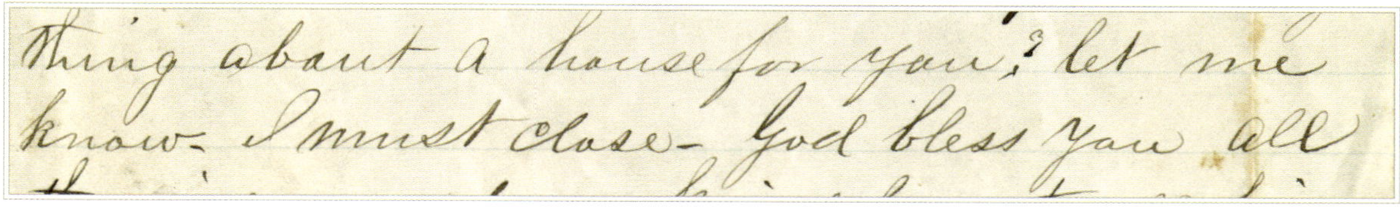

thing about a house for you? Let me know. I must close— God bless you all

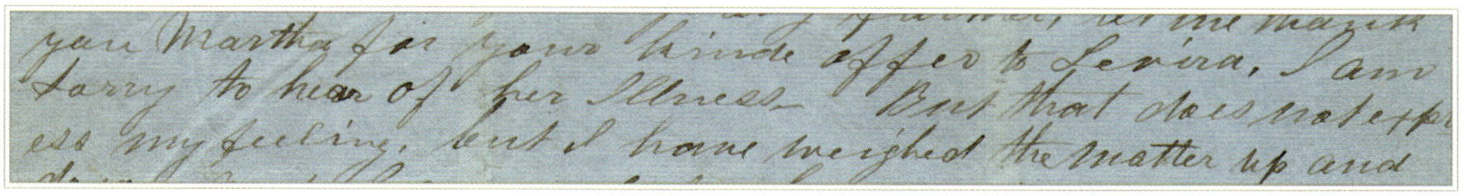

you Martha for your kinde offer to Levira. I am sorry to hear of her Illness— But that does not express my feeling, but I have weighed the matter up and

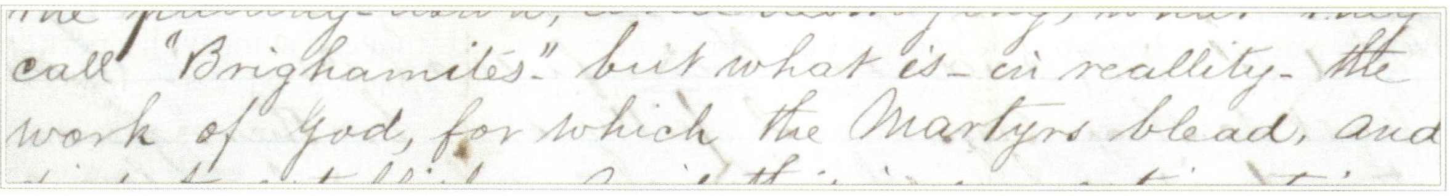

call "Brighamites," but what is—in reallity—the work of God, for which the Martyrs blead, and

SYMBOLS

The following table lists the symbols used to represent elements of the letters that could not be transcribed. Examples from various letters follow.

symbol		description
[*italics*]	italics within brackets	used to describe missing words, partially missing words, or missing letters due to holes, tears, or cuts in the paper; also used to describe illegible portions from strike-through or erasure.
[◊]	diamond within brackets	single illegible letter in a word
[◊̶]	diamond with strike-through within brackets	single illegible letter stricken out in a word
[◊◊]	two diamonds within brackets	two or more illegible letters within a word
< >	angle brackets	readable strike-through, insertion, or correction

[Italics]—Missing Words and Letters

Missing words, partially missing words, or missing letters owing to holes, tears, or cuts in the paper are represented with the dimensions of the missing portion italicized within brackets. One example is found in Joseph F.'s first letter in the collection, dated 17 October 1854, where the upper right-hand corner has been cut.

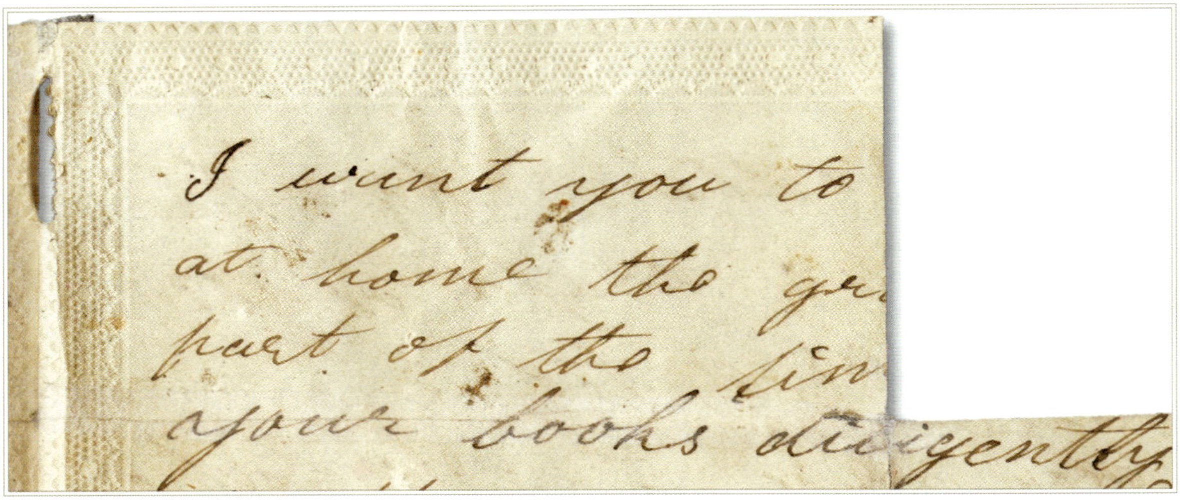
I want you to
at home the gr
part of the tim
your books diligently

I want you to [*2.9 × 3.2 cm cut at top right corner*] at home the gr[*2.9 × 3.2 cm cut at top right corner*] part of the tim[*2.9 × 3.2 cm cut at top right corner*] your books diligently

[◊]—Single Illegible Letter

A single illegible letter in a word is represented by a diamond with brackets. For example, in the 18 October 1855 letter, enough uncertainty existed in identifying the middle letter following the date that we used this notation in transcription.

Wailuku Maui, Sand, Isles,
Oct. $18^{\underline{th}}$ 1855. a.[◊].d.

[~~◊~~]—Single Illegible Letter with Strike-Through

Annotation similar to that mentioned above but with strike-through included is used for a single illegible letter that has been stricken out. An example can be seen in the 25 May 1856 letter.

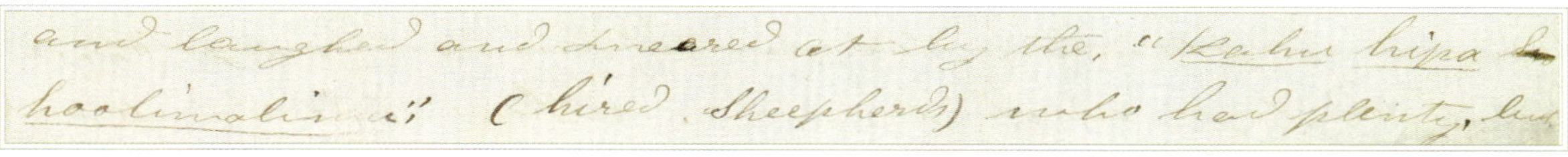

and laughed and sneared at by the, "Kahu hipa ~~h~~[~~◊~~] hoolimalima," (hired sheepherds) who had plenty

[◊◊]—Multiple Illegible Letters in a Word

Two diamonds within brackets represent two or more illegible letters within a single word. For example, in the 14 July 1856 letter, a large smudge obscures the first letters of a word. The bracketed diamonds allow readers to draw their own conclusions regarding the original meaning of the word.

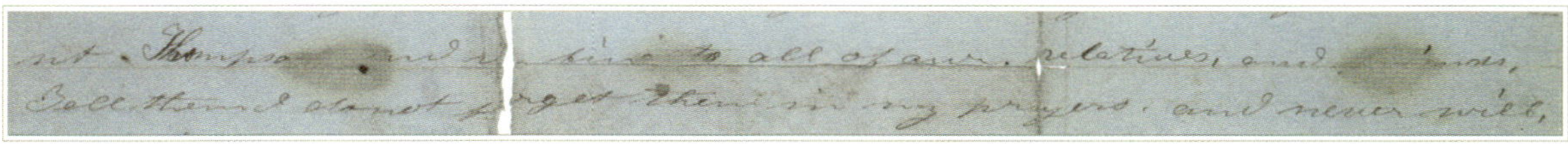

nt Thompson and [◊◊] fine to all of our relatives, and [◊◊]nds. Tell them I donot forget them in my prayers, and never will.

[Italics]—Illegible Strike-Throughs and Erasures

One or more illegible words from a strike-through or an erasure are represented by an italicized description of the strike-through or erasure within brackets, as found in the transcription of the 20 December 1860 letter seen below.

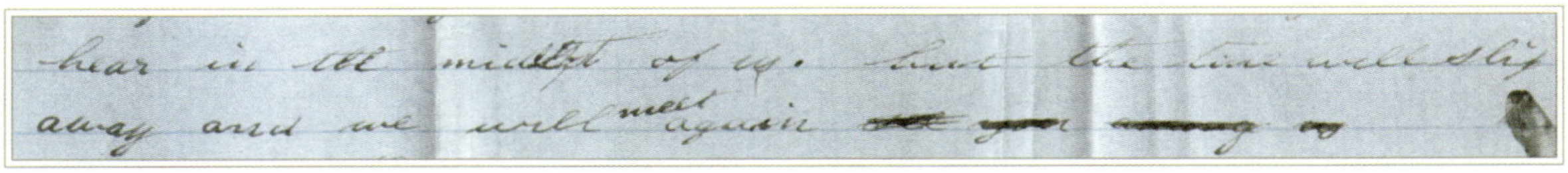

hear in the midst of us. but the time will slip away and we will <meet> again [*illegible strike-through*]

Insertions, Corrections, and Strike-Throughs

Angle brackets are used to represent all insertions and corrections. Words that were corrected by strike-through are transcribed as such, if the words are legible. Where Joseph F. used two lines to strike out a word, a single-line strike-through is used in the transcription. Insertions to letters are transcribed within angle brackets. An example of insertions and corrections can be found in the letter dated 25 July 1857.

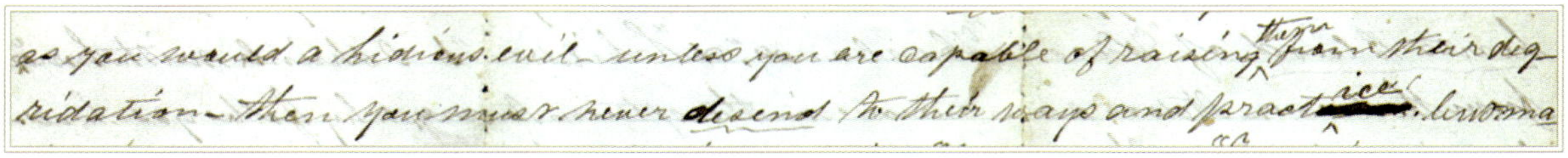

as you would a hidious evil—unless you are capable of raising <them> from their degridation—then you must never <u>desend</u> to their ways and pract<ice>.but ma

Transcription Guidelines Specific to Martha Ann Smith Harris's Letters

The Martha Ann letter collection presents some unique problems in transcription, primarily in Martha Ann's grammar and spelling. It was common to find the same words spelled differently several times, sometimes in the same letter. The following 31 January 1856 letter provides an example of her challenging writing.

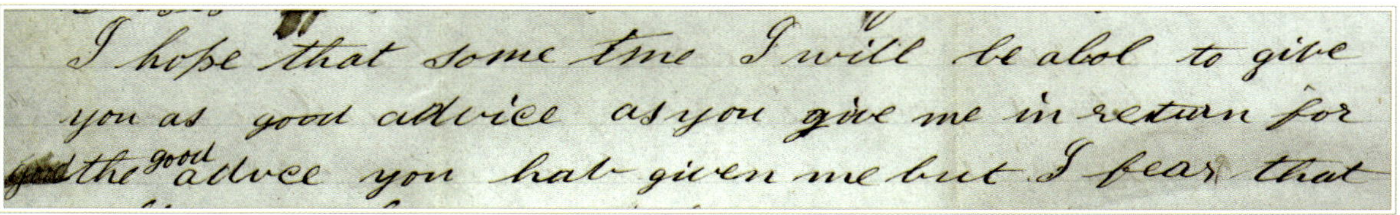

I hope that some tme I will be abol to give you as good advice as you give me in return for good the <good> advce you hav given me but I fear that

Martha Ann at times connected multiple words as a single word. To maintain readability and to accurately reflect the content and meaning, these words were separated, as seen in the letter from 29 July 1856 ("so i went").

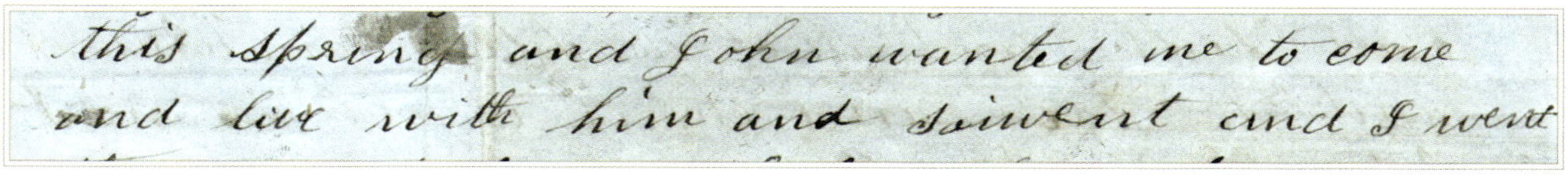
this spring and John wanted me to come
and live with him and soiwent and I went

this spring and John wanted me to come and live with him and so i went and I went

Instances where Martha Ann put spaces within a single word have been corrected for readability. For example, notice the word *cas tis e ments* in the letter dated 3 May 1857.

I would be be afool and would need
castis e ments for it I am thankful to my

I would be be a fool [*illegible strikeout*] and would need castisements for it I am thankful to my

Directions on how to transcribe handwritten letters from the eighteenth and nineteenth centuries vary considerably. By using the guidelines provided above, the editors have chosen to transcribe the letters in a way that helps the reader capture the personality and writing style of Joseph F. and Martha Ann without the distractions of other transcription systems. The guidelines are quite general and are easily understood, with limited changes to formatting, grammar, and punctuation.

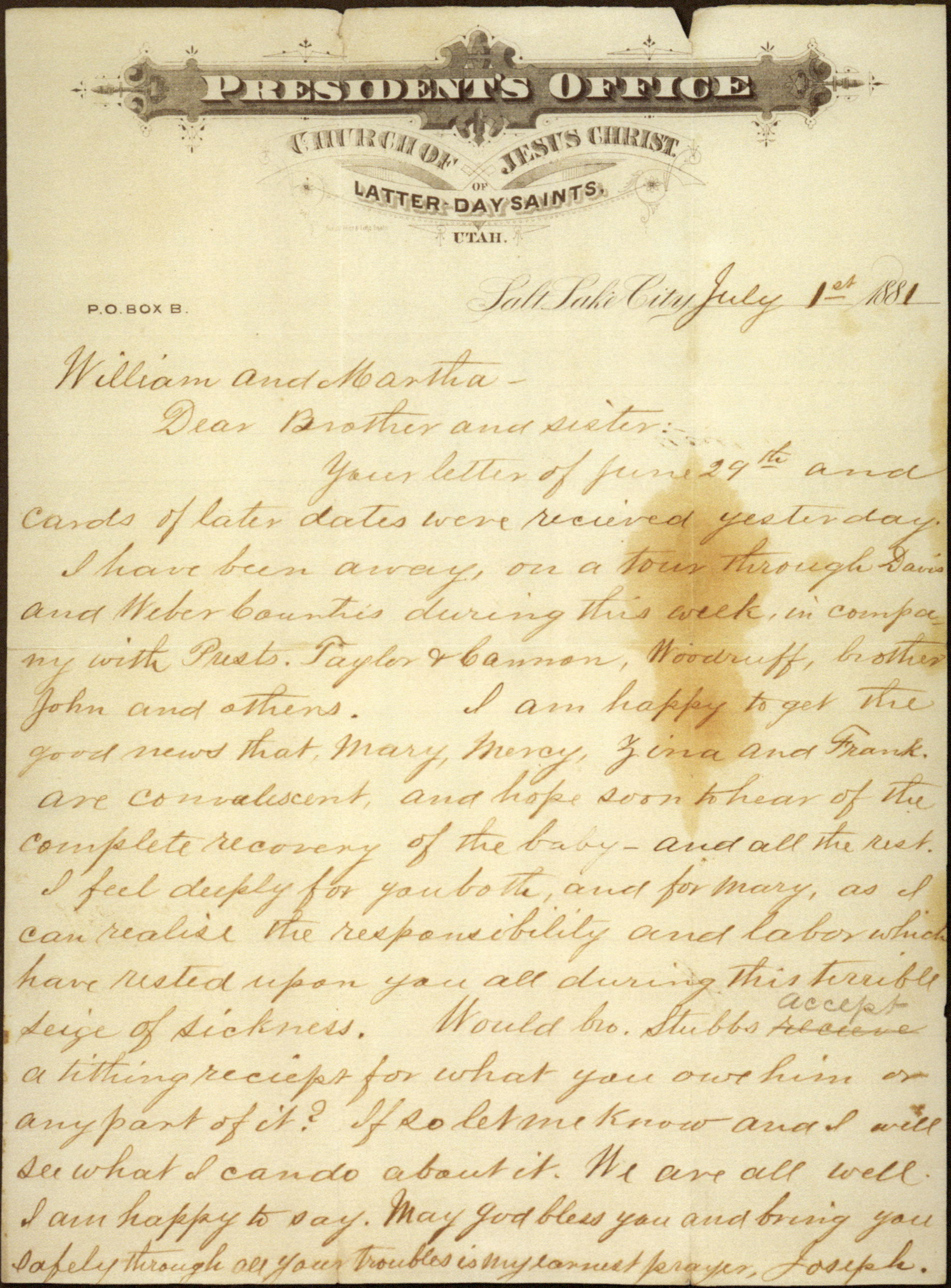
PRESIDENT'S OFFICE

CHURCH OF JESUS CHRIST OF LATTER-DAY SAINTS.

UTAH.

P.O. BOX B.

Salt Lake City, July 1st 1881

William and Martha -

Dear Brother and sister:-

Your letter of June 29th and cards of later dates were recieved yesterday. I have been away, on a tour through Davis and Weber Counties during this week, in company with Prests. Taylor & Cannon, Woodruff, brother John and others. I am happy to get the good news that, Mary, Mercy, Zina and Frank, are convalescent, and hope soon to hear of the complete recovery of the baby - and all the rest. I feel deeply for you both, and for Mary, as I can realise the responsibility and labor which have rested upon you all during this terrible seige of sickness. Would bro. Stubbs ~~recieve~~ accept a tithing reciept for what you owe him or any part of it? If so let me know and I will see what I can do about it. We are all well. I am happy to say. May God bless you and bring you safely through all your troubles is my earnest prayer, Joseph.

Joseph F. to William and Martha Ann, 1 July 1881 (p. 1)

Approaching and Understanding Joseph F.'s and Martha Ann's Letters

Reading Joseph F.'s and Martha Ann's letters is to enter a new world—the historical past, which is like a foreign country in many ways.[1] In the letters we find ourselves in a completely different place and time where we encounter people, practices, and ideas that we may not understand. We may be challenged by unfamiliar geographic locations not easily placed on our mental maps, or we may be less familiar with the time line of the letters (1850s–1910s) than with the Joseph Smith period (1805–44) or with recent Church history—the time in which we live.

Unlike a narrative history, this collection of letters does not contain a story line. The letters, like the letters of Paul found in the New Testament, are preserved without historical context, introductions, or explanations. Joseph F. and Martha Ann did not imagine people living in the twenty-first century reading their letters and as a result did not always provide the kind of information we need today to understand them and their situation.

Many of the letters are preserved in isolation. In this sense, we are hearing only half the conversation, much like listening to someone at the market who is talking on a mobile phone as she or

1. Many people living in Western democratic industrial nations may have a difficult time reconstructing a world with different cultural, political, religious, and social points of view. For example, nineteenth-century attitudes about a husband's legal right to administer corporal punishment to family members, including wives and children, and a schoolteacher's legal rights to punish students would surprise most modern readers.

he stands in line at the cash register. By tone and sometimes by what is said, we can fill in the gaps, but for the most part we are at a loss to fully understand the conversation.[2]

Because many of Joseph F.'s and Martha Ann's letters are lost, we do not have access to the full conversation. Additionally, we miss much of the conversation going on outside the letters—conversations Joseph F. and Martha Ann were having in person and through family and friends. Joseph F.'s journals provide us only some of those interactions. To meet these challenges to some degree, we have provided a historical introduction for each decade and, where possible, annotations identifying the people involved, what was taking place, and where the events occurred in order to establish a context for the letters written during that period.

We also face the challenge of setting aside the version of Joseph F. we have already created in our minds and allowing the sources to challenge our assumptions about him and his world.[3]

Finally, and most importantly, most people living in Western society today face a common problem when examining the past—*presentism*. One definition of presentism is "uncritical adherence to present-day attitudes, especially the tendency to interpret past events in terms of modern values and concepts."[4] In historical analysis, presentism is often identified as the anachronistic introduction of present-day ideas and perspectives into interpretations of the past. Modern historians seek to avoid presentism in their work because they consider it a form of cultural bias and believe it creates a distorted understanding of their subject matter.[5]

Lynn Hunt, former American Historical Association president, argues that presentism does much damage to our understanding of the past: "Presentism, at its worst, encourages a kind of moral complacency and self-congratulation. Interpreting the past in terms of present concerns usually leads us to find ourselves morally superior; the Greeks had slavery, even David Hume was a racist, and European women endorsed imperial ventures. Our forebears constantly fail to measure up to our present-day standards. This is not to say that any of these findings are irrelevant or that we should endorse an entirely relativist point of view. It is to say that we must question the stance of temporal superiority that is implicit in the Western (and now probably worldwide) historical discipline."[6]

Hunt's warnings are especially relevant today with almost unlimited access to historical sources found online—often without context by someone who does not have the academic credentials to illuminate the proper context. This approach is almost like visiting the Roman Forum (*Forum Romanum*) without an authoritative academic guidebook or personal archaeological and historical training. To make matters worse, visitors often are accompanied by guides who have no academic

2. An example is found in a letter written by Joseph F. Smith to Martha Ann in 1875: "Such things as you mention as having occurred at South Willow Creek, are of almost daily occurrence in this country. But that does not lessen the horror of such abominable wickedness." Without Martha Ann's letter, we are unable to reconstruct the events and exact location mentioned in Joseph F.'s response to the letter. See Joseph F. to Martha Ann, 31 March 1875, herein.
3. See Stephen C. Taysom, "The Last Memory: Joseph F. Smith and *Lieux de Mémoire* in Late Nineteenth-Century Mormonism," *Dialogue: A Journal of Mormon Thought* 48, no. 3 (Fall 2015): 1–23.
4. *English Oxford Living Dictionaries*; see https://en.oxforddictionaries.com/definition/presentism.
5. It is not an act of presentism, however, to hold people in the past accountable for their poor choices when those choices were noted by people in the past. See W. Paul Reeve, "'To Save This Fallen Race': Orson Pratt and the Debate over Indian Indenture and Black Servitude at the 1852 Utah Territorial Legislature," unpublished paper delivered at the Mormon History Association Conference, 8 June 2018. Latter-day Saint Apostle and Utah territorial legislator Orson Pratt, for example, called slavery a "great evil" in 1852 and argued that black men be allowed to vote in Utah Territory. It is not presentism to suggest that those who opposed Pratt were on the wrong side of history, because Pratt made that very point in 1852.
6. Lynn Hunt, "Against Presentism," *Perspectives on History*, May 2002, https://www.historians.org/publications-and-directories/perspectives-on-history/may-2002/against-presentism.

training—they have been trained only in guiding people to the major tourist sites in Rome. The tourist is bewildered with the ruins and will more likely than not draw incorrect conclusions and interpretations for what he or she sees in this remarkably rich archaeological site. The experience would be much different if the tourist had studied Roman archaeology or was accompanied by someone who had a PhD in Roman history or Roman archaeology.

In the end, we discover thoroughly interesting and passionate people who lived in a time very different from our own. Their cultural attitudes about women, minorities, children, and other religious faith traditions were different from our own. Joseph F. and Martha Ann were not twenty-first-century Latter-day Saints. Although they believed in many of the core teachings contained in the restored gospel of Jesus Christ, they did not interpret the Word of Wisdom the way we do today, they did not experience temple worship the same way we do today, and they heard sermons about plural marriage, temple adoptions, gathering to specific locations, and so on. Enjoying a visit to the past, like visiting a foreign country, can bring understanding if we learn something about people's lives in context.

Interior view of the Ephraim Tabernacle, ca. 1895, photograph by Matson and Christensen, Ephraim, Utah. Unlike Church practice today, during most of Joseph F.'s and Martha Ann's lives the sacrament was administered by mature men, with the acting priest uplifting both hands as he offered the prayers, as highlighted in this view of the Ephraim North Ward sacrament meeting. Additionally, wine was generally still used as a symbol of Christ's blood, and the practice of first offering the emblems to the presiding leader had not been firmly established. Although the symbolism remains the same, much has changed in the practice over time. Courtesy of CHL.

Hyrum and Mary Fielding Smith portraits, ca. 1842, by Sutcliffe Maudsley. Courtesy of CHM.

Joseph F. and Martha Ann's Parents

Joseph F. and Martha Ann Smith's parents were Hyrum (1800–1844) and Mary Fielding Smith (1801–52).[1] Naturally, Hyrum and Mary Fielding became larger-than-life heroes in the memory of Martha Ann and Joseph F. because of their young ages at the times of their parents' death.[2] Modern Latter-day Saints inherited that memory—a memory that continues to shape our understanding of the past.

Hyrum Smith was born in Tunbridge, Orange County, Vermont.[3] He was the second son of Lucy Mack (1775–1856) and Joseph Smith Sr. (1771–1840). His brother Joseph Smith Jr. (1805–44) was born just before Hyrum's sixth birthday. At the age of about six, Joseph contracted typhoid fever followed by a severe bone infection (osteomyelitis) in his left leg.[4] According to a family tradition, Hyrum, already known for his tender and compassionate nature, helped the family by assuming much of the personal care Joseph required.[5]

1. The two standard family tributes to Hyrum and Mary Fielding are Pearson H. Corbett, *Hyrum Smith, Patriarch* (Salt Lake City, UT: Deseret Book, 1963), and Don Cecil Corbett, *Mary Fielding Smith: Daughter of Britain* (Salt Lake City, UT: Deseret Book, 1966). See also Jeffrey S. O'Driscoll, *Hyrum Smith: A Life of Integrity* (Salt Lake City, UT: Deseret Book, 2003).
2. Their circumstance highlights the challenges and opportunities of using reminiscences to help reconstruct Joseph F.'s life. See Stephen C. Taysom, "The Last Memory: Joseph F. Smith and *Lieux de Mémoire* in Late Nineteenth-Century Mormonism," *Dialogue: A Journal of Mormon Thought* 48, no. 3 (Fall 2015): 1–23.
3. Larry C. Porter, "The Joseph and Lucy Mack Smith Family," in *Mapping Mormonism: An Atlas of Latter-day Saint History*, ed. Brandon S. Plewe et al. (Provo, UT: BYU Press, 2012), 14–15.
4. Richard L. Bushman, *Joseph Smith: Rough Stone Rolling* (New York: Alfred A. Knopf, 2005), 20.
5. Lucy Mack Smith described Hyrum's role in helping his brother Joseph after his surgery: "Hyrum, who was rather remarkable for his tenderness and sympathy, now desired that he might take my place. As he was a good, trusty boy, we let him do so; and, in order to make the task as easy for him as possible, we laid Joseph upon a low bed, and Hyrum sat beside him, almost day and night, for some considerable length of time, holding the affected part of his leg in his hands, and pressing it between them, so that his afflicted brother might be enabled to endure the pain, which was so excruciating, that he was scarcely able to bear it." Lucy [Mack] Smith, *Biographical Sketches of Joseph Smith the Prophet, and His Progenitors for Many Generations* (Liverpool, England: S. W. Richards, 1853), 63.

From this and other experiences, the two brothers developed a deep bond that lasted throughout their lives.[6] Hyrum became one of Joseph's closest advisers, confidants, and co-laborers from the earliest period of the restoration of the gospel of Jesus Christ through the establishment of the Church, and he remained so until his martyrdom at Joseph's side in 1844.[7]

The Smith family eventually moved from Vermont to Palmyra, Wayne County, New York. Joseph Sr. had purchased one hundred acres in nearby Manchester Township by 1820.[8] He and his oldest sons began immediately to clear the land for farming. Additionally, the Smith boys worked as day laborers to supplement the family income in order to pay the annual mortgage on the farm.[9]

Hyrum and several family members, including his mother, became members of the Western Presbyterian Church of Palmyra in the early 1820s.[10] Between 1820 and 1827, many of the founding events of the restoration of the gospel of Jesus Christ took place in New York. Eventually, the family became involved in the coming forth of the Book of Mormon (1827–30) and the organization of the Church of Christ (1830).

During this period, on 2 November 1826, Hyrum married Jerusha T. Barden (1805–37).[11] She was remembered by the family for her "singular beauty and fine character."[12] Her mother-in-law, Lucy Mack Smith, said Jerusha was "one of the most excellent women, with whom I [have] seen much enjoyment."[13] Over the years of their marriage, Jerusha developed a very close relationship with Hyrum's mother and "was so endeared to the family that she enjoyed their greatest confidence."[14]

In 1827 Jerusha gave birth to their first child, a daughter named Lovina (1827–76). Nearly two years later, Hyrum's brother, Joseph Smith, dictated a revelation for him, known today as Doctrine and Covenants 11. Within a month, he was baptized by his brother Joseph Smith in June 1829.[15]

Another girl, Mary, was born (1829–32) to Hyrum and Jerusha on 27 June 1829. Shortly thereafter, Hyrum saw and handled the Book of Mormon plates along with seven other men who became known as the Eight Witnesses.[16] Their testimony is still published with the Book of Mormon.[17]

On 6 April 1830, Hyrum became a founding member of the Church of Christ. Jerusha was baptized shortly thereafter in June 1830.[18] Apparently, Jerusha's family was not supportive of her decision to join the "Mormons."[19]

6. See O'Driscoll, *Hyrum Smith*, 10.
7. Although they were virtually inseparable in life, Joseph and Hyrum were distinct individuals with significant differences in mood and personality. See Stephen C. Taysom's forthcoming biography, *"Like a Fiery Meteor": The Life of Joseph F. Smith*.
8. Larry C. Porter, "Palmyra–Manchester, New York," in *Encyclopedia of Latter-day Saint History*, ed. Arnold K. Garr, Donald Q. Cannon, and Richard O. Cowan (Salt Lake City, UT: Deseret Book, 2000), 889–90.
9. Don Enders, "Palmyra & Manchester," in Plewe et al., *Mapping Mormonism*, 16–17.
10. O'Driscoll, *Hyrum Smith*, 32
11. Smith, *Biographical Sketches*, 40; see also Jerusha T. Barden Smith's biography at http://www.josephsmithpapers.org/person/jerusha-t-barden-smith.
12. Corbett, *Hyrum Smith*, 33.
13. Smith, *Biographical Sketches*, 94.
14. Smith, *Biographical Sketches*, 94.
15. Karen Lynn Davidson, David J. Whittaker, Mark Ashurst-McGee, and Richard L. Jensen, eds., *Histories, Volume 1: Joseph Smith Histories, 1832–1844*, vol. 1 of the Histories series of *The Joseph Smith Papers*, ed. Dean C. Jessee, Ronald K. Esplin, and Richard Lyman Bushman (Salt Lake City, UT: Church Historian's Press, 2012), 312–14.
16. See Terryl Givens, *By the Hand of Mormon: The American Scripture That Launched a New World Religion* (New York: Oxford University Press, 2002), 40.
17. The Book of Mormon: Another Testament of Jesus Christ (Salt Lake City, UT: The Church of Jesus Christ of Latter-day Saints, 2017), vii.
18. Joseph Fielding Smith, "The Patriarch Hyrum Smith," *Young Woman's Journal*, June 1905, 274–77.
19. Jerry C. Roundy, *Jerusha Barden, 1st Wife of Patriarch Hyrum Smith* (Provo, UT: E. H. Peirce 1999), 16.

Hyrum and Jerusha Smith. Each has an inscription on the reverse side. Hyrum's card reads, "Hyrum Smith Patriarh & Martyr from a Likeness taken in his 34th year by 'Webber' of Kirtland." Jerusha's card reads, "Jerusha Barden Wife of Hyruym Smith Patgriach and Mother of John Smith Patrarch." Original spelling retained. Courtesy of CHL.

As conflict and challenges intensified in New York against the Church in 1830, Hyrum and his family joined the Saints gathering in Kirtland, Geauga (renamed Lake) County, Ohio, in early 1831.[20] During the following years, Hyrum was often absent from home, serving and working with his brother Joseph Smith, the President of the Church, as one of the leading elders in the Church.[21]

Tragically, Hyrum and Jerusha's second child, Mary, died on 29 May 1832. In his diary, Hyrum recorded his grief at losing his young daughter: "Not passing mutch tribulation until the 29th of May then I was Cald to view a Scene which Brought sorrw to unto me Sorrow and mourning Even a scene of Death Mary was Cald from time to a ternity on the 29th Day of May She expired in mine arms s Such a Day I never Before exspeirenced and O may god grant that we may meet her again At the greate Day of redemption to part no more."[22]

20. Karl Ricks Anderson, "The Western Reserve," in Plewe et al., *Mapping Mormonism*, 28–29.
21. Bruce A. Van Orden, "Smith, Hyrum," in *Encyclopedia of Mormonism*, ed. Daniel H. Ludlow (New York: Macmillan, 1992), 3:1329–30.
22. Hyrum Smith Papers, 29 May 1832, 19th-Century Mormon and Western Manuscripts, BYU.

Hyrum and Jerusha's first son, John (1832–1911), was born in Kirtland on 22 September1832. Three more children were born to Jerusha and Hyrum in Ohio: Hyrum [sometimes spelled Hiram] Smith (1834–41) on 27 April 1834, Jerusha Smith (1836–1912) on 13 January 1836, and Sarah Smith (1837–76) on 2 October 1837.

The Smith home in Kirtland was described as "affectionate and happy, . . . where culture and refinement were characteristic qualities."[23] It was also the center of considerable activity, as it was often used as a meetinghouse for church services, a gathering place for extended family, and a hospice of sorts for anyone in need of assistance.[24]

During the Kirtland period, Hyrum continued to play a significant role in the Church. For example, in February 1832 he was appointed counselor to Bishop Newel K. Whitney. The following year he was called to be a member of the committee to supervise construction of the Kirtland Temple. Then in September 1834 he was called to the Kirtland high council. Three years later, in September 1837, he was sustained as assistant counselor in the First Presidency, and just two months later he replaced Frederick G. Williams as second counselor in the First Presidency.[25]

During this period, Hyrum received a blessing in which he was promised, "If thou desirest thou mayest bring many souls to Jesus."[26] Tragically, Jerusha died suddenly on 13 October 1837, eleven days after giving birth to Sarah. Hyrum was en route to Missouri on Church business at the time with his brothers Joseph and William. His brothers Samuel and Don Carlos wrote a letter to inform him of her death. They wanted Hyrum to "rest assured that we have done all that we could do to save Jerusha but in vain She is no more, her place can never be supplied! O the scenery, the scenery how afflicting! The funeral I expect will be on the Sabbath at 10 o'clock."[27]

Jerusha's obituary in the local newspaper noted: "She has left five small children together with numerous relatives to mourn her loss, a loss which is severely felt by all. Our sister was beloved and highly esteemed by every lover of truth and virtue."[28] On hearing the news, Hyrum was grief-stricken and shortly afterward left Far West, Missouri, to return to Kirtland.[29] In the meantime, a family friend, Hannah Woodcock Grinnels (1783–1853), took care of the motherless children until he arrived back in Kirtland around December 10.[30]

Before Jerusha's death, a recent convert named Mary Fielding (1801–52) arrived in Kirtland from Toronto, Upper Canada (generally comprising present-day southern Ontario), where she and her brother Joseph (1797–1863) and her sister Mercy (1807–93) had been converted and baptized. The Fieldings had migrated to Canada from England.[31] In Kirtland the Fieldings became acquainted with Hyrum and his family. Mary eventually became part of Hyrum's family.[32]

23. Corbett, *Hyrum Smith*, 147.
24. Corbett, *Hyrum Smith*, 105.
25. See Hyrum Smith's biography at http://www.josephsmithpapers.org/person/hyrum-smith.
26. Kirtland High Council Minutebook, 1 March 1835, 186.
27. Samuel Smith (Kirtland, OH) to Hyrum Smith (Far West, MO), 13 October 1837.
28. "Obituary," *Elders' Journal of the Church of the Latter Day Saints*, October 1837, 16.
29. O'Driscoll, *Hyrum Smith*, 162.
30. Lovina was ten years old, John four, Hyrum three, Jerusha one, and Sarah less than two weeks old when their mother, Jerusha, died. Hannah's last name is spelled differently (e.g., Grennels) in various sources. See O'Driscoll, *Hyrum Smith*, 162.
31. Mary Fielding was English, spoke with an English accent, and reflected many cultural traits found in nineteenth-century British society. See Taysom, *"Like a Fiery Meteor."*
32. See Susan Arrington Madsen, "Mary Fielding Smith," in Ludlow, *Encyclopedia of Mormonism*, 6:1358–59. See also Amanda Hendrix-Komoto, "To Forsake Thy Father and Mother: Mary Fielding Smith and the Familial Politics of Conversion," *Dialogue: A Journal of Mormon Thought* 45, no. 3 (Fall 2012): 26–37.

Mary Fielding was born on 21 July 1801, at Honeydon, Bedfordshire, England.[33] She was the sixth child of John Fielding (1759–1836) and Rachel Abbotson (1767–1828).[34] The Fielding family were strict Methodists—the faith Mary Fielding brought with her to Upper Canada in 1834 when she emigrated to join her brother and sister.[35]

On 24 December 1837, following the death of Jerusha, Mary Fielding (age thirty-six) and Hyrum (age thirty-seven) were married.[36] Mary Fielding effectively became the mother to Jerusha's five children.[37]

In 1838 Hyrum and Mary took their family to the new Church gathering place of Far West, Missouri.[38] Their stay there did not last long. In August tension on the Missouri frontier between Latter-day Saints and some Missourians flared into violent skirmishes. The conflict tragically increased, resulting in a three-month conflict known as the Missouri Mormon War.[39]

Several encounters occurred during the conflict, including the Battle of Crooked River, which left three Latter-day Saints and one Missourian dead, and the Hawn's Mill massacre, which left seventeen Latter-day Saint men and boys dead and another fourteen wounded.[40]

Just days before the Hawn's Mill massacre, after hearing exaggerated reports about a full-scale "rebellion" in northern Missouri, Governor Lilburn W. Boggs (1796–1860) issued Executive Order 44, also known as the extermination order, authorizing the expulsion of all Latter-day Saints from the state.[41] In the end, as word spread of Boggs's executive order, attacks on the Latter-day Saints ended when their enemies realized the Latter-day Saints would now be forced to move beyond state boundaries.

33. Honeydon is a hamlet located in the Borough of Bedford in Bedfordshire, England. See Kenneth Mays, "Picturing History: Honeydon, Bedfordshire," *Deseret News*, 3 October 2012.

34. Also known as Rachel Ibbotson. A recent history of Mary Fielding's early life is found in Jay Parry, "Mary Fielding Smith," in *Women of Faith in the Latter Days, Volume 1: 1775–1820*, ed. Richard E. Turley Jr. and Brittany A. Chapman (Salt Lake City, UT: Deseret Book, 2011), 376–88.

35. Mary Fielding's brother, Reverend James Fielding, was a Methodist minister, as were the husbands of her two sisters in England.

36. As a tutor, Mary Fielding had already become well acquainted with the Smith family before Hyrum's wife had passed away in October 1837. After Jerusha died, Joseph Smith "informed Hyrum that it was the will of the Lord that he marries again and take as a wife a young English convert, Mary Fielding by name." Joseph Fielding Smith, *The Life of Joseph F. Smith: Sixth President of The Church of Jesus Christ of Latter-day Saints* (Salt Lake City, UT: Deseret Book, 1938), 120. Hyrum, according to a family tradition, did not want to simply make this a matter of convenience, so he decided to court Mary in such a way that "his gentlemanly and courtly proposal . . . provided the basis of lasting affection between them." Corbett, *Mary Fielding Smith*, 45.

37. Mary Fielding struggled as a stepmother. In a letter written to Hyrum, she signed, "your faithful companion and friend but unhappy stepmother M. Smith." Mary Fielding Smith to Hyrum Smith, 14 September 1842. Corbett, *Mary Fielding Smith*, 45.

38. Alexander L. Baugh, "Settling Northern Missouri," in Plewe et al., *Mapping Mormonism*, 48–49.

39. Governor Boggs was willing to call out state militia forces to end this conflict. In fact, he had engaged in two other military conflicts during this period. The first was between native peoples and the state of Missouri in 1838 and a second conflict with the state of Iowa in 1839. See Richard Neitzel Holzapfel, "Crossing Borders: Lilburn Boggs and the 1839 Missouri–Iowa War," Mormon Historical Association annual meeting, St. Louis, MO, 2 June 2017, forthcoming in *BYU Studies Quarterly*.

40. The spelling of Jacob Hawn's last name was thought to be have been "Haun" until recent discoveries made it clear that it had been misspelled in modern sources. See Alexander L. Baugh, "Jacob Hawn and the Hawn's Mill Massacre: Missouri Millwright and Oregon Pioneer," *Mormon Historical Studies* 11, no. 1 (Spring 2010): 4.

41. Sean Cannon, "The Mormon–Missouri War," in Plewe et al., *Mapping Mormonism*, 50–51.

Hyrum and Joseph were arrested by state militia officers at Far West, Caldwell County, on 31 October. After a short stop in Jackson County, they were held almost one month (4–29 November) in the Richmond Jail in Ray County and just over four months (1 December 1838—6 April 1839) in Liberty Jail in Clay County.

Liberty Jail, ca. 1878, photograph by J. T. Hicks. Joseph F. received this image on 8 September 1878. An inscription on the back notes, "From Miss Josie Schweich Richmond, Ray Co. MO. grand-daughter of D. Whitmer." Courtesy of CHL.

The conditions in this filthy jail during the winter of 1838–39 were horrific. Joseph and Hyrum were at times lonely, hungry, cold, sick, and despondent. Joseph's description paints a terrible scene:

> Thursday night I sat down just as the sun is going down, as we peak throu the greats of this lonesome prision, to write to you, that I may make known to you my situation. It is I believe <it is> now about five months and six days since I have bean under the grimace, of

a guard night and day, and within the walls grates and screeking of iron dors, of a lonesome dark durty prison. With immotions known only to God, do I write this letter, the contemplations, of the mind under these circumstances, defies the pen, or tounge, or Angels, to discribe, or paint, to the human mind being, who never experiance what I we experience. This night we expect; is the last night we shall try our weary joints and bones on our dirty straw couches in these walls, let our case hereafter be as it may, as we expect to start tomorrow. . . . we cannot get into a worse hole then this is, we shall not stay here but one night besides this if that thank God, we swall never cast a lingering wish after liberty in clay county Mo. we have enough of it to last forever.[42]

On 13 November 1838, two weeks after Hyrum's arrest, Mary gave birth to their first child—Joseph Fielding Smith (1838–1918), but also known as Joseph F. Smith through much of his life.[43] Mary was sickly for much of the next four months.

The separation and the lack of communication between them caused challenges for each.[44] Finally, in January 1839 Mary traveled forty miles on a makeshift bed in the back of a wagon to visit her husband in the Liberty Jail. During her overnight visit, Hyrum saw his son for the first time and may have blessed him.[45]

As their leaders languished in a Missouri jail during the winter of 1838–39, the Latter-day Saints were forced to leave their homes to comply with the extermination order issued by Governor Boggs. Like many other beleaguered Saints, Mary fled to Quincy, Adams County, Illinois, seeking refuge from the violence and persecution in northern Missouri.

In early April 1839, a hearing for Hyrum and the other Latter-day Saint prisoners was held in Gallatin, Missouri. During the proceedings, the judge granted a change of venue and issued an order for Church leaders to be taken to Columbia, Boone County, Missouri. While en route on 16 April, the prisoners were allowed to escape. A few days later, Hyrum and Joseph were reunited with their families in Illinois. Shortly thereafter, Hyrum, Mary, and their children settled in Commerce (later Nauvoo), Illinois, which had been identified as the next major Latter-day Saint gathering place.[46]

During this period in Nauvoo, Hyrum was called to assume Oliver Cowdery's position, as stated in Doctrine and Covenants 124:91–96. As a result, he played an increasingly significant role in the religious, social, political, and economic activities in the Church. While Joseph Smith was in Washington, DC, for example, Hyrum wrote him a lengthy letter, dated 2 January 1840, highlighting his activities while Joseph was absent from Nauvoo.[47]

In Nauvoo, Mary and Hyrum welcomed their second child, Martha Ann (1841–1923), on 14 May 1841. Later that year, Hyrum buried his seven-year-old son, Hyrum Jr. What Joseph F. remembered

42. Joseph Smith to Emma Smith, 4 April 1839, Joseph Smith Papers, Beinecke Rare Book & Manuscript Library, Yale University. See also "Letter to Emma Smith, 4 April 1839," p. [1], The Joseph Smith Papers, http://www.josephsmithpapers.org/paper-summary/letter-to-emma-smith-4-april-1839/1.

43. Stephen C. Taysom suggests even though Joseph F. was an infant during this period, Missouri cast a long and traumatizing shadow during the rest of his life. Mobs were real and dangerous. See Taysom, "Last Memory," 9–10.

44. See Hyrum Smith to Mary Fielding Smith, 20 March 1839; Hyrum Smith to Mary Fielding Smith, 30 March 1839; and Mary Fielding Smith to Hyrum Smith, 11 April 1839.

45. See Alexander L. Baugh, "Was Joseph F. Smith Blessed by His Father Hyrum Smith in Liberty Jail?," *Mormon Historical Studies* 4, no. 1 (Spring 2003): 101–5.

46. Donald Q. Cannon and Brandon S. Plewe, "Commerce, Illinois," in Plewe et al., *Mapping Mormonism*, 52–53.

47. Hyrum Smith, letter, Nauvoo, Hancock County, Illinois, to Joseph Smith and Elias Higbee, Washington DC, 2 January 1840, in Joseph Smith Letterbook 2, pp. 91–94, handwriting of Howard Coray.

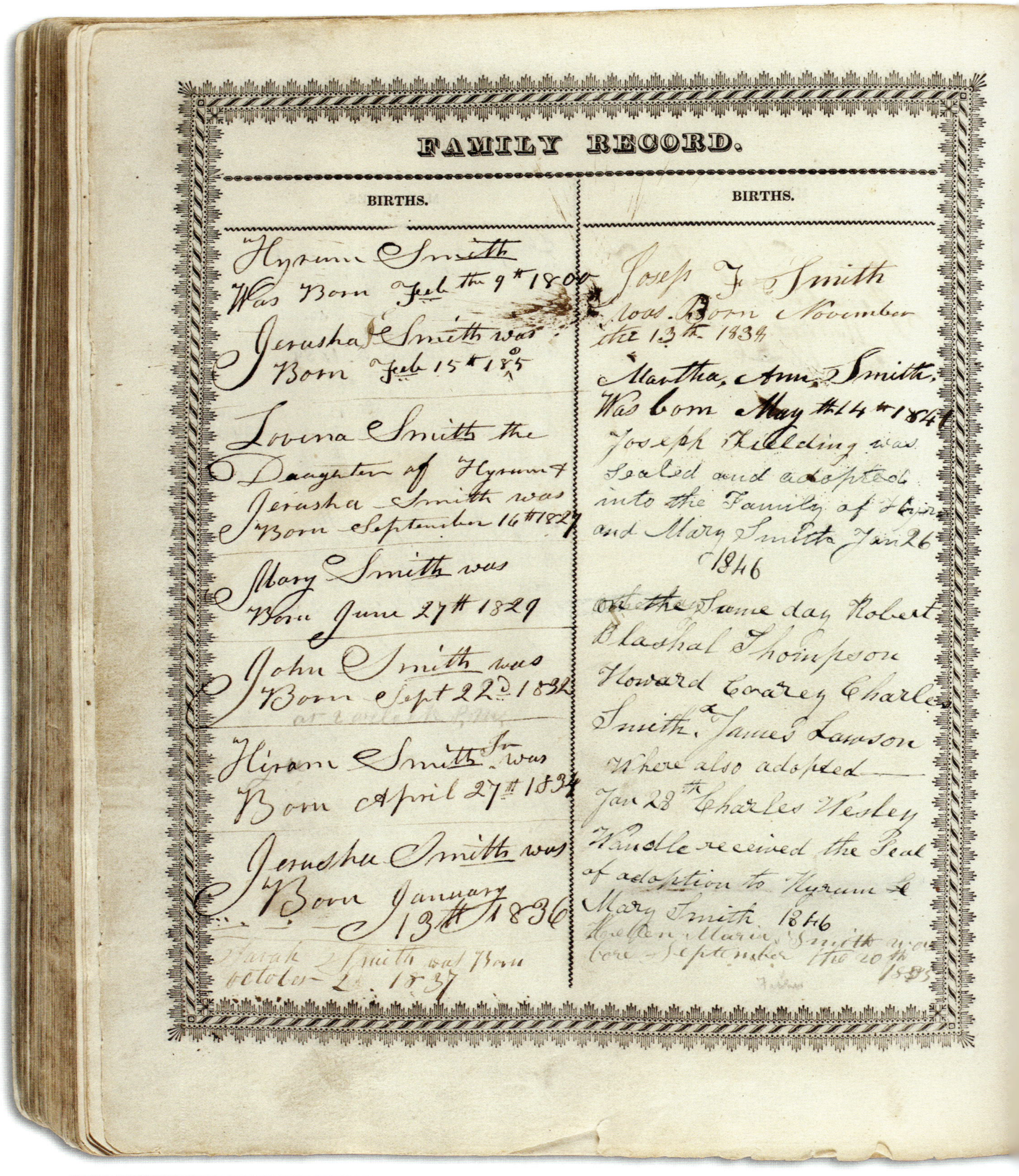

Hyrum Smith family Bible, *The Holy Bible* (Boston: Langdon Coffin, 1834). Like many other large-size Bibles of the day, this one had been printed so that family history information could be recorded. Here someone noted the births of Joseph F. and Martha Ann in a preprinted section titled "Family Record." Courtesy of BYU.

Nauvoo Landscape, ca. 1859, painting by Johann Schröder. Courtesy of CHM.

about that event is not known. It was not, however, the last time Joseph F. witnessed the burial of a young child.[48]

As an increasing number of Saints moved into western Illinois, many local and influential citizens in Hancock County feared Latter-day Saint political and economic power.[49] By 1841 the Anti-Mormon Party had been organized as a political tool. Unfortunately, physical violence—so common in pre–Civil War America and largely aimed at abolitionists, minority ethnic groups, and religious groups—eventually became the main method used to drive the Latter-day Saints from the state.[50]

During this tense period, Hyrum joined in the introduction of new ordinances when on 4 May 1842 he was washed, anointed, and endowed in Joseph Smith's red brick store on Water Street in Nauvoo, along with several other Church leaders.[51] Hyrum and Mary were sealed for time and

48. See Taysom, *"Like a Fiery Meteor."*
49. Brandon S. Plewe and Donald Q. Cannon, "Buying Nauvoo"; and Donald Q. Cannon and Brandon S. Plewe, "Building Nauvoo," in Plewe et al., *Mapping Mormonism*, 54–55, 56–57.
50. Kenneth W. Godfrey, "Conflict in Hancock County," in Plewe et al., *Mapping Mormonism*, 62–63. See also David Grimsted, *American Mobbing, 1828–1861: Toward Civil War* (New York: Oxford University Press, 2003), 3.
51. Andrew H. Hedges, Alex D. Smith, and Richard Lloyd Anderson, eds., *Journals, Volume 2: December 1841–April 1843*, vol. 2 of the Journals series of *The Joseph Smith Papers*, ed. Dean C. Jessee, Ronald K. Esplin, and Richard Lyman Bushman (Salt Lake City, UT: Church Historian's Press, 2010), 53–54n198.

eternity on 29 May 1843.[52] By 23 December 1843, Mary Fielding was administering these ordinances to other women. Bathsheba W. Smith recalled receiving her own blessings when Mary "pour[ed] oil on" her head and "blessed" her.[53]

When the temple was open to the Saints, following the deaths of Joseph and Hyrum, Mary Fielding worked there to help them receive the same temple blessings she had received earlier. Martha Ann recalled, "I went with my mother every day for three weeks while she worked in the Nauvoo Temple. What joy that was to me."[54]

Hyrum and Mary Fielding also participated in plural marriage, which was being taught and practiced by a select group of Saints in Nauvoo.[55] Hyrum married Mercy Rachel Fielding Thompson, Mary Fielding's sister, on 11 August 1843.[56] Plural marriage became a lightning rod for increased antagonism from without and rebellion from within the Church, including by some senior leaders.

In 1844, tension reached a fever pitch. Opposition to Joseph Smith was coming from both within and without the Latter-day Saint community:

> The opposition that Joseph Smith faced stemmed from a variety of sources. Many non-Mormons in the area, for example, felt the Nauvoo Municipal Court had overstepped its authority on 1 July 1843 when it discharged Joseph Smith from his arrest in Dixon. Following the Democratic Party's virtual sweep in the August 1843 county elections, others, especially local Whigs, opposed Smith's growing political influence in western Illinois. In addition, rumors, misunderstandings, and disagreements about the practice and validity of plural marriage turned several influential Latter-day Saints against the Mormon leader. Some church members also turned against him over doctrinal developments—such as those taught in the King Follett discourse—and over concern that his roles as president of the church and mayor of Nauvoo represented a dangerous combination of church and state. Joseph Smith's tendency to speak freely and publicly against his detractors—a habit his brother Hyrum cautioned him about—also probably contributed to the intensity of the opposition against him.[57]

At this time a small but influential group of Latter-day Saint business, political, and Church leaders organized what they denominated the True Church of Jesus Christ of Latter Day Saints (or Reformed Church) as an alternative to Joseph Smith's prophetic leadership. Opponents increasingly felt that Joseph and Hyrum had to be removed.

The conspiracy to kill the Smith brothers centered among influential men in Hancock County. Through a series of events, including the destruction of an opposition newspaper, the *Nauvoo*

52. Andrew H. Hedges, Alex D. Smith, and Brent M. Rogers, eds., *Journals, Volume 3: May 1843–June 1844*, vol. 3 of the Journals series of *The Joseph Smith Papers*, ed. Ronald K. Esplin and Matthew J. Grow (Salt Lake City, UT: Church Historian's Press, 2015), 24n87.
53. Bathsheba W. Smith, "Testimony," in "Respondent's Testimony, Temple Lot Case," 1892, 302, Community of Christ, Library-Archives, Independence, MO.
54. Martha Ann to posterity, 22 March 1881. Because Martha Ann was between four and five years old when these ordinances were performed, one should be cautious when referring to reminiscences of events that occurred decades earlier.
55. See Kathryn M. Daynes, *More Wives Than One: Transformation of the Mormon Marriage System, 1840–1910* (Urbana: University of Illinois Press, 2001).
56. Mercy R. Thompson, Affidavit, Salt Lake County, Utah Territory, 19 June 1869, in Joseph F. Smith, Affidavits about Celestial Marriage, 1:34.
57. Hedges, Smith, and Rogers, *Journals, Volume 3*, xxii–xxiii.

Joseph and Hyrum Smith, image based on a lithograph by Sutcliffe Maudsley, ca. 1842. Courtesy of CHL.

Expositor, in June 1844 Joseph and Hyrum were ordered to appear in Carthage, Hancock County.[58] They were held in the local two-story jail to await trial.

Thursday afternoon, 27 June 1844, was hot and humid. About 5:00 p.m. an organized armed body of men rushed Carthage Jail and within a few minutes of "scuffling, shouts, and shots"[59] murdered Joseph and Hyrum Smith.[60]

Joseph F. and Martha Ann recalled different details about the days following the martyrdom, but the general outlines remain consistent—Mary Fielding and her family experienced shock, dismay, anger, hopelessness, and fear.

The last time young Joseph F. saw his father alive was on a street in Nauvoo before going with his brother Joseph to Carthage Jail in June 1844. Joseph F., during a visit to Nauvoo, recalled, "This is the exact spot where I stood when the brethren came riding up on their way to Carthage. Without getting off his horse father leaned over in his saddle and picked me up off the ground. He kissed me good-bye and put me down again, and I saw him ride away."[61]

Joseph F. recalled, "I heard the voice of Dimmick B. Huntington at the window of the old chamber of my mother's home on the morning after the 27th day of June, 1844, saying to my mother, 'Hyrum is dead!' . . . It was a misty, foggy morning; everything looked dark and gloomy and dismal, not only to me, but I have heard scores of others say the very same thing. Now, these are some of the things I remember."[62]

A non–Latter-day Saint observer of the events in Nauvoo recalled that Mary Fielding "had gathered her . . . children into the sitting room and the youngest [Martha Ann] about four years old sat on her lap. The poor and disabled that fed at the table of her husband, had come in and formed a group of about twenty about the room. They were all sobbing and weeping, each expressing his grief in his own peculiar way. Mrs. Smith seemed stupefied with horror."[63]

Martha Ann and Joseph F. both remembered seeing the lifeless bodies of their father and uncle in the Mansion House in Nauvoo following their murders. Martha recalled, "Oh how I did love them & imagine again how I felt when I saw them laying side by side murdered in cold blood for preaching the gospel. . . . I saw the anguish & the sorrow the heart felt grief of my dear mother My dear brothers & sisters My aged grandmother & cousins & their mother I cannot never forget how dreadful it was."[64]

Joseph F. also recalled the moment when Mary Fielding lifted him up to look at his dead father.[65] Historian Scott Kenney's description captures the pathos of the tragic scene in the Mansion House, located on Water Street in Nauvoo:

58. See Dallin H. Oaks and Marvin S. Hill, *Carthage Conspiracy: The Trial of the Accused Assassins of Joseph Smith* (Urbana: University of Illinois Press, 1975).
59. Davis Bitton, *The Martyrdom Remembered: A One-Hundred-Fifty-Year Perspective on the Assassination of Joseph Smith* (Salt Lake City, UT: Aspen Books, 1994), xvi. Joseph Smith was the first US presidential candidate to be assassinated. Robert F. Kennedy, who was shot in June 1968, is the most famous.
60. See "Extra," *Nauvoo Neighbor*, 30 June 1844, 1; and "Extra," *Nauvoo Neighbor*, 2 July 1844, 1.
61. Preston Nibley, *The Presidents of the Church* (Salt Lake City, UT: Deseret Book, 1959), 228.
62. Joseph F. Smith, "Boyhood Recollections of President Joseph F. Smith," *Utah Genealogical and Historical Magazine*, April 1916, 57–58.
63. B. W. Richmond, "The Prophet's Death," *Deseret Evening News*, 27 December 1875, 3.
64. Martha Ann to Joanna Spears, 1920.
65. See Preston Nibley, *The Presidents of the Church* (Salt Lake City, UT: Deseret Book, 1941), 229.

Left: Carthage Jail, 27 July 2015. Courtesy of the National Register of Historic Places.
Right: Hyrum Smith's blood-stained shirt from when he was shot and killed in Carthage Jail on 27 June 1844. Photograph by Welden C. Andersen, 2010. Joseph F.'s and Martha Ann's memories of their father's murder was intensified by Mary Fielding Smith's decision to preserve his clothing as a physical reminder of the brutality of the event. Courtesy of CHM.

> Peering through the glass, he saw faces once so familiar, now distended and ashen, their jaws tied shut, cotton stuffed into the bullet hole at the base of his fathers' nose. [Joseph F.] retained few memories of his father, but his mother's lifting him to see Hyrum's body was one of them. At five, he could not fully understand the meaning of death. The anguish in his mother's voice, the sight of his father's and Uncle Joseph's barely recognizable bodies, the stench—it was no doubt a traumatic day. And not only on that day, but for many days following, the sorrow, anger, and fear of the entire community reinforced the horrendous nature of his father's murder. How could the experience *not* have a lasting effect?[66]

The sight and smell of death, especially the disfigured face of the father, Hyrum, had a frightful impact on Martha Ann and Joseph F. Stephen C. Taysom observed, "Unlike most children, who learn eventually that there is no monster under the bed, JFS learned early and often that the brutality he feared was very real, and that it would reach out and snatch happiness away from him with shocking caprice."[67]

Martha Ann and Joseph F. struggled to understand the significance of the tragic events during the last days of June 1844, but the memory of those events was engraved in their minds and hearts for the rest of their lives.[68] Martha Ann's great-great-granddaughter recalled, "When I was a child of about six or seven, I was at my grandparents. Grampa [Elbert Startup] talked about how his

66. Scott G. Kenney, "Before the Beard: Trials of the Young Joseph F. Smith," *Sunstone* 120 (November 2001): 22.
67. See Taysom, *"Like a Fiery Meteor."*
68. See, for example, Joseph F., journal, 27 April 1860.

grandmother [Martha Ann] would ask if he had a testimony of the gospel and of her father, Hyrum Smith, and Uncle Joseph's work. Her last memory of her father was being lifted up as a young child and kissing him goodbye for the last time as he lay in his coffin."[69]

Martha Ann wrote, "I can remember many little things of my beloved father's death. How sad and sorrowful my mother would look. She scarcely ever smiled. If we could get her to laugh we thought we had accomplished quite a feat. I never saw her more than smile. . . . I can see that sorrowful look now [1881]."[70]

The deaths of Hyrum and Joseph were immediately followed by the death of Samuel H. Smith (1808–44), Martha Ann and Joseph F.'s uncle, on 30 July 1844.[71] Mary Fielding took in three of his children to help Samuel's pregnant wife for a season. Of course, Mary Fielding's main responsibilities centered on seven children—five older stepchildren (Lovina was married just days before Hyrum's martyrdom) and two young children, Joseph F. and Martha Ann.[72]

During the winter of 1845–46, the Nauvoo Temple was completed to the point that Saints could gather and worship in the limestone building that dominated the bluff overlooking the Mississippi. Martha Ann and Joseph F. entered the temple to participate in a special ceremony on 26 January 1846.[73] They, along with their half siblings, in their turn, knelt at the altar and were sealed to their individual parents—for Joseph F. and Martha Ann that was Hyrum and Mary Fielding. This was the beginning of a lifetime connection to temples and temple worship for Martha Ann and Joseph F.[74]

After a temporary lull in the conflict in Hancock County between the Saints and their neighbors, attacks on outlying Latter-day Saint settlements increased steadily in an effort to dislodge the Saints from western Illinois. Church leaders agreed to abandon Nauvoo beginning in the spring of 1846,

69. Renee Horton, "Reminiscence," as quoted in Ruth Mae Harris, *Martha Ann, Daughter of Hyrum and Mary Fielding Smith* (Orem, UT: published by the author, 2002), 131.
70. Martha Ann to posterity, 22 March 1881.
71. Sometime after Samuel's death, rumors began to circulate that he had been poisoned by Hosea Stout on orders from Willard Richards; see Dean L. Jarman and Kyle R. Walker, "Samuel Harrison Smith," in *United by Faith: The Joseph Sr. and Lucy Mack Smith Family* (American Fork, UT: Covenant Communications, 2005), 234–35. See also D. Michael Quinn, *The Mormon Hierarchy: Origins of Power* (Salt Lake City, UT: Signature Books, 1994), 152–53; and William Smith, "Mormonism: A Letter from William Smith, Brother of Joseph the Prophet," *New York Tribune*, 19 May 1857, 3. William's letter was quickly debunked by Samuel Smith's son, Samuel H. B. Smith; see "Letter to the Editor," *The Mormon*, 6 June 1857. Although the accusation was generally not taken seriously by the members of the family in Utah, the rumor may be part of the basis for the underlying tension found in some of Joseph F.'s letters to his cousin Josephine Donna Smith, the daughter of Don Carlos Smith (she was known as Ina Coolbrith during most of her adult life). Additionally, much of the tensions between Joseph F. and Coolbrith also developed over her rejection of the Church for what Joseph F. saw as ultimately more worldly pursuits and culture. For one interpretation of their relationship, see Aleta George, *Ina Coolbrith: The Bittersweet Song of California's First Poet Laureate* (Suisun City, CA: Shifting Plates, 2015).
72. Mary Fielding filed a petition to the county court to grant her permission as guardian of John, Jerusha, Sarah, Joseph F., and Martha Ann Smith to sell listed Nauvoo properties for the children's support and education. The petition was signed by Mary Fielding Smith and certified by Hancock County justice of the peace Isaac Higbee and filed by Hancock County circuit court clerk D. E. Head, 18 May 1846. See "Mary Smith, Petition, 1846 April 10, Hancock [County] Circuit Court."
73. Devery S. Anderson and Gary James Bergera, eds., *The Nauvoo Endowment Companies, 1845–1846: A Documentary History* (Salt Lake City, UT: Signature Books, 2005), 497.
74. Eventually Martha Ann was endowed, completed family history work, performed proxy ordinances for family members, and spent her adult life making temple clothing for the living and dead. Joseph F. was endowed, worked with the temple records in the Historian's Office, became an ordinance worker in the Salt Lake Endowment House, and served as the president of the Salt Lake Temple.

hoping to provide a window to prepare for the exodus. Brigham Young and a vanguard company of Saints left Nauvoo in February 1846. Latter-day Saints continued to leave the city during the spring and summer. However, by the fall of 1846, pressure for the remaining Saints to depart came to a climax during the "Battle of Nauvoo" in September 1846. Joseph F. remembered the sound of cannon fire as his family camped across the river after fleeing the city.[75]

Martha Ann recalled leaving Nauvoo: "We left our home, just as it was, with all the furniture, in fact everything we owned. The fruit trees were loaded with rosy peaches and apples. We bade goodby to the loved home that reminded us of our beloved father everywhere we turned."[76]

Eventually, Mary Fielding and her family made their way to the settlement at Winter Quarters in present-day Nebraska on the banks of the Missouri River.[77] The family remained in the area until the spring of 1848. During two successive winters on the banks of the Missouri River, the Saints witnessed more than six hundred men, women, and children die from tuberculosis, cholera, scarlet fever, typhus, and other diseases.[78]

Circumstances were such that when the family moved west with other migrating Saints, nine-year-old Joseph F. and his older half brother John were each responsible for driving one of the family wagons to the Great Salt Lake Valley, the new Latter-day Saint gathering place.[79]

On arriving, the Smiths, like many other pioneer families, slept for a short season in the wagons they had used to make the trek west. They survived that first difficult winter on meager rations of bread, butter, cornmeal, parched corn, and milk. Mary added to their diet a variety of local vegetation, including sego lily bulbs that were boiled, roasted, or made into porridge.

Once in Utah, Joseph F. worked herding the family stock (including protecting the animals from predators), cutting and hauling wood from the nearby canyons, irrigating, harvesting and threshing the crops on the farm, and tending to a myriad of other duties.[80] He later reflected: "My schooling had been extremely limited. My mother taught me to read and write, by the camp fires, and subsequently by the greater luxury of the primeval tallow candle in the covered wagon and the old log cabin, 10 x 12 feet in size, where first the soles of our feet found rest, after the weary months of travel across the plains."[81]

Mary continued to nurture and teach her young daughter Martha Ann the skills necessary to survive on the frontier. According to a family tradition, Martha Ann "learned to spin wool, and as a young teenager, she could spin four skeins a day. Mary Fielding also taught Martha Ann to knit, measuring off a specific amount of yarn which Martha had to knit before a meal. As Martha Ann became more skilled, she learned to weave fabric and dye cloth for bedding and clothing. She even learned to weave denim for men's work clothes."[82]

75. Smith, "Boyhood Recollections," 58–59.
76. As cited in Sarah Harris Passey, "Martha Ann Smith Harris" (unpublished manuscript in editors' possession, courtesy of Carole Call King, granddaughter of Sarah Harris Passey).
77. Gail Geo. Holmes, "The Middle Missouri Valley," in Plewe et al., *Mapping Mormonism*, 76–77.
78. See Conrey Bryson, *Winter Quarters* (Salt Lake City, UT: Deseret Book, 1986), 165.
79. See Joseph F. Smith, "Recollections," *Juvenile Instructor*, 27 May 1871, 87–88; 10 June 1871, 91; and 24 June 1871, 98–99.
80. Andrew Jenson, "The Twelve Apostles: Joseph Fielding Smith," *Historical Record* 6, nos. 3–5 (May 1887): 184. Additional reminiscences are found in several sources, including "Reminiscences, 1838–circa 1848," labeled as "Jos. F. Smith's Journal commencing 13 Nov. 1838," ca. 1890s, CHL. See also Smith, "Boyhood Recollections," 52–69.
81. Jenson, "Twelve Apostles," 184.
82. Harris, *Martha Ann*, 81–82.

Salt Lake City Cemetery, Smith family plot, photographs by Richard Neitzel Holzapfel, 12 October 2013. To the left is the original nineteenth-century Mary Fielding Smith grave marker. The photograph above shows modern grave markers for Joseph F.'s children, who were buried next to Mary Fielding, and a new grave maker for Mary Fielding. Courtesy of the editors.

Malnourished and exhausted, Mary Fielding died in 1852, leaving Joseph F. and Martha Ann orphaned.[83] She was only fifty-one years old when she fell ill on the way home from a meeting. She was taken to the home of Heber C. Kimball (1801–68) and Vilate Kimball (1806–67), where she died after eight weeks and two days of watchful care from her sister and members of the Kimball and Young families.[84] Heber C. Kimball said, "I have never seen a person in life that had a greater anxiety to live than she had, and there was only one thing she desired to live for, and that was to see to her family; it distressed her to think that she could not see to them; she wept about it. She experienced this anxiety for a month previous to her death, and she wept and prayed that the diseased place might be opened."[85]

Following Mary Fielding's death, "Martha Ann, who had just turned eleven, raced from the Kimball home and prayed that she too might die. Joseph F., almost fourteen, fainted."[86]

Brigham Young's funeral address was recently discovered, transcribed from the original Pitman shorthand notes, and published. The transcription begins with the following explanation of the setting for this address: "September 23, a company of friends met at President Kimball's to perform their last duties to Sister Mary Smith who departed this life on Wednesday 22 instant at half past 5 p.m. President Young present. The meeting opened with singing and prayer by President Young."[87]

Brigham counseled those present, including Joseph F. and Martha Ann, "I can [say] to my friends and immediate connections of Sister Mary, and to the children: pattern after her; abide in her good work, be faithful, keep together. Let this family keep together, let them love each other, let them pray, serve the Lord and live just as long as [they] can upon the earth and carry out the work commenced by their father and their mothers."[88]

Hannah Grinnels, known by Joseph F. and Martha Ann as "Aunty Grinnells," who had been living with the family since the death of Jerusha in 1837, took the primary responsibility to care for the younger children.[89] Unfortunately, Hannah died a little more than a year after Mary Fielding, leaving Joseph F. and Martha Ann mourning again. Sources are unclear, but it appears that for a time Joseph F. and Martha Ann moved into the home of their aunt, Mercy Rachel Fielding Thompson (1807–93). The next several years were challenging and difficult for both Joseph F. and Martha Ann. Two years later in April 1854, fifteen-year-old Joseph F. was sent as a missionary to Hawai'i, some three thousand miles from his sister. It was during this mission to the Pacific that Joseph F. and Martha Ann began to write to each other—a tradition that spanned six decades.

83. "Died," *Deseret Weekly News*, 11 December 1852, 3; Edward W. Tullidge, *Women of Mormondom* (New York: Tullidge & Crandall, 1877), 249; and Andrew Jenson, *Latter-day Saint Biographical Encyclopedia* (Salt Lake City, UT: Andrew Jenson History Co., 1914), 2:710–11.

84. Following the deaths of Joseph and Hyrum Smith, many of their plural wives were married to other Church leaders in an effort to support and assist them. Heber C. Kimball married Mary as a plural wife in 1844, but they never lived together in a marriage relationship. However, Heber C. and his wife Vilate Kimball were close friends. See "U.S. and International Marriage Records, 1560–1900," database, Ancestry.com (http://ancestry.com, accessed July 2018), Heber Chase Kimball and Mary Fielding. See also Corbett, *Mary Fielding Smith*, 261.

85. Heber C. Kimball, "Funeral Address," 23 September 1852, in *Journal of Discourses* (London: Latter-day Saints' Book Depot, 1854–86), 1:246.

86. Harris, *Martha Ann*, 83. A number of printed sources attribute a dream about Hyrum and his wife, dated ca. 1852 and found in the Joseph F. Smith Papers (CHL), to Martha Ann. Church History Library staff members believe the dream is more likely attributed to Lovina Smith Walker, Joseph F. and Martha Ann's oldest half sister.

87. Brigham Young, "Sermon at the Funeral of Mary Fielding Smith," 23 September 1852, CHL.

88. Young, "Sermon at the Funeral of Mary Fielding Smith."

89. See Richard P. Harris, "Martha Ann Smith Harris," *Relief Society Magazine*, January 1924, 14.

For, Martha.   J. F. S.

scarcely a day to call mine, but I hope you have.

Be attentive Martha to your work, when you are doing any thing confine your mind to that one thing till it is done, and then you will never have too many irons in the fire at once, and you will not be figity and uneasy, and then as soon as you have done your worke and feel like takeing a 'rough and tumble' all right.

You will hear all the news Martha in Charles letter, and also in Johns so I have no need of writing one thing twice over,

You say in your letter Martha that Miss Bolewinkle has been married, also Rachel, and Hellen too, is in a fair way for it by all appearances. Well I hope their enjoyments will be full. I don't begrudge them their situation, nor any one else. I think it is a good plan, I suppose they are not all married yet?

I expect of course that Mary Jane will soon go off as well as your self, paha (perhaps) well I may join you some time, but when I do not know, but make yourselves contented and Joseph will look out for No. One, I guess No. Two. will not suffer till I finde her, Please look out for Martha and be carful when you step that your foot is solid that you may not fall throw,

I want you should allways tender my kinds regards to Aunt Thompson and my love to all of our relatives, and friends, Tell them I donot forget them in my prayers. and never will, I received a letter from Jerusha this Mail she was well when she wrote, but I donot like the idea of them going so far from the City, She said she had just recieved a letter from Sarah stating that you were all well, &c, She said her little girl grows fine, and she his named it Hanah after Aunty,

Well I will have to close, I am just going to attend a meeting with the Saints, pray for me allways, and I will do the same. write often, and I will do the same also, give my love to all the folks and accept the same to yourself, may God bless you and you all that you may ever be strong, is the prayers of your Bro, } Joseph Smith

Be carfull about going among Poison Ova. be a good girl.

Joseph F. to Martha Ann, 14 July 1856

Decade 1

1854–1859

JOSEPH F. TO MARTHA ANN, LAHAINA, MAUI, SANDWICH ISLANDS, 9 JUNE 1855

If you have any triyals to put up with, you must remember that it is to try you and to see whether you are smith grit or not, but sho your smith. and that good too when it comes to the pinch, but have patiance, and long suffering, be a Mormon out, and out, and you will be ~~pl~~ blessed.

MARTHA ANN TO JOSEPH F., SALT LAKE CITY, UTAH, 3 MAY 1857

I am thankful to my father for giving me a brother that cears for mya. wefare for I know that you care for my welfare more than ennyboddy else can ~~feel~~ <care> fore upon this irth O Joseph would to god that I could expres feellings just as they are and [illegible erasure] I express my thanks to you for your kindness to me. I can never for git you for ever no not for an hour I have never forgotts you senc you left me to far away from your home. I have thaught of you in what ever place I have been no matter whare.

William Jasper and Martha Ann Smith Harris, ca. 1857. Courtesy of Carole Call King.

Decade Introduction

Mary Fielding Smith raised Joseph F. and Martha Ann by herself following Hyrum's death in 1844. The influence of the Fielding family on Martha Ann and Joseph F. eclipsed the Smith family's influence once Mary Fielding crossed the Mississippi River to Iowa in 1846—leaving most of the extended Smith family members, including a beloved grandmother, Lucy Mack Smith, in Illinois.

Shortly after Mary and her family arrived in the Salt Lake Valley, they traded the hardships of overland travel for those associated with establishing what they hoped would be their first permanent home. The summer cricket infestations of early pioneer Utah, for example, devastated crop yields, making the winters of 1849–50 and 1850–51 deplorable for the settlers.[1] Nevertheless, Mary and her family worked hard and endured. By 1850 they had completed a two-room, 14′×22′ adobe home on a forty-acre farm located about six miles southeast of Salt Lake City.[2] The year 1852 seemed to be a year of promise for the Smith household, including Joseph F. and his sister Martha Ann.[3]

FORMATIVE EVENTS IN JOSEPH F.'S LIFE

Between 12 May and 21 September 1852, a brief period of less than five months, Joseph F. experienced three important events that shaped his future experience in ways no one could have anticipated, including himself. The first occurred when President Heber C. Kimball (1801–68), a family friend and member of the Church's First Presidency, baptized him in City Creek on 12 May. He recalled:

> I felt in my soul that if I had sinned—and surely I was not without sin—that it had been forgiven me; that I was indeed cleansed from sin; my heart was touched, and I felt that

1. The so-called Mormon cricket (*Anabrus simplex*) is a wingless species of shield-backed katydid. See https://www.britannica.com/animal/shield-backed-katydid.
2. See Frank T. Matheson, *The Mary Fielding Smith Adobe Home* (Boulder, CO: Western Interstate Commission for Higher Education, 1980).
3. See David M. Whitchurch, "Personal Glimpses of Joseph F. Smith: Adolescent to Prophet," in *Joseph F. Smith: Reflections on the Man and His Times*, ed. Craig K. Manscill et al. (Provo, UT: Religious Studies Center, Brigham Young University; Salt Lake City, UT: Deseret Book, 2013), 159–80.

Mary Fielding Smith's home, ca. 1910. Joseph F. Smith (third from left) and other family members at the Smith family homestead in the Sugar House area of Salt Lake City. The home was originally located at 2818 South Highland Drive, the southwest corner of 27th South and Highland Drive, before being moved to its present location at the This Is the Place Heritage Park in Salt Lake City. On the back of the photo mount is a description in Joseph F. Smith's handwriting: "The old home of Mary Fielding Smith, widow of Hyrum Smith, where she and family settled in the early Spring of 1849: They having arrived in Salt Lake Valley Sept. 23rd 1848. And wintered on Mill Creek during the winter of 1848–9. Joseph F. Smith." Courtesy of CHL.

> I would not injure the smallest insect beneath my feet. I felt as if I wanted to do good everywhere to everybody and to everything. I felt a newness of life, a newness of desire to do that which was right. There was not one particle of desire for evil left in my soul. I was but a little boy, it is true, when I was baptized; but this was the influence that came upon me, and I know that it was from God, and was and ever has been a living witness to me of my acceptance of the Lord.[4]

The second event occurred when John Smith (1781–1854), his father's uncle and the Church Patriarch, gave him a patriarchal blessing on 25 June, just over a month after his baptism. Uncle John placed his hands on his head and began, "Brother Joseph in the name of Jesus of Nazareth . . ."[5] As the aged Patriarch spoke during the next few moments, Joseph F. learned about himself and his future: "Thou are one of the House of Ephraim called to push the people together from the

4. *Sixty-Eighth Annual Conference* (Salt Lake City, UT: Deseret News Press, 1898), 65–66. See also Joseph F. Smith, *Gospel Doctrine: Selections from the Sermons and Writings of Joseph F. Smith*, comp. John A. Widtsoe, 5th ed. (Salt Lake City, UT: Deseret Book, 1939), 117–18.
5. John Smith, "Patriarchal Blessing of Joseph F. Smith, 1852." Joseph F. received a second patriarchal blessing on 25 February 1874 under the hands of his older half brother, John Smith (not to be confused with his father's uncle, John Smith, who gave him his first blessing in 1852).

Church Patriarch John Smith, ca. early 1850s, photograph by Marsena Cannon, Salt Lake City, Utah. Courtesy of CHL.

ends of the earth and from the Isles afar off."[6] The Patriarch continued, "You shall lead thousands to Zion." Joseph F. heard many other promises, including "The mantle of thy Father shall be upon thee. . . . Your name shall be had in honorable remembrance among the Saints for ever. . . . Your posterity shall be great. . . . They shall spread upon the Mountains so numerous that they cannot be numbered for Multitudes." The blessing concluded with a solemn "Even so Amen."[7]

The third event occurred when Mary Fielding died on 21 September 1852. Joseph F. was thirteen years old and Martha Ann was eleven. Mary Fielding's stepchildren were older but still relatively young: twenty-five-year-old Lovina was married and living in the Midwest, John was unmarried and one day short of his twentieth birthday, Jerusha was unmarried and sixteen years old, and Sarah was unmarried and fifteen years old. Mary Fielding's death deeply affected all of Hyrum's children, but none more than Joseph F. and Martha Ann.

In successive moves, Martha Ann and Joseph F. lived with Hannah Grinnels, the housekeeper and caretaker; their aunt Mercy Thompson; and their older half brother, John Smith. According to a family tradition, Martha Ann remained with John Smith until she was married in 1857.[8]

Mary Fielding's death occurred less than three months after Joseph F. received his patriarchal blessing. She had been his "strong spirit and wise mind" guide and now she was gone.[9] Like the approaching fall weather, Mary Fielding's death began to cast a long dark shadow over his baptism and patriarchal blessing. During the next two years, Joseph F.'s future seemed less certain than what his patriarchal blessing envisioned.

In 1888 Joseph F. described to a friend, Samuel L. Adams (1856–1910), the turmoil he felt following his mother's death: "After my mother's death there followed 18 months—from Sept 21st, 1852 to April, 1854 of perilous times for me. I was almost like a comet or fiery meteor, without attraction or gravitation to keep me balanced or guide me within reasonable bounds."[10] Just days before he died in 1918, Joseph F. added, "I had to start out in the world without father or mother.

6. See Doctrine and Covenants 58:44–45; Deuteronomy 33:17.
7. John Smith, "Patriarchal Blessing, 1852."
8. Richard P. Harris, "Martha Ann Smith Harris," *Relief Society Magazine*, January 1924, 14.
9. Smith, *Gospel Doctrine*, 646.
10. Joseph F. to Samuel L. Adams, 11 May 1888.

Samuel L. Adams, ca. 1890, photograph by J. J. Booth, St. George, Utah. Adams, one of Joseph F.'s friends, received a letter from Joseph F. that discussed the challenges he faced following his mother's death in 1852. Courtesy of CHL.

. . . Without anything to start with in the world, except the example of my mother, I struggled along with hard knocks in early life."[11]

By his own admission, both in public and private, the "hard knocks" included learning to control his temper, impulsive behavior, tendency to judge people hastily, and proclivity to hold a grudge against anyone he felt had wronged his family. He also experimented with two commonly used products of his day—alcohol and tobacco. Joseph F. eventually overcame these habits and invited others to do the same. In some cases, he strongly warned against their use to avoid the consequences of abusing them.[12] This is not surprising since nineteenth-century Latter-day Saints did not generally observe the Word of Wisdom the way their modern counterparts are required to do today.[13]

Doctrine and Covenants 89, a revelation known as the Word of Wisdom, was originally "sent" as a "greeting" and "not by commandment or constraint" when it was given to the Saints through the Prophet Joseph Smith in February 1833.[14] Martha Ann and Joseph F. lived at a time when waterborne disease, especially cholera, killed tens of thousands of people during several pandemics in the 1800s, including along the Mormon Trail between 1849 and 1855.[15] People in the second half of the nineteenth century faced diseases without the medical advances that have made twentieth- and twenty-first-century epidemics less common and deadly. In this setting, fermented drinks ended up being a safe alternative to local water sources. Later engineering advances eventually provided clean-water delivery systems and took human and animal waste away from human water sources.

Additionally, most Americans believed in the use of alcohol for medical purposes. Even though Latter-day Saints generally believed "the general use of whiskey and liquor was contrary to the principle [of the Word of Wisdom]," they nevertheless generally believed "these beverages had redeeming medicinal qualities. It was drunk by some to help remedy the effects of cholera, and

11. "Minutes of a Meeting Held at the Bee Hive House, 1918 November 10."
12. See Joseph F. to Martha Ann, 14 June 1872, herein.
13. The current requirement to observe the proscriptions mentioned in the Word of Wisdom as a test of fellowship and worthiness was established by President Heber J. Grant in 1921. See Thomas G. Alexander, *Mormonism in Transition: A History of the Latter-day Saints, 1890–1930* (Urbana: University of Illinois Press, 1986), 258–71; and Paul H. Peterson and Ronald W. Walker, "Brigham Young's Word of Wisdom Legacy," *BYU Studies* 42, nos. 3–4 (2003): 29–64. Currently, Latter-day Saints are not required to observe the prescriptions (as opposed to proscriptions) mentioned in the Word of Wisdom.
14. Doctrine and Covenants 89:2; emphasis added.
15. See Charles E. Rosenberg, *The Cholera Years: The United States in 1832, 1849 and 1866* (Chicago: University of Chicago Press, 1987).

evidently was used as an alleviating cure for the effects of other sicknesses."[16] Joseph F. held a similar position.[17]

The use of tobacco in the United States was widespread, increasing almost exponentially from the 1800s to the mid-1960s. In the late nineteenth and early twentieth centuries, Americans consumed tobacco primarily in the form of chewing tobacco and cigars. As one report notes, "The [annual] per-capita consumption of tobacco products in the early 1880s was approximately 6 pounds of tobacco per person aged 18 and older; 56 percent of that tobacco was in the form of chewing tobacco, whereas only 1 percent took the form of manufactured cigarette."[18] Spitting tobacco was publicly acceptable for most common people, and spittoons were ubiquitous.[19]

Historian Jed Woodworth provides context for the gradual acceptance of the Word of Wisdom:

> It required time to wind down practices that were so deeply ingrained in family tradition and culture, especially when fermented beverages of all kinds were frequently used for medicinal purposes. The term "strong drink" certainly included distilled spirits such as whiskey, which thereafter the Latter-day Saints generally shunned. They took a more moderate approach to milder alcoholic beverages like beer and "pure wine of the grape of the vine, of your own make." For the next two generations, Latter-day Saint leaders taught the Word of Wisdom as a command from God, but they tolerated a variety of viewpoints on how strictly the commandment should be observed. This incubation period gave the Saints time to develop their own tradition of abstinence from habit-forming substances. By the early 20th century, when scientific medicines were more widely available and temple attendance had become a more regular feature of Latter-day Saint worship, the Church was ready to accept a more exacting standard of observance that would eliminate problems like alcoholism from among the obedient. In 1921, the Lord inspired President Heber J. Grant to call on all Saints to live the Word of Wisdom to the letter by completely abstaining from all alcohol, coffee, tea, and tobacco.[20]

MISSION TO THE SANDWICH ISLANDS

Sometime during the winter of 1853–54, Martha Ann and Joseph F. were in school when, according to Joseph's own recollection, the teacher pulled out a leather strap to punish Martha Ann.[21]

16. Paul H. Peterson, "An Historical Analysis of the Word of Wisdom" (master's thesis, Brigham Young University, 1972), 24.
17. Joseph F. noted in 1879, "I bought a gallon of Alcohol at the drug store for bathing and medical purposes. Cost. $3.25 paid." Joseph F., journal, 10 October 1879. See also Joseph F. Smith to Martha Ann, 28 July 1881, herein.
18. "Epidemiology of Tobacco Use: History and Current Trends," in *Ending the Tobacco Problem: A Blueprint for the Nation*, ed. Richard J. Bonnie, Kathleen Stratton, and Robert B. Wallace (Washington, DC: National Academies Press, 2007), 41.
19. In the late nineteenth-century United States, spittoons became a very common feature of banks, hotels, railway carriages, stores, and government buildings, including the White House and the United States Capitol building.
20. Jed Woodworth, "The Word of Wisdom: D&C 89," in *Revelations in Context: The Stories Behind the Sections of the Doctrine and Covenants* (Salt Lake City, UT: The Church of Jesus Christ of Latter-day Saints, 2016), 186.
21. There is no record that explains why the teacher, D. M. Merrick, had chosen to discipline Martha Ann on this occasion. Whatever happened following this incident, B. F. Cummings reported, "President Smith speaks highly of [Merrick] as a teacher . . . and states that under him he made more rapid progress than under any other." B. F. Cummings, "Shining Lights: How They Acquired Brightness," *Contributor*, January 1895, 174.

Although corporal punishment in schools[22] was a common practice in the nineteenth century, Joseph F. defended his younger sister and shouted at the schoolmaster, D. M. Merrick, "Don't whip her with that!" When Merrick turned on him, the apparently stronger frontier boy "licked him good and plenty."[23]

This incident reveals the internal conflict Joseph F. faced as a young man in the wake of real persecution, loss, and death.[24] As noted, Joseph F. never seems to have been able to forget or forgive those who he felt wronged his family. Now Mary Fielding was gone and Joseph F. was in trouble.[25]

Joseph F. was expelled from school following the incident with the schoolteacher, ending his opportunity to continue a formal education. Apparently hoping to provide Joseph F. the direction he desperately needed in life, Church leaders decided to act to save the young man. During the April 1854 general conference, President Brigham Young (1801–77) read the names of those "appointed . . . to go on missions," including the list of those called to the "Pacific Isles," three thousand miles away from Salt Lake City.[26] Among those called to the islands was fifteen-year-old "Joseph Smith (son of Hyrum)."[27] Like most of those called that day, Joseph F. had no warning or even suspicion that he would be asked to serve a full-time mission. Called to the Sandwich Islands, he was at the time the youngest missionary ever called to a full-time proselyting mission in the Church.[28] As was the custom, Joseph F. was also endowed at this time.[29]

Joseph F.'s missionary certificate, signed by the First Presidency of the Church, is dated 18 April 1854. Six days later, on 24 April, he received the Melchizedek Priesthood and was ordained an elder by Church Apostle and family relative George A. Smith (1817–75), his father's cousin. On the same day, Joseph F. "received [his] endowments in the old Council House" and was set apart as a missionary by Apostles Orson Hyde (1805–78) and Parley P. Pratt (1807–57), "Parley being mouth."[30]

Years after Joseph F.'s mission to the Hawaiian Islands, George A. Smith visited the home of Ira Ames (1804–69) in Wellsville, Cache County, Utah, with Joseph F., who had just become a member of the Quorum of the Twelve in 1867. Charles W. Nibley (1849–1931), who was present on the occasion, remembered Old Father Ames asking George A. "who of the Smiths was this young Joseph F." George A. replied, "He was Hyrum's son; his mother Mary Fielding Smith." Ames

22. Legal efforts to stop this practice altogether started with Sweden in 1979, followed by Finland in 1983. In the United States it is still legal in nineteen states as of July 2018. The United Kingdom and the Czech Republic still allow teachers to administer physical punishment in certain situations and with certain limitations.
23. Charles W. Nibley, "Reminiscences of President Joseph F. Smith," *Improvement Era*, January 1919, 191–92; see also Smith, *Gospel Doctrine*, 656.
24. Stephen C. Taysom opines that events from Joseph F.'s birth in Far West, Missouri, until his arrival in Utah were defining moments. See Taysom's forthcoming biography, *"Like a Fiery Meteor": The Life of Joseph F. Smith.*
25. Joseph F. reflected on this challenging period, as he did about the other challenges he faced later in life, in public and private, inviting others to learn from his mistakes and his triumphs. For a thoughtful and sympathetic discussion, see Nathaniel R. Ricks, "Triumphs of the Young Joseph F. Smith," in Manscill et al., *Joseph F. Smith: Reflections on the Man and His Times*, 37–51.
26. "Minutes," *Deseret News*, 13 April 1854, 2–3.
27. "Minutes," *Deseret News*, 13 April 1854, 2–3.
28. The Hawaiian Islands were known as the Sandwich Islands at this time. They were so named by the first European visitor, Captain James Cook, after his sponsor, John Montagu, 4th Earl of Sandwich. The Sandwich Islands are composed of eight major islands, several atolls, and numerous islets. In 1854 these islands were an independent kingdom ruled by King Kamehameha III (King Kamehameha the Great). Beginning in the 1840s, the current name, Hawaiian Islands, began to be used and eventually became the common designation.
29. At this time, temple ordinances were being performed in the upper room of the Council House, located on the corner of Main Street and South Temple Street.
30. Andrew Jenson, "The Twelve Apostles: Joseph Fielding Smith," *Historical Record* 6, nos. 3–5 (May 1887): 184.

then observed, "He looks like a likely young fellow." George A. agreed, "Yes, I think he will be alright. His father and mother left him when he was a young child, and we have been looking after him to try and help him along. We first sent him to school, but it was not long before he licked the schoolmaster and could not go to school. We then sent him on a mission, and he did pretty well at that. I think he will make good as an apostle."[31] Joseph F.'s call to serve in Hawai'i when he was a young, inexperienced, and rough fifteen-year-old began a personal journey that would eventually allow him to claim many of the promises he received from his baptism, confirmation, and patriarchal blessing.

George A. Smith, ca. 1856, photograph by Marsena Cannon, Salt Lake City, Utah. Courtesy of CHL.

In May 1854 Joseph F., along with twenty-one other missionaries going to the Pacific Isles, left Salt Lake City.[32] The group traveled to San Francisco by way of San Bernardino,[33] where some of them worked in the nearby mountains making "cut shingles" to help pay for their traveling expenses.[34] Joseph F. and some of the missionaries embarked from San Pedro on a steamer for San Francisco and then departed on the *Vaquero* for the islands on 8 September 1854.[35] They finally arrived in Honolulu, the capital of the Kingdom of Hawai'i, nearly twenty days later, on 27 September 1854.[36]

31. Smith, *Gospel Doctrine*, 655–56. Reminiscences present historians with challenges because memory often influences the way a story is remembered, especially after a long period of time has passed before retelling the story. As a result, historians are careful how they use reminiscences, preferring to use contemporary primary sources instead. However, lacking the kind of primary sources needed to adequately reconstruct Joseph F.'s life before he began to record his thoughts and experiences in letters and personal journals in the mid-1850s, we have exercised caution in drawing on reminiscences.
32. Joseph F. later noted that he departed Salt Lake City "in company with D. M. Merrick, bound for the Sandwich Islands." Joseph F., journal, 5 May 1857. If this was the same schoolmaster that he "licked," there may have been reconciliation rather quickly following the incident at school.
33. This was an important Latter-day Saint agricultural settlement in Southern California founded in 1851. See Edward Leo Lyman, *San Bernardino: The Rise and Fall of a California Community* (Salt Lake City, UT: Signature Press, 1996).
34. Jenson, "Twelve Apostles," 185.
35. Conway B. Sonne, *Ships, Saints, and Mariners: A Maritime Encyclopedia of Mormon Migration, 1830–1890* (Salt Lake City, UT: University of Utah Press, 1987), 193–94.
36. Jenson, "Twelve Apostles," 186.

The Sandwich Islands had been first dedicated for missionary work just four years earlier, in 1850.[37] According to one study, the total Hawaiian population (including those who were part Hawaiian) stood at 71,019 about the time Joseph F. arrived. Christianization was virtually complete with a Protestant membership of 56,840, followed by a Catholic membership of 11,401 and a Latter-day Saint membership of 2,778.[38] The Saints were organized into fifty-three branches scattered around the islands.[39]

CHALLENGES AND OPPORTUNITIES

Joseph F. faced major challenges during his first mission to the islands, including a new language, new culture, new and exotic foods, and exposure to new religious traditions.[40] Biographer John J. Hammond observes, "It is hard to imagine today what a shock it was for New England sailors and missionaries to see the Sandwich Islands (Hawai'i) for the first time: the flora and fauna was different, the food unrecognizable, the customs and language incomprehensible. . . . It was an extreme exercise in faith. They had little funds; there was no support system in case they were without food or lodging; the mission existed in name only and had no assets. . . . Many missionaries could not cope and soon left the islands."[41]

Joseph F. was one of the missionaries who decided to stay in Hawai'i until he was honorably released. He discovered that the people he served "had different habits to anything I had before known, and their food, and dress and houses and everthing were new and strange."[42]

LĀHAINĀ FEVER

Within a few days, Joseph F. was assigned to labor in Maui. He recalled, "On my way to Maui, on board a small schooner, I was attacked with a severe fever, which clung to me for over two weeks."[43] Mary Jane Dilworth Hammond (1831–77), the wife of Elder Francis A. Hammond (1822–1900), took care of him during this critical time and noted his progress in her diary.

> Sat. Oct 7th /54 School half a day . . . Bro. Joseph Sm not very well but he is better than he was . . . about 1, o clock we was waken by the native Brethren from Wailuku with a couple

37. The mission covered several of the islands, but most of the work centered on Hawai'i (for which the island chain eventually took its name), Maui (an important Protestant missionary and New England whaling center), Lāna'i (the Church's gathering place in the 1850s), Moloka'i (where Joseph F. spent the last four months of his mission), O'ahu (where the political capital of the Kingdom of Hawai'i was located at the time), and Kaua'i (an island west of O'ahu). See R. Lanier Britsch, *Unto the Islands of the Sea: A History of the Latter-day Saints in the Pacific* (Salt Lake City, UT: Deseret Book, 1986), 94–95.
38. Robert C. Schmitt, "Religious Statistics of Hawaii, 1825–1972," *Hawaiian Journal of History* 7 (1973): 41–47.
39. Fred E. Woods, "The Palawai Pioneers on the Island of Lanai: The First Hawaiian Latter-day Saint Gathering Place (1854–1864)," *Mormon Historical Studies* 5, no. 2 (Fall 2004): 5.
40. Hawai'i was in transition from a pre-Christian culture to a new, amalgamated Christian culture, one heavily influenced by New England Calvinist missionaries and Anglo-American merchants, traders, and whalers. Their economic, political, religious, and social world had been turned upside down with the advent of British and American explores, whalers, and missionaries. Aspects of precontact Hawaiian culture had been officially banned beginning in 1818. However, some Hawaiians retained certain practices and beliefs or adapted them.
41. John J. Hammond, *Island Adventures: The Hawaiian Mission of Francis A. Hammond, 1851–1865* (Salt Lake City, UT: Signature Books, 2016), ix.
42. Hyrum M. Smith III and Scott G. Kenney, comps., *From Prophet to Son: Advice of Joseph F. Smith to His Missionary Sons* (Salt Lake City, UT: Deseret Book, 1981), vii.
43. Jenson, "Twelve Apostles," 186.

of horses to take the two Brothers over to Wailuku . . . but Joseph did not because he was not able for he has the touch of the Lahaina fever

Sund Oct. 8th /54 This is sunday morning there was no Early morning meeting about 10. oclock there there was 6 gather to meeting Bro Joseph and myself whent in had a little meeting and then dismissed they were very anxious to have Bro Joseph speak they thought surely he could speak the language they seem to have a great deal of love for him.

Tues Oct 10th all quite well I buisy washing untill 9. o clock then called school and sewed a little Bro Joseph is better this morning he has had the Lahaina fever but not heavey.

Frid Oct 13th /54 Early this morning Bro Karren came here from Honolulu on his way to Lahaina he stoped here all day and about 12 o clock he and Bro Joseph and Mr Hammond left for Lanai left me and the family allalone there is 7 ships in harbor.[44]

THE HAWAIIAN LANGUAGE

About three months after arriving in the islands, Joseph F. had not yet spoken in Hawaiian in any meeting even though he had been diligently studying the language. Elder Redick N. Allred (1822–1905) decided that the time had come and invited him, in Joseph F.'s words, to "give out the hymn, then to pray, and then, before the close of the meeting, to speak, all of which I did to the best of my knowledge, and I felt, and so did he, that the 'ice' was now broken."[45] The same day or the next (Joseph F. could not remember) he "accompanied Brother Allred to another branch . . . where I took my part with him in administering the sacrament, blessing some children and baptizing and confirming, all of which I did in the Hawaiian language."[46]

Joseph F. was now fully engaged and was sent on a 125-mile tour of the Church branches on the east end of Maui with a native Hawaiian missionary, Elder Pake (unknown dates). Joseph F. recalled, "We made a sucessful tour, visited all the branches, held meetings and were warmly received and kindly treated by all."[47]

About a month later, Joseph F. reported to Martha Ann, "I am well and Harty. and Have grew conciderable since you saw me last that things were progressing."[48] In March 1855 Joseph F. reported to George A. Smith, "I have been greatly blessed in obtaining a portion of their language, and by the blessings of the Lord I have got so that I can chat quite freely with the natives in their own tongue." He continued "to speak in meetings several times in the native language."[49]

Mission president Francis A. Hammond noted with delight that Joseph F. had spoken in the April 1855 conference, "causing all the saints to rejoice exccedingly. He has only been here 6 months. The Lord has been with him in getting hold of the language. He spoke very feelingly & I rejoiced much to hear his voice in the native language."[50]

44. Mary Jane Dilworth Hammond, journal, vol. 1, 1853–1855, BYU.
45. Quoted in Jenson, "Twelve Apostles," 186.
46. Quoted in Jenson, "Twelve Apostles," 186.
47. Quoted in Jenson, "Twelve Apostles," 187.
48. Joseph F. to Martha Ann, 28 January 1855, herein.
49. Joseph F. to George A. Smith, 19 March 1855, published in "Sandwich Islands," *Deseret News*, 11 July 1855, 143.
50. F. A. Hammond, journal, 8–9 April 1855.

"MY CANDID OPINION"

Joseph F.'s observations about life in the islands are not surprising given the cultural, political, religious, and historical context. In his surviving diaries and letters from his first mission to Hawai'i, he recorded his candid opinions about almost everything he observed and experienced.[51]

In one letter written to his sister from Lāhainā on the island of Maui, Joseph F. observed, "The signs of the times here are about as useual, there is but one Ship in this harbar now. but the streats are sworming with sailors, and prostitutes of the lowest grade. I tell you it is differant here to what it is in the vallyes. Men and Women go about the streats day and night, one party seeking for money and the other seeking to spend it, we can only let them . . . work out their own damnation."[52]

Rear View of Lahaina, showing several ships in the harbor, published in Edward T. Perkins, *Na Motu: or, Reef-Rovings in the South Seas* (New York: Pudney & Russell, 1854).

Joseph F.'s journals and letters are remarkably candid in revealing his personal views on matters, including other Latter-day Saint missionaries and Hawaiian Church members. Not only did missionaries have to deal with Christian ministers who criticized the Church, but they also had to deal with John Hyde, a former Church member and one of the most notorious apostates during the early Utah period. He had been called to Hawai'i as a full-time Latter-day Saint missionary, most likely to rekindle his spiritual commitment to the Church. However, on his way to his mission, Hyde

51. For a good reason, Nathaniel R. Ricks titled his edited edition of Joseph F.'s Hawaiian mission diaries *"My Candid Opinion": The Sandwich Islands Diaries of Joseph F. Smith, 1856–1857* (Salt Lake City, UT: Signature Books, 2011).
52. Joseph F. to Martha Ann, 18 February 1856, herein.

rejected his faith and decided to give lectures critical of the Church in Hawaiʻi.[53] Eventually Hyde published his most influential book critical of the Church, *Mormonism: Its Leaders and Designs*.[54]

Joseph F.'s surviving mission journals highlight the physical, emotional, social, and spiritual challenges he faced as a young teenager, including the struggle to find adequate food during much of his mission. He recorded that on Molakaʻi, for example, most of the people were "afflicted with a scarcity of food."[55]

During this mission, Joseph F. also confronted difficult economic challenges as he labored without "purse or scrip."[56] Many local members were poor themselves, as noted above, and sometimes they were either unable or unwilling to help the missionaries, who in such cases had to find employment.[57] When the members did help, Joseph F. was grateful and noted that such kindnesses and sacrifices "should not be forgotten." For example, he noted in March 1856 that a brother "gave me his shoes from off his feet and went barefooted himself."[58] Given their own situation and their past support of the missionaries, the members' help and support were nothing less than remarkable.

Joseph F. and his fellow missionaries generally lived with the local people in thatched-roof huts and ate the same foods. As a result they were often criticized by British and Anglo-American Protestant missionaries for lowering their standards. The young Joseph F. struggled to adapt to this new environment. "I have slept in places where should my hog sleep my stumiche would forbid me eating of it," he wrote.[59] In other words, the conditions were so poor that he would not eat a pig that lived in the same manner.

Joseph F.'s letters and journals note other challenges he faced that were unlike anything he had experienced before his mission: "I was a little dubious about going into the seas there had been 15 sharks caught . . . the longest was about 6 feet."[60] The very young teenager sometimes struggled with Church members, Latter-day Saint missionaries, and religious leaders and missionaries of other denominations. He welcomed letters from home and was greatly disappointed when a letter did not arrive as expected.

THE GATHERING AT LĀNAʻI

As early as 1831, Latter-day Saint missionaries invited converts to leave their homes wherever they lived and gather to specific geographical areas identified by their leaders. Beginning in 1847, most

53. See, for example, "Utah as It Is," *The Polynesian*, 18 October 1858, 94; and "Lectures on Mormonism," *The Polynesian*, 25 October 1856, 98. Interestingly, a letter to the editor, written by one of the Latter-day Saint missionaries, Edward Partridge, was published in the same issue. See Edward L. Hart, "John Hyde, Junior—An Earlier View," *BYU Studies* 16, no. 2 (1976): 1–7.
54. John H. Hyde Jr., *Mormonism: Its Leaders and Designs* (New York: W. P. Fetridge, 1857).
55. Jenson, "Twelve Apostles," 187.
56. Latter-day Saint missionaries generally relied on members and others for food, housing, and laundry services during their labors. This common nineteenth-century missionary practice was based on Luke 10:4 and Doctrine and Covenants 24:18.
57. The Hawaiian population had been decimated by the introduction of European weapons and disease, including sexually transmitted ones, following the arrival of Captain Cook in 1778. While exact numbers are unknown, the population may have fallen from an estimated 300,000 at the time of European contact to fewer than 80,000 by 1854. The economic situation in the islands eroded significantly during this period, and the culture was in complete disarray. Those living away from Honolulu, the capital of the Kingdom of Hawaiʻi, lived in a variety of conditions, but many lived in what some have described as wretched conditions.
58. Joseph F., journal, 1 March 1856.
59. Joseph F., journal, 4 July 1856.
60. Joseph F., journal, 22 July 1857.

converts were invited to gather in Utah. However, since the laws of the Kingdom of Hawai'i prevented native Hawaiians from emigrating to the United States, Church leaders asked the Hawaiian converts to gather on the island of Lāna'i.[61] Joseph F. also noted this situation in one of his letters to his sister: "The Sandwich Island mission is rather weacker than it has been <for> sone time."[62] In addition to the challenges that the Saints who remained behind experienced, Joseph F. wrote about the difficulty that the gathering caused for those who moved to Lāna'i. "The Natives are verry poor here upon this Island as they have mostly all left their homes and came to this place."[63]

Joseph F. noted while on Hawai'i, "I allmost sometimes dread when sunday comes, for where the fiew saints who are left, are so dull and indifferant as those in my field, it is a hard task to preach to them in plainness." Yet there were times when he felt a "good spirit" among the members of the Church, as he observed: "Where the saints are alive to the work, it is a chearing in sted of a labourious task to address them."[64]

Joseph F.'s success in learning Hawaiian and his persistence in preaching the gospel led to a number of assignments in his mission, including being assigned as a conference president.[65] The first assignment came when at only age sixteen he was called as "President over the Maui Conference," which included forty-one branches with 1,253 members.[66] He also served as president of the Kohala Conference on Maui. He was then sent to preside over the Hilo Conference on Hawai'i, the largest island in the chain, followed by an assignment to direct the work on Molaka'i.

FIRE ON LĀNA'I

On 26 June 1856, Joseph F. received a letter from Edward Partridge Jr. (1833–1900), a fellow missionary, informing him that a fire had destroyed one of the mission buildings on the island of Lāna'i. "The house is burnt to the ground," Partridge wrote, "and what is wors, most of the things that ware in it. four trunks were destroyed—three only saved. yours I am sorry to say was burned with its contents."[67] Joseph F. lost two diaries, presumably covering the period from his arrival in 1854 to the end of 1855, extra clothes, toiletries, books, and letters, including those sent to him by Martha Ann.[68] He added, "Well these dear earned fiew things is gon and not one saved, and now I am destitute, but with old Jobe exclaim, 'The Lord givith and the Lord taketh away, blessed by the name of the Lord' I am confident that he has and will provide for his servants, so all is well."[69]

In the last year of his mission, the Church's stability in Hawai'i had changed dramatically from the early period of rapid conversions and growth. The work not only had leveled off but also had begun a steady decline. The challenges, difficulties, and trials Joseph F. faced on this first mission provided a foundation for his lifelong service in the Church. As many have observed, he left home as a boy but nearly four years later returned to Utah as a man. This manhood was not only in terms

61. Church leaders established the City of "Iosepa," or Joseph, in the Palawai Basin (identified by the Saints as the "Valley of Ephraim") as the gathering place for Hawaiian converts.
62. Joseph F. to Martha Ann, 23 November 1855, herein.
63. Joseph F. to Martha Ann, 25 July 1857, herein.
64. Whitchurch, "Personal Glimpses," 169.
65. Nineteenth-century Latter-day Saint missions were composed of conferences or districts. Each mission conference contained several local congregations identified as branches.
66. Jenson, "Twelve Apostles," 187.
67. Copied by Joseph F. into his journal, letter dated 4 June 1856; see Ricks, *"My Candid Opinion,"* 37–38.
68. See Joseph F. to Martha Ann, 12 December 1856, herein.
69. Joseph F., journal, 26 June 1856.

of his physical size, but also included a more mature spirit, increased administrative acumen, and, most importantly, a new ability to serve as a powerful preacher and teacher of the restored gospel.

THE UTAH WAR AND MISSION RELEASE

On Saturday, 3 October 1857, Joseph F. recorded in his journal that Brigham Young had requested that all missionaries "that could be spared" be released from their missions and return immediately to the Utah Territory.[70]

For weeks in the early spring of 1857, rumors had been spreading in the Latter-day Saint settlements in Utah that the president of the United States, James Buchanan, was sending troops to Utah to put down a "Mormon uprising." Many federally appointed officials in Utah who were not Latter-day Saints felt that the Saints defied their authority and that the territory needed stronger federal control. Brigham Young, who had been the territorial governor since 1850 when the Utah Territory was created by the federal government, received news that mail had been cut off and that a new governor had been appointed to replace him. More alarmingly, various reports also noted that a large military force of twenty-five hundred soldiers was on its way to Utah to establish complete federal authority there.

"We expect to have warm times here," wrote President Young to the missionaries in Hawai'i, "would you not come and help us? if so, hasten to our midst."[71] Accordingly, thirteen missionaries were released from the Sandwich Island Mission and gave farewell addresses during a conference the following day; Joseph F. was among them.[72] He departed Honolulu for California on 6 October aboard the *Yankee*, a 343-ton bark built in 1854.[73]

The *Deseret News* reported that the missionaries "arrived in San Francisco, from the Sandwich Islands, on the 22d October."[74] The report continued, "They were all in good health, and were preparing to prosecute their journey, at as early a date as possible, to their homes from which they have been absent since the spring of '54."[75] The party arrived home in the Salt Lake Valley on 24 February 1858.

After his arrival, Joseph F. immediately enlisted in the territorial militia and spent the next several months performing various duties in defense of the Latter-day Saints during the crisis. Fortunately, the conflict was settled by negotiations in the spring of 1858. However, by that time Brigham Young had been replaced as governor of the Utah Territory with a federal appointee who came from outside Utah, the military had established a permanent headquarters west of Utah Lake in Cedar Valley, and the Saints' lives had been significantly disrupted by the events of 1857–58.[76]

Having served as an elder in the Church during his mission, Joseph F. was ordained "into the 32nd quorum of Seventies" on 20 March 1858.[77] He spent the rest of the year working to support himself. As the harvest season ended, as was customary, many Saints gathered from time to time

70. Joseph F., journal, 3 October 1857.
71. Joseph F., journal, 3 October 1857.
72. Joseph F. borrowed money from Silas Smith to leave immediately. However, because there were two Silas Smiths in the mission at this time, it is not known which one loaned the money. See biographical register, "Smith, Silas" and "Smith, Silas Sanford."
73. Sonne, *Ships, Saints, and Mariners*, 202.
74. "Missionaries," *Deseret News*, 9 December 1857, 317.
75. "Missionaries," 317.
76. See Richard Neitzel Holzapfel, *A History of Utah County* (Salt Lake City, UT: Utah State Historical Society, 1999), 85–94.
77. Jenson, "Twelve Apostles," 189.

at dances and socials during the slower winter months. Apparently Joseph F. participated in these diversions as occasion allowed. Joseph "was ordained a High Priest, and appointed a member of the High Council of the Salt Lake Stake of Zion" on 16 October 1858.[78]

Joseph F. Smith, ca. 1858. This is the earliest-known photograph of Joseph F. Smith, taken shortly after his return from service in the Hawaiian mission. He was between nineteen and twenty years of age. Courtesy of CHL.

COURTSHIP AND MARRIAGE

Joseph F. became romantically interested in his cousin Levira Annette Clark Smith (1842–88).[79] By February 1859 he was willing to reveal his affections to her. "It is with feelings of true emotions that I attempt to address you a few lines this morning," he wrote. Struggling "to deliniate the feelings of my beating heart, in writing," Joseph F. confessed his love for Levira. "I am aware that our acquaintance has been short to you, I do not know how pleasant, but allow me to say, that since I saw you first, the admiration and respect I first concieved for you. have daily grown, till they have changed to something stronger and more fervent." Expressing his uncertainty regarding her feelings, he undertook "to simply aske you, cousin . . . what you think of 'Cousin Joe.'"[80]

78. Jenson, "Twelve Apostles," 189.

79. Before the mid-twentieth century, marriage between cousins was not only legal and socially acceptable in Western culture but also the norm in royal families. Queen Victoria and Prince Albert of the United Kingdom are the most famous examples during this period. In the United States, cousin marriage was legal in every state and territory before the Civil War. It was also legal in Canada, where Sir John A. Macdonald, who became the premier of the province of Canada (1856) and Canada's first prime minister (1867), married his cousin Isabella Cark in 1843. Levira Annette Clark Smith was the daughter of Samuel Harrison and Levira Clark Smith. Her father was a brother to Hyrum Smith, Joseph F. and Martha Ann's father. See biographical register, "Smith, Levira Annette Clark."

80. Joseph F. to Levira, 26 February 1859.

Levira must have reciprocated Joseph F.'s regards because only a few months later, on 5 April 1859, Church President Brigham Young performed the marriage sealing for them in his office in Salt Lake City. The Journal History of the Church adds, "A sumptuous wedding feast was prepared at Alfred Randells and partaken of by their friends and relatives."[81]

CHALLENGING YEARS FOR MARTHA ANN

Following the death of her mother in 1852, Martha Ann's life was in flux. For a time, as noted previously, she remained at the family homestead with Hannah Grinnels, even though John Smith, Hyrum's oldest son from his first wife, had been appointed by Brigham Young to be the family guardian.[82]

Joseph F. left on his mission in late September 1854 while Martha Ann remained with family. Over the next several years, Martha Ann apparently spent some time at the home of her aunt Mercy Fielding (1807–93), her mother's sister, living with her cousin Mary Jane (1838–1901).[83] It is clear from letters between Martha Ann and Hellen Maria Fisher (1835–1907), John Smith's wife, that Martha Ann also lived with John and Hellen in the family homestead from at least 1856 to 1857.[84]

These years continued to be challenging for Martha Ann, as one would expect for such a young child. She often felt alone and isolated. Martha Ann noted in her letters that she did not always get along with John's wife, Hellen, and other members of the family.[85] She often felt that John, her older half brother, was insensitive to her concerns.[86]

Adding to the challenges at home, Martha Ann was unable to attend school as much as Joseph F. encouraged her to because of the demanding nature of farm life and a poor financial situation. As noted, she frequently mentioned her poor writing skills and apologized for them in letters to Joseph F. When he asked her to write Ina Coolbrith (1841–1928) and Agnes Smith (1836–73), their cousins in California, Martha Ann declined, most likely because she felt embarrassed about her rudimentary writing skills.[87]

---

81. Church Historian's Office, Journal History of the Church, 5 April 1859, 1. Alfred J. Randall (1811–91) was a family friend and had accompanied Joseph F.'s father and uncle to Carthage in 1844. Randall was one of the last Latter-day Saints to leave the jail on 26 June, the day before the martyrdom. The Randall family had also been with the Smith family in Winter Quarters and had traveled with the Smiths to Utah in 1848. At the time of the marriage, Randall lived on West Temple just north of the Temple Block.
82. There seems to be some confusion as to exactly what role John Smith took in caring for the family during this period, likely in part because he was serving as the Church Patriarch and appears to have been periodically working away from home. See Joseph F., journal, 31 January 1856.
83. Mercy Fielding (Thompson) is the sister of Mary Fielding Smith, Martha Ann and Joseph F.'s mother. See biographical register, "Thompson, Mary Jane."
84. See Martha Ann to Joseph F., 31 January 1856 and 3 May 1857, herein. See also letter from Hellen Maria Fisher to Joseph F., 5 July 1857.
85. Whatever difficulties existed between Hellen Maria Fisher and Martha Ann were later resolved. Details of when or how the resolution came about are unknown. See Martha Ann to Joseph F., 5 April 1857, herein.
86. See J. B. Haws, "Joseph F. Smith's Encouragement of His Brother, Patriarch John Smith," in Manscill et al., *Joseph F. Smith: Reflections on the Man and His Times*, 133–58.
87. Agnes Moulton Coolbrith married Don Carlos Smith, brother of Hyrum Smith, on 30 July 1835 in Kirtland, Ohio. They were parents of three children, the youngest being Josephine (Ina) Donna Smith. See biographical register, "Coolbrith, Agnes Moulton" and "Smith, Josephine Donna." Joseph F. may have added to Martha Ann's trepidation while attempting to encourage her: "I have received a letter lately from Cousin Josephine," he once wrote. "She said she had written to you but had received no letter in return tolde me to speak to you about it, I would advise you to write to her. do your best to spell and write correct, for she is a good writer, this is what I wish you to progress in, till you are also a good writer." See Joseph F. to Martha Ann, 14 June 1857, herein.

Life on the farm kept Martha Ann quite busy. A family history written by Martha Ann's daughter notes: "Martha had little time for idleness. She did many chores, morning and night, before and after school. She herded sheep on the hills east of home, many times barefooted until her feet would bleed. She spun wool into yarn and wove the yarn into cloth, blankets, sheets, jeans for men's clothing and linen with cotton war[p] and woolen wool for women's clothing." She also gleaned wheat with her friend Jane Fisher, which earned them enough money to purchase their own winter dresses.[88] Throughout the early letters, Joseph F. and Martha Ann wrote on occasion about the family farm animals, often referring to them by name as if they were beloved pets.[89]

When Martha Ann did have free time, much of it was spent with her friend Jane Fisher, the younger sister of John Smith's wife, Hellen Maria Fisher. The Fisher family was apparently very close with the children of Hyrum Smith, as evidenced by several letters between Joseph F. and his sister and by letters between Joseph F. and the Fishers. Letters between Joseph F. and Jane suggest some early budding romantic feelings between them.[90] On at least two occasions, Martha appended brief notes to the end of letters Jane had written to Joseph F.[91]

THE REFORMATION OF 1856–57

In 1856 and 1857, nearly ten years after the Saints began to settle the Great Basin, Church leaders launched a spiritual renewal known as the "Mormon Reformation," or simply the "Reformation."[92] During this time the Saints were asked to join their leaders in personal introspection and soul-searching, the hope being that the Saints would increase their commitment to live gospel principles and heighten their individual spirituality. Martha Ann noted in a letter to her brother, "I hav been looking at myself and noticeing my self and triiy to reform and I see that I need a good deal of tutuing before I can become perfect."[93] While commending his sister for her desires to reform, Joseph F. also advised prudence: "It is a good thing if you commence by degrees, you know this world, though small, cannot be circumscribeed with one huge stride, . . . therefore you see <u>Martha</u> that all our faults cannot be overcome in a moment, but they must be forsaken little by littel."[94]

Perhaps one impact of the Reformation that most profoundly influenced Martha Ann was the increased emphasis on marriage, including participating in plural marriage, which the Church had openly announced in 1852.[95] "There is great excitment among the young folks here about getting married," wrote William Harris, a family friend. "There is from twenty to forty a getting married evry day."[96] The anxiety over marriage even made its way to the Sandwich Islands, where letters warned the missionaries that all the young girls in the territory were being married off.[97] However, Joseph Fisher, in a letter to young Joseph F., wrote that his daughter Jane "& 2 or 3 girls in the

88. Sarah Harris Passey, "Martha Ann Smith Harris" (unpublished manuscript in editors' possession, courtesy of Carole Call King, granddaughter of Sarah Harris Passey).
89. See Joseph F. to Martha Ann, 9 June 1855 and 14 July 1856, herein; and Martha Ann to Joseph F., 17 December 1856, herein.
90. See Martha Ann to Joseph F., 29 July 1856, herein.
91. See Martha Ann to Joseph F., 19 August 1857 and 11 May 1857, herein.
92. Paul H. Peterson, "The Mormon Reformation of 1856–1857: The Rhetoric and the Reality," *Journal of Mormon History* 15 (1989): 59–87.
93. See Martha Ann to Joseph F., 17 December 1856, herein.
94. See Joseph F. to Martha Ann, 17 April 1857, herein.
95. Peterson, "Mormon Reformation of 1856–1857," 71.
96. Martha Ann to Joseph F., 3 February 1857, herein.
97. Joseph Fisher to Joseph F., 24 February 1857.

city are single yet not because they havent had offers but I think they must be waiting for some of the young misionari<e>s to return."[98] Jane was most likely waiting for Joseph F.'s return.[99] Martha Ann had apparently also turned down several proposals of marriage. Joseph Fisher indicated that Martha Ann "frequently has proposials for mariage but none of them soots [suits]."[100] Martha Ann, however, soon found one proposal that did capture her attention.

Mary Fielding Smith's Home, 31 August 2018, photograph by Kate Beasley Holzapfel. This adobe home, built in 1850, was where Joseph F. and Martha Ann lived much of their lives during the 1850s. Martha Ann, following her marriage to William Jasper Harris in 1857, moved away to establish her own home. Courtesy of Kate Beasley Holzapfel.

MARTHA ANN'S MARRIAGE TO WILLIAM JASPER HARRIS

Fifteen-year-old Martha Ann married twenty-year-old William Jasper Harris on 21 April 1857, just as the Reformation was ending. William had been called to serve a mission to the British Isles and reported at the Endowment House, a temporary temple and administrative office on the Temple Block in Salt Lake City, to be set apart as a missionary. A Church leader attending the meeting asked if there was anyone present who would consider marrying before departing for the mission field. William mentioned Martha Ann and was instructed to "go and get her right now and be married."[101]

98. Joseph Fisher to Joseph F., 24 February 1857.
99. See Martha Ann to Joseph F., 29 July 1856, herein.
100. Joseph Fisher was stating that even though Martha Ann had a number of proposals, none were suitable for marriage. Joseph Fisher to Joseph F., 24 February 1857. Hellen Maria Fisher also wrote that Martha Ann "is not maried yet, it is not for want of offers." Hellen M. Smith to Joseph F., 4 April 1857.
101. Harris, "Martha Ann Smith Harris," 15.

When he entered the house, he asked Martha Ann to marry him that day. She turned to William's mother and asked what she should do.[102] Her future mother-in-law responded, "Law me, honey, put on the calico dress and go with him!"[103] Martha Ann did and climbed into the wagon and headed to the Endowment House, where they were married. William left his young bride to begin his mission to England two days later.[104]

Martha Ann may have stayed with John Smith, her older half brother, for a time after William left, but she eventually went to live with her new mother-in-law, Emily Hill Harris Smoot (1815–82). Her son, Richard P. Harris, reported, "Martha lived with her mother-in-law and helped her spin and weave, milk many cows, make butter and cheese, and do all the other household duties. . . . [Emily Hill Harris] sat beside [Martha Ann] in the schoolroom and learned to read and write."[105]

When Martha Ann reunited with Joseph F. is not known. The reunion must have been short-lived because Utah was on the move as the US Army made its way to the territory.

Like many other Salt Lake area residents, Martha Ann moved south with the family and relocated temporarily to Pond Town in Utah County.[106] As peace was established, most of the Salt Lake Valley Saints returned to their homes in the latter part of July 1858. Martha Ann, recalling her trip back to Salt Lake Valley, noted, "As we were travelling along the road I was driving a team of horses. I just drove around the Point of the Mountain[107] when we saw a man riding on a white mule. To my great surprise it was my husband. We had not heard from him for six months so we were not expecting him. It was an agreeable surprise. We reached home safe and found the old house just as we left it."[108]

LIGHTNING STRIKE

Not very long after this reunion, William Harris and Joseph Abbott (1840–59) were struck by lightning while plowing and sowing a field in Salt Lake City near what is now known as Pioneer Park on 18 May 1859.[109] The *Deseret News* reported a few days later, "On Wednesday last, about five p.m., William Harris and Joseph Abbott, engaged in planting corn, on what is commonly known as the 'Old Fort Square,' were struck by lightning and the latter instantly killed. Harris was knocked down, his body badly burned, and was taken up for dead but, by unwearied exertion, was resuscitated and in a fair way to recover. A light shower was passing over the city. Harris was furrowing out the ground and Abbot, a lad about 17 years old, was dropping the corn immediately after the plow and within ten or twelve feet of the other at the time of the occurrence."[110]

According to a family tradition, William was dragged across the field by his frightened team of horses and was found by John Smith, his half brother-in-law. Abbot was an orphan who had been living with the Abraham O. Smoot family.

102. Emily Hill Harris Smoot; see biographical register, "Hill, Almira Emily."

103. According to the *Oxford English Dictionary*, the exclamation *law me* expresses "chiefly astonishment or admiration, or (often) surprise at being asked a question."

104. Harris, "Martha Ann Smith Harris," 15.

105. Harris, "Martha Ann Smith Harris," 16.

106. Pond Town's name was changed to Salem, after Salem, Massachusetts, hometown of Pond Town's oldest living resident at the time.

107. This is the boundary, both geographically and politically, between Salt Lake and Utah Valleys.

108. Carole Call King, "History of William Jasper Harris, 1841–1921" (paper presented at monthly meeting of the Daughters of Utah Pioneers, copy in the editors' possession), 4.

109. A ten-acre park located at 350 South and 300 West in Salt Lake City, site of the first fort built by the Latter-day Saints in Salt Lake Valley in 1847.

110. "A Sad Occurrence," *Deseret News*, 25 May 1859, 1.

William never fully recovered from this accident and struggled physically for the rest of his life as a result. A short time later in August 1859, William and Martha Ann's first child was born, William Jasper Harris Jr. (1859–1926).

THE FINAL LETTER OF THE 1850S

As noted earlier, Joseph F. returned home from his mission in Hawai'i during the Utah War and immediately enlisted in the militia to help defend the Saints from the approaching military force sent by President Buchanan. When Joseph F. wrote his final extant letter to his sister during this decade, she was living temporarily in Utah County following the evacuation of the northern settlements. He was at the family farm in the Sugar House Ward. After the military threat had passed, most of the Saints who had moved south returned to their homes in the northern settlements.

GAINING AN EDUCATION

Though short on formal education, Joseph F. and Martha Ann experienced significant personal growth during this period of their teen years. For Joseph F., informal education came primarily from serving a mission. He recalled in 1875 that it was in the Kingdom of Hawai'i that he wrote his very first letter: "I was 15 years old and had never written a letter in my life, and did not know how to write a duzzen words, but I began to feel the need of education so I studied and practiced and prayed and tried to learn and have been learning at a disadvantage ever sine until now I can just write to be understood."[111] That practice included preparing and sending a prodigious number of letters to missionaries, Church leaders, family, and friends, including his younger sister. Additionally, during this first mission Joseph F. also became a voracious reader, increasing his vocabulary, his knowledge of a variety of subjects, and his interest in the wider world.[112]

SUMMARY

By the end of December 1859, Joseph F. was twenty-one years old and married with no children. Martha Ann was eighteen years old and married with one child.

Joseph F.'s surviving Hawaiian diaries often provide insights on the interconnection with the letters. For example, on 24 May 1856, he wrote, "Spent time reading one letter from my sister Martha. . . . I received good news from home. The folks were all well. Martha was on a visit to her friends in the city."[113] On the following day, 25 May 1856, he recorded, "I wrote two letters today in answer to those received last evening from my Sister and cousin."[114]

This experience in the islands of the Pacific helped shape Joseph F.'s understanding of an expanding worldwide Church and prepared him to hold significant administrative responsibilities as he continued to minister to the Saints and others. Years later, after receiving a copy of the "Hawaiian Annual" for 1907, Joseph F. sent a note to thank the missionary who sent it and reflected,

111. Joseph F. to Robert B. Taylor, 9 March 1875. See Scott G. Kenney, "Before the Beard: Trials of the Young Joseph F. Smith," *Sunstone* 120 (November 2001): 38.

112. See, for example, Joseph F., journal, 21 April 1857, where he notes receiving and reading a number of issues of two Church newspapers, the *Deseret News* (published in Salt Lake City beginning in 1850) and the *Western Standard* (published in San Francisco beginning in 1855): "On going to the Post Office, I received four Nos. of 'D.N.' and 'W.S,' . . . Spent the afternoon reading." Other entries highlight Joseph F.'s wide range of reading material, which included novels, biographies, and national and international newspapers and magazines. See, for example, Joseph F., journal, 1 July 1857. For a brief summary, see Ricks, *"My Candid Opinion,"* xiv–xv.

113. Joseph F., journal, 24 May 1856.

114. Joseph F., journal, 25 May 1856.

“So many years of my youth and early manhood have been spent upon those ‘beautiful Isles of the Sea,’ that I naturally hail with delight the coming of any souvenir or reminder of passed scenes, and circustances of my triple sourines [sojourns], and later visit there.”[115]

Martha Ann, on the other hand, remained in Utah for the rest of her life (except for a few brief visits to California and Texas later in life), caring for family, friends, and neighbors.[116] She saw the world beyond the valleys in Utah largely through her brother’s letters. Martha Ann’s letters to Joseph F. provided him an important window into her life and helped keep him updated on events in Utah. Joseph F. was able to fill in gaps as he read letters from a variety of individuals writing him from home. Later, during his second mission, Joseph F. told Martha Ann that her letters “were my best corispondent on the Islands.”[117]

The surviving letters written between them in this decade reveal their love, loyalty, support, and concern for each other, especially during times when they were separated by long distances.

115. Joseph F. to Abraham Fernandez, 15 May 1907.

116. She did make several trips to Joseph F.’s home in Southern California. See Martha Ann to Joseph F., 7 July 1914, herein.

117. Joseph F. to Martha Ann, 15 December 1860, herein.

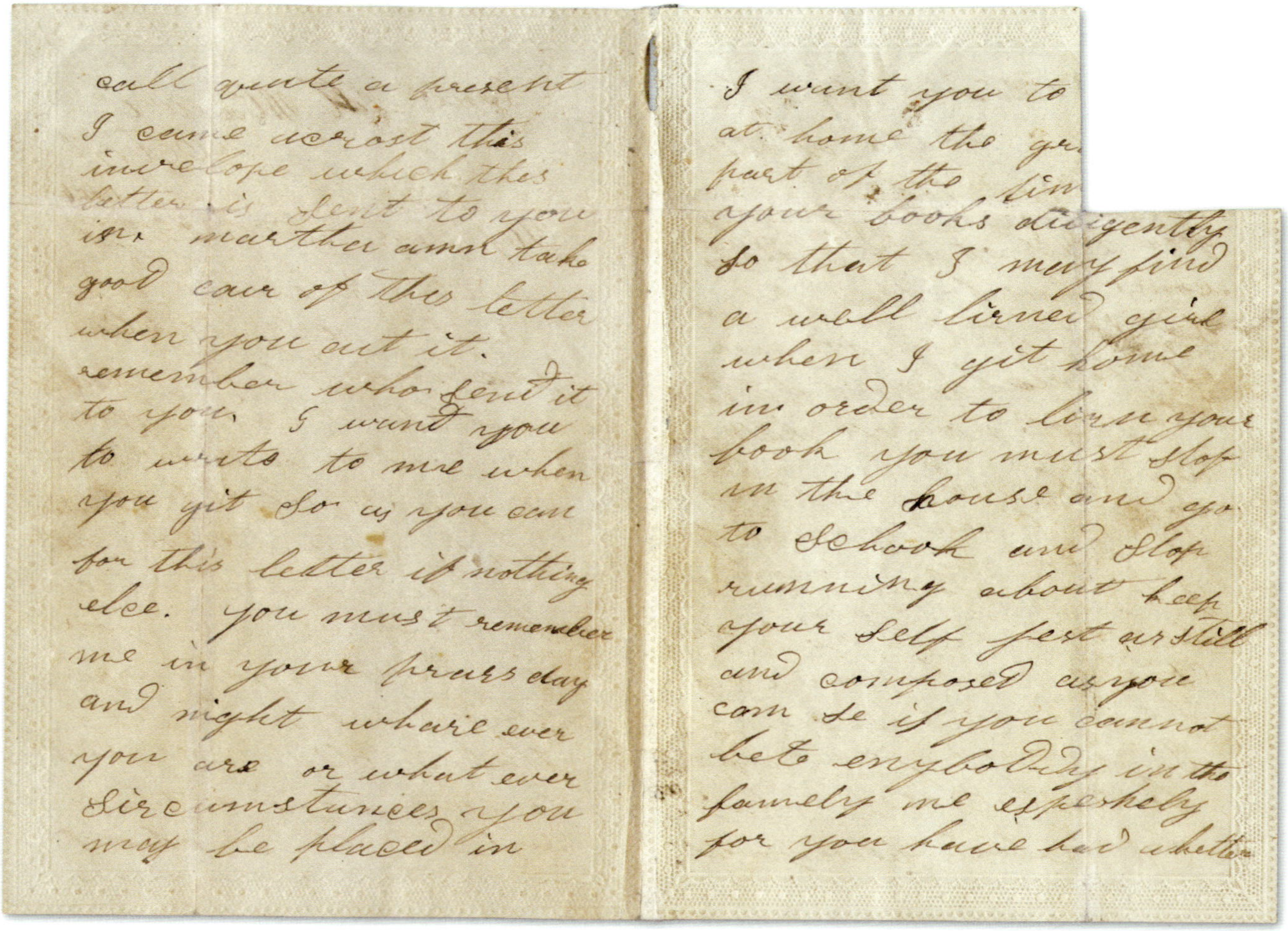
call quite a present
I came acrost this
invelope which this
letter is sent to you
in. marthea ann take
good care of this letter
when you cut it.
remember who sent it
to you. I want you
to write to me when
you git so as you can
for this letter if nothing
else. you must remember
me in your prayrs day
and night where ever
you are or what ever
circumstances you
may be placed in

I want you to
at home the gr
part of the tim
your books diligently
so that I may find
a well lirned girl
when I git home
in order to lirn your
book you must stop
in the house and go
to school and stop
running about keep
your self just as still
and composed as you
can se if you cannot
bete enybody in the
famely me espeshely
for you have had better

Joseph F. to Martha Ann, 17 October 1854 (p. 2; pp. 1 and 4 of this letter are displayed on p. xvi)

Joseph F. to Martha Ann, 17 October 1854 (p. 3)

Letters

JOSEPH F. TO MARTHA ANN, 17 OCTOBER 1854

Lani[1] [*illegible strike-through*] Mauwi[2]
Oct 17th
1854[3]

My dear Sister it is with plesure and with very peculiar feeling that I take my peen in hand to write a fuw lines to you. which I know that you will exept it with the gratest of plesure and you must not git angery with me because I that I did not write to you before this time[4] and this is what I [**p. 2**] call quite a present I came acrost this invelope which this letter is sent to you in. martha ann take good cair of this letter when you cut it. remember who sent it to you. I want you to write to me when you git so as you can for this letter if nothing elce. you must remember me in your prars day and night whare ever you are or what ever sircumstances you may be placed in [**p. 3**] I want you to [*2.9 x 3.2 cm cut at top right corner*] at home the gr[*2.9 x 3.2 cm cut at top right corner*] part of the tim[*2.9 x 3.2 cm cut at top right corner*] your books diligently so that I may find a well lirned girl when I git home in order to lirn your book you must stop in the house and go to school and stop running about keep your self jest as still and composed as you can se if you cannot bete enyboddy in the famely me espeshely for you have had a better [**p. 4**] [*2.9 x 3.2 cm cut at top left corner*]e then I hav had [*2.9 x 3.2 cm cut at top left corner*]m. exept of this [*2.9 x 3.2 cm cut at top left corner*] as a tokun of rememberance and take good cair of it untill I come back then let me se it. take good cair of the duks[5] and se that thay do not go hungery and take notice of my council and you will be blest

1. Lāhainā was the main port town on Maui and the center of Protestant missionary efforts in the islands and also the center of commercial whaling in the Pacific.
2. The first Latter-day Saint baptisms occurred on Maui, and the first branch was established there in 1851.
3. Joseph F. was fifteen, and Martha Ann was thirteen.
4. Joseph F. departed Salt Lake City on 5 May 1854 and arrived in Honolulu on 27 September 1854. This letter was written less than three weeks after his arrival in Hawaiʻi, but nearly five months after he left Utah.
5. The family "duks" (ducks) are mentioned in several letters during this first mission. See Joseph F. to Martha Ann, 9 June 1855, herein; and Martha Ann to Joseph F., 2 October 1856, herein.

giv my love and best respects to all of the folks and exept the same to your self I remain your affectionate brother Joseph Smith may the lord bless you all.[6]

Martha ann Smith
Grate Salt Lake[7]
City Ut teritory[8]

JOSEPH F. TO MARTHA ANN AND JERUSHA SMITH, 1 NOVEMBER 1854

Omopio[9] Maui Novem 1st 1854

My Dear Sister Martha ann[10]

As I had wrote a letter to aunt Thompson[11] and thare was room in the envelope for this so I poot it in, and it jest to let you now my feelings at this time, and I want to tell them in short notice my feelings are there. martha I want you to stop at home as much as posible and keep jerusha[12] company and study your Book with diligence. donot be crose but keepe your temper to yourself. help jerusha all you can, and keep hur in a good humer[13] Now I would say to jerusha my Dear Sister jerusha. remember your god that protects you in times of need. and remember your brother who is fare frome you. remember how I wo[◊]d wish you to do if I was thare to tell you. take good care of martha and for my sake do not be cose to one another but remember you are sisters and remember that you have a brother that hinks of you day and nite. I would say to you boath be one be of one hart and of one mind[14] and all will go rite. may the

6. Enclosed with this letter is a lock of Joseph F.'s blond hair.
7. Great Salt Lake City was the original name for the principal Latter-day Saint settlement in the Great Basin; it was later known simply as Salt Lake City after *Great* was officially dropped in 1868.
8. The Latter-day Saints petitioned to create the state of Deseret soon after they began to settle in the Great Basin. Instead of granting statehood, Congress created a territory in 1850. The territory designation is found on the envelope. Unless otherwise noted, all additional writing in margins and on envelopes is in Joseph F.'s hand.
9. Omopio was in the Kula region of Maui.
10. There are multiple illegible pen marks in the top margin of page 1. The name Martha is legible.
11. Mercy Rachel Fielding (Thompson), sister to Mary Fielding Smith and aunt to Joseph F. and Martha Ann. In letters she is most often referred to as "Aunt Thompson." See biographical register, "Fielding, Mercy Rachel."
12. Jerusha Smith is half sister to Joseph F. and Martha Ann. She is the daughter of Hyrum and his first wife, Jerusha Barden. See biographical register, "Smith, Jerusha."
13. Martha Ann appears to feel some discord in her family relationships, and throughout the letters Joseph F. offers loving advice and encouragement. For example, see Joseph F. to Martha Ann, 28 January 1855 and 9 June 1855, herein; and Martha Ann to Joseph F., 5 April 1857, herein.
14. Latter-day Saints dreamed, prayed, sang, studied, talked, and worked to establish Zion, as described in an important early text: "And the Lord called his people Zion, because they were of one heart and one mind, and dwelt in righteousness; and there was no poor among them" (Moses 7:18). Joseph F. had access to extracts from the Joseph Smith Translation (JST) material through a British publication published in 1851. See Franklin D. Richards, *The Pearl of Great Price: Being a Choice Selection from the Revelations, Translations, and Narrations of Joseph Smith, First Prophet, Seer, and Revelator to the Church of Jesus Christ of Latter-day Saints* (Liverpool: F. D. Richards, 1851), 4. Joseph F.'s personal copy was destroyed in a fire at the mission headquarters in Lāhainā, Maui, in June 1856; see Joseph F., journal, 26 June 1856.

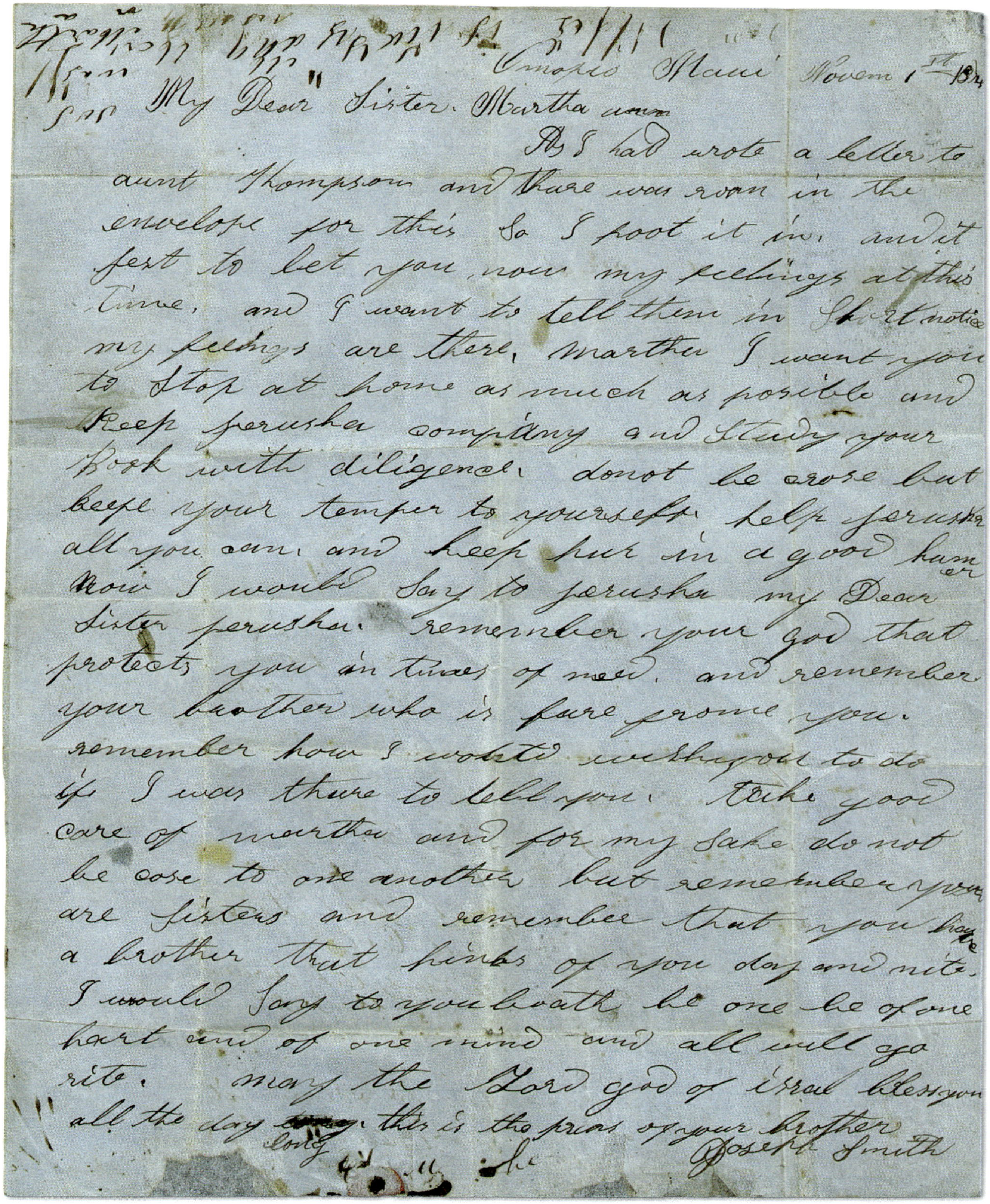
Omopeo Maui Novem 1st 1854

My Dear Sister. Martha ann

As I had wrote a letter to aunt Thompson and thare was room in the envelope for this So I poot it in. and it felt to let you now my feelings at this time. and I want to tell them in Short notice my feelings are there. marthe I want you to Stop at home as much as posible and keep jerusha company and Study your Book with diligence. donot be crose but keep your temper to yourself. help jerusha all you can. and keep her in a good humer now I would Say to jerusha my Dear Sister jerusha. remember your god that protects you in times of need. and remember your brother who is fare frome you. remember how I would wish you to do if I was there to tell you. take good care of martha and for my Sake do not be cose to one another but remember you are Sisters and remember that you have a brother that thinks of you day and nite. I would Say to you boath be one be of one hart and of one mind and all will go rite. may the Lord god of isral bless you all the day ~~long~~ long. this is the prayr of your brother

Joseph Smith

Joseph F. to Martha Ann, 1 November 1854 (p. 1)

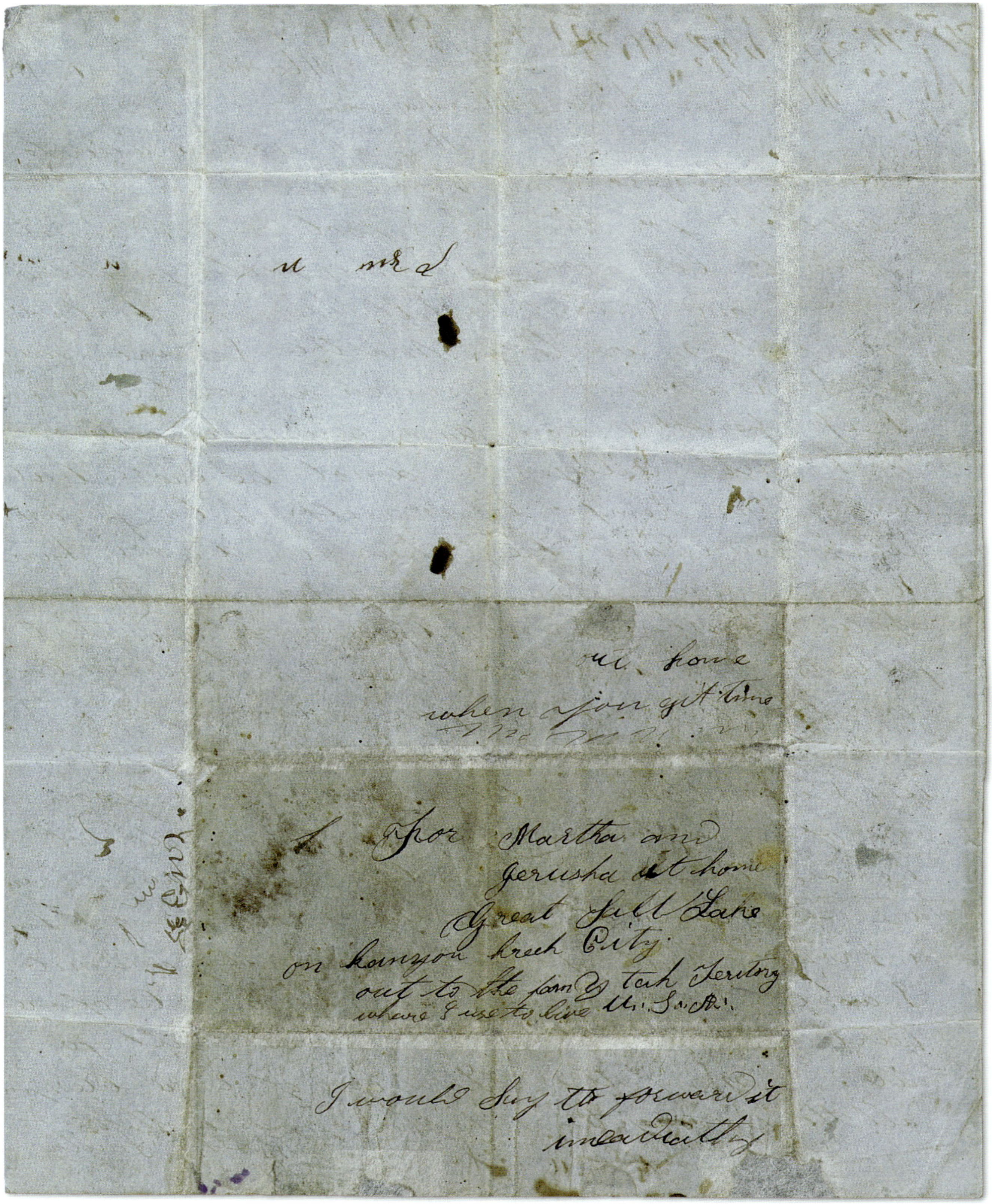

out home
when you get time

For Martha Ann
Jerusha at home
Great Salt Lake
on Kanyon Kreek City
out to the farm Utah Territory
where I use to live U. S. A.

I would say to forward it
immediately

Joseph F. to Martha Ann, 1 November 1854 (p. 2)

Lord god of isral bless you all the day ~~long~~ <long>. this is the prar of your brother Joseph Smith
[p. 2]
out home
when you git time

For Martha and
Jerusha at home
Great Salt Lake
City
Utah Teritory
U. S. A.[15]

on kanyon kreek[16]
out to the farm
whare I use to live
I would say to forward it
imeadiatly

JOSEPH F. TO MARTHA ANN, 28 JANUARY 1855

the 28,th 1855.
Omopio Kula, Maui S. I.[17] January.

My Dear and affectionate <Sister> Martha.

Haveing jest finished writing a letter to Jerusha. I thought that I would try and write one to you also thinking that a fiew lines from me would be acceptibal to you. I am well and Harty. and Have grew conciderable since you saw me last and I have no reasons to doubt but what you have grew much larger you ware when I last saw you. if you have you Have got to be quiet a woman and I supose that you have got so that you can look over the heds of your Sisters.[18] and now I would like to give you some little council, if you will take it and that is this. be Humbel and prayorful, and be kind to your connections and you will Have the Spirit of the Lord abiding with you at all times and the lord will bless you and you will give up in the footsteps of your Mother and you will be blessed with every thing even as your Mother was. and you will neve[*0.5 x 1.8 cm tear*] lack for the comferts of life if you will only growe up

15. The letter was folded to make an envelope with the address written on page 2. The address and the note directing delivery to the farm (found immediately below the address) were originally written side by side, making it difficult to distinguish the directions from the note. The two have been separated here for clarity.
16. Canyon Creek, or Big Canyon Creek, became known as Parley's Creek.
17. Joseph F. frequently uses the initials *S. I.* to refer to the Sandwich Islands (Hawaiian Islands).
18. Martha Ann had been maturing during Joseph F.'s absence and apparently grew taller than her half sisters Lovina Smith, Jerusha Smith, and Sarah Smith. She mentions her height as being five feet seven inches in a letter she wrote fourteen months later; see Martha Ann to Joseph F., 2 March 1856, herein.

in the footstep[*0.5 x 1.8 cm tear*] of our Mother who has gon before us.[19] only be kind to your Sisters and mind what they say to you and never git above them for they are your older Sisters, and it is for them to give council and also for our oldest Brothers.[20] you be kind to them and do what they and donot get cross. and study your books. And stop at home as much as posible and do not think because you have not the priveliges of meny that you are slited but be sober and prayorful, and you will groe up in the footsteps of our Mother. and I would rather groe up in the ways of my Mother than to have all the riches in this world, and be wild and rude, and unprayorful. for if you groe up after your Mother you will never lack for the comferts of life. I will ask you a question. did you ever know the time when we were not provided for by the Hand of our Mother [**p. 2**] I answer, the time never was known. ask those who knows. I could give you much council Moty,[21] that would be benifissial to you as long as you live upon this earth. Only remember what I have alredy sed and se if it will not be good in days to come. I must now bring my letter to close. Preying the Lord to bless you and prosper you all the day long. and I want you to write to me as often as you can and let me know how you are giting along.

One thing more never feel down harted but be merry <in your hart,> and joyful. and keepe a prayorful hand and a thoughtful mind and the Lord will L Bless you. So this is all and may the lord bless you all the day long is the prayors of your affectionate Brother Joseph.

the Woman, of the house[22] sends Hur aloha[23] <love.> to little keiki.[24] <baby.>

N. B.[25] Marty ann write to me ofton. Pray for me ofton. and think of me ofton, and think more ofton of what I have sed in this letter. and think more of Joy in your Hart, than of sorrow in your mind, and keepe it all to your self, and tell it to no body. and you shall be blessed. Joseph Smith.

Miss. Jerush and Martha
Smith
Great Salt Lake City
Utah Te[◊◊]itory[26]

19. Joseph F. and Martha Ann's mother, Mary Fielding Smith, died 21 September 1852, roughly two and a half years before this letter was written. See biographical register, "Smith, Mary Fielding."
20. There were four surviving children from Hyrum Smith and his first wife, Jerusha Barden Smith, and two children—Joseph F. and Martha Ann—from his second wife, Mary Fielding Smith. The sisters and brothers referred to here are the children of Jerusha: Lovina (then living at Florence [Winter Quarters], Nebraska), John, Jerusha, and Sarah. See biographical register, "Smith, Lovina," "Smith, John," "Smith, Jerusha," and "Smith, Sarah."
21. Likely a misspelling of Marty, a nickname for Martha Ann.
22. Most likely Mary Jane Dilworth, wife of Francis A. Hammond, with whom Joseph F. lived during the early months of his mission. See biographical register, "Dilworth, Mary Jane."
23. "Love, affection, compassion . . . ; to greet, hail. Greetings! Hello! Good-bye!" Mary Kawena Pukui and Samuel H. Elbert, *Hawaiian Dictionary*, rev. ed. (Honolulu: University of Hawai'i Press, 1986), s.v. "aloha."
24. "Child, offspring, descendant, . . . youngster." Pukui and Elbert, *Hawaiian Dictionary*, s.v. "keiki."
25. An abbreviation for the Latin *nota bene*, meaning "note well" or "take special notice."
26. The address block runs perpendicular to the rest of the letter on page 2. The letter was folded such that no envelope was necessary. On the front, "coppy to be typed" is written in pencil by an unknown hand.

JOSEPH F. TO MARTHA ANN, 9 JUNE 1855

Lahaina Maui[27]
june the, 9th 1'55.

My Dear and affectionate
Sister, Martha Ann

you may be ashured that I recievd your kind and affectionate letter of March, 31,st with the greatest plesure in the world, Marty[28] I see that you are gaining fast. and I hope and pray that you may improve untill you become pirfect,

you said Marty that you went to Helens[29] to stop. and that things did not go rite so you left, well that is with you, but be kind and mind that you donot do any thing to hurt ot[◊◊] feelings, if they hurt yours, be shure and do that and then you will be blessed and no one can find falt with you make yourself contented whare ever you may be and put up with evry, thing that you can. if you have any triyals to put up with, you must remember that it is to try you and to see whether you are smith grit[30] or not, but sho your smith. and that good too when it comes to the pinch, but have patiance, and long suffering, [**p. 2**] be a Mormon out, and out, and you will be ~~pl~~ blessed, I find that thare is nothing that will try a person so as to tell this world that he is a mormon, but I feel first rate. I am fat, and stout, I feel like I could through all the hays down[31] that thare is in the valeys. (but I donot know how it would be if I should try it)

I am a Preaching (Marty) like a good one, (you had aught to here me) ~~or~~ (or my voys, (I suppose if you wase any whare nee the Islands you could) we had a good meeting this morning, and I was caled upon to Preach, I acordingly, made an attempt, I expect, to go on my third trip around the Island. and if you ask Bro Lawson[32] he will tell you, how fare it is, and how bad the roads is,[33] and what kind of houses we have to sleep in, and what kind of food to eat, &co,[34] and what kind of horses we have to ride also for we have to rid shanks horses[35] most of the time, he knows all about this and it will be interesting for him to tell, it [**p. 3**] to you. and through all

27. In the original letter a number of faded words are written in various places in the top margin of page 1. *Book* and *May 1856* are legible.
28. A nickname for Martha Ann.
29. Likely refers to Hellen Maria Fisher, wife of John Smith, half brother of Joseph F. and Martha Ann. See biographical register, "Fisher, Hellen Maria."
30. Grit is an attribute of individuals who demonstrate courage, determination, and strength, especially when confronted with obstacles and challenges. Joseph F. likely believed that Martha Ann was born with this trait because she was a descendant of the Smith and Fielding families.
31. To throw down hay refers to an aspect in the process of harvesting hay. Once the hay was cut with a hand scythe, either it was bundled and "thrown" (loaded), or it was simply "thrown" without being bundled onto a wagon. Either way, it was a strenuous and demanding job, especially on a long, hot day during the summer harvest.
32. James Lawson was a close friend of the Smith family. He was called on a mission to the Hawaiian Islands in the fall of 1852, beginning his service there in 1853 and serving there until at least the end of 1854. He appears to have been in Utah in 1855, but he returned to Hawai'i with his wife in 1856. See biographical register, "Lawson, James."
33. Joseph F. records in his personal journal the following: "I sliped in the creek, clost to where bro, Lawson fell in the first time I came here[.]" Joseph F., journal, 31 March 1856.
34. The abbreviation *&c.* was commonly used for *et cetera* at this time. The abbreviation *& co.* typically stands for "and company." Joseph F. likely confused the two.
35. *Shanks' mare* or *shanks' horse* was an idiom referring to one's own legs, meaning here that the missionaries generally had to walk. *Oxford English Dictionary*, s.v. "shank."

these difficultyes I get along first rate, and feel well, but If I should tell you the bad side as well as the good I would say that once in a while I got rite down lonesome, and commence to think that I would like to see Marty and the (ducks). besides to see the (rest) of the folks, but it is little that my mind is trubled with these thoughts for I try and drive them away. be patiant and I will come back home some time (if I ever do) and then I will see Marty the ~~ba~~ Babyes and the ducks, and also the Pet lambs, take good care of them and when I come home if I am prosperd like I have been here to fare I will try and give you a Presant, see if I dont, that is if you tend to the books at the same time. and if thare is any differance in tending to those things, be shure and have the ducks in want, and not the book, well this is true but it is simple. and now I will go on to another subject and that is be a mormon <mormon>, but not **[p. 4]** Such a one ase our Cousins, Agnes ~~and~~ and Josephine,[36] for I know what kind they are. but they are not to blame, and I will see and if I can, I will better it some day, I wrote a letter to them yesterday and gave them a rite good mormon sirmon. and intimated strongly to them that California was not a sutible place for them, at present, &co,

Well my dear sister, be good, kind, and Prayerful, and you will be blessed and loved, ~~and~~ go to school, as much as you can, and be attentive to study, for I know what it is to be without it, and you donot, at the Presant but will, when you are cast out into the woarld like I have been, I have jest recievd letters from Charles,[37] Aunt, Thompson, and Mary J.[38] which I have to answer to day as I am a going around the Island. write ofton, and I will reciprocate the favors, give my love to Sarah,[39] and tell hur to write. and also to bro Lawson, and to John[40] and all of the folks, may god allmighty bless you[41] for everr. Joseph Smith
I have answard all of your letters that I have recievd. I also answard Sarahs last. J. S.[42]

I wrote this in a hurrey tharefore it is writtne poor, but I gues that you can read it,[43]

(next time I will take time if I have time and write planer, Joseph Smith)[44]

36. Agnes Charlotte Smith (eighteen years old) and Josephine Donna Smith (fourteen years old), cousins of Joseph F. and Martha Ann, are the daughters of Don Carlos Smith (1816–41), who was the brother of Hyrum Smith (1800–1844), and Agnes Moulton Coolbrith (1811–76). Josephine is also referred to as "Cousin Iney," "Ina," and "Ina Coolbrith" in other letters. After the death of her father, Ina and her family eventually moved to California in 1852. See biographical register, "Smith, Agnes Charlotte" and "Smith, Josephine Donna."
37. Charles Emerson Griffin, Joseph F. and Martha Ann's brother-in-law, husband of Sarah Smith. See biographical register, "Griffin, Charles Emerson."
38. Mercy Rachel Fielding is the aunt mentioned in this letter, and her daughter Mary Jane Thompson was cousin to Joseph F. and Martha Ann. See biographical register, "Thompson, Mary Jane."
39. Sarah Smith is Joseph F. and Martha Ann's older half sister and the daughter of Jerusha Barden and Hyrum Smith.
40. Likely John Smith, son of Hyrum Smith and Jerusha Barden and half brother to Joseph F. and Martha Ann.
41. An indistinguishable word has been written directly below "bless you."
42. Written upside down in the top margin of page 4.
43. Written upside down in the top margin of page 3.
44. Written upside down in the top margin of page 2.

JOSEPH F. TO MARTHA ANN, 18 OCTOBER 1855

Wailuku[45] Maui, Sand, Isles,[46]
Oct. 18th 1855. a.[◊].d.

My dear and affectionate Sister Martha,

it is wit plesure that I seat myself at this time to answer the receipt of your kind letters, which came to hand on the 12th inst.[47] it gave me much joy to here from you, and read your writing. you was saying that you was not going to school, I am sorry, for I was in hopes that you would keepe going.[48] I hope that the school will soon start again that you can keepe going as much as posible. I want to see you improve in writing, and every thing els, when you write take pains and make the letters all plain and destinct, and be shure to spell all of the words right that you can, I suppose if you had a Dictionary it would be a great help, to you, in learning how to spell and what the meaning of the words are. I believe there is anough of ~~the~~ them about the primmisses so you had better get one and take good cair of it, and keepe it by you as much as you can, I wish I could send you a good little one that I have got, but it is to far. I wish I could send you a great many things that would be useful to you but I am so fare away from you at the presant, that it is imposible. I have sent you a great many letters, and some of them had small envellops[49] in side, but you have never said whether you have recievd them or not. I also sent you a small book with virses in it, but I forget the Title of it, it is read coverd, and verry small. I hope you have got it safe, long ear this, I want you to learn it all by heart, and take good cair of it and keepe it to remember me by. Cousin Iney, (Josephine)[50] has got one just like it that was given to her while I was at California, so you have boath **[p. 2]** got one apeas, and I would like to see who kept theirs the best, that is if you get yours.[51] now I must return upon the subject of learning, you know that it is good to have a good education, and you know that many are deprived of that privelige but many are not deprived of the prvelige, but do not improve their

45. Wailuku is located at the mouth of the ʻĪao Valley, about twenty-two miles from Lāhainā.
46. The original letter has four stamps in the top middle of the page, three green and one cream, each commercially printed with a short phrase. The green stamps read "Do not ever think of me," "Fondly and with affection true," and "As innocent as a lamb." The cream-colored stamp reads "Thursday."
47. Abbreviation for *instant*, meaning the current calendar month.
48. Fredrick S. Buchanan observes, "Most [Utah Territory] elementary schools in the 1850s and 1860s were organized on the basis of Mormon Wards with the church meeting house serving as the school house during the week. These ward schools differed widely in their curriculum offerings and the quality of their teaching. They were in essence quasi-public Mormon schools, controlled by local trustees appointed by Mormon bishops; they reflected Mormon community values, used Mormon scriptures as supplemental texts and supported in part by tuition from patrons and local taxes. As early as 1851 the office of territorial superintendent of schools was created, promoting the centralization of school policy and curriculum at least in theory if not in practice. During the pioneer period up to 1869, in the words of John C. Moffitt, 'very little was done in Utah for education beyond the rudiments of learning.'" Fredrick S. Buchanan, "History of Education in Utah," in *Utah History Encyclopedia*, ed. Allan Kent Powell (Salt Lake City, UT: University of Utah Press, 1994), 153–55.
49. Most likely, Joseph F. included letters to friends and family in Martha Ann's letters, counting on her to deliver them.
50. Ina Coolbrith (née Josephine Donna Smith), cousin to Joseph F. and Martha Ann. Ina most likely appreciated the "small book with virses," as she was set to become a well-known poetess in her own right. Ina began publishing her poetry in 1856. She sent Joseph F. a poem in 1857 where she emphasizes a longing for his association. This poem, "We Miss Thee at Home," was published in the *Los Angeles Star*, 12 September 1857, [2].
51. Martha Ann confirmed receipt of this book. See Martha Ann to Joseph F., 31 January 1856, herein.

opertunities and therefore gro up in ignarance, now I donot believe that you are deprived of that privelige, therefore you must improve everry moment of time that you can, you are younger and have a better chance than any of the others, and so if you only knew the blessing of an ed<u>catione you could make a good schooler. now I would like to see you exceede all of us in learning, which you can easly do if you try when you have a chance. now donot think what a great many have thaught and that is, I can get anough learning to morrow for to day and to morrow too, and when tomorrow comes it will still be to morrow, and so on. improve everry moment as they fly by, for time is precious and it waits for no one, and time once past never returns again. so remember that to morrow wont acount for to day, and by thaus thinking, you may improve everry moment in it's right place and time. I want this letter to be a standerd for you to go by. and so, I say, when you go to school, look at your book and not at any thing els, seek for wisdome and it shall be given to you, by an allmighty pour if you cannot get it by your own power, do you not know that there is a God in heven, who has said he that asketh recievth and he that seeketh find'th and he that knocketh it shall be opened, unto him,[52] and again he said, If any one lacketh wisdome let him ask god who giveth liberally **[p. 3]** ~~upbra~~ abraideth none,[53] now I will worant that if you will go to school with a prayerful heart, and your mind on your studies, insted of being upon play and folly, that you will learn faster than ever you did in your life before. the thing of it is be prayerful, pray morning and night and not let your mind run upon foolishness and some little girl for a play mait, or something to that affect, but be stidy and kind to all about you, act wise act knowingly act as though you had been braught up as you ware <was>, by a good and rightous mother, donot take notice of every littl thing that tranpires, but let your mind be upon one subject untill it is proper to move it to nother, then you will not be whimsickle, and nonsensical, with your mind first on one thing and then on another, jumping and twiching about as tho' you was possessed with a leigon of spirits one trying to pull one wey and the other the other way. all these things, you aught to shun, and don't get nervous, nor let your mind be excited, by nothing, be calm, be easy, by quiat, say but little, and what you say have it come to the point, donot gab about nothing, and any thing, but shrude, and canties,[54] picking up exampls from those who are wise, and thaughtful, but take no notice of foolishess, shun all bad sosiety. be not wild, and gidy, when you travel wack[55] thaughtfully, and donot run, carry your body in a good shape but be shure to not be proud, and haughty, give everry their due, and be no respecter of person, but respect good manners and good <sence> actions, and tresure it up in your heart, now I want you to be carful and obsurve all that I have said, **[p. 4]** and you will some day become respected, and your example will be worth gold. and you will be loved and thaught conciderable of. a now I could say a great deal more if there was time and space but you can more fully learn and understand what I have allredy written. I donot write this for your disadvantage, but for your wellfair and prosperity, I want you to go to school and be carful to learn all that you can, you may be with out [*illegible strike-through*] means to pay your school bills, but if you can arange it any way to go to school, it may be that I can help you or settle it when I get home. remember Martha that I am not in a passion whilst writing this, but I am in ded earnest, and mean it all jest as I say it, so you can

52. See Matthew 7:8; Luke 11:10; 3 Nephi 14:8.
53. See James 1:5–6.
54. Possibly the phonetic spelling of the English dialect word *canty*. The *Oxford English Dictionary* defines it as "lively; brisk; in good spirits."
55. Most likely *walk*.

depend upon it all, for a fact. I hope that you will proffit by this and read it as ofton as once a Weak or oftoner, untill it is all wore out. I want you to be sharp and not dull of comprehentions, be prudent in all things, and I want you to be cool and not passionate, nor hasty in all things. I could say more but my paper is full and it is dark and so write to me ofton and take pains in writing, that it may be plain to be understood. be prayerful and wachful and god will bless you in all of your undertakeings I now close by saying God allmighty bless you all the day long. these are the prayers of your affectionate <Brother>

Joseph Smith

PS. I was pleas to hear your thaughts in regard to Jerusha and her husband,[56] Joseph Smith.

JOSEPH F. TO MARTHA ANN, 23 NOVEMBER 1855

Milksop,
Waluku, Maui, S. I.[57]
Nov. 23rd 1'55.

My Dear Sister Martha. Ann.

As I recievd no letters from You the two last Mails I thought that I would write a fiew lines to you in bro. Lawsons[58] letter to let you know how I am geting along. and to remind you of what ~~I want~~ I want you to do and ~~act~~, how I want you to act. Though you may think that I suppose you to be wild, and unprudant, but that is not the case, all that I want of you is to do right and act as neer right as you can. I know that you are large anough to take care of yourself and set good exanples before your young friends. but I think that good Counsul will not eretate an unerritatible mind, neither will good exanples lead one into disrespect, o bad habits, nor will it disaffect a good and stable mind if it is rightly apreciated, and duly conciderd, upon,

I wish you to understand that when I write to you I write as I would like to have John[59] or any of my older friends write to me who is younger, and more inexperianced in the things of this life. so you must duly consider from whence it comes, and remember that it is from one who looks after your intrests and who greatly desires and prays for your well fair.

I am well and feel first rate. though I have felt better or stronger in body than I do now.

The things of this world trubls me but litle.or I try to controle myself and be controled by the things of this life.

The Sandwich Island mission is rather weacker than it has been <for> sone time before, or since the rise of the church on the Lands, but I hope that it will soon take a chance for the

56. Jerusha Smith, half sister of Joseph F. and Martha Ann, married William Pierce in December 1854. See biographical register, "Pierce, William."
57. Wailuku.
58. James Lawson.
59. Likely refers to John Smith, oldest son of Hyrum Smith and Jerusha Barden.

better.[60] I am now stoping with Cousin Silas S. Smith.[61] and you know it is some plesure to be in company with our friends and relativs, [**p. 2**] all the Bretheren that came out when I did are well and are in the enjoyments of the spirit of god, I think.[62]

As for our Cousins in California I can say but little as I have written to them several times but have recievd no letters from them, but I hope that they are well and doing well. when I saw them last they had a great desire to see you all at home.[63] I have no more room so I must close. I want you to continue reading as much as you can, go to school as much as you can, and improve evry that is posible. give my love to all enquireing friends. I have sent you a little book that I hope you will recieve, as I wrote before, I have also writen to you severlal times, write ofton to me and I will do the same, may god bless you is the prayers of Joseph, <Smith>

Care of James Lawson, Deseret,[64]
Pleas foreward this and oblige
me; J. S.
For, Martha Ann. Smith,
Great Salt Lake. Co,
Utah Territory[65]

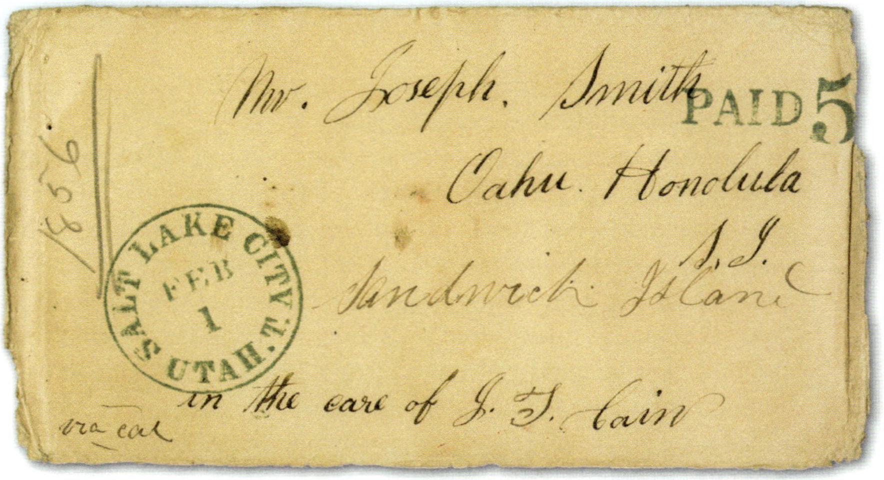

Martha Ann to Joseph F., 31 January 1856 (envelope)

60. The weakness referred to here is likely due to the policy of gathering the Saints to the island of Lānaʻi. After this gathering, the other island branches were strained by the loss of so many dedicated members. Also, many of the Saints who gathered to Lānaʻi did not have money or resources to establish themselves in their new home. R. Lanier Britsch, *Unto the Islands of the Sea: A History of the Latter-day Saints in the Pacific* (Salt Lake City, UT: Deseret Book, 1986), 111–16.
61. Likely refers to Silas Sanford Smith, Joseph F. and Martha Ann's father's uncle, though Joseph F. did have two relatives named Silas Smith serving at this time in the Sandwich Islands. See biographical register, "Smith, Silas Sanford."
62. Of the twenty-one missionaries called to the Pacific Isles who departed from Utah with Joseph F., nine were able to leave San Francisco on the ship *Vaquero* in September 1854. The remaining members of the group arrived a month later.
63. Joseph F. and Martha Ann's cousins Agnes Charlotte Smith and Ina Coolbrith (née Josephine Donna Smith) were living with their mother, Agnes Moulton Coolbrith, in California. Also living with them were Agnes's husband, William Pickett, and her twin sons, Don Carlos and William. Before departing from San Francisco in 1854, Joseph F. visited the family. Eventually, he would receive letters in reply to those he sent, and he would continue his correspondence with Aunt Agnes and Cousin Ina throughout their lives.
64. The location is unknown. Deseret, Millard County, Utah (1860), and Deseret, Fresno County, California (1887), important Latter-day Saint agricultural communities, were not yet established.
65. The original letter was folded in such a way that it was also used as an envelope.

MARTHA ANN TO JOSEPH F., 31 JANUARY 1856

G. S. L County[66] Sugar House ward[67]<U T> Jan 31.st 1856[68]

My dear and affectionate Brother Joseph

it is with pleasure that I set down to write a few lines to you to answer your kind and ~~and~~ affectionate letter. I recieved it this evning with the gratest of pleasure and hapiness. ~~to and to~~ to hear from you. John[69] told me that you was sick and I was sorry to hear that for it will put you back a good <deal> I am aff<r>aid but I hope ere this letter reaches your you will be as well and harty as you ever was.[70] thank the lord ~~for~~ that ~~I~~ he<a>lth is a blessing that I enjoy I havnot been sick so as to be confined to my bed a day sence you left home. and I wish that it had been so wth you but the lord orders all things for the best. I hav been going to school[71] to months now and am learning midling fast and I intend to learn a good deal faster than I have, we have got one of the fineest school housees in salt lake vall<e>y and brother Eldredge[72] keeps school and he is a good school master. I hav got a d<i>ctionary and I am sorry that I hav made mistakes in writing to you and both<e>ring you in reading my letters but you must excuse me this <time> and I will try to do better [*illegible strike-through*] <this [*illegible strike-through*]> time. thare is plenty of dictionary about and ~~thare~~ if you hav got a good one I would advise you to keep it even if you cold send it for I psume that it is an artical that you need your self when you are writeing I hav written one letter to you befor that I gave to John to send and he sent another that I had witten in the hace of it I wrote it when I received the book that you sent me I have ~~sent~~ got all of the thngs you sent me [**p. 3**][73] and I am much oblgeed to you for them[74] I ~~hope~~ have learne severrel of the peases in the book I think that it is the prtteest thing I seen in my and I think as much of it as I [*illegible strike-through*] would of so much gold and a good deal more becaus it is a preasent from a brother~~er~~ tht I love and respect I intend to learn it all by heart as fast as I can and I intend to obey all that you counciled me to do iff it is in my

66. Great Salt Lake County was created in 1850; its name was changed to Salt Lake County in 1866.
67. Created in 1854, the Smith family farm was within the Sugar House Ward boundaries.
68. Joseph F. was seventeen, and Martha Ann was fourteen.
69. John Smith.
70. Joseph F. became quite ill with a high fever the first month of his mission and was nursed on the island of Maui by Mary J. Hammond, the wife of a fellow missionary. See Mary Jane Dillworth Hammond, journal, vol. 1, 1853–1855, BYU.
71. Sugar House first had a log schoolhouse that was built in 1852. This building was replaced by an adobe structure, "then considered the best of the kind in the Territory," in 1855; see *Historical Records Survey (Utah), Historical Sketch of Salt Lake County* (Ogden, UT: Historical Records Survey [Utah], 1941), 25. School districts coincided with ward boundaries at this time; see Linda Sillitoe, *A History of Salt Lake County* (Salt Lake City, UT: Utah State Historical Society; Salt Lake County Commission, 1996), 102. According to a family tradition, "This was a very hard period in Martha's life; comforts, for her were practically non-existent and food was very scarce. Many times, she would go to school with nothing but a biscuit to eat all day long." Richard P. Harris, "Martha Ann Smith Harris," *Relief Society Magazine*, January 1924, 14.
72. Most likely this was Edmond [Edmund] Eldridge, who lived in the Sugar House Ward and was twenty-one years old at the time. See biographical register, "Eldridge, Edmond."
73. This letter originally consisted of two large sheets of paper that Martha Ann cut in half, making a total of four pages. From the alignment of the pinholes in the top corners of the paper, it appears that a straight pin had been used at one point to fasten the sheets of paper together. Martha Ann's letter is written on pages 1, 3, and 4. Page 2, the backside of page 1, was left completely blank. Martha Ann explains why she cut the paper in half in her last paragraph.
74. This was apparently a book of poetry, title unknown. See Joseph F. to Martha Ann, 18 October 1855 and 23 November 1855, herein.

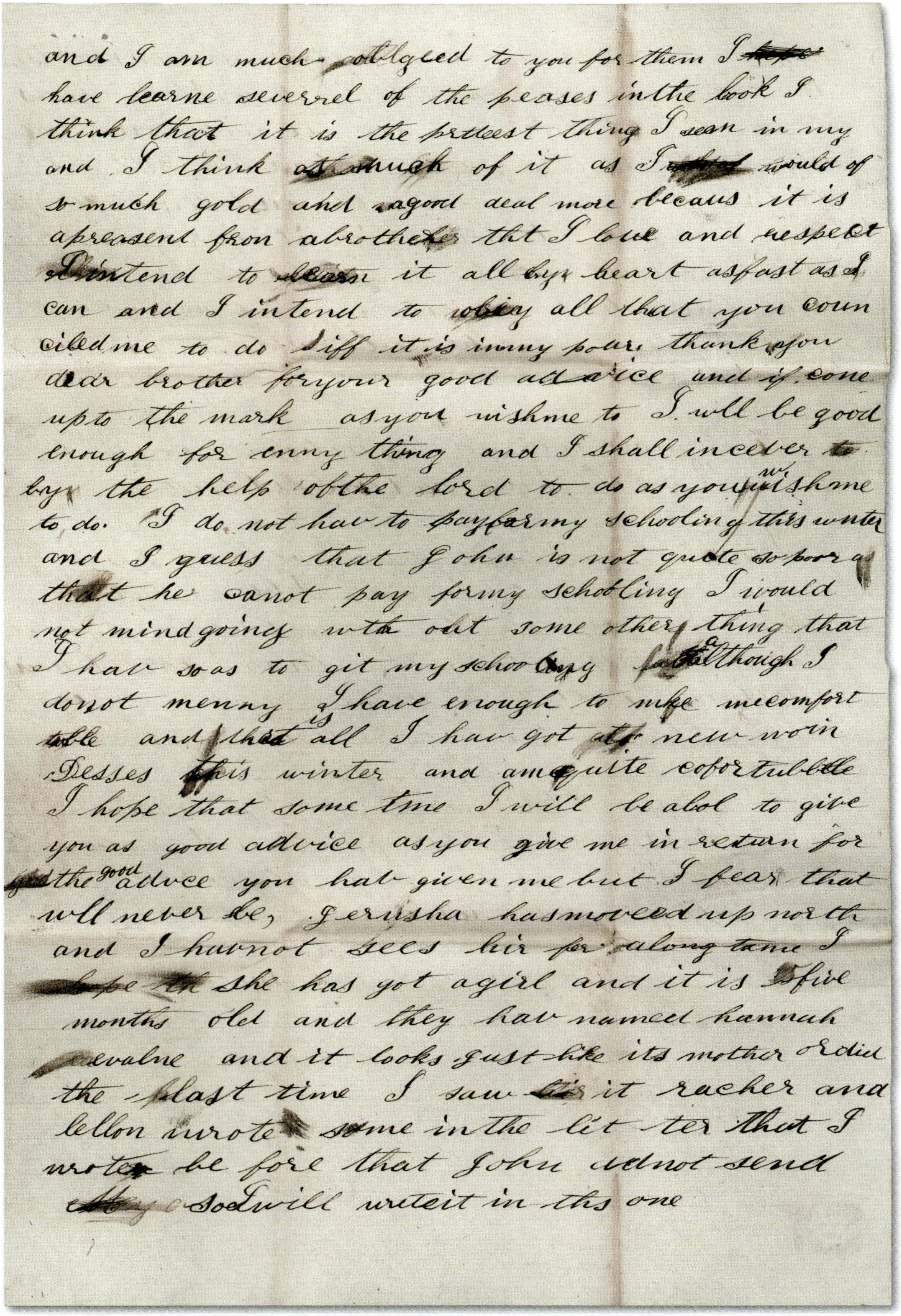

and I am much obliged to you for them I
have learne severel of the peases in the book I
think that it is the prttiest thing I seen in my
and I think as much of it as I would of
so much gold and agood deal more becaus it is
apreasent from abrother that I love and respect
I intend to learn it all by heart asfast as I
can and I intend to obey all that you coun
ciled me to do iff it is inmy poar thank you
dear brother foryour good advice and if come
upto the mark as you wishme to I will be good
enough for enny thing and I shall incever to
by the help ofthe lord to do as you wishme
to do. I do not hav to pay formy schooling this winter
and I guess that John is not quite so poor as
that he canot pay formy schooling I would
not mind going with out some other thing that
I hav so as to git my schooling although I
donot menny I have enough to make meecomfort
able and that is all I hav got two new woin
Desses this winter and amquite cofortubble
I hope that some time I will be abol to give
you as good advice as you give me in return for
the good advice you hav given me but I fear that
will never be, Jerusha has moveed up north
and I havnot seen hir for along time I
hope she has got agirl and it is five
months old and they hav named hannah
evaline and it looks just like its mother or did
the last time I saw it racher and
lellon wrote some in the letter that I
wrote be fore that John did not send
so I will write it in this one

Martha Ann to Joseph F., 31 January 1856 (p. 3; p. 1 of this letter is displayed on p. xvii)

1c My dear cosen as Martha ann was writeng
she gave us the prevledg of writting lines
to you to let you we are all well and enjoy
ing good helth and that we hav not for
goten you we are all well and send our
love to you do not think it hard that
father does not write to you for he is so bussy
all the time that he can not git a chance to
write he says that he will write to you as
soon as he can

We remain ever your affectionate cousins
Rachel and Ellen feldnd

I made a mistake and got my pper
rong so cut it in two I bleeve that I
hav told you all the news at the present
and it is giting late thare fore I must
bring my letter to a close good bye dear
Brother at the present

May the lord god of isrel
bless you in all your under ta
kings is the pray of your
affectionate sister

Martha Ann Smith

Martha Ann to Joseph F., 31 January 1856 (p. 4)

pour. thank you dear brother for your good advice and if come up to the mark as you wish me to I wll be good enough for enny thing and I shall indever ~~to~~ by the help of the lord to do as you <w>ish me to do. I do not hav to pay for my schooling this wnter and I guess that John is not quite so poor as that he canot pay for my schooling I would not mind going wth out some other thing that I hav so as to git my schooling <a>lthough I donot menny I have enough to mke me comforttable and that <is> all I hav got to new worn desses this winter and am quite cofortubbele I hope that some tme I will be abol to give you as good advice as you give me in return for ~~good~~ the <good> advce you hav given me but I fear that wll never be, Jerusha[75] has moveed up north[76] and I hav not sees hir for a long time I ~~hopeth~~ she has got a girl and it is ~~5~~ five months old and they hav named hannah ~~ea~~ evalne[77] and it looks just like its mother or did the last time I saw ~~her~~ it racher and hellon[78] wrote some in the litter that I wrote be fore that John ddnot send ~~My~~ so I will write it in ths one **[p. 4]**[79]

[80]I made amstake and got my pper rong socut it in <⟠>to[81] I believe that I hav tol[d] you all the news at the present and it ~~is~~is giting late thare fore I must bring my letter to a close good bye dear Brother at the present
May the lord god of isrel bless you in all your under takeings is the prar of your affectionate sister ~~is the prar~~
Martha Ann Smith[82]

JOSEPH F. TO MARTHA ANN, 18 FEBRUARY 1856

For Martha.
Lahaina Maui S. I.
Febru<a>ry 18th 1856.[83]

75. Jerusha Smith, older half sister to Joseph F. and Martha Ann.
76. Jerusha Smith and her husband, William Pierce, were living in Brigham City, Box Elder County, in northern Utah at this time.
77. Hannah Eveline Pierce, daughter of William Pierce and Jerusha Smith, is the niece of Joseph F. and Martha Ann. See biographical register, "Pierce, Hannah Eveline."
78. Rachel (1837–1914) and Ellen (1841–1906), daughters of Joseph Fielding and Hannah Greenwood Fielding, were first cousins of Joseph F. and Martha Ann. See biographical register, "Fielding, Rachel" and "Fielding, Ellen."
79. At the top of page 4 is a short paragraph signed by "Rachel and Hellon feldnd." It is unknown, which cousin actually wrote the note, but Rachel is three and a half years older. The note reads, "My dear cosen as Martha ann was writing she gave <us> usthe prviledg of wrtting lines toyou to let you we are all well and enjing good helth and that we hav not fer gotten you we are all wll and send our lo love toy you do not think it hard that father does not write to you for he is sobuessy allthe time hat he can not git achance to write hesas [he says] that he will write to you as soon as he can." The note is signed "We remain ever your affectionate cousins Rachel and Ellen feldnd."
80. Martha Ann's letter is continued on page 4 below the note from her cousins.
81. Martha Ann seems to be saying, "I made a mistake and got my paper wrong so cut it in two."
82. The envelope is addressed to "Mr. Joseph Smith Oahua Honolulu S.I. Sandwich Island in the care of J. T. Cain via Cal." "PAID 5" has been stamped on the right with a postal mark on the left, "SALT LAKE City UTAH. T. FEB 1." Joseph F. wrote on the back, "M. A. Smith Rachel & Hellen."
83. Joseph F.'s journal reveals that this letter was written over a two-day period; see Joseph F., journal, 18–19 February 1856.

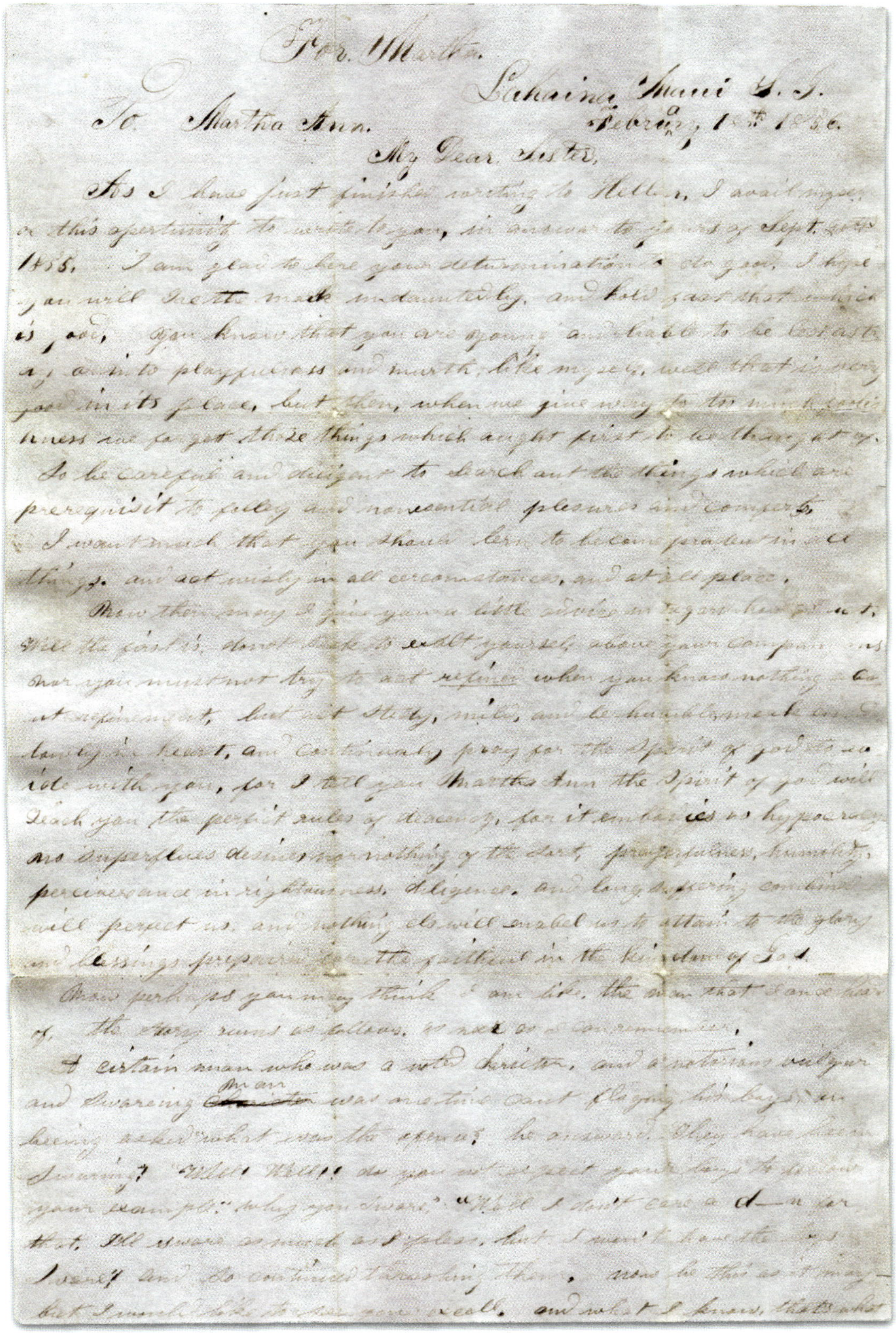
For. Martha.
Lahaina, Maui S. I.
To. Martha Ann. February 18th 1856.
My Dear. Sister,
As I have just finished writing to Hellen, I avail myself
of this opertunity to write to you, in answer to yours of Sept. 20th
1855. I am glad to here your determination to do good, I hope
you will Meet the mark undauntedly, and hold fast that which
is good, You know that you are young and liable to be led astr
ay, or into playfulness and mirth, like myself, well that is very
good in its place, but then, when we give way to too much fooli
shness we forget those things which ought first to be though[t] of.
So be careful and diligent to search out the things which are
prerequisit to folly and nonesential pleasures and comforts.
I want much that you should lern to become prudent in all
things, and act wisely in all circumstances, and at all places.
Now then may I give you a little advice in regard to [illegible] it.
Well the first is, donot seek to exalt yourself above your companions
nor you must not try to act refined when you know nothing abo
ut refinement, but act steady, mild, and be humble, meek and
lowly in heart, and continualy pray for the Spirit of God to a-
bide with you, for I tell you Martha Ann the Spirit of God will
teach you the perfect rules of decency, for it embodies no hypocracy
no superflous desires nor nothing of the sort, prayerfulness, humility,
perciverance in rightiousness, diligence, and long suffering combined
will perfect us, and nothing els will enabel us to attain to the glory
and blessings prepared for the faithful in the kingdom of God.
Now perhaps you may think I am like, the man that I once hear[d]
of. the story runs as follows. as near as I can remember,
A certain man who was a noted character, and a notorious vulgar
and swearing ~~character~~ man was one time caught flogging his boys, on
being asked "what was the offence? he answered "they have been
swearing?" "Well! Well!! do you not expect your boys to follow
your example," why you swear," "Well I don't care a d—n for
that. Ill sware as much as I please, but I won't have the boys
swear! and so continued thrashing them, now be this as it may—
but I would like to see you excell, and what I know, thats what

Joseph F. to Martha Ann, 18 February 1856 (p. 1)

To Martha Ann.
My Dear Sister,

As I have just finished writing to Hellen,[84] I avail myself of this opertunity to write to you, in answar to yours of Sept. 28th 1855. I am glad to here your deturmination to do good, I hope you will Toe the mark undauntedly, and hold fast that which is good.[85] You know that you are Young and liable to be led astray or into playfulnass and murth, like myself, well that is verry good in its place, but then, when we give way to too much foolishness we for get those things which aught first be thought of, so be careful and diligent to Search out the things which are prerequisit to folley and nonesential plesures and comferts. I want much that you should lern to become prudent in all things. and act wisly in all cercomstances, and at all places.

Now then may I give you a little advice in regard how [*illegible word*] act. Well the first is, donot seek to exalt yourself above your companyons nor you must not try to act refined when you know nothing about refinement, but act stedy, mild, and be humble, meak and lowly in heart, and continualy pray for the spirit of god to abide with you, for I tell you Martha Ann the spirit of god will Teach you the perfict rules of deacency, for it embodies no hypocracy, no superflues desines nor nothing of the sort, prayerfulness, humility, percivereance in rightousness, diligence, and long suffering combined will perfect us, and nothing els will enabel us to attain to the glory and blessings prepaired for the faithful in the kingdom of God.

Now perhaps you may think I am like, the man that I once heard of, the story runs as follows, as neer as I can remember.

A cirtain man who was a noted charictor, and notorious vulgur and swareing ~~charicter~~<man> was one time caut floging his boys, on beeing asked "what was the ofense"? he answard. "They have been swaring"! "Well! Well!! do you not expect your boys to follow your example," why you sware," "Well I don't care a d—n for that, I'll sware as much as I pleas, but I won't have the boys sware"! and so continued thrashing them. now be this as it may—but I would like to see you excell. and what I know that's what [**p. 2**] I want you should know. Well, I suppose you would like to know how I am geting a long. My helth is good and I feel well, and hope that I shall ever have strength to continue in well doings. I enjoy myself first rate here so fare from you all. I hope you enjoy the same blessings at home.

The signs of the times here are about as useual, there is but one Ship in this harbar now. but the streats are sworming with sailors, and prostitutes of the lowest grade. I tell you it is differant here to what it is in the vallyes. Men and Women go about the streats day and night, one party seeking for money and the other seeking to spend it, we can only let them wolle[◊] it out, and work out their own damnation.[86] The hare you sent me came to hand in s[◊◊]y. I showed it to the nativs and they said, "Maikai Maoli!" "ai ai"[87] They asked me many questions

84. Hellen Maria Fisher. Joseph F. noted in his journal, "In the evening I wrote a letter to Mrs. H. M. smith, G.S.L." Joseph F., journal, 18 February 1856.
85. 1 Thessalonians 5:21.
86. Prostitution and grog shops—establishments selling alcoholic drinks, primarily rum mixed with beer or water—had been introduced into the islands in the 1840s. They flourished in several Hawaiian port cities during the early and mid-nineteenth century, particularly in Lāhainā, Maui, where whaling ships often docked. See Brij V. Lal and Kate Fortune, eds., *The Pacific Islands: An Encyclopedia* (Honolulu: University of Hawai'i Press, 2000), 207.
87. *Maika'i maoli* means "very good indeed"; *a'ia'i* means "bright as moonlight; fair, white, clear, pure, brilliant, shining; brightness." The phrase *wahine'ili a'ia'i* means "a woman of skin that is fair and clear." Pukui and Elbert, *Hawaiian Dictionary*, s.vv. "maoli," "a'ia'i."

about you. and wanted to know if you could tal[◊] [*illegible word*], they think you know that any body younger than I am, must be verry young, as I am the youngest on the mission, and they ware much surprised to hear of your highth.

They like to here about you folks at "Maunapohaku"[88] (rockey mountains) and they ask a great many questions about you all, and how the countrey looks, and in fact [*illegible strike-through*] how all things appear.

I will write to you again when I have more time, and feel more like writing. Study Martha with all fidelity to obtain wisdome, be humble and prayerful, and you will be blessed. Write to me ofton and I will do the same.

I hear that all the young people of your countrey are geting marred off—and that counsel is that they should continue to marrey. I think it is a good plan, the young folks are becomeing mormons fast. I am glad to here of it. I think it will be my turn next,(!) I hear that little Brigham Young[89] has been marred, thats the Talk, "walk right up like a chicken to the doe and aske for the artickal," that's a good plan. I tell you martha they are going to flud the world with "true blue"[90] or with true borne "Mormons" and I'm glad to here it. give my love to Sister Griffin and also to bro. Griffin, Charley, Sarah, William, Jrusha, John, Hellen,[91] and all enquireing friends. god bless you, as ever your brother, Joseph Smith.

MARTHA ANN TO JOSEPH F., MARCH 1856

G S Ƚ L C Sec March 1856[92]

My dear and affectionate brother I with pleasure take my pen in hand to write a few lines to you to let you know that I am well and all of the folks and I hope that this letter will find you well also. I hav just come from home this morning and I am at [*illegible strike-through*] cousin lucys[93] and she gave me some paper to write to you on and my school was out day before yester day and I thaught that I would gow up in town and visit a while with the folk. I did not git a

88. *Mauna* means "mountain" and *pohaku* means "rock"; the combination of these words, *Maunapohaku*, means "Rocky Mountains" and was often used as a name for Utah. Pukui and Elbert, *Hawaiian Dictionary*, s.vv. "mauna," "pohaku."
89. Brigham Young Jr., son of Brigham Young and Mary Ann Angell, married Catherine Curtis Spencer on 15 November 1855. See biographical register, "Young, Brigham, Jr."
90. Here is the first reference to a phrase used in a story about Joseph F. when he responded to an "inebriated scoundrel" who wanted to know if he was a Mormon as he pointed a gun at him: "Yes, siree; dyed in the wool; true blue, through and through." See Joseph Fielding Smith, *The Life of Joseph F. Smith: Sixth President of The Church of Jesus Christ of Latter-day Saints* (Salt Lake City, UT: Deseret Book, 1938), 189.
91. Sister and Brother Griffin likely refer to Abigail Varney and her husband, Albert Bailey Griffin. Also named here are their son Charles Emerson Griffin and his wife Sarah Smith, William Pierce and his wife Jerusha Smith, and John Smith and his wife Hellen Maria Fisher. See biographical register, "Varney, Abigail" and "Griffin, Albert Bailey."
92. Martha Ann addressed the envelope, "Mr Joseph Smith, Esq in Honalulu Sandwich, Islands in care of John T. Cain." The envelope has a Salt Lake City postal mark, "SALT LAKE CITY UTAH.T. MAR 1." Joseph F. wrote on the back of the envelope, "Received and answerd May 24th & 25th 56 Hilo Hawaii]." Martha Ann wrote on the back of the envelope, "Why don't you write?"
93. Likely refers either to Lucy Brown, wife of Elias Smith, or to Lucy Meserve Smith, second wife of George A. Smith. Both Elias and George A. Smith are first cousins once removed to Joseph F. and Martha Ann. See biographical register, "Brown, Lucy" and "Smith, Lucy Meserve."

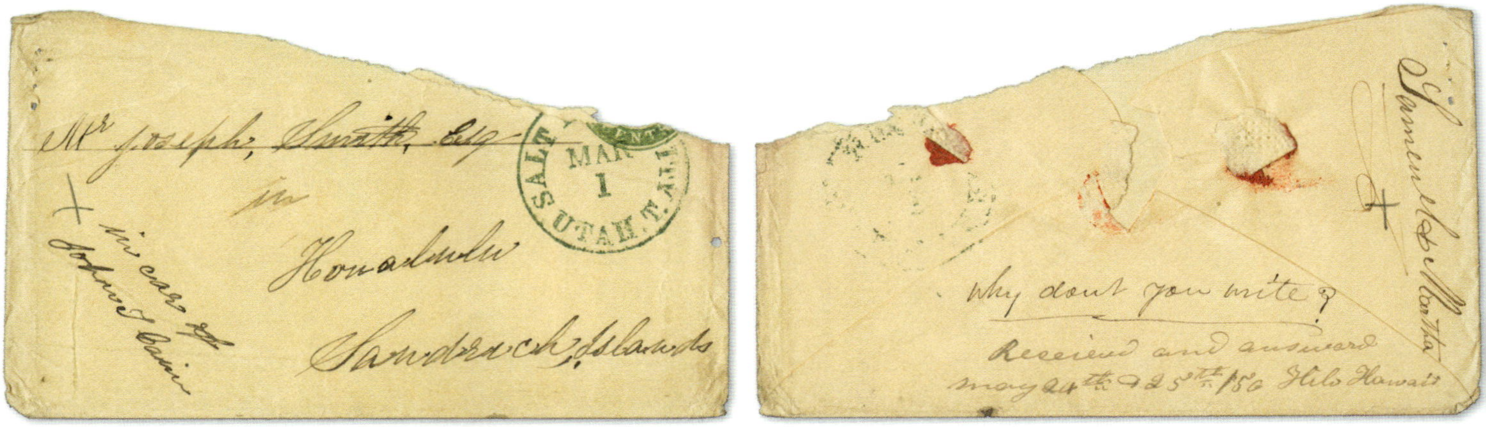

Martha Ann to Joseph F., March 1856 (envelope)

letter from you this male but I have <not> answered <~~not~~> all that you wrote in the last letter you wrote ~~me~~ you may not read the last letter I wrote, for it was wrote in such a hurry I just got it [*illegible erasure*] after schol <and> was out at knight and we was out of candels and I was in such a hurry that I could not half write it. and I expect that thare was lots of mistakes in it but I guess that you can read it [*illegible strike-through*] or at least I hope you can with out much trubbul and <if> [*illegible strike-through*] is not wrote verry good I hope you will git it. I wish that I could write as good as you can and I aught to write better for I hav had a better chance than you have had but I have not opresheated a good chance as I aucht to hav done [*illegible erasure*] O I wish that I could see you Joseph and I could tell you a grate many things that you dont know any thing about you dont know how every thing is here but you will sometime I dare not write every thing just as it is ~~you~~ and wish you ~~would~~ could come home before long and see the folks and see how things are but I wil hav to wait a whille before that time Joseph you would hardley know me ~~I~~ iff you was to see me I am such a grate big girl I ~~seven foot~~ **[p. 2]** ~~G S L C See March~~

five foot and seven inches. but I dont know when I will git marred I wount till you git back enny how I tell you Joseph that it is hard work to sow all of my wild oats[94] yet but I hope that I will make it out ater a while but I have not yet. now I believe I hav ~~ha~~ told you all the news except the indens hav killed a good may of our folks over in sedar valley.[95] now I believ that I will bring my letter to a close preying the lord to bless you and prospr you is the <this is> prear of your sister excuse all mistakes and bad writing for my hand trembles so that I can not hold

94. Martha Ann's use of this phrase most likely did not have the same meaning that it generally has, but she is referring to some kind of youthful behavior.

95. The *Deseret News* reported a "disturbance with Indians" in Cedar Valley, west of Utah Lake. On 21 February 1856, Indians allegedly killed two herdsmen, and another herdsman was reported missing. (These were later identified as Henry Moran, Washington Carson, and Lewis Hunsaker.) The next day, a skirmish broke out between a posse with court writs for the arrest of the supposed perpetrators and a group of unidentified Indians at "an Indian camp near the south fort in Cedar county," resulting in the deaths of George Carson and two unnamed Indians. On 26 February, another skirmish broke out that apparently resulted in the deaths of three more herdsmen and two Indians. See "Disturbance with Indians," *Deseret News*, 27 February 1856, 405; and "Disturbance with Indians," *Deseret News*, 5 March 1856, 413.

my pen still so good by for the present for I cant find enny more to say may the lord bless you
Joseph
Martha Ann Smith

Receivd and answard May 24th 1'56[96]
Hilo[97] Hawaii

MARTHA ANN TO JOSEPH F., CA. APRIL 1856

[CA. APR. 1856]
G S ~~G~~

My Dear Brother Joseph
as I recievd a letter from you the last ma<i>l[⟠] I thaught that I would answer it but I did not recieve till <after> the ma<i>l[⟠] went out and so I thaught that I would answer it this male I recievd your letter and was glad to hear so kind and affectionate a letter it done me good to read it and it alway does do me good to read a letter from you for I alway learn something new that does me good. you said that you had felt stronger in boddy than [*illegible strike-through*] you do now I am sorry that you do not have better helth but I supose the climate does not agree with you as well as it does here in our mountain home it is the helthyest place in the wourld I believ. for I never hav benn sick to speak of sence you left home but I hav been poisoned this spring prity bad with poison iva[98] and i had as live ~~be~~ sick as to be botherd with that but I am gittng better now. and all of the folks are well and sarah has got a girl and it ~~well~~ was five weaks old the twenty first of this month., of aprile.[99] I wll tell you all of the [*illegible strike-through*] <news> now that I know of. rache <fielding> is [*illegible strike-through*] marriad to a ~~man~~ man by the name of william burton[100] and gon up north to live and hellon sais she is going to have him to and rachel sais she wants hur to hav him when she gits old enough.[101] and I forgot to tell you sarahs babys name <it is> allice lovina[102] and it is the picture of its mother.

96. The last two lines are written in Joseph F.'s hand. He noted in his journal, "Saturday, May 14th . . . I went down in town (to the Post Office) . . . and found . . . one letter from my sister Martha." Joseph F., journal, 24 May. He answered Martha Ann on 25 May; see Joseph F., journal, 25 May 1856.
97. Originally, Hilo represented most of the east coast of the island of Hawai'i. Eventually, Protestant missionaries established a community overlooking a large bay, known today as Hilo Bay, that became the modern town of Hilo. Most of Joseph F.'s references to Hilo are references to the Hawaiian villages in the Hilo district, not the town of Hilo.
98. Poison ivy, along with poison oak and sumac, belong to the *Anacardiaceae* family. These plants cause a rash if a person comes in contact with their oily resin.
99. Sarah Smith, daughter of Hyrum Smith and Jerusha Barden, gave birth to Alice Lovina Griffin on 21 March 1856. See biographical register, "Griffin, Alice Lovina."
100. William Burton married Rachel Fielding on 28 March 1856. See biographical register, "Burton, William Walton."
101. William Burton subsequently married Rachel's two younger sisters, Ellen (possibly the "hellon" referred to here) and Sarah Ann, as they each came of age, in 1862 and 1870, respectively. All three women, daughters of Joseph Fielding and Hannah Greenwood, are cousins to Joseph F. and Martha Ann. See biographical register, "Fielding, Ellen."
102. Alice Lovina Griffin.

and little [*illegible strike-through*] rosey[103] is dead she died with the lollor horn[104] and she was poor for last winter was a hard winter and lots of catle ded she s<t>ood it till sprng and then she died I i was sorry but I done my best to save hur but I could not. I expect hur time had come to die you said that I might think that you thaucht I was wild but I donot I know what you want and and I will strive to do the best I can and the best I know how. I do not feel above taking your council but I want you **[p. 2]** to advise me what to do for you are older than I am and hav been tried mor than I hav. I consdder from whence your good advice comes I consider that it comes from a brother who wishes me wel and who I had ~~rather~~ ~~re~~ as live recieve advice from as any boddy in the world. I am glad that all of the bretheren are well and enjoying the sprret of the lord and I onely wish that you could enjoy good helth and then I should be satticefied but they hav sent some mor of our boys to the sandwch isleland and I perhaps they send for you. they hav sent frank young to take Johns place[105] and maby they have sent some one to take your place. if they hav it will <I hope so> be all right. now I wil tell you a little mor new that I did not think of be fore. Sarah Bollwinkel is marriad to a man by the name of nelson and she is second wfe.[106] and I wll be fifteen years old neext month and you wuld scarcely know me if you was to see me now I hav growed a foot sence you seen me I guess I expect that I hav <not> alterd as much as you have sence you left home. I am not ging to school now the school is out and I am staying with sarah[107] yet and I shall hav to learn all I can at home. for I dont expect that schol will beg<i>n again untill winter but I hope it wil. sarah is as good to me as any mother need to be she is kind to me and she will be rewarded for it. my hand is gittng tierd and my paper is ~~git~~ nearly fool and so I wll bring my [*illegible strikethrough*] <scroll> to a close excuse ~~my~~ it for I can not make enny thing else but a scroll. ~~my~~ for my pen is poor and had not got a better one ~~it~~ at the pesent

May the lord bless you and ~~I remain yo~~ prosper you in all of your under takei<n>gs is the prair of your sister Martha Ann Smith

Recieved[108] July 11th and answered July 14th 1856.[109]
Puneonka Hilo Hawaii.[110]

103. Rosey appears to be the name of a cow.
104. Most likely a reference to a cattle disease.
105. Franklin Wheeler Young, nephew of Brigham Young, was probably sent to replace his younger brother John Ray Young. See biographical register, "Young, Franklin Wheeler" and "Young, John Ray."
106. Sarah Bollwinkel married William Nelson on 13 March 1856 in Salt Lake City. See biographical register, "Bollwinkel, Sarah" and "Nelson, William."
107. Sarah Smith.
108. Joseph F. noted, "We also received the mail. I received the 'D News' the 'W. Standard' and two No. of the 'Polynesian.' I also receivd letters from several of the Bretheren, and one from home." Joseph F., journal, 11 July 1856. The *Deseret News* was published in Salt Lake City, and the *Western Standard* was published in San Francisco; both were Latter-day Saint publications. The *Polynesian* was the official publication of the government of the Kingdom of Hawaiʻi and was published in Honolulu.
109. In Joseph F.'s hand; see Joseph F. to Martha Ann, 14 July 1856, herein.
110. Written upside down in the top margin of page 2.

JOSEPH F. TO MARTHA ANN, 25 MAY 1856

For, Martha[111]
Hilo Hawaii Sand. Islands
May 25th 1856[112]

My Dear Sister Martha

[*illegible word due to faded paper*] plesure I receievd & perused your kind note of March, (mind your dates Marty) and with plesure I seat myself to answer the same, tho' I have but little time to write as the mail gos out tomorrow. I shall undoubtedly be engaged most of this day in attending to Church affairs, such as preaching—visiting the saints (and sinners) &c. I allmost sometimes dread when sunday comes, for where the fiew saints who are left, are so dull and indifferant as those in my field, it is a hard task to preach to them in plainness, therefore it makes sundays Work a hard days work for me. where the saints are alive to the work, it is a chearing in sted of a labourious task to address them.[113]

I am Well and happy,—can't help but rejoice everry day,—for the goodness of the Lord. I sometimes think is too good for me, and is more than I realy mer~~r~~it, but I always had a desire to be good anoug<h> to merit the blessing of Heaven at all times, how far I may have fallen short in acting out my own desires, is not for me to say, but as all other people I have no doubt fallen short in may things. but let us be courageous martha in bearing off the duties incumbent upon us, be not ashamed of do[◊◊] good, or any thing pertaining to our duty.— do nothing in secret we would not do in publich, or rather, do nothing in secret that we would be ashamed of in public, and then we will have nothing to doubt, nor fear.

I am geting along verry well at presant, my helth is good and my spirits buoyant, for which I feel to thank the Lord. I have se[◊]n but fiew sick days comparitively since I left home. and I still hope to **[p. 2]** enjoy with you all a continuance of the same good Blessings. I am now on the Largest Island[114] in the group. the greatly renouned volcano[115] is with in 5 or 6 miles from me, the light of its flames by night, and its smoke by day can plainly be seen for miles and miles. this is the Island also upon which Capt. Cook was killed some 70 years ago, by the Natives,[116] I suppose you mind reading of it. this also (which is of greater importance to you and I) is the

---

111. There are multiple indecipherable pen markings in the top left margin.

112. "I wrote two letters to day in answer to those received last evening from my Sister and Cousin, attended meeting. Administered the sacrament etc., we had a great meeting, and the Spirit of the Lord was with us" Joseph F., journal, 25 May 1856. He mailed the letters the following day. Joseph F., journal, 26 May 1856.

113. Joseph F. attributed this apparent apathy on the island of Hawai'i to the policy of gathering the most committed converts to the island of Lāna'i, which created a challenge for work on the other islands. See Joseph F. to Martha Ann, 23 November 1855, herein.

114. Hawai'i is about four thousand square miles and is the largest island in the Hawaiian Island chain.

115. The volcano mentioned here is Mauna Loa, Hawaiian for "Long Mountain." Joseph F. was in Puneo, one of the many small Hawaiian villages, where branches of the Church had been organized in the Hilo District. See Joseph F., journal, 21 May 1856: "Wednes May 21st, We started this morning for Puneio Hilo where we arrived in safely."

116. James Cook served as a member of the British Royal Navy and was an explorer and surveyor in southeast Canada. He became famous for his three voyages to the Pacific, where he was the first to map specific islands throughout the area. Cook was killed in a skirmish with Native Hawaiians during his third voyage to the Pacific in 1779. See biographical register, "Cook, James." See also Vanessa Collingridge, *Captain Cook: The Life, Death and Legacy of History's Greatest Explorer* (London: Ebury Publishing, 2003); and Gananath Obeyesekere, *The Apotheosis of Captain Cook: European Mythmaking in the Pacific* (Princeton: Princeton University, 1992).

Island upon which bro. Lawson and many others ware imprisened for some length of time for truths sake, and where he with many of the Bretheren have been compelled to travel on foot with out a shoe to their feet for days and days and laughed and sneared at by the, "Kahu hipa ~~h~~[◊] hoolimalima," (hired sheepherds)[117] who had plenty, but by their narrow contractedness were so neerly robed of all philanthropey, that they looked upon all such as as Mormons to be wors than inhumain, and degadeing to look upon. I am sorry to say that is exactly the spirit that prevails to day, and the situation in which we are at the presant placed.

You was saying in your letter, that you were going to visit a little up in town, well be a good girl and observe good becomming behaviour where ever you may be, shake off rudeness and thoughtlessness when you are visiting in the midst of your friends.

Write to me ofton Martha and give me all the news, pertaining to the famely and building of Zion &c. &c.

I shall have to close, as I have no time to lengthen out at presant. remember what I have told you ofton to be a good girl.— Learn all you can, and be prayerful, &c. that is one great thing, never be ashamed of praying. May god bless you Martha with all neadful blessings with all of our friend and Reations, is the prayers of your, affectionate brother Joseph Smith

JOSEPH F. TO MARTHA ANN, 14 JULY 1856

Hilo Hawaii Sandwich Islandes
July 14th 1856,[118]

To My Dear Sister Martha Ann.

I recievd your kind but short letter of ____ (date your letters Marta) which came to hand last day before yesterday it found me well and hearty as usual. I was glad to hear from you for you are my most punctual corispondent, and I'll reward you for it some day. I thank you for the information you gave me of home and her situations, the flocks, and the Herds &c. I'm sorry for little Rosy, poor little thing I would like to have seen her again, and another thing what has become of Mager?[119] I suppose he has gon the way of all the Earth before now? I want you to be some what observing and informe me in regard to all the affairs about home. John[120] I suppose will not have time to give me all the particulars, so you can do it. I feel anxious to know about all the folks, from John to all of our connections, so be careful observing, and particular to tell things just as they are nothing under nor over, then there will be no misunderstanding

And again, when you write try and take care of your paper that it may not be blotted. and see if you cannot punctuate your writing, and see that the ending of one word is not joined

117. Joseph F. is most likely referring to other Christian missionaries who he felt were like the individual mentioned by Christ in the New Testament who "fleeth, because he is an hireling, and careth not for the sheep." See John 10:12–13.
118. Joseph F. wrote four letters, including this one, during the morning on Monday, 14 July 1856. See Joseph F., journal, 14 July 1856.
119. Rosy and Mager appear to be the names of farm animals or pets. See Martha Ann to Joseph F., 17 December 1856, herein, where the name "old mager" is also used. Joseph Smith, Joseph F. and Martha Ann's uncle, had a dog named Old Major in Nauvoo. It is possible that Joseph F. refers to a dog or pet named after the Prophet Joseph Smith's dog.
120. John Smith.

on the commencement of another. and be sure to commence all nowns with a capital, as John, Sarah, Rosy, Rachal, House, Ship, Sheep,—&c, &c, &c.

And when you come to the end of a full sentance, o[◊] paragraph, dot it with a period, and commence the next sentance with a Capital letter. Try also to get all the wordes on the line of the paper, and not have to poot it above, as, "I <am> going"—&c it does not look so well. but where you make a mistake and leave out a word, that is the way to fix it. When you commence a letter allways date it, and commence in any stile that sutes your notion, but have it neat. These are my rules, but whether they are acording to grammar, I donot know.

You might ask, why don't you obeserve them, the reason is I have allways to write in a hurry and so I can [◊]ot [*0.3 x 1.3 cm tear along fold*] particular, I have [**p. 2**] scarsely a day to call mine, but I hope you have.

Be attentive Martha to your work, when you are doing any thing confine your mind to that one thing till it is done, and then you will never have too many irons[121] in the fire at once, and you will not be figity and uneasy, and then as soon as you have done your worke and feel like takeing a 'rough-and-Tumble', all right.

You will hear all the news Martha in Charles'[122] letter, and also in Johns' so I have no need of writing one thing twice over.

You say in your letter Martha that Miss Bolewinkle[123] has been married. also—Rachel,[124] and Hellen[125] too, is in a fair way for it by all appearances.Well I hope their enjoyments will be full. I don't begrudge them their situation, nor any one els, I think it is a good plan. I suppose they are not all married yet?

I expect of course that Mary Jane[126] will soon go off as well as your self, paha (perhapes) well I may join you some time, but when I do not know, but make yourselves contented and Joseph will look out for No. One. I guess No. Two, will not suffer till I finde her. <P>pleas look out for Martha and be carful when you step that your foot is sollid that you may not fall throw.

I want you should allways tender my kind regardes to Aunt Thompson[127] and [*0.1 x 6.8 cm tear along fold*] fine to all of our relatives, and [◊◊]nds. Tell them I donot forget them in my prayers, and never will. I recievd a letter from Jerusha[128] this Mail she was well when she wrote, but I donot like the idea of them going so far from the City. she said she had just receievd a letter from Sarah[129] stating that you were all well, &c. she [Jerusha] sais her little girl grows fine and she has named it Hanah after Aunty.[130]

121. An English idiom that refers to having too many duties or obligations at once so that one of them is bound to fail; when a blacksmith had too many irons in his fire, he could not effectively keep track of all of them.
122. Likely Charles Emerson Griffin.
123. Sarah Adelaide Bollwinkel. She married William Nelson on 13 March 1856 in Provo, Utah. See biographical register, "Bollwinkel, Sarah."
124. Rachel Fielding.
125. Likely Ellen Fielding, sister of Rachel Fielding. Ellen would become the second wife of William Burton in 1862. See Martha Ann to Joseph F., April 1856, herein.
126. Mary Jane Thompson, cousin to Joseph F. and Martha Ann, was the daughter of Robert Blashell Thompson and Mercy Rachel Fielding.
127. Mercy Rachel Fielding.
128. Jerusha Smith.
129. Sarah Smith.
130. Hannah Eveline Pierce may have been named after either Hannah Grinnels, who helped with Hyrum Smith and Jerusha Barden's children after the death of Jerusha, or after Hannah Greenwood, aunt to Joseph F. and Martha Ann. See biographical register, "Grinnels, Hannah" and "Greenwood, Hannah."

Well I will have to close, I am just going to attend a meeting with the saints, pray for me allways, and I will do the same. write ofton, and I wi[*0.1 x 6.8 cm tear along fold*] do the same also. give my love to all the folks and accept the same to yourself. may God bless you and you all that you may ever be strong, is the prayers of your Bro. Joseph Smith Be carful about going among Poison Iva. be a good girl.[131]

MARTHA ANN TO JOSEPH F., 29 JULY 1856

G S L utah ter July 29 1856[132]

My dear brother I wth pleasure set [*illegible erasure*] my self down to scribble a few lines to you to let you knonow how I am. and how I am gitting along I am well and enjoying good helth and all of the folks. sarah is well and the baby and chares[133] is well to. and I hope that this letter wll find you [*illegible strike-through*] enjoying the same bessing. I donot feal very well in mind if I do in [*illegible strike-through*] boddy I hav heard that you was [*illegible strike-through*] ~~ingaged~~ enageed[134] to some [*illegible strike-through*] pe<r>son tha is not honnest hearted, and it was not very good news to me now I assure you that for I thaught that one slice of a [*illegible strike-through*] <loaf> was enough. esspecialy of a sour loaf. it is none of my buisness but it hurt my feallings so that I could not help speaking about it. ~~but~~<but> if it is out of the way you must excuse me [*illegible strike-through*] help speaking about it for I must speak as I think <some times> enny how if I dont always o Joseph thare is thousands of things I could tell you but my hand trembles and my heert beats so when I go to write to you that I can not wrte wat I wold like to and what I do wrte is not fit to be red some times I forgit what I am wrting~~s~~ and go to writeting some thng elce but forgiv me [*illegible strike-through*] dear brother and I will [*illegible strike-through*] <con>tinue to do better until I be come pirfect if it is the will of the

131. There are markings at the bottom of page 1. It looks as though Joseph F. was practicing some letters. *I* and *Dear* are the only legible words. At the top of page 2 are the words "For Martha" and three other illegible letters.

132. Joseph F. noted on 12 October 1856, "attended two meetings during the day, in the evening ten of us started for Lahaina on foot, arrived in safty about 'cock crowing' found the brethren well who preceded us in, received two letters from home"; see Joseph F. journal, 12 October 1856. The two letters included this one and one from his brother; see John Smith to Joseph F., 31 July 1856. The envelope that contained this letter was postmarked "Aug 5 Salt Lake City Utah Territory" and addressed to "Mr. Joseph Smith Honolulu Sandwich Islands Care J. T. Caine." For J. T. Caine, see biographical register, "Caine, John Thomas." Joseph F. noted on the back of the envelope, "M. A. Smith Received Oct. 12th Lahaina Maui. 1856. Answered Oct. 20th Hawaii Kohala Kapaliuka"; see Joseph F., journal, 20 October 1856.

133. Sarah Smith, Charles Emerson Griffin, and Alice Lovina Griffin, born 21 March 1856.

134. Apparently, Martha Ann heard that Joseph F. was engaged to marry once he returned to Utah and was not happy about the news. She later apologized for her comments; see Martha Ann to Joseph F., 2 October 1856. For Joseph F.'s reply, see Joseph F. to Martha Ann, 20 October 1856 herein.

lord. I wll ~~tell~~ tell you some news loviana[135] is on her way to the valey and John[136] is going to meat her in about a weak~~s~~ and help her in she has got four children [**p. 2**] and Anney tomson[137] has got mared and got to boys for the first start.

I am not ging to school yet and cant untill winter for I hav so much to do I am stopping at Johns again chares grain fell short this spring and John wanted me to come and live with him and so i went and I went thare in aprile and I hav been thare ever sence[138] helon has treted me better ths time than she did before but they wll tell lies be hind my back and mace fun of your sisters and call them liers and that isnet all neither if you should know them as well as I do you [*illegible erasure*] would not blame me for witing as I do and Johns iyes is blinded and he will not believ. they are hyocrtes they daw near to you wih thir lips but thir hearts is far from you.[139] I will ceac and talk of some thing elce May Jane has been looking is the peap stone[140] for you and she seen you and and I sopose she wll tell you the pticalars for my paper is ~~ner~~ nearely [*illegible strike-through*] full you mst tell me whether you are promised or not that is if you are amnder <to Jane>[141] to you mut not tell enny thing elce. if John knew what I had wrote he would do I do not know what to me you must not mention it in enny of your leters. I will bring my [*illegible strike-through*] scrall to a close for my pper is ~~fool~~ nearely full write to me oftin and [*illegible word*] do the same.

May the [*illegible erasure*] lord bless you in all of you under takng is the prar of your sister Martha Ann Smith

135. Lovina Smith, eldest daughter of Hyrum Smith and Jerusha Barden, married Lorin Walker on 23 June 1844 in Nauvoo, just days before the martyrdom. They had four children at the time this letter was written: Hyrum, Jerusha, Edwina, and Emma. Lovina and Lorin remained in Nauvoo, living with Lovina's aunt Emma Hale Smith. They then moved to live with Lovina's aunts Catherine and Sophronia Smith. The family was preparing for their journey to Winter Quarters at this time. However, they did not arrive in Winter Quarters until 16 March 1857. The family finally made their way to Utah in the spring of 1860 with the help of John Smith, Lovina's young brother. They settled in Farmington, Utah. Brigham Young offered to buy them a home there. See Joseph F. to Martha Ann, 14 June 1872, herein. See also Rodney W. Walker, comp., *Ancestry and Descendants of John Walker* (Kaysville, UT: Inland Printing, 1953), 22–23, 85–86. See also biographical register, "Walker, Hyrum Smith," "Walker, Jerusha Celeste," "Walker, Edwina Mariah," and "Walker, Emma Irene."
136. John Smith, Martha Ann's and Joseph F.'s older half brother.
137. Thompson, Anna or Annie. She married William Samuel Godbe on 15 November 1855.
138. Martha Ann lived with John Smith and Hellen Maria Fisher for a time.
139. Martha Ann, troubled by what she perceived to be Hellen's tendency to gossip, spoke to John about it, but he apparently would not listen to or believe her. Whatever the problems, they seem to have been resolved later. See Martha Ann to Joseph F., 5 April 1857, herein.
140. Mary Jane Thompson's use of a "peepstone" to view Joseph F. in the Sandwich Islands is referred to at least two other times in letters from Elizabeth Jane Fisher to Joseph F. See Elizabeth Jane Fisher to Joseph F., 20 July 1856 and 11 May 1857. For Joseph F.'s response regarding the matter, see Joseph F. to Martha Ann, 20 October 1856, herein.
141. Elizabeth Jane Fisher. See biographical register, "Fisher, Elizabeth Jane."

MARTHA ANN TO JOSEPH F., 2 OCTOBER 1856

G S L C Utah T Oct the <second 1856>[142]

My dear brother Joseth

with pleasure I received your too last kind and affectionate letters of may 25[143] and <of> Aprile 17 I did not received eather of them untill the ma<i>le went out and so I could not write before now I am not very well to day in boddy nor in spirets I hav nothng much to chear me now for you are gon and John[144] is gon. he ~~is~~ <has> not got home yet. and helon[145] ~~is~~ has got a very bad tooth ache and she sends her love to you and sais she could not write to you this time. sister griffin and Sarah[146] is over hear to day and sister <griffin> is the same womern she alway was. she sends her love to you and ~~sar~~ she sais that she is to old <to write> to you <you> know in her joke I am livving at [*illegible strike-through*] <Johns> yet and sarah sends hir love to you and sais she has not forgotton you but she has got a baby to worry wth and you must excuse hir. I [*illegible strike-through*] suppose you will wonder what has beecome of the ducks for I hav not said enny thing about ~~it that~~ it. last foll when I <went> to stay with Jerusha a while something cot them and I felt so sorry about it that I could not tell you enny thing about it but I could not help ~~is~~ it. Joseph you must e<x>cuse what I said in my last letter for I suppose you think it is none of my busness.[147] but out of the abncec of th heart the mouth speaketh but dear brother I thought I would giv you a timely [**p. 2**] worning and you must excuse my [*illegible erasures*] writing for my pen is poor and my ink is not thee best in the world and I am in a hurry for I hav got to send it to town to night or not atoll for a boy is going to town to night and I can send it wth him. I am not going to schol now but I think that I wil go this wnter. I hope so enny hoow you said you was on the island that capt cook was murded on[148] I rememberd readdng of it very well. and i hope that you wll be treatted different to when the elders ware. you say that you could not write enny thing sensubbul to me when you was in a hurry but I onely wsh that I could write enny thing half as sesuble as[◊] you can ~~for~~ when in a hurry. ~~you~~ O Joseth i wish i could see you and then I could tel you my fealling better than I could write them. the hand cart company has come in to the valley and they said that that the company that John is in is thre weaks behind and hey came in last [*illegible erasure*] friday.[149] wal I mist bring my scroll to a close for it is gitting dark and my papper is ~~fool~~ nearly fool excuse all mstakes and bad writing

May the lord bless you is the prayr of your own sister Martha Smith

142. Martha Ann apparently had someone address the envelope, "Joseph. F. Smith Esq Honolulu Sandwich Islands." The postmark for this envelope is dated "OCT 8 SALT LAKE CITY UTAH." On the reverse Joseph F. has written "M. A. Smith Received Dec. 19th 1856. Kukuiahuhia. Answered Dec. 22nd Pololu Kohala, Kohala Hawaii."
143. See Joseph F. to Martha Ann, 25 May 1856, herein.
144. John Smith seems to have already departed from Salt Lake for Florence (Winter Quarters), Nebraska, to help his sister Lovina and her family move to Utah Territory. See Martha Ann to Joseph F., 29 July 1856, herein, note 135.
145. Hellen Maria Fisher.
146. "Sister griffin" probably refers to Sarah's mother-in-law, Abigail Varney, wife of Albert Bailey Griffin.
147. See Martha Ann to Joseph F., 29 July 1856, herein.
148. See Joseph F. to Martha Ann, 25 May 1856, herein.
149. Though Lovina and her family were not prepared to make the trek at this time, John returned to the Salt Lake Valley with another group instead and went back for Lovina in 1860. He appears to have been on the return trail from his first visit when this letter was written. Martha Ann reported his return in Martha Ann to Joseph F., 17 December 1856, herein.

JOSEPH F. TO MARTHA ANN, 20 OCTOBER 1856

For Martha / Sandwich Islands
Oct. 20th 1856.[150]

Dear Sister Martha

It is with plesure that I seat myself at this time to answer your kind letter of July the 29th which came to hand in safety on the 12th of this month.[151] it found me well and hearty as usual. I was glad to hear from you, and I should write you a good long letter but I have not the means at presant. I must tell you one thing which bothers me, (and all of us) to write, they have passed a law, that all letters to and from the Sandwich Islands are to be taxed 7 cts each, it has formerly been 5 cts, a letter but now you see it is much harder, but for all that I donot want any of you to stop writing, but if you are some times deprived (if it may so be called) of reading letters from me you must not be surprised, nor discouraged, but continue with your writing to me.[152]

I suppose you have learned that Elder John T. Ca[*1 x 3.4 cm tear*][153] has returned home, and all letters directed here of [*1 x 3.4 cm tear*] must be as follows, Honolulu Oahu S. I.[154] Care of Silas Smith.[155] Now dont forget, be presise.

Well marty Two of the Bretheren ware released last conferance to go home, viz. O. K. Whittney and Washington B. Rogers.[156] but there are no signs of my being released for some time yet, but I am perfictly contented, and I donot feel as tho' I had done my mission as yet and I donot want, [**p. 2**] to go home till then. You ware saying that you was living with John,[157] I hope you enjoy your self, all I have to say is, Marth be a good girl dont trubel yourself about other folkses business and then if they bother you and your business, you will have one consolation, that is you are not in the wrong. be sober martha, and, in fine try and cary yourself as streight as you can, and then if folks impose on you tell them in a sober way just what you think of them, and then let them alone, that is "moral courage" and it is the best thing on

150. Joseph F. noted that he "spent the day writing to my bro. John and sister Martha Ann." Joseph F., journal, 20 October 1856.
151. It took over two months for Martha Ann's letters to reach Joseph F.
152. Postal prices were based on destination. For example, San Francisco and "Inland California, Oregon, and Utah Ter" were five cents, and other destinations were higher. Mail to Hawai'i required a twelve-cent US stamp and a five-cent Hawaiian stamp. Joseph F. seems to refer to an additional Hawaiian tax on outgoing and incoming letters. See "Post Office Notice," *The Polynesian*, 8 November 1856, 108.
153. John Thomas Caine was part of the company of missionaries called to the Sandwich Islands in 1854 along with Joseph F. He was called as counselor to the mission president, Silas Smith (Joseph F.'s father's uncle), in July 1855. He returned home in 1856. See biographical register, "Caine, John Thomas."
154. Sandwich Islands.
155. Refers to Silas Smith, who served as president of the Sandwich Islands Mission from 1855 to 1857.
156. The conference referred to was probably held in October 1856. At this conference Joseph F. was transferred to preside over the Kohala Conference, still on Maui. Orson Kimball Whitney was called as a missionary in 1852 and arrived in the Sandwich Islands on 16 April 1854. See Kate B. Carter, comp., *Our Pioneer Heritage* (Salt Lake City, UT: Daughters of Utah Pioneers, 1958), 2:596–97. Washington Bolivar Rogers was part of the company of missionaries called to the Sandwich Islands Mission in 1854. He traveled on the *Vaquero* along with Joseph F., arriving on the islands on 27 September 1854, and labored with Joseph F. in Maui at the beginning of their missions. See biographical register, "Whitney, Orson Kimball" and "Rogers, Washington Bolivar."
157. John Smith.

earth. never be afraid of any one, but calmly tell them if you think they insult you, and have an understanding about it, and then let them alone. that is all I have to say about that. you will understand me, and I am willing everry body els should, sute yourself about maters and things, as best you can.

In regard to my being indebted or obligated to any person on Earth, I am not. Thank the Lord [*1 x 3.4 cm tear*] am perfictly "free, and easy," and contented, and [*1 x 3.4 cm tear*] owe no more than respect to my fellow man, I am indebted no other way.[158] you will pleas show or let brother John read this, and write to me as often as you can also John must write as often as is posible, and give me all the news. I have no more to write at presant, but wish you all good luck and many blessings. I pray God to bless you all
Joseph Smith

Bro. Franklin Young[159] and the rest of the Bretheren wish a kind rememberance to you all.[160]

For Martha[161]

MARTHA ANN TO JOSEPH F., 17 DECEMBER 1856

G ~~G~~ S G S Utah terrtory Dsemb<er the [*illegible erasure*] 17 1866[162]>
the 17

[*illegible erasure*] Dearest Brother

I received your kind letter of july the 14 and it gaave me mutch joyy to read your writing and to know that you wrote it with your own hand gave me cumfort I thaught that I would answer it the best I could and that wi~~ll~~ell not be very good. I am well and harty and strong I can be or as enny one need wish to be and I hope and pray that this letter will find you the same. you thanked me for the information I gave you of home. you are p<i>rfectelly welcome Joseph for <all> th~~at~~<e> good that I can do you you speak of a reward but to read a letter from you is all the reward I want they allways do me more good than eny thing else I know of you wanted to know what had become of <old> mager[163] and so I wll tell you. he is well and harty ~~and~~ <and he> is mager yet and he wll be as long as sarah[164] keeps him, some times he is at

158. This seems to be the response to a comment made by Martha Ann about rumors regarding Joseph F. being engaged or "promised" to Elizabeth Jane Fisher. See Martha Ann to Joseph F., 29 July 1856, herein, note 134.
159. Franklin Wheeler Young. John R. Young, Franklin's older brother, was called with Joseph F. to the Sandwich Islands in 1854. Franklin was called to the same mission two years later and arrived on 7 May 1856; he served under Joseph F. in the Kohala District.
160. Written in bottom left margin.
161. Cross-written in the middle of page 1. In cross-writing, rather than continuing the letter on another piece of paper, additional text was written on top of and perpendicular to the first portion of the letter. This technique may have been used to conserve paper and to save on postage costs.
162. The letter is dated 1866, but the content shows that it was actually written in 1856. Martha Ann mentions her sixteenth birthday and says she received a letter from Joseph F. dated 14 July 1856.
163. One of the family's farm animals; see Joseph F. to Martha Ann, 14 July 1856, herein.
164. Sarah Smith.

sarahs and some times he is hear but his home is at sarahs, old watch[165] is alive yet to, and lives [*illegible strike-through*] hear to Johns, I also live to Johns[166] yet, and ~~and~~ expect to this winter and go to school. school commenced last monday and I did not go then for I did not have enny shoos and I intend to start next mnday. John has gon up north he started last satturday ~~and~~ on buisness and Hellon[167] has been up to ~~her~~ her mothers and I have been over to sarahes all <the> weak and I just came home to day and I hav been alone all day and I got lonesome and so I thaugh that I wold write a little to keep me company but I git along so slow that I cnnot finnish it to night [**p. 2**] I expect John home to night. you said in charles~~es~~[168] letter that you had had some bad luck wth your things I am sory for that and I thank my he<a>venly fother that I hav got a brother that can bare such thngs with paciencs [*illegible erasure*] I w<i>sh that such things had not happed ~~but~~ but I suppose it was to try you, and perhaps all for the bst ~~did~~ <did> you git~~t~~ your letters all burnt up[169] or did you save enny of them. pleas tell me about it in the next letter you write to me. I thank you for the kind advice you gave me in my last letter from you you spoke of [*illegible erasure*] Marry Janes[170] gitting ~~m~~ married and also me it may be so with her but not w<i>th me at present I am to ignorant to think of such things yet I ~~hav not~~ I want more lirning than I have got before I git married when I take that step I want to get some boddy that is of some account I can not the smartes in the world in intellect tharefore I would like to git some boddy that was smarter than I am that can [*illegible strike-through*] take me through this world in safety. can you blame me for that Joseph I do not think you can, I hav been looking at my self and noticeing my self and triiy to reform and I see that I need a good deal of tutuing before I can become perfect. I hav ~~been~~ <been> on a visit up north to Jrushas[171] and I must side wih you in not likng the idear of them goi<n>g up north so far.[172] but as the saying is all that is is [*illegible erasure*] writ and so it is not for me to complain. I allso hird Jerushas letter [*illegible erasure*] I was up north when she [*illegible erasure*] recie<v>d it [**p. 3**] she was well when I left thare she did not have enny paper when I was hare and so I was obligad to wte untill I could git home before I could write in answer to it and after I got home I detaind writing thou mistake that the ma<i>le sarted out sooner than common. but I hav got more neus to to you now than I had then. for John came home last night and told me that Isic bullock was marred to a young lady[173] from up north I have forgotten her name. [*illegible strike-through*] ~~you~~ enny how she has got a good man worthy of enny girls notice. such a man as him would suit me. if I got a man to my likeing he has got the pincipals about him them are the knd Joseph dont you think so. they war marr<i>ed twoo weaks agoo this is the frst time that I spoke of marry to you about my self but I am gitting faeuer[174] than I hav been I am in my

165. Likely a pet dog.
166. John Smith.
167. Hellen Maria Fisher.
168. Charles Emerson Griffin.
169. See Martha Ann to Joseph F. 17 December 1856 letter, herein.
170. Likely refers to their cousin Mary Jane Thompson.
171. Jerusha Smith (born 13 January 1836) was the daughter of Hyrum Smith and Jerusha Barden. She was the half sister of Joseph F. and Martha Ann.
172. Jerusha Smith and her family were living in Brigham City, Box Elder County, in northern Utah. See Martha Ann to Joseph F., 31 January 1856, herein.
173. Isaac Bullock married Electa Wood on 14 December 1856. See biographical register, "Bullock, Isaac" and "Wood, Electa."
174. Possibly *fairer*.

sixteenth year but I am motly yet I am well aware of that you may tell that by the simple way that I write but it is naturel to me to be simpol althow I am sriving is over come it evry day, I suppose that it does not become a large girl like me but I hope I shall over come it and become noble minded afer a while and all of my other faults. John hass gon afer ~~lelon~~ hellon and the babys and I am olone again they all say that hyrum looks like you but [*illegible erasure*] that is fishers folks.[175] but I thin that he is the picture of elon only his eiyes are are a dark blue he has got a nose like hellen and mouth **[p. 4]** and chin like her a<l>so Elisebath[176] has as got large lite blue eyes and rosey cheeaks and lite ~~heir~~ hairr she looks like Jony sarahs baby[177] is a sweet little dear it has large blieu eys rosy cheeks and broun hare and dubble chin and very fat and Jerishas baby[178] is not very fleshey it has hare like Jerusha it looks like Jerusha. now I hav told you about the chldren I love them all. I feall first rate in [*illegible erasure*] sirets Josiph fisher[179] has just this minute come and told me that John and helon is not comeing home to night that they had gon down to cotton wood[180] to a meettng, and I think I wll gow to meeting to nigt to but I will hav to walk insted of riding in a slay like they hav I must go alone to but no matter, the snow is very deep but the evning is plasant when I hear enny boddy complaining I can not help thnking about you and of what you are going through for truths sake, I dar not complain but dear brother I isupose that it is all for the best. I hope that it will not injorre your helth by staying thre in that hot climate I hope it wll not. all of the flks is wel and harty we hav lost a fatthul friend in brother Grant[181] I supose that you will hear all about that in the nuse paper tharefore I w<i>ll not tell you enny thing about it for my paper is fool nearly and I must bring my letter to a close exuse all bad writing and mstakes for my pen is poor good by for the pesent may the lord bless you is the prar of your sister Martha ann Smith

MARTHA ANN SMITH AND WILLIAM JASPER HARRIS TO JOSEPH F., 3 FEBRUARY 1857

G S L C~~ounty~~ utah terry <feb the 3 1857>[182]

Dear and affecttionate brither Joseph I did not git a letter from you in neither of the last mails and I thaught that I would write wth out one for it is through my own neglect for I donot

175. Hyrum Fisher Smith, son of John Smith and Hellen Maria Fisher, was born on 10 January 1856. He is the nephew of Joseph F. and Martha Ann. See biographical register, "Smith, Hyrum Fisher."
176. Elizabeth Maria Smith, eldest child of John Smith and Hellen Maria Fisher, is a niece to Joseph F. and Martha Ann. See biographical register, "Smith, Elizabeth Maria."
177. Alice Lovina Griffin.
178. Hannah Eveline Pierce.
179. Possibly Hellen's father, Joseph Fisher, or Hellen's younger brother Joseph Armstrong Fisher. See biographical register, "Fisher, Joseph" and "Fisher, Joseph Armstrong."
180. Cottonwood was the first settlement established outside Salt Lake City proper. Founded in 1849, it was located about three miles below the mouth of Big Cottonwood Canyon. On 15 November 1856, David Brinton was ordained the bishop, and from 19 November to 21 December 1856 a series of meetings was held to fully organize the ward. See "Big Cottonwood Ward," *Historical Record* 6, no. 9 (December 1887): 284.
181. Jedediah Morgan Grant, counselor to Brigham Young who died on 1 December 1856; see "Remarks" and "Obituary," *Deseret News*, 10 December 1856, 316–17. See biographical register, "Grant, Jedediah Morgan."
182. Joseph F. was eighteen, and Martha Ann was fifteen.

blame you for not writing when you ~~a~~ hav no promter.[183] I am expectting a letter this next [*illegible word*] from you wth all the patienc I hav got. I am well and am going to school I am at sister Harris~~es~~[184] to day. school has just let out and I am going to write a few lines to <you> and tell you how the folks is gitting along they are all well and they all send thir love to you sister smoot[185] sends her love to you al<l>so [*illegible strike-through*] Diana[186] sends her love to you. I live with Johs[187] yet I am gittng along as well as can be expected

I hav been on a visit with [*illegible erasure*] <aunt> thompson and mary Jane[188] up north to Rachels and she has got a fine little girl[189] nearly six weaks old they are well and in good helth. all of the folks are gitting marryed but me and Mary Jane.[190] <Mary Smthes is> marryed to brother kimbol[191] but ~~th~~ I supose my turn will come some time if it ever does but I do not know when that wll be yet I ope that you wll [*illegible word*] home wth you when you come home. I wll bring my [*illegible strike-through*] scrall to a close for I can not think of eny more to write at present I wll write mor the next time I write. pleas excuse all mistaks for it was wrote in <a> hurry write often and I wll do the same good by for the ~~pr~~ pesent

May the lord bles you in all your undertakngs is the prar of your sister
Martha Ann Smith [**p. 3**][192]

Great Salt L City feb[th] 3, 157

Dear friend[193]

I am happy to have this opportunity of writing you a few lines to let you kow that I am still alive and kicking and hope that this will finde you the same Martha ann was here a writing she asked me if I had any thing to write to you I told her that I would write a little in her letter if

183. Most likely a reference to the fact that Martha Ann had not written Joseph F. and therefore he did not have a letter from her that would have prompted him to respond.
184. Perhaps Emily Hill, widow of Zachariah Harris, who would become Martha Ann's mother-in-law in 1857 when Martha Ann married William Jasper Harris. After the death of her first husband, Emily Hill married Abraham O. Smoot in 1846 and may be referred to as "Sister Smoot" at times in the letters. See biographical register, "Hill, Almira Emily."
185. Likely refers to Margaret Thompson McMeans, first wife of Abraham O. Smoot. According to the 1860 US census, Abraham O. Smoot's household consisted of several children and Abraham's wives, Margaret, Emily Hill, Diana Tanner Eldredge (likely the three women mentioned here), as well as Anna Morris. In letters "Sister Smoot" may refer to another of Abraham O. Smoot's wives, and this ambiguity is maintained throughout the letters. However, in most cases, Sister Smoot clearly refers to Margaret Thompson. See biographical register, "Thompson, Margaret."
186. Likely Diana Tanner Eldredge, fourth wife of Abraham O. Smoot. See biographical register, "Eldredge, Diana Tanner."
187. John Smith.
188. Mercy Rachel Fielding and Mary Jane Thompson.
189. Rachel Fielding, wife of William Walton Burton, was living in Ogden. Her first daughter, Isabella Burton, was born 26 December 1856. See biographical register, "Burton, Isabella."
190. Mary Jane Thompson.
191. Mary Smithies married Heber C. Kimball on 25 January 1857. See biographical register, "Smithies, Mary" and "Kimball, Heber Chase."
192. William Jasper Harris, who married Martha Ann three months after the date of this letter, enclosed a letter on a separate piece of paper along with this letter from Martha Ann. At the conclusion of William's letter, Martha Ann wrote another note, which she began on page 3 and concluded on the back of the first page. The flow of the letter, as this transcription indicates, moves successively in the following page order: 1, 3, 4, 2.
193. This portion of the letter was written by William Jasper Harris, a family friend of Martha Ann and Joseph F. See biographical register, "Harris, William Jasper."

there was room I wrote a letter to you be fore but did not get it in the mail in time I very often think of you and have intended to write but through neglect I have not done it I hope that you will save us all the trouble of writing for I think you will be a coming home some of these days there is great excitment among the young folks here about getting married but still more among the old ones there is from twenty to forty a getting married evry day there is a great many old men that <think> they will be cut off from the church and be damned if they dont get another wife[194] I believe that Gim[195] is a going to take a ribe[196] I dont know but I shall have to have you bring me some of them native girls well I dont that I have much more to write the folks are a reforming and waking up from their sleep and begining **[p. 4]** to live a new life and these poor deviles are getting in a hurry and leaving[197] and them that cant take the hint will take you know what well the boys are on hand for any thing will I hope that you will excuse me for this short note but remember that it is from a friend I hope that you will be reliesed and be caled home be fore long the folks are all wel~~l~~ as far as I know Martha ann can tell you more about them than I can so no more at present. From
Wm J Harris to
[*illegible strike-through*] Joseph Smith

[198]Dear brother I did not git a chance to write the last mail and I wrote one the mail before last, and did not git it in in time to send it Willim Harris wrote a few lines in my letter and I thaught that I would write some more in it and tell you how it was I did not <git> now chance to send it in to town the last mail and so I did not write nor send this letter [*illegible strike-through*]. I would not hav sent <this> letter if William harris had not been sent on a missin to ingland.[199] and he will not have a chance to write to you be fore he gows he has got the same trial as you had and worse if enny thing for he has a mother[200] to leave a kind and affectionate mother which I suppose would have been a greate triel to you but alass, dear brother you had no mother to leave and I dar say that you hav felt the want of **[p. 2]** ~~the~~ Mother[201] hundreds of times sence you left your home at enny rate if you havent I have felt the want of her more than folks think I have I was young when she was taken away from me and I did not realise as much about it as you did becaus you was older than I was but I have realised it sence more so for the last to years. wal dear brother Im just waking up to the reffrmatinon I ~~am~~ hav been

194. Many Latter-day Saints believed the practice of plural marriage was necessary for exaltation. See, for example, Brigham Young, in *Journal of Discourses* (London: Latter-day Saints' Book Depot, 1854–86), 18:249. After his call to the apostleship, Joseph F. also taught this idea. See "Colfax and 'Mormon' Doctrines," *Deseret News*, 11 July 1878.
195. Likely referring to James Madison Fisher, who married Edith Evelina Pierce on 12 February 1857. See Martha Ann to Joseph F., 5 April 1857, herein; see also biographical register, "Fisher, James Madison" and "Pierce, Edith Evelina."
196. Possibly a slang term for or misspelling of *bride*.
197. William refers to the Reformation of 1856–57 (see section introduction). Apparently, some less-committed Saints, perhaps the "poor devils" William refers to here, chose to leave the territory at this time instead of participating in what Paul H. Peterson described as "a short but highly spirited reform movement." The Reformation was the result of Church leaders' desire to increase faith among the members. See Paul H. Peterson, "The Mormon Reformation" (PhD diss., Brigham Young University, 1981); and Paul H. Peterson, "The Mormon Reformation of 1856–1857: The Rhetoric and the Reality," *Journal of Mormon History* 15 (1989): 61.
198. Martha Ann continued her letter on page 4.
199. William Jasper Harris left on his mission to England on 23 April 1857, two days after he and Martha Ann were married.
200. Emily Hill.
201. Mary Fielding Smith was the mother of Martha Ann and Joseph F. See biographical register, "Fielding, Mary."

baptise~~d~~d[202] and am commenc<e>ing ~~to~~ to live my religion I am just beginning to [*illegible strike-through*] see my faults and mend my ways may my god enable me to continue striving that I may always be [*illegible strike-through*] <found> in the line of my duty I am well and harty and donot know whether I have stopped growing or not I do fell thankfull to my hevenly father for [*illegible strike-through*] <blessings> unto me for preserveing my life. I have had a trial la<i>tely thhat ~~that~~ has dampend my feeling some but I am gitting over it now, that is I am striveing to overcome it I will tell you what it is but do not say enny thing about it [*illegible strike-through*] in any of your letters exept [*illegible strike-through*] mine and tell me what you think about it. do not hint it him that wrote in this letter ~~is~~ is the one that I love my hand tembls when I say love but it is so verly so he is a good young man and has gaind my affections John thinks a good deal of him and he sais that thare is not a young man in the valleys of the mountains that he thinks more of than he does of William harris ~~do not tell~~ he is sent on a mission and I suppose it is all rite good by for the pesent may the lord bless you is the prarr <of> your <sister>

Martha Ann to Joseph F., 5 April 1856 (envelope)

MARTHA ANN TO JOSEPH F., 5 APRIL 1857

Geat Salt <~~G L~~> Couty Utah teritory Apr the 5 <1857>[203]

Dear brother Joseph
[*illegible strike-through*]
it is with a degree of no [*illegible strike-through*] ordenary plaure as you say, that I seat my self at this time to answer your kind and affectionate letters <of ~~which came to hand~~> nov

202. Martha Ann is most likely referring to a rebaptism, which was common during the Reformation period in Utah, 1856–57, when members demonstrated their desire to recommit to living their faith.

203. The envelope is addressed to "Joseph Smith Honolulua Oahu S.I. in care of S. Smith." The cover is stamped "PAID 5" with a postal mark "SALT LAKE CITY UTAH. T. APR 5." Joseph F. wrote on the envelope, "Received June 14th Answered June 14th 1857 Kolae Molokai S.I." On the reverse Joseph F. wrote, "Martha A. Smith & Wm. J. Harris Miss Smith From Miss Martha Ann Smith."

the 13 and Oct th 18 1856 which came to hand on 8 of Jenuary it gave me joy and sttisfaction to hear from you that you was [*illegible strike-through*] well and enjoying your self as well as you are. theey found me well and enjoying my self first rate. I was sorry to hear that you was botherd to write to us hear and I am going to send you a qarter dollar gold peace and prhaps it will help you some. you said that the lord had, had an eiye on you ever sense you left home and I believe it I know he has on me and why not on one that is far more worthy than I am for I feel that you have [*illegible strike-through*] deserveed the blessings of the lord more han I have I know that I am a poor weak and earing ceature and need the assistence of a brother and a friend to help me along and the lord my god to bare me up. I am witing to bare enny thing that is to prove me to see what I can bare. I do thank you for your [*illegible strike-through*] kind and fatherly advice thahat you give me from time to time I do feel that it is a privledge to write you letters and read your letters it is the gratest comfort that I have to hear from you and read your writing but [*illegible strike-through*] I hop to see you in a short time and that will be far more joy than reading ~~all~~ a letter from you you told me is stop my thnking about <your> <~~your~~> comeing home but I am afraid I will have to disobay you in that for I can~~d~~ not help it. I do hope to see in a year from now at enny rate you said that you had, had some sollid triels sence you lef home and know <you> [*illegible strike-through*] m<u>st have [**p. 2**] a grat men<n>y. you said that <you suposed> I had, <h>ad some trials sence you left. True it has not been a smooth sea with my feelings all the time but I need not say trublels side of you let alone trials. you was saying that the brethein some of them had been releaced wal I am glad to hear it and would be still gladder if it had been you to. but I will try to have patence and wait untill I <see> you. my school is out Horice ~~berde~~ <Burdlick>[204] taught it I do not know whether school will keep this summer or not yet [*illegible erasure*] if it does I will gow and if not I will try to learn all I can at home. I did not let John[205] see that letter for I thaught it was not best for the folks are reforming and they treat me well now and so I did not say ennay thing about it. we are all good friends now I can forgive but I cannot forgit[206]

[*illegible erasure*] you have said that you supposed that all of the girls wo<u>ld be married off when you git home but you need not think so for they is plenty of girls a waiting for you untill you come home and have been ever sence you left home and they will wait till you come home you will have no truble at all in gitting wves a plenty[207] I wll assure you of that I suppose thhat helon[208] has told you about John gitting him another wife.[209] and mr stratton has got him another wife[210] and William burrous has got him a wife also by the name of catherine louder[211]

204. Horace Burdick was a schoolteacher in the Salt Lake City area at this time. See biographical register, "Burdick, Horace."

205. John Smith.

206. On Martha Ann's family trials, see Martha Ann to Joseph F., 29 July 1856, herein.

207. Plural marriage was first introduced privately to a small group of Church members, which expanded over time. Church leaders publicly announced the practice on 29 August 1852; see David J. Whittaker, "The Bone in the Throat: Orson Pratt and the Public Announcement of Plural Marriage," *Western Historical Quarterly* 18, no. 3 (1 July 1987): 293–314.

208. Hellen Maria Fisher.

209. John Smith married his second wife, Nancy Melissa Lemmon, on 18 February 1857, in Salt Lake City. See biographical register, "Lemmon, Nancy Melissa."

210. Likely refers to James Stratton and Eliza Briggs, who were married on 2 February 1857. See biographical register, "Stratton, James" and "Briggs, Eliza."

211. William Creeland Burrows married Catherine Lowder on 1 January 1857. See biographical register, "Burrows, William Creeland" and "Lowder, Catherine."

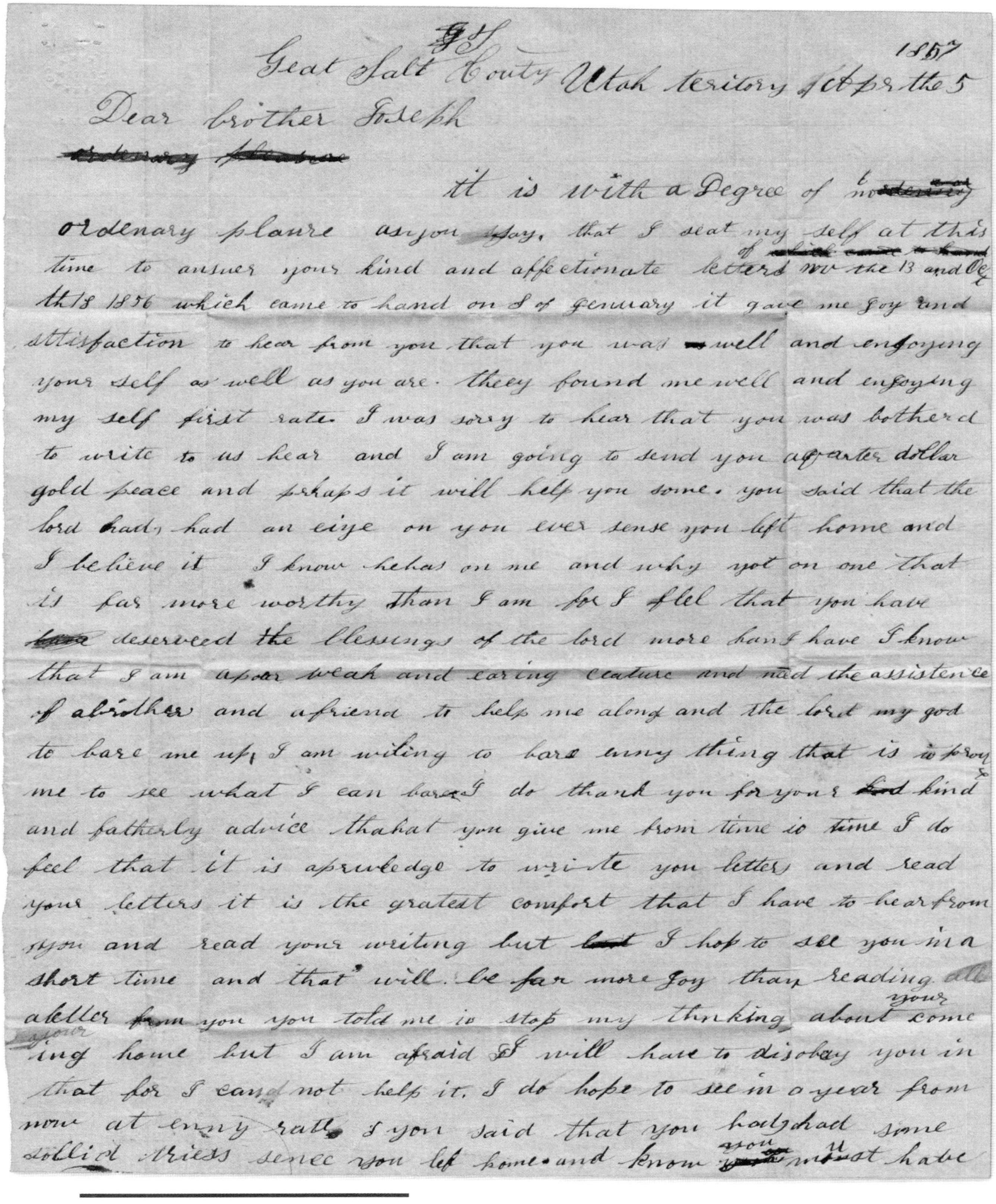

G S
Geat Salt Couty Utah teritory Apr the 5 1857

Dear brother Joseph

[illegible]

it is with a Degree of not ordenary plaure as you say, that I seat my self at this time to answer your kind and affectionate letters of the 13 and Dec th18 1856 which came to hand on 8 of Jenuary it gave me Joy and sattisfaction to hear from you that you was well and enjoying your self as well as you are. they found me well and enjoying my self first rate. I was sorry to hear that you was botherd to write to us hear and I am going to send you a quarter dollar gold peace and prhaps it will help you some. you said that the lord had, had an eiye on you ever sense you left home and I believe it I know he has on me and why not on one that is far more worthy than I am for I feel that you have deserveed the blessings of the lord more than I have I know that I am a poor weak and earing creature and need the assistence of a brother and a friend to help me along and the lord my god to bare me up, I am wiling to bare enny thing that is to prove me to see what I can bare I do thank you for your kind and fatherly advice thahat you give me from time to time I do feel that it is a prwiledge to write you letters and read your letters it is the gratest comfort that I have to hear from you and read your writing but I hop to see you in a short time and that will be far more Joy than reading a letter from you you told me to stop my thinking about your comeing home but I am afraid I will have to disobey you in that for I can not help it. I do hope to see in a year from now at enny ratt I you said that you had had some sollid trials sence you left home and know you must habe

Martha Ann to Joseph F., 5 April 1857 (p. 1)

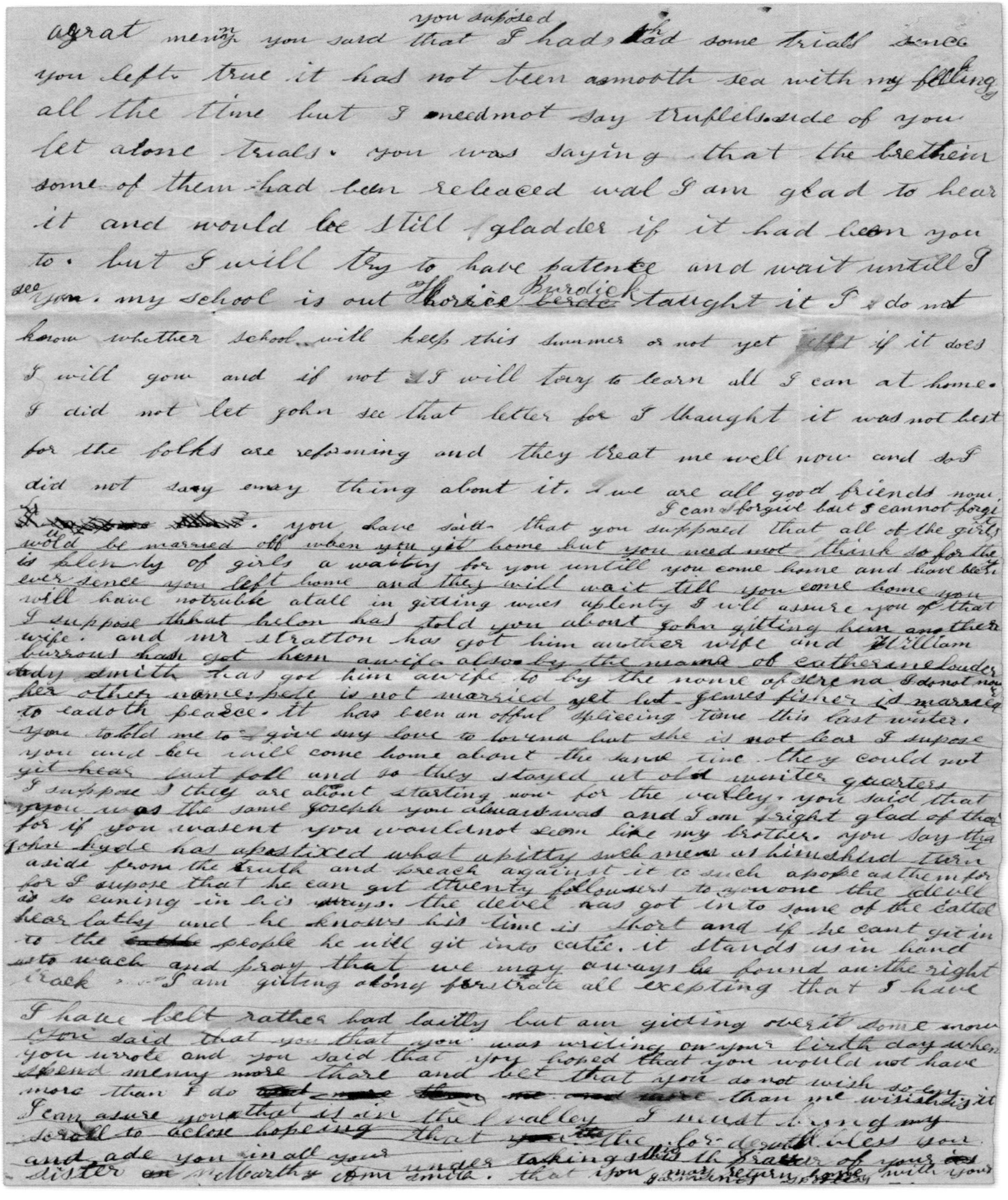

agrat meny you said that I had you supposed had some trials sence
you left. true it has not been asmooth sea with my feelings
all the time but I needmot say trufles side of you
let alone trials. you was saying that the brethern
some of them had been releaced wal I am glad to hear
it and would be still gladder if it had been you
to. but I will try to have patence and wait untill I
see you. my school is out Horice Burdick taught it I do not
know whether school will help this summer or not yet but if it does
I will you and if not I will try to learn all I can at home.
I did not let john see that letter for I thaught it was not best
for the folks are reforming and they treat me well now and so I
did not say eney thing about it. we are all good friends now.
I can forgive but I cannot forgit
[illegible]. you have said that you supposed that all of the girls
would be married off when you git home but you need not think so for the
is plenty of girls a waiting for you untill you come home and have been
ever sence you left home and they will wait till you come home you
will have notrubble atall in gitting wives aplenty I will assure you of that
I suppose that helon has told you about john gitting him another
wife. and mr stratton has got him another wife and William
burrows has got him awife also by the name of catherine louder
tody smith has got him awife to by the nome of serena I do not no
her other name; pete is not married yet but james fisher is married
to cadoth peazce. it has been an offul splicing time this last winter.
you told me to give my love to lorena but she is not hear I suppose
you and ben will come home about the same time. they could not
git hear last fall and so they stayed at old winter quarters
I suppose they are about starting now for the valley. you said that
you was the same Joseph you always was and I am right glad of that
for if you wasent you wouldnot seem like my brother. you say that
John hyde has apostized what apitty such men as him shud turn
aside from the truth and preach against it to such apope as them for
for I supose that he can git twenty followers to you one the devil
is so cuning in his ways. the devel has got in to some of the cattel
hear latly and he knows his time is short and if he cant git in
to the [illegible] people he will git into cattle. it stands us in hand
to wach and pray that we may always be found on the right
track I am gitting along firstrate all excepting that I have
I have felt rather bad laitly but am gitting over it some now
you said that you that you was writing on your birth day when
you wrote and you said that you hoped that you would not have
spend meny more there and bet that you do not wish so eny
more than I do [illegible] than we wish it
I can asure you that if in the valley I must bring my
scroll to aclose hopeing that the lord will bless you
and ade you in all your under takings this the prayer of your
sister Martha Ann smith. that you may return home with your
[illegible]

Martha Ann to Joseph F., 5 April 1857 (p. 2)

dody Smith has got him a wife to by the name of serena[212] I do not now her other name. pete[213] is not married yet but Jemes fisher is married to eadoth pearce.[214] it has been an offul spliceing[215] time this last winter. you to told me to give my love to lovina but she is not hear I supose you and her will come home about the same time they could not git hear last foll and so they stayed at old winter quarters I suppose they are about starting now for the valley.[216] you said that you was the same Joseph you alwais was and I am right glad of that for if you wasent you would not seem like my brother. you say that John hyde[217] has apostixed what a pitty such men as him shud turn aside from the truth and preach against it to such a pope as them for for I supose that he can git twenty followers[218] to you one the devel is so cuning in his ways. the devel has got in to some of the cattel hear latly and he knows his time is short and if he cant git in to the [*illegible strike-through*] people he will git into catle. it stands us in hand to wach and pray that we may aways be found on the right track I am gitting along first rate all exepting that I have I have felt rather bad laitly but am gitting over it some now you said that you that you was writing on your birth day when you wrote and you said that you hoped that you would not have spend menny more thare and bet that you do not wish so eny more than I do [*illegible strike-through*] more than me wisishis it I can asure you that is in the valley I must bring my scroll to a close hopeing that the lorde will bless you and ade you in all your undertakings this <is> th prauar of your [*illegible strike-through*] sister [*illegible strike-through*] Marthy Ann smith. that you may return home with your garments spotless

212. Likely Andrew McLean Smith, here referred to as "Dody," who married Serinna Thompson on 14 August 1857 in Salt Lake City. See biographical register, "Smith, Andrew McLean" and "Thompson, Serinna."
213. Unknown individual.
214. James Madison Fisher, brother-in-law to John Smith, married Edith Evelina Pierce on 12 February 1857. See Martha Ann to Joseph F., 3 February 1857, herein.
215. *Splice* was a nineteenth-century slang term for marriage.
216. Lovina Smith, half sister of Joseph F. and Martha Ann, married Lorin Walker on 23 June 1844 in Nauvoo, three days before the martyrdom of her father, Hyrum. Lovina and her family would not actually arrive in Utah until 1860. See Martha Ann to Joseph F., 29 July 1856, herein, note 135.
217. John Hyde, a British convert who had immigrated to Utah in 1853, was called by Church leaders to serve in the Sandwich Islands Mission in 1856 in hopes that a mission would rekindle his commitment to the faith. When he arrived in the Sandwich Isles later that year, however, he spoke against the Church in several public meetings and was excommunicated in 1857. See biographical register, "Hyde, John."
218. The Honolulu Second Evangelical Church reported, "Mormonism is at a pretty low ebb among us. It was rapidly declining before the arrival of Mr. John Hyde and his associates last fall, some six or seven Mormon missionaries, who were sent here from Utah by Brigham Young, to establish a newspaper in the native language, and to do their best to convert this entire nation into Mormonism. But on arriving here, Mr. Hyde, their leader, fully and freely renounced Mormonism, not only in private conversation, but in two public lectures in the Seaman's chapel, and in several native congregations, and also through the medium of the press. I think his tract has done our people good; quite a number have returned to our congregation, confessing their *kuhi hewa* in going after those blind leaders of the blind." See *Minutes of the Meeting of the Hawaiian Evangelical Association Held at Honolulu, May, 1857* (Honolulu, HI: Press of H. M. Whitney, 1857), 15.

JOSEPH F. TO MARTHA ANN, 17 APRIL 1857

Sandwich Islands, Lahaina
April 17th 1857.[219]

My Dear Sister Martha Ann:—

It is with no ordinary feeling that I seat myself this morning to reciprocate your favor of December 17th '56, it graced my presence on the 28th ultimo,[220] but I have had no oppertunity of answering it untill now, owing to my travels to Conference, &c. which came off on the 7th, 8th and 9th of this month.[221] We had a good time togather. I am well and hearty at the present, altho' I feel verry sore and and dull this morning becaus of sleeplessness, and labor for the last three days and nights.

Eight of us started from the Island of Lanai on Wednesday, and on acount of contrary and high winds we ware compelled to return to port, here we slept out doors with nothing but a verry thin mat for a bead, and another one for a covering, our carpet-sacks serving for pillows, at moon rise in the morning, (1 o clock) we went on board of our little Boat and started for this Island. Martha it would make you wonder if you could see us being tossed and driven by the waves of the mighty Paciffic, when every wave seemed like it was the next moment going to engulf us in ~~the~~ its auful surge, yes, to see us in an open Boat, with a tract of Ocean before us of some 15 miles, and only a one fourth inch of pine boards between us and the tremenduous, dreadful, yawning grave of thousands of poor ill-fated beings, who ware not so fortunate as ourselves; when you get with in a quarter of an inch of death itself, then who can save you?[222] Marth, the arm on which we trusted is that which hath delivered, it is ever willing to deliver, and will deliver all who lean upon it, and put all their trust on it, therefore lets be faithful. **[p. 2]** Well, we arived at this place, at 10 o clock in the morning of the next day, after we started.— and this morning several of the Brethren started for Wailuku leaving three of us at this place. I have been appointed to preside over the Molokai,[223] conference, which is about 15 miles from this place, and on another Island, so you see I have to cross another strip of Ocean before I get to my field of labor.[224] When we arived at this place we found that 33.50$ of money recieved for Books of Mormon, that has been solde to the Native Saints had been stolen, who the perpetrator of this dead was, we are at loss to know or finde out. certain, it is we are in distress because of it, and that any person who would take money from us, who knew our situation, is wors than a murderor! but it seems that the Devil exerts his utmoste power to thwart every thing that we attempt to do for the prosperity and emelioration of this people. the Lord only knows what will take place next. to impede his moste holy work, who could endure what we have to, but mormon Elders? I do not believe, that man lives outside of the kingdom of God

219. Joseph F. noted, "I wrote to my sister M. A. Smith, and to Jerusha Pierce." Joseph F., journal, 17 April 1857.

220. *Ultimo* means "of last month."

221. A mission conference was held at Kohalapalaoa on the southeastern shoreline of the island of Lāna'i, 7–9 April 1857. See Joseph F., journal, 6–9 April 1857.

222. Joseph F.'s experience in the ocean likely influenced his later counsel in 1864 to a group of his brethren not to attempt to land their smaller boat in a harbor under similar conditions. Their refusal to heed his counsel resulted in a capsized boat and the near drowning of Apostle Lorenzo Snow.

223. Moloka'i is an island located between O'ahu and Maui.

224. Joseph F. noted, "We have had no opportunity of geting to Molakai. plenty of Boats, too high prises." Joseph F., journal, 17 April 1858.

that would begin to endure to allmoste indurable trials and privations that seem to beset us on every hand, and that we have to pass thro' evry day of our lives on these degraded lands, yet it is all for the best. I feel to rejoice, Martha, all the day long. I feel buoyant & hopeful, and like pressing forward, notwithstanding the hardships I have to encounter, because I know what I am doing, and for whom I am laboring, it is not as though I was seaking for gane, or secularly striving for the vain things of this world. if it was so, no one could have escaped despondancy, provided this was his dernier[225] <prospects> for [**p. 3**] advancement.— Well, now for your letter; you asked me if all my letters ware burnt, or if any were remaining. all those I recieved before the misfortune ware burned,[226] but no axident has yet happened to those I've recieved since. I am glad that you manifest a desire to reform, you speak of observing yourself &c. well it is a good thing if you commence by degrees, you know this world, though small, cannot be circumscribeed with one huge stride, neither does the Eagle soar to the heavens with one fears flap of the wings, neither does the hour pass, with <out> the minutes, or even the seconds, therefore you see Martha that all our faults cannot be overcome in a moment, but they must be forsaken little by littel, with assiduous and and untireing exertion, but you must not look at all your faults at once, nor any ones elses, but look at them little by little, or they will discourage you. it is not the long, and ravishing strides that bring us to our journies end, but the stedy, slow-and-sure, the undigressive, and undeviating from the streight ahead course, that is what will accomplish the dead! I know sometimes when I look at my journies, my little privations, coupled with my inexperiance and incapability, it makes me allmoste sink under the burthen of my thoughts, it is not my inexperiance nor my incapability, neither my deprivations, but just the mear thaught, the Idea, of it, that is what weighs heavy on the mind, therefore it is well to bare in mind that all our inabilities, insufficiencies, defaults, soon &c. are not to be emeliorated at once, neither can we become perfect at once, but in time:—by picking up a little here and a little there, by gaining step by step. do not get discurraged, Dear Sister, nor weary in well-doing, but continually press forward, in the work of progression for there is a vast field lieing before us, and we ware not born in [**p. 4**] to existance for nothing. No! you speak of being inefficient, inept, &c, who is wise that was not foolish? who is erudite, or where is an adept, that was not ignorant,? why even the Lord Jesus Christe was once an infant, so ware we all, therefore be mindful that the wisest and moste learned was once ignorant, and as inept as you and I are, and never get discouraged, but press onward. You expressed a desire to know if the climate hurt or injured my helth. I am happy to inform you that it agrees verry well with me, since I have partially become inured to it, altho' I do not enjoy the strength that is custommary for me, and I think I never would as long as I stop here, because the atmosphere, climate, food, and the elements in general, are not so nutritious and strengthing, as at our peasful, happy mountain home. I suppose Martha, in about 8 months or a year I shall be released from the mission with the privelige of returning home as soon as I can make necessary arangements. therefore in about two years from now I will see you all again if the Lord spairs our lives untill then, it may be however before that, and it may be longor, I cannot tell. you must be patient, and do the best you can. you must be prayrful, and studious, and you will be blessed. improve in every thing you can, and ocupy ever moment and oppertunity in improveing, use the moments as they fly, for they are precious, particals of time which, when passed, never will return.— I have nearly

225. *Dernier* means "last; ultimate, final." *Oxford English Dictionary*, s.v. "dernier."

226. In the June 1856 fire at the mission storehouse in Palawai, Lānaʻi, where Joseph F.'s trunk was destroyed. See Martha Ann to Joseph F., 17 December 1856, herein.

filled my sheat, so I will have to close. Tell John[227] I wish the Deseret News to be stoped, also the "Mormon"[228] appropriated to his own use, tho' I spoke of it in his letter. write ofton, give me all the news, give my love to all the little Children, to all our folks, not excepting yourself, and recieve me ever your moste affectionate Bro. Joseph Smith
To Martha Ann Smith.[229]

MARTHA ANN TO JOSEPH F., 3 MAY 1857

G S G city utah Ty may the 3 1857[230]

Most dear and affectionate brother Joseph I take my pen in hand to write you a few lines [*illegible strike-through*] to answer your to last kind and affectionate letters. the last note came to hand last night and ~~and~~ the other came to hand about three weeaks ago the mail had gon out and so I did not git a chance to write to you but I will try to write enough to make it up this time if you will except of it. I have just come down from Janes[231] this morning and they are all well and we are all well allso. Jane was writeing to you when [*illegible strike-through*] I started away from thare about an hour agoa. she got [*illegible strike-through*] <her> letters last evning and I [*illegible strike-through*] <hird> of it and so I went up thare ~~to git it~~ to see if thare was one in it for me. and [*illegible strike-through*] it hapned to that thare was one and I was glad to [*illegible strike-through*] <git> ~~it~~ git it ~~for~~ if it was nothng but a note. it done me as much good as though it had have been more. you was sayig in your last letter but ~~the~~ <one> th that you was destetute off the comforts of life and it greaved me very much to hear it it set me a thinginking about you and I have thaughh more about you <[*illegible strike-through*]> ever sence than I ever did befor my mind was trubled and have wished that I could send you a good loaf of bread and some butter over to you. and some paper so that you could write to me and the rest of the folks with out robing you of the coforts that you might have if you had plenty [*illegible strike-through*] but I trust in my god and in your [*illegible strike-through*] god [*illegible erasure*] that he will ~~all~~ open the way before you as he has opened the way before me from time to time. I was glad to hear that you was well and [*illegible erasure*] under such circomstanses not onely glad but thankfull for it. you say that you presume you will live through it. dear brother I would not think for a moment that you would not **[p. 2]** I could not thnk for a moment that you would not for I have srong hopes and ardent desiers as you say to see you before long. you say in Janes letter she sais that you expect to be relieced in about nine months I hope and pray that it wil be so if not sooner if your mission is competed and I hope it will ~~be~~ be before long for I think that you have sufferd enough for one 3 years and it would not be more than fair if some one took your place and let you come home and stay wih your friends and relations a

227. Likely John Smith.

228. *The Mormon* was a periodical published by John Taylor in New York between 1854 and 1856. John Smith, Joseph F.'s half brother, was apparently forwarding these periodicals to Joseph F.

229. Written at the end of the letter below Joseph F.'s signature.

230. Martha Ann had someone address the envelope, "Joseph Smith Honolulu Sandwich Island care of Silas Smith." Postmark: SALT LAKE CITY UTAH T. May 5. Also, a stamp mark, "PAID 5." On the reverse, Joseph F. wrote, "Martha A. Harris Received July 13 '57 Lahaina Answered July 25, Lanai Sandwich Islands."

231. Likely Martha Ann's friend Elizabeth Jane Fisher or one of Joseph F. and Martha Ann's relatives.

G S L city utah T.y may the 3 1857

Most dear and affectionate brother joseph

I take my pen in hand to write you a few
lines to answer your to last kind and
affectionate letters. the last note came to hand last
night and the other came to hand about three
weeks ago the mail had gon out and so I did not
git a chance to write to you but I will try to
write enough to make it up this time if you will
except of it. I have gust come down from James
this morning and they are all well and we are all
well allso. Jane was writeing to you when I started
away from there about an hour ago. she got her letter
last evenig and I heard of it and so I went up there
to see if there was one in it for me. and it
hapned to that there was one and I was glad to git
it git it if it was nothing but a note. it done me
as much good as though it had have been more. you
was saying in your last letter but one ch that
you was destetute off the comforts of life and it
greaved me very much to hear it It set me
a thingking about you and I have thought
more about you ever since than I ever did befor
my mind was trabled and have wished that I
could send you a good loaf of bread and some butter
over to you. and some paper so that you could write
to me and the rest of the folks with out robing
you of the coforts that you might have if you had
plenty but I trust in my god and in your
god that he will open the way
before you as he has opened the way before
me from time to time. I was glad to hear that
you was well under such circomstanses
not onely glad but thankfull for it. you say that
you presume you will live through it. dear brother
I would not think for a moment that you would not

Martha Ann to Joseph F., 3 May 1857 (p. 1)

I could not think for amoment that you would not
for I have strong hopes and ardent desiers as you say
to see you before long. you say in Janes letter she sais
that you expect to be releisett in about nine months
I hope and pray that it will be so if not sooner if
your mission is compteted and I hope it will be
before long for I think that you have sufferd enough
for one 3 years and it would not be more than fair
if some one took your place and let you come home
and stay with your friends and relations awhile
at least. yes I am still living at johns and am
there to day writing heare and am doing the
best I can. Dear Brother I have an Item of news
To write to you and my hand trembles when I go to
write it for my concience is gilty before my brother
for I fear that he will think I have slited him
but forgive me dear brother if I say that I have
but I fear that It will dampen your feelings
but I can not help it now I must say it enny
how I am marriett – to William harris. I suppose
that this will shock you to hear it. it almost
shocks me to think of it my sellf when I think of it
but it is really so now I must tell you the whis
and the wharefors and then I hope you will not blame
me so much he had been keeping company with me john
gave him leave to do so and I had no objection to it
and I began to think considderable of him and he
be gan to think considerable of me. to tell the of the
matter my thaughts has been that way for
some time for 2 years at the least and my mind
has not been among studys as you can plainly se
my heart was young and tender and I let it
go to far and John notised it for I did not tell it
to enny boddy not even to you who is my nearest
and dearst friend and I tried to conceal my
all I could but John found it out in site of me

Martha Ann to Joseph F., 3 May 1857 (p. 2)

while at least. yes I am sill living at Johns and am thare to day writing heare and am doing the best I can. ~~B~~ Dear b<rother> I have an itam of news to write to you and my hand trembles when I go to write it for my concence is gilty before my brother for I fear that he will think I have slited him but for give me dear brother if I say that I have [*illegible erasure*] but I fear that it will dampen your feelings but I can not help it now I must say it enny how I am married—to William harris.[232] I suppose that this will shock you to hear [*illegible strike-through*] <it>, it almost shocks me to thnk of it my sellf when I thnk of it but it is really sow now I must tell you the whis and the whare fors[233] and then I hope you wll not blame me so much he had been keepping companey with me John gave him leave to do so and I had no objection to it and ~~my~~ I began to think considderable of him and he began to think considerrabe of me. to tell the of the matter my [*illegible strike-through*] thaughts has been that way for some time for 2 years at the least and my mind has not been among studys as you can plainly se my ~~mind~~ heart was young and tender and I let it go to far and John notesed it for I did not tell it to enny boddy not even to you who was my nearest and dearst friend and I tr<i>ed to concal my all could [*illegible erasure*] but John found it out in site of me [**p. 3**] for he could se that I did not learn much and he had to know the resoning and I had to tell him and [*illegible erasure*] John went to brother kimbol[234] about it and he said that we had better git married be fore he went away and John thaught that it would [*illegible erasure*] be the best and then my mind would be setteld and then I could learn some thing but other wse I could not. and ~~wll~~ william went up to git his parting blesings[235] and I did not know for certain that I should git married befor he went away. and brother Kimible[236] sent him after me and told [*illegible erasure*] him that he had better ~~git~~ have it all done up that day and he came and I went and was seald over the alter. and he started to ingland ~~to drag~~ on a mission to drag a hand cart acrosst the plains we was married on tusday and he started on thursdas so you see that I did not stop long with him and I am glad of it for if he had not have going ~~to~~ away money could not have herd me to have ben married untll you come home for I have long wished for your <re>turn with a longing heart that I mght be the same when you come back as I was when you went away. but allas things can not be just as the huane[237] heart would desire. I am just the same as I was onely I am married I will be free for three years yet.[238] and dear brother I beseach of you to ~~is~~ treat me as you always did if you dont it will almost break my heart give me council and I wil try to abid it I am not perfect yet and I shall thank you for your coun~~cil~~<cil> and I am not ofended to you if I was I thinks I would ~~be~~ be a fool [*illegible strike-through*] and would need castisement~~s~~ for it I am thankful to my [**p. 4**] father for giving me a brother that cears for mya. wefare for I know that you care for my welfarre more than enny boddy else can ~~feel~~ <care> fore upon this irth O Joseph would to god that I could expres feellings just as they are and [*illegible erasure*] I express my thanks to you for your kindnes to me. I can never for git you for ever no not for an hour I have never

232. Martha Ann and William Jasper Harris were married on 21 April 1857.
233. Most likely the phonetic spelling of *whys and wherefores*.
234. Heber C. Kimball, a member of the First Presidency. See biographical register, "Kimball, Heber Chase."
235. Likely refers to both the reception of temple endowments and William's setting apart as a missionary.
236. Reflecting a common nineteenth-century practice in which a proper name was spelled phonetically and with variety, even in the same letter, Martha Ann spelled the name Kimball two ways: Kimbol and Kimible.
237. Possibly *human* or *humane*.
238. It would appear from this comment that Martha Ann assumed that William's mission would last three years. Due to the Utah War, however, which temporarily brought an end to most missionary work at the time, he was called home after only sixteen months.

for he could se that I did not learn much
and he had to know the resoning and I had to
tell him and so John went to brother Kimbal
about it and he said that we had better
git married be fore he went away and John
thaught that it would be be the best and then
my mind would be setteld and then I could
learn some thing that other wise I could not. and
william went up to git his parting blesings
and I did not know for certain that I should
git married befor he went away. and brother
Kimble sent him after me and told him that
he had better have it all done up that day
and he come and I went and was sealed over
the alter. and he started to ingland to day
on amission to drag ahand cart across the
plains we was married on tusday and he star
ted on thursday so you see that I did not stop
long with him. and I am glad of it for if
he had not have going to away money could
not have herd me to have ben married untill
you come home for I have long wished for your
return with alonging heart that I might
be the same when you come back as I was
when you went away. but allas things
can not be just as the human heart would
desire. I am just the same as I was onely
I am married I will be free for three year
yet. and dear brother I beseach of you to
treat me as you always did if you dont
it will almost break my heart give me coun
cil and I will try to abide it I am not per
fect yet and I shall thank you for your coun cil
and I am not offended at you if I was I thin
k I would be be afool and would not
cast it e ments for it I am thankful to my

Martha Ann to Joseph F., 3 May 1857 (p. 3)

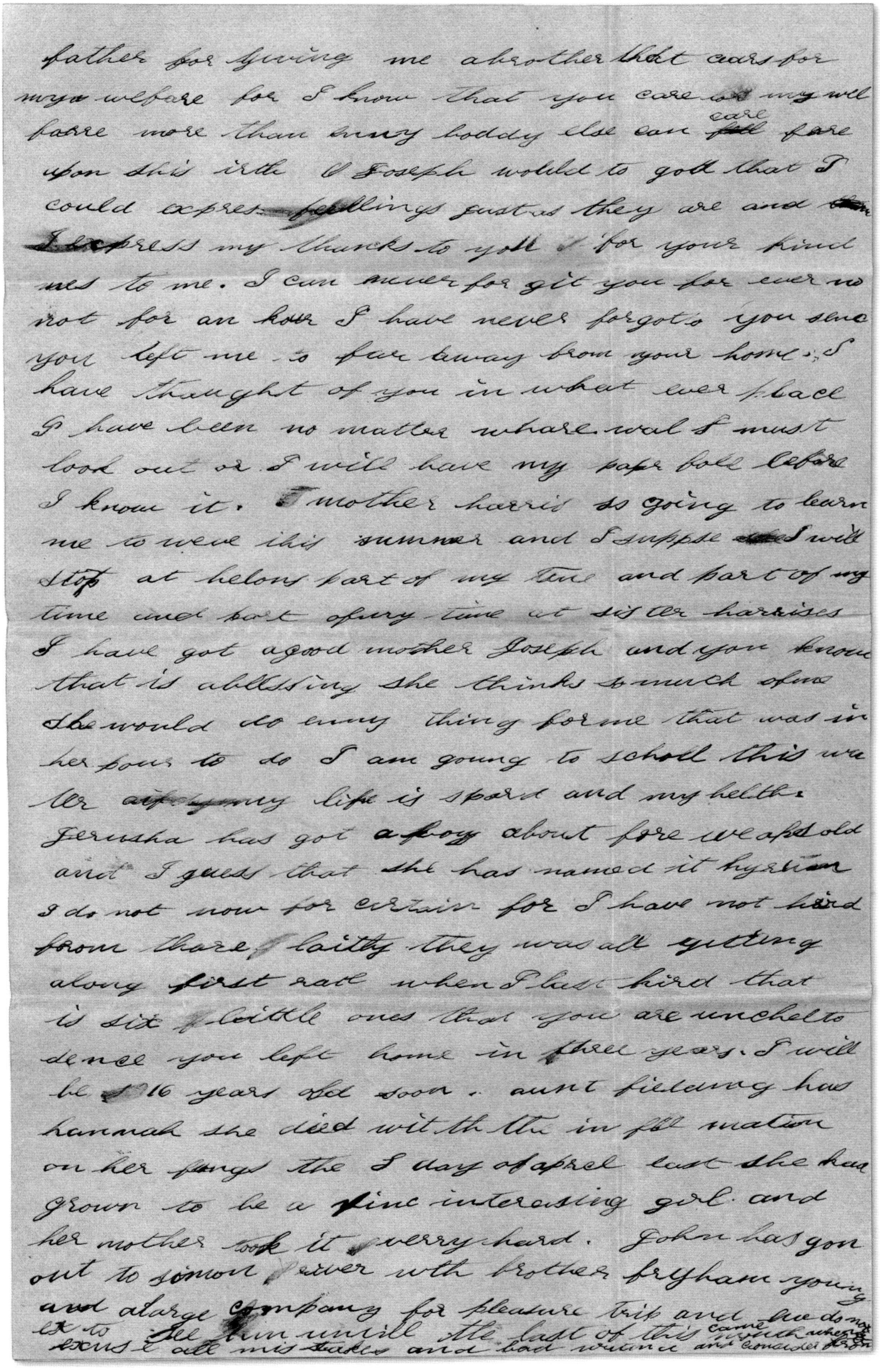

father for giving me abrother that cars for
myo welfare for I know that you care or my well
farre more than enny boddy else can ~~fell~~ care fare
upon this irth O Joseph wolld to god that I
could expres ~~fellings~~ jast as they are and ~~I~~
~~I express~~ my thanks to yoll I for your kind
nes to me. I can never for git you for ever no
not for an hour I have never forgotis you senc
you left me to far away from your home; I
have thaught of you in what ever place
I have been no matter whare wal I must
look out or I will have my paper foll before
I know it. mother harris is going to learn
me to weve this summer and I suppse ~~she~~ I will
stop at helens part of my time and part of my
time and part of my time at sister harrises
I have got agood mother Joseph and you know
that is ablessing she thinks so much of me
she would do enny thing for me that was in
her powr to do I am going to scholl this win
ter ~~if~~ my life is spard and my helth.
Jerusha has got aboy about fore weaks old
and I guess that she has named it hyrum
I do not now for certain for I have not hird
from thare laitly they was all getting
along first rate when I last hird that
is six little ones that you are unchel to
sence you left home in three years. I will
be 16 years old soon. aunt fielding has
hannah she died with the in flamation
on her lungs the 5 day of april last she has
grown to be a fine interasting girl and
her mother took it verry hard. John has gon
out to simons river with brother brigham young
and alarge company for pleasure trip and we do not
ex to see him untill the last of this month when they came
excuse all mistakes and bad writing and consider the son

Martha Ann to Joseph F., 3 May 1857 (p. 4)

forgotts you senc you left me to far away from your home. I have thaught of you in what ever place I have been no matter whare. wal I must look out or I will have my papr fole before I know it. mother harris[239] is going to learn me to weve this summer and I suppse ~~she~~ I will stop at helons[240] part of my time and part of my time and part of my time at sister harrises I have got a good mother Joseph and you know that is a blessing she thinks so much of me she would do enny thing for me that was in her pour to do I am going to scholl this winter if [*illegible strike-through*] my life is spard and my helth. Jerusha has got a boy about fore weaks old and I guess that she has named it hyrum[241] I do not now for cirtain for I have not hird from thare laitly they was all gitting along first rate when I last hird that is six little ones that you are unchel to sence you left home in three years. I will be 16 years old soon. aunt fielding[242] has hannah[243] she died witth the inflemation on her lungs the 8 day of aprel last she had grown to be a fine interasing girl and her mother took it verry hard. John has gon out to samon river[244] with brother brgham young and a large company for pleasure trip and we do not ex to see him untill the last of this month[245] exuse all mistakes and bad writing and consider from whence it <came>

MARTHA ANN TO JOSEPH F., 11 MAY 1857

[Great Salt Lake County
May 11th 1857.][246]

Most dear and afectionate Brothr Joseph. as thare was room in Janes[247] letter I thaught I would write a word or to as she gave me leaf I can not say much for thare is not room I am well and feel first rate and I hope that this note will find find you the same I am verry buisey this weak for I am. thinking of going up north with jerusha and william[248] when they go they start next fryday and they want me to go with them and stay a [*illegible strike-through*] weak or to and then come home and I think I will go. we all had the pleasure of meeting to gather last su<u>nday and the 5 little neaces and nphew ware [*illegible strike-through*] <all> <to> gether

239. Emily Hill, mother-in-law of Martha Ann.
240. Hellen Maria Fisher, wife of John Smith.
241. Hyrum Robert Pierce, son of William Pierce and Jerusha Smith, was born on 9 April 1857. See biographical register, "Pierce, Hyrum Robert."
242. Hannah Greenwood.
243. Hannah Alice Fielding, daughter of Joseph Fielding and Hannah Greenwood, died at the age of seven on 8 April 1857. See biographical register, "Fielding, Hannah Alice."
244. With headwaters in the mountains of central and eastern Idaho, the Salmon River eventually empties into the Snake River on the current Oregon-Idaho border.
245. President Brigham Young and a group of 142 people, traveling with fifty-four wagons and two boats, left Salt Lake City on 24 April and returned on 26 May. In addition to visiting the settlement of Fort Limhi, the purpose of the trip was "to rest their minds, to invigorate their bodies and to examine the intermediate country." See "Excursion to Fort Limhi," *Deseret News*, 10 June 1857, 108–9.
246. This paragraph by Martha Ann was appended to the end of one of Elizabeth Jane Fisher's letters to Joseph F. The date and location were written by Elizabeth Jane.
247. Elizabeth Jane Fisher.
248. Jerusha Smith and her husband, William Pierce.

and a sweetter little band never was. I know you would think so if you had saw them. from Martha Ann

JOSEPH F. TO MARTHA ANN, 14 JUNE 1857

Sandwich Islands
June 14th 1857[249]

Martha Ann; My Dear Sister:—

I recieved your kinde letters of Feb. 3rd <also April 5th> also of April 5th this morning about an hour since; I was glad to hear from you again. once more Dear Martha, I attempt to address you a fiew lines—altho' I do not feel verry much like writing, my hand feels verry stif and clumsy this morning. but I [*1.7 x 0.8 cm tear along folds*] you will look over and over-look all mistakes. if many there be. I feel this way, Martha, this morning.— God Bless you— what makes me feel so? because I read your letters with a brothers love, and with sympathy, Dearest Sister. one short sentence in your letter, struck me like the mighty surge of Occeans tempestuous swell! what was it?— "I feel that I am a weak and frail being—& why should not God bless you, who is much more worthy than I am, for, he has blessd me"— martha, do not tempt me. that language, tho' simple—speaks louder than the bolts of Heaven, that you do love me. and that you do desire to live humbe, and prayerful. Oh! humility! how beutious are thy influances. how profoundly, deep thy serenity and bliss! this subject, subdews—it melts me!— Martha what you said admonished me. I kindely accept its chastening influance, although quite undirected. when I read it something seemed to whisper gently in my minde, Joseph? "understandest thou what thou readest"?[250] "let him that readeth understand,"[251] these ~~th~~ admonishing thoughts came to my minde with the words, "wake up more fully to your duty!" I can look back and see where I might have bettered my course. where I might have been more dilegent in descharge of my duty. but then, these thoughts are dispelled by the strictly varacious adage "time once past never will return, the moment lost, is lost for ever"![252] therefore why morne for things we cannot help. or in the words of Dear **[p. 2]** Cousin Josephine, why, "sigh o'er the plesures now faided. And the joys time can never restore?"[253] there is no use, I am fully resolved to take things as they come, and as they fleet along by with [*1.7 x 0.6 cm tear along fold*] unchangible

249. Joseph F. noted in his journal, "this morning when I arose from my bead I was met in the door with my by a native who had the mail. I was glad to receive, some four or five letters from home, the Deseret News, and Standard. I spent the day writing to Martha, and Hellen in answer to theirs, also wrote to Charley good news from home, folks all well." Joseph F., journal, 14 June 1857.
250. See Acts 8:30.
251. See Mark 13:14.
252. The quotation is from "Robbery of Time," an essay by Dr. Samuel Johnson (1709–84), a prolific English writer famous for his contributions as a poet, essayist, and lexicographer. The essay appeared in *The Idler* (no. 14, 15 July 1758), a series of essays published in London's weekly *Universal Chronicle*.
253. Josephine Donna Smith (Ina Coolbrith), daughter of Don Carlos Smith and Agnes Moulton Coolbrith. She was Joseph F. and Martha Ann's first cousin, and she would become the first poet laureate of California in 1915. Though Joseph F. disapproved of Josephine's choice to remain in California and of her opposition to plural marriage, he still respected and admired his cousin, as this letter demonstrates.

goings of time, I feel to say, farewell, thou hurring time. thou industrious time, that wateth not for the sluggard, neither can man stay thy speading progress. but do thy duty in hastening the period when all creation shall reach the end for which they were created.— I wish now to give you a fiew words of advise. Martha, I have had [*1.9 x 0.6 cm tear along folds*] opertunity of accepting the hand, and heart of many by mear sugjestion, I know it. for I can read the heart as well as moste any one. well, now am I bound to any one? No, I am not. is any one bound to me, by her sacred vows for life No, there are non. now what is the reason?— I will reveal the secret. I have not my life ensured, only by my own goodness, my own true merrit. then God will, or has ensured my life to enjoy many great blessings. therefor if I am spaired to join my life with one in whome there is a spark of heavenly fire, that beams and blazes in the dark hour of adversity and that is willing to shair the humble lot of One whome God knows loves the humble and honest heart. then I will say to God be the glory, what hour is mine? what moment is my own? at what time may God say, Joseph, thy soul is required of thee—? can I say no? I cannot, then I say thank the Lord no soul is bownd to mine at stake of houer. varasity, and vertue, no, I am free as the air, so ~~are~~ <is> avery one free from me, I wish to be tied to no one till I am able to provide and take care of her, untill then hear ye O—fair ones, ye are free from me,—where no vows are made no hearts are broken. now the whole amount of this is, when sumed up. I do not want you to make any vows, with any one if you can avoid it.[254] I have seen too many such things, and they [**p. 3**] they are allways attended with more or less disappointments, you know Martha where there is a law, then you are under the [*1.3 x 0.2 cm tear along fold*] Law, as long as you obey it,—when you become aggressor to that Law, then you are condemnable, and become liable to be punished by that Law, whereas, if there is no Law, how can you become punishable by that which is not? the words of Paul are more consise upon this point, he sais, "if one dies with out the Law he is judged with out the Law, if [*1.8 x 2.6 cm tear along fold*]ies with the Law then he shall be judged with that Law".[255]— sp[*1.8 x 2.6 cm tear along fold*] the reserection I write this for an example to you, if you [*1.8 x 2.6 cm tear along fold*] vows you can break no vows, and therefore are not guilty, but if you make vows then you live in constant fear of breaking those vows, the guilt of the guilty allways condemns them, so also the fear of the fearful, or those in fear <allways betr[*1 x 0.9 cm tear along fold*] them> it exc[*1 x 0.9 cm tear along fold*],—it discomposes them and they are more liabl to do what they moste dreaded. these are my thoughts upon this subject. I read Williams'[256] letter with respect and notwithstanding his peculiar mode of address, I thought it was first-rate. I hope his mission will bring him out of the bud into a full blooming flower, and make a man of him. I wish also to say to you Martha keep trying to improve, especially in writing, for you have had a good chance to learn, be sure to spell right, in writing—observe your capitals, I wrote to you and before about this. and then I did not excactly understand the affair myself, conciquently I made some mistakes. you will learn with casual observation that the names of the Deity aught allways to be comenced with a capital letter, also all proper nouns—or names as of John, Sarah &c—should be commenced with a capital, also in commencing new sentances, allways commence with a capital,—all these little difficulties may be easly obviated if you look

254. As the opening line of this letter indicates, Joseph F. had not yet received the letter of 3 May 1857 that informed him of Martha Ann's marriage to William Jasper Harris on 21 April 1857, roughly two months before this letter was written.

255. See Romans 2:12.

256. William Jasper Harris.

earnestly into your grammar. all this counsel I take [**p. 4**] to myself—but my Dear sister I have all moste given up, <the idea of> ever becom[*0.4 x 0.2 cm tear along fold*] chiro[*1.3 x 0.2 cm tear along fold*]pher[257] m[*1.5 x 1 cm tear along folds*] hand has been too badly straned with hard work in its young days. you have not as much excuse, so improve the time— in writing Martha be sure to stile yourself genteelly, and polite,—at the same time do not get swollowed up in the Idea that you are polite, genteel &c—& thus neglect your cautions. I have recieved a letter from Charly[258] that has been opened, by some slipery-fing[*1.6 x 2.3 cm tear along fold*] Post-master of inqu[*1.4 x 0.3 cm tear along folds*]s[*1.4 x 0.3 cm tear along folds*]ive nature, I do not know how it [*1.6 x 2.3 cm tear along fold*] I would rather folks would let my letters alone, especial[*1.6 x 2.3 cm tear along fold*] for whome they were not designed—

I have recieved a letter lately from Cousin Josephine, also some poetry she composed on my absence from home. I would write it to you but I think I have not room if I write it to any one of the folks you will see it, it is splendid. in real poetic stile. she said she had written to you but had recieved no letter in return tolde me to speak to you about it, I would advise you to write to her. do your best to spell and write correct, for she is a good writer, this is what I wish you to progress in, till you are also a good writer.— I shall hav[*2.1 x 0.6 cm tear along folds*] to write several letters to day, some on rather peculiar subjects, which will probably take some more reflection than writing to any one, on common and every-day affairs. At generally takes me about two hours to write such a letter as this altho' I believe I have been writing about an hour on this may be a little more, so you will overlook mistakes and bad writing— I shall have to close for this time, for my sheet is full, and I have other letters to write, as I said before, give my love to Dear Bro. John, Hellen & Malissa, to Sarah—Charles.[259] Sister Smoot,[260] and all enquireing friends. I should write to William but donot know where to direct. to my affectionate Sister M. A. Smith— from your affectionate Brother, God Bless you— Joseph Smith

P.S. also give my love to Aunt Thompson, to Mary Jane,[261] and be sure to give my love to our Dear Sister Jerusha, to Uncle and Aunt Fieldings[262] and finally to All Joseph[263]

N. B. you mentioned something about sending some money, but said nothing definate, so, I am not certain how it stands. if you sent it, ts is lost, but if you did not send it—you nead not bother about it, for the lord has been with me & I have never wanted neither will I, so rest unconcerned about me. as ever Joseph.[264]

257. A chirosopher is someone learned in palmistry, or telling fortunes from reading the lines on the palms of the hand.
258. Likely Charles Emerson Griffin.
259. John Smith, Hellen Maria Fisher, "Malissa" (likely John's second wife, Nancy Melissa Lemmon), Sarah Smith, and Charles Emerson Griffin.
260. This likely refers to Margaret Thompson McMeans, first wife of Abraham O. Smoot, though it could refer to Emily Hill, mother-in-law of Martha Ann and third wife of Abraham O. Smoot.
261. Mercy Rachel Fielding and Mary Jane Thompson.
262. Jerusha Smith, Joseph Fielding, and Hannah Greenwood. See biographical register, "Fielding, Joseph."
263. Written upside down in the top margin of page 4.
264. Written upside down in the top margin of page 3.

MARTHA ANN TO JOSEPH F., 3 JULY 1857

G S L Co utah Try Julie the 3 857[265]

Most Dear and affectiona Brother Joseph

it is with a trembling hand and a palptating heart that I again take my pen in my hand to write a few lines to you to let you know ~~how~~ how I am gitting along and the rest of the folks. I am gittng long very well and feel first rate in bod<d>y but some troubled in mind. I can not help thinking about you away of thare alone fear from your fri<e>nds and relatons all that is dear to you with out enay of the comforts of life and I suppose not heardley enough to sustain life, for I hear thare is a fammnie[266] thare. O that I could have shareed it with you, [*illegible strike-through*] or could have known for moment what you have suferd <I mean in my own mind> it would have done me good and made me feel lots better I never ralised your sittuation untill laitellly ~~of~~ or not near so much I ~~I~~ do <[*illegible strike-through*]> noow. I have been allmost sensless sence you left it seems to me like a dreem and I some times think and all most loose myself in thaught and I say is thare such a boy as Joseph F smith in the wourld ~~and~~ it seams like you had ben gon an age of most. to look back on the changees that has took place sence yo left home bu to look at years and months it looks like a s~~h~~hort time sence **[p. 2]** we all stood round in a ring and bid you gooby, that was a sean that can not be forgotton by me. O Joseph I do look forward to that day when we shall aain meet. Would to god that it was now that I could meet you and be encirked in your arms and recieve that [*illegible strike-through*] warm kiss that I so ofton receive in dreams and it be in reality O dearest brother it would be the happest hour that ever I pent in my life O I can scarcelly wait for that day. but when you return home you will not see that little slender girl that you ~~you~~ left but a tall girl of some 5 foot and 8 inches tolerable light complctted dark [*illegible strike-through*] blue eyes and light [*illegible strike-through*] hare and a <g>rate big nose with a bone shticking upon it. I am not in the least hansm. but that does not hurt my goodness if I am good but I am not as good as I would like to be. I am not pirfect yet but I do desire to do right with all my heart, and improve my self all in my power. I have ben to meeting to day and enjoyd the best spirret that I ever enjoyd in my ~~life~~ life that I can remember off. it is fast day and I fasted untill 2 ~~o~~ O clock pm and I went to meeting 27 min<u>its ten O clock we have ~~had~~ got the finest shool house you ever saw in your life or not in your **[p. 3]** life one of the fineest in the in the valley at enny rate I now not how menny you have seen sence you left home of splended school housees. Joseph you must excuse my ill manner of composeing my letters if you pleas. and be like the man when <when> the jack ass kicked him you mus considder from whence it comes or they come. O Joseph I do not sopose that I have ~~not~~ got quite as good intellect as some folks has or elce I have not got the powers of collectting my fee~~l~~ling arite to bring up everry point ~~like~~ as I would [*illegible strike-through*] <like> to but ~~you~~ every booddy is not alik, and I must be

265. The envelope is addressed to "Jos. F. Smith Esq. Honolulu Sandwich Islands" and stamped "PAID 5" with an additional postage mark, "SALT LAKE CITY UTAH.T. JUL 5." Joseph F. wrote on the front cover in pencil, "Martha A Harris Received Sept." He also wrote several vocabulary words on the reverse side of the envelope in pencil, including *onslaught*, *misnomer*, and *delightful*. This habit of making lists of vocabulary words continued throughout his life.

266. An evangelical minster reported, "We have great cause for praise and thanksgiving that our people, after having suffered so long from drought and famine, are now abundantly supplied with 'food of the earth.'" See *Minutes of the Meeting of the Hawaiian Evangelical Association*, 9.

contented with it. I have not got good memory ~~as I would like to have~~ or I might have been a good schallar. dearst brother you may have thaught that I was distant in my way of writing but thare ~~thare~~ is whare is whare my fault lays I can not convey my idars in a ways that can be under stood. but I prey god that he will enable me so to do. O Joseph you do not know my love for you my God onelly my love for you and <my> weell <~~my~~> wishes <for> your welfare. my dearst brother I never in my life done a little mean trick to you but what I have thaught of it a thousand times sence you left home with regret and sorrow. my heart is lots warmmer than it youst to be Joseph and thare is not a girl in the world that loves [**p. 4**] her brothers and sisters and friends and relations than I do and nothing in the world cold have inticeed me me to have got married if things had ~~have~~ not have been just as they ~~my~~ was. I can not tell you how it was with me, by leter. but I will tell you when you ~~when~~ come home. and I do not believe you will blame me for doing as I have done. when you come home I will tell you all. and do not condemn me untill you know all and then you will not blame me. I am learning to weve real well and when you come home I can [*illegible strike-through*] weave you a pair of pants. ~~and~~ weaving is the best trade that a womern can have in this country. and I am gld that I have got the chanc~~h~~ to learn. I ~~have not~~ went to meeting last night and Sarah[267] [*illegible strike-through*] stayd with me all and she is hear now and sister harris sent for sister griffin and emmoely[268] and they came over and they are all thare and sarah has got one of the prttyest little girls[269] you ever set eyes on I do believe. they are all pritty I think Sarah tels me to give her love to you and sais she will not write to you for she is no writer but it is not becaus she has forgotton you in the least. I migh might say the same but I love to write to you when I can git the chance. I must bring my letter to close and I will not have a chance to write [*illegible strike-through*] <to you enny more> to and I am glad of it for I do want to see you if you believe me [*illegible strike-through*] good by dear brother Martha ann

JOSEPH F. TO MARTHA ANN, 25 JULY 1857

Lanai, Sandwich Islands
July 25th 1857—[270]

Dear Sister Martha Ann:— I recieved your long letter of May 3rd—about a week ago, and was verry glad indeed to hear from you; I was somwhat surprised on hearing of your marriage.[271] but as I was not there to partisipate in the ~~in the~~ scene, I can only wish you much joy;—and happy life You have now taken the moste important step of your life—or existance—under the

267. Sarah Smith.
268. Emily Hill, Abigail Varney, "emmoely" (likely Laura Emily Beebe, sister-in-law of Sarah Smith). See biographical register, "Beebe, Laura Emily."
269. Alice Lovina Griffin.
270. Joseph F. wrote two short lines in his journal on this day, "Saturday 25th this day I wrote to my sister Mrs. Martha Ann Harris. Also one to Cousin George Gee." Joseph F., journal, 25 July 1857.
271. Joseph F. noted in his journal, "We went to the Office this morning and I found quite a package of papers for. On opening them I found I had three letters from home—one from Aunt Thompson—Martha Ann and Cousin George Gee. I learned by Martha's letter that she had been married to Mr. W.m. Harris sometime in the latter part of April or the first of May. Good news generally." Joseph F., journal, 13 July 1857.

Bonds of the Gospel. upon the step you have just taken is pending all the social enjoyments—and happiness of your present existance—and the Blessings of a happy and chearful home. as well as an obediant and God-like posterity,—or the misories and heart-rending scenes: of discontent,—discord & bitter unhappiness;—I almoste quake when I think upon this all obsorbing subject—to the center. when I look around me and reflect upon the many direful circumstanses accuring from day to day,—among the great and the Learned, the Small and the Ignorant, as well as the Rich and the Poor;—of "heart-Broken" women, distracted husbands, "Jealousy" in all its hideous formes—suspicion with all his train of poisonous rancour. with his drawn daggar and un-cheathed vengense. ready to spill the hearts Blood of "Wives", "Husbands", & "Children"! I shrink with horro<u>r from the scene:— It does seem curious in the extreem to me, why folks go so head-long into business that so greatly concerns their future prosperity and happiness on the other hand will bring down upon them ponderous grieveancies, and a world of truble,—from which they may never extract themselvs—and inverriably a Bad name—however—with all these conciderations—before us—it is not with us, as it is with the World at Learge—we have the the light of the Gospel the—influance of the Holy Spirit—the teachings of the Prophits & servants of God, to "Lead us into all truth"[272] and teach us our duty— If you have adhered to counsel—it is all right—and you will come off victorioous. You will certainly leave off Girl-ism now. I hope you will remem[**p. 2**]ber your possition, and let your actions and conduct in all things, and at all times be such as will store up for you Respect, Esteem, and Friendship in the heart of every honest and good person. now, do you want me to tell you the way to attain to this desireable possition?— prayer—with faith, and hope on Jesus and his Gospel, will alone do it. a person that holdes your stateon in the True Kingdom of God, need never fear the face of "Clay". be determined and resolute in prayer and the Gospel, so that you could see Joseph John—Jerusha—Sarah—and every one els go [*0.5 x 0.5 cm tear along folds*] Heel and be damned[273]—and never shake your faith! "lean not upon the arm of flesh".[274] I can never save you, neither can I be saved by aught but my own good faith and works—now if you are sinceerly prayrful, the spirit of prayer is the spirit of God and it will lead you "into all truth"[275] & will never ~~urr~~ <err>. you will never yeald to temptations, and allurements, but will stand fast, and ever True to him with whome you have covenented to abide through all the vicissittudes of Life and death. you can never suffer by scandal, defamation, pique and misrepresentations, for none but miserable wretches would ever indulge in such meanness, be sure you are true and guiltless, and then be calm and quiet—and let the world roal on just as it may never head or listen—nor associate with the Law and vulgar—eschew them as you would a hidious evil—unless you are capable of raising <them> from their degridation—then you must never desend to their ways and pract<ice>. but make them assend to yours. never indulge in "tale-Bearing"—"Tatteling" &c.—this is the moste miserable and outragious evil that is extant—hear the words of Bro. Brigham on this subject—Read the Deseret News—the

272. See John 16:13.

273. May refer to Joseph Fisher, John Smith's father-in-law, or to Joseph Armstrong Fisher, John Smith's brother-in-law. The others are John Smith, Jerusha Smith, and Sarah Smith. In several letters during this decade, Martha Ann and Joseph F. make reference to relationship difficulties between Martha Ann and her stepbrothers and stepsisters.

274. See 2 Chronicles 32:8; 2 Nephi 4:34; Doctrine and Covenants 1:19.

275. See John 16:13.

"discourses" at least, and lay them at heart,[276]—adhibit yourself, Marth Ann, to sobriety—and taciturnity[277]—be studious with all—learn every thing you can—but when you have learned do not tell it—but "wear your knowledge like a watch, in a private pocket, and if you are asked what time it is, tell it—" but do not tell it before you are asked,[278]—I feel deeply for your intrest, and allways remember you in my prayers—feel for me the same. Martha Ann? **[p. 3]** Mormonism is the verry life of my soul—I love it—would die for it without a groan. when ever I bare my testimony to it—I feel as though I could sink the world—hurl the eternal Hills into perpetual space, or shake the verry heavens with my strength! by this I know that the Spirit of the Lord Bears record of the Latter Work, and I never can deny its truth unless I lie! yet, am I a perminent Rock which the fluds of Hell may <overwhelm> yet never shake? is it imposible for Saten to overcome me? no—when I look at the mighty Men that have rent the vail of Heaven and viewed the mansions of eternal Bliss, beheld the Throne of Almighty God—and yet have fallen!![279] never more to rise! my soul burns with-in me, and I fear and tremble. but those who have the same thoughts will know that feelings of this kind are easier experiansed than expressed— O! that we may "live our Religion!"

I recieved a letter from Cousin Josephine not long ago—but I believe I told you of it when I wrote before,—she was well—she did not say any thing about Agnes,—said her Mother[280] she feared was "sewing herself to death," they are living at a town Called Las Angelos[281]—some distance from San Bernardino,[282] and about 600 miles from San Francisco—they seem to be anxious for me to return. she says she has written to you several times, but has recieved no answers—just emulate her hand write, Martha—as neer as posible—she writes first rate. devote as much time as posible in learning to write. I have often tolde you I never expect to be a good writter, I've worked too much, at hard labor. I suppose you remember a certain ocasion on which I was lain up with a Broken Bone in my right hand,[283] I have never fully regained my usual agility in that hand, nor do I ever expect to;— It cramps my hand to write—so I am allways compelled to write as fast as posible—hence many mistakes and a bad hand-write.— I am verey careless too in writing—as I do not take much pride in it,—you should be more

276. In a sermon given 15 June 1856, Brigham Young stated: "I am wearied with seeing the conduct of some of these people, their thieving, lying, tattling, deceiving." George D. Watt, "Discourse by President Brigham Young," *Deseret News*, 25 June 1856, 123–24. Joseph F. received copies of the *Deseret News* from his brother John. See Joseph F. to Martha Ann, 17 April 1857, herein.

277. Naturally quiet.

278. Joseph F. is alluding to a Lord Chesterfield quote: "Wear your learning, like your watch, in a private pocket; and do not pull it out and strike it merely to show that you have one. If you are asked what o'clock it is, tell it; but do not proclaim it hourly and unasked like the watchman." See Lord Mahon, ed., *The Letters of Philip Dormer Stanhope, Earl of Chesterfield* (London: Richard Bentley, 1847), 1:115.

279. The words *have fallen* are written considerably larger than the rest of the text. Joseph F. may be alluding to prominent Church members who had fallen away or, possibly, those who were viewed as sons of perdition. See Doctrine and Covenants 76:25–38.

280. Josephine Donna Smith (Ina Coolbrith), Agnes Charlotte Smith, Agnes Moulton Coolbrith. See biographical register, "Coolbrith, Agnes Moulton."

281. Los Angeles was incorporated as a city in April 1850. See Lynn Bowman, *Los Angeles: Epic of a City* (Berkeley: Howell-North Books, 1974), chapter 5.

282. Located about sixty miles from Los Angeles, San Bernardino was an important Latter-day Saint settlement in Southern California.

283. Joseph F. broke a bone in his hand when he hit a hired farmhand who was chasing his older brother John with a pitchfork.

careful,—in writing—just say what you have to say—and then quit! take no round about course to tell any-thing—and make no apologies for what you are going to say [**p. 4**] but after you've said it—if necessary—smothe it over a little—in writing to me I do not want you to smothe any thing over—let it come indigenious and unsoffisticated with fals modisty, and it will relish well anoug.— if by taking this course your minde is not "Big" anough to fill three or four fools Cap[284] sheats, get some good piec[◊] of poetry—a "patent sermon"[285]—ore a good interresting moral story—a striking Historical event, a philological or philosophical problem, or any thing els—something that will help pass a lonly moment, or chear up a sad-fraught hour,—but do not exaust a hundred words to express just one Idea—like I do!— you must excuse me seeing I'm a learner like yourself=[286] the Idea of it, is, I scarcely know when to stop, when I get to writing to my folks at home,—I feel as though I would like to tell them the depths of my heart=[287] although they do not call me any way loquacious— Only when I write home!

I wrote a long letter to Aunt Thompson[288] yesterday-evening—gave her a short history of my travels for the last three or four months, it may ~~b~~ be interresting to you, if you have an oppertunity of hearing it. The 24th of July passed uncerimoniously with us here. I am now stoping with Bro. S. M. Molen[289] on the Island of Lanai, as you will see by the heading of this letter. I left my field of Labour on the 11th instent, expect to return in a short time. The Natives are verry poor here upon this Island as they have mostly all left their homes and came to this place, consonant with the Counsels of the President[290]— Bro. Molen and I are living on Boild Pumpkins and Squashes—with a little Goat meat which we are thankful to get. I think <we> will ~~soon~~ have more to subsist upon before long— I must now close.— I am short of poastage Stamps, so I will enclose a letter to Cousin Georg Gee[291] in this, you will pleas forward it to him, present my love and esteem to Sisters Smoot, & Harris, to Bro John,[292] his family and to all enquiring friends my cordial rememberance— may God Bless you allways is my prayr. your Bro, Joseph Smith

284. *Foolscap* or *fool's cap* is a long sheet of writing or printing paper that comes in various sizes. It receives its name from the "fool's cap" used as a watermark.
285. Patent sermons were a very popular genre during the nineteenth century and were "short" and "comic, although they were clearly intended to edify." John Bryant, *Melville and Repose: The Rhetoric of Humor in the American Renaissance* (New York: Oxford University Press, 1993), 127. One of the most famous collections of patent sermons was J. R. Dow, *Dow's Patent Sermons* (Philadelphia: T. B. Peterson and Brothers, 1857). J. R. Dow was the pen name of Elbridge G. Paige.
286. In the original letter Joseph F. used a double dash mark, here represented by an equals sign.
287. In the original letter Joseph F. used a double dash mark, here represented by an equals sign.
288. Mercy Rachel Fielding.
289. Simpson Montgomery Molen was serving as a missionary in the Sandwich Islands at this time. See biographical register, "Molen, Simpson Montgomery."
290. Brigham Young. See Joseph F. to Martha Ann, 23 November 1855, herein, note 60.
291. George Washington Gee was a second cousin of Joseph F. and Martha Ann. See biographical register, "Gee, George Washington, II."
292. Margaret Thompson McMeans, Emily Hill, and John Smith.

MARTHA ANN TO JOSEPH F., 19 AUGUST 1857

[August 19, 1857][293]

Dear Brother I will write a word or to more as thare is room in Janes[294] letter I am ashamed of that I wrote in the other but I could not cut it out with out cuting some of hers of and so I had to send it but you will excuse the bad writng this time for this ink was made of gunpouger and vinager and you mist not git to near the fire when you read it or it may blow you up if you are not carefull. aint you afraid of it. Jane made it yester day and we have both wrote with it we had no other kind and so we had to. May the lord bless you is the prayer of your sister

MARTHA ANN TO JOSEPH F., [1857?]

[1857?][295]
worst kind *[illegible mark]* I am going to write you twice in return for them you wrote to me [*illegible erasure or mark*] theme is <so> pretty I am going to c[◊]aser then thank you for them. william[296] would have wrote but he had time and he told me to give me his love to you and sister smoot[297] and [*illegible erasure or mark*] sister harris[298] wishes to be remena and [*illegible erasure or mark*] you write to me often for

For when far apart
Twill cheas the lonely hous
T shed asunshine on the heart

Whare haply clongs might lovr
O write to me often that they
Cerished love may never fade
Away but like the plar[299] star
Above may shine whare e[◊][◊] I stay
May the lord bless you
And prosper you in all of
Your undertakings[300] and give you patence helth and strength

293. This paragraph is appended to the end of a letter from Elizabeth Jane Fisher to Joseph F. The letter is dated simply "Teusday 19th." By textual comparison with other letters written by Elizabeth Jane, this letter was likely written on 19 August 1857.

294. Elizabeth Jane Fisher.

295. The surviving fragment of this letter does not have a date and greeting and is written on blue paper by Martha Ann. The tone, content, and style appear to reflect the time period between the late 1850s and early 1860s.

296. William Jasper Harris.

297. Most likely one of Abraham Owen Smoot's wives.

298. Emily Hill Harris.

299. The Polar Star, known as the North Star or Polaris, which is used for navigation because of its consistent location in the night sky. Often used as a metaphor for the idea of consistency.

300. Martha Ann uses a similar phrase in a letter dated 5 April 1857.

as I could not finnish my letter on the other peace of paper I thaught that I would finnish it on this you said in in your letter ~~that you~~ to mind my own buisness and not meddle with others folkes buisness that is what I have always done so far. ~~you~~ I do not think you are allway finding fault they ~~thaught~~ never such athaught entred my head. thare is no part that I would select for it is all good advice and thank you for it. I am not above being chastised and I have not forgotton your disposition and it is agood deal like mine I have got as much grit as the most of folks but I have had to grind my grit down considerable to the finest pouder in some caes send you left home. you said that you was all alone when you wrote my last letter. O how I wish I could be with you and share with you your trials I could do it as free as I could eat ameal of vitles when I am hungry if it was [illegible] was done that I should. but it can not be so. I do not believe that midion is endearing all things & if you was to stay away away ten years from home it would not in dear it to me one bit for I would not git used to it I would rather have you at home if it was the best your hopes are not lively stronger to be home than our hopes are to see you I do not think for I want to see you the

worst kind. I am going to write you verse in return for them you wrote to me the theme is pretty I am going to learn them thank you for them. william would have wrote but he had time and he told me to give me his love to you and sister smoot and sister harks wishes to be remembered to you

O write to me ofton for
~~For when far apart~~
~~Twill cheer the lonely hour~~
I shed asunshine oer the heart
Whare hapley clouds might low
O write to me ofton that thy
cherished love may never fade
Away but like the blue star
Above may shine whare ~~ere~~ I stray
May the lord bless you
and prosper you in all of
your undertakings and give
you patience helth and strength
to doyour duty to the praise of
yr affectionate Sister Martha Ann

O my friend I do breathe
a wish that thou might
spend thy hy life in
love and peace May cares
Shal hand near tuch thy Brow
~~Brow~~
But age sed joys as years increace
and I would wish
That visions fair might ever
Glide oer thy thaughts of
me that thou might sometimes
breathe a prair for
one that ever thinks of thee

Martha Ann to Joseph F., [1857?]

To do your duty so the price of
You affection [*illegible erasure or mark*] sister Marth Ann

O my friend I do breathe
A wish that thou might
Spend thy hy lifle in
Love and peace cores
Thie hand near tuch <Brown> thy [*illegible erasure or mark*]
[*illegible erasure or mark*]
But age send guys as years in
crease and I would wish
That visions fair might <ever>
Glide they thoughts of
Me that thou might some
times breathe a praer for
One that ever thinks of thee

As I could not finnish my letter on the other pease of paper I thought that I would finnish it on this you said[301] in your letter <that> <you> to mind my own buisness and not meddle with others folks bi<u>sness that is what I have always done so far. [you] I do not think you are always finding fault they [*illegible strike-through*] <was> never such athought entered my head. Thare is no part that I would select for it is all good advice and thank you for it. I am not above being chastsed and I have not forgotten your dispi[◊]to[◊] and it is a good deal like mine I have got as much eait as the most of folks but I have had to grind my grit[302] <to> down considerable to the finest powder in some caces sence your left home. You said that you was all alone[303] when you wrote my last letter [◊] O how I wish I could be with you and share with you your trials I could do it as far as I could eat a meal of vites when I am hungry if it was [*illegible strike-through*] [*illegible strike-through*] [*illegible strike-through*] wis dom that I should. but it can not be so. I do not believe that mation [◊] onsearing all <thanks> for [◊] if you was to stay [*illegible strike-through*] away ten years from home it would not in dear it to me one bit for I would not git used to it I would rather have you at home if it was the best your hopes are not being <stronger> to be home thank our Lord for believe me dear brother are to be you I do not think I want to see you the[304]

301. It is characteristic of Joseph F. to give Martha Ann advice in many of his letters during his time in Hawai'i. Here Martha Ann responds to several pieces of advice he had given her.
302. Joseph F. speaks of "smith grit" in his letter dated 9 June 1855, herein.
303. In her letter from 3 July 1857, Martha Ann expresses similar concern about Joseph F. feeling alone.
304. The surviving fragment of this letter ends midsentence with *the*.

JOSEPH F. TO MARTHA ANN, 20 MAY 1858

S. H. W.[305] May 20th 1858[306]

Dear Sister Martha,—

I am happy to improve this, the first favorable oppertunity, of writing to you a few lines.[307] I would not have you think that I am cold and indiferant towards you, for nothing is more foreign from my minde than to once forget my sister. Mary Jane,[308] called here the other day, and said you were about to have made us a visit down here, but was persuaded not to come, I wish you had, have come. we are all well here, now, little Allis[309] was very sick last night. She was taken with a warm fit, last night about 8 O'clock which lasted her about 10 minutes. Mary Jane was there, and sat up by turns, with Sister Griffin and Sarah[310] watching her all night. She appears to be very well to day again. I hope she will never have another.

I am doing little or nothing here now.[311] I have to appear in the City every \ other morning at 6 O'clock, to answer to my name in Ranks.[312] John[313] was here a few days since but I started the morning after he arived, to Grants' Ville in Toweele,[314] he started on his return to Provo before I got back.

The City, houses, and Countrey, look deserted & **[p. 2]** lonely, every thing wears a lonesome, dreary aspect.[315]

I have heard nothing from "East,"[316] lately, of importance. I have no doubt, however, that it will be some time yet, before many of the Brn[317] get in from that Quarter.

I am glad that William and Jerusha[318] have gon so near where you stop, they will be company for you.

Keep up good Spirits Marty, and do not get down hearted, what use is there of it?— You know, it takes seperation and devision, to affect unicon and oneness, in these days.

305. Sugar House Ward in Salt Lake Valley.

306. Joseph F. was nineteen, and Martha Ann was seventeen.

307. In anticipation of possible military attack or occupation, as many as thirty thousand residents in the northern Latter-day Saint settlements in Utah, including Salt Lake City, relocated to shared or temporary housing in Utah County and points farther south. Known as the "Move South," the evacuation began in March 1858 and continued into early June. When this letter was written, some Saints were still in the process of preparing to leave their homes, but a majority had already left.

308. Likely Mary Jane Thompson.

309. Alice Lovina Griffin. The final letter could be either an *s* or an *e*.

310. Abigail Varney and her daughter-in-law Sarah Smith.

311. Joseph F. continued his militia duties by remaining in the Salt Lake Valley with other men who had been assigned to burn everything to the ground if the military attempted to enter the valley. Later, when negotiations had settled the conflict, the army was allowed to pass through the Salt Lake Valley on 26 June 1858 on their way to establish Camp Floyd on the western side of Utah Lake in Utah County.

312. Likely a reference to roll call as a member of the militia when the soldier stood in rank and file.

313. Likely refers to John Smith.

314. Grantsville, Tooele County, is located thirty-six miles southwest of Salt Lake City.

315. Salt Lake City was abandoned before US Army troops marched into the city on 26 June 1858.

316. Possibly a reference of the peace negotiations being held between leaders of The Church of Jesus Christ of Latter-day Saints and the new governor, Alfred Cummings.

317. A mark above the *n* indicates that this is an abbreviation for *Brethren.*

318. William Pierce and Jerusha Smith.

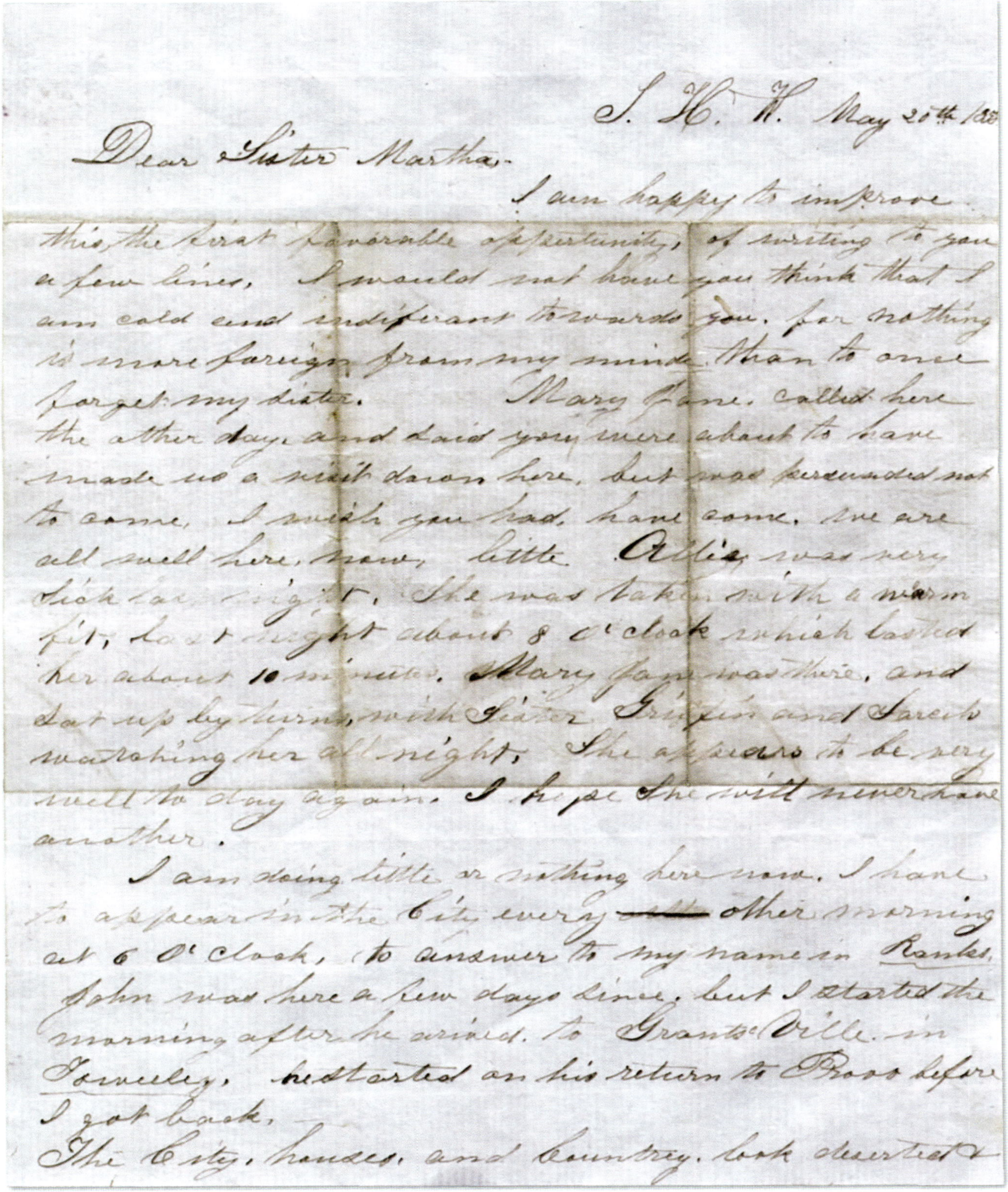
S. H. H. May 20th 185[8]

Dear Sister Martha

I am happy to improve this, the first favorable opportunity, of writing to you a few lines, I would not have you think that I am cold and indifferent towards you. for nothing is more foreign from my mind than to once forget my sister. Mary Jane. called here the other day, and said you were about to have made us a visit down here, but was persuaded not to come, I wish you had, have come, we are all well here, now, little Allie, was very sick last night, She was taken with a worm fit, last night about 8 O'clock which lasted her about 10 minutes. Mary Jane was there, and sat up by turns, with Sister Griffin and Sarah watching her all night, She appears to be very well to day again. I hope she will never have another.

I am doing little or nothing here now. I have to appear in the City every ~~all~~ other morning at 6 O'clock, to answer to my name in Ranks. John was here a few days since, but I started the morning after he arrived. to Grants Ville in Towelley, he started on his return to Provo before I got back, —
The City, houses, and country. look deserted &

Joseph F. to Martha Ann, 20 May 1858 (p. 1)

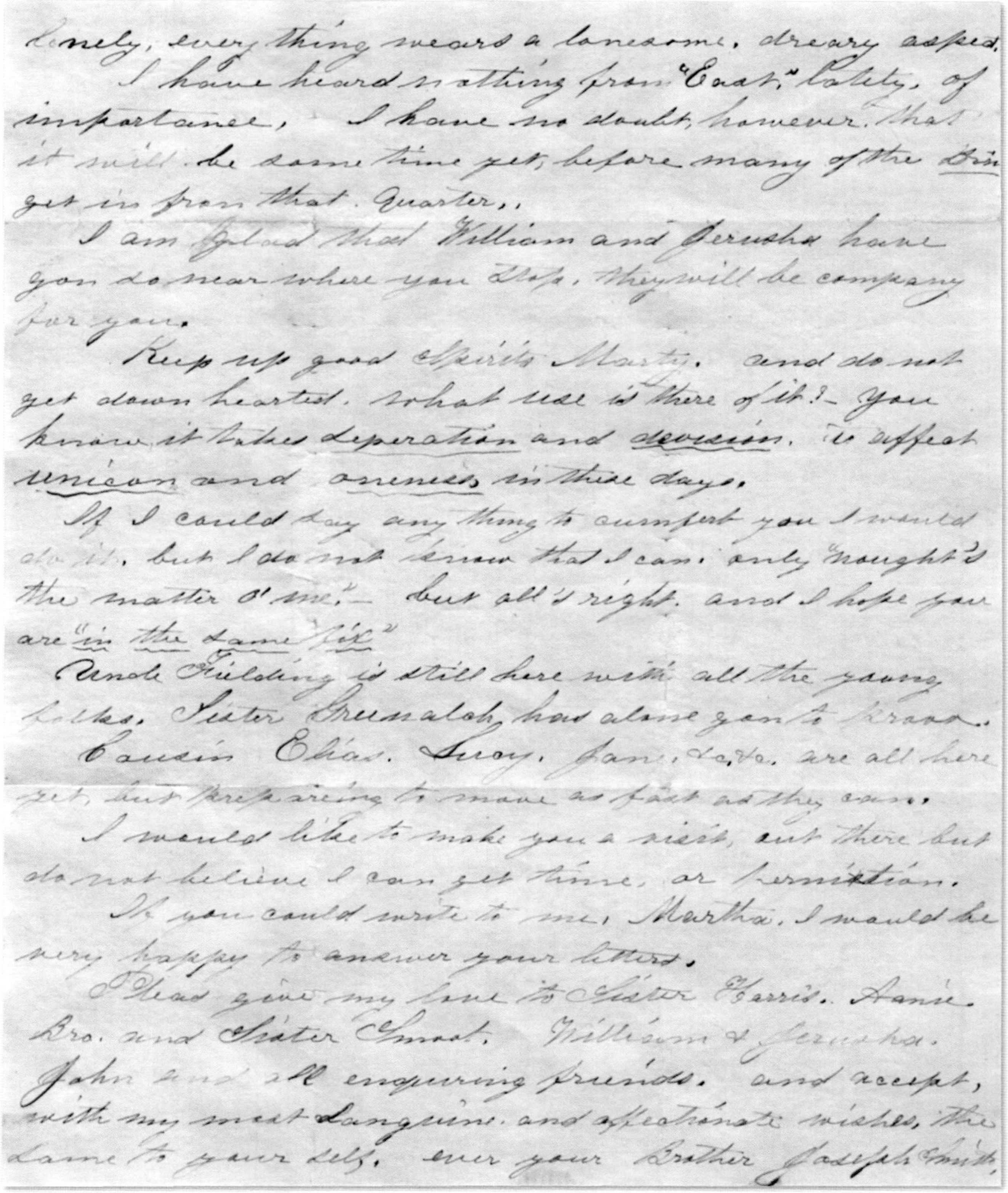
lonely, every thing wears a lonesome, dreary aspect.
I have heard nothing from "East," lately, of importance, I have no doubt, however, that it will be some time yet, before many of the Brn get in from that Quarter,.
I am glad that William and Jerusha have gon so near where you stop, they will be company for you.
Keep up good spirits Marty, and do not get down hearted, what use is there of it?– You know it takes seperation and devision, to effect union and oneness in these days.
If I could say any thing to cumfort you I would do it, but I do not know that I can, only "nought's the matter o' me."– but all's right, and I hope you are "in the same fix"
Uncle Fielding is still here with all the young folks. Sister Greenalch has alone gon to Provo.
Cousin Elias, Lucy, Jane, &c, &c, are all here yet, but prepareing to move as fast as they can,.
I would like to make you a visit, but there but do not believe I can get time, or permittion.
If you could write to me, Martha, I would be very happy to answer your letters.
Please give my love to Sister Harris, Annie, Bro. and Sister Smoot, William & Jerusha, John and all enquiring friends. and accept, with my most sanguine and affectionate wishes, the same to your self. ever your Brother Joseph Smith,

Joseph F. to Martha Ann, 20 May 1858 (p. 2)

If I could say any thing to cumfert you I would do it, but I do not know that I can, only "nought's the matter o' me,"—but all's right. and I hope you are "in the same fix"

Uncle Fielding[319] is still here with all the young folks. Sister Greenalch[320] has alone gon to Provo.

Cousin Elias, Lucy, Jane,[321] &c. &c. are all here yet, but prepareing to move as fast as they can.

I would like to make you a visit, out there but do not believe I can get time, or permistion.

If you could write to me, Martha, I would be very happy to answer your letters.

Pleas give my love to Sister Harris, Aanie, Bro. and Sister Smoot, William & Jerusha, John[322] and all enquring friends. and accept, with my most sanguine, and affectionate wishes, the same to your self, ever your Brother Joseph Smith.

319. Joseph Fielding.

320. Mary Ann Peake. See biographical register, "Peake, Mary Ann."

321. Likely refers to Elias Smith and two of his wives, Lucy Brown and Amy Jane King. See biographical register, "Smith, Elias" and "King, Amy Jane."

322. Likely Emily Hill; "Aanie" possibly refers to Abraham O. Smoot's fifth wife, Anne Kirstine Mauritzen; Abraham O. Smoot; Margaret Thompson McMeans; William Pierce; Jerusha Smith; and John Smith. See biographical register, "Smoot, Abraham Owen" and "Mauritzen, Anne Kirstine."

Salt Lake City
Tues. Dec. 1st. 1868

My Dear Sister:—

Your's of 19th. ult. came safely to hand I though I would just now—in the midst of labor and unperformed duties—stop a moment and drop you a line.

Julina, Sarah, Baby and Edward are all well, as usual, Edward is slowly recovering from a spell of sore eyes. Baby for sometime has been a little restless of nights, and she is such a little talker! She will repeat almost any simple word after me or her mother, and say them plain too. She is as blessed as ever; I have comfort with my little one.

My birthday present was a long law-document styled "Levira A. Smith vers. Joseph F. Smith", an action, brought before the 4th Judicial District Court of San Francisco for "divorce" and "Relief" for the "crime of adultery" in which Levira swears that I have committed adultery with one "Julina Lambson" "Mary Ellen Richards and other women, in Salt Lake City & Provo—in Utah Territory—and in San Francisco Cal. and other places"!! Aunt Thompson, Mary Jane & Robert are usually well. Jones moves out of your house this week and another family moves in. so I understand. Please to forward the inclosed to bro. Jensen the Taylor, and oblige me. With kind love to William & the Children and all friends I am your affectionate Brother Joseph

The girls send love—Edward sends love to the children.

Joseph F. to Martha Ann, 1 December 1868 (p. 1)

Decade 2

1860–1869

JOSEPH F. TO MARTHA ANN, LEEDS, YORKSHIRE, ENGLAND, 29 JANUARY 1861

My little experiance has proven this Latter day work, to be of good material, and I am now content, let what will come, and I trust I shall for ever be able to keep my ground and be found among the faithful and the doing, of Gods People. I have partly learned one thing, i.e. I am mighty small, and don't know much—if anything. and I see a great deal more to learn every day and still experiance is such a slow-and-sure School Teacher that I do not seem to make scarcely any proggress in my lessons, but I hope—"in patience to possess my soul" and struggle unceasingly t[*0.6 x 2.7 cm vertical tear along fold*] the end.

It is but an easy matter to make good resolutions, the duce of it is to carry them out.

MARTHA ANN TO JOSEPH F., SALT LAKE CITY, UTAH, 30 MAY 1861

O yo do not know how mutch good it does me to read your letters Joseph. to know that I have one brother that does not forgit me is a great consolation. I hardly knowe how to be thankfull enough for the goodness of my heavenly father to me a weak and frail being that I am for giving me such kind friendes. as I have and such kind husband. and a home. O how sweet that name does sound to me. would that you ware as comfotuble as I am Joseph, but god will grant that you shall be rewarded for the toils and privations that you have passed thre for the gospil sake.

Joseph F. Smith in Liverpool, England, 1861. Joseph F. mentions having his "likeness taken" on several occasions during this mission (as in his 30 July 1860 journal entry). Courtesy of CHL.

Decade Introduction

One year after his marriage to Levira Annette Clark (1842–88), Joseph F. was called in 1860 to serve a second mission, this time to the British Isles.[1] He departed Salt Lake City with Levira's half brother, Joseph F.'s cousin Samuel H. B. Smith (1838–1914), on 27 April 1860, just two days before Levira's eighteenth birthday. Joseph F. noted in his journal, "This day I baid my wife & numirous friends farewell, and started upon my mission to England."[2] He, along with several other missionaries, traveled across the plains with a wagon train, apparently working as teamsters to pay their passage. They arrived in Florence, Douglas County, Nebraska, on 8 June 1860. There Joseph F. met his older half brother, John Smith, who had been visiting his Smith cousins (children of Emma Hales Smith and Joseph Smith Jr.) in Nauvoo and had stopped on his return trip to Utah to help his sister, Lovina Smith Walker (1827–76), and her family move to Salt Lake City.[3] For Joseph F., it had been fourteen years since he had seen his half sister.[4]

JOSEPH F.'S VISIT TO NAUVOO

From Florence, the missionaries continued on to Nauvoo, Hancock County, Illinois, arriving in late June. Returning to his boyhood home, Joseph F. recalled those days in a letter to Levira: "It looked as natural to me as tho' I had lived there my life time. There stood our old Barn and Brick Office as they did 14 years ago. Uncle Joseph's Big Brick store looked as it did when I saw it last, in fact I could pick out nearly every spot that I had known in Childhood."[5]

1. Levira was the daughter of Samuel Harrison Smith and his second wife, Levira Clark; Samuel and Levira had two additional children, but both died at the time of birth in 1841 and 1843.
2. Joseph F., journal, 27 April 1860.
3. Lovina Smith Walker was the oldest child of Hyrum Smith and Jerusha Barden. She and her family left Florence one week after Joseph F.'s visit. Her brother, John Smith, was appointed company leader responsible for 359 people making the trek to Salt Lake City. See biographical register, "Walker, Lovina Smith." For details of John Smith's reunion with his cousins, see Buddy Youngreen, "Sons of the Martyrs' Nauvoo Reunion—1860," *BYU Studies* 20, no. 4 (Summer 1980): 351–70.
4. Joseph F., journal, 27 April 1860.
5. Joseph F. to Levira, 28 June 1860.

Joseph F. noted in his journal, "Here we found cousins—Joseph, Fredrick, Allexander, and David, and Aunt Emma."[6] The immediate family of the Prophet Joseph Smith (1805–44) remained in Illinois when the Saints left Nauvoo in 1846. They included Emma Hale Smith (1804–79)—the aunt of Joseph F. and Martha Ann and the widow of the Prophet—and her children Joseph Smith III (1832–1914), Frederick Granger William Smith (1836–62), Alexander Hale Smith (1838–1909), and David Hyrum Smith (1844–1904).[7]

This joyful reunion was somewhat overshadowed by Joseph Smith III's recent call to be the first prophet-president of the "New Organization," or the Reorganized Church of Jesus Christ of Latter Day Saints (RLDS).[8] Espousing an alternative interpretation of the Restoration, the RLDS Church challenged the leadership of Brigham Young (1801–77) and the Twelve Apostles.

Although these cousins held differing opinions and interpretations of Church history, doctrine, and practice, Joseph F.'s visit with Joseph III was friendly. Joseph F. noted, "I think [Joseph III] felt unfeigned pleasure at seeing us."[9] However, the goodwill and cordial disagreement between cousins did not last long. By the decade's end, the doctrinal divides between Joseph F. and his cousins had widened and feelings had turned acrimonious as each defended his own interpretation of the past.

After their brief stop in Nauvoo, the missionaries continued east, allowing Joseph F. an opportunity to visit his aunts Sophronia Smith McCleary (1803–96) and Lucy Smith Milliken (1821–82) in nearby Colchester, McDonough County, Illinois.[10] The missionaries arrived in New York City on the Fourth of July[11] and soon thereafter boarded the *Edinburgh*, a ship bound for England.

Emma Hale Smith, ca. 1870. This image is found in the Joseph F. Smith photograph collection. Included in that collection are images of Joseph Smith III and other family members who did not gather to Utah. Courtesy of CHL.

6. Joseph F., journal, April 1860, [4].
7. See Youngreen, "Sons of the Martyrs' Nauvoo Reunion," 351–70.
8. Known today as the Community of Christ, with headquarters in Independence, Jackson County, Missouri.
9. Hyrum M. Smith III and Scott G. Kenney, comps., *From Prophet to Son: Advice of Joseph F. Smith to His Missionary Sons* (Salt Lake City, UT: Deseret Book, 1981), 14.
10. These aunts were children of Joseph and Lucy Mack Smith.
11. See Joseph F. to Martha Ann, 28 July 1861, herein.

THE BRITISH ISLES

Joseph F. and his companions arrived in Liverpool, Lancashire, England, on 27 July 1860.[12] As with his first mission to the Sandwich Islands, Joseph F. (still young at age twenty-one) encountered a new culture, diet, and social and religious world. His journal records his perceptions of the squalor in an industrial city shortly after his arrival: "This evening . . . we took a walk thro' the principle thoroughfares of the town, and the sites we saw defy description. They were simply horrible!"[13] He also faced a variety of English dialects. Curiously, he undertook to learn sign language, noting in 1861, "Took a lesson in 'deaf & dumb' getting quite expert."[14]

Certain habits that Joseph F. acquired during his first mission were conducive to his personal growth in Britain: keeping a journal; communicating with family, friends, associates, and Church leaders through numerous letters; practicing handwriting; making vocabulary lists; reading voraciously; visiting natural, cultural and historical sites; sending items home, including newspapers; and widening his circle of friends and associates. He always gave special attention to his wife Levira, his younger sister Martha Ann, and other Smith family members in Utah.

Joseph F. was always grateful to receive news from home and disappointed when he did not receive a letter. For example, he noted in his journal that he had not received a "letter from, Sarah [Smith Griffin] nor John [Smith] since I left home, and only one from Charlie [Charles Emerson Griffin]. I can hardly tell what has come over them but I suppose it's all right— if so— why— all right— it is."[15]

As before, Joseph F.'s mission to the British Isles provided him an opportunity to communicate with his sister and others through letters. In a record book of expenses for this particular mission, he noted an example of costs associated with his efforts to keep in touch with family and friends.[16]

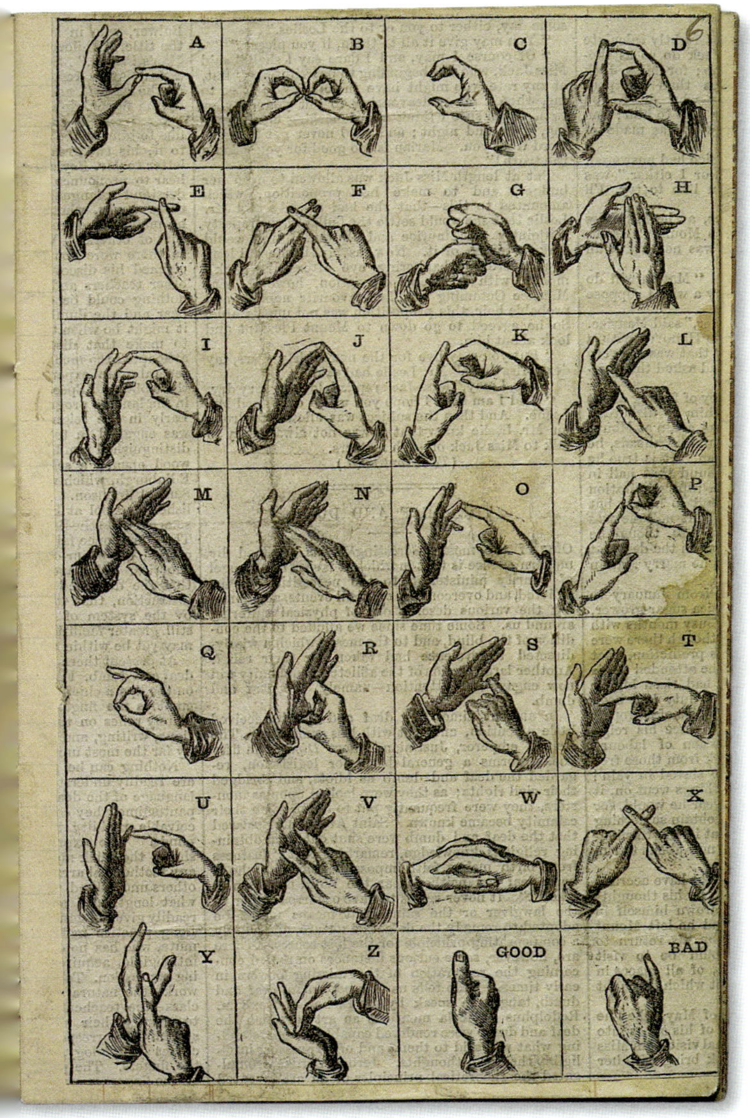

Joseph F. cut and pasted a sign language chart in his journal. Joseph F. Smith, journal, 27 April 1860 to 22 September 1860. Courtesy of CHL.

12. Joseph F., journal, 27 July 1860.
13. Joseph F., journal, 28 July 1860.
14. Joseph F., journal, 18 November 1861.
15. Joseph F. to Martha Ann, [spring 1861?], herein.
16. Joseph F., 2–3 November 1860, [9]; notebook, 31 July 1860–8 August 1862.

1860		For What Expenses	Ł[17]	S.[18]	D.[19]
Nov.	2nd	letter home		1	
"	3rd	Stamps		1	
"	"	For Paper			2
"	"	letters overweight			2[20]

It is fortunate that Joseph F. took care to record his efforts to communicate with others, because many of his letters from this period have not survived. His journal attests to the time-consuming efforts he expended in this regard. For example, one entry notes, "I mailed two parcels off of papers to Vira and Martha."[21] Another entry records, "I wrote to Levira sent her some verses and my likeness, also Martha Ann."[22] When the famous *London Illustrated* published drawings based on daguerreotypes taken in Salt Lake City, along with a balanced article about the Church, Joseph F. collected several copies and sent them home to family members. He noted in his journal, "Got the 'Elustrated London News' for Saturday 16th with a photograph of Br. Brigham, and his houses in G.S.L. City and a short history of his life since the Death of Joseph—very good."[23] On the following day, he recorded, "Mailed 3 Nos. of the 'London Journal' and 'Elustrated London News' to Leveria . . . to Bro. William [Jasper] Harris."[24]

Joseph F. often shared his activities with loved ones back home, especially Martha Ann, who he thought would likely never have the kind of experiences he was having serving missions across the world.

In an 1862 letter to Martha Ann, Joseph F. described the historical sites he visited in London and asked for her patience: "I do not wish to impase an good nature, So I will prescribe the limits of your portion to this remaining half sheet. Which I hope you will have patiance to read."[25]

Joseph F.'s journals also contain insights into his personality. One such entry reads, "On awakening this morning I found my watch had stopped about the time I wound it up on going to bed. The hands standing at 11:15 minuets. I feel as if I had lost a friend!!!"[26] His letters could be similarly lighthearted. To Levira he wrote:

> I think you would hardly know whether it was Joseph or not. Let me describe him as he sits. Here he is, hair "shinggaled,"[27] tall "stovepipe" hat, stiff collar, and in full English Style, all set and in full trim to go forth a regular English Mormon preacher! And in fact I must

17. Ł was the symbol for the British pound. It was divided into twenty shillings.
18. S, from Latin *solidus* (a Roman coin), was the symbol for the British shilling. It was divided into twelve pence, or pennies.
19. D, from Latin *denarius* (a Roman coin), was the symbol of the British pence or penny.
20. Yorgason, *From Orphaned Boy to Prophet of God*, 214–15.
21. Joseph F., journal, 21 September 1861.
22. Joseph F., journal, 28 February 1862.
23. Joseph F., journal, 18 November 1861.
24. Joseph F., journal, 19 November 1861.
25. Joseph F. to Martha Ann, 10 April 1862, herein.
26. Joseph F., journal, 7 August 1862.
27. Likely a misspelling for *shingled*, meaning to be covered with shingles; that is, his hair was combed neatly.

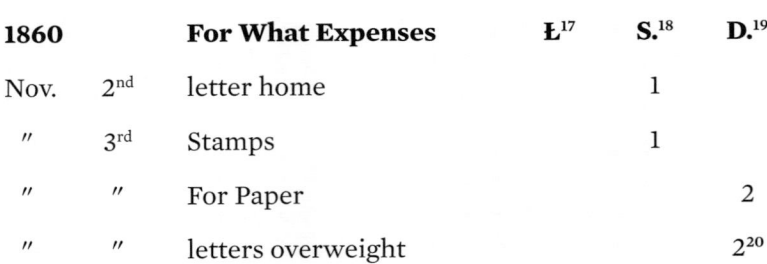

"The Great International Exhibition of 1862." Joseph F. Collection. Joseph F. discusses this visit in a letter to Martha Ann, 10 April 1862. Courtesy of CHL.

> confess that I think myself with the rest of the boys appear very respectable, fair examples of the hail, hearty, rugged mountain boys of deseret. . . . We stand quite a show even if they did take us to be wilde beasts and monkeys when we first came.[28]

In letters home Joseph F. mentioned his plans to visit his extended Fielding relatives in "Ould England."[29] Levira conveyed a message from Mercy Rachel Fielding Thompson (1807–93), Joseph F.'s aunt, suggesting that he visit Martha Ibbotson Fielding Watson (1803–72), who "could tell you all about the rest of the relitives and whare to find them."[30]

As good fortune would have it, Joseph F. did meet some of his mother's siblings, including his uncle James Fielding (1793–1877), a Methodist minister; another uncle, Thomas Fielding (1795–1882); his aunt Ann Fielding Matthews (1799–1884); and another aunt, Martha Ibbotson Fielding

28. Smith and Kenney, *From Prophet to Son*, 15.
29. See, for example, Joseph F. to Martha and William Harris, 28 June 1860, herein.
30. Levira to Joseph F., undated letter.

Levira Annette Clark Smith, ca. 1867, photograph by Edward Martin, Salt Lake City, Utah. Joseph F. and Levira were married on 5 April 1859 and divorced on 9 July 1869. See Joseph F. to Martha Ann, 1 December 1868, herein. Courtesy of CHL.

Watson (1803–72).[31] Both of these aunts were married to Methodist ministers. Joseph F. maintained contact with his aunt Martha Watson through a significant letter correspondence in the years that followed.

The British Mission was progressing in the early 1860s, and Joseph F. was seeing the fruits of his labors. He observed in a letter to William Jasper Harris, his brother-in-law, "We are prospering finely. We baptize frequently and only seldomly have to cut anyone off."[32]

LEADERSHIP IN GREAT BRITAIN

Church leaders in the British Isles, like those in Hawai'i, gave Joseph F. more and more responsibilities. He was appointed president of the Sheffield Conference, which included the cities of Barnsley, Doncaster, Rotherham, and Sheffield. The *Millennial Star*, the Church's newspaper in the British Isles, reported, "The Sheffield Saints are warm-hearted and full of good works, under the Presidency of Joseph F. Smith, who though young is like a father to them. He is esteemed very highly by the Saints."[33] During the fall of 1862, Joseph F. was also given a charge to supervise the emigration of hundreds of European Church members to Zion.[34]

It was during this mission that Joseph F. became better acquainted with George Q. Cannon (1827–1901), who helped open the Sandwich Islands Mission.[35] Cannon had recently been called to the Quorum of the Twelve Apostles and had been sent to England by President Brigham Young to preside over the British Mission, which also included administrative responsibilities for the European Mission.

In addition to performing his duties, Joseph F. decided to use sixty dollars to help a four-year-old orphan named Edward Arthur (1858–1911) make the journey to Utah. Edward lived in Utah with Joseph F.'s cousin Rachel Fielding Burton (1837–1914) until Joseph F. returned home in April 1863 and took Edward in as a member of his personal family.[36]

RETURN TO UTAH

Once he and his traveling companions arrived in New York on 6 July 1863, Joseph F. began arranging for the transit of Latter-day Saint emigrants to Florence, Douglas County, Nebraska, the staging ground for the trek west to Salt Lake City. His first duty in this assignment was to assist the Saints with whom he had traveled from England to America. He then awaited the arrival of other emigrant ships before making his way to Utah.

31. See Nathaniel R. Ricks, "'Shameful Inconsistency': Joseph F. Smith Encounters the British Fieldings" (lecture at Mormon History Association conference, 2013), in editors' possession.
32. Joseph F. to William Jasper Harris, 24 October 1861.
33. "Sheffield Conference," *Millennial Star*, October 25, 1862, 685.
34. Blaine M. Yorgason, *From Orphaned Boy to Prophet of God: The Story of Joseph F. Smith* (Ogden, UT: Living Scriptures, 2001), 214. See Joseph F. to Martha Ann, 1 March 1862, herein.
35. George Quayle Cannon served in the Quorum of the Twelve Apostles and eventually was called as a counselor in the First Presidency. He had served as a missionary in the Sandwich Islands from 1850 to 1854 and had been ordained an Apostle on 26 August 1860. See biographical register, "Cannon, George Quayle."
36. See Kevin Folkman, "Letters from Joseph F. Smith to His Adopted Son Edward Arthur Smith," in *Joseph F. Smith: Reflections on the Man and His Times*, ed. Craig K. Manscill et al. (Provo, UT: Religious Studies Center, Brigham Young University; Salt Lake City, UT: Deseret Book, 2013), 114–32.

In New York Joseph F. stayed at the Stevens House, a hotel located at 25 Broadway, with John W. Young (1844–1924). There Joseph F. witnessed the draft riots[37] breaking out across the city as the US Civil War (1861–65) moved into its third year.[38]

On arriving in Salt Lake City in late September 1863, Joseph F. found Levira extremely ill and spent the next six weeks tending to her needs day and night.[39]

ANOTHER MISSION TO THE SANDWICH ISLANDS

Five months after Joseph F. returned from England, President Young sent Apostles Ezra T. Benson (1811–69) and Lorenzo Snow (1814–1901) to Hawai'i to resolve a problem created by a Latter-day Saint convert named Walter Murray Gibson. Three former Sandwich Island missionaries—Joseph F. Smith (1838–1918), Alma L. Smith (1831–87), and William W. Cluff (1832–1915)—were sent to assist Benson and Snow.

It will be recalled that several years earlier, in the early spring of 1857, rumors had begun swirling about an impending showdown between the US government and the Church. Brigham Young had called for missionaries preaching abroad to return to Salt Lake City. In a matter of a few months, all of the Utah missionaries serving in Hawai'i had left the islands, with Joseph F. departing on October 6, 1857. Their absence had left the indigenous members exposed to the cunning designs of Walter Gibson, who had arrived in Hawai'i in 1861. Gibson had identified himself to the members as their newly appointed leader.

For nearly three years Gibson controlled the Church and its members by raising money through various means, including selling priesthood offices. When word finally reached Salt Lake City, Brigham Young dispatched Elders Benson and Snow, along with Joseph F. and two other former Hawaiian missionaries, to investigate and set matters right. They reached the islands on 27 March 1864.

Joseph F. described the scene on Lāna'i to Levira in a letter home as one of "considerable pomp" but confessed he did "not find any fault with [the] arrangement" of organized meetings and classes for children. Ultimately, Gibson did not recognize the Apostles' authority and was excommunicated.[40] When Gibson refused to reassign the property deeds to the Church, the Church lost six thousand acres on Lāna'i.[41]

---

37. The New York City draft riots took place in Lower Manhattan on 13–16 July 1863, leaving nearly 120 dead (mostly black Americans) and 2,000 injured. The riots broke out following the passage of a law by the US Congress to draft men to fight in the American Civil War. See Nathaniel Ricks, "Joseph F. Smith and the New York City Draft Riots, Part 1: Background," *Juvenile Instructor: Organ for Young Latter-day Scholars*, 10 July 2013, https://juvenileinstructor.org/joseph-f-smith-and-the-new-york-city-draft-riots-part-1-background/; "Part 2: 13 & 14 July 1863," *Juvenile Instructor*, 12 July 2013, https://juvenileinstructor.org/joseph-f-smith-and-the-new-york-draft-riots-part-2-13-14-july-1863/; and "Part 3: 15–18 July 1863," *Juvenile Instructor*, 16 July 2013, https://juvenileinstructor.org/joseph-f-smith-and-the-new-york-city-draft-riots-part-3-15-18-july-1863/.
38. No letter from Joseph F. to Martha Ann exists from his stay in New York City in July 1863, most likely because he determined that he would arrive home about the same time as any letter that made its way to Utah. His journal provides a vivid picture of the draft riots.
39. Yorgason, *From Orphaned Boy to Prophet of God*, 218.
40. See Gwynn Barrett, "Walter Murray Gibson: The Shepherd Saint of Lanai Revisited," *Utah Historical Quarterly* 40, no. 2 (Spring 1972): 142–62. Joseph F.'s and Gibson's paths crossed again in Hawai'i when Joseph F. sought refuge in the islands from the judicial crusade against the Latter-day Saint practice of plural marriage during the 1880s.
41. For additional details about Walter Murray Gibson, see R. Lanier Britsch, *Unto the Islands of the Sea: A History of the Latter-day Saints in the Pacific* (Salt Lake City, UT: Deseret Book, 1986), 118–24.

Following the Apostles' departure, Joseph F. Smith remained for six months and worked with Elders Cluff and Smith as his assistants and with local members to reestablish order in the Church.[42] The task was daunting since membership—peaking at around four thousand during Joseph F.'s first mission—now stood at about five hundred. He led the effort to reorganize and revitalize the branches on the islands and to identify a new gathering place. Eventually, having made significant progress, Joseph F. departed on 12 October 1864 for Utah, having completed another mission assignment for the Church.

Joseph F. Smith, ca. 1866, about the time he was ordained an Apostle. Courtesy of CHL.

LIFE IN UTAH AND ORDINATION TO THE APOSTLESHIP

After returning from his second mission to the Sandwich Islands, Joseph F. was elected to the Utah Territorial House of Representatives and found employment at the Church Historian's Office, where he worked under the supervision of his father's cousin George A. Smith (1817–75), an Apostle and Church Historian. In addition to his work at the Church Historian's Office, Joseph F. was also employed at the Endowment House as a recorder and served as an ordinance worker.

One of Joseph F.'s responsibilities at the Historian's Office included keeping minutes of Brigham Young's weekly prayer circle meetings. At the conclusion of one meeting on Sunday, 1 July 1866, President Young said: "Hold on, shall I do as I feel led? I always feel well to do as the Spirit

42. See Eric Marlowe and Isileli Kongaika, "Joseph F. Smith's 1864 Mission to Hawaii: Leading a Reformation," in Manscill et al., *Joseph F. Smith: Reflections on the Man and His Times*, 52–72.

First Presidency and Quorum of the Twelve, 9 October 1869, photograph by C. R. Savage, Salt Lake City, Utah. The first photograph of the combined First Presidency and Quorum of the Twelve includes Joseph F. Smith on the far right. Courtesy of USHS.

constrains me. It is my mind to ordain Brother Joseph F. Smith to the Apostleship, and to be one of my counselors."[43] After receiving approval of those present, including four members of the Twelve Apostles, the ordination proceeded: "We then offered up the signs of the Priesthood, after which Bro. Jos. F. Smith knelt upon the altar and taking off his cap, we laid our hands upon him. Bro. Brigham being mouth and we repeating after him in the usual form." Joseph F. was twenty-seven.[44]

43. Brigham Young instructed John Taylor, Wilford Woodruff, George A. Smith, and George Q. Cannon to record the ordination but did not want it "written in a way to lead others to think that this mode [during a prayer circle with participants dressed in temple robes] is essential or the only way in which such ordinations can be performed." Journal History, 1 July 1866, 2–3.
44. See Patrick A. Bishop, "The Apostolic Succession of Joseph F. Smith," in Manscill et al., *Joseph F. Smith: Reflections on the Man and His Times*, 249–64.

Since there was no current vacancy in the Quorum of the Twelve at the time, President Young asked that the ordination remain confidential.[45]

Almost a year later, in preparation for being set apart as a member of the Twelve Apostles, Joseph F. recorded, "26 day of June 1867. I was re-baptized[46] in the font at the Endowment House and confirmed at the same time and place by Elder Geo. Q. Cannon."[47]

Eventually the ordination was made public when, in the October 1867 general conference, Joseph F. was sustained as a member of the Quorum of the Twelve Apostles, filling the vacancy created by the apostasy of Amasa Lyman.[48] In October 1867 Joseph F. noted in his journal that he was "set apart in the upper room at the E. H. as one of the twelve Apostles" with Brigham Young as voice.[49]

A MISSION TO PROVO CITY

In oder to strengthen the Saints in Utah against those who hoped to separate members of the Church from their leaders, the First Presidency and Quorum of the Twelve Apostles made personal visits, preached the restored gospel of Jesus Christ during their visits, and appointed local leaders who would direct the spiritual and temporal work of building the kingdom of God in their appointed places.

As part of this effort, in February 1868 President Brigham Young traveled to Provo, a Latter-day Saint settlement about forty-five miles south of Salt Lake City. During this visit President Young said, "I am happy in the privilege [of] meeting with you. . . . As far as I am acquainted with the inhabitants of Provo I think they are as good a people as those who dwell in Salt Lake City or in any other settlement in Utah Territory. I think much of Provo; it is a very favored locality."[50] However, Church leaders felt they could help resolve some of the issues facing the community. "While cogitating upon this matter," President Young continued, "it came to me very forcibly to make a proposition for a few men to go to Provo and comfort the hearts of the brethren here, to show them the necessity of becoming one, of laying aside all individual bickerings, of overlooking and forgiving the weakness of one another, and of uniting our faith together to make this one of the most beautiful and lovely cities of Zion."[51]

Brigham Young assigned former Salt Lake City mayor and businessman Abraham O. Smoot, Apostle Wilford Woodruff, Joseph F. Smith, and several others "to go to Provo and make homes there, and live there a portion of the time." He promised the Saints "if the brethren of the city of Provo are willing for us to dictate and guide them, and make our homes with them, we will try to do them good, and teach them the ways of life and salvation, and show them how to overcome the

45. Joseph F. said many years later that the decision to keep the ordination confidential hurt the feelings of Heber C. Kimball, counselor in the First Presidency. See Edward Leo Lyman, *Amasa Mason Lyman: Mormon Apostle and Apostate* (Salt Lake City, UT: University of Utah, 2009), 367–68.

46. Rebaptism was a common practice in the nineteenth century required for major events, including on arrival in Zion after gathering to Utah, as a prerequisite to receiving an endowment and sealing, and before joining a united order. See Joseph F. to Thomas Rasband, 19 March 1883; also D. Michael Quinn, "The Practice of Rebaptism at Nauvoo," *BYU Studies* 18, no. 2 (1978): 226–32.

47. Joseph F., notebook, November 1866–December 1871, 26 May 1867.

48. For an insightful and reflective story about the connection between Amasa Lyman and Joseph F. Smith and the apostleship, see Lyman, *Amasa Mason Lyman*, 367, 404–5, 420, 491–94.

49. Joseph F., notebook, November 1866–December 1871, 6 October 1867.

50. Brigham Young, "School of the Prophets, Improvements of Provo City, Litigation, Injudicious Trading," in *Journal of Discourses* (London: Latter-day Saints' Book Depot, 1854–85), 12:157, delivered at Provo, 8 February 1868.

51. Young, "School of the Prophets," 159.

darkness so natural to the human mind, and give them extended ideas on the building up of the kingdom of God on the earth."[52]

A week later, President Young told an audience in Salt Lake City about his visit to Utah Valley, "There are good Saints in Provo, and they want to be better Saints; they may have committed errors, but when you arrive at the truth of the matter, they wish to be Saints."[53]

Elder Ezra T. Benson (1811–69) updated fellow Apostle Franklin D. Richards (1821–99), who was directing the work in England at the time: "On Friday, Feb. 7, 1868, President Young, accompanied by Elders Heber C. Kimball, Wilford Woodruff, E. F. Sheets, Joseph F. Smith, A. O. Smoot and others, started for Provo. A great change has taken place in the administration of that locality. Brother A. O. Smoot is elected mayor of Provo, and presiding Bishop of the whole county; Wilford Woodruff, Joseph F. Smith, George Bywater, A. F. McDonald, and Daniel W. Cluff, City Councillors; E. F. Sheets, Wm. Miller, and Myron Tanner, Alderman. They report the spirit of the people in that region as very good."[54]

Emily Harris Smoot, Martha Ann's mother-in-law and a plural wife of Elder Smoot, was among the first of his families to move to Provo from Salt Lake City. Apparently William Jasper, Emily's son, arrived in Provo with his wife Martha Ann and their five children[55] about the same time.

Joseph F. followed his sister and arrived in Utah County in mid-March, writing, "Provo, Wednesday, Mar. 11th 1868, last night, we moved into one of bro. Cluff's houses, it took all day Tuesday to whitewash, and clean it. So that it was fit to stop in."[56] To help supplement his income while away from Salt Lake City that year, Joseph F. worked for David Cluff in Provo.[57]

The following year, Joseph F. returned to Salt Lake City and resumed many of his duties, including those of a clerk, secretary, and recorder. In October 1869 he returned to Provo on assignment with Brigham Young and recorded, "Baby was unwell all night with a fevor. Left home this morning at 7. . . . reached Provo at 5.20 p.m. I felt low spirited when I left home this morning. Martha Ann and family well."[58] On the following day, he noted, "Felt some better this morning. . . . visited Martha Ann and the [County] Fair."[59]

PLURAL MARRIAGE

Plural marriage had been privately practiced in the Church since the 1840s but was publicly announced as a practice in 1852 after it had become widely known in Utah. Despite negative reactions by people of other faiths and some members, Church leaders vigorously defended plural marriage.

52. Young, "School of the Prophets," 159.
53. Brigham Young, "Object of the Gathering, Necessity of a Temple, Trails of the Saints, Sealing, Visit to Provo," in *Journal of Discourses*, 12:167, delivered at Salt Lake City, 16 February 1868.
54. Ezra T. Benson to Franklin D. Richards, 16 February 1868, as published in "Correspondence. America," *Millennial Star*, 21 March 1868, 188–89.
55. William Jasper Jr., Joseph Albert, Hyrum, Mary Emily, and Franklin Hill.
56. Joseph F., notebook, 11 March 1868.
57. See Joseph F., account book, May 1868. Additionally, entries from 28 July through 17 September 1868 provide dates, hours, and salary ("14 days at $3.00 [total] $42.00"). David Cluff Jr. is identified as a "cabinet maker and turner" in G. Owens, comp., *Salt Lake City Directory, Including a Business Directory of Provo, Springville, and Ogden, Utah Territory* (Salt Lake City, UT: G. Owens, 1867), 125.
58. Joseph F., journal, 1 October 1869; see also "Local and Other Matters," *Deseret Evening News*, 1 October 1869, 3.
59. Joseph F., journal, 2 October 1869.

Joseph F. and Julina Lambson Smith about the time of their marriage in 1866. Courtesy of Miriam Taylor Meads.

Within a decade, the US federal government took its first step to curb the practice when Congress passed the Morrill Anti-Bigamy Act on 8 July 1862. Nevertheless, Church leaders viewed the practice of plural marriage as protected by the US Constitution's religious freedom clause and continued teaching and practicing the principle.

In the face of government efforts to stop plural marriage, Church leaders encouraged an increasing number of members to begin the practice, and those already living in plural families were urged to expand the practice. It appears that Brigham Young counseled Joseph F. to enter into plural marriage. In response to a letter from his cousin Samuel H. B. Smith inquiring about rumors that Joseph F. had entered into plural marriage, Joseph F. wrote that he "had no other object in view other than to obey counsel."[60] Moreover, his plural wife Julina Lambson (1849–1936) recalled as much: "He had never paid any special attention to me, and I do not think that he had thought of getting another wife, but President Young advised him and he had told him a number of times, so he thought he should obey." She also recalled that when her mother warned her not to expect a great deal of affection from a man who already had a wife he loved, she had replied, "Mother, I love him and if I am good, he will learn to love me. He is the only man I have ever seen that I could love as a husband."[61]

60. Joseph F. to Samuel H. B. Smith, 13 June 1866.

61. Scott Kenney, "Joseph F. Smith," in *The Presidents of the Church: Biographical Essays*, ed. Leonard J. Arrington (Salt Lake City, UT: Deseret Book, 1986), 190. Joseph F. was introduced to sixteen-year-old Julina Lambson (George A. Smith's niece) while he worked at the Historian's Office. They were married on 5 May 1866 in the Endowment House. Brigham Young ordained Joseph F. an Apostle two months later in July 1866.

Joseph F. and Sarah Ellen Richards, ca. 1868. Courtesy of CHL.

Two years later, Joseph F. was sealed to his third wife, Sarah Ellen Richards (1850–1915), on 1 March 1868.[62] Sarah Ellen was the daughter of Willard Richards (1804–54), a close associate of Joseph and Hyrum Smith and a counselor to Brigham Young in the First Presidency before his death.

Two children were born to Joseph F. during this period: Mercy Josephine, a daughter of Joseph F. and Julina born on 14 August 1867, and Sarah Ella, a daughter of Joseph F. and Sarah Ellen Kimball born on 5 February 1869.

A TRAGEDY

Joseph F.'s participation in plural marriage created additional burdens and tests, including additional strains in his first marriage with Levira. Although entering into a plural marriage may not have been the main cause of the dissolution of his marriage to Levira, taking a second wife in 1866 seems to have exacerbated what was apparently an increasingly challenging and volatile relationship. It appears that Levira's mental state had been deteriorating and that she may have suffered from a major depressive disorder, which is mentioned in the letters as an "an<y>xity of mind."[63]

By December 1868, nine months after Joseph F.'s third marriage, Levira brought legal action against him, suing for divorce in a California court.[64] One factor in the dissolution of the marriage

62. See biographical register, "Richards, Sarah Ellen." Joseph F.'s first wife, Levira, had moved out of the home and was living with her parents before Joseph F. married Sarah Ellen. He was therefore a monogamist again. Sometime after Levira's departure, Brigham Young asked Joseph F. to marry another wife. See Stephen C. Taysom's forthcoming biography, *"Like a Fiery Meteor": The Life of Joseph F. Smith.*
63. For more information regarding Levira's health and circumstances, see Martha Ann to Joseph F., 12 January 1862 and 3 February 1862, herein.
64. The action was submitted to the Fourth Judicial Court in San Francisco, San Francisco County, California, on 30 October 1868. The divorce was finalized on 9 July 1869; see Joseph F. to Martha Ann, 1 December 1868, herein.

besides plural marriage was Joseph F.'s long absences from home. He recorded in his journal, "4 years today since I was married 3 of which time I have been from home."[65] It is also evident that his temper and his personal failures as a young, inexperienced husband played a role.[66] Another factor was the pressure from Levira's extended family in California to leave her husband, the Church, and Utah. Levira was also disappointed in not having children after eight years of marriage.

Given Joseph F.'s personal struggle to "guard" his temper and his tendency to be "too quick to resent a wrong," one historian remarks that Joseph F.'s management of his increasingly challenging relationship with Levira "was a herculean effort, emotionally and physically."[67] The end of that marriage was certainly one of Joseph F.'s lifelong regrets. Even though he went on to establish five successful family relationships thereafter, the dissolution of his marriage to Levira was a tragedy for a man who was committed to the Church's teachings on the essential role of family. Subsequently Joseph F. rarely talked about Levira.

Joseph F. Smith, Julina Lambson, Sarah Ellen Richards, and Edna Lambson, ca. 1860s–70s. Typical of many large family Bibles, Joseph F.'s Bible had a section for family photographs. Courtesy of Mary Lou Walker.

ANOTHER TRAGEDY

In addition to ending his relationship with Levira, Joseph F. experienced another heartbreak when his daughter Sarah Ella died on 11 February 1869, shortly after birth.[68] A funeral was held at 2:00 p.m. the following day at the "Homestead," the name of the Smith family home located at First North between Second and Third West.[69] Little Sarah Ella was buried next to Mary Fielding Smith, her grandmother, in the Salt Lake City Cemetery.[70]

65. Joseph F., journal, 5 April 1863.
66. In an exchange of letters with Brigham Young, Levira and Joseph F. told their versions of the incidents that played a role in the dissolution of their marriage. See Joseph F. Smith to Brigham Young, 25 August 1864; Levira to Brigham Young, undated; and Joseph F. to Brigham Young, 25 August 1867. See Scott G. Kenney, "Before the Beard: Trials of the Young Joseph F. Smith," *Sunstone* 120 (November 2001): 30–34.
67. Kenney, "Before the Beard," 31.
68. "Died," *Desert News*, 17 February 1869, 31.
69. E. L. Sloan, comp., *The Salt Lake City Directory and Business Guide for 1869* (Salt Lake City, UT: E. L. Sloan & Co., 1869), 138.
70. The Salt Lake Cemetery was established in 1848, soon after the Saints arrived in the Salt Lake Valley.

View of Salt Lake City Cemetery, located northeast of the city, 1868, photograph by Charles W. Carter, Salt Lake City, Utah. The Wells Fargo Stable is seen in the foreground with the white fence that enclosed the cemetery clearly visible in the background on the bench above the buildings. Courtesy of CHL.

STRAINED RELATIONSHIP WITH SMITH FAMILY RELATIVES

During the second half of the 1860s, Joseph F. defended the Church against attacks by his cousins, the sons of Joseph Smith Jr. and Emma Hale Smith. Alexander Hale Smith and David Hyrum Smith had come to Utah as missionaries for the RLDS Church. Joseph F. reported in a letter to Martha Ann that they were "on their way out here to preach against polygamy and convert the Brighamit's."[71]

The cousins' relationship grew strained in a public meeting when Alexander denounced Brigham Young and plural marriage and Joseph F., now an Apostle and an influential member of Hyrum Smith's family, stood and firmly defended Young's succession to the Presidency and the Church's practice of plural marriage.[72] An RLDS missionary in attendance reported to Joseph Smith III what happened next in the exchange. "After he [Joseph F.] sat down Bro. Alexander followed

71. See Joseph F. to Martha Ann, 21 June 1869, herein.

72. See Charles W. Turner, "Joseph Smith III and the Mormons of Utah" (PhD diss., Graduate Theological Union, 1985), 264; and Roger D. Launius, *Joseph Smith III: Pragmatic Prophet* (Urbana: University of Illinois Press, 1988), 224–25. Surprised at how little evidence existed regarding the origins of plural marriage in Nauvoo, Joseph F. began collecting statements affirming that the Prophet Joseph Smith taught and practiced plural marriage. See "Affidavits about Celestial Marriage, 1869–1915."

him and gave him one of the worst castigations that I ever saw any person receive."[73] The public war of words had begun, and during this first decade of interaction between the two churches, there appeared to be no way to heal the divide.

As his letters to Martha Ann indicate, Joseph F. felt that his two cousins, "however much we may love them and pray for their good," were in "the clutches of vile apostates" and were being influenced by the same spirit that led mobs to murder their father and uncle.[74] After bidding them goodbye, Joseph F. noted that they had "treated me very coldly" and had "lied about me to boot."[75] The two Smith brothers had hoped to persuade many of the Utah Saints to see the error of their ways and to unite them with the "purified" form of belief and practice.[76] Much to their disappointment, however, Alexander and David's visit had little impact on the Saints in Utah.[77]

The decade ended with both families vigorously and passionately attempting to define the legacies of their martyred forebears.

Joseph F. Smith, Martha Ann Smith Harris, Mercy Rachel Fielding Thompson, and Mary Jane Thompson Taylor, ca. 1868. Courtesy of Carole Call King.

73. "Pres. Smith," *True Latter Day Saints' Herald*, 15 December 1866, 177.
74. See Joseph F. to Martha Ann, 17 August 1869, herein.
75. Joseph F., journal, 23 November 1869.
76. See Launius, *Joseph Smith III*, 220–21.
77. See Turner, "Joseph Smith III and the Mormons of Utah," 273; and Launius, *Joseph Smith III*, 227.

MARTHA ANN'S GROWING FAMILY

Martha's husband William completed his mission to England in 1858. In the ensuing decade, Martha Ann gave birth to four children: Joseph Albert (1861–1911) in Provo, Hyrum Smith (1863–1924) in Salt Lake City, Mary Emily (1865–1947) in Salt Lake City, and Franklin Hill (1867–1947) in Salt Lake City. Joseph F.'s journals are filled with references concerning Martha Ann's family. Three such entries appear below, the first two referring to the birth of Joseph Albert.

> 6 October 1861: "This morning I received a letter from Mary Jane Taylor and Sister Randall. Good news. All are well. Martha An has another Boy they call him Joseph."[78]

> 21 October 1861: "Came to Sheffield by the first Train found a letter awaiting me from Bro. William Harris grand news from home. Martha Ann has another fine Son."[79]

> 26 October 1861: "I mailed my Letter to William Harris."[80]

In one of his account books six years later, he noted the birth of another nephew: "1867. Wednesday. Sep. 11—Martha Ann gave birth to a fine boy—weighing 10 lbs. and 14 oz. 5.58. a.m."[81]

Always keen to support his sister, Joseph F. took an opportunity to remind William Jasper that Martha Ann was a "faithful and affectionate" wife:

> Your much desired, welcome and interesting letter of Sept 6th came duly to hand last Saturday. It was about one month and 13 days on the way. If this makes the trip as readily, it will reach you about the 1st of December or at Christmas. So trusting its lucky God will guard and guide it. I will suppose you to receive it then and will say, when you are surrounded by merriment and real enjoyment, engaged in the merry dance, perhaps and above all, at your own fireside with little joseph on your knee, and prattling Willie by your side with faithful and affectionate Martha at your elbow preparing delicacies for the usual Christmas enjoyments.[82]

William Jasper provided for his family during this decade by working at a number of different jobs, including stints as a police officer[83] and as a freighter moving goods from Salt Lake City to forts and communities along the Salmon River in Idaho. He also served for three months in the Black Hawk War (1865–72) as second lieutenant in Heber C. Kimball's company.[84] In 1867 William Jasper

---

78. Joseph F., journal, 6 October 1862.
79. Joseph F., journal, 21 October 1862.
80. Joseph F., journal, 26 October 1862.
81. Joseph F., notebook, November 1866–December 1871.
82. Joseph F. to William Jasper Harris, 24 October 1861.
83. Joseph F. mentioned William Jasper in an entry in the Historian's Office journal during this period and identified him as a policeman: "Specimans of red sand, rock of various kinds were brought in by Bros. Jacobs & Mr. Harris (policeman) from the reported diggings up City Creek, which has made some excitement for a day or two. These brethren reported they only found one man digging who owned he had not found any gold yet." See Historian's Office journal, 1 June 1866–1 June 1868, 26 August 1866, 52.
84. See Carole Call King, "History of Martha Ann Smith Harris, 1841–1923" (unpublished manuscript in the editors' possession), 4; and Carole Call King, "History of William Jasper Harris, 1841–1921" (paper presented at monthly meeting of the Daughters of Utah Pioneers, copy in the editors' possession), 4.

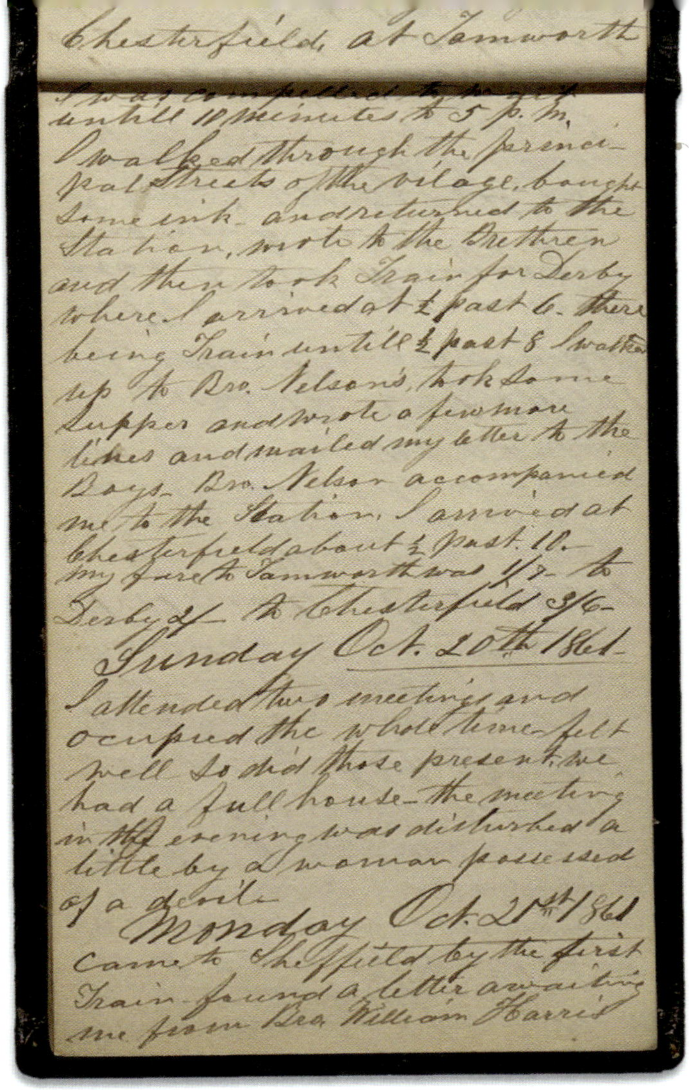

Chesterfield, at Tamworth

I was compelled to wait untill 10 minutes to 5 p.m. I walked through the principal Streets of the village, bought some ink and returned to the Station, wrote to the Brethren and then took Train for Derby where I arrived at ½ past 6. there being Train untill ½ past 8 I walked up to Bro. Nelson's, took some Supper and wrote a few more lines and mailed my letter to the Boys. Bro. Nelson accompanied me to the Station. I arrived at Chesterfield about ½ past 10. my fare to Tamworth was 1/7 to Derby 2/- to Chesterfield 3/6-

Sunday Oct. 20th 1861-

I attended two meetings and occupied the whole time felt well so did those present. we had a full house—the meeting in the evening was disturbed a little by a woman possessed of a devil

Monday Oct. 21st 1861

Came to Sheffield by the first Train found a letter awaiting me from Bro. William Harris

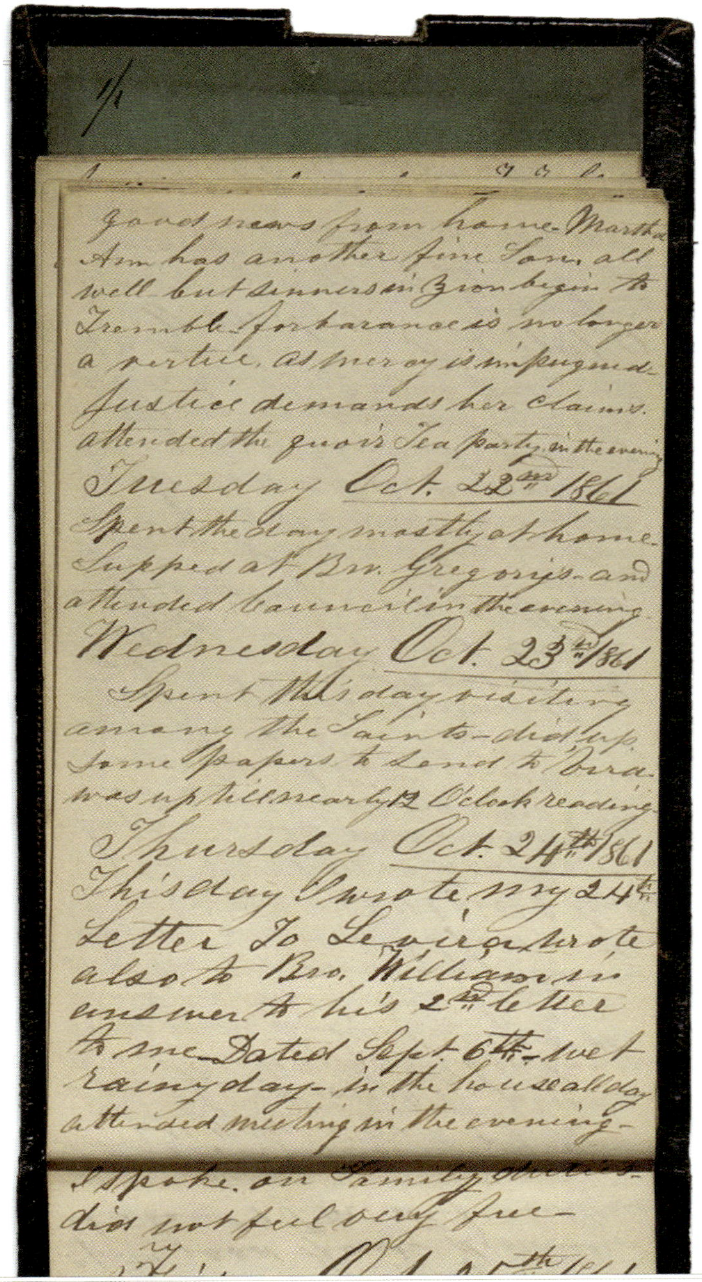

good news from home Martha Ann has another fine Son. all well but sinners in Zion begin to Tremble forbearance is no longer a virtue. as mercy is impugned justice demands her claims. attended the quoir Tea party in the evening

Tuesday Oct. 22nd 1861

Spent the day mostly at home. Supped at Bro. Gregory's and attended Council in the evening

Wednesday Oct. 23rd 1861

Spent this day visiting among the Saints—did up some papers to send to [illegible] was up till nearly 12 Oclock reading

Thursday Oct. 24th 1861

This day I wrote my 24th Letter to Levira. wrote also to Bro. William in answer to his 2nd letter to me Dated Sept. 6th—wet rainy day—in the house all day attended meeting in the evening—

I spoke on family duties did not feel very free

Joseph F.'s journal entry for 21 October 1861. He mentions receiving a letter from his brother-in-law, William Jasper Harris, announcing the birth of Martha Ann's second child, Joseph Albert Harris, who was born on 19 August 1861. Courtesy of CHL.

was listed in the Salt Lake City directory as living within the Sixteenth Ward boundary: "Harris Wm. Policeman, res 16th wd, w s 2nd W Bet 1st N and N Temple."[85]

Martha Ann, like most other pioneer women, played a significant role in the family economy. One such contribution was sewing gloves, a skill she learned in Salt Lake City after paying for a six-week course. Martha Ann's children remembered that after her move to Utah County, she purchased buckskin (deer hides) and beaver furs from Native Americans, who often visited Provo to engage in trading. Sometimes she prepared the hides herself, but she often hired that work out to

85. G. Owens, comp., *Salt Lake City Directory, Including Business Directory, Provo, Springville, and Ogden, Utah Territory* (Salt Lake City, UT: G. Owens, 1867), 61.

Joseph Albert, Martha Ann (holding Hyrum), and William Jr., summer 1864. See the letter herein from Martha Ann to Joseph F., July 1864. Courtesy of Carole Call King.

Provo Woolen Mills,[86] especially for her finer gloves. Martha Ann was able to make forty to fifty pairs per year, selling them for as much as seven dollars each.

NEW HOME AND FAMILY CHALLENGES

William and Martha Ann moved to Provo sometime after the birth of young Franklin Hill.[87] They and their five children settled into a two-room adobe home owned by William's stepfather, A. O. Smoot, located on the southwest corner of Second South and Third West. After their arrival in Utah Valley, William Jasper participated in discovering the Mammoth Mine in the Tintic Mining District in Juab County. He and his sons mined there, among other locations, for many years without any significant success.

Martha Ann experienced poor health during much of the 1860s. This was particularly hard for her young family when William Jasper was away from home for long periods of time. On one such journey, William Jasper wrote to Martha Ann, "I assure you that I will come Just as soon as I can for I feel uneasy about you and am afraid you are not well and I know how scantily you are provided

86. Provo Woolen Mills, established in 1872, was Utah's first large factory. See Joseph F. to Martha Ann, 9 February 1875, 26 November 1875, 11 July 1876, and 5 February 1915, herein.
87. The family's move may have coincided with the move of William Jasper's mother to Provo in early 1868.

for food and I realize how good & patient you are and our dear little ones are content with what we set before them God bless you and them and keep you from sickness my thoughts day and night is how I can better our condition."[88]

William Jasper worked hard to provide for his family, and his letters to his wife show fatherly concern for his children and the well-being of Martha Ann. For example, in August 1869 he advised his wife to have their children vaccinated against a smallpox outbreak that occurred in Jordan, Salt Lake County, Utah. To the children he wrote, "Willie and Jody and Hyrum be good boys and minde Ma help her and tend to your pig and cut wood and don't run away and get in the watter and Mary be a good girl and Frank if you ain't a good boy Pa will attend to you when he comes home."[89]

Homes of William Jasper and Martha Ann Smith Harris on the southwest corner of Second South and Third West in Provo, Utah County, Utah Territory, ca. 1895. Left to right (adults): Sarah, William Jasper, Martha Ann, and Zina holding baby. Their first home in Provo was the adobe structure on the right. They eventually built the larger home on the left in about 1890. Although substantially remodeled, the second home still stands today at 214 South 300 West in Provo. Courtesy of CHL.

88. William Jasper Harris to Martha Ann, 7 August 1869, transcribed in Ruth Mae Harris, *Martha Ann, Daughter of Hyrum and Mary Fielding Smith* (Orem, UT: published by the author, 2002), 141–42.
89. William Jasper Harris to Martha Ann, 7 August 1869, transcribed in Harris, *Martha Ann*, 141–42.

SUMMARY

By December 1869, Joseph F. was thirty-one years old, married to Julina Lambson and Sarah Ellen Richards and the father of three living children and one adopted son, Edward Arthur. Joseph F. and Sarah Ellen had buried an infant, Sarah Ella, who died only days after her birth in February 1869. He and his families lived in Salt Lake City in a single-family dwelling known as the "Homestead."

Martha Ann was twenty-eight years old at the end of the decade. She and William Jasper were the parents of five living children. The family resided in Provo and established roots in this frontier community that lasted until they died.[90]

Mary Emily, Martha Ann, and Franklin Hill Harris, ca. 1868. Courtesy of Carole Call King.

Joseph F.'s journal during the 1860s reveals a remarkable and prodigious correspondence effort. For example, he noted in 1862, "I wrote to President Kimball, and, also, a letter of 12 pages to Uncle Fielding, Aunt Hannah Fielding, Aunt Thompson, Mary Jane Taylor, and Martha Ann Harris. Descriptive of my visit to my relatives at Preston, Also mailed 6 nos. of the 'Star' with a drawing of the Great International Exibition building to Leavira."[91]

Interestingly, no envelopes from this decade have survived. Additionally, no letters between Joseph F. and Martha Ann exist for the period September 1864–May 1868, inclusive. One partial explanation may be that Joseph F. did not serve a mission during this period, making it easier for them to communicate in person.

Though their individual and family responsibilities changed, Joseph F. and Martha Ann continued to express their love and support for each other through the letters written between them during the 1860s. Since Joseph F.'s responsibilities were often focused on the public affairs of the time, some of his letters to Martha Ann provide a window into the political, social, and religious affairs of the period. In contrast, Martha Ann's responsibilities were almost exclusively focused on her family and home life, and as might be expected, her letters provide a remarkable window into pioneer life on the Latter-day Saint frontier.

90. The Harrises also resided in Pleasant Grove, north of Provo in Utah County, for a brief period; see the 1880 US Census, C, 296. At the beginning of the twenty-first century, some of their descendants still lived in Utah Valley.
91. Joseph F., journal, 29 April 1862.

Letters

JOSEPH F. TO MARTHA ANN AND WILLIAM, 28 JULY 1860

William Harris[1]
42 Islington Liverpool England[2]
July 28th 1860[3]

Dear Bro. & Sister:—

William & Martha.— You must excuse me for writing to boath at once. and upon the same sheet,—but you know ye "twane one,"[4] so I shall address you as such. I shall not be able to write much, but you must make allowances for time distance, the number I have to write to &c &c. I would like to write to every one of my filks, and am going to some time, just to get them to write to me, in return.—

I expect that "Ould England" is about the same as it was when you were here,[5] this place is fully as nice a place as I had expected it to be. I like it better than I do N. Y.— I expect to start tomorrow for Leeds, Sheffield pasterate,[6] with Samuel,[7] we have recieved no deffinate

1. William Jasper Harris and Martha Ann lived in Salt Lake City at this time. Their first son, William Jasper Harris Jr., was born on 4 August 1859 in Salt Lake City. While *Jr.* was not part of his birth name, the editors have used it to clarify the relationship between father and son. The abbreviation *Jr.* appears on his headstone in the Provo City Cemetery. See Carole Call King, "History of William Jasper Harris, 1841–1921" (paper presented at monthly meeting of the Daughters of Utah Pioneers, copy in the editors' possession), 4.
2. Church headquarters in the British Isles and the publication office for the *Millennial Star* between 1855 and 1905.
3. Joseph F. was twenty-one, and Martha Ann was nineteen. This letter was written the day after Joseph F. arrived in England; see Joseph F., journal, 27 July 1860.
4. See Matthew 19:5.
5. William served in the England Mission for about sixteen months in 1856–57.
6. Franklin D. Richards, one of the Twelve Apostles, created the position of pastor in 1852 during the time he served as the president of the British Mission. This new and unique administrative position, limited to the British Isles, placed a mature missionary between the mission president and the conference president. Pastors presided over a "pastorate," which included several mission conferences or districts. A mission conference included several congregations known as branches. Branch presidents presided in the local congregations. See William G. Hartley, "LDS Pastors and Pastorates, 1852–55," in *Mormons in Early Victorian Britain*, ed. Richard L. Jensen and Malcolm Thorp (Salt Lake City, UT: University of Utah Press, 1989), 194–95.
7. Samuel Harrison Bailey Smith was the cousin of Joseph F. and Martha Ann and a brother-in-law to Joseph F. following his marriage to Levira. He was born to Samuel Harrison Smith and Mary Bailey, making him Levira's half brother. See biographical register, "Smith, Samuel Harrison Bailey."

appointments, and will not I suppose, till Conferance. I calculate to visit all I can till then. I want to see my folks,[8] the Country, the Brethren all feel well. [**p. 2**] I am glad to hear that you have got the sheep togather. I hope they will be prospered and you too, and I believe you will be. keep up good courage any how. our good times may perhaps come yet.

I hope you may have ~~go~~ good luck in trading Fanny[9] to advantage.[10] I told John[11] if you did not—or could not trad her—he could have the use of her when he needed her if you, were not useing her. but trade her if you can, to advantage. tell, William Freeman[12] to try and finde my Cow~~s~~s and I will see that the Cows shall pay him for his trouble.[13] keep an eye out for them yoursilf. who ever finds them shall be entitled to Calvs enough to well pay them for their trouble, you may set that down.

Give my love to your Mother Bro. and Sister Smoot,[14] to all enquireing friends, John Vance[15] and kiss little Willie,[16]—bless him—for me. I am ever faithfully & affectionately your brother Joseph

MARTHA ANN TO JOSEPH F., 26 SEPTEMBER 1860

G S L City Utah Teritory Sept 26 1860[17]

My dear brother it is with the pleasure that I take my pen in hand to write you a few lines to let you know how we are all gitting along at the preasent time we are all tolerable well at preasant and hope that this scroll will find you enjoying the bleasing of health. we have been vry poorly along back for fore or five weaks but we are some better now. Williams[18] health is not very any of the time[19] yet he keps at work early and lately he is getting in his pradce hay and wood. he thinks of going down to Californa this winter. thare fore he will have a great deal to do before he starts. I am allmost ashamed that I have not written to you before this time but I thaught

8. Fielding family members.
9. Likely one of the family farm animals.
10. Martha Ann's husband eventually made the trade. See Joseph F. to Martha Ann, 15 December 1860, herein.
11. Likely refers to John Smith.
12. William Hamblin Freeman was a nephew of Abraham O. Smoot. See biographical register, "Freeman, William Hamblin."
13. Most cattle in Utah Territory roamed on unimproved land, foraging at will. Local Utah newspapers often contained advertisements about lost cattle. See, for example, "Come Get your Cattle," *Deseret News*, 13 February 1861, 400. Owners typically branded their cattle to help identify the animals belonging to them.
14. Emily Hill, Abraham O. Smoot, and Margaret Thompson McMeans.
15. Likely John Vance, a bishop in Salt Lake City. See biographical register, "Vance, John."
16. William Jasper Harris Jr. was born on 4 August 1859. See biographical register, "Harris, William Jasper Jr."
17. Earlier in the month, Joseph F. wrote Martha Ann a letter: "Spent the afternoon writing to Levira, Martha Ann, Heber, & Joseph Fielding." Joseph F., journal, 5 September 1850; the letter is not extant. He continued writing on the following day, "Left Hull this morning for Sheffield traveled per Packet 30 miles then took train changed three times and arrived safely about 1 p.m. spent the afternoon writing to Levira, Martha Ann, and Heber and Joseph Feilding." Joseph F., journal, 6 September 1860.
18. William Jasper Harris.
19. Apparently William was still suffering from effects of the lightning strike that nearly took his life on 18 May 1859. See "A Sad Occurrence," *Deseret News*, 25 May 1859, 1.

Martha Ann to Joseph F.,
26 September 1860 (p. 1)

G S L City Utah Territory Sept 26 1860

My dear Brother it is with the pleasure
that I take my pen in hand to write you a few lines
to let you know how we are all getting along at
the present time we are all tolerable well at present
and hope that this scroll will find you enjoying
the blessing of health. we have been very poorly [illegible]
back for four or five weeks but we are [illegible] better
now. William's health is not very [illegible] of the time
yet he keeps at work early and late. he is getting in
his winter hay and wood. he thinks of going down to
California this winter. therefore he will have a great
deal to do before he starts. I am allmost ashamed
that I have not written to you before this time
but I thought I would wait untill you got to England
and then I would know where to write to. so you
must excuse my carelessness, or as you might call it,
[illegible] to make me rejoice. She stayed
[illegible] days and [illegible] nights with me I was truly glad
to see her here safe. and in as good spirit as she
manifests. Jerusha has been down to my house she
was confined [illegible] she had a daughter and named it
[illegible] Martha [illegible] after sister [illegible] and
[illegible] the name by waiting
[illegible]
on her through her sickness however I did not like
the name [illegible] I done the best I could for her
and she went home when the baby was three weeks
old. I have not herd from them since that time.
we received your letter the last week and was
glad to hear that you had crossed the great ocean
in safety and was in good health and spirits
I was not only glad [illegible] thankful
to my heavenly father for his kindness to you.
William cannot write this time to you

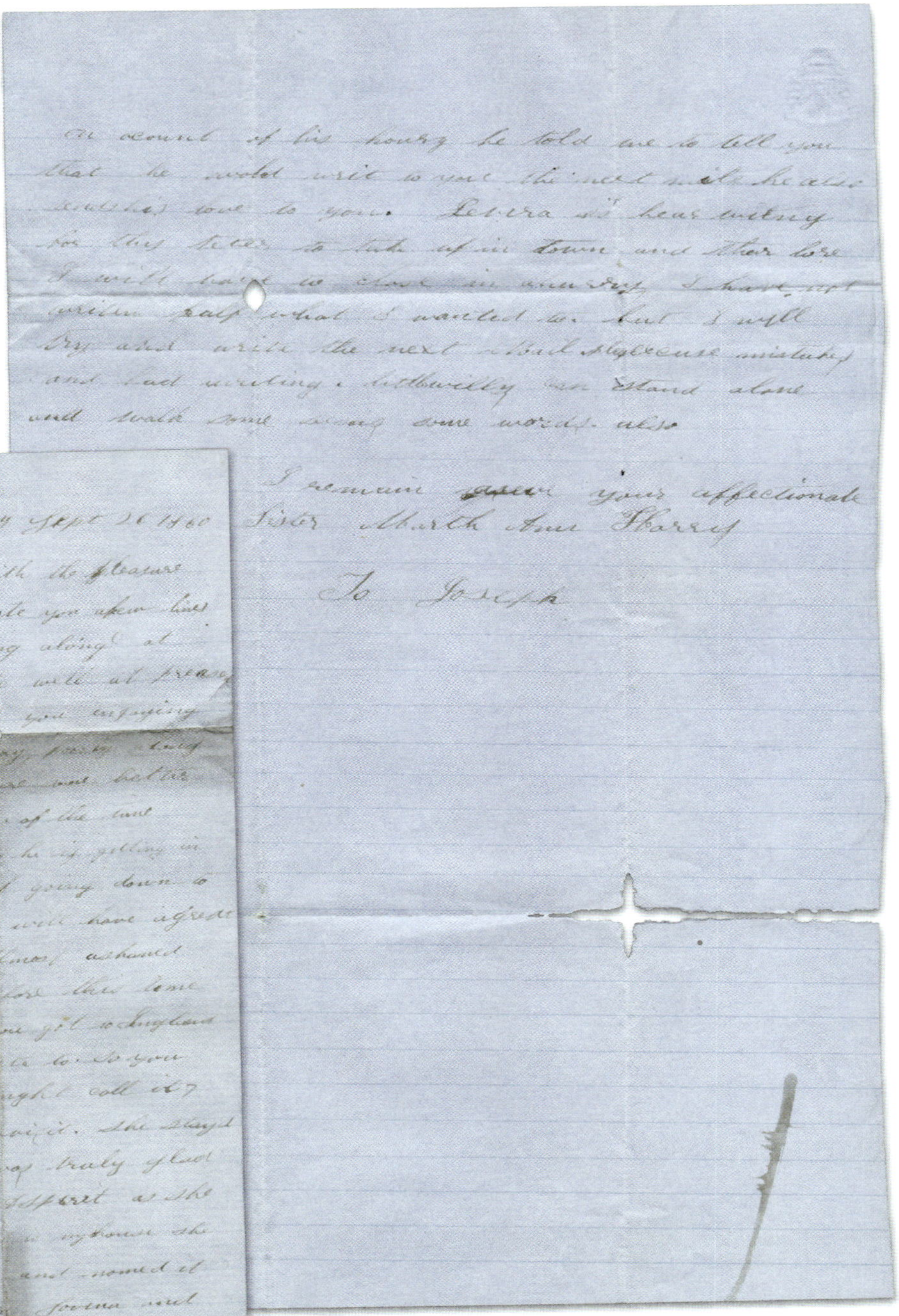
on acount of his hurry he told me to tell you
that he would write to you the next mail he also
sends his love to you. Levira is here waiting
for this letter to take up in town and therefore
I will have to close in a hurry. I have not
written half what I wanted to. but I will
try and write the next mail. please excuse mistakes
and bad writing. little Willy can stand alone
and walk some and say some words also

I remain ~~[illegible]~~ your affectionate
Sister Martha Ann Harris

To Joseph

Martha Ann to Joseph F.,
26 September 1860 (p. 2)

would write untill you got to Ingland and then I would know whare to write to. so you must excuse my carlessness on as you mght coll it, Lovina[20] has been hear to make me a visit. She stayd to days and too nights with me I was truly glad to see her hear safe and in a good as spirit as she manifests. Jerusha[21] has ben down to my house she was confine hear she had a daughter and named it ~~after me~~ Martha Lovina[22] after sister Lovina and [*16.5 x 3.2 cm tear along fold*] yet I earnd the name by waiting on her there in [*16.5 x 3.2 cm tear along fold*] her sicknes however I did not like the nome wich I done the best I could for her and she went home when the baby was thre weaks old. I have not herd from them sence that time we [*illegible strike-through*] recived your letter[23] the last maile and was glad to hear that you had crossed the great ocin in saifly. and <was ~~in~~> in good healh and spirrets I was not ~~oy~~ only glad Joseph but thankfol to my heavly father for his kindness to you.

William cannot write this time to you [**p. 2**] on acount of his houry he told me to tell you that he wold writ to you the next male he also sends his love to you. Levira[24] is hear witng for this letter to take up in town and thar fore I will have to close in a hurry I have not writen half what I wanted to. but I will try and write the next mail. ples excuse mistakes and bad writing. little willy[25] can stand alone and walk some sesas some words also

I remain as eve your affectionate Sister Marth Ann Harris

To Joseph

JOSEPH F. TO MARTHA ANN, 15 DECEMBER 1860

Martha Ann.[26]
Leeds[27] England Dec. 15th 1860

My Dear Sister Martha Ann:—

Yours of the 26th of September came to hand yesterday. and I nead scarcely to say that I was very much pleased to hear from you. it being the first scratch of a pen that I have recieved from any of my Relatives but Levira[28] and Cousin George A.[29] I guess you have all been waiting to get "a good ready". and I shall have it <all at> once by-and-by. Levira has been a good Girl

20. Lovina Smith.
21. Jerusha Smith.
22. Martha Lovina Pierce was born on 23 August 1860. See biographical register, "Pierce, Martha Lovina."
23. See Joseph F. to William Harris, 26 July 1860. Joseph F. noted that he had written another letter on 6 September, which is not extant: "I spent the afternoon writing to Levira, Martha Ann, and Heber and Joseph Fielding." Joseph F., journal, 6 September 1860.
24. Joseph F. married Levira Annette Clark Smith on 5 April 1859. See biographical register, "Smith, Levira Annette Clark."
25. William Jasper Harris Jr.
26. Written in large bold letters.
27. Leeds is located about seventy-three miles from Liverpool.
28. Levira Annette Clark Smith.
29. Letters from George A. Smith and Levira dated 28 and 22 June 1860 were sent in the same envelope. A subsequent letter from George A. is dated 11 October 1860. Joseph F. reported, "Recieved letters from Cousin G. A. Smith & Levira." Joseph F., journal, 8 August 1861. See biographical register, "Smith, George Albert."

Martha Ann

Leeds England Dec. 15th 1860

My Dear Sister Martha Ann:—

Yours of the 26th of September came to hand Yesterday. And I need scarcely to say that I was very much pleased to hear from you. it being the first scratch of a pen that I have received from any of My Relatives but Levira and Cousin George A. I guess you have all been waiting to get "a good ready," and I shall have it all at once by-and-by. Levira has been a good Girl in writing to me, she has given me an item of nearly all the news. And so you see I have been kept posted. but I am glad to hear from you. You were my best correspondent on the Islands. but of course Levira is expected to fill that place now. Nevertheless you must not suppose you are wholly exhonorated, which I hope I will be able to make all understand ere long.

My helth is good. as is also the case with Samuel who is here, I came to this place from Sheffield last night. by Rail. a distance of over 40 miles. I was only about 2½ hours coming the whole distance. including all the stoppages. So you see we travel fast in this country. Cousins John L. And Jesse N.— Wm W. Cluff. and some 7 or 8 more have arrived in Liverpool but I have not seen them yet. but I believe they are all in good helth. And they had a speady passage.

I am very thankful that Lovina has at last got safely in the valley. I hope the blessings of the Allmighty will attend them. that all their Efforts to do good may be crowned with success.

Joseph F. to Martha Ann, 15 December 1860 (p. 1)

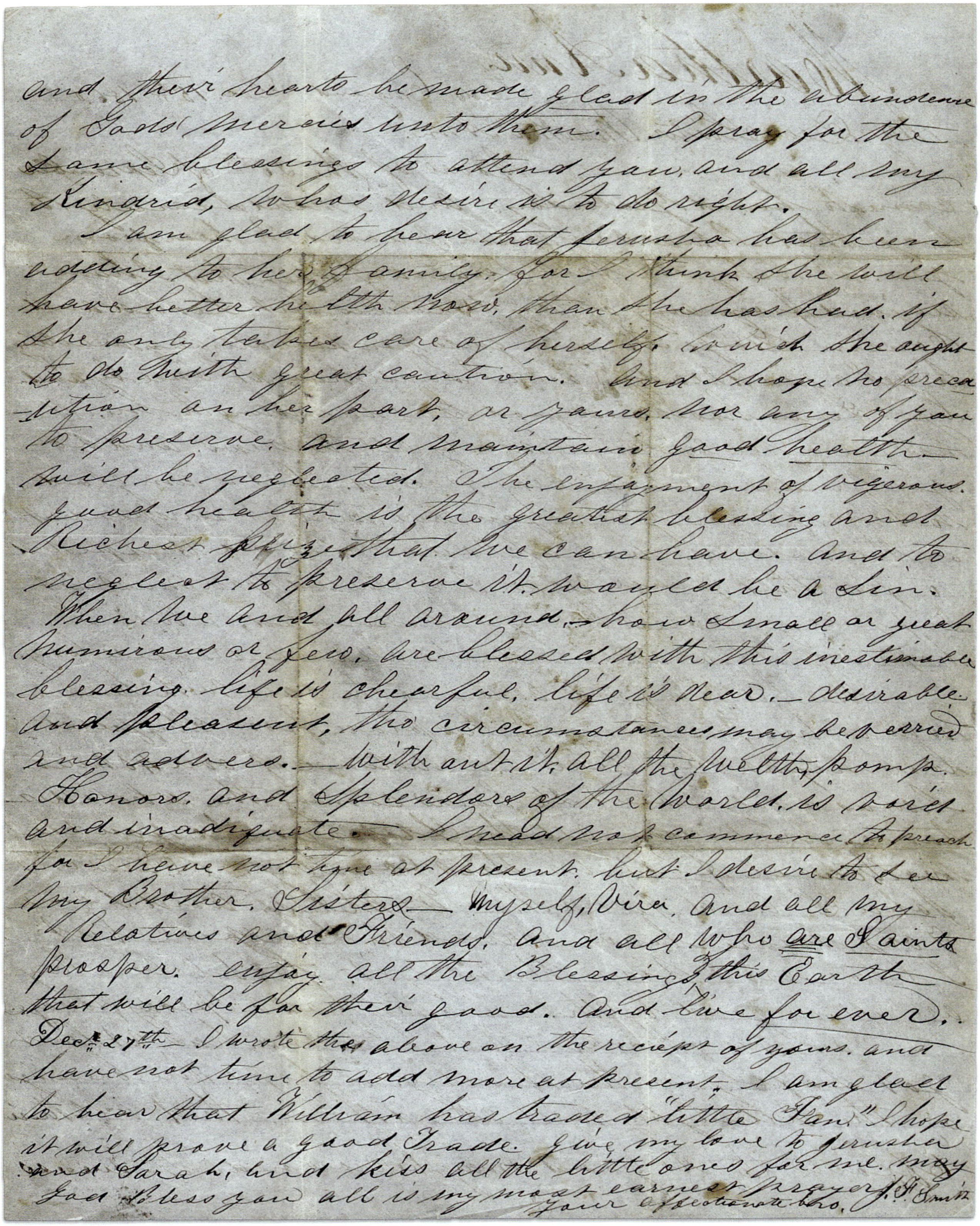

and their hearts be made glad in the abundance
of Gods mercies unto them. I pray for the
same blessings to attend you, and all my
Kindred, who has desire is to do right.
I am glad to hear that Jerusha has been
adding to her family, for I think she will
have better helth now, than she has had. if
she only takes care of herself, which she ought
to do with great caution. And I hope no preca-
-ution on her part, or yours, nor any of you
to preserve and maintain good health
will be neglected. The enjoyment of vigerous
good health is the greatest blessing and
Richest prize that we can have. And to
neglect to preserve it, would be a sin.
When we and all around,— how small or great
numerous or few, are blessed with this inestimable
blessing, life is cheerful, life is dear,— desirable
and pleasant, tho circumstances may be varried
and advers.— without it, all the welth, pomp,
Honors, and Splendors of the world, is void
and inadiquate.— I need not commence to preach
for I have not time at present. but I desire to see
my Brother, Sisters— myself, Vira, and all my
Relatives and Friends, and all who are Saints
prosper, enjoy all the Blessings this Earth
that will be for their good, and live for ever.
Dec. 27th— I wrote the above on the receipt of yours, and
have not time to add more at present. I am glad
to hear that William has traded "little Fan." I hope
it will prove a good Trade. give my love to Jerusha
and Sarah, and kiss all the little ones for me. may
God bless you all is my most earnest prayer. J. F. Smith
Your affectionate bro.

Joseph F. to Martha Ann, 15 December 1860 (p. 2)

in writing to me. She has given me an item of nearly all the news. and so you see I have been kept posted. but I am glad to hear from you. You were my best corispondent on the Islands. but of course Levira is expected to fill that place now. nevertheless you must not suppose you are wholly exhonorated, which I hope I will be able to make all understand ere long.

My helth is good, as is also the case with Samuel[30] who is here. I came to this place from Sheffield[31] last night by Rail, a distance of over 40 miles. I was only about 2½ hours coming the whole distance, including all the stopages. so you see we travel fast in this country. Cousins John L.[32] and Jessa N.[33]—Wm W. Cluff,[34] and some 7 or 8 more have arrived in Liverpool but I have not seen them yet. [*illegible strike-through*] I believe they are all in good helth. and they had a speady passage.

I am very thankful that Lovina[35] had at last got safely in the Valley. I hope the blessings of the Allmighty will attend them. that all their Efforts to do good may be crowned with success. [**p. 2**] and their hearts be made glad in the abundence of Gods' mercies unto them. I pray for the same blessings to attend you, and all my Kindrid, whos desire is to do right.

I am glad to hear that Jerusha[36] has been adding to her family, for I think she will have better helth now, than she has had. if she only takes care of herself, which she ought to do with great caution. and I hope no precaution on her part, or yours, nor any of you to preserve, and maintain good health—will be neglected. The enjoyment of vigerous, good health is the greatest blessing and Richest Prize that we can have. and to neglect to preserve it would be a sin.

When we and all around,—how small or great numirous or few, are blessed with this inestimable blessing, life is chearful, life is dear,—desirable and pleasent, tho' circumstances may be verried and advers.— with out it, all the welth, pomp, Honors, and Splendors of the world, is void and inadiquate. I nead not commence to preach for I have not time at present, but I desire to see my Brother, Sisters—myself, Vira[37] and all my Relatives and Friends, and all who are[38] Saints prosper. enjoy all the Blessings <of> this Earth that will be for their good. and live for ever. Decr 27th— I wrote the above on the reciept of yours, and have not time to add more at present. I am glad to hear that William has traded "little Fan."[39] I hope it will prove a good Trade. give my love to Jerusha and Sarah,[40] and kiss all the little ones for me.[41] may God Bless you all is my most earnest prayer J. F. Smith
your affectionate bro.

30. Samuel Harrison Bailey Smith, first cousin once removed. See biographical register, "Smith, Samuel Harrison Bailey."
31. Sheffield in Yorkshire was an important industrial town at the time.
32. Likely refers to John Lyman Smith, first cousin once removed to Joseph F. See biographical register, "Smith, John Lyman."
33. Jesse Nathaniel Smith, first cousin once removed to Joseph F., was on his way to preside over the Scandinavian Mission. See biographical register, "Smith, Jesse Nathaniel."
34. William Wallace Cluff, a close friend of Joseph F., was passing through England with Jesse Nathaniel Smith en route to the Scandinavian Mission. See biographical register, "Cluff, William Wallace."
35. Lovina Smith, Joseph F. and Martha Ann's older half sister, and her family arrived in the Salt Lake Valley in 1860.
36. Jerusha Smith, half sister of Joseph F. and Martha Ann.
37. Levira Annette Clark Smith, Joseph F.'s wife.
38. The word *are* is underlined four times.
39. Likely refers to the "Fanny" mentioned in Joseph F.'s previous letter, probably a farm animal. See Joseph F. to Martha Ann, 28 July 1860, herein.
40. Sarah Smith.
41. This would have included Martha Ann's own son, William Jasper Harris. Jr., born on 4 August 1859.

MARTHA ANN TO JOSEPH F., 20 DECEMBER 1860

G S L City Utah Dec 20 1860

My Dear brother Joseph

it is with [*illegible strike-through*] pleasure that I take my pen in han to write you a few lines to let you know how we are giting along. wer are all toolerable well at preasent and I hope that this may find you enjoying the same blessing. your letter came to hand the other day. and I can asure you that I was glad to hear from you for I had been very oneasy, about you on acont of a dream <that> I had. you said you had been sick but that you was some better when you <wrote> our letter. I feel to say Joseph, thank God that it was no worse with you than it was. I have been troubeld ~~with the~~ [*illegible strike-through*] wih the Disppey[42] this fall but I am better now

I am at home all alone to day with the exceptuon of little Willy[43] he has ben runing about the floor playing for the last to or thre ours he does not give me a chance to be lonesome. never. he is so good naturede and playfull that he would amuse alloste any pirson in the world. William[44] has gon to Richards Maxfields[45] on buisness to day if it is Sondays we all have to be governd by sircumstances you knowe. I have wrote to letters to you and we have recived to from you. William has not written any to you yet but he calculates to this mail I believe he will tell you all the patic<u>lars when he wrtes. Jerusha[46] has just gon home fom hear she has been down on visit [**p. 2**] <she was well> when she started home with the exception of a bad cold she has a sweet little girl[47] it is growing finely. Jerusha and her children Sarah[48] and her children, and sister Griffin.[49] Richard and Artimissa.[50] and allso Charles[51] ware all hear ~~last~~ weak agoe last Siturday on a visit they all happy hear at once. that was the day we got your letter I have not had a chance to writ to you sence untill to day I have been so busy I have fore [*illegible word*] famoly to do for now besides [*illegible strike-through*] ~~and~~ considerable company and so I hav enough to do to keep me out of mischief you see. I have been to see Levira twice Sarah twice Aunt fieldng[52] once Aunt Tompson[53] to or three times sence you have been gon. I think I have staiyd at home tolerable well and minded my own business I have not written to you very ofton I have but it is not becaus I do not think of you Joseph. for I do think of you both night and day and prey that my heavnly father may [*illegible strike-through*] gard and proptect you from all harm and danger and help you as it ware in the hollw of his hand. I do calculate to write more ofton when I git my hury over a little I have been a making up my

42. Likely dyspepsia (indigestion).
43. William Jasper Harris Jr.
44. William Jasper Harris.
45. Richard Dunwell Maxfield, brother-in-law to William Jasper Harris. See biographical register, "Maxfield, Richard Dunwell."
46. Jerusha Smith.
47. Probably referring to Martha Lovina Pierce, born on 23 August 1860.
48. Sarah Smith.
49. Likely Abigail Varney, mother-in-law to Sarah Smith.
50. Richard Maxfield and his wife Artimissa Ann Harris. See biographical register, "Harris, Artimissa Ann."
51. Likely Charles Emerson Griffin, husband of Sarah Smith.
52. Likely Hannah Greenwood, wife of Joseph Fielding.
53. Mercy Rachel Fielding.

winter clothng and knittng my stockings and gitting ready for winter. Levira has been to me sister and a friend in your absence both in sicness and in helth she has never for saken me and the more I git acqainted with her the better I like [**p. 3**] her. I am some like an i[⟠]nden I do not forgit kindnesses. nor mean treatment. rather, I have had three real ~~sick~~ sick spels during the fall a summer Levira was with me twice andone <the> best she could for me, so i ced to say whare thare is good mettle the more you <rub it> the briter it will shine

But I fear that I am growing tedious and not writing any thing that will eddefy you eather but you must do like the man did just consider from whence it came. O Joseph I do miss you so, I had no idear how much I would mis you untill you was gon. I can not help hinking of the good times that we had when you ware hear in the midst of us. but the time will slip away and we will <meet> again [*illegible strike-through*]

I sappoe you will have hird of the cruil death of little Gorge A[54] before this letter reaches you I could not posable believe it at first but was obliged to at last. I do pitty his poor mother she took it so very haar at first but she is more recacled now.[55]

I do not know that I have any thing more to write to you at preasent ~~so~~ and so I will bring my letter to a close please excuse all mistakes and ba ~~wr~~ writing. give <my> love to Samueel and tell him that I have not forgoten him and that I will write to him the first chance I git

May God bless you is the prayr of yor

Affectionate <sister> Martha Ann Harris [**p. 4**]

Rec$^{\underline{d}}$ & Ans$^{\underline{dpo}}$

JOSEPH F. TO MARTHA ANN AND WILLIAM, 29 JANUARY 1861

Jan. 29$^{\underline{th}}$ 1861
<u>Leads.</u>[56]
William Harris / Leeds Yorkshire England[57]
Marha Ann / January 29$^{\underline{th}}$ 1861[58]

My Dear Brother And Sister
William and Martha:—

54. George Albert Smith Jr. was killed on 2 November 1860 while serving as a missionary among the Navajo people with Jacob Hamblin in New Mexico Territory, present-day Arizona. See biographical register, "Smith, George Albert, Jr." See also Jacob Hamblin, *Jacob Hamblin: A Narrative of His Personal Experience, as a Frontiersman, Missionary to the Indians and Explorer*, ed. James A. Little, 2nd ed. (Salt Lake City, UT: Deseret News Press, 1909), 72–73. Joseph F. did not receive this letter until 29 January 1861 but had, as Martha Ann assumed, heard of the death beforehand. On 11 January he noted in his journal, "I heard a report that Cousin George A. Smith Jr. had been killed by the Indians somewhere near the 'great Desert.' I hope it is not true." On 16 January he noted in his journal that this report was confirmed by a *Deseret News* article.
55. Bathsheba Wilson Bigler.
56. Phonetic spelling for *Leeds*. Joseph F. noted that he spent ten shillings and eight pence on train fares from Leeds the next day. See Joseph F., 30 January 1861, [10]; notebook, 31 July 1860–8 August 1862.
57. "Tuesday, Jan 29th I wrote to George Gee and William and Martha Ann. . . . Attended a meeting at the pottery fields." Joseph F., journal, 29 January 1861.
58. Joseph F. was twenty-two, and Martha Ann was nineteen years old.

I am happy to say that your kinde favors of December 20th has just come to hand, and to say I was glad to hear from you would not express the feeling, nor do I expect to finde the word that will suffice to say I am now going to write you a long letter in return. In the first-place I am glad to hear that you are well.

God Bless you, and may you ever pro[*0.3 x 0.3 cm tear*]per, is the prayer of my heart.

I am happy to say that I am well, and I am getting along first-rate, for me. I am very thankful to get the desired information of my folks,[59] and shall not be long before I learn something of them. although at present I shall not be able to visit them, in conciquence of a scarcity of means. ~~it~~ It is hard times in England, and especially for the saints, and the encouraging (?)[60] fact is, there is no prospects of times brightening. The Difficulties of the U. S. only tends to increas the darkness, and the Blackness of the cloud of Trouble that hangs over England.[61] The intrests of the Two "worlds" are so closly connected, and so interwoven, that Sickness to one is pain to the other. and they can but feel <too> keenly the sorrows of each-other[62] **[p. 2]** I am rejoiced to hear that Cattle and Horse Thieves, are growing scarse in.[63] It is high time that they were gon where they belong.—[64]

I am glad that you have got along as well as you have, but sorry that you have lost your Mule, I hope you will find him again. It seems too Bad that animels are so un-safe on the range, but so it is, and I see no way of remidying the thing, unless, we can get pastures, and keep things constantly under our Eyes,—that you know requires a great deal of Means and Laber, or in other words, it wants "Capital"! I wish we had it, William, but the fact is, we have not, and if we ever do have it, we have got to make it. There is on[*0.2 x 0.4 cm tear along fold*] consolation William, if we ever do Make it we will know how to appreciate it, and enjoy it, I hope. There is no telling what Latter day saints will have to do; if they stick to the ship all will be right whether we have much or little.[65] If we can only learn to feel reconsiled to the will of the Almight, and do as we are told I do not fear but all will come out right.

My little experiance has proven this Latter day work, to be of good material, and I am now content, let what will come, and I trust I shall for ever be able to keep my ground and be found among the faithful and the doing, of Gods People. I have partly learned one thing, i.e. I

---

59. Joseph F. is referring to his mother's family, the Fieldings.
60. In his letters, Joseph F. sometimes included a question mark in parentheses, apparently to indicate uncertain spellings or to signal irony.
61. Tension continued to build in the United States as a result of the election of Abraham Lincoln on 6 November 1860 to the office of president. South Carolina seceded from the Union in December, and by the end of January 1861, six more states followed. In April the US Civil War began when Confederate forces fired on the federal fortification at Fort Sumter in Charleston Harbor in South Carolina.
62. See Amanda Foreman, *A World on Fire: Britain's Crucial Role in the American Civil War* (New York: Random House, 2011).
63. In 1860 there were 34,094 head of cattle in Utah Territory, with 5,126 in Salt Lake Valley alone. See Donald D. Walker, "The Cattle Industry of Utah, 1850–1900: An Historical Profile," *Utah Historical Quarterly* 32, no. 3 (Summer 1964): 182–97.
64. Several waves of migrations swept across the landscape in Utah Territory during the second half of the nineteenth century, including a larger number of religiously devout and hardworking people, primarily Latter-day Saints. Another group of immigrants was composed of gunfighters, outlaws, cattle rustlers, and horse thieves. It has been observed that some outlaws became Latter-day Saints and some baptized members of the Church became outlaws, the most famous being Robert LeRoy Parker (1866–1909?), known as Butch Cassidy.
65. Brigham Young often referred to the Church as the "Old Ship Zion." See, for example, Brigham Young, "Discourse," *Deseret News*, 27 January 1858, 373; and Brigham Young, "Remarks," *Deseret News*, 18 November 1857, 291.

am mighty small, and don't know much—if anything. [**p. 3**] and I see a great deal more to learn every day and still experiance is such a slow-and-sure School Teacher that I do not seem to make scarcely any proggress in my lessons, but I hope—"in patience to possess my soul"[66] and struggle unceasingly t[*0.6 x 2.7 cm vertical tear along fold*] the end.

It is but an easy matter to make good resolutions, the duce[67] of it is to carry them out.

Well, I'll quit preaching, and talk about something els— I have been writing to cousin Silas S.[68] and George Gee,[69] till I recieved your letter, and I am getting tired of writing, but I will try and weary your patience before I quit. You say that you were having a little snow for Christmas. That sounds encouraging, for there will be a chance to have a sleigh-ride any how! something that I have not seen in the country.

The people here are very industrious, they never have a chance of enjoying the pleasure of a sleigh-ride. The Rich can find scar[*4.1 x 0.9 cm tear along folds*] [*4.1 x 0.9 cm tear along folds*]nough time to lay plan[*1.7 x 1.3 cm tear along folds*] to amass their glit[*4.1 x 0.9 cm tear along folds*]ring pile, and count their dust, and reccon up the results of pending evils, and bind beneath their iron yoke of Tyrany, their less fortunate, but equally as noble; fellow man, and compell them to li[◊]e from "hand to mouth," and utterly dependant upon them, without the value of a foituites' food to call their own! O! land of liberty! "Enlightened," "Christian England!" Give me the free air of our mountain Home, to all the musty [**p. 4**] glories of this christian Land! I had rather roam the Hill tops—breath the pure air, and associate with the Loved ones at—mountains, than roal in "Englands clover" and enjoy (?) all the luxuries of this free (?) and easy (?) world. I mean England, of course we are apt to have peculiar notions of our own, about things.

Martha speakes of little Willie,[70] sais he is a little busy fellow, no one could get lonesome where he was; I am glad of that I would like to see him, and all the rest of you, but "yet a little" longer, "and th[*0.3 x 0.3 cm tear on fold*]n"! I hope you will enjoy your selves a little for me, as I have none here only such as are congenial to older and more sober heads.— Tho' I get along first-rate.

William, pleas give my love to all enquiring friends, you must excuse prolixity,[71] and bad writing, and mistakes, and all that sort of thing. I hardly know what I have said, as I have written extempore,—without much re[*2.5 x 1 cm tear along fold*]tion. Any thing to fill up the paper and tire you out, [*1.6 x 1.3 cm tear along fold*] matter whether it is interresting or not. Kiss little Will, for me, and the rest of the little ones and take care of yourselves. My kinde love to your Mother, Sister Smoot,[72] and all the family. God Bless you all,—and you William in particular to enable you to read this! Well, my heart is good, my Desire is good, if I am not always Sane. no more this time, I am ever your Bro. J. F. Smith

66. See Luke 21:19.
67. *Duce* is a variant form of the word *deuce*, which is often used in "exclamatory and interjectional phrases . . . as a mere expression of impatience or emphasis." *Oxford English Dictionary*, s.v. "deuce."
68. Likely Silas Sanford Smith, first cousin once removed to Joseph F. and Martha Ann.
69. George Washington Gee II was second cousin to Joseph F. and Martha Ann.
70. William Jasper Harris Jr.
71. A word meaning "extended to great, unnecessary, or tedious length; long and wordy." Dictionary.com, s.v. "prolixity."
72. Likely refers to Emily Hill, mother-in-law to Martha Ann and Margaret Thompson McMeans, both wives of Abraham O. Smoot.

MARTHA ANN TO JOSEPH F., 12 MARCH 1861

G S L City Utah Teritory March the 12 <1861>

My dear Brother Joseph ~~I take my~~

Onse again I take the pen in hand to write you a few lines but I hardly know what will bee the most intersting to you. however we are all to begin with, and doing the best we can under the circumstancs that we are placed. we are [*illegible strike-through*] living in the same place we ware when you left home. and we do not know whare we shahall move to yet cirton. but we shall have to moove some whare and that before long. for the folks wants to moove in. they are now wating to come in.[73] I am gitting tierd of renting houses for it is like throwing mo<n>ey away we will try to bye us a place the next time.[74] he talks of byeing a little house of brother Houtses[75] but that is not setled yet. I was to leviras one day last weak I spent the day with her and enjoyd my self first rate came home in the evnig. William is one of the poliece and has been for over 2 months he has onley been home to git his meals threw the day. so you see that I have spend spent the winter alone with the exption of little Willey he is so [*illegible word*] mischevioses that he does not give me mutch chance to be lonesom for as fast as he git out off one peace of mischief he is in to another. he is as quick as a flash. that is some of his writing above I was writing and I got up to turn a lof of bread in the oven and he was in my [**p. 2**] chair in a moment and had the pen[76] he is so fat and harty now <with> red cheaks but he does not talk mutch yet I think the will before long though. he trys hard enoug at eny rate.

William has not got cows yet for the stove ~~yet~~ but he is trying to all the time now ~~he will~~ <he> ~~as you wish as he can~~ William is is honnest Joseph do not think he would is cheat you. it has been a very hard winter on cattle and he thaught it best not to git cows to kep over I do hope that you will not loose any thing by letting us have the stove for he wil eather git cows that have calvs or those that are that way.

John[77] has moved in town I sapose ~~E~~ Levira has told you though she wrote last weak Aunt T[78] to I was to have written but I did not git ink enor pen in time to git it in the mail ~~in time~~ and now I have got it it is all most imposable to write wih it. it is to poor how ever you must excuse it this time as fine paper is scarse. and I can not wat to git another pen. we have been to 5 partys this winter and enjoyd our selves first rate Vira[79] has been to 2 with us one to the Seventys hall[80] and one to your Corum[81] party at the court house[82] we had a very nice party thare [**p. 3**]

---

73. William and Martha Ann were living in Salt Lake City at this time.
74. Within a short time, William and Martha Ann bought a home. See Martha Ann to Joseph F., 30 May 1861, herein.
75. Jacob Houtz. See biographical register, "Houtz, Jacob."
76. In the original letter, faint childish scribbles are visible in the lower right corner and center of the page.
77. John Smith.
78. Likely Mercy Rachel Fielding.
79. Levira Annette Clark Smith.
80. Located on the west side of First East (currently State Street) between First and Second South Streets, the Seventy Hall was built in the 1850s. See E. L. Sloan, comp., *The Salt Lake City Directory and Business Guide for 1869* (Salt Lake City, UT: E. L. Sloan & Co., 1869), 72, 75.
81. Quorum. William was ordained a Seventy on 8 April 1855 by J. S. Scofield.
82. Located on the northeast corner of the intersection of Second West (currently Third West) and Second South Streets, the Salt Lake County Court House was built in the 1850s. See Sloan, *Salt Lake City Directory*, 71, 74.

We also have been to one in the Asembly rooms the 13th Ward Schooll House [83]and 2 too <the> Social Hall.[84] We had a party[85] for the handcart boyz[86] those that drew the Cart back you know. this was in the Socal Hall we had a splended party Bro Brigham and Bro Cimbol[87] ware thare to chear the hand carts they said. I had the privlag of dancng with them both. they feel first now. they are very lvly and chearfull Bro Weells[88] was thare but he did not join in the dance. he has been very sick all all winter but he is better now. so Bro B gave us a breaf discourse but every word came to the point it was sirtinly very good O how I have longed to see you my brother in our social partys this past winter. but that was not to be. but I do hope and prey that the time will not be long eare we can meat in such places and by the fire side allo. but the will of the lord be done in all things and I have all confidence in you Josseph that you will do wrigh so near as you can. if we ~~of~~ all do as near ~~wrin~~ rite as we know how we are prity shure of salvation but I fear that I do not do that all the time allthough it is ~~yay~~ my desire to do so but humane nature is prone to go astray from the path~~s~~ truth and virtue [**p. 4**]

The trials of the present day ~~re~~
Require the saints to watch and prey
That they may keep the narrow way
To the Selestuel glory[89]
this is verley so

William traided of that larg span of horses for a yoak ~~ch~~ cattle and a horse last fal and turned them out on the range and one of the cattle died in the cold weather. and ~~t~~he has never found his mule yet so you see we have some bad luck with the rest of our fellow creatures however we must not complain for God is good and knnd

William sends his best respects to you ~~well I do not~~

I am ashamed to send this scroll to you Joseph. you must not show it to any boddy I will try and do better next time. we have received 3 letters from you one to W[90] and 2 to mee

May ~~G~~ [*illegible strike-through*] God bles you for ever is the prair of your Sister ~~M~~ Martha Ann Harris

give my love to Samuel[91] <and tell him to me>

83. Located on the north side of Second South between First and Second East, the Thirteenth Ward Assembly Rooms building was constructed during the 1850s. See E. L. Sloan, *Gazetteer of Utah and Salt Lake City Directory* (Salt Lake City, UT: Salt Lake Herald and Publishing Company, 1874), 176.
84. Located on the east side of First East (current designation State Street) between South Temple and First South, the Social Hall was built in the early 1850s. See Sloan, *Salt Lake City Directory*, 72, 75.
85. A "social party" was given by President Brigham Young on 6 February 1861 at the Social Hall, where there was dancing, musical performances, recitations, and some remarks by President Young. "President Young's Social Party," *Deseret News*, 13 February 1861, 396.
86. Some twenty-seven rescuers helped at the Sweetwater crossing on 4 November 1856. See Chad M. Orton, "The Martin Handcart Company at the Sweetwater: Another Look," *BYU Studies* 45, no. 3 (2006): 4–37.
87. Brigham Young and Heber Chase Kimball.
88. Likely Daniel Hammer Wells, Second Counselor to President Brigham Young in the First Presidency. See biographical register, "Wells, Daniel Hammer."
89. Martha Ann is quoting from Eliza R. Snow's poem "Celestial Glory." See Eliza R. Snow, *Poems: Religious, Historical, and Political* (London: Latter-day Saints' Book Depot, 1856), 139; and Jill Mulvay Derr and Karen Lynn Davidson, "Eliza R. Snow's Poetry," *BYU Studies* 48, no. 3 (2009): 267.
90. Presumably William Jasper Harris.
91. Possibly Joseph F. and Martha Ann's cousin Samuel Harrison Bailey Smith, son of Samuel H. and Mary Bailey Smith.

JOSEPH F. TO MARTHA ANN, [SPRING 1861?]

[Spring 1861?][92]

Well Marth[93]— about "flitting" so much [*edge of fragment*] I do not like the [◊uoi], and I wish thare was some way of avoiding the necessity of it. O! I wish but wishing is vain. Well do the best we can and then be satisfied, that is the best way to secure happiness, that I know. The old woman thought so that labored hard for <u>years</u> for a conten[◊◊◊◊] [**p. 2**] [*back side of fragment*] she to write to me I have hath receive a letter from, Sarah[94] nor John[95] since I left home, and only one from Charlie.[96] I can hardly tell what has come over them but I suppose it's all right— if so— why— all right— it is— kiss Willie[97] for me, give my love to William,[98] to Sarah Jerusha, Lovina[99] and everybody— God bless you, Your Bro. J. F. Smith

MARTHA ANN TO JOSEPH F., 30 MAY 1861

Ans$^{\underline{d}}$ Aug. 3$^{\underline{rd}}$[100]
Leeds, 1861.

G S L City Utah Teritorry May the <30th 1861>

My Dear brother ~~L~~ Joseph
I onse more take my pen in hand to write you a few lines. all though I am all most ashamed of my self for not writng to you before. but I supose it is better late than never. Is it

92. This letter is missing the top portion, which most likely contained a date and salutation. The remaining portion contains material written on the front and reverse. The reverse page is signed by Joseph F., who arrived in England on 27 July 1860. Martha Ann's son Willie, mentioned in the letter, was born on 4 August 1859; and the next son, Joseph Albert, who is not mentioned in the letter, was not born until 19 August 1861. This provides a window for possible composition between 27 July 1860 and 4 August 1861. Additional internal evidence closes the window more. For example, Joseph F.'s letter, dated 15 December 1860, mentions that he had not received any letters from relatives besides his wife Levira and cousin George A. Smith. Because this letter mentions a letter received from Charlie Griffin, the date must be after 15 December 1860. Joseph F. mentions in this letter that Charlie Griffin wrote him once. Martha Ann notes, "Charles has moved his famoly out to Weber. But I guess he has writen to you sence that" (Martha Ann to Joseph F., 30 May 1861, herein). Because it is unlikely that she would have included this line if she had received this letter earlier, the composition date can be narrowed to spring 1861. Joseph F.'s request to "kiss Willie for me" is a phrase he used in his letters to Martha Ann on 28 July 1860 and 29 January 1861, suggesting this letter comes from this time period.
93. Martha Ann refers to herself as "Marth" in an earlier letter. See Martha Ann to Joseph F., 26 September 1860, herein. Joseph F. refers to Martha Ann by various names, including Marth. See Joseph F. to Martha Ann, 20 October 1856, herein, for example.
94. Most likely Sarah Smith (Griffin), an older half sister.
95. Most likely John Smith, an older half brother.
96. Most likely Charles Emerson Griffin, a brother-in-law married to Sarah Smith Griffin.
97. William Jasper Harris Jr, Martha Ann's firstborn son, was born on 4 August 1859.
98. William Jasper Harris, Martha Ann's husband.
99. Most likely, Sarah Smith (Griffin), Jerusha Smith [Pierce], and Lovina Smith [Walker], older half sisters.
100. Joseph F. wrote the first two lines in pencil, "Ans$^{\underline{d}}$ Aug. 3$^{\underline{rd}}$ Leeds, 1861."

Ans'd Aug 2nd
Leeds. 1861.

G S L City Utah Territory May 30th 1861

My Dear brother J Joseph

I once more take my pen in hand to write you afew lines: all though I am all most ashamed of my self for not writing to you before. but I supose it is better late than never. Is it not. do not think that I forgit you brother becaus I do not write ofton thare are other resons than that to attribute it to. one reson is lack of confidece in my self to write to you and another thing is that I am so stupid as to not learn to write better than I do. I am so ruff coarse and such a big awkward thing as the women said about me the other day. that you cannot expect me to write such letters as Ezra writes to you.. however you must make allowences for me. for you know that some times whare thare is a rough hand thare is a warm heart

I have been ashamed of the last letter that I wrotte to you ever sence I wrote it and have all most wished you would not get it. and I do not know that you ever did for we have not received one sence the one you wrote on Jan the 29th we was glad to get it I can asure you. and to hear that you was well was another comfort to me. O you do not know how mutch good it does me to read your letters Joseph. to know that I have one brother that does not forgit me is agreat consolation. I hardly know how to be thankfull enough for the goodness of my heavenly father to me a weak and frail being that I am for giving me such kind friends. as I have and such

Martha Ann to Joseph F., 30 May 1861 (p. 1)

have Husband. and ahome. O how sweet that
name does sound to me. would that you ware as
compfortuble As I am Joseph. but god will grant
you shall be rewarded for the toils and privations
that you have passed thro for the gospel sake. for
than I have. and O how match greater will be your re
but my trials will have to come yet I expect when he gi
me another wife I will have human nature to wrestel with
awhile untill I over come, and I hope that will n
be long god being my helpper for he helps thos
that helps them selves you know.
William has baught brother Shurtlefs place it is a
but very comfortuble thare are fore rooms in the ho
a good sellar one large square rome and 2 bed roo
plenty of room for my family at any rate
there is not match land belongs to it we have
small space of garden ground. alarge correll agood chi
house and Carrage shed all of lumber and ast
that would hold about 8 horses our carrage s
will do to put acarage into when we get one you know
perhaps that will be some time yet I expect it
Our place is just 2 and half blocks ~~Lovinas~~
from Lovinas so you see weare close neighbors she
offten runs down to see me when she get lonesome
~~Willim~~ William is still on police both night and
day and so I have agirl to stop with me this summer
as my health is not very good at present And I am no
able to do match house worke. I have done consider
spinning for Lovina this Spring I can spin better

Martha Ann to Joseph F., 30 May 1861 (p. 2)

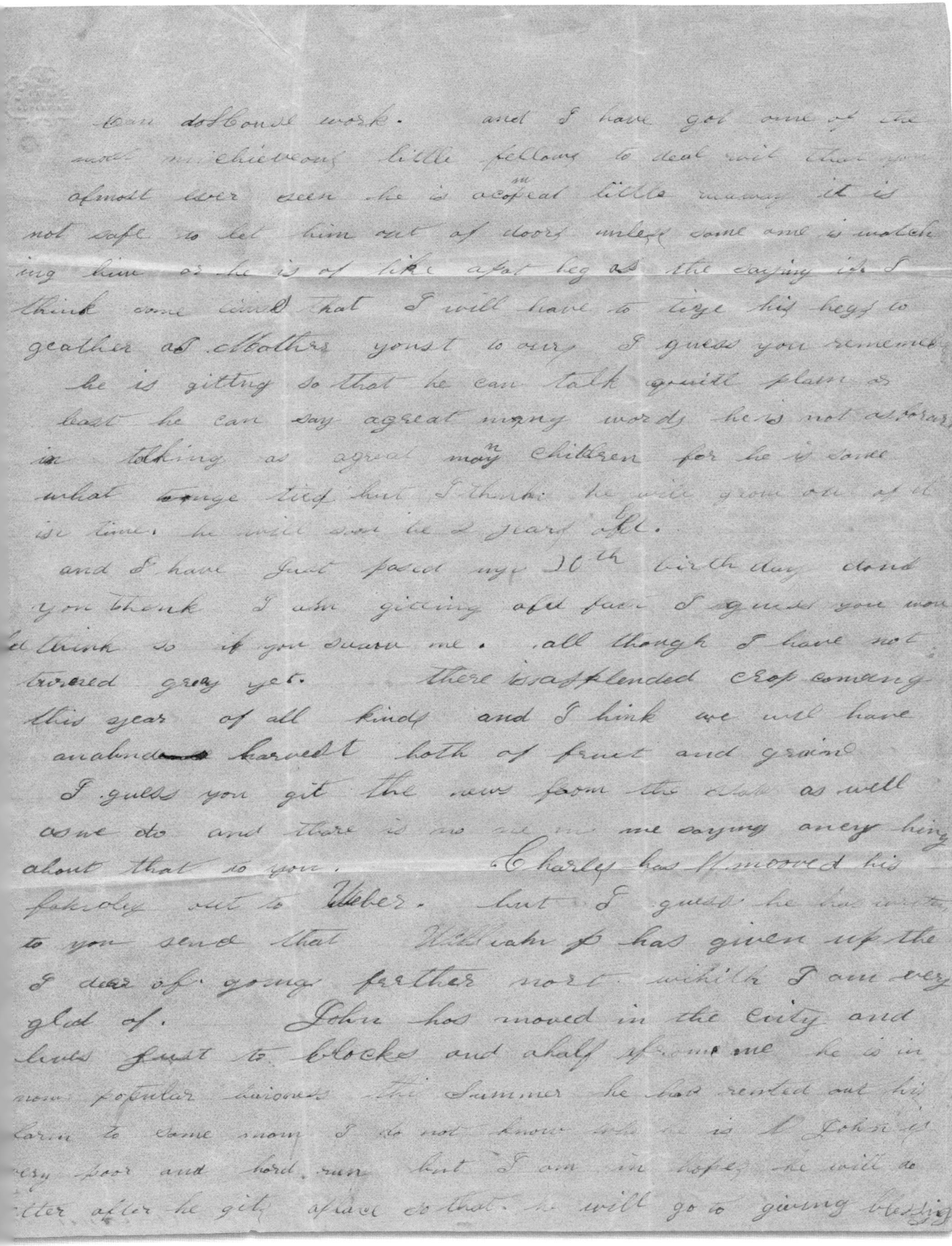
can do some work. and I have got one of the
most mischievous little fellows to deal with that you
almost ever seen he is a great little man it is
not safe to let him out of doors unless some one is watch
ing him as he is of like a pot leg as the saying is I
think some times that I will have to tie his legs to
geather as Mother yoused to say I guess you remember
he is gitting so that he can talk quite plain at
least he can say agreat many words he is not as forward
in talking as agreat many children for he is some
what tongue tied but I think he will grow out of it
in time. he will soon be 2 years old.
and I have just pased my 20th birth day dont
you think I am gitting old fast I guess you would
think so if you seen me. all though I have not
turned gray yet. there is asplended crop coming
this year of all kinds and I think we will have
anabundant harvest both of fruit and grain
I guess you git the news from the state as well
as we do and there is no use in me saying aney thing
about that to you. Charley has moved his
family out to Weber. but I guess he has written
to you send that William J has given up the
I dear of going farther north which I am very
glad of. John has moved in the city and
lives just to blocks and ahalf from me he is in
now popular business this Summer he has rented out his
farm to some man I do not know who he is John is
very poor and hard run but I am in hopes he will do
better after he gits aplace so that he will go to giving blessings

Martha Ann to Joseph F., 30 May 1861 (p. 3)

not. [*illegible strike-through*] Do not think that I forgit you brother becaus I do not write ofton thare are other resons than that to attribute it to. one reson is lack of confidece in my self to write to you and another thng is that I am so stupid as to not learn to wrte better than I do. I am so ruff cowon[101] and such a big awkward thing as the women said about me the other day. that you cannot expect me to write such letters as Vira[102] writes to you. howeve you must make allowneces for me. for you know that some times whare thare is a a ruff <hand> thare is a warm heart

I have been ashamed of the last letter that I wrotte to you ever sence I wrote it and have all most wished you would not git it. and I do not know that you ever did for we have not recieved one sence the one you wrote on Jan the 29th we was glad to git it I can asure you, and to hear that you was well was another cumfert to me. O yo do not know how mutch good it does me to read your letters Joseph. to know that I have one brother that does not forgit me is a great consolation. I hardly knowe how to be thankfull enough for the goodness of my heavenly father to me a weak and frail being that I am for giving me such kind friendes. as I have and such [**p. 2**] kind husband. and a home. O how sweet that name does sound to me. would that you ware as comfotuble as I am Joseph, but god will grant that you shall be rewarded for the toils and privations that you have passed thre for the gospil sake. far more than I have. and O how mutch <greater> will be your reward but my trials will have to come yet I expect when he gits another wfe I will have human nature to rassel with for a while untill I over come, and I hope that will not be long god being my helpper for he helps those that <tries> helps them selves you know.

William has baught brother Houtses[103] place it is smal but very comfortuble thare are fore rooms in the house a good sellar one large square roome and 2 bed roomes plenty of room for my famoly at aney rate there is not muctch land belonges to it we have a small peace of garden grond, a large correll a good chicken house and carrage shed all of lumber and a stable that would hold about 8 horsees our carrage shed will do to put a carage into when we git one you know. perhaps that will be some time yet I expect it will

Our place is just 2 and half blocks ~~Leviras~~ from Leviras so you see we are close neighbors she ofton runs down to see me when she git lonesome. ~~W Willial~~ William is still on polece[104] both night and day and so I have a girl to sop with me this summer as my healh is not very good <at> preasent aand I am not able to do mutch house worke. I have done considerable spinning for Lovina this spring I can spin better [**p. 3**] can do House work. and I have got one of the most mischieveous little fellows to deal wit that you almost ever seen[105] he is a co<m>peat little ruaway it is not safe to let him out of doors unless some one is watching him or he is of like a pot leg as the saying is.[106] I think some times that I will have to tiye his legs to geather as Mothrs youst to ours I guess you rememebr he is gittng so that he can talk quite plain or least he can say a great many words he is not as forard in talking as a great ma<n>y children for he is some what to[⟠]nge tied but I thnke he will grow out of it in time. he will soon be 2 years old.

101. Possibly *cowan*, which means "uninitiated, outside," or "profane." *Oxford English Dictionary*, s.v. "cowan."
102. Levira Annette Clark Smith.
103. William Jasper Harris and Jacob Houtz. See Martha Ann to Joseph F., 12 March 1861, herein.
104. William Jasper Harris worked for the Provo Police Department at this time. See King, "History of William Jasper Harris," 4, 6.
105. William Jasper Harris Jr. was a year and a half old.
106. "Off like a pot-leg" was a common saying during the nineteenth century, equivalent to "off like a shot" or "in a hurry."

he has been very wild sence he came home but
he has reformed considrable and I think he is doing better
now. sence I comenced to write this Charley and
Sarah has been hear they have just came in from
Weber they are all well and they have been so buisy
fitting there house up that they have not had
time to write to you sence they went out there. but
Charles sais when he git threw with his hurry he is
going to. Sarah told me to tell you that she had
not forgotton you. and for me to write to you for her
for she could not doit for her self she is a poor hand
to write you know to aney person. worse than I am
for you know I will write if it is no better than
agoose scratch. Sister Griffin is living Whare Sarah
lived when you went away and Bro Griffin and E. Emo
ley has gon out there to. along with Sarah.
well I guess I have told you enaugh about them
for this time I am going to write to Samuel
and inclose it in this letter you will forward to him
if you pleas Sister Smoot wishes me to Send
her best respects to you ~~with~~ and all the rest of the
famoley Amey Diana Mother all and all the rest
William sends his respects to you also and
sais he would have written to you if he had have had
time but he is very buisey just now his hand
trembles so that he can not hold his pen still so you
see there is an excuse for them all. I guess
I have told you all the news that would be intersting
and more to. may God bless you my dear Brother
is the prayr of your Sister Martha Ann Harris

Excuse bad writing and do not let any body see it for pity sake

Martha Ann to Joseph F., 30 May 1861 (p. 4)

and I have just pased my 20th birth day[107] dont you think I am gitting old fast I guess you would think so if you saaw me. all though I have not turned grey yet. there is a splended crop comeing this year of all kinds and I hink we wil have an abundence harvest both of fruit and grain

I guess you git the news from the states as well as we do and thare is no [*illegible word*] me saying aney hing about that to you. Charles[108] has mooved his famoly out to Weber.[109] but I guess he has writen to you sence that William P[110] has given up the idear of going frrther nort wihith I am very glad of. John[111] has moved in the city and lives just to blocks and a half frome me he is in now popular buisness this summer he has rented out his farm to some man I do not know who he is John is very poor and hard run but I am in hopes he will do better after he gits a place so that he will go to giving blessings[112] [**p. 4**] he has been very wild sence he come home but he has reformed cosidrable and I think he is doing better now. sence I comenced to write this Charles and Sarah[113] has been hear they have just came in from Weber they are all well and they have been so buiey ptting thirn house up that they have not had time to write to you sence they went out thare. But Charles sais when he git threw with his hurry he is going to. Sarah told me to tell you that she had not forgotton you. and for me to write to you for her for she could not do it for her self she is a poor hand to write you know to aney person. worse than I am for you know I will write if it is no better than a go<o>se scratch. sister griffin[114] is living whare Sarah lived when you went away and Bro Griffin and ~~E~~ emoly[115] has gon out thare to. along with sarah. wall I guess I have told you enough about here for this time I am going to write to Sameul[116] and inclose it in this letter you will foreward to him if you pleas sister Smoot wishes me to send her best respects to you ~~with~~<and> all the rest of the famoley Anney Diana Mother[117] [*illegible erasure*] and all the rest

William sends his respcts to you also and sais he would have written to you if he had have had time but he is very buisey just now his hand trembles so that he can not hold his pen still so you see thare is an excuse for them all. I g<u>ess I have told you all the news that would be intersing and more to. may [*illegible strike-through*] God bless you my dear brothr to the praryr of your Sister Martha Ann Harris

Excuse bad writing and do not let any body see it <for pity sake>[118]

107. Martha Ann was born on 14 May 1841.
108. Charles Emerson Griffin.
109. Possibly Weber County, Utah, which is located north of Salt Lake City. Established in 1850, Ogden is the county seat and has been the largest city in the county.
110. William Pierce, husband of Jerusha Smith.
111. John Smith.
112. John Smith was serving as Church Patriarch at this time.
113. Sarah Smith.
114. Abigail Varney.
115. Likely Albert Bailey Griffin and his third wife, Laura Emily Beebe.
116. Samuel Harrison Bailey Smith.
117. Margaret Thompson McMeans, Anne Kristine Mauritzen, Diana Tanner Eldredge, and Emily Hill, all wives of Abraham O. Smoot.
118. Written sideways in the left margin of page 4.

MARTHA ANN TO JOSEPH F., 8 DECEMBER 1861

Ansd March 1st
Hul[◊][119]

G S L, City Utah T <Decembr the 8 1861>

My dear brother it so a long time sence wrote to you I am allmost ashamed of my self if not quite. for not writing to you before, this time but you will ex<c>use me I think when I tell you the resons. sence I last wrote to you which I think was in May last God has intrusted to my care one more little charge,[120] which I hope may some day become a man of God and do mutch good in his generation in helping to build up the kingdom of our heavenly Father may he give me wisdome to trane them up in truth honesty and virtue is my prair from day to day. if they are trained in this way while young they will not depart from it whin older **[p. 2]** we receivd your kind letter of ~~ast~~ October 24th last evning and was glad to hear from you you may depend upon it. we also recieved to bunches of papers I am very thankfull to you for beeing so thaughtfull in sending me those papers they are very interesting and allso very edefying and I am alone so mutch they keep me from beeing lonesom they are a great comfert to me all though I do not git mutch time to read them for I have been so buisey this fall makng up my winter clothing and spining, I have spun 24 pounds of roles since the first of september, knit 5 pare of stockings and done lots of sewing besides taking care off my babys[121] so you see I have not been idle now my helth is good with the exc<e>ption of a lame back it is so bad some times that I can **[p. 3]** scarcly raise up when I stoop down but I am in hopes it will git better before long [*illegible strike-through*] the children are well and groing fine my dear little Joseph[122] is such a fine little fellow I wish you could see him you would give him shuch a shaking I know he is not very littler eather I can asure you of that for when he was 2 munthes old he wayd 18 pounds he is nearly 6 muths old now and when I write again I I will tell you how much he wayd then. they say he looks like you his I <eyes> are so dark theyr are blue but very dark his hare parts on the same side that yours does. well I guess you will think I have writen enough about that at enny rate. Willey[123] sais he would like to see his ~~un~~ Uncle Joseph he is a very m<i>sceiveous boy but he does not mean any [*illegible strike-through*] <[*illegible strike-through*] harme> by it **[p. 4]**

You spoke of Christimas and of us enjoying our selvs so mutch togther I hope we m[◊]ay but we would enjoy our selvs <mutch ~~better~~> better iff you ware hear to enjoy it with us and Jerusha and Sarah[124] they are so far off that I scarcly ever git to see them now they ware all

119. The first two lines were written by Joseph F. Kingston. Hull is located at the confluence of the River Hull and the Humber Estuary in Yorkshire, England. Most Scandinavian Saints passed through Hull on their migration to America during the second half of the nineteenth century. See Fred E. Woods and Nicholas J. Evans, "Latter-day Saint Scandinavian Migration through Hull, England, 1852–1894," *BYU Studies* 4, no. 4 (2002): 75–102.
120. Joseph Albert Harris, Martha Ann's second child, was born on 19 August 1861 in Provo, Utah County, Utah Territory. See biographical register, "Harris, Joseph Albert."
121. Most likely William Jasper Harris Jr. (born 1859) and Joseph Albert Harris (born 1861).
122. Joseph Albert Harris.
123. William Jasper Harris Jr.
124. At this tim Sarah Smith was living in Weber County, about ninety miles north of Utah County, and Jerusha Smith was living in Box Elder County, about two hundred miles north of Utah County.

well when I hird from them last all but Jerushas little Martha[125] she had the canker and was cutting her teeth. but I hope that next year at this time we will have the pleasure of s<p>ending the Christimas togeather if it pleases Good that we should. our dear brother John has at last comensed to perform his duty which I feel very thankfull for.[126] they ware ~~all~~ all very well when I saw them last Vira was very sick the last time I saw her but I have hird sence that she is better. Aunt levira[127] has allso ben <very> sick but I hope she is better now I have not been up thare sence weak be fore last for it has been such bad weather that I could not take the baby out. good by for the preasent may God bless [*illegible word*] <you> for ever ~~Martha~~

Martha Ann Harris pleas write to me as often as you can.[128]

William[129] sends his love to you and sais he will write be fore long[130]

give my love to Samuel[131] and tell him to write to me[132]

MARTHA ANN TO JOSEPH F., 12 JANUARY 1862

Ans$^{\underline{d}}$ March 1$^{\underline{st}}$
Hull—[133]

G S L city Jan. the 12 1862[134]

My Dear and beloved Brother
as no one was sendng a letter when I wrote I I thaught that I would wait untill I could have some thing more to write that would be worth your notice. Christimas and new years <day> is over and we are all alive yet thank the Lord and as far as my my fameoly is consirned we are all well and your famoly I think is on the mend they have had a long seige of it Aunt Levira[135] has been very low for a long time and she is very low yet but she is mut<c>h better than she has been I was thare yesterday to see them Vira[136] has been passing threw a very

125. Martha Lovina Pierce.
126. Likely refers to their half brother John, fulfilling his duties as Church Patriarch.
127. Levira Clark, widow of Samuel Harrison Smith and also Joseph F.'s mother-in-law. See biographical register, "Clark, Levira."
128. Written sideways in the right margin of page 4.
129. William Jasper Harris.
130. Written upside down in the top margin of page 4.
131. Samuel Harrison Bailey Smith.
132. Written sideways in the left margin of page 4.
133. Joseph F. wrote the first two lines indicating when and where he answered Martha Ann's letter. He noted in his journal on 22 February 1862, "Came to Hull by 2.25 train, found letters awaiting me from Prest. Cannon. John Clark, Samuel H and one from Martha Ann dated January 12th Levira and Mother were very Ill. I feel very unwell myself. I took a bath in the evening."
134. Joseph F. was twenty-three, and Martha Ann was twenty years old.
135. Levira Clark Smith was married to Dustin Amy at this time. See biographical register, "Smith, Levira Clark."
136. Joseph F.'s wife, Levira Smith.

severe trial for her to endure with her weak consteution. she is very poorly nearly worn out with the caare that she has had on her mind with regard to her mothers[137] safety and comfort she has had hardly thaught of her own wellfare. she has been low pirrited some of the time but she has done excedingly well considering the stuation she hase been placed in. she has got a strong nerve and I think her nerve is stronger than her ~~than her~~ boddy is able to bare. M N An<e>y[138] has been so mean to them he grows worse and & worse Vira sais she does not know but he will go crasey if he keps on as he has been he sais that [**p. 2**] Aunt Levira is not sick. that it is nothig but ~~damd~~ d d laisenes and that she is just as able to work as he is and that is the way that he gows and he will scarcly let them have what they want to eat he is so stingy and he will scarslly let them have any one to waite on her. he is afraid he will come to want and I am afraid he will unless he does nearer right. but do not wory Joseph perhaps it will all turn out for the best ~~if Levira would~~ [*illegible strike-through*] allthough we cannot se how that can bee now. perhaps we may some time. I would like to have Levira come and live with me when her mother git better iff she would have her. ~~Mother~~ but I do not expect she will I have made her the offer and she can do ashe[139] likes about comeing you know. William[140] is still on polise duty he has been very buis<e>y for the last few weaks both knight and day. John[141] is in the Legeslature this winter.[142] he all so gives blessings on Mondays and Satturd[143]

I was up to M N Smoots[144] on Saturday last to see the new comers thare Dians has got a girl five weaks old and Anna had a sun born last thursday.[145] Sister Smoot[146] send her best respectes to you with the rest of the famoly. they all so thank you for your kind rememberence to them all. I must bring my scroll to a close as my paper is fooll. I have not hird from Sarah nor Jerusha[147] sence I wrote. Considder from whense ths comes may the Lord bless you for ever and bring you safe home is <ever> my prayr I remain as ever your sister

Martha Ann H[148]

---

137. Levira Clark Smith.
138. Dustin Amy was married to Levira Clark Smith, Samuel H. Smith's widow, at this time. He eventually abandoned his three wives in Utah and returned to Iowa. The designation *M N* is uncertain. See biographical register, "Amy, Dustin."
139. Martha Ann has combined *as* and *she*.
140. William Jasper Harris.
141. John Smith.
142. John Smith served as the sergeant-at-arms for the Legislative Council of the Territory of Utah during the Eleventh Session, 1861–62. As such, his role was to maintain order and execute commands during the meetings.
143. As Church Patriarch, John Smith (Joseph F. and Martha Ann's older half brother) gave blessings to the Saints from 1855 until his death in 1911, a practice mentioned both in the Bible and Book of Mormon; see Genesis 48:14; 49; and 2 Nephi 4:3–11. According to Martha Ann, at this time he did so on Mondays and Saturdays.
144. Abraham O. Smoot. The designation *M N* is uncertain.
145. Diana Tanner Eldredge, Abraham O. Smoot's plural wife, gave birth to Elizabeth Smoot on 7 December 1861. Anne Kirstine Mauritzen, Abraham O. Smoot's plural wife, gave birth to Reed Smoot on 10 January 1862. See biographical register, "Smoot, Elizabeth" and "Smoot, Reed."
146. Likely Emily Hill Harris Smoot.
147. Sarah Smith and Jerusha Smith.
148. Written sideways in the right margin.

MARTHA ANN TO JOSEPH F., 29 JANUARY 1862

G S L City Utah Teritory Jan the 29 1862

Joseph F Smith
my dear brother as I had an appernity of sending ~~of sending~~ you a few lines I thaught I would improv it Charles[149] has just been hear and he told me that he was going to send a letter to you and that I could put a few lines inn with him. we are all better than we have been William[150] has had a very bad cold and I have had a large boil on my brest which has been very painfull for the last weak but it broke day before yester day and it is gitting better. the children are ~~better~~ well and groing fine. Aunt Thompson and Mary J & David[151] was hear one day this weak and spent the after noon with me they ware all tolerable well. you told Charls you had only recieved 3 letters from me. but I think I have writen <more> often~~er~~ than that to you if I mistake not perhaps [**p. 2**] you have not recieved all off them.[152]

you say in your litter to Charles that you are better of your cold for which I feel very thankfull for I have been very uneasy about you. dear brother I often think of you when set down to a good meal of vitules and wonder if my dear brother has enough to eat and when I lay me down to rest on my comforttable bed I allso wonder what kind of a bed that he has is so near and derr to me has to lie down upon to rest his weary boddy. I some times think that I am not worthy of ~~of~~ all Gods kindness to me for I feel my smallness more and more every day of my life I feel more and more the nessaty of prayr for I feel that thare is a great responcability resting upon me that is in trainng up my children in the right way you must pray for the lord to give me wisdom and that I may be found worthy at the last day to meet those that are gone before us this is my prayr for you and for me and for all that is honnest in hart may God bless you forever I remain as ever

your sister Martha A Harris[153]

MARTHA ANN TO JOSEPH F., 3 FEBRUARY 1862

G S L City Feb the 3 1862

My dear Brother

149. Charles Emerson Griffin.
150. William Jasper Harris.
151. Mercy Rachel Fielding, Mary Jane Thompson, and Mary's husband, David Taylor. See biographical register, "Taylor, David."
152. Martha Ann wrote several letters to Joseph F. in the first half of 1862. In one case he notes in his diary, "Received a letter from C. D. Griffin and Martha Ann, mailed some papers home." Joseph F., journal, 13 March 1862.
153. Written sideways in the right margin.

I went to see Leviras[154] yesterday and she requested me to write and tell you how she is and whare she is she is at Brother Brigham Youngs[155] in the care of ~~Aunt~~ Aunt Zina Young[156] she has been very sick but she was some better yesterdy she thaught she would be more comfortable thare than at my house and I supose she will Aunt Zina knows what to do for her better than I do you know she is older and more experenced than I am ~~you know~~ and understands her disease better. she has been with her mother so long that she has pertaken of her complaint care and an<y>xity of mind has helped to bring it on. but B Br Brigham[157] layd hands on her last fryday and comanded [**p. 2**] helth to return to her boddy.[158] and wih good care and nursing I think she will soon regain her strength ~~again~~ she told me to tell you that she would write to you just as soonn as she was able. and for you not to be uneasy about ~~you~~ her for she was in trusty hands. I feel so thankful she is whare she is. her ~~mot~~ mother is a great deal better she can set up for some time in a chare. William pe[◊]rce[159] was hear the other day and he wanted me to write for him I told him he had better write him self but he was going home the next morning and he coud not he said he sends his love and says they are all in all well. Jerusha[160] did not come down with him I supose that some of the folks have told you in their letters of the death of Lot hntington A <r>one Clawson & a John Smith which was done weak before last.[161] and also about the ~~M~~ man that has been robing the dead[162] this is ~~the no~~ all the

154. Levira Annette Clark Smith.
155. Brigham Young's residences, the Beehive House (1854) and Lion House (1856), are located one block east of Temple Square in Salt Lake City.
156. Zina Diantha Huntington, who was sealed to Joseph Smith Jr. in 1841, making her an aunt to Levira Annette Clark (through marriage) as well as to Joseph F. and Martha Ann. However, in Utah culture at this time *Aunt* was also used in nonbiological relationships as a title of respect and endearment, especially in plural marriage families. See biographical register, "Huntington, Zina Diantha."
157. Brigham Young was affectionately known as "Brother Brigham" by the Latter-day Saints.
158. A Latter-day Saint practice rooted in the Bible; see James 5:14.
159. William Pierce, Jerusha Smith's husband.
160. Jerusha Smith.
161. Lot Huntington, Moroni Clawson, and John P. Smith were accused of stealing horses and assaulting Utah territorial governor John W. Dawson, which occurred on 31 December 1861. Dawson had recently been appointed governor of Utah Territory by Abraham Lincoln in early December and was fleeing the territory after making inappropriate proposals to Albina Merrill Williams, a Latter-day Saint widow. Orrin Porter Rockwell led the posse to arrest Clawson, Huntington, and Smith. Huntington was shot and killed in Rush Valley, Utah, when he resisted arrest on 16 January 1862. Rockwell delivered Clawson and Smith to authorities in Salt Lake City. They were also shot and killed in Salt Lake City on 17 January 1862 as they attempted to escape. See "Governor Dawson's Statement," *Deseret News*, 22 January 1862, 234; and "Exciting and Terrifying Occurrences," *Deseret News*, 22 January 1862, 237. See also Andrew Jenson, *Church Chronology: A Record of Important Events Pertaining to the History of the Church of Jesus Christ of Latter-day Saints*, 2nd ed. (Salt Lake City, UT: Deseret News Press, 1899), 66. Interestingly, Dawson was a childhood friend of John Chapman, better known as Johnny Appleseed, and was his first biographer. Dawson's article in the *Fort Wayne Sentinel*, 21 and 23 October 1871, is the basis of biographical information on Chapman. See also biographical register, "Huntington, Lot Elisha," "Clawson, Moroni, Sr.," and "Smith, John P."
162. Clawson, noted above, was buried in "potter's field," a section in the Salt Lake City Cemetery reserved for unknown or indigent persons. Later, family members arrived to arrange for his reburial at the family plot in Draper, Utah. When the body was exhumed, the family discovered that Clawson was naked in the casket. This began an investigation to determine who was responsible for removing his clothing after burial. During a visit to the home of Jean Baptiste, the Salt Lake City Cemetery gravedigger, officers discovered boxes of what appeared to be burial clothing. Baptiste was eventually charged with robbing some three hundred graves in the Salt Lake City Cemetery in January 1862 and was banished to Fremont Island in the Great Salt Lake as punishment. See John Devitry-Smith, "The Saint and the Grave Robber," *BYU Studies* 33, no. 1 (1993): 7–52. See also biographical register, "Baptiste, Jean."

news that I know of I could say more but my paper is fool excuse bad writing and mistakes for the a baby[163] is crying on my lap & I am in a hury

Martha Ann Harris[164]

JOSEPH F. TO MARTHA ANN, 1 MARCH 1862

[*10.8 x 6.4 cm diagonal tear*][165]oline Street[166] Hull, Yorkshire England
March 1st 1862.—
[*diagonal tear*]ter Martha Ann:—

I am happy to have the privilige of answering [*diagonal tear*]lcome letters of Dec. 8th and Jan. 12th—[*diagonal tear*]d.[167] I am always glad to hear from you [*diagonal tear*] family who take the panes to write. [*diagonal tear*]end this enclosed in a letter to Levira,[168] instead of sending it in John's,[169] as I at first intended, the reason I did not send it in John's's, was because his was full.

I am glad to hear that you are getting along so well, and before I go any farther, let me thank you Martha for your kinde offer to Levira. I am sorry to hear of her Illness— But that does not express my feeling, but I have weighed the matter up and down and I can only see how vain any attempts of mine would be to administer the necessary relief unaided by some higher Power.[170] I feel my weakness, and dependance upon God as much in this thing as any that has come across me, and am reconciled to my fate. I can but excersise my faith, in prayer and supplication, for my own, and the welfair of my friends while so far away from them. My faith is:—all is right!

I have not heard a word from Levira for a long time If she is so Ill that she cannot write I want you to tell me so!—for I want to know.—

My health is very good at present, although I am never free from cold, and cough, altogether.—

163. Probably Martha Ann's second child, Joseph Albert, born on 19 August 1861, less than six months before Martha Ann wrote this letter to Joseph F.
164. Written sideways in the right margin.
165. The top left corner of page 1 (the top right corner of page 2) is torn diagonally. Subsequent references to this tear will hereafter be referred to in this letter as "diagonal tear."
166. Caroline Street, a two-block-long road located between Cannon Street train station (no longer in existence) and Christ Church near Kensington Square at the time. According to the 1860 census, the Jackson family, which included two daughters, had a boarder living with them at 11 Caroline Street. The family most likely continued to rent rooms to boarders in subsequent years. Joseph F. provided the exact address, 11 Caroline Street, Hull, Yorkshire, England, in a letter addressed to Levira (see Joseph F. to Levira Annette Clark Smith, 1 March 1862) and mentions the address on several occasions in his journal (see Joseph F. to Levira Annette Clark Smith, 1 March 1862; and Joseph F., journal, 15 and 22 November 1861).
167. See Martha Ann to Joseph F., 8 December 1861 and 12 January 1862, herein.
168. Levira Annette Clark Smith.
169. John Smith.
170. Martha Ann invited Levira to live with her because of the poor living arrangements Levira had with a new stepfather, Dustin Amy. See Martha Ann to Joseph F., 8 December 1861; and Martha Ann to Joseph F., 12 January 1862, herein.

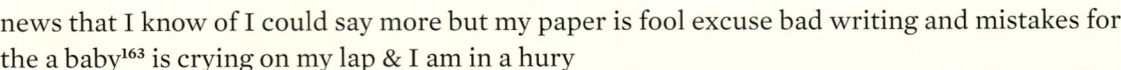

I was glad to hear ~~from~~ about the little ones, my blessing upon them.[171] May the Lord bless them, and preserve them from Death, axident, disease, and sin. May they live, and grow, and prosper, and become, noble and great—and always remain good—may the foundation and the whole fabric of their greatness be, wisdom and their Honor Truth—may they possess meakness and humility forever **[p. 2]** May they become shining lig[*diagonal tear*] of Eternal Truth, may they be [*diagonal tear*]iant in the Armies of Zion, and [*diagonal tear*] and them that fight against God [*diagonal tear*] Peace watch over them, and the j[*diagonal tear*] and intelligence, never be close [*diagonal tear*] May they be the Joy of their Mother, an[*diagonal tear*] happiness of their Father, and the comfort [*diagonal tear*] of their declining years, may Thousands call them Blessed, and Isreal speak their Praize,—amen.

You must not forget me to Jerusha and Sarah and their little ones[172]—my prayer is for them, and my blessing is upon them,—I remember them always—

I will say here for William's[173] benifit—or rather information, that the first ship, with emigrating saints, this season will sail on or about, the 20th of April.— I am not sure but, the Danish Saints will sail from Denmark direct—instead of coming thro' England—which will be a saving, I think, but I am not sure of this—there has been some talk of it, but it has never before been tryed.—[174]

Please remember me kindly to Sisters Smoot, Harris—Annie, Diena,—Bro. Smoot and all enquiring friend.[175] I remember them all with kindly feelings, always.

Take care of yourselves. I am trying do the same,—tho' I am very careless, or neglectful of my own good sometimes. But one must take Care of one's self—or suffer the conciquences.

I would like to hear from you when ever you have time to write. Glad that William gets on so well.

I think Prest Rich, (C. C. Rich) will return to the valley this year, and Perhaps Prest. Amasy M. Lyman[176] as well,—of this I am not sure. Several of the Brethren are expecting to return Home on account of Illness, and some because business requires, or they think so—we are very short of help.— May God Bless you all— I am as ever faithfully your Brother, well-wishes

J. F. Smith

---

171. A reference to Martha Ann's children William Jasper Jr. (born 4 August 1859) and Joseph Albert (born 19 August 1861).
172. Jerusha Smith had three children at this time, and Sarah Smith had four children.
173. William Jasper Harris.
174. Three hundred twenty-four Scandinavian Saints sailed on the German ship *Humboldt*, departing Hamburg on 9 April 1862 and bypassing England. Previously, all Latter-day Saint emigrants from Europe passed through the British Isles on their way to America.
175. Margaret Thompson McMeans, Emily Hill, Anne Kirstine Mauritzen, and Diana Tanner Eldredge, plural wives of Abraham O. Smoot.
176. Charles Coulson Rich and Amasa Mason Lyman had been serving as mission assistant and president, respectively, in the British Mission. See biographical register, "Rich, Charles Coulson" and "Lyman, Amasa Mason."

JOSEPH F. TO MARTHA ANN, 10 APRIL 1862

[10 April 1862][177]

Page, 9 I do not wish to impase an good nature, So I will prescribe the limits of your portion to this remaining half sheet. Which I hope you will have patiance to read. I visited London:[178]— Well. I went to the Great International Exhibition,[179] again. (for I was thare once before) and also to the Crystle Palace.[180] London Tower,[181] Saw the Queen's Crown, worth a Milion Pounds Sterling. And other juelry and Gold plates and Ceptor valued at 3 Millions More. And all under an glass case! Saw the Block and ax which Severed the heads of Ann Bolyn[182] and Several others from their bodies. also the dungon where many notable individuals have been confined to await the Block, Guillitine, or Scaffold.[183] Visited Hampton Court built by Cardenal Woosy and presented to a Jealous King to tame his head.[184] This palace is magnificent. Also The House of Parliament, or as it is called The New Westminister Palace, it is the finest building in London.[185] At least I think so. Saw the House of Lords and the house of commons and the identical **[p. 2]** Table on Which Cromwell Stood and dismissed the "Mock Parliament." The House of Lords is concidered the finest Specimen of architecture in Europe. It is certainly Grand. Visited the Thames Tunnell. D^{r}. Kahn's Anotomical Museum, Madam Truesaus and Sons' Bazar. or Wax Works.[186] Sat in two of Napolians Carriages. Saw the Duke of Wellington's funeral Car. Weighing [*illegible erasure or fading*] and [*illegible erasure or fading*] 20 Thousand Pounds Sterling. Been on the Tower of St. Pauls Cathedral. In West Minister Abby. And a

177. We assume this letter is the one noted in his diary: "I wrote to David Taylor, Aunt Thompson, and Martha Ann." Joseph F., journal, 10 April 1862. He wrote a longer letter later in the month: "I wrote to President Kimball, and, also, a letter of 12 pages to Uncle J. Fielding, Aunt Hannah Fielding, Aunt Thompson, Mary Jane Taylor, and Martha Ann Harris." Joseph F., journal, 29 April 1862; the signature on this letter is on page 10.
178. London was the capital of the British Empire. During the nineteenth century, an increasing number of railways and roads connected London to the rest of Britain. See Aldon D. Bell, *London in the Age of Dickens* (Norman: University of Oklahoma Press, 1967).
179. See John A. Hollingshead, *Concise History of the International Exhibition of 1862: Its Rise and Progress, Its Building and Features and a Summary of all Former Exhibitions* (London: n.p., 1862).
180. Originally erected in Hyde Park, the Crystal Palace was a cast-iron and plate-glass structure built to house the Great Exhibition of 1851. By 1862, when Joseph F. visited the building, it had been moved to Penge Common, an area of South London.
181. Officially known as "Her Majesty's Royal Palace and Fortress of the Tower of London," this structure is a historic castle located on the north bank of the River Thames in central London.
182. Anne Boleyn was the second wife of King Henry VIII and was the queen of England from 1533 to 1536. She was beheaded on 19 May 1536 in the Tower of London.
183. A person laid his or her head on a block as part of beheading by guillotine. The scaffold was a raised platform used in public executions.
184. Built by Cardinal Thomas Wolsey, Hampton Court Palace is a royal palace located about twelve miles southwest and upstream of central London on the River Thames. Henry VIII took possession of it after Wolsey fell out of favor.
185. After a fire destroyed an earlier building in 1834, the "New Westminster Palace" was built to host the two houses of the United Kingdom Parliament—the House of Commons and the House of Lords.
186. Thames Tunnel was completed under the River Thames in 1842 and was the first tunnel constructed underneath a navigable river. Established in 1851, Dr. Joseph Kahn's Anatomical and Pathological Museum was the most famous and most visited public museum of anatomy in the nineteenth century. Established in 1835, Madame Tussauds and Sons' Bazaar featured wax sculptures by Anna Maria "Marie" Tussaud.

hoste of other places.[187] Visited Covent Garden opara House,[188] the finest I ever saw, but, her Magesties Theatre is concidered the Second best in the World. The best known is a new Theatre in Russia.[189] Went to the Hay Market Theatre.[190] Witnessed Some Scenes in London life at mid-night in the Streats and Lanes. Which you can better immagin than I can discribe. Visited the British Museum.[191] Where there is one of the largest libraries in the World. Well I must Stop, O! for a peep at you all. But adieu, God Bless you. J.F. Smith

MARTHA ANN TO JOSEPH F., 30 SEPTEMBER 1862

Rec^{d} and Ans^{d} Nov. 12th 1862[192]
Sheffield—[193]

Great Salt Lake City Sep 30th 1862

My Dear Brother Joseph

after so long a silence I once more take my pen in hand to pay my debts. or to let you know how we are gitting along. your to kind letters came duley to hand and we was truley glad to hear from you to hear that you are well and doing well is allways a great comfort to me I can asure you. but I have not had an opportunity off answering them before this for severel reasons, I have had no paper sutable to write to you onn and I could not git any in town. this for one. ~~and~~ my baby[194] has ben very sick and I have had no one to help ~~to~~ <me> do any thing and William has been from home a great deal of the time and I have had every thing to atend to in his absence. my babey is better now or at least onn the mend for he is so cross that I scarcely know what to do with him the rest of us are all well at present and I sincerly hope this may find you enjoying the same blessings. I had pleasure of gitting dinner for Sister Jackson[195] day before yester day she arived in the citty last Thursday evning with all off her children and her self in good health and spirets she requested me to give her love to you and tell you she never felt better in her life. I was very mutch pleased to see some one that had been knd to you it

187. St. Paul's Cathedral is an Anglican cathedral constructed at the highest point of the City of London. Westminster Abbey is the site where all coronations of English and British monarchs have been held since the coronation of William the Conqueror in 1066. It is located just to the west of the Palace of Westminster.
188. Covenant Garden Opera House was rebuilt after a fire destroyed the earlier building in 1858.
189. Most likely referring to the Bolshoi Theatre in Moscow.
190. Haymarket Theatre, or the Little Theatre, dates back to 1720 and is in the Haymarket in the City of Westminster.
191. The British Museum, located in the Bloomsbury area of London, remains the largest library in the world.
192. Written sideways in the top left margin of page 1 and circled.
193. First two lines written by Joseph F.
194. Joseph Albert Harris had just turned one year old on 19 August 1862.
195. Sarah Smith Jackson, with her nine children, left England on the *John J. Boyd* in April 1861, eventually arriving in Salt Lake City on 24 September 1862 with the Homer Duncan Company.

done my sowl good you may dpend upon it.[196] I have ingaged her little girl to come and live with me this winter to help me take care of my children. I need some <one> to asist me very [*illegible strike-through*] <mutch> she is fifteen years old I forgit her name now I suppos you will know whch of them it is.[197] she is to come to morrow I have not seen her yet I hope she will bee agreable. I had intended to send you my babyes likeness[198] but he looks so poor and bad that I could not have it taken but he is very pritty [**p. 2**] iff he is my child, when he is well I wish you could see him he is a sweet little dear at least I think so perhaps I am saying to mutch in prais of my own but it is if you Joseph and to you is not to strangers you know I love my little ones dearley they are my dayly care. my comfort in my lonely hours. may God grant me wisdom to train them aright is my constant desire <and prayr> every day of my life. Willey[199] is growing very tall and slim he is not a very ruggd boy. he is very mutch like you was when you was little he loves milk dearly but he will not touch any kind of fruit no matter what it is he never would eat any candy nor sugar ~~en~~ untill latlly he eats a very little I hope he will out grow his pcular ways after ~~I~~ a while. ~~I~~ the baby ~~is~~ has just woke up and so good night

Dear brother it is just one weak to night sence I wrote the above it is is now Conference time[200] and and Mary Jane[201] was hear this evnng and she told me that Jerusha had just got in town to day she is at sister peirces,[202] now I have not seen her yet I have not seen her for some time ~~it is~~ never sence last March and I can scarcly wait to see her now that she is so near ~~she is~~ they are tolerable wll she sais. Charles[203] is going to moove inn from the Weber this weak I believe he was in with a lode of coal ~~this~~ <last> weak he said they was all well when he left them. the fair[204] came off last weak it lasted three [*illegible strike-through*] days. I do not know whethr it iis any youse for me to say any thing about Levira.[205] for I supose you have got all the news from her self she was well or at least better when she was hear last weak she has been very poorley for sometime back she has not come back to live with me and I do not know wheather she is going to or not. the girl that was going to come and stop with me could not come the reeson why I do not know I was very much disapointd about it but perhaps it is all for the best I must close for my paper is full <pleas excuse all mis>takes and dirty paper[206] it is the best I could git may God bless you for ever is my praryr

196. Joseph F. mentions Sarah Smith Jackson several times in his journal, including a specific reference to having a meal with her and receiving a "silk neck Tie" from a family member; see Joseph F., journal, 5 September 1861. Additional references to being in her home are found in Joseph F., journal, 17 December 1861, 24 December 1861, 30 January 1862, 3 February 1862, 24 March 1862, and 3 April 1862. In November 1861, Joseph F. confirmed Elizabeth Jackson, Sarah's daughter; see Joseph F., journal, 15 November 1861.

197. Emma Jane Jackson, born on 28 April 1848, was fourteen years old in 1862.

198. Because the basic goal of portrait photography was to capture the likeness of the subject, the term *likeness* became a substitute word for *photograph* in the nineteenth century.

199. William Jasper Harris Jr.

200. The 32nd Semiannual General Conference began on 6 October 1862 in Salt Lake City. For a report, see "Semi-annual Conference," *Deseret News*, 15 October 1862, 124–25.

201. Mary Jane Thompson, cousin to Martha Ann and Joseph F.

202. Probably Hannah Harvey, mother-in-law of Jerusha Smith. See biographical register, "Harvey, Hannah."

203. Charles Emerson Griffin.

204. The fair was the annual exhibition of the Deseret Agricultural and Manufacturing Society. See "The Annual Fair," *Deseret News*, 1 October 1862, 105.

205. Levira Annette Clark Smith.

206. Old rags were used to make paper in Utah during this early pioneer period. As a result, depending on the colors present in old clothing, paper color varied.

I remain as ever your Sister Martha Ann Harris[207]

brother Smoots folks[208] join in love to you with thanks for your kind rememberence to them Unchehel fielding folks[209] also send thir love to you thare is a letter for Samuel[210] pleas forward it to him[211]

JOSEPH F. TO MARTHA ANN, [FALL 1862?]

[Fall 1862?][212]

my kind regards to her. I hope she will always love her Religion more and more so long as her Religion is the Gospel. Which I have every reason to believe in the case. I bilieve I apreciate the principles of the gospel more to day than I ever did before, and I hope to be able to appreciate them better tomorrow [*end of page*] paper I would not advise you to send them, as, Tin plates[213] are so liable to be bent and spoilled, as are I have of Levira.[214] besides they will cost as much as a better, that would contain several of the other kind, I have the promis of going home next spring,[215] if every thing moves right. [*end of page*] here, at most, is short. I am convinced the Lord has sent us here to do good. The longer, then, we live, the better we shall be able to fill the design of our creation. We require but little, to supply the real wants of life so that much else than the mear supplying of our wants may be done, by us, for our comfort and the good [*end of page*] Must, write again. And please give my love to William,[216] and the babies,[217] and To Jerusha and William and their family,[218] and to Aunt Thompson,[219] David,[220] Mary Jane,[221] Uncle

207. Written sideways in the right margin.
208. Abraham O. Smoot and his family.
209. Joseph Fielding, uncle to Joseph F. and Martha Ann, and family.
210. Samuel Harrison Bailey Smith.
211. Cross-written on page 2.
212. Date and greeting are missing from this letter. However, internal evidence suggests it was written after the letter from Martha Ann to Joseph F. dated 30 September 1862 (herein) and after his return home to Utah Territory in September 1863.
213. A popular art form in the 1860s and 1870s, a tintype photograph was made by creating a direct positive image on a thin sheet of metal. Martha Ann mentions wanting to send a "likeness" of her sons to Joseph F. See Martha Ann to Joseph F., 30 September 1862, herein.
214. Levira Smith.
215. Joseph F. returned home from a mission to the British Isles on 28 September 1863.
216. William Jasper Harris.
217. William Jasper Harris Jr. and Joseph Albert Harris.
218. Older half sister Jerusha Smith Pierce and her husband, William Pierce.
219. Aunt Mercy Rachel Fielding.
220. Joseph F. and Martha Ann's cousin-in-law David Taylor, husband of Mary Jane Thompson.
221. Cousin Mary Jane Thompson, daughter of Mercy Rachel Fielding.

Fielding,[222] and family, to Bro. Smoot and family.[223] And— Every body. May God bless you My Dear Sister, Marth William and all the faithful, I am truly, J. F. Smith[224] [*end of page*]

MARTHA ANN TO JOSEPH F., 22 FEBRUARY 1863

Ans$^{\underline{d}}$ April 8$^{\underline{th}}$ [225]
1863—
Sheffield[226]

G S L C
1863[227]
[*illegible strike-through*]
Feb the[◊] 22

My dear kind mutch beloved brother it would been hard matter to disscribe to you the feelings with whichich I read your kind letter of Nov the 12 itis is a great privelege to me to receive a lettr from you but perhaps you do no think this is so for I am so long in answering them but it is not ths that is the cause of my long silence but itis becus I could not git papr that was sutable to write to you on it is very scarce you can hardly git hold of fine paper atall. we are all tolerable well at present and hope hat this may find you [*illegible strike-through*] enjoyng the same blessing I do hope you have got <[*illegible strike-through*] that> hatefull caulf you spoke off cuerd ere this. I have ben very oneasy about you on acount of it I am verry ancious to hear how you are. I hope you wll git strong and well before you start home O Joseph I hardley know how to <wait> for the <time> to slip away for you to start [**p. 2**] home and then the time you are crossing the mighty deep O may our father in heave spare your life while crossing that dreade<d> Sea and then the wery miles you have to cross before we can again met with you it has been a long wery time to wait for your return but may it slip quickely an[*0.6 x 2.5 cm tear*] way that we may meet again and O what a happy metting it will be. so be ware of thy self and cake care of thy self, dear brother and you shall hav our united prayr from day to day for your safe return to <your> home.[228]

I do not know that I have anythng mutch ~~to~~ write to ~~you~~ that will be news to you warever I will do my best william[229] has been on poliece dutey for fore or five weaks back but has sence

222. Uncle Joseph Fielding, Mary Fielding's brother.
223. Abraham O. Smoot, William Jasper Harris's stepfather.
224. Cross-written on page 2.
225. Joseph F. noted receipt of this letter on 2 April, "Returned to Sheffield. Found awaiting me letters from Martha Ann. E. L. Sloan, Samuel [Smith], Hewitson Steenforth, and others also the [Millennial] Star. And a Deseret News." Joseph F., journal, 2 April 1863.
226. Written sideways and circled in the top left margin.
227. Joseph F. was twenty-four, and Martha Ann was twenty-one years old.
228. Joseph F. was not officially released to return home until 15 April 1863, arriving in the Salt Lake Valley in October 1863 with the John W. Woolley company, where he served as chaplain. Martha Ann's comments suggest that he knew of his pending release and had made it known to his family.
229. William Jasper Harris.

been relieved he is now garding a man in the coart house who had some words with anothr man by the name of Greenlief Gre<e>nlief[230] beat him over the head with hs pistol severly **[p. 3]** and the lef him he was arested and taken to th stasion house where he remained uder williams care and some others of the polices [*illegible strike-through*] william came home to git hs dnnr and while he was gon they took Holaday wihch was beten over head to the stacion house to have thir triel and when he got in they told him to take a chair which he refuesed to do Greenlief sat aparte hm in a chare and he drew out his pistole and shot him threw the heart before any one could hinder him he never spoke aftr it they ware both gentiles we do not know how it will torminate yit I must now stop to git the lit ones[231] thir dinnrs. I have satesfied thir litle wones and now they are quiet it is no little matter to to write where they are <near> one pulls me on one side and the other on the other Mothr I want a peace of bread and butter Mother look hear and the pritty Jody[232] sas Mah Mah Mah a lttle louder and a little <louder> untll he makes me hear him then I must look rownd at him and then he sais ba bur for bread and buter **[p. 4]** I have to git up and wait on them well perhapes this is not interesting so I will stop and tell somethng else the children in the valley have all had the hooping caugh[233] mine have escaped so far they have not had it a great many little ones have ded w[*1.1 x 2.6 cm tear*] it. Jerusha[234] was down hear a weak ago she left her too oldest ones at home and brought the too younges with her[235] she went to ~~the~~ <the> theater[236] saturday night and I kept the babey while they ware gon ~~whle they were~~ <while they ware> thear I took thir teem & Jerusha and I went down to Sarahs[237] she lives in Johs[238] house now they mooed in from waber last fall they ware all well I have not seen Levira sence we took her to the social hall[239] to a party she was well as comon there she has ben out severrel times thiss winter to the theater and to party she looks rather poor and thin she needs you at home to cumfort her up sadly O I wish you was hear as fervently as she does I am quite sure but we must wait with paciens untill you come & may God sppead you is my prayr Lovina Jerusha Sarah Brothr Sister Smoots[240] all send thir love and best respects to you. excuse this short scroll God bless you for ever

Martha Ann Ha

230. This altercation between Silas C. Greenleaf and Joseph Holladay, as well as Holladay's initial trial for manslaughter, was reported in "Another Homicide," *Deseret News*, 18 February 1863, 268. Holladay's trial was repeatedly postponed over the course of two years, during which time he eventually skipped town. On the development of the extended trial, see the Third District Court reports in *Deseret News*, 1863–65. See biographical register, "Greenleaf, Silas C." and "Holladay, Joseph."
231. Martha Ann and William had two children at the time of this letter.
232. Joseph Albert Harris, nicknamed Jody.
233. Whooping cough is a highly contagious bacterial disease known today as pertussis. The *Deseret News* reported the deaths of the two children from whooping cough. See "Died," *Deseret News*, 25 February 1863, 280.
234. Jerusha Smith.
235. Hannah Evaline Pierce and Hyrum Robert Pierce were eight and six years old, respectively. Martha Lavinia Pierce and Margaret Jerusha Pierce were two years and two months old, respectively.
236. The theater was the Salt Lake Theatre built on the corner of 100 South State Street with a seating capacity of fifteen hundred people and dedicated on 6 March 1862 by Brigham Young. See Charles L. Metten, "Salt Lake Theatre," in *Encyclopedia of Mormonism*, ed. Daniel H. Ludlow (New York: Macmillan, 1992), 4:1255.
237. Sarah Smith.
238. John Smith.
239. See Martha Ann to Joseph F., 2 March 1861, herein.
240. Abraham O. Smoot and likely Margaret Thompson McMeans.

MARTHA ANN TO JOSEPH F., [23–24 FEBRUARY 1863?]

Ans$^{\underline{d}}$ Apr. 3$^{\underline{rd}}$[241]
1863[242]

for Joseph

Dear brother excuse this little dirty peas of paper and alow me to say a few more things to you which I left out of my letter which will be sent with this. for there was not room in it it to write all that I wanted to I am realy ashamed to send what I have writen it looks so bad but I have no papr to coppy it on and so you must considder from whenhense it comes and make alouences acordingly. the children botherd me while writing and I had a dreadfull pain in my shouder which was very disagreable, in short I am not a very good writer which you are well aware off but what I write ill composed as it is comes from my heart and I mean it I may not not have the languege of some nor the talent for writing that this will ed<e>fye a preson say ferinstence <that> Levira[243] has but my life has been far differenty spent to what hrs has been I have [**p. 2**] had to earn my bred by hard labor ever sence my m<o>thr died[244] I have ben obliged to work hard and it does not have a tendencey to refine any ones mind to such things. onely ~~in such things~~ as we are awkupied in the most we lirn how to be usefull in some thngs and in others we are ig<no>ront [*illegible strike-through*] if you spoke of my arousing your desire to see the likenesses[245] of my little ones and I am very sorry that I cannot grattify your wish but we have not the means, to git them at present but you shall have them when you return iff I can git them for you I would like very mutch to have a likeness of you iff I could git one I have never had that privlege yet I have asked Levira to give me even the worst one she had off you severrel times but she refused to do so and so I have been obliged to look at you threugh my minds eye or beg the privolege off seeing ~~it~~ you I should like to have you git me one iff you can conveniently but do not rob your self ~~to do so~~ of any comfort to git it I would rather you would wait untill you git home an I would pay for it myself for I am viry ancious to have one I got one of Johns[246] be fore I let him go it is a very good one I am going to send a note to ~~hi~~ John in this will you pleas to forward it to him. and allso to Samuel.[247] William[248] sends his love to you and says he is so busy that he can not write hiss time so you will pleas to excuse him your cows are

241. Joseph F.'s journal indicates that he received a letter from Martha Ann on 2 April 1863 and then mailed a letter to Martha Ann on 9 April 1863. See Joseph F., journal, 2 April 1863 and 9 April 1863.
242. Written sideways and circled in the top left margin of page 1. This letter is not dated; however, it was likely written on 23 or 24 February 1863 and included with the letter dated 22 February 1863, as Martha Ann states here. See also Joseph F. to Martha Ann, 3 April 1863, herein, in which Joseph F. confirms the receipt of letters from 22–24 February.
243. Levira Annette Clark Smith.
244. Mary Fielding, Joseph F. and Martha Ann's mother, died on 21 September 1852.
245. *Likeness* was a common nineteenth-century term for a photograph. Although photography had seen significant technological advances that lowered costs, many pioneer families still could not afford to divert resources to purchase photographs. See Martha Ann to Joseph F., [July] 1864, herein.
246. John Smith, Joseph F. and Martha Ann's half brother.
247. Samuel Harrison Bailey Smith, Joseph F. and Martha Ann's cousin.
248. William Jasper Harris.

all alive and well all though it is very hard on them this winter there is lots of cattle dying of on the rang write to me be fore you start home and let us know when it will be may God bless you

Martha Ann Harris[249]

JOSEPH F. TO MARTHA ANN, 3 APRIL 1863

Page 1[250]
103 Hodgson St.[251] Sheffield
YorkshireEng. April 3rd 1863[252]

My Dear Sister MarthaAnn:—

Yours of Feb. 22nd, 23rd& 24th has come duly to hand.[253] I see by the marks on the Envellope that it was mailed on the 27th which made it a little over a month coming to hand. I am pleased that you have written to me. I had almost begun to think you did not intend to write to me again. and yet I could not tell what I had done amiss. but all is right.— This letter will be my last one to you—while I am in England, I hope. My—time is drawing rappidly to a Close.[254] before this reaches you I shall be on my way home if all goes on well. The first vessel—the "John J. Boyd"[255]—will Sail from Liverpool[256] on the 29th of this month, and vessels will continue to leave untill May the 20th or there abouts. when the Emigration will close[257] for this Season. very many intend Emigrating from this Country and from Scandinavia this Season, if the way continues open, which I hope may be the <case> [**p. 2**] I shall not be able to finish writing this letter for two or three day, as I am very busy just now. and shall have to leave the Town on Sunday. I shall therefor write a little now and then as I have oppertunity, untill it is done. I will

249. Written sideways in the left margin.
250. Written on top right corner of the letter.
251. See Joseph F. to Levira, 17 January 1862.
252. Joseph F. delayed finishing the letter because of an obligation he had in Woodhouse, a farming village and now a suburb of Sheffield, on Sunday, 5 April. See Joseph F., journal, 5 April 1863.
253. Joseph F. noted, "Returned to Sheffield. Found awaiting me letters from Martha Ann. E. L. Sloan, Samuel, Hewitson Steenforth, and others. Also the [Millennial] Stars and a Deseret News." Joseph F., journal, 2 April 1863. During the next few days and weeks, Joseph F. mentioned Martha Ann in his journal several more times. "I mailed letters to Martha Ann [and others]." Joseph F., journal, 9 April 1863. "I wrote to Parley, and mailed 18 Stars home. 6 to Martha Ann, 6 to Sarah & 6 to D. Taylor." Joseph F., journal, 12 June 1863.
254. Joseph F. had been in England for almost three years. After a brief trip to France, he departed England aboard the *City of Washington* on 24 June 1863. Joseph F. arrived in New York on 6 July and witnessed the famous draft riots there before making his way to the Latter-day Saint staging ground in Florence, Douglas County, Nebraska. He finally arrived in Salt Lake City in October 1863.
255. The *John J. Boyd* departed Liverpool on 30 April 1863 and arrived in New York on 29 May with 767 Latter-day Saint immigrants onboard.
256. See Fred E. Woods, "The Tide of Mormon Migration Flowing through the Port of Liverpool, England," *International Journal of Mormon Studies* 1 (2008): 60–86.
257. Some ninety thousand Latter-day Saints crossed the ocean during the nineteenth century. Latter-day Saint leaders organized emigration to fit a specific window that generally opened during the spring months of April and May to ensure that converts arrived at the Latter-day Saint staging grounds in the United States to make the trek across the Mormon Trail during the best weather.

send you a likeness by this letter,[258] and I will take one of the little Boys'[259] when I get home that is—"I will if I can—but if I can't—of course—how can I ?"—

I don't mean to say I will take one of them, because I expect you could not spare one—if you had a dozen. but a likeness of them both, now you can understand me. there's nothing like being plain, at a weding!

God Bless my little Strainger Relatives.[260] I think much of them, and I pray for them. Oh! may they each grow up in wisdomes pathes and their lives be crowned with long-years, and happiness. May they be equel to the days in which they shall live, and to the great work which lies before them. do your [**p. 3**] duty to your's. Walk in the foot-steps of our Mother, and be wiser and better if you can, and in the memory of your offspring, and posterity yet unborne,[261] your name shall be honoured and your memory reviered, as is hers.[262]

I believe you will teach your children to love, not fear you.

Inspire their youthful hearts to love virtue and dispise vice. Encourage and succor every noble and Godly aspiration of their Souls, and check with a kind and motherly affection, but with a firm, unwavering hand every tendancy to disobedience, or wrong. never praise them for doing right, nei[*13.2 x 7 cm diagonal tear*][263] them nor behind the[*diagonal tear*] they will do, to be [*diagonal tear*] them that, to d[*diagonal tear*] for which no[*diagonal tear*] is as easy [*diagonal tear*] thousan[*diagonal tear*] please[*diagonal tear*] [**p. 4**] will grow up in the nurture and admonition of God, disinterrestedly good, which is true nobility, & Godliness.

Never—No! Never!! Scold them. — It is the greatest folly in the world to Scold. if any thing needs to be said, it may be said calmly, and affectionatly, not in a passion. Scolding of any kind is usless, and worse, it is a folley, and a crime. reason, counsel, instruct, but never scold. Never box or Slap them, not even in calmness. if you need to whip, do as mother did to me. talk, and reason, till the quck[264] is thoroughly probed, then apply the healing balm of birch or raw-hide, & do it well. Mother has corrected [*diagonal tear*] I have looked forward [*diagonal tear*]ing, kind reproof [*diagonal tear*] far less pain[*diagonal tear*] can punish [*diagonal tear*]roof to the [*diagonal tear*] do not [*diagonal tear*]sel.—

258. Unknown photograph. An image survives from this early mission to England that may be the photograph mentioned in the letter.

259. Martha Ann's two sons, William Jasper and Joseph Albert. Martha Ann was pregnant at the time and delivered another son, Hyrum Smith, four months later on 15 August 1863.

260. William Jasper Harris Jr. (born 1859) and Joseph Albert Harris (born 1861). This is an allusion to the fact that the boys were rather unfamiliar with their uncle because he had been away so long.

261. Whether Joseph F. was referring to Martha Ann's pregnancy (she was five months pregnant at the time) or simply alluding to future children in general is unknown.

262. Mary Fielding Smith, Joseph F. and Martha Ann's mother. She had already become a larger-than-life figure without flaws or human weakness.

263. The bottom right corner of page 3 (the bottom left corner of page 4) is torn diagonally. Subsequent references to this tear will hereafter be referred to in this letter as "diagonal tear."

264. According to the *Oxford English Dictionary*, *quick* means a "tender" or "sensitive . . . part."

MARTHA ANN TO JOSEPH F., 12 JUNE 1864

leter no 1
G S L City Utah T June 12 1864[265]

My dear and ever beloved brother Joseph it would be a hard mater to me to describe to you my feelings while reading your kind & welcome letter[266] of aprael the 20th and the reason I have not answerd it before now is becaus we have all been very poorly for some time back hyrum[267] has had the mesels & willey[268] has had the sweled face he has been very bad for a weak that he coul not eat any thing he could drink a little he is better now I have had the tooth ache ever sence you left home[269] I have just got <too of> them pulled out and I hope ~~you~~ I will git some peace now.[270] William[271] has gon to the States[272] on buisness and I know how to simpathise with levira[273] for I am alone as well as her but I have far more care than her upon my mind but I feell to cary my burdens with a chearfull heart and say I thank the heavnly father thou hast given me something [**p. 2**] smething to love to encurage me to do right that I may ~~not~~ <recive that> which I would most desre to have and that is the good will of my heavnly father and his approbation O may I have wisdom gven to me that I may train my little ones up in nutre and admonnetion of thir God I feel more and more the re<s>ponsibelity that rests upon me every day that I live I feel that it is a very great one. I thank you my dear <brother> for your kind advice to me as regards to my children any thing that you can see amis is ~~my~~ the training of my children will be thankfulley recieved from you[274] do not be friiend you will you will ofend me for I could not feel bad to you for I love you to well for that you do not know the ancious days and nights that I have spent thinking of my dear brothr while crossing the mighty deep and how hankfull I felt when herd you had got ~~thire~~ safe threw the [**p. 3**][275] dangers you have passed any one can se thhat the arm of God was out streched to save you from distruction I feel to thank him for the presurvation of your lives O Joseph I can not pen my feelings to you iff you could see my heart laid bare & read it then you would know how I feel toords you O he <may ~~be~~> still preserve your life and keep you from harm while you are on those Ilands and

265. Joseph F. was twenty-five, and Martha Ann was twenty-three. Joseph F. arrived in Hawai'i on 27 March, nearly seven years after completing his first mission there (1854–1857).
266. A nonextant letter written within a month of Joseph F.'s arrival in Hawai'i.
267. Hyrum Smith Harris, Martha Ann's third child, was born on 15 August 1863 in Salt Lake City, Salt Lake County, Utah Territory. See biographical register, "Harris, Hyrum Smith."
268. William Jasper Harris Jr.
269. Joseph F. left Salt Lake City on 2 March 1864 for a second mission to Hawai'i. See Joseph F., journal, 2 March 1864.
270. On Utah dentistry, see "Pioneer Dentistry," *Utah Historical Quarterly* 10 (1942): 32–33, which discusses Alexander Neibaur, a German Jewish convert to the Church, one of the more prominent surgeon-dentists in Utah Territory, having studied dentistry at the University of Berlin. See also Kate Carter, comp., *Treasures of Pioneer History* (Salt Lake City, UT: Daughters of Utah Pioneers, 1952), 1:333–40.
271. William Jasper Harris.
272. William Jasper, accompanied by William Henry Hooper, made his way to the eastern United States to purchase oxen, dry goods, and hardware on behalf of his stepfather, Abraham O. Smoot. Such trips were dangerous because the men carried a significant amount of money. See King, "History of William Jasper Harris," 4.
273. Levira Annette Clark Smith. Even though Brigham Young had given permission for Joseph F. to take his wife, Levira remained behind in Utah, most likely because of her continued ill health.
274. Joseph F. had given advice before. See Joseph F. to Martha Ann, 3 April 1863.
275. "[12 JUN 1864]" is written in the top right margin in an unknown hand.

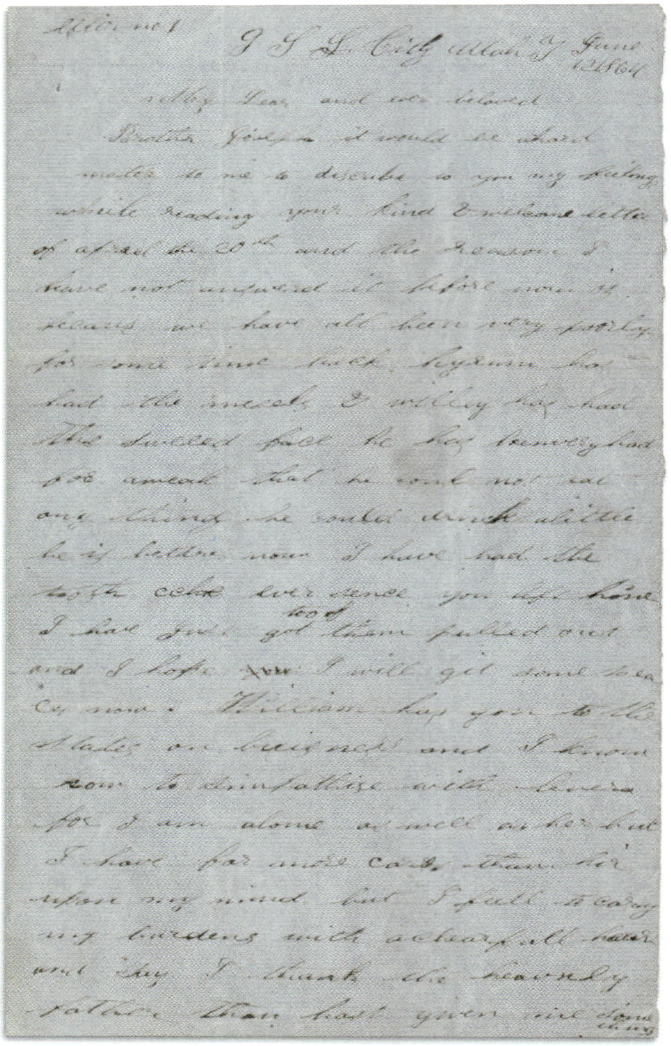
Letter no 1

G S L City Utah Ty June 12 1864

My Dear and ever beloved
Brother Joseph it would be a hard
matter for me to describe to you my feelings
while reading your kind & welcome letter
of april the 20th and the reason I
have not answered it before now is
because we have all been very poorly
for some time back Hyrum has
had the measels & willey has had
the swelled face he has been very bad
for a week that he could not eat
any thing he could drink a little
he is better now I have had the
tooth ache ever sence you left home
I have just got them pulled out too
and I hope ~~xxx~~ I will get some sleep
now. William has gone to the
States on business and I know
how to simpathise with Levira
for I am alone as well as her but
I have far more cares than her
upon my mind but I feell to cary
my burdens with a chearfull heart
and say I thank the heavenly
father that hast given me some thing

Martha Ann to Joseph F., 12 June 1864 (p. 1)

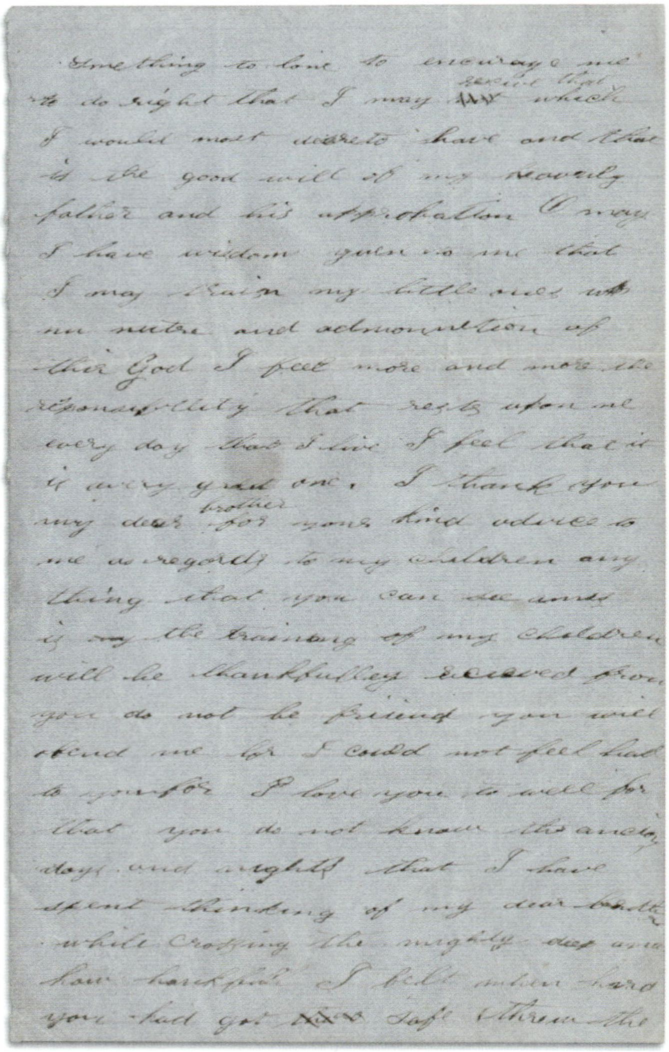
some thing to love to encourage me
to do right that I may ~~xxx~~ receive that which
I would most desire to have and that
is the good will of my heavenly
father and his approbation O may
I have wisdom given to me that
I may train my little ones up
in the nurture and admonition of
their God I feel more and more the
responsibility that rests upon me
every day that I live I feel that it
is a very grand one. I thank you
my dear brother for your kind advice to
me in regards to my children any
thing that you can see amiss
in ~~my~~ the training of my children
will be thankfully received from
you do not be fearing you will
offend me for I could not feel bad
to you for I love you to well for
that you do not know the anxious
days and nights that I have
spent thinking of my dear brother
while crossing the mighty deep and
how thankfull I felt when I heard
you had got ~~xxx~~ safe through the

Martha Ann to Joseph F., 12 June 1864 (p. 2)

enable you to acomplish the work he has sent you to do we will all pray for you tha you may have strength given you acording to your day. I have been to see Levira or at least made severl calls on her sence you left home she is begining to look ~~look~~ like her sef now I hardly think she will have to go to Californa to improve her helth I realy hope she will not go but that is none of my buisness you know but I feell intersted in her wellfare & I can not help saying it you must excuse me [**p. 4**]

I can not tell you when William will be home the waters[276] is so high that they can not git thir goods from new york and that will keep them longer than they would be iff they ware not hinderd he was to have been hear by the 10 ~~J~~ July but he will not be heare that soon. Mr Smoot[277] famely are all gittng better of the meesels, it [*illegible word due to cross-writing*] will soon be be 27 of June and our visit will come off up thare you must tell us off what you are

276. Most likely referring to swollen rivers owing to high spring runoff that year.
277. Abraham O. Smoot.

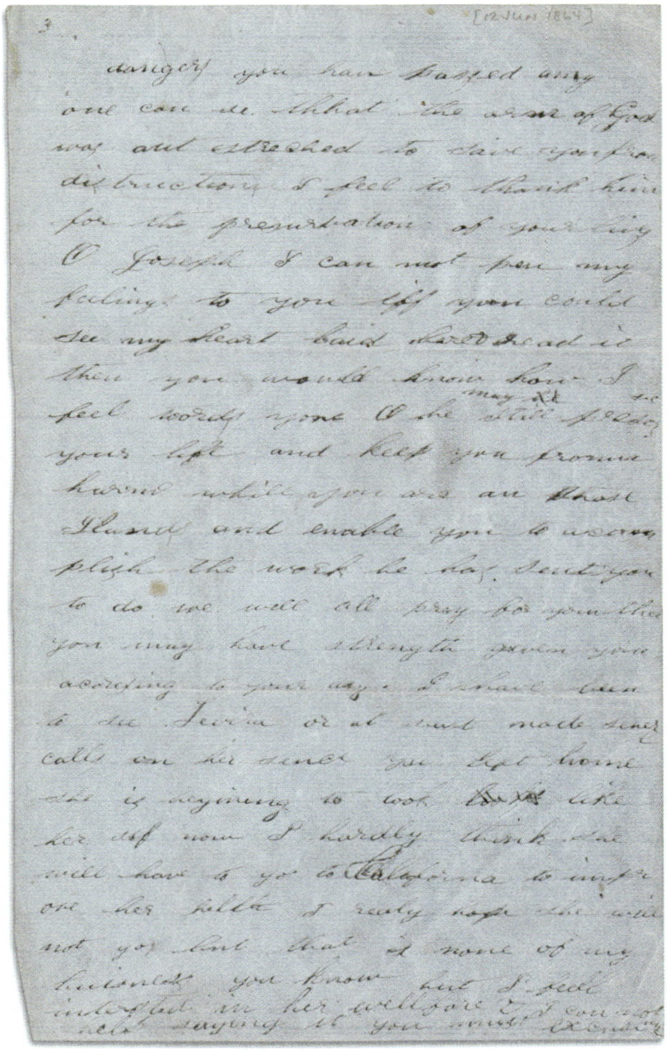

Martha Ann to Joseph F., 12 June 1864 (p. 3)

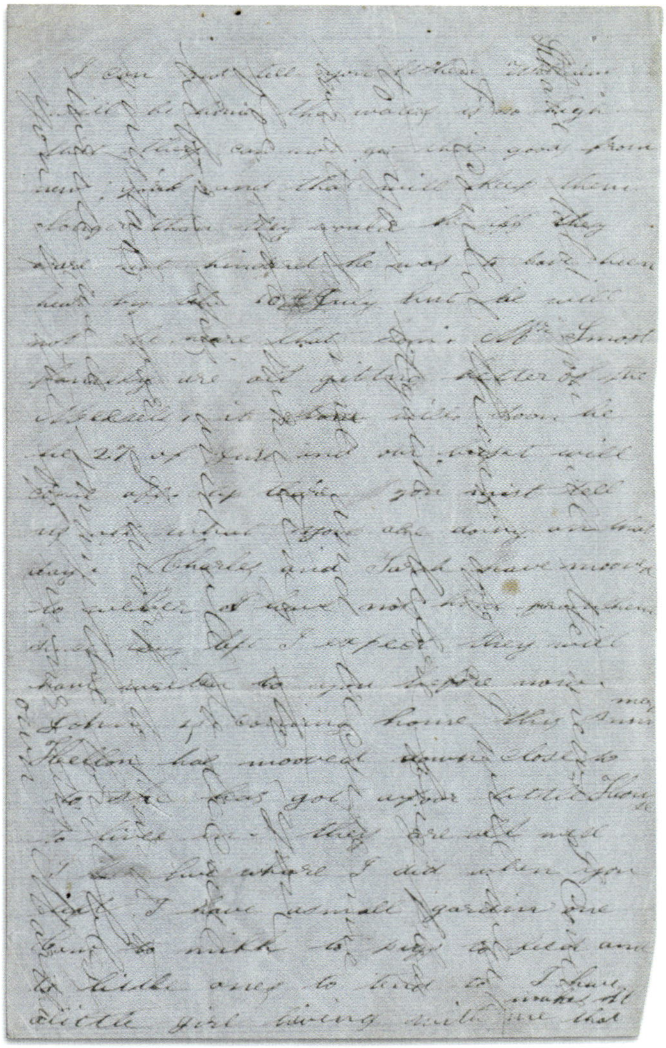

Martha Ann to Joseph F., 12 June 1864 (p. 4)

doing on that day.[278] Charles and Sarah[279] have mooved to weber[280] I have not herd from them sence they left I expect they will have writen to you before now. John[281] is coming home this summer Hellon[282] has mooved down close to to she has got a poor little house to livee in. they are well I [*illegible erasure*] live whare I did when you left I have a small gardin one cow to milk to pigs to feed and to little ones to tend to I have a little girl lving with me that makes [*illegible word*]

278. The anniversary of the martyrdom of Joseph Smith Jr. and Hyrum Smith, who were killed on 27 June 1844 in Carthage, Illinois.
279. Charles Emerson Griffin and Sarah Smith.
280. Weber City, in Morgan County, Utah Territory, located eighty-one miles from Provo, was first settled in 1855. The name was later changed to Peterson in honor of an early settler, Charles Shreeve Peterson.
281. John Smith, Joseph F. and Martha Ann's older half brother, was serving a mission in Denmark at the time.
282. Hellen Maria Fisher, John Smith's wife.

I have told you all the news I could I could think off I will write to you again before long pleas write to me and excuse me for not writing to you before this and all so excuse mistaks for I work to hard to write well may the lord bless you is the of your <own> sis Martha[283]

JOSEPH F. TO MARTHA ANN, 22 JUNE 1864

My address Box 54 Honolulu Oahu S. I.
June 22nd 1864

My Dear Sister Martha Ann:—

I have not heard from you since I left, only that Hyrum[284] was sick, but mending. And that William had gon to the States.[285] Well that is something to hear—away out here where news and friends, are like pearls—few and greatly prised.

I sincerely hope that little Hyrum is better. I can hardly bear to think of seeing him changed in any way from his little, picture in my minde. I can always see him, streight and portly, strung up to the highest point of nerve, full of animation and life—& in a commanding manner & tone issuing weighty orders, that cannot be regarded lightly—or slighted with impunity, by the most majestic of his small but growing Empire! As he stands—in photograph—upon the tablet of my memory—he "is monarch of all he surveys,"[286] he knows no fear, no equel, he commands and—is obeyed, or woe! befall us!!! well he is my ideal—of male baby perfection! of genuine infantile nobility, & magnanimity!!

You well know I love the babies, they are all interresting to me from two months old, ~~and~~ upward.[287] I wonder of Willie and Joseph[288] will forget me, I guess not. kiss all of them for me, & tell them that I think of & pray for them ofton. that they may grow up—worthy of the great mercies of Him whos Image they so nobly bear.[289] I think you have great cause to be proud of your boys. If they are not good men, it will not be their fault. The soil is your own, see that it lacks not cultivation.

I hope you are well, I have no doubt you will be very busy while William is gon. try to be cautious of your health, and that of the babies, theirs often depends much upon the state of your own. I hope you can spare a few moments once in a while to call upon Levira,[290] she complains that she is lonesome, and the folks do not call very ofton. I presume you are always far [**p. 2**] more home-tied, than she is. and perhaps she can finde strength & time to visit with

283. This paragraph is cross-written on page 4. To conserve paper, a portion of a letter could be written over at a perpendicular angle to what had already been written on a page.
284. Hyrum Smith Harris.
285. On William Harris Sr.'s trip, see Martha Ann to Joseph F., 12 June 1864, herein.
286. Joseph F. may be referring to William Cowper's poem "The Solitude of Alexander Selkirk," which begins, "I am monarch of all I survey." It was published in 1782.
287. Married since 5 April 1859, Joseph F. and Levira had no children together during their marriage.
288. William Jasper Harris Jr. and Joseph Albert Harris.
289. Likely referring to a verse in the Bible, "So God created man in his own image, in the image of God created he him" (Genesis 1:27).
290. Levira Annette Clark Smith.

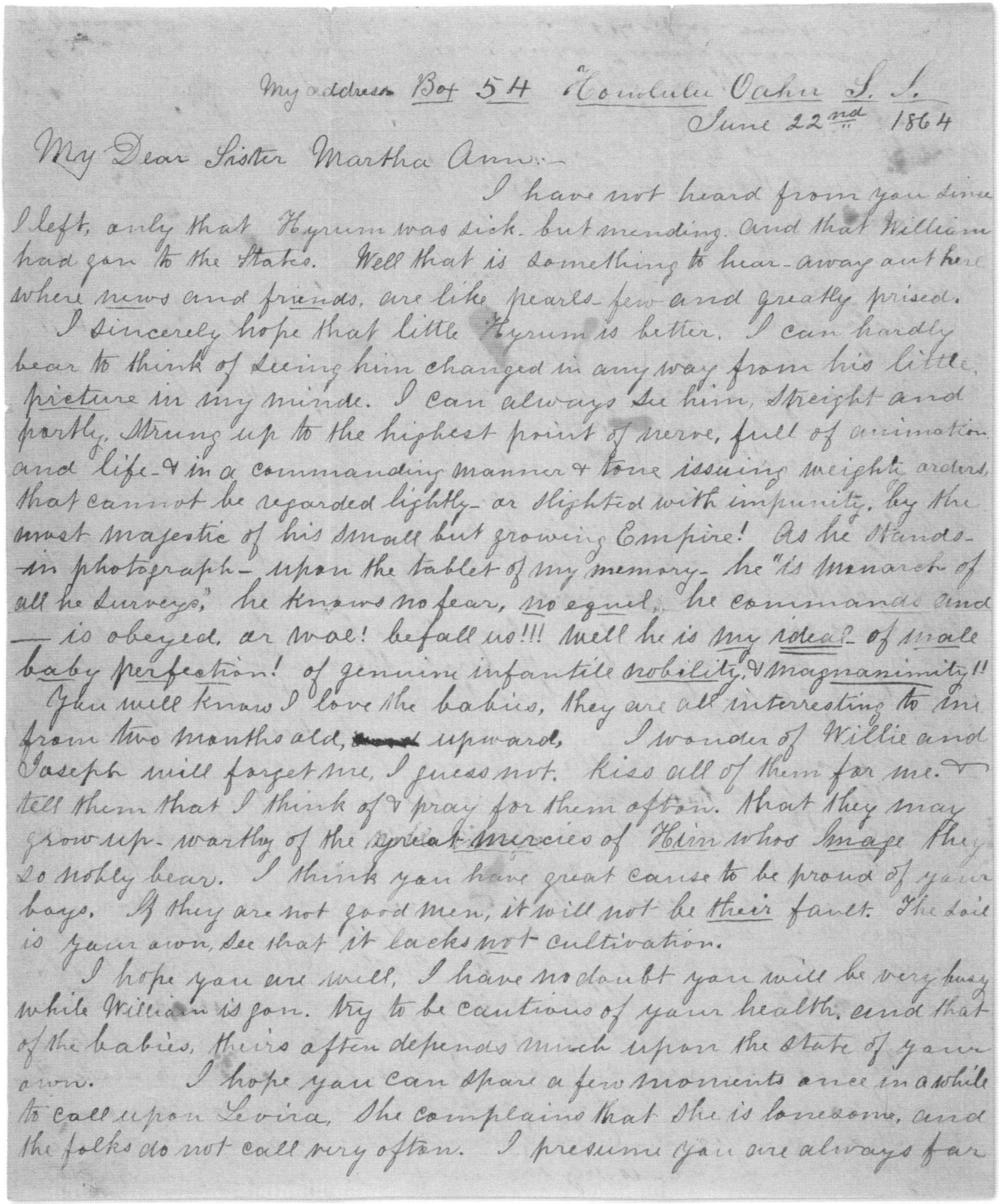
My address Box 54 Honolulu Oahu S. I.
June 22nd 1864

My Dear Sister Martha Ann:—

I have not heard from you since I left, only that Hyrum was sick. but mending. And that William had gon to the States. Well that is something to hear—away out here where news and friends, are like pearls—few and greatly prised.

I sincerely hope that little Hyrum is better. I can hardly bear to think of seeing him changed in any way from his little picture in my minde. I can always see him, streight and portly, strung up to the highest point of nerve, full of animation and life—& in a commanding manner & tone issuing weighty orders, that cannot be regarded lightly—or slighted with impunity, by the most majestic of his small but growing Empire! As he stands—in photograph—upon the tablet of my memory—he "is monarch of all he surveys," he knows no fear, no equel, he commands and—is obeyed, or woe! befall us!!! Well he is my ideal of male baby perfection! of genuine infantile nobility, & magnanimity!!

You well know I love the babies, they are all interresting to me from two months old, upward. I wonder if Willie and Joseph will forget me, I guess not. kiss all of them for me & tell them that I think of & pray for them often. that they may grow up—worthy of the great mercies of Him whos Image they so nobly bear. I think you have great cause to be proud of your boys. If they are not good men, it will not be their fault. The soil is your own, see that it lacks not cultivation.

I hope you are well, I have no doubt you will be very busy while William is gon. try to be cautious of your health, and that of the babies, theirs often depends much upon the state of your own. I hope you can spare a few moments once in a while to call upon Levira, she complains that she is lonesome, and the folks do not call very often. I presume you are always far

Joseph F. to Martha Ann, 22 June 1864 (p. 1)

P.S. I am going to write to Robert Joseph [illegible] [illegible] to [illegible]
If you see any of them tell them to enquire at the office—very truly J. F. S.

more home-tied, than she is. and perhaps she can finde strength & time to visit with her Aunt, when the same fatigue could not be endured to visit you. Never minde such things, Martha Ann, if such things there be. Often the heart may be good when the head is wrong. We should always bear with each other, and ever try to remidy a wrong by a right; knowing, wrong is not righted by wrong, but by the oposite.

Inclosed is a letter to Charles E. & Sarah, and another to William & Jerusha, will you please send them, as soon as you can. You can read them if you think they will be interresting enough. I should be pleased to write to Lovina but I have not time nor space at present. I wrote you a few lines in a letter to Vira a few weeks ago. You have doubtless received it before this time. I wrote to Vira, Aunt Thompson, David and Samuel, and sent the letters by the last vessel. Another vessel go's out in a few days. I have no news to write.

Gibson is going down, everybody that knew him begins to despise him. Some did so from the first. the natives have all left him, but 3 or 4 – but he has the land, & the money he has gathered from the Natives, and intends to keep it – if he can! he is a firm believer in the – "good old rule & simple plan "That they shall take who have the power & they shall keep who can!" The natives have entered a suit against him, but it is a slow opperation, and I do not know that they will succeed, but I sincerely hope they may.

You will see by Charles' half sheet how we are getting along. Please give my love to Brother Smoot and his family. and tell them I shall recollect my last visit for some time – if not longer, – and the 27th of June – near at hand – I do not intend to forget. Give my love to Bro. Hoglend, & to sister Cannon if you should see her. to Aunt Thompson, Mary Jane, Aunt Zina – Geo. A. – Elias & families & every body – God bless you my dear sister – is my earnest prayer – yours – J. F. Smith

Joseph F. to Martha Ann, 22 June 1864 (p. 2)

her Aunt,[291] when the same fatigue could not be endured to visit you. Never minde such things, Martha Ann, if such things there be. Ofton the heart may be good when the head is wrong. We should always bear with each other, and ever try to remidy a wrong by a right, knowing, wrong is not righted by wrong, but by the oposite.

Inclosed is a letter to Charles E. & Sarah,[292] and another to William & Jerusha,[293] will you please <to> send them, as soon as you can. you can read them if you think they will be interresting enough. I should be pleased to write to Lovina[294] but I have not time nor space at present. I wrote you a few lines in a letter to Vira[295] a few weeks ago. You have doubtless recieved it before this time. I wrote to Vira, Aunt Thompson, David and Samuel,[296] and sent the letters by the last vessel. another vessel go's out in a few days. I have no news to write.

Gibson[297] is going down, every body that knew him begins to dispise him. some did so from the first. the natives have all left him, but 3 or 4—but he has the land, & the money he has gathered from the Natives, and intends to keep it—if he can![298] he is a firm believer in the—"good old rule & simple plan "That they shall take who have the power & they shall keep who can!"[299] The natives have entered a suit against him, but it is a slow opperation, and I do not know that they will succeed, but I sincerely hope they may.

You will see by Charlies' half sheet how we are getting along.[300] Please give my love to Brother Smoot and his family. and tell them I shall recollect my last visit for some time—if not longer,—and the 27th of June—neer at hand—I do not intend to forget.[301] give my love to Bro. Hoglend, & to sister Cannon[302] if you should see her. to Aunt Thompson, Mary Jane, Aunt Zina—Geo. A.—Elias[303] & families & every body—God bless you my dear sister—is my earnest prayer—yours—J. F. Smith.

P.S. I am going to write to Heber & Joseph Fielding[304]—Shall direct to Heber If you see any of them tell them to enquire at the office—very truly J. F. S.[305]

291. Possibly Zina Diantha Huntington.
292. Charles Emerson Griffin and Sarah Smith.
293. William Pierce and Jerusha Smith.
294. Lovina Smith.
295. Nickname for Joseph F.'s wife, Levira Annette Clark Smith.
296. Mercy Rachel Fielding. The name David likely refers to Mercy Rachel's son-in-law David Taylor; the name Samuel likely refers to Samuel Harrison Bailey Smith, Joseph F. and Martha Ann's cousin, Levira's half brother.
297. Walter Murray Gibson. See biographical register, "Gibson, Walter Murray."
298. See Matthew Kester, *Remembering Iosepa: History, Place, and Religion in the American West* (New York: Oxford University Press, 2013), 63–65, 70, 82.
299. Both quotations come from William Wordsworth's poem "Rob Roy's Grave," written after his visit to Scotland in 1803.
300. This most likely refers to the letter written to Charles Emerson Griffin mentioned earlier in this letter. Joseph F. asked Martha Ann to get additional information about Charles's activities through that letter.
301. The anniversary of their father's martyrdom on 27 June was always remembered. See Martha Ann to Joseph F., 12 June 1864, herein.
302. Possibly Abraham Lucas Hoagland or one of his sons; "Sister Cannon" likely refers to Elizabeth Hoagland, daughter of Abraham L. Hoagland and wife of George Q. Cannon. See biographical register, "Hoagland, Abraham Lucas" and "Hoagland, Elizabeth."
303. Mercy Rachel Fielding, Mary Jane Thompson, Zina Diantha Huntington, George Albert Smith, and Elias Smith, first cousin once removed to Martha Ann and Joseph F.
304. Heber and Joseph Fielding, sons of Joseph Fielding and Hannah Greenwood and Joseph F. and Martha Ann's cousin. See biographical register, "Fielding, Heber G." and "Fielding, Joseph Greenwood."
305. Paragraph written upside down in the top margin of page 2.

MARTHA ANN TO JOSEPH F., JULY 1864

letter no 2
G S L City Utah Ter 1864[306]

My own dear brother it is wih feelings of graitetude to my heavenly father that I seat my self down to write you a few lines in return for your very kind letter to me. I have read it over and over again for I love to hear or read your letters bettr than any thing I can think off they do me more good than you have any idear off. my health is is not muth to brag on this summer but I manage to keep joging and do my work nursing a gret big baby like mine pulls me down this hot weather and having the carrs all on my sholers and my work to do all help you know I do not git much time to gosop neether with friends nor neighbors but that keeps me out of mischief William[307] has not got home yet he sent a telacraph [**p. 2**] on fryday last that he was at Larina[308] he has been on the plains six weaks he has had very bad luck they have had very bad storms sense they started from th states they have had 3 three stampeeds one break down & one tip over & lost 2 yolk of cattle so you se has got ~~his~~ his hans full his helth is good and he will be hear in one month iff nothing happns more than we know of the Idens are very bad they have r<o>bed severel trains of emagrants this year[309] but they have not dis turbed our people yet & I hope they will not they are in the hans of the Lord he knows all things and does all things for the good off his saints.

I went up to Brothr Brigaham yesterday I thaught I would let him know how you was gitting along but I did not git to see him [*illegible word*] was [**p. 3**] went home with a heavy heart for it greaves me to the very hearts core to hear <w>hat my poor brothre has to pass threw Mother[310] sent for me to come up thare with the wagon I thaugh I would go and I am up hear to day they went to the Teatre last night black Eyed Susen was the name of the play[311] they come home at twelve O clock & what do you think they told me when they come—they said that you and all the rest ware released from that mishon[312] I can scarsley contain my self for joy O my you return home safe you shall have my prayrs at least I dread the great watters you have

306. The envelope provides evidence that this letter was written in July 1864; the postmark is "Salt Lake City U July 64." Additionally, Joseph F. wrote on the cover, "Ans 1864 Aug 30 Honolulu." Finally, Martha Ann mentions in the letter that her children will have birthdays "next month." All three children were born in August: William Jasper Jr. on 4 August 1859, Joseph Albert on 19 August 1861, and Hyrum Smith on 15 August 1863.

307. William Jasper Harris.

308. Possibly Fort Laramie, Albany, Wyoming. Located at the confluence of the Laramie and North Platte Rivers in southeast Wyoming, the site was established as a fur trading post and then as a military garrison. The fort witnessed successive waves of trappers, traders, Native Americans, missionaries, migrants, soldiers, miners, ranchers, and homesteaders for fifty-six years.

309. Conflict with native peoples increased after 1861. One of the most well-known confrontations was the attack on the Kelly-Larimer Wagon Train in July 1864 by mostly Oglala Sioux, with a scattering also from Hunkpapa, Yankton, and Blackfoot Sioux bands. See Randy Brown, "Attack on the Kelly-Larimer Wagon Train," *Overland Journal* 5, no. 1 (Winter 1987): 16–40.

310. Possibly Emily Hill Harris, William Jasper's mother. However, as can be seen later in this same letter, Martha Ann identified several other women as "Mother."

311. *Black-Eyed Susan; or All in the Downs* was a nautical play written by British playwright Douglas Jerrold, first performed in 1829. See John Russell Stephens, *The Profession of the Playwright: British Theatre, 1800–1900* (Cambridge: Cambridge University Press, 1992), 42. The Salt Lake Theatre was constructed in 1861–62.

312. Joseph F. was not released in July 1864.

to cross but the hand that preserved you when you went can protect you when coming home. I have not been to Viras[313] to make a visit for some time for I have ben so buisey but I shall coll on her as soon as I can posable do so [**p. 4**] I do hope she will not go to C<a>liforna[314] for iff she goes it may detain you thare and I should not like that for I would like to see you come hom. Sister Smoot[315] sends her love and best wishis to you and sais she would write to you iff you was not coming home but she prays that the way my open up that you my have a speedy delivery from tohose landchs land she sends you one of her Roses in this letter pleas except of it. She has some butiful ones this year ~~Anna~~. Mother Diana & Anna[316] sends ther lovee to you they all rember you in thir prayrs continualy Mr Smoot also sends his best respecs to you he just came in they hav thir new hous finnished it looks very nice Sister Smoot has the new part. It is not much [**p. 5**][317] like the one I live in I live whare I did wen you left I hope I will have a bettr one when you git home.

My children are all tolerable well hyrum is just lining to stand alone he is very trresum in to every thing he comes to up to his eyes he is even now tugging at my dress and squeling wih great forse I can not write very god under such sircumstances he looks just as he did onely he is 5 munth older than he was he will soon be a year old thir birh days all come off next month Wi 4 J A on th 19 H S on the 15 one 5 one 3 one 1 years old[318] I have had our likenesses[319] taken for you and one for me my famaly groupe [**p. 6**] So I fullfilled my promise at last[320] better late than never is it not Iff I was inclined to be vain you would help me to be so but iff my children are as good as thy ar good looking it will be all i ask it will be thir goodness that will make me proud and no thir looks I will send the girls thir letters I was hley interested with ~~you~~ thir letters

I have not ha<r>d from Jerusha for some time William is building her a house this sumer I am glad of that for her sake

Aunt Zina[321] sends her love to you she than you for your kind remembence to her. I have writen all I can at this time excuse mistakes I will write again iff I can you will have a hard job to read this may God ~~Gog~~ bless you is my prayer I remain Martha

313. Levira Annette Clark Smith.
314. Levira traveled to San Francisco, where she met Joseph F. as he returned home from this mission. However, Levira decided to remain in California.
315. Likely Margaret Thompson McMeans.
316. Diana Tanner Eldredge and Anna Kirstine Mauritzen, plural wives of Abraham O. Smoot.
317. "[P.5—1864]" is written in the top left margin by an unknown hand.
318. Martha Ann's three sons all had August birthdays: William turned five on 4 August, Joseph Albert turned three on 19 August, and Hyrum turned one on 15 August.
319. Most likely the photograph printed in the decade introduction for this chapter (p. 108).
320. See Martha Ann to Joseph F., 3 April 1863.
321. Zina Diantha Huntington.

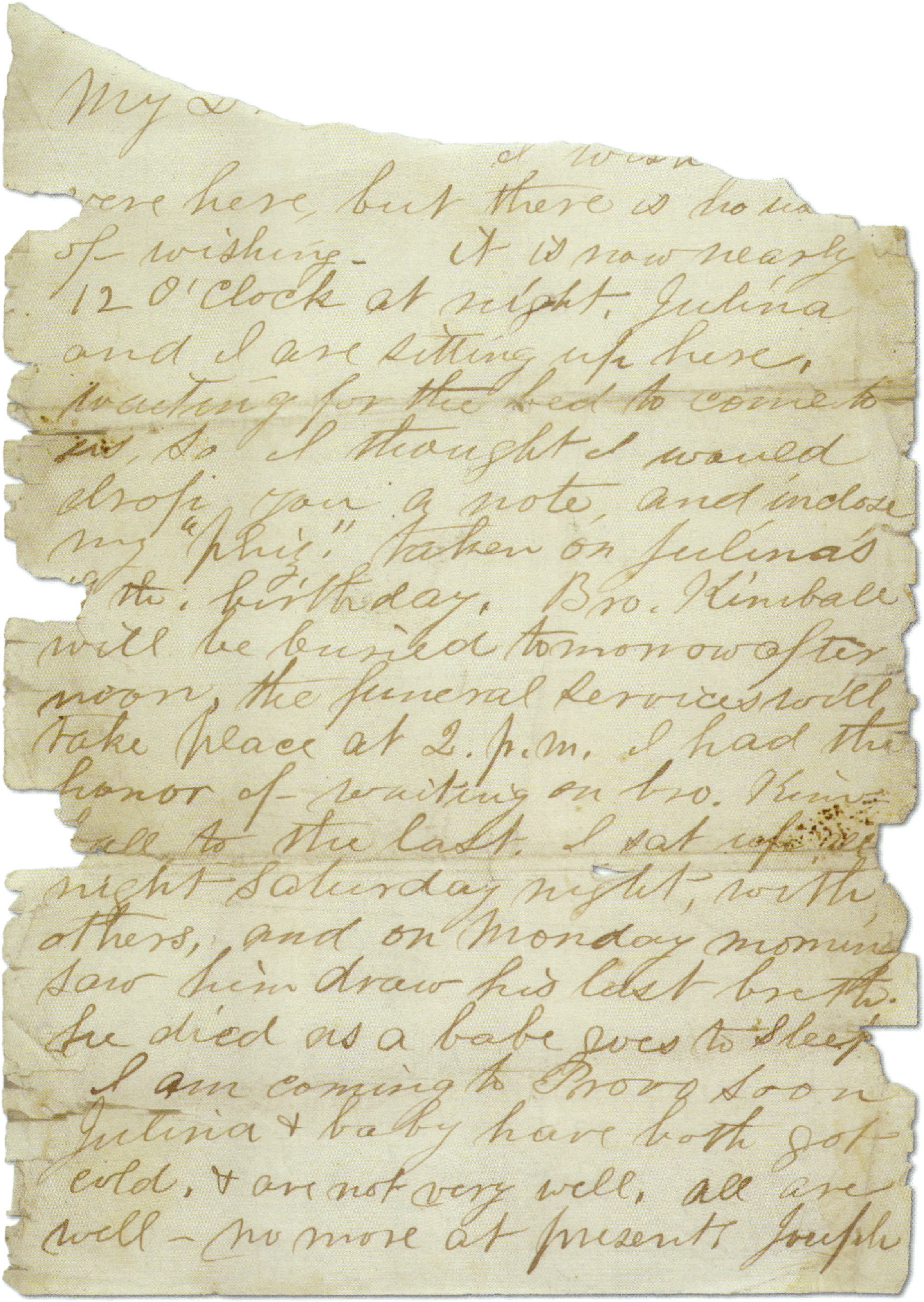

My D[ear] ... I wish ... were here, but there is no use of wishing. It is now nearly 12 O'Clock at night. Julina and I are sitting up here, waiting for the bed to come to us, so I thought I would drop you a note, and inclose my "phiz." taken on Julina's 9th. birthday. Bro. Kimball will be buried tomorrow after noon, the funeral services will take place at 2. p.m. I had the honor of waiting on bro. Kimball to the last. I sat up [all] night Saturday night, with others, and on Monday morning saw him draw his last breath. He died as a babe goes to sleep. I am coming to Provo soon. Julina & baby have both got cold, & are not very well. all are well — no more at present. Joseph

Joseph F. to Martha Ann, 23 June 1868

JOSEPH F. TO MARTHA ANN, 30 AUGUST 1864

To Martha.[322]
Aug. 30. 1864
Honolulu

"Is there on this cold selfish earth
"One heart so cruel as to scold
"A roguish boy. brim-full of mirth
"And like my pet just one[323] year old?"[324]

Or should his little heart be grieved
And tears bedim his pretty eyes
Coldly pass him unperceived
Regardless of his pitious cries?
If such a heartless wretch could be
On earth produced. He'd have no <friend.>
No home, no peace nor sympathy,
And grief should haste his timely end![325]

JOSEPH F. TO MARTHA ANN, 23 JUNE 1868

[23 June 1868][326]
My D[*12.7 x 3.4 cm tear*][327]

I w[*diagonal tear*] were here, but there is no us[*diagonal tear*] of wishing— it is now nearly 12 o'clock at night, Julina[328] and I are sitting up here, waiting for the bed to come to us, so I thought I would drop you a note, and inclose my "phiz",[329] taken on Julina's [*diagonal tear*]9 th,

322. From Joseph F.'s journal, 30 August 1864, original not extant. Joseph F. copied three letters into his journal at this point: Joseph F. to Family, 2, 3, and 4 August 1864; Joseph F. to Martha Ann, 30 August 1864, herein; and Joseph F. to Samuel H. B. Smith, 14 September 1864.
323. Joseph F. changed the word *two* in the original poem to *one* at this point, most likely as a reference to Hyrum Smith Harris, Martha Ann's one-year-old son.
324. Four lines from Rosa Vertner Johnson Jeffrey's sixty-four-line poem "Two Years Old." See *Poems* (Boston: Ticknor and Fields, 1857), 79. An American poet from Mississippi, she was considered the first widely known Southern female poet.
325. The letter ends at this point.
326. Although this letter is undated, the reference to Heber C. Kimball's death in Salt Lake City (22 June 1868) and his scheduled funeral (24 June 1868) suggests a date of 23 June 1868. Joseph F. was twenty-nine, and Martha Ann was twenty-seven.
327. There is a tear of 12.7 by 3.4 centimeters from the top left corner to five centimeters below the top right corner. The edges are worn, and some words are indecipherable. Subsequent references to this tear throughout this letter will be indicated by the words "diagonal tear."
328. Joseph F. married Julina Lambson on 5 May 1866. See biographical register, "Lambson, Julina."
329. Photograph.

birthday.[330] Bro. Kimball will be buried tomorrow after noon, the funeral services will take place at 2. p.m. I had the honor of waiting on bro. Kimball to the last. I sat up all night Saturday night, with others, and on Monday morning saw him draw his last breth. he died as a babe goes to sleep[331]

I am coming to Provo soon[332] Julina & baby[333] have both got cold, & are not very well. all are well—no more at present Joseph

JOSEPH F. TO MARTHA ANN, 1 DECEMBER 1868

Salt Lake City
Tues. Dec. 1st. 1868[334]

My Dear Sister:—

Your's of 19th. ult. came safely to hand I though I would just now—in the midst of labor and unperformed duties—stop a moment and drop you a line.

Julina, Sarah, Baby[335] and Edward[336] are all well, as usual, Edward is slowly recovering from a spell of sore eyes. Baby for some time has been a little restless of nights, and she is such a little talker! She will repeat almost any simple word after me or her mother, and say them plain too. She is as blessed as ever; I have comfort with my little one.

My birthday[337] present was a long law-document styled "Levira A. Smith vers. Joseph F. Smith", an action, brought before the 4th Judicial District Court of San Francisco for "divorce" and "Relief"—. for the "crime of adultery". in which Levira Swears that I have committed adultery with one "Julina Lambson" "Mary Ellen Richards"[338] and "other women,"[339] in Salt Lake City & Provo—in Utah Territory—and in San Francisco Cal. and other places"!! Aunt

330. Julina Lambson turned nineteen on 18 June 1868.

331. Heber C. Kimball married Joseph F. and Martha Ann's mother, Mary Fielding, in 1844 and baptized thirteen-year-old Joseph F. in May 1852; he remained interested and concerned about Joseph F. throughout his life.

332. Joseph F., Wilford Woodruff, Abraham O. Smoot, and several others were sent to reside in Provo by Brigham Young as part of an effort to bring about a "Reformation" in the community. Joseph F. apparently moved there in March 1868 but had been absent from Provo on various assignments, including a speaking tour with other Church leaders in May. Joseph F. was still in Salt Lake City on 27 June, for he "borrowed, till harvest, from Aunt Thompson two sacks of flower weighing 98 lbs. each." He commenced working in Provo again on 28 July.

333. Mercy Josephine Smith was born to Julina and Joseph F. on 14 August 1867. See biographical register, "Smith, Mercy Josephine."

334. Joseph F. was thirty, and Martha Ann was twenty-seven.

335. Julina Lambson and Sarah Ellen Richards. Sarah Ellen had recently married Joseph F. on 1 March 1868. Mercy Josephine Smith was born on 14 August 1867 and is referred to as "Baby." See biographical register, "Richards, Sarah Ellen."

336. Joseph F. took charge of Edward Arthur Smith during his first mission in England. Eventually, Joseph F. adopted Edward and raised him in the Smith household. See biographical register, "Smith, Edward Arthur."

337. Joseph F. celebrated his thirtieth birthday on 13 November 1868.

338. Levira may have confused this name with that of Sarah Ellen Richards.

339. At this point, Joseph F. had married two women in addition to Levira and had two children, Mercy Josephine and Edward Arthur (adopted). Since the federal government did not recognize Latter-day Saint plural marriages, Levira charged Joseph F. with adultery as grounds for divorce.

Thompson, Mary Jane & Robert[340] are usually well. Jones[341] moves out of your house this week and another family moves in, so I understand. please to forward the inclosed to bro. Jensen the Taylor,[342] and oblige me. with kind love to William & the Children[343] and all friends I am your affectionate Brother Joseph

The girls[344] send love— Edward sends love to the children. [**p. 2**]

P.S. The Juvenile[345] reaches you safely—it goes in my name. I hope you get it all right. I will send you a paper once in a while— Joseph

JOSEPH F. TO MARTHA ANN, 21 JUNE 1869

S. L. City, June 21st. 1869[346]

My Dear beloved Sister
Martha Ann:—

Your's of 19th inst. has this moment come to hand;[347] I have been very busy since the telegram come announcing the sickness of "Jodie",[348] the same day a letter came to Julina[349] informing us of your own poor health and also of the sickness of 'Jodie', I can assure you my Dear Sister, some earnest prayers assended from the Alter of our family circle,[350] from three kind hearts for you, your little ones and for William,[351] the night after the telegram came,—I felt sorry that I could not get to see William, I hunted all over town, but unfortunately I could not find him. Aunt Thompson[352] had a few dollars—rent-money, on hand and I advised her to send it to you, part of ~~a t~~ it at a time, for I thought perhaps you would need it. I hope you will ~~g~~ be able to get what you need for the children. I do not think it is wisdom to give a great deal of Medicine of <u>any kind</u>, make a <u>little</u> do. Wash often, keep the body, and clothes clean, and

340. Mercy Rachel Fielding, Mary Jane Thompson, and Robert Blashel Thompson Taylor, son of David Taylor and Mary Jane Thompson. See biographical register, "Taylor, Robert Blashel Thompson."
341. Possibly Joseph C. Jones. The 1870 US Census lists Jones and his family living near Martha Ann in Provo. See biographical register, "Jones, Joseph C."
342. Unknown individual. From the context of the letter, Jensen was a tailor by profession living in Provo in 1868.
343. William Jasper Harris and Martha Ann had five children at the time.
344. Joseph F.'s wives, Julina Lambson and Sarah Ellen Richards.
345. The *Juvenile Instructor*, published by George Q. Cannon beginning in 1866, was a monthly publication directed to children and youth. It was purchased by the Church in 1901 and became the official circular of the Church's Sunday School until 1929, when it was replaced by the *Instructor* magazine.
346. Joseph F. was thirty, and Martha Ann was twenty-eight.
347. Nonextant letter from Martha Ann.
348. Joseph Albert Harris.
349. Julina Lambson.
350. A possible euphemism for a simple family prayer or a more formal prayer circle around an altar in a private residence, in a meetinghouse, or in the Endowment House. See D. Michael Quinn, "Latter-day Saint Prayer Circles," *BYU Studies* 19, no. 1 (Fall 1978): 79–105.
351. William Jasper Harris.
352. Mercy Rachel Fielding.

breath plenty of fresh air both night and day, do not sleep in closed **[p. 2]** rooms, but breath pleantifully and freely of the fresh, pure air.

Tell William, that Richard[353] called upon me and we made arrangements for him to lift that note. I think a trade can be made that will be satisfactory to William and all concerned, as far as possible.

The folks will be very thankful that Jodie is better. I cannot write much more. David and Alexander[354] are on their way out here to preach against polygamy and convert the Brighamit's.[355] John[356] is up north at Box Elder. Jerusha[357] was down on a visit a short time ago, but only came a few moments ~~at~~ <to> our house. We are all well, the Baby[358] has most excellent health, for which we are most thankful I assure you.

With kind love and prayer for your safety and health, and speady recovery from all sickness. I am your brother

Jos. F. Smith

If I can do any thing for you, be sure to let me know, and do not be backword or timid about telling us your necessities. I send this by bro. Smoot.[359] Joseph

JOSEPH F. TO MARTHA ANN, 13 JULY 1869

S. L. City
July 13th. '69

My Dear Sister:—

Yours of 10th has just reached me.[360] I am always glad to hear from you, and more particularly so when your letters bring good tidings &c.—

My health is good, Julina and Baby[361] are well, Sarah is not well, nor has she been since baby died,[362] her health is poor all the time and now and again wors than ever. A few days since

353. Possibly Richard D. Maxfield, William Jasper Harris's brother-in-law.
354. David Hyrum Smith and Alexander Hale Smith, sons of Joseph and Emma Hale Smith, who were missionary-leaders for the RLDS Church. See Joseph F. to Martha Ann, 13 July 1869 and 17 August 1869, herein. See also biographical register, "Smith, David Hyrum" and "Smith, Alexander Hale."
355. Brighamites, a nickname used by RLDS members to identify those who sustained Brigham Young and the Twelve. For additional information, see Joseph F. to Martha Ann, 17 August 1869, herein.
356. John Smith.
357. Jerusha Smith.
358. Likely Mercy Josephine Smith, born 14 August 1867. She was almost two years old at this time.
359. Abraham O. Smoot, Martha Ann's father-in-law and an important businessman and Church and civic leader in Utah Valley, evidently had been in Salt Lake City and brought this letter to Martha Ann with him as he returned home to Provo.
360. Nonextant letter from Martha Ann.
361. Julina Lambson and Mercy Josephine Smith.
362. Sarah Ellen Richards, Joseph F.'s wife, gave birth to Sarah Ellen Smith on 5 February 1869. "Little Ella" died six days later on 11 February 1869. This was the first of thirteen children's deaths that Joseph F. had experienced by 1918; nine died at very young ages. See biographical register, "Smith, Sarah Ellen."

she put some concentrated lye[363] on the poarch floor to take out some greece spots, and then hastily stepped upon it and slipped down, bruising her some and causing quite a severe spell [**p. 2**] of sickness. And then women are so foolish to worrie and fret—and stew about little or nothing that it ofton times makes it worse for them, such an one is Sarah. She got out of bed the other day, and to day I suppose she did her washing—I remonstrated but to no effect, she must do out a few things—because she needed them!!!

Edward[364] is a good boy and keeps well.

Edwina Walker[365] has been stopping at our house for some time, the Docters have straightened her leg for her—but the Knee joint is so grown out of shape I fear she will not be able to use it. the foot and ankle [**p. 3**] is also very small and slender from long disuse—since she was a child—the lower part of the leg not growing in proportion to the rest of her body.

We give Endowments every Monday and every Wednesday—& sometimes two days a week we baptized for the dead, in the font.[366] the rest of the time I am very busy in the office. I am busy all the time; I want to come down <to Provo> the latter part of this month if I possibly can. Alexander and David Smith are expected in town daily—they are coming full of bitterness & hatered toward polygamy & the Utah Mormons.[367]

You must excuse haste if I had not written now, I might not have got another chance [**p. 4**] William I suppose is in town but he seems to avoid me for he does not come to the house[368] only when he cannot avoid it—I have never done any thing to injure William—I should not think he would shun us—I am sorry to see him part with his place—but I cannot help it—and it is all right with me—I suppose he feels bad.

Please give my love to the Children and to all friends. write again—

May god Bless you and yours—and William and his efforts to extricate himself from every embarrasment[369] is my prayer most cincerely— from your affectionate bro. Joseph

JOSEPH F. TO MARTHA ANN, 17 AUGUST 1869

Salt Lake City
Aug. 17th. 1869

My Dear Sister

363. Lye is a powerful cleaning agent that contains largely potassium carbonate (potash) and was traditionally obtained by leaching ashes.
364. Edward Arthur Smith.
365. Edwina Mariah Walker, a daughter of Lorin Walker and Lovina Smith born in 1850, was Joseph F. and Martha Ann's niece.
366. Some temple ordinances such as baptisms for the dead, endowments, and sealing ceremonies for the living were performed primarily in the Endowment House, located on the northwest corner of the Temple Block in Salt Lake City. See A. William Lund, "History of the Salt Lake Endowment House," *Improvement Era*, April 1936, 213.
367. See Joseph F. to Martha Ann, 21 June 1869 and 17 August 1869, herein. See also section introduction.
368. Known as the "Homestead," Joseph F.'s home was located in the Sixteenth Ward on First North between Second and Third West. See Sloan, *Salt Lake City Directory*, 138.
369. Most likely a reference to an unpaid debt. In 1868 William Jasper Harris was a defendant in a debt collection case. See William J. Harris, 3 March 1868, box 12, folder 119, Salt Lake County, Utah Civil and Criminal Case Files, 1852–1887.

Martha Ann

Yours of 15th inst. came to hand this morning, and I hasten to reply.[370] My health is improving, I have had an attack of the urticaria or hives, which made me rather unwell for a day or two, but I am now all right again. Julina and baby are well, as also is Edward, but Sarah[371] has had another little sick spell, from which she is recovering nicely.

I am sorry you have so many taxes upon your time and strength, I pray God that you may have strength sufficient for your day, and that ere long scenes may change materially in your favor—in every particular. I do not know when Alex, and David[372] will go to the South.[373] David has had a sick spell, from which he was just emerging, when Alex was taken with the complaint which troubled me a few days ago, but I had it very light.

Let me say, that the <u>Salvation</u> of the "<u>Gurleyites</u>"—(for they are <u>not</u> Josephites)—depends upon the pulling-down, and destroying, what they call "Brighamites,"[374] but what is—in reallity—the work of God, for which the Martyrs blead, and died to establish.[375] And this in my estimation places the Prophets Sons, and all their fo[*15.9 x 10.2 cm diagonal tear*][376] on the same platforme, and lev[*diagonal tear*] who have shead the blood of [*diagonal tear*] stoned those who ~~I~~ were [*diagonal tear*] the message of life, i[*diagonal tear*] and this grieves me. [*diagonal tear*] [**p. 2**] from limb, be tortured on the rack, and hetchelled[377] into shreads, or burned at the stake, than to stand in the shoes of our Cousins, <if they continue.> however much we may love them and pray for their good. O! that God may have mercy upon them and deliver them from the clutches of vile apostates and from the cumpass of that Spirit which persecuted their Father, and ours, to death, would have obliterated all trace of Gods holy work from the earth had it the power, and that Spirit still lives in the bosoms of apostates who have rallied around the Sons of the Martyr, and hedged them about, until works of destruction, malice, and

370. Nonextant Martha Ann letter to Joseph F.

371. Julina Lambson, Mercy Josephine Smith, Edward Arthur Smith, and Sarah Ellen Richards.

372. Alexander Hale Smith and David Hyrum Smith, sons of Joseph and Emma Hale Smith and cousins to Joseph F. and Martha Ann, were in Utah Territory as missionary-leaders for the RLDS Church (which followed the leadership of Joseph Smith III). See Joseph F. to Martha Ann, 21 June 1869 and 13 July 1869, herein, and section introduction.

373. *South* was a common name for the Latter-day Saint settlements south of Salt Lake City.

374. Several individuals attempted to replace Joseph Smith as the leader of the Church before his death; for example, William Law was appointed by dissenters of the Church to replace Joseph Smith as Church president and eventually organized a new church in 1844. See Lavina Fielding Anderson, ed., *Lucy's Book: A Critical Edition of Lucy Mack Smith's Family Memoir* (Salt Lake City, UT: Signature Books, 2001), 835. Efforts to assume Joseph Smith's role as the leader of the Church increased following the martyrdom, in what has been identified as the "Succession Crisis." A significant majority of Latter-day Saints followed the Quorum of the Twelve Apostles. Eventually, the Quorum of the Twelve reorganized the First Presidency, appointing Brigham Young as the President of the Church in 1848. During the nineteenth and early twentieth centuries, it was rather common to identify a Restoration church by the name of the group's leader; for example, RLDS Church members who followed Joseph Smith III were identified as "Josephites," and Latter-day Saints who chose to follow Brigham Young were identified as "Brighamites." Joseph F. used "Gurleyites" rather than "Josephites" in referring to RLDS Church members to argue that RLDS members did not actually follow Joseph Smith the Prophet; instead, he argued, they actually followed Zenos H. Gurley, one of the primary individuals responsible for creating the Reorganization Movement that eventually became the RLDS Church. See Roger D. Launius, *Joseph Smith III: Pragmatic Prophet* (Urbana: University of Illinois Press, 1988), 86–92.

375. Joseph and Hyrum Smith.

376. A large portion of the bottom right corner of page 1 (the bottom left corner of page 2) is torn out diagonally. Subsequent references to this tear throughout this letter will be indicated by the words "diagonal tear."

377. A hetchel, or hatchel, is an instrument for combing flax or hemp, so "hatchelling" is the process by which flax or hemp is combed and separated. *Oxford English Dictionary*, s.v. "hatchel."

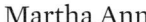

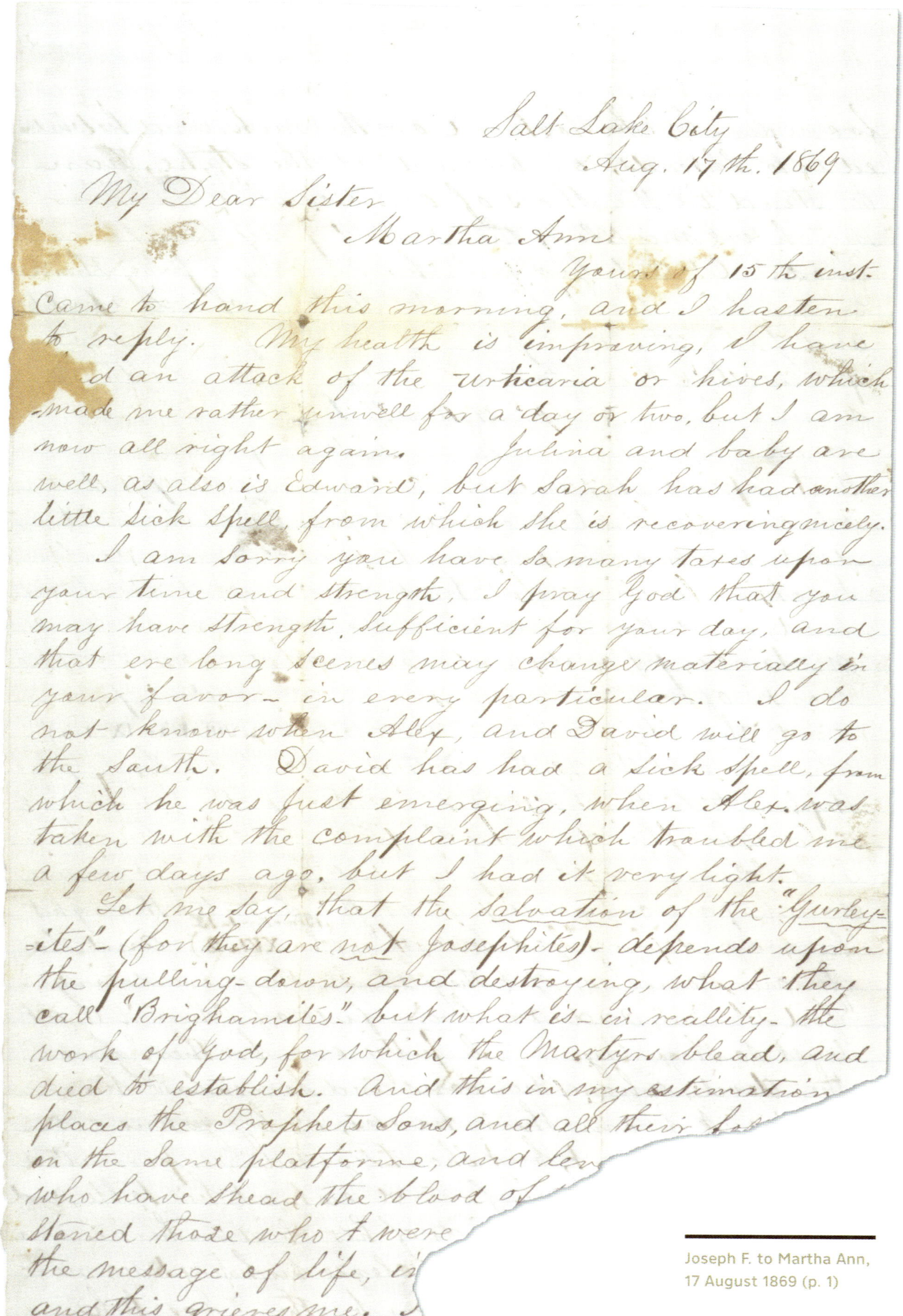
Salt Lake City
Aug. 17th. 1869

My Dear Sister
Martha Ann

Yours of 15th inst.
Came to hand this morning, and I hasten
to reply. My health is improving, I have
d an attack of the urticaria or hives, which
made me rather unwell for a day or two, but I am
now all right again. Julina and baby are
well, as also is Edward, but Sarah has had another
little sick spell, from which she is recovering nicely.
I am sorry you have so many taxes upon
your time and strength, I pray God that you
may have strength sufficient for your day, and
that ere long scenes may change materially in
your favor – in every particular. I do
not know when Alex, and David will go to
the South. David has had a sick spell, from
which he was just emerging, when Alex was
taken with the complaint which troubled me
a few days ago, but I had it very light.
Let me say, that the salvation of the "Gurley-
-ites" – (for they are not Josephites) – depends upon
the pulling-down, and destroying, what they
call "Brighamites" but what is – in reallity – the
work of God, for which the Martyrs blead, and
died to establish. And this in my estimation
places the Prophets Sons, and all their fo
on the same platforme, and len
who have shead the blood of
stoned those who were
the message of life, i
and this grieves me. I

Joseph F. to Martha Ann, 17 August 1869 (p. 1)

hatred against the Priesthood, and the Lord's Annointed, have become metamorphosed unto them, and to many—into works of righteousness, love and compassion, and charity. Paul (Acts. 7–58—VIII–1–3—IX–1–4) when he held the clothes of those who stoned the Prophet Stephen to death, being associated with murderers, and when he dragged the Saints from their houses and sc<o>urged and imprisoned them, and wrought much persecution against the Saints, thought he was doing "God Service" (John. XVI–2 <1 Timothy.1–13.>) and so do our cousins, yet they think they are doing "God service",[378] and are brim full of charity (?) at least so they say. I pitty our brother, for the devil, whom her Sons and Son-in-law have [*diagonal tear*]t from their houses, is by John's[379] liberral [*diagonal tear*]t, but short-sightedness, permitted [*diagonal tear*]oof and eat at his table, and [*diagonal tear*]ds of his children her venom [*diagonal tear*] clense his house![380] no more [*diagonal tear*]ur brother Joseph

[*5.2 x 9.5 cm diagonal tear on bottom left corner*]ay night—

JOSEPH F. TO MARTHA ANN, 23 DECEMBER 1869

[23 December 1869][381]
City Dec. 24th. 1869[382]

Martha Ann
My Dear Sister:—

It has been some time if not more since we heard from you directly. I hope you all have good health, which is the greatest of blessings, provided there is something to eat—the drink is always sure—(unless frozen up—) in Provo. I am greatful for the many blessings which we all enjoy up here excepting Aunt Thompson[383] who has been for some time complaining of rheumatism: but she is getting over it.

Julina and Sarah[384] are both well, as usual, Sarah has a bad cold, so also had Julina, from which she has pretty much recovered. Edward[385] and my little ones are all well, the

378. See John 16:2.
379. John Smith.
380. John Smith, Martha Ann and Joseph F.'s older half brother and Patriarch to the Church from 1855 until his death in 1911. Church leaders, including Joseph F., were unhappy with John's decision to host his cousins David Hyrum Smith and Alexander Hale Smith, RLDS missionary-leaders, while they were proselyting in Salt Lake City. See Irene M. Bates and E. Gary Smith, *Lost Legacy: The Mormon Office of Presiding Patriarch* (Urbana: University of Illinois Press, 1996), 128–31. John's efforts to maintain family relationships with his cousins, including Joseph Smith III, president of the RLDS Church, should be balanced with his long-term commitment to the Church, including serving the longest as Patriarch to the Church (fifty-six years), fulfilling missions, participating in plural marriage, and vigorously inviting extended family members to join the Church in Utah and to keep those already in Utah from gravitating to the RLDS movement.
381. Joseph F. wrote the letter on 23 December 1869; see contents of the letter.
382. Joseph F. was thirty-one, and Martha Ann was twenty-eight.
383. Mercy Rachel Fielding.
384. Julina Lambson and Sarah Ellen Richards.
385. Edward Arthur Smith.

baby—Mary S.[386] is growing like a wead, she is a much stronger child than Mercy[387] was, but such a little thing! and ~~shuch~~ such a head of hair! Josephine[388] is a prefect box of chatter and grave questions she says, "mama what are you for?" mama cannot answer! and it is "papa what is that for—& this for? and soon. It is a great pitty she is so ~~toung~~ tongue-tied!! [**p. 2**] her eyes are still like two little Jets, while the baby has blew eyes. Julina has gon to the Theatree, I am tending babies.[389]

Sarah getting breakfast ready. I have dated this for tomorrow morning.[390] Sarah gets things ready over night, and in the morning gets breakfast in 3/4 of an hour. I wish you could come and see us, and that I know how you are getting along. I have felt considerable anxiety for you, but I have not known how to avoid it, or in other words how to change fate. I feel condemned sometimes when I see the comfortable situation of my family and know that my own sister does not enjoy as much. I wish it were otherwise, but who can change it? Cheer up my sister something whispers to me it will not always be thus with you, and it may not even with me. There is allways a bright hope for the good, and a sure promis of reward. God bless you and yours. I will send you some paper and pens the first chance.

Your brother Joseph

Happy Christmas[391]

All send you cincere love![392]

386. Mary Sophronia Smith was born on 7 October 1869 to Joseph F. and Julina Lambson. See biographical register, "Smith, Mary Sophronia."
387. Mercy Josephine was apparently ill or weak at this time. She died on 6 June 1870, six months after this letter was written. See Joseph F. to Martha Ann, 25 June 1870, herein.
388. Mercy Josephine Smith.
389. Joseph F. noted in his journal, "Julina . . . took Mary Richards to the Theatre. I tended babies." Joseph F., journal, 23 December 1869.
390. 24 December 1869.
391. Written upside down in the top margin of page 1.
392. Written upside down in the top margin of page 2.

42 Islington Liverpool Eng.
Dec. 8th 1874

Martha Ann Harris

My Dear Sister:-

Your kind favors of Oct. 17th and Nov. 16th are both received, the first Nov. 10th and the other Dec. 7th I wrote Nov. 6th enclosing a letter to Bro. N. Muhlestein and others, which you will long ere this have received. Since my last writing I have been to London, Brighton, Birmingham, and other places attending public meetings, and I have been rather busy.

My health is good, as a general thing, much better than when at home, indeed my labors here have been of a less wearing kind, upon my lungs than they were at home. Nothing can be more trying to weak lungs or throat weaknesses, or bronchial affections than such work as has to be done in the E.H. and more especially in the font room, from such labors I have been free since leaving home, and I am much relieved and better for it, as my Photograph will show, and for which I am very thankful. I even have not the opportunity of doing as much preaching here as I had at home, altho' my mission is for the purpose of preaching the gospel. So that really I am having a rest from toil, and am improving under it in health, for all of which - so far as I know how to be - I am very grateful. I have more than this to be grateful for, for since my departure from home, my family have been blessed even as I have, and so far have got along very comfortably, and happily. This to me personally is the

Joseph F. to Martha Ann, 8 December 1874 (p. 1)

Decade 3

1870–1879

JOSEPH F. TO MARTHA ANN, LIVERPOOL, ENGLAND, 8 DECEMBER 1874

[S]ince my departure from home, my family have been blessed even as I have, and so far have got along very comfortably, and happily. This to me personally is the greatest source of my comfort and happiness in my separation from them, and in my sojournings in strange lands, among strangers. If the Lord will only preserve my family,—my little ones, from harm, continue <unto> them shelter, comfortable beds, food and raiment, then I can face the wold with a brave heart, and faithfully try to do my duty in the Kingdom of God.

MARTHA ANN TO JOSEPH F., PROVO CITY, UTAH, 15 AUGUST 1874

[T]he Lord has been good to me after all he has so far spar<e>d the lifes of my little ones they are all alive and in the enjoyment good health and that is saying a good deal whare thare are so many and we . . . have enough to eat such as it it is it plain but healthy and good prospects ahead.

Sarah Ellen Richards Smith and Mercy Josephine Smith, 15 August 1869, photograph by C. R. Savage, Salt Lake City, Utah. Sarah Ellen Richards, Joseph F. Smith's plural wife, poses with Mercy Josephine, the daughter of Joseph F. Smith and Julina Lambson. Sarah Ellen Richards had lost her first and only child in February 1869, just five months earlier. Courtesy of Elaine Cannon Nichols.

Decade Introduction

In 1870 Joseph F. and Julina Lambson (1849–1936) suffered a devastating blow when their two-year-old, Mercy Josephine (1867–70), fell deathly ill. Joseph F. tenderly cared for his young daughter; his journal records the toll it took on him. "I have no apetite," he wrote. "[M]y sympathy & solicitude for my darling little Josephine, has greatly bowed my spirit. . . . She is a sensitive, delicate, and tender little creature and loves her 'papa.'"[1] On 6 June, Joseph F. attended to his duties at the Endowment House during the day, but when he returned home later that afternoon, he found that little Josephine had passed away. He was grief-stricken.

In all, Joseph F. would lose thirteen children before his own death.[2] Julina noted, "He loved them all, but never got over losing [Mercy Josephine]. . . . He never got to where he could talk of his 'Dodo'[3] without tears in his eyes."[4] For the rest of his life, whenever his children were sick, Joseph F. could not help but worry. "I am, as you well know," he once wrote to Julina, "almost useless when anything ails the children."[5] Joseph F.'s letters from this decade demonstrate the depth of his grief over his children's death, as well as his love for and devotion to the rest of his family.

Despite such tender moments in which Joseph F. mourned the loss of a child, life continued in the Smith family, with work at the Historian's Office and Endowment House, church meetings, family gatherings, and special celebrations. For example, in July 1870 Joseph F. noted in his diary, "Friday, July 15, 1870. at H.O. copying S. Record. Got Edward's like ness taken at John Olsens."[6]

Edward Arthur Smith (1858–1911) was the adopted son of Joseph F., who found him in England without family or support. It was a special day for Joseph F. and Julina to have Edward's likeness taken to record and celebrate the life of a young child.

1. Joseph F., journal, 5 June 1870.
2. See appendix A, "Joseph F. Smith's Family."
3. Dodo was Joseph F.'s pet name for his daughter Mercy Josephine Smith.
4. Julina Lambson, journal, 1912, as cited in Joseph Fielding Smith, *The Life of Joseph F. Smith: Sixth President of The Church of Jesus Christ of Latter-day Saints* (Salt Lake City, UT: Deseret Book, 1938), 458–59.
5. Joseph F. to Julina Lambson, 2 April 1888.
6. Joseph F., journal, 15 July 1870. The "H.O." was the Historian's Office, where Joseph F. worked. That day he was most likely copying the sealings performed in the Endowment House in what he identified as the "S. Record" book.

On the first day of the following year, Julina accompanied her husband and her younger sister, Edna (1851–1926), to the Endowment House on the northwest corner of the Temple Block in Salt Lake City on Sunday, 1 January 1871. There, in the structure built for sacred ordinances, she witnessed Joseph F. and Edna's marriage sealing. There were now three sister wives and three children living in a house not far from the Historian's Office and Temple Block.[7]

At the end of his journal for 1871, Joseph F. listed the things for which he was grateful but made one last observation: "I have buried two little girls."[8]

Edward Arthur Smith, 15 July 1870. See Joseph F. to Martha Ann, 23 February 1871, herein. Courtesy of Wilburta Moore.

JOSEPH F.'S SECOND EUROPEAN MISSION

In the 1873 October general conference, Joseph F. was called to preside over the European Mission, which included Great Britain, Holland, Germany, Scandinavia, and Switzerland. At the time he was only one year short of a five-year commitment that would secure him nearly 160 acres of farmland.[9] Leaving for the mission meant forfeiting his claim, but he did not object. "I felt that I was engaged in a bigger work than securing 160 acres of land," he said. "I went as I was called, and God sustained and blessed me in it."[10] Additionally, his call also temporarily ended his career in the territorial legislatures, which had begun in 1865.[11]

Joseph F. departed Salt Lake City on 28 February 1874, leaving three wives—Julina, Sarah Ellen, and Edna—and seven children behind. Edna was pregnant. En route he stopped in Washington, DC, and visited George Q. Cannon for two days. During his stay, Cannon took him to "the White House, and called on & shook hands with President U. S. Grant."[12] Joseph F. also visited the War Department, Treasury, Patent Office, Capitol, and Washington Monument. Joseph F. continued his journey to New York City, where he boarded the steamship *Idaho* and sailed to England.

7. Julina Lambson (married 5 May 1866), Sarah Ellen Richards (married 1 March 1868), and Edna Lambson (married 1 January 1871).
8. Joseph F., journal, 31 December 1871.
9. This was part of the 1862 Homestead Act in which Congress granted land to homesteaders virtually free of charge if they improved it and occupied it for five years. According to the National Park Service, there were 16,798 homesteads in Utah, or about 7 percent of the total territorial land area; see https://www.nps.gov/home/learn/historyculture/statenumbers.htm.
10. Joseph F. Smith, "Discourse," *Deseret Weekly News*, 2 May 1896, 2–3.
11. Joseph F. served again in the 1880 and 1882 session and was the council president in 1882.
12. Joseph F., journal, 7 March 1874.

Joseph F. Smith, 1874, photograph by Charles W. Carter, Salt Lake City, Utah. During the 1870s, Joseph F. was called to preside over the European Mission in 1873 and again in 1877. He was also called to accompany Orson Pratt on a special Church history mission, visiting New York, Ohio, Illinois, and Missouri in 1878. Courtesy of CHL.

Joseph F. Smith, 27 May 1874, Lauritz Olsen, Kjøbenhavn (Copenhagen), Demark. Courtesy of CHL.

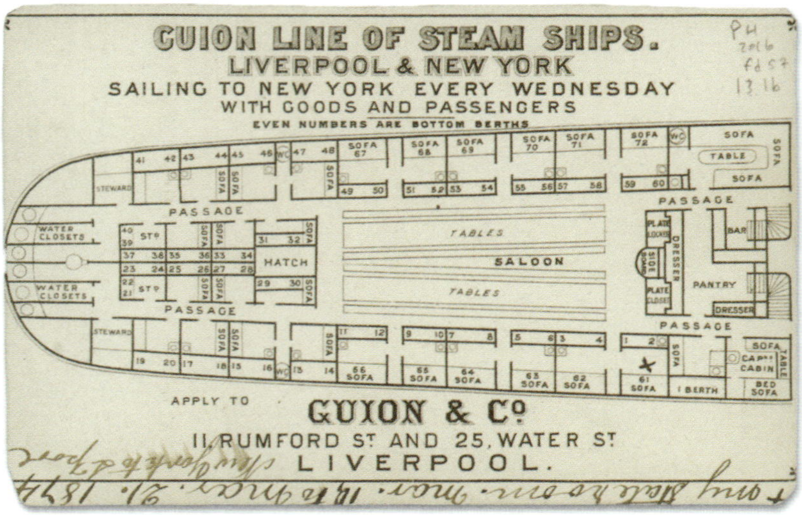

Front: "Steam Ship Idaho, Guion Line." Reverse: "Guion Line of Steam Ships." Joseph F. noted in his journal on 10 March 1874, "Came to Peir 46. At the foot of Huston ST. N. River. And came on board the Idaho . . . set sail for Liverpool." Joseph F. identified where he stayed during his voyage to England: "My State room. Mar. 10, to Mar. 21. 1874 New York to L. pool." He placed an *X* on stateroom sixty-one. Courtesy of CHL.

When his ship came into port on 21 March 1874, he reported, "bros. John C. Graham & Geo. F. Gibbs met me on board and ascorted [escorted] me to 42,"[13] the British Mission headquarters. He had traveled 2,740 miles by train and 3,050 miles by ship to get to his assignment. Although thirty-five-year-old Joseph F. had held significant positions on previous missions, this assignment would be his first major administrative position.

13. Joseph F., journal, 21 March 1874. The notation "42" was the affectionate nickname for the Church's headquarters at 42 Islington Street in Liverpool.

When he arrived, Joseph F. faced a number of challenges in Europe. First, there were only a handful of missionaries to help administer the work.[14] Second, he was responsible for the Church's massive and highly successful emigration efforts.[15] Finally, he served as editor of the *Millennial Star*, the Church's oldest continuous English-language publication.[16]

During this second mission, Joseph F. expressed concern about the poverty he confronted in England. In a letter to his sister, he observed, "I cannot bear to see suffering and poverty, I see sights which grieves me every time I go out in the streets."[17] The never-ending demands of his important assignment and Liverpool's dreary weather often made him miss his family and home in Utah.[18] In addition to writing letters, when time and circumstance allowed, he sent packages containing small gifts to his family with returning missionaries.[19]

During this mission, he had what he termed "one of the most memorable days of my life."[20] He recounted: "I have traveled in the world for twenty years, meeting and passing through all classes of people. I am now over 35 years of age. Today for the first time in my life I was robbed of £17.10 by a gang of thieves between Liverpool and Crewe.[21] No man can know my mortification, Shame, and chagrin. I blame nobody so much as myself. I was caught off my guard, but I am all most stifflied with Shame. . . . This day let me not forget."[22] On this mission Joseph F. had additional photographs taken as well. In one case he noted, "I am in excellent health as you will see by my Photo, which I inclose, it is the last one of a dozzen I had taken while in Denmark."[23]

After nearly twenty months of service in Europe, Joseph F. learned that fellow Apostle George A. Smith (1817–75), his father's cousin, had died in Utah. Joseph F. had worked with Elder Smith in the Historian's Office since 1865. Additionally, George A. had become a father to Joseph F. and was his closest friend among the Apostles.[24] Shortly after receiving this news, Joseph F. was released from his missionary service and made his return home.[25]

After his arrival home from England, Joseph F. was assigned to preside over the Davis County Stake, an ecclesiastical area north of Salt Lake City.[26] This made him directly responsible for both the spiritual and the economic well-being of the Saints throughout the county. With the completion of the First Transcontinental Railroad in 1869, Utah witnessed a large influx of non–Latter-day Saints—changing forever the economic, social, and religious landscape there.[27]

14. See Joseph F. to Martha Ann, 15 July 1874, herein.
15. See Joseph F. to Martha Ann, 7 September 1874, herein.
16. Blane M. Yorgason, *From Orphaned Boy to Prophet of God* (Ogden: Living Scriptures, 2001), 266. The *Latter-day Saints' Millennial Star* began publication in 1840 and was suspended in 1970, when the *Ensign* magazine became the English-language publication for the entire Church.
17. Joseph F. to Martha Ann, 15 July 1874, herein.
18. Francis M. Gibbons, *Joseph F. Smith: Patriarch and Preacher, Prophet of God* (Salt Lake City, UT: Deseret Book, 1984), 98.
19. See Martha Ann to Joseph F., 24 November 1874, herein.
20. Joseph F., journal, 15 May 1874.
21. Crewe was a railway town in Cheshire, England, that included an important locomotive works.
22. Joseph F., journal, 15 May 1874.
23. Joseph F. to Martha Ann, 15 July 1874, herein.
24. Yorgason, *From Orphaned Boy to Prophet of God*, 270; Gibbons, *Joseph F. Smith*, 104.
25. Joseph F. to Martha Ann, 15 July 1874, herein.
26. Located in Davis County, Utah, the Davis Stake was an important early Church unit.
27. For additional readings into the economic circumstances of the Saints during the 1870s, see Leonard J. Arrington, *Great Basin Kingdom: An Economic History of the Latter-day Saints, 1830–1900* (Chicago: University of Illinois Press, 2005), 234–56.

Brigham Young responded to these challenges with a well-directed program encouraging self-sufficiency that included an all-out effort for the Saints to grow their own crops and produce their own goods, all to be sold through Church-established wholesale trading businesses like the Zion's Cooperative Mercantile Institution.[28] Joseph F. was made president of the Davis County Cooperative, one of the many institutions established during this period to assist the Saints in remaining economically independent. He served in this capacity for the next year and a half.[29] He also continued working at the Historian's Office and Endowment House in Salt Lake City.

THIRD EUROPEAN MISSION AND DEATH OF BRIGHAM YOUNG

Just a few weeks before the April 1877 general conference, Joseph F. lost another child—Heber John (1876–77), the son of Sarah Ellen Richards. He was less than a year old at the time of his death on 3 March 1877. Since no photograph had been taken before he died, the family chose to remember him by having his photograph taken following his death; this type of photograph, known as a post-mortem photograph or memorial portraiture, was popular in the nineteenth century.

At the April 1877 general conference, which coincided with the dedication of the St. George Temple in southern Utah, Joseph F. was once again called to preside over the European Mission. This would be his fifth international mission.[30] Because this assignment was expected to last for several years, Joseph F. took Sarah Ellen[31] and their four-year-old son Joseph Richards (1873–1954) with him, leaving Julina, Edna, and eight children in Utah.[32]

Just three months after his arrival, Joseph F. received word that Brigham Young had died on 29 August 1877, cutting short this mission. He immediately made the necessary arrangements so that he and his family could return to Utah. Once in Salt Lake City, Joseph F. took on a more active leadership role in the general affairs of the Church, including responding to the increasing government pressure against plural marriage, settling Brigham Young's complicated estate, and tackling various other assignments as a member of the presiding Council of the Twelve until the First Presidency could be reorganized.[33]

CHURCH HISTORY MISSION

In the summer of 1878, Joseph F. was asked to accompany fellow Apostle Orson Pratt (1811–81) on a brief Church history mission to the eastern United States to gather information that would be helpful in completing a history of the early Church. Pratt had been appointed Church historian in place of John Taylor (1808–87). Now senior Apostle following the death of Brigham Young in 1877, Taylor had assigned Elders Pratt and Smith to this unusual Church mission. On their journey east, Pratt and Smith visited sites associated with the early history of the Restoration (1820–44), including Independence in Jackson County, Missouri, where they met with several members of the RLDS Church and with Latter-day Saints who had not moved to Utah. After visiting William E. McLellin

28. For more information on the United Order, see Arrington, *Great Basin Kingdom*, 327–41.
29. Yorgason, *From Orphaned Boy to Prophet of God*, 270; see also Martha Ann to Joseph F., 31 May 1874, herein.
30. The previous four missions were to the Sandwich Islands (1854–58), Great Britain (1860–63), the Sandwich Islands again (1864–65), and the British Isles and Europe (1874–75).
31. Sarah Ellen Smith was twenty-six years old and was set apart by Brigham Young on 7 May 1877. She returned home on 27 September 1877.
32. Son Joseph Fielding Smith suggested that Joseph F. may have chosen to bring Sarah since Julina had a young baby at the time and Sarah had just been through the death of her young child; he may have thought the trip would help take her mind off the recent tragic events.
33. Gibbons, *Joseph F. Smith*, 111–12.

Heber John's postmortem photograph, 3 March 1877. Courtesy of Mary Lou Walker.

(1806–83), one of the original members of the Quorum of the Twelve Apostles,[34] Joseph F. reflected, "I never saw the sad effects of apostasy more plainly manifested."[35] Despite this disappointment, Joseph F. began a friendly correspondence with McLellin, maintaining it until McLellin's death.[36]

34. See Reid L. Neilson and Mitchell K. Schaefer, "Excavating Early Mormon History: The 1878 History Fact-Finding Mission of Apostles Joseph F. Smith and Orson Pratt," in *Joseph F. Smith: Reflections on the Man and His Times*, ed. Craig K. Manscill et al. (Provo, UT: Religious Studies Center, Brigham Young University; Salt Lake City, UT: Deseret Book, 2013), 359–78.
35. Joseph F. Smith, "Reminiscences by the First Presidency: My Missions," *Deseret News*, 21 December 1901, 57.
36. See Jan Shipps and John W. Welch, eds., *The Journals of William E. McLellin, 1831–1836* (Provo, UT: BYU Studies, 1994), 353–55.

Following up on information provided by William McLellin, the Apostles traveled to Richmond in Ray County, Missouri, where they met with David Whitmer (1805–88), one of the Three Witnesses of the Book of Mormon. Although Whitmer had been excommunicated from the Church in 1838, he maintained faith in the founding revelations of the Restoration and in his testimony and witness of the Book of Mormon (his testimony is still published in current editions of the Book of Mormon). Joseph F. reported that David Whitmer "bore to us his usual strong and undeviating testimony to the truth of the Book of Mormon. . . . Nothing could be more earnest, more sincere, than that aged man's solemn affirmation that he saw the angel and heard his voice declaring that the characters upon those plates were divinely translated."[37]

After making numerous stops throughout Missouri, Elders Smith and Pratt went on to various cities in Illinois to visit members of the Smith family. They then traveled to Kirtland, Lake County, Ohio, the site of the first Latter-day Saint temple; Palmyra, Wayne County, New York, the site where the Book of Mormon was first printed; and New York City. On their return trip, Joseph F. visited Joseph Smith III in Plano, Kendall County, Illinois, the headquarters for the RLDS Church. During this visit, Joseph F. asked to see the manuscript of Joseph Smith's translation of the Bible (JST). Although denied access to the manuscript, he was presented with a published copy of the translation, known as the *Inspired Version,* released in 1867.

Elders Smith and Pratt returned to Salt Lake City in time for the October 1878 general conference. Once back at home, Joseph F. continued his busy schedule with family, work, and Church responsibilities.

On 6 July 1879, Joseph F. witnessed another death in his family—his daughter Rhoda Ann. He wrote Martha Ann the following day: "It has become my painful duty to inform you, that we have this day laid away—in the great city of the dead upon the hill—another of my precious little pets."[38]

As he dealt with that tragedy, Joseph F. faced continued opposition in the local press, primarily in the *Salt Lake Tribune.*[39] He noted in his journal in August 1879, "p.m. at meting in the Large Tabernacle. The congregation was large & many Strangers being present. . . . I followed 45 minutes. And had very good liberty. . . . For once I think I have spoken in the Tabernacle and have given the Anti-Mormon papers nothing to say."[40]

One of the earliest public attacks occurred earlier in the decade when he was a member of the Salt Lake City Council. The *Salt Lake Tribune* described Joseph F. as having "a bad temper and worse taste . . . a bitter and narrow minded fanatic . . . [whose] affectation of superiority and sometimes positive insolence" rendered him "most unworthy" of a place on the city council.[41] During the following year in 1873, the *Salt Lake Tribune* published Joseph F.'s likeness as a woodcut with a caption that read, "Elder Joseph F. Smith, how he appears in his sublunary state, the champion of the Church and the opponent of free speech, the man whose zeal outruns his discretion."[42]

37. Smith, "My Missions."
38. Joseph F. to Martha Ann, 7 July 1879, herein.
39. Richard Neitzel Holzapfel and R. Q. Shupe, *Joseph F. Smith: Portrait of a Prophet* (Salt Lake City, UT: Bookcraft, 2000), 1–9, 143–47. We thank Stephen C. Taysom for the specific *Tribune* references mentioned in this section.
40. Joseph F., journal, 31 August 1879. Reports of his sermons often appeared in the press, including the *Salt Lake Tribune.* In 1882, for example, the *Tribune* described him as a "natural ruffian and outlaw whose fanaticism leads him to distort all the images in the world's kaleidoscope, and to imagine that [all] others are robbers and rogues." See "The Conference," *Salt Lake Tribune,* 5 October 1882, 2.
41. "Our City Council and the Public," *Salt Lake Tribune,* 2 August 1872, 2.
42. "Elder Joseph F. Smith," *Salt Lake Tribune,* 28 September 1873, 4.

These public attacks in the 1870s were some of the mildest of Joseph F.'s life. Unfortunately, in the decades ahead, Joseph F. was the specific target of the local, national, and international press in ways that John Taylor, Wilford Woodruff, and Lorenzo Snow never experienced.

MARTHA ANN'S PERSEVERANCE

Martha Ann continued to dedicate her life to her growing family. The 1870 US Census reached their neighborhood on 12 August 1870. Martha Ann and William Jasper were living in the Provo First Ward at the time.[43] The family consisted of eight members: William Jasper, age thirty-two; Martha Ann, twenty-nine; William Jasper Jr., twelve; Joseph Albert, nine; Hyrum Smith, six; Mary Emily, four; Franklin Hill, two; and Lucy Smith, two months old. Martha's occupation was listed as "Keeping House."[44]

Four more children were born to Martha Ann and William Jasper after the 1870 census was completed: Lucy Smith Harris (1870–1903), John Fielding Harris (1872–1946), Mercy Ann Harris (1874–1905), Zina Christine Harris (1876–1958), and Martha Artimissa Harris (1879–1961).

Martha Ann continued to face financial challenges during this decade. Joseph F. in the fall of 1879 wrote, "My sister is in very straitened circumstance. Her husband is unthrifty."[45] A few weeks later, he noted after a personal visit, "[Martha Ann] is in very low circumstance, but in good health."[46] To help provide for her growing family, Martha Ann continued to make gloves and also sewed temple clothing used in Latter-day Saint temple worship and burial practice. She became a known authority on temple aprons, producing about six per week and sending them to the Relief Society Burial Clothes Department in Salt Lake City.[47] She also often helped with the dressing of deceased members in their temple clothing. Because many of her aprons were intended for burial, she would quip with her daughters that most of her work was "underground."[48] Granddaughter

43. When the Provo First Ward boundary changed in April 1902, Martha Ann and her family became members of the Provo Sixth Ward.
44. 1870 US Census, Provo City First Ward, Utah County, Utah Territory, 8.
45. Joseph F., journal, 13 October 1879.
46. Joseph F., journal, 29 November 1879.
47. Many decades after Martha Ann's death, polygamist break-off groups began claiming that she was involved in the transmission of knowledge about the "revealed pattern" of temple clothing. According to one version of this story, Emma Smith crossed the Mississippi River in 1846 to where Mary Fielding's family was camped after their exodus from Nauvoo and handed Mary Fielding a package and said, "You will have more use of these than I; they are the original garments cut out by the two Angels and given to Joseph." The temple clothing was eventually handed down to Martha Ann Smith. Later, before her death, Martha Ann met with Minnie Ellen Raymond (born on 5 September 1874 in Black Rivers Falls, Wisconsin) and Joseph F. Smith to pass along the full history of temple clothing and the original garments to Minnie. In this greatly expanded version of the story, a divine messenger commanded Minnie to make one hundred temple robes and garments following the exact pattern Martha Ann had given her and then took the original clothing that had been passed to her by Martha Ann. The story of a "revealed pattern" of temple clothing is late and continued to develop over time. There are no primary sources, including any documentation from Minnie before her death on 21 August 1946 or in the Harris family tradition to substantiate even the earliest versions of the story as told by Lorin C. Woolley beginning in the late 1930s and recorded by Joseph W. Musser. See Drew Briney, ed., *Joseph W. Musser's Book of Remembrance* (Salt Lake City, UT: Hindsight Publications, 2010), 187–92. Minnie died an active member of the Church and was described an "an ardent temple, genealogist and Relief Society worker and had served as home missionary in the Liberty LDS Stake. At one time she was a former member of the Tabernacle Choir." See "Obituaries," *Salt Lake Telegram*, 21 August 1946, 17.
48. Ruth Mae Harris, *Martha Ann, Daughter of Hyrum and Mary Fielding Smith* (Orem, UT: published by the author, 2002), 136.

Edna Mae Simmons (1899–1986) recalled: "Grandmother worked her fingers to the bone. She'd sit and embroider temple aprons all day long until she could hardly stand it. I think she used glasses to embroider with. . . . Grandmother would sit in her chair and embroider temple aprons. . . . Some of the aprons had each green leaf embroidered and appliquéd onto white satin. . . . Grandmother made beautiful temple robes, too. She worked very hard pleating the robes in fine linen. Linen was a fabric she loved."[49] Martha Ann earned $1.50 for each apron and would continue this work to the end of her life.

Like many other nineteenth-century Latter-day Saint pioneers, Martha Ann lived in modest and humble circumstances throughout much of her life. There were critical moments in Provo when Martha Ann and her family were in desperate need of help. For example, in a letter written in 1874 to George A. Smith, Joseph F. asked for assistance to help his sister and her family: "I am sorry to say that William Harris is in a very bad fix. On Friday last he had five fits from 5 am to 7 pm. His family and friends thought he would never survive them. He is now perfectly helpless and dependent on charity. The family is destitute of necessaries. Smoot can supply them. Can Tithing Office send provisions, boots, shoes for children?"[50]

In a tender letter to his sister written in 1874, Joseph F. commended Martha Ann for her perseverance and compared her to their saintly mother, who had become, within the Latter-day Saint community, a singular example of faith and dedication: "[I]ndeed, yours has been a thorny path in this world, as mothers was, your patience and endurance are almost if not quite equal to hers."[51] In response she wrote: "I have had so much to contend with first on one side and then on the other one would say why do you put up whith what you do I would not. and other sais you are a fool and so on I could not tell you half I have had to contend with it is very easy to talk but not so easy to perform I feel like leaving it all in the hands of the Lord and when he sees I have born enough he will ease my burdon and all will come out right in the end if I do my dutey in all things & bare all things with so with paciense which I hope I may bee inabled to do. the Lord has been good to me."[52]

The primary sources support the family traditions that Martha Ann spent long hours day after day, week after week, month after month, and year after year, sewing or mending items to use or to give away or to sell, including gloves, burial clothing, and temple aprons.[53]

Martha Ann found time to serve her family, friends, and neighbors despite her own physical hardships. In June of 1871, for example, while suffering with boils and a toothache, she went to Salt Lake City to assist Joseph F.'s wife Sarah in childbirth. While she was away, Martha Ann's thoughts frequently turned toward home and her own family. In a letter to William, she wrote instructions to keep the boys out of the water, "for that will make them Sick."[54] On another occasion Sarah was left weak and ill after her baby died, and Martha Ann traveled to Salt Lake City to help her recover. During her absence from home, she confessed in a letter to William, "I cannot stay away from [the children] mutch longer I want to see my little Frank so bad I can hardly stand it."[55]

49. Harris, *Martha Ann*, 135–36.

50. Joseph F. to George A. Smith, 26 January 1874, CHL; see Joseph F. to Martha Ann, 27 February 1874, herein.

51. Joseph F. to Martha Ann, 5 August 1874, herein.

52. Martha Ann to Joseph F., 15 August 1874, herein.

53. See, for example, Joseph F. to Martha Ann, 15 July 1915 and 20 March 1916, herein.

54. Martha Ann to William Jasper Harris, 23 June 1871; in Harris, *Martha Ann*, 143.

55. Martha Ann to William Jasper Harris, 23 June 1871; in Harris, *Martha Ann*, 142.

MARTHA ANN'S NEW HOME

A few years after Martha Ann was born in 1841, her family abandoned their home in Nauvoo when residents in Hancock County forced them to evacuate the city in 1846. During the next several years, Martha Ann and her family lived as pioneers as they made their way to Utah, eventually arriving there in 1848. The first winter in the valley, they continued living in the wagons that had brought them to the Great Basin. Finally, in 1850, the Smith family moved into a small adobe home they hoped would become a permanent dwelling place.

However, as noted earlier, the death of Martha Ann's mother in 1852 and her brother's call to a mission in 1854 brought about another period of instability, with Martha Ann moving from house to house. Her rootlessness continued when she married William Jasper Harris in 1857, when William Jasper left on a mission, and when the Saints moved south during the Utah War.

Returning to Salt Lake City in 1858, Martha Ann met her husband, who was returning from his mission in England, at the Point of the Mountain. Reunited, they began to raise a family in Salt Lake City. In 1861 Martha Ann wrote her brother, "I am gitting tierd of renting houses for it is like throwing mo<n>ey away we will try to bye us a place the next time."[56] Within a short time, William Jasper and Martha Ann bought a house very near Joseph F.'s home in Salt Lake City.[57]

In the spring of 1868, Martha Ann and her husband, along with their five children, moved again. This time they relocated to Provo, about forty-five miles south of Salt Lake City, and moved into a small adobe house located on lot 6, block 41. The lot was in the name of A. O. Smoot, her stepfather-in-law. We do not know the arrangement made between Smoot and William Jasper and Martha Ann for the house, but they did not have title to it during this period.

William Jasper and Martha had six more children while living in this humble home over the next fourteen years: Lucy Smith (born in 1870), John Fielding (1872), Mercy Ann (1874), Zina Christine (1876), Martha Artimissa (1879), and Sarah Lovina (1882). Granddaughter Edna Mae Hedquist (1899–1986) recalled that the "south door never did have any steps to it."[58] As one would expect, there was no indoor plumbing.

Joseph F. wrote Martha Ann in December 1870, "Has the Bishop done any thing about a house for you? let me know."[59] Four months later he wrote, "bro. Dusenberry, told me he was living near you, & that he thought you were intending to move again. I enquired if you had succeeded in getting a better place, but he did not know. I am fearful that you do not have sufficient air in that little tucked up place, which may be the cause of your ill health."[60] In May 1871 Joseph F. lamented and advised, "I wish you had a comfortable home. You had better take the deed of the place, if you can get no better one, and then try to enlarge your dwelling or build anew when ever you can. or if <you> should have it to exchange for or towords another and better place it would not be amiss."[61]

For many Utah residents, land ownership was problematic until 1870.[62] In June 1870 A. O. Smoot, Provo City mayor, purchased about 2,240 acres for approximately twenty-eight hundred

56. See Martha Ann to Joseph F., 12 March 1861, herein.
57. Martha Ann to Joseph F., 30 May 1861, herein. See also G. Owens, *Salt Lake City Directory, Including Business Directory, Provo, Springville, and Ogden, Utah Territory* (Salt Lake City, UT: G. Owens, 1867), 61.
58. David J. Harris and Ruth B. Harris, ed. and comp., *Harris Heritage* (n.p.: self-published, 1977), 157.
59. Joseph F. to Martha Ann, 7 December 1870, herein.
60. Joseph F. to Martha Ann, 21 April 1871, herein.
61. Joseph F. to Martha Ann, 26 May 1871, herein.
62. See Thomas G. Alexander, "Conflict and Fraud: Utah Public Land Surveys in the 1850s, the Subsequent Investigation, and Problems with the Land Disposal System," *Utah Historical Quarterly* 80, no. 2 (Spring 2012): 108–31.

Provo Train Station, ca. 1878, C. R. Savage, Salt Lake City, Utah. Martha Ann and Joseph F. took advantage of the train connection between Salt Lake City and Provo as soon as that line was in operation. Joseph F. refers to the station in Utah County in letters and his diary. Courtesy of BYU.

dollars.[63] Later that month, Smoot was deeded the land "In trust" for the residents by President Ulysses S. Grant (1822–85).[64]

In 1872, when A. O. Smoot divided lots in Provo, the lot where Martha Ann was living was transferred to Brigham Young.[65] Following Brigham Young's death, Joseph F. helped get the property transferred from Brigham Young's estate to Martha Ann.[66] In the spring of 1878, Martha Ann was deeded a three-quarter-acre parcel identified as lot 6 in block 41 of plat A of the Provo City Survey of Utah County, Utah Territory, owned by Brigham Young according to his will.[67]

63. Utah County Abstract Company, entry 1, 1 June 1870.
64. Utah County Abstract Company, entry 2, 20 June 1872, Certificate 141.
65. August 1872, transfer of mortgage deed of lot 6, block 41 (214 S. 300 W.) from A. O. Smoot to Brigham Young, Utah County Deed Record, Book B, p. 376, Utah County Administration Building, Recorders Office, Provo, Utah.
66. See Joseph F. to Martha Ann, 22 April 1878, herein.
67. Utah County Abstract Company, entry 6, 25 April 1878.

PERSONAL VISITS

As in other decades, Martha Ann and Joseph F. communicated not only through letters in the 1870s but also in person and through family members. For example, in March of 1879 Joseph F. noted, "William J. Harris came in from Provo and put up with us for the night."[68] Ten days later he noted, "W.m. J. Harris and his son Willie and teams with us since Saturday night."[69]

At the end of the month, Joseph F. made his way to Provo. "I took the 7 a.m. to Provo. . . . Afternoon and evening I visited 'Aunt' Hanna & family . . . and my sister Martha Ann and family [were there] . . . took dinner at Pres. Smoots. Supper at Martha Anns & put up at Aunt Lucys. I bought 25c worth of candy for Marthas children. Her little Mercy will be 5 years old tomorrow."[70] On the following day, Joseph F. recorded, "I dined at Joseph A. Harris with Aunt Zina Young. Zine & M. J. Thompson, & my sister & family. Took the train at 2.2-0pm for home."[71]

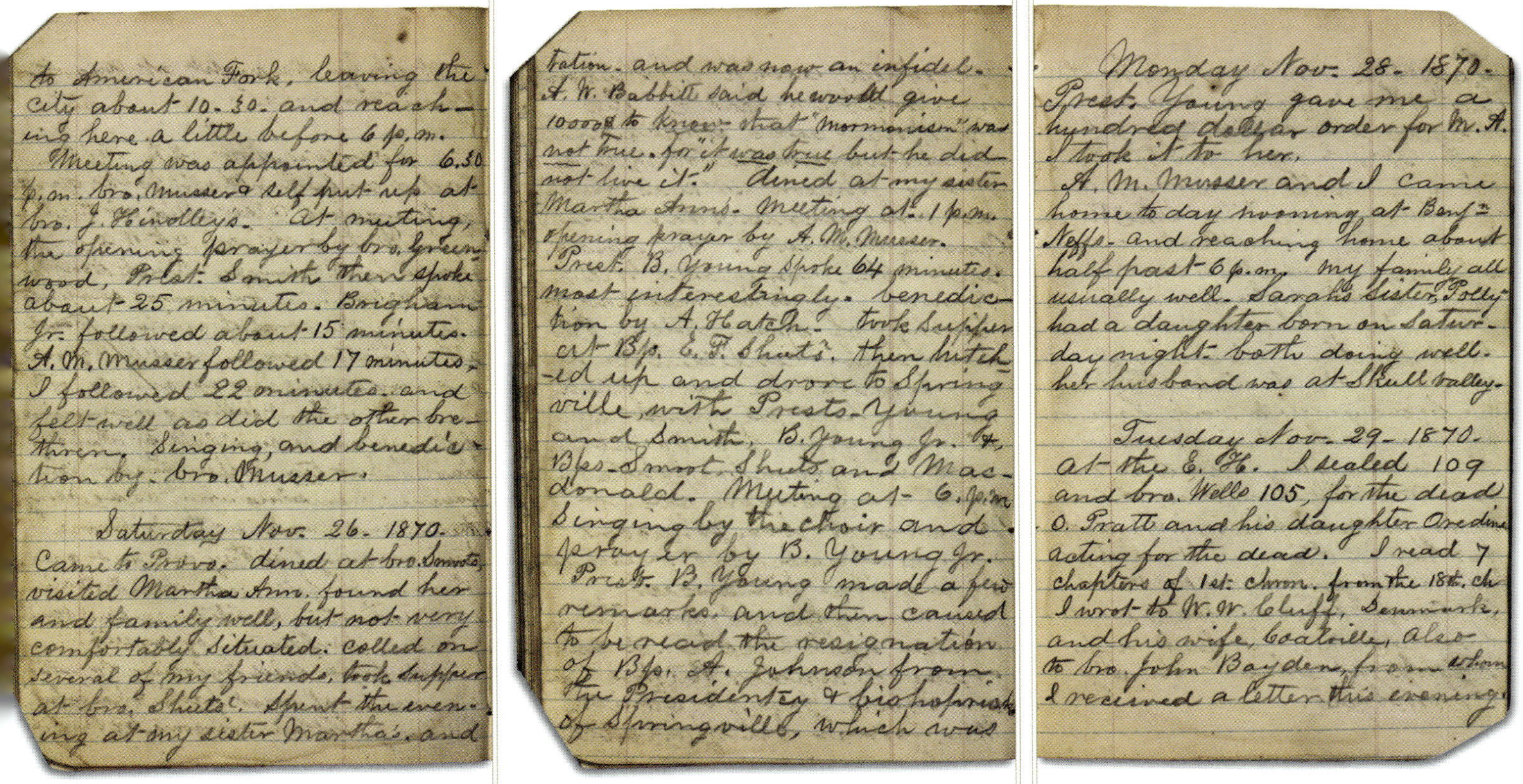
to American Fork, leaving the city about 10.30. and reaching here a little before 6 p.m. Meeting was appointed for 6.30 p.m. bro. Musser & self put up at bro. J. Hindley's. At meeting, the opening prayer by bro. Greenwood, Prest. Smith then spoke about 25 minutes. Brigham Jr. followed about 15 minutes. A. M. Musser followed 17 minutes, I followed 22 minutes. and felt well as did the other brethren, Singing, and benediction by. bro. Musser.

Saturday Nov. 26. 1870.
Came to Provo. dined at bro. Smoots, visited Martha Ann. found her and family well, but not very comfortably situated. called on several of my friends, took supper at bro. Shuts. Spent the evening at my sister Martha's. and

tation. and was now an infidel. A. W. Babbitt said he would give 1000$ to know that "Mormonism" was not true. for "it was true but he did not live it." dined at my sister Martha Anns. Meeting at 1 p.m. opening prayer by A. M. Musser. Prest. B. Young spoke 64 minutes. most interestingly. benediction by A. Hatch. took supper at Bp. E. F. Shuts. then hitched up and drove to Springville, with Prests. Young and Smith, B. Young Jr. &, Bps. Smoot, Shuts and Macdonald. Meeting at 6. p.m. Singing by the choir and prayer by B. Young Jr. Prest. B. Young made a few remarks. and then caused to be read the resignation of Bp. A. Johnson from the Presidentcy & bishopric of Springville, which was

Monday Nov. 28. 1870.
Prest. Young gave me a hundred dollar order for M. A. I took it to her.
A. M. Musser and I came home to day nooning at Benjn. Neffs. and reaching home about half past 6 p.m. my family all usually well. Sarah's Sister "Polly" had a daughter born on Saturday night. both doing well. her husband was at Skull valley.

Tuesday Nov. 29. 1870.
at the E. H. I sealed 109 and bro. Wells 105, for the dead. O. Pratt and his daughter Oredine acting for the dead. I read 7 chapters of 1st. chron. from the 18th. ch. I wrot to W. W. Cluff, Denmark, and his wife, Coalville, also to bro. John Bayden, from whom I received a letter this evening.

Joseph F.'s journal entries, dated 26, 27, and 28 November 1870. In separate entries covering three days when he visited Provo, Utah, on Church assignment with President Brigham Young, Joseph F. mentions being with Martha Ann, her economic challenges, Brigham Young's desire to provide her a permanent home, and Brigham Young's gift of one hundred dollars to help her. Courtesy of CHL.

68. Joseph F., journal, 7 March 1879.
69. Joseph F., journal, 17 March 1879.
70. Joseph F., journal, 29 March 1879.
71. Joseph F., journal, 30 March 1879.

William Jasper Harris, ca. 1876, photograph by Ad. Anderson, Provo, Utah. Courtesy of Carole Call King

After Joseph F. arrived home from Provo, Martha was not far from his mind. He mentioned, "I brought a "dress pattern" and trimmings for my sister Martha A. Harris. I paid $4.00 for the same."[72]

When in October 1879 Joseph F.'s wife Edna Lambson delivered a baby, named Edna Melissa, Martha Ann came to Salt Lake City to help. She remained until the ninth.[73] In November 1879 Joseph F. was back in Utah County on assignment to speak at the Utah Stake Conference in Provo. Joseph F. recorded, "Sarah and I took supper at my sisters Martha Anns" and, on the following day, "Dined at Sister Emily Smoots. Joseph A. Harris & wife, & baby were with us. Martha Ann also came in with W. Harris."[74]

SUMMARY

At the end of the decade, Joseph F. was forty-one years old, married to three wives (he and Edna Lambson had been sealed in 1871), and the father to eleven living children. He buried four children during the 1870s: Julina's daughter, Mercy Josephine (1870); Sarah's son, Heber John (1877); Edna's son, Alfred Jason (1878); and Sarah's daughter, Rhoda Ann (1879).[75] In 1879 Martha Ann was thirty-eight years old and married to William J. Harris. They were the parents of ten living children, five of whom had been born during this decade. The Harris family continued to reside in Provo, Utah County, Utah.

Although in the 1870s the quality of life was changing drastically in the settlements along the Wasatch Front, Provo and Salt Lake City's financial underpinnings were still highly dependent on the barter system. In a real sense, pioneering continued during the 1870s.[76] Martha Ann and Joseph F. were living in two worlds—the declining years of the pioneer period and the advent of premodern urbanization. However, each was experiencing this transformation in Utah rather differently.

The 1870s were full of challenges and opportunities for Joseph F. and Martha Ann. Both experienced sorrow at the loss of children and close friends and extended family members. Joseph F. once again spent time away from his family as he fulfilled the increasing demands of Church responsibilities. His travels away from home during this decade totaled nearly three years, taking him to Europe on two occasions and to the eastern United States on a special Church history assignment. For Martha Ann, the 1870s were a time of caring for her family and dealing with increased health and economic challenges in a more limited sphere than her brother's.[77]

72. Joseph F., journal, 3 April 1879.
73. See Joseph F., journal, 6 October 1879 and 9 October 1879.
74. Joseph F., journal, 29 and 30 November 1879.
75. Joseph F. had buried Sarah's daughter Sarah Ella in 1869, so by 1879 he had buried five children.
76. Ronald W. Walker and Doris Dant, eds., *Nearly Everything Imaginable: The Everyday Life of Utah's Mormon Pioneers* (Provo, UT: Brigham Young University Press, 1999).
77. Additional letters written during this decade have not survived. For example, in 1870 alone Joseph F. noted several nonextant letters from Martha Ann in his diary. He mentioned in August 1870, "I got letters from Aunt Thompson & Martha Ann" (Joseph F., journal, 23 August 1870). In a letter written in September 1870 he noted, "Received a letter from Martha Ann went to the Drug Stowre and got two porous plasters for her hoping they may do her good" (Joseph F., journal, 22 September 1870). He recorded in October 1870, "I wrote to John Boyden, and to Martha Ann this evening having recived a letter from her this morning" (Joseph F., journal, 27 October 1870). In December 1870 he recorded, "I received a letter from Martha Ann which had been advertised" (Joseph F., journal, 7 December 1870). A final example comes from December 1870: "a.m. at H.O. received letters from W. W. Cluff—and Martha Ann. Wrote to William" (Joseph F., journal, 16 December 1870).

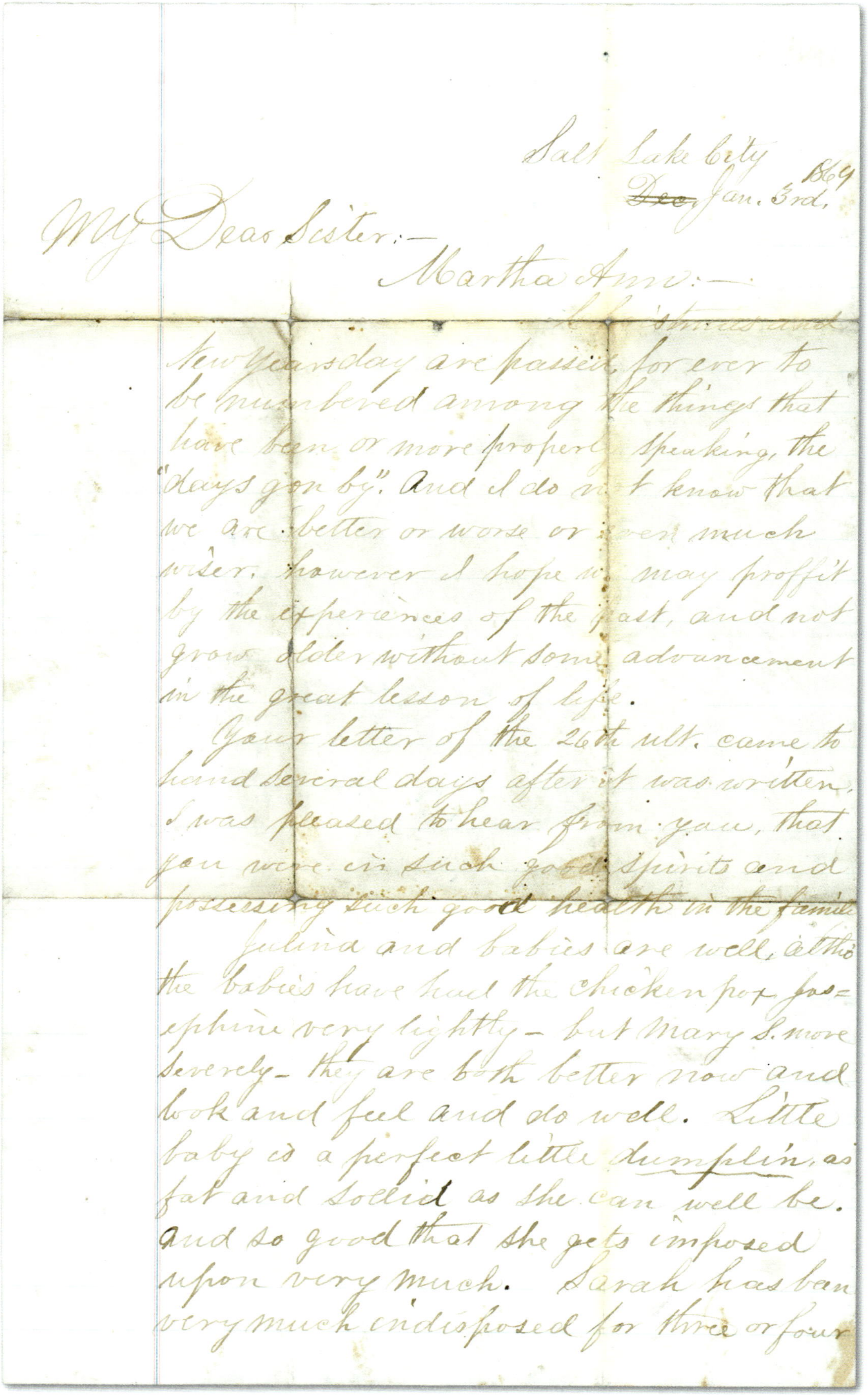

Salt Lake City
~~Dec~~ Jan. 3rd, 1869

My Dear Sister:—
Martha Ann:—

Christmas and New Years day are passed, for ever to be numbered among the things that have been, or more properly speaking, the "days gon by". And I do not know that we are better or worse or even much wiser, however I hope we may proffit by the experiences of the past, and not grow older without some advancement in the great lesson of life.

Your letter of the 26th ult. came to hand several days after it was written. I was pleased to hear from you, that you were in such good spirits and possessing such good health in the family.

Julina and babies are well, altho' the babies have had the chicken pox, Josephine very lightly— but Mary S. more severely— they are both better now and look and feel and do well. Little baby is a perfect little <u>dumplin</u>, as fat and solid as she can well be. and so good that she gets imposed upon very much. Sarah has been very much indisposed for three or four

Joseph F. to Martha Ann, 3 January 1870 (p. 1)

Letters

JOSEPH F. TO MARTHA ANN, 3 JANUARY 1870

Salt Lake City
~~Dec~~. Jan. 3rd. 1869[1]

My Dear Sister:—
Martha Ann:—

Christmas and New Years day are passed, for ever to be numbered among the things that have been or more properly speaking, the "days gon by". And I do not know that we are better or worse or even much wiser, however I hope we may proffit by the experiences of the past, and not grow older without some advancement in the great lesson of life.

Your letter of the 26th ult. came to hand several days after it was written. I was pleased to hear from you, that you were in such good spirits and possessing such good health in the family

Julina and babies[2] are well, altho' the babies have had the chicken pox Josephine very lightly—but Mary S. more severely—they are both better now and look and feel and do well. Little baby is a perfect little dumplin, as fat and sollid as she can well be. and so good that she gets imposed upon very much. Sarah[3] has been very much indisposed for three or four **[p. 2]** days, but is—I am thankful to say, now much better. She is writing to you. She was surprised to learn that you had written to her for she had received no communication, and began to be anxious to know whether you had received a little parcel which she had sent to you, I think by "Alex", or "Elleck".[4]

1. The date is 3 January 1870 as noted in Joseph F.'s journal: "Wrote to Martha Ann. Sarah enclosed a note." Joseph F., journal, 3 January 1870. Additionally, internal evidence suggests the same date since it refers to "Mary S[ophronia]," who was born 7 October 1869. Joseph crossed out "Dec." and wrote "Jan." and most likely simply forgot to correct the year. In January 1870 Joseph F. was thirty-one, and Martha Ann was twenty-eight.
2. Julina Lambson's babies are Mercy Josephine Smith and Mary Sophronia Smith.
3. Sarah Ellen Richards.
4. Unknown individual.

Aunt Thompson and ~~My~~ Mary Jane[5] are well, the latter is teaching School. Mary Catherine and Edward[6] are among her pupils. The girls[7] have talked some of going, but I presume they will reach no farther. I have not seen John[8] since the day after his arrival. he found all well.

I am glad your pig did so well. I will make you a "New Years" gift of my shair. we do not need it. I killed old "cherry"[9] this fall so we have plenty of beef. I intend to kill my pig in a short time. We have thus far plenty to eat—& wear, and we are very comfortable and no reason why we should not be happy and I think we are. And I know we would be if our Dear kindred were all as comfortable as we are. Our ward party comes off tomorrow night in the Social Hall.[10] I wish you could enjoy a visit there with us. Martha Ann I wish you a "happy new year"—and Millions of happy—blissful years to come!! God grant them happy is my prayer— give my love to William[11]—and all friends—not forgetting the little folks—& yourself. more anon— Joseph

JOSEPH F. TO MARTHA ANN, 18 JANUARY 1870

S. Lake City
Jan. 18th. 1870[12]—

My Dear Sister:—
Martha Ann:—

Your's of 16th.inst. came to hand this morning and I hasten to write you a few words in answer while I have a few moments to spare.[13] I am now in the Legislative Hall.[14] I do not go home to dinner as it is too far and the days are two short. The meeting of the Legislative body will resume in 3/4 of an hour.

5. Mercy Rachel Fielding and Mary Jane Thompson.
6. Mary Catherine is an unknown individual. Edward Arthur Smith is the adopted son of Joseph F.
7. Joseph F.'s wives.
8. John Smith.
9. Joseph F. mentioned, "Butchered my old cow 'Cherry' today. She is good beef. It seems as tho' I had lossed a member of my family or an old friend. She was about 17 years old. I raised her." Joseph F., journal, 8 December 1869. A few days later, Joseph F. wrote, "At home cutting up and salting beef." Joseph F., journal, 11 December 1869.
10. For more information on the social hall, see Martha Ann to Joseph F., 12 March 1861, herein, note 84.
11. William Jasper Harris.
12. Many of these letters do not refer to major historical events. For example, five days before Joseph F. wrote this letter, Salt Lake City witnessed a national news event as thousands of Latter-day Saint women gathered in the Old Tabernacle in a mass "Indignation Meeting" to protest the passage of the Cullom Bill in the United States House of Representatives. One historian notes, "If the Senate concurred, the government would soon have the power to confiscate Mormon property, deprive wives of immunity as witnesses, and imprison their husbands." Laurel Thatcher Ulrich, *A House Full of Females: Plural Marriage and Women's Rights in Early Mormonism, 1835–1870* (New York: Alfred A. Knopf, 2017), xi. The bill did not pass the Senate in large part owing to Latter-day Saint women's mobilizing to oppose the law.
13. Joseph F. noted receipt of Martha Ann's letter: "I recd a letter from Martha A and answered it." Joseph F., journal, 19 January 1870.
14. Joseph F. served in the territorial legislature from 1865 to 1874. He was an active supporter of the locally organized and Church-sanctioned People's Party after it was formed in 1870 in response to the anti-Church Liberal Party.

The girls are both very well, and so are the babies[15]— Edward has got the Mumps, and of course I suppose the babies will have their turn at it next, and that probably soon, they got over the Chicken pox very comfortably, and both—and Edward[16] too, are growing like weeds. Edward is also going to school; to Mary Jane[17] who teaches at her own house, but I am sor<r>y to say he cannot come so near writing a letter as "Willie"[18] has done, why did he not write to Edward, and that would show him how he should study to keep up with his cousins? I am real pleased to see 'Willie' make so good an attempt at writing, it is almost as good as I could do when I started on my mission to the Sandwich Islands. [**p. 2**] I hope he will continue to improve. I will send him two or three pens in this, and as soon as I can get a chance I will send him some more, and a pen- holder, and you must tell him to be a good boy and learn all he can. In relation to the ham, you will do nothing of the kind, but you will keep it and use it for your self, now remember this is premtory![19] we shall be pleased to see you any time. I went to Ogden on Sunday last by rail and returned the same evening. I took dinner at Aunt Fieldings or more Properly—at William Burtons, they are all well.[20] You will see the account of our trip in the Des. News[21] which I will send you with this.

The snort of the Iron horse[22] wakes up the echos of the hills and resounds through the broad-ways of our once isolated city, vibrating through the very dwellings and bed-chambers irreverant of the slumbering quiet <of> eve or early dawn!! A grand institution, well worthy of a visit when you can make it convenient. Aunt Thompson and Mary Jane and Robert[23] are all very well, and all the folks would send you love did they know I was writing— Please give my love to all enquiring friends— May God bless you and your little ones is the ever ernest prayer of Joseph

JOSEPH F. TO MARTHA ANN, 29 MARCH 1870

City, Mar. 29th. 1870

Dear Sister, Martha Ann:—

15. Julina Lambson and Sarah Ellen Richards. Joseph F. and Julina had two living children at this time.
16. Edward Arthur Smith.
17. Mary Jane Thompson.
18. William Jasper Harris Jr.
19. Most likely, the word is *peremptory*, which means "not open to appeal or challenge, leaving no opportunity for refusal."
20. Joseph F. and Martha Ann's aunt Hannah Greenwood was apparently living with her daughter and son-in-law, Rachel Fielding and William Burton, in Ogden at this time.
21. According to the *Deseret News*, the purpose of this trip was to hold a funeral for Bishop Chauncey W. West. See "Obsequies of Bishop C. W. West," *Deseret News*, 19 January 1870, 553.
22. The term *iron horse* referred to a train. Joseph F. is commenting about a new railroad line from Salt Lake City to Ogden, Utah. Even before the First Transcontinental Railroad was completed on 10 May 1869 at Promontory Summit, Utah, Church leaders began a railroad line from Salt Lake City that would connect it to Ogden, Utah, and the national rail system. That line was completed in January 1870, the same month this letter was written. See Leonard J. Arrington, *Great Basin Kingdom: An Economic History of the Latter-day Saints, 1830–1900* (Chicago: University of Illinois Press, 2005), 270–75.
23. Robert Blashel Thompson Taylor, son of David Taylor and Mercy Rachel Fielding, and first cousin to Joseph F. and Martha Ann.

I thought I would write you few words this morning as I have not written for some time. I am happy to inform you that our health is good, that is the health of my family. Sarah[24] has just recovered from one of her bad spells,[25] which however has not been so sever nor so protracted as usuel, and has this morning commenced to do the house-work. Julina[26] has had her hands full for some time past—thro' Sarah's being unwell. Tell Aunt Thompson, that Mary Jane[27] is about as usual. Edward[28] has stayed with her almost night and day since she left, and you know he is a very good boy for company, and is handy about chores &c. also there has not a day passed but Julina or I have called on her, so that we think she is getting along first rate considering she is such a "Mama's" girl and so apt to get home-sick if she is away. If she has any wants she has only to make them known and if in our power they shall be supplied. She had a nice little childrens party on Friday evening, for her school children. Julina and I were there,[29] she was afraid the party [**p. 2**] would have a bad effect upon her, and that she would be sick after it. I administered to her, by her request, and the next day she felt better than the day before. She has dismissed school for a week, which I think ~~would~~ will give her a little rest and do her good. President Young and party will reach home about the 17th. of April, all being well.[30] A mass meeting will be held in the Old Tabernacle[31] next Thursday[32] to show reasons for resisting the execution of the "Cullom Bill" should it become a law.[33]

Things begin to assume rather a fearful aspect. Congress seems bent on offering us one of two alternatives viz. to deny God & Revelaton and our religion in toto, or to become serfs and meniels to petty tyrants, whormungers, drunkerds & Cut~~s~~ throats sent to rule over us and despoil our goods and bring us under abject slavery & bondage, such as the negro of the South never experienced in the palmiest days of slavery!

I think the Government will find that Americans whether American born or Naturalized, after drinking at the fount of liberty caused to flow by the fathers of our Country and for which they staked their "lives, their fortunes and their sacred honors,"[34] so long as the Latter Day saints have, that they wold rather [**p. 3**] die free than live bound or in jeopardy. For my part I

24. Sarah Ellen Richards.
25. Referring to a variety of medical conditions that impair a person's physical activity.
26. Julina Lambson.
27. Mercy Rachel Fielding and Mary Jane Thompson.
28. Edward Arthur Smith.
29. Joseph F. recorded, "At childrens party at Mary Janes. Played a game of checkers with Willard and beat him." Joseph F., journal, 25 March 1870.
30. Brigham Young, along with a party of other Saints, had been on a two-month preaching tour of the southern settlements in Utah Territory. See "Return of President Young," *Deseret News*, 20 April 1870, 125.
31. The Old Tabernacle stood at the present-day site of the Assembly Hall on Temple Square in Salt Lake City. It was constructed in 1852 and razed in 1877. See C. Mark Hamilton, "Temple Square," in *Utah History Encyclopedia*, ed. Allan Kent Powell (Salt Lake City, UT: University of Utah Press, 1994), 547.
32. Joseph F. prepared the resolution presented at the meeting. See Joseph F., journal, 29 March 1870; see also *Deseret News*, 31 March 1870, for full report.
33. The Cullom Bill was one of several antipolygamy bills proposed to the federal government during the 1860s and 1870s. It was introduced in 1867 in an attempt to enforce the prior Morrill Act, which outlawed plural marriage, disincorporated the Church, and placed restrictions on the Church's ability to own property. Though the Cullom Bill did not pass, many of its provisions later became law in Utah Territory. See Jessie L. Embry, "Polygamy," in *Utah History Encyclopedia*, 428–30.
34. Joseph F. here quotes from the conclusion of the Declaration of Independence: "And for the support of this declaration, with a firm reliance on the protection of Divine Providence, we mutually pledge to each other our lives, our fortunes and our sacred honor."

am ready for the worst in my own mind. But, I do not know as there is any cause for fear or necessity for trouble, "God and one good man is a great Majority."[35] I would have no trouble in my mind, were it not for the fact, that I do not believe As a people we have lived as near to God as we should have done. And it may be the Lord has a scourge prepared for us on this account. But what ever is, <u>or</u> <u>will</u> <u>be</u>, will be for the best, for His saints for God is at the helm. We are engaged in His work, He must defend it—we cannot, of ourselves. But He has offered us freedom and deliverence from our enimies, seperated us from them, And said "Now try me, and see if I will not Bless you, multiply you, & your substance until there is not room to contain your blessings!"[36] but we have invited in the stranger & the wicked, we have <u>drunk</u> and <u>sworn</u> with them, and patronized them until we were lik potaoes in a sack. now we may have to endure the consequences. God <u>only</u> can deliver us from our enimies. No more at present, you must excuse haist & scribbling. All send love to you. we are glad to hear you are well & improving— from Joseph [**p. 4**]

N. B. Mary Jane was taken worse the day I wrote this so I did not send it—but telegraphed for Aunt Thompson to come home by stage.

This is Thursday Mar. 31—we are expecting Aunt Thompson [*illegible strike-through*] today—we got Sister Smoots[37] tilegram last night— Aunt Zina[38] sat up with Mary Jane last night—Julina and Sarah the night before—she has a bad cough—I hope she will soon recover— your brother Joseph F.——

JOSEPH F. TO MARTHA ANN, 31 MARCH 1870

City Mar. 3rd. '70[39]

My Dear Sister,
Martha Ann:—

We are all together (i. e.) Aunt Thompson, Mary Jane[40] and the rest of us, we are some of us grunting[41] and some of us very well. Aunt Thompson is not very strong—she feels the effects of her journey home, <u>under</u> <u>the</u> <u>circumstances</u> I will have to charge Bp. Smoot[42] with

35. This was a common saying of the time; for example, see Brigham Young, in *Journal of Discourses* (London: Latter-day Saints' Book Depot, 1854-86), 18:234.
36. Compare Malachi 3:10.
37. Likely Margaret Thompson McMeans.
38. Zina Diantha Huntington.
39. This letter should probably be dated 31 March 1870. Joseph F.'s journal for 31 March 1870 reads, "Aunt Thompson got home from Provo, nearly worn out. Bp. Smoot passed her on the way, altho' he had a light (<u>load two men & a little girl</u>) in a good strong two seated carriage. I hold this against him as an ungenerous act." The similarity between this passage and the content of the letter suggests that the letter was misdated.
40. Mercy Rachel Fielding and Mary Jane Thompson.
41. A term referring to abnormal, short, deep, hoarse sounds in exhalation that often accompany severe chest pain. The sound occurs because the glottis briefly stops the flow of air, halting the movement of the lungs and their surrounding or supporting structures. Grunting is most often heard in a person who has pneumonia, pulmonary edema, or fractured or bruised ribs.
42. Abraham O. Smoot.

an ungenerous act, when he drove past her on the way, but perhaps it is a small account which will be overballanced by generosity in other quarters.

Mary Jane is quite unwell, but is, I think improving. Robert[43] is also quite unwell, Sarah[44] has had another bad spell but is now much better and will soon be all right again. Julina, and Babies, Myself and Edward[45] are all well. My Darling little girls and their good "Mama,"[46] enjoy excellent health, and I am very thankful for it, I assure you. I hope you and your family will see no more sickness for some time to come. I think you have had your share. No more at present I have broken up two pens since I commenced writing this and the third deserves to be broken—for it is <of> no account— from your affectionate brother J. F.

JOSEPH F. TO MARTHA ANN, 25 JUNE 1870

City June 25—1870.[47]

My Dear Sister Martha Ann.

Yours of date ~~da~~ forgotten, because I left it at home—has come to hand—not however till this morning. I was pleased to hear from you, that you found all well, and that you were able to do your work. You left quite a number of things as usual which we will send first opportunity, it is said "two moves are equal to a burn",[48] reconing from these premisies I calculate about four of your visits would equal two moves—hense "four visits—equal to one fire"! I do not see how you get along after a short visit—but never mind—I am glad you can visit once in a while. for generally, I hope, what you forget and leave falls into good hands, and may stand a chance to be returned, as I am proud to say you keep good company!! We have been most lonely without our one sweet cottage flower—faded and gon.[49] My feelings are not yet settled— I am dull, stuped—inert, my ambition seems gon—for the present—and my heart sick! O! for a lease of life for my children! O! when will the Millenium come—and will I be worthy to stand? for then the children of Zion shall "live to the age of a trea",[50] and there shall be no "death", but the natural sleep—the rest of [**p. 2**] weary age! I am infidel to the belief that it is the "Will of God", that children—perfect—in body and mind—or complete in organism—should die! my heart and reason tells me no. God is not the author of death, among His Saints—God wills not the defeat of His own great, mighty purpose and plan.[51] But true to the prediction of the

43. Robert Blashel Thompson Taylor.
44. Sarah Ellen Richards.
45. The children referred to are Mercy Josephine Smith (age two), Mary Sophronia Smith (six months), and Edward Arthur Smith (eleven).
46. Likely refers to Julina since Sarah did not have any living children at this time (her daughter Sarah Ellen died on 11 February 1869).
47. Because Salt Lake City was the economic, political, and religious capital of the Utah Territory and the Latter-day Saint core area, it was simply known as the "City" and was often referred to as such in talks, letters, and diaries of the period.
48. A variant of the more common expression "Two moves are equal to a fire," popular in the British Isles.
49. Mercy Josephine, Joseph F. and Julina's oldest daughter, died on 6 June 1870, about three weeks before this letter. She was not quite three years old at the time of her death. See Joseph F. to Martha Ann, 6 August 1870, 3 May 1872, and 14 June 1872, herein.
50. See Doctrine and Covenants 101:30; compare Isaiah 65:20–22.
51. See Joseph F. to Martha Ann, 26 July 1902, herein, about the death of her seventeen-month-old granddaughter.

Prophet—or the truth—foretold by him. There is One—aye Millions under the control of the great "father of lies"—the "Prince of darkness"—"the Enemy of ~~G~~[◊] Christ," "The foe of truth", "the spoiler of peace", "the worker of death"—who will "leave no stone unturned to destroy the children of the saints"—so said Joseph Smith the Prophet.[52] and in this way can I account for the death of children—like mine—perfect in form and being—bright, pure and heavenly—I have need of such—the Kingdom of God has need of such—they are spirits from God—"of such is the Kingdom of Heaven"—[53] Earth—and man—are better for them—and are purified by the possession of them! I am not one to complain of "rest to the weary"— I regret not the "going down to the grave like a shock of corn fully ripe"—but children should, <u>live</u>—ripen—fill the measure of earth—& when weary with age—rest—! this is my doctrine—God help me to see it eternally established among the Saints—is the prayer of your Brother Joseph[54]

JOSEPH F. TO MARTHA ANN, 5 JULY 1870

City, July 5—1870

Dear Sister Martha Ann

I hasten to drop you a few lines to let you know that we are all well. Hyrum[55] is enjoying himself hugely[56] he went to the menagerie,[57] and to the Sunday School, in the morning & to meeting in the after noon, with Edward,[58] then with the Sunday Shool children (with Edward) went with the Prosession to the Tabernacle on the 4th.[59] then amused himself in the evening shooting cannons and pistols which I loaded for the boys to celebrate the great day of National Independence and to conclude with went with Julina Sarah, Aunt Thompson, Edward,

52. Joseph Smith Jr. See biographical register, "Smith, Joseph, Jr." Following his death in 1844, many people recounted Joseph Smith Jr.'s words and acts. Without extant contemporary sources, the collected memories of those who knew him present a challenge to historians as they attempt to reconstruct his life. In some cases the only evidence is a reminiscence. To ascertain what people close to Joseph Smith Jr. knew about certain topics or events, Joseph F. made it a point to collect affidavits. The subject of children who die was one such topic that interested him, and it appears here that he was quoting what he had heard someone say on that topic, for which there is no known contemporary source.
53. Matthew 6:11.
54. A few weeks later, Joseph F. was still struggling with Josephine's death: "It is one month yesterday since my little loved cherished darling Josephine died. O! that I could have saved her to grow up to womanhood. I miss her every day and I am lonely. My heart is sad. God forgive my weakness if it is wrong to love my little one as <u>I</u> love them & especially my first darling babe." Joseph F., journal, 7 July 1870.
55. Hyrum Smith Harris.
56. It appears that Martha Ann's son Hyrum was staying with Joseph F.'s family.
57. A nineteenth-century American menagerie was usually a traveling exhibition of caged exotic animals, similar to a circus.
58. Edward Arthur Smith.
59. The Fourth of July celebration in Salt Lake City, as reported in the *Deseret News*, commenced with a thirteen-gun salute at daybreak, which signaled an unfurling of flags from all public and many private buildings in the city. At 8:00 a.m. a three-gun salute called children to their schoolhouses and civil officers to City Hall and on to the Lion House, where they were met by Presidents Joseph F. and Daniel H. Wells. From there everyone proceeded to the Tabernacle, where "Hail Columbia" was played by a brass band and a "National Hymn" was sung, after which George Q. Cannon delivered an oration. This was followed by the singing of "The Star-Spangled Banner," remarks by George A. Smith, music by the Tenth Ward, toasts and sentiments read by the marshal, a patriotic hymn, and closing remarks by President Brigham Young. See "The Celebration," *Deseret News*, 6 July 1870, 258.

Robert[60] and myself to see the Fireworks at night, all of which he enjoyed very much with the rest of us bigger children. This afternoon we had company[61] and this evening the boys have been eating nuts and rasens, and have now just gon to bed. I asked him if he wanted to see his mother, he said "yes," do you want to go home? "no", he would like to see you but does not want to come home. We are all well, but lazier than "Jacks Mule"[62]—the girls will have to get somebody to chew for **[p. 2]** them soon if they keep on. I got Hyrum linnen for a duster today, which will soon be made laziness permitting— The weather is extremly hot. The grasshoppers have made us another visit, done considerable damage to our trees, and some other vegitation but left us the next day—I never saw them so thick before. I will not lengthen out this any more tonight, as it is late, and Sarah and I were at the Ball in the Theatre last night till 12 o'clock i.e. before we got to bed. The girls send you love and want you to write. Give our kind regards to all enquiring friends and excuse scribbling, for I have written with poor pen and poor ink, and am a poor writer at that God Bless you all is the prayer of your affectionate Brother
Joseph F. Smith

JOSEPH F. TO MARTHA ANN, 6 AUGUST 1870

City, Aug. 6th. 1870[63]

Martha Ann
My Dear Sister:—

Mary Jane and Aunt Thompson[64] having written to you, I thought I would say a few words, and enclose it with theirs. I am pleased to be able to say that we are all measurably well. Sarah's brother Joseph,[65] has returned from his mission from Eng. land, arriving to day in the City.

The weather is very oppressive, and the atmosphere sultry and merky, as tho' impregnated with smoke. Much as it was on the days memorable as the 27th, of June 1844. And the 21st. and 22nd of Sept. 1852—the day of fathers death, and the death and burial of Mother,[66] I recollect

60. Julina Lambson, Sarah Ellen Richards, Mercy Rachel Fielding, Edward Smith (son of Joseph F.), and Robert Blashel Thompson Taylor (grandson of Mercy Rachel Fielding).

61. George Nebeker and family; see Joseph F., journal, 5 July 1870. Nebeker had been called, along with Francis S. Hammond, to preside over the Sandwich Islands Mission after Joseph F. was released in 1864. See R. Lanier Britsch, *Unto the Islands of the Sea: A History of Latter-day Saints in the Pacific* (Salt Lake City, UT: Deseret Book, 1986), 126. See also biographical register, "Nebeker, George."

62. Jack mules are the offspring of a female horse (mare) and a male donkey (jack) and are often characterized as being stubborn or lazy. Unlike horses, mules will not allow an owner to work them to death or put them in danger.

63. Joseph F. noted, "I wrote to my Sister Martha Ann, Provo" (Joseph F., journal, 6 August 1870). He also recorded during the month, "I wrote to Martha Ann" (Joseph F., journal, 18 August 1870, herein) and "I got letters from Aunt Thompson & Martha Ann" (Joseph F., journal, 23 August 1870). Martha Ann's letter is not extant.

64. Mary Jane Thompson and Mercy Rachel Fielding.

65. Sarah Ellen Richards; Joseph Smith Richards was Joseph F.'s brother-in-law. See biographical register, "Richards, Joseph Smith."

66. 27 June 1844 was the day Joseph Smith Jr. and Hyrum Smith were martyred at Carthage Jail. 21 and 22 September 1852, as Joseph F. indicates, were the death and burial dates of Mary Fielding Smith, Joseph F. and Martha Ann's mother. See biographical register, "Smith, Hyrum."

them distinctly. It is two months to day since my own sweet babe[67] joined her grand father and mother in the spirit world, leaving in my hearts affections a void and broken space that time nor earth can ever fill. I mourn the earthly loss of the brightest, purest, dearest, treasure God ever gave me. the one, I prized and cherished most, within the great circle of that greatest gift of God "Eternal Life", [**p. 2**] which is incomparable, being "All in All," and yet as if to compensate in some degree, for my bereavement, fresh sweetness and beauty, increasing inteligence, and love daily developes in my precious, cheerful, merry little "rose bud", left me to bloom and blossom in my cottage "alone." O! in the midst of sorrow, I can say, I thank God for my three sweet, perfect little gifts, "one on earth and two in heaven",[68] the centre of my love, my own sweet "Jode".[69] The fountain of my tears has never closed when I have permitted them to flow, but I complain only of my own weakness and ignorence. but I should not trouble you with these thoughts. And I hardly know why I have done so, but enough. I hope this will find you in good health and your dear little family, and William. Samuel is expecting an increase at his house this week, he predicts that it will be a "boy."[70]

Sarah's health has been better of late and still improves. she is in extacies over her brother's return.[71] Rhoda[72] was at our house today, her children are not very well just now. William Burton was down today[73] I saw him just a moment, said all the folks were well. Robert is getting along nicely. David is expected down daily—wants to take M. Jane up home with him,[74] with kind love to all, I am as ever your affectionate brother Joseph F.——

JOSEPH F. TO MARTHA ANN, 18 AUGUST 1870

City, Aug. 18th. 1870[75]

My Dear Sister Martha Ann

Yours of Aug. 7th. came duly to hand, and I do not know or remember whether I answered it or not, but fearing I did not I now sit down to do so. The warm weather seems to affect almost every body—but I am sorry to hear of the illness of the babies, I hope long ere this they have recovered. You should try to take care of your ow[*8.5 x 1.7 cm horizontal tear along fold*] ch depends upon it [*3.8 x 1.75 cm tear along fold*] only the health of baby[76] but the proper

67. Mercy Josephine Smith.
68. The two children in heaven that Joseph F. makes reference to are Mercy Josephine (born 14 August 1867, died 6 June 1870, daughter of Julina Lambson) and Sarah Ellen (born 5 February 1869, died 11 February 1869, daughter of Sarah Ellen Richards Smith).
69. "Jode" may be another nickname for Mercy Josephine Smith, Joseph F.'s recently deceased daughter, or it may be a simple spelling error. In other letters she is referred to as "Dode." See Joseph F. to Martha Ann, 25 June 1870, herein.
70. Joseph Bailey Smith would be born to Mary Catherine and Samuel Harrison Bailey Smith on 9 August 1870. See biographical register, "Smith, Joseph Bailey."
71. Sarah Ellen Richards, as mentioned in note 65 previously.
72. Likely refers to Rhoda Ann Jennetta Richards, sister of Joseph F.'s wife Sarah Ellen Richards. See biographical register, "Richards, Rhoda Ann Jennetta."
73. William Burton, husband to Joseph F.'s cousins, lived in Ogden, Utah, at this time.
74. Robert Blashel Thompson Taylor and his parents, David Taylor and Mary Jane Thompson.
75. Joseph F. noted, "I wrote to Martha Ann and Aunt Thompson." Joseph F., journal, 18 August 1870.
76. Lucy Smith Harris, born on 10 March 1870. See biographical register, "Harris, Lucy Smith."

care of all the rest of the children, but I am aware that ~~where~~ so large a family, and so many inconveniences as you have, requires all the energy you can summon or obtain to carry you through. I am glad to hear that the boys can earn something to assist their father and mother and their little brothers and sisters. I hope they will always be industrious, good boys and earn and save all they can for themselves and the family. Sorry to hear of the accident[77] to William's horse, which has thrown him back so long.

The Lord says he will have a "tried people",[78] all that [**p. 2**] is dross must sooner or later be consumed, for only the "gold" will remain.[79] I hope for the sake of parantage as well as for our own sake, and the sake of our children, we may be proven to be the pure mettal. I must say that Mormonism, or the Gospel in all its parts grows brighter and brighter with me, & this will inevitably be the case the more it is rubbed, and the Devil and all his imps seem bent on polishing ~~us~~ <it> up. There is one consolation, that is, the wicked can do nothing against, but for the cause of truth. My family are well, [*4.5 x 1.9 cm tear along fold*]y has had several [*8.7 x 1.9 cm horizontal tear along fold*]s of diarhea but nothing serious. Julina[80] is very careful, "burnt child dreads the fire", we dread sickness or even the slightest illness of baby.[81] O! may God spare here for my sake. Aunt Thompson and Mary Jane, Robert, and all, have gon to Bear Lake with David.[82] have been gon about a week, bro. John[83] is also in Rich County, or in the land of the "Monsters".[84] Julina and Sary[85] would send love if they knew I was writing. I have written this in a great hurry, I want to write to Aunt Thompson, and also to Julina's Mother,[86] & tomorrow I am going to Coalville,[87] from Yours truly Joseph

JOSEPH F. TO MARTHA ANN, 27 OCTOBER 1870

1—

77. Accidents involving horses were ubiquitous in the nineteenth century; for example, see Martha Ann to Joseph F., 5 October 1874, herein.
78. Zechariah 13:9.
79. Joseph F. may be referring to a statement by Joseph Smith Jr.: "And now beloved brethren, we say unto you, that inasmuch as God hath said that he would have a tried people, that he would purge them as gold, now we think that this time he has chosen his own crucible, wherein we have been tried." This statement is an excerpt from the letter that Joseph Smith Jr. wrote on 20 March 1839 from Liberty Jail. Parts of the same letter later became Doctrine and Covenants 121–23. See also "History of Joseph Smith," *Deseret News*, 26 January 1854, 222; Job 23:10; Zechariah 13:9; and Doctrine and Covenants 136:31.
80. Julina Lambson.
81. Mary Sophronia Smith was Julilna Lambson's only child living at this time.
82. Mercy Rachel Fielding, Mary Jane Thompson, Robert Blashel Thompson Taylor, and David Taylor. In his journal for 18 August 1870, Joseph F. noted that they had "gon to Bear Lake on a visit."
83. John Smith.
84. Rich County in northern Utah had become known as the "land of monsters" because of a legend about a sea monster in Bear Lake, popularly known as the "Bear Lake Monster." This legend was popularized by Joseph C. Rich in an article he published, "Correspondence: Monsters of Bear Lake," *Deseret Evening News*, 5 August 1868, 204, evening edition. See also Bonnie Thompson, *Folklore in the Bear Lake Valley* (Salt Lake City, UT: Granite, 1972), 35–48.
85. Probably a nickname for Sarah Ellen Richards.
86. Melissa Jane Bigler was the mother of Julina Lambson. See biographical register, "Bigler, Melissa Jane."
87. Joseph F. traveled to Coalville, Summit County, Utah Territory (forty miles east of Salt Lake City), for the weekend in order to attend and speak at meetings there; he also visited several family members and fellow Saints. See Joseph F., journal, 19–21 August 1870.

City, Oct. 27, 1870[88]

My Dear Sister
Martha Ann.

Yours of 18th inst. came to hand this morning. the mail must have slept on the way to this city, as your letter was more than a week coming. I am sorry to hear that the children are or have been sick I hope and trust they are or soon will be better. I am happy to tell you that our little Mary[89] is much better than she has been for some time. She was very sick, so much so that I almost got alarmed. but by faith and the assistence of Dr. Meek[90] she is getting quite well again.

The pears came all safe & sound and were very delicious, I gave one to the President.[91] please give my kind regards to bro. & sis. Mecham,[92] and all the family & kindly neighbors. I thank bro. Mecham very kindly [**p. 2**] the pears, and for many acts of kindness. I do not see John very often, and I have not been at his house for several months. I have no affiliation for John's wife nor her Mother,[93] nor their Spirit I am sorry to say. The last I heard from Lovina[94] she was very sick I should rather think she was better than worse, or we should have heard form her. Lorin[95] was here at Conference,[96] Jerusha[97] also gave us a call, but did not stop long. She staid over night however at Johns. I have got so now, I do not urge my kindred to visit, or stop with me, they know they are welcome, and they can do as they please. I can therefore judge from their actions the Society they choose. The atmosphere of my house is very different from that of Johns I acknowledge but it is not for the worse! Joseph F.

JOSEPH F. TO MARTHA ANN, 7 DECEMBER 1870

City Dec. 7.th. 1870.

My Dear Sister

88. Joseph F. noted, "I wrote to John Boyden, and to Martha Ann this evening, having received a letter from her this morning." Joseph F., journal, 27 October 1870.
89. Mary Sophronia Smith.
90. Likely Dr. Priddy Meeks, a practitioner of Thomsonian herbal medicine and founder of the Society of Health in Salt Lake City. See biographical register, "Meeks, Dr. Priddy."
91. Brigham Young.
92. Likely refers to Edward Mecham and his wife Sophia Barrows, neighbors of William and Martha Ann according to the 1870 US Census. There were also several other Mecham families living in Provo at this time; Joseph F. possibly refers to one of them here. See biographical register, "Mecham, Edward" and "Barrows, Sophia."
93. John Smith, Hellen Maria Fisher, and Evaline McLean. See biographical register, "McLean Evaline." Hellen and her mother were opposed to plural marriage, and though John was married to Nancy Melissa Lemmon as a second wife, he was apparently ambivalent toward plural marriage. Their attitude toward plural marriage, which Joseph F. attributes to Hellen's mother, is probably what he refers to here as "their Spirit." See Irene M. Bates and E. Gary Smith, *Lost Legacy: The Mormon Office of Presiding Patriarch* (Urbana: University of Illinois Press, 1996), 127.
94. Lovina Smith.
95. Lovina Smith's husband, Lorin Walker. See biographical register, "Walker, Lorin."
96. The 40th Semiannual General Conference was held on 6–9 October 1870 in Salt Lake City.
97. Jerusha Smith.

Martha Ann

Your very kind letter of nearly a month ago came to hand last evening—it having been advertized in the papers.[98] Splendid Post Office regulations ours! And dutiful & intelligent clerks to attend to business. Mary Jane[99] has written I do not know what— I have not time to write much. I am in a hurry. Julina, Sarah, Rose bud, Edward[100] and myself are all well, for which I am thankful, baby has got two double teeth through & is complaining some of others on their way.[101]

Edna,[102] Julina's Sister is with us, she has had a severe attack of pluricy,[103] but is now nearly well again. John[104] is away from home, William Pierce[105] was in town yesterday, said the folks were all well. I have not heard from Lovina[106] for some time. Has the Bishop[107] done any thing about a house for you?[108] let me know. I must close— God bless you all the girls send love, kind love to all friends.

from your affectionate brother in haste J. F. S.

98. A letter for "JF Smith" was advertised in the local Salt Lake newspaper in November 1870; see "List of Letters," *Deseret News*, 2 November 1870, 10. Joseph F. noted in his journal, "I received a letter from Martha Ann, which had been advertised." Joseph F., journal, 7 December 1870. If letters were not claimed from the local post office within a certain amount of time, they were advertised in the newspaper under the heading "List of Letters," with the explanation that if they were not claimed within one month of being advertised, they would be sent to the Dead Letter Office in Washington, DC. Located on the second floor of the General Post Office building in the nation's capital on F Street, the Dead Letter Office received 4,152,460 letters in 1870. See Louis Baggar, "The Dead-Letter Office," *Appletons' Journal: A Magazine of General Literature* 10, no. 243 (8 November 1873): 594.

99. Mary Jane Thompson.

100. Julina Lambson, Sarah Ellen Richards, Mary Sophronia "Rosebud" Smith, and Edward Arthur Smith.

101. Mary Sophronia, born on 7 October 1869, was twenty-six months old.

102. Edna Lambson became Joseph F.'s fourth wife on 1 January 1871. See biographical register, "Lambson, Edna."

103. Pleurisy is an inflammation of the lining of the lungs with symptoms of sharp chest pain and coughing. Joseph F. noted in his journal, "Edna is much better." Joseph F., journal, 7 December 1870.

104. Likely John Smith.

105. William Pierce, son of Jerusha Smith and William Pierce, was born on 26 May 1868. He was a nephew of Joseph F. and Martha Ann.

106. Lovina Smith, Joseph F. and Martha Ann's older half sister.

107. It is uncertain which bishop Joseph F. is referring to in this letter. A. O. Smoot, the Utah Stake president and city mayor, was also assigned as the Regional Presiding Bishop for Utah Valley, responsible for the temporal affairs and economic development in Utah County. Martha Ann's local ward bishop was John Peter Rasmus [Johannesen] Johnson, who was serving as the Provo First Ward bishop at the time.

108. On 26 November, Joseph F. noted, "Came to Provo . . . visited Martha Ann, found her and family well, but not very comfortably situation. . . . Spent the evening at my sister Marth's." Joseph F., journal, 26 November 1870. On the following day, Joseph F. reported a conversation he had with Brigham Young in Provo when they were attending a stake conference together in Utah Valley: "The President told me . . . that my sister Martha Ann should have comfortable place provided for her in Provo." Joseph F., journal, 27 November 1870. Finally, on 28 November, Joseph F. recorded, "Prest. Young gave me a hundred dollar order for M.A. I took it to her."

JOSEPH F. TO MARTHA ANN, [AFTER 1870?]

[After 1870?][109]

uired as to your curcomstances, I told him[110] you were living in the little house,[111] &c— that you had built another room &c—and that you liked the place, So he said that he would deed it to you. He then asked me about your [*illegible strikeout*] <condition> — [*end of fragment*] We got home all right, and found babies not very well but they are all right now. Give my love to all friends, and accept the same yourself— Your Brother in haste — Jos. F. Smith. [*end of fragment*]

JOSEPH F. TO MARTHA ANN, 26 JANUARY 1871

City, Jan. 26, 1871[112]

Dear Sister:—

Yours of Jan. 8— and 19th. are both before me,[113] I have just re-read them to see what questions I had to answer. I saw William[114] the day I received your last[115] he had the buck-skins you mentioned and was going to the office to send them to you. He took them to Worley himself.[116]

The reason the girls[117] do not write, is that they would rather cook a week or make a suit of close than write half an hour. In one sence this is a high recommendation, but in the real sence, it is a disgrace! for I wish they would use their pen more. I did not suppose you would think that I would invite you to some body els' wedding. You must be obtuse, let every body do his own inviting!

I am much obliged for Lucy's "photo", it is very good.[118] we have no good likeness of our little bundle of mischief and roguery,[119] or I would send you one with pleasure, I may even

109. The top half of this letter has been lost, so there is no date or greeting. However, the salutation reveals that this is a letter from Joseph F. to Martha Ann. This letter was most likely written after Joseph F.'s discussion in the late fall of 1870 with Brigham Young regarding property for Martha Ann. See Joseph F., journal, 27 November 1870. Property was finally deeded to Martha on 25 April 1878 after the settlement of Brigham Young's estate.
110. Most likely Brigham Young.
111. The "little" adobe house was located at 214 South 300 West, Provo.
112. Joseph F. was thirty-two, and Martha Ann was twenty-nine. "At the H.O. all day wrote to Geo. A. sent him W. W. Cluff's letter. Wrote to Mary Straw, and my sister Martha Ann. . . . Warm pleasant weather." Joseph F., journal, 26 January 1871.
113. Joseph F. received several letters from Martha Ann between 7 December 1870 and 26 January 1871. See, for example, Joseph F., journal, 16 December 1870, for a nonextant letter he received during this period.
114. William Jasper Harris.
115. Joseph F. noted on 23 January that he received a "letter from Martha Ann." Joseph F., journal, 23 January 1871.
116. Unknown individual. Two men living in Salt Lake City could be the person mentioned: Kleber Worley (1800–75) and John Mansfield Worley (1836–1913). Although less likely, another person living in Logan, Cache County, Utah, may be the one mentioned by Joseph F.: Henry Worley (1827–1914).
117. Joseph F.'s daughters or wives, or both.
118. Lucy Smith Harris was born to William Jasper Harris and Martha Ann on 7 October 1869.
119. Joseph F. and Julina Lambert's daughter, Mary Sophronia Smith, was born on 7 October 1869.

send one of such as we have, she has been very sick for a week, cutting four double teeth at once! and her mother[120] has not been very well which may have augmented the baby's troubles. but they were both much better this morning. Sarah[121] continues in excellent health, but has charge of Sister Rhoda's little boy,[122] who is so full of mischief that with Mary, Sarah's nerves are fearfully **[p. 2]**[123] wrought up once in a while. Rhoda and her husband[124] have both been very sick for some time, the former with gathered brest,[125] the latter with plura-pneumonia. and very ill. Aunt Thompson[126] and family are all usually—or rather un-usually well at present. they were very much pleased with little Lucy's likeness. indeed so were we all, I do not hear any more about house and lot &c. for you. I hope the Bp.[127] in the multiplicity of his onerous duties and cares will yet be able to seccure you a comfortable home, if the one you have does not suit you. I think with, sore heads &c. toothache gathered finger and the like you must have been excrusiatingly comfortable for some time past. You need more room and fresh air. that will prevent or cure those irruptions on the children. that is, with wholesome food.

Edna is taking care of her sister, (A. Davis' wife) and family,[128] they are all sick and have been all winter with chills and fever. Edward[129] is not going ~~home~~ but Edna gives him lessens each day, and he is getting so that he reads pretty well. by the way tell Maggie[130] not to dispond, for if that young gentleman does not walk up to the mark, "here am I, Staunch & true,"[131] and I am very[132]

120. Julina Lambson.
121. Sarah Ellen Richards.
122. Probably Benjamin Franklin Knowlton Jr., who was about four years old at the time. Joseph F., journal, 9 January 1871: "Sarah & I went to the Theatre & took little Frank Knowlton." See biographical register, "Knowlton, Benjamin Franklin, Jr."
123. Indecipherable markings at the top of the page.
124. Probably refers to Rhoda Ann Jennetta Richards and her husband, Benjamin Knowlton. See biographical register, "Knowlton, Benjamin Franklin."
125. Mastitis, an inflammation of the breast, is often due to bacterial infection in the mammary gland that makes it difficult and painful to nurse a baby.
126. Mercy Rachel Fielding.
127. Likely Bishop Abraham O. Smoot.
128. Melissa Jane Lambson, wife of Albert Westley Davis, was Edna Lambson's sister. Melissa and Albert had two children at this time, and Melissa was about two weeks away from delivering their third. See biographical register, "Lambson, Melissa Jane" and "Davis, Albert Westley."
129. Edward Arthur Smith.
130. May refer to Margaret West Smith, Joseph F. and Martha Ann's second cousin. See biographical register, "Smith, Margaret West."
131. Apparently a popular phrase, "staunch and true" has the same meaning as "firm and steadfast" or "loyal and true." Mark Twain used the phrase to describe the Latter-day Saints in 1872: "Then for years the enormous migration across the plains to California poured through the land of the Mormons, and yet the church remained *staunch and true* to its lord and master. Neither hunger, thirst, poverty, grief, hatred, contempt, nor persecution could drive the Mormons from their faith or their allegiance; and even the thirst for gold, which gleaned the flower of the youth and strength of many nations, was not able to entice them! That was the final test. An experiment that could survive that was an experiment with some substance to it somewhere." Mark Twain, *Roughing It* (Hartford, CN: American Publishing Co., 1872), 573; emphasis added.
132. The rest of this letter is missing.

JOSEPH F. TO MARTHA ANN, 23 FEBRUARY 1871

City Feb. 23.rd. '71

My Dear Sister
Martha Ann

Yours of 15th—is received, for which accept thanks. Always pleased to hear from you you deserve credit for being a faithful correspondent. I never get a linee or scarcely a word from Jerusha or Sarah.[133] Julina and Mary[134] made a visit to Coalville[135] a couple of weeks ago, and had an excellent time. we found Sarah and family enjoying excellent health—Sarah is much better than for years past, and showes it in her looks. Charlie[136] is doing pretty well, at carpentering and they all appear comfortable.

Alice[137] is the prettiest, best-behaved [**p. 2**] and most beloved of any young lady in Coalville. All speak well of her, and admire her as a modist womanly young lady. but her health is not very good. I proffered to send her to school if they would let her come to town. but I do not think they want to part with her company. The other children were well.

We have all been suffering with the prevailing distemper of the city. terrific colds. Except Edward,[138] he has escaped so far. And Sarah[139] has not suffered much. Julina and Mary S. are just recovering (we hope) rapidly— Edna[140] is well again, and as for myself, this is the third day that I have been confined to the house. but I am much better and shall be ready to go to work in the morning.[141] Our little Leonora,[142] is gro<w>ing like a wead—[**p. 3**] but she sufferes very much with the colic. otherwise she is perfectly healthy. Sarah enjoys her little charge, as such as she, only can. it would do you good to see her take such solid comfort, yet she takes it to heart sadly when it cryes with the colic. She is not as pretty a baby as Ella[143] was, but will grow prettier, no doubt.— we are perfectly satisfied at all events. She has the making of an inteligent woman, that is the best of all.

Aunt Thompson & Mary Jane[144] are also suffering with bad colds—or, the epidemic. I am sorry to learn that you are or have been suffering with colds, but I am in hopes you will all be well again ere this reaches you.

I send inclosed photographs of Mary S. and Edward,[145] such as they are. You must excuse [**p. 4**] this scribbling for I am <in> very bad trim for writing. rather tremulous. my pants are at least four inches larger arround the waist than they were four days ago!

133. Jerusha and Sarah Smith.
134. Julina Lambson and Mary Sophronia Smith.
135. Coalville, Summit County, Utah, about forty-five miles northeast of Salt Lake City.
136. Charles Emerson Griffin, husband of Sarah Smith. They were living in Coalville at the time of this letter.
137. Alice Lovina Griffin, daughter of Sarah Smith and Charles Griffin, was fourteen years old at this time.
138. Edward Arthur Smith.
139. Sarah Ellen Richards.
140. Edna Lambson.
141. Joseph F. was still employed in the Historian's Office and as a recorder in the Endowment House.
142. Leonora Smith, the second and at that time the only living daughter of Sarah Ellen Richards, was born on 30 January 1871. See biographical register, "Smith, Leonora."
143. Sarah Ellen Smith, who died on 11 February 1869, six days after her birth.
144. Mercy Rachel Fielding and Mary Jane Thompson.
145. See Edward's photograph in the decade introduction for this chapter (p. 170).

Edna is living at Melissa Janes.[146] left me allready you see!! our little "Mayõ"[147] is always all sunshine whether it rains or storms, or fair! she just now found her way into the sugar sack and the first thing we knew here she came with a lump half the size of her head! she will make mischief out of lawful play.

I must conclude. The girls send love to you and all the children and all friends.

Always remember me kindly to bro. & sis. Mecham.[148] John[149] just called, got a letter from you but had not had time to read it— God bless you all Joseph F.

Mary Gray[150] has twins—girls—8 lbs each— Melissa Jane has a girl[151]— Sister Evans had three girls[152]— Polly—has a girl[153]— Rhoda has a girl.[154] of course Sarah has a girl— Julina hopes to have a girl (some day—) & perhaps you may hear of me having one some day—no more room.[155]

JOSEPH F. TO MARTHA ANN, 21 APRIL 1871

S. L. City, April 21st 1871

My Dear Sister Martha Ann,

I believe I have not answered your two last letters to me, not because I have not thought of you, but because I have been pressed somewhat with other matters,[156] and therefore neglected to write. I heard from you at Conference,[157] and at several times from those, who were up from

146. Melissa Jane Lambson. Edna likely visited to help with the birth of Edna May Davis, Melissa's third child, born on 15 February 1871. See Joseph F. to Martha Ann, 26 January 1871, herein.
147. Apparently a nickname for Mary Sophronia, who was seventeen months old.
148. Edward Mecham and Sophia Barrows. See Joseph F. to Martha Ann, 27 October 1870, herein, note 92.
149. John Smith.
150. Mary Elizabeth Russell gave birth to Sarah Ellen Russell Gray and Jennie Isabell Gray on 14 February 1871. See biographical register, "Russell, Mary Elizabeth," "Gray, Sarah Ellen Russell," and "Gray, Jennie Isabell."
151. Melissa Jane Lambson, sister-in-law to Joseph F., gave birth to Edna May Davis on 15 February 1871. See biographical register, "Davis, Edna May."
152. Mary Elizabeth Jones Evans had triplets—Cora, Eva, and Ruth—on 21 February 1871. Tragically, they died and were buried on the same day they were born. Only four of Mary Evans's eleven children lived to adulthood. See biographical register, "Jones, Mary Elizabeth."
153. Possibly refers to Pauline Richards, older sister of Joseph F.'s wife Sarah Ellen Richards. Her daughter Cora Doremus was born on 26 May 1870. See biographical register, "Richards, Pauline" and "Doremus, Cora."
154. Rhoda Ann Jennetta Richards, half sister to Sarah Ellen Richards, gave birth to Harriet Knowlton on 23 November 1870. See biographical register, "Knowlton, Harriet."
155. The list of names, beginning with Mary Gray, is written vertically in the top margin of page 1. Joseph F. appears to be writing in jest, as Julina does have a young daughter, just not a new baby girl like so many other women at that time.
156. During the previous four weeks, Joseph F. worked in the Historian's Office and at the Endowment House; attended the School of the Prophets and ZCMI stockholders meetings; spoke in several meetings, including at the recent general conference, at the Nineteenth Ward's Sabbath meeting, and at a funeral; wrote a lengthy article for the *Juvenile Instructor*; attended another funeral and various other meetings, including a ceremony connected with the Salt Lake railroad line; observed a medical operation; set apart a missionary and administered to several sick people; and attended to various family duties, including babysitting, going to the theater with different wives on separate nights, working in the garden, building a beehive, and cleaning up his yard. See Joseph F., journal, 21 March–21 April 1871.
157. The 41st Annual General Conference was held on 6–9 April 1871 in Salt Lake City.

Provo. I am sorry you have had to suffer so much with sickness, but I trust you are all better. bro. Dusenberry,[158] told me he was living near you, & that he thought you were intending to move again. I enquired if you had succeeded in getting a better place, but he did not know. I am fearful that you do not have sufficient air in that little tucked up place, which may be the cause of your ill health.[159] Air is esential to health, as much so as wholsome food. I hope the boys are learning well, and that they will be good to their mother & little sisters,[160] and take care of the lot or garden, and raise some vegetables and fruit for themselves and the family. Edward is a good boy—he works like a little man in the garden, digging the ground helping to plant peas beans, radishes, turnips, and other seads. he gathers up the rocks and wheels them off in the wheel-barrow, and is a real good boy.

Besides he helps the folks all the time, draws their water, cuts the wood, makes the fires, cleans out the stoves, brings in the coal and does all the chores, and errends for the folks. I know Willie, Jodie and Hyrum[161] can be just as good as Edward and can anticipate every <want> [**p. 2**] of their mother and save her hundreds of steps and a great deal of hard work, and care. Edward never runs away to play with the boys—unless he gets permission, and we are always willing he should have time to play when he has done his work, and been a good boy.

We are all well, for which I am thankful, some of us have slight colds but nothing serious. Sister Ann Cluff[162] and children are stopping with us for a little while on a visit. They are well. I never hear from William J.[163] What is he doing? I have bought Aunt Fieldings[164] portion of city lot—which enlarges my front eight rods more, I have paid $\$300^{\underline{00}}$ towards it out of my own pocket, and have borrowed $\$100^{\underline{00}}$ more towards it— I am still owing $\$200^{\underline{00}}$ which I shall also have to borrow until I can raise it by selling some other property. I had to draw my int<e>rest out of the Cooperative store,[165] which amounted to $\$200^{\underline{00}}$ which I very much regretted, but I could not afford to let some body else buy—for I needed it. I am writing some articles for the Juvenile Instructor, headed "Recollections".[166] giving some sketches of our Journey from Nauvvo—to the valley. I thought I would draw your attention to them as they may be interesting to you, and the children.

Aunt Thompson and Mary Jane, (and their "baby")[167] are very well. and as good as ever—there are not many better folks than they with all their peculiarities.

The girls would all send love if they knew I was writing if you should write to Edna[168] she would correspond with you. May God Bless You all, with kind love I am ever Joseph F. Smith

---

158. Warren N. Dusenberry and Wilson H. Dusenberry were both prominent educators in Provo at the time; Joseph F. may be referring to either of them here. See biographical register, "Dusenberry, Warren Newton" and "Dusenberry, Wilson Howard."
159. William and Martha Ann lived in a two-room adobe house on the corner of 200 South and 300 West in Provo. See Carole Call King, "History of Martha Ann Smith Harris, 1841–1923" (unpublished manuscript in editors' possession), 3.
160. At this time, Martha Ann had four boys and two girls.
161. William Jasper Harris Jr., Joseph Albert Harris, and Hyrum Smith Harris.
162. Ann Whipple was the wife of William Wallace Cluff, who was presiding over the Scandinavian Mission at this time. See Joseph F. to Martha Ann, 26 May 1871, herein. See also biographical register, "Whipple, Ann."
163. William Jasper Harris.
164. Hannah Greenwood.
165. Zion's Cooperative Mercantile Incorporation (ZCMI). See Martha Sonntag Bradley, *ZCMI: America's First Department Store* (Salt Lake City, UT: ZCMI, 1991).
166. Joseph F.'s "Recollections" was published in the 1871 *Juvenile Instructor*, pp. 37, 87, 91, 98–99.
167. Mercy Rachel Fielding and Mary Jane Thompson. The phrase "their 'baby'" likely refers to Mary Jane's son Robert Blashel Thompson Taylor. At the time of this letter, Robert would have been about ten.
168. Edna Lambson.

JOSEPH F. TO MARTHA ANN, 26 MAY 1871

City, May, 26—1871[169]

My Beloved Sister Martha Ann.

I am in the mood of corresponding this afternoon. I have written to Geo. Nebeker on the Sandwich Island,[170] to William Cluff in England,[171] and now I will scribble you a few lines in haste, you must excuse them for I am in a hurry— I must write still another to a native on the Islands in answer to one from him,[172] and then I shall be thro' with letter writing till I get some more to answer. I am pleased that the President[173] called to see you while in Provo. I wish you had a comfortable home. You had better take the deed of the place, if you can get no better one, and then try to enlarge your dwelling or build anew when ever you can. or if <you> should have it to exchange for or towords another and better place it would not be amiss.

My family are all tolerably well just now, little Mary S[174] has been very sick for some time but is [*30.5 x 1.6 cm cut along bottom*] [**p. 2**] they are determined to help me out of debt by economy &c. My little Leonora,[175] is a pretty, fat—good—black-eyed little baby, and hitherto, with the exception of colic once in a while, is as healthy as a child could be. And Sarah[176] was never happier in her life. Little Mary S. with her long hair, way down on her shoulders—and her little prattle is the life of our home. God Bless the babies! I will renew your subscription to the Juvenile;[177] and will have it sent at once. I had forgotten that the year was up. Aunt Thompson, Mary Jane and Robert[178] are all well, but they write to you so I need not particularise. The Lord is blessing us on every hand. we have a fair amount of health, our share of peace, contentment and happiness. We try to live our Religion and do right, and we are blessed. we will have a new milch cow[179] in a few days all being well, and I hope will be able to [*29.2 x 1.3 cm cut along bottom*] and [*29.2 x 1.3 cm cut along bottom*][180]

169. Joseph F. "met with bro. Eli Bell, recently returned from the Sandwich Island" on this day, which may explain why Joseph F. wrote letters to a Hawaiian Saint and a missionary assigned to the Hawaiian Mission. Joseph F., journal, 26 May 1871.
170. George Nebeker.
171. William Wallace Cluff served as president of the Scandinavian Mission during 1870–71 and may have spent some time in, or could have been contacted via, England. See Joseph F. to Martha Ann, 21 April 1871, herein, note 163.
172. Joseph F. noted, "wrot to G. Keoeoe, a native Elder at Laie. Oahu." Joseph F., journal, 26 May 1871.
173. Probably refers to Brigham Young.
174. Mary Sophronia Smith.
175. Leonora Smith.
176. Sarah Ellen Richards.
177. The *Juvenile Instructor* was published beginning in 1866 by George Q. Cannon and Sons for the benefit of the Sunday School children and youth of the Church.
178. Mercy Rachel Fielding, Mary Jane Thompson, and Robert Blashel Thompson Taylor.
179. Joseph F. had his old milk cow, Cherry, slaughtered earlier; see Joseph F. to Martha Ann, 3 January [1870], herein.
180. The rest of this letter is missing.

JOSEPH F. TO MARTHA ANN, 14 SEPTEMBER 1871

City Sept. 14. 1871

My dear Sister

Martha Ann, Yours of the 9th inst came duly to hand, but for hurry and bustle I should have answered it immediately. Julina[181] got some concentrated lie[182] in her eye and she is suffering considerably with it, but it is not dangerous. Sarah is well, "Nonie"[183] is cutting teeth and rather fretful of nights, has four through and others coming. Mamie[184] has been very poorley ever since you saw her except a few days at Sodah Springs,[185] until now. We all feel and believe she has now taken a turn for the better, & begins to look very different, tho' she is still almost a little skelaton. Edna has been sick for six weeks or more, perhaps you might guess the cause,[186] if you were a Yankey, even a Succor even might. poor girl I never saw any one who had to suffer so much, withall she has been very much troubled with pluricy[187] in her left **[p. 2]** side, an old complaint with her.

Our early peach crop is gon, and the late crop has now come on so that the girls are very busy drying fruit, I am in hopes you will have some fruit this year, for winter use. I was very sorry to hear of little Lucy's[188] illness I hope she is all right ere this.

Julina spent two weeks at black-rock[189]—Salt Lake—with Mamie, and Mary Jane & Robt[190] one, for their health but mamie did not seeme to be improved by it—except the first week.[191]

Aunt Thompson[192] and family are all well. and they are all as full of care and business as ever. There is a vast amount of sickness among children, and the Tiphoid fever is almost epedemic, among grown persons. several have died of it lately[193]— I am very busy—or should be—so you will please excuse this brief note— I will try to do better next time. God Bless you always Joseph

181. Julina Lambson.
182. Lye is a highly corrosive alkali leached from hardwood. It is an essential ingredient for making certain types of soap. Both wet lye and dry lye are highly caustic and may cause chemical burns, permanent scarring, and blindness.
183. Sarah Ellen Richards and Leonora Smith.
184. Possibly Mary Sophronia Smith.
185. Soda Springs is located in present-day Caribou County in southeastern Idaho. The site was a well-known stop for native peoples, trappers, and Oregon Trail emigrants who enjoyed bathing in the natural mineral springs that bubble out of the earth there. Later, Brigham Young established a permanent settlement, including a summer home for his use, at Soda Springs in 1870; the settlement was modeled on the plat of Zion grid system. Joseph F. noted, "Saturday Aug. 6, 1870. a.m. at office copying & p.m. at School [of the Prophets]. Prest. Spoke of making a settlement at Soda Springs." Joseph F., journal, 6 August 1870.
186. Joseph F.'s wife Edna Lambson was about three months pregnant; Hyrum Mack Smith would be born on 21 March 1872.
187. Pleurisy, also known as pleuritis, is an inflammation of the pleura, the thin layers of tissue covering the chest walls and lungs.
188. Lucy Smith Harris.
189. Black Rock was one of Utah's earliest swimming resorts, located on the east side of the Great Salt Lake. See David Eugene Miller, "The Great Salt Lake: Its History and Economic Development" (PhD diss., Brigham Young University, 1947), 241.
190. Mary Jane Thompson and Robert Blashel Thompson Taylor.
191. A Salt Lake newspaper reported some theatrical and musical entertainment at this time. See "Pic-Nic at Black Rock," *Deseret News*, 6 September 1871, 353.
192. Mercy Rachel Fielding.
193. A local newspaper reported that "considerable sickness prevails in the city and vicinity . . . with some cases of typhoid fever." See "Sickness," *Deseret News*, 13 September 1871, 369.

JOSEPH F. TO MARTHA ANN, 21 NOVEMBER 1871

City Nov. 21—1871[194]

My Dear Sister
Martha Ann.

I now take a moment or two to answer your kind letter of Sept. 30th which came duly to hand, and I have carried it in my pocket ever since. Am always glad to hear from you, but sorry when any of the children are sick. It has been a long time since receiving your letter, in it you mentioned the baby's being sick,[195] I trust she soon got better, and that you are all well now. I made enquiry about your shawl but could learn nothing. I think there are some little things that you left, but I am not sure what they are. I do not know but I shall make a visit to Provo sometime soon, & then I can bring them down, unless some of you come up here first. Our health's are very good at presant—except colds from which none of us are free. Little Mary S.[196] is much better than she has been since last May, begins to look plump and fat, and [**p. 2**] is as lively as a cricket. Leonora[197] is cutting four teeth & is fretful, but is pretty as a picture ~~and~~ and dearer than life.

Since Aunt Thompson left for Canada[198] Mary Jane[199] has rented the only room left and turned herself out of doors to cook and up stairs to sleep, she has said nothing to me about it, nor I to her, but I thought it the most absurd, but I had no need to tell you oft it—so keep it to yourself. The weather is very wintery, hard frosts; &c. All is peace in the city, excepting the incroachments of "civilization", & the District Court, an institution that deserves damnation, more than Belzibub its father, because it is a nondescript—notwithstanding its paternal origin![200] Tell sister Jaques[201] that I have 182$ received from bro. Staines,[202] for her, & will send it first <good> chance.[203] Give my love to the children, & to William[204] if at home, and to any Enquiring friends. May God bless you my Dear Sister, giving you strength sufficient for your day is my prayer, Jos F. Smith

194. Joseph F.'s journal for this period ends on 1 November 1871 and begins again on 1 January 1872, making his letters written during this time important sources for reconstructing this period of his life.
195. Lucy Smith Harris was the youngest of Martha Ann's children at this time.
196. Mary Sophronia.
197. Leonora Smith.
198. Mercy Rachel Fielding lived in eastern Canada before joining the Church. She returned there in 1871 to visit her relatives. From there, she traveled to England the following year to visit other relatives.
199. Mary Jane Thompson.
200. There was significant anti-plural marriage sentiment in local and federal courts at the time.
201. Most likely Louisa Adelada Phillips Jacques, a resident of Provo. See biographical register, "Phillips, Louisa Adelada."
202. Possibly William Carter Staines, an assistant to Brigham Young; see 1870 US Census. See also biographical register, "Staines, William Carter." The funds had come to Joseph F. through J. P. R. Johnson. See Joseph F., journal, 13 December 1871.
203. Joseph F. sent the amount a few weeks later. See Joseph F., journal, 13 December 1871.
204. William Jasper Harris.

JOSEPH F. TO MARTHA ANN, 12 DECEMBER 1871

Page 1—S.L. City
Dec. 12th 1871

My Dear Sister
Martha Ann,

Yours of 20th inst. came to hand duly. and found us all measurably well—we are a little troubled with colds nothing more. I am sorry to hear of William's[205] illness, not only on his own account but yours also. It would seem that you had more than your share of troubles in this life, and I wish it could be otherwise, were it in my power I would certainly releave you, and that gladly.

I am gratified however to hear that you have a little more room,[206] may you enjoy even that little fully—[p. 2] (2) I ment to have made a visit to Provo—but the weather and roads came on so bad that I think I shall postpone <it> until some more favorable time. Dec. 14th 1871[207]—I got this far with this note the other evening and was obliged to quit for more pressing duties.[208] I have sent my team away for the winter, in care of Willard Richards,[209] as I could not afford to keep them. Edward[210] not being able to work it—and besides I want him to go to school this winter is possible. We are all about as well as usual. Uncle Sam's[211] minion's made another onslaught yesterday by arresting three or four of the special police, on the charge of the murder of Dr. Robinson. one of them, J. L. Blythe,[212] who by the way[213]

---

205. William Jasper Harris.
206. Martha Ann was living in Provo at this time. Six months earlier, Joseph F. had written to Martha, "I am pleased that the President called to see you while in Provo. I wish you had a comfortable home. You had better take the deed of the place, if you can get no better one, and then try to enlarge your dwelling or build anew when ever you can. or if <you> should have it to exchange for or towords another and better place it would not be amiss." Joseph F. to Martha Ann, 26 May 1871, herein. It appears that Martha Ann had taken his advice and added to the adobe home by this time.
207. Joseph F. wrote four people on this date, "Geo. A., John Hopkins, Knute Peterson and Martha Ann." Joseph F., journal, 14 December 1871.
208. In addition to his work at the Endowment House and Historian's Office and attending sessions of the School of the Prophets during this period, Joseph F. was also erecting a barn on his property. See Joseph F., journal, 12 December 1871.
209. Willard Brigham Richards, son of Sarah Longstroth and Willard Richards and brother to Joseph F.'s wife Sarah Ellen Richards. Richards had worked as a rancher in Skull Valley, Utah, for several years by this time and was in charge of the Utah Livestock Company ranch. Skull Valley is located approximately seventy miles northwest of Salt Lake City. See biographical register, "Richards, Willard Brigham."
210. Edward Arthur Smith.
211. Based on the initials *US*, "Uncle Sam" is still a common national personification of the United States government. Its usage traces to the beginning of the nineteenth century.
212. Between 13 December and 19 December 1871, four Latter-day Saints were arrested in connection with the murder of Dr. J. King Robinson, who was killed in October 1866. These four suspects—James Toms, John L. Blythe, Alexander Burt, and Brigham Y. Hampton—were convicted on the testimony of Charles W. Baker. One month later, Baker confessed to having fabricated his testimony. Surprisingly, the innocent men remained in custody until 30 April 1872. For more information, see Edward William Tullidge, *History of Salt Lake City* (Salt Lake City, UT: Star Printing, 1886), 573–74; see also "Another of Those Indictments," *Deseret News*, 20 December 1871, 533; and Andrew Jenson, *Church Chronology: A Record of Important Events Pertaining to the Church of Jesus Christ of Latter-day Saints*, 2nd ed. (Salt Lake City, UT: Deseret News Press, 1899), 86–88. See also biographical register, "Robinson, John King" and "Blyth, John Law."
213. The rest of this letter is missing.

JOSEPH F. TO MARTHA ANN, 3 MAY 1872

Salt Lake City
May 3rd 1872[214]

My Dear Sister Martha Ann

Your letter of Apr. 3rd came duly to hand, and you will see by the dates that it is just one month today since it was written and I have carried it in my pocket ever since awaiting a favorable opportunity to answer.

I am happy to say that we are all usually well with slight colds among the babies. we are getting quite a respectable show of them now, and in greater variety than heretofore. We have three babies—God Bless them for ever, they are bright, hansome, and good.[215] The beauty—of course since we had to part with our little black-eyed Josephine,[216] is our little black eyed Leonora. Still they are all pretty—and beloved. our little boy[217] has manifested so far the Sweet disposition of our "dode",[218] and if his eyes were black, and hair darker he would remind me of her looks. but he is blue eyed, and light, and grows like a "wead." he is large beside of the rest of the babies, Bathshebas, Sarah's—(John's, Sarah) and even Susan's.[219]

Edna is here at Geo. A.'s,[220] Sarah[221] has gon to the store & will be here soon, and Julina[222] is attending Retrenchment Meeting[223] after which she will also be here, it is "Aunt" Bathsheba's 50th Birth day,[224] and so the Girls are out on a visit. Our Sarah spent six week at Skull Valley,[225] I **[p. 2]** I went for her and returned just a week ago yesterday.[226] The City begins to look beautiful, trees beginning to get green and all in blossom, but the roads are already dusty,

214. Joseph F. was thirty-three, and Martha Ann was thirty.
215. Joseph F.'s three surviving infants at this time were Mary Sophronia, Leonora, and Hyrum Mack.
216. Mercy Josephine Smith. See Joseph F. to Martha Ann, 25 June 1870, herein.
217. Hyrum Mack Smith was born to Edna Lambson on 21 March 1872. See biographical register, "Smith, Hyrum Mack."
218. Mercy Josephine Smith.
219. Likely refers to Bathsheba Smith, second cousin to Joseph F. and Martha Ann. She gave birth to Margaret May Merrill on 5 February 1872. Sarah Farr, second cousin to Joseph F. and Martha Ann and wife of John Henry Smith, gave birth to Lorin Farr Smith on 22 April 1872. Susan Elizabeth West, wife of George A. Smith, Joseph F. and Martha Ann's first cousin once removed, gave birth to Emma Pearl Smith on 19 April 1871. See biographical register, "Smith, Bathsheba Kate," "Merrill, Margaret May," "Farr, Sarah," "Smith, John Henry," "Smith, Lorin Farr," "West, Susan Elizabeth," and "Smith, Emma Pearl."
220. Edna Lambson and George A. Smith, who is Joseph F. and Martha Ann's first cousin once removed.
221. Sarah Ellen Richards.
222. Julina Lambson.
223. The Young Ladies' Mutual Improvement Association was originally organized by Brigham Young as a retrenchment society for his daughters. It eventually became a Churchwide organization for young women. Alice Ann Kimball was its treasurer in 1905 and a board member beginning in 1806. See Susan Young Gates, *History of the Young Ladies' Mutual Improvement Association* (Salt Lake City, UT: Deseret News Press, 1911), 294–98. See also Joseph F. to Martha Ann, 3 May 1872, herein.
224. Bathsheba Wilson Bigler, wife of George A. Smith, was born on 3 May 1822. Joseph F. attended a "supper in honor of Aunt Bathsheba's birthday. All the girls present. Their mother, and several others." Joseph F., journal, 3 May 1871. See biographical register, "Bigler, Bathsheba Wilson."
225. See Joseph F. to Martha Ann, 12 December 1871, herein.
226. Joseph F.'s wife Sarah and their two-year-old daughter Leonora apparently stayed at Hooper Ranch in Skull Valley, Utah. Joseph F. traveled to Skull Valley to escort them home between 23 and 25 April 1872. See Joseph F., journal, 23–25 April 1872.

notwithstanding the recent storms. I hope the health of yourselfe and little family ~~are~~<is> all well and good.

Prest. Young and all the prisoners are enjoying their liberty again, and McKean[227] is enjoying his much merrited scorn, contempt, and degredation. He is down and everybody is now ready to give him a Kick![228] but it serves him right it is in answer to prayer.

Aunt Thompson and her Children[229] are usually well. They are stopping at our house this after noon to take care of Mamie[230] who is suffering with a severe cold & cough, & we thought we dare not risk the exposure of a visit up here. You know it was from here[231] we carried home our sweet little Josephine to bid her that long farewell, it has made us cautious. I was pleased to learn from some friends from Provo that little Lucy[232] was better— How is William?[233] and where is he & what doing? give my love to all friends. The Girls[234] all join in love to you—all. You must excuse this hastily written letter— Ever Truly Joseph

JOSEPH F. TO MARTHA ANN, 17 MAY 1872

City May 17th 1872

My Dear Sister
Martha Ann,

227. Chief Justice of the Utah Territorial Supreme Court James B. McKean. He placed Brigham Young under house arrest for four months for violation of the law against the practice of plural marriage. Brigham was released in mid-April when the US Supreme Court ruled that Justice McKean had allowed juries to be drawn illegally. At this time many Saints who had been tried by McKean in the eighteen months preceding this ruling were released. See Leonard J. Arrington, *Brigham Young: American Moses* (Urbana: University of Illinois Press, 1985), 371–73. See also Jenson, *Church Chronology*, April 1872. McKean is mentioned in another letter; see Joseph F. to Martha Ann, 15 May 1875, herein. See also biographical register, "McKean, James B."
228. As noted in the *Deseret News*, McKean and his "political intriguers and anti-Mormon religious sects" were denounced by the *San Francisco Newsletter*, the Cincinnati *Commercial*, and the Louisville *Courier Journal* for "twist[ing] and distort[ing] the law to carry out their own purposes," thus "prov[ing] themselves to be even more fanatical than the Mormons." These papers reportedly celebrated the Supreme Court's decision to overturn some of McKean's decisions as proof that the country "will be governed by law, and not by passions and prejudices." See "That Decision," *Deseret News*, 1 May 1872, 171. While the Saints had reason to be pleased with the Supreme Court's decision, it should be recognized that Judge McKean was responding to national pressure to end plural marriage. In 1871 US president Ulysses S. Grant believed that Utah was a barbarous territory with little regard for the laws of the United States. When President Grant appointed McKean to Utah's judiciary, McKean believed it was a calling from God to eradicate plural marriage. See Edwin Brown Firmage and Richard Collin Mangrum, *Zion in the Courts: A Legal History of the Church of Jesus Christ of Latter-day Saints, 1830–1900* (Urbana and Chicago: University of Illinois Press, 1988), 138–41.
229. Mercy Rachel Fielding and her daughter, Mary Jane Thompson. Joseph F. may also be including Mary Jane's son, Robert Taylor, since Mercy Rachel had only one child of her own.
230. Mary Sophronia Smith.
231. Joseph F. is writing from George A. Smith's house.
232. Lucy Smith Harris.
233. William Jasper Harris.
234. A reference to Joseph F.'s wives, Julina Lambson (married 1866), Sarah Ellen Richards (married 1868), and Edna Lambson (married 1872).

Yours of 13th inst. came duly to hand and I take the present opportunity to write you a few words in a hurried manner, as I am at city council.

I was not requested to go to provo so I remained at home I might have gon, if I had been requested. But I have plenty to do at home, and more than I can do, except I had more to do with but I have no cause to complain, nor would I for a slight one.

The health of the family is again very good, our [**p. 2**] our precious little black eyed "Nonie"[235] is teathing and some what puney but, but she is doing nicely, she has been weaned from her mother and has taken to nursing Edna.[236] But I am rather glad of it, for she has plenty of milk, and if she does not wean easily by-and bye we will let her pass the summer. I am fearful for the children this summer, our experience last we have not forgotten, with our little Mary S.[237] She is now hearty and well. The Girls are very busy sewing rags for another carpet. and they do seem to work harder and more hours than any body else that I know. and I cannot prevent it, some way they seem to be overwhelmed with work all the time. I ofton say "what will you do when you get as many to do for each as MarthaAnn has"? but it is no use—I believe the Lord has blessed us with more than we can well take care of—and yet I know of nothing that we can well do without, and we are all the time desiring, and seeming to need more. One of John Sharp's[238] daughters[239] died recently of what the Docters call spotted fever, a very virulent and fatal desease. it is said no one recovers from it, who takes it.[240]

I am pleased to hear that your little ones are so well. [**p. 3**] and that you are getting your little home so comfortable I was very sorry to hear that William[241] had had another bad spell, tell him for a friend & a brother, and one who has more than one tie of sympathy and friendship, that when he quits wholly and entirely the use of Ardent,[242] or Stimulous drink, and will take proper rest and excercise, he will be a well man once more, and not till then.[243] And I know what I say, and I do not mince it. That he drank while here, some little time ago, I do know, and it grieved me. Now I say this, perhaps at the expense of friendship, but I have said it, with an earnest solicitude

for William and his precious family—of wife & little ones. and I only speak of what I know, but I have been worried about him. God Bless you all, yours ever true Joseph.[244]

235. Leonora Smith was fifteen months old at this time.

236. Edna Lambson.

237. Mary Sophronia Smith. See Joseph F. to Martha Ann, 26 May 1871 and 14 September 1871, herein.

238. John Sharp was bishop of the Twentieth Ward in Salt Lake City and was superintendent of the Utah Central Railroad. See biographical register, "Sharp, John."

239. Most likely Cecilia Sharp, who "died at 5:30 p.m. on Thursday, May 16, and her age was 11 years 5 months and 20 days." "Funeral," *Deseret Evening News*, 18 May 1872, 3. See biographical register, "Sharp, Cecilia."

240. Rocky Mountain spotted fever is a tick-borne rickettsial illness characterized by widespread rash and fever.

241. William Jasper Harris.

242. Ardent drink was usually identified with strong distilled alcoholic liquors such as whiskey, brandy, or gin.

243. In the 1860s and 1870s, Church leaders encouraged the Saints to obey the Word of Wisdom, but its "observance was not mandatory and Brigham Young never made it a test of fellowship." See Paul H. Peterson, "An Historical Analysis of the Word of Wisdom" (PhD diss., Brigham Young University, 1971), 68.

244. Written upside down in the top margin of page 3.

JOSEPH F. TO MARTHA ANN, 14 JUNE 1872

S. L. City June 14th 1872

My Dear Sister
Martha Ann.

Yours of May 25—th came duly to hand, I am always pleased to hear from you, especially so when I can learn of your welfare. It is rather strange but I never hear from either Jerusha or Sarah,[245] there seems to be a strange indifference, almost coldness, in the brests of them both towards me, and I may say the rest of the family, for I daresay I hear from them almost as often as any one of the family. who would have thought that our family could have grown up to become strangers, to each other. Lovina[246] never calls except thro' a sort of courticy, but Lorin[247] is sociable and friendly. But that I am not surprised at—by the way, President Young has bought Lovina a very good home at farmington[248] at a cost of over three housand dollars. Leonard Rice's[249] place. House, city lots, pasture & farm. [**p. 2**] I cannot but feel grateful to, and say God Bless President Young, at the same time either of the other girl's were quite as worthy. Not but what President Young would as readily assist either of them ~~as soon~~ as he would her if it was in his power. He has certainly dealt kindly and liberally with our Father's house, and with Samuel.[250] He has proven himself a father to the fatherless in our cases at least—and he has been no less liberal to many others, aye many![251] the demands on his bounty are numirous, and he seldom sends away empty. He has sent Aunt Catherine,[252] some $\$400^{00}$ in cash to help her build a house, and make herself comfortable. I hope we will never for get his kindness, it would be ungrateful.

My family are all well, for which I am very thankful, our little blackeyed Leonora[253] is cutting her double teeth and is just being weaned, she is therefore a little fretful, but we hope—yes believe she will get along all right. Mamie[254] is growing like a weed, she is taller than [**p. 3**] Josephine[255] was when she died, altho' not quite so old. her health is good. our little Hyrum Mack[256] is growing nicely, and is a sweet little fellow, fat—blue-eyed and good. Today is mary Jane's birth day she is 34, tomorrow is Aunt Thompsons.[257] I do not know her age. I just happened to think—she was born in 1807 which makes her 65—to~~day~~ morrow, and if she had nobody's troubles but her own to bear she would be good for many years— (you must excuse

245. Jerusha and Sarah Smith.
246. Lovina Smith.
247. Lorin Walker.
248. Farmington, Davis County, Utah, about seventeen miles north of Salt Lake City.
249. Leonard Gurley Rice was still in Farmington in 1880, according to the US census records. See biographical register, "Rice, Leonard Gurley."
250. Samuel Harrison Bailey Smith.
251. The word *many* is written twice as large as the other words on the page.
252. Katherine Smith was the younger sister of Hyrum and Joseph Smith Jr. When the Saints moved west, she remained in Illinois with her family, where she was living at the time of this letter. See biographical register, "Smith, Katherine."
253. Leonora Smith.
254. Mary Sophronia Smith.
255. Mercy Josephine Smith.
256. Hyrum Mack Smith.
257. Mary Jane Thompson and Mercy Rachel Fielding.

my writing my pen is very bad) Julina[258] is 24 this month. I forget the day.[259] it is two years on the 6th of this month since our one best beloved little angel Josephine left us, it will not be long till we shall go to meet those that have gon behind the veil! "where the wicked cease from troubling, and the weary are at rest"![260] O! glorious release, yet I want to finish my work here before I go, and tho' it were a century it would be short! My health is good, and my spirits tolerable.

George A.[261] who has been east for about a month, and Geo. Q. Cannon, who has been at **[p. 4]** Washington several months & Capt. Hooper are expected home tomorrow.[262]

The weather is very hot and dry & the Kanyon streems are decreasing. I hope we shall have rain before long.

I sympathise with you my dear sister—I would to God that William would see and stop the folly of his past course in regard to that one terrible thing.[263] it is the curse of Millions, and it has desolated tens of thousands of homes, it would ruin an Angel, it would defuse and <impovish> a millionair, it ruins health, happiness and honor. it degrades, destroys and damn's it votaries—broadcast over the whole earth. But it is still worse for those who have drunk at the fountain of God's spirit. who have labored in the vineyard of souls, and reaped the blessings of the Priesthood in the House of God. O! may he think of this before it is too late! Look at Furguson,[264] Nixon, & Macintosh, remember the fate of J. R. Long,[265] James Meyers, and __ Luce,[266] all the same. Look at O. K. Whitney,[267] & others. O! God deliver me & my kindred from their fates! Yours in love & eternal fraternaty— Jos. F. Smith

258. Julina Lambson.

259. Julina Lambson was born on 18 June 1849.

260. A line from H. H. Milman's popular funeral hymn "Brother, Thou Art Gone Before Us," published in 1830.

261. George Albert Smith.

262. George Q. Cannon and William Henry Hooper were in Washington, DC, petitioning for Utah's statehood, a measure that failed at that time. They would return to Ogden on 16 June to be greeted by a great crowd that rode with them by train to Salt Lake City. See Joseph F., journal, 16 June 1872. See biographical register, "Cannon, George Quayle" and "Hooper, William Henry."

263. Likely a reference to William's use of alcohol. See Joseph F. to Martha Ann, 17 May 1872, herein.

264. Possibly refers to James Ferguson, a prominent member of the Church who died young because of excessive drinking. See biographical register, "Ferguson, James."

265. John Varah Long, known as a heavy drinker, was found dead in a ditch in Salt Lake City on 14 April 1869. The news report of his death ended, "How sad a finish to a life that might have been so useful." "Found Dead," *Deseret News,* 21 April 1869, 132. See biographical register, "Long, James Varah."

266. Stephen Luce died in April 1872 after falling into a water sec (a drainage ditch generally lined in stone that could hold a significant amount of water, especially during the spring runoff) on the corner of Third South and Third East. The newspaper reports that he "was about seventy-two years of age, a resident of the 10th ward, and occasionally of rather intemperate habits." See "Coroner's Inquest," *Salt Lake (UT) Herald,* 30 April 1872, 3.

267. Orson Kimball Whitney. His obituary states, "His worst enemy was strong drink and it finally overcame his iron constitution." See "A Pioneer Passed Away," *Ogden Daily Herald,* 2 August 1884, [3]. See biographical register, "Whitney, Orson Kimball."

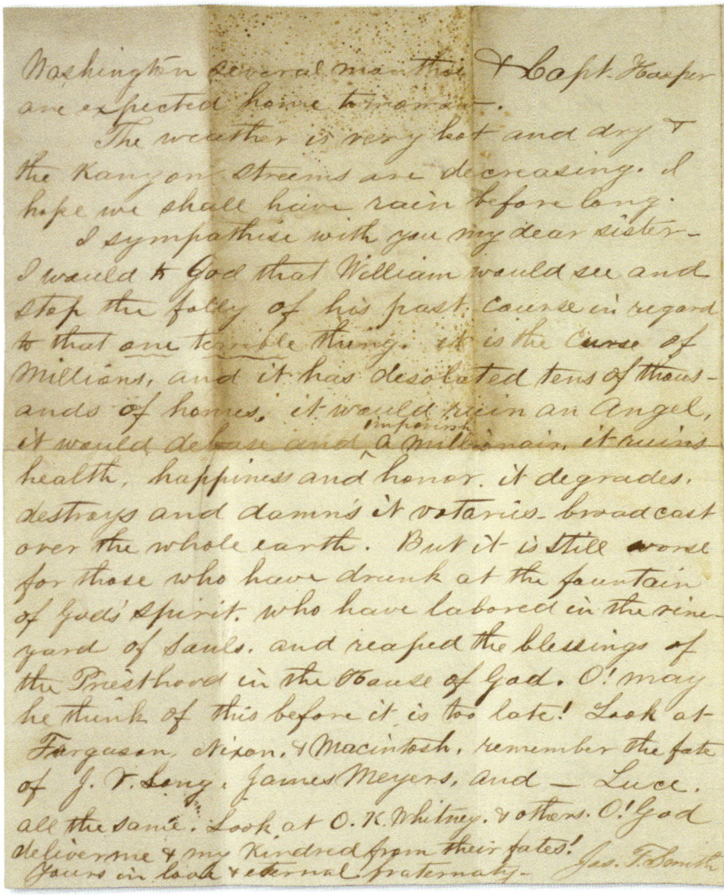

Washington several months, & Capt. Hooper are expected home tomorrow.

The weather is very hot and dry & the Kanyon Streams are decreasing. I hope we shall have rain before long.

I sympathise with you my dear sister— I would to God that William would see and stop the folly of his past course in regard to that one terrible thing. it is the Curse of Millions, and it has desolated tens of thousands of homes. it would ruin an Angel, it would debase and impoverish a millionair. it ruins health, happiness and honor. it degrades, destroys and damns it votaries broadcast over the whole earth. But it is still worse for those who have drunk at the fountain of God's Spirit. who have labored in the vineyard of Souls. and reaped the blessings of the Priesthood in the House of God. O! may he think of this before it is too late! Look at Ferguson, Nixon, & Macintosh, remember the fate of J. T. Long, James Meyers, and — Luce. all the same. Look at O. K. Whitney. & others. O! God deliver me & my kindred from their fates! Yours in love & eternal fraternity— Jos. F. Smith

Joseph F. to Martha Ann, 14 June 1872 (p. 4)

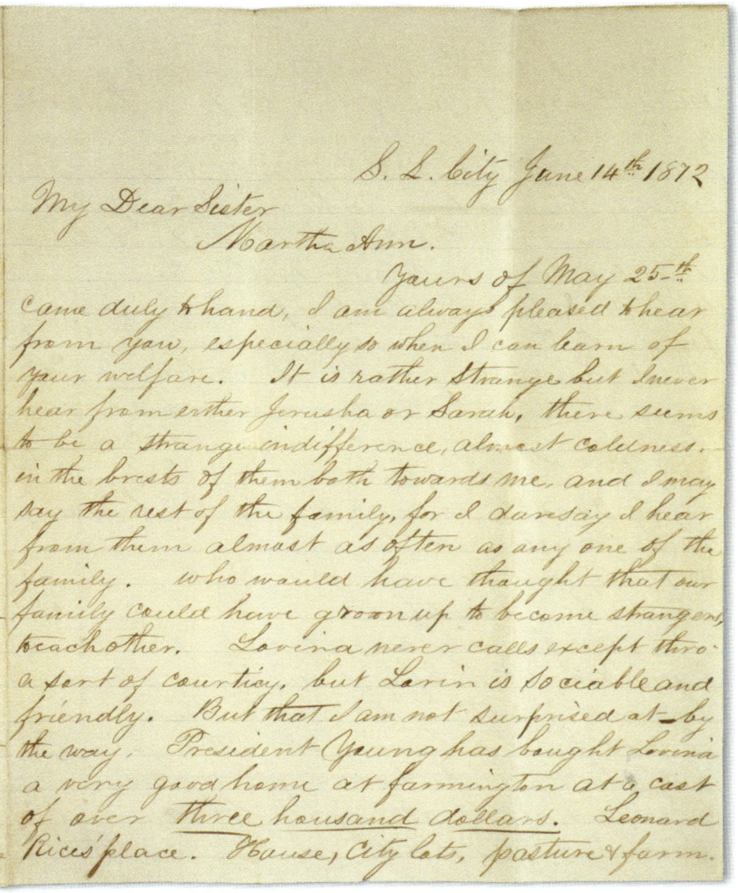

S. L. City June 14th 1872

My Dear Sister
Martha Ann.

Yours of May 25th came duly to hand, I am always pleased to hear from you, especially so when I can learn of your welfare. It is rather Strange but I never hear from either Jerusha or Sarah, there seems to be a strange indifference, almost coldness, in the brests of them both towards me, and I may say the rest of the family, for I darsay I hear from them almost as often as any one of the family. who would have thought that our family could have groon up to become strangers to each other. Lovina never calls except thro' a sort of courtesy, but Lorin is sociable and friendly. But that I am not surprised at—by the way. President Young has bought Lovina a very good home at farmington at a cost of over three housand dollars. Leonard Rice's place. House, City lots, pasture & farm.

Joseph F. to Martha Ann, 14 June 1872 (p. 1)

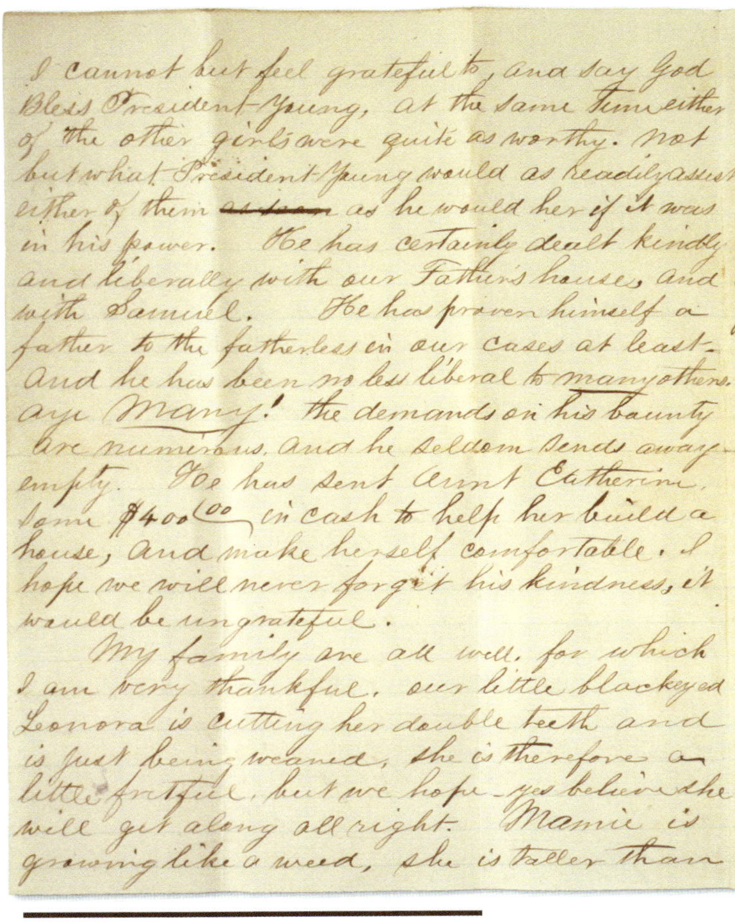

I cannot but feel grateful to, and say God Bless President Young, at the same time either of the other girls were quite as worthy. not but what President Young would as readily assist either of them ~~as~~ as he would her if it was in his power. He has certainly dealt kindly and liberally with our Father's house, and with Samuel. He has proven himself a father to the fatherless in our cases at least. And he has been no less liberal to many others, aye Many! the demands on his bounty are numerous, and he seldom sends away empty. He has sent Aunt Catherine Some \$400.00 in cash to help her build a house, and make herself comfortable. I hope we will never forget his kindness, it would be ungrateful.

My family are all well, for which I am very thankful. our little blackeyed Leonora is cutting her double teeth and is just being weaned, she is therefore a little fretful, but we hope—yes believe she will get along all right. Mamie is growing like a weed, she is taller than

Joseph F. to Martha Ann, 14 June 1872 (p. 2)

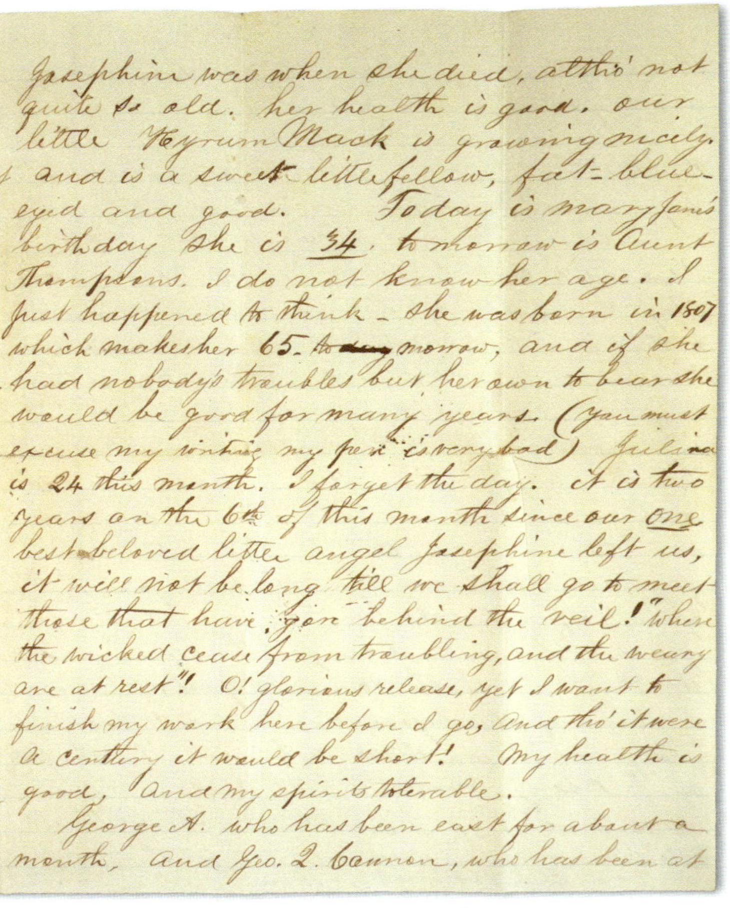

Josephine was when she died, altho' not quite so old. her health is good. our little Hyrum Mack is growing nicely and is a sweet little fellow, fat—blue-eyed and good. Today is Mary Jane's birthday She is 34. to morrow is Aunt Thompsons. I do not know her age. I just happened to think—she was born in 1807 which makes her 65 to ~~day~~ morrow, and if she had nobody's troubles but her own to bear she would be good for many years. (you must excuse my writing my pen is very bad) Julina is 24 this month. I forget the day. it is two years on the 6th of this month since our one best beloved little angel Josephine left us, it will not be long till we shall go to meet those that have gone behind the veil! "where the wicked cease from troubling, and the weary are at rest"! O! glorious release, yet I want to finish my work here before I go, and tho' it were a century it would be short! My health is good, and my spirits tolerable.

George A. who has been east for about a month, and Geo. Q. Cannon, who has been at

Joseph F. to Martha Ann, 14 June 1872 (p. 3)

JOSEPH F. TO MARTHA ANN, 26 JULY 1872

City, July 26th 72[268]

My Dear Sister
Martha Ann
President Young[269] [rest of page missing]
[**p. 2**] Gave directions to David McKenzie[270] to notify Bp. Smoot[271] accordingly; [rest of page missing]

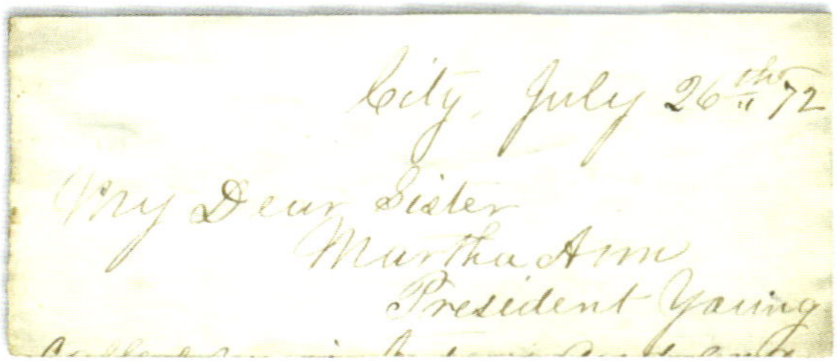
City, July 26th 72
My Dear Sister
Martha Ann
President Young

Joseph F. to Martha Ann, 26 July 1872 (p. 1)

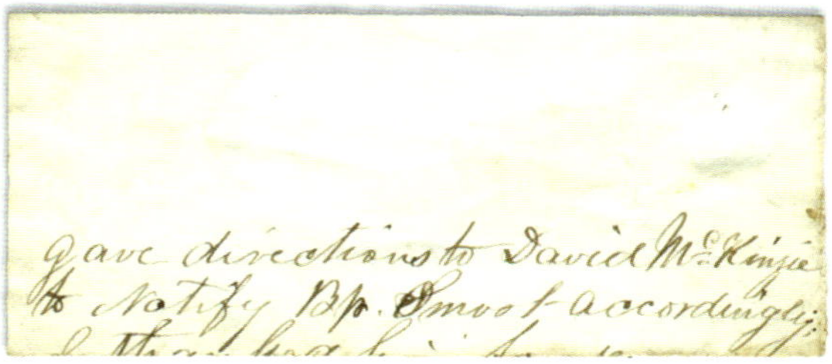
Gave directions to David McKenzie
to notify Bp. Smoot accordingly;

Joseph F. to Martha Ann, 26 July 1872 (p. 2)

JOSEPH F. TO MARTHA ANN, 18 JANUARY 1873

Salt Lake City
Jan. 18th 1873.[272]

My Dear Sister
Martha Ann
Provo.

Your letter of Nov. 24th is before me and has never been answered. I was glad to hear from you as I always am. And now, although I have no news, I thought I would send you a few lines. We are now all in the enjoyment of tolerable health. the children have all had a seige of the epedemic influenza, cold or pneumonia that has been going the rounds of late, but fortunately they have all escaped any serious results. And those of us that are older have not entirely

268. On Friday, 26 July, Joseph F. "Went up town this morning with Sarah" to make some purchases amounting to $21.33. See Joseph F., journal, 26 July 1872.

269. Brigham Young was the President of the Church and was particularly busy during the summer of 1872. He had been arrested in March 1872; closed the School of the Prophets on 3 August, shortly after Joseph F. had written this letter to his sister Martha Ann; met Leopold Bierwirth, a New York merchant who kept a diary of his travels from New York to San Francisco, with a detailed account of his visit to Salt Lake City and Brigham Young; and reorganized the school on 4 November 1872, limiting it to about 234 leaders.

270. David McKenzie was a private secretary to Brigham Young and manager of the Salt Lake Theatre.

271. Most likely a reference to A. O. Smoot, who had been a bishop in Salt Lake City.

272. Joseph F. was thirty-four, and Martha Ann was thirty-one.

escaped. we have all had our turn; except myself and now I feel as though mine had come, or was coming.

Julina[273] and I were at a Ball at the City Hall last night in honor of the Fire Brigade.[274] And the night before we spent a few hours at our own ward School House,[275] which has just been built. a very fine stone building with galary, Entrance Hall, Vestry and upper room over Vestry, connected to main Hall by a draw partition, nearly the whole width, a very neet and useful arrangement. the whole building will cost not less than $12,000^{00/100}$

William[276] called on us and stopped over night. I was pleased to have him as it seemed a little more friendly than usual, of late. But he would not stop to eat with us having promised to breakfast at Mary Janes.[277] **[p. 2]**[278] There is no reason why he should not make his home with us when he is in the city, as we have pleanty of room and beds. speaking of that, I will say the girls have just got each a new fether bed. so that now we have two spare ones for our friends when they come to see us. for which I am very thankful for I like to make my friends and especially my Kindred comfortable when they favor us with a call. we can now do this, and they can share with us in the other blessings which we enjoy. I have sold my wagon, harness, and remaining horse for $220^{00/100}$ and I have put the money into the Coôp. so that now I have a small interest, once more, in that Institution.[279] I am out of imployment just now, there being nothing for me to do in the office.[280] this makes me feel uneasy, as always, you know the expence goes on. whether there is much, little or nothing coming in. The girls are earning more than I am now. Sarah[281] is dress making, and we are boarding sister E. Pratt[282] and son, School teachers in our ward. Edward[283] is going to School and is doing well. Aunt Fielding[284] has sold her farm on Mill creek for $1000^{00/100}$ cash down, the money will do her much more good at interest, than the farm would in her possession. Mary Jane has not been very well of late, but is much better now. The girls all joine in love to you and all the family.

God bless you and yours and continue to open your way and strew blessings upon your wearisom path is my constant prayer Jos. Fielding S.

---

273. Julina Lambson.
274. This was followed one week later by a police reunion ball. Both balls were reported in the local newspaper. See "Police Re-Union," *Deseret News*, 29 January 1873, 793.
275. Though Utah had not established a public, tax-supported school system at this time, there were public schools in most towns and in each ward of the larger cities. See Thomas G. Alexander, *Utah: The Right Place* (Salt Lake City, UT: Gibbs Smith, 2003), 183.
276. William Jasper Harris.
277. Mary Jane Thompson.
278. There are scribbles written in a dark black ink at the top of the page. There is also what appears to be a child's drawing of a bird in the middle of the letter.
279. Zion's Cooperative Mercantile Institution.
280. Church Historian's Office.
281. Sarah Ellen Richards.
282. Likely Eleanor Jane McComb, wife of Parley P. Pratt, and her son Albert McLean, who is listed in the 1870 US Census as a schoolteacher. This person could also be any number of the Pratt relatives. See biographical register, "McComb, Eleanor Jane" and "McLean, Albert."
283. Edward Arthur Smith.
284. Likely Hannah Greenwood, wife of Joseph Fielding and aunt of Joseph F. and Martha Ann.

JOSEPH F. TO MARTHA ANN, 28 APRIL 1873

Salt Lake City
April 28th 1873.

My Dear Sister
Martha Ann:—

I am now in city council and I thought I would drop you a few lines. We are all well, except Edna,[285] she is very sick. Was taken sick on tuesday last, flooding,[286] and has been suffering very much since, but I think she is now some better. But we have had our hands full for two or three days I assure, <you> with five babies and only two mothers,[287] babies more or less cross—some teathing &c. &c. But I have no fears that we shall not live through it. We have to have our little troubles once in a while, to remind us of our infirmities and helplessness. For if our course through life was all pleasant, we should loose, the best portion, for we should not know how to apreciate the good, for however good,—if not apreciated, there can be no enjoyment. Mary Jane and Robert[288] are well. I hope these few lines [*illegible strike-through*] hastily scribbled may find you and all the family well, give my love to all good friends not forgetting William[289] & the Children,[290] and your self— May God bless you all— from your affectionate brother— Jos. F. Smith

JOSEPH F. TO MARTHA ANN, 1 JULY 1873

S. L. City
1st July 1873

My Dear Sister
Martha Ann,

I find in my pocket your letter of Apr. 3th 1873— I do not know whether I have ever answered it or not—but I thought on a venture it would do no harm to write a few lines by way of acknowledgement— I am in city council and will have to do two things at once—as I must listen to business as I write—

My family are all usually well— Some of the Children have colds, and our little Joseph Richards[291]—is fretful and I think beginning to cut teeth.

Aunt Thompson[292] and some of her English friends took Supper with us this evening. She is looking very well—looks but little older and must have enjoyed her visit very well.[293]

---

285. Edna Lambson.
286. A nineteenth-century term for uterine hemorrhage.
287. Joseph F. had three wives at this point, each with one or two children; his reference to "only two mothers" likely refers to the fact that only two of his wives were doing all the mothering for the five young children because of Edna's illness.
288. Mary Jane Thompson and Robert Blashel Thompson Taylor.
289. William Jasper Harris.
290. Martha Ann had seven children at the time of this letter.
291. Joseph Richards Smith was born to Sarah Ellen Richards on 22 February 1873. See biographical register, "Smith, Joseph Richards."
292. Mercy Rachel Fielding.
293. Mercy Rachel Fielding had just returned from a trip to England that day.

I returned form Cache Valley[294] [**p. 2**] Yesterday morning— Somewhat tired as I had been travelling most of the night without sleep— Geo. A.[295] looks well and, except a rheumatic pain, in his right arm, is feeling first rate.

My health is not quite as good as I could wish—and for several days I have had something like the blues[296] on a small scale— Sarah Ann Whitney Kimball[297] is very low with sickness—I have been twice to lay hands on her. We are in hopes she will get well. I saw Aunt Lucy[298] this morning, and had a long talk with her— She talks of building a boarding house in Provo. I advised her to be very cautious about getting in debt—and paying interest on money.

Give my love to William[299] and the little ones—and all friends and excuse haste and scribbling, Affectionately Joseph

JOSEPH F. TO WILLIAM AND MARTHA ANN, 10 NOVEMBER 1873

S. L. City
Nov. 10. 1873—

William and Marth—

Next Thursday is my thirty-fifth birth day,[300] I am trying to get the family together on that day at my house— I desire your presence.[301]

If William cannot come with his team, please take the train & come immediately.[302] I do not want to be disappointed. If you want R. R. tickets—telegraph to me & I will send them.

We are all well— I will tell you the rest when I see you, try & get here on Wednesday[303] if you can—but on Thursday sure—

Your affectionate brother
Jos F. Smith

---

294. Cache Valley was an important agricultural valley in Utah and Idaho, about seventy miles northeast of Salt Lake City, with several important Latter-day Saint settlements, including Logan, Cache County, Utah.
295. George Albert Smith.
296. Most likely a reference to his feelings.
297. Sarah Ann Whitney was a plural wife of Joseph Smith Jr. and subsequently married Heber C. Kimball. See biographical register, "Whitney, Sarah Ann."
298. Possibly refers to Lucy Walker, a plural wife of Joseph Smith Jr. who later married Heber C. Kimball. Joseph F. and Martha Ann also had an aunt Lucy Smith, sister of Hyrum and Joseph Smith Jr., who was living in Colchester, Illinois. See biographical register, "Walker, Lucy."
299. William Jasper Harris.
300. Joseph F. celebrated his thirty-fifth birthday on Thursday, 13 November 1873.
301. This was an important gathering of the Hyrum Smith family, including other extended Smith family members. Joseph F. noted on Thursday, 13 November, "that for the first time in over 27 years my fathers children were once more all together, at my house. . . . We spent the day and evening together in a very pleasant visit and reunion, feasting on the good things that we could afford, having an excellent good time. In evening we had Songs and recitations, and dissolved about 9.30 pm. All from a distance remaining with us for the night." Joseph F., journal, 13 November 1873.
302. The Utah Southern Railroad ran from Salt Lake City through Utah Valley and southward.
303. Joseph F. wrote on Wednesday, 12 November, "William & Martha Ann arrived from Provo by the 7 p.m. train." Joseph F., journal, 12 November 1873.

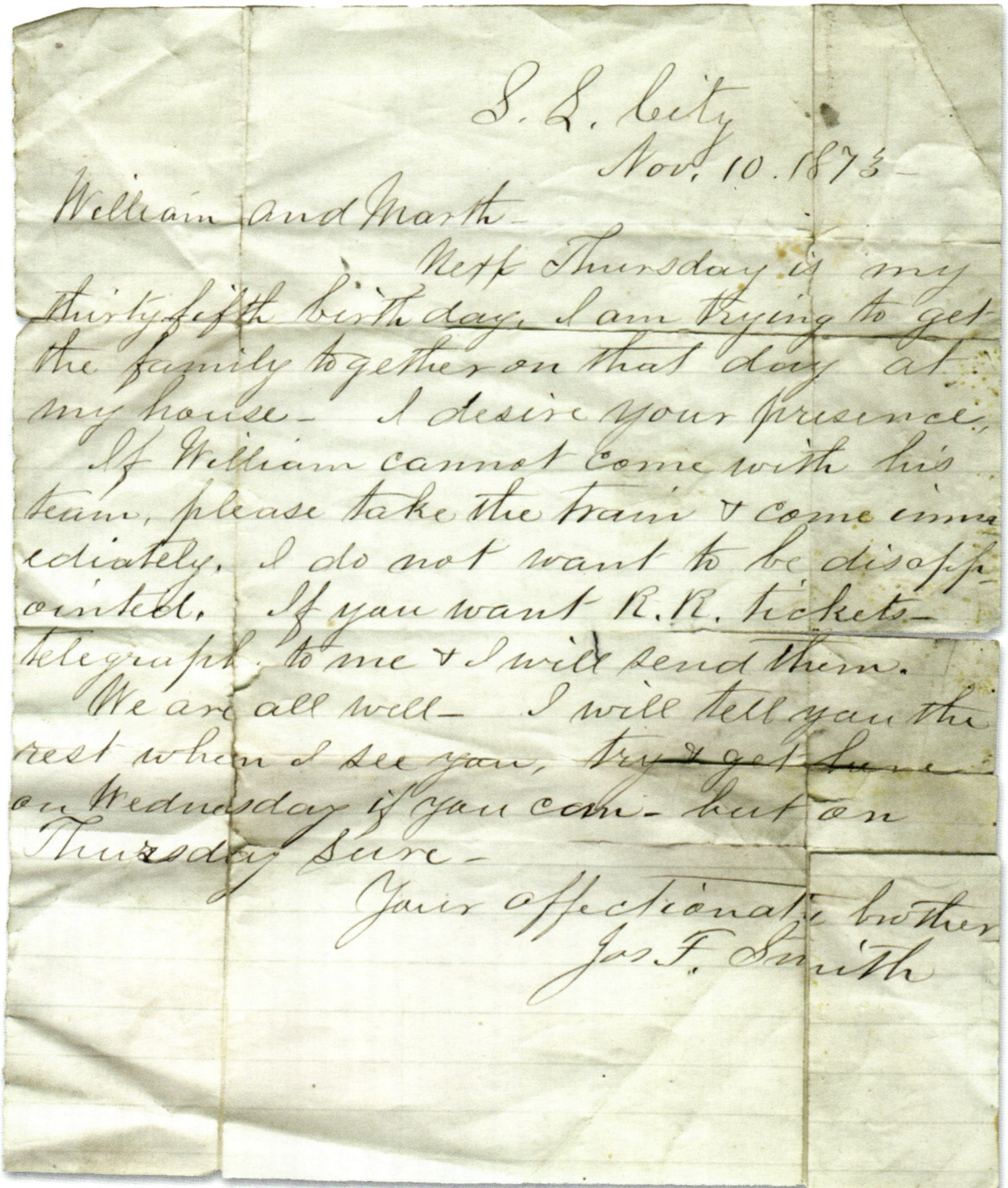

S. L. City
Nov. 10. 1873—

William and Marth—

Next Thursday is my thirty fifth birthday. I am trying to get the family together on that day at my house— I desire your presence, If William cannot come with his team, please take the train & come immediately. I do not want to be disappointed. If you want R.R. tickets— telegraph to me & I will send them.

We are all well— I will tell you the rest when I see you, try & get here on Wednesday if you can— but on Thursday sure—

Your affectionate brother
Jos. F. Smith

Joseph F. to William and Martha Ann, 10 November 1873

JOSEPH F. TO MARTHA ANN, 27 FEBRUARY 1874

S. L. City
Feb. 27. 1874[304]

My Dear Sister
Martha Ann:

I have heard that your children have got the whooping cough, I am sorry to hear it, and I hope they will mend all right with the coming warm weather—if it ever does come! It does seem as though you were bound to pay the penelty of all your sins—in this world—and life. Certainly if suffering and trials are entitled to reward, you will have nearly as good and great an one as your mother[305] before you, and if you continue a little longer you will fill up your cup as full as hers—provided you continue as faithful.

I wrote to President Smith,[306] St. George, and asked him to autherise Bp. Smoot[307] to furnish you with such necessaries as you may require. inclosed you will find his telegram to me on the subject. You can keep it, and if necessary present—or shew it to Bp. Smoot. ~~My~~ **[p. 2]** I do not want you to go without, any thing you need, if it can be had by asking for it. and the way is open for you, I think, to get what you need. I want also to advise you in regard to one thing—never promise any thing you cannot fulfill. as I have noticed that whenever any one showed you a kindness you would surely pledge yourself to return the measure in full. now, I have no objections to any one showing or expressing thanks, and gratitude for kindness, but I donot like to see you feel obliged to make promises you cannot fulfill. never do it.

My family are all well. excepting slight colds, and little Dannie[308] is not altogether recovered from her sick spell—but is improving.

I expect to start tomorrow—Saturday—morning for the East.[309] When this reaches you I shall be on my way.[310] I hope you will find time to write to me once in a while, and also to the folks at home, and I hope they will write to you often as I will keep them posted.

Please give my kind love to Sister (Harris—) Smoot,[311] to the Bishop,[312] and all his Excellent family, I am Your Brother. Jos. F. Smith. God Bless You.

---

304. Joseph F. was thirty-five, and Martha Ann was thirty-two.
305. Mary Fielding Smith.
306. George A. Smith was in St. George, Utah, at this time.
307. Abraham O. Smoot.
308. Donnette Smith was born to Julina on 17 September 1872. See biographical register, "Smith, Donnette."
309. The eastern United States were often referred to as the "States" or the "East" by residents in Utah Territory during this period.
310. During the 43rd Semiannual General Conference held in October 1873, Joseph F. was called to preside over the European Mission; see "General Conference," *Deseret News*, 6 October 1873, [2]. He left Salt Lake City on 28 February 1874, arriving in Liverpool on 21 March.
311. Likely refers to Emily Hill.
312. Bishop Abraham O. Smoot.

MARTHA ANN TO JOSEPH F., 31 MAY 1874

Rec^d^ June 20. 1874
Ans^d^ July 15."[313]

Provo City[314] May the 31 1874

My Dear brother ~~and~~ [*illegible strike-through*]

Joseph it is a long time sence I have writen to you but is not becaus I have haveforgoton you. no I could never forget my brother who has been so kind to me as you have been I have been waiting untill my head got a little stronger be fore I dare to write to you and even now I fear to make the attempt when the body is weak we are all weak from head to foot I have had a great deal to contend with sence I last saw you both in body and mind[315] but the Lord has sustained me threw it all and I am sill in the land of the living and able to write once more to my truest most faithfull friend that I have had sence the death of my dear Mother[316] you have never forsaken me you have been more than a brother to me you have filled as near as could bee the plase of a Father I do feel greatfull to you for all you have done and may the God we try to sirve reward you for I never can more than bee greatfull. I have had threw my sickness while laying in my bed of suffering time to thnk and reflect I wish I could write you one tenth of the thaughts that has passed threw my mind perhaps it might interest you and then it might not. Sence this new order[317] has been made known I have thaught still more and have had great caus to think for we all do not think alike nor see things in the same light I had never thaught that thare would bee [**p. 2**] so great a test of our fidelity to our religeon as as this new order will brng to light it is the deviding line beteen those that is faithful and those that are wavering they have got to do one thing or the other and it is a sore trial for many, they feel as though they cannot bare it and some as though they will not. My heart is sad whin I think that any one should hesetate for one moment to step forward at the command of those that are plased over us to lead and guide our footstepps why not have faith in our father in heaven and put our trust in him that he will not for sake us if we will try to do his will. O when I think of the care and the responcibillity that is restng upon parrents the anxiety of mind we are bound more or less to have as our children grows older we do not know how they will indure wheather they will bee faithfull or not and what could bee so sore a grief as to see them fall away from the true path and let go of the rod of iron that leds to life etirnel thare are many that are having this trial now but I hope and prey that those that are in darkness may see thir foley and turn in the

313. Written sideways in the top left margin of page 1.
314. Provo, in Utah County, Utah, was the county seat and an important Latter-day Saint community located forty-five miles south of Salt Lake City. Martha Ann lived there from 1867 until her death in 1923.
315. Martha Ann and William were busy raising their eight children, the youngest born on March 1874. In addition, Martha Ann was apparently quite ill before writing this letter.
316. Mary Fielding.
317. During the 1870s, Brigham Young instituted several United Orders based on revelations and earlier orders instituted by Joseph Smith Jr. These were related to the cooperative movement instituted in 1869. See Leonard J. Arrington, Feramorz Y. Fox, and Dean L. May, *Building the City of God: Community and Cooperation among the Mormons* (Salt Lake City, UT: Deseret Book, 1976). The United Order had been emphasized during the 44th Annual General Conference, held on 7–8 May 1874 in Salt Lake City. For Brigham Young's address, see "Forty-fourth Annual Conference," *Deseret News*, 13 May 1874, 225.

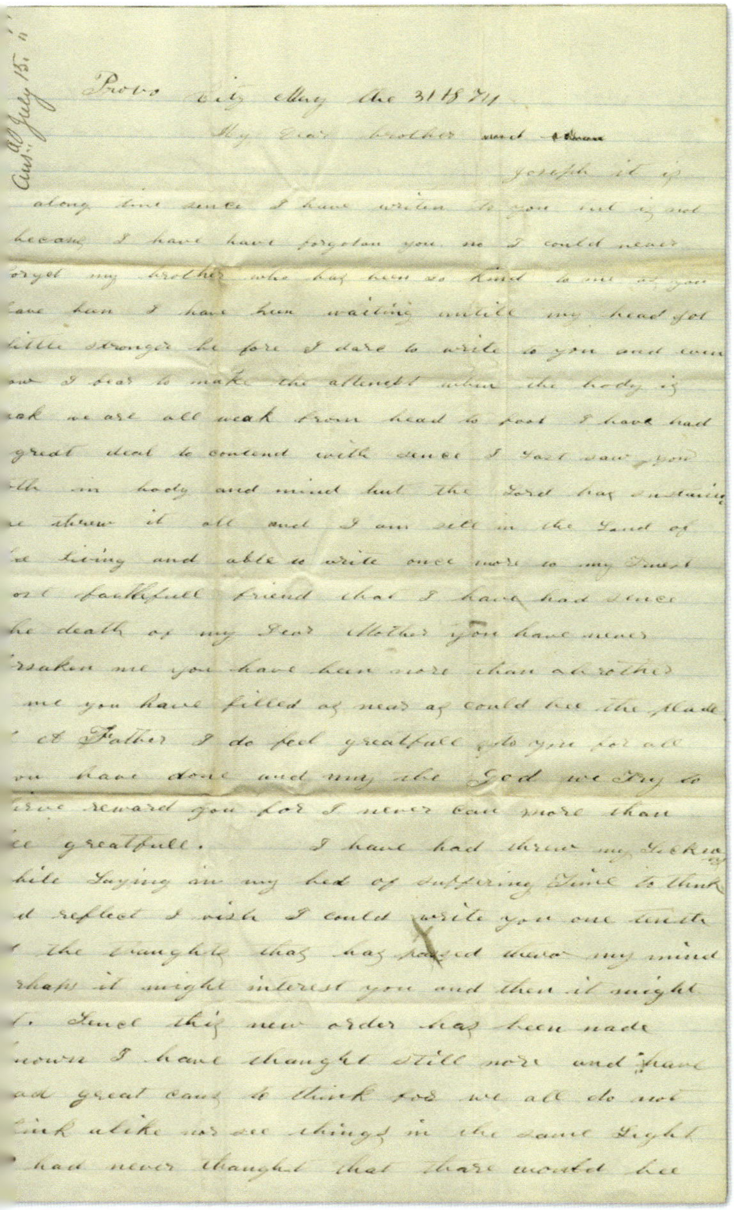

Ans'd July 15 '74

Provo City May the 31 1874

My Dear brother and

Joseph it is along time since I have writen to you but it is not because I have forgoten you no I could never forget my brother who has been so kind to me as you have been I have been waiting untill my head got little stronger before I dare to write to you and even now I fear to make the attempt when the body is weak we are all weak from head to foot I have had great deal to contend with since I last saw you ... in body and mind but the Lord has sustaind me threw it all and I am still in the Land of the living and able to write once more to my truest most faithfull friend that I have had since the death of my Dear Mother you have never forsaken me you have been more than a brother to me you have filled as near as could bee the place of a Father I do feel greatfull to you for all you have done and may the God we try to serve reward you for I never can more than be greatfull. I have had threw my sickness while laying in my bed of suffering time to think and reflect I wish I could write you one tenth of the thoughts that has passed threw my mind perhaps it might interest you and then it might not. Since this new order has been made known I have thought still more and have had great caus to think for we all do not think alike nor see things in the same light I had never thought that there would bee

Martha Ann to Joseph F., 31 May 1874 (p. 1)

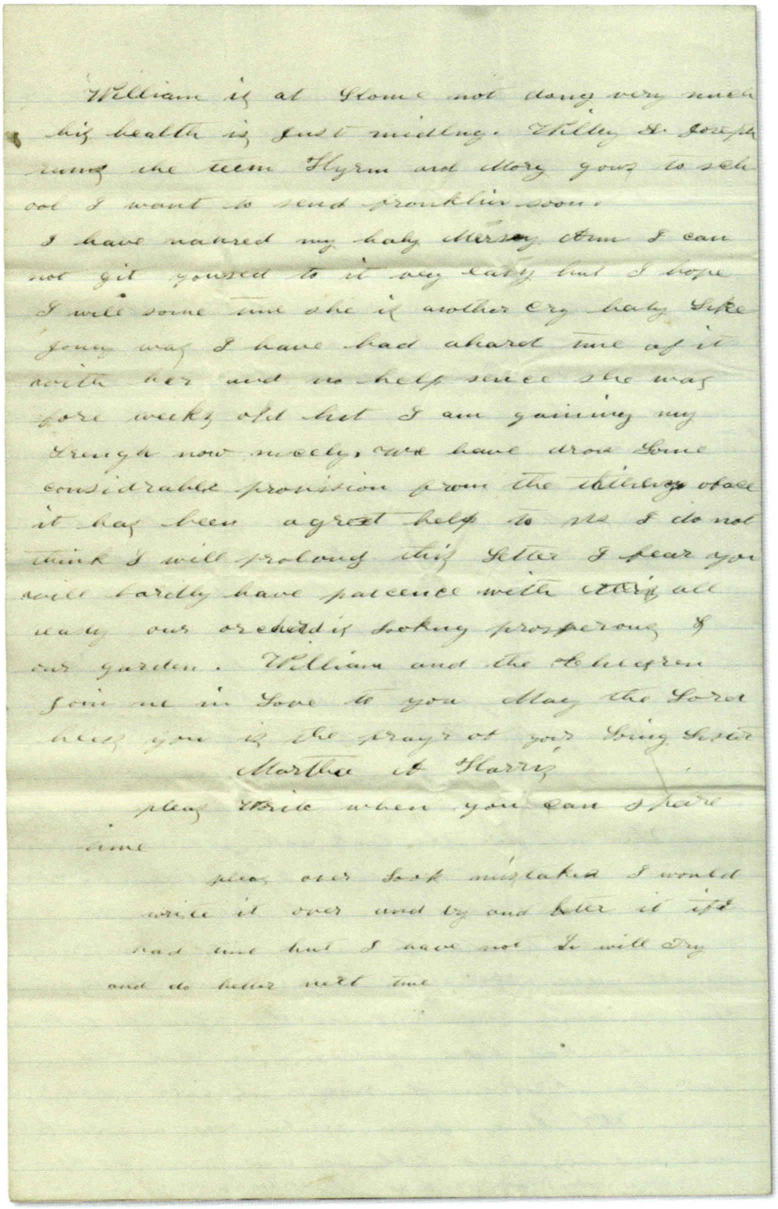

William is at Home not doing very much his health is just midling. Willey & Joseph runs the teem Hyrum and Mary goes to school I want to send Franklin soon. I have named my baby Mersy Ann I can not git youse to it very easy but I hope I will some time she is another cry baby like Jenny was I have had a hard time of it with her and no help since she was fore weeks old but I am gaining my strength now nicely we have drew some considrable provision from the tithing office it has been a great help to us I do not think I will prolong this letter I fear you will hardly have patience with it as it all ready our orchard is looking prosperous & our garden. William and the Children join me in Love to you May the Lord bless you is the prayr of your loving Sister

Martha A Harris

pleas write when you can spare time

pleas over look mistakes I would write it over and try and better it if I had time but I have not I will try and do better next time

Martha Ann to Joseph F., 31 May 1874 (p. 4)

right path. I could say much on this subject but I can not fooley explain my fears and ancious thoughts on paper it would not do but O my brother prey for me and myne that we <may> not bee waid in the balance and found wantng that his call we may all obey like Abraham of old not knowing our way but faith make us bold [**p. 3**] we have a good guide and trust in all dangers the Lord will povde but I fear I will wery you on this subgect so I will turn to something else.

When I think you are so far from me & that great & mghty osion betwen us[318] I can hardly think it posable. yit it is verly so I but I know you are trying to do good you are on the Lord

318. Joseph F. was presiding over the European Mission at this time.

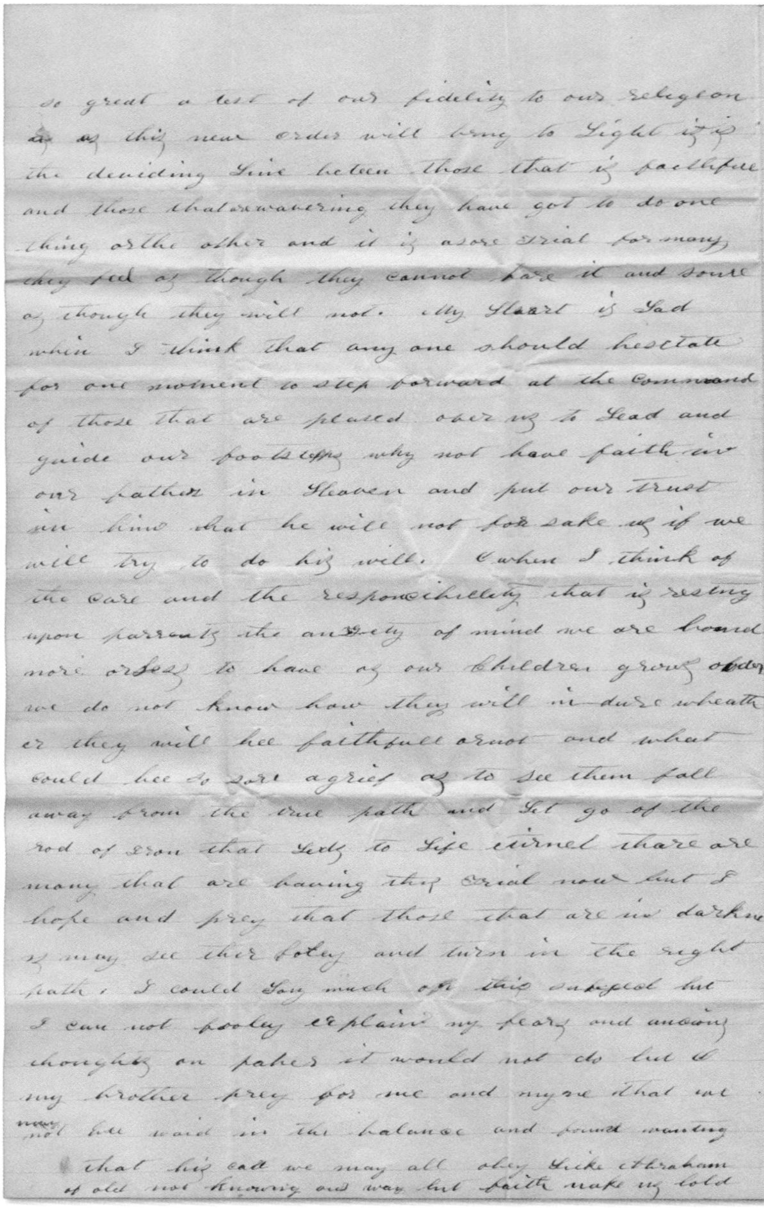

so great a test of our fidelity to our religion as this new order will bring to light it is the deviding line beteen those that is faithfull and those that are wavering they have got to do one thing or the other and it is a sore trial for many they feel as though they cannot bare it and soure as though they will not. My Heart is sad when I think that any one should hesitate for one moment to step forward at the Command of those that are placed over us to lead and guide our footsteps why not have faith in our father in Heaven and put our trust in him that he will not forsake us if we will try to do his will. When I think of the care and the responsibility that is resting upon parents the anxiety of mind we are bound more or less to have as our Children grows older we do not know how they will indure wheather they will bee faithfull or not and what could bee so sore a grief as to see them fall away from the true path and let go of the rod of iron that leds to life eternel there are many that are having thir trial now but I hope and prey that those that are in darkness may see thir foley and turn in the right path. I could say much of this subject but I can not fooly explain my fears and anxious thoughts on paper it would not do but dear my brother prey for me and myne that we may not bee waid in the balanse and found wanting that his call we may all obey like Abraham of old not knowing our way but faith make us bold

Martha Ann to Joseph F., 31 May 1874 (p. 2)

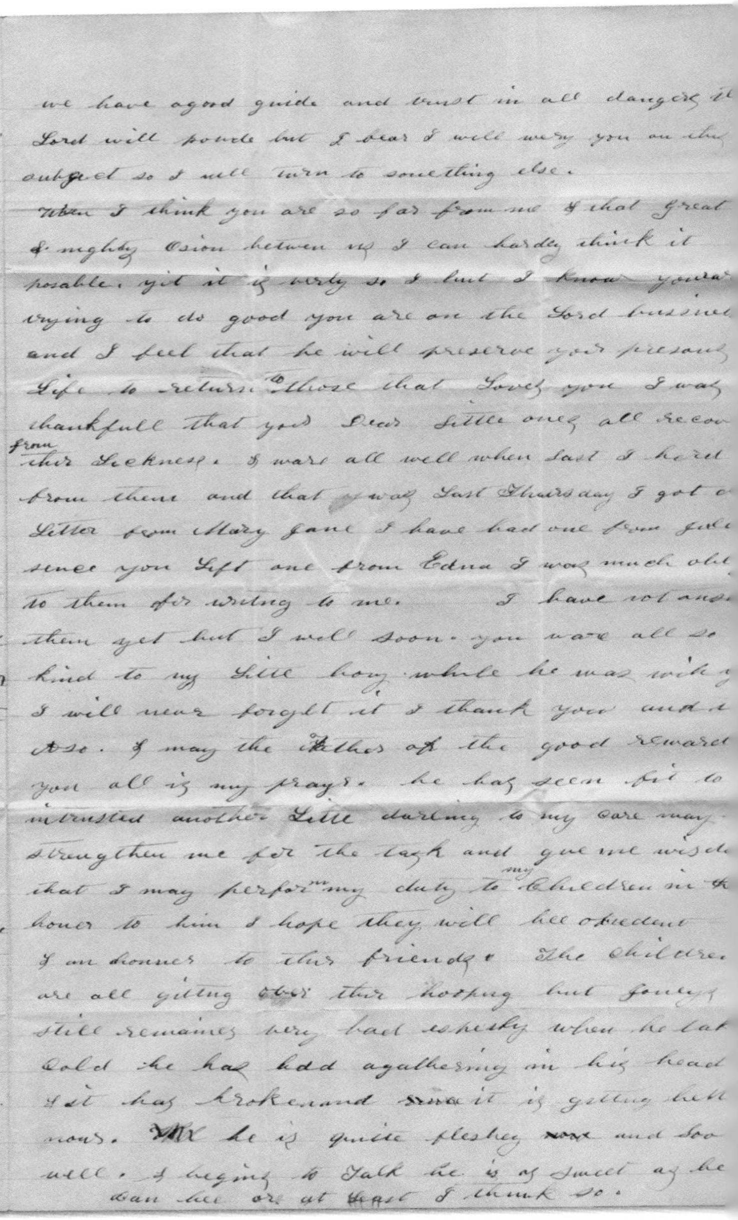

we have a good guide and trust in all dangers the Lord will provide but I fear I will wery you on this subject so I will turn to something else. When I think you are so far from me & that great & mighty Osion between us I can hardly think it posable. yet it is verly so. but I know you are trying to do good you are on the Lord busness and I feel that he will preserve your presous life to return to those that loves you I was thankfull that your dear little ones all recoverd from thir sickness. & ware all well when last I herd from them and that was last Thursday I got a letter from Mary Jane I have had one from Julina sence you left one from Edna I was much obligd to them for writing to me. I have not answrd them yet but I will soon. you ware all so kind to my littl boy while he was with you I will nevr forget it I thank you and them aso. & may the Father of the good reward you all is my prayr. he has seen fit to intrusted another little darling to my care may he strengthen me for the task and give me wisdom that I may perform my duty to my Children in the honor to him I hope they will bee obedient & an honner to thir friends. The children are all getting over thir hooping but Joney still remaines very bad especially when he takes cold he has had a gathering in his head & it has broken and since it is getting better now. he is quite fleshey now and looks well. & begins to talk he is as sweet as he can bee or at least I think so.

Martha Ann to Joseph F., 31 May 1874 (p. 3)

business and I feel that he will preserve your presous life to return <to> those that loves you I was thankfull that your dear little ones all recoverd <from> thir sickness, & ware all well when last I herd from them and that was last Thursday I got a letter from Mary Jane[319] I have had one from Julina[320] sence you left one from Edna[321] I was much obligd to them fer writng to me. I have not answrd them yet but I will soon. you ware all so kind to my littl boy while he was wih you I will nevr forget it I thank you and them aso. & may the Father of the good

319. Mary Jane Thompson.
320. Julina Lambson.
321. Edna Lambson.

reward you all is my prayr. he has seen fit to intrusted another littl darling to my care[322] may he strengthen me for the task and gve me wisdom that I may perfor<m> my duty to <my> children in th[◊◊]ne honer to him I hope they will bee obiedent & an honner to thir friends. The children are all gittng over thir hoopng but Joneys[323] still remaines very bad espesly when he takes cold he has had a gathering in his head & it has broken and [*illegible strike-through*] it is gittng better now. [*illegible strike-through*] he is quite fleshey ~~now~~ and look well, & begins to talk he is as sweet as he can bee or at least I think so. [**p. 4**]

William[324] is at home not dong very much his health is just midlng. Willey & Joseph runs the teem Hyrm and Mary gows to school I want to send franklin soon.[325]

I have named my baby Mersey Ann[326] I can not git yoused to it very easy but I hope I will some time she is another cry baby like Joney[327] was I have had a hard time of it with her and no help sence she was fore weeks old but I am gaining my srengh now nicely. We have drove some considrable provision from the tithe<n>g oface it has been a great help to us I do not think I will prolong this letter I fear you will hardly have paicence with [*illegible strike-through*] all ready our orcherd is lookng prosperous & our garden. William and the chldren join me in love to you May the Lord bless you is the prayr of your loving sister
Martha A Harris

pleas write when you can spare time

pleas over look mistakes I would write it over and try and beter it if I had time but I have not I will try and do better next time

MARTHA ANN TO JOSEPH F., 20 JUNE 1874

Recd July 26. 1874
Ansd Aug. 5.[328]

Provo City June the 20th 1874[329]

My Dear ~~brother~~ brother Joseph

322. Mercy Ann Harris was born on 30 March 1874.
323. John Fielding Harris was almost two years old at this time. See biographical register, "Harris, John Fielding."
324. William Jasper Harris.
325. William Jasper Harris Jr. was fourteen years old, Joseph Albert Harris twelve, Hyrum Smith Harris ten, Mary Emily Harris eight, and Franklin Hill Harris six. See biographical register, "Harris, William Jasper, Jr.," "Harris, Joseph Albert," "Harris, Hyrum Smith," "Harris, Mary Emily," and "Harris, Franklin Hill."
326. Mercy Ann Harris was born on 30 March 1874. See biographical register, "Harris, Mercy Ann."
327. John Fielding Harris was born on 28 June 1872.
328. Written sideways in the top left margin of page 1.
329. Martha Ann addressed the envelope, "Mr. Joseph F. Smith 42 Islington Liverpool England." On the reverse, Joseph F. wrote, "Rcd. July 26. 1874 & Ans Aug 5. Martha Ann."

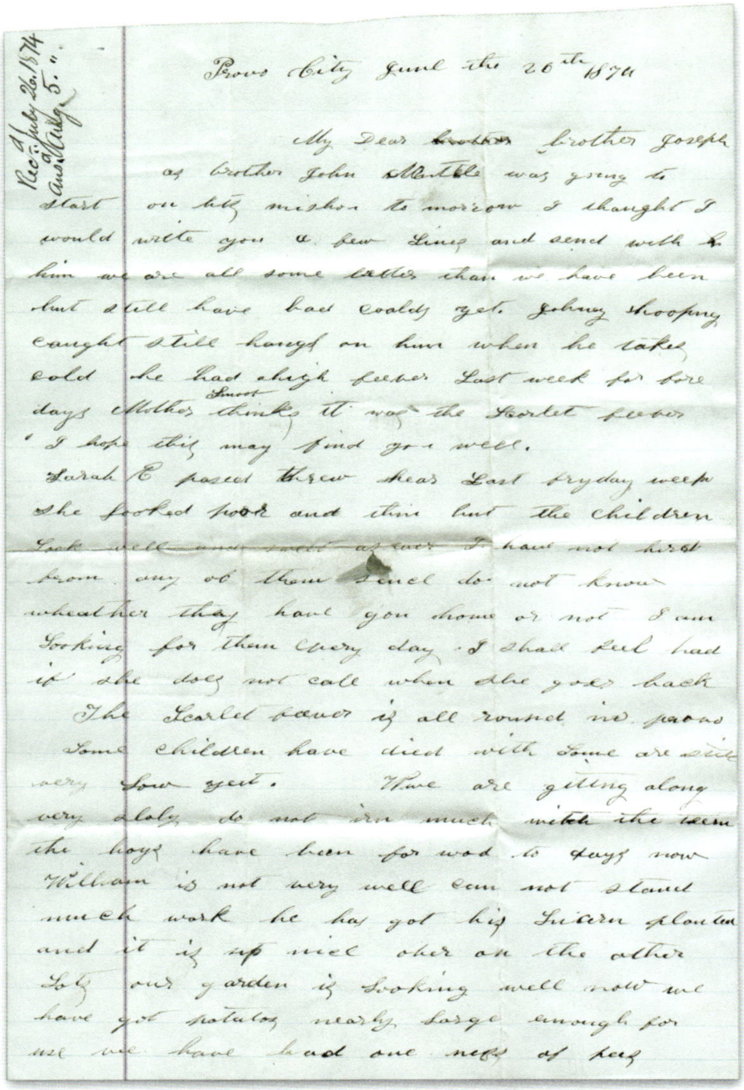

Rec^d July 26, 1874 Ans^d Aug 5.

Provo City June the 20th 1874

My Dear ~~brother~~ brother Joseph

as brother John Nuttele was going to start on his mishon to morrow I thaught I would write you a few lines and send with h him we are all some better than we have been but still have bad coalds yet. Johney hoopng caught still hangs on him when he takes cold he had a high feever last week for fore days Mother Smoot thinks it was the Scarlet feever I hope this may find you well.

Sarah E pased threw hear last fryday week she looked poor and thin but the children look well and sweet as ever I have not hird from any of them sence do not know wheather they have gon home or not I am looking for them every day I shall feel bad if she does not call when she goes back

The Scarlet feaver is all round in provo some children have died with some are still very low yet. We are getting along very sloly do not irn much with the team the boys have been for wod to days now William is not very well can not stand much work he has got his Lucern plantin and it is up nice ober on the other Lots our garden is looking well now we have got potatos nearly large enough for use we have had one ness of peas

Martha Ann to Joseph F., 20 June 1874 (p. 1)

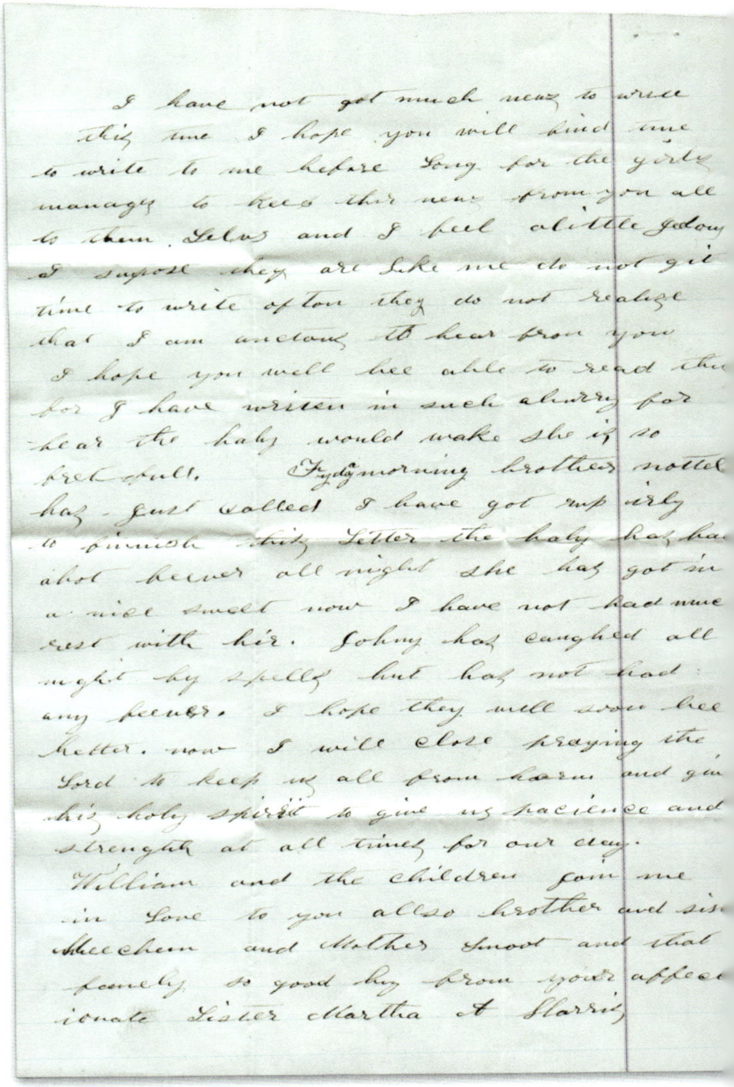

I have not got much news to write this time I hope you will find time to write to me before long for the girls manages to keep the news from you all to them. Selas and I feel a little jelous I suppose they are like me do not git time to write ofton they do not realize that I am anctious to hear from you I hope you will bee able to read this for I have writen in such a hurry for fear the baby would wake she is so fretfull. Frydy morning brother Nottel has just called I have got up irly to finish this letter the baby has had a hot feever all night she has got in a nice sweat now I have not had much rest with her. Johny has caughed all night by spells but has not had any feever. I hope they will soon bee better. now I will close praying the Lord to keep us all from harm and give his holy spirit to give us pacience and strength at all times for our day. William and the children join me in Love to you allso brother and sister Meechem and Mother Smoot and that famely so good by from your affectionate Sister Martha A Harris

Martha Ann to Joseph F., 20 June 1874 (p. 2)

as brother John Nuttele[330] was going to start on his mishon to morrow I thaught I would write you a few lines and send with ~~h~~ him we are all some better than we have been but still have bad coalds yet. Johney[331] hoopng caught still hangs on him when he takes cold he had a high feever last week for fore days Mother <Smoot>[332] thinks it was the Scarlet feever I hope this may find you well.

Sarah E[333] pased threw hear last fryday week she looked poor and thin but the children look well and sweet as ever I have not hird from any of them sence do not know wheather they have gon home or not I am looking for them every day I shall feel bad if she does not call when she goes back

330. Leonard John Nuttall served a mission in England from 1874 to 1875. See biographical register, "Nuttall, Leonard John."

331. John Fielding Harris.

332. Likely Emily Harris or Margaret Thompson McMeans.

333. Sarah Ellen Richards.

The Scarlet feever is all round in provo some children have died with some are still very low yet. Wwe are gittng along very sloly do not irn much with the teem the boys have been for wod to days now William[334] is not very well can not stand much work he has got his lucern[335] planted and it is up nice over on the other lots our garden is looking well now we have got potatos nearly large enough for use we have had one ness of pees **[p. 2]**

I have not got much news to write this tme I hope you will find tme to write to me before long for the girls[336] manages to keep thir news from you all to them selvs and I feel a little jeelous I supose they are like me do not git time to write ofton they do not realise that I am anctous to hear from you I hope you will bee able to read this for I have writen in such a hurry for fear the baby[337] would wake she is so fretfull. Fyd<a>y morning brother nottele has just called I have got up irly to finnish this letter the baby has had a hot feever all night she has got in a nice sweet now I have not had much rest with hir. Johny has caughed all night by spells but has not had any feever. I hope they will soon bee better. now I will close praying the Lord to keep us all from harm and give his holy spirrit to give us pacience and strength at all times for our day.

William and the children join me in love to you allso brother and sister Meechem[338] and Mother Smoot and that famely so good by from your affectionate sister Martha A Harris

JOSEPH F. TO MARTHA ANN, 15 JULY 1874

42, Islington, Liverpool[339]
July 15th 1874

Martha Ann
My own Dear Sister

Your long and welcome letter of May 31.st reached me June 20. I would have written sooner but I have been very busy.

I often think of my poor dear sister and her almost helpless little family, and breathe but one earnest prayer, O! Lord Bless them, and provide for their every need. I am afraid I should not write tonight for I am a little lonely, and sober in my feelings. Sometimes we cannot help feeling so. I think the reason is I have just had a visit from a poor brother,[340] who about six weeks ago called on me to borrow 5/— (five shillings) to release his effects from bondage, I lent him the money. And last evening he called again with a little girl not quite so large as **[p. 2]** your little Mary,[341] and I thought he was crazy, he seemed to want to tell me something and could not—but gave me his address and went away. I never saw a more writched looking

334. William Jasper Harris.
335. Alfalfa.
336. At the time of this letter, Joseph F. was married to three wives, whom he affectionately called his "girls."
337. Mercy Ann Harris.
338. Edward Mecham and Sophia Barrows.
339. Written on letterhead from the Latter-day Saints' European Printing, Publishing and Emigration Office. "42 Islington Street, Liverpool, England" was the address of mission headquarters in the British Isles and Europe.
340. The man's last name was Taylor. See Joseph F., journal, 14 July 1874.
341. Mary Emily Harris was eight at the time of this letter.

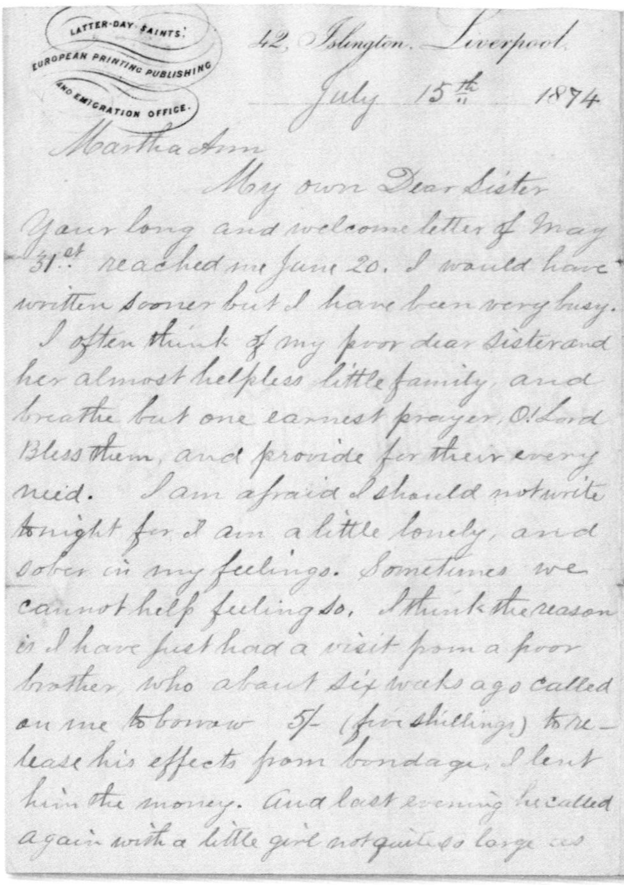

LATTER-DAY SAINTS' EUROPEAN PRINTING PUBLISHING AND EMIGRATION OFFICE.

42, Islington. Liverpool.
July 15th 1874

Martha Ann

My own Dear Sister

Your long and welcome letter of May 31st. reached me June 20. I would have written sooner but I have been very busy.

I often think of my poor dear Sister and her almost helpless little family, and breathe but one earnest prayer, O! Lord Bless them, and provide for their every need. I am afraid I should not write tonight for I am a little lonely, and sober in my feelings. Sometimes we cannot help feeling so. I think the reason is I have just had a visit from a poor brother, who about six weeks ago called on me to borrow 5/- (five shillings) to release his effects from bondage. I lent him the money. And last evening he called again with a little girl not quite so large as

Joseph F. to Martha Ann, 15 July 1874 (p. 1)

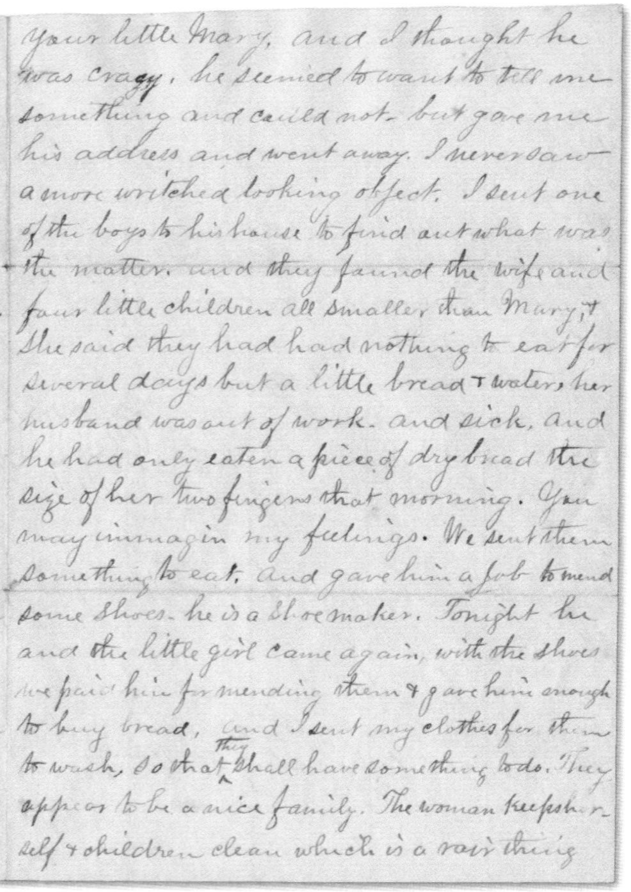

your little Mary, and I thought he was crazy, he seemed to want to tell me something and could not, but gave me his address and went away. I never saw a more wretched looking object. I sent one of the boys to his house to find out what was the matter, and they found the wife and four little children all smaller than Mary, & She said they had had nothing to eat for several days but a little bread & water, her husband was out of work, and sick, and he had only eaten a piece of dry bread the size of her two fingers that morning. You may immagin my feelings. We sent them something to eat, and gave him a job to mend some shoes, he is a Shoemaker. Tonight he and the little girl came again, with the shoes we paid him for mending them & gave him enough to buy bread, and I sent my clothes for them to wash, so that they shall have something to do. They appear to be a nice family. The woman keeps herself & children clean which is a rare thing

Joseph F. to Martha Ann, 15 July 1874 (p. 2)

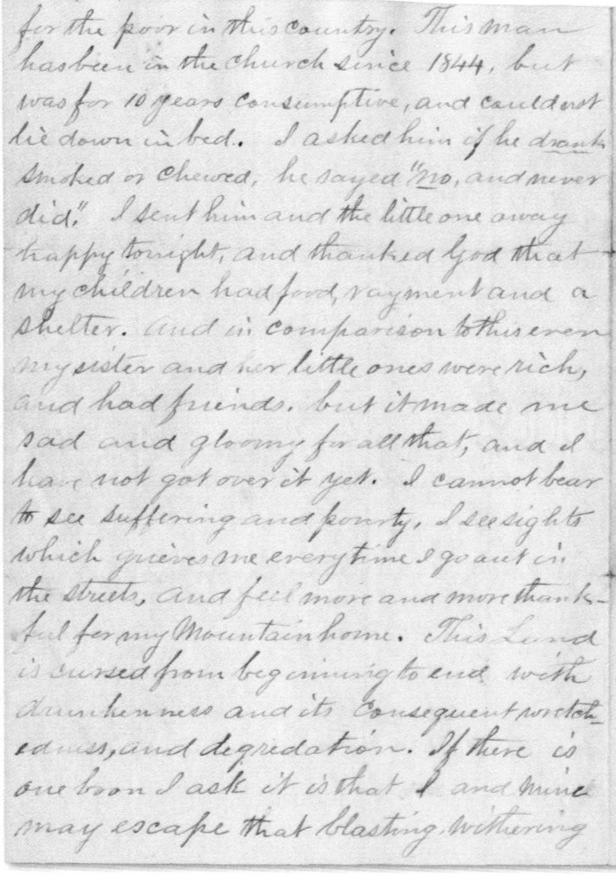

for the poor in this country. This man has been in the church since 1844, but was for 10 years consumptive, and could not lie down in bed. I asked him if he drank Smoked or Chewed, he sayed "No, and never did." I sent him and the little one away happy tonight, and thanked God that my children had food, rayment and a Shelter. And in comparison to this even my sister and her little ones were rich, and had friends, but it made me sad and gloomy for all that, and I have not got over it yet. I cannot bear to see suffering and poverty, I see sights which grieves me every time I go out in the streets, and feel more and more thankful for my Mountain home. This Land is cursed from beginning to end with drunkenness and its Consequent wretchedness, and degredation. If there is one boon I ask it is that I and mine may escape that blasting withering

Joseph F. to Martha Ann, 15 July 1874 (p. 3)

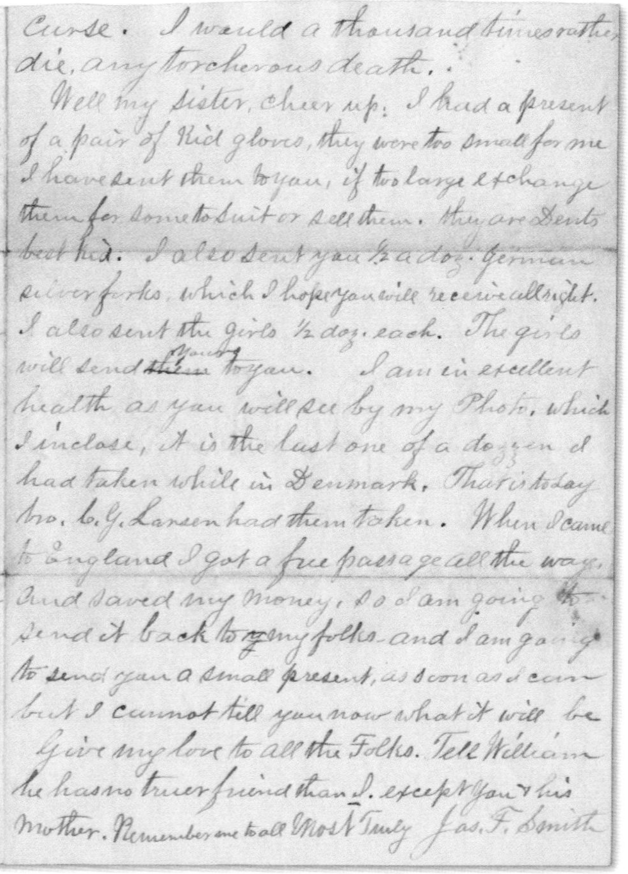

curse. I would a thousand times rather die, any torcherous death.

Well my Sister, cheer up; I had a present of a pair of Kid gloves, they were too small for me I have sent them to you, if too large exchange them for some to suit or sell them. they are Dents best kid. I also sent you ½ a doz. German silver forks, which I hope you will receive all right. I also sent the girls ½ doz. each. The girls will send ~~them~~ yours to you. I am in excellent health as you will see by my Photo, which I inclose, It is the last one of a dozen I had taken while in Denmark. That is today Bro. C. G. Larsen had them taken. When I came to England I got a free passage all the way, and saved my money, so I am going to send it back to my folks and I am going to send you a small present, as soon as I can but I cannot tell you now what it will be

Give my love to all the Folks. Tell William he has no truer friend than I. except You & his Mother. Remember me to all Most Truly Jos. F. Smith

Joseph F. to Martha Ann, 15 July 1874 (p. 4)

object. I sent one of the boys to his house to find out what was the matter, and they found the wife and four little children all smaller than Mary, & she said they had had nothing to eat for several days but a little bread & water, her husband was out of work—and sick, and he had only eaten a piece of dry bread the size of her two fingers that morning. You may immagin my feelings. We sent them something to eat, and gave him a job to mend some shoes—he is a shoe maker. Tonight he and the little girl came again, with the shoes we paid him for mending them & gave him enough to buy bread, and I sent my clothes for them to wash, so that <they> shall have something to do. They appear to be a nice family. The woman keeps herself & children clean which is a rair thing [**p. 3**] for the poor in this country. This man has been in the church since 1844, but was for 10 years consumptive,[342] and could not lie down in bed. I asked him if he drank, smoked or chewed, he sayed "no, and never did." I sent him and the little one away happy tonight, and thanked God that my children had food, rayment and a shelter. And in comparison to this even my sister and her little ones were rich, and had friends, but it made me sad and gloomy for all that, and I have not got over it yet. I cannot bear to see suffering and poverty, I see sights which grieves me every time I go out in the streets, and feel more and more thankful for my Mountain home. This Land is cursed from beginning to end with drunkenness and its consequent wretchedness, and degredation. If there is one boon I ask it is that I and mine may escape that blasting, withering [**p. 4**] curse. I would a thousand times rather die, any torcherous death.

Well my sister, cheer up. I had a present of a pair of Kid gloves,[343] they were too small for me I have sent them to you, if too large exchange them for some to suit or sell them, they are Dents best Kid.[344] I also sent you ½ a doz. German silver forks, which I hope you will receive all right. I also sent the girls ½ doz. each. The girls[345] will send ~~them~~<yours> to you. I am in excellent health as you will see by my Photo, which I inclose, it is the last one of a dozzen I had taken while in Denmark.[346] That is to say bro. C. G. Larsen[347] had them taken. When I came to England I got a free passage[348] all the way, and saved my money, so I am going to send it back to ~~y~~ my folks—and I am going to send you a small present, as soon as I can but I cannot tell you now what is will be

Give my love to all the Folks. Tell William[349] he has no truer friend than I. except You & his mother.[350] Remember me to all Most Truly Jos. F. Smith

342. *Consumption* was a nineteenth-century term for either any general disease or sometimes specifically for tuberculosis.
343. Made from young goat (kid) leather.
344. Founded by John Dent in 1777, Dents is a company in England still world-renowned for its leather gloves.
345. Joseph F.'s three wives, whom he affectionately referred to as the "girls."
346. Joseph F. wrote on Tuesday, 26 May 1874, "I went with bro. Larsen & Wells to Mr. Olsens, Ostergade [a neighborhood in Copenhagen], and had my likeness taken" (Joseph F., journal, 26 May 1876). Later he noted, "I called at Mr. Olsens, and sat again for a picture, the first not being good" (Joseph F., journal, 27 May 1874). Finally, he recorded on 29 May, "I also go my Photos. 1 doz. And one large one cost 4 Rd, & 4 Rd" (Joseph F., journal, 29 May 1874). During his presidency, Joseph F. traveled from England to Scandinavia, Germany, Switzerland, and France.
347. Christian Greis Larsen was a Danish convert who was presiding over the Scandinavian Mission at this time. See biographical register, "Larsen, Christian Greis."
348. Although it is uncertain how Joseph F. obtained "free passage" back to England, it may have been a courtesy extended by the passenger shipping line because of the large number of Latter-day Saint passengers who used its services.
349. William Jasper Harris.
350. Emily Hill.

JOSEPH F. TO MARTHA ANN, 5 AUGUST 1874

42 Islington L'pool
Aug. 5th 1874

My Dear Sister
Martha Ann

Brothers Nuttall, John Henry and McKenzie,[351] arrived here on Sunday July 26, in more than usual good health. Bro. Nuttall was looking better than I expected to see him, and thought he had improved in health since his departure from home. I hope this climate will agree with him for he is a usful man. He brought me your welcom letter of June 26th I was pleased to hear from you and of any good news from home.

I wrote to you some little time ago and I hope that and this will find you and the family all well. I am very sorry to hear of so much sickness among the children at home, I hope your little Pets ~~are~~ are all well. You so far have been very fortunate with your children, God grant that you may continue to be so to the end. There is nothing to me **[p. 2]** so painful and hard to bear as sickness and deaths of children I trust that I have suffered my share of bereavment. I want my children to lay me away next.

I do not mean by this that I am tired of life and want to go—by any means, but that my children may live and grow up to be usful and in the end to bury me if I am to buried—as was the custom of old. I do not believe in the doctrine that the Lord designes for Parents to bury their children but children their parents. But we are so near the latter days, we may not have to sleep but a few moments, or an instant, until the great change from death to life, when I hope we shall be worthy "to come forth in the morning of the first resurrection clothed with glory, immortality, and eternal lives,"[352] according to the promises which have been sealed upon our heads, by that divine authority which God **[p. 3]** has restored to the earth. The scriptures say "blessed and holy is he, that hath part in the first resurrection, for on such the second death hath no power"[353]— I desire to be numbered with that throng, for then I shall enjoy my rewards, my family—and the "gift of the endless lives". "which is the greatest gift of God".[354] How little indeed do people realize or even know of this great gift and blessing.

We may know many things, the worth and value of which we do not realize, and therefore pass lightly by. But a day of rec<k>oning will come, and an awakening, who then will have oil in their lamps?[355] but I need not preach to you, I hope you are not one of the forgetful, you certainly have enough cares and duties, indeed yours is a thorney path in this world as mothers[356] was, your patience and endurence are almost if not quite equal to hers. I only wish you had her education and her bold and firm decision, from which when once the **[p. 4]** the

351. Leonard J. Nuttall. See Martha Ann to Joseph F., 20 June 1874, herein. John Henry Smith, a second cousin to Joseph F. and Martha Ann, served in the European Mission from July 1874 to July 1875, during which time he traveled significantly with Joseph F. David McKenzie served in Great Britain from 1874 to 1876. See biographical register, "McKenzie, David."
352. One of the promises received in the temple sealing; the phrase was quoted publicly by Joseph F. on several occasions. See, for example, *Journal of Discourses*, 19:258 and 22:353.
353. See Revelation 20:6.
354. See Doctrine and Covenants 14:7; 132:22, 24, 55.
355. See Matthew 25:1–13.
356. Mary Fielding.

aim was fixed, in truth & right—neither prayers, nor tears, nor sympathy could move it. I wish I had these qualities myself, as she had them. We would both be better off. We will hope for the best and and do what we can to bring it about. I send this enclosed to Aunt Thompson,[357] as I have been writing to her. She or Julina[358] will forword it to you

I hope you will remember me very kindly to Bros. and Sisters Mecham, and Jones.[359] To Aunt Lucy Kimball[360] and family, George Gee Sophina and their Mother.[361] To Bp. Smoot[362] and family, bro. S. S. Jones[363] and family and to all friends.

When you write tell me if you need anything, to make you or the children comfortable. I charge you not to allow yourself or family to suffer for fear of telling your true condition. I am not there to see for myself. Give my kindest wishes for his welfare to William[364] & kiss the babies for Uncle Joseph. with prayers for your prosperity I am Joseph F.

MARTHA ANN TO JOSEPH F., 15 AUGUST 1874

Recd Sep. 7. 1874
Ansd " —"" —"[365]

Provo City Aug the 15th 1874

Joseph F

My dear and much beloved brother I recieved your long looked for and very welcom letter <of the 18th July> with the greatest pleasure and from the botom of my heart I thanked my heavenly fathar for the blessing of haveing so good and kind a brother your good kind littery helps to sustain me in my deapest hours of triels for I have all ways known you was a true friend to me and may god grant that I may ever proove my sellf worthy of that blessed friendship ~~my~~ I thank you most sincerly for every kind word you utter in your letter I have needed every scrap of comfort that I could get and have caught at [*illegible strike-through*] <it.> Like a drown[◊◊]ing man for I felt if it ware not for som aid I shoud sink I have had so much to contend with first on one side and then on the other one would say why do you put up whith what you do I would not. and other sais you are a fool and so on I could not tell you half I have had to contend with it is very easy to talk but not so easy to perform I feel like leaving it all in

357. Mercy Rachel Fielding.
358. Julina Lambson.
359. Likely Edward Mecham and his family, and possibly Joseph Jones and his wife, Emma Buxton. The 1870 US Census lists Joseph and Emma as neighbors of Martha Ann. See biographical register, "Jones, Joseph C." and "Buxton, Emma."
360. Lucy Walker, wife of Heber C. Kimball.
361. George Washington Gee II was married to Sophina Alcesta Fuller. "Their Mother" likely refers to Mary Jane Smith, mother of George Gee and first cousin once removed to Joseph F. and Martha Ann. See biographical register, "Fuller, Sophina Alcesta" and "Smith, Mary Jane."
362. Abraham O. Smoot served as a bishop in Provo at this time.
363. Samuel Stephen Jones was a prominent Provo businessman. See biographical register, "Jones, Samuel Stephen."
364. William Jasper Harris.
365. Written sideways in the top left corner of page 1.

the hands of the Lord and when he sees I have born enough he will ease my burdon and all will come out right in the end if I do my dutey in all things & bare all things ~~with~~ so with paciense which I hope I may bee inabled to do. the Lord has been good to me **[p. 2]** after all he has so far spar<e>d the lifes of my little ones they are all alive and in the enjoyment good health and that is saying a good deal whare thare are so many and we are not like that poor famely you mension[366] we have enough to eat such as it it is it plain but healthy and good prospects ahead we had traided our old cow of for a nice new chicks <one> onely fore years old we have raised some potatos will have too nice pigs to kill in the winter and a small one to keep over we had eleven small pigs which we payd some of our small debts with that helped us some Willey[367] has been runing the teem all summer he has irnt enough to git us some clothng he just got home from the City[368] yesterday he went with a load of fraight Willey is a very good boy to work and so is Joseph[369] when they have a steady job Joseph is hired out to a man to help him harvest he gits wheet for his pay. Willey saw that new boy of yours[370] he sais it is a great big fellow they ware all doing well you will soon have as many boys as me we are even in children now I am so glad for your sake for I know you love them all so dearly & I hope you may all ways have plenty to make them comfortable and suply all thir little wants and I know you will have for you diserve **[p. 3]** all the Lord can gve you my dear brother you spoke of sending me some presents I hope you will not rob your [*illegible strike-through*] self and famely for my sake what can I <say> to you for so much kindness in rembering me how will I evr repay it all I know now other way than to prey the Lord to bless you with fore fold and to greatfulley remember you both me and mine

Sarah[371] called when she went home with those <too> sweet little black eyed darlings[372] just as prity as they can be the baby was not very well. I got the picture all right I was so pleased with it I have not seen you look so well for years as you do in that I am much obliged to you for it. Our little Johns[373] caugh still hangs on him but it does not keep him from beeing mischevous I had <to> stot writing just now to go and look after him he had found the creem jare and was in to it with his arm to his elbow and such a sight as he was I know you would have laughed to see him he is just as fat as he can well bee and so heavy I can hardly lift him he begins to talk and he ticles the children so. the baby is growing nicely she is a sober thaughtfull little thing and very small the smallest of any of my children at her age.[374] **[p. 4]**

Well this is the last page I fear I will tire you out so I must bring my letter to a close. Brother Sammeul Jones[375] wished me to kindly remember to you also brother & sister

366. See Joseph F. to Martha Ann, 15 July 1874, herein.
367. William Jasper Harris Jr.
368. Salt Lake City.
369. Joseph Albert Harris.
370. Edna gave birth to Alvin Fielding Smith on 19 July 1874. Joseph F. noted that he had received a letter from home informing him that "Edna had had a boy." "This makes me 8 children," he continued, "two deceased. 3 boys and three girls living." Joseph F., journal, 27 August 1874. A few days later, he wrote, "Good news. my boy is named Alvin Fielding. god bless him, and may his name be held in honorable and everlasting remembrance with the rest of my sons." Joseph F., journal, 1 September 1874. See biographical register, "Smith, Alvin Fielding."
371. Sarah Ellen Richards.
372. Leonora Smith and Joseph Richards Smith.
373. John Fielding Harris.
374. Mercy Ann Harris, Martha Ann and William's eighth child, was born on 30 March 1874. See biographical register, "Harris, Mercy Ann."
375. Samuel Stephen Jones.

Meechem[376] he is in very poor health very feeble this summer not able to do much the baby is frettng and I have got a large ieroning to do. William[377] and the children join me in love to you may the Lord bless you is the prayr of your affectonate sister
Martha A Harris

JOSEPH F. TO MARTHA ANN, 7 SEPTEMBER 1874

42 Islington Liverpool Eng.
Sept. 7th 1874

My Dear Sister Martha Ann

I am happy to let you know I am in receipt of your favor of Aug. 15.th which has just come to hand. I am always pleased to hear from you, but more especially so when I can learn of your welfare from your own hand. I am in good health, and perhaps would have been in better spirits had I received, this morning, my usual quota of letters from my own dear home.[378] I only hope all is well with my family. I have never missed before receiving a line from some one of them with the Sunday mail.

I generally get my mail matter from home on Sunday. but some times, the mail is a little late in chich case it lays over until monday, for there is but one delivery on the Sabath. I certainly am a little disappointed this morning, but I shall rest in the assurence that all is well, till I hear.[379]

On last Wednesday we sent off our 5th company;[380] it numbered 553 souls. not all of them by any means good Latter day Saints. Some of our people at home are sending for some of the meanest specimens of humanity, drunken apostates, some of them, on account [**p. 2**] of relationship. Some could not do worse if they should send for his Satanic Majesty's lowest imps, and would be gainers by odds to send for beelzebub himself.[381] Perhaps this

376. Edward Mecham and Sophia Barrows.

377. William Jasper Harris.

378. Joseph F. wrote in his journal later in the evening, "Monday Sep. 7. 1874 Got letters from my Sister Martha Ann, Jos. S. Richard & Lorin Farr. None from home. Some fears of Sickness, but no all Shall be well. I wrot to Martha Ann. . . . Evening I got a long letter from Edna and answered it, filling one Sheet of letter paper. She reports all tolerably well. God bless my family." Joseph F., journal, 7 September 1874.

379. Joseph F. noted that he received some additional letters the following day: "This morning received another letter from Edna and one from Sarah." Joseph F., journal, 8 September 1874.

380. The ship *Wyoming* sailed from Liverpool on Wednesday, 2 September 1874, and arrived in New York on 27 October 1874. There were 553 Latter-day Saint immigrants on board—320 from the British Isles, 224 from other European countries, and 9 returning missionaries—under the leadership of John C. Graham. The majority of the group continued on to Utah Territory by train, arriving there on 23 September. While aboard the *Wyoming*, John C. Graham wrote to Joseph F. on 13 September, describing the seasickness experienced by most passengers onboard but also indicating that "the utmost good order and behavior have prevailed. A willing acquiescence has been accorded by the Saints to all the requirements of those in charge of the company, the result of which has been that the most perfect harmony has prevailed." See *Mormon Immigration Index*, "Wyoming," September 1874; and Joseph F., journal, 19 August–10 September 1874.

381. First mentioned in 2 Kings 1:2–3, 6, 16, Beelzebub had become one of the names for the devil. See Mark 3:22; Matthew 10:25; 12:24, 27; Luke 11:15, 18–19.

<is> stretching the thing a little, but I have been so anoyed at such downright folly if not wickedness, that if <I> should go to a little extreme in my expressions on the subject, it might be pardonable. I am pleased to hear that Willie[382] is such a help, as also Jodie I hope they, and Hyrum, Frankie and Johnnie[383] will all grow up to be industrious, prudend and icomomical, and honorable men. And take good care of their mother, and sisters. You certainly have been blessed with boys, and I hope they will be an honor to you and themselves, following every good example and shunning all the bad. How great the responsibility that rests upon the parents, of children who are depending upon them for their characters which to them is the bread of life or of death. May God bless you <with> good fruit for your toil. and abundently reward all your labors and sufferings.

I would like to know that William[384] felt and realized these things as I do; that would be my crowning happiness respecting him and you. O! that it may be so ere it is too late. The inclosed bit is from a dress pattern of 14 yards,[385] which I have sent you by bro. Charles Sansom,[386] who will leave it at my house for you. give my love to bro. Smoot[387] and all the family and accept the same richly, I am Joseph

JOSEPH F. TO MARTHA ANN, 7 SEPTEMBER 1874

42 Islington Eng.
Sept. 7. 1874

My Dear Sister

Since writing the foregoing I thought I would drop a few lines to bro. S. S. Jones,[388] and I wish you would enclose it in an envelope, and send it to him as soon as you can. There is one other person in Provo, I feel a sympathy for, it is bro. Stubbs.[389]

382. William Jasper Harris Jr.

383. Joseph Albert Harris, Hyrum Smith Harris, Franklin Hill Harris, and John Fielding Harris.

384. William Jasper Harris.

385. Joseph F. indicated that he had included in this parcel "32 yds dress goods. for M. A. Harris 14 yds. do." Joseph F., journal, 2 September 1874.

386. Charles Sansom served a mission in England from 1873 to 1874, apparently returning on the *Wyoming*. In his autobiography and journal, Charles Sansom noted that during this passage he lost track of one of his bags that contained, among other things, "a parcel belonging to President Joseph F. Smith." Fortunately, however, William C. Staines, who was in the following company, found the bag and forwarded it to Charles, who then apparently delivered it successfully to Joseph F.'s family. See *Mormon Immigration Index*, "Wyoming," September 1874. See also biographical register, "Sansom, Charles."

387. A. O. Smoot.

388. Samuel Stephen Jones.

389. This is likely Peter Stubbs, a resident of Provo, according to the 1870 US Census. Peter lived in the same ward as Martha Ann at this time. Another possibility is Richard Stubbs, Peter's brother who lived in the neighboring ward in Provo. See biographical register, "Stubbs, Peter."

He was a true friend to me when I was in Provo,[390] and I cannot forget a kindness, I have heard that he was not feeling exactly right but I hope for his sake and his families, it is not so~~w~~. I want you, when you see him, to give him my best compliments, and wish him, for me to hold fast for ever his possition and priveleges in the gospel. I respect him sincerely for his kindness to me, and I want to see him prosper and stand firm in the kingdom of God. I do not [**p. 2**] forget my good friends bro. and sister Mecham,[391] give them my kind regards and best wishes. May the Lord bless them with long life and plenty. and finally crown them with everlasting life and rewards. Another of my best and dearest Provo, Friends is bro. Madsen, the fisherman,[392] he was a true friend to me in my temporary exile or sojourne at Provo. and I shall ever remember him with respect. give him my my very best wishes & regards.

I also remember the kindness of my cousin George Gee,[393] while I was there. I think of these things now that I am absent from my home again, and feel my dependence upon the Lord, he being my only friend except those who are as friendless, among strangers as myself. God bless the good every where is the prayer of your bro. Joseph

MARTHA ANN TO JOSEPH F., 8 SEPTEMBER 1874

Provo City Sep ~~8.~~<8th 1874>

Nicholas Muhlesteen.
Christion Shony. & John Liethy.[394]

My Dear brother Joseph

the three above named bretheren called on me the other day to know whether I would interseed for them to you and give them an interduction to you allso, by letter what thir object is I know not they have been very kind to me in sending me choise bits of fruit severel times

390. Joseph F. spent a short time living in Provo during part of 1868–69. He was sent there, along with Wilford Woodruff and Abraham O. Smoot, by Brigham Young. They were instructed to stay there long enough to be elected to the city council and to correct the lawlessness that largely prevailed in Provo at the time. In addition to performing public service, Joseph F. worked in a cabinet shop during his time in Provo. See "Shining Lights," *The Contributor: Representing the Young Men's Mutual Improvement Associations of the Latter-day Saints* 16, no. 3 (January 1895): 172.
391. Edward Mecham and Sophia Barrows.
392. Peter Madsen, a Danish migrant and pioneer fisherman, lived in the Provo Third Ward at this time. He began commercial fishing in Utah Lake in 1854. See biographical register, "Madsen, Peter." See also Martha Ann to Joseph F., 24 November 1874, herein.
393. George Washington Gee II was second cousin to Joseph F. and Martha Ann.
394. Nicholas Muhlestein, Christian Schoeni, and John Liechty, convert immigrants from Switzerland, wanted their families to be sealed to Joseph F. according to the law of adoption. See Nicholas Muhlestein, Christian Schoeni, and John Liechty to Joseph F., 25 August and 13 November 1874. This practice was later discontinued by Wilford Woodruff in 1894. See Gordon Irving, "The Law of Adoption: One Phase of the Development of the Mormon Concept of Salvation," *BYU Studies* 14, no. 3 (Spring 1974): 291–314. See also Richard E. Bennett, "'Line upon Line, Precept upon Precept': Reflections on the 1877 Commencement of the Performance of Endowments and Sealings for the Dead," *BYU Studies* 44, no. 3 (2005): 62–66; Richard E. Bennett, "Which Is the Wisest Course?": The Transformation in Mormon Temple Consciousness, 1870–1898," *BYU Studies Quarterly* 52, no. 2 (2013): 4–43; and biographical register, "Muhlestein, Nicholas," "Schoeni, Christian," and "Liechty, John."

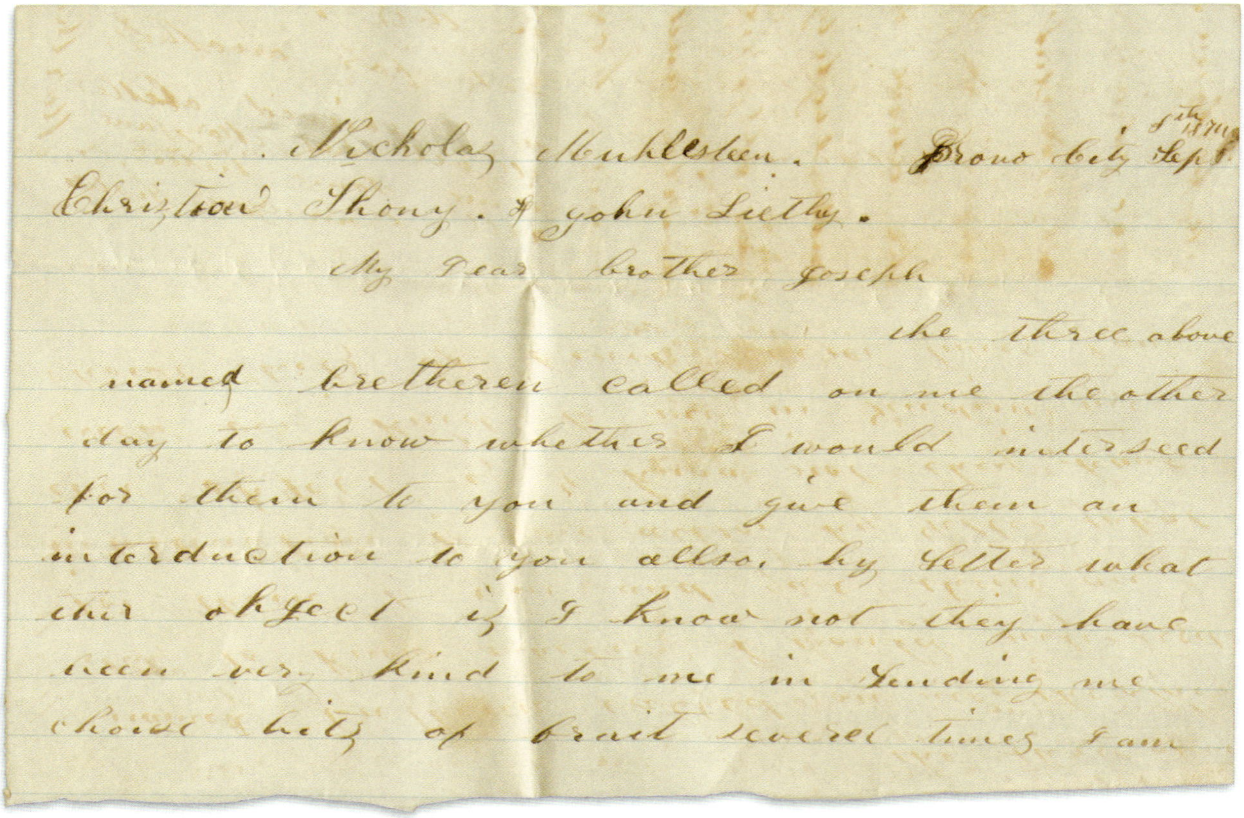

Nicholas Muhlestien. Provo City Sept 8th 1874
Christian Shony. & John Lietly.
My Dear brother Joseph
the three above named bretheren called on me the other day to know whether I would intersead for them to you and give them an interduction to you allso. by letter what thier objcet is I know not they have been very kind to me in sending me choise bits of fruit several times I am

Martha Ann to Joseph F., 8 September 1874 (p. 1)

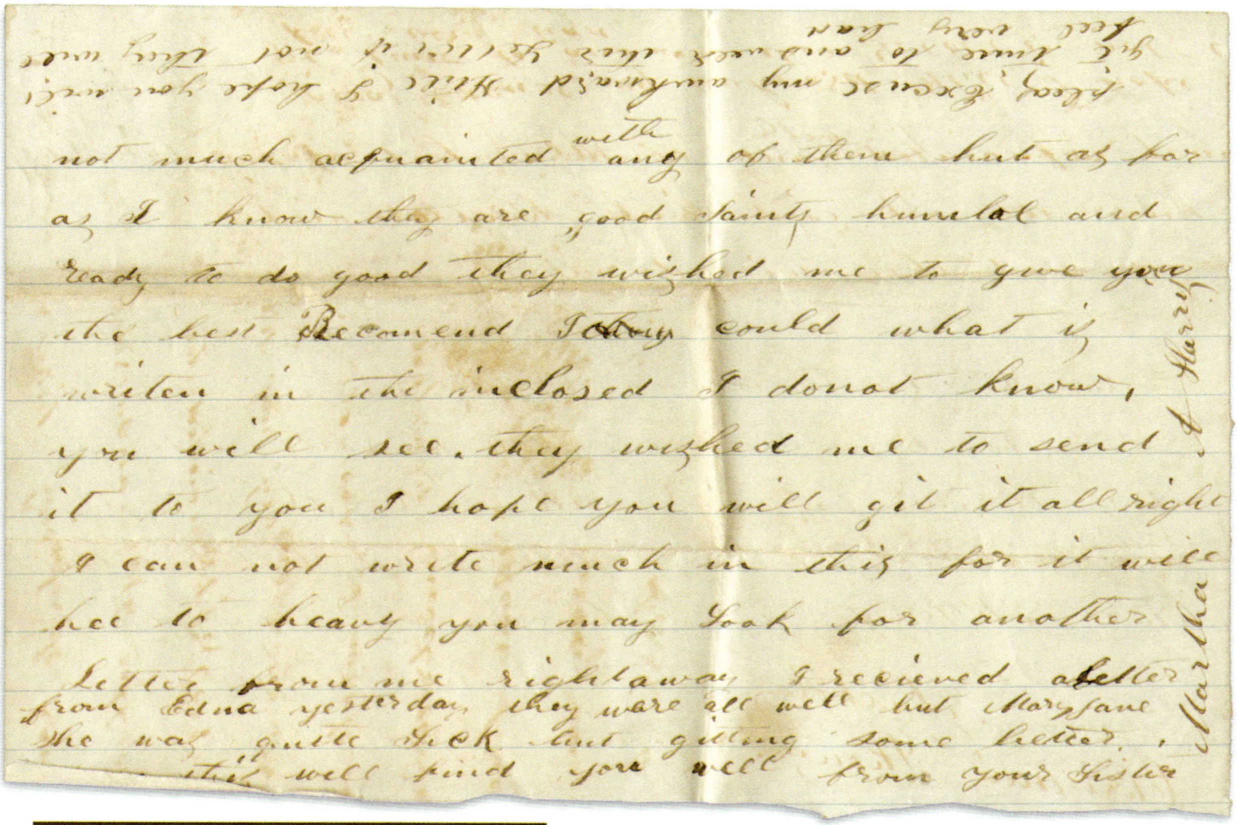

not much acquainted with any of them but as far as I know they are good saints humbal and ready to do good they wished me to give you the best Recomend I could what is writen in the inclosed I donot know, you will see. they wished me to send it to you I hope you will git it all right I can not write much in this for it will bee to heavy you may look for another letter from me rightaway I received a letter from Edna yesterday they ware all well but Mary Jane she was quite sick but gitting some better, this will find you well from your Sister Martha A Harris

pleas Excuse my awkward Hill I hope you will git time to answer this letter if not they will feel very bad

Martha Ann to Joseph F., 8 September 1874 (p. 2)

I am [**p. 2**] not much acquainted <with> any of them but as far as I know they are good Saints humbol and ready to do good they wished me to give you the best recomend I [*illegible strike-through*] could what is writen in the inclosed I donot know, you will see. they wished me to send it to you I hope you will git it all right I can not write much in this for it will bee to heavy you may look for another letter from me right away I recieved a letter from Edna[395] yesterday, they ware all well but Mary Jane[396] she was quite sick but gitting some better. [*6.1 x 0.6 cm fold along bottom*] this will find you well from your sister

Martha A Harris[397]

pleas excuse my awkward stile I hope you will git time to answer thir letter if not they will feel very bad[398]

MARTHA ANN TO JOSEPH F., 10 NOVEMBER 1874

Recd Nov. 10. 1874
Ansd Dec. 8." [399]

Provo City Octtober the 5th 1874

My dear good kind jenerous noble hearted brother, Joseph. what can I say to you for all your kindness to me, my poor way of expressing my self does not do my feelings justice I have recieved too of your dear welcome letters but have not answerd them yet becaus it has been such buisy times wth fruit drying and cross sick babyes ~~my~~ my mind has been to confused and my nirves to harrowd up to wrte or collect my thaughts I am very near tierd out with all my work that I have to perform Joney[400] has been cuttng teeth allso the baby[401] they have been very fretfull. [*illegible erasure*] but they are gittng better now [*illegible erasure*]
Sunday the 17th

sence I wrote the above I have travled one hundred and eighty miles and am home again finding all right I went to the City[402] partly on a visit and partly on buisness I got thare to your house on fry day [**p. 2**] week evning found Sarah[403] at home all alone with the children Julina and Edna[404] ware gon to the house[405] I stoped at your house untill Saturday enving

395. Edna Lambson.
396. Mary Jane Thompson.
397. Written sideways in the right margin of page 2.
398. Written upside down in the top margin of page 2.
399. Written sideways in the top left margin of page 1.
400. John Fielding Harris.
401. Mercy Ann Harris was born on 30 March 1874.
402. Salt Lake City.
403. Sarah Ellen Richards.
404. Julina Lambson and Edna Lambson.
405. Most likely the "Homestead," Joseph F.'s home located at 333 West First North (now 200 North), Salt Lake City.

and John[406] came after me and took me to his house he then went and got a pass for thre to Ogdon[407] we started at six <o clock> on sunday morning got to sarahs[408] just as they ware asking the blessing on thir breakfast I got to see all the folks had a nice visit and started home at six in the evning and got hom at eight or <at> Aunt Thompson[409] I went over to your house found the girls all in bed but they let me in I stayd thare all night and started home on monday morning at seven o clock got home at a quarter to ten. I was so tierd out that I had to go to bed the rest of the day I have been very buisy ever sence I got the gloves <and forks> all right for which my dear <brother> pleas except of my warmest thanks[410] **[p. 3]** how I would love to return the complement in some way or another you are so kind to me I fear you are robing your self for my sake I was sorry the dresses got lost for it is such a loss for you[411] I got the letter with the <peas> in it I thaught it was so nice the gloves fit me nicely they came very accptable for I did not have a pare of any kind I will make me a pare of common ones to save them I shall not forget your kindess to me and may the Lord bless you for it intill every desire of your heart shall bee granted unto you for I know you would have no evle desir. Wiliam[412] has been to the canyon and got to loads of logs [*illegible strike-through*] and made lumber for his grainery he is gitting on real well with it has got the adobes baught and paid for and allso the shingles. we will have a little more room when we git that done. Williey[413] has been **[p. 4]** going [*illegible erasure*] with the thrashng mashene[414] he got a job when he could that has helped us considrable Joseph[415] and William runs the teem and irn what they can we all try to help a litle I want to git Willy in school as soon as posable Joseph will have to lirn at home this winter Wiliams health is good now he is not very strong though can not stand it to work very stady We have dryed considrable fruit enough to do us and some to sell the boys talk of going to canyon this week for wood one of the horses have been very lame for severrel weeks that has throon them behind considrable he is still very lame I hope he will soon git better we have had to hire a horse for some <time> which quite an expence. the weather has been very faverable for canyon work but thir wagon is not stronge enough for canyon work they have to hire one or borrow when they go we have had sevrrel deaths in provo of late brother Jonson the Bishop

406. Likely John Smith.

407. Train ticket to Ogden, Weber County, about thirty-eight miles north of Salt Lake City.

408. Sarah Smith.

409. Mercy Rachel Thompson.

410. See Joseph F. to Martha Ann, 15 July 1874, herein. Joseph F. notes in his journal on 2 September 1874 that he sent items home from England with people who were sailing to America aboard the *Wyoming*: "I sent the following things. by J. C. Gram. For John. 1 doz. Knives, ivory handles, carver fork & steel. 1 doz. Best plated forks. and an overcoat. for Mary J. Taylor. An umbrella. for my folks, 9 yds. of b. b. velvet. by C. Sansom, for my folks, 32 yds dress goods for M. A. Harry's 14 yds. do. By. R. W. Heyborne for my folks, 1 doz. knives self tips, & 1 doz. best plated forks. and pair of clogs (4/6) for J. Cottam. By. Anna M. Thorp. For my folks 1 doz. knives & ½ doz. best plated forks. for M. J. T. a suit of clothes (for R. B. Taylor)."

411. Charles Sansom apparently lost his luggage containing gifts from Joseph F., but it was later found and returned by William C. Staines, who was in the following company. See Joseph F. to Martha Ann, 6 November 1874; and Martha Ann to Joseph F., 16 November 1874, herein.

412. William Jasper Harris.

413. William Jasper Harris Jr.

414. A threshing machine is used to separate grain from stalks and husks.

415. Joseph Albert Harris.

has lost his second wife[416] she died in child bed and left 4 small children allso Bishop Scot[417] of the second ward of earica[◊]l[◊]s[418] in the arm. I have not seen brother Stubs[419] yet but I will call on him as soon as posable I hope you will bee able to read this scrool pleas excuse all mistakes and bad wrtng I will write again before long William and the children join me in love

from your ever greatfull and loving sister Martha A Harris this is the third letter I have begon to you and I have not wrote this [*illegible word*] now[420]

JOSEPH F. TO MARTHA ANN, 6 NOVEMBER 1874

42 Islington Liverpool Eng.
Nov. 6. 1874

My Dear Sister Martha Ann,

Your favor of Provo. Sep. 8th enclosing a letter from N. Muhlesteen C. Sheeny, & J. Leihty,[421] came to hand Oct. 6. one month today, as you will see by dates. I have answere[*0.5 x 1.3 cm triangular tear along fold*] theirs, and will enclose it for you to forward. You can read it if you wish, and then close it in an envelope and seal and forward it. I have to be economical, as I do so much corrisponding my postage is prodigeous.[422] Your letter was over weight, as it was. Always in such cases they charge us double postage, besides the amount already paid, so be a little more careful in the future.

I would not mention it, only I have so many such circomstances to meet, and "many mickles macks a muckle". as the scotch say.[423] I am so grieved and disappointed about the loss [**p. 2**] of your dress and those of the girls', at New York, that I feel bad whenever I think of it. Still I cling to the hope that you will yet get them.[424] At all events I sincerely hope so. Yours cost £2.14.10 or about $15^{00/100}$ in green backs,[425] and I do not want you to loose it. I sent you ½ a doz. german silver forks I hope you got them all right. I heard about your visit to the City and

416. Maren Poulsen, wife of Bishop John Peter Rasmus Johnson, died on 5 October 1874 in Provo. See biographical register, "Poulsen, Maren" and "Johnson, John Peter Rasmus."
417. Andrew Hunter Scott, bishop of the Provo Second Ward, died on 11 October 1874 in Provo. See biographical register, "Scott, Andrew Hunter."
418. Possibly erysipelas, a bacterial skin infection often accompanied by fever, chills, and nausea that sometimes leads to gangrene and necrosis and can, in severe cases, be fatal. See Robert Hooper, *Lexicon Medicum; or Medical Dictionary* (New York: Harper & Brothers, 1841), 337–38.
419. Likely Peter Stubbs. See Joseph F. to Martha Ann, 7 September 1874 (second letter), herein, note 389.
420. Written upside down in the top margin of page 4.
421. Nicholas Muhlestein, Christian Schoeni, and John Liechty. See Martha Ann to Joseph F., 8 September 1874, herein, note 394.
422. The 1874–75 journals reveal the "prodigeious" number of letters that Joseph F. wrote and received during his mission. See, for example, Joseph F. to Martha Ann, 7 September 1875, herein, note 526.
423. A Scottish saying, though garbled from its original form ("Many a mickle makes a muckle"), meaning "Many small amounts accumulate to make a large amount."
424. See Martha Ann to Joseph F., 16 November 1874, herein.
425. US paper currency notes were first issued during the American Civil War beginning in 1862. They became known as "greenbacks" because the backs were printed in green.

Ogden, both from the girls, Charlie Griffin, and from John.[426] the first time either of them have written to me since I left home.

I will send enclosed a letter to aunt Lucy[427] in answer to hers to me, please forward it. John informs m[*0.6 x 0.3 cm tear along fold*] that William[428] is much, much better, I am more than thankful. You must excuse this short bit, I go to London in the morning, or tomorrow some time, & must answer several letters. My health is good. and the Lord is blessing me in my labors, God bless You & Yours Kind love to Bp. Smoot[429] & family bro. L. J. N. Joins.[430]
Joseph

MARTHA ANN TO JOSEPH F., 16 NOVEMBER 1874

Provo City november the 16th 1874

My Dear brother Joseph

I wrote a few lines inclosed in a letter of brothor Mulisteen[431] we have not recieved any answr yet they are ancious to know wheather you got it or not[432] I hope you are well I want to hear from you very much we are all better than we have been I have had a bad spell of the chills and a gatherd thumb[433] on my right thumb or I should have writen to you before now I can not hardly youse it now I have <not> herd from your famely for ovr a w<e>ek they ware all well then I have writen once sence conference. but have not rcieved any <letter> from you sence [**p. 2**] the one with the peas of the dress patrin in it ~~I was~~ I was glad to hear from Julina[434] that they ware found all right[435] I went to see Aunt Jane Gee[436] yester day she was very sick they hardly know wheth[◊] she will git well or not she is very low in deed I feel[◊] so sorry for her poor womern she seems to suffer so much I hope she will soon git better.

I wrote a few lines in brother Mulisteen letter and gave you an introduction and a rcomend pleas wrte to them in answ<e>r for theiy seem very ancious to hear from you I will close hopng you will excuse this short note for I am in a hurry for he is waitng. ever your sister
M A Harris

I will soon write again pleas write when you can[437]

426. "The girls" most likely refers to Joseph F.'s three wives. The other two people mentioned are Charles Emerson Griffin and John Smith. Charles wrote to Joseph F. on 13 October 1874: "John, Hellen Martha Ann and their Babies came up here day before yesterday morning stayed through the day and went back in the evening." John wrote to Joseph F. on 15 October 1874: "Martha Ann came down last Friday the 9th and Hellen and myself went with her up to Ogdon on sunday and she went home on monday herself and family were all well and william was doing better much better."
427. Lucy Walker.
428. William Jasper Harris.
429. Abraham O. Smoot.
430. Leonard J. Nuttall.
431. Nicholas Muhlestein.
432. See Joseph F. to Martha Ann, 6 November 1874, herein.
433. *Gathered* refers to having a purulent infection. *Oxford English Dictionary*, s.v. "gather."
434. Julina Lambson.
435. This may be in reference to the missing dresses Joseph F. sent home. See Martha Ann to Joseph F., 5 October 1874; and Joseph F. to Martha Ann, 6 November 1874, herein.
436. Mary Jane Smith, mother of George Washington Gee II. See biographical register, "Gee, George Washington, II."
437. Written upside down in the top margin of page 2.

Martha Ann to Joseph F., 24 November 1874 (envelope front and back)

MARTHA ANN TO JOSEPH F., 24 NOVEMBER 1874

Recd Dec. 14. 1874
Ansd Feb. 9. 1875[438]

Provo City Nov the 24 1874[439]

My Dear brother Joseph

Joseph Albert[440] just came in from his work with his fase all over smiles & handed me your letter of nov the 6th I commenced one to you last evning but did not finnish it so I will begin another one. it contained your dear potogrape I could not supress the tears that would gush forth with grattude and thankfullness for so kind and good a brother the constant expresion of my heart is may the Lord bless him and all that pertains to him I cannot express half I feel to the donor of so much kindness I thank you for sending it to me I think it is splendid I am so thankfull to see you look **[p. 2]** so well I think it is better than the othher one you sent me I got a letter to day all so ~~a~~ from Aunt Thompson[441] saying that they had got the dress patrons all right I was so pleased to hear it she said they ware all well at home both them and your famely I wish you could see your little Alvin[442] bless his little heart he is such a great fine noble little fellow and seemed to know every word you said to him I quite fell in love with him. your children are all sweet and prity and that dear little Donny[443] she said her papa was in Liverpool she is so cuning I love them all they are very dear to me I hardly know how you can **[p. 3]** stand away so long from them I juge yous by my own feelings but you~~r~~ are keeping the comandments of God to love him first and obey his comandments I know it must bee hard to tare your self

438. Written sideways in the top left margin of page 1.
439. Martha Ann addressed the envelope, "Mr Joseph F Smith 42 Islington Liverpool England." It is postmarked "PROVO CITY UT" and also "NEW YORK DEC 5." Joseph F. wrote, "M. A. Harris—Recd Dec. 14 1874. Ansd Feb. 9. 1874." On the reverse, Joseph F. wrote, "M. A. Harris Recd Dec. 14 1874. Ansd Feb. 9."
440. Joseph Albert Harris.
441. Mercy Rachel Fielding.
442. Alvin Fielding Smith, born to Edna on 19 July 1874.
443. Donnette Smith, born to Julina on 17 September 1872.

from your famely who are so dear to you but he will reward you for all your sacrefises. I got the forks you sent to me and all so the gloves they fit me nicely they are to nice I fear for my suroundngs but I can keep them perhaps I will have better some time I live in hopes at any rate that it will be better some day with me and mine my dear brother I hope you have not curtailed your **[p. 4]** self from comforts to send them to me Sarah[444] sint me that butifull nect tie you sent me I thnk it is lovly I shall never forget no never. may I ever proove worthy and greatfull. William[445] is doing real well he has not drank any for five months he works all he is abole he sais he will try and wrte to you be fore long it is hard work to git him to writng he has got the griainery built and coverd with shingls and the flore layed it lack the doors yet and then it will bee done I am so glad to have it now we can take care of what we have it will be a valuable little place I can put lots of things in it and make[446] more room in my little house we are crowded now that the children are [◊◊]ng lar[◊]e **[p. 5]**

William talks of building a bed room for the boys next sumer he has subscribed for the juvnile instructer[447] for the children and we have got the children all shod round and hope soon to git them all clothng for the winter it has pinched us some to build the grainery for provisions we have drawn some from the thything offase William is workng thare to pay for it all he can Willey[448] is going to school and is lirnng nicely Joseph and Hyrm[449] are rinng the teem they have plenty to do and when I compare ~~oo~~ our situation to what it was a year ago I see thare is a great change **[p. 6]** for the better. I told brother Stubbes[450] what you wrote he said some one had been mischef makng that he hoped he was all right he said he was nevr a very religous man told me to give his kind regards to you and thank you~~r~~ for your intrest in his welfare I allso saw bro Matson[451] and gave your respects to him he told me thare was not a man living that he loved more than you he thanked you kindly for remembering him also his sun[452] wished to be rememberd to you. Brother meechem[453] is not very well I read your note to them and they both shed tears they ware so thankfull ~~they~~ they both thank you for your kind blessing.[454] poor Aunt Jane she is very low ~~I~~ I sent to know **[p. 7]** how she was and she sent me word her time had come[455] it made me feel quite sad I can asure you Gorge[456] sais he is going to write to you he feels bad poor boy about his Mother you and I konow how to simpathse with him for we know what it is to lose a Mother but was thare evr a Mother like ours[457] I feel greatfull that we had such a Mother as we had you said you wished I had her abelites and her education I cincerly wish I ha but I have not I know it to my sorrow neather have I her

444. Sarah Ellen Richards.

445. William Jasper Harris.

446. The following sentence is written sideways in the margin between page 4 and page 1.

447. A monthly periodical for children and youth, the *Juvenile Instructor* was a private publication from 1866 until 1901, when it was purchased by the Church and became the official publication of the Sunday School organization.

448. William Jasper Harris Jr.

449. Joseph Albert Harris and Hyrum Smith Harris.

450. Likely Peter Stubbs. See Joseph F. to Martha Ann, 7 September 1874 (second letter), herein, note 389.

451. Possibly Henning Madsen.

452. Peter Henning Madsen. See Joseph F. to Martha Ann, 7 September 1874, herein.

453. Edward Mecham. See Joseph F. to Martha Ann, 7 September 1874, herein.

454. See Joseph F. to Martha Ann, 7 September 1874, herein.

455. Mary Jane Smith lived until March 1878.

456. George Washington Gee II, son of Mary Jane Smith and George Washington Gee, is second cousin to Joseph F. and Martha Ann.

457. Mary Fielding Smith.

firmness I would gve any thing that I posess if was half as smart as our dear Mother was yet Mother never had such things to contend with as I have or I do not know how she would have born them [**p. 8**]

Magey Smoot just called to tell me that this was the last day of grace with her as she gows to bee married to morrow to Wilson Dosenbery[458] I hope she will bee hapy. Mah Mother and Dieana[459] sends thir kind love to you with thanks for your kindness in rem<em>berng theim

I was sorry <to hear> the letter they sent was so heavy I never thaugh of thir writng any ~~thing any~~ thing of that kind to you or I would not have had any thing to do with it[460] I think you gave them a splendid answer any how.[461] I did not like to refuse their request they was afraid you did not git it so I had to write again to you last week. I have had a gatherd thumb[462] for some time it is not well yet I must close for the present I remain as ever your greatfull sister Martha Harris

I hope this will not bee to heavy I will write again before long William and the children join me in love pleas give our respects to [*illegible word*] Nuttel[463]

please<when you> write to us again give the boys a word of advise not to asocate with bad swaring boys they will lison to you better than they to me[464]

JOSEPH F. TO MARTHA ANN, 8 DECEMBER 1874

42 Islington Liverpool Eng.
Dec. 8th 1874

Martha Ann Harris
My Dear Sister:—

Your kind favors of Oct.17th and Nov.16th are both received, the first Nov. 10.th and the other Dec. 7th I wrote Nov. 6th enclosing a letter to bro. N. Muhlestein and others,[465] which you will long ere this have received. Since my last writing I have been to London, Brighton, Birmingham, and other places attending public meetings, and I have been rather busy.

458. Margaret Thompson Smoot, sister-in-law to Martha Ann, married Wilson Howard Dusenberry on 25 November 1874. See biographical register, "Smoot, Margaret Thompson."
459. Emily Hill and Diana Eldredge, wives of Abraham O. Smoot.
460. Martha Ann here refers to the letter she forwarded to Joseph F. from Nicholas Muhlestein, John Liechty, and Christian Schoeni. It was apparently too heavy, and Joseph F. had to pay the extra postage. See Martha Ann to Joseph F., 8 September 1874; and Joseph F. to Martha Ann, 6 November 1874, herein.
461. Joseph F.'s reply is not extant, but a subsequent letter sent to Joseph F. from Nicolas, John, and Christian indicates that they received a positive response to their request. See Nicholas Muhlestein, John Liechty, and Christian Schoeni to Joseph F., 29 December 1874.
462. See Martha Ann to Joseph F., 16 November 1874, herein.
463. Likely refers to Leonard J. Nuttall or possibly his wife Elizabeth Clarkson. See Joseph F. to Martha Ann, 5 August 1874, herein. See also biographical register, "Clarkson, Elizabeth." Written upside down in the top margin and left side of page 8.
464. Written upside down in the top margin of page 5.
465. John Liechty and Christian Schoeni.

My health is good, as a general thing, much better than when at home, indeed my labors here have been of a less wearing kind, upon my lungs than they were at home. Nothing can be more trying to weak lungs or throat weaknesses, or bronchial affections than such work as has to be done in the E. H.[466] and more especially in the font room,[467] from such labors I have been free since leaving home, and I am much relieved and better for it, as my Photograph will show, and for which I am very thankful. I even have not the opportunity of doing as much preaching here as I had at home, altho' my mission is for the purpose of preaching the gospel. So that really I am having a rest from toil, and am improving under it in health, for all of which—so far as I know how to be—I am very grateful. I have more than this to be grateful for, for since my departure from home, my family have been blessed even as I have, and so far have got along very comfortably, and happily. This to me personally is the **[p. 2]** greatest source of my comfort and happiness in my separation from them, and in my sojournings in strange lands, among strangers. If the Lord will only preserve my family,—my little ones, from harm, continue <unto> them shelter, comfortable beds, food and raiment, then I can face the wold with a brave heart, and faithfully try to do my duty in the Kingdom of God. But should affliction come, as in the past, I should meet it with the best grace, fortitude and manliness I could. My family is to me as the "apple of my eye",[468] and no affliction could be so great, nor hard to bear, as affliction upon them. God grant them preservation, and peace, and I am happy. yet I feel keenly for all my Fathers[469] House—and were it in my power would shield them from every power of darkness, from the consequence of every folly or sin, and from all <u>enemies</u> both without and within. I do not feel selfish, I do not <u>live</u> for self—but "for those who love me, for those who'r kind and true, For the heaven, that smiles above me, And the good that I can do." as the poet says.[470] When I have finished this work, completed this object, fulfilled this mission satisfactorily, I am done with this world and am ready to go hence. ¶ I was pleased to learn from your last that you were all some better, that William[471] was getting along so well. Sorry Aunt Jane Gee[472] was suffering so, please give my kind love and regards to them all. I hope she is better. Am pleased the dress patterns were found for your sake as well as for my own, I hope you will receive yours safely and will enjoy it. I only wish it had been a better one. I hope to see you wear it some day, have it made nice. I would be proud to see you clothed in the best rayment, with all neatness, equal to any. had I the power you should be. I am Your Brother. Joseph F.

P.S. please forward the enclosed by one of the boys to bro—Muhlestein or any one of them.[473] You can read it if you wish[474]

466. Endowment House. See Joseph F. to Martha Ann, 13 July 1869, herein, note 366.
467. Baptismal font room, located in the Endowment House.
468. Proverbs 7:2.
469. Hyrum Smith.
470. This poem has been attributed to George Linnaeus Banks under various titles, first appearing as "Life" in the *London Family Herald* in 1848. See J. F. Cosgrove, "Answers from Readers," *New York Times*, 21 March 1920. See also *The Columbia World of Quotations* (New York: Columbia University Press, 1996), no. 5531.
471. William Jasper Harris.
472. Mary Jane Smith.
473. See Martha Ann to Joseph F., 8 September 1874; Joseph F. to Martha Ann, 6 November 1874; and Martha Ann to Joseph F., 24 November 1874, herein.
474. Written upside down in the top margin of page 2.

JOSEPH F. TO MARTHA ANN, 9 FEBRUARY 1875

42 Islington Liverpool Eng.
Feb. 9. 1875[475]

My Dear Sister
Martha Ann.

Your welcome letters came duly to hand. That of Nov. 24. on Dec. 14th and that of Jan. 13 & 17, on yesterday. (Feb. 8th) I should have answered yours of Nov. 24th long ere this but I must plead, that I have been a little busy and a little neglectful hence my delay—but it is to be hoped "it is better late than never".

I was extremely sorry for the sickness of Sarah.[476] and some surprised at the news of the sudden death of sister Griffin,[477] but poor old soul, she has gone to rest, peace be to her ashes. When I called at charlies, a week before leaving home, I wondered if I should ever see her again, in this world. and I never will. [**p. 2**]

I received a letter from Charlie to day, dated Jan. 19.th in which he gives me the particulars. I am thankful that Sarah escaped, & that Alice[478] was there to wait upon her. The Lord preserve my Kindred from sickness and death until they have finished a good work on the earth. and I would that the way might be opened up for greater temporal prosperity for them, inasmuch as they would continue true and faithful to their covenants, but I would rather, continue poor always than deny the faith for prosperity. and I have just as good wishes for my Kindred. I have often thought, it would be a good idea for Willie[479] to get a situation in the Factory[480] and learn a trade. Or if he prefers it, some other business, as I think a good trade will one day be almost [**p. 3**] if not entirely indispensible to our children. I think Willie is not very strong, Factory work is not generally hard work, tho' continuous and confining. but get the children as soon as possible into some steady employment, if possible, and let them grow up to steady and industrious habits. for their own sakes, as well as for yours.

This whiffling about, at something and nothing, without any definite idea of business or labor; much valuable time is frittered away, and bad habits of shiftlessness and irrisponsibllity are contracted, in youth which is the ruin of manhood.

It is getting so dark I cannot see my lines. Please tell sisters Smoot and Mecham,[481] that my Photos all went like hot cakes,[482] and I have none left. should I get any more I will remember them with pleasure.

475. Joseph F. was thirty-six, and Martha Ann was thirty-three.
476. Sarah Smith, half sister to Martha Ann and Joseph F.
477. Abigail Varney, mother-in-law to Sarah Smith, died on 5 January 1875 in Ogden, Utah.
478. Alice Lovina Griffin.
479. William Jasper Harris Jr.
480. Most likely the Provo Woolen Mills, built between 1870 and 1872. It was a significant manufacturing enterprise in Utah Valley, employing around 150 people during this early period. See Sharon S. Arnold, "The First Large Factory in Utah," *Beehive History* 6 (1980): 22–23.
481. Likely Margaret Thompson McMeans and Sophia Barrows.
482. A popular idiom beginning in America about 1839 indicating that an item was in great demand and easily disposed of like pancakes at a church or community fair, where they were sold as fast as the cooks could make them.

I am pleased to hear Aunt Jane[483] is [**p. 4**] better. I will drop her just a line in this for you to hand to her.

Make your dress neat and nice. and, enjoy it the best you can. I am glad it reached you in safety at last. I think it should be well lined. but make it to suit yourself; I am abundently suited that you have it, I only wish it had been more, and better, but poor missionaries cannot always do what they would like. I think there can be but one expression, respecting "T's" choice, if indeed it was a choice.[484] I have heard nothing but surprise in regard to it. but I hope she is happy. Please remember me kindly to Bp. Smoot[485] and family, especially to sister Harris,[486] I was pleased that the Bp. had the benefit of a short respite from care and laborious responsibilities. I know it did him good. Kind regards to William,[487] and all the dear little ones—not forgetting neighbors and friends I am yours affectionately Jos. F. Smith

JOSEPH F. TO MARTHA ANN, 31 MARCH 1875

42 Islington Liverpool
Mar. 31. 1875[488]

My Dear Sister
Martha Ann.

Your very welcome letter of Feb. 20. came to hand Mar. 15.

I was and am very sorry you had been so poorly. And I hope you are all right again long ere this. I feel extreme sympathy for you in your afflicted condition. I think you are paying the debt of your sins as you go along. or in otherwords you must be among those whos "sins go before unto Judgement."[489]

I am very thankful you have had the courage and strength to bear it so far, and I sincerely hope these qualities will prove more than equal to your trials at last.

I owe gratitude to your kind neighbors for their attentions towards, and sympathy for you during your illness. [**p. 2**]

Please remember me kindly to them one and all without my calling their names. I will mention however, Sister Smoot (Harris)[490] bro. & sister Mecham,[491] and all your good neighbors and friends.

483. Mary Jane Smith. See Martha Ann to Joseph F., 24 November 1874, herein.
484. This may be in reference to the marriage between Margaret Thompson Smoot and Wilson Howard Dusenberry, mentioned by Martha Ann in Martha Ann to Joseph F., 24 November 1874, herein.
485. Abraham O. Smoot.
486. Emily Hill.
487. William Jasper Harris.
488. This is the first letter for which the original is extant, and a copy preserved in a letterpress copybook is also extant. See Joseph F., letterpress copybook, 7 January–20 July 1875, 246–47. This letterpress copybook is labeled "Private Letter Book No. 2. B." (see p. xx).
489. See 1 Timothy 5:24.
490. Emily Hill.
491. Edward Mecham and Sophia Barrows.

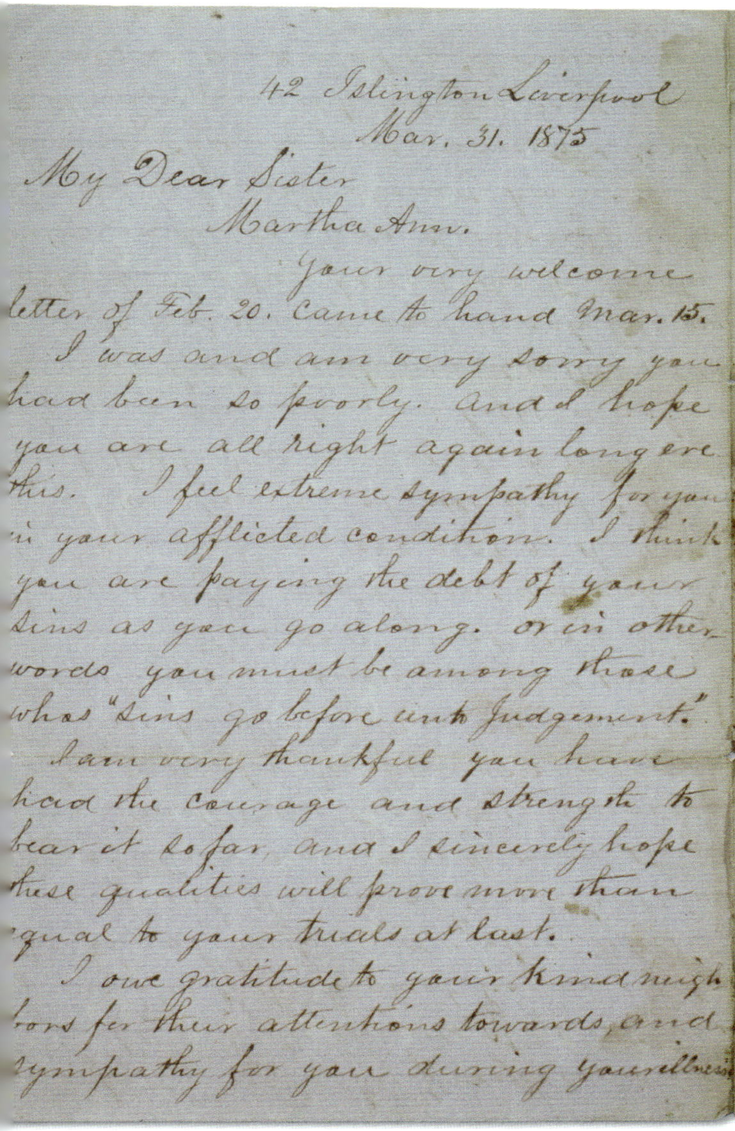

42 Islington Liverpool
Mar. 31. 1875

My Dear Sister
Martha Ann.

Your very welcome letter of Feb. 20. came to hand Mar. 15.

I was and am very sorry you had been so poorly. and I hope you are all right again long ere this. I feel extreme sympathy for you in your afflicted condition. I think you are paying the debt of your sins as you go along. or in other words you must be among those whos "sins go before unto judgement."

I am very thankful you have had the courage and strength to bear it so far, and I sincerely hope these qualities will prove more than equal to your trials at last.

I owe gratitude to your kind neighbors for their attentions towards, and sympathy for you during your illness

Joseph F. to Martha Ann, 31 March 1875 (p. 1)

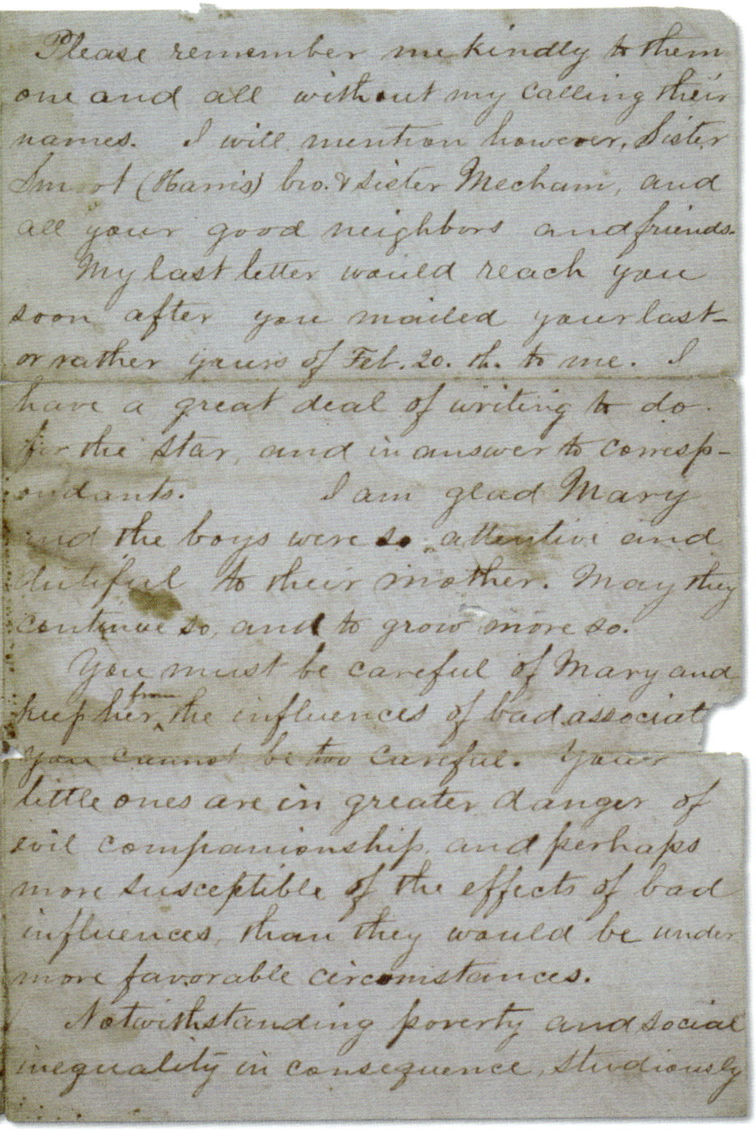

Please remember me kindly to them one and all without my calling their names. I will mention however, Sister Smoot (Harris) bro. & Sister Mecham, and all your good neighbors and friends.

My last letter would reach you soon after you mailed your last— or rather yours of Feb. 20. th. to me. I have a great deal of writing to do for the Star, and in answer to correspondants. I am glad Mary and the boys were so attentive and dutiful to their mother. May they continue so, and to grow more so.

You must be careful of Mary and keep her from the influences of bad associat[es] You cannot be too careful. Your little ones are in greater danger of evil companionship, and perhaps more susceptible of the effects of bad influences, than they would be under more favorable circumstances.

Notwithstanding poverty and social inequality in consequence, studiously

Joseph F. to Martha Ann, 31 March 1875 (p. 2)

My last letter would reach you soon after you mailed your last—or rather yours of Feb. 20. th. to me. I have a great deal of writing to do for the star,[492] and in answer to correspondants. I am glad Mary and the boys[493] were so attentive and dutiful to their mother. May they continue so, and to grow more so.

492. The *Latter-day Saints' Millennial Star* was a Church-run publication printed in England. The mission president in England typically served as its editor. See Stanley A. Peterson, "*Millennial Star*," in *Encyclopedia of Mormonism*, ed. Daniel H. Ludlow (New York: Macmillan, 1992), 2:906. One of Joseph F.'s articles appeared in the following issue of the *Star* as well as in the *Sheffield Daily Telegraph*. See "Mormonism Defended by Joseph F. Smith," *Millennial Star*, 6 April 1875.

493. Martha Ann had three daughters and five sons at the time of this letter. Mary Emily Harris was the oldest girl.

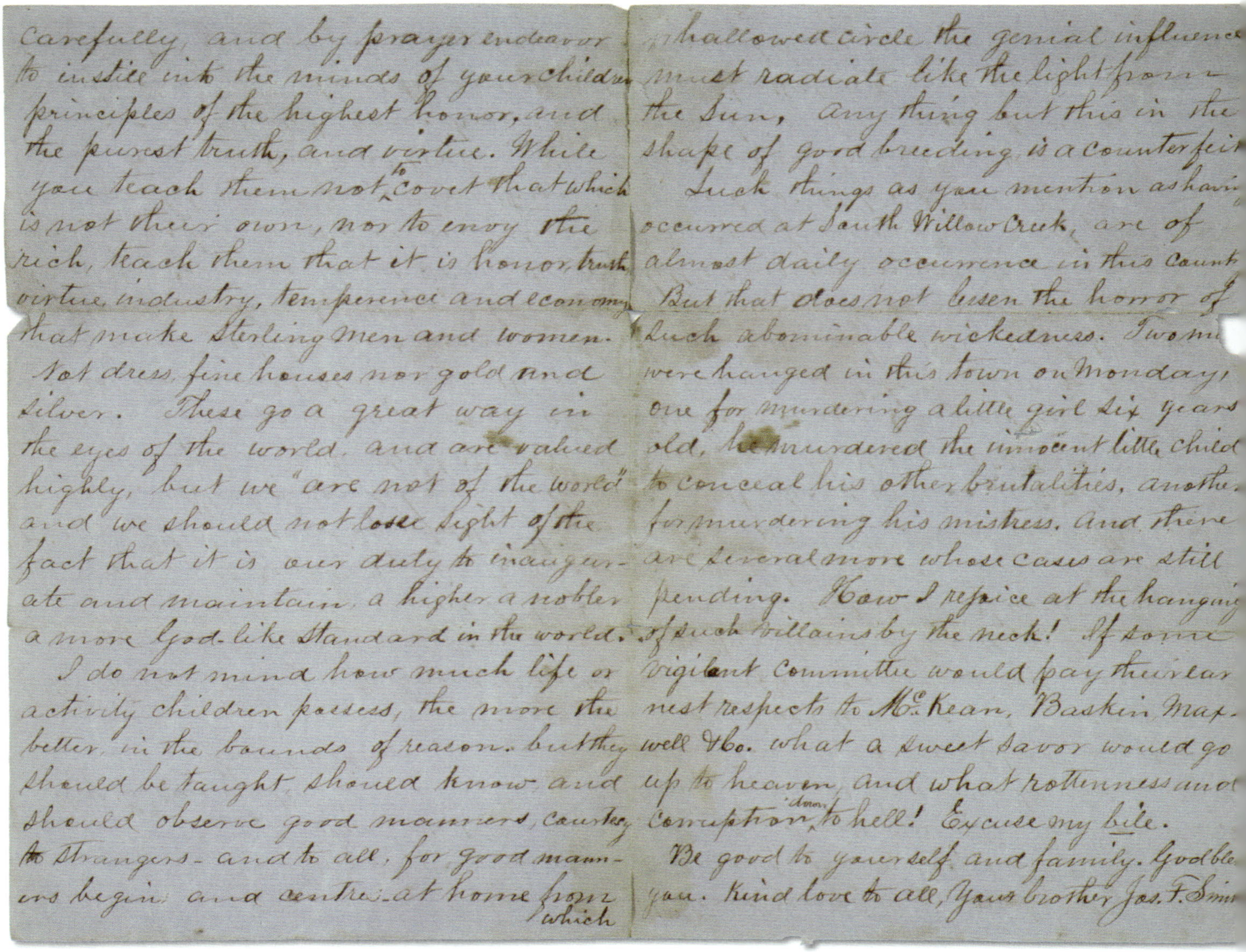
carefully, and by prayer endeavor
to instill into the minds of your children
principles of the highest honor, and
the purest truth, and virtue. While
you teach them not to covet that which
is not their own, nor to envy the
rich, teach them that it is honor, truth
virtue, industry, temperence and economy
that make Sterling men and women.
Not dress, fine houses nor gold and
silver. These go a great way in
the eyes of the world, and are valued
highly, but we "are not of the world"
and we should not loose sight of the
fact that it is our duty to inaugurate and maintain a higher a nobler
a more God-like Standard in the world.
I do not mind how much life or
activity children possess, the more the
better, in the bounds of reason. but they
should be taught, should know, and
should observe good manners, courtesy
to strangers - and to all, for good manners begin and centre at home from
which

hallowed circle the genial influence
must radiate like the light from
the Sun, any thing but this in the
shape of good breeding is a counterfeit
Such things as you mention as having
occurred at South Willow Creek, are of
almost daily occurrence in this County
But that does not lessen the horror of
such abominable wickedness. Two men
were hanged in this town on Monday,
one for murdering a little girl six years
old, he murdered the innocent little child
to conceal his other brutalities, another
for murdering his mistress. And there
are several more whose cases are still
pending. How I rejoice at the hanging
of such villains by the neck! If some
vigilant Committee would pay their ear
nest respects to McKean, Baskin, Maxwell & Co. what a sweet savor would go
up to heaven, and what rottenness and
corruption down to hell! Excuse my bile.
Be good to yourself and family. God bless
you. Kind love to all, Your brother Jos. F. Smith

Joseph F. to Martha Ann, 31 March 1875 (p. 3)

Joseph F. to Martha Ann, 31 March 1875 (p. 4)

You must be careful of Mary[494] and keep her <from> the influences of bad associat[*0.9 x 0.91 cm tear*][495] you cannot be too careful. Your little ones are in greater danger of evil companionship, and perhaps more susceptible of the effects of bad influences, than they would be under more favorable circumstances.

Notwithstanding poverty and social inequality in consequence, studiously [**p. 3**] carefully, and by prayer endeavor to instill into the minds of your children principles of the highest honor, and the purest truth, and virtue. While you teach them not <to> covet that which is not their own, nor to envy the rich, teach them that it is honor, truth, virtue, industry, temperence

494. Mary Emily Harris was nine years old at this time.
495. The original letter has a tear at this point. However, the letterpress copybook preserves a complete copy of the letter, allowing for a complete transcription at this point, "associates."

and economy that make sterling men and women. Not dress fine houses nor gold and silver. These go a great way in the eyes of the world, and are valued highly, but we "are not of the world"[496] and we should not losee sight of the fact that it is our duty to inaugurate and maintain, a higher a nobler a more God-like standard in the world.

I do not mind how much life or activity children possess, the more the better, in the bounds of reason. but they should be taught, should know, and should observe good manners, courtesy to strangers—and to all, for good manners begin, and centres—at home from <which> **[p. 4]** hallowed circle the genial influence must radiate, like the light from the Sun, any thing but this in the shape of good breeding is a counter feit.

Such things[497] as you mention as having occurred at South Willow Creek,[498] are of almost daily occurrence in this country. But that does not lessen the horror of such abominable wickedness. Two m[*0.6 x 1.3 cm tear*][499] were hanged in this town on Monday, one for murdering a little girl six years old, he murdered the innocent little child to conceal his other brutalities, another for murdering his mistress.[500] And there are several more whose cases are still pending.[501] How I rejoice at the hanging of such villains by the neck! If some vigilant committee[502] would pay their earnest respects to McKean, Baskin, Maxwell & Co.[503] what a sweet savor would go up to heaven, and what rottenness and corruption <down> to hell! Excuse my bile.[504]

Be good to yourself and family. God bless you. Kind love to all, Your brother Jos. F. Smith

496. John 17:16.
497. An unknown incident.
498. Ebenezar Brown came to South Willow Creek, a tributary stream of the Jordan River, in 1849 to graze cattle, and during the following year he established his family in the area. Additional settlers arrived, and by 1850 about twenty families had built homes along South Willow Creek. Four years later in 1854, a post office was established named Draperville after the local bishop, William Draper. The name was shortened to Draper thereafter.
499. The original letter has a tear at this point. However, the letterpress copybook preserves a complete copy of the letter, allowing for a complete transcription at this point: "Two men were hanged."
500. There were thirty-seven executions in England in 1875, many of them reported in newspapers throughout England and the United States. A Liverpool newspaper reported the execution of Richard Coates, age twenty-one, for the murder of "six year old girl [Alice Boughen] on Monday [29 March]." See "The Purfleet Murder," *Liverpool Mercury*, 30 March 1875, [6]. See also the report under the same title on 29 March 1875, [7], for more details about the crime. The paper reports other executions at this time, but not for a man who killed his mistress. See, for example, "Stafford Murder," *Liverpool Mercury*, 31 March 1875, 6; and "Executions and Murders," *The Times* [London], 31 March 1875, 10.
501. The Liverpool paper reported that Robert Searle was awaiting execution for a murder in Hull, England, at the time. See "Two of the Visiting Justices of York Castle," *Liverpool Mercury*, 27 March 1875, [7].
502. Vigilance Committees were organized in many states and territories in the western United States before and after the Civil War to maintain law and order and administer summary justice when citizens believed governmental law enforcement was unable to protect people. These committees attempted to provide safety, security, and stability. See Roger D. McGrath, *Gunfighters, Highwaymen and Vigilantes* (Berkeley, CA: University of California Press, 1984).
503. Utah chief justice James B. McKean, attorney Robert N. Baskin, and territorial marshal George R. Maxwell, influential leaders in the anti-Church Liberal Party. See also biographical register, "Baskin, Robert N." and "Maxwell, George R."
504. A word that means anger or irritability.

JOSEPH F. TO MARTHA ANN, 15 MAY 1875

May[505] 15th. 75[506]

My Dear Sister;
Martha Ann:

Your kind favor of Apr. 2d. and 8th came to hand Apr. 29th. and found me enjoying my usual health, and many other blessings. I wish you could say as much for yourself. I hope your health will improve, but while you and all the children are clustered up in one small room to sleep, I cannot see how you can have health, nor how you can live long.

There should not more than two persons **[p. 2]** sleep in ~~in~~ your small bed room at a time—indeed it would be better for only one person; but to have your whole family crowded into it to sleep it is almost as sure a destruction of health and life as strychnine itself. There is one consolation, you can spread out more in the summer. And I hope William[507] can put up an addition this summer with all those boys to help him which will relieve you from the necessity of crowding so closely to gether to sleep.

All hands of them could make adobes enough in a week to build a mansion almost. one mason and one good carpenter would be all the help necessary to **[p. 3]** hire, against which there would be the time and labor of William and all of the boys who can work, and even Frankie,[508] could help his Papa build a house. Lumber, nails, glass, locks and paint, would not be much for your present necessity. and all the rest adobes, rocks, sand, clay, and labor, you have in your own hands. You remember the adobe hole in front of the old house on the farm.[509]

How much <u>money</u> did it cost Mother[510] to build the old farm house?[511] we hauled the rocks, sand, clay, made the adobes out of the very door yard, cut logs in the cañons, made the lumber and shingles on shares—hauled them—and did all the labor, except making the sash[512] and **[p. 4]** doors, and laying up the walls. We even put on the roof and hung the doors fitted in the sash, put in the glass and paid for hired help in labor—teaming, and the products of the farm, no money! "Where there's a will there's a way"![513]

---

505. Written on official Church letterhead, 42 Islington, Liverpool.
506. The blue plain envelope is addressed to "Mrs. Martha A. Harris Provo, Utah Co. Utah Territory, U.S.A." with the word *America* in the upper left corner. The letter has a Liverpool postmark, "15 MY 75." There are three "Penny Red" stamps that depict Queen Victoria, with cancellation marks across each one. A watermark on the right side of the stamp reveals the printing plate number, "175." The red color made it easier to see a black cancellation mark. There is an additional New York City postmark located in the center of the letter.
507. William Jasper Harris.
508. Franklin Hill Harris was only seven at the time of this letter.
509. Mary Fielding Smith built an adobe cabin in 1850 on the forty-acre farm shortly after she arrived in Utah. Given the lack of trees in the Salt Lake Valley, adobe was a popular building material. Bricks were fashioned by combining sand, clay, water, and a fibrous material and then drying them in the sun. Apparently a pit was dug at the Smith property as a source for the clay or sand used to make the adobe bricks.
510. Mary Fielding.
511. This house was located at what is now 2700 South Highland Drive, Salt Lake City.
512. The sash is the frame that holds the glass in a window.
513. An English proverb that means a way can be found to accomplish a task if someone has desire to do so despite any obstacles.

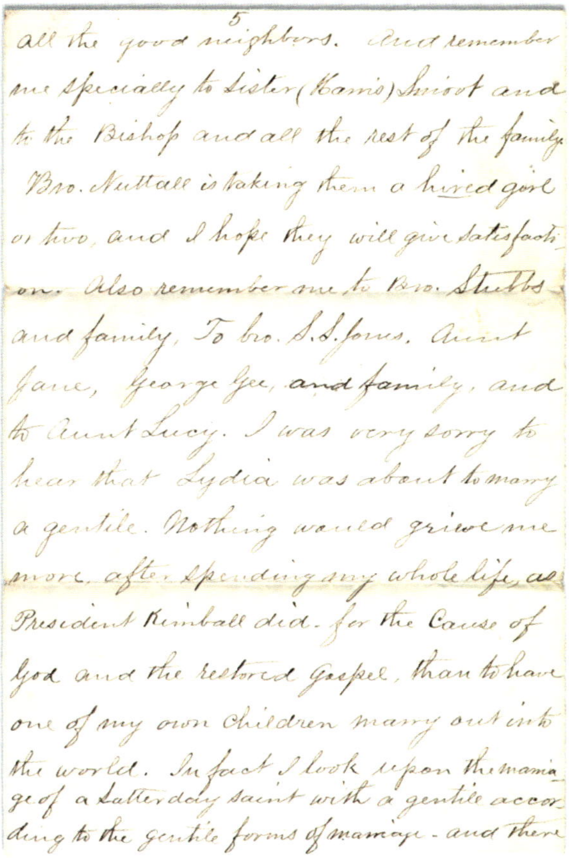

5
all the good neighbors. And remember me Specially to Sister (Harris) Smoot and to the Bishop and all the rest of the family. Bro. Nuttall is taking them a hired girl or two, and I hope they will give satisfacti-on. Also remember me to Bro. Stubbs and family, To bro. S.S. Jones. Aunt Jane, George Gee, and family, and to Aunt Lucy. I was very sorry to hear that Lydia was about to marry a gentile. Nothing would grieve me more. after spending my whole life, as President Kimball did. for the Cause of God and the restored Gospel, than to have one of my own Children marry out into the world. In fact I look upon the marria-ge of a Latterday saint with a gentile accor-ding to the gentile forms of marriage - and there

Joseph F. to Martha Ann, 15 May 1875 (p. 5)

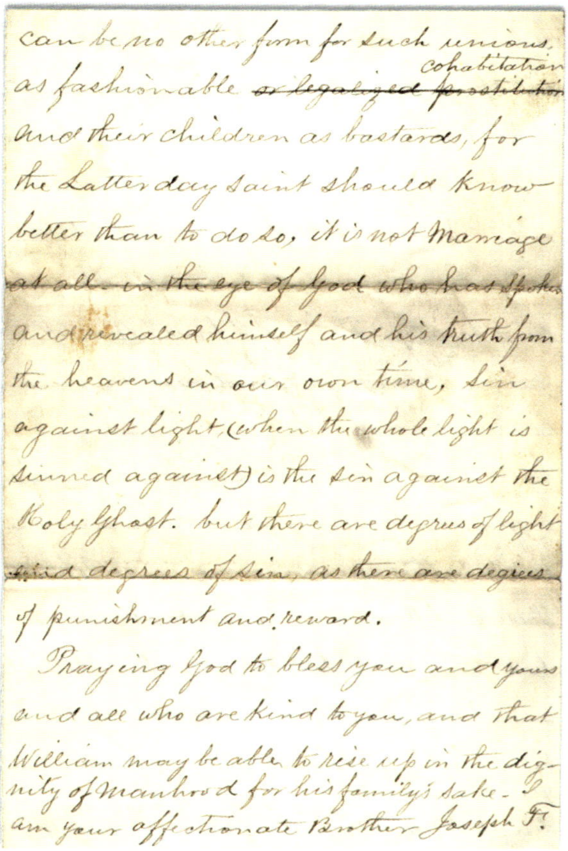

can be no other form for such unions. as fashionable ~~or legalized prostitution~~ cohabitation And their children as bastards, for the Latter day Saint should know better than to do so, it is not Marriage at all in the eye of God who has spoken and revealed himself and his truth from the heavens in our own time, Sin against light, (when the whole light is sinned against) is the sin against the Holy Ghost. but there are degrees of light and degrees of sin, as there are degrees of punishment and reward.

Praying God to bless you and yours and all who are kind to you, and that William may be able to rise up in the dignity of manhood for his family's sake. I am your affectionate Brother Joseph F.

Joseph F. to Martha Ann, 15 May 1875 (p. 6)

I sent you by bro. L. John Nuttall[514] a dress piece—14 yards—like the enclosed bit for a good strong summer dress for you. It is half wool and half cotton. and is said to wear well. I do not think you will admire the color very much but it will wash, and is strong.

I go to London to day, all being well, attend Conference[515] tomorrow, and then go to Denmark. I shall return to England in about 15 or 20 days. Remember me kindly to bro. and sister Mecham,[516] and [**p. 5**][517] all the good neighbors. And remember me specially to sister (Harris) Smoot and to the Bishop[518] and all the rest of the family.

Bro. Nuttall is taking them a <u>hired</u> girl or two, and I hope they will give satisfaction. Also remember me to Bro. Stubbs and family, To bro. S. S. Jones, Aunt Jane,[519] George Gee, and

514. L. John Nuttall was serving as a missionary in the British Mission and returned home on 4 June 1875. See biographical register, "Nuttall, Leonard John."

515. Joseph F. presided at the London Conference held in the Horn's Assembly Rooms, Kennington Park Road, on Sunday, 16 May 1875. See London Conference," *Millennial Star*, 31 May 1855, 337–40; and "London Conference," *Millennial Star*, 7 June 1875, 353–57.

516. Edward Mecham and Sophia Barrows.

517. Pages 1–4 were located in Joseph F.'s letter book in the CHL. Pages 5 and 6 come from the letters found by Carole Call King. See introductory material.

518. Emily Harris and her husband, Bishop Abraham O. Smoot.

519. Mary Jane Smith, mother of George Washington Gee II.

family, and to Aunt Lucy.[520] I was very sorry to hear that Lydia was about to marry a gentile.[521] Nothing would grieve me more, after spending my whole life, as President Kimball did—for the Cause of God and the restored Gospel, than to have one of my own children marry out into the world.[522] In fact I look upon the marriage of a Latter day saint with a gentile according to the gentile forms of marriage—and there [**p. 6**] can be no other form for such unions, as fashionable ~~or legalized prostitution~~ <cohabitation> and their children as bastards, for the Latter day saint should know better than to do so, it is not Marriage at all—in the eye of God who has spoken and revealed himself and his truth from the heavens in our own time, sin against light, (when the whole light is sinned against) is the sin against the Holy Ghost. but there are degrees of light and degrees of sin, as there are degrees of punishment and reward.

Praying God to bless you and yours and all who are kind to you, and that William[523] may be able to rise up in the dignity of manhood for his family's sake— I am your affectionate Brother Joseph F.

JOSEPH F. TO MARTHA ANN, 7 SEPTEMBER 1875

42, Islington, Liverpool,[524]
Sept. 7th. 1875[525]

My Dear Sister,
Martha Ann:—

I have been very neglectful in not answering your letter of ~~July 3^{d}~~ June 9. which reached me July 3$^{d.}$ but I have been busy as well—so you must excuse me. and when you answer this, direct to P.O. Box 321. Salt Lake City. I received yesterday a letter from Pres. B. Young. releasing me to return home Sept. 15th from this port—with our company that sails at that time. Bro. Carrington[526] being on the way to relieve me.

520. Likely Lucy Walker, wife of Heber C. Kimball. See Joseph F. to Martha Ann, 1 July 1873, herein, note 298.
521. In nineteenth-century Latter-day Saint usage, *Gentile* was a person who was not a Latter-day Saint. The term could be used pejoratively, or it could be used fondly to describe a friendly person who was not a Latter-day Saint.
522. Though the marriage was apparently delayed, Lydia Holmes Kimball, daughter of Heber C. Kimball and Lucy Walker, married Frances Xavier Loughery, who was not a Latter-day Saint, on 12 June 1875. See biographical register, "Kimball, Lydia Holmes."
523. William Jasper Harris Jr.
524. Written on official letterhead of the Latter-day Saints' European Printing, Publishing, and Emigration Office.
525. Joseph F. noted, "I wrote to the following named persons. F. M. Lymn, B. H. Watts, James Payne, John Woodhouse, C. E. Griffin, Peter Sinclair, The Capital Publishing Company, Julina & Sarah, J. U. Stucki, Fred Theurer, Mercy. R. Thompson, Jesse N. Smith, Martha Ann Harris, L. John Nuttall, S. H. B. Smith, H. H. Cluff, N. C. Tlygare & H. J. Richards, very busy today." Joseph F., journal, 7 September 1875.
526. Albert Carrington presided over the European Mission three separate times during his life: 1871–73, 1875–77, and 1880–82. He departed Utah Territory for England with his wife and son on 25 August 1875. See "Local and Other Matters: Departure," *Deseret News*, 1 September 1875, 488. See also biographical register, "Carrington, Albert."

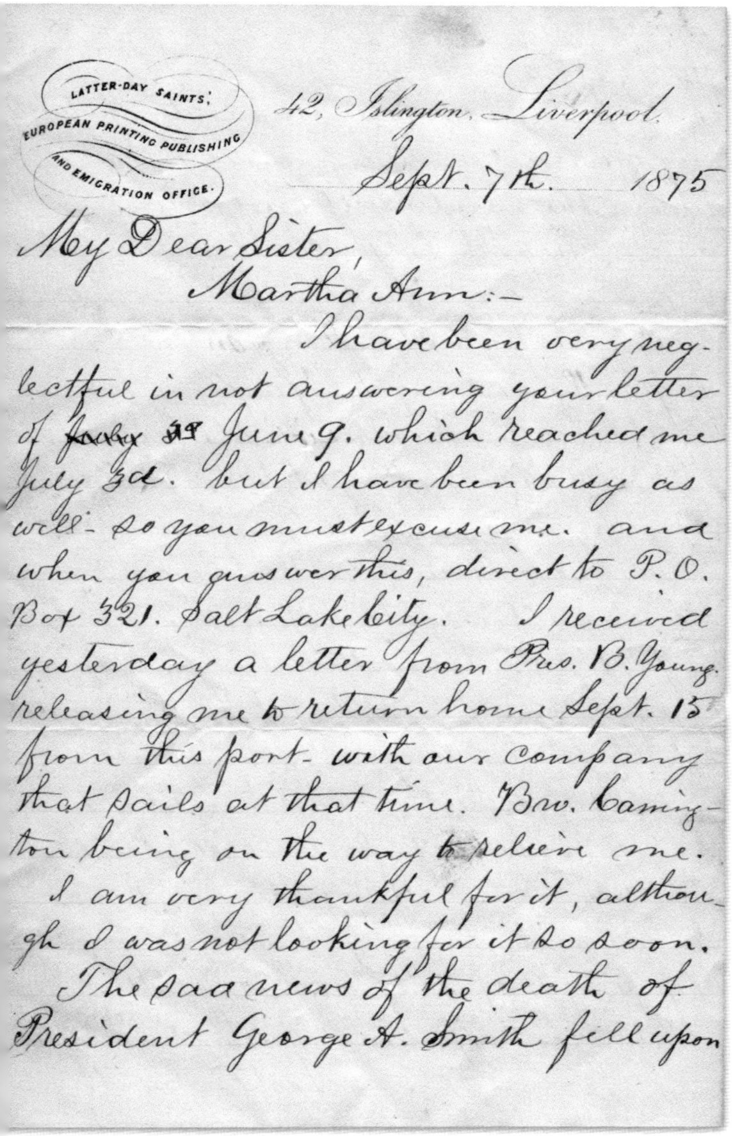

LATTER-DAY SAINTS' EUROPEAN PRINTING PUBLISHING AND EMIGRATION OFFICE.

42, Islington, Liverpool.
Sept. 7th. 1875

My Dear Sister,
Martha Ann:—
I have been very neglectful in not answering your letter of ~~July 29~~ June 9. which reached me July 3d. but I have been busy as well—so you must excuse me. and when you answer this, direct to P.O. Box 321. Salt Lake City. I received yesterday a letter from Pres. B. Young. releasing me to return home Sept. 15 from this port—with our company that sails at that time. Bro. Carrington being on the way to relieve me. I am very thankful for it, although I was not looking for it so soon. The sad news of the death of President George A. Smith fell upon

Joseph F. to Martha Ann, 7 September 1875 (p. 1)

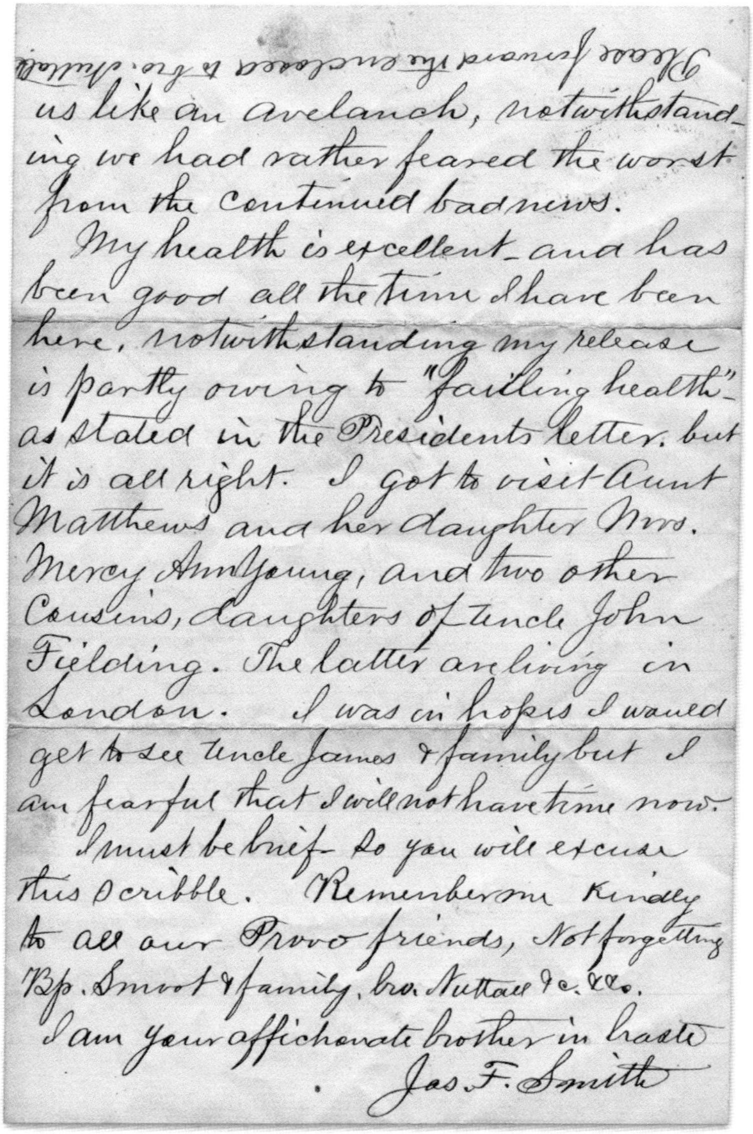

us like an avelanch, notwithstanding we had rather feared the worst from the continued bad news.
My health is excellent—and has been good all the time I have been here, notwithstanding my release is partly owing to "failing health"—as stated in the Presidents letter. but it is all right. I got to visit Aunt Matthews and her daughter Mrs. Mercy Ann Young, and two other Cousins, daughters of uncle John Fielding. The latter are living in London. I was in hopes I would get to see uncle James & family but I am fearful that I will not have time now.
I must be brief—so you will excuse this scribble. Remember me kindly to all our Provo friends, Not forgetting Bp. Smoot & family, Bro. Nuttall &c. &c.
I am your affectionate brother in haste
Jas. F. Smith

Joseph F. to Martha Ann, 7 September 1875 (p. 2)

I am very thankful for it, although I was not looking for it so soon.

The sad new of the death of President George A. Smith[527] fell upon [**p. 2**] us like an avelanch, notwithstanding we had rather feared the worst from the continued bad news.

527. George A. Smith, counselor in the First Presidency, died 1 September 1875 after an illness of several months, which had begun as a cold contracted during one of his several trips from St. George to Salt Lake City. Joseph F. filled pages of his journal with thoughts on the occasion, of which the following, from 2 September 1875, is a sampling: "This evening I received a cable dispatch from Elder W. C. Staines, saying. 'President Geo. A. Smith died yesterday.' I cannot tell with what terrible weight this melancholy intelligence fell upon my soul. . . . The world has lost a bright light, and an honest man The Saints a wise and faithful counseller, a Prophet, Seer and Revelator. and as true a friend as Christ the Lord. As for myself, I feel as though he were my own father, and my greatest Earthly benefactor."

My health is excellent—and has been good all the time I have been here, notwithstanding my release is partly owing to "failling health"—as stated in the Presidents letter.[528] but it is all right. I got to visit Aunt Matthews and her daughter Mrs. Mercy Ann Young,[529] and two other Cousins, daughters of Uncle John Fielding.[530] The latter are living in London. I was in hopes I would get to see Uncle James[531] & family but I am fearful that I will not have time now.

I must be brief—so you will excuse this scribble. Remember me kindly to all our Provo friends, Not forgetting Bp. Smoot & family, bro. Nuttall &c. & &[◊].[532]

I am your affichonate brother in haste
Jos. F. Smith

Please forward the enclosed to bro. Nuttall[533]

JOSEPH F. TO MARTHA ANN, 26 NOVEMBER 1875

Salt Lake City
Nov. 26th 1875

My Dear Sister,
Martha Ann:

I learned with deep[◊◊] regret day before yesterday of the accident which befell Hyrum[534] (I suppose) in the factory the day before. I was in hopes to have learned the particulars ere this, but seeing nothing more than the notice which appeared in the Herald[535] I thought I would drop you a line expressive of my sympathy, and that of the girls,[536] for you under your trying misfortune, and also to express the hope that the injurie[◊] to Hyrums hand [*illegible word*] so severe as at first feared.

528. Joseph F., journal, 6 September 1875: "[Brigham Young] had been informed that my health was impaired and it was thought best for me to return home and recruit. I am happy to say my health is and has been good, equal to what it is at home. Nevertheless I am thankful for the privilege of going to my family."
529. Ann Fielding (the sister of Mary Fielding Smith) and her daughter Mercy Ann Matthews. See biographical register, "Fielding, Ann" and "Matthews, Mercy Ann."
530. John Osborn Fielding, brother of Mary Fielding Smith, had four daughters. Dorothy Rachel Fielding lived with her husband and children in London by at least 1881, according to the England census. She is likely one of the daughters referred to here. Joseph F. is also likely referring to Mary Fielding in 1878. See biographical register, "Fielding, John Osborn," "Fielding, Dorothy Rachel," and "Fielding, Mary" (cousin of Joseph F. and Martha Ann).
531. James Ibbotson Fielding, brother of Mary Fielding Smith. See biographical register, "Fielding, Rev. James Ibbotson."
532. Abraham O. Smoot and Leonard J. Nuttall. See Joseph F. to Martha Ann, 5 August 1874, herein.
533. Written upside down in the top margin of page 2.
534. Hyrum Smith Harris.
535. The *Salt Lake Daily Herald* reported the following on 24 November 1875: "Accident. Yesterday morning a boy about 13 years of age, a son of Wm. Harris, of Provo, at work in the Provo woolen factory, had his hand badly mangled by being caught in the cogs of a carding machine. The wounds were dressed, and all hopes are entertained that no very serious consequences may ensue."
536. "The girls" refers to Joseph F.'s three wives.

I have just returned from the funeral of Uncle Elias' last twin baby, which died yesterday and was buried today by the side of his little twin brother this makes three children buried for them.[537]

Nearly [◊◊]y body is suffering from terrible cold [*illegible word*] "epizootic",[538] probably to speak more c[◊◊]tly influenza. I am [**p. 2**] sorry to say that Sarah is considera[*1.3 x 4 cm tear*] "under the weather" with that or some other ailment just now. The children are so far all well, and my own health is excellent. Aunt Thompson[539] is also sick with the "bad cold." Julina and Edna[540] are well, and as cross as ever, which, when translated, means that they are charmingly good natured.

I hope you reached home in safety and found all well on your arrival.

Remember us kindly to all our friends you may chance to meet in Provo. and try to take care of yourself, do not [*1 x 0.3 cm fold*]orry over what is unavoidable, continue to look on the bright side of life—if it has but a <u>shadow</u> of ~~the~~ brightness, and trust in the providence of God.

Praying for your comfort and prosperity, and with kindly regards to William[541] and all the children in which the family joine, I am your friend and brother Joseph

JOSEPH F. TO MARTHA ANN, 27 FEBRUARY 1876

Sunday Morning
Salt Lake City
February 27th 1876[542]

My Dear Sister Martha Ann

Your very Welcom favor bearing date of Feb. 23 Came duly to hand. I glad to hear from you, It is true that it has been a long time since I wrote to you, but notwithstanding all this I have not forgoten you neither do I forget any of my conections or friends although is may seen so by my negligence, I am glad to learn that you and yours are in the Enjoyment of a Moderate degree of good health as your found us. We all have a turn of very bad colds combined with sore throats with a slight lever. [**p. 2**] The children have been the worst in that respect. and Hellen[543] is all most worn out with hara most and care of the children.

but we are now all out of danger and the children are playing abbout as well as usual. as reg~~p~~ards my health is as good as I can expect until the weather gets better, I have been very lame this winter with my knee. but it is much better now and I feel very well only a Cold

537. Thomas King Smith and Edward Hunter Smith were born to Amy Jane King and Elias Smith on 5 August 1875. Thomas died on 12 August and Edward on 25 November 1875. They had previously lost another son, Albert William Smith. See biographical register, "Smith, Thomas King" and "Smith, Edward Hunter."
538. Also known as Canadian horse disease. The illness was signaled by a dry cough, labored breathing, and mucus discharge from the nostrils. See "The Epizootic and How to Treat It," *Deseret News*, 6 November 1872, 597.
539. Mercy Rachel Fielding.
540. Joseph F.'s wives Julina Lambson and Edna Lambson.
541. William Jasper Harris.
542. Joseph F. was thirty-seven, and Martha Ann was thirty-four.
543. Perhaps referring to Sarah Ellen Smith or to Joseph F. and Martha Ann's half sister Hellen Maria Fisher.

which makes me cough some but I shall be all right when warm weather comes Libby's[544] baby (Manny) is well and harty all right now and Libby has **[p. 3]** another baby born on Valintyne's day (14th Feb.) all doing well. (a girl)

I recieved a letter from Charley[545] yesterday all was well up there,[546] Hyrum[547] was up to Jerusha's about three weeks ago all were well there And all were well at Levina's[548] on Hyrum's return, Joseph's folks[549] are also well although the children have had the Scalet fever

As regard the Crow you may have to pick with me that is all right I can stand you off any time. so pitch in. for I would rather fight a little than write a letter. Well Martha ann I realize your feelings **[p. 4]** in regards to being away off seperated from the rest of the family. I know what it is to be from home and and how one feels when they are homesick and a little cry for those who com cry gives a relief to the mind and makes one feel better after we get over it. Well, I could write oftener but I don't that is all the reason I have to offer, Well My sister when our long financiel lone takes a turn and we (if we ever should) get hold of something to make our selves comfortable and have enough to make a show a few ruffles, frills, Gold and diamond rings fine horses with Eymppages Etc. Etc. then we shall have all the new friends we want and more too

JOSEPH F. TO MARTHA ANN, 11 JULY 1876

S. L. City July 11. 1876[550]

My Dear Sister
Martha Ann

Yours of Mar. 5th is still before me. I thought I would answer it even now. I am always glad to hear from you but sometimes it is not convenient for me to answer at the time of receiving a letter and then it is laid away until a more convenient time, and thus days—weeks and months pass by before that convenient time comes.

I have no news to write except that we are all well once more, and corrispondingly happy. Our little Heber John[551] is a fine boy, his mother is congratulating herself this morning, that this is her last day in bed.

She has done well so far, and the baby is strong and healthy, and has a large nose.

544. Possibly Libby Raymond. She and her husband, William M. Raymond, lived at 144 North 200 West in Salt Lake City, very near Joseph F's home in 1880. They do not appear in any other records except the 1880 census and 1873 and 1874 city directories. See biographical register, "Raymond, Libby."

545. Charles Emerson Griffin, brother-in-law to Joseph F. and Martha Ann.

546. Weber County, Utah.

547. Maybe Hyrum Mack Smith or Hyrum Fisher Smith, nephew of Joseph F. and Martha Ann.

548. Lovina Smith Walker.

549. Presumably the Fishers.

550. From Joseph F.'s letterpress copybooks; original not extant. Joseph F. was thirty-seven, and Martha Ann was thirty-four.

551. Heber John Smith was born to Sarah Ellen Richards on 3 July 1876.

Julina[552] expects to continue arround for a day or two longer, when we all look for an improvement on her part. She will probably [**p. 2**] be some worse before she is much better.

Sister Smoot can give you an account of Edna,[553] as she saw her yesterday.

Bro. Taylor[554] informed me yesterday that a two days' meeting will be held at Provo on Saturday and Sunday next,[555] and I am expected to be there, so I shall get to see you soon, all being well. It may be rather an awkward time for me on Julina account.

I suppose Aunt Thompson[556] was somewhat disappointed in the naming of our new boy yester day, for as usual, she had a "name" selected for him.

Samuel H. B.[557] received a letter from Uncle William Smith[558] yesterday. I heard it read.

He was 65 years old last mar.,[559] he writes a very good hand. and seems friendly.

The weather is delightful since the late showers, but the worms are destroying the fruit and there is a blight upon the trees, and vermin of multifarius kinds abound.

Inclosed find $1.25 on the Provo Factory,[560] which you will please use at your discretion.

I am as ever your brother Joseph F.——

JOSEPH F. TO MARTHA ANN, 25 AUGUST 1877

42 Islington Liverpool England[561]
Aug. 25th 1877[562]

My Dear Sister
Martha Ann

Your welcome favor of July 31st came duly to hand. I was glad to hear from you, as I always am. We are all well here, and getting along the best we can, so far from home, and family and the people of God. There are a great many indifferent and inimical[563] people among us at home, I am well aware, but there we at least expect the majority we meet are friendly to us.

Here to meet a friend is so rare that when we do we are surprised, as much as delighted. For some cause the world of mankind are filled with not only unfriendly feelings towards us, but with actual hatered and enmity, and yet not one of the whole world can give a valid

552. Julina Lambson.
553. Likely Edna Lambson.
554. Likely John Taylor. See biographical register, "Taylor, John."
555. See "Provo Meetings," *Deseret News*, 19 July 1876, 392.
556. Mercy Rachel Fielding.
557. Samuel Harrison Bailey Smith.
558. William Smith, uncle of Joseph F. and Martha Ann, had been excommunicated from the Church in 1845. He eventually joined the RLDS Church in 1878. See biographical register, "Smith, William."
559. William Smith was born on 13 March 1811.
560. The Provo Woolen Mills.
561. Joseph F. was called to preside a second time over the European Mission, with Elders Alma L. Smith and Charles W. Nibley as counselors during the 47th Annual General Conference on 7 April 1877. Joseph F. took his wife Sarah and their four-year-old son, Joseph Richards, with him, arriving in Liverpool on 27 May 1877. This mission was cut short, however, when Brigham Young died on 29 August 1877.
562. Joseph F. was thirty-eight, and Martha Ann was thirty-six.
563. In this context, *inimical* refers to an unfriendly or hostile person.

reason for such a condition of mind. The spirit of Christ was "peace on earth, and good will to man",[564] these enlightened (?) nations loudly profess their love for him, and their faith in his doctrine, yet they hate their neighbor without a cause, and their hearts are filled with enmity toward their fellow creatures for no other reason than because they are called "Mormons". I am convinced there is something in a name. yet it is not the name, for if we were called Angels and professed and practiced the precepts and doctrins of the scriptures and of truth as we do, it would be all the same. This generation cannot endure sound doctrine, their ears are turned unto fables, they fall a ready and willing prey to delusions and doctrines of Devils, having **[p. 2]** their consciences seared as with a hot iron.[565] The pivilege and blessing of friends and neighbors are denied us here, therefore our hearts are where our treasures are,[566] in Heaven and at home. I wish you were as strong and healthy as I am, and as well or better clad. I am neither sick nor pale nor ragged, so your dream must have come from a late supper, over fatigue or some other disorder of your own stomache or immagination. The Lord will take care of me, wherein I lack the ability myself, so long as I am true to my covenants, never fear. He has done it so far, and I'll trust him for the future. I was sorry to hear that the boys had such bad luck with their farming operations. They must not be discouraged with trifles. Remember the motto—"try—try again".[567]

Sarah[568] gets along very well. She thinks it will not take her long to get ready to start, when the time comes to go home, nor do I.

I do not wonder at the girls not writing, they scarcely get time to write to me. They have everything to do themselves, which is no small task with so many little folks to care for all the time, cows to feed and milk and house work to do, and no man at home to lighten their cares. I donot see how they could get time to visit much, very far from home. I hope the way will open for you to be comfortable this winter and that you will lack nothing necessary to this end.

I suppose Owen and Willie Smoot will return home this fall, but not before October.[569] I want to keep them as long as I can. They are good boys—and I dislike to part with them.

Remember me kindly to Pres. Smoot[570] and family, to William[571] and all the Children, in which request Sarah joines.[572] May God bless you all. And believe me ever your affectionate brother Joseph F.——

P.S. five cents is all that is needed to send a letter not over 2 oz. to England[573]

564. Luke 2:14.
565. See 1 Timothy 4:1–2; 2 Timothy 4:3–4.
566. See Matthew 6:21; Luke 12:34.
567. Published as early as 1840 in Thomas H. Palmer's *Teacher's Manual* but popularized by Edward Hickson's "Moral Song" published in 1857. See Gregory Y. Titelman, *Random House Dictionary of Popular Proverbs and Sayings* (New York: Random House, 1996), 154.
568. Likely Sarah Ellen Richards.
569. Abraham Owen Smoot Jr., son of Abraham O. Smoot and Diana Eldredge, and William Cochran Adkinson Smoot, adopted son of Abraham O. Smoot and son of Margaret Thompson McMeans. They were serving in the European Mission at this time. See biographical register, "Smoot, Abraham Owen, Jr." and "Adkinson, William Cochran."
570. Brigham Young asked Abraham O. Smoot to move from Salt Lake City to Provo in 1868 to serve as stake president over all of Utah Valley. Martha Ann's mother-in-law, Emily Hill Harris Smoot, A. O. Smoot's plural wife, was the first Smoot family member to relocate to Provo from Salt Lake City in 1868. Martha Ann and family arrived in Provo about the same time.
571. William Jasper Harris.
572. Joseph F.'s wife, Sarah Ellen Richards.
573. Written upside down in the top margin of page 2.

JOSEPH F. TO MARTHA ANN, 29 NOVEMBER 1877

City, Nov. 29, 1877[574]

My Dear Sister
Marth Ann
Provo. Utah Co—

Your favor of 17th inst came to hand yesterday. It must have been waiting for me sometime somewhere. It did not find us all well, our little Joseph F.[575] had been suffering for several days with a high-intermittent fever and sore throat, with a sevier coald. Yesterday we were very much alarmed about him, but today the little cheerful lively soul is playing around as merrily as ever—but somewhat weak and tottering.

We are all happy tonight however [**p. 2**] at the cheering prospects of his final recovery, and of the future good health of all the rest. as well as he. We have enjoyed this thanksgiving day at the House of the Lord,[576] and at home. and have had a general good time, without thanksgiving dinner, holiday, or friends to see us.

It has been like Sunday.

I saw bro. Smoot[577] and L. John Nuttall[578] yesterday after getting your letter, and bro. Smoot promised me to take a day on his return home to make a thorough search for the deed of your property in Provo.[579] I think it will be found, if not, I will see what else can be done. Still [**p. 3**] I would like you to enquire for it, and continue to importune until you see it cannot be found. I am informed the deed is made out for both pieces of land in one. As soon as you get it, have it recorded and then have the deed deposited in some safe place, where it cannot be lost or destroyed.

I am glad to hear William[580] is building a barn. I hope he will be eminantly successful in his enterprise, and that he will come out square at the finish of it. A good barn is the next thing to a good house—indeed, where a team is the main dependence for a family, a good barn should receive the first consideration, and the good house the secondary. for the good barn will save more in proportion than the house, and will therefore do more towards assisting to build a house, than a house would do towards building a barn. Still I think you need both. I wish I had it in my power to help you in them.

Aunt Thompson[581] has received a letter from Cousin Mary Lupton[582]—(I think is her name) now residing in London, asking for means to help her and her daughter to emigrate to Utah, She is the daughter of Uncle John Fielding if I recollect rightly. The are in very poor circumstances. I do not know what will be done for her yet. My family are all well. I am glad to

574. Joseph F. was thirty-nine, and Martha Ann was thirty-six.
575. Joseph Fielding Smith was born to Joseph F. and Julina Lambson on 19 July 1876. See biographical register, "Smith, Joseph Fielding, Jr."
576. Joseph F. worked in the Endowment House. See L. John Nuttall, diary, 29 November 1877, BYU.
577. Abraham O. Smoot.
578. L. John Nuttall. See biographical register, "Nuttall, Leonard John."
579. See Joseph F. to Martha Ann, 22 April 1878, herein.
580. William Jasper Harris.
581. Mercy Rachel Fielding.
582. Mary Fielding, first cousin of Joseph F. and Martha Ann.

hear your baby[583] is better. You must excuse this scribble—I have, hastily scratched it off while waiting for the children to get ready to go out with me—with love Jos F. Smith

JOSEPH F. TO MARTHA ANN, 6 APRIL 1878

"DESERET TELEGRAPH CO."] "DESERET TELEGRAPH CO."] "DESERET TELEGRAPH CO."]

From Salt Lake Apr. 6th 1878[584]

To Mrs. M. A. Harris
Provo

Edna's baby[585] died this morning funeral tomorrow

JOSEPH F. TO MARTHA ANN, 22 APRIL 1878

Salt Lake City
Apr. 22. 1878[586]

My Dear Sister
Martha Ann,

Your kind and welcome favor came duly to hand— I read and passed it over to Edna,[587] and have not seen it since. We miss our sweet little "red" headed boy, so affectionate and tender hearted and so much beloved.[588] Why I lose so many of my children is a mystery to us all, they have all seemed, and were strong and healthy children, the two boys even more so than any we have had, yet it has pleased Father to suffer them to be taken from us.[589] Lung fever[590] seemes

583. Zina Christine Harris was eighteen months old at the time of this letter. See biographical register, "Harris, Zina Christine."

584. Joseph F. was thirty-nine, and Martha Ann was thirty-six.

585. Alfred Jason Smith (13 December 1876–6 April 1878).

586. From Joseph F.'s letterpress copybooks; original not extant. Joseph F. was thirty-nine, and Martha Ann was thirty-six.

587. Edna Lambson.

588. Alfred Jason Smith was born to Edna on 13 December 1876 and died on 6 April 1878. He was Joseph F.'s third child to die in infancy. See biographical register, "Smith, Alfred Jason."

589. Shortly before his death in 1918, Joseph F. reflected, "I struggled along with hard knocks in early life, and believe, perhaps, my wives and I were responsible to some degree, for the loss of some of our children, who were the most beautiful and perfect children that were ever born, because we did not have the nourishment nor the convenience nor the comforts that were necessary to take care of them and to preserve their lives." "Minutes of a Meeting Held at the Bee Hive House, 1918 November 10."

590. Pneumonia.

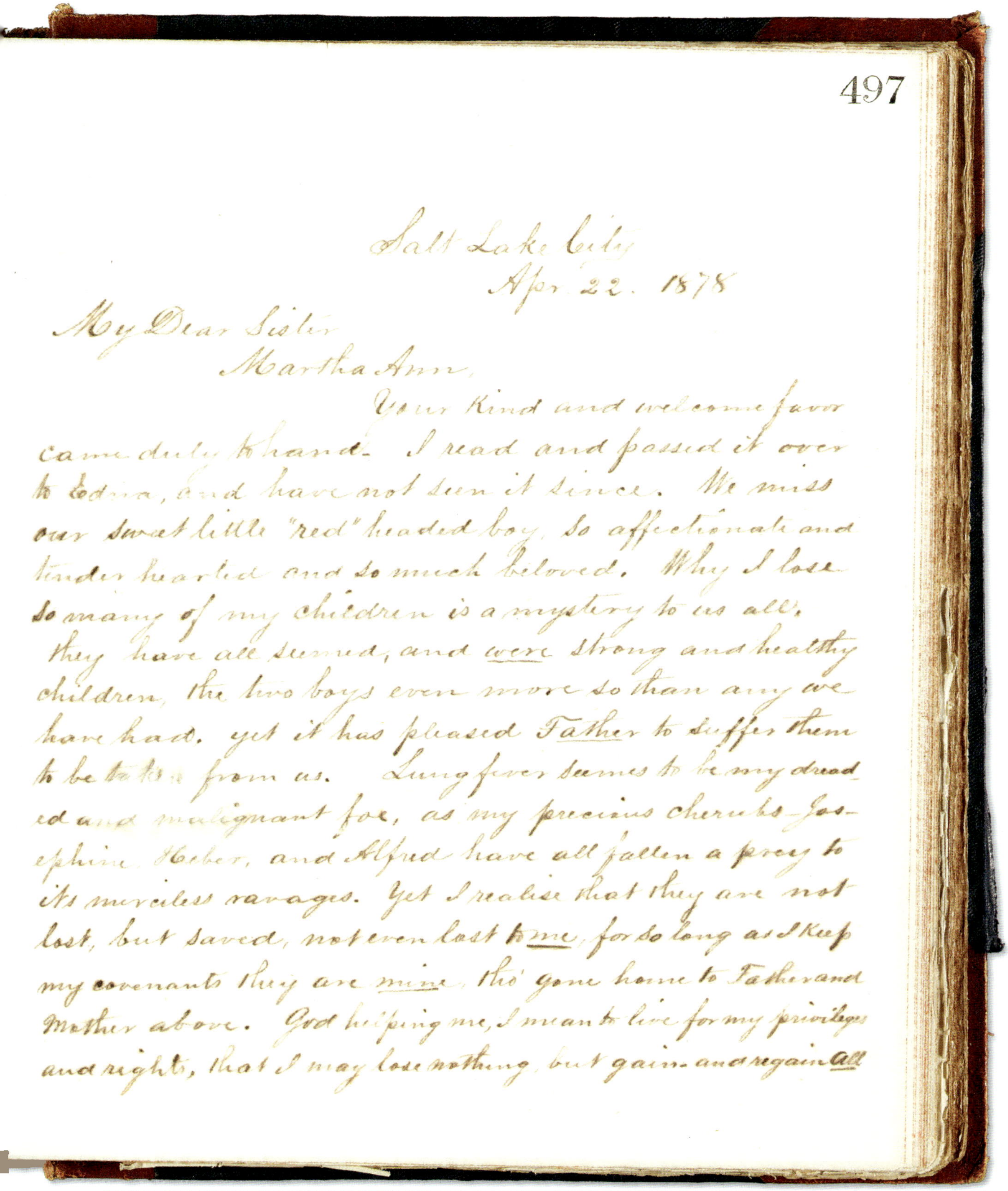

497

Salt Lake City
Apr. 22. 1878

My Dear Sister
Martha Ann.

Your kind and welcome favor
came duly to hand. I read and passed it over
to Edna, and have not seen it since. We miss
our sweet little "red" headed boy, so affectionate and
tender hearted and so much beloved. Why I lose
so many of my children is a mystery to us all.
they have all seemed, and were strong and healthy
children, the two boys even more so than any we
have had. yet it has pleased Father to suffer them
to be taken from us. Lung fever seems to be my dreaded and malignant foe, as my precious cherubs—Josephine, Heber, and Alfred have all fallen a prey to
its merciless ravages. Yet I realise that they are not
lost, but saved, not even lost to me, for so long as I keep
my covenants they are mine, tho' gone home to Father and
Mother above. God helping me, I mean to live for my privileges
and rights, that I may lose nothing, but gain and regain all

Joseph F. to Martha Ann, 22 April 1878 (p. 1), copy found in Joseph F.'s letterpress copybooks under that date.

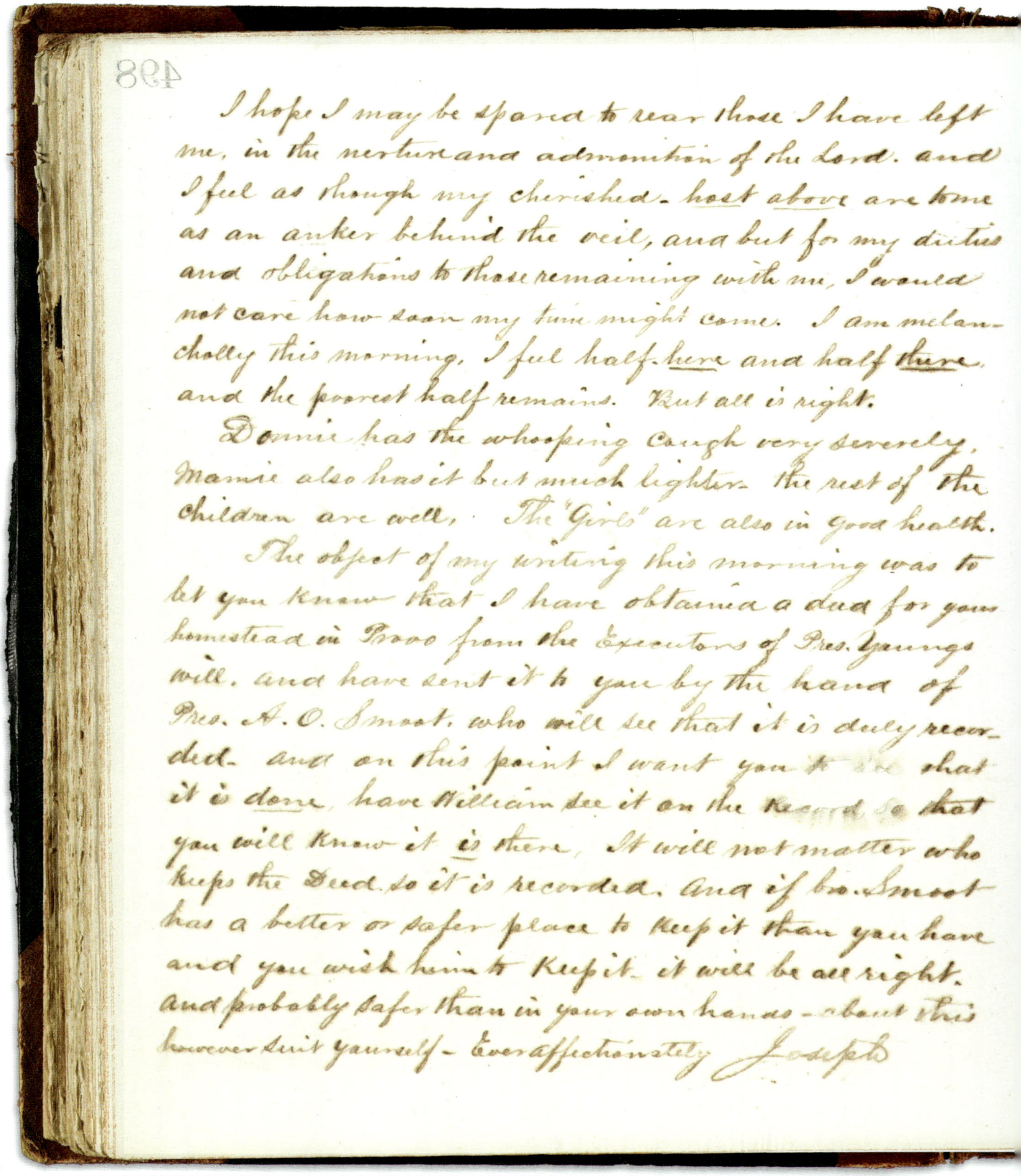
498

I hope I may be spared to rear those I have left me, in the nerture and admonition of the Lord. and I feel as though my cherished host above are to me as an anker behind the veil, and but for my duties and obligations to those remaining with me, I would not care how soon my time might come. I am melancholly this morning. I feel half here and half there. and the poorest half remains. But all is right.

Donnie has the whooping cough very severely. Mamie also has it but much lighter. the rest of the children are well, The "Girls" are also in good health.

The object of my writing this morning was to let you know that I have obtained a deed for your homestead in Provo from the Executors of Pres. Youngs will. and have sent it to you by the hand of Pres. A. O. Smoot. who will see that it is duly recorded. and on this point I want you to see that it is done, have William see it on the Record so that you will know it is there, It will not matter who keeps the Deed so it is recorded. and if bro. Smoot has a better or safer place to keep it than you have and you wish him to keep it. it will be all right. and probably safer than in your own hands. about this however suit yourself. Ever affectionately Joseph

Joseph F. to Martha Ann, 22 April 1878 (p. 2), copy found in Joseph F.'s letterpress copybooks under that date.

to be my dreaded and malignant foe, as my precious cherubs—Josephine, Heber,[591] and Alfred have all fallen a prey to its merciless ravages. Yet I realise that they are not lost, but saved, not even lost to me, for so long as I keep my covenants they are mine, tho' gone home to Father and Mother above.[592] God helping me, I mean to live for my privileges and rights, that I may lose nothing, but gain—and regain All [**p. 2**]

I hope I may be spared to rear those I have left me, in the nerture and admonition of the Lord.[593] and I feel as though my cherished—host above are to me as an anker behind the veil, and but for my duties and obligations to those remaining with me, I would not care how soon my time might come. I am melancholly this morning, I feel half-here and half there, and the poorest half remains. But all is right.

Donnie[594] has the whooping cough very severely, Mamie[595] also has it but much lighter—the rest of the children are well. The "Girls"[596] are also in good health.

The object of my writing this morning was to let you know that I have obtained a deed for your homestead in Provo from the Executors of Pres. Youngs will, and have sent it to you by the hand of Pres. A. O. Smoot, who will see that it is duly recorded[597]—and on this point I want you to see that it is done, have William[598] see it on the Record, so that you will know it is there. It will not matter who keeps the Deed so it is recorded. And if bro. Smoot[599] has a better or safer place to keep it than you have and you wish him to keep it—it will be all right. And probably safer than in your own hands—about this however suit yourself— Ever affectionately
Joseph

JOSEPH F. TO MARTHA ANN, 14 AUGUST 1878

S. L. City Aug. 14th 1878[600]

My Dear Sister
Martha Ann,

591. Mercy Josephine Smith died on 6 June 1870 (see Joseph F. to Martha Ann, 25 June 1870, herein), and Heber John Smith died on 3 March 1877.
592. Hyrum and Mary Fielding Smith or possibly a reference to heavenly parents. See Eliza R. Snow, "My Father in Heaven," later titled "Invocation, or the Eternal Father and Mother," now used as the lyrics in the popular Latter-day Saint hymn "O My Father," *Hymns* (Salt Lake City, UT: The Church of Jesus Christ of Latter-day Saints, 1985), no. 292.
593. Ephesians 6:4, Enos 1:1.
594. Donnette Smith was five years old at this time.
595. Mary Sophronia Smith was eight years old at this time.
596. "The girls" refers to Joseph F.'s three wives: Julina Lambson, Sarah Ellen Richards, and Edna Lambson.
597. This was accomplished a few days later; see 25 April 1878, Transfer of deed of lot 6, block 41 (214 S. 300 W.) from Est. of Brigham Young to Martha A. Smith Harris, Utah County Deed Record, Book G, 602, Utah County Administration Building, Recorders Office, Provo, Utah County, Utah.
598. William Jasper Harris.
599. A. O. Smoot.
600. From Joseph F.'s letterpress copybooks; original not extant.

Your letter without date came safely hand, on my return from the cañon where we had been several days with the children, servis-berrying,[601] and to get a breath of cool, fresh air. We got about two bushels of berries, and had a good time. The family are all well, for which I am very thankful, I am fearful of the fruit season, and the prevalent summer complaints which generally accompany the same. There is considerable sickness of that kind all 'round us, but I hope we shall escape. I am sorry the grass-hoppers have troubled you this season, and I am surprised at it, as I had not heard of there being any in that section of the country.

With regard to Mrs. Cunninghams[602] brother, I can only say, if she has not male relative in the Church, she could send her brothers name, date [**p. 2**] of birth, and place of brrth, with father and Mothers (maiden) name, to Elder John D. T. M^c^Allister[603] at St. George, with the request that he get some one to be baptized, ordained &c.[604] for him,when the Temple is again opened.[605] It is now closed for the present. When it will be opened again I do not know. If she knows of any woman dead—(or other wise) who would have been married to him when living, if dead, her name &c—could also be sent with his, to to recieve such ordinances as would prepare them to be sealed &c. if living the woman would have to attend to the matter in person. We are not performing any ordinances for the dead in the Endowment House hence the necessity of applying to those in charge of the Temple.[606] If she did not want to send particulars to the temple, she ought to make a full Record of her desires and carefully preserve the same, or hand it to some one to do the work, for her brother, when opportunity affords. We are all well the Girls[607] are hard at work—all the time. The weather is very [**p. 3**] oppressively hot—and uncomfortable.

Our new girl[608] is a very-verry little doll—and as sweet as she is little, and as good as she can be Sarah and baby are both well and happy.

Our plumbs and peaches are now getting ripe, our appricots are all gon, Apples nearly all destroyed by worms; I think however we will have a few good apples—this fall.

Aunt Thompson[609] and family are all usually well. Annie Luptons little boy[610] is suffering with the summer complaint,[611] Mary-Jane and Robert[612] are well—so far as I know.

601. Serviceberries have a flavor similar to that of blueberries and were harvested for pies and jams.
602. Mary Hopper Cunningham was the "postmistress" in Provo at this time. See *Utah Directory and Gazetteer for 1879–1880* (Salt Lake City: H. L. A. Culmer & Co. Publishers, 1879), 212. See biographical register, "Hopper, Mary."
603. John Daniel Thompson McAllister was a counselor in the St. George Temple presidency at the time. See biographical register, "McAllister, John Daniel Thompson."
604. These ordinances are preformed vicariously with someone standing in the place of the deceased person.
605. The St. George Temple is located in St. George, Washington County, Utah. Opened in 1877, this was the only fully functional temple operating at the time. The Logan, Manti, and Salt Lake Temples were under construction. Vicarious work for the dead was first performed in the St. George Temple on 11 January 1877. See Bennett, "Line upon Line, Precept upon Precept," 39–67.
606. Built as a temporary structure for sacred temple ordinances, the Endowment House, located on the Temple Block in Salt Lake City, was reserved for living ordinances, the exception being baptisms for the dead.
607. This is a reference to Joseph F.'s wives.
608. Rhoda Ann Smith was born to Sarah Ellen Richards on 20 July 1878. See biographical register, "Smith, Rhoda Ann."
609. Mercy Rachel Fielding.
610. Ann Jane Lupton, daughter of Mary Fielding Lupton, is the first cousin once removed of Joseph F. and Martha Ann. See Joseph F. to Martha Ann, 29 November 1877, herein. She had two sons at this time: Harry Heward, two years old, and Joseph Fielding Heward, one month old. See biographical register, "Lupton, Ann Jane," "Heward, Harry," and "Heward, Joseph Fielding."
611. "Summer complaint," also known as cholera infantum, is an often deadly illness characterized by severe diarrhea.
612. Mary Jane Thompson and Robert Blashel Thompson Taylor.

Willie[613] called to see us on the 4th of July, but only stopped a few minutes, I think he stopped at Johns.[614] While he was here I was very busy answering letters, and had not much chance to visit with him. I hope he will be successful in his work in the cañon, and will get out of there before winter.[615] The life one leads in such places is invariably a rough one, not very elevating to the general moral character. I hope Willie will keep straight. I think he will—

With kind love, in which the Girls[616] joine, and praying God to bless you all, I am Your Brother Joseph

JOSEPH F. TO MARTHA ANN, 23 OCTOBER 1878

S.L. City
Oct. 23d 1878[617]

My Dear Sister
Martha Ann-

Yours of the 20th came to hand this evening. I was very glad to hear from you and to learn you were all well— at least as usual. Sorry to hear Williams[618] health continues feeble— I hope Willie[619] will succeed well in his labors in the canyon,[620] but would like to hear of his getting some good employment down in the valley. as coald weather will make can.yon labor very disagreeable, + it may be dangerous. I hate to see you in debt and having [◊◊] **[p. 2]** pay interest on borrowed money. for my part I cannot afford it. Like yourselves we have too many little feet to shoe— backs to clothe and mouths to feed, to pay interest on money. No man can prosper who has it to do to any extend. and I sincerely trust that with the help of the boys and continued health you will soon be bey[◊◊]d that evil. We are all well, for which I am very thankful I assure you. Aunt T— and M. J.[621] are also usually well. Aunt T[622] is fast growing old now. The girls[623] joine in kind love to you and all. give my kind regards to Joseph Albert.[624] I wish him a long prosperous and happy <life> and a most honorable career. Excuse haste. I have been very busy today— + it is now late— Ever Truly your affectionate Brother Joseph.

613. William Jasper Harris Jr.
614. Likely John Smith.
615. The work referred to here is probably mining or lumbering. Mining in particular was generally viewed in a negative light by some Church leaders.
616. Joseph F.'s wives: Julina Lambson, Sarah Ellen Richards, and Edna Lambson.
617. From Joseph F.'s letterpress copybooks; original not extant.
618. William Jasper Harris.
619. William Jasper Harris Jr.
620. Latter-day Saint settlers exploited the nearby canyons for food, wood, and stone.
621. Mary Jane Thompson.
622. Mercy Rachel Fielding was seventy-one years old.
623. Joseph F.'s wives, Julina Lambson, Sarah Ellen Richards, and Edna Lambson.
624. Martha Ann's son Joseph Albert Harris.

JOSEPH F. TO MARTHA ANN, 22 APRIL 1879

S. L. City
Apr. 22d 1879[625]

My Dear Sister
Martha Ann—

Yours of the 20th inst. came to hand last evening. I was somewhat surprised at the manner of your letter, and am left—after perusing it—as much in ignorence as before as to the nature of your trouble or the cause of your heaviness of heart.

I do not know when I shall be at Provo again, perhaps at the next stake conference[626]—but I cannot tell.[627] I hope there is nothing very serious the matter. For my own part I—and my family are very much troubled just at this time. Our little Rhoda—Sarahs baby,[628] is a very sick child—we fear she has lung fever[629]—that terrible monster which has already carried off three [**p. 2**] of our precious little ones—and we are all very much alarmed about the safety of our darling little Rhoda. I hope we will have your earnest faith and prayers for her safety.

Willie[630] started for home on Friday last but got only to Richard Maxfields, and yesterday he was in the city again. William[631] was here—Friday, Saturday and Sunday nights but was not here last night, we look for him again to night.

Tell me your troubles—by letter—if not otherwise convenient—and if I can do any thing for you I will do my best. Dont borrow trouble! This is good counsel altho' coming from a poor source—

My God bless you and your family— I was at Ogden on Sunday— All were well— Ever faithfully your affectionate brother— Jos. F. Smith

625. From Joseph F.'s letterpress copybooks; original not extant. Joseph F. was forty, and Martha Ann was thirty-seven.

626. In addition to the Church's general conferences held in April and October, local conferences were also held in the individual stakes (geographical units composed of several individual congregations) on a regular basis with general officers of the Church, such as Apostles, attending, presiding, and speaking at these gatherings.

627. The Utah Stake held a quarterly conference 31 May and 1 June 1879, but Joseph F. was not present; see "Utah Stake Conference," *Deseret News*, 11 June 1879, 291. Another quarterly conference was held on 30–31 August 1879, but Joseph F. was not present; see "Local and Other Matters: Utah Stake Conference," *Deseret News*, 10 September 1879, 1. He finally attended the Utah Stake quarterly conference held on 29 November 1879; see "Utah Stake Conference," *Deseret News*, 17 December 1879, 722.

628. Rhoda Ann Smith is Sarah Ellen Richards's youngest child.

629. Pneumonia.

630. William Jasper Harris Jr.

631. William Jasper Harris.

JOSEPH F. TO MARTHA ANN, 7 JULY 1879

S. L. City
July 7, 1879—[632]

My Dear Sister
Martha Ann,

It has become my painful duty to inform you, that we have this day laid away—in the great city of the dead upon the hill[633]—another of my precious little pets.[634]

This time—as heretofore, the victim of the "fell monster" was a shining, beautiful star in my little constellation, the luster of whose presence has been removed for ever from our dreary pathway, and sorrowing circle to cheer and gladden the purer circle and brighter pathway of a holier sphere.

Did they need her more than we? was her presence to them more welcome? were they, without her, as lonely as we are now? could she make them more happy than she did us?

If so, then they are welcome to her, but oh! who can answer the burning quearies **[p. 2]** of our stricken souls—and who can stop the aching void occasioned by her absence from us? This we know—their claim was stronger than ours— We could not keep her—for oh! how we struggled to do so, and yet we could not! how we prayed—and plead—and wept and plead again and again, and our prayers did not prevail and our petitions returned unto us void!

When I think of my beautius, lovely babes whose remains we have deposited in yonder silent, slumbering city—of the dead, my heart in anguish asks why should I lose all the diamonds from my crown of posterity in this life?

God knows best! indeed he only knows, for I do not, nor can I tell. I can think of some reasons why—but others volunterily spring up which overbalance them, so I am left to queary still. In grief we send our love—and I remain your bro— Jos. F.[635]

632. From Joseph F.'s letterpress copybooks; original not extant. Joseph F. was forty, and Martha Ann was thirty-eight.

633. Now comprising about 120 acres, the Salt Lake City Cemetery is located on the east bench between "N" and "U" Streets and 4th Avenue and 11th Avenue. At the time of this letter it comprised 20 acres.

634. Rhoda Ann Smith died on 6 July 1879 "of pleuro-pneumonia, after a painful illness of eight days, at the residence of the parents, 16th Ward of this city [Salt Lake City], Rhoda Ann, infant daughter of Joseph F. and Sarah E. Smith, aged 11 months and 17 days." "Died," *Deseret News*, 16 July 1879, 384.

635. Martha Ann responded to this letter, but the letter is not extant: "I received letters from my Sister Martha A. Harris and Bp. Niels Aagaard of Levan." Joseph F., journal, 10 July 1879.

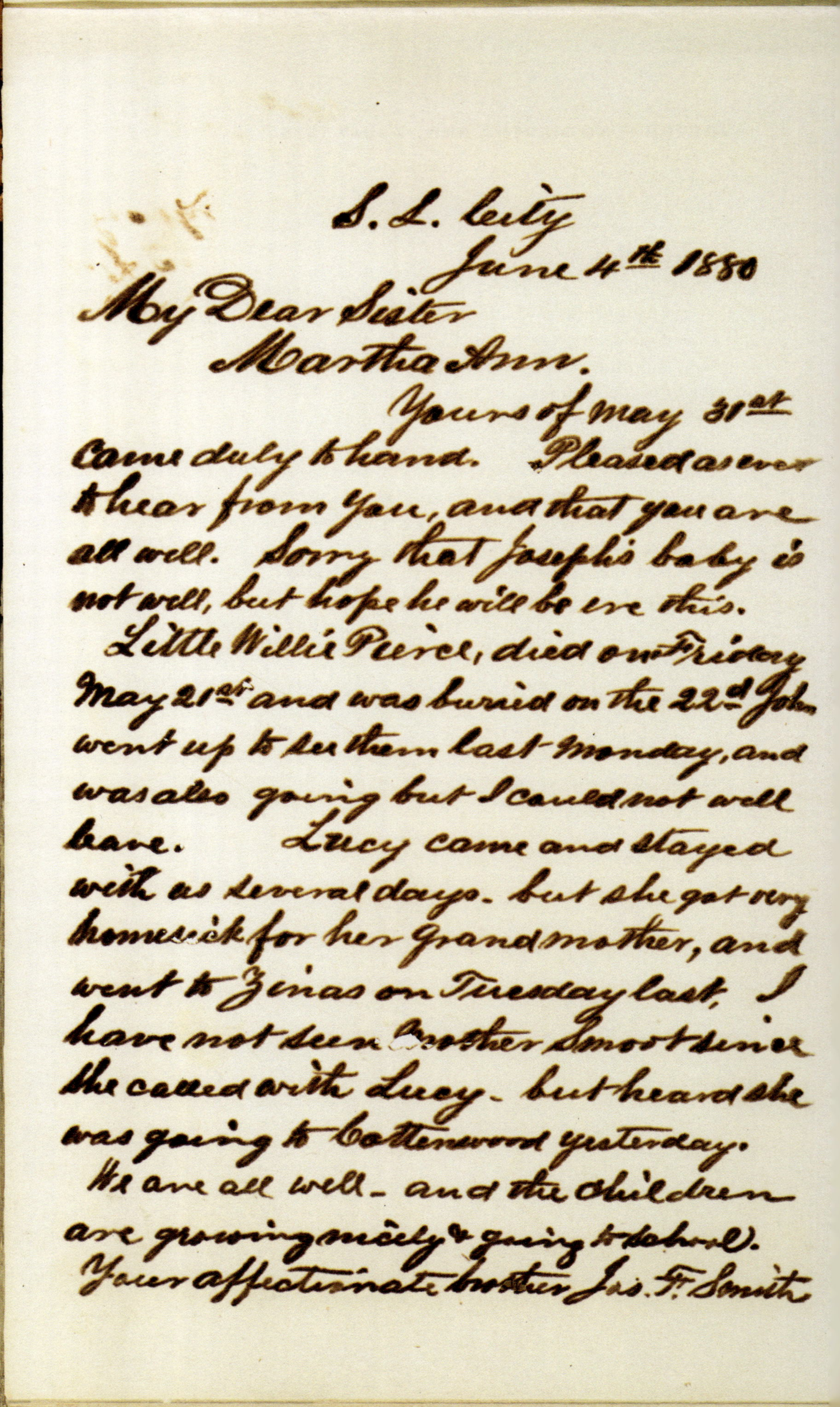

S. L. City
June 4th 1880

My Dear Sister
Martha Ann.

Yours of May 31st came duly to hand. Pleased as ever to hear from you, and that you are all well. Sorry that Joseph's baby is not well, but hope he will be ere this.

Little Willie Peirce, died on Friday May 21st and was buried on the 22d. John went up to see them last Monday, and was also going but I could not well leave. Lucy came and stayed with us several days. but she got very homesick for her Grandmother, and went to Zinas on Tuesday last, I have not seen Brother Smoot since she called with Lucy. but heard she was going to Cottonwood yesterday.

We are all well. and the children are growing nicely & going to school.

Your affectionate brother Jos. F. Smith

Joseph F. to Martha Ann, 4 June 1880, copy found in Joseph F.'s letterpress copybooks under that date.

Decade 4

1880–1889

JOSEPH F. TO MARTHA ANN, HONOLULU, O'AHU, SANDWICH ISLANDS, 18 MARCH 1885

With me it is the Kingdom of God or nothing. My only course is onward and, I trust, upward. I can yeald to nothing but the will and pleasure of the Almighty. It is my delight to serve the Lord and the people of God. . . .

. . . [M]y family have been scattered I hardly know where and I am thousands of miles away from them with out power to look after them. I look and long for my liberty once more, not but what I should be and am content to labor where I am sent and do all I can for good where ever I may be.

MARTHA ANN TO JOSEPH F., PROVO, UTAH, 11 MARCH 1887

[M]y continual prayr for my dear berother is for his safty & I know you~~a~~re in the hands of our Father in Heaven & also are our enimys O may they not have pour to ingure you never & they will not unless it is his will that ~~you~~ they should.

The First Presidency with George Q. Cannon, John Taylor, and Joseph F. Smith, ca. 1880. Courtesy of CHL.

Decade Introduction

The First Presidency of the Church was reorganized in the October 1880 general conference, three years after the death of Brigham Young (1801–77). Joseph F.'s notes, taken at a meeting of the Quorum of the Twelve held in the Endowment House on 9 October, simply stated: "The Twelve met at 6 p.m. in the E. H. when the motion of C. C. Rich & seconded by O. Pratt that we organize the 1st Presidency was put and carried. Then a motion of W. Woodruff John Taylor was chosen President. He then chose G. Q. C & Joseph F. as councillors."[1]

A day later, at a historic Sunday afternoon conference session, John Taylor (1808–87) was sustained as President of The Church of Jesus Christ of Latter-day Saints, with George Q. Cannon and Joseph F. Smith chosen as counselors in the First Presidency.[2] Joseph F. was forty-one years old when called and would serve as a member of the presidency until his own death in 1918, thirty-eight years later.

THE CAMPAIGN AGAINST THE CHURCH

Following the Church's first public acknowledgment on 29 August 1852 that it practiced plural marriage, an increasing number of religious and political leaders in the United States began a campaign to eradicate the practice, primarily through enacting laws against it and the institutional Church that supported it.[3] The general population in the United States was firmly opposed to the practice and supported the government's effort, which became more intense after 1884, to end it.

Between 1862 and 1887, Congress enacted four antipolygamy laws directed specifically at the Church and its members: the Morrill Act (1862), the Poland Act (1874), the Edmunds Act (1882), and the Edmunds-Tucker Act (1887). The Edmunds and Edmunds-Tucker Acts were especially detrimental to Church members because they allowed a separate crime to be charged for each day a person lived with or supported more than one wife. Additionally, the Edmunds-Tucker Act gave the federal government the added authority to disincorporate the Church, escheat its property and

1. Joseph F., journal, 9 October 1880.
2. Fiftieth Semiannual General Conference, 10 October 1880. See John Taylor, "The Organization of the First Presidency, Etc.," in *Journal of Discourses* (London: Latter-day Saints' Book Depot, 1854–86), 22:38–41.
3. Orson Pratt of the Quorum of the Twelve announced that plural marriage was an official practice of the Church. See *Deseret News*, "Extra," 4 September 1852, 15.

financial assets, and disenfranchise women voters.[4] The Edmunds-Tucker Act also made plural marriage a felony and set the punishment at six months in prison and a three-hundred-dollar fine, while simultaneously depriving anyone participating in its practice, including wives, of the right to vote. A whirlwind of prosecution was about to break out across the Latter-day Saints' religious landscape in the western part of the United States. In 1879 the US Supreme Court had affirmed the arrest and conviction of George Reynolds (1842–1904), a secretary to the First Presidency who had originally volunteered to act as a test case regarding the extent of the "free exercise clause" of the US Constitution. He had been prosecuted for cohabitation under the 1862 Morrill Act. Basically, the court ruled that the Constitution guaranteed protection of religious belief but not religious practice. A few days after the beginning of the new year in 1879, Joseph F. had noted in his journal, "We got news that the Supreme Court had decided in the Reynolds case, against Reynolds."[5] This short entry belies the significance of the news for fellow member George Reynolds, the Church, and its members, including Joseph F. and his family. Latter-day Saints were surprised and shocked by the decision, believing the US Constitution protected their marriage practice because it was based on their religious belief. This historic case opened the way for increased legal actions against the Church and individual members.[6]

PLURAL MARRIAGE

Various studies have attempted to identify how pervasive the practice of plural marriage was in the Church during the nineteenth century. Some have examined the adult male population, which would naturally result in smaller numbers. Others have included wives and children, which would dramatically increase the numbers and therefore the percentage of participation. Whichever category one chooses to use, the percentage of Latter-day Saints involved in plural marriage apparently hit its peak during the Reformation in the 1850s.[7]

As one would suspect, the percentage of those involved in the practice changed over time and varied from community to community. However, if one counts "closest monogamous relatives—parent, sibling, married children, and in-laws—one could argue that by 1880 close to a majority of the Mormon population was directly or indirectly affected by a practice much more prevalent than generally acknowledged."[8]

Most studies also reveal that males who participated in the practice were generally married to two wives, making Joseph F.'s situation an exception to the general rule. Already by 1880, he

4. In 1890 the US Supreme Court upheld the legality of the Edmunds-Tucker Act. See US Supreme Court, 140 US 665, *Late Corporation of the Church of Jesus Christ of Latter-day Saints v. United States*, 19 May 1890. For a recent summary, see Andrew H. Hedges and Richard Neitzel Holzapfel, eds., *Within These Prison Walls: Lorenzo Snow's Record Book, 1886–1897* (Provo, UT: Religious Studies Center, Brigham Young University; Salt Lake City, UT: Deseret Book, 2010). For examinations of the antipolygamy legislation, see Gustive Olof Larson, *The "Americanization" of Utah for Statehood* (San Marino, CA: Huntington Library, 1971); Edward Leo Lyman, *Political Deliverance, The Mormon Quest for Utah Statehood* (Urbana: University of Illinois Press, 1986); Edwin Brown Firmage and Richard Collin Mangrum, *Zion in the Courts: A Legal History of the Church of Jesus Christ of Latter-day Saints, 1830–1900* (Urbana: University of Illinois Press, 2001), 139; and Edwin Brown Firmage, "The Judicial Campaign against Polygamy and the Enduring Legal Questions," *BYU Studies* 27, no. 3 (Summer 1987): 96.
5. Joseph F., journal, 7 January 1879.
6. For a brief overview of the federal campaign to end plural marriage, see Holzapfel and Hedges, *Within These Prison Walls*, xvii–xxvi.
7. See Lowell C. Bennion, "Plural Marriage," in *Mapping Mormonism: An Atlas of Latter-day Saint History*, ed. Brandon S. Plewe et al. (Provo, UT: BYU Press, 2012), 122.
8. Bennion, "Plural Marriage," 124.

was married to three wives. During this decade, he married two more times. Alice Ann Kimball (1858–1946) was Joseph F.'s fourth wife, married on 6 December 1883. She was the daughter of Heber C. Kimball (1801–68), a member of the First Presidency at the time of his death and a personal associate of Joseph F.'s father, Hyrum Smith (1800–44). Joseph F. married his fifth wife, Mary Taylor Schwartz (1865–1956), the niece of John Taylor (1808–87), on 13 January 1884.

Alice Ann Kimball, ca. 1888. Joseph F. Smith was sealed to Alice on Thursday, 6 December 1883, in Salt Lake City. Alice had three children—Alice May (1877–1920), Heber Chase (1881–1971), and Charles Coulson (1881–1933)—from a previous marriage. These children became part of Joseph F.'s family. Courtesy of CHL.

ON THE UNDERGROUND OR EXILED

As the government's efforts to end plural marriage intensified, especially after 1884, Church leaders chose to go into hiding (on the "underground") or leave Utah as exiles to avoid arrest and incarceration rather than submitting to what they considered to be unjust laws.

President John Taylor was particularly concerned with Joseph F.'s personal safety because of his position in the First Presidency and his work at the Endowment House. Both assignments gave him particular knowledge about the Church's marriage practices, something the federal government would surely want to obtain if possible. Additionally, as noted above, Joseph F. was practicing plural marriage himself and therefore was also subject to arrest. Joseph F., attempting to lighten the mood during this challenging period, wrote to Martha Ann, "It seems I am in some demand in certain quarters."[9]

Joseph F. began his life on the underground on 29 August 1884, when he departed with his wife Edna Lambson (1851–1926) and one of their children on a tour through Utah, Colorado, New Mexico, and Arizona, visiting members and conducting Church business. Joseph F. had to be constantly vigilant to avoid arrest. Informers and spies were hired by government officials to locate Church leaders in order to arrest them. Apparently, movement in and out of the territory was particularly difficult. In a letter to Susa Young Gates in 1889, Joseph F. noted that he had left Utah for Washington, DC: "This makes the 4th time, in a year, that I have run the gauntlet getting out and in, the territory."[10] He continued, "I have seen none of my family for several days— Some of my <u>friends</u> are very anxious to interview me— But owing to the circumstances over which I <u>now have no control I am not anxious for the honor! I may be in</u> stripes <u>however by the time you get home</u>."[11] He would basically remain out of the public eye until September 1891, seven years later, when President Benjamin Harrison granted him amnesty.

Joseph F.'s life on the underground was often challenging. In addition to the constant fear of possible detection and arrest, he was worried about his family's welfare. Of this experience his wife Edna wrote, "We are living at our poorest now. No butter, no meat, but imported bacon, and we women folks cannot eat that. . . . Some of us are almost starved."[12] Additionally, the homes of Joseph F.'s wives were under constant surveillance by federal marshals and without warning they were raided.[13] At various times, Joseph F. traveled to Salt Lake City to visit his wives and children. However, with such a large family, he found it difficult to remain incognito. "I am getting quite an experience," he wrote. "It is rather funny to try to conceal oneself at home with so many little prattlers, so happy to see their papa."[14]

Finally, President Taylor decided that Joseph F. needed to leave Utah for a longer season and called him to return to Hawai'i. Joseph F. and Julina Lambson (1849–1936), along with their daughter, Julina Clarissa (1884–1923),[15] departed on 2 February 1885, beginning an exile in the islands under the pseudonyms "Mr. and Mrs. Speight" (see letter envelope on p. 271).

---

9. Joseph F. to Martha Ann, 18 March 1885, herein.
10. Joseph F. to Susa Young Gates, 21 March 1889. To "run the gauntlet" was an English phrase that recalls a military punishment when the guilty party was forced to run between two rows of soldiers who would strike them with fists, switches, and weapons.
11. Joseph F. to Susa Young Gates, 21 March 1889.
12. Scott Kenney, "Joseph F. Smith," in *Presidents of the Church: Biographical Essays*, ed. Leonard J. Arrington (Salt Lake City, UT: Deseret Book, 1986), 196–97.
13. See Joseph F. to Martha Ann, 22 May 1885, herein.
14. Joseph F., journal, 7 December 1884.
15. They had left five other children at home, Mary Sophronia (born 7 October 1869), Donette (born 17 September 1872), Joseph Fielding (born 19 July 1876), David Asael (born 24 May 1879), and George Carlos (born 14 October 1881).

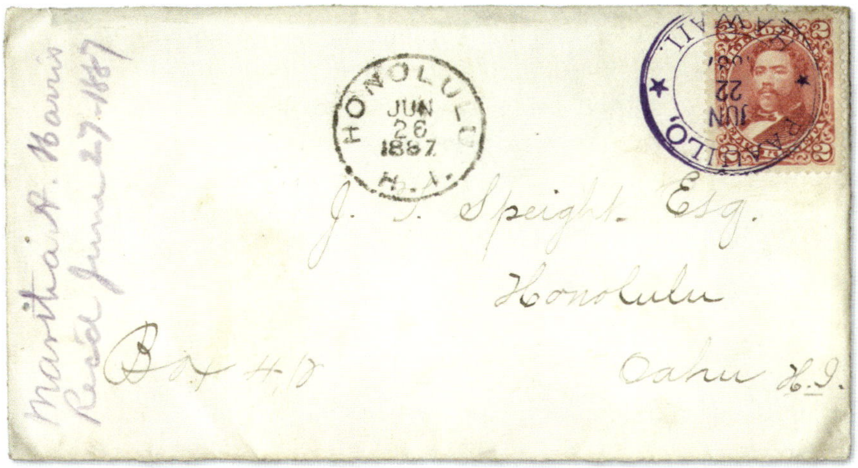

Envelope addressed to J. S. Speight (Joseph F.'s alias). The first postmark (to the right) features a two-cent stamp depicting King David Kalākaua and is dated "Jun 22 1887 Paauilo, Hawaii." The second postmark (center) is dated "26 June 1887 Honolulu H.A." Joseph F. wrote on the envelope, "Martha A. Harris Rec'd June 27 1887," with a purple pencil. A few days later, Joseph F. was on his way home to Utah. Courtesy of CHL.

During his exile in Hawai'i, Joseph F. was able to visit Martha Ann's son Hyrum Smith Harris (1863–1924), who was serving a mission in the islands at the time. He wrote Martha Ann about visiting his nephew: "I arrived in these lands on Feb—9th ~~and~~ and the following day came out here—where I met our boy, Hyrum, looking and feeling well, and seemingly as happy as he could be so far from home, and surrounded by so many circumstances foreign to his customs of youth. He is making very good progress in the study of the language."[16]

In January 1886 Julina, who was five months pregnant, noted in her journal, "One year this morning Since I left my home and precious children little did I think of being away from them so long oh how my heart yearns for their presence. When O when can we go home."[17] In addition to the pain of separation, Joseph F. and Julina experienced heartache when they received word that Joseph's son Robert (1883–86) had died in February 1886. Edna Lambson (1851–1928), his mother, was Julina's sister, in addition to being one of her husband's plural wives. Julina recorded:

> Albert came early [from Honolulu] in the evening bringing the Sad news of little Roberts death, Joseph met him at the barn. I Stepped out of the door I cold See by their

Hyrum Smith Harris, 1886, photograph by J. A. Gonsalves, Honolulu, Hawai'i. Courtesy of CHL.

16. Joseph F. to Martha Ann, 18 March 1885, herein. Julina Lambson mentions him several times in her journal; for example, see "Hyrum took Ina [Julina Clarissa] to Sunday School." Julina Lambson, journal, 28 March 1886.
17. Julina Lambson, journal, 29 January 1886.

looks that Something was rong they both looked so Sad, I asked what is the matter you have brought bad news, Albert answered "Your children are all right. I thought he ment all of Josephs children, So I said is it ours Albert "no." is it mothers "no." it is Robert he is dead, I burst into tears. I felt that it was too hard, Oh my poor Sister Edna in her touching letter She Says. "I am So lonesome no baby to love." Poor girl how my heartaches for her, and poor papa to See his grief seems more than I can bear. O. Lord comfort thier heart.[18]

Two weeks later, Julina finally decided to write in her journal again: "Jos has fretted So much and felt So very bad over the loss of his little Robert one of the nicest children we had, at first I thought it was no comfort to him my being hear with little Ina [Julina Clarissa], but I can now See that if he had been here along, it would have been harder, it Seems that he can not Stand it to be alone."[19]

Julina delivered a baby boy, Elias Wesley Smith (1886–1970), on 21 April 1886, while in exile (see photograph on p. 273). Years later Wesley was called to serve a mission in Hawai'i. In a letter dated 12 May 1907, Joseph F. told his son about some of his activities in Lā'ie just before Wesley was born: "You mentioned helping to white wash the fences, barns, etc. at Laie. Did you realize that I helped to build the barn and carriage house, and the square 4 roomed house nearest the barn when I was there, before you were born?"[20]

In November 1886 Joseph F. became seriously ill and dangerously emaciated. Julina's teenage daughter Donnette (1872–1961) came to the islands to take care of Joseph F. and help Julina with her baby. In March 1887, after his recovery, Joseph F. sent Julina and Donnette back to Utah. As they set sail, he wrote: "I took the last look at the receding forms of my loved and loving ones until God in his mercy shall permit us to meet again. When the ship passed the line of sight, I . . . climbed Puuoina to look again at the speeding steamer. . . . When once alone, my soul burst forth in tears and I wept their fountains dry and felt all the pangs and grief of parting with my heart's best treasures on earth."[21]

When Joseph F. received a letter from Martha Ann on 27 June 1887, momentous changes were under way in the Kingdom of Hawai'i.[22] Just one day later, Walter M. Gibson[23] (1822–88) and other cabinet members in the government of King David Kalākaua (1836–91) resigned under pressure of antimonarchists who supported the annexation of Hawai'i by the United States.[24]

According to Joseph Fielding Smith, "Joseph F. Smith said that he met Gibson several times after his excommunication from the Church [in 1864] and when he was a man of power in the

18. Julina Lambson, journal, 21 February 1886.
19. Julina Lambson, journal, 7 March 1886.
20. Joseph F. to E. Wesley Smith, 12 May 1907.
21. Joseph F., journal, 15 March 1887.
22. See Martha Ann to Joseph F., May–June 1887, herein.
23. As discussed earlier, Gibson had arrived in the islands in 1861 as a Latter-day Saint missionary, but disturbing reports about his behavior and activity on the island of Lāna'i (the Church's gathering place for the Hawaiian Saints at the time) eventually reached Church headquarters in Salt Lake City, leading to his excommunication in 1864. Gibson continued to live in Hawai'i for many years, and he was offered a position in King Kalākaua's government as premier and minister of foreign affairs in 1882. Gibson wielded significant influence and power in Hawaiian political affairs between 1882 and 1887. See Gwynn Barrett, "Walter Murray Gibson: The Shepherd Saint of Lanai Revisited," *Utah Historical Quarterly* 40, no. 2 (Spring 1972): 142–62.
24. On 6 July 1887, a few days later, King Kalākaua signed a new constitution, known as the "Bayonet Constitution," that curtailed his authority, disenfranchised as many as two-thirds of the formerly eligible Native Hawaiians from voting, and extended voting rights to noncitizens, including foreign residents of American and European background.

Lā'ie, O'ahu, Hawai'i, ca. 1885. Joseph F. and Julina Smith lived at the Lā'ie Church plantation on the island of O'ahu from 1885 through 1887. The individual residences and store in the plantation compound were numbered and identified. The building indicated with #3 was the home where Joseph F. and Julina's son, Elias Wesley Smith, was on 21 April 1886. Courtesy of CHL.

Hawaiian Islands, and that he never seemed to hold a spirit of bitterness. . . . [Apparently] there were even occasions when he befriended the Saints when he exercised power as Prime-minister to King Kalakaua."[25] It is possible that Joseph F. was personally a recipient of that kindness during his exile in Hawai'i between 1885 and 1887.

CHURCH RESPONSIBILITIES BACK HOME

Joseph F. was planning to remain in Hawai'i for a while longer, but his exile was cut short by news that Church president John Taylor was near death.[26] As a result, he sailed home on 1 July 1887 on the steamer *Mariposa*, a ship owned by the Oceanic Steamship Company.[27]

25. Joseph Fielding Smith, *The Life of Joseph F. Smith: Sixth President of The Church of Jesus Christ of Latter-day Saints* (Salt Lake City, UT: Deseret Book, 1938), 224.
26. The Kingdom of Hawai'i no longer existed when Joseph F. returned to the islands in 1899. It had become a US Territory in 1898 by the same forces that had brought about the constitutional changes and the downfall of Walter M. Gibson in 1887.
27. Conway B. Sonne, *Ships, Saints, and Mariners: A Maritime Encyclopedia of Mormon Migration, 1830–1890* (Salt Lake City, UT: University of Utah Press, 1987), 139.

Joseph F. Smith, ca. 1884, photograph by C. R. Savage, Salt Lake City, Utah. Courtesy of CHL.

As soon as he was back in Utah, Joseph F. hurried to the home of Thomas F. Roueche (1833–1903) in Kaysville, Davis County, where President Taylor had been in hiding from federal officers.[28] George Q. Cannon, Joseph F.'s fellow counselor in the First Presidency, arrived shortly thereafter, on 18 July. This was the first time the First Presidency had been together since 1884.[29] President Taylor died a week later, on 25 July 1887. Due to possible arrests, only five Apostles were able to attend the public funeral.

In February 1888 Wilford Woodruff, the senior Apostle of the Quorum of the Twelve, sent Joseph F. on a brief mission to Washington, DC, to help manage Church finances, supervise the missionary effort and immigration affairs, and garner political favor for the beleaguered Latter-day Saints. Joseph F. and Charles W. Penrose (1832–1925) traveled together under the pseudonyms "Jason Mack" and "Charles Williams," respectively. They returned to Utah in June for six months before returning to Washington, DC, again in December. This short mission ended in March 1889, when Joseph F. returned to Utah in preparation for the annual general conference of the Church.[30]

In April 1889 the First Presidency was reorganized with Wilford Woodruff as President. He called George Q. Cannon and Joseph F. Smith, who had been counselors in the previous First Presidency, to be his counselors.

PACIFIC ISLANDERS IN UTAH

At this same time, Joseph F.'s connections with the Hawaiian Saints reemerged, but this time in Utah.[31] While serving his first mission in Hawai'i in the 1850s, Joseph F. often mentioned Jonathan Napela (1813–79), one of the earliest Hawaiian converts in the islands.[32] Eager to receive his temple blessings, Jonathan came to Utah for a visit in 1869. During his time in Utah, he met Church leaders, attended the annual Pioneer Day celebration, spoke to local Latter-day Saint congregations, received his temple endowment, and had his photograph taken at Edward Martin's studio in Salt Lake City.[33]

Napela's reports to the Hawaiian Saints in the islands increased interest among many of them to make the journey to Utah to receive their own temple blessings. Within five years, small groups of Native Hawaiian Latter-day Saints began settling in Utah.

In 1888 Joseph F. noted in a letter to Wilford Woodruff, "They come to Utah believing it to be the gathering place for the Saints—the Zion of the latter days—and while they are ignorant of

28. Thomas F. Roueche was a prominent citizen of Davis County, being the first mayor of Kaysville. He and John Taylor both served on the Legislative Assembly of the Territory of Utah, albeit in different years. Additionally, he was a trusted member of the Church. Andrew Jenson, *LDS Biographical Encyclopedia* (Salt Lake City, UT: Deseret Book, 1901), 1:464.
29. Blane M. Yorgason, *From Orphaned Boy to Prophet of God* (Ogden: Living Scriptures, 2001), 307–8.
30. Francis M. Gibbons, *Joseph F. Smith: Patriarch and Preacher, Prophet of God* (Salt Lake City, UT: Deseret Book, 1984), 158.
31. For a detailed discussion, see Stephen C. Taysom's forthcoming biography, *"Like a Fiery Meteor": The Life of Joseph F. Smith*. We appreciate Taysom's willingness to share his research for this section.
32. For example, see Joseph F., diary, 10 February 1856. See also Fred E. Woods, "Jonathan Napela: A Noble Hawaiian Convert," in *Regional Studies in Latter-day Saint Church History: The Pacific Isles*, ed. Reid L. Neilson, Steven C. Harper, Craig K. Manscill, and Mary Jane Woodger (Provo, UT: Religious Studies Center, Brigham Young University, 2008), 23–36.
33. The image in the CHL is identified as "J. H. Napela" (written on the image itself), photograph by Edward Martin, 1869, Edward Martin portraits 1860, PH 1600, folder 3, item 4.

our language and customs and will appear awkward and dependent somewhat at first, they are naturally bright."[34]

These Hawaiian pioneers to the Great Basin were among the first minority groups to settle in what was still a European-American dominated society. Although he had some reservations about an effort to establish a permanent presence of Hawaiian Saints in Utah, Joseph F. supported and encouraged efforts to provide Church help to these Saints and was involved in the decision to create a Church-owned joint-stock company (the Iosepa Agriculture and Stock Company) that led to the establishment of a Hawaiian gathering place in Skull Valley, about seventy-five miles southwest of Salt Lake City.[35] Named in honor of the Prophet Joseph Smith and Joseph F., Iosepa became the home of several hundred Hawaiian converts beginning in 1889.[36]

Joseph F. was pleased to see the new settlement become the gathering place for the Hawaiian Saints and continually sought to support and help the Hawaiian Saints, who he believed were members of the house of Israel through Father Lehi, mentioned in the Book of Mormon.

Counter to prevailing views of many American and European explorers, colonizers, and others at the time, Joseph F. believed the Hawaiian people "have souls to save."[37] Joseph F. opined that "the long experience I have had upon those islands and the intimate acquaintance I formed with that people in the days of my childhood [have given me] a particular warmth of friendship in my heart towards them."[38]

As a result of his earlier experiences in Hawai'i and his scriptural understanding, Joseph F. supported the Hawaiian Saints' temporal and spiritual advancement through his Church assignment as a counselor in the First Presidency, letters to Church leaders in Utah and Hawai'i, and personal visits to Iosepa.[39]

MARTHA ANN'S BLESSINGS AND STRUGGLES

Martha Ann and William had been married twenty-five years when their eleventh and last child was born on 8 December 1882. Sarah Lovina (1882–1961) was welcomed into the Harris home in Provo, Utah County, Utah Territory.

Joseph F. acknowledged the birth of Martha Ann's daughter in a letter to his brother-in-law, William Jasper Harris, six days later: "Yours of the 9th inst. Containing information of your family increase on the 8th is duly received." Joseph F. added, "I am thankful that Martha Ann and daughter are or were at your writing so well." He then asked William Jasper if Martha Ann might be willing to "swap her girls for boys!"[40] Martha Ann's last four babies were girls, Mercy Ann (born on 30 March 1874), Zina Christine (born on 13 May 1876), Martha Artimissa (born on 27 June 1879), and Sarah Lovina (born on 8 December 1882). Joseph F. observed and proposed, "[H]er preponderance of

34. Wilford Woodruff, journal, 16 May 1889.
35. Now a ghost town identified with a historical marker, Iosepa was inhabited between 1889 and 1917. See Matthew Kester, *Remembering Iosepa: History, Place, and Religion in the American West* (New York: Oxford University Press, 2013).
36. See Harold S. Davis, "The Iosepa Origin of Joseph F. Smith's 'Laie Prophecy,'" *BYU Studies* 33, no. 1 (1993): 81–108.
37. Joseph F. to Wilford Woodruff, 19 May 1888.
38. Joseph F. to Alice Smith, 13 September 1899. Nevertheless, Joseph F. lived in a culture and time when attitudes and actions did not always match the high expectations announced in Latter-day Saint scripture; see, for example, 2 Nephi 26:33.
39. For example, see Joseph F. to Marriner W. Merrill, 20 October 1890, in which he recommends a Hawaiian couple to receive the highest temple blessings in the Church.
40. Joseph F. to William J. Harris, 14 December 1882.

girls is now getting noticeable. . . . Let us have this thing put right next time. With love. Yours Truly. Joseph."[41]

Given the infant and childhood mortality rate in the United States during the nineteenth century, it is rather remarkable that Martha Ann lost none of her children during their infancy or childhood, in stark contrast to her brother's experience with losing young children.[42]

While Martha Ann celebrated Sarah Lovina's birth, two challenges remained constant for Martha Ann: the economic struggles she experienced as she cared for a large family and her health concerns.

In a letter to his brother-in-law, William Jasper Harris, written in 1881, Joseph F. responded to a report about Martha Ann: "I am extremely sorry to hear of Martha's continued illness. What can be done for her? If I can do anything please let me know what and I will endeavor to do it. . . . Do you need anything that I can get for you? Please let me know. We are all well. With love and prayers for Martha Ann, I am as ever Joseph F." [43]

Nearly half of Joseph F.'s letters written to Martha Ann in the 1880s make reference to Martha Ann's humble circumstances.[44] For example, in a letter dated 23 November 1881, he wrote:

> I herewith send you an order, (No. 1497) on the Provo Woollen factory for $50.00 I send you this on condition that you will get with it such things as you may need to clothe yourself and the little children, as far as possible, for the winter. And this is all I ask. I also send you order No. 775: for $10.00 for shoes for yourself and little ones, so far as it will go. and as every little helps, if wisely used this may do you a little good in the face of the present and future cold weather.[45]

In another letter written four years later, Joseph F. lamented to his sister: "Why should my poor—dear sister and her family ever be bound down by the strong cords of poverty and want? Perhaps it is all right, but it seemes to me there is a screw loose some where. I do not think it is your fault. surely you have ever worked hard

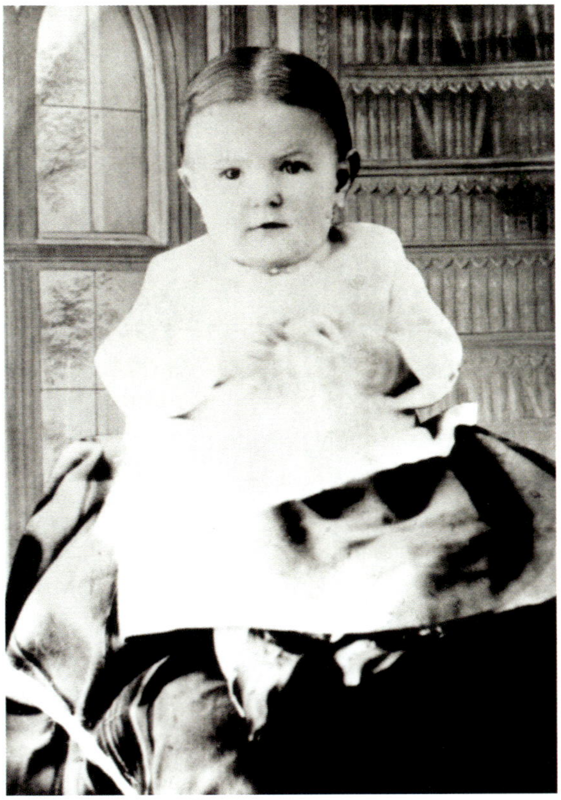

Sarah Lovina Harris, ca. 1883.
Courtesy of Carole Call King.

41. Joseph F. to William J. Harris, 14 December 1882.
42. Three grown children—Lucy Smith (died 1903), Mercy Ann (died 1905), and Joseph Albert (died 1911), ranging between twenty and fifty years of age—died before Martha Ann's death in 1923.
43. Joseph F. to William Jasper Harris, 5 January 1881.
44. See Joseph F. to Martha Ann, 1 July 1881, 28 July 1881, 23 November 1881, 13 March 1883, 12 November 1883, 15 August 1884, 30 November 1885, 11 February 1887, and 11 March 1887, herein.
45. Joseph F. to Martha Ann, 23 November 1881, herein.

enough and have deserved better fare."[46] This pattern of helping Martha Ann would continue not just during the 1880s but throughout the remainder of Joseph F.'s life.

In 1881 Martha Ann wrote one of her most important letters, identified herein as "Martha Ann to her Posterity, 22 March 1881."[47] It is an autobiographical letter reaching back to her birth in Nauvoo and covering the major events in her life, including the death of her father, leaving Nauvoo, arriving in Utah, the death of her mother, her marriage to William Jasper, his mission to England, her move to Utah County during the Utah War, her move to Provo, and an update on her membership in the Provo First Ward Relief Society.[48]

Martha Ann went on to counsel her posterity, to express gratitude for her neighbors and friends in Provo (who "have helped me in times of sickness and need") and for a merciful Heavenly Father, and to plead that she and her family would be saved in the kingdom of heaven:

> Now my dear children, never be ungrateful. Always be sure to pay your tithing, for by so doing I have, and you will, receive a great many favours and blessings. . . . I feel to sincerely thank my Heavenly Father for His mercies to me. Ingratitude is a very great sin. Through privations and hardships, my load has seemed at times more than I could shoulder, but I tried to do my duty, have tried to be a good Latter-day Saint. My Father in Heaven knows how hard it has been. He has seen my struggles, has heard and answered my prayers, that have been offered for the welfare of those I love. Though many times I have fallen short through my weakness, my desire is to do the will of the Lord and live so while I remain here on the earth to strive to keep his commandments, that at the last day He may say "Well done, my faithful handmaid." This is the desire of my heart. I DEDICATE MYSELF AND ALL I HAVE ON THIS EARTH INTO THE HAND OF MY HEAVENLY FATHER, asking him in the name of Jesus Christ to grant me that me and my companion and my children and those I love may be saved in the Kingdom of Heaven. Even so, Amen.[49]

Towards the end of the letter she predicted, "When [her family] read this letter I shall have passed away very likely."[50]

In addition to her own challenges, Martha Ann was also concerned with her brother's safety during the last half of the decade. Joseph F.'s prominence in the Church leadership was one factor for concern because federal law enforcement officials targeted Church leaders—in particular Joseph F., George Q. Cannon, and John Taylor—and their families for special prosecution.

46. Joseph F. to Martha Ann, 30 November 1885, herein.
47. Other early Latter-day Saint converts prepared similar letters at this time. For example, Helen Mar Kimball Whitney wrote a letter on 30 March 1881 to her family covering the same key themes Martha Ann does in this letter. See Jeni Broberg Holzapfel and Richard Neitzel Holzapfel, eds., *A Woman's View: Helen Mar Whitney's Reminiscences of Early Church History* (Provo, UT: Religious Studies Center, Brigham Young University, 1997), 481–87.
48. Later in life, Martha Ann wrote another letter in which she provided recollections of her early life in Nauvoo, especially the martyrdom of her uncle Joseph Smith and her father, Hyrum Smith. See Martha Ann to Joanna Spears, 1920. Spears lived in Cookeville, Tennessee, and had provided some kindness to Martha Ann's grandson J. C. Harris during his labors in the Southern States Mission.
49. Martha Ann to her posterity, 22 March 1881.
50. Martha Ann to her posterity, 22 March 1881. Helen Mar Kimball Whitney has a very similar phrase at the end of her 1881 letter: "Before ["my children"] have broken this seal the writer of these few lines will most likely have passed onto another stage of action, but I shall live until I have finished my Earthly mission and rejoice in the day of salvation & may all my loved ones enjoy these blessings is the prayer of your affectionate mother. Helen Mar Kimball Smith Whitney." Holzapfel and Holzapfel, *A Woman's View*, 487.

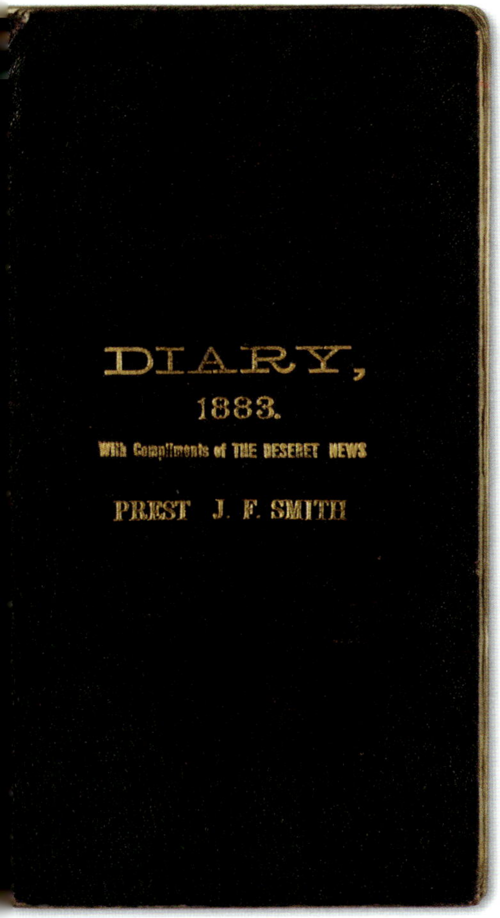

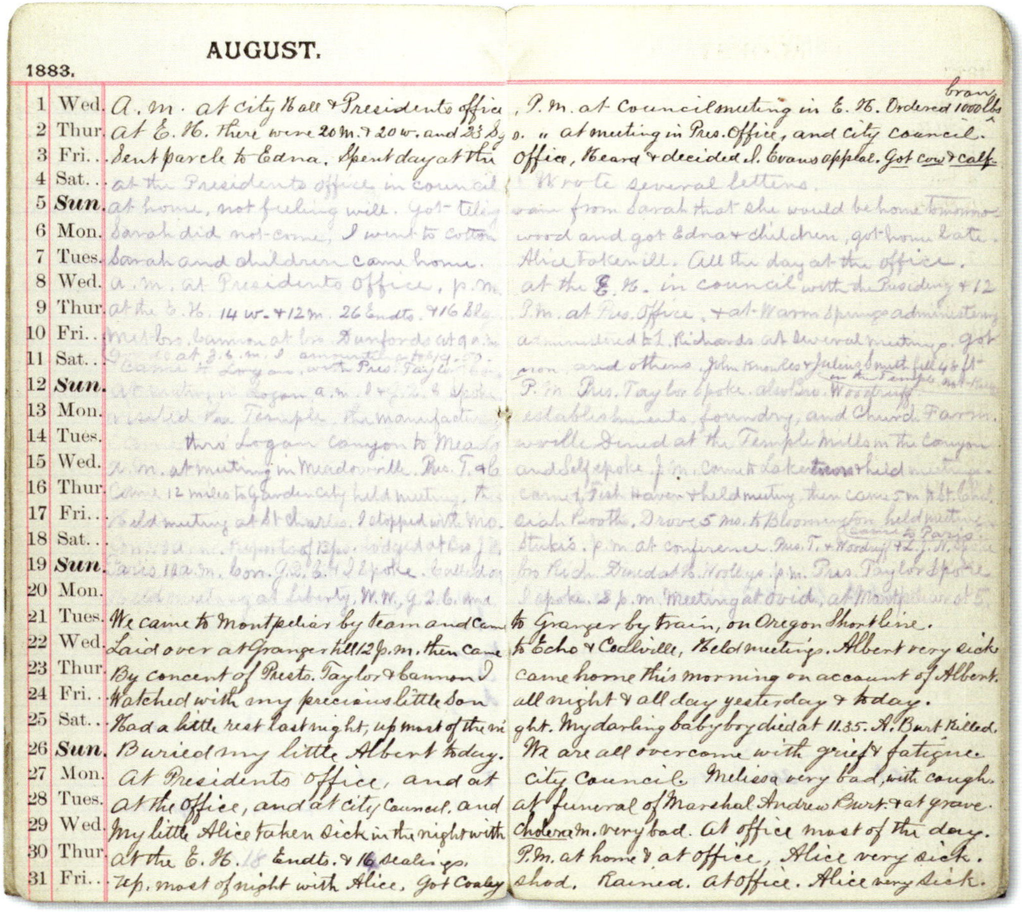

Joseph F.'s journal for August 1883. This 1883 journal was kept in a complimentary diary provided by the *Deseret News* with his name embossed in gold on the cover. This particular journal did not allow extensive writing per day, basically giving a single line across two pages for daily entries. These images highlight August 1883. Although this particular journal did not allow extensive comments, his entries for the twenty-fourth, twenty-fifth, and twenty-sixth are poignant: "Watched with my precious little Son all night & all day yesterday & today. Had a little rest last night, up most of the night. My darling baby boy died at 11.35. Buried my little Albert today. We are all overcome with greif & fatique." Courtesy of CHL.

SUMMARY

At decade's end, fifty-one-year-old Joseph F. was supporting five families living in separate households with twenty-one living children (one had been adopted in the 1860s, and another three had been adopted when he married Alice Ann Kimball in 1883). Tragically, he buried three young children in the 1880s. Never before had family life been so complicated for him. His opportunities to visit his family when he wanted were limited because spies and law enforcement officers were monitoring his homes in an effort to arrest him.

Martha Ann was forty-eight years old at the end of the decade. She and William were the parents of eleven living children, one born in 1882. The family residence remained in Provo, Utah.

Financial hardship continued to plague Martha Ann and her family. In a letter written to Joseph F.'s wife Julina Lambson, Martha Ann mentioned her efforts to augment the family budget: "I have been busiy all the fall making gloves and taking in anything I could git to do." In closing the

Martha Ann and William Jasper Harris family, ca. 1889, photograph by William Hill, Provo, Utah. Front row: Mary, Martha, William Jasper, Martha Ann, Sarah, and Zina. Back row: William, Joseph, Mercy, Hyrum, Lucy, Frank, and John. Courtesy of CHL.

letter, she wrote with some remorse, "Love to send them [her nephews and nieces] something more substantial than a kiss but they will have to take the will for the deed intill my Ship Came in."[51]

The letters written during this decade reveal Joseph F. and Martha Ann's deep affection and concern for each other. More tellingly, they attest to their unflinching determination to overcome obstacles in order to serve the Lord in any capacity or station in which they found themselves and to support and strengthen their cherished family relationships.

51. Martha Ann to Julina Smith, 21 December 1889.

Letters

JOSEPH F. TO MARTHA ANN, 21 MAY 1880

May 21st 1880[1]—
S. L. City—
Martha Ann Harris—[2]

My Dear Sister:—

It has been a long time since I wrote to you, and I have received several letters for which I am indebted to you. I hope however you will pardon me when I assure you it is not from any forgetfulness or lack of brotherly and friendly regard that I have neglected so long to write; but I have been waiting for a favorable opportunity to accomplish some other matters before I should write. I have never been able, as yet, to present your T. O.[3] accounts to the Council, because of the multitude of other matters which have occupied their attention. Besides I desire to present them at a time when I think nothing will prevent favorable action.

Perhaps I should have done it sooner **[p. 2]**[4] but to the best of my understanding I have had no right favorable chance. I now think I begin to see the way opening and am in hopes soon to be able to report to you favorably, which I will do as soon as I possibly can.

I suppose you are aware that Sarah has another little girl. Mary Jane[5] informed us that you had been notified. They are both doing exceedingly well. The baby—whom we call Minerva[6]—is growing nicely and as usual is a very pretty, sweet little one. The rest of the family are well. Aunt Thompson[7] and Mary Jane, ditto, so far as I have heard. Aunt T.[8] was here this morning. She is never real happy unless she can make herself uncomfortable for the

1. Joseph F. was forty-one, and Martha Ann was thirty-nine.
2. In addition to writing Martha Ann on this day, Joseph F. also wrote, "Emily d. Hepworth, Geo. Anderson, R. Maeser, Wm. Price, P. O. Hansen, Jacob Jacobsen, James I. Steel and Danl M. Bell." Joseph F., journal, 21 May 1880.
3. Tithing Office.
4. Page 2 is on the reverse side of page 1.
5. Mary Jane Thompson, daughter of Mercy Rachel Fielding Thompson and Robert Blashell Thompson.
6. Minerva Smith was born to Sarah Ellen Richards on 30 April 1880. See biographical register, "Smith, Minerva."
7. Mercy Rachel Fielding Thompson, sister of Mary Fielding.
8. Mercy Rachel Fielding Thompson.

welfare of somebody else. She is now trudging every where with a subscription list; soliciting subscriptions to help a poor family out from England She has raised nearly 100 $[9]

JOSEPH F. TO MARTHA ANN, 4 JUNE 1880

S. L. City
June 4th 1880

My Dear Sister
Martha Ann.

Yours of May 31st came duly to hand. Pleased as ever to hear from you, and that you are all well. Sorry that Joseph's baby is not well, but hope he will be ere this.[10]

Little Willie Pierce,[11] died on Friday May 21st and was buried on the 22d John[12] went up to see them last Monday, and was also going but I could not well leave. Lucy[13] came and stayed with us several days—but she got very homesick for her grand mother, and went to Zinas[14] on Tuesday last. I have not seen Mother Smoot since she called with Lucy[15]—but heard she was going to Cottenwood[16] yesterday.

We are all well—and the children are growing nicely & going to school.

Your affectionate brother Jos. F. Smith

JOSEPH F. TO MARTHA ANN AND WILLIAM, 1 JULY 1881

Salt Lake City July 1st 1881[17]

William and Martha—
Dear Brother and sister:—

Your letter of June 29th and cards of later dates were recieved yesterday.

9. The letter ends at the bottom of page 2. The rest of the letter is missing.
10. Joseph Albert Harris Jr., son of Johanna Patten and Joseph Albert Harris, was Martha Ann's grandson.
11. William Harvey Pierce, Joseph F. and Martha Ann's nephew. His death was reported in the local paper: "At Call's Fort, Box Elder County, on the 23d inst., by the effects of an accident, WILLIAM H., son of William and Jerusha Pierce, aged about 12 years." "Fatal Accident," *Deseret News*, 2 June 1880, 273. See biographical register, "Pierce, William Harvey."
12. Possibly John Smith.
13. Lucy Smith Harris, Martha Ann's sixth child, was ten years old at this time.
14. Likely Zina Diantha Huntington, a plural wife of Brigham Young.
15. Margaret Thompson McMeans and likely her granddaughter Lucina Smoot. See biographical register, "Smoot, Lucina."
16. Located in the eastern part of Salt Lake Valley.
17. Written on official letterhead of the Church from the Office of the President. Joseph F. was forty-two, and Martha Ann was forty.

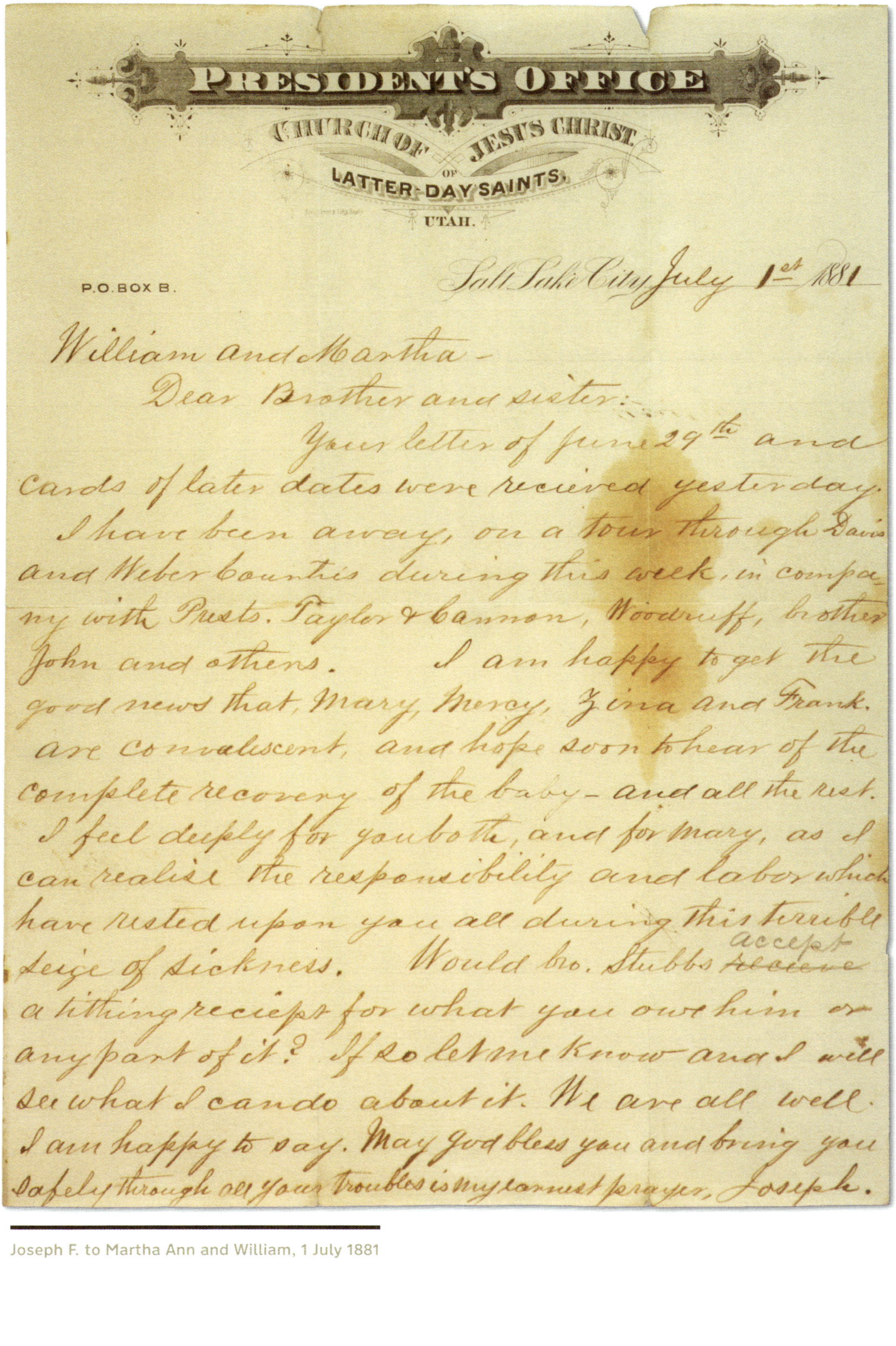

PRESIDENT'S OFFICE
CHURCH OF JESUS CHRIST OF LATTER-DAY SAINTS,
UTAH.

P.O. BOX B. Salt Lake City, July 1st 1881

William and Martha –
Dear Brother and sister:
Your letter of June 29th and cards of later dates were recieved yesterday. I have been away, on a tour through Davis and Weber Counties during this week, in company with Prests. Taylor & Cannon, Woodruff, brother John and others. I am happy to get the good news that, Mary, Mercy, Zina and Frank. are convalescent, and hope soon to hear of the complete recovery of the baby – and all the rest. I feel deeply for you both, and for Mary, as I can realise the responsibility and labor which have rested upon you all during this terrible seige of sickness. Would bro. Stubbs ~~recieve~~ accept a tithing reciept for what you owe him or any part of it? If so let me know and I will see what I can do about it. We are all well. I am happy to say. May God bless you and bring you safely through all your troubles is my earnest prayer, Joseph.

Joseph F. to Martha Ann and William, 1 July 1881

I have been away, on a tour through Davis and Weber Counties[18] during this week, in company with Prests. Taylor & Cannon, Woodruff, brother John and others.[19] I am happy to get the good news that, Mary, Mercy, Zina and Frank.[20] are convalescent,[21] and hope soon to hear of the complete recovery of the baby—and all the rest.

I feel deeply for you both, and for Mary, as I can realise the responsibility and labor which have rested upon you all during this terrible seige of sickness.[22] Would bro. Stubbs[23] ~~receive~~ <accept>[24] a tithing reciept for what you owe him or any part of it? If so let me know and I will see what I can do about it. We are all well. I am happy to say. May god bless you and bring you safely through all your troubles is my earnest prayer, Joseph.

JOSEPH F. TO MARTHA ANN, 28 JULY 1881

July 28th[25]

My Dear Sister, Martha Ann

Your favor of yester day and Williams[26] Telegram, are duly recd

I am indeed sorry for Joseph,[27] and was greatly surprised when recd Wms Telegram yester day announcing the fact.

We do hope and pray that he may soon recover his health. The good spirit, I trust, suggests to me that he will get over it all right. I would give him freely of the iron we sent you, if you have not already exhausted it. Alcohol taken freely I believe to be an excellent remidy for that desease.[28] Still depricate works without faith, for I believe faith and the ordinance of anointing and laying on hands, of faithful men to be one of the most powerful agencies for the healing of the sick. Gods promise is that the prayer of faith shall save the **[p. 2]** sick, and the Lord shall

18. Davis County is immediately north of Salt Lake City, Salt Lake County, and Weber County is immediately north of Davis County.
19. This tour was reported in a Salt Lake City newspaper: "Presidents John Taylor and George Q. Cannon, Apostle Wilford Woodruff, Patriarch John Smith, and Elders George Reynolds and Geo. F. Gibbs, returned yesterday from a preaching tour through Davis and Weber Counties, upon which, with President Joseph F. Smith, who came back on Wednesday afternoon, they started last Saturday morning." "The Presidents' Tour," *Deseret News*, 6 July 1881, 357. See biographical register, "Woodruff, Wilford."
20. Martha Ann's children at the time: Mary Emily Harris, Mercy Ann Harris, Zina Christine Harris, and Franklin Hill Harris.
21. *Convalescing* is most likely the word Joseph F. was trying to spell.
22. The "terrible siege of sickness" he mentions may be when Martha Ann was convalescing in bed for six months from a broken knee, followed by another eighteen months on crutches. See Carole Call King, "History of Martha Ann Smith Harris, 1841–1923" (unpublished manuscript in editors' possession).
23. Likely Peter Stubbs. See Joseph F. to Martha Ann, 7 September 1874 (second letter), herein, note 390.
24. The insertion is written in pencil and may not be in Joseph F.'s handwriting.
25. Judging from the sequence of letters in the Joseph F. copybook in the CHL, the year is likely 1881.
26. William Jasper Harris.
27. Likely Joseph Albert, the second son of Martha Ann and William Jasper Harris.
28. In the early days of the Church, "while the general use of whiskey and liquor was contrary to the principle [of the Word of Wisdom], many Saints felt these beverages had redeeming medicinal qualities. It was drunk by some to help remedy the effects of cholera, and evidently was used as an alleviating cure for the effects of other sicknesses." Paul H. Peterson, "An Historical Analysis of the Word of Wisdom" (master's thesis, Brigham Young University, 1972), 24.

raise them up."[29] You have been wonderfully blessed through all your afflictions, in losing none of your children. Still you have had a hard "row to hoe"[30] Some are blessed in one thing and some in another. Johns little "Birdie"[31] has had another attack of the desease, but is now thought <to> be slowly recovering. I am happy to say that at present we are all well, which is a great deal to say for one with such a family as I have. I pray God to continue his mercies unto all of us. I have not been able to send you an order as you desired, as yet, for the reason that the girls have been drawing heavily on me of late for sewing machines and one thing and another, which has draned me very closely. I hope soon to be able to send it. We will surely remember Joseph in our prayers. and all the rest of you I had Joseph prayed for yesterday in our prayer circle,[32] and I beseech God to hear our prayers. Remember me kindly to all. If M[◊◊]i[◊]h Holt[33] gets a divorce she can marry again. Affectionately Joseph

JOSEPH F. TO MARTHA ANN, 18 SEPTEMBER 1881

Sept. 18, 1881[34]

Dear Sister Martha Ann,

On Friday, 16th inst. Edna gave birth to a fine boy,[35] weighing 8lbs and 4 ounces. They are both, up to date doing very nicely. We are all usually well, and sincerely hope you and all ditto.

I am very sorry to have to report that Robert B.[36] has got the Typhus or Typhoid fever, and is very sick. Mary Jane is still very feeble and poor Aunt Thompson is nearly worn out. I sat up with them till 2 o'clock this morning. Edna is in bed. Julina getting ready for the same,[37] Sarah with nursing baby,[38] and no help—so we [*illegible*] do much [*illegible*] from home. [*illegible*] With love, Joseph

29. See James 5:14–15.
30. An American idiom meaning a difficult task or situation to deal with.
31. Likely Hellen Jerusha Smith, eight-year-old daughter of John Smith. She died of diphtheria two days later, on 30 July. See "Died," *Deseret News*, 3 August 1881, 432.
32. See D. Michael Quinn, "Latter-day Saint Prayer Circles," *BYU Studies* 19, no. 1 (Fall 1978): 79–105. See also Joseph F. to Martha Ann, 21 June 1869, herein.
33. Likely refers to Maria Mabey, who married Albert Holt in 1862 in Salt Lake City. See biographical register, "Mabey, Maria."
34. From Joseph F.'s letterpress copybooks; original not extant.
35. Albert Jesse Smith.
36. Unknown individual.
37. "In bed" was a euphemism for the time a woman was delivering a baby, including postbirth. "Julina getting ready for the same" refers to the upcoming birth of George Carlos. He was born on 14 October 1881, less than a month later.
38. Sarah is most likely nursing Minerva Smith, born 30 April 1880.

JOSEPH F. TO MARTHA ANN, 23 NOVEMBER 1881

Nov. 23^{d} 81[39]

My Dear Sister Martha A. Harris

I herewith send you an order, (No. 1497) on the Provo Woollen factory[40] for $50.00 I send you this on condition that you will get with it such things as you may need to clothe yourself and the little children, as far as possible, for the winter. And this is all I ask. I also send you order No. 775: for $10.00 for shoes for yourself and little ones, so far as it will go. and as every little helps, if wisely used this may do you a little good in the face of the present and future cold weather.

We are all well, Julinas baby[41] is fretful, and cries a great deal, but seemes strong and healthy, and grows "like a weed." Edna has got the best baby she ever had.[42] Hoping this with the inclosed orders, may find you and yours all well and as happy as possible. I am as ever your ~~your~~ <affectionate> brother and friend in the bonds of kindred love, in which my family joine.
Jos. F. Smith

JOSEPH F. TO MARTHA ANN, 13 MARCH 1883

Salt Lake City, U.T. Mar. 13th 1883[43]

My Dear Sister
Martha Ann

I meant to have written you on monday 5th inst. after returning from Provo,[44] but so many duties, cares and responsibilities have been pressing upon me of late that I could not, it seemed, get a chance. My little folks—that is, George C., Albert J. and Melissa,[45] were taken, about the time I was at Provo, with alarming symptoms of the croup, one after another, and little Albert is still in a very dangerous condition and none of them fully recovered. At the same time both of Sarahs babies[46] are suffering with colds, teathing and general uneasiness. So you see I have had enought to worry my mind with about home.

39. From Joseph F.'s letterpress copybooks; original not extant.
40. Opened in 1872, Provo Woolen Mills was one of Utah Territory's largest and most successful nineteenth-century enterprises.
41. George Carlos Smith was born to Julina Lambson on 14 October 1881. See biographical register, "Smith, George Carlos."
42. Albert Jesse Smith was born to Edna Lambson on 16 September 1881. See biographical register, "Smith, Albert Jesse."
43. Written on official letterhead of the Church from the Office of the President. Joseph F. is forty-four, and Martha Ann was forty-one. Joseph F.'s journal for 1883 consists of a preprinted daily date book, "With Compliments of THE DESERET NEWS," allowing only one-line entries for each day across two pages. For example, for this date, Joseph F. had room to note only, "Paid Taylor, Romney & Co. $11.54 for [unknown word]. $11.50 for 1000 bran. Paid [Carl Christian] Asmussen 75¢ for watch ring." Joseph F., journal, 13 March 1883.
44. Joseph F. participated in the Provo Stake's quarterly conference on 4 March 1883. See Joseph F., journal, 4 March 1883.
45. George Carlos Smith (seventeen months old), Albert Jesse Smith (eighteen months old), and Edna Melissa Smith (three years old). See biographical register, "Smith, Edna Melissa."
46. Sarah Ellen Richards's babies, Alice Smith and Minerva Smith, were born on 27 July 1882 and 30 April 1880, respectively. See biographical register, "Rich, Alice May" and "Smith, Minerva."

I had to attend the Davis Conference on Saturday and sunday last.[47] and on my return, I received word from William W. Burton, Ogden that they buried their little Parley[48] on Saturday last—who died the day previously with croup. Aunt Thompson and Mary Jane[49] are in the same feeble condition and without help. They are so peculiar in their fancies and notions that it is with difficulty that they can get any [**p. 2**] help to remain long with them. They seeme to think their work is light, that any little girl, half smart could do it. but when it comes to waiting on two invalids, very peculiar in their notions, and hard to please, and do house work, and a hundrid and one other things required by a family, it is no small or triffling matter. I felt very much grieved at not being able to call on you on sunday, the 4th inst. Sarahs baby[50] not having had the measles—and as we already had so much sickness—and of a kind that we have had so much cause to dread, I did not think it wise for the little girls[51] to call—and as I had no time myself I could not. between meetings we were occupied every moment in council, except bearly time to get dinner,[52] and the conference meetings occupied the rest of the time. As you know I am a public servant, and absolutely have no time of my own. My folks feel this as much as any body, and my own children get as little of my company as many strangers. or in otherwords, I am so much from home, engaged in public duties, that comparative strangers get about as much of my compay as my own family, yet I am sure it is no where more welcome than at home. I cannot tell you my feelings about your circumstances. I often upbraid myself for my inability to make you as comfortable as my own family. Your life has been a hard one as was that of our ever dear and precious Mother.[53] Surely there is a noble reward awaiting you after your trials. Cheer up. If I live and prosper I shall not forget you. My heart is full, my eyes moist. I am ever truly Joseph F.——

JOSEPH F. TO MARTHA ANN, 27 MARCH 1883

Mar. 27th 83[54]

My Dear Sister, Martha Ann:—

47. The Davis Stake's quarterly conference was held in Bountiful, Davis County, on 9–10 March 1883. See Joseph F., journal, 9–10 March 1883.
48. Parley Parson Burton, four-year-old son of Sarah Ann Fielding and William Burton, died on 8 March 1883. See biographical register, "Burton, Parley Parson."
49. Mercy Rachel Fielding and Mary Jane Thompson.
50. Alice Smith was born on 27 July 1882.
51. Joseph F. noted, "The three little girls accompanied me." Joseph F., journal, 4 March 1883. Sarah's daughters were Leonora (born on 30 January 1871), Minerva (born on 30 April 1880), and Alice (born on 27 July 1882).
52. The midday meal was called "dinner," and the later evening meal was called "supper."
53. Mary Fielding.
54. From Joseph F.'s letterpress copybooks; original not extant.

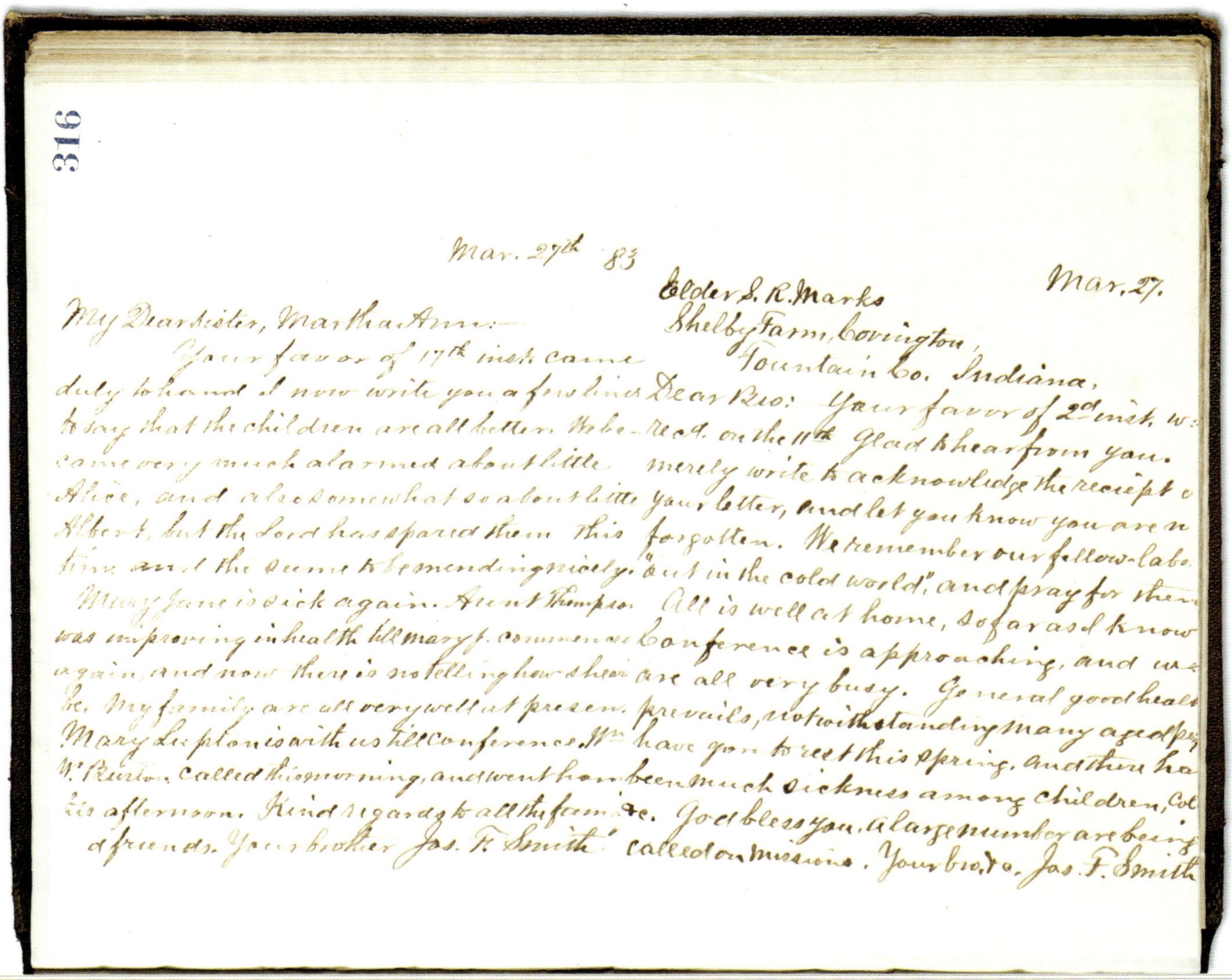

Joseph F. to Martha Ann, 27 March 1883, copy found in Joseph F.'s letterpress copybooks under that date.

Your favor of 17th inst. came duly to hand I now write you a few lines to say that the children are all better. We became very much alarmed about little Alice,[55] and also somewhat so about little Albert,[56] but the Lord has spared them this time and the seeme to be mending nicely.[57]

Mary Jane is sick again. Aunt Thompson[58] was improving in health till Mary J. commenced again, and now there is no telling how she wi[◊◊] be. My family are all very well at present Mary Lupton[59] is with us till conference. Wm W. Burton[60] called this morning, and went hom[◊◊] this afternoon.[61] Kind regards to all the fam[◊◊] [◊◊]d friends. Your brother Jos. F. Smith

55. Alice Smith. Joseph F. noted, "At home attending Alice, very bad" (Joseph F., journal, 18 March 1883) and "up till 2 am with my little Alice" (Joseph F., journal, 20 March 1883).
56. Albert Jesse Smith, who died on 25 August 1883. See Joseph F. to Martha Ann, 26 August 1883, herein.
57. Joseph F.'s journal highlights his concern during this period for his children's well-being. For example, he noted, "Children very sick. I am worried." Joseph F., journal, 17 March 1883.
58. Mary Jane Thompson and Mercy Rachel Fielding.
59. Mary Eliza Fielding, first cousin to Joseph F. and Martha Ann.
60. William W. Burrton, married Joseph F. and Martha Ann's cousins (Rachel Fielding, Ellen Fielding, and Sarah Ann Fielding).
61. Ogden, Weber County, Utah Territory.

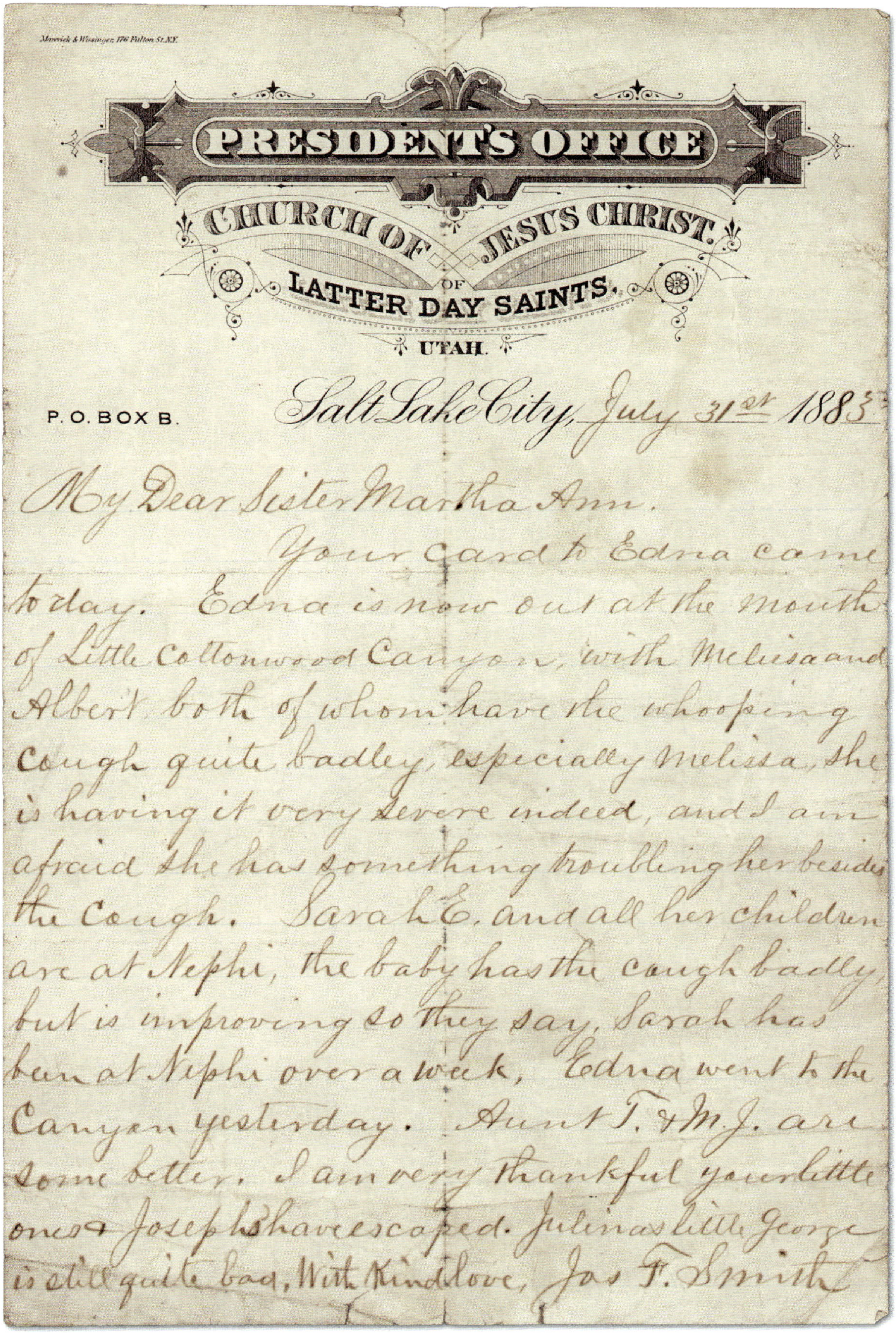

Maverick & Wissinger, 176 Fulton St. N.Y.

PRESIDENT'S OFFICE

CHURCH OF JESUS CHRIST OF LATTER DAY SAINTS,

UTAH.

P. O. BOX B. Salt Lake City, July 31st 1883

My Dear Sister Martha Ann.

Your card to Edna came today. Edna is now out at the mouth of Little Cottonwood Canyon, with Melissa and Albert, both of whom have the whooping cough quite badley, especially Melissa, she is having it very severe indeed, and I am afraid she has something troubling her besides the cough. Sarah E. and all her children are at Nephi, the baby has the cough badly, but is improving so they say, Sarah has been at Nephi over a week, Edna went to the Canyon yesterday. Aunt T. & M. J. are some better. I am very thankful your little ones & Joseph's have escaped. Julina's little George is still quite bad, With kind love, Jos F. Smith

Joseph F. to Martha Ann, 31 July 1883

JOSEPH F. TO MARTHA ANN, 31 JULY 1883

Salt Lake City July 31st 1883[62]

My Dear Sister Martha Ann.

Your card to Edna[63] came to day. Edna is now out at the mouth of Little Cottonwood Canyon,[64] with Melissa and Albert[65] both of whom have the whooping cough quite badley, especially Melissa, she is having it very severe indeed, and I am afraid she has something troubling her besides the cough. Sarah E. and all her children[66] are at Nephi,[67] the baby[68] has the cough badly but is improving so they say, Sarah has been at Nephi over a week,[69] Edna went to the Canyon yesterday. Aunt T. & M. J. are some better.[70] I am very thankful your little ones & Josephs'[71] have escaped. Julinas little George[72] is still quite bad. With Kind love, Jos F. Smith

JOSEPH F. TO MARTHA ANN, 26 AUGUST 1883

Salt Lake City U.T. Aug. 26th 1883[73]

My Dear sister Martha Ann,

Once more, and now for the sixth time, by the inexorable will of an inscrutible providence we have been called upon to part with one of our dearest, most preacious treasures.[74]

This time the pitiless monster, death, has chosen for his "shining mark" our beautiful, inteligent, bright and lovely little Albert Jesse. His death occurred yesterday at 11.35 a.m. after an illness of about 13 days, most of which time I was absent from home, travelling thro' the settlements north with Pres. Taylor. I arrived home on thursday morning having been sent for, and being honorably released by the President. I had the [**p. 2**] sorrowful pleasure of watching and waiting upon him, my darling boy, for 52 hours, with heart-felt prayers and scalding tears

62. Written on letterhead from the "President's Office The Church of Jesus Christ of Latter-day Saints Utah P.O. Box B. Salt Lake City, ________ 188__."
63. Edna Lambson.
64. Little Cottonwood Canyon is located southeast of Salt Lake City. Joseph F. noted, "I took my team and conveyed Edna & children to Granite, and returned, very tired." Joseph F., journal, 30 July 1883. He recorded a week later that he "went to cotton wood and got Edna & children." Joseph F., journal, 6 August 1883.
65. Edna Melissa Smith and Albert Jesse Smith.
66. Sarah Ellen Richards had four children living at the time of this letter.
67. Nephi, Juab County, Utah, is located eighty-four miles from Salt Lake City.
68. Likely refers to Alice Smith, who was a year old at this time.
69. Joseph F., journal, 21 July 1883: "Went to Nephi, Sarah & Jos. R & baby accompanied me." On 23 July he returned home but "left Sarah & children at Nephi." They returned home on 7 August.
70. Mercy Rachel Fielding and Mary Jane Thompson.
71. Likely refers to Joseph Albert Harris.
72. Julina Lambson and George Carlos.
73. Written on letterhead from the "President's Office The Church of Jesus Christ of Latter-day Saints P.O. Box B."
74. In his journal of the same date, Joseph F. wrote, "Buried my little Albert today. We are all overcome with grief & fatigue." Joseph F., journal, 26 August 1883.

not a few, but the heavens were brass over our heads.[75] our crys and tears fell alike to the earth and all were buried this day with the lifeless, beautious form of our hearts' treasure in the grave! and yet not all were buried, for still our cry would assend, why is it so? O. God why had it to be? and still our tears seak the earth to releave if not to bury our heart-aches in its feelingless bosom.

If for the sorrows of parting with our little, innocent ones in this world, we are to be rewarded with joy in the near or distant future, then may I not hope for a rich reward hereafter! Have I not laid up treasures in heaven? Sarah Ella, Mercy Josephine, Heber John, Alfred Jason, Rhoda Ann, and now Albert Jesse, all hold out their loving arms to "Papa," from the other side.[76] What a happy meeting awaits me! and I trust, that in that ransomed [**p. 3**] throng no hearts nor hands will welcome me more warmly than those of Father, Mother, Hyrum, Mary, (whom we knew not) and Sarah, and Lovina,[77] and hosts of Kindred dead who being "dead yet live", they having tasted of the living waters of christ, and died in Him. By far the greatest number are beyond the vail, the ties which draw us thither are fast becoming stronger than those which bind us here. Yet I look upon my little flocks now drawing upon me for their daily food, and none in store, but trusting in providence, and depending upon my mortal life for <their> help and protection ~~and~~ I breathe the earnest prayor, O! let me stay to battle with the ills and ups and downs of life yet a little longer in the world for their dear sakes. Were it not for this, now while my soul is cleansed by poignant grief I would rather go than stay. and yet I half feel that I am neither good enough to go or stay. It seemes not [**p. 4**][78] always an easy task to acknowledge the hand of God in All things. yet I will do it. and my heart says, "tho' He slay me yet will I trust in Him,"[79] for "The Lord giveth and the Lord taketh away, blessed be the name of the Lord".[80] I would rather have to pass through ~~the~~ the scenes of the past few days, harrowing as they have been, to the heart and soul, time and time again than never to have had my precious boy. Our aim can be no higher or nobler than to aspire to be worthy of an eternal union with, and possession of the pure, innocent trusting and loving little souls, such as those with whom God has blessed me only for ~~so~~ such short and happy periods of time. God help us to be worthy of them. Joseph[81]

75. Albert Jesse Smith, nearly two years old, succumbed to diphtheria on 25 August 1883. See "Died," *Deseret News*, 29 August 1883, 512. In his journal that allowed for one-line entries only, Joseph F. recorded the events leading up to Albert's death: Joseph F. returned home early from a speaking tour "on account of Albert" on Thursday, Joseph F., journal, 23 August 1883. Two days later on Saturday, he noted, "Had a little rest last night, up most of the night. My darling baby boy died at 11.35." Joseph F., journal 25 August 1883. See also see Joseph F. to Martha Ann, 13 March 1883, herein.

76. Sarah Ella (died 11 February 1869), Mercy Josephine (died 6 June 1870), Heber John (died 3 March 1877), Alfred Jason (died 6 April 1878), Rhoda Ann (died 6 July 1879), and Albert Jesse (died 25 August 1883).

77. Hyrum Smith Jr., Mary Smith, Sarah Smith, and Lovina Smith were deceased children of Hyrum Smith and Jerusha Barden. Sarah and Lovina had both died in 1876.

78. This page is also written on official letterhead of the Church from the Office of the President, but the official heading has been crossed out.

79. See Job 13:15.

80. See Job 1:21.

81. In a letter written on the following day to W. W. Cluff, Joseph F. remarked, "I stood by the brave little fellow almost constantly for 52 hours, but had to give up to the inexorable will of that inscrutable providence which I suppose must remain a mistery in this life to most of us mortals." Joseph F. to W. W. Cluff, 27 August 1883.

JOSEPH F. TO MARTHA ANN, 12 NOVEMBER 1883

Nov. 12th 1883[82]

My Dear Sister Martha Ann.

Your favor of the 11th is received I am pleased to hear of the improvement of your children, and those of Joan,[83] and I hope all of you will pull through safely.

My family are generally well, some of the children have slight colds, but nothing serious I trust. Tomorrow I shall be 45 if I live, nearly a year older than father was when taken home.[84]

Cousin Ina[85] is very high-toned, highly educated, well read and talented, she has out grown her fathers religion, and surpassed all her kindred, especially those in Utah. She is ~~tal~~ gifted in music [**p. 2**] and poetry, is a good writer, and resides in Oakland, California. I think a letter addressed Miss. Ina Pickett,
Oakland Library
Oakland, California
would find her. If you write take paines with your hand and spelling, for she is somewhat critical. I think she would like to hear from you, but she will not answer my letters, I have written several times. I send you herewith General Tithing office order #701 on Provo Coôp-store for my birth day present, to get shoes and other necessary articles for you and the children. It calls for 25$ in merchandise.[86]

You must excuse haste and give my love to the children There is a letter at my house for William[87] Your affectionate brother Joseph

JOSEPH F. TO MARTHA ANN, 22 NOVEMBER 1883

Nov. 22 83[88]

Dear Sister Martha Ann—
Provo, Utah Co.
Dear Sister:—

82. From Joseph F.'s letterpress copybooks; original not extant.
83. Possibly refers to Martha Ann's daughter-in-law Johanna Patten, wife of Joseph Albert Harris. Johanna and Joseph were the parents of two children at this time, Joseph Albert Jr. (four years old) and Frank Ernest (eight months old). See biographical register, "Patten, Johanna."
84. Joseph F.'s father, Hyrum Smith, was martyred in Carthage, Illinois, on 27 June 1844 and was forty-four years old at the time of his death.
85. Ina Coolbrith (née Josephine Donna Smith).
86. During the 1870s and 1880s, the General Tithing Office was used as a community accounting and exchange facility. When a Church member had paid more than what he owed in yearly tithing, the "accumulated credits could be transferred to others by a written order on the tithing office resembling in every aspect the modern check." It appears that Joseph F. was drawing on credit he had with the Deseret Co-op for Martha Ann to purchase needed goods at the Provo store. Quotation from Leonard J. Arrington, *Great Basin Kingdom: An Economic History of the Latter-day Saints, 1830–1900* (Urbana: University of Illinois Press, 2005), 143–44.
87. William Jasper Harris.
88. From Joseph F.'s letterpress copybooks; original not extant.

Yours of the 14th reached me on tuesday 20th inst. on my return from San Pete.[89] I have failed to notify you that on Monday Nov. 12th at 8.30p.m. my ninet[◊]enth child and tenth son was born. both mother and boy have done well so far, for which I am very thankful. We have named him Robert, after our first american ancestor, Robert Smith.[90] He is a fine healthy little fellow, and weighed just 8lbs and 14oz. Hoping this will find you and yours well I am in haste
Joseph

JOSEPH F. TO MARTHA ANN, 11 FEBRUARY 1884

Feb. 11st 1884[91]

My Dear Sister
Martha Ann Harris.

I write to inform you that our tenth daughter[92] and twentieth child was born yesterday at 20 minutes to 2, O'clock—a.m. Julina and baby are comfortable and we are all once more happy. Of course mothers always think their babies are the prettiest, sweetest and best, but we all think we have never had a prettier one than this one <is> at the beginning.

Ednas last boy[93] is a regular bouncer, and a fine, noble little fellow, but he means to be taken notice of in this world, at least while he is or will be an attachee of the "brest-works", he therefore manages to keep his mother busy, and sometimes all that branch of the family are not too many for him!

I think he (Robert)[94] is one of the very finest infantile specimens of the genus-homo.[95]
With love, Your brother Joseph F.——

JOSEPH F. TO MARTHA ANN, 1 AUGUST 1884

S. L. City Aug. 1st 1884[96]

My Dear Sister

Yours of 16th ult. was duly recd Should have answered it right-away but as you desired to know who was coming to conference, I thought I would wait until I could send you word.

89. San Pete County, Utah.
90. Robert Smith was Joseph F.'s and Martha Ann's fourth-great-grandfather. He arrived in America as an indentured servant in 1638.
91. From Joseph F.'s letterpress copybooks; original not extant. Joseph F. was forty-five, and Martha Ann was forty-two.
92. Julina Clarissa Smith was born to Julina Lambson on 10 February 1884. See biographical register, "Smith, Julina Clarissa."
93. Edna Lambson gave birth to Robert Smith on 12 November 1883. See biographical register, "Smith, Robert."
94. Reference to Robert Smith, as noted in note 94.
95. *Homo* is the genus that includes modern humans and their close relatives. In this context, Joseph F. meant *Homo sapiens*.
96. From Joseph F.'s letterpress copybooks; original not extant.

And not until yesterday did I learn the conclusions reached. I learn that Pres. Taylor, and Cannon, F. M. Lyman, L. J. Nuttall[97] and some of their women folks and a few others, names not remembered—are going to take a trip into the north country, calling at Paris to attend the "Bear Lake" Conference on their way.[98] I was in hopes another of your friends would be invited, but other duties have been enjoined, so it will not be. Yours of 30$^{\underline{th}}$ is just rec$^{\underline{d}}$ Very sorry you were disappointed at the P. O.[99]— Hope it will not occur again—but you will see the reason. Was pleased to hear of the pleasant rec[◊◊] [*illegible word*] [ ][100] [**p. 2**] by you on every hand. You must have enjoyed the company of Sr. Priscindia & Co. from Cache. Look out for Z. Y. W[101]—some folks' tongues run at both ends, loose very active and rattling. I have no fears on this head, for where "nothing is concealed nothing can pop out"[102]—as "Margery" told her "cousin Joe".[103] The best way to retain ones thoughts is to lock them up and lose the key—where it cannot be found, then one can treat friends and foes alike without exception.

In the fire is a good place to lose certain kinds of keys. Your friend has not seen your aunt Amanda[104] since her return, so I am informed. which is rather singular. You ask what would be thought of your stopping till Oct. I do not think there can be any objections, provided you feel like doing so. You are safe out there among your relatives, and I am sure your friend-s would be pleased to have you enjoy yourself however pleasing it would be to see you safe home again. Bp. L. W. Hardy died yesterday,[105] & Elder W. W. Taylor died today,[106] also Orson Whitney.[107] poor fellow, with him it is good ridance.[108] Your neighbors are all well. Sister Ed.[109] and children are in the canyon. God bless you & yours. With sincere regards I am truly [ ][110]

97. President John Taylor, George Q. Cannon, Francis Marion Lyman, and Leonard John Nuttall. See biographical register, "Lyman, Francis Marion."
98. Paris, Bear Lake County, Idaho, is the county seat and the site of the impressive Bear Lake Stake Tabernacle, built between 1884 and 1889.
99. Post office.
100. Bottom line missing.
101. Possibly Zina Presendia Young, wife of Thomas Williams. See biographical register, "Young, Zina Presendia."
102. A popular saying found in the play *The Rough Diamond: A Comic Drama in One Act*. See John Baldwin Buckstone, *The Rough Diamond* (New York: Samuel French & Son, Publishers, 1847), 17. The play was first performed at the Royal Lyceum Theatre in London on Monday, 8 November 1847.
103. Two main characters in the play *The Rough Diamond*. In the original cast (1847), Margery was played by Frances "Fanny" Elizabeth Fitzwilliam, a British actress, and Cousin Joe was played by John Baldwin Buckstone, a British actor, playwright, and comedian who wrote 150 plays, including *The Rough Diamond*.
104. Possibly referring to Amanda Barnes, former plural wife of Joseph Smith. See biographical register, "Barnes, Amanda Melissa."
105. Leonard Wilford Hardy died on 31 July 1884. See "From Friday's Daily, August 1" and "Local News: Obsequies," *Deseret News*, 6 August 1884, 457, 461. See also biographical register, "Hardy, Leonard Wilford."
106. William Whittaker Taylor died on 1 August 1884. See "President William W. Taylor," *Deseret News*, 13 August 1884, 470. See also biographical register, "Taylor, William Whittaker."
107. Orson Kimball Whitney died on 31 July 1884. He was a Hawaiian missionary sent to the islands in 1854 at the same time Joseph F. was sent there. Joseph F. mentions him several times in his journals. See biographical register, "Whitney, Orson."
108. His death notice noted, "Like all mortals, he had his faults and weaknesses. . . . His worst enemy was strong drink, and it finally overcame his iron constitution." See "Death of a Pioneer," *Deseret Evening News*, 1 August 1884, [3].
109. Likely refers to Edna Lambson.
110. Bottom line missing.

JOSEPH F. TO MARTHA ANN, 15 AUGUST 1884

S. L. City, Aug. 15—1884[111]

My Ever Dear Sister,

Your favor the 9th is just recd and I hasten to drop you a line in return.

We are very sorry for your affliction with rheumatism, but hope sincerely that you are wholly relieved from it before now. We do pray for you and remember you and yours constantly before the Lord. Any thing in reason that we can do to help you or to comfort you you may confidently expect if you will only let us know, so far as we may fail to see. The Lord bless and heal you and preserve both you & yours and all who are dear to you we humbly pray.

The family and your friend's are all well. S. E.[112] with six of the family are in the Canyon.[113] The weather has been much cooler for a week, since the showers a week ago. The nights are very pleasant but the days are warm. It is perhaps as well your friends was not there at the Con. [**p. 2**] as it could have been little more or less than an agravation. We cannot say any thing against your remaining till cooler weather, altho' we would be pleased to see you safely and soundly in our midst once more. When you get ready to come to the city if you will let us know we will assist you on your journey. We send herein (10$) ten dollars for you which you can credit up on a/c. as you may need a little money for present necessities or for travelling expenses. Bro. E. Snow,[114] and others expect to leave the city about the latter part of this month for a visit to Colorado and the Sanjuan country[115] to be gon nearly a month, will return in time for conference all being well.[116] The Presidency are expected to return to Salt Lake about the 27th of this month.[117] You will have heard the sad news of the assassination of two Elders & two

111. From Joseph F.'s letterpress copybooks; original not extant.
112. Sarah Ellen Richards.
113. Most likely Little Cottonwood. See Joseph F. to Martha Ann, 31 July 1883, herein.
114. Erastus Fairbanks Snow. See biographical register, "Snow, Erastus Fairbanks."
115. Latter-day Saint pioneers, after passing through Hole-in-the-Rock, established the community of Bluff in the spring of 1880, at which time San Juan County was created.
116. Joseph F. and his wife Edna, along with other leaders, left Utah Territory for a time so they could avoid federal prosecution. See Joseph Fielding Smith, *The Life of Joseph F. Smith: Sixth President of The Church of Jesus Christ of Latter-day Saints* (Salt Lake City, UT: Deseret Book, 1938), 131–33. Joseph F. recorded in his journal regarding this trip, "1884 Colorado, & Arizona trip. names of party, Jos. F. Smith & wife Edna & baby, E. Snow & wife, and John Morgan, accompanied to Emery Co. by bro. Andrew Jenson. / August 29th 1884 left Salt Lake city at 11 a.m. by D. & R. G. Ry."
117. The First Presidency and a few other Church leaders were on a tour of the northern territories. See "Local News: A Tour in the North," *Deseret News*, 13 August 1884, 465.

or more Saints in Tennessee.[118] It is too horrible to contemplate.[119] Excuse brevity, and believe me ever— [ ][120]

JOSEPH F. TO MARTHA ANN, 23 AUGUST 1884

Salt Lake U.T. Aug. 23d 1884[121]

My Dear Sister
Martha Ann Harris:—

Yours of the 18,th was duly received. I am sorry you do not enjoy good health. and that the boys are so often out of work, I hope things will change with them for the better, and permanently so.

We are all usually well. Aunt T. and M. J.[122] have just returned from Logan[123] where they have been doing Temple work for some of their dead Kindred.[124] M. J. is not very well.

I send you a list of names &c. for sister Beesley,[125] Son and daughter; which I hope will prove satisfactory.

You must excuse haste as I am sorely pressed for time. Your affectionate brother
Jos. F. Smith

JOSEPH F. TO MARTHA ANN, 26 JANUARY 1885

Sacramento, Jan 26. 85[126]

My Dear Sister

118. On 10 August 1884, a mob attacked the home of Church member James Conder in Cane Creek, Tennessee. The mob wounded Conder's wife and killed his son William Martin Conder, his stepson John Riley Hudson, and two missionaries, Elders John Henry Gibbs and William Shanks Berry. See "The Murdered Elders," *Deseret News*, 20 August 1884, 481; and "An Atrocious Deed," *Deseret News*, 20 August 1884, 488. This event came to be known as the Cane Creek Massacre. A week later, assistant mission president B. H. Roberts traveled in disguise to Tennessee to retrieve the missionaries' bodies. See Marshall Wingfield, "Tennessee's Mormon Massacre," *Tennessee Historical Quarterly* 17 (March 1953): 19–36. See also biographical register, "Conder, William Martin," "Hudson, John Riley," "Gibbs, John Henry," and "Berry, William Shanks."
119. For a broader context, see Patrick Mason, *The Mormon Menace: Violence and Anti-Mormonism in the Postbellum South* (New York: Oxford University Press, 2011).
120. Bottom line of the letter is missing.
121. Written on official letterhead of the Church from the Office of the President.
122. Mercy Rachel Fielding and Mary Jane Thompson.
123. Logan, Cache County, Utah, is located about eighty-three miles northeast of Salt Lake City.
124. The Logan Temple was dedicated on 17 May 1884.
125. Possibly Mary Leese Miller, an elderly woman and the wife of John Beesley. She likely lived in Provo at the time. See biographical register, "Miller, Mary Leese."
126. The original letter is found in the Joseph F. Smith family papers, Annie Clark Tanner Western Americana Collection, Special Collections Department, J. Willard Marriott Library, University of Utah, Salt Lake City.

Martha Ann:—

Months have come and gon since I saw or heard from you. I trust that time is dealing with you with a friendly hand. I am pleased to say that I am well, but too far from home to be entirely comfortable.[127] My lot seemes to be somewhat peculiar. I am apparently doomed to wander upon the earth for a season as a missionary, having the word of life, and the light of the Comforter only as my companion and guide. Still I might be more dependent upon the cold charity of the world, as yet my lot has fallen among friends good and true, and I have not lacked for any thing needful. When I write to you again I may be able to send you some good news. At least I hope so. Twenty one years ago next March, I first visited this city, I was then on my way to the Sandwich Islands for the 2d time.[128] I returned a little less than a year later, and met Levira[129] [**p. 2**] in San francisco, She returned with me to the Sierie Nevadas some 60 miles further east where we got snowed in for two or three days and she went back to San Francisco and I went home. This was the first break and downward move she made from which she never recovered.[130] And now, poor creature <I believe> she is an object of pitty. I expect to visit San Francisco in a few days, and will if possible call and see if Ina[131] has returned. I rather think she has not or I should have heard of it. I have been travelling since Aug. 29th when I left home with E. Snow and J. Morgan[132] to visit the Saints in Colorado New Mexico, Arizona and S. E. Utah.[133] Since then I have been to Oregon in the north and Mexico in the south and the Golden gate[134] in the west_ and east almost to the Missouri.[135] I cannot boast of having <done> much good either to the world or myself still I am confident neither is any the worse for it. I heard thro' the folks that Mary was married.[136] I wish her present and eternal happiness. I regret my absence from home at the time. Give my best love to her & to all the children and friends. I will write again & send you my address. Your Brother.

127. The "Mormon Underground" period had begun. At this point, Joseph F. was in Sacramento, Sacramento County, California, awaiting the arrival of his wife Julina and their infant daughter Julina Clarissa, who were to accompany him to the Sandwich Islands (Hawai'i). Joseph F. was sent to the Islands as a missionary in exile because of the federal prosecution.

128. Joseph F. wrote, "Wednesday Mar. 9th Arrived at Sacramento, took breakfast & dinner at 'the Golden Eagle,' Washed, changed, purchased hats & boots . . . One week from home." Joseph F., journal, 9 March 1864.

129. Joseph F. refers to Levira Annette Clark Smith, his first wife. See introductory material to the 1860–69 chapter. See also Martha Ann to Joseph F., 12 June 1864; and Joseph F. to Martha Ann, 1 December 1868, herein.

130. Joseph F. and Levira's divorce was finalized on 10 July 1869.

131. Ina Coolbrith (née Josephine Donna Smith). See Joseph F. to Martha Ann, 22 May 1885, herein.

132. Erastus Fairbanks Snow was an Apostle, and John Hamilton Morgan was in the Presidency of the Quorum of the Seventy. See biographical register, "Morgan, John Hamilton."

133. See Joseph F. to Martha Ann, 15 August 1884, herein.

134. Connecting the Pacific Ocean and the San Francisco Bay, the Golden Gate is a deep channel. Later it was spanned by the famous bridge in 1937 that took its name.

135. This tour was to keep Church leaders out of Salt Lake City to avoid subpoena and arrest for practicing plural marriage. See Joseph F. to Martha Ann, 15 August 1884, herein.

136. Martha Ann's daughter Mary Emily Harris married Walter Sutton Corbett on 12 November 1884 in Logan, Cache County, Utah Territory.

JOSEPH F. TO MARTHA ANN, 18 MARCH 1885

Private.
P.O. 410 Honolulu, Oahu, S. I.[137]
Mar. 18th 1885[138]

My Dear Sister Martha Ann,

I wrote you last at Sacramento,[139] you will not therefore be surprised to hear from me from these distant lands.[140] What I write you I shall expect will be kept to yourself. Also as to my whereabouts. It seemes I am in some demand in certain quarters.[141] I heard that Ray Davis, Johns precious son in law,[142] has been trying to get me indicted for living with and supporting my family, and has succeeded but not satisfied with that he has been trying to bring me into further trouble upon a rumor of my having married somebody—goodness only knows who—and for this purpose he gave to the Grand Inquisition the name of my niece Mary E.[143] in hopes they could wring something out of her, as he knew she had been for some time living with us. I am of the opinion that Rays Mother-in-law[144] is but little better than he, as Mary informed the "girls"[145] that she had quizz'd her very carefully about my family matters while she (Mary) was stopping with us. I say this much to you to put you on your guard, and that you may put others on their guard against associations with Ray Davis or his aforesaid Mother-in-law. I do not blame John—but I sympathise with him in his unfortunate associations and relations.

I am aware that the children sometimes visit at Johns & hence with his family whom I, at least, cannot trust. They do not have good feelings for me or mine, because they do not feel as I do, nor have they the same faith,[146] besides I have been kind to Melissa,[147] and it was thro' me that she has been able to get a little support from John. For this some of them—and I do not know but John himself has feelings towards me. But I have only done my duty in this matter and I know it is right therefore I do not fear the consequences, nor would I change it if I could.

We have heard that Mary had been before the Inquisition (fallsly called a "Grant Jury",) where she had been quizzed in relation to my family affairs. I have no fears that she would intentionally give any evidence against me, but her inexperiance and the natural timidity one feels who is unacquainted with such matters, when brought in contact with such an infernal Machine as this inquisition is, makes possible results very uncertain. I am **[p. 2]** very sorry that

137. Joseph F. departed for Hawai'i with his wife Julina and their daughter Julina Clarissa in early February 1885 aboard the *Mariposa*.
138. Joseph F. was forty-six, and Martha Ann was forty-three.
139. See Joseph F. to Martha Ann, 26 January 1885, herein.
140. The islands were still part of the Kingdom of Hawai'i at this time.
141. Concerned about detection and arrest, Joseph F. marked the letter "Private" and asked Martha Ann to keep information about him, his family, and present location confidential.
142. Ray Leroy Davis married Lucy Smith, daughter of John Smith. See biographical register, "Davis, Ray Leroy."
143. Martha Ann's nineteen-year-old daughter, Mary Emily Harris, was examined before a grand jury regarding her relation to Joseph F. and his plural marriage relationships.
144. Hellen Maria Fisher.
145. Joseph F.'s wives.
146. Joseph F.'s relationship with his half brother John was strained at this time by differing views about plural marriage.
147. Probably Nancy Melissa Lemmon, John Smith's plural wife with whom he did not live and apparently did not have a close relationship, owing in part to his first wife's opposition to plural marriage. See Irene M. Bates and E. Gary Smith, *Lost Legacy: The Mormon Office of Presiding Patriarch* (Urbana: University of Illinois Press, 1996).

she was put to the annoyance of such an unsaught and unwelcome interview, and I hope also they had only their trouble for their pains, and that Mary came out first best. And tell her she has my confidence and love and blessing, that she will always remain true and faithful to her kindred and friends and to the Kingdom of God. I am sorry for Lucy[148] and for John and their unfortunate connection with that miserable, "cussed" little traitor Ray Davis. And if he does not get his deserts it will not be because of a lack of faith on my part.

I arrived in these lands on Feb—9th ~~and~~ and the following day came out here—where I met our boy, Hyrum,[149] looking and feeling well, and seemingly as happy as he could be so far from home, and surrounded by so many circumstances foreign to his customs of youth. He is making very good progress in the study of the language, but feels the lack of early training in study. I am sure he will urge his brothers, and especialy the younger ones to apply their minds to study, every moment they can, so that when any of them are called to fill a mission they will be better prepared, and in a measure quallified to apply their minds to study. Hyrum is doing well and will improve himself—and be able to do good to others while on his mission. Altho' he is not quite so young as I was when I first started out, he is in quite as good a position to learn. Robert[150] is also here, and is doing first rate so far. He has more confidence in himself than Hyrum has in himself, and therfore makes a little better showing in his study of the language. But when Hyrum gets down to study, and gains self relians he will not be far behind.

Aunt J.[151] is here with me, she takes great interest in the boys—and will look after their mending and making so far as needed while she remains. But we hope that our release may come soon, for we are needed at home.

When I heard that S. & E[152]—and all my little ones had been forced to leave home, in the dead of winter, to seek shelter among friends and neighbors, from the venum and bigotry of a mob of deputy marshals, and U. S. office-holders, I felt that somebody was about ready for the wrath of God.[153] Not that it is any worse for me and my **[p. 3]** family to suffer than for others, but of course it came nearer home and I could not but feel it all the keener.

It is no triffling matter for Mothers who are nursing babis and who have a number of other little helpless ones clinging to their skirts besides, to be driven from their comfortable homes in the most inclement season of the year—with no certain shelter or convenience for their protection and comfort to become a burden upon others. And as I live I will hold somebody responsible for this act of cruelty and barbarism before the judgement seat of God. And among the guilty ones I shall not forget that damnable little pup, Ray Davis, as one of the principals in this fiendish move. The least spark of manliness on their part would at least have suggested

148. Lucy Smith.
149. Martha Ann's son Hyrum Smith Harris was serving as a missionary in the Sandwich Islands at this time.
150. Robert Blashel Thompson Taylor, son of Mary Jane Thompson.
151. Julina Lambson.
152. Sarah Ellen Richards and Edna Lambson.
153. Joseph F. wrote about this incident in his journal on 12 February 1885: "Sam. Gilson and three other deputy marshals made a raid on my houses on Saturday, Feb. 7th. They found Aunt Melissa L. Smith and Albert J. Davis and subpoenaed them to appear before either commissioner McKay or the grand jury, which was not stated, but I suppose the grand jury. Bertie refused to give his name, he was subpoenaed as 'John Doe,' but up to the 12th he did not appear. Five of my children were at home at the time; three of Julina's and one each of Sarah's and Edna's, whom the deputies interrogated but could get no information from them; they refusing to give their name, telling the marshals it was 'none of their business.' Sarah and Edna and the children had to leave home to avoid being subpoenaed. Where they went was not stated. This was but one of many raids. Well and long will they be remembered by those children who were home and forced to listen to the abuse and threats of the occasion."

the propriety of waiting for my return home, before making a raid upon my defensless family. I might not have been so healthy for some one—even if it had been only for myself, if I had been nearby. It is perhaps well that I was not.

But this is only vain talk—and I am getting sick of talk. I would like to see some lighning from the other side soon. I had the pleasure of reading Joseph A.'s[154] letter of Feb. 15th to Hyrum, and was pleased with the spirit of it. I would write to him and to Willie[155] and Mary, but I do not care to make myself so conspicuous just now. You can tell them all, that you have heard from me, and that I am well and as usual engaged in the duties of my calling as a messenger of the Gospel to the people of the Earth. I am as useful here at present as I could be any where. And when my labors will be more useful somewhere else I hope to be found there. With me it is the Kingdom of God or nothing. My only course is onward and, I trust, upward. I can yeald to nothing but the will and pleasure of the Almighty. It is my delight to serve the Lord and the people of God. The Lord has made me instrumental in bringing at least two souls into the church by baptism since my arrival on this Island. I hope others will follow. The language is coming back to me rapidly and I can speak quite fluently again in the native tongue, but not as I could once, and perhaps never can again as I could and did in my youth. But adding my experiance [**p. 4**] to or in the place of what I have forgotten in the language I do not know but I can do as much good now as I could when I was here before.

I have often thought of you and your children in the last six or seven months. It has been that long practically since I have been absent from home. My little Willard is now about four month old and I have scarcely seen him or his mother in that time.[156] And yet it is for no offence or crime that I have committed that I have been thus, in a manner, banished from my home and little ones.

Edna accompanied me from home in August and traveled with me for a month[157]—since then she and her little ones have been separated from me, so that I have scarcely seen them. And now my family have been scattered I hardly know where and I am thousands of miles away from them with out power to look after them. I look and long for my liberty once more, not but what I should be and am content to labor where I am sent and do all I can for good where ever I may be. Give my love to William and all the children. I pray for you all—and I trust I am remembered by them and you. Remember me kindly to bro. and sister Mecham. Tell them I am on a mission, preaching the Gospel, but you need not say where, for I am here to day, there tomorrow—and elsewhere the next day, and I may be in the Southern States or England, or Mexico next month, and you do not know where I am. Except that I maybe somewhere in the South.

J. sends love to you. Baby is well, and we would all be happy and enjoy ourselves if we only knew that our loved ones at home were safe and well. Hyrum will send this to you, and should you write send it to him, you know his address. It is at the top of this letter. I trust you can read this. I have scribbled hurridly. I saw your last letter to Hyrum, but you did not mention any thing about Mary being dragged before the Inquisition.

154. Joseph Albert Harris.

155. William Jasper Harris Jr.

156. Willard Richards Smith was born to Sarah Ellen Richards on 20 November 1884. See biographical register, "Smith, Willard Richards."

157. See Joseph F. to Martha Ann, 15 August 1884, herein.

I hope all is well with you and the family and that God will bless you all. Tell Willie & Jos. and Frank, and John[158] that their Uncle expects them to be Men of honor and of truth, and faithful to the Cause of Zion[159] always. Hoping to see you all again some day I am your affectionate brother.

JOSEPH F. TO MARTHA ANN, 13 APRIL 1885

Apr. 13th 1885[160]

My Dear Sister
Martha Ann.

I had the pleasure of reading a letter from you and some of the rest of the folks lately, in which mention was mad of Marys[161] appearance before the Grand Jury in Salt Lake City, I was somewhat worried about the matter for fear that she said something which could be used against me. I would like to know what she did say so that I could prepare myself before hand to meet my accusers. I do not suppose for a moment that she would intentionally "give me away". But knowing her inexperience in such matters I am fearful she has unwittingly told about all they wanted to know— Of course what is done cannot be helped. And perhaps she is not aware of the fact that when she is again brought upon the witness stand she will have to face everything she has said to the Jury. and what she did say will be brought out in open court. I do not know whether you knew this or not, or if you did, whether you thought of it. Now I am going to ask you some questions—which were no doubt put to Mary in the Jury room—and I would like you to get her answers and **[p. 2]** let me know—sending your letter to H.[162] so that I can get it from him. In the first place they would ask her name and relationship. Then they would ask about as follows.

Did you ever live at your uncles?
1 How long did you live there?
2 How many wives has he?
3 What are their names?
4 How many children have they?
5 What are the ages of the youngest ones?
6 Did he stay with them all, eat & sleep &c. &c?
7 Did you ever hear him call them his wives?
8 Did you ever hear him call the children his?
9 Is he the father of these children?
10 Does he support them?
11 What are the names of his children?

158. William Jasper Harris Jr., Joseph Albert Harris, Franklin Hill Harris, and John Fielding Harris.
159. See Doctrine and Covenants 6:6; 11:6; 12:6; 21:7.
160. Joseph F. did not specify where the letter was written, perhaps because he was in hiding.
161. Mary Emily Harris. See Joseph F. to Martha Ann, 18 March 1885, herein.
162. Hyrum Smith Harris, also serving as a missionary in Hawai'i at the time.

Now what I want to know is—what answers did M. make to each and all of these questions? It is very importent to me to know just what answers were given for on the answers given the whole matter depends. and what other questions were asked her, and what her answers were. All that she did say was taken down by a reporter, and when she is brought into court, which she will be—~~should~~ when I am obliged, to meet the indictment against me, she will have it to [**p. 3**] face, and unless she meets it squarely—she will be liable to prossecution for perjury. Therefore I would like you to get the exact truth so far as possible. Again, when she went to the city did she not go to Johns?[163] Did she go to our house? Please tell me where she stopped while in the city and as far as possible who she talked with while there. How many days was she in the city? and any other particulars you can get. I am afraid I am asking of you something that will be quite a task, but it is very important that I should know, my liberty is at stake. I prefer not to go to the Pen.[164] if I can help it, and if I can learn what the evidence is upon which an indictment was found it may be in my power to advise M. for her good and mine too. But unless I can get the streight of these matters, I can do nothing but await the issue. I think it was Ray Davis who gave Ms—name to the Jury—and I think too that he got his information from Helen, at least in part.[165] Ray himself knows nothing only what he has heard. His testimony is worthless, no matter how bitter the little Villain may be, but M. was an inmate of my house, saw and knew for herself, and what they got out of her would be evidence, and will be used in the trial. Therefore she will be to them a very imp[**p. 4**]ortant witness in the case. I am very sorry to trouble you, with these matters— I do not want you to feel worried or get nervous about it. nor feel bad. I do not censure, M. nor blame her. I believe she would not intentionally do anything to hurt me, but she is the only witness they had in my case that knew anything personally. Hence my anxiety about what she did say.

I know you will do all you can for me, you might get Joseph A.[166] to assist you. My whereabouts must be kept to yourself— The enemy is on the alert they want to find somebody very badly, but so far they have failed. Do not trust any body—or they will trust somebody else, and so on, from one to another. These are serious matters. And in this instance they come home to yourself as well as to me. I have written twice to you and the same to John, but so far have received not a line from either of you. I am sorry for John—he has been nursing a viper[167] in his confidence who has struck at hime thro' me—but I doubt if he can see it. If I had a creature about me that would betray him, I would feel like wringing its miserable neck— I may not be as good as I ought to be, but I am not a traitor to my kindred or friends. We are all well, and send love, We hope you are also well. From your Brother

163. John Smith.

164. Known as the "Pen," the Utah Territorial Penitentiary was established in 1855 in what became known as the Sugar House Ward, an area about six miles south of Salt Lake City. The prison was federally operated by US Marshals beginning in 1871 and was enlarged in the 1880s to accommodate an increasing number of Latter-day Saints incarcerated there for violations of antipolygamy laws being enacted in Washington, DC.

165. Hellen Maria Fisher. See Joseph F. to Martha Ann, 18 March 1885, herein.

166. Joseph Albert Harris.

167. Likely refers to John Smith's son-in-law Ray Davis or possibly to John's wife Hellen Maria Fisher.

JOSEPH F. TO MARTHA ANN, 22 MAY 1885

Lanihuli,[168]
May 22d 1885

My Dear Sister Martha Ann

I am pleased to acknowledge the receipt on the 8th inst. of yours of Apr. 19th, which was the first I have received from you since I left home. You are aware that I left home on the 29th of Aug. 1884. and, practically, I have not been home since.[169] And you are also no doubt aware that my folks also left home in the fore part of Feb. '84, and were absent, knocking about, from pillar to post, for over eleven weeks, with their little ones, the mother of part of them being thousands of miles away and unable to do one thing to help them in their wanderings, and all on account of persecutions and some of our friendly (?) neighbors, and pretended friends.[170]

You may depend upon it I do not feel very lamb-like towards some of them for the officious part they have taken in some of these matters. But I can afford to wait the due course of God's Judgement when just compensation shall be meted out to each, according to the intents and purposes of the heart and the acts performed. I do not censure Mary for I am satisfied that she would not intentionally do me a wrong, or injure me or mind.[171] I do not believe I have a <blood> relative in Utah who is so unnatural or heartless as to desire me evil, but I am [**p. 2**] sure the grand "inquisition" would get all they could out of her, and make the most possible of it. In my last I sent you some questions, which I supposed, had been put to her, which I desired you to return with the answers she gave so that I might see and judge for myself the extent of facts or information elicited from her. For, as you are aware, they will depend upon her as a witness in court, and will compell her to substantiate her evidence before the "inquisition".

I have not seen anything in Hyrums letters,[172] which give any light on this subject, and I think he has shown me all his letters from you, and from Joseph and Mary.[173] But if you succeed in answering my last I shall be satisfied. I am sorry you have to continue in such straitened circumstances, but I hope and pray with all my heart that it will not be for always. I

168. Lanihuli was the name of the mission compound at the Church's plantation in Lā'ie on the island of O'ahu. Joseph F. recommended to Brigham Young that the Saints gather at Lā'ie on the island of O'ahu in 1864, following the Walter Gibson crisis on Lāna'i. See Joseph F. to Martha Ann, 22 June 1864, herein. See also Riley M. Moffat, Fred E. Woods, and Jeffrey N. Walker, *Gathering to Lā'ie* (Lā'ie, HI: Jonathan Napela Center for Hawaiian and Pacific Island Studies, 2011), 73–75.

169. On 29 August 1884, Joseph F. departed from his home with his wife Edna and several other Church leaders on a tour of Colorado and other southern territories. The main purpose of the tour was to get Joseph F. and others away from Salt Lake City in order to avoid court subpoena or prosecution for plural marriage. Joseph F. was continually "on the underground," or in exile, between 1884 and 1891. See Joseph F. to Martha Ann, 15 August 1884, herein, and section introduction.

170. Joseph F. laments that neighbors and "pretended" friends in Salt Lake City assisted federal officers in their prosecution against him. Sometimes Joseph F.'s wives and children, who remained in Salt Lake City, were compelled to leave their homes in order to avoid subpoena by federal marshals. See Joseph F. to Martha Ann, 18 March 1885, herein.

171. Mary Emily Harris. See Joseph F. to Martha Ann, 18 March 1885 and 13 April 1885, herein.

172. In a previous letter, Joseph F. instructed Martha Ann to enclose a letter to her son Hyrum Smith Harris, who was serving as a missionary in the Sandwich Islands at this time. See Joseph F. to Martha Ann, 13 April 1885, herein.

173. Joseph Albert Smith and Mary Emily Harris.

am also sorry that Willie has to work under-ground,[174] I hope he will be able to find—or "turn up" something better before long. I am very thankful that Mary has got so good a husband,[175] and they both have my blessing and my earnest prayers for their present and future prosperity and happiness.

I have received one letter from Hyrum, since we parted and have written to him twice. He was doing well. You must not mention where I have been. I expect to leave here soon, but I do not want my friends (?) who are so much interested in my whereabouts to be put to the trouble of keeping track of me. A hint to the wise is sufficient. We are are all well, except Ina,[176] she is troubled with 8 big teeth all at once. She is some better. I called on Cousin Ina at her home in Cal.[177] but did not let her know my lodgings or my destination. She thought it very strange but I knew it was for the best. Remember me kindly to Wm[178] & believe me, yours,[179]

JOSEPH F. TO MARTHA ANN, 30 NOVEMBER 1885

Lanihuli Retreat[180]
Nov. 30th 1885

My Dear Sister,

Your welcome favor of Oct. 6th came to hand Nov. 25th. It was a long time on the way, I received it from Hyrum.[181] He is on Hawaii the farthest Island to the South-east from here.[182] He wrote me quite a letter in "Native", accompanying yours, and I see that he is improving very nicely in the language. I regret very much that he has not had better opportunities at School before coming on a mission, he feels the need of it now, and it would be a help to him beyond every other consideration. I hope the other boys—and girls too—may have greater advantages than he has had. I wish I could help you in regard to this matter. Your children should have a chance to go to School. Why should my poor—dear sister and her family ever be bound down by the strong cords of poverty and want? Perhaps it is all right, but it seemes to me there is a screw loose some where. I do not think it is your fault. surely you have ever worked hard enough and have deserved better fare. I am sorry to say that I notice in Hyrum a lack of carefulness in regard to his clothes and means. but I hope as he gets older he will be more prudent. I was **[p. 2]** careful and economical to a fault, I never liked to make a bad

174. William Jasper Harris Jr. was probably working in mining, a major industry at the time. Brigham Young and some other Church leaders, however, typically discouraged mining in favor of agricultural work and other industries. William Harris Sr. was apparently involved in the discovery of the Mammoth Mine in the Tintic Mining District in northeastern Juab County, Utah Territory. See Carole Call King, "History of William Jasper Harris, 1841–1921" (paper presented at monthly meeting of the Daughters of Utah Pioneers, copy in the editors' possession), 6.
175. Mary Emily Harris married Walter Sutton Corbett on 12 November 1884 in Logan, Cache County, Utah Territory.
176. Likely a nickname for Joseph F.'s one-year-old daughter, Julina Clarissa Smith, who was with him in Hawai'i.
177. Ina Coolbrith (née Josephine Donna Smith) lived in San Francisco at this time.
178. William Jasper Harris.
179. The final paragraph is written upside down in the top margin of page 2. There is no signature.
180. See Joseph F. to Martha Ann, 22 May 1885, herein.
181. Hyrum Smith Harris.
182. The Hawaiian Islands were named after Hawai'i, known as the Big Island.

trade—hence I never did much trading—preferring to stick to what I had—and make the best of it to risking the possibility of getting something worse in a trade. And I cannot bear wastefulness nor untidiness— Hyrum is not untidy in his appearance, but very much so in putting away and taking care of what he has. I have talked to him like a Father on the subject, and will do all I can to help him. He is a good boy—and my interest is no less for him because he is your son, I can assure you. I would be as proud of his success, as I could be if he was my own son. His beginning, altho' a little older than I was, is as good as mine was, when I first came to these lands in my childhood. I hope he will improve his opportunities better than I did, and make a wiser and a better man of himself—by the help of the Lord. There seemes to be no reason why he should not. I shall be as happy and pleased to see it, if my life is spared, as you will yourself, or any one else could. I was greatly pleased with one of Joseph A's.[183] letters to Hyrum. The spirit of it was good and the mechanical part was almost faultless. I should have said that the Spirit of his letter was faultless, indeed excellent, and the chirography[184] was good. He might have improved it a little, grammatically, but otherwise

Dec. 11th 1885. We wish you a merry christmas and a happy new year. This leaves us all well—and in very good spirits. J[185] joines me in love to you all.[186]

JOSEPH F. TO MARTHA ANN, 11 FEBRUARY 1887

In Exile, Feb. 11th 1887[187]

My Very Dear Sister
Martha Ann.

Your welcome favor of Jan. 9th is rec'd. I read your letter with more than ordinary interest, being exceedingly pleased and grateful for the kindness of Pres. A. O. Smoot[188] towards your children, in assisting them to school.

I scarcely need say I hope the children will fully appreciate their opportunity and their "Grandpa's"[189] kindness towards them, and put in their very best licks to improve their minds, and lay a foundation for inteligence and usefulness in the future. I am sorry for Lucys[190] delicate health, and still pray that she may permainently recover. I hope Mary is all right by

183. Joseph Albert Harris.
184. Penmanship.
185. Julina Lambson.
186. Written upside down in the top margin of page 1.
187. Joseph F. was forty-eight, and Martha Ann was forty-five.
188. Abraham O. Smoot, president of the Utah Stake in Utah Valley.
189. Because Martha Ann's mother-in-law was married to Abraham O. Smoot, he was considered to be a grandfather to Martha Ann's children, even though they were not biologically related.
190. Lucy Smith Harris.

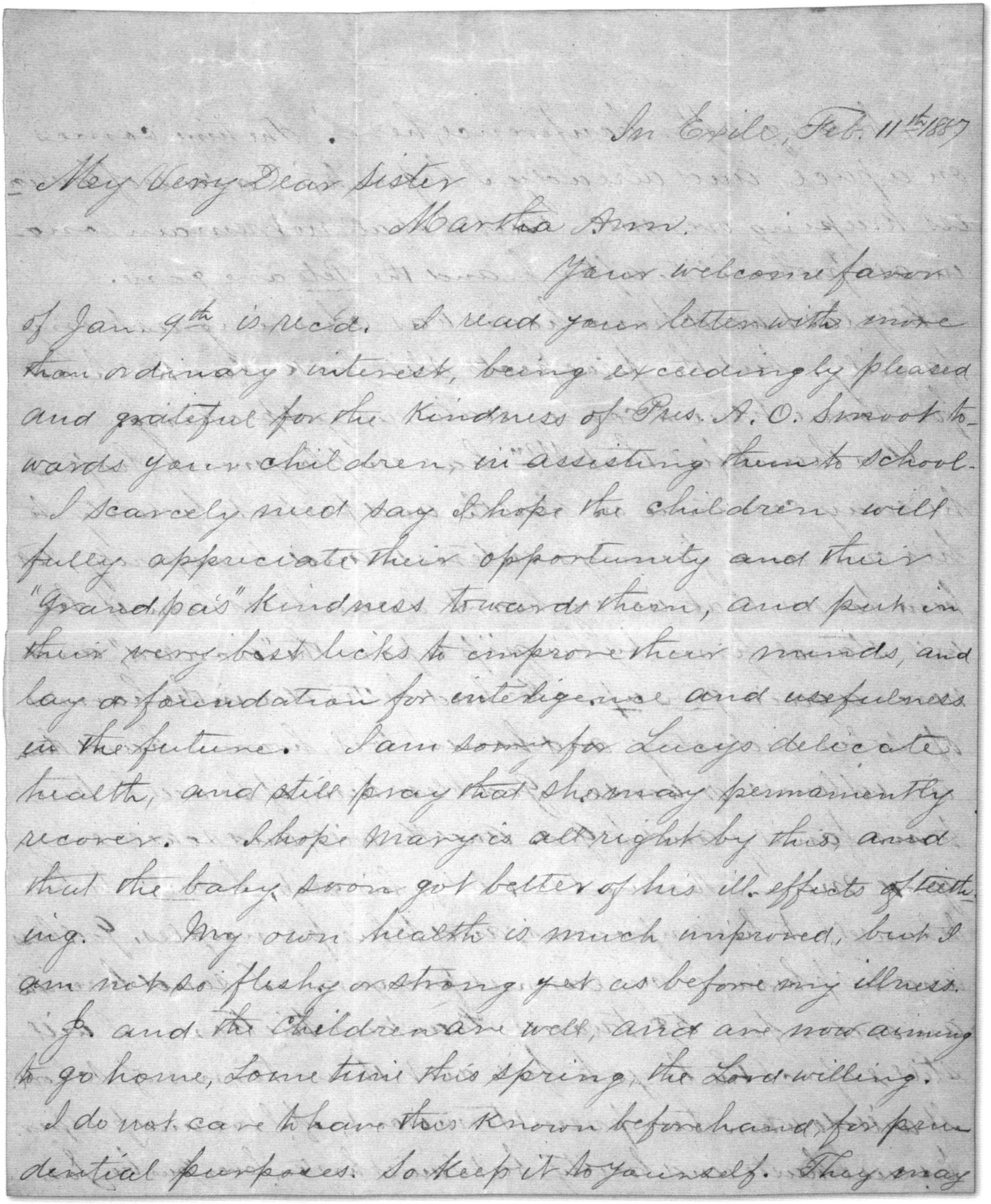
In Exile, Feb. 11th 1887

My Very Dear Sister
Martha Ann.

Your welcome favor of Jan. 9th is rec'd. I read your letter with more than ordinary interest, being exceedingly pleased and grateful for the kindness of Pres. A. O. Smoot towards your children, in assisting them to school. I scarcely need say I hope the children will fully appreciate their opportunity and their "grandpa's" kindness towards them, and put in their very best licks to improve their minds, and lay a foundation for intelligence and usefulness in the future. I am sorry for Lucy's delicate health, and still pray that she may permanently recover. I hope Mary is all right by this, and that the baby soon got better of his ill-effects of teething. My own health is much improved, but I am not so fleshy or strong yet as before my illness. J. and the children are well, and are now aiming to go home, some time this spring, the Lord willing. I do not care to have this known beforehand, for prudential purposes. So keep it to yourself. They may

Joseph F. to Martha Ann, 11 February 1887 (p. 1)

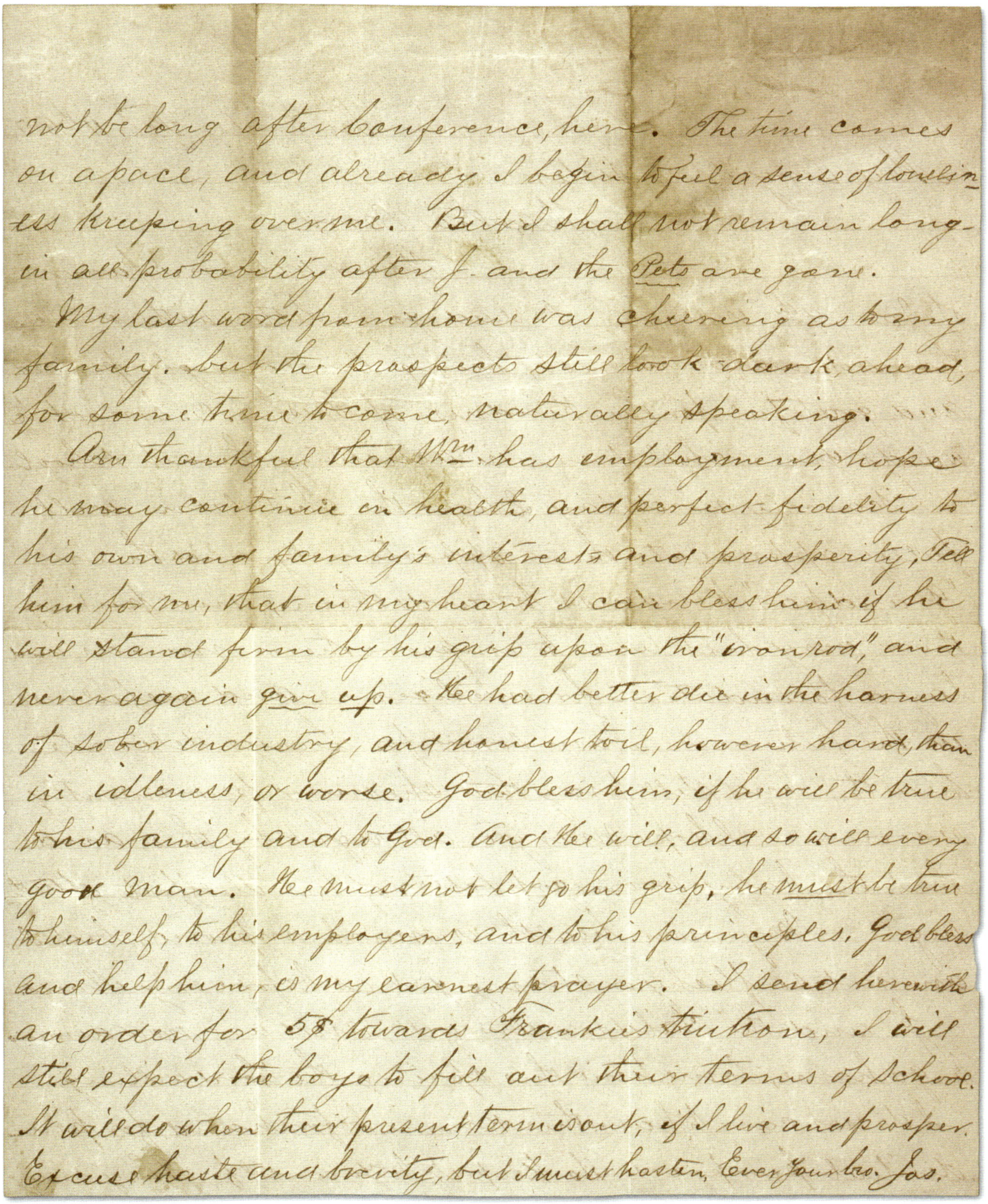
not be long after Conference, here. The time comes
on apace, and already I begin to feel a sense of loneliness kreeping over me. But I shall not remain long-
in all probability after J. and the <u>Pets</u> are gone.
My last word from home was cheering as to my
family. but the prospects still look dark ahead,
for some time to come, naturally speaking.
Am thankful that Wm. has employment, hope
he may continue in health, and perfect fidelity to
his own and family's interests and prosperity, Tell
him for me, that in my heart I can bless him if he
will stand firm by his grip upon the "iron rod," and
never again <u>give up</u>. He had better die in the harness
of sober industry, and honest toil, however hard, than
in idleness, or worse. God bless him, if he will be true
to his family and to God. And He will, and so will every
good man. He must not let go his grip, he <u>must</u> be true
to himself, to his employers, and to his principles. God bless
and help him, is my earnest prayer. I send herewith
an order for 5$ towards Frankie's tuition, I will
still expect the boys to fill out their terms of School.
It will do when their present term is out, if I live and prosper.
Excuse haste and brevity, but I must hasten, Ever your bro. Jos.

Joseph F. to Martha Ann, 11 February 1887 (p. 2)

this, and that the baby soon got better of his ill-effects of teething.[191] My own health is much improved, but I am not so fleshy or strong yet as before my illness.

J. and the children[192] are well, and are now aiming to go home, some time this spring, the Lord willing. I do not care to have this known before hand, for prudential purposes. So keep it to yourself. They may **[p. 2]** not be long after Conference, here. The time comes on apace, and already I begin to feel a sense of loneliness kreeping over me. But I shall not remain long—in all probability after J. and the Pets are gone.

My last word from home was cheering as to my family, but the prospects still look dark, ahead, for some time to come, naturally speaking.

Am thankful that Wm[193] has employment, hope he may continue in health, and perfect fidelity to his own and family's interests and prosperity. Tell him for me, that in my heart I can bless him if he will stand firm by his grip upon the "iron rod," and never again give up.[194] He had better die in the harness of sober industry, and honest toil, however hard, than in idleness, or worse. God bless him, if he will be true to his family and to God. And He will, and so will every good man. He must not let go his grip, he must be true to himself, to his employers, and to his principles, God bless and help him, is my earnest prayer. I send herewith an order for 5$ towards Frankies[195] tiution, I will still expect the boys to fill out their terms of school. It will do when their present term is out, if I live and prosper. Excuse haste and brevity, but I must hasten, Ever Your bro. Jos.

MARTHA ANN TO JOSEPH F., 11 MARCH 1887

Ans'd Apr. 27 1887[196]

Provo Mar 11[197]

belovd brother your welcome favor of Feb the 11th came safely to hand last week & I thank you for writing to me for I am always glad to hear from you I was glad to hear you were some better & that you were all well as useuel. but it brought a heavey sence of care when you told me the news I can not blame you but O do bee care full there has so maney dreemed such ugly dreems about you I dremt one my self about you [*illegible strike-through*] ~~but~~ but my continual prayr for my dear berother is for his safty & I know youare in the hands of our Father in

191. Mary Emily Harris gave birth to Walter Harris Corbett on 28 October 1885, five days before Martha Ann wrote the letter to which Joseph F. is responding. Joseph F. likely refers to this baby here. See biographical register, "Corbett, Walter Harris."
192. Joseph F.'s wife Julina Lambson and their daughter Julina Clarissa had accompanied Joseph F. to Hawai'i. Another of Joseph and Julina's daughters, Donnette, arrived in Hawai'i with her aunt Melissa Davis in October 1886. While in Hawai'i, Julina gave birth to Elias Wesley Smith on 21 April 1886. See biographical register, "Smith, Elias Wesley."
193. William Jasper Harris.
194. 1 Nephi 15:23–24.
195. Franklin Hill Harris.
196. Joseph F. wrote this in ink sideways in the top left margin of page 1.
197. "[1887]" was written in pencil by an unknown hand, most likely an archivist at the CHL, above "Provo Mar 11," which was written between the first and second lines of the letter by Martha Ann.

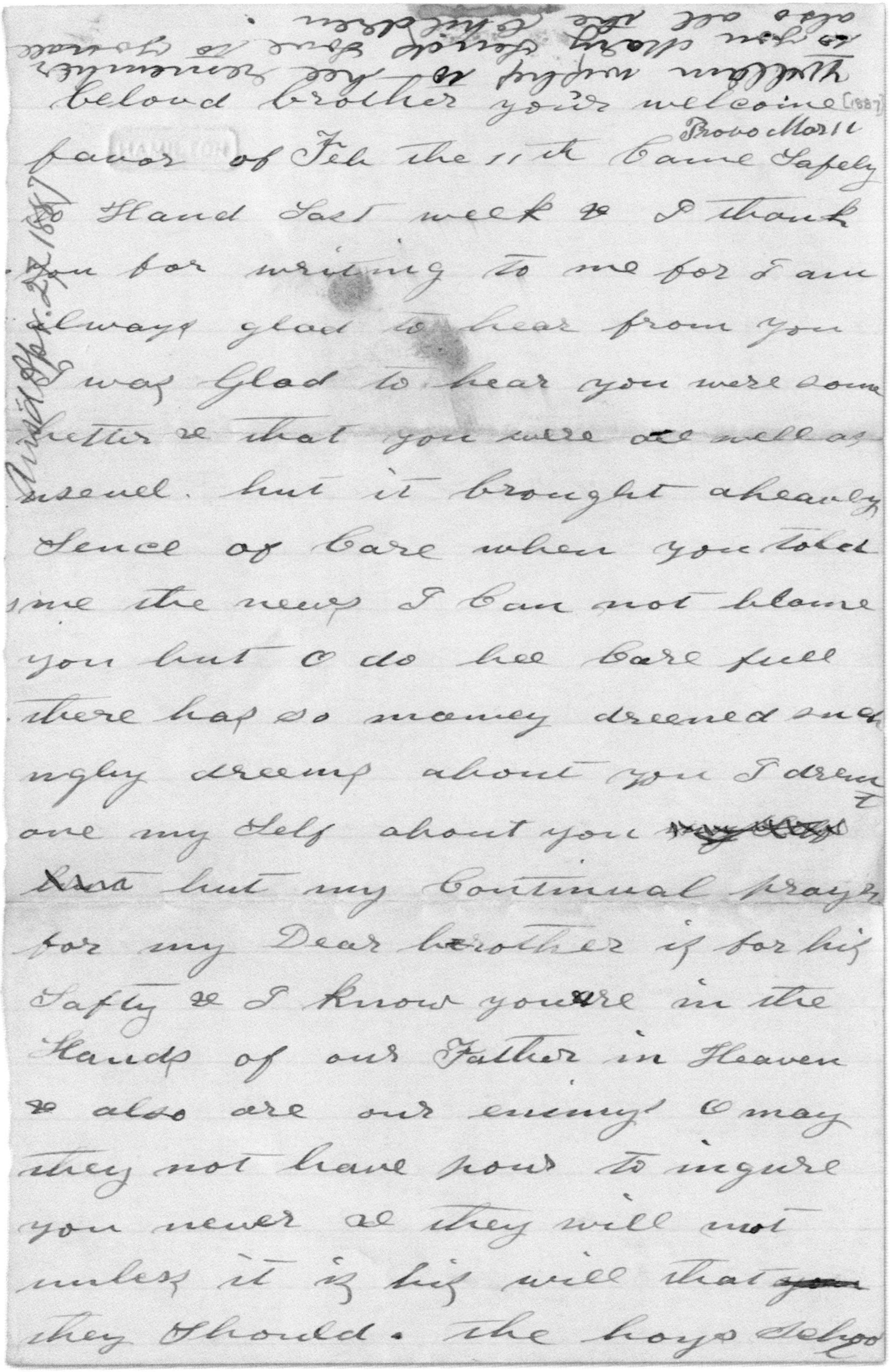

William wishes to be remembered to you Molly sends love to Julina also all the children.

beloved brother your welcome [1887] Provo Mar 11

favor of Feb the 11th Came Safely

to Hand last week & I thank

you for writing to me for I am

always glad to hear from you

I was Glad to hear you were some

better & that you were all well as

useual. but it brought a heavy

Sence of Care when you told

me the news I Can not blame

you but O do bee Care full

there has so maney dreemed such

ugly dreems about you I dream^t

one my Self about you ~~myself~~

~~ther~~ but my Continual prayer

for my Dear brother is for his

Safty & I know you are in the

Hands of our Father in Heaven

& also are our enemys O may

they not have pour to ingure

you never & they will not

unless it is his will that ~~you~~

they Should. the boys Scho[ol]

Rec'd Apr. 2d 1887

Martha Ann to Joseph F., 11 March 1887 (p. 1)

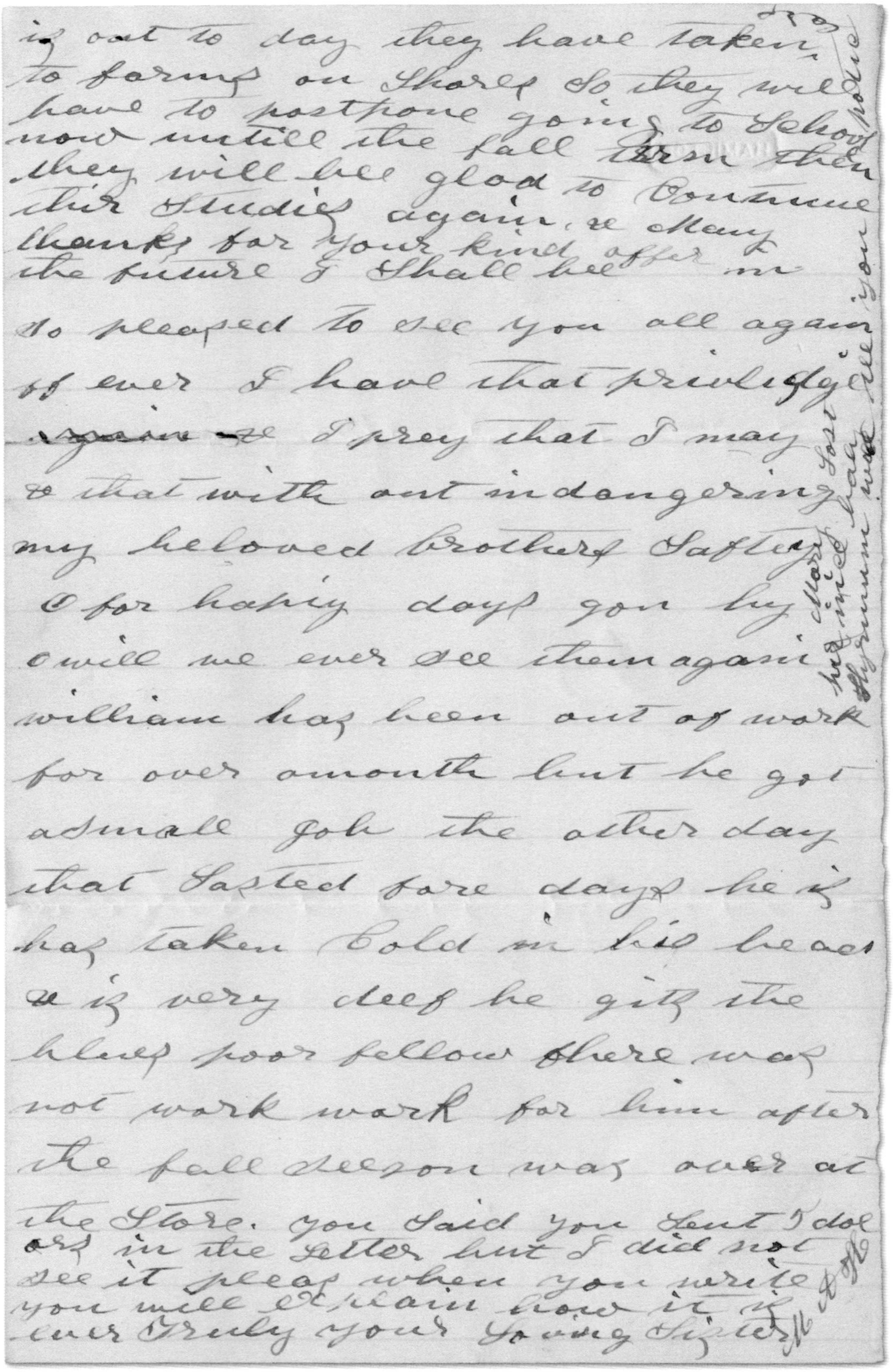
is out to day they have taken
to farms on Shares So they will
have to postpone going to School
now untill the fall term then
they will bee glad to Continue
their Studies again. & Many
thanks for your kind offer in
the future I Shall bee
so pleased to see you all again
if ever I have that priviledge
again & I prey that I may
& that with out indangering
my beloved brothers Saftey
O for happy days gon by
O will we ever see them again
william has been out of work
for over amonth but he got
asmall Job the other day
that lasted fore days he is
has taken Cold in his head
& is very deef he gits the
blues poor fellow there was
not work work for him after
the fall season was over at
the Store. you said you sent 5 dol
ars in the letter but I did not
see it pleas when you write
you will explain how it is
ever Truly your loving Sister M A H

Mary has lost her ... Hymn book ... if you notice

Martha Ann to Joseph F., 11 March 1887 (p. 2)

Heaven & also are our enimys O may they not have pour to ingure you never & they will not unless it is his will that ~~you~~ they should. the boys school [**p. 2**] is out to day they have taken to farms on shares so they will have to postpone going to school now untill the fall term then they will bee glad to continue thir studies again & many thanks for your kind offer in the future I shall bee so pleased to see you all again if ever I have that privledge ~~again~~ & I prey that I may & that with out indangering my beloved brothers saftey O for hopiy days gon by O will we ever see them again william[198] has been out of work for over a month but he got a small job the other day that lasted fore days he is has taken cold in his head & is very deef he gits the blues poor fellow there was not work work for him after the fall seeson was over at the store. you said you sent 5 dolors in the letter but I did not see it pleas when you write you will explain how it is ever truly your loving sister M A H

Mary lost her nice baby[199] Hyruum [*"will see"*][200] you poticlars[201]

Willam wishes to bee remember to you Mary sends love to you all also all the children.[202]

Martha Ann to Joseph F., ca. May–June 1887 (envelope front and back)

198. William Jasper Harris.
199. Joseph Smith Corbett was born to Mary Emily Harris on 29 January 1887 and died two days later. See biographical register, "Corbett, Joseph Smith."
200. The two illegible words here could be "will see." Martha Ann's son Hyrum Smith Harris was serving in Hawai'i at the time.
201. Written sideways in the right margin of page 2.
202. Written upside down in the top margin of page 2.

MARTHA ANN TO JOSEPH F., CA. MAY–JUNE 1887

[Ca. May–June 1887][203]

My dear brother[204] your wecome favor of <march> the 11 came to hand on the 20 of may it was detained some how I was so thankfull to hear from my my dear brother it always gives me pleasure to hear from you. I did not know whether to write to you any more or not until I hird from you again. I am thankfull to hear that you are as well as you say you are. I know your anxiety must be intence the mind being worried is wors than bodily suffering I find it so in my experience at least, & I know or at least I can imagin some little how you must feel away from your loved ones so long as you have been[205] I do not know whether I could bee as brave as Julina[206] was or not she sirtenly is brave to do what she done I have not seen her yet but William went to the City[207] not long ago & he seen her also frank[208] called there they **[p. 2]** were better of thir coalds I recieved a short note from hir yester evning with the five dolars in it you sent for the school bill I will take it to brothir Maiser[209] to day & I cincerly thank you for it untill I can do somethng more substancial for your kindness Franklin started to the park yester day to run the brick mashiene for brother Cook[210] of this town he is a good man & an honest one & will pay his hands Hyrum has worked for him he will tell you what kind of a man he is he sais he wishes he had Hyrum to run it for him he youst to run it for him when he was here he sais he never had nor would ask for any better boys to work for him than Hyrum & Frank was. he will give him too dolars & 50 <a> day & bourd for all sumer if he wants it. the boys hear at home will have thir hands full to keep things moving **[p. 3]** they have thirty achers f lucern[211] to tend to. & fore achors of wheet in three achors oats thre achors potatos one of squashes one corn thre of cain & some melons he sids[212] the lots here at home we will not have any fruit this year so we will have to b<u>y all we have of that. there is one or to trees that have aples on if the worms can bee kept of them the peaches & pears ar all killed, with the frost the worms

---

203. The envelope is addressed to "J. S. Speight. Esq. Honolulu Oahu H.I. Box 412" by an unknown person, not Martha Ann. Interestingly, the envelope was sent from Hawai'i. The two-dollar Hawaiian postal stamp features King David Kalākaua, with a Hawaiian postal mark stamped across it: "PAAUILO, HAWAII JUN 22." A second postal mark, "HONOLULU H.I. JUN 26 1887," suggests the day the letter arrived at the post office in Honolulu. Joseph F. noted on the cover in purple pencil that he had received the letter the following day: "Martha A. Harris Rec'd June 27 June—1887." The best explanation for the information on the envelope is that Martha Ann sent her letter to Hawai'i and someone, most likely a missionary, placed the letter into a new envelope addressed to "J. S. Speight, Esq."

204. Joseph F. was forty-eight, and Martha Ann was forty-six.

205. Martha Ann mentioned similar sentiments earlier in a letter to Joseph F.'s wife Julina in 1884: "I Sincerely hope you are all well & that you will have a merry Chrismas as much so as you Could in the absence of your beloved Husband it must be Lonely for you all to have him don So Long I hope the <day> will soon bee here when he Can retourn to his home & family & friends." Martha Ann to Julina Lambson Smith, 21 December 1884.

206. Julina Lambson.

207. Salt Lake City.

208. Franklin Hill Harris.

209. Karl G. Maeser was the schoolmaster of Brigham Young Academy. See biographical register, "Maeser, Karl Gottfried."

210. Unknown individual. The 1880 US Census lists three Mr. Cooks living in Provo: Fredrick Cook (laborer), Luke Cook (butcher), and Thomas Cook (farmer). See biographical register, "Cook."

211. *Lucerne* is a term for alfalfa.

212. Seeds.

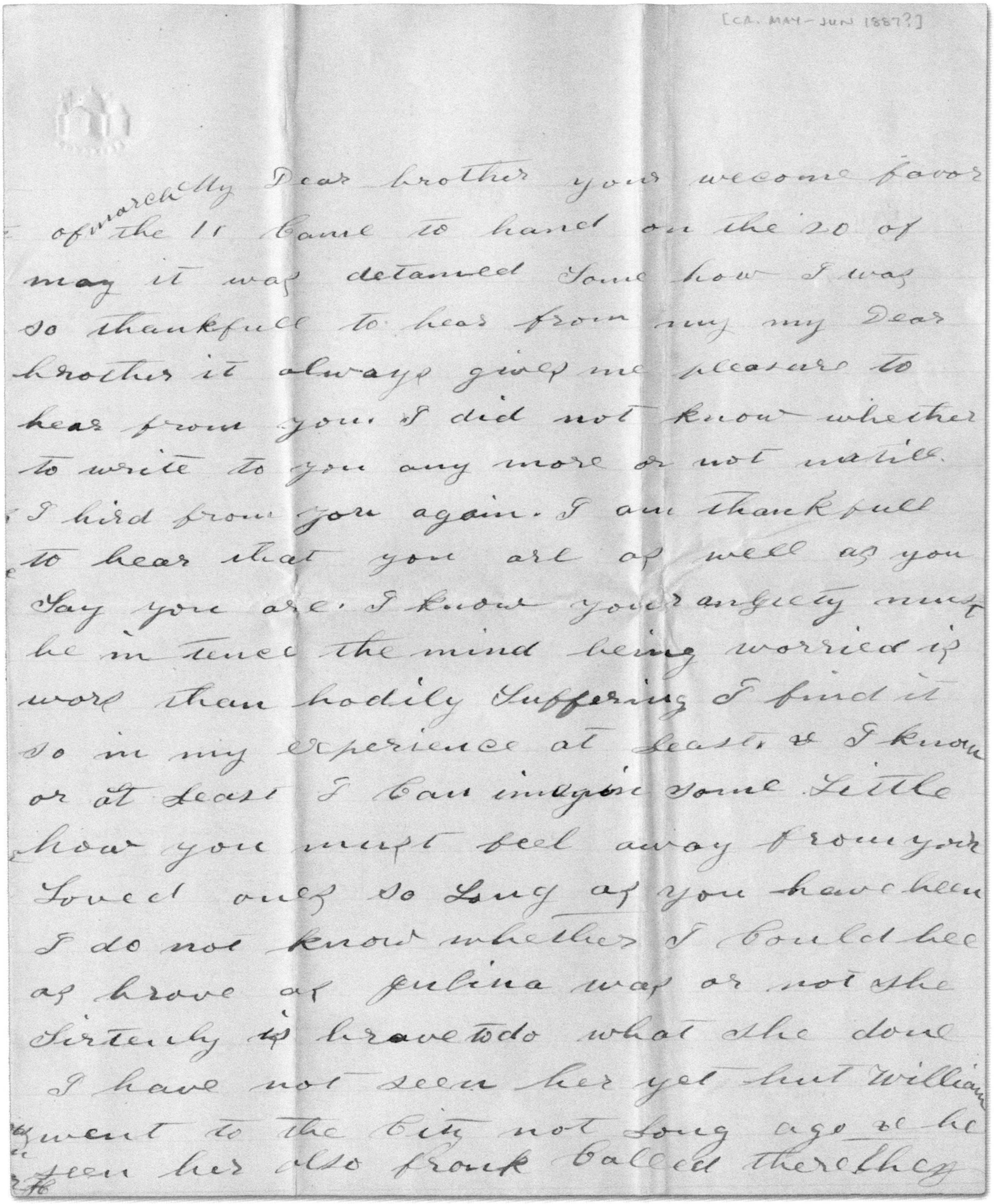
[CA. MAY–JUN 1887?]

My Dear brother your wecome favor
of march the 11 Came to hand on the 20 of
may it was detamed some how I was
so thankfull to hear from my my Dear
brother it always gives me pleasure to
hear from you I did not know whether
to write to you any more or not untill
I hird from you again. I am thankfull
to hear that you are as well as you
say you are. I know your angiety must
be in tence the mind being worried is
wors than bodily suffering I find it
so in my experience at least. & I know
or at least I can imagine some little
how you must feel away from your
loved ones so long as you have been
I do not know whether I could bee
as brave as Julina was or not she
sirtenly is brave to do what she done
I have not seen her yet but William
went to the City not long ago & he
seen her also frank called there they

Martha Ann to Joseph F., ca. May–June 1887 (p. 1)

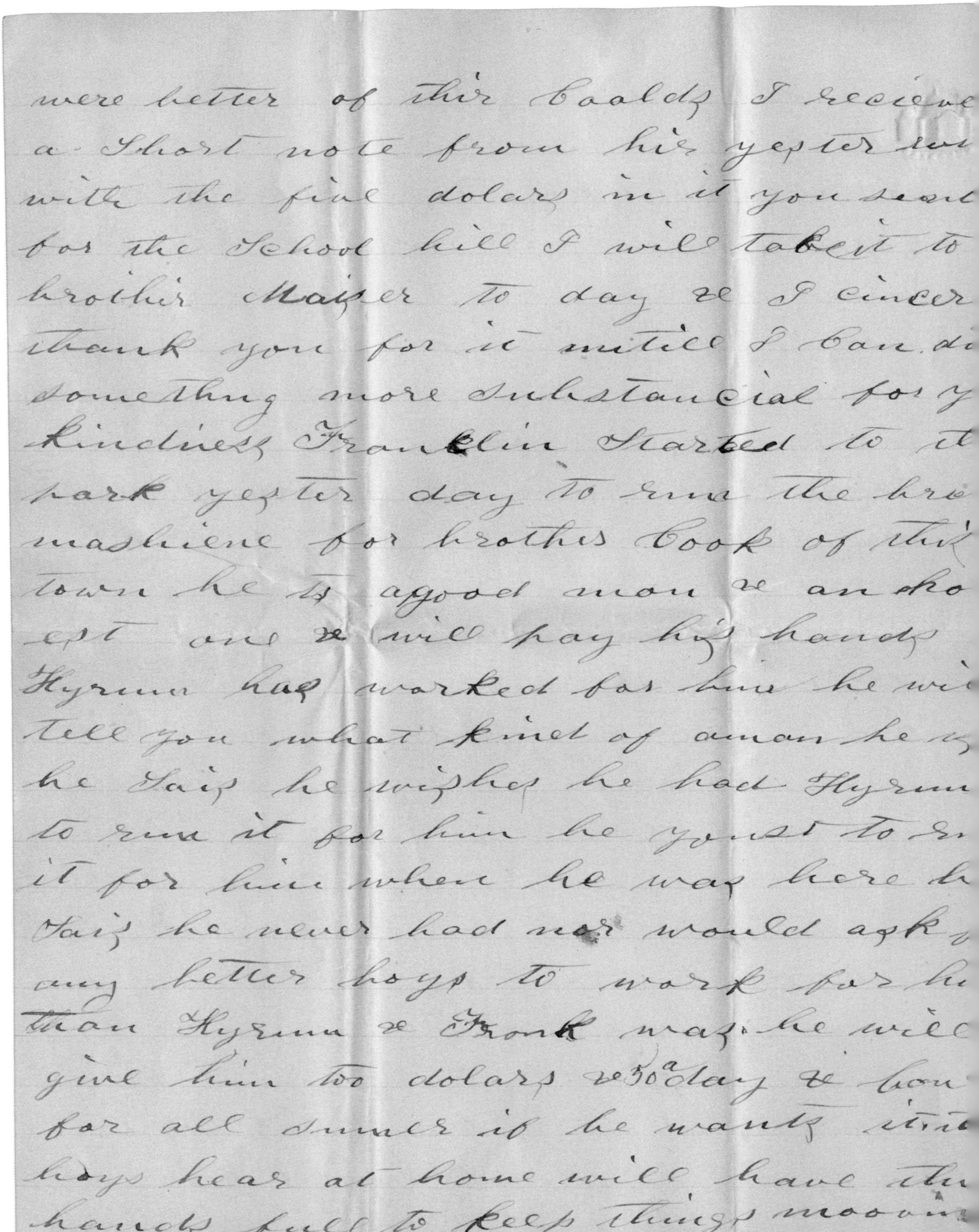

were better of thir coalds I recieve
a Short note from his yester day
with the five dolars in it you sent
for the School bill I will take it to
brother Maiser to day & I cincer
thank you for it until I can do
something more Substancial for y
kindness Franklin Started to the
park yester day to run the bro
mashiene for brother Cook of this
town he is agood man & an ho
est one & will pay his hands
Hyrum has worked for him he wi
tell you what kind of aman he is
he Sais he wishes he had Hyrum
to run it for him he youst to ru
it for him when he was here he
Sais he never had nor would ask f
any better boys to work for hi
than Hyrum & Frank was. he will
give him too dolars & 50 a day & boa
for all sumer if he wants it the
boys hear at home will have thi
hands full to keep things mooving

Martha Ann to Joseph F., ca. May–June 1887 (p. 2)

hey have thirty achers of Lucern to
tend to. & fore achors of wheet in
three achors oats thre achors potatoy
e of Squashes one Corn thre of Cain
Some melons be sids the boys here
t home we will not have any fru
t this year so we will have to buy
ll we have of that. there is one or
trees that have aples on if the
orms Can bee kept of them the
eaches & pears or all killed.
ith the frost the worms are very
ad this year but not quite as
ad as they were last year. William
not in work but he tends to
he gardin & helps the boys all
e can he is not very strong but
e keeps doing all the time & if noth
ng hapens to any of us & if all is
ell I think we will have enough
Live on next winter & make is
mfortable the boys have got the rock
sand halled towards building they are
ing to hall the clay & make the adobys

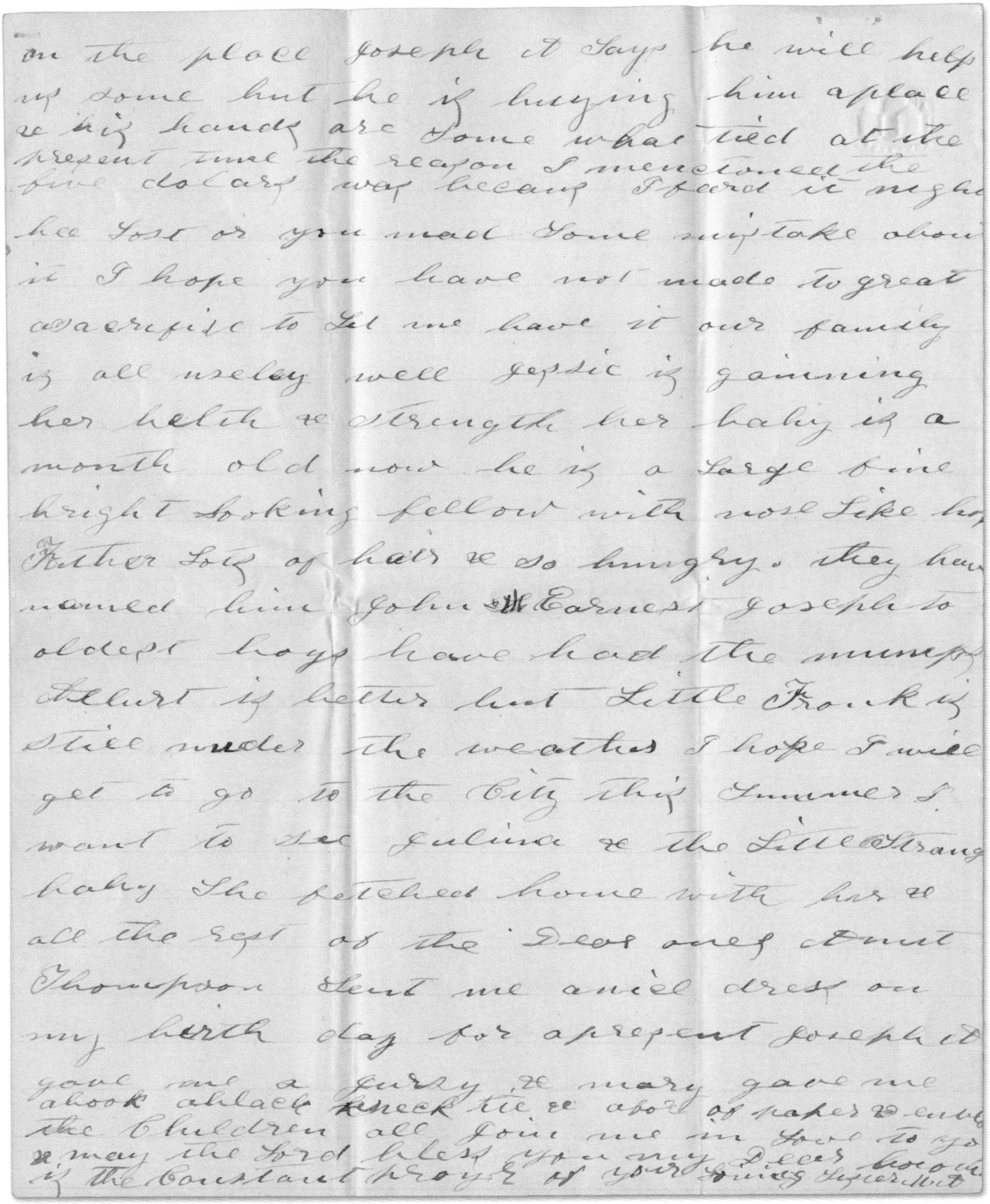
on the place Joseph it says he will help
us some but he is buying him a place
& his hands are some what tied at the
present time the reason I mentioned the
five dolars was becaus I feard it might
bee lost or you mad some mistake about
it I hope you have not made to great
a sacrifise to let me have it our family
is all useley well Jessie is gaining
her helth & strength her baby is a
month old now he is a large fine
bright looking fellow with nose like his
Father lots of hair & so hungry. they have
named him John Earnest Joseph's too
oldest boys have had the mumps
Albert is better but Little Frank is
still under the weather I hope I will
get to go to the City this summer I
want to see Julina & the Little Strang
baby she fetched home with her &
all the rest of the Dear ones Aunt
Thompson sent me a nice dress on
my birth day for a present Joseph
gave me a purse, & Mary gave me
a book a black neck tie & a box of paper & envl
the Children all Join me in love to you
& may the Lord bless you my Dear brother
is the constant prayer of your loving sister M

Martha Ann to Joseph F., ca. May–June 1887 (p. 4)

are very bad this year but not quite as bad as they were last year. William is not in work but he tends to the gardin & helps the boys all he can he is not very strong but he keeps doing all the time & if nothing hapens to any of us & if all is well I think we will have enough to live on next winter & make is comfortable the boys have got the rock & land halled towards building they are going to hall the clay & make the adobys **[p. 4]** on the place Joseph A[213] says he will help us some but he is buying him a place & his hands are some what tied at the present time the reason I mencioned the five dolars was becaus I feerd it might bee lost or you mad some mistake about it I hope you have not made to great a sacrifise to let me have it our family is all useley well Jessie[214] is gainning her helth & strength her baby is a month old now he is a large fine bright looking fellow with nose like his Father lots of hair & so hungry. they hav named him John [*illegible strike-through*] Earnest[215] Joseph to oldest boys have had the mumps Albert is better but little Frank[216] is still under the weather I hope I will get to go to the City this summer I want to see Julina & the little strang baby she fetched home with hir[217] & all the rest of the Dear ones Aunt Thompson[218] sent me a nice dress on my birth day for a present Joseph A gave me a jursy[219] & mary[220] gave me a book a black kneck tie & I a box of paper & env[◊◊] the children all join me in love to you & may the Lord bless you my dear broth[◊◊] is the constant prayr of your loving sister M A

213. Joseph Albert Harris.
214. Jessie Lena Freckleton, Martha Ann's daughter-in-law and wife of William Jasper Harris Jr. See biographical register, "Freckleton, Jessie Lena."
215. John Ernest Harris was born on 19 April 1886 according to family records and his gravestone. However, he was most likely born in 1887 based on the cancellation date on the envelope for this letter, Martha Ann's comments in this letter, and his age listed in the 1910, 1930, and 1940 US Census records. The discrepancy of John Ernest Harris's birth year is likely due to some confusion stemming from his being born at home and from inaccurate record keeping. In the letter Martha Ann seems to indicate that Julina has been away and is now back in Salt Lake City. Julina left Salt Lake City on 28 January 1885 and traveled with her husband from San Francisco to Hawai'i, where they would remain for the next two years. She returned to Salt Lake City in March of 1887. See Joseph F. to Martha Ann, 11 February 1887, herein, and biographical register, "Freckleton, Jessie Lena" and "Harris, John Ernest."
216. Joseph Albert Harris's sons Joseph Albert Harris Jr. and Frank Ernest Harris.
217. Elias Wesley Smith.
218. Mercy Rachel Fielding.
219. Jersey is a popular breed of small dairy cattle that originated in the channel island of Jersey.
220. Mary Emily Harris.

Recd and ans'd Feb. 9. 1891.

Provo City Feb the first 1891

Mr Joseph F Smith

My very Dear brother
your welcome favor of 16th in Came Safly to hand I was pleased to hear from you that you ware all usen ly well & I hope you will forgive me for not answer ing before now I was called away to see a Sick Child was gon from home for three days & when I retur ned I was Sick in bed two days more, then I had to make asuit of grave Clothes for brother Holbrooks Little Soon 5 years old as Soon as that was done I had to make asuit for another Little one that Died on the bench. Last ~~Saturday~~ Fryday Mary Sent for me to Come in hast that her Little walter had got the Croop very bad I went & Stayd too days & nights & worked faithfully with him Came home yester day he was some better but he is very bad yet but we hope he is over the worst of it. So you see how my time is taken up. I have seen so mutch Sickness & death this winter that it has been auffull to Contemplate it gives me the blues & makes me feel Sad. you Said you had hird that I had Ignord your Council to my boys that is not So for I have always been will ing to Lisson to your Counsil & to obey it as far as it Layd in my pour & I also thank you for any advise you might give to my Children for I know you would not give them advise that would doo them harm, but what I did Say was this I thaught that every thing Considerd the way it Came about ~~&~~ you was alittle Severe in Some things you wrote in your Letter & I thaught when you hird both Sides of the Question you would see things in a different Light I told the boys not to have any thing to do with that younion if they had Lisso ned to me they would ~~have~~ hav

Decade 5

1890–1899

JOSEPH F. TO MARTHA ANN, SALT LAKE CITY, UTAH, 18 JUNE 1890

God has blessed me with good wives, and my children with good mothers; and O, how I feel to bless them, and to thank God. How all hell would grin <with delight> and the Devils laugh to see me "go back" on them! And well they might! but I have not the remotest idea of gratifying them in that regard. Exilement for the remainder of my life, or imprisonment till death, would be meat and drink to my soul, if necessity compelled me to suffer it for their sakes. They have been true to me, by Gods help I will be true to them in time and throughout all eternity!

MARTHA ANN TO JOSEPH F., PROVO CITY, UTAH, 15 JANUARY 1891

I thank you ever so mutch for <your> kind rememberance of me it seems so nice to think that one has a dear beloved brother who thinks once in a while of thuem it helps to lighten the heavy burden that I carry. I love to look on your dear fase it is better than gold to me.

Joseph F., 6 April 1893, photograph by Charles Johnson, Sainsbury & Johnson Co., Salt Lake City, Utah. Courtesy of CHL.

Decade Introduction

In 1890 the Church and its members were still feeling the onerous effects of the Edmunds-Tucker Act, passed by the US Congress in 1887. Many Latter-day Saints had been incarcerated, and others, like Joseph F., had been on the underground in an effort to avoid arrest. The combined effects of the federal campaign to change Utah society were the disruption of family, community, religious, political, and economic life in the Latter-day Saint settlements throughout the Intermountain West. Additionally, the Church had been disincorporated in 1887, and the government was considering confiscating Church properties, including the temples. Finally, the Church had also been encumbered with a massive debt as it attempted to fulfill its mission to preach the gospel, gather the poor to Zion, and meet the financial obligations to fight the legal campaign against it and its members.

During this difficult period, Church leaders continued to minister to the Saints as best they could, despite the political and economic challenges facing them and the Church. Joseph F. accompanied Wilford Woodruff, George Q. Cannon, and other Church leaders on a tour to visit members in Arizona, Colorado, and New Mexico in the late summer of 1890. Joseph F. wrote his sister Martha

Envelope addressed to Jason Mack (Joseph F.) and postmarked "May 19, 1890." Still concerned about possible arrest, Joseph F. continued to use aliases during this period to avoid detection. This particular alias was the name of Lucy Mack Smith's brother Jason Mack (1760–1835). Courtesy of CHL.

Ann on 9 August, "I expect to leave here tomorrow or monday, on a mission to be gone some little time."[1]

During the tour, they stopped for a multiday conference in Manassas, Conejos County, Colorado.[2] Joseph F. recorded in his journal details regarding a Sunday School conference, priesthood meeting, and stake conference they attended together and noted, "I spoke with good liberty" during the concluding meeting held on Monday, 18 August.[3]

By the time President Woodruff had returned to Utah from this and another short trip to California in September, he had reached an important "point in the history" of his life.[4] During this pivotal period, he had come to the conclusion that the Saints could continue practicing plural marriage and face even more pressure from the government or they could "safeguard and nourish their expanded vision of temple work" by ending the practice.[5] As a result, President Woodruff released the Manifesto in September 1890, announcing to the world that the Church was going to comply with the laws of the land by ending new plural marriages in the United States.[6]

While some Church members were relieved, others were confused about how the practice of plural marriage could simply be stopped in light of the Lord's initial commands regarding it. Wilford Woodruff responded to some of the concerns in a stake conference in northern Utah:

> The Lord has told me to ask the Latter-day Saints a question. . . . Which is the wisest course for the Latter-day Saints to pursue—to continue to attempt to practice plural marriage, with the laws of the nation against it and the opposition of sixty millions of people, and at the cost of the confiscation and loss of all the Temples, and the stopping of all ordinances therein, both for the living and the dead, and the imprisonment of the First Presidency and Twelve and the heads of families in the Church, and the confiscation of personal property of the people . . . or, after doing and suffering what we have through our adherence to this principle to cease the practice and submit to the law, and through doing so leave the Prophets, Apostles and fathers at home, so that they can instruct the people and attend to the duties of the Church, and also leave the Temples in the hands of the Saints, so that they can attend to the ordinances of the Gospel, both for the living and the dead?[7]

---

1. Joseph F. to Martha Ann, 9 August 1890, herein.
2. Manassas was an early Latter-day Saint settlement located directly north of the New Mexico border in the San Luis Valley.
3. See Joseph F., journal, 18 August 1890.
4. Wilford Woodruff, journal, 25 September 1890, in *Wilford Woodruff's Journal: 1833–1898 Typescript*, ed. Scott G. Kenney, vol. 9, *1 January 1889 to 2 September 1898* (Midvale, UT: Signature Books, 1985), 112–14; spelling corrected for readability.
5. Richard E. Bennett, "'Which Is the Wisest Course?' The Transformation in Mormon Temple Consciousness, 1870–1898," *BYU Studies Quarterly* 52, no. 2 (December 2013): 8.
6. The intent and scope of the 1890 Manifesto was discussed during the administrations of Wilford Woodruff and Lorenzo Snow. Eventually, Joseph F. issued the Second Manifesto in 1904, which announced that no new plural marriages would be authorized, even outside the boundaries of the United States. It also stated that any person who performed or participated in new plural marriages would be subject to Church discipline, including excommunication. By October 1905, Latter-day Saint Apostles John W. Taylor and Matthias F. Cowley were forced to resign from the Quorum of the Twelve in the wake of the Smoot hearings. Taylor was eventually excommunicated in 1911 for continued opposition to the Second Manifesto.
7. Cache Stake Conference, Logan, Cache County, Utah Territory, 1 November 1891. See "Remarks," *Deseret Weekly News*, 14 November 1891, 658. Further excerpts from this conference are contained in Official Declaration 1 in the Doctrine and Covenants.

Joseph F. Smith family members at their home located at 333 West First North Street (200 North), Salt Lake City, ca. 1890. Joseph F. (far right) and several family members, including wives, stand in the front of the home on a winter day. This was the center of Joseph F.'s world until he became President of the Church in 1901 and moved into the Beehive House. Courtesy of CHL.

Although the Manifesto did not immediately put an end to all of the legal and financial challenges that the Church faced, it did allow Church leaders to appear in public for the first time in a number of years. The Saints rejoiced when, in October 1891, the entire First Presidency was present and on the stand together at the semiannual general conference in Salt Lake City. It was the first time this had happened in more than seven years.[8]

RELIEF SOCIETY JUBILEE

On 17 March 1892, Joseph F. participated in the historic jubilee celebration of the founding of the Female Relief Society of Nauvoo, which fell on Thursday, the same day of the week as when the Prophet Joseph Smith met with the sisters in Nauvoo on 17 March 1842 to organize them into a group dedicated to saving souls and relieving the poor.[9] For the jubilee celebration, the Salt Lake Tabernacle was filled with Saints and decorated with bunting, flags, flowers, and portraits. General

8. Joseph F. was greeted with a warm welcome and recorded, "I shook hands with my friends until my hand and arm felt lame." Joseph F., journal, 4 October 1891.
9. See "The Relief Society Jubilee," *Woman's Exponent*, 15 January and 1 February 1892, 108.

Relief Society officers and Church leaders attended and participated in the special program. In a remarkable effort to unify the sisters throughout the pioneer core area, each participating congregation offered a prayer at noon—the very same time Joseph F. prayed in the Salt Lake Tabernacle.[10]

The record is silent about Martha Ann's participation in the jubilee celebrations in Salt Lake or Provo. However, she participated in at least one aspect of the jubilee. Local Relief Societies prepared individual Relief Society jubilee boxes for their wards on the occasion. The sisters in the local Relief Societies deposited various items, including letters written by those who had known the Prophet Joseph Smith.[11]

Martha Ann apparently deposited a letter into a jubilee box as indicated in a newspaper report in 1933: "An enjoyable time was spent by members of Camp Bonneville, Daughters of Utah Pioneers at the home of Mrs. Sarah Passey[12] Thursday afternoon. An interesting Program furnished as follows: Community singing, led by Mrs. Theresa Morgan; letters from the Relief Society Jubilee box, written by Martha Ann Smith Harris[13] and Mercy Rachel Fielding Thompson[14] 50 years ago read by Mrs. Mary H. Hafen.[15] . . . Delicious refreshments were served to 35 members and guests."[16]

For Joseph F. and Martha Ann, this was the first of several important churchwide celebrations held during the decade. Within a month of the Relief Society jubilee celebration, the Saints celebrated again by witnessing the capstone laying for the Salt Lake Temple in April 1892. Another joyous event calling for Churchwide celebration was the dedication ceremonies for the completed Salt Lake Temple in April 1893.

SALT LAKE TEMPLE

As prosecution and government intervention in Church affairs decreased, Church leaders were able to focus more attention on other significant matters, including the completion of the Salt Lake Temple, a project that had begun in 1853.

Almost four decades later, Wilford Woodruff presided at the capstone ceremony held on 6 April 1892. During this special outdoor meeting, President Woodruff invited the Saints to complete the temple in one year so it could be dedicated on 6 April 1893. It was with a sense of celebration, then, that the Saints gathered on 6 April 1892, thirty-nine years from the time the cornerstones were

10. General Relief Society leaders Zina D. H. Young, Jane S. Richards, and Bathsheba W. Smith invited the Relief Society sisters to participate in the celebration "at 12 o'clock p.m. (high noon) let all join in a universal prayer of praise and thanksgiving to God." "Letter of Greeting," *Woman's Exponent*, 15 January and 1 February 1892, 108. See "The Relief Society Jubilee," *Deseret Weekly*, 26 March 1892, 483–86.
11. Later, when the box was opened, some of the items were given to family members. For example, Tamma Durfee Miner wrote a long letter for the Relief Society jubilee box of the Utah Stake Relief Society (copy in possession of the editors). Hannah Sorensen wrote a brief autobiographical sketch as a letter addressed to her youngest son and included a "picture as I look now, and a little relic for your wife, or your daughter, also a lock of my hair." As cited in Robert S. McPherson, *Life in a Corner: Cultural Episodes in Southeastern Utah, 1880–1950* (Norman: University of Oklahoma Press, 2015), 68. Another ward Relief Society jubilee box was donated to the Daughters of the Utah Pioneers Museum in Springville, Utah. "Jubilee Box donated to DUP museum," *Springville Herald*, 31 March 1993, 4.
12. Martha Ann's daughter Sarah Harris Passey.
13. A document in the CHL dating from about fifty years before the time of the 1933 report may be the one mentioned in the article: "Martha Ann Smith Harris to Posterity," 22 March 1881.
14. Mercy Rachel Fielding prepared an autobiography with instructions that it be given to her oldest female descendant in 1930. See "Mercy F. Thompson Autobiographical Sketch, 1880."
15. Mary H. Hafen was Martha Ann's granddaughter and the daughter of Franklin Hill Harris and Josie Parkes Harris.
16. "Pioneer Daughters at Regular Meeting," *Sunday Herald* (Provo, UT), 12 February 1933, 5.

laid, to rejoice together in the laying of the capstone. President Woodruff, who had pounded in the marking stake forty-five years earlier, wrote impressively in his diary that it was "the greatest day the Latter-day Saints ever saw in these mountains."[17]

The city, already crowded for the semiannual conference, received thousands more who came for this historic event. Fifty thousand people jammed the Temple Block, while thousands more watched from adjoining rooftops, windows, and even power poles. Many more thronged the streets.

After the capstone-laying ceremony, many people remained to see the unveiling of the statue of the angel Moroni. The statue, designed by Utah-born sculptor Cyrus Dallin, was made of hammered copper covered with 22-karat gold leaf. Before nightfall, the massive figure was lowered into position on the stone ball of the 210-foot-high central east spire.

In the year that followed, carpenters, painters, plasterers, and other skilled craftsmen worked unstintingly to complete the interior of the temple. The inside of the temple was adorned with fine wood and plaster ornamental carvings, beautiful murals and paintings, mirrors, elegant curtains and draperies, the best carpets and furniture available, fine light fixtures, chandeliers, and specially ordered stained glass art windows. All things were made ready for the dedication ceremonies, which were to begin on 6 April 1893. In an effort to complete the temple on time, workers labored even on holidays. On Thanksgiving Day 1892, "nearly all the men were at work as usual," one worker noted.[18]

The evening before the first dedication service, President Woodruff conducted nonmember guests through the building on a first-of-its-kind tour. This act was a step in reconciliation by Church leaders eager to rebuild harmony with non–Latter-day Saint neighbors after decades of hostility. Even federally appointed Utah Territorial Supreme Court justice Charles S. Zane, a long-time critic of the Church, was impressed by the quality of design, decorations, and craftsmanship. "The building is furnished opulently," he noted in his journal after attending the open house.[19]

Wilford Woodruff, George Q. Cannon, and Joseph F., the First Presidency at the time, went to Charles Johnson's studio for a series of group and individual photographs on this historic occasion.

Finally, the culmination of forty years of effort and sacrifice climaxed when President Woodruff entered the temple the morning of 6 April 1893. "The Temple Block gates opened at 8:30, and the street was packed long before that hour," one priesthood leader noted. Two hours were required "to admit, one by one, the 2200 people" into the large upper assembly hall of the temple.[20]

Thomas Griggs, a member of the Tabernacle Choir, arrived at the south gate at 8:20, but the line was so long that "it was 9:55 A.M. when I was 10 feet from the [gate]," he wrote. "Wind, dust and a little rain had come and it was very uncomfortable, to be ended by the door keeper announcing . . . 'No more can be admitted.' . . . Being well known as a member of the choir [I was] . . . soon at the south west entrance and hurriedly passed through."[21]

The focus of the service was the prayer of dedication offered by the aged prophet, "kneeling on a plush covered stool provided for the purpose" and reading the prayer he had prepared that would be read in each successive service of the many sessions.[22]

Following the conclusion of the dedication sessions, Joseph F. reported, "We all had a most precious time during the dedication services."[23]

17. Wilford Woodruff, journal, 6 April 1892.
18. Samuel W. Richards, journal, 24 November 1892.
19. Charles S. Zane, journal, 5 April 1893, Charles S. Zane Papers, Illinois State Historic Library, Springfield, Illinois.
20. Joseph Henry Dean, journal, 6 April 1893.
21. Thomas C. Griggs, journal, 6 April 1893.
22. Joseph Henry Dean, journal, 6 April 1893.
23. Joseph F. to Jesse B. Martin, 27 April 1893.

Zina Christine Harris and George Thomas Furner, 23 April 1894, photograph by T. E. Daniels Jr., Provo, Utah. Joseph F. performed their marriage ceremony on 18 October 1893 in the Salt Lake Temple. Zina wrote on the reverse side, "To Uncle Joseph F." Courtesy of CHL.

In October 1893 Joseph F. had the distinct privilege of performing the marriage sealing of Martha Ann's daughter Zina Christine Harris (1876–1958) and George Thomas Furner (1868–1903) in the Salt Lake Temple.[24]

Additionally, the work to redeem the dead increased as many more members were able to take advantage of attending the newly dedicated temple in the largest metropolitan area in Utah. Joseph F. and Martha Ann were among those who did work for their own ancestors. Their enthusiasm can be seen in a letter Joseph F. wrote to Martha Ann in 1897: "We have agreed to meet at the Temple in this city on Wednesday, September 1st, to attend to the sealing of all the children living and dead to their father and mothers. . . . We have had a glorious time in the Temple today. I sealed sixteen couples, including our seventh great grandfather and mother . . . and Grandfather and mother Joseph and Lucy Mack Smith, and the work of sealing of children is nearly all completed. I am very anxious to have father's work done."[25]

The newly completed and dedicated temple in Salt Lake City became a central focus of Joseph F.'s life for the next twenty-five years as he visited the upper rooms in the Salt Lake Temple for weekly meetings with the First Presidency and Quorum of the Twelve Apostles.[26] Additionally, he served as the Salt Lake Temple president from 1898 to 1911.

CHURCH AND POLITICS

A new political landscape appeared following the publication of the Manifesto as some former enemies of the Church threw down their weapons of war and collaborated with the Saints to promote the economic welfare of the Utah Territory. More importantly, they also now freely promoted statehood, which had been denied at every turn since the Saints began to settle the Great Basin in 1847. Church leaders knew statehood would provide greater independence in local affairs by

24. Salt Lake Temple "Living Sealing Book A," vol. 1, entry 206.
25. Joseph F. to Martha Ann, 25 August 1897, herein.
26. Francis M. Gibbons, *Joseph F. Smith: Patriarch and Preacher, Prophet of God* (Salt Lake City, UT: Deseret Book, 1984), 190–91.

Above: Mary F. Smith, Ida Bowman, Donette Smith, and Maggie Bowman, 17 February 1894. The individuals in the photograph are identified by numbers one through four. The reverse side reads, "To Papa. From Mamie & Donnie. Apr. 2d 1894. Taken Feb. 17. 1894. 1 Mary F. Smith – 24 2 Ida Bowman 21 3 Donnette Smith 21 4 Maggie Bowman 23." Ida Bowman married Joseph F. Smith's oldest son, Hyrum Mack, on 15 November 1895, less than two years after this photograph was taken. On the day of Hyrum Mack's temple sealing, Heber J. Grant set him apart as a missionary to serve in Great Britain. He departed on his mission the next day, 16 November 1895, and returned on 7 March 1898. Courtesy of CHL.

Left: Joseph F. and John Smith, 14 June 1895, photograph by C. R. Savage, Salt Lake City, Utah. John and Joseph F. Smith were half brothers, sons of Hyrum Smith. Later, when Joseph F. Smith became President of the Church in 1901, it was only the second time in the Church's history that two brothers occupied the positions of President and Patriarch at the same time (the first time being Joseph Smith Jr. and Hyrum Smith). On the photograph, "Jos. F. Smith & John Smith. Taken June 4 1895" is written in Joseph F.'s hand. Courtesy of CHL.

allowing Utah residents to elect their own state officers, answerable to the local electorate, rather than potentially unsympathetic territorial appointees selected by the federal government.

There appeared to be two main obstacles preventing the people of Utah from receiving statehood. The first was the Church's position on plural marriage, which had been largely resolved when the 1890 Manifesto was announced.[27] The other impediment was the political solidarity of Church members that was often viewed as antidemocratic.[28] To overcome this barrier, Church leaders decided to disband the People's Party and encourage Latter-day Saints to join one of the two

Mary Schwartz and Joseph F. family, 19 December 1896, photograph by C. R. Savage, Salt Lake City, Utah. From left: Mary Schwartz, Calvin, James, Samuel, and Joseph F., who identified himself as "Papa." Courtesy of CHL.

27. For several years following the 1890 Manifesto, some Church leaders and members remained confused about how it was to be interpreted. Eventually, Joseph F. issued a Second Manifesto in 1904 to make it absolutely clear that the Church would no longer sanction or permit new plural marriages. Church leaders and members who refused to comply with the Second Manifesto were disciplined. See Brian C. Hales, *Modern Polygamy and Mormon Fundamentalism: The Generations after the Manifesto* (Salt Lake City, UT: Greg Kofford Books, 2006), 51–74. See also Thomas G. Alexander, *Mormonism in Transition: A History of the Latter-day Saints, 1830–1890* (Urbana: University of Illinois Press, 1986), 60–73, 328–31.
28. Edward Leo Lyman, "Utah Statehood," in *Encyclopedia of Mormonism*, ed. Daniel H. Ludlow (New York: Macmillan, 1992), 4:1502–3.

national parties, the Republican and Democratic Parties. The political party system in Utah had previously been divided almost exclusively along lines of religious affiliation, with most Latter-day Saints supporting the People's Party and most others supporting the local Liberal Party (distinct from the national Democratic Party).

As the People's Party was disbanded, many Latter-day Saints were attracted to the Democratic Party because the Republican Party had led the effort to end plural marriage in Utah and was seen as less sympathetic to the desires and aspirations of the members of the Church.

In order to create greater political balance among members, Church leaders encouraged some members to also join the Republican Party. Several Church leaders volunteered, including John Henry Smith (1848–1911) and Francis M. Lyman (1840–1916), both members of the Quorum of the Twelve Apostles. Joseph F. also joined the Republican Party and became a major supporter of it for the rest of his life. The Church then released a statement in local newspapers: "The Church will not assert any right to control the political action of its members. As officers of the Church they disclaim such right. . . . All that is asked for the Church is that it shall have equal rights before the law."[29] Ultimately, their efforts for home rule succeeded when in January 1896 Utah was made the forty-fifth state.

TRAVELS AND A NEW PROPHET

Economic demands and heavy administrative responsibilities continued to press on Church leaders, particularly President Woodruff. In 1895 he traveled to Alaska to seek relief from an increasing number of health concerns. His counselors, George Q. Cannon and Joseph F., accompanied him.[30] Joseph F. mentioned this trip in his letter to Martha Ann, dated 27 September 1895: "Our recent trip to the north was a rest and a change, such as I seldom get, but which was a gracious boon to me both physical and mental and I am very thankful for it."[31]

President Woodruff again sought relief when he traveled to the California coast in 1898. While there, in the home of a friend, he died quietly in his sleep on 2 September 1898. Eleven days later on 13 September 1898, President Lorenzo Snow was sustained as the new President of the Church. He selected George Q. Cannon and Joseph F. as his counselors.[32]

Two months after the reorganization of the First Presidency, Joseph F. celebrated his sixtieth birthday in November 1898. During the following year, Joseph F. made another trip to Hawai'i. He took his ailing wife Sarah Ellen (1850–1915) with him, feeling that the trip would improve her health.[33] Joseph F., Sarah, and two of their daughters left for Hawai'i on 7 January 1899.[34]

Although Joseph F.'s letters to Martha Ann make no mention of the financial burdens confronting the Church, the First Presidency was greatly concerned. The enormous debt resulted partly from government confiscation of Church property and members' limited means in donating to the Church.

29. "They Have Neither Truth Nor Shame," *Deseret Evening News*, 6 July 1891, 4.
30. Richard Neitzel Holzapfel, "New Photographs of Wilford Woodruff's Trip to Alaska, 1895," *BYU Studies* 39, no. 2 (2000): 144–49.
31. Joseph F. to Martha Ann, 27 September 1895, herein.
32. See Richard Neitzel Holzapfel and Ronald Fox, "Photographs of the Fourteen Apostles of The Church of Jesus Christ of Latter-day Saints, September and October 1898," *BYU Studies Quarterly* 56, no. 4 (2017): 68–92.
33. Joseph F. alludes to Sarah's poor health in a letter to Martha Ann. See Joseph F. to Martha Ann, 13 October 1898, herein.
34. See Brian William Sokolowsky, "Photographs of Joseph F. Smith and the Laie Plantation, Hawaii, 1899," *BYU Studies* 41, no. 4 (2002): 47–63.

Joseph F. (seated in the center) and Sarah Ellen Smith (seated to his right) and party, Lāʻie Plantation Mission Home, 3 February 1899, photograph by Otto Hassing, Honolulu, Hawaiʻi. Courtesy of CHL.

Immediately after being sustained as President of the Church, President Snow commenced a campaign to revitalize the practice of paying tithing. He held a special solemn assembly about tithing in July 1899, and the October general conference that year was dedicated to the theme. In that conference Joseph F. told the Saints:

> We are not talking to you about paying your tithing because it is a pleasure to do so, or because we desire to harp upon that principle; but we are doing it because the necessities of the people are such that it becomes obligatory upon the leaders of the Church to say something upon this principle, that not only the people may do their duty in regard to this law, but that there may be something in the storehouse of the Lord with which to meet the necessities of the people; for the necessities of the Church are the necessities of the people.[35]

As a result of this increased emphasis, tithing revenue more than doubled from 1898 to 1899.[36] As a member of the First Presidency, Joseph F. played a particularly important role in helping extricate the Church from debt. In fact, later as President of the Church he would pay off the final debt.

35. Joseph F. Smith, in Conference Report, October 1899, 41.
36. Gibbons, *Joseph F. Smith*, 203–4.

As the decade ended, Joseph F. confided in his son Joseph Fielding Smith about his continuing struggle to manage his correspondence demands, both ecclesiastical and personal: "I am so busy during office or working hours that I cannot get a moment to dictate to our typewriter. And she loves working promptly at quitting time, and I am so unfortunate as to have no son or daughter qualified to write short hand or take dictation on typewriter nearly everyone of president's cannons boys and Leroi Snow can both write short hand and typewrite. I feel condemned that I have not given my children more time for study and greater opportunities to learn. Still I do not know how I could have done more with my large responsibilities and limited means."[37]

CONTINUING HEALTH CHALLENGES

The letters between Joseph F. and Martha Ann frequently mention Martha Ann's ill health. In 1894, for example, Martha Ann fell and splintered her knee. The injury confined her to bed for six months and required her to use crutches for another year and a half.[38] One of her grandchildren remembered that during this time their "aunt" Zina Young (1821–1901) came from Salt Lake to care for Martha Ann. While there, Zina promised Martha Ann that she would be healed and "told her that she would walk again and be made well, with many other grand promises, which were surely fulfilled."[39]

Martha Ann did recover, but within only a few years she fell again, this time breaking her right arm. In addition to all her injuries, she suffered from severe rheumatism. Despite her injuries and ailments, however difficult, Martha Ann used the time confined to her bed to sew, embroider temple aprons, and make other items of clothing for her family, grandchildren, friends, and neighbors.[40] Joseph F. alludes in one of his letters to his sister's devotion to family and her dedication to service: "How you can 'wait on the sick', 'make Temple clothing for one and another' and take care of your own family is almost a mystery. I am thankful, however that the Lord gives you the strength to do it."[41]

Most letters during this decade focus almost entirely on news of family and friends. For example, in a letter dated 25 October 1898, Joseph F. informs his sister of the birth of his grandson, George Smith Nelson.[42]

Interestingly, nothing is said in the known surviving letters from this decade about the 1890 Manifesto, the completion and dedication of the Salt Lake Temple in 1893, or Utah's achieving statehood in 1896 after decades of effort.

Increasingly, rituals of birth, marriage, sickness, and death intertwined in Martha Ann and Joseph F.'s

Mary Emily, Martha Ann, and Lucy Smith Harris, ca. 1890. Courtesy of Carole Call King.

37. Joseph F. to Joseph F. Smith Jr., 8 August 1899.
38. Carole Call King, "History of Martha Ann Smith Harris, 1841–1923" (unpublished manuscript in editors' possession).
39. Ruth Mae Harris, *Martha Ann, Daughter of Hyrum and Mary Fielding Smith* (Orem, UT: published by the author, 2002), 137.
40. Harris, *Martha Ann*, 137.
41. Joseph F. to Martha Ann, 22 May 1890, herein.
42. Joseph F. to Martha Ann, 25 October 1898, herein.

Joseph Smith Nelson and George Smith Nelson, 22 April 1899. Photograph by C. R. Savage, Salt Lake City, Utah. Joseph F.'s daughter Leonora Smith Nelson provided information on the back of this photograph: "To Grandpapa with our affections Joseph S. Nelson born Feb. 22 99. George S. Nelson Oct. 20, 98. Photographed April 22, 99." Joseph F. added, "Grandpa's own little boys." Courtesy of CHL.

Jonathan and Lucy Smith Harris Simmons, 15 June 1898, photograph by Ad. Anderson, Provo, Utah. This photograph was taken on the day they were married. Courtesy of Carole Call King.

lives. For example, Joseph F. mentioned the pain of losing his eighth child when four-year-old Ruth (1893–98) died in March 1898:

> We have, as you perhaps know, for a long time been passing under most trying ordeals of sickness. Aunt Sarah E. was taken with Typhoid fever—then Emily, with Scarlet fever, then Alice M. with Typhoid fever, then Rachel with scarlet fever—then Edith, and next our Dear little Ruth—who—in spite of all we could do by faith and prayer and skill, on the 17th inst—passed away—leaving us heart-broken and bowed down to the dust in grief & sorrow

for our irreparable temporal loss.[43] You will no doubt remember our sweet little Ruth—to be loved—she needed only to be seen. To be admired she had but to be heard—for she was one of the brightest little Souls I ever saw. But O! my Soul, we have had to yield her spirit up to God who gave her, and her sweet little body to the grave. She was buried to day. I should have written you sooner but to tell the truth my poor heart has been in the icey chamber with the cherished lovely form of my darling babe! I could not write.[44]

Ruth Smith, daughter of Edna Lambson and Joseph F., 16 May 1897. Ruth was born on 21 December 1893 and died on 17 March 1898, ten months after this photograph was taken. Joseph F. mentions her death in a letter to Martha Ann, 19 March 1898. On the reverse side Joseph F. wrote, "Ruth May 16th '97. My Darling little Ruth! Papa." Courtesy of CHL.

For Martha Ann, the joy of celebrating the marriage of her daughter Lucy Smith Harris to Jonathan Simmons in Utah County on 15 June 1898 was followed by a tragedy when a grandson

43. Ruth Smith, Edna's daughter (born on 21 December 1893), died on 17 March 1898. See Joseph F. to Martha Ann, 19 March 1898, herein, note 243.

44. Joseph F. to Martha Ann, 19 March 1898, herein.

died after falling from a chair in 1898.[45] As Joseph F. noted earlier, "Your life has been a hard one as was that of our ever dear and precious Mother.[46] Surely there is a noble reward awaiting you after your trials. Cheer up. If I live and prosper I shall not forget you. My heart is full, my eyes moist. I am ever truly Joseph F."[47]

A NEW HOME IN PROVO

Martha Ann and William Jasper built a larger two-story home sometime around 1890 on the same lot where the adobe home had been built. Their daughter Sarah Harris noted, "Thirteen in the family lived in these two rooms [in the adobe home] until the youngest child (myself) was nine years old, when a larger and better house was built."[48] The new home provided the family with a parlor and additional bedrooms, but it lacked a kitchen, dining room, and bathroom at first. The basement remained unfinished for years. Laundry was still being done outside during the summer, and water came from an artesian well near the north door of the old adobe house. The family continued to cook and eat in the small adobe home, and the outhouse in the backyard continued to be used for some time. Despite building a house, Martha Ann's economic situation remained difficult.[49] Eventually, to bring in much-needed income, Martha Ann rented the adobe home and moved into the large home full-time.[50] In the big house, a bedroom on the main floor was converted into a kitchen to accommodate the new arrangement. When, after some time, an indoor bathroom was installed by utilizing part of the parlor space, Martha Ann was elated. Her granddaughter Edna Mae recalled, "I remember her saying when the bathroom was finished, she went in there and fell on her knees and offered a prayer of thanksgiving. At last, she didn't have to go way out to the outhouse in the cold."[51] Around this time, Martha Ann and William Jasper took in "BY Academy students as boarders" to help augment their family income.[52]

SUMMARY

By the end of December 1899, Joseph F. was sixty-one years old. His five wives had borne forty children between 1858 and 1899: Julina had borne eleven children and buried one child; Sarah had borne eleven children and buried four children; Edna had borne ten children and buried three children; Alice had borne three children; and Mary had borne five children, of which one had died. Additionally, four more children were part of the family in 1899—one had been adopted, and three others became part of the family when Joseph F. married Alice in 1883.

Martha Ann was fifty-eight years old by the end of this decade. Between 1852 and 1882, she had given birth to eleven children, with all remarkably still alive in 1899. She and William had raised

45. Martha Ann to William Harris, 20 November 1898, transcription in Harris, *Martha Ann*, 143–44. Though the letter was misdated, the envelope is clearly postmarked 22 November 1898.
46. Mary Fielding.
47. Joseph F. to Martha Ann, 13 March 1883, herein.
48. Sarah Harris Passey, "Martha Ann Smith Harris," manuscript, 7; in possession of the editors.
49. In 1892 the Provo City Council abated Martha Ann's city taxes because of her "indigent" state. "Taxes Remitted," *Daily Enquirer*, 9 August 1892, 4. However, Martha Ann's name continued to appear in the local newspaper for failure to pay taxes during the decade. See for example, "Delinquent Taxes," *Evening Dispatch*, 5 December 1894, 3; "Delinquent Taxes," *Evening Dispatch*, 7 December 1895, 2; "Delinquent Taxes," *Daily Enquirer*, 15 December 1896, 5.
50. See Martha Ann to Joseph F., 3 March 1913, herein.
51. Interview by Mary Harris Hafen, as cited in David J. Harris and Ruth B. Harris, ed. and comp., *Harris Heritage* (n.p., self-published, 1977), 158–59.
52. Harris, *Martha Ann*, 225.

Joseph F. Smith family portrait, 13 November 1898, photograph by Fox and Symons, Salt Lake City, Utah. Group photograph taken on his sixtieth birthday with his five wives and his children. Courtesy of CHL.

the family in a two-room adobe home in Provo but had finally built a second larger home on the same lot. With each generation of grandchildren and great-grandchildren, of course, the family continued to enlarge. Joseph F. often made mention of his sister's growing family in his letters to her during this decade—for example, "Hoping You and William are well, and all the children, & childrens children, I am Your brother Joseph."[53]

The letters written in the 1890s still show Martha Ann living in Provo in very humble circumstances. As noted above, in addition to her family's challenging economic situation, she was plagued by poor health throughout the decade. Joseph F. understood and appreciated the differences in their lives and tried to comfort and honor his sister Martha Ann for her goodness and faithfulness:

> What a comfort it is to know that all will be rewarded, eventually, according to their works, and the intents of their hearts. The noblest, and therefore in the true sense, the highest ideas that men can entertain are those of "faith, hope and charity", and in all these I award you credit of being superior to most women, else you would have succumbed to your

53. Joseph F. to Martha Ann, 2 May 1890, herein.

Sarah Lovina Harris, ca. 1899. Born in 1882, Sarah was Martha Ann and Williams's last child. Courtesy of Carole Call King.

misfortunes long ago. but your hope, your charity for others, and your faith in providence have sustained you. In temporal things God has dealt more mercifully with me than with you, as it now seems, but who can tell what the end may be?[54]

The letters of this decade also reveal the challenges of having a conversation with another person through written correspondence. In a series of five letters written between 17 April and

54. Joseph F. to Martha Ann, 22 May 1890, herein.

22 May 1890, Joseph F. and Martha Ann misunderstand each other on almost every point.[55] We cannot always discern the meaning and intent in every letter. Joseph F. and Martha Ann shared a common human dilemma in misunderstanding each other from time to time. Adding to the complex and interconnected aspects of their letter-writing relationship was the fact that they also communicated with other family members and friends through letters that were often part of their dialogue.[56] This naturally increased the number of people in the conversation and also the possibility of misunderstanding.

As discussed earlier, Joseph F. sometimes felt dutybound to counsel his sister's children. For example, Franklin Hill Harris (1867–1947) and his brother Hyrum Smith Harris (1863–1924) were working in Salt Lake City, and Joseph F. wrote a letter expressing his wish that they be fully engaged at Church and accept a call to become home missionaries.[57] In reply Frank (the name he was known by) reported that he had gone to Provo and "got my recommend from the Bishop and was roled in to the Ninttheen ward tonight. I will go up and get ordained a Elder tomorrow night." Frank added to his report, "Mother Says when I wrote to you to give her Love to you. I every remain your Loving Nephew."[58] Joseph F. received the letter on 25 March and responded to it on the same day.[59]

In a series of letters written in 1891, Joseph F. provided counsel intended directly for Martha Ann's sons. He began his letter, "I feel interested in the welfare of your family, for their welfare is yours."[60] He added, "My understanding of Joseph's course, gives me confidence in him. I like his continuity and steadiness and persistance in his purpose, I like the spirit and disposition I have seen of John, I believe them both to be good boys. and I feel in my heart to bless them. Willie and Hyrum and Frank have my love and my most earnest faith and prayer, I love them because they are my sisters boys, because they are my Nephews, and because I feel in my heart that they are good boys, but we have all much to learn."[61]

Joseph F. later provided additional counsel and direction for two of Martha Ann's daughters. He cautiously justified his intervention: "You may think it is 'none of my business', to worry over your affairs, but, I cannot help it."[62] Obviously, Joseph F. felt he should provide advice to Martha Ann's children, and while the advice was not always accepted or appreciated, he developed a warm relationship with his nephews and nieces as they continued to write him asking for advice and help, requesting that he perform their temple sealings, visiting him in Salt Lake City, and sending him photographs and warm salutations.

55. See Joseph F. to Martha Ann, 17 April 1890; Martha Ann to Joseph F., 29 April 1890; Joseph F. to Martha Ann; 2 May 1890; Martha Ann to Joseph F., 18 May 1890; and Joseph F. to Martha Ann, 22 May 1890, herein.

56. Throughout their lives, Joseph F. and Martha Ann communicated with other family members at the same time they were writing each other. See, for example, Joseph F. to Martha Ann, 3 March 1870, herein; Joseph F. to William Jasper Harris, 18 March 1870; and Joseph F. to Martha Ann, 29 March 1870, herein.

57. In the 1850s, Brigham Young began calling home-based missionaries, who would travel in pairs throughout the Utah Territory, speaking in meetings and visiting members' homes to call them to repentance and greater levels of commitment. See Paul Edwards Damron, "Home Missionaries," in *Encyclopedia of Latter-day Saint History*, ed. Arnold K. Garr, Donald Q. Cannon, and Richard O. Cowan (Salt Lake City, UT: Deseret Book, 2000), 508.

58. Franklin Hill Harris to Joseph F., 23 March 1890.

59. Joseph F. to Franklin H. Harris, 25 March 1890.

60. Joseph F. to Martha Ann, 11 February 1891, herein.

61. Joseph F. to Martha Ann, 11 February 1891, herein.

62. Joseph F. to Martha Ann, 7 June 1891, herein.

Martha Ann and William Jasper Harris's sons, ca. 1898. Seated, left to right: William Jasper Harris Jr. and Franklin Hill Harris. Standing, left to right: Hyrum Smith Harris, Joseph Albert Harris, and John Fielding Harris. Courtesy of Leland Harris.

Letters

JOSEPH F. TO MARTHA ANN AND WILLIAM, 17 APRIL 1890

Apr. 17th 1890.[1]
Mr. & Mrs. Wm J. Harris
Provo, Utah Co.[2]

Dear Brother and Sister:—

Your card of invitation to the wedding Reception of Hyrum S. and Miss Delia Tweedie,[3] held on the 11th inst. reached me on the 12th—the day following the Reception; Thus being a day too late and not having heard of the event before, will be sufficient excuse for my not having been present, if no other were to be given.

I sincerely wish Hyrum and his Bride a prosperous, peaceful, long and happy voyage thro' life.

As a small token of good will please find enclosed $5^{00} toward the expenses of the Reception, from your brother Jos. F.

1. Preprinted envelope with return address in the upper left-hand corner, "IF NOT DELIVERED IN 10 DAYS, RETURN TO P.O. BOX B, SALT LAKE CITY, UTAH." The envelope is addressed, "Mrs. Martha Ann Harris, Provo, Utah" with a blue-ribbon typewriter. The postmark, "SALT LAKE CITY UTAH APR 2 5:30 PM 01" has a United States two-cent George Washington stamp.
2. Joseph F. was fifty-one, and Martha Ann was forty-eight. Joseph F. had returned to Utah Territory from Washington, DC, but was still keeping a low profile.
3. Hyrum Smith Harris married Delia Sarah Rebekah Twede in the Manti Temple on 9 April 1890. See biographical register, "Twede, Delia Sarah Rebekah."

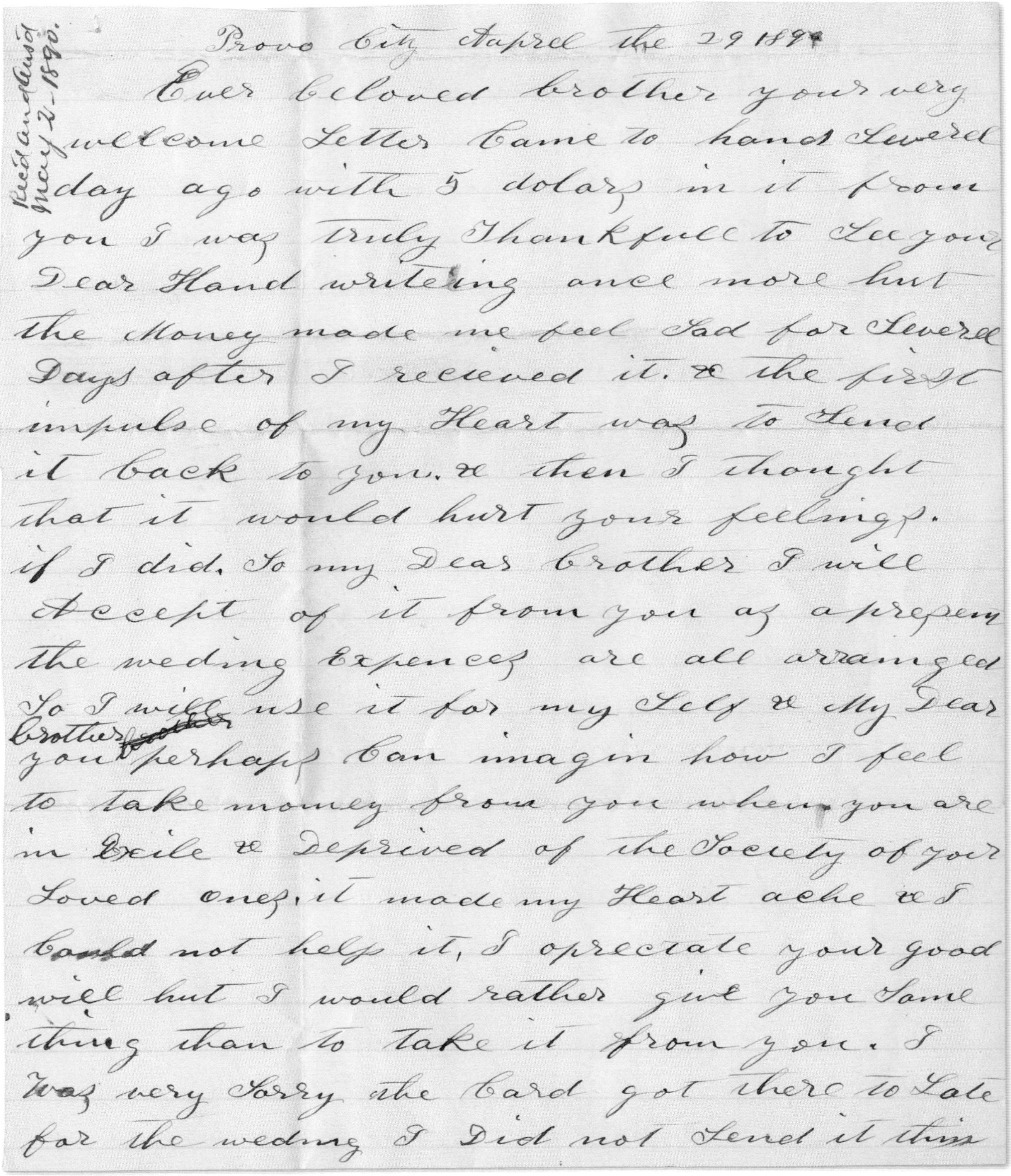

Rec'd and Ans'd May 2 - 1890.

Provo City Aprel the 29 1890

Ever beloved brother your very welcome Letter Came to hand Several day ago with 5 dolars in it from you I was truly Thankfull to See your Dear Hand writeing ance more but the Money made me feel Sad for Several Days after I recieved it. & the first impulse of my Heart was to Send it back to you. & then I thought that it would hurt your feelings. if I did. So my Dear brother I will Accept of it from you as a presen[t] the weding Expences are all arranged So I will use it for my Self & My Dear brother ~~father~~ you perhaps Can imagin how I feel to take money from you when you are in Exile & Deprived of the Society of your Loved ones, it made my Heart ache & I could not help it, I oprecíate your good will but I would rather give you Same thing than to take it from you. I was very Sorry the Card got there to Late for the weding I Did not Send it this

Martha Ann to Joseph F., 29 April 1890 (p. 1)

I hope to hear from you again soon
and how I would like to see you once more

king to obtain any thing. & I knew
you Could not Come your Self. but
my Dear Brother we Sent it to Let you
know we had not forgoton you. but
I thought Some of your Family would
Come at Least. but I supose they
Did not think it worth while but
we had avery nice pleasent time of
it. I am Sorry Hyrum did not Let
you know about it before he was
Married. but his girl got amisund
erstanding Some how. & got ready
nearly a whole week be for Hyrum
~~had~~ made arrangements with us to
be ~~there~~ So it took us by Surprise
& Crouded things Sadly hence the
caus of your Card Coming to Late
but he did not Like to tell her the
mistake becaus he was afraid it
might make her feel bad I hope
you have not robed your Self to Send
me the money. I thank you for your kind
wishes to Hyrum & I prey they may all Come
to pass. praying the Lord to bless you I am
your Sister M A H

Martha Ann to Joseph F., 29 April 1890 (p. 2)

MARTHA ANN TO JOSEPH F., 29 APRIL 1890

Rec'd and Ans'd
May 2—1890[4]

Provo City Aaprel the 29 1890[5]

Ever beloved brother your very welcome letter came to hand severel day ago with 5 dolars in it from you I was truly thankfull to see your dear hand writeing once more but the money made me feel sad for severel days after I recieved it. & the first impulse of my heart was to send it back to you. & then I thought that it would hurt your feelings. if I did. So my dear brother I will accept of it from you as a present the weding expences are all arrainged so I will use it for my self & my dear <brother> you <~~brother~~> perhaps can imagin how I feel to take money from you when you are in exile & deprived of the society of your loved ones. it made my heart ache & I could not help it. I opreciate your good will but I would rather give you some thing than to take it from you. I was very sorry the card got there to late for the weding I did not send it thin[**p. 2**]king to obtain any thing. & I knew you could not come your self. but my dear brother we sent it to let you know we had not forgoton you. but I thought some of your family would come at least. but I supose they did not think it worth while but we had a very nice pleasent time of it. I am sorry Hyrum[6] [*illegible strike-through*] did not let you know about it before he was married. but his girl[7] got a misunderstanding some how. & got ready nearly a whole week be for Hyrum had made arrangements with us to be thear so it took us by surprise & crouded things sadly hence the caus of your card coming to late but he did not like to tell her the mistake becous he was afraid it might make her feel bad I hope you have not roobed your self to send me the money. I thank you for your <kind> wishes to Hyrum & I prey they may all come to pass. praying the Lord to bless you I am your sister M A H

I hope to hear from you again soon ~~&~~ & O how I would to see you once more[8]

JOSEPH F. TO MARTHA ANN, 2 MAY 1890

Salt Lake City, U.T. May 2d 1890[9]

Mrs. Martha A. Harris,
Provo.

4. Written sideways in the top left margin.
5. Martha Ann addresses the envelope, "Mr. Jason Mack Salt Lake City Box B." Joseph F. wrote on the front, "M.A. Harris Recd May 2d 1890. Ansd " " " ". Postmark: MAY 1 1890 UTAH." There is a US George Washington two-cent stamp in the upper right-hand corner.
6. Hyrum Smith Harris.
7. Delia Sarah Rebekah Twede.
8. Written upside down in the top margin of page 2.
9. From Joseph F.'s letterpress copybooks; original not extant. This letter is written on official letterhead of the Church from the Office of the President.

My Dear Sister Martha:— Your letter of the 29th ult. is received. I am glad to hear from you.

The little matter of $5^{00} in honor of the wedding supper of Hyrum[10] is nothing here nor there, unless you feel like ridiculing me because it was not more.[11] This is a day of small things with me and I cannot reach the high and mighty ideas some people entertain. But I and mine are much blessed and lack for no absolutely needful thing. I am glad to hear a good report about Hyrums wife,[12] they say she is a neat, tidy housekeeper, and a good housewife, I certainly wish them every prosperity. I wrote **[p. 2]** to Hyrum a short time before his marriage but have not heard whether he received it or not.[13]

I was thankful when Frank was called to home missionary[14] duties, and I hope he will strive to honor the calling.[15] It will be much better for him to get his hand in here among the saints than to go out into the world, raw and unprepared. I would like it if Hyrum could also engage in home missionary work. Or Willie or John.[16] The family are all as well as usual. They all work hard and have but very little leisure to visit, or go any where. I have no doubt several of them would have enjoyed a visit to Provo, could they have spared the time to go. Sarah[17] has had three children down with Scarlet fever but they have got over it nicely—she has had a hard time of it, nevertheless.

They are all pretty well now. I am in very good health— Hoping You and William are well, and all the children, & childrens children, I am Your brother Joseph

MARTHA ANN TO JOSEPH F., 18 MAY 1890

Rec'd May 20/90
Ans'd 5/22/90.[18]

Provo City May the
18th 1890

Mr Joseph F Smith beloved brother your very welcome favor[19] came to hand some time sence, but this is the first time I have had a chance to answer. I have been very busy waiting on the sick & making temple cloths for one & another. I was pleased to hear from you that your health was good & that the children had recouverd from the dreaded diseas scarlet feeever I sincerly hope that there will no more take <it>. we are all tolerable well Williams[20] is feeble but he keeps round

10. Hyrum Smith Harris.
11. See Martha Ann to Joseph F., 13 May 1890, herein.
12. Delia Sarah Rebekah Twede.
13. See Joseph F. to Hyrum S. Smith, 25 March 1890.
14. In the 1850s, Brigham Young began calling home-based missionaries, who would travel in pairs throughout the Utah Territory, speaking in meetings and visiting members' homes to call them to repentance and greater levels of commitment.
15. See Joseph F. to Franklin H. Harris, 25 March 1890.
16. William Jasper Harris Jr., John Fielding Smith.
17. Sarah Ellen Richards.
18. Written sideways in the top left margin of page 1.
19. See Joseph F. to Martha Ann, 2 May 1890, herein.
20. William Jasper Harris.

& [**p. 2**] does all he can you spoke about me rideciling[21] you, my dear brother I, think ~~my dear brother~~ you know me better than to think such a thing of me I do not wish to ridicule you nor any one else I have always ben thankfull for small favors & did not expect large ones & as far as high idars[22] are consirned I never did entertain very high idars my self. I have allways been very humble in my idars I have never expected mutch & I do not wish to do any thing rong you spoke about the boys going on home misions but I [**p. 3**] am afraid that the work that they are ingaged in that it will bee awkward for them to do mutch at it I wish thir work was different. I should like very mutch to have them ingaged in the good work. I feel greeved to the heart that my boys are so backward in theese things. I am thinking very strongly of trying to go to the Temple[23] before long to bee baptised for my health[24] & doing the work for some of my kindred Aunt Louisa Lovina mack they were[25] [**p. 4**] good folks and cousin Joulya[26] who died not long ago in the City[27] now will you tell me who else you think of O yes Aunt Ann Mathues[28] & I want to do all I can. pleas write & tell me what you think about my going if you think of any one else pleas put me in mind of them. pleas give my love to all your family & take a large share your self & may my Father in heaven bless you is my prayr allways from your loving sister Martha Harris

William & the children all join me in love to you[29]

JOSEPH F. TO MARTHA ANN, 22 MAY 1890

Salt Lake City, U.T. May 22^d 1890[30]

To Mrs. M. A. Harris
Provo—

My Dear Sister Martha:—

21. Joseph F. thought Martha Ann may have considered his five-dollar gift for Hyrum Harris's wedding too little. See Joseph F. to Martha Ann, 2 May 1890, herein.
22. "Ideals." See Joseph F. to Martha Ann, 2 May 1890, herein.
23. Because the Salt Lake Temple was still under construction at this point, Martha Ann may have been referring to the Logan Temple (dedicated 1884), Manti Temple (dedicated 1888), or St. George Temple (dedicated 1877).
24. Though discontinued in 1922, baptisms for health, most likely based on 2 Kings 5:1–14 and John 5:2–4, were practiced during the nineteenth and early twentieth centuries. See Jonathan A. Stapley and Kristine Wright. "'They Shall Be Made Whole': A History of Baptism for Health," *Journal of Mormon History* (Fall 2008): 69–112.
25. Lovisa Mack and Lovina Mack were sisters of Joseph F. and Martha Ann's grandmother Lucy Mack. The sisters were very close and died within a short time of each other. See Lavina Fielding Anderson, ed., *Lucy's Book: A Critical Edition of Lucy Mack Smith's Family Memoir* (Salt Lake City, UT: Signature Press, 2001) 167, 236–46; and Lucy Mack Smith, *Biographical Sketches of Joseph Smith, the Prophet, and His Progenitors for Many Generations* (Liverpool: Orson Pratt, 1853), 27–29. See also biographical register, "Mack, Lovisa" and "Mack, Lovina."
26. Unknown individual. Likely Julia, a relative of Mary Fielding.
27. Salt Lake City, Salt Lake County, Utah Territory.
28. Ann Fielding, wife of Rev. Timothy Richard Matthews.
29. Written upside down in the top margin of page 4.
30. The original letter, written on official letterhead of the Church from the Office of the President, is incomplete. A copy of the full letter is found in Joseph F.'s letterpress copybooks.

Your letter of the 18th came to hand on the 20th inst. How you can "wait on the sick", "make Temple clothing for one and another" and take care of your own family is almost a mystery. I am thankful, however that the Lord gives you the strength to do it.

There seems but little leisure or pleasure in this world for some of us, but we may stand a chance for a more liberal share in the next, provided we can endure to the end in this. I am in no degree impressed with the beauties of the world by the knowledge I have gained of it—nor of its <u>glories</u> either. I am satisfied it is but a probation at best.

There is always satisfaction, however in trying to **[p. 2]**[31] do good, and there is a degree of joy in the accomplishment thereof, but the good we do seems infinetisimel in comparison to what is needed to be done. What a comfort it is to know that all will be rewarded, eventually, according to their works, and the intents of their hearts. The noblest, and therefore in the true sense, the highest ideas that men can entertain are those of "faith, hope and charity,"[32] and in all these I award you credit of being superior to most women, else you would have succumbed to your misfortunes long ago. but your hope, your charity for others, and your faith in providence have sustained you. In temporal things God has dealt more mercifully with me than with you, as it now seems, but who can tell what the end may be? I have buried 8 of my children, you, not one of yours. Yours are mostly grown, and should be able to take care of themselves—and look after their parents—mine are mostly young and dependent still. **[p. 3]** I think your children all love you—and will do all they can for your comfort in your coming days— Your boys are tall, strong men—and if they feel toward <u>their</u> mother as I have always felt, and still feel, towards mine—(and I see no reason why they should not—) then they will <u>see</u> <u>to</u> <u>it</u> that <u>you</u> will not <u>lack</u> if it is in their power to prevent it. When I see young men—or hear of them—spending their means for pleasure and amusement, and to gratify a taste for appearances, and pride, or any such things, while <u>mother</u> is toiling at home and lacking home comforts, I cannot help but think there is something wrong. Boys should think of Mother <u>first</u>—and self afterwards, is the way it looks to me. No doubt <u>your</u> boys do so. **[p. 4]**

In regard to doing Temple work for our Kindred, when it comes to Mothers folks[33] it would be well for you to consult with Aunt Mercy R. Thompson.[34] I do not know whether any thing has been done for Grand Mother Lucy Mack Smith's[35] Sisters or Kindred or not. Until very recently—Solomon Mack, Grand Mothers brother was living—and a member of the church—but never came to Utah.[36] He may be living yet for ought I know. But our Grand Aunts and Unkles should be looked after. Did you ever say any thing to John[37] about them. <u>He</u> should lead out in such matters. I donot know who you mean by "Cousin Julia, who died not long ago in the City". Whoever she was, the question arises in my mind is this, if she "died in the city" why was she not baptised for herself? I would like you to go to the Temple and do all you can for our departed Kindred, and I will help you all I can. Before you go, consult with brother John and with Aunt Thompson. I am your brother Joseph

31. Page 2 is also written on official letterhead of the Church from the Office of the President.
32. See 1 Corinthians 13:13.
33. The family of Mary Fielding.
34. Mercy Rachel Fielding.
35. Lucy Mack, grandmother to Martha Ann and Joseph F. See biographical register, "Mack, Lucy."
36. Solomon Mack, maternal uncle to the Prophet Joseph Smith Jr. and Hyrum Smith, died in 1851. See biographical register, "Mack, Solomon."
37. John Smith.

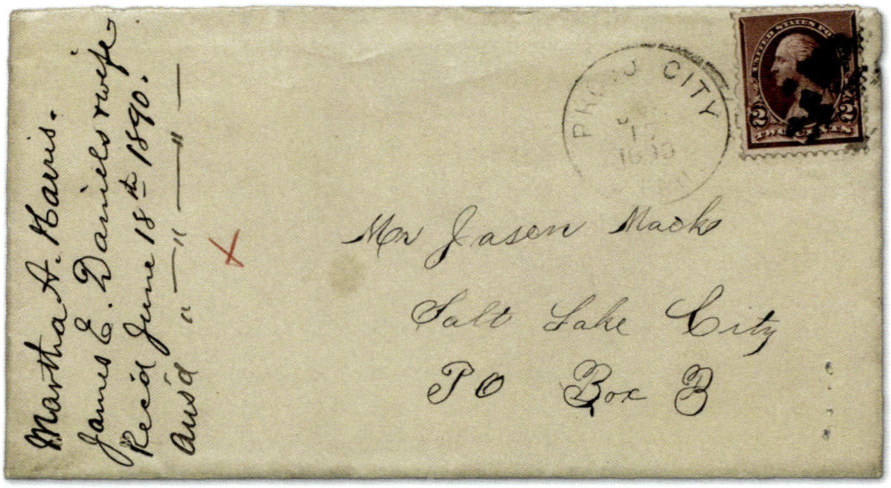

Martha Ann to Joseph F., 16 June 1890 (envelope)

MARTHA ANN TO JOSEPH F.,[38] 16 JUNE 1890

Recd June 18.1890[39]
Ans d ″— ″— ″—[40]

Provo City June
the 16 1890

Ever Dear & mutch beloved brother Joseph Sister Danelly[41] wished me to Send this Letter to you She is avery Dear friend to me & has been very kind to me in deed Sence I have been in provo & I ~~Can~~ Can recommend them to you as good faithfull Latter day Saints worthy any blissing. I Sincerly hope you are all well. I am Coming to the City before many days & I would like very mutch to see you when I Come I hope I Can have that privlige we are all [**p. 2**] tolerable well I have been very poorly so I got adminsterd to & I have felt better ever Sence I recieved your kind & very welcome favor of may the 27 I was thankfull to hear you were all well ~~the~~ when I Come I will go & See brother John[42] & I thank you for your kind advice the folks have just come in to spend the Day Mary & Charley Smiths wife so I will draw my letter to aclose The children all join me in love to you & yours ever truly your Loving Sister Martha A Harris

38. Written in pencil by someone other than Martha Ann is the following: [COVER TO: JAMES E. DANIELS, 11 JUN 1890]. The letter was in an envelope addressed to "Mr Jasen Mack Salt Lake City PO Box B." Written sideways on the left side of the envelope in what appears to be Joseph F.'s handwriting is "Martha A. Harris. James E. Daniels & wife Recd June 18th 1890. Ans d ″— ″— ″—." In the top right-hand corner of the envelope is a two-cent postage stamp with an image of George Washington. The postmark is from "PROVO CITY," dated "J[◊◊] 17 1890."
39. Written sideways in the top left margin of page 1.
40. Written directly under note 1.
41. Unknown individual.
42. John Smith, Joseph F. and Martha Ann's older half brother.

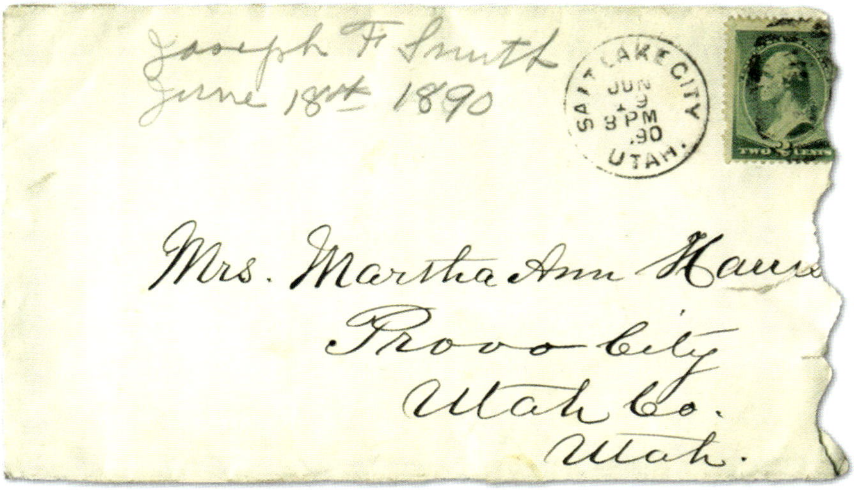

Joseph F. to Martha Ann, 18 June 1890

JOSEPH F. TO MARTHA ANN, 18 JUNE 1890

Salt Lake City, U.T. June 18th 1890[43]

My Dear Sister,[44]
Martha Ann Harris—

Your favor of the 16th inst. with inclosure from James E. Daniels and wife,[45] have come to hand. I have answered bro. Daniels, which you will find herewith, and will please forward, with the caution that my name is not to be used except in the Temple. and that my letter is not to be shown to any one except the proper authorities.

I shall be able to see you, I think, when you come. This is Julinas 41st birth day.[46] She is better than gold, more precious than diamonds. She is a jewel of the first water, and of the greatest value—judged by the standard of the companionship of quarter of a century![47] God has blessed me with good wives, and my children **[p. 2]** with good mothers; and O, how I feel to bless them, and to thank God. How all hell would grin <with delight> and the Devils laugh to see me "go back" on them![48] And well they might! but I have not the remotest idea of gratifying them in that regard. Exilement for the remainder of my life, or imprisonment till death, would

43. This nonextant letter, written on official letterhead of the Church from the Office of the President, is from Joseph F.'s letterpress copybooks. It was found in a plain envelope addressed to "Mrs. Martha Ann Harris Provo City Utah Co. Utah." The envelope has two postmarks. The one on the front indicates it was sent from Salt Lake City on 19 June at 3:00 p.m. There is a green two-cent Washington postal stamp on the front. On the backside is a postal mark: "PROVO CITY UTAH JUN 20 1890."
44. This letter is written in response to Martha Ann's letter dated 16 June 1890 and received on 18 June 1890, herein.
45. James E. Daniels was married to Marilla Johnson, and according to the 1900 US Census, they lived in Provo at about this time. See biographical register, "Daniels, James Ephraim" and "Johnson, Marilla Lucretia."
46. Julina Lambson.
47. Joseph F. and Julina Lambson were married on 5 May 1866.
48. During the legal and political struggles of the 1880s and early 1890s, Latter-day Saint men were forced to consider ending all connections, including financial support, with their plural wives or face possible imprisonment, fines, or self-imposed exile. In this letter, Joseph F. indicates that he will not abandon his wives.

be meat and drink to my soul, if necessity compelled me to suffer it for their sakes. They have been true to me, by Gods help I will be true to them in time and throughout all eternity!

John[49] has got some work to do for Father,[50] with our old friend Lizzie Hawkins (Wilcox)[51] She has been divorced from Wilcox, and has permission to be sealed, with her children, to Father.[52] John is slow about such matters. I wrote to Jerusha[53] a few days ago, but have never heard from her for 5 years.

Hoping you and yours are well, and with kind love to all, I am your affectionate brother. Joseph——

MARTHA ANN TO JOSEPH F., 4 AUGUST 1890

Rec'd & Ans'd—
Aug. 9. 1890.[54]

Provo City Augest[55]
the 4th 1890

beloved brother.

Joseph it is with pleasure that I take my seat to write you a few lines hoping it may find you all well as it leaves us at this time to day thirty one years ago my willey[56] w~~a~~as born he came home yester day from the railroad & went back to day he sais he has got a good job & I hope he has but he looks very thin in flesh & worn out he is not very strong & can not stand very mutch hardships **[p. 2]** he suffers very severly at times with the cramping in his sthomack but he keeps at work all the time poor boy. I hope he will bee able to wether it threw. brother meechem[57] is very low I went in to day & set down on the side of his bed he can not speak above his breath only in a whisper he looked at me & said O how I would love to see your dear brother once more be fore ~~you~~ I go for said he I shall not bee hear with you long I wish he could **[p. 3]** come & see me O if he could wouldent I ask him for an interest in his faith & prayrs in my behalf so I thaught I would write & tell you what he ~~said~~ he said if I ever seen you to

49. John Smith.
50. Hyrum Smith.
51. Elizabeth Hawkins married Walter Eli Wilcox on 4 September 1853. She was the second of his five plural wives. See biographical register, "Hawkins, Elizabeth" and "Wilcox, Walter Eli."
52. Posthumous sealings and adoptions into the families of General Authorities or temple presidents were practiced during the nineteenth century until 1894. See Richard E. Bennett, "'Line upon Line, Precept upon Precept': Reflections on the 1877 Commencement of the Performance of Endowments and Sealings for the Dead," *BYU Studies* 44, no. 3 (2005): 62–67. See also Joseph F. to Martha Ann, 25 August 1897, herein.
53. Jerusha Smith Pierce was Joseph F. and Martha Ann's older half sister. See biographical register, "Smith, Jerusha."
54. Written sideways in the top left margin of page 1.
55. Martha Ann addresses the envelope, "Mr Jason Mack Salt Lake City Utah Box B." Joseph F. wrote, "M. A. Harris Recd Aug. 9. 1890 Ansd " " " "." There is a US two-cent stamp in the upper left-hand corner. Postmark: "PROVO CITY UTAH AUG 1890."
56. William Jasper Harris Jr.
57. Likely Edward Mecham.

pleas tell you that he loved you dearly & he hoped to soon meet our dear Father & Uncle[58] & many more that had gon before I hate to see him go & leave us but he may raley yet but I think it will bee a hard matter if he ever does he is 80 7 years [**p. 4**] old he cryed like a child I tried to comfort him all I could he seems to cling to life so hard pleas give my love to all your dear ones & do not forget to take a big share for your self Frank[59] was home to make us a short visit came monday night went back Tuesday morning bless his soal he is a dear good boy if he is myne [*illegible strike-through*] pleas excuse this scroll for my <pen> is poor & you know I cannot write worth tupence[60] I will write again soon ever truly your loving sister Martha A Harris I would copy this if I had time

JOSEPH F. TO MARTHA ANN, 9 AUGUST 1890

Aug. 9th 1890[61]

My beloved Sister:
Martha Ann:— Your welcome favor of the 7th inst. is just rec'd, and I hasten to reply. I congratulate Willie[62] on his attainment of 31 years. and I deeply sympathise with him in his lack of sound health. Let me here say—that for some time Julina[63] was sorely afflicted with severe cramps suddenly attacking her in the stomache. Dr. Jos—S. Richards[64] recommended, and gave to her, in one of her bad spells, a common tumbler two thirds full of the best olive oil, (consecrated) at one dose; from which she realized the very best results.[65] I believe her cramps arose from the abnormal condition of the liver and gall. She was relieved entirely by this treatment. Some time after wards, when attacked, she treated [**p. 2**] herself in the same way with the same good results. but she has never suffered since anything like what she did before, either in the severity or the frequency of the attacks. It might be worth Willie's while to try the remedy when again attacked.

I want you to say to Brother Meecham[66] for me, God Bless him, and that I bless him with all my heart. And I feel assured that he is and shall be blessd whether in this life or the better life to come. His integrity, his sincerity, his love for God and his truth, his unwavoring fidelity to the Cause of Zion, his goodness of heart and soul and all his faithfulness, throughout, are all established and known and acknowledged by those who know him, and are accepted of

58. Hyrum Smith and Joseph Smith.
59. Franklin Hill Harris.
60. A tuppence equals two English pennies, hence something of very little value.
61. From Joseph F.'s letterpress copybooks; original not extant.
62. William Jasper Harris Jr.
63. Julina Lambson.
64. Joseph Smith Richards went to medical school in New York and was a practicing physician and surgeon as well as the director of the Dr. W. H. Groves LDS Hospital in Salt Lake City.
65. Though discontinued later, applying consecrated oil to the affected area or ingesting it for health and healing was practiced during the nineteenth and early twentieth centuries. See Lester E. Bush, *Health and Medicine among the Latter-day Saints: Science, Sense & Scripture* (New York: Crossroads, 1993), 78–80, 100–103.
66. Edward Mecham.

God— He has made his calling and his election sure[67] and whether in time or in eternity all is and will be well and glorious with father Meecham. God bless him now and forever, is the prayer of your affectionate brother, (with all the faithful—) Joseph——

P.S. I expect to leave here tomorrow or monday, on a mission to be gone some little time.[68] My family are all well so far as I know. Sarah[69] and family are out in the canyon[70]— Joseph—[71]

MARTHA ANN TO JOSEPH F., 15 JANUARY 1891

Rec'd & Ans'd Jan. 16—1891[72]

Provo City
January the 15th
1891[73]

My dear beloved brother Joseph I take pleasure in setting down to write you a few lines to let you know how we are at the present time we are all well as useuel but I have been away from home taking care of the sick. was absent when your pcture came to hand. I <was> very mutch pleased with it & I thank you ever so mutch for **[p. 2]** <your> kind rememberance of me it seems so nice to think that one has a dear beloved brother who thinks once in a while of thuem it helps to lighten the heavy burden that I carry. I love to look on your dear fase it is better than gold to me. I am not ashamed to own that I love my brothers & sisters & kindred they are all dear to me but there are onely a feew that seems to care for me you are about the onely <one> that **[p. 3]** cares to answer a letter from me <only my children> when I write to them. it some times makes me feel sad but then if they do not care for me I can not help, it I sincerly wish you a hapy new year in return for your kind wish to me & many of them & my prayr is that you may soon have your freedom to mingle with your loved ones once more I never for get to prey for my brothers <sisier> & my kindred I have not been able to go to the temple yet **[p. 4]** for want of means & I do not think I will now untill spring & then I shall make a big effort to go. I am botherd very mutch with a lame back & side when I over do. I supose you have hird we lost Willeys little baby[74] too months old it died Christmas night or rather the

67. Latter-day Saints believe that having one's calling and election made sure means that the Day of Judgment is advanced so that one would know in this life that he or she is saved and exalted in the kingdom of God. See Robert L. Millet, Camille Fronk Olson, Andrew C. Skinner, and Brent L. Top, "Calling and Election," in *LDS Beliefs: A Doctrinal Reference* (Salt Lake City, UT: Deseret Book, 2011), 88–90.
68. The First Presidency left Utah Territory on 11 August 1890 to meet with Church members and political and business leaders in Arizona, Colorado, and New Mexico.
69. Sarah Ellen Richards.
70. Most likely at the Smith family's summer cabin in Little Cottonwood Canyon, southeast of Salt Lake City.
71. Written upside down in the top margin of page 2.
72. Written sideways in the top left margin of page 1. A flower is embossed and outlined in black ink in the top left margin of page 1.
73. Joseph F. was fifty-two, and Martha Ann was forty-nine.
74. Delia Jessie Harris, daughter of Jessie Lena Freckleton and William Jasper Harris Jr., was born on 20 October 1890 and died on 26 December 1890. See biographical register, "Harris, Delia Jessie."

morning after Chiristmas half past 5 it threw a gloom over us all it had lung feever & it turned to congestion I hope this will find you

<all> well & in the enjoyment of good health there is lots of sickness[75]

May the Lord bless you all with kind love. I am your affectionate sister
M A H[76]

I should be pleased to hear from you when convenient[77]

JOSEPH F. TO MARTHA ANN, 16 JANUARY 1891

Salt Lake City, U.T. Jan. 16th 1891[78]

Mrs. Martha A. Harris.
Provo.

My Dear Sister Martha Ann. Your favor of the 15th is rec'd, and read with pleasure. I am glad you received the Photo. all right. not having heard for so long I began to doubt its safe arrival. I sent one to Jerusha[79] at the same time but have heard nothing from her. I also wrote her a letter several months ago but she has never deigned a reply. I heard however that she called to see some of my folks when last in the city, some three weeks ago. John[80] also called with Jerusha, but he seldom calls on my folks—and never comes to see me. I cannot go to see him. I hear that Helen is up north somewhere with **[p. 2]** Lucy,[81] and John is "batching it."[82] I would rather be in exile than that. I have often thought that my own kindred, that is our own family, except you alone, care nothing for me. I wrote a kind spirited letter to Hyrum Walker,[83] nearly two years ago, but he never, replied to it. I have written several times to Hyrum and Frank,[84] but they have never penned a line to me in return, and I have heard that you made unfavorable

75. Written upside down in the top margin of page 3.
76. These two lines were written upside down in the top margin of page 2.
77. Written upside down in the top margin of page 4.
78. Written on official letterhead of the Church from the Office of the President.
79. Jerusha Smith.
80. John Smith.
81. Hellen Maria Fisher and Lucy Smith.
82. Referring to being temporarily single because a partner is away. In this context, Joseph F. was referring to the fact that John Smith's wife, Hellen Maria Fisher Smith, was away from Salt Lake City.
83. Joseph F. and Martha Ann's nephew.
84. Martha Ann's sons Hyrum Smith Harris and Franklin Hill Harris. See Martha Ann to Joseph F., 1 February 1891, herein.

comments on one of my letters to the boys.[85] Condemning my advice and approving their course.[86] I am quite sure you would not have taken that view if you had properly understood my motive.

Next to my own children, I hold yours in esteeme and love. I would not advise your children <u>other</u> than I would my own. And I would as gladly see them prosperous and happy.[87] We are all usually well, so far as I know. God bless you my Sister, and all your children, and William.[88] With love to you and them I am as ever your affectionate brother. J. F. Smith

Martha Ann to Joseph F., 1 February 1891 (envelope)

85. Joseph F. sent a letter to three of Martha Ann's sons in September 1890 after reading in the local newspaper about their possible involvement in a streetcar drivers' strike in Salt Lake City. His advice to them was frank, including his feelings that "the spirit of combinations, 'strikes,' strife and contention is rife in the world just now. It is most deplorable to see that spirit fall upon the people of Utah, where Zion and the Spirit of Zion should prevail." Joseph F. to Hyrum, Frank, and John Harris, 26 September 1890. This discussion continues in a series of letters. See Martha Ann to Joseph F., 1 February 1891; and Martha Ann to Joseph F., 9 February 1891, herein.
86. This strike was the result of failed negotiations between the streetcar company and a labor union. The increase in labor issues and strikes during this period in American history has led historians to refer to the general unrest as "the crisis of the 1890s." See Richard Schneirov, Shelton Stromquist, and Nick Salvatore, eds., *The Pullman Strike and the Crisis of the 1890s: Essays on Labor and Politics* (Urbana: University of Illinois Press, 1999).
87. A few days later, Joseph F. received a four-page letter, dated 18 January 1891, from W. J. Harris Jr. seeking advice and counsel from his uncle, Joseph F. See W. J. Harris Jr. to Joseph F., 18 January 1891.
88. William Jasper Harris.

MARTHA ANN TO JOSEPH F., 1 FEBRUARY 1891

Rec'd and Ans'd Feb. 9. 1891.[89]

Provo City Feb
the first
1891

Mr Joseph F Smith

My very dear brother your welcome favor of 16th <in> came safly to hand I was pleased to hear from you that you ware all useuely well & I hope you will forgive me for not answering before now I was called away to see a sick child was gon from home for three days & when I returned I was sick in bed **[p. 2]** two days more, then I had to make a suit of grave clothes for brother Holbrooks little so~~o~~n 5 years old[90] as soon as that was done I had to make a suit for another little one[91] that died on the bench.[92] Last ~~Saturday~~ <Fryday> Mary sent for me to come in hast that her little walter[93] had got the croop very bad I went & stayd too days & nights & worked faithfully with him came home yester day he was some better **[p. 3]** but he is very bad yet but we hope he is over the worst of it. so you see how my time is taken up. I have seen so mutch sickness & death this winter that it has been auffull to contemplate it gives me the blues & makes me feel sad. you said you had hird that I had ignord your council to my boys[94] that is not so for I have always been willing to lisson to your counsil & to obey it as far as it layd in my pour & I also thank **[p. 4]** you for any advise you might give to my children for I know you would not give them advise that would doo them harm, but what I did say was this I thaught that every thing considerd the way it came about ~~&~~ you was a littl severe in some things you wrote in your letter & I thaught when you hird both sides of the question you would see things in a different light I told the boys not to have any thing to do with that younion if they had lssoned to me they would hav ~~saved~~ **[p. 5]**[95] saved all that trouble but perhaps the hand of the Lord was in it we must acknolege his hand in all things & I do not think Hyrum[96] would have stud it very long, to have worked on those cars. I am sorry Hyrum is out of work just now it is

89. Written sideways in the top left margin. A flower is embossed and outlined in black ink in the top left margin of page 1.
90. Emmett Gordon Holbrook, son of Emily Angelina Hinckley and Lafayette Holbrook, was born on 23 March 1886 and died on 14 January 1891; see "City and County Jottings," *Daily Enquirer* (Provo), 15 January 1891, 4. The article says that he was three years old and that he died of membranous croup and was the second child of Mr. and Mrs. Holbrook that had succumbed to the disease within a very short time.
91. Unknown individual. Between the death of the Holbrook child on 14 January and this letter, dated 9 February 1891, several children's deaths were mentioned in the local paper, including an eight-month-old baby of Mr. and Mrs. Nicholas Everett on 20 January, a five-year-old daughter of M. R. William Probert and a daughter of Edwin Honey on 22 January, an infant son of Edward Stewart on 31 January, an eight-year-old daughter of Mamie Kershaw on 2 February, a daughter of Mr. and Mrs. John Grier on 5 February, and Jessie T. Lewis on 6 February.
92. Known today as Orem (a city bordering Provo City), the Provo Bench was an area where Latter-day Saint pioneers attempted to establish farms in the 1850s but failed because of lack of water. It was not until 1877, with the development of irrigation and channel systems, that permanent residents had established themselves.
93. Walter Harris Corbett, son of Mary Emily Harris and Walter Sutton Corbett, was Martha Ann's grandson.
94. See Joseph F. to Martha Ann, 16 January 1891 herein.
95. "[P.5, 1 FEB 1891 ?]" is written in the top right margin of page 5 in an unknown hand.
96. Hyrum Smith Harris.

very unfortunate for him just at the present time.[97] John has a job with his brother Joseph[98] they git along fine to geather & he helps us & is very kind he is a dear good boy to us **[p. 6]** all. Hyrum was home last week he is thinking some of mooveing to provo & gitting working here I do not know how it will bee yet Williams[99] health is improving & I sincerly hope he will bee able to do something to help his family with before long. The reason the boys shuns writing to you I think is they do not feel compitent to write to you that is Franklin[100] & John. I can not speak for Hyrum but I do not think he has any thing against you my dear brother I am very **[p. 7]** sorry that any of my children should slight my beloved brother. I am sure they all love you or they seem to as far as I know. we are having some very coald weather now hear winter in irnest. I mus tell you I have just got a nice new milch cow & I feel very thankfull for I had now milk all last summer only what I baught. I baught a pig with my work about three months old, it is doing nicely now I am very comfortable **[p. 8]** this winter more so than I have been for a long time or I may say I have never ~~have~~ been so comfortable in my maried life the Lord has truly been good to me though my health is poor some of the time but I hope to weather the storm & out live my weeknesses well I must fetch my letter to a close or you will wery of reading it the children all join me in love to you & may all bee well with you ever is the humble prayr of your loing sisier M A H

I had such a sweet dreem the other night I thaught uncle Joseph[101] the prophet came to see me & he spoke & looked so kindly to me he said God bless you you have done the best[102]

you could it made me feel so hapy[103]

JOSEPH F. TO MARTHA ANN, 9 FEBRUARY 1891

Salt Lake City, U.T. Feb. 9th 1891[104]

Mrs. Martha Ann Harris[105]
Provo, Utah Co.

My Dear Sister Martha Ann:— Your letter of 1st inst. (so headed) came to hand this morning, and I hasten to acknowledge its receipt, and to make a brief response. I am much pleased to hear that you are so comfortable as you represent yourself to be, and that after the great strain upon your physical endurence, <which> you mention, through waiting upon the sick, that you are in as good health and bodily condition as your are. I deeply sympathise with you in the

97. It appears that most of the strikers lost their jobs.
98. Likely John Fielding Harris and Joseph Albert Harris.
99. William Jasper Harris.
100. Franklin Hill Harris.
101. Joseph Smith Jr.
102. Written upside down in the top margin of page 5.
103. Written sideways in the bottom right margin of page 5.
104. Written on official letterhead of the Church from the Office of the President.
105. Joseph F. was fifty-two, and Martha Ann was forty-nine.

mental sorrow you feel for the afflicted and suffering ones. If you are going to follow nursing, as a profession, I would advise you to take a leaf from the book of the average physician—that is—[**p. 2**][106] never to allow your sympathy for the afflicted, to cause you any mental anguish. Doctors never borrow trouble, nor grieve except at "funerals" of their own. You will have to take this "leaf from their book", in order to make a successful nurse, as to enduring long at the trade.

You need never borrow any trouble over delaying to answer my letters. Write to me when you want to, or need to, and not because I write to you. Take your own time about this matter. And don't worry.

I sincerely hope that Mary's little boy[107] will soon be better. I hope it is not Croup. I don't know that I ever heard of a genuine case of croup ever being cured. That which is mostly called croup, is not croup, but only resembles it in some respects. A bad cold, with hoarseness, and the apparent closing of the bronchial tubes with phlegm, is often taken for croup. The latter <i. e. hoarseness &c—> is not always dangerous, if taken in time. it may easily be remidied. But croupe proper, is a fatal disease. True, or membraneous croup, is inflamation of the larynx, with fiberous exudations which form a <false> mem[108]

JOSEPH F. TO MARTHA ANN, 11 FEBRUARY 1891

Salt Lake City, U.T. Feb. 11th 1891[109]

Mrs. Martha Ann Harris,
Provo.

My Dear Sister Martha:— I feel impressed to write you this morning, not that I have any thing out lined in my mind to say, not because I have nothing else to do, for I have no time to be idle, and none to spare, indeed my time is not sufficient for the duties required.

I feel interested in the welfare of your family, for their welfare is yours. You cannot feel prosperous nor happy unless they are prospered and are moving in the line of duty, and faithful to their callings and true to their principles, to their religion and to God and man. neither can they be happy and successful unless they are walking in these pathes.

First and foremost we owe allegience to Him [**p. 2**] who is the giver of life, and all other good things. No Latter day Saint can enjoy the spirit of God without sincerely acknowledging Him, remembering him, honoring him in their lives and in the first fruits of all their increase. Merely living, or living only for the present life, to make money, to accumulate riches, and to be admired, is not true prosperity, is not the part of wisdom, is not true inteligence, is not manly great nor good, but it is sordid, carnal, groveling and contemptible in the sight of God. Nor is it the true way to ordinary prosperity for a good Latter-day Saint.

106. The numeral 2 is written in the top center margin of the page and is circled.
107. Mary Emily Harris's son Walter Harris Corbett.
108. The original letter is missing the final two pages. Fortunately, a Joseph F. Smith letterpress copybook preserved those pages.
109. Written on official letterhead of the Church from the Office of the President.

Those who have never saught riches in this Church, but have been faithful to their callings, have realized most fully the injunction of the Redeemer:—"Seek ye first the Kingdom of God and His righteousness and all other things shall be added unto you."[110]

While those who have not lived their religion, while they may have succeeded in gathering means to some extent, in some cases, they are destitute ~~of the~~ of the riches of eternal truth and of the love of God, and have **[p. 3]** only a little of the dross and reffuse of the world which at best can only serve a temporary purpose, and cannot possibly avail them anything on the death bed, nor in the great eternity before them. Then, Oh! then they will be poor indeed! The poverty you have suffered all your life would not be a drop in the Ocean, not a single atom in the limitless world of matter, compared with the destitution—the abject poverty of him who has made—or will make worldly gain his God, and the goal of his ambition.

God has said, "I will be enquired of by my people."[111] "If ye seek me early, ye shall find me."[112] "Seek and ye shall find, knock and it shall be opened unto you, ask and ye shall receive."[113] But he that asketh, must do so in faith—or he will ask amiss— He that doubteth will not receive. To ask right—one must be right—to receive one must be worthy to receive; therefore "first seek the Kingdom of God and His righteousness", obtaining that we shall "find"—if we "seek",—"receive" if we "ask", and the door will be opened to us when we knock. And not other wise. **[p. 4]** I do not want to weary you, but I want—or would like you to let the boys read this letter, and for you to impress upon them these principles. of cours I can only slightly touch upon them in a letter. But these truths lie at the root of the matter. I like firmness to purpose, provided the purpose is right and good. firmness in wrong, is only obstinasy and wickedness. I like integrity to the truth, in all men; integrity to business depends upon a mans integrity to good principles, but integrity to any purpose is essential to success therein. My understanding of Joseph's[114] course, gives me confidence in him. I like his continuity and steadiness and persistance in his purpose, I like the spirit and disposition I have seen of John,[115] I believe them both to be good boys. and I feel in my heart to bless them. Willie and Hyrum and Frank[116] have my love and my most earnest faith and prayer, I love them because they are my sisters boys, because they are my Nephews, and because I feel in my heart that **[p. 5]** they are good boys, but we have all much to learn. Sometimes young men, and sometimes old ones too, think they know a great deal, and are much mistaken.

In last nights "News" there is an editorial on the silent force of truth, which I commend to all the boys, and wish they would study it well.[117] It bears upon the subject of my letters to the boys. And for fear you may not see it, I will quote an extract, taken from a Gentile Paper.[118] which seems to be waking up in dead earnest to the great necessities of men. It says:—"Freedom will not come until the people unite; but the people will never unite until

---

110. Matthew 6:33.
111. Possibly an allusion to Ezekiel 36:37.
112. Proverbs 8:17.
113. See Matthew 7:7; Luke 11:9; Doctrine and Covenants 88:63.
114. Joseph Albert Harris.
115. John Fielding Harris.
116. William Jasper Harris Jr., Hyrum Smith Harris, and Franklin Hill Harris.
117. See "The Silent Force of Truth," *Deseret Evening News*, 10 February 1891, 4.
118. The excerpt, which Joseph F. quotes in full, is from a publication titled *The Remedy*, which is described as "an exchange . . . published in the interest of working people." The excerpt in the newspaper is followed by an editorial on the unity of the Latter-day Saints, most likely written by the editor, Charles W. Penrose.

they know what they unite for, and they can never know that until they fully learn certain grand truthes: Political parties cannot unite them—old parties nor new parties. Trades unions cannot unite them, Knights of labor[119] cannot unite them. Alliances and confederations can not unite them, for parties and organizations have power only as they have truth. It is the power of truth, and that only, that can ever unite the people nothing else. Yet few men really understand this [**p. 6**] Good men who will really spend days and dollars to organize, to build and to make a noise and a show, will very grudgingly spend minutes and cents to quietly spread—(or even learn)[120] the truth. As yet men know little of the silent, irresistable power of truth, and in their ignorance make little use of it."[121]

The above is a key to the whole situation. The world has not got "the truth", therefore how can they unite? and when will liberty come to them, for they have rejected "the truth", and prefer to believe a lie, and to depend upon man rather than upon God. that is why we have "strikes", and "lock outs" in the world, and why the working people are distracted, poor and comparatively helpless. God has revealed the truth, and the Spirit of it—he has organized the most perfect system of union ever known to men on earth. A system of perfect union, of perfect liberty—and what we need is to study it, learn it, and live by it—then we will have no need for "Trades unions," or combinations of any kind, other than that which God has established— With love, I am your affictionate brother Joseph

JOSEPH F. TO MARTHA ANN, 7 JUNE 1891

June 7th 1891

Mrs. Martha Ann Harris—
My Dear Sister Martha:—

I hope you and yours are enjoying good health.

Our little Franklin R.[122] was the last to come down with measles, and is the 8th one of the children who have taken the desease this spring. And in order that it might last longer, not more than two have had it at once;—generally only one at a time! Two of the little ones have had whooping cough, and nearly all—old and young have had a turn—more or less heavy of la grippe.[123] We are all in pretty good health now, except Frankie who commenced yesterday with measles. none of them have had it very severely, and all—so far—have got over it nicely—for which we feel exceedingly thankful. We now have only four more liable to take the desease. Having not heard from you for some time, I thought I would just drop you a line or two to say we have not forgotten you, and we hope you are all well and comfortable.

119. The Knights of Labor was one of the largest labor unions in the United States during the 1880s. By the early 1890s, its membership had dramatically dropped. The union promoted numerous social and cultural ideals seen by Joseph F. and others as antithetical to Church principles. See J. Kenneth Davies, "The Secularization of the Utah Labor Movement," *Utah Historical Quarterly* 45, no. 2 (Spring 1977): 108–35.

120. Joseph F. inserted this parenthetical phrase into the quote.

121. As quoted in "Silent Force of Truth," 4.

122. Franklin Richards Smith was three years old at the time of this letter. See biographical register, "Smith, Franklin Richards."

123. *La grippe* was a common French term used to describe various types of influenza.

By the way—I heard lately that Lucy[124] was going—or had gone to Provo on a visit and that Zina[125] was here taking care of her boarders. You may think it is "none of my business", to worry over your affairs, but, I cannot help it—all the same. I think it is bad enough for Lucy to have to keep gentile boarders **[p. 2]** in Salt Lake City, as I am informed she does; but I consider it still worse for Zina to do so.

Lucy is older than Zina, and I have confidence in her as a sensible, good girl. She also hase some experience. Zina may be just as good and true as Lucy, but she is younger and less experienced. The history of boarding gentiles, from the beginning in this Territory, has no variations from its natural results. Circumstances have varied but the result has been invariable—and it has been evil. The nature, character and extent of the evil have varied—but Evil has been and is the common result—whatever the character, extent or nature of that result might be. It can only be a question of time—when the results—bad or worse—never good—will be apparent. I sincerely hope your girls will quit the business in time. And I think it is exceedingly unwise for Zina to be left alone with boarders—whether gentiles or not. If one of the boys was with her, I should not see the same cause for fear—either for Zina or Lucy. You may not thank me for my suggestions, counsel or interference in your children's affairs, but I must sound a note of warning, and leave the result with you and providence. If the girls must keep a boarding house—let one of the boys be near, and if possible chose their lodgers. Your brother Joseph.

JOSEPH F. TO MARTHA ANN, 17 JUNE 1891

June 17th 1891—

My Dear Sister,
Martha Ann Harris:—

Your favor of the 14th inst. came to hand yesterday, and has been read with much interest, for I can realize, to some extent at least, the trying circumstances under which you are placed.

I feel sorry for Adelia,[126] and for Hyrum.[127] I do not know what the trouble is with Adelia, or what the nature of her desease, which you speak of, but it is hard for any one to be sick, and confined to bed. I sincerely hope she will soon be better, so that she can take care of her baby[128]

124. Lucy Smith Harris. Lucy was twenty-one years old, unmarried, and living in Salt Lake City. Later, she married Jonathan Simmons in 1898 and died in 1905.
125. Zina Christine Harris is Lucy's sister. Zina Christine was fifteen years old, unmarried, and living in Provo, but she apparently had gone to Salt Lake City to help her sister. Zina eventually married George Thomas Furner in 1893 and lived in Nephi, Juab County, Utah; see Joseph F. to Martha Ann, 28 January 1895, herein. Following her husband's death in 1903, Zina lived in Provo, where she raised four children and did washing and sewing and took in boarders to make ends meet; see Zina Christine Harris Furner, journal, 1905–7, copy in editors' possession. Later she married John Thomas Dennis, widower husband of her sister Mercy Ann Harris in 1909.
126. Delia Sarah Rebekah Twede, also known as Adelia in some sources.
127. Hyrum Smith Harris.
128. Mercy Rachel Harris, daughter of Delia Sarah Rebekah Twede and Hyrum Smith Harris, was just a few months old. See biographical register, "Harris, Mercy Rachel."

and relieve you. What is Hyrum doing at "Fish Creek"?[129] Has he tried to get a position again on the street car line? Would not a position there if steady—be better than his work at "Fish Creek"? My motto has always been that steady work with moderate wages are better than unsteady Jobs, altho' the latter might make better short returns.

If a man can get steady work and regular wages he knows what to depend upon and can make honest calculations for the present and future. Not so with unsteady and uncertain jobs. I think if Hyrum could get employ [**p. 2**]ment here on the street-care line,[130] or in some store or other steady business it would be the best thing he could do, unless he took up some land some where and went to fruit raising, market gardening,—farming and stock raising—or something of that kind. Of course, I do not know what his natural inclinations are, nor what his tastes and talants are best adapted to. I am satisfied that it is well for young men to start at something good—or reasonably so—and stick to it.

How is Joseph[131] getting along? What is he doing now? I sincerely hope he is prospering. Also John, and Willie, I sometimes hear of Frank.[132]

I cannot but regret that the Girls[133] are compelled to keep boarders—but if they must, may God preserve them from harm and keep them from all evil.

I have great confidence in the natural intigrity of your girls, as I also have in my own, yet I would keep them all as far away from the precipice of ruin as I possibly could, until, at least, they were old enough to understand and know for themselves. There is one good safe-guard against evil for our girls, and that is prayer and trust in God! no girl with that Spirit thoroughly in her heart, can easily be over come. May God bless, and preserve our children from harm. With love to all, I am, as ever, your brother Joseph.

JOSEPH F. TO MARTHA ANN, 13 AUGUST 1891

Salt Lake City, U.T. Aug. 13th 1891[134]

My Dear Sister
Martha Ann Harris:— Your favor of June 27th came duly to hand. It needed no immediate answer, so I have not hurried to reply. You did not say how old Arta was on June 27?[135] nor was I aware that she was born on that ever memorable day. How well I remember the early morning of June 28th, 47 years ago. When D. B. Huntington announced at Mothers bed-room

129. There are several Fish Creeks in Utah, among them one in Carbon County and another in Piute and Sevier Counties.
130. Salt Lake City had the largest network of streetcar lines in Utah Territory at the time. Several rapid-transit companies established in the 1890s made much of the city and beyond accessible by streetcar. The last streetcar line in Salt Lake City was closed in 1946.
131. Joseph Albert Harris.
132. John Fielding Harris, William Jasper Harris Jr., and Franklin Hill Harris.
133. Zina Christine Harris and Lucy Smith Harris.
134. Written on official letterhead of the Church from the Office of the President.
135. Martha Artimissa Harris, known as Artie or Arta. 27 June was Artimissa's birthday and also the day that commemorated the martyrdom of Joseph Smith Jr. and Hyrum Smith in 1844. See biographical register, "Harris, Martha Artimissa."

window that sad news of the murder's, the day before![136] While memory holds its sway, that day can never be forgotten by me. But let that pass. I hope our children may never have an experience such as we have had. Since I received your letter, Hyrums baby[137] has passed away. In life we are in the midst of death. I hope the mother is doing better.

I happened to be where I saw Lucy[138] last sunday morning. I learned that Frank[139] was going to leave Clark, Eldridge &c.[140] and go to work on the Rail Road [**p. 2**] some where. This surprised me, for I supposed he had steady work, and was doing well. I am afraid the change will not result in great good to him, altho' for Lucys sake I am not sorry for it.[141]

We have had lots of sickness since last winter.[142] We commenced with the grip[143]—filled in with the measles and I hope we can end off—for a few years, at least, with the whooping Cough which we are having now. Eight of the children at the same time are having it—some light—some very severe. We have had them all up in the Canyon[144] for about a month, when they came home much improved, but some of them soon took the summer complaint,[145] and to day, Edna[146] and little ones had to return to the Canyon.

My own health is very good, but I do not relish the extreme heat as well as I would like.

Edna had her house broken into on Wednesday the 5th inst. and rummaged by thieves. Her <gold> watch, locket, finger ring, sleeve buttons, ear-rings, and other things were taken away. No trace of the burglar.

Hoping this will find you and yours well and that the future may smile upon you more abundently than in the past. I remain as ever your affectionate brother Joseph.

136. Dimick Baker Huntington was city marshal ad interim and the First Ward high constable in Nauvoo in 1844. According to this letter, it was he who told Mary Fielding of her husband Hyrum's death. He was one of three men who washed and prepared Joseph Smith Jr.'s and Hyrum's bodies for burial. See Von Wymetal and Wilhelm Ritter, *Joseph Smith the Prophet: His Family and His Friends* (Salt Lake City, UT: Tribune Printing and Publishing, 1886), 317. See also biographical register, "Huntington, Dimick Baker."
137. Mercy Rachel Harris, daughter of Hyrum Smith Harris and Delia Sara Rebekah Twede, died on 29 July 1891.
138. Lucy Smith Harris.
139. Franklin Hill Harris.
140. Located at 141 West First South in Salt Lake City, Clark, Eldredge, and Company was one of the largest wholesalers in the Intermountain West, established in 1881.
141. Perhaps Joseph F. hoped this meant that Frank would be able to look after Lucy at the boarding house. See Joseph F. to Martha Ann, 7 June 1891, herein.
142. See Joseph F. to Martha Ann, 7 June 1891, herein.
143. Shortened form of *la grippe*. See note 123 above.
144. At the Smith family home in Cottonwood Canyon. See Joseph F. to Martha Ann, 15 August 1884, herein.
145. A term used in the nineteenth century for *cholera infantum*, or summer diarrhea of infants.
146. Edna Lambson.

JOSEPH F. TO MARTHA ANN, 20 JUNE 1892

June 20—1892[147]

Martha Ann Harris
Provo—

My Dear Sister Martha:— Your letter of June, came to hand yesterday—Sunday and I could not then answer it. Little Zina[148] passed the fatal turning point on the eleventh or twelfth day of her fever and since then has been slowly recovering. but she is still a very sick child and needs constant care—night and day. Her mother[149] and others have been almost worn out with watching. Several others have been ailing, with slight attacks of bronchitis, bad colds, teething &c. Little Emily[150] is quite poorly just now—but not seriously so, we trust.

I am sorry for your continued weakness and sincerely hope you will soon get well.

I am willing for bro. "John Leathy"[151] to be adopted to Father[152] and will send him an authorization— In haste I am your brother Jos. F. Smith

JOSEPH F. TO MARTHA ANN, 16 MAY 1893

May 16th 1893[153]

Mrs. Martha A. Harris
Provo—

My Dear Sister:—

John[154] sends you 6$ and Lucy[155] 4$—making $10^{00} which please find herewith, and on receipt of this please drop me the enclosed card and oblige.

We are all well, and hope you are all the same.

Your brother,
Jos. F. Smith

147. From Joseph F.'s letterpress copybooks; original not extant. Joseph F. was fifty-three years old, and Martha Ann was fifty-one.
148. Zina Smith, born to Joseph F. and Edna Lambson on 11 October 1890. See biographical register, "Smith, Zina."
149. Edna Lambson.
150. Emily Jane Smith, born to Joseph F. and Julina Lambson on 11 September 1888. See biographical register, "Smith, Emily Jane."
151. John Liechty. See Martha Ann to Joseph F., 8 September 1874; Joseph F. to Martha Ann, 6 November 1874; and Martha Ann to Joseph F., 16 November 1874, herein.
152. Hyrum Smith. See Joseph F. to Martha Ann, 25 August 1897, herein.
153. From Joseph F.'s letterpress copybooks; original not extant. Joseph F. was fifty-four, and Martha Ann was fifty-two.
154. Likely John Fielding Harris, Martha Ann's son, or possibly Joseph F. and Martha Ann's half brother John Smith.
155. Lucy Smith Harris.

JOSEPH F. TO MARTHA ANN, 7 MARCH 1894

Mar. 7th 1894[156]

Mrs. Martha Ann Harris,
Provo—&c.

My Dear Sister Martha:— I did not see Lucy[157] until last evening when I gave her your letter—and thinking it would relieve her for me to attend to the Exponent matter,[158] I said nothing to her about it, but when I came up Town saw to it myself, and herewith send you the receipt, which I trust will be all right. I have before me two letters from you, neither of which have been answered; one was received Oct. 8th 1892—a year ago last Oct. and the other on the 7thult—or a month ago. In yours of Oct. 92—you speak of a matrass & [**p. 2**] syringe and your broken knee—those things are now of the past, and I am glad you are able to walk to the Depot[159] and back again without crutches, as you did on Monday last.[160] I am also glad you did not have to over-draw your a/c—at the T. O.[161] more than $2^{50} I hope to live to see the day when your noble sons can provide for their Mother and sisters at home so that they will be comfortable. In the mean-time if <u>you</u> or the children should need more than you have or can get please let me know, and if in my power I will help you. My own burdens are pretty heavey for me—these hard times. I have 35 Souls[162] to feed, clothe, and educate, and it keeps me busy.

We are all usually well—Lucy[163] seems all right. We had a pleasant visit at Roberts[164] last evening—I wish you had been there. God bless you my sister—is the prayer of your brother Jos. F.——

[*illegible strike-through*] not fail to look at the Deseret news of tonight— It contains a statement of the Martyrdom at Carthage.[165] Jos F. Smith[166]

---

156. From Joseph F.'s letterpress copybooks; original not extant. Joseph F. was fifty-five, and Martha Ann was fifty-two.
157. Likely Lucy Smith Harris.
158. The *Woman's Exponent* was a periodical first published in 1872. It was established by and oriented toward Latter-day Saint women. It ran until 1914, when it was succeeded by the *Relief Society Magazine*.
159. The train depot. In this context Joseph F. could have been referring to the Provo or Salt Lake depots.
160. Carole Call King wrote, "At one time [Martha Ann] was confined to her bed for six months because of a splintered bone in her knee. It was broken and reset twice and put in a cast. When she was able to get up, she walked with crutches for 18 months." Carole Call King, "History of Martha Ann Smith Harris, 1841–1923" (unpublished manuscript in editors' possession).
161. Tithing office. Tithing offices were centers of economic activity and served as "community warehouses, general stores, banks, weighing stations, relief and employment agencies, and communication centers." See Leonard J. Arrington, *Great Basin Kingdom: An Economic History of the Latter-day Saints, 1830–1900* (Urbana: University of Illinois Press, 2005), 142.
162. Joseph F.'s family consisted of five wives and thirty living children.
163. Lucy Smith Harris.
164. Unknown individuals.
165. Col. M. B. Darnell of Sheldon, O'Brien County, Iowa, claimed to have been present at the martyrdom of Joseph and Hyrum Smith on 27 June 1844. See "The Assassination," *Deseret Evening News*, 7 March 1894, 1.
166. Written upside down in the top margin of page 2.

JOSEPH F. TO MARTHA ANN, 24 DECEMBER 1894

Dec. 24th 1894[167]

My Dear Sister—
Martha Ann Harris—
Provo—Utah Co.—

Your letter of the 22d inst. came to hand this afternoon. I regret that the necessities of my own family, which now numbers 36 souls[168]—including myself—and excluding Leonora,[169] not one of them in employment—and many of them going to school—make it impossible for me to render such help as I would like to do to my sister and her dear good girls. I would gladly provide for you and them if I could. If it were in my power to make you all, and my own family also, perfectly happy and comfortable, nothing would give me greater pleasure.

As it is, the little I can do—or have done, is not worth an expression of thanks, much less that of gratitude. However I send you here with my cheque for 10$ with my best wishes and the complements of the Season. With love—I am your brother
Jos. F. Smith

JOSEPH F. TO MARTHA ANN, 28 JANUARY 1895

Jan. 28th 1895[170]

Mrs. Martha Ann Harris
Provo—

My Dear Sister Martha Ann.

I passed Provo on Saturday morning[171] on my way to Nephi to attend the Juab stake conference, and I returned last evening.

While at Nephi I called at Zinas place[172] expecting to see her there, but the paths were un-swept and trackless, almost, and in response to my repeated loud rapps at the door there came back only the echo's of the empty hall.

I hope you are all well— I heard you had been suffering again from your injured knee.[173] but I hope it is better.

167. From Joseph F.'s letterpress copybooks; original not extant.
168. Since writing Martha Ann in March 1894, James Schwartz Smith was born on 13 November 1894, adding one more child to his family. See Joseph F. to Martha Ann, 7 March 1894, note 162, herein.
169. Joseph F.'s daughter Leonora Smith had married Joseph Nelson the previous year on 14 June 1893.
170. From Joseph F.'s letterpress copybooks; original not extant. Joseph F. was fifty-six, and Martha Ann was fifty-three.
171. Saturday, 26 January 1894.
172. Zina Christine Harris and her husband, George Thomas Furner, were living in Nephi, Juab County, Utah Territory, at this time.
173. See Joseph F. to Martha Ann, 7 March 1894, herein.

I write now, more particularly, to say to you that we are thinking of having a family gathering at Julinas[174] on the 9th February next, in memory of Father's birth day,[175] and to invite you and William[176] to attend it if possible.

Hoping to hear from you soon, and favorably on this matter, I am as ever affectionately your brother
Jos. F. Smith.

On Friday last Ina[177] fell on the ice and broke her arm.)[178]

JOSEPH F. TO MARTHA ANN, 20 FEBRUARY 1895

Feb. 20th 1895[179]

"Aunt Martha",
My Dear Sister Martha Ann:— Your favor of the 15th inst. announcing the birth of Zinas baby[180] on the 14 th came duly to hand. Now if Zina had written it I would not have been surprised at the omission of a statement indicating the gender of her "Valentine", but for you to write and not tell us it was a "boy"—I am surprised. unless it was a "girl"!

Well I hope the little stranger—(boy or girl) as the case may be—will meet a hearty welcome from all sides, and enjoy a prosperous voyage through life. I am thankful the Mother and baby were well—and happy.

God bless them now and for ever—is the earnest prayer of Uncle
Jos. F Smith

JOSEPH F. TO MARTHA ANN, 6 AUGUST 1895

Remember me most kindly to Sister Meacham[181] and any of the family who may know me. May the Lord bless and comfort her as only the merciful Father of us all can do _ is my prayer.
Joseph.

Aug 6 1895[182]

174. Julina Lambson.
175. Hyrum Smith was born on 9 February 1800.
176. William Jasper Harris.
177. Julina Lambson Smith's home, located at 333 West First North (now 200 North), Salt Lake City. See photograph of this home in the decade introduction for this chapter.
178. Written in the bottom left, before the signature.
179. From Joseph F.'s letterpress copybooks; original not extant.
180. Merilla Furner, daughter of Zina Christine Harris and George Furner, was born on 14 February 1895. See biographical register, "Furner, Merilla."
181. Possibly Sophia Burrows Mecham or Hannah Eliza Phillips Freshwater Mecham.
182. From Joseph F.'s letterpress copybooks; original not extant.

Mrs. Martha Ann Harris
Provo_

My Dear Sister Martha. On looking through the Provo Enquire[183] of this date, I saw the notice of the funeral in Friday, Aug 2d inst. of our dear old friend and brother, Edward Meacham[184] This is the first word I had received of his demise. And it is a mere accident or incidences that I saw the notice of his funeral. I do not much time to read the papers and am kept so busy otherwise. I cannot mourn that Father Meachams earthly part is finally at rest for a little season. He was aged and had been infirm and helpless for such a long time that to him, at least, death must have been a happy release. I regret I did not know of his funeral in time to have been present. But it is just as well, no doubt as I am sure all was said and some that could have been comfort of his wife and relatives. God blessed them! All is well with that good man, bro. Meacham. Hoping you and family are well. I am as ever Your affectionate Brother Jos F. Smith

JOSEPH F. TO MARTHA ANN, 27 SEPTEMBER 1895

Sept. 27th 1895[185]

My Dear Sister Martha Ann

Your favor of the 22d inst. Came to hand on the 23d inst. I did not expect an answer to my letter, therefore to hear from you was an unexpected surprise. In former years we corresponded once in a while, but of late this practice seems to have gone into disuse. The same with Jerusha;[186] I have written her once or twice, but without response. In the days of our youth it would have been a hard task to have convinced me that time or circumstance <would> would or ever could bring about so great a change. However strange it seems, or however impossible we at one time would have thought it to be, the spell has come, and has caught us in its grasp. On my part I find no fault nor cast any blame. I am perhaps the cause of the change and yet if this is true, I have not been conscious of it. True, my life has been a busy one, my time has been consumed by public duties and **[p. 2]** foreign missions until in some degree I am a stranger to many of my former, best of friends. I have no time to visit, as a rule, or to be sociable eve in the midst of my own family. With me it is almost a constant round of work, from day to day, and very little play. Our recent trip to the north[187] was a rest and as change, such as I seldom get <but> which was a gracious boon to me both physical and mental. and I am very thankful for it.

183. Funeral for "Edward Meacham was held in the Second ward meeting house at 2 o'clock this afternoon. There was a large attendance." "City and County Jottings," *Daily Enquirer* (Provo), 2 August 1895, 4.
184. Edward Mecham was a next-door neighbor of Martha Ann and William J. Harris. See 1870 US Census, Provo First Ward, Utah, Utah Territory, 267.
185. From Joseph F.'s letterpress copybooks; original not extant.
186. Jerusha Smith, Joseph F.'s and Martha Ann's older half sister.
187. See Richard Neitzel Holzapfel, "New Photographs of Wilford Woodruff's Trip to Alaska, 1895," *BYU Studies* 39, no. 2 (2000): 144–49.

John[188] and I live with in a short distance of each other, yet neither of us ever darken the others doors. Still we are on the best of terms, so far as I know. His children and mine are perfectly strangers to each other. And why I cannot tell. My children are good home loving children my boys[189] neither drink nor smoke, nor swear. and they have faith in the gospel and in the divine mission of Joseph Smith.[190] My daughters[191] are as good as gold but lovers of home and earnest toilers in domestic life. It is true we are poor in this world's goods- and yet we do not lack for the necessaries of life and are blessed above many of our fellow beings. I feed, clothe, house, warm lodge, and educate. So far as I can. with my own hands and efforts. 36 souls now at home. besides many callers and friends. and occasionally keep others besides. and would do more if I could. Well. Excuse this scribble. Your brother, J. F. Smith

JOSEPH F. TO MARTHA ANN, [1 NOVEMBER] 1895

1895[192]

My Dear Sister
Martha Ann Harris:
Provo.

Your letter of yesterday, conveying to us the sad news of the death of Mary's[193] little son, Franklin Nephi Corbett,[194] reached me to day; The unwelcome tidings not only filled my heart with deep sympathy for the bereaved parents,[195] grand parents and immediate kindred, but is awakened sorrowful memories of the past <of similar scenes> within my own house hold, and the sweet faces and cherished names of my own loved children came to tr[◊◊]ping up before me till I counted eight of them laid away in the silent grave. My first sweet little one claimed by death was Sarah Ella[196] then followed all the brightness and heaven of our home, our Mercy Josephine,[197] then our little heros Heber[198] and Alfred,[199] both beautiful, lovely boys then followed our precious little Rhoda,[200] next were Albert J[201] and Robert.[202] and then

188. John Smith, Joseph F.'s and Martha Ann's older half brother.
189. Joseph F. has sixteen living sons at this date.
190. Joseph F. and Martha Ann's uncle.
191. Joseph F. has eighteen living daughters at this date.
192. From pages 169–70 of one of Joseph F.'s letterpress copybooks; original not extant. Because the letters immediately preceding and following this one are dated 1 November 1895, we assume it was written on the same date.
193. Mary Emily Harris.
194. Martha Ann's grandson. See biographical register, "Corbett, Franklin Nephi."
195. Mary Emily Harris and Walter Sutton Corbett.
196. Sarah Ella died in 1869.
197. Mercy Josephine died in 1870.
198. Heber John died in 1877.
199. Alfred Jason died in 1878.
200. Rhoda Ann died in 1879.
201. Albert Jesse died in 1883
202. Robert died in 1886.

OFFICE OF
The First Presidency
of the
Church of Jesus Christ
of
Latter-day Saints

P.O. Box B.

Salt Lake City, Utah. Mar. 23rd 1896

My Dear Sister Martha Ann:

It has been a long time since I wrote to or have received a letter from you. I hope you and the Children and William are all enjoying good health, and good peace, and good plenty. The object of this writing is to inform you that we are all usually well, except Joseph R. who a week ago yesterday was stricken down with what the Doctors call "Appendicitis", and the next day – Monday – one week ago to day – he was subjected to an Operation, and the "apendix vermiformus" removed. It was a most severe and dangerous operation, but I am happy to say, he has now passed the imminent danger line and is progressing favorably towards convallscence. His mother and I – (especially his mother –) have watched with him constantly since the attack and the operation, and have been greatly blessed with strength and fortitude to endure the strain. I trust this, as all other afflictive providences of the past, may prove to be a blessing in disguise designed to chasten and humble, and draw us nearer to the Lord – God bless you all, with love I am &c. Jos. F. Smith

Joseph F. to Martha Ann, 23 March 1896 (p. 1)

John,[203] all of them most lovely, bright and fair. They were perfect [**p.2**] in their day, and they each one brought and left with us joyous hopes and precious memories, with which we would not part for all this world. They are ours still![204] both they and all their sweetness and the joyous hopes they brought us; for they are not lost! nor can they fail! They rest with God and await our coming unto them when faithfully we shall have finished our earthly work, and are prepared to meet them. This beyond <a> doubt is true, and I wish I could say as much for all the rest who have been left to battle with the ills and dangerous of this world. I would be but doing my duty to go to you tomorrow, and mingle my tears and sorrows with yours, and add what consolation my presence might bring; but I am not well. I have a cold and cough, and am not in a condition to use my voice or lungs. besides important duties require my presence here tomorrow and next day I will have to go north. So— God bless and comfort you and heal the broken hearts. Affectionately [◊◊] Jos. F. Smith.
P.S. The folks all joine in deepest sympathy for the parents— and children— and you all— Again, May the Merciful Father of us all, bless and comfort you. Joseph

JOSEPH F. TO MARTHA ANN, 23 MARCH 1896

Salt Lake City, Utah. Mar. 23d 1896[205]

My Dear Sister Martha Ann:

It has been a long time since I wrote <to> or have received a letter from you. I hope you and the children and William[206] are all enjoying good health, and good peace, and good plenty.

The object of this writing is to inform you that we are all usually well, except Joseph R.[207] who a week ago yesterday was stricken down with what the Doctors call "appendicitis", and the next day—Monday—one week ago to day—he was subjected to an operation, and the "appendix vermiformus" removed.[208] It was a most severe and dangerous operation, but I am happy to say, he has now passed <the> imminent danger line and is progressing favorably towards convalescence.[209] His mother[210] and I—(especially his mother—) have watched with him constantly since the attack and the operation, and have been greatly blessed with strength

203. John Schwartz died in 1889.

204. According to Latter-day Saint practice, "a temple marriage or sealing refers to the ceremony in which a man and woman are married (sealed) to each other for time and eternity in a temple by the authority of the holy priesthood. Children born to the couple after this marriage are automatically sealed to their parents eternally and are spoken of as having been born in the covenant." Ralph L. Cottrell Jr., "Born in the Covenant," in *Encyclopedia of Mormonism*, ed. Daniel H. Ludlow (New York: Macmillan, 1992), 1:218.

205. Written on official letterhead of the Church from the Office of the President. Joseph F. was fifty-seven, and Martha Ann was fifty-four.

206. William Jasper Harris.

207. Joseph Richards Smith.

208. The term *vermiform* comes from Latin and means "worm-shaped." See Hyrum M. Smith III and Scott G. Kenney, comps., *From Prophet to Son: Advice of Joseph F. Smith to His Missionary Sons* (Salt Lake City, UT: Deseret Book, 1981), 34.

209. The operation cost three hundred dollars, adding to the financial strain Joseph F. experienced at this time. See Smith and Kenney, *From Prophet to Son*, 36.

210. Sarah Ellen Richards.

and fortitude to endure the strain. I trust this, as all other afflictive providences of the past, may prove to be a blessing in disguise designed to chasten and humble, and draw us nearer to the Lord. God bless you all, with love I am &c. Jos. F. Smith

JOSEPH F. TO MARTHA ANN, 28 MARCH 1896

Mar. 28th 1896[211]

My Dear Sister
Martha Ann Harris.

Your welcome favor of the 25th inst. came to hand the following day. I write you hurriedly now, to say that Joseph R.[212] is progressing nicely, and will, with the blessing of the Lord, in answer to our prayers, be on his feet again a few weeks. He is beginning to take some food now, the wound is healing slowly but surely from appearances and everything looks encouraging & hopeful. Mamie[213] and Donnie[214] as I suppose you know are going to the Pratt Institute[215] in Brooklyn, N.Y. our last from them was not so cheerful. as Donnie had a severe cold and was feeling poorly. We hope better new will come next mail. Hyrum M.[216] was doing well in England when he last wrote. The rest of our family are usually well. Hoping this will find you & yours in good hope and spirits. I am as ever affectionately your brother Jos. F. Smith.

JOSEPH F. TO MARTHA ANN, 21 APRIL 1896

Apr. 21st 1896[217]

Mrs. Martha Ann Harris—
Provo. Utah Co.

My Dear Sister Martha Ann: —

Your favor of the 20th has just been received. I cannot tell what kind of a contract you have made with the Dentist about <u>fitting</u> you. Teeth are not like shoes or clothing. if the teeth don't

211. From Joseph F.'s letterpress copybooks; original not extant.
212. Joseph Richards Smith.
213. Mary Sophronia Smith.
214. Donnette Smith.
215. One of the first institutions that admitted all people regardless of gender and color, the Pratt Institute is a private, nonsectarian, nonprofit institute of higher learning established in 1887. The most popular major at the time was domestic arts.
216. Hyrum Mack Smith was set apart by Heber J. Grant on 15 November 1895 to labor in the British Mission until he was released on 7 March 1898.
217. From Joseph F.'s letterpress copybooks; original not extant.

fit the mouth they are made for they will fit no other, and are a dead loss! Still they do not suit— or fit the mouth, you should not pay for them. A workman should make a fit. I sincerely hope Mr. F.F. Reed[218] the Dentist will make a good job of his work for you. Of course I do not know him; it is better to get a good job no matter what the cost than a poor one. for however much or little a set of teeth may cost, if they are not good it is so much thrown away. I intended to have sent my check, for the money, but have concluded to send you the enclosed (10$) Ten dollar bill, which I hope will reach you safely, and get you a set of good teeth. My family are all getting along nicely. With kind love to you and all, I am your brother Jos. F. Smith

Please acknowledge the receipt of this letter and contents by return mail. for which please find herewith a stamped Envelope. and oblige your brother. Joseph F.

JOSEPH F. TO MARTHA ANN, 18 NOVEMBER 1896

Nov. 18th 1896[219]

My Dear Sister—
Martha Ann Harris—

I have obtained transportation for yourself and one—from Provo to Mamoth[220] and return.[221] I got one ticket good for four persons—and Julina[222] and one of the children will go which with you and William[223] will make the four. Frank[224] has written to aunt Julina Saying they—the boys—would send you a ticket—or the means to get one. If they do you might let one or more of the girls use it—as the case may be. They—the boys expected you to start on Friday next—but we cannot go until Saturday. Should you & William get ticks from the boys—in time to go on ~~Saturday~~ <Friday>, you might go right on, and leave word for a coupel of the girls to go with us on our ticket on Saturday. On account of getting transportation at special cheap rates, they made the ticket for 4 persons on the one ticket. We are all usually well— With kind love yours Joseph F.

Excuse haste, I have written in a great hurry. Joseph.[225]

218. Dentist F. F. Reed claimed to have "all modern instruments for the practice of operative and prosthetic dentistry, artificial crowns, and bridgework." His practice was located in the Excelsior block. "Advertising," *Daily Enquirer* (Provo), 22 January 1895, 4.

219. From Joseph F.'s letterpress copybooks; original not extant.

220. Mammoth, Juab County, Utah, is near Eureka, about forty-five miles southwest of Provo.

221. Joseph F. dedicated the Mammoth meetinghouse on Sunday, 22 November 1896: "President Smith gave a very interesting sketch of the exodus of his mother's family from Nauvoo to Winter Quarters, and from there across the Plains to Salt Lake City in 1847–8. We noticed among the congregation his sister Martha Harris of Provo and a number of her children. . . . Brother and Sister Harris from Provo are both advancing in years yet they look hearty and healthy and have raised a large family of boys and girls, eleven in number, and strange to say, they have never had a death in their family." "Meetings at Mammoth," *Deseret Weekly*, 28 November 1896, 756.

222. Julina Lambson.

223. William Jasper Harris.

224. Franklin Hill Harris.

225. Written upside down in the top left margin.

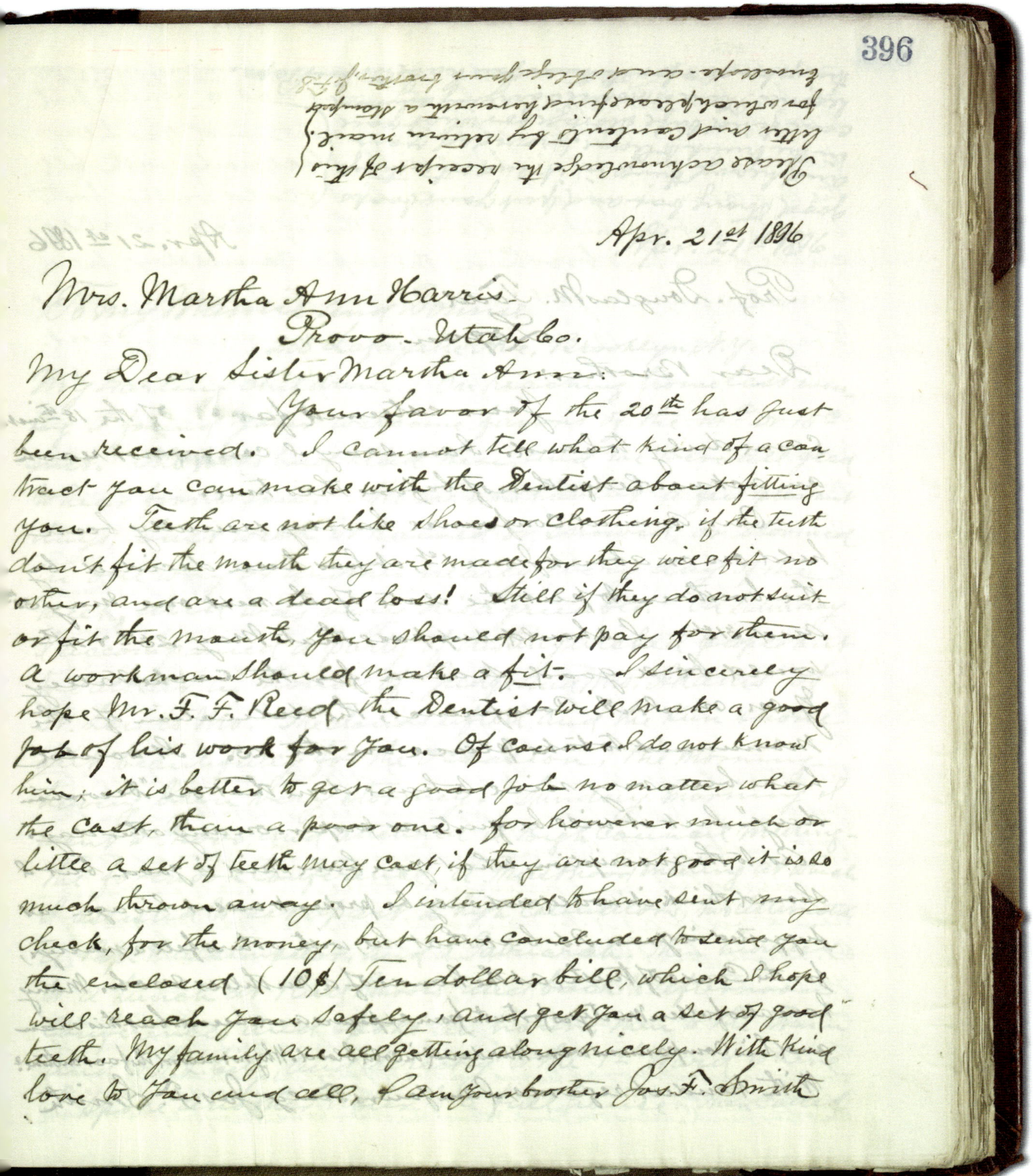

396

Please acknowledge the receipt of this letter and contents by return mail; for which please find herewith a stamped envelope - and oblige yours truly J.F.S.

Apr. 21st 1896

Mrs. Martha Ann Harris.
Provo. Utah Co.

My Dear Sister Martha Ann:-

Your favor of the 20th has just been received. I cannot tell what kind of a contract you can make with the Dentist about fitting you. Teeth are not like shoes or clothing, if the teeth don't fit the mouth they are made for they will fit no other, and are a dead loss! Still if they do not suit or fit the mouth, you should not pay for them. A workman should make a fit. I sincerely hope Mr. F. F. Reed the Dentist will make a good job of his work for you. Of course I do not know him; it is better to get a good job no matter what the cost, than a poor one. for however much or little a set of teeth may cost, if they are not good it is so much thrown away. I intended to have sent my check, for the money, but have concluded to send you the enclosed (10$) Ten dollar bill, which I hope will reach you safely, and get you a set of good teeth. My family are all getting along nicely. With kind love to you and all, I am your brother Jos. F. Smith

Joseph F. to Martha Ann, 21 April 1896 (p. 1), copy found in Joseph F.'s letterpress copybooks under that date.

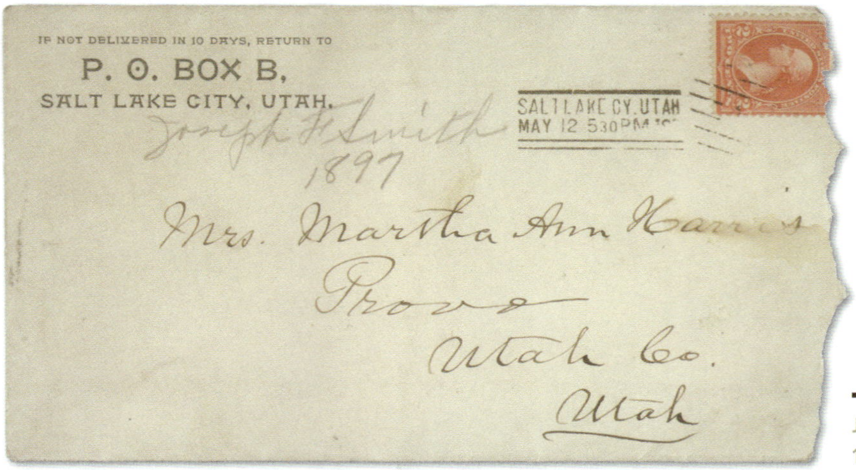

Joseph F. to Martha Ann, 12 May 1897 (envelope)

JOSEPH F. TO MARTHA ANN, 12 MAY 1897

Salt Lake City, Utah. May 12, 1897.[226]

Mrs. Martha Ann Harris,
Provo.

My dear sister Martha:

Your favor of the 8th is just received. I am glad to hear that the family are all enjoying usual health, and I hope Sarah will be successful in her examination at school.[227] I am also glad that you felt pleased with my discourse, although I regret exceedingly that I had not time to complete it.

The boil on my neck developed in to a first class carbuncle.[228] I have been suffering with it ever since, although it is now healing rapidly. My visits to Provo always seem to be hurried, indeed, my visits there are no exception to the rule, for I am always in a hurry. I do not know when I shall visit Provo again, but hope when I do I shall have a little more time to visit with you. You inquire about Hyrum and Donnie.[229] They were both well and prospering nicely when we last heard from them. All of my family, except myself, are in usual good health, and I have to report to you in addition to Aunt Sarah's nicest little baby[230] in the world, last night another came to visit us which promises to be the peer of her sister.[231] This time the addition is in Aunt Edna's family. I am going to Ogden today on business and will return this evening if I can.[232]

226. Typewritten on official letterhead of the Church from the Office of the President. Joseph F. was fifty-eight, and Martha Ann was fifty-five.
227. Sarah Lovina Harris, fourteen years old at this time, would have likely been attending Brigham Young Academy in Provo. See biographical register, "Harris, Sarah Lovina."
228. A group of boils.
229. Probably Hyrum Fisher Smith and Donnette Smith, children of Joseph F.
230. Asenath Smith, Sarah Ellen Richards's youngest daughter, was born on 28 December 1896. See biographical register, "Smith, Asenath."
231. Martha Smith, Edna's youngest daughter, was born on 12 May 1897. See biographical register, "Smith, Martha."
232. Ogden, Weber County, Utah, located about thirty-eight miles from Salt Lake City.

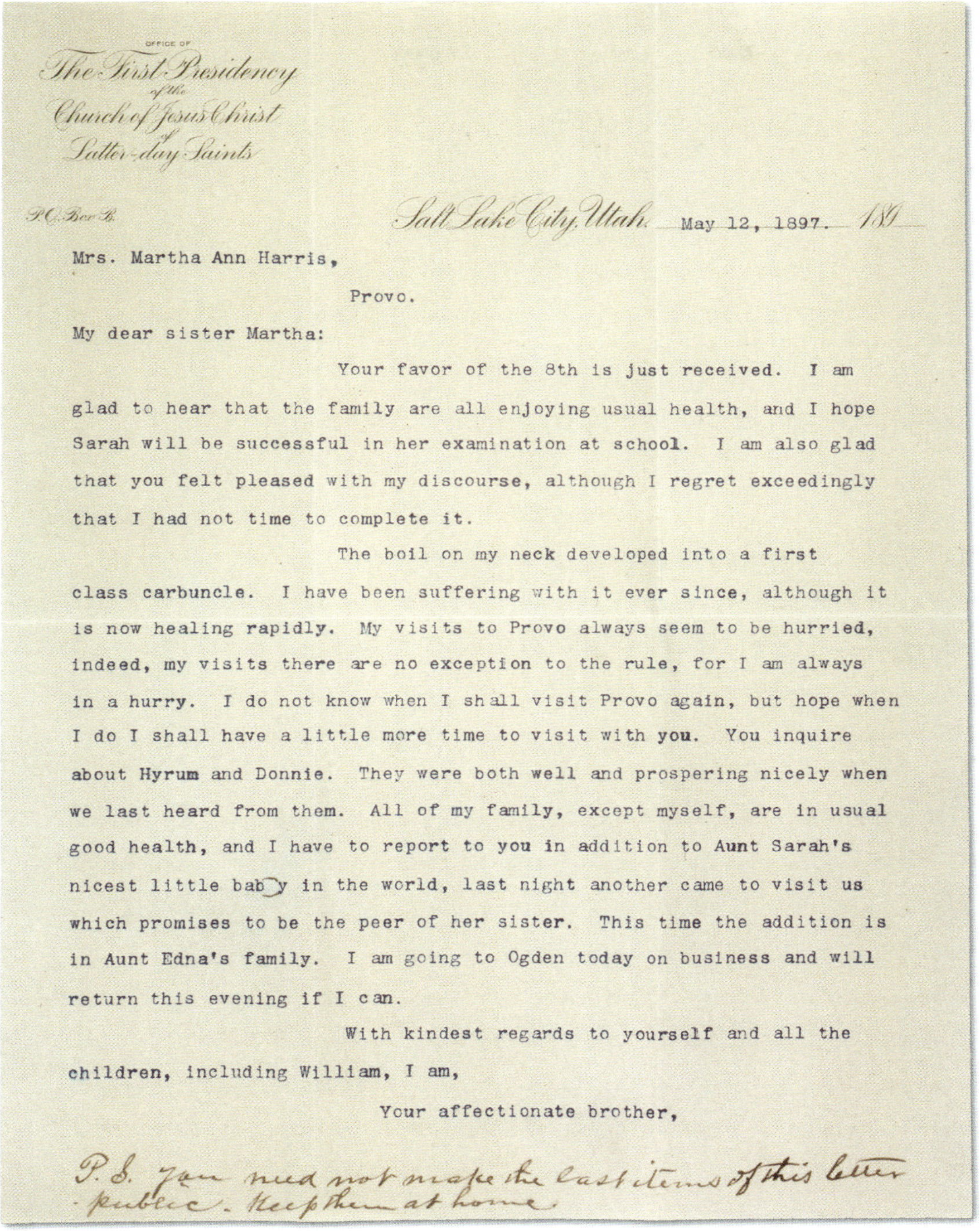

OFFICE OF
The First Presidency
of the
Church of Jesus Christ
of
Latter-day Saints

P.O. Box B.

Salt Lake City, Utah. May 12, 1897. 189

Mrs. Martha Ann Harris,

Provo.

My dear sister Martha:

Your favor of the 8th is just received. I am glad to hear that the family are all enjoying usual health, and I hope Sarah will be successful in her examination at school. I am also glad that you felt pleased with my discourse, although I regret exceedingly that I had not time to complete it.

The boil on my neck developed into a first class carbuncle. I have been suffering with it ever since, although it is now healing rapidly. My visits to Provo always seem to be hurried, indeed, my visits there are no exception to the rule, for I am always in a hurry. I do not know when I shall visit Provo again, but hope when I do I shall have a little more time to visit with you. You inquire about Hyrum and Donnie. They were both well and prospering nicely when we last heard from them. All of my family, except myself, are in usual good health, and I have to report to you in addition to Aunt Sarah's nicest little baby in the world, last night another came to visit us which promises to be the peer of her sister. This time the addition is in Aunt Edna's family. I am going to Ogden today on business and will return this evening if I can.

With kindest regards to yourself and all the children, including William, I am,

Your affectionate brother,

P.S. You need not make the last items of this letter public. Keep them at home.

Joseph F. to Martha Ann, 12 May 1897 (p. 1)

With kindest regards to yourself and all the children, including William,[233] I am,
Your affectionate brother,

P.S. You need not make the last items of this letter public— Keep them at home.[234]

233. William Jasper Harris.
234. This note was handwritten below the typed letter.

Office of
The First Presidency
of the
Church of Jesus Christ
of
Latter-day Saints.

P.O. Box B.   Salt Lake City, Utah,   Aug. 25, 1897.

Mrs. Martha Ann Harris,

Provo.

My dear Sister Martha:-

For some time past Cousin Silas has been at work here in the Temple for our dead kindred. The work has proceeded so far that most of the children have already been adopted to their parents. The principle branch of the family which is lacking in this regard is our father's family. We have agreed to meet at the Temple in this city on Wednesday, September 1st, to attend to the sealing of all the children living and dead to their father and mothers. It will be necessary for you and Jerusha to be here to help do the work. You will have to reach this city not later than Tuesday evening, August 31st. Write me immediately on receipt of this whether you can come on Tuesday or not, and I will make arrangements for your transportation. We have had a glorious time in the Temple today. I sealed sixteen couples, including our seventh great grandfather and mother, Robert and Mary, who came from England, and Grandfather and mother Joseph and Lucy Mack Smith, and the work of sealing of children is nearly all completed. I am very anxious to have father's work done. Come without fail. We are all usually well.

Affectionately, your Brother,

Jos. F. Smith

P.S. I would like you to bring with you a record of your marriage and the names and births of all your children for the family Record.

Joseph F. to Martha Ann, 25 August 1897 (p. 1)

JOSEPH F. TO MARTHA ANN, 25 AUGUST 1897

Salt Lake City, Utah, Aug. 25, 1897.[235]

Mrs. Martha Ann Harris,
Provo.

My dear Sister Martha:—

For some time past Cousin Silas[236] has been at work here in the Temple[237] for our dead kindred. The work has proceeded so far that most of the children have already been adopted to their parents.[238] The principle branch of the family which is lacking in this regard is our father's[239] family. We have agreed to meet at the Temple in this city on Wednesday, September 1st, to attend to the sealing of all the children living and dead to their father and mothers. It will be necessary for you and Jerusha[240] to be here to help do the work. You will have to reach this city not later than Tuesday evening, August 31st. Write me immediately on receipt of this whether you can come on Tuesday or not, and I will make arrangements for your transportation. We have had a glorious time in the Temple today. I sealed sixteen couples, including our seventh great grandfather and mother, Robert and Mary,[241] who came from England, and Grandfather and mother Joseph[242] and Lucy Mack Smith, and the work of sealing of children is nearly all completed. I am very anxious to have father's work done. Come without fail. We are all usually well.

Affectionately, your Brother,
Jos. F. Smith

P.S. I would like you to bring with you a record of your marriage and the names and births of all your children for the family Record.[243]

235. Written on letterhead from the "Office of the First Presidency of the Church of Jesus Christ of Latter-day Saints P.O. Box B. Salt Lake City, Utah." The body of the letter is typed with a handwritten postscript by Joseph F.
236. Silas Sanford Smith.
237. The Salt Lake Temple was completed and dedicated in 1893.
238. Joseph F. seems to be using the term *adopted* synonymously with *sealed*. On the practice of adoption, see Gordon Irving, "The Law of Adoption: One Phase of the Development of the Mormon Concept of Salvation," *BYU Studies* 14, no. 3 (Spring 1974): 291–314. See also Bennett, "'Line upon Line, Precept upon Precept,'" 62–67. See also Joseph F. to Martha Ann, 18 June 1890, herein, note 53.
239. Hyrum Smith.
240. Jerusha Smith.
241. Joseph F. and Martha Ann's seventh great-grandparents through Lucy Mack were Robert Lee and Mary Atwood. See biographical register, "Lee, Robert" and "Atwood, Mary."
242. Joseph Smith Sr.
243. The postscript is handwritten below the typed letter.

JOSEPH F. TO MARTHA ANN, 19 MARCH 1898

143 North 2d West St—
Salt Lake City
Mar. 19th 1898.[244]

My Dear Sister
Martha Ann Harris:—

We have, as you perhaps know, for a long time been passing under most trying ordeals of sickness. Aunt Sarah E.[245] was taken with Typhoid fever—then Emily,[246] with Scarlet fever, then Alice M.[247] with Typhoid fever, then Rachel[248] with scarlet fever—then Edith,[249] and next our Dear little Ruth—who—in spite of all we could do by faith and prayer and skill, on the 17th inst—passed away—leaving us heart-broken and bowed down to the dust in grief & sorrow for **[p. 2]** our irreparable temporal loss.[250] You will no doubt remember our sweet little Ruth—to be loved—she needed only to be seen. To be admired she had but to be heard—for she was one of the brightest little Souls I ever saw. But O! my Soul, we have had to yield her spirit up to God who gave her, and her sweet little body to the grave. She was buried to day. I should have written you sooner but to tell the truth my poor heart has been in the icey chamber with the cherished lovely form of my darling babe! I could not write.

Aunt Sarah and Alice M. are slowly improving in health—Julinas[251] children **[p. 3]** are <u>well</u> and convellescing, and now our little Zina[252] is down with the scarlet fever, and the yellow flag[253] is nailed to our front wall. But we hope soon to be free from all these troubles. Little Andrew and Jesse[254] have got the whooping cough—and so, you see, we are not without our troubles.

244. Joseph F. was fifty-nine, and Martha Ann was fifty-six.
245. Sarah Ellen Richards.
246. Emily Jane Smith.
247. Likely Alice May Smith.
248. Rachel Smith.
249. Edith Eleanor Smith.
250. Ruth Smith, Joseph F. and Edna Lambson's daughter (born on 21 December 1893), died on 17 March 1898. "Ruth, the 4-year-old daughter of President Joseph F. Smith and wife, died at 7:40 o'clock last evening from scarlet fever and bronchitis. Other children in the family have been afflicted with the former trouble, but are now convalescent. In the case of little Ruth, however, bronchitis came to complicate the already serious condition, and she was unable to withstand the combined ravages of both ailments. She was a bright, winsome and affectionate child, and her death is a serious blow to her parents and friends." "Little Ruth Smith Dead," *Deseret Evening News*, 18 March 1898, 2. See biographical register, "Smith, Ruth."
251. Julina Lambson.
252. Zina Smith.
253. A Utah Board of Quarantine ruled in 1875 that "if any person or persons shall be found in an unhealthy condition from any contagious disease" deemed a public hazard, they should be quarantined and their quarters marked with a yellow flag. See Kate B. Carter, comp., *Our Pioneer Heritage* (Salt Lake City, UT: Daughters of Utah Pioneers, 1958), 4:342.
254. Andrew Kimball Smith and Jesse Kimball Smith, sons of Joseph F. See biographical register, "Smith, Jesse Kimball" and "Smith, Andrew Kimball."

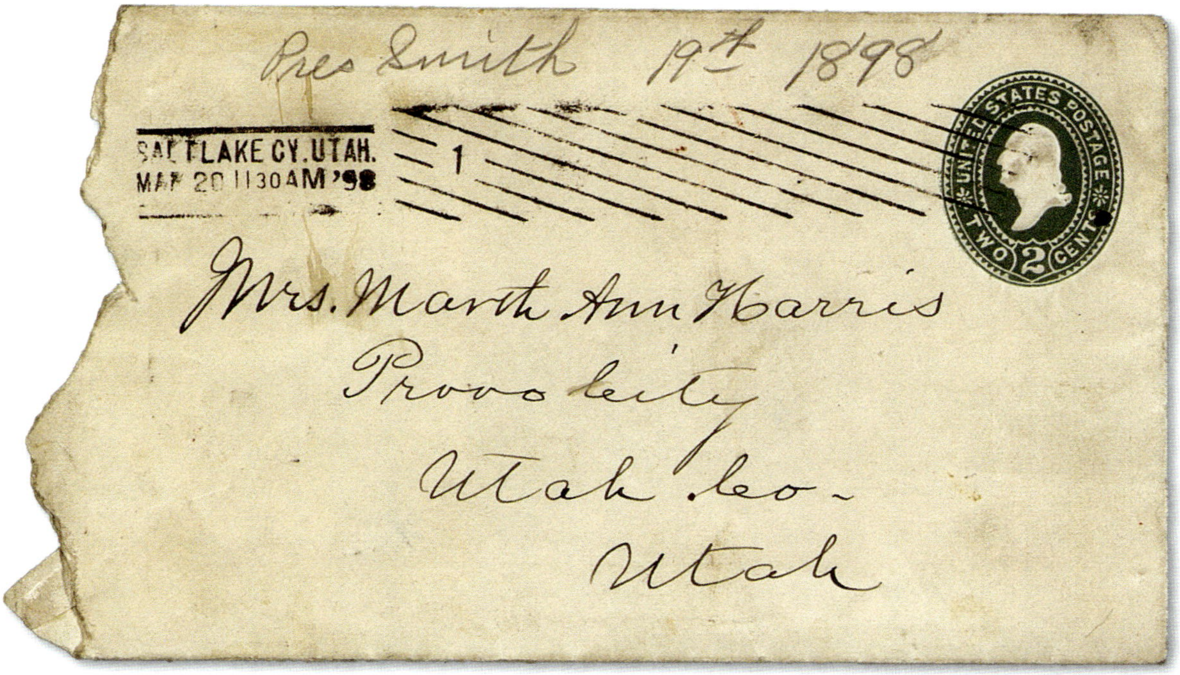

Joseph F. to Martha Ann, 19 March 1898 (envelope)

Little Nettie[255] has also been quite poorly for a week but she is better now. We thought she was coming down with the fever—but if she did she had it so light, we did not know it was scarlet fever.

Our sweet little Ruth took bronchitis on the top of her Scarlet fever—and the darling could not resist them both. Oh! [**p. 4**] She was such a lovely—intelegent little child— She possessed a wit and wisdom far beyond her years—and far beyond all her little playmates. "The glory of God is intelligence", therefore she must have been a part of His glory! for she was indeed inteligent!

Inscrutible are the ways of providence. But one thing we know—She was sinless—pure, redeemed by the Savior of the world from before the foundations thereof— And she will not have to feel the pangs that we have felt in losing her for time. God help us to bow to His will—and to see his providence in all things. We all send you our love—and remain as ever your brother Jos. F. Smith

P.S. I suppose you know that our Hyrum M.[256] got home from his mission on the 7th inst. in good health and spirits. We are thankful he found us all well when he came.[257]

255. Probably referring to Jeanetta Smith, Sarah Ellen Richards's daughter, who was six years old at the time. See biographical register, "Smith, Jeanetta."

256. Hyrum Mack Smith, Joseph F. and Edna Lambson's oldest son, had been serving a mission in England since November 1895. He departed on his mission on 16 November, the day after he married Ida Bowman.

257. Written upside down in the top margin of page 1.

OFFICE OF
The First Presidency
of the
Church of Jesus Christ
of
Latter-day Saints.

I send you herewith two or three
Stamped Envellopes.

P.O. Box B.

Salt Lake City, Utah, Oct. 13th 1898

Martha Ann Harris,
Provo – Utah –

My Dear Sister Martha:– I just drop you a line to let you know we are all usualy well. Little Rachel seems to be as well as ever and Aunt Sarah is about the same. I was very sorry you left us so abruptly on the morning you went away. It was so unnecessary – but of course we are all free agents, and will only be held for our voluntery acts. I did not follow you to the Depôt – for the reason you made it unwise if not impossible for me to do so. You had a full half hour, I should think, to wait at the Station before the train started. We were all sorry to have you leave us feeling as you did. I hope your feelings may change when you know us better.

We had some material for a "comforter" which we wanted you to take with you. If you did not need it yourself, you might have taken it for Mercy or Sarah – or both. We love you very much – we pray for you always, and we wish you ever increasing prosperity, Affectionately, Your brother

Jos. F. Smith

Joseph F. to Martha Ann, 13 October 1898 (p. 1)

JOSEPH F. TO MARTHA ANN, 13 OCTOBER 1898

Salt Lake City, Utah, Oct. 13th 1898[258]

Martha Ann Harris,
Provo—Utah—

My Dear Sister Martha:— I just drop you a line to let you know we are all usually well. Little Rachel[259] seems to be as well as ever and Aunt Sarah[260] is about the same. I was very sorry you left us so abruptly on the morning you went away. It was so unnecessary—but of course we are all free agents, and will only be held for our voluntery acts. I did not follow you to the Depot—for the reason you made <it> unwise if not impossible for me to do so. You had a full half hour, I should think, to wait at the station before the train started. We were all sorry to have you leave us feeling as you did. I hope your feelings may change when you know us better.

We had some material for a "comforter" which we wanted you to take with you. If you did not need it yourself, you might have taken it for Mercy or Sarah[261]—or both. We love you very much—we pray for you always, and we wish you ever increasing prosperity, affectionately, your brother Jos. F. Smith

I send you herewith two or three Stamped Envellopes.——[262]

JOSEPH F. TO MARTHA ANN, 25 OCTOBER 1898

Oct. 25, 1898.[263]

Mrs. Martha Ann Harris,[264]
Provo.

My dear Sister Martha:—

I have been absent from the city for a week.[265] On returning this morning to the office I find awaiting me your favor of the 18th inst. which I hasten to acknowledge, although with

258. Written on official letterhead of the Church from the Office of the President.
259. Likely Rachel Smith.
260. Sarah Ellen Richards.
261. Mercy Ann Harris and Sarah Lovina Harris.
262. Written in the top margin.
263. From Joseph F.'s letterpress copybooks; original not extant.
264. This letter is typewritten except for Joseph F.'s signature.
265. The First Presidency—Lorenzo Snow, George Q. Cannon, and Joseph F.—left Salt Lake City on 18 October 1898 to attend the Trans-Mississippi Exposition and International Exposition, a world's fair held between 1 June and 1 November 1898 in Omaha, Douglas County, Nebraska; see Journal History, 18 October 1898, 2. They were present for "Utah Day," held on 20 October 1898; see "Utah Day at Exposition," *Salt Lake Tribune*, 24 October 1898, 3. They returned to Utah on 24 October 1898 and were in their office on Tuesday morning, 25 October 1898; see Journal History, 25 October 1898, 2.

some regret that you are still troubling your mind, somewhat, over matters which should be received and considered as valuable lessons in experience, which if properly heeded will lead to very great improvement in habits and conscience, and especially in matters of conversation and friendly associations. However, I will not attempt to reply <to> that [*illegible strike-through*] portion of your letter now, may do so at some other time in person when I have an opportunity to converse with you.

I am very glad to hear that you reached home in safety, and that "Artie"[266] was at the depot to meet you with the buggy to take you home, and I hope, too, that your health continues to be good, and that William's[267] health is better than when you reached home, and I also very sincerely hope that the health of the children generally is good. We are all about the same as when you were here. Little Rachel[268] has had two or three days of stomach trouble since you left, but is now going to school again. Leonora has a beautiful little boy, born on the 20th inst.[269] Both she and the baby are progressing nicely, and we are all very happy for her success. Being pressed for time at present, I will write you at greater length at some time in the future. With love to all.

Affectionately your brother,
Jos. F. Smith

JOSEPH F. TO MARTHA ANN, 23 DECEMBER 1898

Salt Lake City, Utah, Dec. 23$^{\underline{d}}$ 1898[270]

Martha Ann Harris:
Provo—

My Dear Sister Martha:—

This is the 83 anniversary of the Birth of the Prophet Joseph Smith.[271] We expect to have a little gathering in the 16$^{\underline{th}}$ ward this evening in his honor. I have been thinking of you, and concluded, altho' my needs are great and my resources comparitively few—that I would divide a little with you— I send you therefore my check for <u>five dollars</u>, in hope it will reach you in time for you to get a Christmas <u>Turkey</u> for your Christmas dinner.

I wish you all the compliments of the season. And pray God to bless you, heal you, and prosper you and yours.

We are not all of us well—but we are gaining. With love in which all would joine if they could, I am sincerely, lovingly and truly your Brother,
Jos. F. Smith

266. Probably Martha Artimissa Harris.
267. William Jasper Harris.
268. Rachel Smith.
269. Joseph F. and Sarah's daughter Leonora Smith, wife of Joseph Nelson, gave birth to George Smith Nelson on 20 October 1898. See biographical register, "Nelson, George Smith."
270. Written on official letterhead of the Church from the Office of the President.
271. It was actually the ninety-third anniversary of the Prophet Joseph Smith's birth. This celebration was noted in Andrew Jenson, *Church Chronology: A Record of Important Events Pertaining to the History of the Church of Jesus Christ of Latter-day Saints*, 2nd ed. (Salt Lake City, UT: Deseret News Press, 1899), 222.

JOSEPH F. TO MARTHA ANN, 16 JUNE 1899

June 16th 1899[272]

Mrs. Martha Ann Harris
Provo Utah Co.

Want to do Temple-work next week for the Fieldings. Expect Rachel Burton[273] down next Monday. Can you come? Let me know by Deseret wire.[274]

All well here.

Jos. F. Smith

JOSEPH F. TO MARTHA ANN, 6 SEPTEMBER 1899

Sept. 6th [ ]9[275]

Mrs. Martha Ann Harris
Provo.
We are anxious to hear how Sarah[276] is? Please answer by the mes[◊◊]nger—on my order.[277]
Aunt Alice[278] is quite poorley, also Melissa,[279] all others about as usual.
Jos F. Smith

272. From Joseph F.'s letterpress copybooks; original not extant. Joseph F. was sixty, and Martha Ann was fifty-eight.
273. Rachel Fielding.
274. Deseret Telegraph Company.
275. From Joseph F.'s letterpress copybooks; original not extant. The sequencing with other correspondences makes it quite clear that the year was 1899. See Joseph F. to Martha Ann, 4 October 1899, herein.
276. Likely Sarah Lovina Harris, daughter of Martha Ann.
277. The US transcontinental telegraph system was completed in October 1861, joining at Salt Lake City. However, the Western Union system was oriented east–west generally along railroad rights-of-way, while the Latter-day settlement pattern was oriented north–south. To connect Latter-day Saint settlements with Salt Lake City, the Deseret Telegraph Company was established in January 1867, even though construction on the lines had already begun much earlier. Delivery of telegraph communications by a "messenger" soon became ubiquitous. Most likely, this communication was sent by telegraph since no copy of the letter was found in the Carole C. King Collection. If so, Joseph F. may have instructed Martha Ann to respond to his question about Sarah's health immediately by the messenger who delivered this telegraph. Additionally, Joseph F. instructed her to charge it to "my order," his personal account.
278. Alice Ann Kimball married Joseph F. on 6 December 1883. See biographical register, "Kimball, Alice Ann."
279. Likely refers to Joseph F.'s daughter Edna Melissa Smith.

JOSEPH F. TO MARTHA ANN, 4 OCTOBER 1899

October 4th, 1899,[280]
Mrs. Martha Ann Harris,
Provo.
My Dear Sister Martha:

Finding that the railroad people are averse to selling tickets at this end of the Line for places at a distance, I came to the conclusion I would send you money to pay your fares from Provo to Salt lake and return at regular conference rates which is $1.90 each.[281] I will be able I think to get them extended at this end to any length of time you may desire to remain with us. Simply call for the regular conference ticket and come and see us as soon as you feel like it. I hope Sarah[282] is gradually gaining her strength and that all of you are well. I am happy to say that our sick ones are improving slowly so far as we can discern.

With kindest regards, I remain,
Affectionately your Brother,
Jos. F. Smith[283]
I send you herein[284]
$5[00] green back.

JOSEPH F. TO MARTHA ANN, 5 OCTOBER 1899

Oct. 5th 1[◊◊]9[285]

Martha Ann Harris:
Provo—Utah.

Hope Sarah[286] is rapidly improving, and will accompany you & Mercy[287] to Conference.[288] Wrote you yesterday Let us know when you will arrive here by O. S. L.[289]
Jos. F. Smith

280. From Joseph F.'s letterpress copybooks; original not extant. The letter is typewritten using blue ink.
281. Railroad agents provided a variety of ticket discounts for Church leaders, missionaries, and those attending general conference. The 69th Semiannual General Conference was scheduled for 6–8 October 1899.
282. Sarah Lovina Harris; see Joseph F. to Martha Ann, 5 October 1899, herein.
283. Name is signed, not typed.
284. The last two lines of the letter are written by hand.
285. From Joseph F.'s letterpress copybook indicating that the year is 1899; original not extant.
286. Likely refers to Sarah Lovina Harris.
287. Likely refers to Mercy Ann Harris.
288. The 69th Semiannual General Conference was held on 6–8 October 1899.
289. The Oregon Short Line Railroad was a large railway system in Utah at the time.

JOSEPH F. TO MARTHA ANN, 16 OCTOBER 1899

Oct. 16th 1899[290]—

Martha Ann Harris
Provo—
Girls start home by five-thirty train, Oregon Short-Line. Meet them with conveyance. Melissa[291] accompanies them. All usually well.
Jos. F. Smith

JOSEPH F. TO MARTHA ANN, 23 DECEMBER 1899

Dec. 23d 1899[292]—

Martha Ann Harris—
Provo.
Look out for letter to morrow. We are all usually well—
Jos. F. Smith

JOSEPH F. TO MARTHA ANN, 23 DECEMBER 1899

Dec. 23d 1899[293]

My Own Dear Sister[294]
Martha A. Harris—
Provo.—

This is the anniversary of Uncle Joseph's[295] Birth—94 years to day since he was born. We celebrate the occasion to night in the 16th ward. I wish you and all of yours a merry Christmas and a happy New Year—and many—of them. I send you a small token of my devoted love— I wish it was a hundred—instead of only $5 00/100. But I can only do what I can. The Lord has been merciful to me and mine all through the years until now, and although my family is large—and my cares many and my responsibilities great—Father[296] has so far fitted my back to my burdens, and has made me what I am.

God bless my sisters—my brother—and their families—With love to you all, I am your brother, Joseph F.——

290. From Joseph F.'s letterpress copybooks; original not extant.
291. Edna Melissa Smith, daughter of Joseph F.
292. From Joseph F.'s letterpress copybooks; original not extant. The following text is a telegram.
293. From Joseph F.'s letterpress copybooks; original not extant.
294. Martha Ann was fifty-eight, and Joseph F. was sixty-one.
295. Joseph Smith Jr.
296. Referring to God as Heavenly Father.

W. WOODRUFF, Pres. GEORGE M. CANNON, Cashier.

OFFICE OF
ZION'S SAVINGS BANK AND TRUST COMPANY.
CAPITAL $200,000.
SURPLUS $200,000.

Salt Lake City, Mar. 8th 1906

My Dear Sister-
Martha Ann Harris.

We got the word to day that Cousin Ellen F. Burton, died at Ogden this morning. and the funeral will be held in their ward meeting house on Sunday next at 12-O'clock.

William desired me to get the word to you, but I have been Kept so busy all the after-noon, since we got the word, that I could not do it until now, and it is now bed time and I must write a few words to William and the folks before I retire.

We are all about as we were when you were here. All busy, all hard worked, not a moment to spare, even for sympathy or condolence.

Affectionately your brother. Joseph F.

Joseph F. to Martha Ann, 8 March 1906

Decade 6

1900–1909

JOSEPH F. TO MARTHA ANN, SALT LAKE CITY, UTAH, 26 JULY 1902

Look at the life of Joseph, the Prophet and our own Father, and the hundreds who laid down their lives in Missouri, Illinois and on the plains for Conscience sake. God suffered all these things—and the persecution unto death of His only begotton Son in the Flesh, that they and He might obtain far more exceeding and eternal weight of Glory in the World to Come.

Martha Ann Smith Harris, 14 May 1901, photograph by Adam Anderson, Provo, Utah. Courtesy of CHL.

Decade Introduction

As the twentieth century dawned, the Church witnessed changes in leadership that would influence its course for years to come. When George Q. Cannon died on 12 April 1901, Joseph F. was called by President Lorenzo Snow to be the First Counselor in the First Presidency. Joseph F. served in this capacity until the death of President Lorenzo Snow later that year. He was then sustained as the sixth President of the Church during the general conference in November 1901.[1] President Joseph F. Smith chose as counselors a native of England, John R. Winder (1821–1910), and a native of Denmark, Anthon H. Lund (1844–1921). A hallmark of his presidency was that he raised the status of his counselors to near equals with him in decision making. President Smith mentions the importance of this relationship in several sermons.[2]

In his new role, President Smith worked energetically to improve the Latter-day Saints' image, retire the Church's debt, meet the needs of a growing international membership, and preserve the early history of the Restoration with the purchase of historical sites associated with the founding events of the Church.[3]

During this time of increased responsibilities, President Smith was often weighed down by a desire to accomplish more despite his continual strenuous efforts. In a letter to Martha Ann's daughter and son-in-law, Naomi and Walter Startup, he noted, "I need more time, more endurance, more ability and more help to meet all my obligations, and to perform more promptly my duties."[4]

1. Joseph F. moved into the Beehive House, which had become the Church President's home in 1889, after being set apart as President of the Church. He maintained the other homes in Salt Lake City that had been built for each of his wives.
2. We acknowledge Stephen C. Taysom's insight on this important point.
3. See Justin R. Bray, "Joseph F. Smith's Beard and the Public Image of the Latter-day Saints," in *Joseph F. Smith: Reflections on the Man and His Times*, ed. Craig K. Manscill et al. (Provo, UT: Religious Studies Center, Brigham Young University; Salt Lake City, UT: Deseret Book, 2013), 457–69; Howard D. Swainston, "Tithing," in *Encyclopedia of Mormonism*, ed. Daniel H. Ludlow (New York: Macmillan, 1992), 4:1480–82; Jennifer L. Lund, "Joseph F. Smith and the Origins of the Church Historic Sites Program," in Manscill et al., *Joseph F. Smith: Reflections on the Man and His Times*, 342–58.
4. Joseph F. to Elder Walter Startup and Dear Little Naomi, 25 January 1908.

The First Presidency, 19 November 1907, photograph by Charles E. Johnson, Salt Lake City, Utah. From left to right: Joseph F. Smith, Anthon H. Lund, and John R. Winder. One of the secretaries in the office of the First Presidency is seated behind the group. Note the large stack of correspondence on the desk near President Smith's left hand. In most cases he dealt with official Church correspondence during the day and personal correspondence after work until late. Courtesy of CHL.

THE LATTER-DAY SAINTS' PUBLIC IMAGE

The number of new plural marriage sealings being performed began to drop rapidly in 1889. This trajectory continued following the decision by Church President Wilford Woodruff (1807–98) to publicly issue a statement, known as the 1890 Manifesto, that the Church would comply with United States law.

However, the scope and interpretation of the Manifesto was not universally agreed upon by Church leaders and members. Many believed new plural marriages could be performed in Mexico and Canada without violating the intent of the 1890 Manifesto. The question of continuing cohabitation by those who had entered into the practice before 1890 was not addressed in an authoritative manner at this time. As a result, some men with plural families chose to live monogamously, while others chose to continue to support and live with their plural families. Nevertheless, the 1890 Manifesto represented a significant shift in Church teachings regarding plural marriage and began the process of ending new plural marriage sealings in the Church.

At the beginning of the twentieth century, the American public demanded clarification of the issues surrounding alleged new plural marriages being performed by Church authorities and continuing cohabitation by its members. When Apostle Reed Smoot (1862–1941)[5] was elected to the United States Senate as one of Utah's two senators in 1902, these issues came to a head.

By the time Smoot arrived in Washington, DC, on 20 January 1903, a group of Utah citizens had written a letter to the president of the United States protesting Smoot's seating as a senator by virtue of his conflict of interest as a Latter-day Saint Apostle and his views on plural marriage.[6] They also believed Smoot's allegiance to his church would supersede his allegiance to the country.[7]

In response, the Senate organized a series of hearings to determine the propriety of the appointment. Among many other witnesses, President Smith was subpoenaed as one of the chief witnesses, becoming the first President of the Church to appear before a Senate committee hearing.[8] During the ensuing months, President Smith testified before Congress about the Church's doctrines and practices. He was asked probing questions regarding not only Smoot's appointment to Congress but also details about his own personal life, including his continued cohabitation with his plural wives after the 1890 announcement of the Manifesto.

Though the hearings purportedly concerned the seating of Senator-Elect Smoot, it became clear that the Church was on trial not only in the US Congress but also in the press.[9] Never before had the Church been so thoroughly investigated by an official federal government body and criticized and lampooned in public lectures, newspaper articles, editorials, and political cartoons.[10] It was a particularly challenging time for the Church. President Smith personally felt humiliated by the experience.[11]

In Washington, President Smith promised the committee that he would clarify the Church's position on new plural marriage sealings, including those performed in Mexico and Canada. As a result, he issued another official statement on plural marriage at the Church's general conference in the fall of 1904. The statement, known as the Second Manifesto, broadened the scope of the 1890 Manifesto throughout the world, including in Canada and Mexico, and is considered a watershed event in Church history.

President Francis M. Lyman (1840–1916), President of the Quorum of the Twelve Apostles at the time, explained, "When [the 1890 Manifesto] was given, it simply gave notice to the Saints that they need not enter plural marriage any longer, but the action taken at the conference held in Salt Lake City on the 6th day of April 1904 [the Second Manifesto] made that manifesto prohibitory."[12] The First Presidency directed President Lyman to send letters to each member of the Quorum

5. Reed Smoot was a prominent businessman, member of the Utah state legislature, United States senator from 1903 to 1933, and a member of the Quorum of the Twelve Apostles from 1900 until the time of his death in 1941. See Milton R. Merrill, *Reed Smoot: Apostle in Politics* (Logan: Utah State University Press, 1990).
6. It should be noted that while Smoot was a monogamist himself, he still accepted the principle of plural marriage as divinely inspired.
7. Milton R. Merrill, "Reed Smoot, Apostle in Politics" (PhD diss., Columbia University, 1950), 27–28. See also Harvard S. Heath, "Smoot Hearings," in Ludlow, *Encyclopedia of Mormonism*, 3:1363–64.
8. Joseph F., as President of The Church of Jesus Christ of Latter-day Saints, was subpoenaed to appear before a Senate hearing "to testify of the power the Church exerted over its members in general and over General Authorities in particular." While other Apostles were questioned as well, Joseph F. received "especially harsh treatment" throughout the hearings. See Heath, "Smoot Hearings," 3:1363–64. See also Harvard S. Heath, "Reed Smoot: The First Modern Mormon," 2 vols. (PhD diss., Brigham Young University, 1990), 1:113.
9. See Kathleen Flake, *The Politics of American Religious Identity: The Seating of Senator Reed Smoot, Mormon Apostle* (Chapel Hill: University of North Carolina Press, 2004).
10. See Gary L. Bunker and Davis Bitton, *The Mormon Graphic Image, 1834–1914: Cartoons, Caricatures, and Illustrations* (Salt Lake City: University of Utah Press, 1983), 57–70.
11. See Michael Harold Paulos, "Under the Gun at the Smoot Hearings: Joseph F. Smith's Testimony," *Journal of Mormon History* 34, no. 4 (Fall 2008): 181–225.
12. "President Lyman Very Emphatic," *Deseret Evening News*, October 31, 1910, 1.

of the Twelve informing them that they planned to "strictly enforce" the intent and scope of the Second Manifesto as they had outlined.[13]

Despite this effort to end new plural marriage sealings, some leaders at the local, stake, and general level continued to authorize new plural marriage sealings after 1904. By October 1905, two Church Apostles, John W. Taylor[14] and Matthias F. Cowley,[15] resigned from the Quorum of the Twelve because of their continued opposition to the Second Manifesto.[16] Taylor and Cowley continued to be "out of harmony" with Church leaders following being dropped from the Quorum of the Twelve and were eventually disciplined for performing unauthorized new plural marriage sealings outside the temple.[17]

In the end, the Church had turned a corner regarding its efforts to end new plural marriage sealings, and Senator Smoot was able to retain his seat.[18] Finally, despite the embarrassment of the lengthy Smoot hearings and the painful resignations of two Apostles, this period of Church history provided the Saints an opportunity to tell its own story.[19]

THE CHURCH'S DEBT

Though Lorenzo Snow made significant progress in retiring the Church's massive debt before his death in 1901, President Smith continued to address this pressing need once he became Church President.[20] As President Snow before him, Joseph F. continued to stress the sacred opportunity and blessing every member had to pay tithes and offerings. He taught the promised blessings that would come from doing so. As a result of increased donations to the Church and careful debt management, President Smith could make a triumphant announcement at the 1907 April general conference: "Today the Church of Jesus Christ of Latter-day Saints owes not a dollar that it cannot pay at once. At last we are in a position to pay as we go. We do not have to borrow any more, and we won't have to if the Latter-day Saints continue to live their religion and observe the law of tithing."[21]

A WORLDWIDE CHURCH

For some time, the Church had asked members to remain where they lived, instead of immigrating to the Latter-day Saint core area as had been the practice since 1831. During President Smith's

13. Francis M. Lyman letter to John W. Taylor, May 3, 1904, Francis Marion Lyman Papers; Francis M. Lyman letter to Matthias F. Cowley, May 6, 1904, in Francis M. Lyman journal, May 6, 1904; as cited in "The Manifesto and the End of Plural Marriage," Gospel Topics, https://www.lds.org/topics/the-manifesto-and-the-end-of-plural-marriage.
14. John Whittaker Taylor was the son of the third President of the Church, John Taylor, and a member of the Quorum of the Twelve Apostles until he resigned in 1905. See Andrew Jenson, *Latter-day Saint Biographical Encyclopedia: A Compilation of Biographical Sketches of Prominent Men and Women in the Church of Jesus Christ of Latter-day Saints* (Salt Lake City, UT: Andrew Jenson History, 1901–36), 1:151–56.
15. Matthias F. Cowley was a member of the Quorum of the Twelve Apostles until he resigned in 1905. Cowley was the father of Apostle Matthew Cowley and also of well-known FBI agent Samuel P. Cowley. See Jenson, *Latter-day Saint Biographical Encyclopedia*, 1:168–72.
16. See Victor W. Jorgensen and B. Carmon Hardy, "The Taylor-Cowley Affair and the Watershed of Mormon History," *Utah Historical Quarterly* 48 (January 1980): 4–36.
17. Taylor was eventually excommunicated in 1911 for his continued involvement in new plural marriages. Cowley was also disciplined in 1911 for the same reason, but he eventually returned to full fellowship before he died in 1940.
18. This affirmative decision from the Senate hearings was not issued until 20 February 1907.
19. See commentary by Harvard S. Heath in his introduction to Michael Harold Paulos, ed., *The Mormon Church on Trial: Transcripts of the Reed Smoot Hearings* (Salt Lake City, UT: Signature Books, 2008), xix.
20. The debt owed had reached more than two million dollars by 1898.
21. Joseph F., in Conference Report, April 1907, 5–6.

Joseph F. Smith and party at British Mission home, 1906. A group portrait of Joseph F. Smith, his wife Edna, and four of his sons, along with Charles W. Nibley and two of his daughters and Heber J. Grant, his wife Emily, and two of his daughters. Courtesy of CHL.

administration, the Church increased efforts to expand beyond the traditional borders of the Intermountain West by building chapels in areas where the Church hoped to grow and stay.

To emphasize his vision of an international Church, President Smith and his wife Edna (1851–1926) departed Salt Lake City on a trip to Europe to strengthen and encourage the Saints living there. As a result, he became the first Church President to visit members outside the United States.[22] During his trip, he visited Belgium, England, France, Holland, Germany, and Switzerland, where he attended various conferences and instructed the Saints and missionaries before returning home to prepare for general conference in October.

A few years later, in the early spring of 1909, President Smith returned to the Hawaiian Islands with his wife Julina Lambson (1849–1936) and several family members. Again, this was a historic trip because no Church President had yet traveled to Hawai'i to minister to the people.[23] President Smith received a warm welcome from the Saints and missionaries. He thanked them for their dedication and sacrifices over and over again. It was a tender time for him, as he reflected on his

22. See map "Travels of Joseph F. Smith," in *Mapping Mormonism: An Atlas of Latter-day Saint History*, ed. Brandon S. Plewe et al. (Provo, UT: BYU Press, 2012), 131.
23. An extant journal for the period 17 February through 1 April 1909 highlights Joseph F.'s trip to Hawai'i.

ministry among the people he loved there, beginning in 1854. As President Smith and his party departed for home in late March, he noted that they were met at the wharf by "many of the good Hawaiian Sisters who fairly Smothered us with flowers and leis of a great variety."[24]

CHURCH HISTORY

As he looked toward the future, President Smith also made efforts to remember the past. During his administration, the Church began to buy sites associated with its beginnings.[25] In 1903 President Smith authorized the purchase of Carthage Jail, where his father, Hyrum, and uncle Joseph were martyred in 1844. This was followed by the purchase of the Vermont farm where Joseph Smith had been born in 1805.

In 1905, to celebrate the centennial anniversary of Joseph Smith's birth, President Smith traveled to Vermont in late December to participate in the unveiling and dedication of a monument.[26]

This was not the first year President Smith had promoted the observance of the Prophet's birthday among the Saints.[27] However, because of the historic nature of the centennial, the First Presidency underscored the importance of the celebration this particular year by inviting all Church members to participate in special services to honor the Prophet throughout the Church on Sunday, 24 December 1905. The official announcement stated, "Memorial services will be held on Sunday, the twenty-four of December, in all the Assemblies of the Latter Day Saints throughout the world. You are cordially invited to attend these services wherever most convenient to join in honoring the memory of one who was honored of God and is beloved by his people."[28] Most congregations and communities complied with the request and gathered on Sunday, December 24, to celebrate the birth of the Prophet. Before returning to Salt Lake City, President Smith and family members toured many Church historical sites in New York and Ohio.

FAMILY LIFE

Joseph F.'s large family remained the center of his life. He rejoiced at the birth of four children and many grandchildren during this decade. He also experienced heartbreak when family members, including his own children, died. In early 1901, Joseph F.'s daughter Alice Smith (1882–1901) passed away at the age of eighteen. A local Salt Lake paper reported, "The parents and friends have stood by her for a year and helplessly watched her life gradually ebb away. . . . There was nothing that love or skill could suggest that was not done, but the bloom faded from her beautiful cheeks and the silent working of the disease went on without abatement."[29]

24. Joseph F., journal, 24 March 1909.
25. James A. Davis, "Historical Sites: 1903–present," in Plewe et al., *Mapping Mormonism*, 136–39.
26. The broader context of this story is outlined in several important articles by Keith A. Erekson; see Keith A. Erekson, "The Joseph Smith Memorial Monument and Royalton's 'Mormon Affair': Religion, Community, Memory, and Politics in Progressive Vermont," *Vermont History*, 73 (Summer/Fall 2005): 117–51 and "'Out of the Mists of Memory': Remembering Joseph Smith in Vermont," *Journal of Mormon History*, 73 (Summer/Fall 2005): 117–51. See also Richard Neitzel Holzapfel and Paul H. Peterson, "New Photographs of Joseph F. Smith's Centennial Memorial Trip to Vermont, 1905" *BYU Studies* 39:4 (2000), 107–14.
27. Beginning in 1894, Joseph F. Smith "called for wider celebrations of his uncle's birth. . . . In 1901, [he] became president of the Church and directed local congregations to hold commemorative services on the Sunday nearest Joseph Smith's birth each December"; see Erekson, "Memories, Monuments, and Mormonism," 134.
28. "First Presidency Invitation," *Deseret Evening News*, December 21, 1905, 1.
29. "Beautiful Girl Dead," *Deseret Evening News*, 29 April 1901, 1.

Home of Joseph F. and Sara Ellen Richards Smith, 25 September 1906, Shipler Photographers. Alice Smith returned home from school in 1900 to convalesce but died here in April 1901. Courtesy of USHS.

During the sickness, Joseph F. kept Martha Ann updated on Alice's condition: "I am happy to say that we are all better with the exception of Aunt Sarah's Alice, who is still quite poorly."[30] The newspaper noted that she had returned home from school a year earlier, but "she failed gradually from then on. The affliction was so deeply rooted that nothing seemed to be able to control it. So that the pall of her impending fate has been hanging over the home on Second West street for several weeks." The news report concluded, "This morning, at 10:30, surrounded by her father and mother, and other members of the family, her sweet soul was released, and nothing was left but the wasted form and sorrowing hearts."[31]

Joseph F. also supported his sister Martha Ann in her times of trouble and loss. A year following his daughter's death, Joseph F. took an opportunity to write a letter to his wife Edna Lambson to update her on family matters: "I got a letter this morning from Aunt Martha telling how little Mary Corbett was suffering, and while I was reading it, I got a message thru the phone that she passed away last night or this morning at about 1 o'clock."[32]

30. Joseph F. to Martha Ann, 2 April 1901, herein.
31. "Beautiful Girl Dead," 1.
32. Joseph F. to Edna Lambson, 26 July 1902.

A local Salt Lake City newspaper reported: "Provo July 26 Mamie Corbett, the 11 year old daughter of Mr. and Mrs. W S Corbett, died last night, after several weeks of severe illness, commencing with periostitis, caused by taking cold, and for which an operation was performed. This was followed by pleurisy pneumonia, and finally meningitis, which was the immediate cause of the child's death."[33]

Joseph F. wrote a short letter to Josephine Harris, Martha Ann's daughter-in-law, and mentioned he had attended the funeral. "My Dear Niece: I got your letter of 25th on the 26th but I have been so driven with crowding duties that I could not get to your affairs. I was at Provo on Monday attending the funeral of little Mary Corbett."[34]

Each death brought great sorrow to Joseph F. In a tender letter to Martha Ann on 22 November 1905, he recorded his feelings at the loss of his six-month-old grandson Alfred William Peterson Jr. (1905): "Yesterday morning at about 2 o'clock My precious Mamies Sweet little boy[35] passed into the great beyond from whence he so recently came. He was a most inteligant, attractive, beautiful little man. . . . We are all broken up. To my beloved and noble Mammie death could not have come in a more cruel way. He was her very hope, joy and life!"[36]

Writing and receiving letters continued to be an important means for Joseph F. to keep in touch with family members even though it was challenging to do so. For example, he noted in a letter to his wife Sarah Kimball, "This is Sunday night. I am a little tired. I have been at work all day with my accounts, which have been neglected of late, having been so much away from home, and so busy when at home, that I let my own affairs go behind. And then have, with Joseph's help, got a lot of correspondences off my hands, today. Thus I have been busy all day. My eyes begin to ache, and my head swim, so I must stop pretty soon, I also prepared an article for the Era today, so you may guess I have not been idle."[37]

By 1900 Joseph F. had started to use his children to help him with his correspondence. In some cases, they were learning how to help him. After a letter had been typed with multiple corrections, Joseph F. would pick up a pen and add a note to the letter, "P.S. I dictated the foregoing to one of my boys who is just learning to typewrite, therefore you will kindly excuse its in-artistic appearance."[38]

His letterpress copybooks during this period are filled with letters to his missionary children. As noted earlier, between 1895 and 1914, Joseph F. sent twelve sons on missions.[39]

In addition to the letters between Joseph F. and his missionary sons, his letters to Martha Ann provide important information about his life and ministry during this period. Additionally, they are one of the few primary sources to help reconstruct Martha Ann's world during this decade.

33. "Provo News Notes," *Salt Lake Herald*, 27 July 1902, 5.
34. Joseph F. to Josephine Harris, 30 July 1902.
35. Mamie is a nickname for Mary Sophronia Smith, daughter of Joseph F. and Julina Lambson. Mary Sophronia married Alfred William Peterson on 17 December 1901. Their son Alfred William Peterson Jr. (born 25 May 1905) died on 21 November 1905.
36. See Joseph F. to Martha Ann, 22 November 1905, herein. Joseph F. suffered another loss in 1907 when Leonora Smith died, leaving behind a husband and six young children (the oldest was just ten years of age).
37. Joseph F. to Sarah Kimball, 18 August 1907.
38. Joseph F. to C. C. Bush, 18 February 1900. See also Joseph F. to Jos. H. Dean, 21 June 1900, where Joseph F. signs his name and adds in his own handwriting, "This was dictated to my son David, who is just learning to use the typewriter. Please excuse errors."
39. See Hyrum M. Smith III and Scott G. Kenney, comp., *From Prophet to Son: Advice of Joseph F. Smith to His Missionary Sons* (Salt Lake City, UT: Deseret Book, 1981), viii.

Old and New Provo Tabernacles, ca. 1886, photography by F. I. Monsen and Company, Salt Lake City, Utah. View looking east showing side and rear of old tabernacle (1861–1919) and back of new tabernacle (1898–2010). Construction of the new tabernacle, known as the Provo Stake Tabernacle, began in 1883. The April 1886 general conference of the Church was held in the new tabernacle. However, it was not dedicated until 1898. Joseph F. Smith participated in various meetings in both buildings during his ministry. Martha Ann also attended meetings in these historic buildings, and in 1923 friends and family gathered in the Provo Stake Tabernacle to honor Martha Ann during her funeral services. Courtesy of CHL.

MARTHA ANN SMITH HARRIS

Joseph F. and Martha Ann continued to face the deaths of loved ones during this period. Martha Ann's thirteen-month-old granddaughter, Lucy Jane Corbett, was tragically killed by a train on 21 March 1901.[40]

It is hard to imagine how Martha Ann's daughter Mary Emily Harris (1865–1947) and her husband, Walter Sutton Corbett (1857–1912), felt after losing two children within such a short time. That Joseph F. and Martha Ann also felt deeply about these deaths is manifested in the letters written during this period.

The natural rhythms of life continued to flow through Martha Ann's family. For example, nearly a year later, Martha Ann and William celebrated a daughter's wedding when Mercy Ann Harris (1874–1905) married John Thomas Dennis (1866–1929) in June 1903. Again, Martha Ann's brother Joseph F. was able to perform the marriage sealing in the Salt Lake Temple.[41] To have the President

40. See Joseph F. to Martha Ann, 2 April 1901, herein.
41. Salt Lake Temple "Living Sealings Book A," 1:311, entry 5581.

John and Mercy Ann Harris Dennis on their wedding day, 25 June 1903, photograph by Anderson, Provo, Utah. Courtesy of Carole Call King.

of the Church participate was certainly appreciated, but the fact that he was her brother made the wedding ceremony even more meaningful for Martha Ann and her family.

One month after celebrating this special occasion, Martha Ann and William Jasper's daughter Lucy Smith Harris Simmons (1870–1903) died from complications during delivery on 26 July 1903. Her baby, Lucy, also died at the same time. Martha Ann chose to raise Lucy's two young children, Edna Mae (1899–1986) and John Arthur (1900–1961). Joseph F. was worried about that decision, and in a letter dated 10 April 1907 he wrote, "I have been thinking about you and Dear Lucy's children. I feel it is too much for you to try to take care of them alone. And Even if you could and did succeed in doing so for a while, the moment you cannot do it any longer the children would have to do without you—or without your help."[42]

42. See Joseph F. to Martha Ann, 10 April 1907, herein.

Martha Ann and daughters, ca. 1904. This photograph was taken sometime after the death of Lucy Smith Harris Simmons in 1903 and before the death of Mercy Ann Dennis in 1905. Courtesy of Carole Call King.

Joseph F. reached out to his nephew Hyrum Smith Harris and his wife Delia Twede Harris to encourage them to adopt the children.[43] At the time, Hyrum and Delia had no children since their only child, Mercy Rachel Harris, had died within a few months of her birth in 1891. In the end, Martha Ann decided to raise these two grandchildren as her own children. Later, still childless, Hyrum and Delia adopted a daughter, Julina Harris, who was born on 3 July 1909.

Delia Twede Harris and her adopted daughter, Julina Harris, ca. 1913. Courtesy of Carole Call King.

Mercy Ann Dennis lost her first child, George A. Dennis, on the day of his birth in 1904. The next year was even more tragic for Martha Ann's family when Mercy Ann gave birth to another stillborn child, Marguerite, on 9 January 1905.[44] Little Marguerite was buried on 11 January. Twelve days later, on 23 January 1905, Mercy Ann died too, at the age of thirty. Martha Ann had taken care of her at the Harris home in Provo during this difficult time. Zina, Martha Ann's daughter who had lost a child in 1899 and her own husband in 1903, wrote the following:

To Mother on the death of her girls, Mercy & Lucy:

Break the news gently to Mother dear heart, tell her oh gently
That she is now called with a dear living daughters to past
Speak gently words to her pray for her too
Show her the tranquil sweet peace she has gained
And the rest, oh so blissful, now spirit so free.[45]

Funerals brought the family together as they gathered to mourn and support one another. For example, when Hellen Fisher Smith, the wife of Martha's older half brother John Smith, died in September 1907, Martha Ann made her way to Salt Lake City to help Joseph F.'s wives make burial clothes; she also attended the funeral.[46]

Despite such hard times, Martha Ann celebrated the births of grandchildren and enjoyed being a grandmother, as when her son Franklin Hill Harris and his wife, Josephine P. Robinson (1868–1965), had their first child, Franklin Hyrum (1898–1971). This couple added four more children to their family in the first decade of the twentieth century: Richard Parkes (1900–1976), Mary Harris (1903–91), Carl Joseph (1906–87), and Leonora Harris (1909–76). For Martha Ann, these were joyous blessings straight from heaven.

43. See Joseph F. to Hyrum S. Harris, 10 April 1907.
44. Death Certificate for Marguerite Dennis, 9 January 1905, file no. 16520, Utah State Board of Health.
45. A copy of this poem is in the editors' possession courtesy of David J. and Ruth B. Harris.
46. Joseph F. to E. Wesley Smith, 3 September 1907.

Frank and Josephine Harris family, October 1906, Olson & Hafen, Provo, Utah. From left: Franklin Hyrum, Carl Joseph, Josephine Robinson, Richard Parkes, Franklin "Frank" Hill, and Mary Harris. Courtesy of CHL.

ECONOMIC CHALLENGES

Although Martha Ann was the major contributor to the family economy for some time as the decade began, she continued to struggle financially for the remainder of her life. As their letters so often demonstrate, Joseph F. helped his sister whenever he could. For example, in December 1901 he wrote, "I send you here with my check No. 24. for ten dollars, which please accept as a small token of remembrance for your Christmas dinner."[47]

In June 1904 Joseph F. offered to replace the home's roof and make needed repairs. He recorded the work done in an account book: "June 1 to 30. Paid E. D. Partridge for shingling and repairing my sister, Martha Ann. Harris' house."[48] In December that year, Joseph F. sent her a check for ten dollars to cover a Christmas meal. During the next month, he handed her cash on two separate occasions. In February 1906 he presented her with a gift of "dress goods, Sheeting, etc." costing

47. Joseph F. to Martha Ann, 23 December 1901, herein.
48. Joseph F., Account Book, June 1904.

fifteen dollars. During the decade, Joseph F.'s account books reveal numerous gifts in addition to cash, including shoes, linen, dress patterns, slippers, pillows, tablecloths, and a subscription to the *Deseret Semi-Weekly News*.[49]

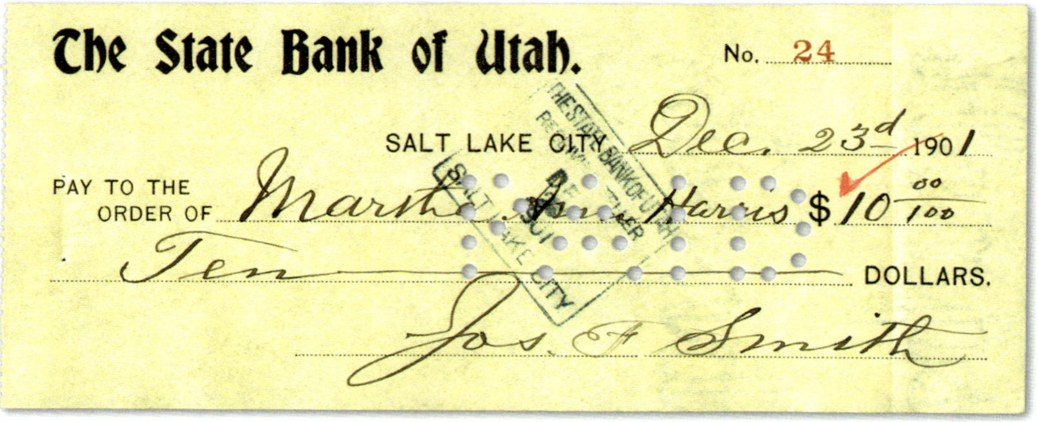

Joseph F. Smith's check, drawn on an account with the State Bank of Utah, dated 23 December 1901. Martha Ann countersigned the back of the check to cash it. Courtesy of CHL.

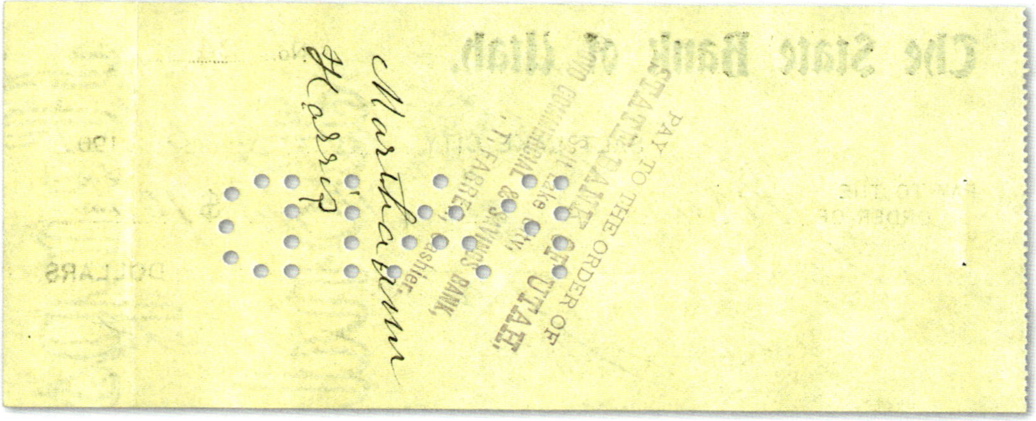

WILLIAM HARRIS'S DEATH

As the decade ended, Martha Ann experienced another heartbreak when her beloved husband, William Jasper Harris, was killed in an accident in 1909. He and his son John Albert (1872–1946) attended a Black Hawk War veterans' celebration at the Opera House on Center Street in Provo on Friday, 23 April 1909.[50] As they crossed the street while walking home after the event, an out-of-control horse and buggy driven by a family friend struck William. He suffered severe injuries to the head and died in his home early the next morning.[51] Martha Ann and William had celebrated their fifty-second wedding anniversary just three days before the accident.

49. Joseph F., Account Book, February 1906. Joseph F. was generous to a large circle of family and friends throughout most of his life.

50. The Black Hawk War was a conflict between the settlers in southern Utah and some of the native peoples in that region. See John Peterson, "Black Hawk War," in *Encyclopedia of Latter-day Saint History*, ed. Arnold K. Garr, Donald Q. Cannon, and Richard O. Cowan (Salt Lake City, UT: Deseret Book, 2000), 106–7.

51. See "Racing Teams Kill Pioneer," *Deseret News*, 24 April 1909, 1.

Martha Ann ironing at home in Provo, Utah, ca. 1909. Family members describe her wearing a white apron and recall how she used the apron to wipe tears from her eyes at tender moments. Courtesy of Carole Call King.

To his son Franklin Richards Smith (1888–1967), who was serving a mission in the British Isles at the time, Joseph F. wrote, "This morning Uncle William Harris died, from being knocked down and run over by a team and wagon late last night. The time for the funeral has not yet been set."[52] The funeral was held on 29 April.[53] Joseph F. attended the funeral, as noted in a letter written late that evening: "It is now 8 p.m., I have just come into the office from attending the funeral of Wm. J. Harris, my sister's husband, at Provo." Apostles Orson F. Whitney (1855–1931) and Francis M. Lyman (1840–1916) had delivered the eulogies.[54]

52. Joseph F. to Franklin Richards Smith, 25 April 1909.
53. Joseph F. helped Martha Ann with some of the funeral expenses. See Joseph F. to Martha Ann, 6 May 1909, herein.
54. Joseph F. to Will G. Farrell, 29 April 1909.

Mary and Donette Smith, ca. 1900, photograph by Charles W. Symons, Fox & Symons, Salt Lake City, Utah. The photograph was colorized by the photographer in the studio in an effort to capture the natural colors of clothing, eyes, and hair. As Joseph F.'s family grew, more and more photographs were being taken at studios in Salt Lake City in an effort to document his personal family life and to share that life with his friends and family, including Martha Ann. See, for example, the letter from Joseph F. to Martha Ann, 16 January 1891, herein. Courtesy of CHL.

A few days later, Joseph F. wrote his sister, "I spoke to Frank when he was here about it, and I told him I would help him out on the Expenses of the Undertaker. I will enclose in this letter a note for you to hand or send to mr. Edward L. Jones, the Undertaker, as I do not know his address. All you need to do will be to send it to him by one of the Children, or any person who can deliver it to him."[55] In that note, Joseph F. asked the undertaker to "kindly send" him a status on the funeral expenses, as he wanted to help pay for the "burial of Wm. J. Harris."[56]

Martha Ann made her way north to Salt Lake City to stay with her brother during this time of mourning. On 4 July 1909, Joseph F. wrote his nephew Hyrum Smith Harris, "Your mother is here. Adelia's little baby girl [Julina was born in Salt Lake City and taken to Provo by Martha Ann. Hyrum and Adelia, who were childless after their first child died in July 1891, adopted and raised Julina], as pretty as a picture, was born yesterday (July 3r). Your mother starts for Provo with 'it' in a few minutes by the San Pedro Rwy. You should come at once to Provo, or send Adelia to take care of her baby. Your mother is as pleased she would be with one of her own. She acts just like a young mother. We all feel sure that Adelia will be proud of it too, and if she doesn't come quickly for it, I fear Aunt Martha will not want to give it up. Now you see the situation and you will govern yourself accordingly. We all send love and congratulations for the baby and best wishes for Adelia. Affectionally, your Uncle Joseph F."[57]

CONTINUING HEALTH ISSUES

Martha Ann continued to suffer from sickness and injuries throughout much of the decade. She was in a great deal of pain from a second break to her knee sometime following her daughter Martha Artimissa's marriage in 1903. Martha Ann's grandson Elbert remembered that before her injury, Martha Ann would walk to Artimissa's house for a home-cooked meal each day. After her injury, she was unable to make the trip, so Elbert would drop off a tin of food for her, which he would hang from the handlebars of his bicycle on his way to school. That routine continued for some time until the family got a dog and trained it to carry a container of mush in his mouth to Martha Ann's house every day.[58]

SUMMARY

In 1909 Joseph F. was seventy-one years old. He and his five wives, thirty-seven living children, and increasingly large third-generation family enjoyed time together whenever possible during the time he led the church to which he had dedicated his life since he was fifteen years of age.

Reflecting on life's opportunities and challenges in 1906, Joseph F. wrote a man in Chicago who was not a member of the Church, "I would not have you think we have no cares, no sickness, anxieties, no ups and downs. Of these incidents of life we have and share, but 'the fruit of righteousness is sown in peace of them that make peace,' we pull together in love and confidence and hope of the glorious promise of immortality and eternal life and union now and forever."[59]

Joseph F. knew personally about tragic losses and the compensating eternal promises of the gospel. The same held true for Martha Ann. Although by 1909 she had lost her husband, two children, and several grandchildren, she and her nine living children, along with their spouses and children, continued to build strong family relationships as they began the next decade.

55. Joseph F. to Martha Ann, 6 May 1909, herein.
56. Joseph F. to Elder S. Jones, 6 May 1909.
57. Joseph F. to Hyrum S. Harris, 4 July 1909.
58. Ruth Mae Harris, *Martha Ann, Daughter of Hyrum and Mary Fielding Smith* (Orem, UT: published by the author, 2002), 139.
59. Joseph F. to Jos. S. Sohott, 28 November 1911.

Like the letters written to Martha Ann during the previous decade, Joseph F.'s known 1900–1909 letters to his sister were similarly brief and usually written in haste. On 6 May 1909, he noted, "I need not say that I have been very busy since I saw you last. I have had no time for writing letters—but have thought many times I aught to drop you just a line or two."

The brevity and family focus of the letters from this period do not hide the great love that existed between Joseph F. and Martha Ann. Every missive begins with "My own Dear Sister" or "My Dear Sister" and ends with such tender phrases as "With love to all I am affectionately your brother" and "Lovingly, I am your brother." While these expressions might initially appear to be routine elements of courteous written correspondence, they ring true, evidenced by many years of ongoing affection and personal interest in each other's lives as expressed in hundreds of letters between them, Joseph F.'s personal journal entries about Martha Ann and her family, and letters they wrote to extended family members and friends in which they mention each other. This devotion is also apparent in the historical record.

William Jasper Harris Jr., ca. 1900, photograph by Goldsmith Studio, St. Louis, Missouri. William was Martha Ann's oldest son. During his lifetime he had frequent interaction with Joseph F., his uncle. In some instances during the 1890s and early 1900s, Joseph F. gave strong counsel to his nephew that sometimes affected Martha Ann's relationship with her brother. Fortunately, family loyalty trumped moments of passion and momentary discord. Courtesy of Carole Call King.

Letters

JOSEPH F. TO MARTHA ANN, 26 JULY 1900

July 26th 1900[1]

Marth Ann Harris
Provo—

My Dear Sister Martha.

I am in receipt to day of a letter from Ernest A. Griffin,[2] of Escalante Garfield Co. Utah, bringing the sad news of the death of his father, Charles E. Griffin, at "Coyote"[3] on the 17th inst—and was burried on the 19th

I have [*illegible strike-through*] written to Ernest and the children giving them what poor comfort I could. A line to him from you would no doubt be appreciated.

We are all usually well— I have written the news to Jerusha,[4] and will send word to John[5] this evening. Mary Jane[6] is quite feeble. Julina[7] has gone to Wasatch[8] to bring home the children who have been there two or three weeks. It is very hot weather. I called on Jerusha a short time ago.

I expect to start for Mexico to morrow—on a special mission.[9] With love to all— I am affectionately your brother Jos. F.——

1. From Joseph F.'s letterpress copybooks; original not extant. Joseph F. was sixty-one, and Martha Ann was fifty-nine.
2. Ernest Adelbert Griffin is the son of Sarah Smith and Charles Emerson Griffin and a nephew of Joseph F. and Martha Ann. See biographical register, "Griffin, Ernest Adelbert." His father, Charles Emerson Griffin, a brother-in-law of Joseph F. and Martha Ann, died on 18 July 1900.
3. Coyote, later renamed Antimony, was a small town in Garfield County in southern Utah.
4. Jerusha Smith.
5. John Smith.
6. Mary Jane Thompson.
7. Julina Lambson.
8. Located 1½ miles up Cottonwood Canyon, Wasatch was a summer resort.
9. Joseph F. left for Mexico in early August 1900 to meet with Anthony W. Ivins (president of the Juarez Stake). He also took time to dissuade Benjamin Cluff Jr. (acting president of Brigham Young Academy) from continuing an expedition he was leading to discover Book of Mormon lands and artifacts in Mexico and Central America. See Thomas G. Alexander, *Mormonism in Transition: A History of the Latter-day Saints* (Urbana: University of Illinois Press, 1986), 166–67.

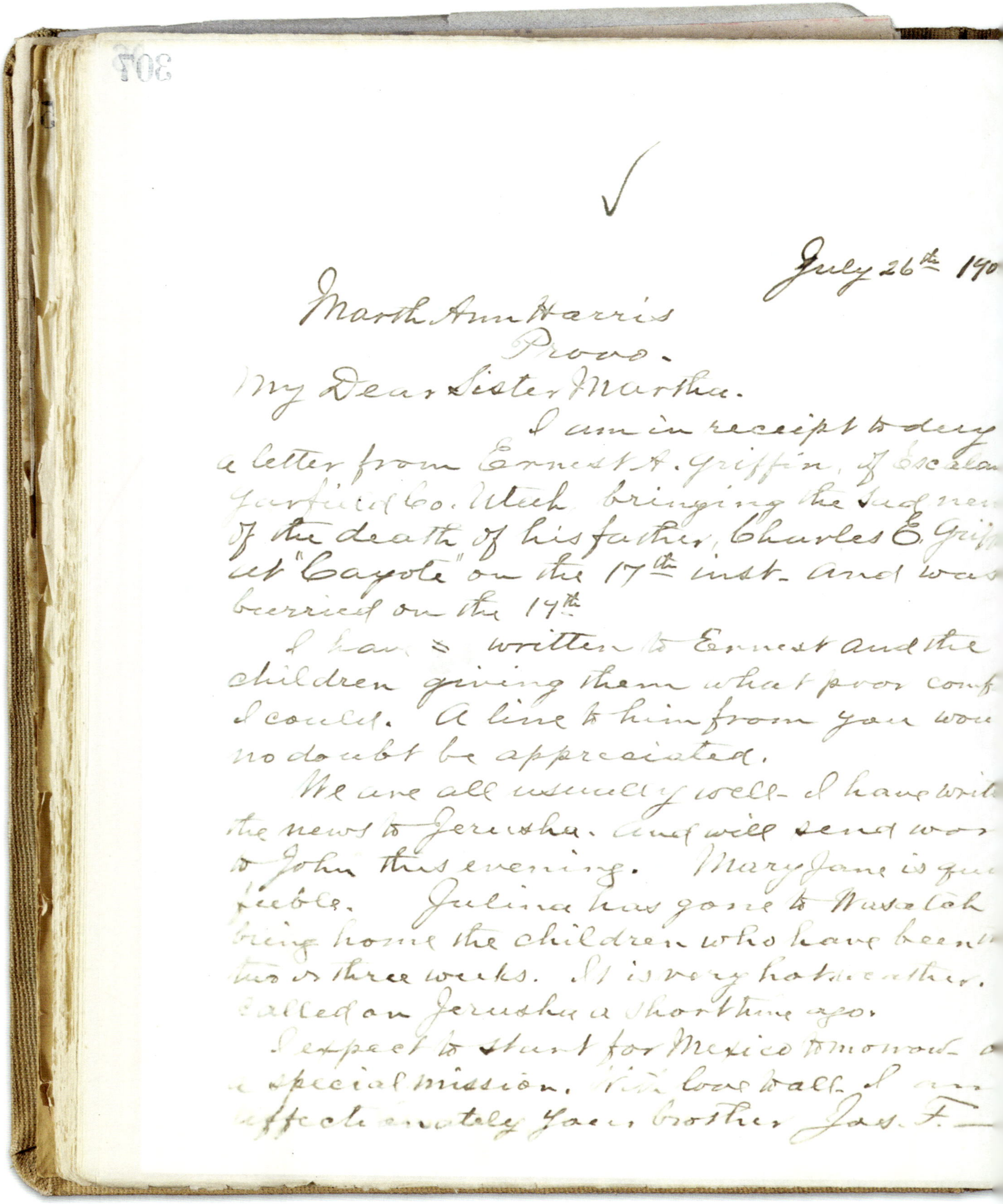
July 26th 190

Marth Ann Harris
Provo.

My Dear Sister Martha.
I am in receipt to-day
a letter from Ernest A. Griffin, of Escalan
Garfield Co. Utah, bringing the sad new
of the death of his father, Charles E. Griff
at "Cayote" on the 17th inst. and was
buried on the 17th.
I have written to Ernest and the
children giving them what poor comf
I could. A line to him from you wou
no doubt be appreciated.
We are all usually well. I have writ
the news to Jerusha. And will send wor
to John this evening. Mary Jane is qui
feeble. Julina has gone to Wasatch
bring home the children who have been
two or three weeks. It is very hot weather.
Called on Jerusha a short time ago.
I expect to start for Mexico tomorrow o
a special mission. With love to all, I am
affectionately your brother Jos. F. —

Joseph F. to Martha Ann, 26 July 1900, copy found in Joseph F.'s letterpress copybooks under that date.

JOSEPH F. TO MARTHA ANN, 26 JANUARY 1901

Jan. 26th 1901[10]

My Dear Sister,
Martha Ann Harris
Provo—Utah—

I was sorry I did not get to see you on or just before your departure for home. I got you a ticket for Provo and return, as better rates can be got for a return trip than for single fare one way.

I did not notice how long the return was good for—but if you want to use it before the time expires, do so. If you do not use it—you can return it to me, and if needed within a reasonable time I may get it extended and return it to you. I hope you got home in safety and found all well. We had a sad funeral[11] at poor Mary B's.[12] I wish you had gone—we go back in time for you to have gone home by the 5 p.m. Train. I hope Mercy[13] is all right—and that William[14] & all the rest are well as also yourself. We are all about as usual.

With love to all I am affectionately your brother Joseph F.—

JOSEPH F. TO MARTHA ANN, 7 FEBRUARY 1901

Feb. 7th 1901—[15]

My Dear Sister
Martha Ann.

Your letters of Jan. 29th & Feb.__ inst. are before me. Glad you got home safely, and found all us well at home as you did— Sorry you had to walk from the Depot—and the bereaved families you mention have my sympathy.

David and Donnette[16] have been quite ill since you were here. The latter has moved into their new house—and are very comfortable, except for her sickness. She will be confined to her bed for a day or two longer. Aunt Mary Jane[17] is just about the same as when you were here. All the rest are usually well. Now, I would like to know how soon you would like that ticket

10. From Joseph F.'s letterpress copybooks; original not extant. Joseph F. was sixty-two, and Martha Ann was fifty-nine.
11. John J. Norman died on 24 January 1901. His funeral was held on 25 January at his residence in North Salt Lake; he was buried in the Salt Lake City Cemetery. Joseph F. wrote: "I attended the funeral of Norman, at North Salt Lake, he is the husband of cousin Mary B. Smith. I, and my brother John and Saml. H. B. spoke. John Henry Smith dedicated the grave." Joseph F., journal, 25 January 1901. John Henry Smith noted, "I went to the City Cemetery with the funeral procession for J. J. Norman. I offered the dedicatory prayer." John Henry Smith, journal, 25 January 1901.
12. Mary Bailey Smith, Joseph F. and Martha Ann's cousin. See biographical register, "Smith, Mary Bailey."
13. Likely Mercy Ann Harris.
14. William Jasper Harris.
15. From Joseph F.'s letterpress copybooks; original not extant.
16. Likely children of Joseph F., David Asael Smith and Donnette Smith. Donnette had recently married Alonzo Kelser on 26 December 1900.
17. Mary Jane Thompson.

returned to you. It can only be extended for a short time, and only once. I must therefore hold it until within a few days of the time you need it for use. You can let me know—when that will be— With love—and hoping you are all well, I am affectionately &c. Joseph F.—

JOSEPH F. TO MARTHA ANN, 2 APRIL 1901

April 2, 1901.[18]

Martha Ann Harris,
Provo.

My dear Sister:—

Your letter of the 27th reached me on the 29th, and I have been too busy to answer until now. I am happy to say that we are all better with the exception of Aunt Sarah's Alice, who is still quite poorly.[19] The quarantine at Aunt Alice's[20] has been removed, the folks are all right. The death of little Lucy is too sad for utterance.[21] We saw the accounts of it in the paper and feared the worst, but we tried to make ourselves believe it was not our little Lucy. It would have been sad for anybody, and we regret the terrible accident as keenly as you do. I hope it will be a dreadful warning for all time to come to keep the little children from the railroad tracks. Give our heartfelt sympathy to Mary[22] and the family. I sincerely hope the Lord will give you all sufficient strength to endure the sorrow into which you have all been so suddenly plunged. I understand that Artie[23] expects to come to the city.[24] I will send her a ticket by the next mail.[25] Let her wait until she receives it.

In great haste, I am,
affectionately your brother,

18. From Joseph F.'s letterpress copybooks; original not extant. This letter is typewritten except for the signature.
19. Alice Smith, daughter of Joseph F. and Sarah Ellen Richards, died at age eighteen on 29 April 1901, four weeks after this letter was written. The funeral was held on the following day. John Henry Smith noted, "The funeral of Allice Smith today. She was the daughter of Joseph F. and Sarah Ellen Richards Smith. Prest. Lorenzo Snow, Myself, George Brimhall, Heber J. Grant, M.F. Cowley, Abraham O. Woodruff and Brigham Young spoke. The attendance was large and many carriage followed the remains to the grave." John Henry Smith, journal, 30 April 1901. See Jean Bickmore White, ed., *Church, State, and Politics: The Diaries of John Henry Smith* (Salt Lake City, UT: Signature Books, 1990), 468.
20. Alice Ann Kimball.
21. Martha Ann's thirteen-month-old granddaughter Lucy Jane Corbett (born on 28 January 1899), daughter of Mary Emily Harris and Walter Sutton Corbett, was killed in a train accident on 21 March 1901. She was incorrectly identified as "little Susie Corbett" in "Little Girl Killed," *Salt Lake Herald*, 22 March 1901, 5. See biographical register, "Corbett, Lucy Jane."
22. Mary Emily Harris.
23. Martha Ann's daughter Martha Artimissa Harris.
24. Salt Lake City.
25. Joseph F. was a director of the Salt Lake, Garfield & Western Railway. Through this association and others, he was able to obtain train passes on a number of lines.

JOSEPH F. TO MARTHA ANN, 23 DECEMBER 1901

Dec. 23d 1[◊]901[26]
Martha Ann Harris
Provo—Utah Co.
My Dear Sister Martha.

I send you here with my check No. 24. for <u>ten dollars</u>, which please accept as a small token of remembrance for your Christmas dinner. I wish you all the compliments of the Season in which all the family joine. We are usually well. I hope you are <u>all</u> in good health. God bless my beloved sister and all your children, not forgetting William J.[27] Mamie[28] is married and is busy with her husband in the Bee Hive House.[29] I can get my lunch now early.

We shall be pleased to see you any time. You can endorse this check and get to Reed Smoot Bank[30] and cash it.

Affectionately your brother
Joseph F.

JOSEPH F. TO MARTHA ANN, 23 JULY 1902

July 23rd 1902[31]
My Dear Sister

Martha Ann Harris: A few days ago I sent Hyrum M. to Provo to see how you were all getting along in the midst of sickness and sore afflictions.[32] We were gratified to hear that little Marys condition was such as to give promise and hope of her recovery.[33] The causes for such sudden and unexpected attacks upon our dear little children, are often completely hidden in mystery. And yet, no doubt, when we shall see the facts by the superior light of faith, the causes may be very plain to us.

---

26. From Joseph F.'s letterpress copybooks; original not extant. Joseph F. had recently been set apart as the sixth President of the Church on 17 October 1901, ratified by a special conference and solemn assembly on 10 November 1901.
27. William Jasper Harris, Martha Ann's husband.
28. Mamie is a nickname for Mary Sophronia Smith, daughter of Joseph F. and Julina Lambson. She married Alfred William Peterson just a few days earlier on 17 December 1901.
29. Joseph F. had moved into the Beehive House, the official residence of the President of the Church at the time, shortly after writing this letter. He lived there until his death on 19 November 1918.
30. A. O. Smoot organized First National Bank of Provo in 1882 and constructed a building on the northeast corner of Academy [now University] Avenue and Center Street in 1884. His son Reed Smoot established Provo Commercial and Savings Bank in 1890 and took over First National Bank of Provo in 1894. A new bank building replaced the original in 1904 and still stands today.
31. From Joseph F.'s letterpress copybooks; original not extant. See Joseph F. to Martha Ann, 26 July 1902, herein.
32. Hyrum Mack Smith, Joseph F.'s son.
33. Martha Ann's eleven-year-old granddaughter Mary Elizabeth Corbett, daughter of Mary Emily Harris and Walter Sutton Corbett, died a few days later on 26 July 1902. See Joseph F. to Martha Ann, 26 July 1902, herein. Also see biographical register, "Corbett, Mary Elizabeth."

We often cannot tell when or how we take cold, but we do it, and we have to suffer the consequences and no one is to blame for it. Although we had sufficient knowledge we would discover that we ourselves were responsible!

Providence is often blamed for our own follies or ignorance. I feel that little Mary will pull through, with proper care, and if she does I shall thank the Lord. She should be kept quiet & all noise should be hushed. I hope Lucys husband[34] is better and that all of you are blessed. Ever etc. Jos. F. Smith

JOSEPH F. TO MARTHA ANN, 26 JULY 1902

Salt Lake City—
July 26—1902[35]

My own Dear Sister—
Martha Ann—

Your letter dated the ("5th") 25th inst came to hand this morning and I was reading it when called to the Phone, to hear of little Mary's death—at 1 o'clock last night.[36] The news of her passing away—beyond this vail of tears was was indeed sad news—but scarcely worse than your discription of her terrible suffering before she died.[37]

God's will be done! In this I do not confess that it was His design or <u>will</u> that <u>she</u> should suffer <u>so</u> and in the midst thereof find relief—in death—but that He suffered it to be so—perhaps to <u>prove</u> and test the faith and confidence of those who remain in Him. God has said he would try his people <u>even</u> [**p. 2**] unto death if need be in order to prove their integrity— See D. &. C. Sec. v.

Look at the life of Joseph, the Prophet and our own Father,[38] and the hundreds who laid down their lives in Missouri, Illinois and on the plains for Conscience sake.[39] God suffered all these things—and the persecution unto death of His only begotton Son in the Flesh, that they and He might obtain far more exceeding and eternal weight of Glory[40] in the World to Come.

Think of the many who <u>fall</u> from Grace by the way and the comparitively few who stem the tide of Sin in the world!

34. Jonathan Simmons, Martha Ann's son-in-law, was married to Lucy Smith Harris. See biographical register, "Simmons, Jonathan."
35. From Joseph F.'s letterpress copybooks; original not extant. Joseph F. was sixty-three, and Martha Ann was sixty-one.
36. Mary Elizabeth Corbett died on 26 July 1902.
37. See "Provo News Notes," *Salt Lake Herald*, 27 July 1902, 5.
38. Joseph Smith Jr. and Hyrum Smith.
39. The total number of Latter-day Saints who lost their lives as a direct result of violence or from the result of being forced from their homes in Missouri and Illinois is not known. However, an estimated 1,909 died on the Mormon Trail between 1847 and 1868, before the railroad arrived in Utah. Additional loss of life occurred on sea voyages and rail travels as the Saints made their way to the Latter-day Saint staging grounds for the trek west during the nineteenth century. See Melvin L. Bashore, H. Dennis Tolley, and the BYU Pioneer Mortality Team, "Mortality on the Mormon Trail, 1847–1868," *BYU Studies* 53, no. 4 (2014): 109–23.
40. See 2 Corinthians 4:17.

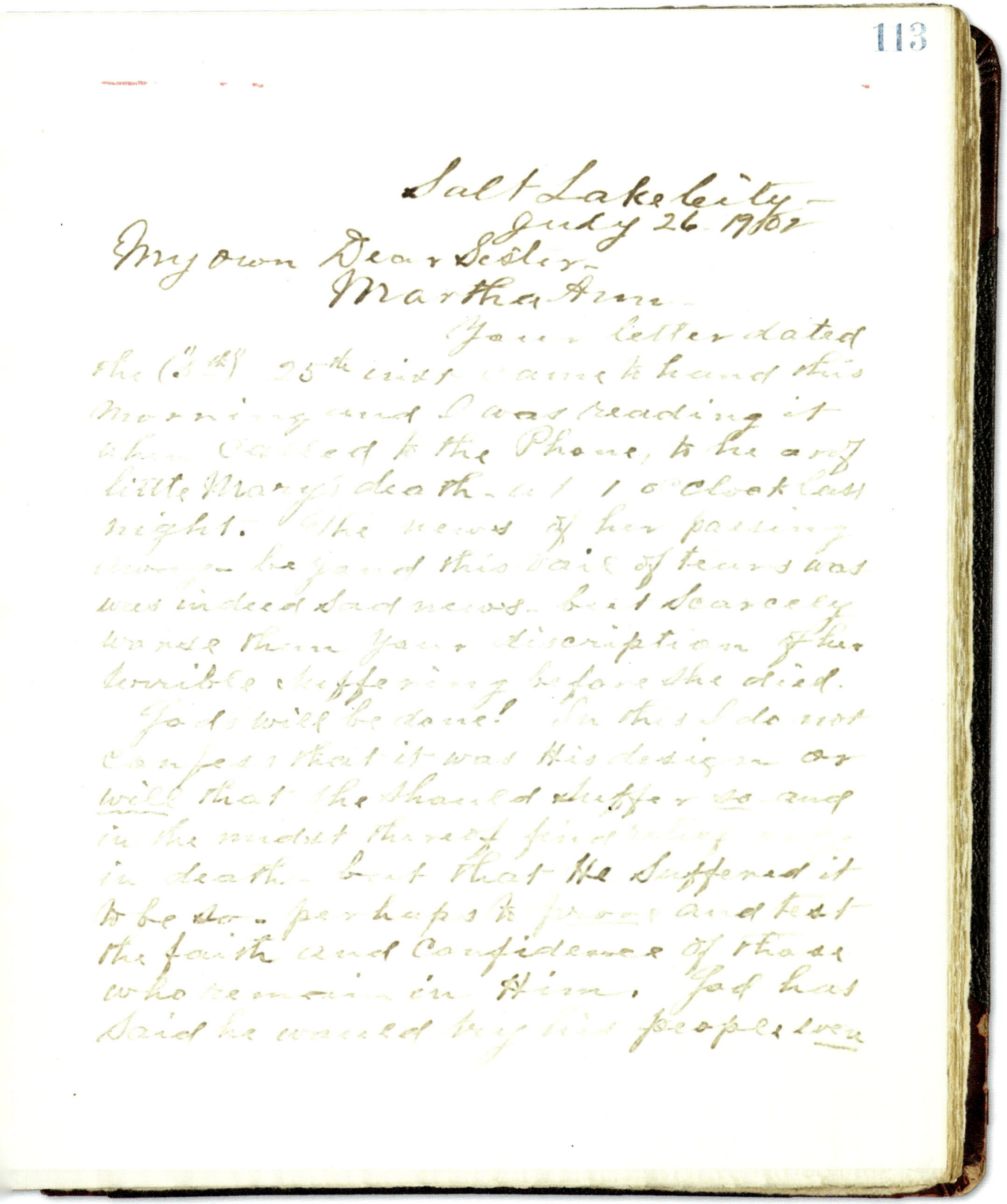

113

Salt Lake City—
July 26. 1902

My own Dear Sister—
Martha Ann—

Your letter dated
the (8th) 25th inst. came to hand this
morning and I was reading it
when Called to the Phone, to hear of
little Mary's death at 1 o'clock last
night. The news of her passing
away— beyond this vail of tears was
was indeed sad news. but scarcely
worse than your discription of her
terrible suffering before she died.
God's will be done! In this I do not
confess that it was His design or
will that she should suffer so and
in the midst thereof find relief [illegible]
in death— but that He Suffered it
to be so— perhaps to prove and test
the faith and Confidence of those
who remain in Him. God has
Said he would try his people even

Joseph F. to Martha Ann, 26 July 1902 (p. 1), copy found in Joseph F.'s letterpress copybooks under that date.

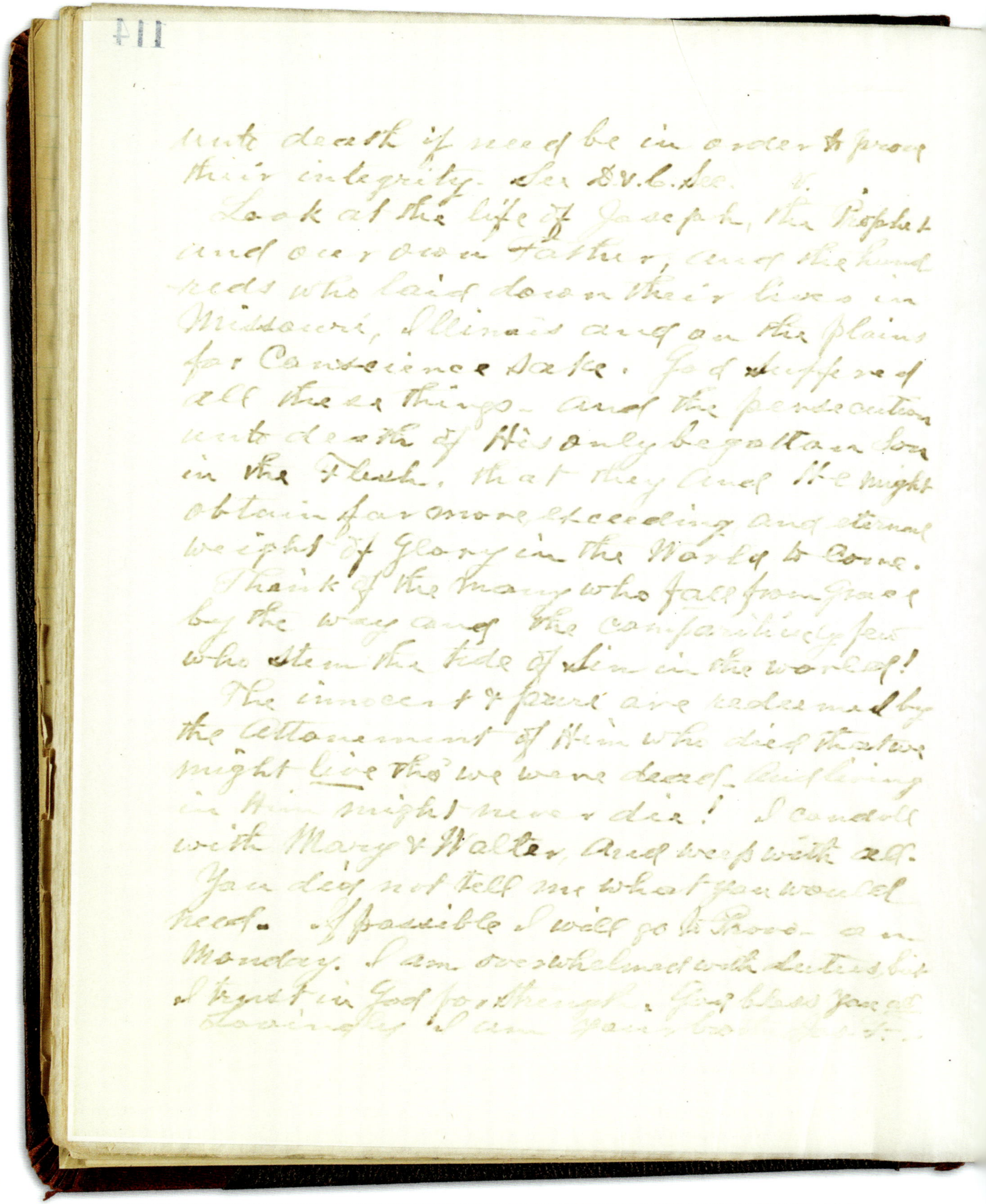
411

unto death if need be in order to prove
their integrity. See D.&C. Sec.
Look at the life of Joseph, the Prophet
and our own Father, and the hundreds who laid down their lives in
Missouri, Illinois and on the plains
for Conscience sake. God suffered
all these things—and the persecution
unto death of His only begotten Son
in the Flesh, that they and He might
obtain far more exceeding and eternal
weight of Glory in the World to Come.
Think of the many who fall from Grace
by the way and the comparatively few
who stem the tide of sin in the world!
The innocent & pure are redeemed by
the Atonement of Him who died that we
might live tho' we were dead, and living
in Him might never die! I condole
with Mary & Walter, and weep with all.
You did not tell me what you would
need. If possible I will go to Provo on
Monday. I am overwhelmed with duties but
I trust in God for strength. God bless you all
Lovingly I am your bro. J.F.S.

Joseph F. to Martha Ann, 26 July 1902 (p. 2), copy found in Joseph F.'s letterpress copybooks under that date.

The innocent & pure are redeemed by the Attonement of Him who died that we might live tho' we were dead—and living in Him might never die! I condoll with Mary & Walter,[41] and weep with all.

You did not tell me what you would need— If possible I will go to Provo—on Monday.[42] I am overwhelmed with duties, but I trust in God for strength.[43] God bless you all

Lovingly I am your bro Joseph F.—

JOSEPH F. TO MARTHA ANN, 24 DECEMBER 1903

Dec. 24th 3[44]

My Sister Martha Ann Harris
Dear Sister Martha:—

I send you herewith my cheque No. 30. for $10.00 as a Christmas gift. I am sorry it is so late in the day— but I have been driven with my work until I scarcely knew which way to turn, or whether I was standing on my heels or head.

I wish you a merry Christmas and a happy, prosperous New Year, and greatly improved health. We are all about as usual— Some have colds, more or less severe. Aunt Edna[45] has a touch of Sciatica.[46] And I am getting old.[47] Not in my feelings, but physically. My spirit still seems young and willing but the flesh is weak.[48]

With love and best wishes to all I am your affectionate brother
Jos. F. Smith

41. Mary Emily Harris and her husband, Walter Sutton Corbett. See biographical register, "Corbett, Walter Sutton."
42. A Salt Lake City newspaper reported, "President Joseph F. Smith and Patriarch John Smith were in Provo today attending the funeral of Miss Mamie Corbett, their grand-niece." "News from Four States," *Salt Lake Telegram*, 29 July 1902, 2. See also Anthon H. Lund, journal, 29 July 1902. Joseph F. wrote, "I was at Provo on Monday attending the funeral of little Mary Corbett." Joseph F. to Josephine [Parkes] Harris, 30 July 1902.
43. Joseph F. was "overwhelmed with duties" as he participated in a special conference for Scandinavian Saints in Brigham City, Box Elder County, on Sunday, 27 July 1902. See "Conference of Scandinavians," *Deseret News*, 28 July 1902, 1. Some four thousand people gathered for the conference that concluded with a "Sacred Band Concert" on Sunday evening. Joseph F. and other Church leaders departed Brigham City at 11:00 p.m. and arrived in Salt Lake City at 2:00 a.m. on Monday morning, the day of the funeral. See Anthon H. Lund, journal, 27 July 1902.
44. From Joseph F.'s letterpress copybooks; original not extant.
45. Edna Lambson.
46. Sciatica is a medical condition generally caused by a herniated disk that presses a nerve root. The pain is usually felt from the lower back down the leg.
47. Joseph F. celebrated his sixty-fifth birthday on 13 November 1903.
48. See Matthew 26:1.

JOSEPH F. TO MARTHA ANN, 8 FEBRUARY 1904

Feb. 8th 1904[49]

Martha Ann Harris
Provo, Utah Co.

My Dear Sister Martha:—
I received this morning, too late for trains, your letters— telling of the death and of the burrial of our Dear little Martha Corbitt.[50] The loss of another little girl is a sad, sad loss to poor Mary and her husband. They have our most sincere and heartfelt sympathy in their lamentable bereavement. I hope the comforting thought will fill their hearts with joy— that she "is not dead but sleepeth,"[51] and will come forth in the morning of the First Resurrection clothed with immortal glory. "Suffer little children to come unto me, and forbid them not"[52] was the loving admonition of the Son of God, "for of such is the Kingdom of Heaven."[53] They must indeed remember that "God giveth and taketh away"[54]—and they are bound to sayin their hearts, "blessed be the name of the Lord."[55] God bless and comfort them and you and make you all strong to bear the grief you all must feel for the temporal loss of one of our number. I sent you **[p. 2]** a telegram this morning as soon as I could, after receiving your letters, to let you know that we did not know soon enough to get ready and catch the morning train.

I am sorry that such a gloom should fall upon us, just on the eve of Father's birthday.[56] as it will sadden all hearts. Cousin Joseph of Lamoni,[57] Iowa has sent his eldest son, Frederick M.[58] to be with us tomorrow evening in the celebration of the 104th Anniversary of Fathers birth.[59]

We were in hopes that you and the children would be with us tomorrow. And we still hope you may. If I could learn that you were coming, and at what time we would meet you at the Depot. We should know what train you may come by.

Our little David J.[60] has been very sick with La grippe[61]—but is now turning for the better

49. From Joseph F.'s letterpress copybooks; original not extant.
50. Daughter of Mary Emily Harris and Walter Sutton Corbett.
51. Matthew 9:24.
52. Mark 10:14.
53. Mark 10:14.
54. See Job 1:21.
55. See Job 1:21.
56. Hyrum Smith was born on 9 February 1800.
57. Joseph Smith III, Joseph F. and Martha Ann's cousin and oldest son of Joseph Smith Jr. At this time the RLDS Church was headquartered in Lamoni, Decatur County, Iowa.
58. Frederick Madison Smith was serving as a counselor in the RLDS Church's First Presidency and would later become President of the RLDS Church on 5 May 1918 after his father, Joseph Smith III, died.
59. The celebration was held on 9 February 1904: "This being the anniversary of Patriarch Hyrum Smith's birthday. The Smith family had a reunion at the Beehive house. Frederik Smith was there. There was much entertaining matter on the program—comic and seris. The spinster's convention was a laughable farce. 15 of the Smith sisters acted. 'Oh that manifesto' was sung with much gusto. Frederik Smith spoke well. President Smith closed with a fine testimony." Anthon Lund, journal, 9 February 1904.
60. Joseph F.'s grandson.
61. *La grippe* was a French term commonly used to describe various types of influenza.

Our Minerva,[62] who was married to Matthew Miller last April—has a beautiful boy,[63] who weighed 8½ lbs. at his birth. It happened on Saturday Feb. 6th at 12.35p.m.

May the Lord bless and comfort you all— and help Mary to bear her burden of grief is my most earnest prayer. I am affectionately your brother Joseph F.—

JOSEPH F. TO MARTHA ANN, 25 JULY 1904

July 25. 1904[64]
Marth Ann Harris
Provo City, Utah Co.

My Dear Sister:—

Your letter of the 20th inst. came duly to hand. (on the 22d inst.) I went that day to Richmond, Cache Co. to attend the ceremony of laying the Corner Stone of the Richmond Tabernacle.[65] And I returned last evening. Lucy M.[66] is just getting over the Mumps. and now her three little brothers, Andrew,[67] Jesse,[68] and Fielding[69] have taken the desease. So that Aunt Alice is having her hands full just now. I was sorry about John's[70] Sickness, I sincerely hope he is better, and will soon be well. [**p. 2**] The enlargement of the liver is a very serious ailment. And the lungs are also vital organs and it is a serious thing to have any of these parts of the body deseased. But I hope he will soon be all right. He shall have my faith and prayers.

I am only happy and well pleased that you have the roofs repaired[71] over your heads and that once more you are sheltered <alike> from the sun and the rain. And I can only feel gratitude to God that he has blessed me with the means to do it.

With love to all. and especially to John and the girls—and prayer for you and Wm I am you Brother, Jos. F. Smith

---

62. Joseph F. and Sarah Ellen Richards's daughter.
63. Joseph F.'s grandson.
64. From Joseph F.'s letterpress copybooks; original not extant.
65. The Benson Stake Tabernacle was built in Richmond, Cache County, Utah, between 1902 and 1904. A detailed description of the building is found in Heber J. Grant, "Favorite Hymns," *Improvement Era*, June 1914, 781. A list of items discovered in the cornerstone is found in the "Benson Stake Tabernacle Collection," Annie Clark Tanner Western Americana Collection, Special Collections Department, J. Willard Marriott Library, University of Utah, Salt Lake City. The building was condemned after an earthquake on 30 August 1962 and demolished three months later.
66. Lucy Mack Smith (born 1890).
67. Andrew Kimball Smith (born 1893).
68. Jesse Kimball Smith (born 1896).
69. Fielding Kimball Smith (born 1900). See biographical register, "Smith, Fielding Kimball."
70. John Fielding Harris (born 1872).
71. Joseph F. noted, "1904 June 1st to 30. Paid E. D. Partridge for shingling and repairing my Sister, Martha Ann. Harris' house." Joseph F. Account Book, 1904–7. Additionally, Joseph F. wrote Partridge, "I send you here with my check for $78.50 (no. 40) as pr bill rendered and I would like it if you would kindly make out a bill to me for the whole job, specifying the roofs shingled, stairs repaired, etc. and oblige your brother in the cause. Jos. F. Smith" Joseph F. to Bishop E. D. Partridge, 22 June 1904.

JOSEPH F. TO MARTHA ANN, 23 DECEMBER 1904

Salt Lake City
Dec. 23d 1904[72]
Martha Ann Harris
Provo Utah Co.

My Dear Sister Martha:—

Please accept the enclosed check for $10^{00} as a small remembrance for Christmas 1904.

I hope you will all have good health and good apitites and good digestion, and good cheer, and excellent Spirits for the one great Christmas day of the year now drawing to a close, in which the birth of Gods own Son, the Redeemer and of God's younger[73] Son, Joseph<the Restorer>, will be celebrated on the self same day.[74]

I wish you all the compliments of the Season. And all joine me in love to you and the children.

I congratulate William[75] on the Irish victory[76] of his darling Chum,[77] O.W.P.!

Affectionately yours
Jos. F. Smith

JOSEPH F. TO MARTHA ANN, 23 JANUARY 1905

Jan. 23^d 1905[78]

My Dear Sister—
Martha Ann Harris. Provo.

The sad word has just reached me over the wire[79] that our precious, beloved Mercy,[80] passed to the reward of the good and true at 2 o'clock today. It was not all together unexpected to me, for after my visits to her yesterday, I was strongly impressed that her mortal end seemed all

72. From Joseph F.'s letterpress copybooks; original not extant.
73. Latter-day Saint teachings identify Jesus Christ as the firstborn spirit child of God and state that every human being is a son or daughter of God. See Corbin Volluz, "Jesus Christ as Elder Brother," *BYU Studies* 45, no. 2 (2006): 141–58.
74. Joseph Smith Jr., Joseph F. and Martha Ann's uncle, was born on 23 December 1805. In 1904, 23 December was a Friday and 25 December (Christmas) was a Sunday. Apparently, the decision was made to celebrate both events on Sunday.
75. William Jasper Harris.
76. Most likely a reference to an unknown horse-racing event.
77. According to family tradition, William owned "a beautiful white riding horse." Carole Call King, "History of William Jasper Harris, 1841–1921" (paper presented at monthly meeting of the Daughters of Utah Pioneers, copy in the editors' possession), 2.
78. From Joseph F.'s letterpress copybooks; original not extant.
79. Apparently, Joseph F. received a telegram informing him of the event.
80. Mercy Ann Harris (born 1874) died on 23 January 1905.

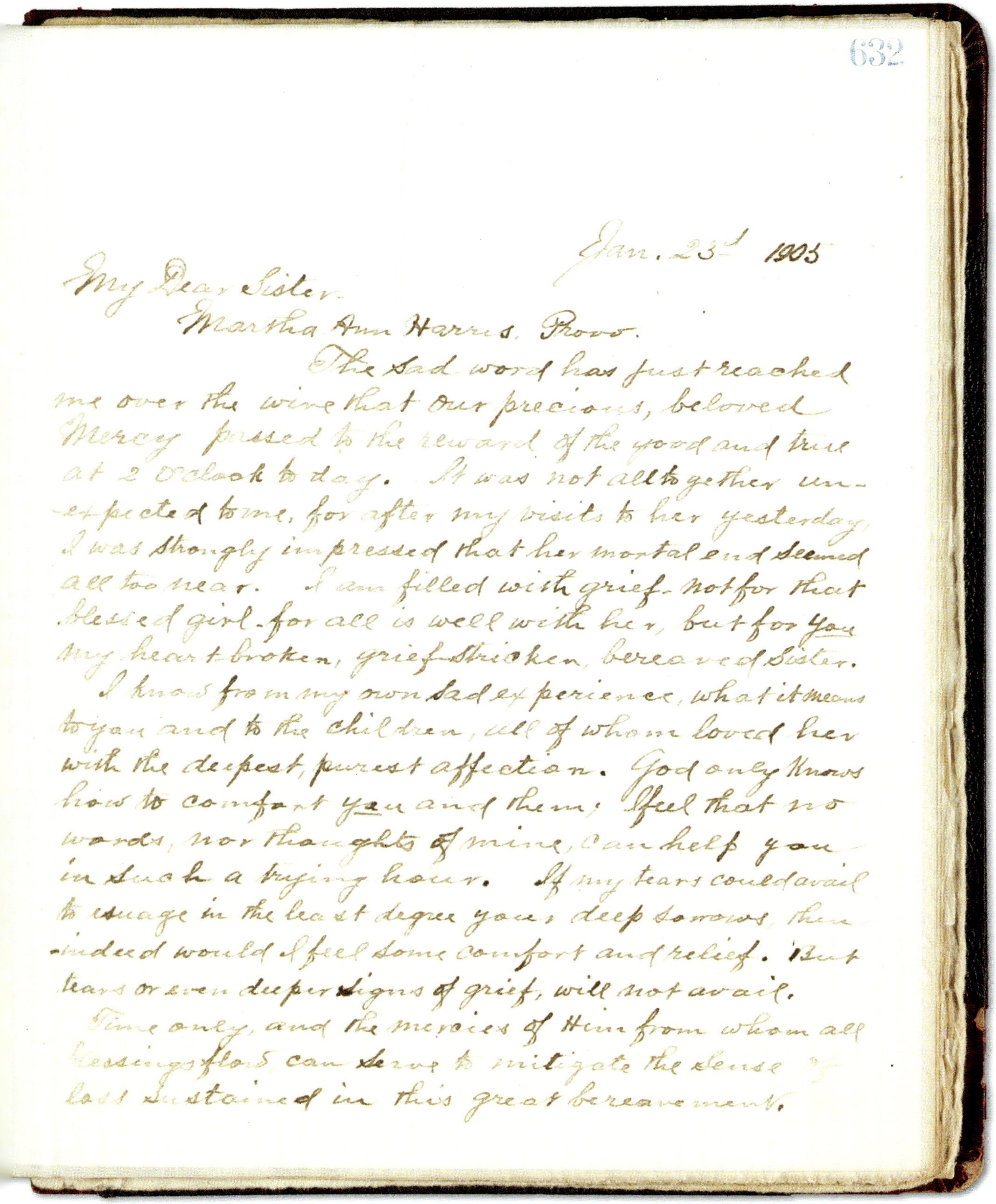

632

Jan. 23rd 1905

My Dear Sister.

Martha Ann Harris. Provo.

The sad word has just reached me over the wire that our precious, beloved Mercy passed to the reward of the good and true at 2 O'clock to day. It was not alltogether unexpected to me, for after my visits to her yesterday, I was strongly impressed that her mortal end seemed all too near. I am filled with grief-not for that blessed girl-for all is well with her, but for you my heart-broken, grief-stricken, bereaved Sister.

I know from my own sad experience, what it means to you and to the children, all of whom loved her with the deepest, purest affection. God only knows how to comfort you and them; I feel that no words, nor thoughts of mine, can help you in such a trying hour. If my tears could avail to esuage in the least degree your deep sorrows, then indeed would I feel some comfort and relief. But tears or even deeper signs of grief, will not avail.

Time only, and the mercies of Him from whom all blessings flow, can serve to mitigate the sense of loss sustained in this great bereavement.

Joseph F. to Martha Ann, 23 January 1905 (p. 1), copy found in Joseph F.'s letterpress copybooks under that date.

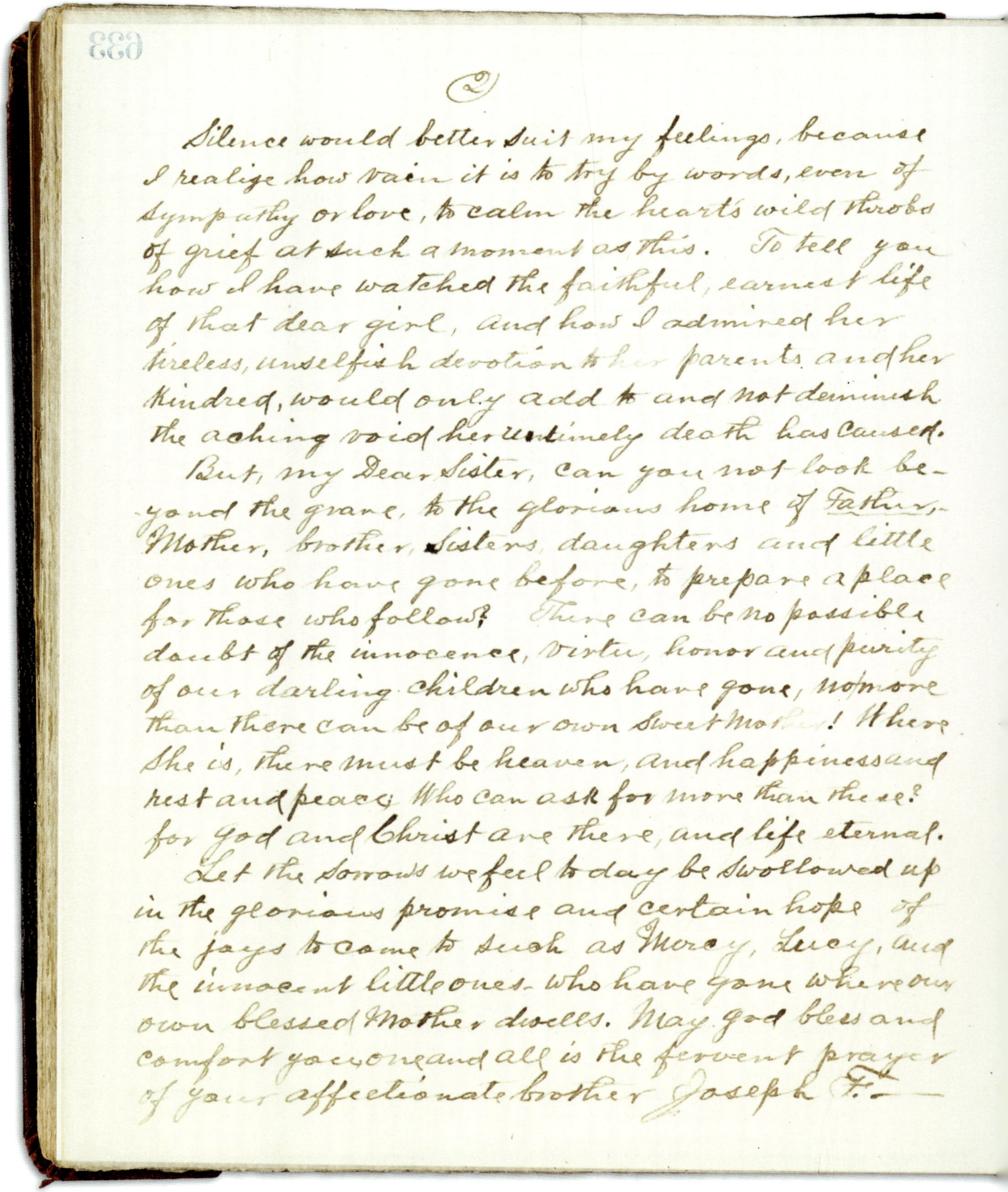
633

(2)

Silence would better suit my feelings, because I realize how vain it is to try by words, even of sympathy or love, to calm the heart's wild throbs of grief at such a moment as this. To tell you how I have watched the faithful, earnest life of that dear girl, and how I admired her tireless, unselfish devotion to her parents and her kindred, would only add to and not diminish the aching void her untimely death has caused.

But, my Dear Sister, can you not look beyond the grave, to the glorious home of Father, Mother, brother, sisters, daughters and little ones who have gone before, to prepare a place for those who follow? There can be no possible doubt of the innocence, virtu, honor and purity of our darling children who have gone, no more than there can be of our own sweet Mother! Where she is, there must be heaven, and happiness and rest and peace; Who can ask for more than these? for God and Christ are there, and life eternal.

Let the sorrows we feel today be swollowed up in the glorious promise and certain hope of the joys to come to such as Mercy, Lucy, and the innocent little ones who have gone where our own blessed Mother dwells. May God bless and comfort you, one and all is the fervent prayer of your affectionate brother Joseph F.—

Joseph F. to Martha Ann, 23 January 1905 (p. 2), copy found in Joseph F.'s letterpress copybooks under that date.

to near. I am filled with grief—not for that blessed girl—for all is well with her, but for <u>you</u> my heart broken, grief stricken, bereaved Sister.

I know from my own sad experience, what it means to you and to the children, all of whom loved her with the deepest, purest affection. God only knows how to comfort <u>you</u> and them; I feel that no words, nor thoughts of mine, can help you in such a trying hour. If my tears could avail to esuage in the least degree your deep sorrows, then indeed would I feel some comfort and relief. But tears or even deeper signs of grief, will not avail.

Time only, and the mercies of Him "from whom all blessings flow,"[81] can serve to mitigate the sense of loss sustained in this great bereavement. [**p. 2**] Silence would better suit my feelings, because I realize how vain it is to try by words, even of sympathy or love, to calm the heart's wild throbs of grief at such a moment as this. To tell you how I have watched the faithful, earnest life of that dear girl, and how I admired her tireless, unselfish devotion to her parents and her kindred, would only add to and not deiminish the aching void her u[◊]timely death has caused.

But, my Dear Sister, can you not look beyond the grave, to the glorious home of <u>Father</u>,— Mother, brother, Sisters, daughters, and little ones who have gone before, to prepare a place for those who follow? There can be no possible doubt of the innocence, virtu, honor and purity of our darling children who have gone,[82] no/more than there can be of our own Sweet Mother![83] Where she is, there must be heaven, and happiness and rest and peace; Who can ask for more than these? For God and Christ are there, and life eternal.

Let the sorrows we feel today be swallowed up in the glorious promise and certain hope of the joys to come to such as Mercy, Lucy, and the innocent little ones—who have gone where our own blessed Mother dwells. May God bless and comfort you, one and all is the fervent prayer of your affectionate brother Joseph F.—

JOSEPH F. TO MARTHA ANN, 2 APRIL 1905

April 2nd. 1905.[84]

Mrs. Martha Ann Harris,
Provo City, Utah Co.,
Utah.

My Dear Sister:—

81. Perhaps an allusion to the hymn "Praise God, from Whom All Blessings Flow," written by Thomas Ken in 1674. The hymn was part of Latter-day Saint worship beginning at least in 1840, when it was printed in *A Collection of Sacred Hymns: For the Church of Jesus Christ of Latter-day Saints, in Europe* (Manchester: W. R. Thomas, Spring Gardens, 1840), 149.
82. By 23 January 1905, Joseph F. had lost nine children and Martha Ann had lost two children, Lucy Smith Harris (died 1903) and this child, Mercy Ann Harris (died 1905), mentioned in the last paragraph of this letter.
83. Mary Fielding Smith, who had died in 1852.
84. From Joseph F.'s letterpress copybooks; original not extant. Joseph F. was sixty-six, and Martha Ann was sixty-three. This letter was typed with blue ink.

Your letter of February 19th., over a month ago, was duly received and read with great interest. After reading it, I handed it over to Aunt Julina[85] to read and she laid it aside and it escaped my attention for quite a long while; I afterwards found it lying on the dresser, and I remembered that I had not acknowledged the receipt of it. You will remember you wrote it soon after you returned from a short visit with us. you reported that on reaching home, you "found William[86] nearly laid up with a swelled foot and a very bad cold". As I have never heard anything more from him since, I hope he recovered from those ailments without much delay, and is now enjoying his usual health. I hope your strength held out to the completion of the work you found awaiting your return home. I am sorry you have so much to do.

You would scarcely believe that Wesley[87] is still only slowly recovering his health. He has had one of the most tenacious attacks of Lagrippe[88] that I ever witnessed, but he is slowly overcoming it. Our little Emily[89] has also had quite a heavy attack of the same disease and is still coughing very severely. Julina has also been laid up with a very bad cold which threatened to devalop into Lagrippe; but a few days of quiet, taken in time, I think prevented a more **[p. 2]** serious attack.

Whenever memory recalls the dear name of our beloved Mercy,[90] we cannot help feeling the shades of sadness which come over us, and still feel as though it was scarcely possible for one so good and true to have been called home so suddenly in her very youth. She was indeed a lovely girl and no one can possibly doubt that all is well with her. Now in the companionship of her precious sister, Lucy,[91] and their martyr Grandfather and Grandmother,[92] who were there awaiting their arrival on the other side.

It has now been over a month since the death and burial of Grandfather Lambson.[93] His son, Alfred,[94] returned home soon after his father's funeral.

85. Julina Lambson.
86. William Jasper Harris.
87. Elias Wesley Smith, Joseph F. and Julina Lambson's son, born on 21 April 1886.
88. *La grippe* was a French term for influenza.
89. Emily Jane Smith, Joseph F. and Julina Lambson's daughter, born on 11 September 1888.
90. Martha Ann's daughter Mercy Ann Harris died on 23 January 1905 at the age of thirty. A Salt Lake City newspaper reported, "Provo, Jan. 24.—Mrs. Mercy Dennis, wife of John F. Dennis of Marysvale, died last evening in this city at the home of her parents, Mr. and Mrs. William J. Harris, after about two weeks' severe illness resulting from childbirth. Mrs. Dennis was born in this city [Salt Lake City] thirty-one years ago." "Death of Mrs. Dennis," *Salt Lake Herald*, 25 January 1905, 3.
91. Martha Ann's daughter Lucy Smith Harris died on 26 July 1903. While an obituary indicated that she "died suddenly from heart disease," a later family history indicated that she died during childbirth. See Carole Call King, "History of Martha Ann Smith Harris, 1841–1923" (unpublished manuscript in editors' possession), 5. Her funeral service, at which Joseph F. spoke, was held on 31 July; see "Provo: Funeral of Mrs. Simmons," *Deseret Evening News*, 1 August 1903, 7. She was married to Jonathan Simmons and was living in Mammoth, Utah, at the time. Martha Ann raised Lucy's two surviving children. At the time of this letter, Edna Mae was six years old and John Arthur was four. See Joseph F. to Martha Ann, 26 July 1902 and 10 April 1907, herein.
92. Hyrum Smith and Mary Fielding.
93. Joseph F.'s father-in-law Alfred Boaz Lambson Sr., father of Edna and Julina, died on 26 February 1905 at the age of eighty-four. See biographical register, "Lambson, Alfred Boaz, Sr."
94. Alfred Boaz Lambson Jr., brother-in-law of Joseph F. See biographical register, "Lambson, Alfred Boaz, Jr."

Four of my boys, Alvin, George, Willard and Chase, expect to start on their missions about the 19th. of April.[95] their absence will make quite a hole in the family for the time that they may be absent. Alvin's and George's wives and little ones are all in excellent health and spirits. You will not be surprised to learn that on the 29th. instant Alice May Sant gave birth to a nice little boy,[96] and on the morning of the 30th. instant, our Melissa followed suit in a royal style.[97] Both of them are rejoicing in the posession of their new-comers.

These are days of house cleaning and turmoil among all my folks: but the hottest fight is being made upon me by the dastardly apostate and degenerate son of my life-long companion and friend Prest. George Q. Cannon.[98] He has exhausted his vocabulary of invective and abusive slanders upon me and my associates. What the end may be, we cannot just now forsee; but we know that all will be well with Zion.

With kind love to all from all here, I am,

Your Affectionate Brother, Joseph F. Smith

JOSEPH F. TO MARTHA ANN, 22 NOVEMBER 1905

Nov. 22d 1905[99]

My own Dear Sister Martha

Yesterday morning at about 2 o'clock My precious Mamies Sweet little boy passed into the great beyond from whence he so recently came.[100] He was a most inteligant, attractive, beautiful little man. so much so that he drew every body to him and fixed himself in the very centre of all our hearts. He was about 5 months old, and sat in his high chair at the table giving his precious Mamma and others pleanty to do. We are all broken up. To my beloved and noble Mammie death could not have come in a more cruel way. He was her very hope, joy and life! And I feel

95. Alvin Fielding Smith (thirty years old), George Carlos Smith (twenty-three), Willard Richards Smith (twenty), and Heber Chase Smith (twenty-three) left for England on 19 April 1905. From there they were assigned by mission president Heber J. Grant to separate mission areas in the European Mission. Alvin was assigned to London, England; George to Sundsvall, Sweden; Chase to Cheltenham, England; and Willard to Trondheim, Norway.

96. Alice May Rich Smith was born on 11 October 1877 to Alice Ann Kimball and David Patten Rich. After her father died and her mother married Joseph F., Alice was adopted into the Smith family and had her surname changed from Rich to Smith. She married Robert Roscoe Sant on 16 June 1900 and gave birth to Robert Smith Sant on 29 March 1905. See biographical register, "Rich, Alice May" and "Sant, Robert Smith."

97. Edna Melissa Smith, wife of John Fife Bowman, gave birth to Richard Smith Bowman on 30 March 1905. See biographical register, "Bowman, Richard Smith."

98. Franklin Jenne Cannon publicly renounced the Latter-day Saint faith in January 1905 and was excommunicated in March 1905. As editor of the *Salt Lake Tribune*, he wrote scathing articles condemning Joseph F., Reed Smoot, and other Church leaders. In 1911 he published a highly critical exposé titled "Under the Prophet in Utah." See Kenneth W. Godfrey, "Frank J. Cannon: Declension in the Kingdom," in *Differing Visions: Dissenters in Mormon History*, ed. Roger D. Launius and Linda Thatcher (Urbana: University of Illinois Press, 1998), 241–61. See also biographical register, "Cannon, Franklin Jenne."

99. From Joseph F.'s letterpress copybooks; original not extant.

100. Mamie is a nickname for Mary Sophronia Smith. She married Alfred William Peterson. Their son Alfred William Peterson Jr. (born on 25 May 1905) died on 21 November 1905 at six months old. See biographical register, "Peterson, Alfred William, Jr."

like one who stands within reach of her he loves more than his own life, just falling into the yawning abyss of death but is utterly powerless to save her! O! my soul how weak is man!

We were all so completely overwhelmed all day yesterday that we could not collect our thoughts. I telephoned Sister Smoot[101] last night, asking her to send you the sad news [**p. 2**] which she promised to do. I did not send word to Jerusha,[102] nor any any of our kindred. I may go to Brigham[103] next Saturday and if I do I will perhaps see her. She was here, in the city, a short time ago, but was in such a hurry as usual she could not make us more than a moments call.

There is a great deal of sickness here at this time. Our Calvin[104] is quite sick. We do not know just what ails him. We hope it is nothing worse than a severe cold and indigestion. The Dr. feared he was taking typhoid fever. But we hope not. All our little ones and some of the big ones have had and are having colds and hard coughs. I hope you and yours are all well. I feel ashamed that I have been to Provo two or three times since Artie had her little baby,[105] and I have not yet seen it. Give all the children our kindest love.

I saw John[106] and family at Saltair[107] the other day. They were all well. John weighs over two hundred pounds.

Well, Martha—we burried our little treasure to day—and our homes and hearts are empty for the want of him! The Lord have mercy on my Mamie! With love to all— I am affectionately your brother Joseph F.—

JOSEPH F. TO MARTHA ANN, 3 JANUARY 1906

January 3^{d} 1906[108]

Martha Ann Smith Harris
Provo, Utah Co.

My Dear Sister Martha:—

I send you herewith my cheque No. 3. for \$15$^{\underline{00}}$ as a small remembrance for your Christmas and New Year gifts.

101. Possibly Diana Tanner Eldredge, the eldest living widow of Abraham O. Smoot at this time.
102. Jerusha Smith.
103. Brigham City, Box Elder County, Utah, is about sixty miles north of Salt Lake City.
104. Calvin Schwartz Smith was born on 29 May 1890 to Joseph F. and Mary Taylor Schwartz. See biographical register, "Smith, Calvin Schwartz."
105. Martha Artimissa Harris, wife of Harry Walter Startup, gave birth to Naomi Startup on 10 August 1905. See biographical register, "Startup, Naomi."
106. Likely refers to John Smith, half brother of Martha Ann and Joseph F.
107. Saltair was a popular resort located about eighteen miles west of Salt Lake City on the Great Salt Lake. It was built in 1893 and was co-owned by the Church and the Salt Lake and Los Angeles Railroad Company.
108. From Joseph F.'s letterpress copybooks; original not extant. Joseph F. was sixty-seven, and Martha Ann was sixty-four.

I have been away from hem for over two weeks, hence the delay.[109] While it is too late to wish you a "merry Christmas" it is yet in time to wish you a "Happy New Year," and as many of them as you can desire. I am well, and the family are enjoying usual good health

Joseph Albert[110] is here with us this morning, he stayed with us last night, and is going over to Saltair Beach this morning.[111] He is well. The folks here all joine in love to you and all the family. Give my love to the girls,[112] and my best wishes to William.[113]

God bless you my sister Martha. We are hastening on to that time when we shall cross the dark river from whence no traveller returns, but on the other side our loved ones will welcome us I hope. I am your brother Joseph F.——

P.S. Do you have postal delivery—and if you do what is your Number and proper address?[114] Please let me know— Affectionately, Joseph F.[115]

JOSEPH F. TO MARTHA ANN, 1 FEBRUARY 1906

Feb. 1$^{\underline{st}}$ 1906[116]

Martha Ann Harris
214 South 3$^{\underline{d}}$ West St. Provo.

My Dear Sister Martha.

Edna[117] informed me that you had broken you <u>Truss</u>[118]—and had to send for another. I send you herewith my cheque No. 17. for $\$5^{\underline{00}}$ to help you out on your loss.

109. Joseph F. and other Church leaders had just returned from dedicating a granite monument in Vermont to celebrate the one hundredth anniversary of the birth of Joseph Smith Jr. See Richard Neitzel Holzapfel and Paul H. Peterson, "New Photographs of Joseph F. Smith's Centennial Memorial Trip to Vermont, 1905," *BYU Studies* 39, no. 4 (2000): 107–14. For a discussion of the effort to celebrate the Prophet's birthday in Utah, see Richard Neitzel Holzapfel and Ronald L. Fox, "Photographs of the Tabernacle in 1905," *BYU Studies* 57, no. 2 (2018): 52–70.
110. Joseph Albert Harris.
111. Nancy D. McCormick and John S. McCormick, *Saltair* (Salt Lake City, UT: University of Utah Press, 1985).
112. Martha Ann's daughters. Ten days later, Joseph F. attended a stake conference in Provo where his niece Zina Christine Harris Furner was able to personally greet him, as noted in her journal: "I also attended afternoon meeting on Sunday. I listened to a fine sermon from Uncle Jos. F. Smith upon the experience of the recent journey East. After which I met him with loving greetings. I also met my dear Mother, Sisters Artie & Sarah & others of my kindred and friends. I introduced my boarder Silas Rowley, Thomas Allred & Walter Hilbert to Uncle Jos." Zina Christine Harris Furner, journal, 14 January 1906, in private possession.
113. William Jasper Harris.
114. Martha Ann apparently provided the mailing address of her home in Provo because, beginning with the next letter in this collection, Joseph F. used it. See Joseph F. to Martha Ann, 1 February 1906, herein.
115. Written upside down in the top margin.
116. From Joseph F.'s letterpress copybooks; original not extant.
117. Possibly Edna Lambson.
118. A hernia truss is a beltlike apparatus used to prevent a hernia from enlarging. *Oxford English Dictionary*, "truss."

I am sorry you need to use such a thing, but I suppose we must put up with the ills we have and avoid as far as possible flying to others that we know not of.[119]

I think you have ills enough of your own, without any of my folks going there with theirs. I refer to Edna and Annie.[120] However I am sorry for Annie and hope she will soon be herself again. I hope you get your Semi-Weekly News[121] all right. David Allen Cousin Bathshebas grand son, was killed yesterday by his team.[122] We are all well— Affectionately your brother Joseph F.——

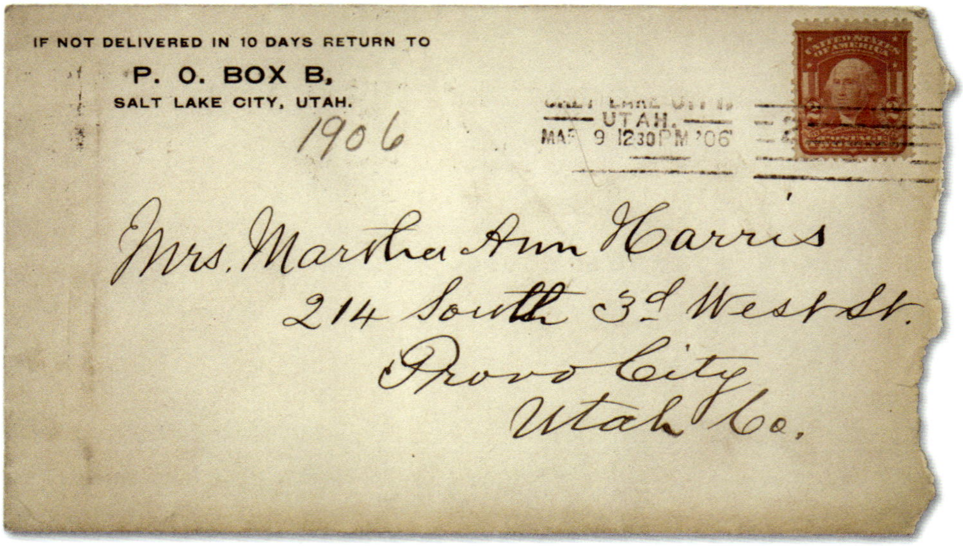

Joseph F. to Martha Ann, 8 March 1906 (envelope)

JOSEPH F. TO MARTHA ANN, 8 MARCH 1906

Mar. 8th 1906[123]

My Dear Sister—
Martha Ann Harris.

We got the word to day that Cousin Ellen F. Burton,[124] died at Ogden this morning. And the funeral will be held in their ward meeting house on Sunday next at 12-o'clock.

119. An allusion to Shakespeare's *Hamlet*, act 3, scene 1: "But that the dread of something after death, / The undiscover'd country from whose bourn / No traveller returns, puzzles the will / And makes us rather bear those ills we have / Than fly to others that we know not of."

120. Edna Lambson. The name Annie likely refers to Alice Ann Kimball. Both were wives of Joseph F.

121. The *Deseret Semi-Weekly News* was published in Salt Lake City between 1865 and 1922. Apparently, Joseph F. provided Martha Ann a subscription to this newspaper.

122. David Robert Allen Jr. was the grandson of Bathsheba Smith. As indicated, he died on 31 January 1906. See biographical register, "Allen, David Robert, Jr."

123. Written on letterhead from Zion's Savings Bank. Joseph F. served on the board of trustees for Zion's Savings Bank.

124. Ellen Fielding, wife of William W. Burton and first cousin to Joseph F. and Martha Ann, died of heart disease at the age of sixty-five. See "Mrs. Burton Dead," *Ogden Standard Examiner*, 8 March 1906, 6; and "Impressive Obsequies Held," *Deseret Evening News*, 12 March 1906, 3. See biographical register, "Fielding, Ellen."

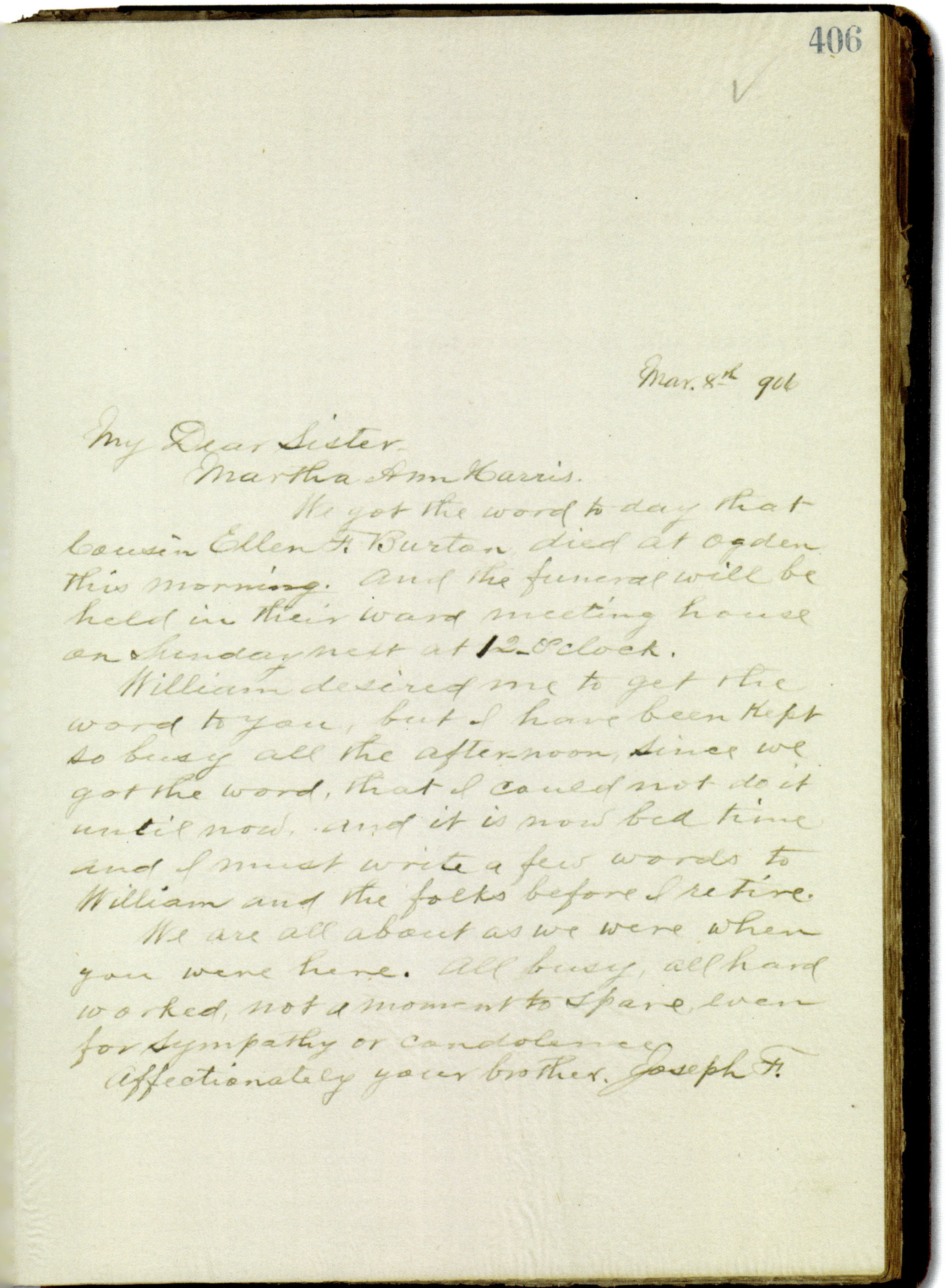

406

Mar. 8th 906

My Dear Sister
Martha Ann Harris.
We got the word to day that Cousin Ellen F. Burton, died at Ogden this morning. And the funeral will be held in their ward meeting house on Sunday next at 12 O'clock.

William desired me to get the word to you, but I have been kept so busy all the after-noon, since we got the word, that I could not do it until now, and it is now bed time and I must write a few words to William and the folks before I retire.

We are all about as we were when you were here. All busy, all hard worked, not a moment to spare, even for sympathy or condolence.

Affectionately your brother, Joseph F.

Joseph F. to Martha Ann, 8 March 1906, copy found in Joseph F.'s letterpress copybooks under that date.

William[125] desired me to get the word to you, but I have been kept so busy all the afternoon, since we got the word, that I could not do it until now, and it is now bed time and I must write a few words to William[126] and the folks before I retire.

We are all about as we were when you were here. All busy, all hard worked, not a moment to spare, even for sympathy or condolence.

Affectionately your brother, Joseph F.

JOSEPH F. TO MARTHA ANN, 26 NOVEMBER 1906

Nov. 26th 1906[127]

Martha Ann Harris.
214 South Third West St.
Provo, Utah Co. Utah.

My own Dear Sister Martha Ann:—

"grass" is a little short with me just now, as I have had to pay "\$300.00 and costs," for my last baby.[128] But I thought I would send you the enclosed \$5 00/100 bill, No B. 14534932/ which may help out a little for your thanksgiving dinner on Thursday next.

I hope this will reach you safely and find you well, to gether with all the rest of the family. We are all usually well. Aunt Julina[129] is still going on the rush, no time for anything only work—Work, WORK! This is the case with all my precious Mammas. They have mighty little time for play or rest. But the Lord is good to them and to me. Four days ago I did not know but I would to day be a prisoner in the county jail—and for What? Because in my old age I have had a son born to me![130] But I am free from prison and from bonds. Thank God. Your brother Joseph F.

125. William W. Burton.
126. William W. Burton.
127. From Joseph F.'s letterpress copybooks; original not extant.
128. Joseph F.'s sixth wife, Mary Taylor Schwartz, gave birth to Royal Grant Smith on 21 May 1906. See biographical register, "Smith, Royal Grant."
129. Julina Lambson.
130. Joseph F. had married each of his plural wives before the 1890 Manifesto and continued his marital relationships after 1890. This was in accordance with the view held by most Latter-day Saints—a view accommodated by federal officials at the time—that the Manifesto signaled the process to end new plural marriages but did not require husbands to abandon their plural families begun before 1890. However, when Joseph F. had a child by his wife Mary Taylor Schwartz in May 1906 (see note 128), he was charged with "unlawful cohabitation." Although the jail sentence was waived, he nevertheless was fined three hundred dollars.

JOSEPH F. TO MARTHA ANN, 24 DECEMBER 1906

Dec. 24th 1906[131]

Martha Ann Harris
214 South 3d West Street
Provo, Utah Co. Utah—

Dear Sister Martha:

We are all usually well, except Coulsen,[132] who is in the Hospital,[133] having been operated upon for Apendicitis—

I wish you a merry Christmas, at least to the extend of the enclosed $500 bill Numbered A 62548728/—which I hope will reach you in time for dinner

Affectionately your brother (in great haste)

Joseph F. Smith

JOSEPH F. TO MARTHA ANN, 8 MARCH 1907

Mar. 8th 1907[134]

Martha Ann Harris:—
214 South 3d West St. Provo.

My own Dear Sister Martha Ann.

I have not heard from you for what seemes to me, a long time. Perhaps I have neglected to write to you as often as I should. Last month your allowance was raise from $12.50 to $1500 pr. month, you know "every little helps." It will be $15—hereafter.[135]

I hope you are well, and that all the children and "little ones,"[136] are also well. How is Sarah[137] getting along? I hope she will keep well. Also Artie and baby and husband.[138] Nor do I forget Zina and her little ones,[139] nor Mary and hers.[140] Nor do I forget the dear departed—Lucy and "Mertie"[141] nor any of the boys and theirs. The Lord bless them all, and open their way.

131. From Joseph F.'s letterpress copybooks; original not extant.
132. Charles Coulson Rich Smith is the son of Alice Ann Kimball, Joseph F.'s fifth wife, from her first marriage to David Patten Rich. See biographical register, "Rich, Charles Coulson."
133. Located in Salt Lake City, the Dr. W. H. Groves LDS Hospital opened in 1905.
134. From Joseph F.'s letterpress copybooks; original not extant. Joseph F. was sixty-eight, and Martha Ann was sixty-five.
135. When Joseph F. began helping Martha Ann with a monthly check is unknown.
136. Martha Ann's grandchildren.
137. Sarah Lovina Harris.
138. Artie is a nickname for Martha Artimissa Harris. She married Harry Walter Startup, and they had one child, Naomi Startup, at this time. See biographical register, "Startup, Harry Walter."
139. Zina Christine Harris had four children at this time.
140. Mary Emily Harris had eleven children at this time.
141. Lucy Smith Harris died on 26 July 1903. Mertie is a nickname for Mercy Ann Harris, who died on 23 January 1905. See Joseph F. to Martha Ann, 2 April 1905, herein.

I am about as usual, in health, but grow older each day. Aunts Julina, Sarah, Edna, Alice and Mary[142] are all usually well— They have commenced House cleaning, and I pity them. The children are all prety well. I have a dollar green back, all the cash in my pocket. I sent it to you. With love to all. I am affectionately your brother Joseph F. —

JOSEPH F. TO MARTHA ANN, 10 APRIL 1907

Apr. 10th 1907[143]

My Dear Sister
Martha Ann Harris:— Conference is over, and we are winding up the business connected with it. We have had a good conference.[144] The spirit of the Lord has been with us. I am hoarse yet from much speaking, but hope to be all right again soon.[145] I have been thinking about you and Dear Lucy's children.[146]

I feel it is too much for you to try to take care of them alone. And Even if you could and did succeed in doing so for a while, the moment you cannot do it any longer the children would have to do without you—or without your help.

Hyrum and Adelia[147] are childless, but they are young and able-bodied. The children are almost like their very own—Hyrum and Adelia—could and would love them as no strangers could. They would love them as their own dear sisters babes. Now I wish you would let them have the children to protect and raise. [**p. 2**]

There are many good reasons why you should consent to this, and why it would be best. Hyrum and his wife would take care of them and guard them against falling into the hands of their un-[◊◊] father, and some strange, heartless, loveless step-mother. You may live many years yet, so may I, but at our time of life, that is a matter of grave doubt. William[148] would be no help to you nor the children in your care for them. Without the labor, care, and anxiety incident to the keeping of the dear little children, your own life and health would be prolonged.

142. Joseph F. was married to five wives at this time: Julina Lambson, Sarah Ellen Richards, Edna Lambson, Alice Ann Kimball, and Mary Taylor Schwartz. Traditionally, family members who were not their own children addressed plural wives by the honorific title "Aunt." See biographical register, "Schwartz, Mary Taylor."

143. From Joseph F.'s letterpress copybooks; original not extant.

144. The 77th Annual General Conference was held on 5–7 April 1907 in Salt Lake City. Joseph F. and his counselors presented to the conference a response to questions raised during the Smoot hearings. See "An Address. The Church of Jesus Christ of Latter-day Saints," *Improvement Era*, May 1907, 481–95.

145. Joseph F. spoke several times during this historic conference, held in the Tabernacle on Temple Square in Salt Lake City. See *Seventy-Seventh Annual Conference of The Church of Jesus Christ of Latter-day Saints April 5, 6, 7* (Salt Lake City, UT: Deseret News Press, 1907), 1–9, 25, 39, and 118–19.

146. After Martha Ann's daughter Lucy Smith Harris died on 26 July 1903, Martha Ann raised Lucy's two surviving children; at the time of this letter, Edna Mae Simmons was eight years old and John Arthur Simmons was six. See Joseph F. to Martha Ann, 2 April 1905, herein. See also biographical register, "Simmons, Edna Mae" and "Simmons, John Arthur."

147. Hyrum Smith Harris and his wife, Delia Sarah Rebekah Twede. Joseph F. wrote them on the same day: "My Dear Nephew. I have just written to your mother about Lucy's little children. I would like you to read it. And I hope you and Dear Adelia will agree with my view as expressed in my letter to your mother." Joseph F. to Hyrum S. Harris, 10 April 1907.

148. William Jasper Harris.

And Hyrum, and Adelia would be most happy in taking care of them, and they would be most contented and happy with their own Uncle, their own Darling Mother's brother, and their Aunt Adelia.

Now Martha I know what a trial this will be to you, but it is wise counsel, and as I do not advise you very much—I hope you will see your way to do as I say.[149]

Affectionately your brother

Joseph F. Smith

JOSEPH F. TO MARTHA ANN, 16 JULY 1907

July 16th 1907[150]

My Dear Sister,

Martha S. Harris, Provo.

William J. called to see me this morning.[151] I listened for more than an hour to his recital of the story he had to tell.[152] To say the least I was surprised at the tale he told, and I expressed myself in terms which I think were unmistakable, and that even he could not fail to understand. I simply judged him by his own statements to me. He went away much dissatisfied and I believe much displeases but I only tried to do my duty as I understood it. He said he went to the place of business of the bishop[153] and told him deliberately three times over that he (the Bps.) was "a liar." And further that he did it intending to provoke him to a quarrel and violent excitement, "but he was too cowardly" to resent it by force <he said>. This conduct on the part of William I condemned. I told him it was not only wrong, but unchristian but he stoutly justified himself in it. He said he refused to "shake hands with the Bp." After an attempt was made to reconcile the trouble. That was also not only wrong, but foolish. He said "President John[154] advised him to drop it." This he refused to do, and [**p. 2**] condemned his course in [*illegible due to ink smear*] and

149. Martha Ann decided to raise these children in her home and did so until they were "grown and married." See King, "History of Martha Ann Smith Harris," 5.

150. From Joseph F.'s letterpress copybooks; original not extant. Unfortunately, the wet ink smeared when the copy was made, creating a long diagonal smudge from the top of page 2 through the middle of the letter. Pages 1, 3, and 4 are preserved in the letterpress copybook without any smudges.

151. William Jasper Harris Jr.

152. In 1881 William Jasper Harris Jr. raised another issue with his uncle. Joseph F. expressed, "In your letter you say, you have been 'robbed of your pay.'" Joseph F. to William Jasper Harris Jr., 9 November 1881. Joseph F. had promised to help him in this earlier situation.

153. William Jasper Harris Jr. was living in the Provo Second Ward in 1910. If he was there in 1907, then his bishop was Lars Lovendall Nelson, who had been called to serve in 1902 and was released in 1929. According to a city directory in 1904, Nelson was the deputy county treasurer. See *R. L. Polk & Co's Provo City and Utah County Directory, 1904–1905* (Salt Lake City, UT: R. L. Polk & Co., 1904), 138. However, by 1911 he was listed as a farmer in the local city directory. See *R. L. Polk & Co's Provo City and Utah County Directory, 1911* (Salt Lake City, UT: R. L. Port & Co., 1911), 158. Nelson died on 15 September 1933; see "Pay Tributes to L. L. Nelson," *Evening Herald*, 18 September 1933 [1, 3]. The other Provo bishops serving at the time were Ole H. Berg, bishop of the First Ward and a funeral director; Thomas N. Taylor, bishop of the Third Ward and the president of Farmers & Merchants Bank; Alfred L. Booth, bishop of the Fourth Ward and a local attorney-at-law; Albert Manwaring, bishop of the Fifth Ward and a barber; and Ralph Poulton, bishop of the Sixth Ward and an employee at the Bishop's Storehouse. See *R. L. Polk & Co's Provo City and Utah County Directory, 1911*, 207, 60, 149, 173.

154. David John, president of the Utah Stake.

pointed out to him that he was not only making war on his bishop, but was ignoring the counsel of his President, and was placing himself in [*illegible due to smudge*] authorities of the Church. He attacks President Joseph Keeler,[155] and that, [*illegible due to smudge*] of him. I resented [*illegible due to smudge*] that anything evil be [*illegible due to ink smear*] say against Prest. [*illegible due to smudge*], would [*illegible due to smudge*] himself and not bro. Keeler. The latter [*illegible due to smudge*] will know [*illegible due to smudge*] to suffer form anything he [*illegible due to ink smear*] say against him. He said he would not go to meeting nor take the sacrament until the bishop made things right." This I also denounced as wrong, and if he kept up that course long enough it would "take him to hell." But he did not think so. I told him if he had called me a liar, as he had done the bishop, I would have "knocked him down." For I did not think I could have controlled my temper as the bishop did his. I certainly commend the Bp. For his patience and coolness. I cannot recall in the course of my experience any man, claiming [*illegible due to smudge*] intelligence, whoever [*illegible due to smudge*] more [*illegible due to smudge*] or who could be more devoid of [*illegible due to smudge*] or true Christian spirit than William J. Harris. I was so [*illegible due to smudge*] for him. After my [*illegible due to smudge*], I do not want to would your feelings by [*illegible due to smudge*] you [**p. 3**] this miserable stuff, and unless it is necessary I hope you will not mention the contents of this communication to him. I simply wanted to know my views of William's visit to me this morning. I was sorry because, I am sorry I did not simply refer him to the local authorities who's duty it is to settle all such matters in the wards and stakes. With them is the right and the power to deal with all such matters. But I could not even do that unit I had heard his story, and when I hear tit I would have been under to myself and to my brethren if I had let it pass without reproof. I told him to go to his Bishop and apologize for his conduct and ask his forgiveness. And to make it right with President John for ignoring and refusing to take his counsel, and repent and he would do right. But my counsel was than President Johns. He said, "I differ with you," and boasted of his wonderful independence and freedom! Well I am sorry to trouble you with such foolish things!. I hope you [ ] I do not think it will do any good to tell him what I have written, but you can do [**p. 4**] as you please about it. I do not justify wrong doing in anybody, and much less in my relations, or in myself. The author of our Salvation taught hat it was better to suffer wrong than to do wrong. Read His Sermon on the Mount, commencing with <St. Matthew> Ch. 5. When did William read it? And what does he know about it? I want you to read verse 9 in Sec. 64 Doctrine & Covenants. "Wherefore I say unto you that ye ought to forgive one another, for he that forgiveth not his brother his treaspass, standeth condemned before the Lord, for there remaineth in him the greater sin." And again, v. 10. "I the Lord will forgive whom I will forgive but of <u>you it is required to forgive all men</u>! etc. Please read all the verses from 1 to 17. And try to impress the lessons taught upon the mind. It is astonishing that any man with a life-long connection in the Church should be so sense as to put himself into the very jaws of apostacy and hug to himself bitterness, and wrath, and repentance, toward his brethren, when he should know his is doing more injury to himself, and those foolish enough to sympathize with him, than he can possibly to to his object of hate. Some men can nurse the Tribune & Herald, Judge Powers[156] and other bitter enemies of their brethren and

155. Joseph B. Keeler was the first counselor in the Utah Stake presidency.

156. The *Salt Lake Tribune*, originally known as the *Mormon Tribune*, was founded by a group of former members of the Church in 1871. The *Salt Lake Herald* was founded in 1870 by two Latter-day Saints and reflected Church policy during most of the nineteenth century but was purchased by a non-LDS businessman in 1898, at which time the paper's tone changed and Judge Orlando W. Powers was appointed associate justice of the Third District of Utah in 1885 by President Grover Cleveland. Powers was the leader of the Liberal Party, the opposition party in Utah, beginning in 1888.

their Church, and feel that they are serving god by doing so. My God help them, for they need it.
Affectionately your brother
Joseph F.

JOSEPH F. TO MARTHA ANN, 27 NOVEMBER 1907

Nov. 27th 1907[157]

Martha Ann S. Harris
214 South 3d West St. Provo, Utah Co.

My Dear Sister Martha:

I should have written you yester day but did not have the time.

We are all usually well— I have had a bad attack of indigestion of late—but am feeling much better. Julina[158] is working as hard as ever. Edna[159] has had a bad cold—and is still laid up with it—but is improving. Several of the Grand children have the Measles—all doing well so far.

Hope you and the rest of the family are well— Give my love to all the children—

I send you herewith a slight memento for Thanks-giving a Five d. bill—No. D 16323172[*illegible mark at the end of the serial number*]

I hope it will reach you all right, and I am sorry I could not have sent it in time for your dinner to morrow. I have just written to Emma and Melissa[160] in [*illegible word*]—signed my name [◊]24 times[161] since I quit work in the office, and I am <u>almost</u> [*illegible word*]!

I am sincerely your brother Joseph F.—

JOSEPH F. TO MARTHA ANN, 27 DECEMBER 1908

Dec. 27th 1908[162]

My Dear Sister, Martha Ann Harris

214 South 3rd West St. Provo City.

157. From Joseph F.'s letterpress copybooks; original not extant.
158. Julina Lambson.
159. Edna Lambson.
160. Emma Smith and Edna Melissa Smith are Joseph F. and Edna Lambson's daughters. See biographical register, "Smith, Emma."
161. Joseph F. sometimes mentioned to family, friends, and Church leaders how many times he signed his name as he transacted business during the day. See, for example, the letter written on the same day mentioned in this letter: Joseph F. to Emma Smith, 27 November 1907.
162. From Joseph F.'s letterpress copybooks; original not extant.

I wish you a happy New Year and a turkey for a new year's dinner, and to ensure the fulfillment of my wish I send you herewith a 5$[163] bill which bears the number R136321 and E733 and under Pres. Harrison[164] 478001. I hope it will reach you safely, and that you may make good use of it, which I have no doubt you will. I am partly laid up with a lame back, but this makes the 10th letter I have dictated and written this afternoon.[165] We are all usually well. Mamies[166] little new son is a beauty, and she is correspondingly happy. Aunt Julina[167] & child join me in love to all,
Every your brother
Joseph F.

JOSEPH F. TO MARTHA ANN, 24 APRIL 1909

Apr. 24th 1909[168]

My Dear Sister Martha:

The announcement by telephone this morning of the accidental and sudden death of William[169] came all unexpected[170] and with its full measure of sadness to us all. I have been so completely occupied thro' the day with office duties that I have not had a moment to myself until now, 8.10 p.m. Bro. John[171] called me by telephone this morning and said that he intended to go to Provo this afternoon. I do not know what help you may need, or whether I could do anything to help you or not, if I were there; but what ever you would like or need, which may be within my power only let me know and you shall have it.[172] It seems very strange and sad that William should have been stricken down so suddenly and so unawares. I hope you will have courage and strength to bear this terrible shock it **[p. 2]** must have been to you. My whole sympathy and sorrow goes out to you in your bereavement. Of course poor William is beyond the reach of our sympathy or help. Neither tears nor sorrow, nor anguish can now avail aught for his good; he has gone to his reckoning and reward. Peace be to his earthly remains, and sweet rest to his soul, but many the merciful Father sustain you and all the children in the sorrow of parting with him for

163. Five dollars in 1908 is basically equivalent to between USD $120 and $130.
164. One of the 1908 five-dollar bills featured President Benjamin Harrison on the front.
165. Joseph F. distinguishes between dictated letters and a letter he wrote by hand. The dictated letters include those to his missionary sons, E. Wesley Smith in Hawai'i and Franklin R. Smith in England; Elder Abraham Fernandez, a missionary serving in Hawai'i; R. Wells, the general manager of the San Pedro, Los Angles, and Salt Lake Railroad Company; M. W. Cooley, the general manager of the Uintah Railway Company; William H. Bancroft, vice president of the Oregon Short Line Railroad; Bishop Thomas R. Cutler, general manager of the Utah–Idaho Sugar Company; Simon Bamberger, president and general manager of the Salt Lake and Ogden Railway Company; and Becky Smith Murphy, a cousin who had sent him a box of seedless raisins. The tenth letter was handwritten to Martha Ann.
166. Mary Sophronia Smith. The son born in 1908 is George Smith Peterson.
167. Julina Lambson Smith, Joseph F.'s wife. The child is most likely Marjorie Virginia Smith, an adopted child born in 1906.
168. From Joseph F.'s letterpress copybooks; original not extant.
169. William Jasper Harris.
170. William was trampled by the horses on Center Street in Provo on 23 April 1909 about 11:00 p.m. and died the following morning, 24 April 1909, at 3:30 a.m.
171. John Smith, Joseph F.'s and Martha Ann's older half brother.
172. Joseph F. paid the funeral expenses for William. See Joseph F. to Martha Ann, 24 May 1909, herein.

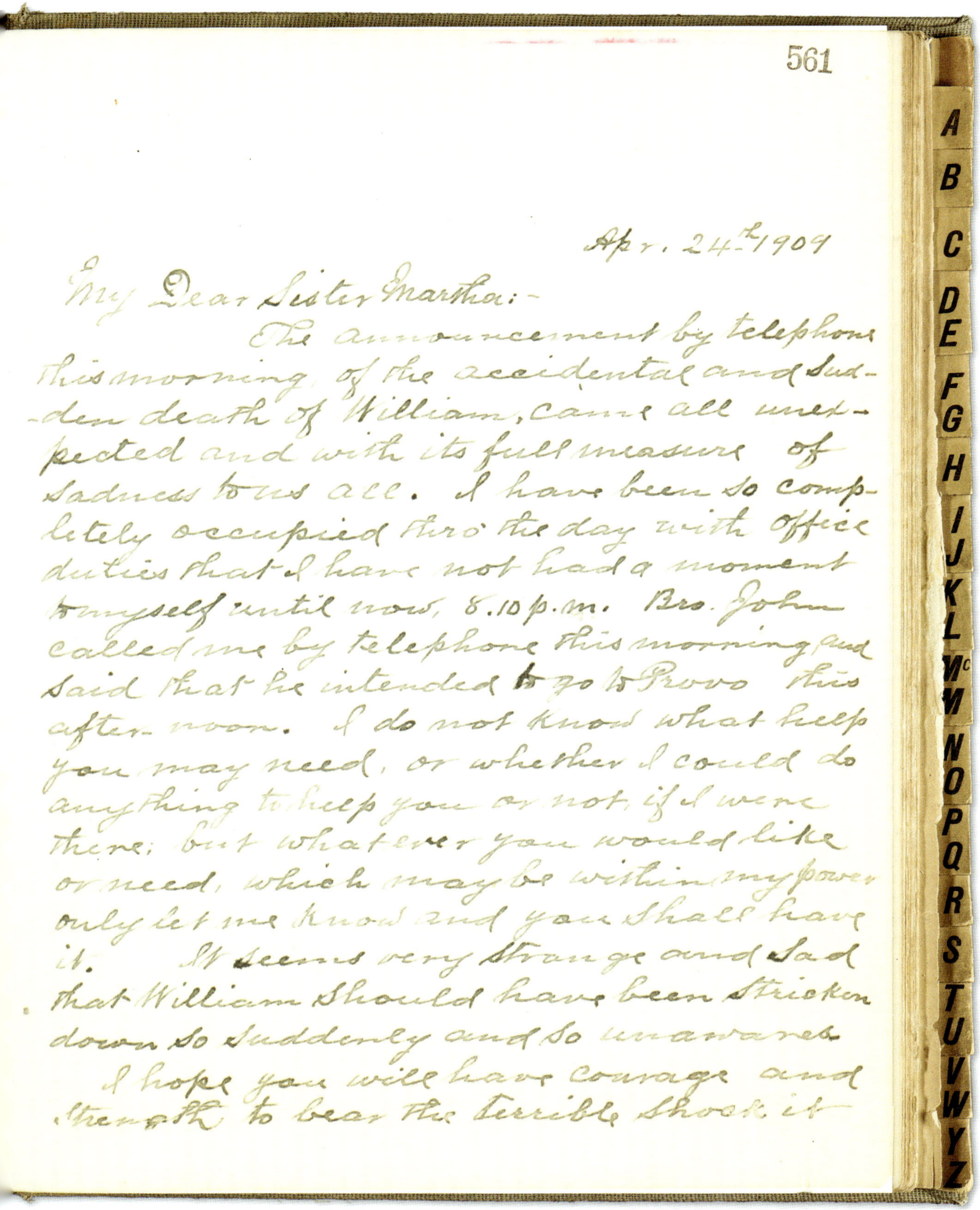

561

Apr. 24th 1909

My Dear Sister Martha:-

The announcement by telephone this morning, of the accidental and sudden death of William, came all unexpected and with its full measure of sadness to us all. I have been so completely occupied thro' the day with office duties that I have not had a moment to myself until now, 8.10 p.m. Bro. John called me by telephone this morning and said that he intended to go to Provo this after-noon. I do not know what help you may need, or whether I could do anything to help you or not, if I were there; but whatever you would like or need, which may be within my power only let me know and you shall have it. It seems very strange and sad that William should have been stricken down so suddenly and so unawares.

I hope you will have courage and strength to bear the terrible shock it

Joseph F. to Martha Ann, 24 April 1909 (p. 1), copy found in Joseph F.'s letterpress copybooks under that date.

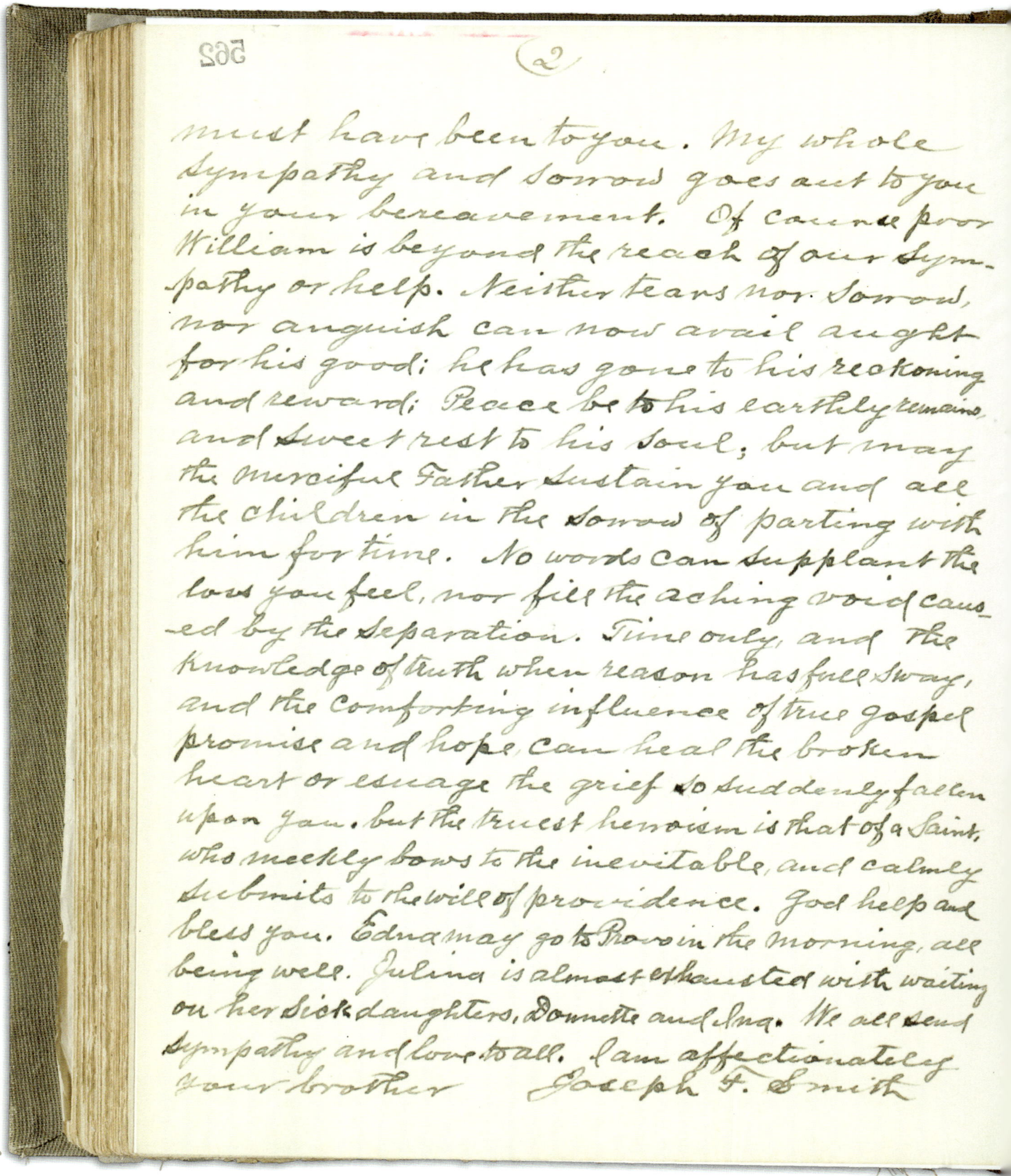

562

(2)

must have been to you. My whole sympathy and sorrow goes out to you in your bereavement. Of course poor William is beyond the reach of our sym-pathy or help. Neither tears nor sorrow, nor anguish can now avail aught for his good: he has gone to his reckoning and reward: Peace be to his earthly remains, and sweet rest to his soul; but may the merciful Father sustain you and all the children in the sorrow of parting with him for time. No words can supplant the loss you feel, nor fill the aching void caus-ed by the separation. Time only, and the knowledge of truth when reason has full sway, and the comforting influence of true gospel promise and hope, can heal the broken heart or esuage the grief so suddenly fallen upon you. but the truest heroism is that of a Saint, who meekly bows to the inevitable, and calmly submits to the will of providence. God help and bless you. Edna may go to Provo in the morning, all being well. Julina is almost exhausted with waiting on her sick daughters, Donnette and Ina. We all send sympathy and love to all. I am affectionately Your brother Joseph F. Smith

Joseph F. to Martha Ann, 24 April 1909 (p. 2), copy found in Joseph F.'s letterpress copybooks under that date.

time. No words can supplant the loss you feel, nor fill the aching void caused by the separation. Time only, and the knowledge of truth when reason has full sway and the comforting influence of true gospel promise and hope can heal the broken heart or esuage the grief so suddenly fallen upon you, but the truest heroism is that of a Saint, who meekly bows to the inevitable, and calmly submits to the will of providence. God hel and bless you. Edna[173] may go to Provo in the morning, all being well. Julina[174] is almost exhausted with waiting on her sick daughters, Donnette and Ina.[175] We all send sympathy and love to all. I am affectionately your brother.
Joseph F. Smith

JOSEPH F. TO MARTHA ANN, 6 MAY 1909

May 6th 1909[176]

Martha Ann Harris.
Provo, City—Utah Co.

My Dear Sister Martha:—

I need not say that I have been very busy since I saw you last.[177] I have had no time for writing letters—but have thought many times I aught to drop you just a line or two.

We are still complaining somewhat of poor health. Ina[178] is some better, but Donnette[179] has not been getting along right well since her confinement and she is here at the Beehive,[180] now under her mother's care. Emily has been having a seige of tonsilitus—and these ailments—mixed with house-cleaning has made it very hard on Julina, who has not been right well herself.[181]

I feel that we are all improving some and that we will soon be all right again.

I hope you and Jerusha[182] are well and having a good visit together. [**p. 2**]

The main purpose, however, of this letter is to enquire how the boys got along over the funeral expenses.[183] I spoke to Frank[184] when he was here about it, and I told him I would help him out on the Expenses of the Undertaker. I will enclose in this letter a note[185] for you to hand or send to mr. Edward L. Jones,[186] the Undertaker, as I do not know his address. All you need to do will be to send it to him by one of the Children, or any person who can deliver it to him.

173. Edna Lambson Smith, Joseph F.'s wife and sister to Julina Lambson Smith.
174. Julina Lambson Smith, Joseph F.'s wife and sister to Julina Lambson Smith.
175. Donnette Smith and Julina Clarissa Smith were Joseph F. and Julina Lambson Smith's daughters.
176. From Joseph F.'s letterpress copybooks; original not extant. Joseph F. was seventy, and Martha Ann was sixty-seven.
177. Most likely at the funeral of Martha Ann's husband, William Jasper Harris, held in Provo on 29 April 1909.
178. Julina Clarissa Smith.
179. Donnette Smith. Joseph F. moved Julina's family into the Beehive House on Temple Square in 1905.
180. The Beehive House was built between 1855 and 1858 and was Joseph F.'s main residence in 1909.
181. Emily Jane Smith and her mother, Julina Lambson.
182. Jerusha Smith, half sister of Joseph F. and Martha Ann.
183. Martha Ann's husband, William Jasper Harris, died on 24 April 1909, after being hit by a runaway team of horses.
184. Martha Ann's son Franklin Hill Harris.
185. See Joseph F. to Edward L. Jones, 6 May 1909.
186. Edward L. Jones of Graham & Jones Undertaking, located on Center Street in Provo.

Uncle John[187] told me yesterday that he intended to go to Provo sometime this or next week, and if Jerusha[188] was ready to come back with him, he would bring her; with yourself also if you could and would come. I told him if he would let me know before he went I would try to arrange your transportation for you. Give my love to all the children, and to Aunt Jerusha, and accept the same for yourself. Have your heard from your son John[189] yet? Where are the boys now? I am affectionately, Joseph F.

JOSEPH F. TO MARTHA ANN, 24 MAY 1909

May 24th 1909—[190]

My Dear Sister Martha Ann.

I have received your letters of—21st and of May 19th. I have sent, today, my cheque for $85.00/100 to Graham & Jones,[191] Undertakers, Provo; in payment of their bill for the burial of William.[192]

I enclose you a card from the Deseret News, acknowledging payment for the "Semi Weekley" from Jan. 22d 1907. to July 22d 1909.[193] I hope you have received the paper regularly, and I will renew the subscription when necessary, if you desire the paper. I commenced sending the paper to William in 1906.

I was glad to hear from you, and I hope your health and strength will soon be restored and continued to you for many—many years to come. I am glad the children have fixed up the house a little for your comfort. When you were here I was pretty closely run for means as I had to pay our some five or six hundred dollars for Coulsen's[194] debts and expenses **[p. 2]** to the Islands.[195] These obligations of Coulsen were entirely unknown and unexpected to me until just before his departure from home. But these are only my own little family troubles and I need not bother you with them. My trip, recently, to the Islands also cost me seven or eight hundred dollars, which came pretty close to "running me ashore," so to speak, financially, before having to meet Coulsen's demands. But I am right again now and if you need anything within my power, to give, please let me know.

---

187. John Smith, Joseph F. and Martha Ann's older half brother.
188. Jerusha Smith, Joseph F. and Martha Ann's older half sister.
189. John Fielding Harris.
190. From Joseph F.'s letterpress copybooks; original not extant.
191. "Graham & Jones. Funeral Directors and Licensed Embalmers. Phones: Bell, 340-Z, 95 and 28 Black; Ind., 49-D, 184-A and 158-A. 162-166 W. Center St." *Business Directory of Salt Lake City* [and Provo] (Chicago: Stemmer & Co's, Superior Inc., 1909–10), 161.
192. In a letter to the undertaker, Joseph F. wrote, "I send you herewith my cheque No. 13. On the State Bank of Utah for $85.00/100, which covers the bill. . . . Yours very truly Joseph F. Smith. P.S. I thank you very much for all your kindness to my Sister. Mrs. Harris." Joseph F. to Edward L. Jones, 24 May 1909.
193. *Deseret Semi-Weekly News*, published in Salt Lake City; this newspaper was meant for those living outside Salt Lake City.
194. Charles Coulson Rich Smith was the third child of Alice Ann Kimball and David Patten Rich. Joseph F. married Alice in 1883, at which time Joseph F. took responsibilities for her three children.
195. Charles Coulson Rich Smith was called to the Sandwich Islands and set apart on 16 April 1909 by John Henry Smith, a member of the Quorum of the Twelve Apostles and a second cousin of Joseph F. and Martha Ann.

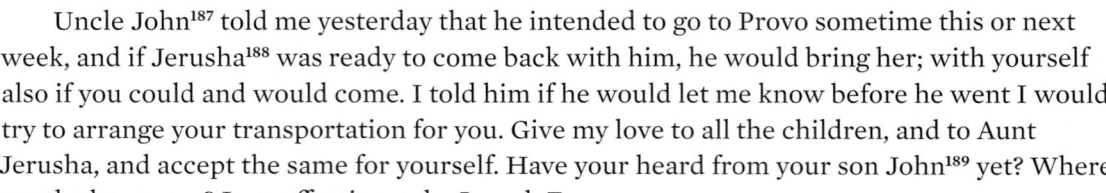

Donnette, spent a little more than a week at the Hospital and improved some. She is now here, with her Mother, confined to her bed; and so far we can tell she is slowly improving. Julina is not real well herself and has no keep but that of her girls.

What with Ina's recent severe illness, and Emily's recent attack of Tonsillitis, and Donnies illness, Julina has been very severely taxed and it is a wonder she has been able to endure it all. With love to you and the children and praying sincerely for your welfare I am as ever you affectionate brother, Jos. F.

JOSEPH F. TO MARTHA ANN, 22 DECEMBER 1909

Dec. 22d 1909[196]

Martha Ann Harris
214 South 3d West St. Provo City.

My Dear Sister[197] Martha:—

I wish you a pleasant and joyous Christmas and a happy and prosperous new year. We are not all well yet by long way. Aunt Alice[198] and my little Martha[199] are better, and enjoying themselves at home. But now two of our Donnies children are sick. Little Donnie has typhoid fever and little Henry the grippe[200] and an attack of bronchitis.[201] Joseph's little Julina[202] is getting along nicely—and excepting slight colds the rest are quite well. I hope you and the children are all well and comfortable.

Wesley[203] left the Hospital, in Honolulu, yesterday. I hope he will get along all right.

I send you my cheque for five dollars so that you may have a turkey for dinner on Christmas day if you want it. Ina is to be married tomorrow.[204] All send love— Affectionately & c. Joseph F. Smith

196. From Joseph F.'s letterpress copybooks; original not extant.
197. Martha Ann was sixty-eight, and Joseph F. was seventy-one.
198. Alice Ann Kimball.
199. Martha Smith was twelve years old.
200. The French word for influenza, usually referred to as "la grippe." See Joseph F. to Martha Ann, 2 April 1905, herein.
201. Joseph F. and Julina Lambson's daughter Donnette Smith married Alonzo Pratt Kesler on 26 December 1900. Donnette Kesler was born on 13 March 1902, and Henry Smith Kesler was born on 24 April 1907. See biographical register, "Kesler, Donnette" and "Kesler, Henry Smith."
202. Julina Smith, daughter of Joseph Fielding Smith Jr. See biographical register, "Smith, Julina."
203. Elias Wesley Smith. Wesley was serving a mission in Hawai'i and had recently been "in the hospital with typhoid fever." See Joseph F. to E. Wesley Smith, 22 December 1909.
204. Joseph F.'s daughter Julina Clarissa Smith married Joseph Strass Peery on 23 December 1909.

OFFICE OF
The First Presidency
of the
Church of Jesus Christ
of
Latter-day Saints.

P.O. Box B.

Salt Lake City, Utah, Feb. 28th 1913

Martha Ann Smith Harris
214 South 3rd West St. Provo.

My Dear Sister Martha.

I hope this will find you all well, that William is himself again, and that the rest of the children are happy and prosperous. We are all pretty well at present, for which we are most grateful.

Some of the grand children are troubled with colds, but, so far as we know, none of them, are in serious condition.

Your Cousin Ina "Coolbrith" sends her love and sympathy to you, and hopes the grand-children you are raising will always remember with gratitude your services and sacrifices for them. I saw a notice in the News that you had met with a loss by fire, but have heard nothing more about it. I send you herewith my cheque No. 19. for \$19.00/100. (nineteen dollars.) as follows: \$9.00/100 from Julina to pay for some work you did. and \$10.00/100 from your brother as a gift. Ever true, Joseph F. Smith

Joseph F. to Martha Ann, 28 February 1913

Decade 7

1910–1916

JOSEPH F. TO MARTHA ANN, BEEHIVE HOUSE, SALT LAKE CITY, UTAH, 14 MAY 1911

[I] know you have been compelled to pass through many narrow places, and your path has been—all too—rough and thorney, yet we cannot fail to see the hand of Providence has not deserted you allways. Your life has been spared—your faith unimpaired, your hopes have not failed you, you have learned to kiss the hand that held the rod of your afflictions, and dealt out mercies in the hour of need, and to say from your heart "He doeth all things well".

You have had experience to prove that God is more kind and loving to ward His children than is Man.

MARTHA ANN TO JOSEPH F., PROVO CITY, UTAH, 27 MARCH 1916

[I now have] 70 one gran children . . . & thirty ~~3~~ 4 great grand children. . . . I can join in with you in saying god bless the babyes for ever.

Martha Ann Smith Harris and Joseph F. Smith, 5 May 1916. Courtesy of Carole Call King.

Decade Introduction

When Joseph F. became President of the Church in 1901, he had served in the First Presidency since 1880. No other Church President had been a member of the First Presidency before being called to preside over the entire Church. Additionally, Joseph F. had served more missions overseas than his predecessors, a record that has not been broken since his time.[1] He also visited the Saints around the world and was the first Church President to visit members outside the Latter-day Saint core area while serving in that capacity.

A FOUNDATION FOR THE TWENTIETH AND TWENTY-FIRST CENTURIES

During President Joseph F. Smith's administration, the Church was beginning to establish a permanent presence throughout the world that would become the basis for its explosive growth in the second half of the twentieth century.[2] Membership increased significantly, from 283,765 in 1901, when Joseph F. became President, to 495,962 at the time of his death in 1918.[3] His presidency set the course for the Church in the next six decades and beyond.[4]

As the Church continued to retire its debts and began the process of moving from tithing-in-kind to cash donations, it was positioned to strengthen the infrastructure at its Salt Lake City headquarters

1. See Stephen C. Taysom's forthcoming biography, *"Like a Fiery Meteor": The Life of Joseph F. Smith.*
2. "The Church in 1910," in *Mapping Mormonism: An Atlas of Latter-day Saint History*, ed. Brandon S. Plewe et al. (Provo, UT: BYU Press, 2012), 132–33.
3. See *Church Membership Statistics* (Provo, UT: Brigham Young University, 1973), 2.
4. Joseph F.'s long-term impact is also seen in those he called to serve in the Quorum of the Twelve. Among them were mostly monogamist brethren, including Hyrum Mack Smith (1901), George Albert Smith (1903), David O. McKay (1906), George F. Richards (1906), Anthony W. Ivins (1907), Joseph Fielding Smith (1910), James E. Talmage (1911), Stephen L Richards (1917), and Richard L. Lyman (1918). This was an important and significant departure from the earlier practice of calling men who practiced plural marriage. Three of those called by Joseph F. became Presidents of the Church—George Albert Smith in 1945, David O. McKay in 1951, and Joseph Fielding Smith in 1970. Several of those called, including David O. McKay, Joseph Fielding Smith, Hyrum Mack Smith, and James E. Talmage, wrote important doctrinal and inspirational books. Elder John A. Widtsoe compiled Joseph F.'s sermons and writings in 1918, and the resulting book was published in early 1919 within a few months of the latter's death. See Joseph F. Smith, *Gospel Doctrine: Selections from the Sermons and Writings of Joseph F. Smith*, comp. John A. Widtsoe, 5th ed. (Salt Lake City, UT: Deseret Book, 1939), v–vi.

Joseph F. during a visit to Mexico in the last decade of his life. Courtesy of CHL.

by completing the Bureau of Information (1910), Bishop's Building (1910), Business Building (1910), Deseret Gymnasium (1910), Hotel Utah (1911), and Church Administration Building (1917).[5]

President Smith encouraged the Saints to remain where they lived in order to help build up the Church internationally. In February 1911 the First Presidency noted, "It is desirable that our people shall remain in their native lands and form congregations of a permanent character to aid in the work of proselyting."[6] As he continued to meet the needs of a burgeoning membership outside Utah, President Smith participated in the groundbreaking and site dedication of two historic temples.[7]

"Cardston Temple Site Souvenir," 27 July 1913, photographs by Arthur Thomas Henson, Cardston, Alberta, Canada. Henson's photomontage of temple groundbreaking ceremonies features images of Joseph F. Smith and local Church leaders and members, including a view of Joseph F. Smith and his party taken at the dedication (top left). Courtesy of CHL.

5. See W. Ray Luce, "Joseph F. Smith and the Great Mormon Building Boom," in *Joseph F. Smith: Reflections on the Man and His Times*, ed. Craig K. Manscill et al. (Provo, UT: Religious Studies Center, Brigham Young University; Salt Lake City, UT: Deseret Book, 2013), 320–41.
6. Quoted in James R. Clark, comp., *Messages of the First Presidency* (Salt Lake City, UT: Bookcraft, 1965), 4:222.
7. See Gary L. Boatright Jr., "'We Shall Have Temples Built': Joseph F. Smith and a New Era of Temple Building," in Manscill et al., *Joseph F. Smith: Reflections on the Man and His Times*, 303–19.

The first one was dedicated in Cardston, Alberta, Canada (1913),[8] and the other in Lā'ie, O'ahu, Hawai'i (1915).[9]

During President Smith's administration, numerous local meetinghouses were planned, built, and dedicated throughout the Church—many beyond Utah's borders—to accommodate and bless the lives of the Saints.[10] President Smith highlighted this effort in his 1911–12 journal:

20 November 1911 — Meeting House for Los Angeles, Cal. Cost as estimated by bro. Jos. E. Robison & architect.

Meetinghouse	$16,000.00
Parsonage	3,500.00
Elder's Home	3,000.00
Estimated Total Cost	$22,500.00

19 May 1912 — Brigham City . . . Dedicated 3 ward's Meeting House. Fine Building. Cost 31,700

17 August 1912 — In the Office as usual. Many calls for help to build meeting houses. We granted several appeals today.

17 November 1912 — Reached Boise this morning & came to Nampa. Breakfast at bro. Horton. At meeting, dedicated house. Returned to Boise for evening Meeting.[11]

President Smith also supported the erection of many other Church-owned buildings in Utah. For example, he noted in May 1912, "Council at the Temple. Dedication Maeser building. To Provo at 4:30 p.m."[12] He had presided over the cornerstone-laying ceremonies for the Karl G. Maeser Building in October 1909. The Maeser Memorial Building was the first building constructed on "Temple Hill," the present-day site of Brigham Young University's main campus.[13]

During this time of Church growth, new programs and organizational changes, such as the modern stake and ward structures, were being introduced.[14] Additional developments included the publication of the *Children's Friend* (1902), a restructuring of the Mutual Improvement Associations (1903), Sunday School classes for adults (1906), weekly priesthood meetings (1909), the adoption of the Boy Scout program (1911), the beginning of the seminary program (1912), the publication of the *Relief Society Magazine* (1915), and the introduction of "Home Evenings" (1915).

8. See Richard Neitzel Holzapfel, "New Photographs of the Alberta Canada Temple Site Dedication, 1913," *BYU Studies* 39, no. 1 (2000): 204–8. The Cardston Alberta Temple was dedicated in 1919 by Heber J. Grant.
9. The temple in Lā'ie was dedicated in 1923 by Heber J. Grant.
10. See Smith, *Gospel Doctrine*, 650.
11. Joseph F., journal, 20 November 1911, 19 May 1912, 17 August 1912, and 17 November 1912.
12. Joseph F., journal, 30 May 1912.
13. "Corner Stone Laid at B.Y.U.," *Deseret Evening News*, 16 October 1909, 2.
14. See Richard O. Cowan, "Church Programs in Transition," in Manscill et al., *Joseph F. Smith: Reflections on the Man and His Times*, 418–33; and Scott C. Esplin, "Joseph F. Smith and the Shaping of the Modern Church Educational System," in Manscill et al., *Joseph F. Smith: Reflections on the Man and His Times*, 401–17.

Joseph F. Smith at the Maeser Memorial Building cornerstone-laying ceremony, 16 October 1909, photograph by Olson-Hafen, Provo, Utah. Joseph F. is standing to the right of the US flag. Courtesy of BYU.

During this decade, President Smith, along with members of the First Presidency and Council of the Twelve Apostles, issued major doctrinal statements.[15] For example, a statement issued on 30 June 1916 titled "The Father and the Son: A Doctrinal Exposition by the First Presidency and the Twelve" explains how the term *Father* is used in scripture as it relates to God.[16] Along with an earlier statement issued by the First Presidency in 1909, this important document demonstrates President Smith's effort to clarify Church doctrine for the twentieth-century Church.[17]

A PERSONAL MINISTRY

While presiding over an increasingly large Church membership scattered around the world, President Smith nevertheless took time to minister to individuals. In 1912 he wrote, "Office all day. Called at Melissas and prayed for her."[18] In 1913 he recorded, "I baptized Robert S. Sant and

15. For a wider view of Joseph F.'s doctrinal contributions, see Joseph Fielding McConkie, "Doctrinal Contributions of Joseph F. Smith," in Manscill et al., *Joseph F. Smith: Reflections on the Man and His Times*, 17–35.
16. "The Father and the Son: A Doctrinal Exposition by the First Presidency and the Twelve," *Improvement Era*, August 1916, 934–42.
17. See Joseph F. Smith, John R. Winder, and Anthon H. Lund, "The Origin of Man," *Improvement Era*, November 1909, 75–81.
18. Joseph F., journal, 28 May 1912.

confirmed him today in Font at Tabernacle, S.L.City. He is 8 years old today. I also baptized & confirmed Eloise Leilani Fernandez who will be 8 years old tomorrow."[19] His journals and letters highlight this personal one-on-one attention generously extended to many people, including his beloved sister Martha Ann, throughout his ministry.

President Smith's letters became an important way for him to extend his outreach to many more people than otherwise possible. This included people close by, such as his sister Martha Ann in Provo, as well as those farther away from Church headquarters. When he left Utah for an extended visit to California in 1912, President Smith recorded addresses of people he wanted to write while he was away from Utah—Martha Ann, two sons serving as missionaries in Europe, and other people not related to him, such as President Melvin J. Ballard (1873–1939), who was presiding over the Northwestern States Mission at the time.[20]

When President Smith returned home from any trip, many letters awaited his attention. After a trip to California, he noted, "Found all well at home and piles of letters to answer."[21] A few days later, he recorded, "A.M. going over my personal letters."[22] His journals and letters reveal a man dedicated to reading and writing letters on an almost daily basis. By 1912 he began receiving help with this increasing responsibility. He noted, "Read Letters. Met bro. Wally. At Temple. Prayed for Geo. Albert [Smith], C. W. & M Co. Meeting. I dictated letters."[23]

TIME MARCHES FORWARD

The decade of 1910 began with the death of John R. Winder (1821–1910), first counselor in the First Presidency, on 27 March 1910. Winder had been a close associate of President Smith for decades. His work as a counselor in the Presiding bishopric during the challenging days of the 1880s when the U.S. government pressured the Church to conform to the country's protestant values were much appreciated. Additionally, his work in completing the Salt Lake Temple in time for it's dedication in April 1893, was also highly valued.

President Smith called Anthon H. Lund (1844–1921), his second counselor, to replace Winder as first counselor in the presidency on 7 April 1910. Like Winder, Lund was was an immigrant (born in Denmark). Additionally, Lund was among the few monogamist Church leaders. Increasingly, but not exclusively, President Smith called monogamist to fill vacancies in the Church's leadership moving the the Saints into a new world.

At the same time, President Smith called his cousin, John Henry Smith (1848–1911), who had been serving as the President of the Quorum of the Twelve, as the new second counselor.[24]

19. Joseph F., journal, 29 March 1913. Baptism of children in the nineteenth century took place around eight years of age. For many Latter-day Saint families this special event did not take place on a child's eighth birthday.
20. President Ballard's address was recorded as 264 E. 25th Street, Portland, Oregon. President Smith and President Ballard developed a very close relationship. The latter began his service as mission president in 1901, the same year President Smith was sustained as Church President. President Ballard continued in that assignment until 1919, when he was called to fill the vacancy in the Quorum of the Twelve created when President Smith died. Later, in 1926, Elder Ballard's son married Hyrum Mack Smith's daughter, forging an even greater bond between the Ballard and Smith families.
21. Joseph F., journal, 15 August 1912.
22. Joseph F., journal, 18 August 1912.
23. Joseph F., journal, 23 May 1912.
24. John Henry Smith was Joseph F.'s second cousin. His father, George A. Smith, was Hyrum Smith's cousin. George A. Smith's father, John Smith, known as Uncle John, was Joseph Smith Sr.'s brother and gave Joseph F. his patriarchal blessing in 1852. At the time of John Henry Smith's call to the First Presidency, his son George Albert Smith was also serving in the Quorum of the Twelve, the only time a father and son had served in that quorum simultaneously.

The First Presidency, ca. 1910, photograph by Charles William Symons, Salt Lake City, Utah. From left to right: Anthon H. Lund, Joseph F. Smith, and John Henry Smith. The First Presidency was reorganized on 7 April 1910 when Anthon H. Lund was called as First Counselor and John Henry Smith was called as Second Counselor following the death of the former First Counselor, John R. Winder, on 27 March 1910. Courtesy of CHL.

President Smith often called individuals who had a much different temperament and personality than himself. John Henry Smith was one such individual. He was affable and easily maneuvered in circles with individuals who held different political, religious, and social views. His diaries, like Anthon Lund's diaries, are remarkable for their frankness and candor. In this, he followed President Smith's admonition that "I must keep an accurate history of facts as they occur."[25]

A year and half later, on 13 October 1911, President John Henry Smith died, creating a vacancy soon filled by Charles W. Penrose (1832–1925). For a second time in Joseph F. Smith's administration, the First Presidency consisted of two members born outside the United States (Lund was born in Denmark and Penrose in England).

25. Jean Bickmore White, ed. *Church, State, and Politics: The Diaries of John Henry Smith* (Salt Lake City, Utah: Signature books, 1990) 33.

In the time between his first and last letters of this decade to Martha Ann, Joseph F. experienced personal losses in his immediate family, beginning with the death of his adopted son Edward Arthur (1858–1911) on 17 July 1911. Four years later, Joseph F.'s beloved wife Sarah Ellen Richards (1850–1915) died on 22 March 1915. Her passing was followed by the death of his daughter Zina (1890–1915) on 25 October 1915. Extended family members also died during this period, giving Joseph F. additional cause to weep and mourn for those close to him.

Edward A. and Cytha Ellen Smith, known as Ella Smith, January 1901. Ella Smith married Edward Arthur on 3 March 1881. They were the parents of eleven children. Edward, the adopted son of Joseph F., died on 17 July 1911. Joseph F. wrote on this card, "Edward A. and Ella Smith taken Jan. 1901." Courtesy of CHL.

On the international scene, another death indirectly influenced the lives of Joseph F. and other Church members worldwide. The assassination of Archduke Franz Ferdinand of Austria on 28 June 1914 plunged Europe into war. In response to the outbreak of hostilities, that same year President Smith closed the missions in Europe, where the conflict was raging. Latter-day Saints living in Canada, particularly those from settlements in the western province of Alberta, and in the British Isles were immediately affected as husbands and sons marched off to join the conflict in Europe. With great anxiety and alarm, the European Saints witnessed the battles raging close to home.

When the United States officially entered World War I in April 1917, a large number of American Latter-day Saints from the western United States were sent to the battlefront in France. Six of President Smith's own sons served during the war, which ended just days before his death in November 1918.

During his last year of life, President Smith experienced the heartache of death again and again when his son Hyrum Mack Smith[26] died in January following an appendectomy, his son-in-law Alonzo Pratt Kesler[27] died in February after falling from a ladder, and his daughter-in-law Ida Bowman[28] died in September after childbirth.

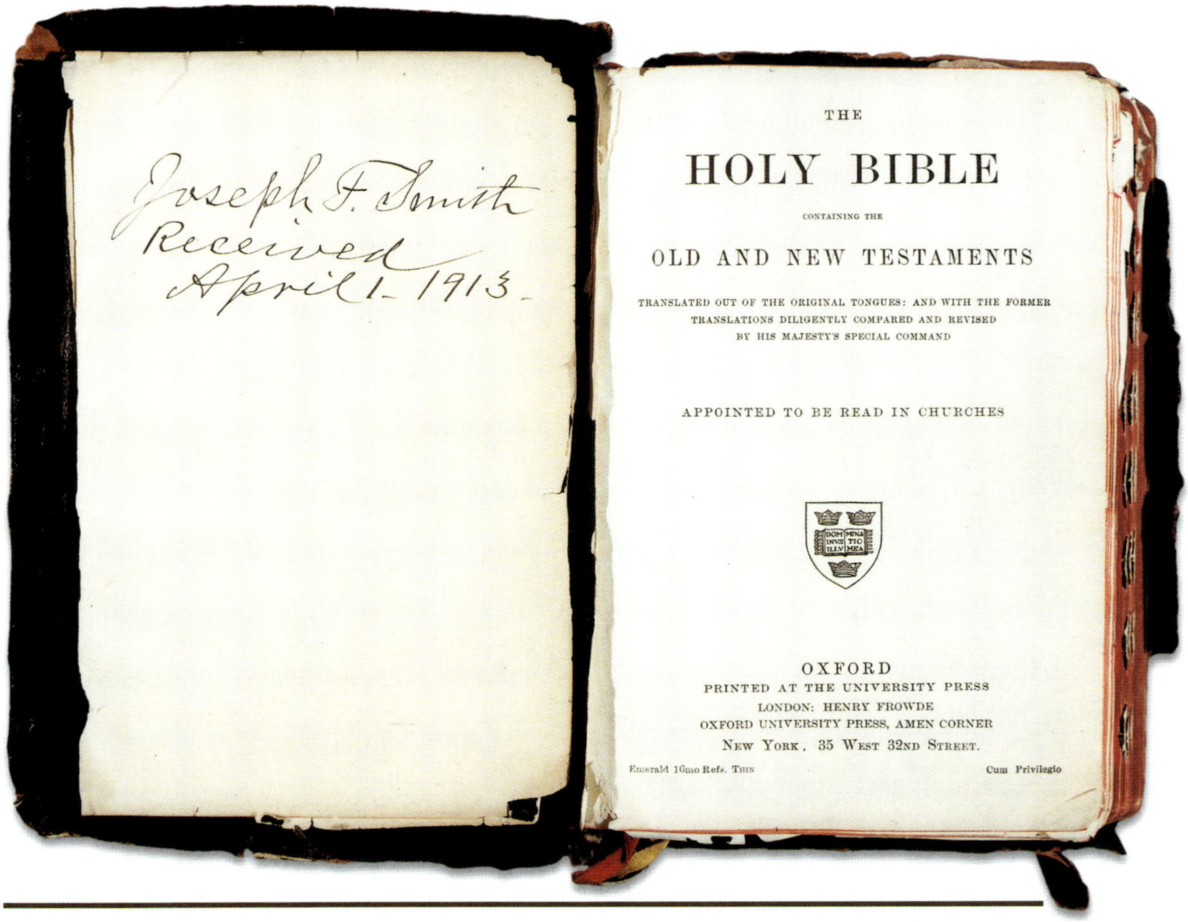

Joseph F.'s King James Version Bible, "Received April 1. 1913." This may have been the Bible he was studying in October 1918 when he beheld a vision of the redemption of the dead. Courtesy of CHL.

26. "Apostle H. M. Smith, Eldest Son of President Smith of Mormon Church, Is Dead," *Ogden Standard*, 24 January 1918, 2.
27. "A. [P.] Kesler Is Killed in Fall from a Building," *Ogden Standard*, 5 February 1918, 5.
28. "Ida Bowman Smith," *Salt Lake Herald-Republican*, 26 September 1918, 4.

During the last few months of his life, President Joseph F. Smith was mostly confined to the Beehive House, his home in Salt Lake City. It was in this setting that he beheld on 3 October 1918 a magnificent vision of the redemption of the dead.[29]

The vision came to Joseph F. at a terrible personal cost through decades of burying family members one by one. One scholar noted the following:

> One of the things that becomes obvious almost immediately is that Joseph F. Smith was acutely acquainted with death from the time of his father's murder [in] 1844 until the death of JFS's favored son in 1918, just months before JFS himself died. The decades in between were liberally sprinkled by the loss of many children. JFS grieved deeply the loss of each one. On August 26, 1883, JFS wrote to his sister Martha Ann that "Once more, and now for the sixth time, by the inexorable will of an inscrutable providence, we have been called upon to part with one of our dearest, most precious treasures. This time the pitiless monster, death, has chosen for his 'shining mark,' our beautiful, intelligent, bright and lovely little Albert Jesse [2 years old]. . . . [Despite] scalding tears, the heavens were brass above our heads. Our cries and tears fell alike to the earth and were buried this day with the lifeless form of our hearts treasure in the grave! And yet not all were buried, for our cry would ascend: why is it so? Why, God, did it have to be? And still our tears soak the earth to releave, if not to bury, our heartache in its lifeless bosom."[30]
>
> This would not be the last time that JFS buried a child who had died in his arms. It would not be the last time that he found the heavens as brass over his head. I think now of what we know as Doctrine and Covenants 138. The Vision of the Redemption of the Dead. We've studied its theology; we've contextualized it and given a nod to the role of World War One and Smith's own impending death. But we have not, I think, yet reckoned with the full cost of that revelation. It seems to me that the gift we were given in that text was extruded from Joseph F. Smith, dead child by dead child, over the course of decades. God did not kill those children so that we could have this revelation. But God certainly used those experiences to deepen the well of yearning that a prophet seems to need in order to see beyond himself and into the heart and mind of God. That revelation cost this prophet dearly. . . . I cannot look at that revelation the same way anymore. In it resides the buried treasures lost by a prophet. In it we see the brass heavens break. Finally.[31]

The vision was grand and comforting for Joseph F. On a deeply personal level he mentions seeing his father, Hyrum Smith, who had been murdered in 1844.[32] Within two months after receiving this momentous revelation for the Church, Joseph F. was dead, five days after his eightieth birthday.[33]

29. Found in Doctrine and Covenants 138.
30. This quotation is from a letter included in this collection. See Joseph F. to Martha Ann, 26 August 1883, herein.
31. Stephen Taysom, "Bob Dylan, Joseph F. Smith, and the Price of Revelation," *By Common Consent*, 5 September 2013.
32. See Doctrine and Covenants 138:53, 56–57.
33. Because of the flu pandemic, no public funeral was held. However, people lined the streets to pay their respects as the solemn funeral procession made its way from the Beehive House to the Salt Lake City Cemetery. Martha Ann, along with her family, was present, as reported in a local Salt Lake City newspaper. See "Impressive Tribute Paid Church Head," *Salt Lake Tribune*, 23 November 1918, 2.

MARTHA ANN'S MIXED EXPERIENCES

The conflict in Europe also affected Martha Ann's life in Provo. For one thing, her grandson John Alvin Corbett (1897–1962), like several other Smith extended family members, was a soldier in France during the war. In a letter from "somewhere in France" and written to his grandmother Martha Ann, John wrote, "No one realizes what the world is till he gets out and gets into a place like this."[34] He further reflected, "Of course, we have to consider that France has had 4 yrs of careless war and the flower of her youth have surely suffered. Only the women left you might say to do the work with the old and the young." He then opined, "The people have brought this terrible thing on themselves through their disobedience to the laws of God and not listening to his teachings. Only something like this can bring them to their senses."[35]

Before the outbreak of World War I, Martha Ann celebrated the birth of another granddaughter, Ann Adalaide Dennis (1910–2008). She was the daughter of Martha Ann's daughter Zina Christine (1876–1958) and John Thomas Dennis (1866–1929). Zina and John's marriage in 1909 was unique and must have given Martha Ann additional reasons to celebrate. John had previously married Martha Ann's third daughter, Mercy Ann (1874–1905). Four years after her death in 1905, John married her younger sister, Zina Christine Harris Furner, Martha Ann's fourth daughter. Zina Christine's first husband, George Thomas Furner (1868–1902), had died in 1902, leaving her a widow with four young children: Merrilla (1895–1967), Zina May (1897–1934), Pearl Irene (1900–1987), and Sarah Rachel (1902–77). Zina and John had three children together; Ann Adalaide was the first, born on 12 July 1910.[36]

John Alvin Corbett, ca. 1918. Courtesy of Carole Call King.

Martha's son Joseph Albert died during the spring of 1911. According to a family tradition, Joseph Albert was robbed and severely beaten on a train on his way home from Texas where he had been visiting his brothers. "When he arrived at the Provo depot, he was put in a strait jacket and taken to the Utah State Mental Hospital. He didn't recognize any of his family when he arrived."[37] Upon hearing of Joseph Albert's death, Joseph F. wrote his sister: "My Dear Sister Martha Ann:— I got the sad word last evening thro' Julina, that Joseph Albert

34. John Alvin Corbett to Martha Ann, 13 October 1918. Courtesy of Carole Call King.
35. John Alvin Corbett to Martha Ann, 13 October 1918.
36. Following John's death in 1929, Zina Christine married Irving Llewelly Pratt in 1942.
37. Based on conversation between Naomi Startup Biggs and Carole Call King, December 1993.

Zina Christine with her daughter, Ann Adalaide Dennis, 1910. Courtesy of Carole Call King.

had passed over the dark river to the great majority beyond. While it is always sad and sorrowful to pass thro' the gloomy shadows of the dark valley of death, there are some things much worse than death itself. A living death is more to be dreaded than the final sleep, and rest from the fatal ills of mortality. Joseph is all right now. He is beyond the power of death."[38]

Joseph Albert Harris and Johanna Patten with "Burt" and "Frank," ca. 1883. Courtesy of Carole Call King.

Joseph Albert Harris, 1904, photograph by A. E. Clodfelter, Versailles, Missouri. Courtesy of CHL.

In July 1912, Martha Ann accompanied her brother to Southern California for a monthlong vacation. Joseph F. recorded in mid-July, "Edna L., Emma, and Martha, Lucy, Edith and I Started for Ocean Park Cal. We have 2 trunks & Satchels."[39] The group traveled by train in a sleeping car, making the journey south through the desert a pleasant one. Joseph F. noted, "a.m. cool and pleasant p.m. warm."[40] Wanting Martha Ann to enjoy her time in Southern California without any financial worries, Joseph F. took care of the expenses.[41]

Martha Ann went fishing, apparently became seasick, and, along with everyone else, did not catch any fish. Sometimes Joseph F. and Martha Ann remained alone at the cottage while everyone

38. Joseph F. to Martha Ann, 29 May 1911, herein.
39. Joseph F., journal, 13 July 1912.
40. Joseph F., journal, 14 July 1912.
41. A few days after arriving in California, Joseph F. noted in his cash account record that he paid five dollars for a "Bathing Suit [for] Martha." Additionally, he gave Martha Ann, Emma, Lucy, and Edith five dollars each. See Joseph F., cash accounts, 1911–12, 73–74.

Joseph F. Smith at Santa Monica Beach, Los Angeles County, California, ca. 1910. When he traveled to Southern California, Joseph F. found time to swim, visit tourist sites, golf, and visit with family and friends. Courtesy of UU.

else traveled somewhere nearby. On one occasion, Joseph F. noted in his journal, "I was writing letters all day."[42] A day after arriving home in Salt Lake City on 14 August, Joseph F. briefly noted, "Found all well at home and piles of letters to ans[wer]."[43] Overall, the trip to California provided Martha Ann with a well-deserved respite from the crush of daily work and other obligations in Provo.

Less than a year later, Martha Ann's son-in-law Walter Sutton Corbett (1857–1912) died on 2 February 1912 at his home in Pleasant View.[44] The following month, Joseph F. noted in a letter to the local stake president in Provo that Mary Emily Harris (1865–1947), Walter's wife, owed about two hundred dollars "for the burial of her husband and two children" and "a mortgage of some $600 or more on her house."[45] Joseph F. had interceded to help his niece reduce her expenses and coordinate a final settlement of the bills by a group of friends and family members.

Tragedy struck again just months later when Mary Emily lost a daughter-in-law, Irene Colvin Corbett (1881–1912). Irene was married to Walter Harris Corbett (1885–1917), Mary's son and Martha Ann's grandson. At the time of her death, she was the mother of three children: Walter Colvin (1906–2002), Kady Roene (1908–73), and Mark Colvin (1910–76).

Irene had earned a degree at Brigham Young Academy in Provo, Utah, and then desired to continue her education by attending school in England. Her husband and some close Harris family

42. Joseph F., journal, 5 August 1912.
43. Joseph F., journal, 15 August 1912.
44. "Funeral Notice," *Provo Daily Herald*, 6 February 1912, 8.
45. Joseph F. to Joseph B. Keeler, 10 March 1912.

members opposed her choice. Undeterred, she traveled to Salt Lake City with her father, Levi Alexander Colvin (1857–1928), to obtain a blessing from Joseph F., her great uncle-in-law, before departing. To her surprise, President Smith advised her to go to school on the East Coast instead of in England.[46] Nevertheless, with her parents' help and support, Irene decided to go forward with her plans and made her way to England. The *Salt Lake Tribune* reported that Irene "went to England last October to study obstetrics."[47] She spent 1911–12 in London training at the General Lying-In Hospital, where a photograph was taken, the last known image of Irene.

Concluding her studies there in 1912, Irene sent Martha Ann the photograph of herself and the other nurses taken in London and a poignant note in which she mentioned the challenges she faced when she decided to leave Utah to attend school in England the year before. Irene still felt hurt by her husband's opposition and President Smith's counsel: "In Going through the struggle here alone in the world I felt to resent Walter's [her husband] and Pres. Smith's remarks toward my father [Levi Colvin, who had mortgaged his farm to pay for her travel and school expenses] who is doing so much for me and has done for us all along. . . . My [nursing] course here has just about been 'all work and no play.'" As is sometimes the case in history, she then penned what would become a tragic and ironic line, "*But expect to enjoy my trip home better.*"[48]

Tragically, three weeks after writing this note and sending the photograph, she took passage on the RMS *Titanic*, which sank in the North Atlantic on 15 April 1912, less than three hours after colliding with an iceberg.[49]

Walter married again in November 1914, but a year later he and his wife, Annie Dean (1884–1960), lost their first baby, Mary. A year later, on 30 November 1916, Annie delivered twin girls, Lora (1916–2006) and Dora

Irene Colvin Corbett (standing, second row on left), London, England, ca. 1911–12. This image was sent to Martha Ann by her grandson's wife Irene just weeks before she began her journey back to the United States. Courtesy of Don Corbett.

46. Joseph F. reported to Irene's husband the visit he had with Irene and her father, indicating that he had recommended an alternative but that she was determined to travel to England. See Joseph F. to Walter H. Corbett, 19 December 1911.
47. "Memorial in Provo for Titanic Victim," *Salt Lake Tribune*, 22 May 1912, 7.
48. Irene Colvin Corbett to Martha Ann, 1 April 1912, emphasis added; as cited in Carole Call King, *Verna Passey Call: Her Place in the Line of Extraordinary Women* (n.p., 2018), 52.
49. See Richard E. Bennett and Jeffrey L. Jensen, "'Nearer, My God, to Thee': The Sinking of the *Titanic*," in *Regional Studies in Latter-day Saint Church History: The British Isles*, ed. Cynthia Doxey, Robert C. Freeman, Richard Neitzel Holzapfel, and Dennis A. Wright (Provo, UT: Religious Studies Center, Brigham Young University, 2007), 109–27.

(1916–75). This double joy was replaced with sadness when Walter died in February 1917 at the age of thirty-one.

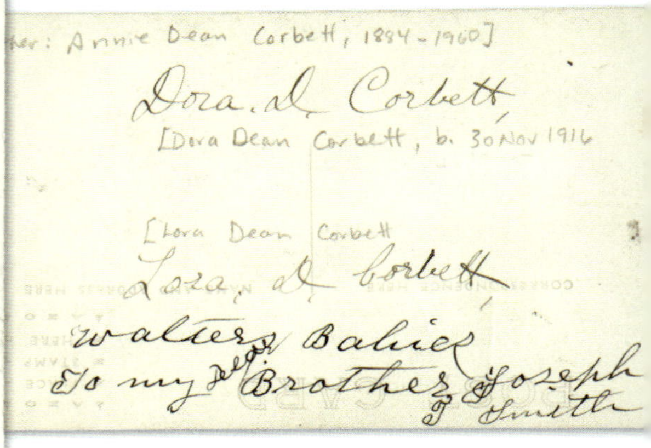

Annie Dean Corbett and her twins, Lora and Dora, ca. 1917. Martha Ann wrote, "Walter's babies To my Dear Brother Joseph F Smith." Courtesy of CHL.

In 1913 Martha Ann informed Joseph F. of a fire at her home.[50] This setback, along with other challenges, required Martha Ann to move back into the adobe home.[51] Letters between her and

50. Joseph F. read in a local paper about a fire that damaged Martha Ann's home; see Joseph F. to Martha Ann, 28 February 1913, herein. Martha Ann provided details in early March; see Martha Ann to Joseph F., 3 March 1913, herein.

51. Later, on 16 October 1918, Martha Ann transferred the lot to the Church for one dollar. With the agreement, she could apparently remain in the home until her death. See Utah County Deed Record Book No. 180, entry number 5812.

Joseph F. during this period often mention concerns with the annual property tax payment.[52] Martha Ann was unable to make the full payment in 1916, resulting in a tax sale. She obtained a mortgage release on 23 September 1918, and the following month, just weeks before Joseph F. died, the property was transferred to the Provo Sixth Ward Corporation of The Church of Jesus Christ of Latter-day Saints.[53]

An event that brought much joy to Martha Ann during this period was the publication of an article about her mother, Mary Fielding Smith, that included photographs of Joseph F.'s and Martha Ann's families in the Church's Relief Society publication.[54] In January 1916 Martha Ann received a letter from Susa Young Gates (1856–1933), founder and editor of the *Relief Society Magazine*:

> Dear Aunt Martha: I am just now sending you the picture which you lent me of your little family. Aunt Edna let me have your other group, and we are now working on the magazine. I hope to have it out in a week or ten days, when I will try and remember to send you a copy. . . . I wrote a little something about yourself, which I hope will prove satisfactory. President Smith has gone over the article very carefully and approved of it all. There is a very beautiful picture of your mother beside the other family groups. I hope you will like it all. May the Lord bless you and heal your body and comfort your spirit, is the prayer of, your living friend and sister, Susa Young Gates.[55]

When the March issue of the *Relief Society Magazine* appeared, readers were introduced to Mary Fielding Smith, Joseph F., and Martha Ann, along with information about their children.[56] Two photographs of Martha Ann and family members appeared in the article: (1) "Mrs. Martha A. Smith Harris, daughter of Mary Fielding Smith, and her three eldest boys" and (2) "William J. Harris and Martha A. Smith-Harris with their children."[57]

The article acknowledged, "The people are not so well acquainted with Martha Ann Harris, the daughter of Mary Fielding Smith. For, like her mother, she is modest, retiring, and gentle. She is frugal and very industrious. . . . She has reared her family in the fear of the Lord and they have risen up to bless her in the gates."[58]

During this decade, Martha Ann's health continued to plague her as she aged. Her multiple accidents over the years had taken a toll. Joseph F. noted in a letter to their cousin, "Martha is still at her little home in Provo, in rather feeble health, but carrying the responsibility of maintaining her home, and caring for her two motherless grandchildren."[59] A letter of hers in 1914 mentions some of the health problems she was facing at that time: "I am gaining sloly . . . while I have been here I have sufferd quite a bit with my knee & other ailments that I have to contend with. but I am very

52. See Martha Ann to Joseph F., 26 December 1911; Joseph F. to Martha Ann, 22 November 1912; and Joseph F. to Martha Ann, 14 November 1916, herein.
53. Following Martha Ann's death in October 1923, the property was again transferred—this time to Martha Ann's son-in-law Harry Walter Startup, who was married to Martha Artimissa Harris. The adobe home is now gone, and the larger home, which was still standing at 214 South Third West in Provo in 2018, has been remodeled beyond recognition and is occupied by people who are not related to Martha Ann and William Jasper.
54. Susa Young Gates, "Mothers in Israel," *Relief Society Magazine* 3, no. 3 (March 1916): 122–48.
55. Susa Young Gates to Martha Ann, 31 January 1916.
56. See "Genealogy of William J. Harris and Martha Ann Smith," *Relief Society Magazine* 3, no. 3 (March 1916): 146–48.
57. Gates, "Mothers in Israel," 141, 147.
58. Gates, "Mothers in Israel," 140–41.
59. Joseph F. to Ina D. Coolbrith, 23 October 1911.

thankfull that I am as well as I am, at the present & hope & pray I may <still> be improving I got a pare of crutches & have yoused them some but I have been very week I could not get round mutch."[60]

In February 1919 Vivian Clyde Safford (1896–1919), the husband of Martha Ann's granddaughter Edna Mae, died, leaving behind his young wife and a newborn baby, Virginia Safford (1919–98). To support the family, Edna Mae worked during the day while seventy-eight-year-old Martha Ann watched the baby, performing as she had done so often before an act of service that revealed her innate gift of charity and reflected her unstinting devotion to her family throughout her life.[61]

During the latter part of her life, Martha Ann visited Salt Lake City whenever she could for general conference during President Smith's administration. As her granddaughter Edna Mae

President's Home (Beehive House), ca. 1912. Martha Ann visited her brother at his home in Salt Lake City on numerous occasions, including at the annual and semiannual general conferences held in the spring and fall of each year. Courtesy of CHL.

60. See Martha Ann to Joseph F., 7 July 1914, herein.
61. See Carole Call King, "History of Martha Ann Smith Harris, 1841–1923" (unpublished manuscript in editors' possession).

Harris family reunion, 11 April 1917, photograph taken outside the Provo Sixth Ward building by George Edward Anderson, Provo, Utah. Front row: Mary Corbett, Martha Ann Harris, and William Harris Jr. Back row: Sarah Passey, Martha Startup, Zina Dennis, John Harris, Franklin Harris, and Hyrum Harris. This is one of four photographs taken by Anderson at the reunion. Courtesy of CHL.

Simmons recalled, "Grandmother went to Salt Lake for Conference every year—spring and fall—and stayed in the Beehive House where Uncle Joseph lived. There we had our own room and a bath to ourselves. Oh, how wonderful I thought it was! Then we ate in the large dining room at a big long table with Uncle Joseph at the head."[62] During one visit, Martha Ann fell on the front steps of the Beehive House. Her granddaughter who had accompanied her recalled, "She went 'a flying' and broke her ribs. She convalesced in the Beehive House for several weeks."[63]

As Martha Ann neared the end of her life, she remained close to her extended family. Her children, grandchildren, and great-grandchildren recalled her uncanny ability to know when someone in her family was in trouble. "There seemed to be a thin veil between her and the Spirit World," wrote one of her descendants. "When one of her sons was injured by a premature blast [probably while mining], his family decided to keep the news from her until he was well again, so she would not worry." However, she wrote and asked them to tell her what the matter was because she knew something was wrong and could not rest until she knew what it was. After several similar instances that confirmed Martha Ann's prescience, family learned to tell her immediately when anything of moment happened to any member of her family.[64]

A WITNESS OF THE RESTORATION

Martha Ann often related her memories of Hyrum and Joseph the Prophet to her grandchildren and urged them to gain testimonies of the gospel's truthfulness for themselves.[65] In one such instance, Elbert Startup (1912–99), a grandson, recorded Martha Ann's recollection of the aftermath of the

62. Ruth Mae Harris, *Martha Ann, Daughter of Hyrum and Mary Fielding Smith* (Orem, UT: published by the author, 2002), 147.
63. Harris, *Martha Ann*, 148.
64. Harris, *Martha Ann*, 131.
65. In one case, Martha Ann wrote a letter to a person in Tennessee to witness the truth of the Restoration. See Martha Ann to Joanna Spears, 1920.

Martha Ann and a group of sisters, 24 March 1914. Left to right: Margaret Allen Harris, Marinda Knapp Glazier, Martha Ann Smith Harris, Marilla Lucretia J. M. Daniels, Eunice Billings Snow, Johanna H. Patten, Alice M. B. Wilkins, Sarah L. Fausett Turner, Pericia Grover Bunnell, Hannah Carter Robbins, and Sarah Topham Clark. Courtesy of the Pioneer Museum, Provo, Utah.

martyrdom: "I saw them bring in the bodies of Uncle Joseph, and of my father, and I remember that everyone was weeping. I remember that someone lifted me up to kiss my father's lips for the very last time. I was only three years old, but I knew that something very important had happened that night."[66]

To share her testimony beyond her family circle, Martha Ann joined ten other Provo women in signing an affidavit officially witnessing that they had seen the Prophet Joseph Smith. The special occasion was captured in a photograph taken at the time.[67] The notarized document states, "Provo, Utah Mar. 24, 1914. We the undersigned with joy and heartfelt gratitude to God, Our Heavenly Father, hereby testify that we saw the Prophet Joseph Smith and declare unto all that he was a Prophet of God." The eleven women signed their names and added their ages and birthplaces. Martha Ann was the ninth person to sign the document: "My name is Martha Ann Smith Harris."[68]

66. Harris, *Martha Ann*, 131.

67. The photograph and affidavit are displayed at the Provo Daughters of Utah Pioneers Museum in Provo, Utah. See Katherine Thatcher Brimhall, *The Testifiers of the Prophet Joseph Smith: Biographical Vignettes of Mormon Pioneer Women* (n.p., 2011).

68. "March 24, 1914 Affidavit," Provo Daughters of Utah Pioneers Museum, Provo, Utah.

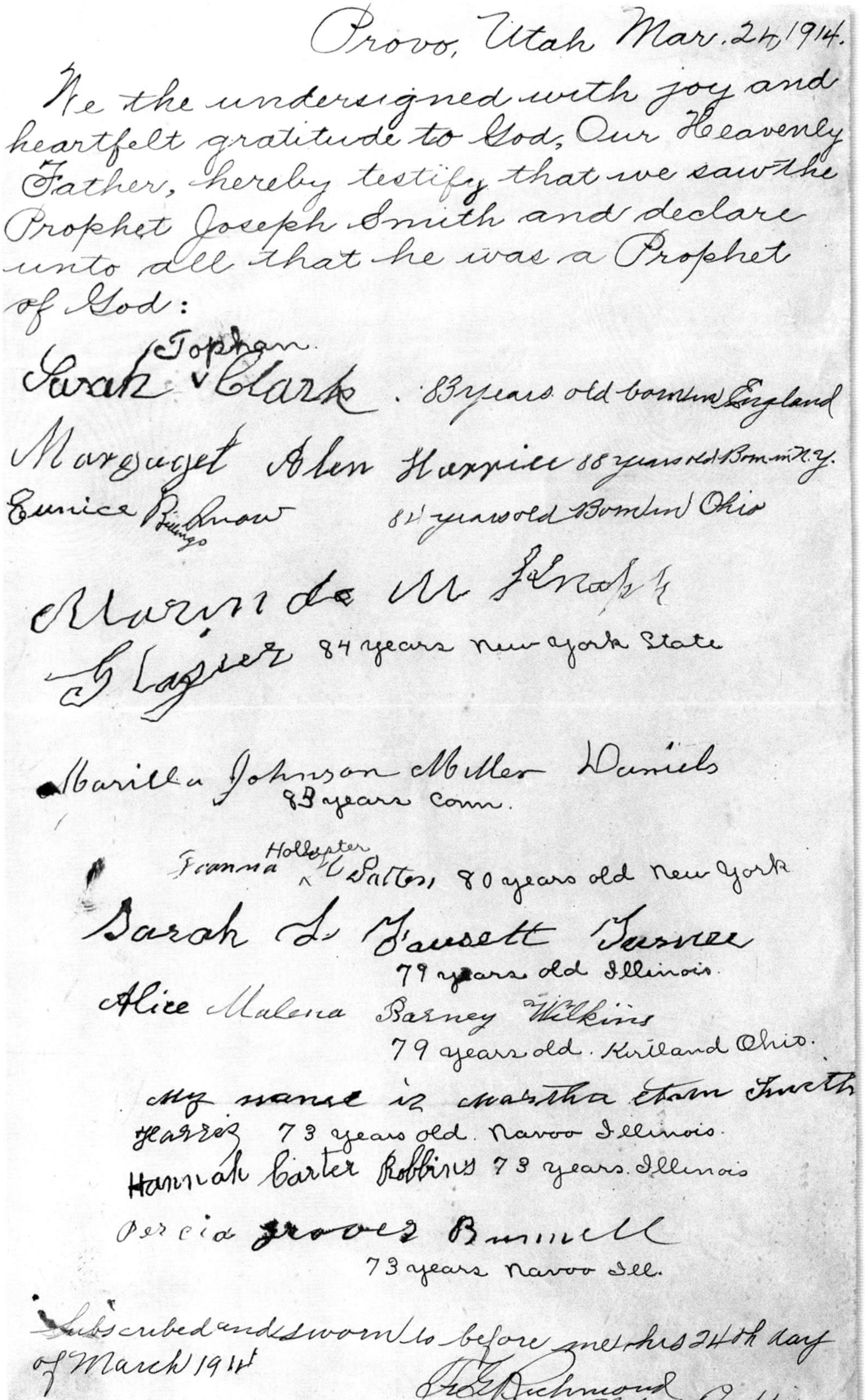
Provo, Utah Mar. 24, 1914.

We the undersigned with joy and heartfelt gratitude to God, Our Heavenly Father, hereby testify that we saw the Prophet Joseph Smith and declare unto all that he was a Prophet of God:

Sarah Topham Clark . 83 years old born in England
Margaget Alen Harriss 88 years old Born in N.Y.
Eunice Billings Snow 84 years old Born in Ohio
Mary Ada M Knapp Glazier 84 years New York State
Marilla Johnson Miller Daniels 83 years Conn.
Joanna Hollister Patten 80 years old New York
Sarah L Fausett Fausee 79 years old Illinois.
Alice Malena Barney Wilkins 79 years old. Kirtland Ohio.
My name is Martha Ann Smith Harris 73 years old. Navoo Illinois.
Hannah Carter Robbins 73 years. Illinois
Percia Groves Bunnell 73 years Navoo Ill.

Subscribed and sworn to before me this 24th day of March 1914
F. E. Richmond
Notary Public

Martha Ann and ten other women signed their names to their testimony of having seen the Prophet Joseph Smith. Martha Ann is the ninth signer: "My name is Martha Ann Smith Harris." Someone has added "73 years old. Navoo Illinois." Courtesy of the Pioneer Museum, Provo, Utah.

Joseph F. and Julina Lambson Smith and family, 5 May 1916, Thomas Studio, Salt Lake City, Utah. Joseph F. inscribed a note on the mount for his sister, "Martha A. Smith Harris May 5th 1916. Golden Wedding Day." Courtesy of CHL.

SUMMARY

Joseph F. was seventy-eight years old when he sent Martha Ann his last letter in December 1916. Four of his wives were still living, along with thirty-four children. In the end, Joseph F. was the father of forty-eight children, including two who had been adopted and three who had come into his family when he married Alice Ann Kimball. The year 1916 held special meaning for Joseph F. because he celebrated his fiftieth wedding anniversary with Julina. On 5 May that year, about two hundred fifty people joined in a celebration at the Beehive House. The following day the family gathered at the Thomas Studio in Salt Lake City for what has become a famous family photograph, with him and Julina dressed in white.

Later, family members gathered for "moving pictures," which have not survived.[69] At this time Joseph F. and Martha Ann were photographed together—apparently for the last time—in at least two poses, one outdoors and one indoors.

Joseph F. and Martha Ann visiting, 5 May 1916, during the "Golden Wedding Reception given by President and Mrs. Joseph F. Smith in commemoration of their fiftieth wedding anniversary Friday evening, May the fifth from eight until eleven o'clock at the Beehive House, Salt Lake City."[70] Courtesy of Carole Call King.

69. Joseph F., journal, 5–6 May 1916.
70. Invitation, "1866–1916," Golden Wedding Reception, Joseph Smith Family Papers, CHL.

Martha Artimissa Harris Startup with children, ca. 1913. From left: Naomi, Norell, Martha Artimissa with Elbert Harris on her lap, and LaRue. Courtesy of Carole Call King.

Martha Ann was seventy-five years old when she received the last letter from her brother in 1916. She was the mother of eleven children, eight of whom were living in 1916. Her husband William Jasper had been dead seven years. She and Joseph F. were matriarch and patriarch over large, multigenerational families. Joseph F. wrote to her in 1916 about a family gathering where 125 members were present, including 65 of his 79 grandchildren.[71] Writing to him that same year, Martha Ann spoke of her 71 grandchildren and 34 great-grandchildren.[72]

Martha Ann and her granddaughter Naomi Startup, ca. 1913. Courtesy of Carole Call King.

Martha Ann enjoyed the company of family members who lived close by, giving her an opportunity to spend time with grandchildren and great-grandchildren. On one occasion in 1913, the family's efforts to gather and celebrate Martha Ann's birthday was mentioned in a Salt Lake City newspaper: "Mrs. Walter Startup entertained at her home Wednesday evening in honor of her mother, Mrs. Martha Harris, who had reached her seventy-second birth anniversary."[73] At some point during the decade, the family expanded the birthday celebration into a Harris family reunion held near Martha Ann's birthday. These reunions were generally held in the Provo Sixth Ward building (see photos on p. xxvi, p. 459, and p. 520). As mentioned earlier, this tradition continued after Martha Ann's death in 1923.

In these family gatherings, the stories of Martha Ann and William Jasper were retold to new generations.[74] Fortunately, Many descendants of Martha Ann who had known her firsthand shared their reminiscences of her on paper and in voice recordings. In these stories Martha Ann is described as a loving, kind, thoughtful, faithful, and hardworking mother, grandmother, and great-grandmother.

Family and health concerns are once again highlighted in the final letters between

71. See Joseph F. to Martha Ann, 14 November 1916, herein.
72. See Martha Ann to Joseph F., 27 March 1916, herein.
73. "Social Events in Utah," *Salt Lake Herald*, 18 May 1913, 40.
74. In 1935 a gathering that included swimming, games, singing, eating, and a special visit from Martha Ann's sister-in-law Julina Lambson Smith took place with more than one hundred family members present. A Provo newspaper reported, "Remarks were then made by Mrs. Julina L. Smith, of Salt Lake, the eldest surviving wife of the [Church] president Joseph F. Smith. She gave a splendid talk on her acquaintances with and her love of Martha Ann and William [Jasper] Harris." "Harris Family Reunion at Saratoga," *Daily Herald*, 17 June 1935, 2. Her visit was timely since Julina died less than seven months later on 10 January 1936.

Joseph F. and his sister. Beyond the usual common maladies, they both confronted the increasing effects of aging. Joseph F. wrote with a touch of humor, "We are all usually well—but growing older at an excellerated pace, like the cart-wheel rolling down the hill, which gains speed as it nears the bottom!"[75]

Near the end of 1916, Joseph F.'s usual vigor took a permanent turn for the worse. Extracts from his journal show some of the health problems he faced near the end of his life:

> I had a very painful, restless night; I could not rest.

> I passed a most sleepless and uncomfortable night, with great difficulty to get full breath.

> My heart was throbbing with rapid violence, and my head swam, and my eyes dimmed until I could scarcely see.[76]

From the thirty-five surviving letters from this decade, it appears that Joseph F. and Martha Ann visited each other from time to time, particularly during general conferences of the Church and family celebrations. Joseph F.'s already-rigorous schedule as a Church leader took on even more demands, a workload he maintained until health issues forced him to slow down in 1916.

Throughout this decade, Martha Ann continued to care for her children, grandchildren, and great-grandchildren. As much as possible, she worked at home and continued making temple clothes. She expected to die long before her brother would,[77] but as it turned out, she lived five years beyond his death.[78]

Martha Ann always treasured her brother's letters. On 3 March 1913 she penned these words:

> I cirtenly do opricate your kindness to me poor old cripled up woman that I am I dont know what ever I would do if it was not for my dear good noble grand ~~dear~~ beloved generous harted even more than I could ever expect & I feel in my heart to say God bless you for ever. for you have helped me to bare my burdons helped to lighten the load that has rested on me if it had not have been for you I surly would hav sunk under the load I feel truly greatfull to you mor than I can express.[79]

The known letters between them of this final decade make few references to local and world events. The family is by far the predominant focus—a fitting finale to nearly six decades of correspondence between Joseph F. Smith and his "Dear Sister."

75. See Joseph F. to Martha Ann, 30 September 1916, herein.
76. Quoted in Joseph Fielding Smith, *The Life of Joseph F. Smith: Sixth President of The Church of Jesus Christ of Latter-day Saints* (Salt Lake City, UT: Deseret Book, 1938), 472.
77. See introduction to the 1880–89 letters.
78. Martha Ann passed away in Provo on 19 October 1923 at the age of eighty-one.
79. See Martha Ann to Joseph F., 3 March 1913, herein.

Letters

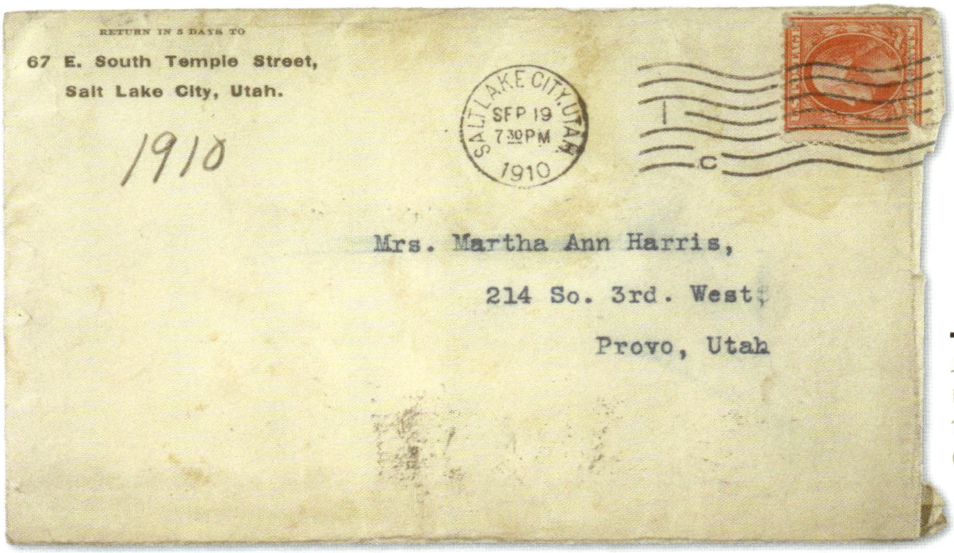

Joseph F. to Martha Ann, 19 September 1910 (envelope)

JOSEPH F. TO MARTHA ANN, 19 SEPTEMBER 1910

Sept. 19, 1910.[1]

Martha Ann Harris,
214 So. 3rd. West St.,
Provo City, Utah.

My Dear Sister[2] Martha:

1. The postmark on the envelope indicates that it was processed at 7:30 p.m. at the Salt Lake City Post Office on the day it was written. Typewritten in blue ink on official letterhead of the Church from the Office of the Trustee-in-Trust.
2. Martha Ann was sixty-nine, and Joseph F. was seventy-one.

Church of Jesus Christ of Latter-day Saints
Office of
Trustee-in-Trust
Salt Lake City

JOSEPH F. SMITH
TRUSTEE-IN-TRUST

Sept. 19, 1910.

Martha Ann Harris,
214 So. 3rd. West St.,
Provo City, Utah.

My Dear Sister Martha:

It has been some time since I heard from you or you from me. On the 4th. of July I started on a tour, in company with Bishop Nibley and family, in the hope that it would be beneficial to my health. We followed this delusive hope to New York, across the sea to Dover, England, and Antwerp, Belgium, thence to Holland, thence to Scandinavia through Germany and back to Germany again, thence to Switzerland and France and back again to England, the native land of our dear mother, thence returning to New York and this city, arriving here on September 3rd, two weeks ago last Saturday, during which time I have been confined to my bed with sciatic-rheumatism, Many times during the past two weeks or more I have been wondering how it was with you and all your children and with our sister Jerusha who I so seldom see; so I thought I would just write you a line so say "Howdy" and express the wish that you may all be in the enjoyment of good health and still in the pursuit of happiness.

I was very much grieved on noticing in the paper

Joseph F. to Martha Ann, 19 September 1910 (p. 1)

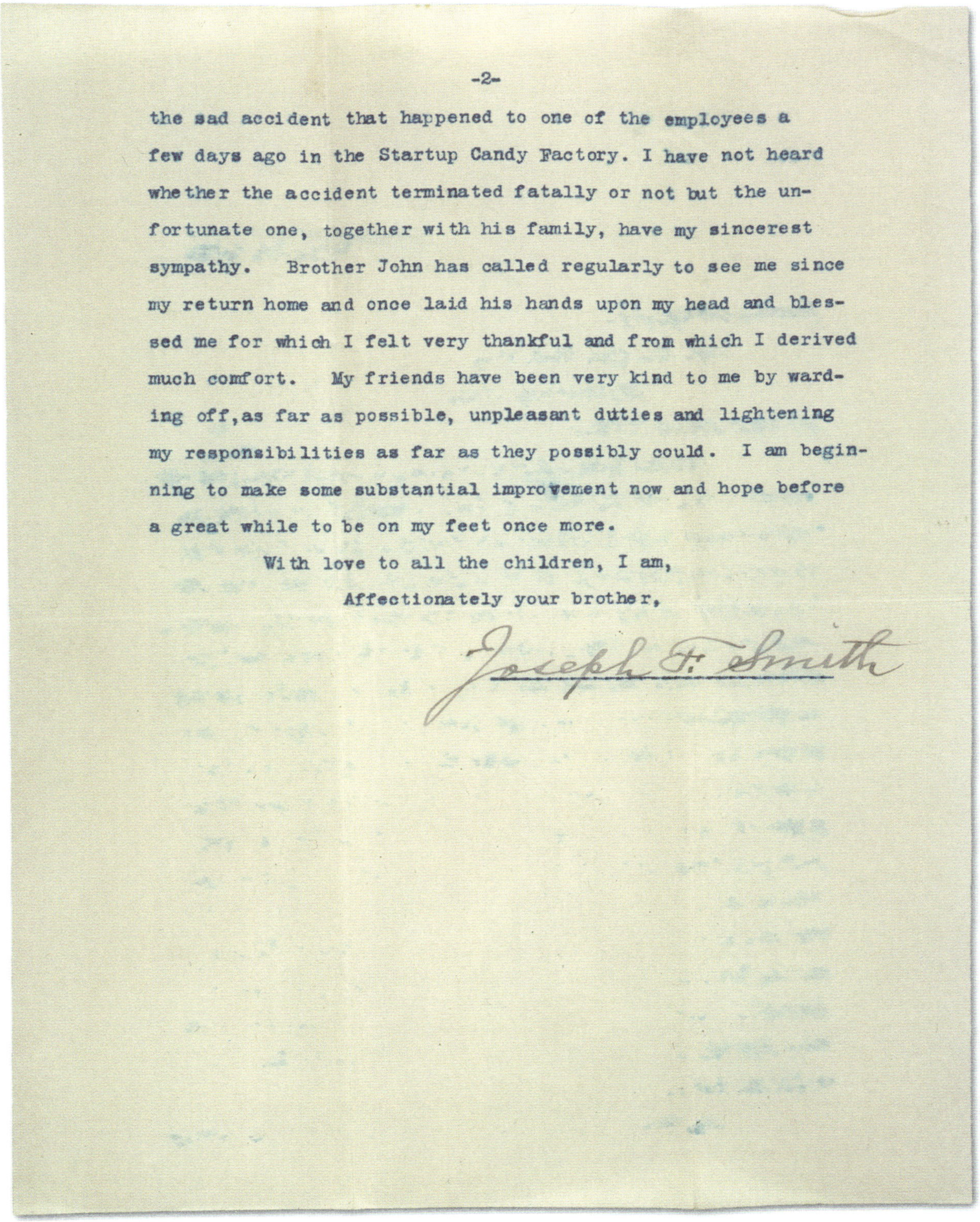

-2-

the sad accident that happened to one of the employees a few days ago in the Startup Candy Factory. I have not heard whether the accident terminated fatally or not but the unfortunate one, together with his family, have my sincerest sympathy. Brother John has called regularly to see me since my return home and once laid his hands upon my head and blessed me for which I felt very thankful and from which I derived much comfort. My friends have been very kind to me by warding off, as far as possible, unpleasant duties and lightening my responsibilities as far as they possibly could. I am beginning to make some substantial improvement now and hope before a great while to be on my feet once more.

With love to all the children, I am,

Affectionately your brother,

Joseph F. Smith

Joseph F. to Martha Ann, 19 September 1910 (p. 2)

It has been some time since I heard from you or you from me. On the 4th. of July I started on a tour, in company with Bishop Nibley[3] and family,[4] in the hope that it would be beneficial to my health. We followed this delusive hope to New York, across the sea to Dover, England, and Antwerp, Belgium, thence to Holland, thence to Scandinavia through Germany and back to Germany again, thence to Switzerland and France and back again to England, the native land of our dear mother,[5] thence returning to New York and this city, arriving here[6] on September 3rd, two weeks ago last Saturday, during which time I have been confined to my bed with sciatic-rheumatism.[7] Many times during the past two weeks or more I have been wondering how it was with you and all your children and with our sister Jerusha[8] who I so seldom see;[9] so I thought I would just write you a line so say "Howdy" and express the wish that you may all be in the enjoyment of good health and still in the pursuit of happiness.

I was very much grieved on noticing in the paper **[p. 2]** the sad accident that happened to one of the employees a few days ago in the Startup Candy Factory.[10] I have not heard whether the accident terminated fatally or not but the unfortunate one, together with his family, have my sincerest sympathy. Brother John[11] has called regularly to see me since my return home and once laid his hands upon my head an blessed me for which I felt very thankful and from which I derived much comfort. My friends have been very kind to me by warding off, as far as possible, unpleasant duties and lightening my responsibilities as far as they possibly could. I am beginning to make some substantial improvement now and hope before a great while to be on my feet once more.

With love to all the children, I am,

Affectionately your brother,

Joseph F. Smith[12]

---

3. Charles Wilson Nibley was the presiding bishop of the Church at the time. See biographical register, "Nibley, Charles Wilson."
4. Joseph F.'s wife Mary Taylor Schwartz accompanied him on this trip. Joseph F. spoke to missionaries and Church members in each of the countries he visited and also did some sightseeing. See Richard Neitzel Holzapfel and R. Q. Shupe, *Joseph F. Smith: Portrait of a Prophet* (Salt Lake City, UT: Bookcraft, 2000), 177–79.
5. Joseph F. and Martha Ann's mother, Mary Fielding Smith, was born in Bedfordshire, England, on 21 July 1801.
6. Salt Lake City.
7. Sciatica, also known as sciatic rheumatism, occurs when the sciatic nerve at the base of the spine is compressed, making it painfully difficult to sit, stand, or walk. Anthon H. Lund visited Joseph F. on the day he returned from his European tour: "In the afternoon we went in to see the President. He has suffered with Sciatica the whole distance from here and back again on his European trip. He says when he lies down he is all right but when he is up he is suffering much pain." Anthon H. Lund, journal, 3 September 1910. See John P. Hatch, ed., *Danish Apostle, The Diaries of Anthon H. Lund, 1890–1921* (Salt Lake City, UT: Signature Books, 2006), 437.
8. Jerusha Smith.
9. The semicolon is written in pencil.
10. A Salt Lake newspaper reported, "Provo, Sept. 17.—William F. Dunn, engineer at the Startup candy factory discovered something wrong with the belting last evening, and while endeavoring to adjust the trouble, was terribly injured by the machinery. He was dragged on to the shaft, which performed several revolutions before it could be stopped. The unfortunate engineer sustained a dislocation of the right knee, his collar bone was broken, and a screwdriver which he carried in his hip pocket was driven through his side, protruding from his back. However, it is believed that he is not injured internally, and hopes are therefore entertained for his early recovery." "Serious Accident," *Deseret News*, 17 September 1910, 9.
11. John Smith.
12. Signed in pencil and underscored with typewriting.

JOSEPH F. TO MARTHA ANN, 7 NOVEMBER 1910

Salt Lake City, Utah—
Nov. 7th 1910[13]

Martha Ann Harris
214 South 3d West Street,
Provo City, Utah Co. Utah

My Dear Sister Martha:—

I hope you are well, and that you are having a good visit with Jerusha.[14]

I was sorry you went off so unceremoniously the last time you were here, or just after the close of conference;[15] I expected you to remain here another day or two at least, and was surprised to learn you had gone without even saying goodby.

I have no news to write. I am gaining a little, but very slowly, in strength. My trouble has by no means entirely left me. I am still lame.[16] I send you my cheque for $10.00—, which may come in handy for a few trifling things you may need.

Tomorrow will be a day of good fortune or of calamity and disaster for Utah, and especially for this city. If the Republican Party shall win—there will be prosperity and peace. Every democratic vote cast will be in favor of the so-called American Party—and against my friends![17] Affectionately your Brother. [**p. 2**]

Let no man decieve or wheedle[18] you or any body you can influence to the contrary—to vote for Tom Kearns' party.[19] and the Salt Lake Tribune.[20] Every democratic vote cast in Utah will be in the interest—more or less of the bitterest foes of Utah and of the mormon people, in the combination known as "The American Party". Any Republican who will desert his party at this election—in Utah—for any cause—I don't care what it is, is either a traitor to his party or is sadly deceived or in error. If my party had faults I desired to amend or eradicate from it, I would not fly to my enemies to do it but would stay with my party and benefit it if I could.[21]

---

13. The postmark on the envelope indicates that it was processed at Salt Lake City Post Office on 8 November 1910 at 9:30 a.m.
14. Jerusha Smith.
15. The 80th Semiannual General Conference was held on 6–7 and 9 October 1910.
16. See Joseph F. to Martha Ann, 19 September 1910, herein.
17. The American Party, organized in September 1904, was largely composed of local non–Latter-day Saint citizens and disaffected Latter-day Saints. See Thomas G. Alexander, *Mormonism in Transition: A History of the Latter-day Saints* (Urbana: University of Illinois Press, 1986), 29. See also biographical register, "Kearns, Thomas."
18. *OED* defines *wheedle* as "to use influence or flattery to persuade someone to do something."
19. Thomas Kearns, a prominent Catholic businessman and politician.
20. The *Salt Lake Tribune* had been an anti–Latter-day Saint newspaper from the time it was first published in 1870 but had become less strident when Kearns purchased it in 1901. Nevertheless, it was still often the voice of opposition against the Church.
21. Anthon H. Lund reported the election results: "I was anxious about the result as it has been a very hard fought campaign with much bitterness and personal abuse. . . . It was pleasing to learn that the Americans were beaten. The country seems to have gone Democratic." Anthon H. Lund, journal, 8 November 1920; quoted in Hatch, *Danish Apostle*, 443.

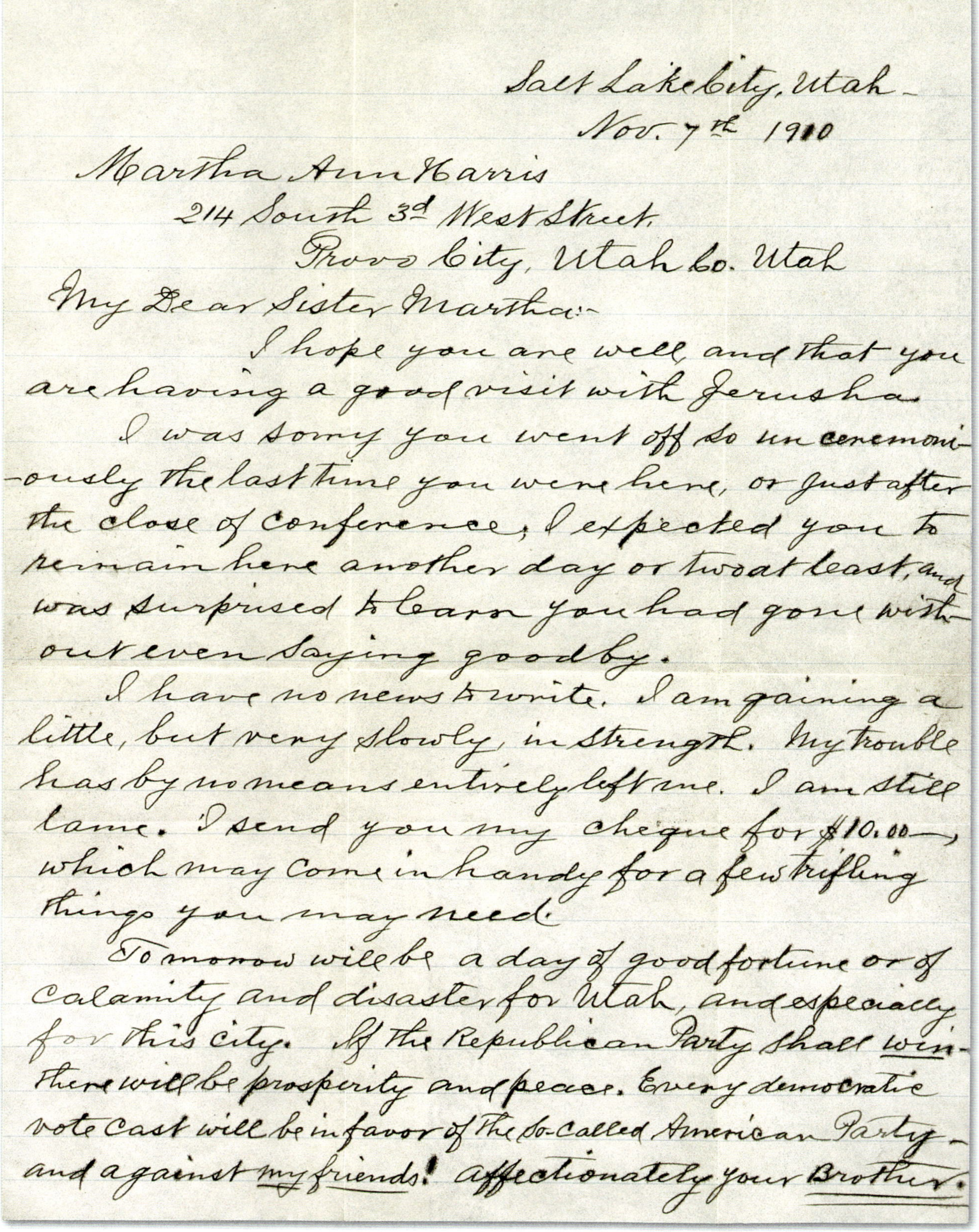
Salt Lake City, Utah.

Nov. 7th 1910

Martha Ann Harris
214 South 3d West Street.
Provo City, Utah Co. Utah

My Dear Sister Martha:-

I hope you are well, and that you are having a good visit with Jerusha.

I was sorry you went off so unceremoniously the last time you were here, or just after the close of conference; I expected you to remain here another day or two at least, and was surprised to learn you had gone without even saying goodby.

I have no news to write. I am gaining a little, but very slowly, in strength. My trouble has by no means entirely left me. I am still lame. I send you my cheque for $10.00, which may come in handy for a few trifling things you may need.

Tomorrow will be a day of good fortune or of calamity and disaster for Utah, and especially for this city. If the Republican Party shall win there will be prosperity and peace. Every democratic vote cast will be in favor of the so-called American Party – and against my friends! affectionately your Brother.

Joseph F. to Martha Ann, 7 November 1910 (p. 1)

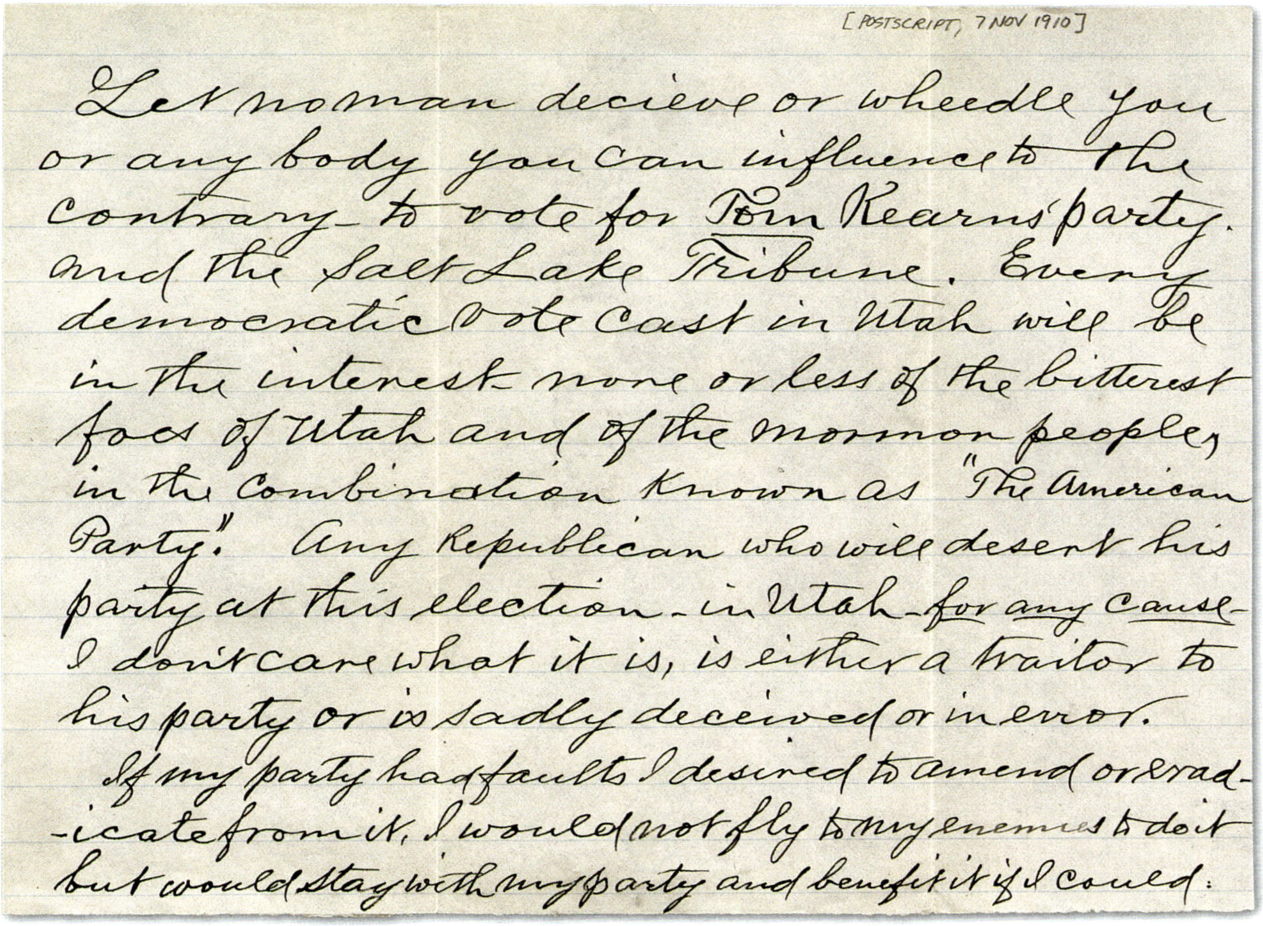
[POSTSCRIPT, 7 NOV 1910]

Let no man decieve or wheedle you or any body you can influence to the contrary to vote for Tom Kearns' party. and the Salt Lake Tribune. Every democratic vote cast in Utah will be in the interest more or less of the bitterest foes of Utah and of the mormon people, in the Combination known as "The American Party". Any Republican who will desert his party at this election - in Utah - for any cause - I don't care what it is, is either a traitor to his party or is sadly deceived or in error.

If my party had faults I desired to amend or erad-icate from it, I would not fly to my enemies to do it but would stay with my party and benefit it if I could.

Joseph F. to Martha Ann, 7 November 1910 (p. 2)

JOSEPH F. TO MARTHA ANN, 24 DECEMBER 1910

Dec. 24—1910[22]

Martha Ann Harris
214 South 3d West St. Provo City.

My Dear Sister Martha:—I certainly wish you a cheerful joyous Christmas and a happy, prosperous New Year and an endless succession of them.

I send you herewith my cheque No. 59—for $10.00 which I hope will bring you at least ten dollars worth of good.

Julina[23] is still suffering with rheumatism but keeps on her feet, and never stops from morning till night. Alice K.[24] is also troubled with rheumatism. I am some better. The rest

22. From Joseph F.'s letterpress copybooks; original not extant.
23. Julina Lambson.
24. Alice Ann Kimball.

of the folks are usually well. John is not well, Jerusha[25] is with him—We celebrated Uncle Joseph's[26] birth day anniversary yesterday, and would have been glad if you had been with us[27]

I hear that Joseph Albert[28] is not much better in health. I hope he will soon be himself again. All send love. Affectionately your brother
Joseph F. Smith

JOSEPH F. TO MARTHA ANN, 3 APRIL 1911

Salt Lake City, Utah, Apr. 3d 1911[29]

Martha Ann Harris
Provo, Utah Co.

My Dear Sister Martha:—

I send you herewith my cheque for $20.00 which accept with my compliments and love.

Your letter of Feb. 26th came to me Feb. 28th. I have been so busy that I have neglected my correspondence. In fact I have no time for myself—nor for my family or friends.

I can only attend to my public duties imperfectly for the want of more time and strength and ability. My kindred will therefore not have much pleasure nor profit in me. I am grieved over Joseph's condition.[30] We pray for him every day <at home,> and every week in the Temple[31]—and yesterday in our Fast meeting.[32] God only can give relief. Conference is on us.[33] We are all moderately well. With love, your brother Joseph F.

25. John Smith and Jerusha Smith.
26. Joseph Smith Jr.
27. John Henry Smith reported, "In the evening the party who went to Vermont to dedicate the Monument at the Birth place of Joseph Smith about 75 persons were present. We had an elegant meal, some good singing and reciting and speaking." John Henry Smith, journal, 23 December 1910; quoted in Jean Bickmore White, *Church State and Politics: The Diaries of John Henry Smith* (Salt Lake City, UT: Signature Books, 1990), 662.
28. Joseph Albert Harris.
29. Written on official letterhead of the Church from the Office of the First Presidency.
30. Joseph Albert Harris died on 28 May 1911, about two months after this letter was written. See Joseph F. to Martha Ann, 29 May 1911, herein.
31. Latter-day Saint practice includes special prayers held in temples as part of the ordinances performed therein and during the meetings of Church leaders in the Salt Lake Temple.
32. Generally held on the first Sunday of each month. See Mary Jolley, "Fast and Testimony Meeting," in *Encyclopedia of Mormonism*, ed. Daniel H. Ludlow (New York: Macmillan, 1992), 2:502.
33. The 81st Annual General Conference was held on 6–7 and 9 April 1911.

JOSEPH F. TO MARTHA ANN, 14 MAY 1911

Beehive House[34]
Salt Lake City, Utah
May 14—1911

My Dear Sister—
Martha Ann.

We have not forgotten that you have reached your Seventieth mile stone on your life's journey today.[35] And while we know you have been compelled to pass through many narrow places, and your path has been—all too—rough and thorney, yet we cannot fail to see the hand of Providence has not deserted you allways. Your life has been spared—your faith unimpaired, your hopes have not failed you, you have learned to kiss the hand that held the rod of your afflictions, and dealt out mercies in the hour of need, and to say from your heart "He doeth all things well".[36]

You have had experience to prove that God is more kind and loving to ward His children than is Man. God does not err—nor fail but Man is full of weakness. I send you $20.00 for a little birth-day gift. Affectionately your brother Joseph [**p. 2**]

May 16th 1911

P.S. I got a card from cousin Josephine Fielding Heath,[37] from Smithfield, Cache Co.[38] last evening informing us that her daughter Seraph[39] died the day before, i.e. on Sunday the 14th inst. So you will see she died on your birth-day anniversary. Julina[40] had to go off somewhere to day with "Aunt Em".[41] on mission work for the Relief Society[42]—so she is away from home.[43]

Josephines daughter will be burried to day, at Smithfield.

Our folks are all pretty well just now for which we are all very thankful.

Give our love to the girls and all friends, and reserve your share to yourself.

Affectionately your—brother

Joseph F.

---

34. See Joseph F. to Martha Ann, 6 May 1909, herein, note 165.
35. Martha Ann was born on 14 May 1841.
36. Based on Mark 7:37, the line comes from Elisha A. Hoffman's hymn "He Doeth All Things Well," published in 1879.
37. Josephine Fielding, wife of Orson Omer Heath, was Joseph Fielding's daughter. See biographical register, "Fielding, Josephine."
38. Located ninety miles north of Salt Lake City and seven miles north of Logan, Smithfield was originally known as Summit Creek when it was founded in 1857.
39. Seraph Celestia Heath. See biographical register, "Heath, Seraph Celestia."
40. Julina Lambson.
41. Emmeline B. Wells, affectionately known as "Aunt Em," had been the Relief Society General President since 3 October 1910. See biographical register, "Woodward, Emmeline Blanche."
42. Julina Lambson had been the second counselor in the Relief Society General Presidency since 3 October 1910.
43. Emmeline Wells noted on 16 May 1911, the day Joseph F. added a postscript to his unfinished 14 May letter, "Came up early and went off to Jordan Stake. Clarissa and Julina with me, called at President H. H. Larson's and had some refreshment fine strawberries, I spoke in the morning but gave Clarissa the most time as she was going away and could not speak in the afternoon, however it came about that Julina had to go too, Afternoon Julina spoke a few minutes & I had all the time." Emmeline B. Wells, journal, 16 May 1911, BYU.

N. B. We have just got word that Abraham Cannon's son, now in Holland—or France died to day—of apendicitis.[44] This is sad news. I have been so busy I neglected to send this as I should.

JOSEPH F. TO MARTHA ANN, 29 MAY 1911

May 29th 1911[45]

My Dear Sister Martha Ann:—

I got the sad word last evening thro' Julina,[46] that Joseph Albert had passed over the dark river to the great majority beyond.[47]

While it is always sad and sorrowful to pass thro' the gloomy shadows of the dark valley of death, there are some things much worse than death itself.

A living death is more to be dreaded than the final sleep, and rest from the fatal ills of mortality.

Joseph is all right now. He is beyond the power of death. Let me know what you need, and when the funeral will be—Ever—your Brother, Joseph F.

P.S. Julina and all the folks send you their love and sympathy in your hour of trial and sorrow. You must bravely sustain your trial—for Joseph is at rest, and is much better off than he has been for months, or possibly could have been if he had lived.[48]

JOSEPH F. TO MARTHA ANN, 6 NOVEMBER 1911

Nov. 6th 1911[49]

Martha Ann Harris—
214 South 3d West St. Provo,

My Dear Sister Martha:—

44. Lester Jenkins Cannon, son of Sarah Ann Jenkins and Abraham H. Cannon, was serving a mission in the Netherlands when he suffered from appendicitis complicated with peritonitis. He died on 16 May 1911 in Lille, France. See biographical register, "Cannon, Lester Jenkins."
45. From Joseph F.'s letterpress copybooks; original not extant.
46. Julina Lambson.
47. Martha Ann's son, Joseph Albert Harris, died on 28 May 1911 at age forty-nine, leaving behind his wife, Johanna Patten, and six children. A Provo newspaper reported that he died of "nervous exhaustion after several months' illness." See "Former Provo Man Dead," *Daily Herald* (Provo), 30 May 1911, 1. See also Joseph F. to Martha Ann, 3 April 1911, herein.
48. Written upside down in the top margin.
49. From Joseph F.'s letterpress copybooks; original not extant.

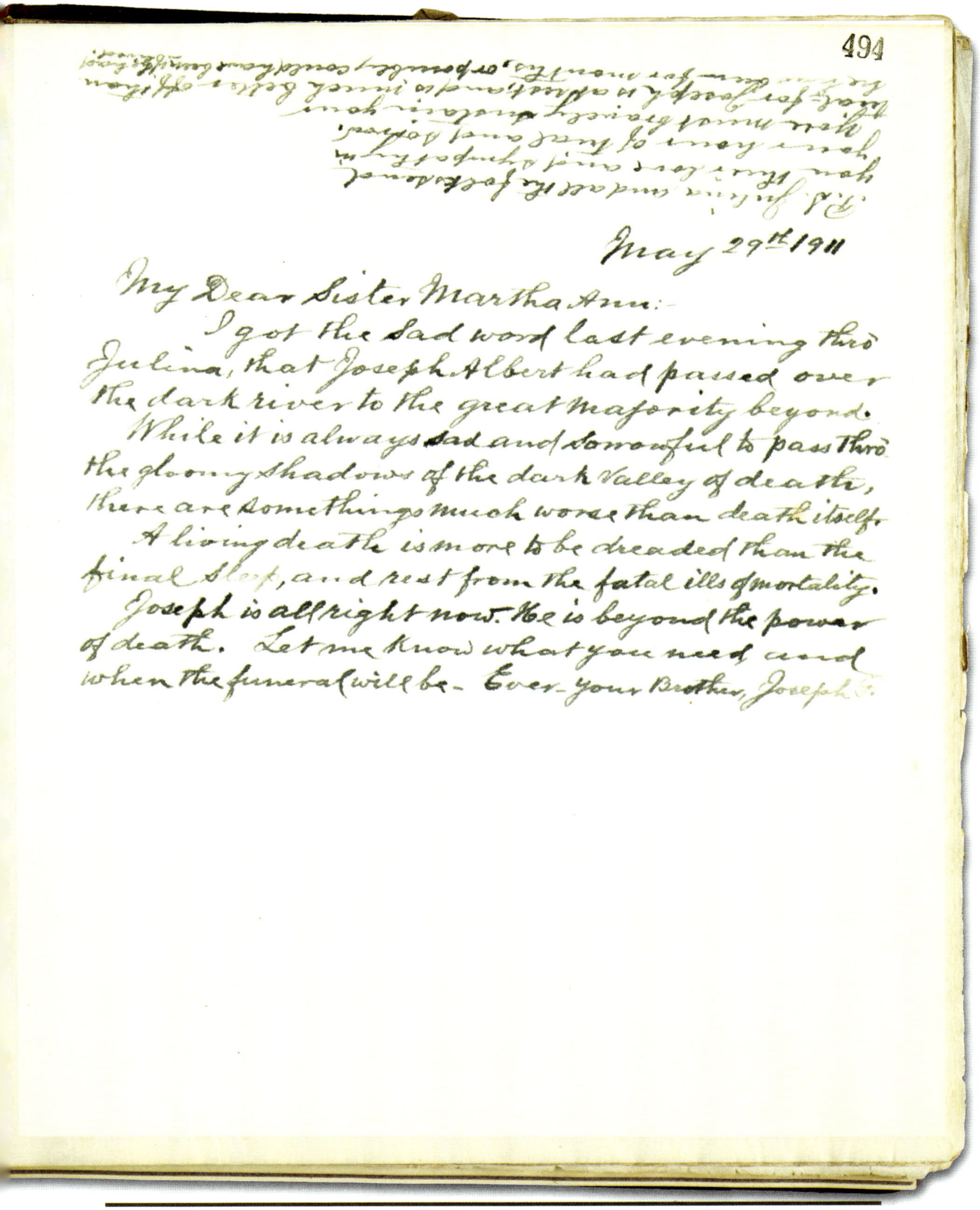
494

May 29th 1911

My Dear Sister Martha Ann:-

I got the sad word last evening thro' Julina, that Joseph Albert had passed over the dark river to the great majority beyond.

While it is always sad and sorrowful to pass thro' the gloomy shadows of the dark valley of death, there are some things much worse than death itself.

A living death is more to be dreaded than the final sleep, and rest from the fatal ills of mortality.

Joseph is all right now. He is beyond the power of death. Let me know what you need and when the funeral will be- Ever your Brother, Joseph F.

Joseph F. to Martha Ann, 29 May 1911, copy found in Joseph F.'s letterpress copybooks under that date.

I write to inform you that our brother, John, is in exceedingly bad health.[50] Last thursday he returned from a visit to Ray Davis,[51] up north with a severe cold, which immediately developed into pneumonia—or lung-fever. He has been confined to his bed, under the care of a trained nurse since last friday morning, without any symptoms so far as can be discerned, of improvement or relief. The general impression being, that he has steadily grown weaker.

The Doctor[52] gives no hope for his recovery, but we are all hoping and praying for his recovery.[53] His age is against us, and his heart seems very weak.

We will keep you posted by letter or phone as to his condition. I have a cold myself—but we are generally well. With love your brother
Joseph F.

Joseph F. to
Martha Ann,
22 December 1911
(envelope)

JOSEPH F. TO MARTHA ANN, 22 DECEMBER 1911

Salt Lake City, U.T. Dec. 22d 1911[54]

Martha Ann Harris
Provo, Utah—

50. John Smith died at 11:35 p.m. after a six-day battle with pneumonia. See "Patriarch Smith Summoned Home," *Deseret News*, 7 November 1911, 1, 6.
51. Ray Davis, John Smith's son-in-law, lived in Preston, Franklin County, Idaho. See biographical register, "Davis, Ray Leroy."
52. Dr. C. F. Wilcox, "Physical and Surgeon, Both Phones 367. 407 Templeton Blk." See *Business Directory of Salt Lake City, Utah* (Salt Lake City, UT: n.p., 1909), 108.
53. Joseph F. spent an hour with his older half brother before writing this letter.
54. The envelope includes a postal department stamp in the upper left-hand corner that reads, "Delivery delayed on account of insufficient time" (the delay most likely caused by the increased volume of mail during Christmastime). The postal stamp indicates that it was processed at the Salt Lake City Post Office at 12:00 p.m. Joseph F. has written Martha Ann's address as well as the word *Personal*, most likely because he has included a ten-dollar check. The letter is written on official letterhead of the Church from the Office of the President.

My Dear Sister Martha:—

I send you herein, my cheque for Ten—(10) dollars as a small remembrance of Christmas.[55]

I hope this will enable you to prepare a nice little christmas dinner for yourself and the two little grand children[56] who are keeping their Grand Mother Company in her widowhood.

We had a glorious meeting this morning[57] in the T. Annex[58] in honor of Uncle Joseph's[59] birth-day anniversary, tomorrow.[60] I have written our poor, proud Cousin Ina[61] and sent her enough for her christmas dinner—Hoping you are well I am your bro. Joseph F.——.

MARTHA ANN TO JOSEPH F., 26 DECEMBER 1911

RECEIVED
DEC29'11
PRESIDENT'S OFFICE[62]

Provo City December the
26 1911

Mr Joseph F Smith,

55. Joseph F. sent several people checks to cover Christmas dinners at this time. See, for example, Joseph F. to Ina D. Coolbrith, 20 December 1911; Joseph F. to Bishop Franklin S. Tingey [17th Ward, Salt Lake City], 21 December 1911; and Joseph F. to Jerusha Smith Pierce, 22 December 1911.
56. Refers to Edna Mae Simmons and John Arthur Simmons. See Joseph F. to Martha Ann, 2 April 1905 and 10 April 1907, herein.
57. The journals of most of those who likely participated, including Joseph F., Francis M. Lyman, Heber J. Grant, and Joseph Fielding Smith, are held in the Church History Library and are closed to researchers, so additional information about this gathering is unknown. The meeting is not mentioned in the Journal History of the Church.
58. The Salt Lake Temple Annex was designed by Joseph Don Carlos Young in 1866, constructed in 1888, and demolished in 1962 and replaced by a temporary annex that was replaced in 1966 with the annex currently in use. The annex accommodated three hundred people in the main assembly hall, which featured a podium for speakers. See James E. Talmage, *The House of the Lord: A Study of Holy Sanctuaries Ancient and Modern* (Salt Lake City, UT: The Church of Jesus Christ of Latter-day Saints, 1912), 255–59.
59. Joseph Smith Jr.
60. Another celebration was held on Saturday, 23 December 1911. James E. Talmage noted, "This evening wife and I were among the invited guests at the Smith anniversary gathering of the Centennial Memorial party in the celebration of the dedication of the Joseph Smith monument. The party was given by Prest. Smith, at the Lion House." James E. Talmage, journal, 23 December 1911, BYU. The printed program, included in Talmage's journal, indicates the gathering was held in the "Assembly Rooms at 5 p.m. Sharp." An extended report of the event appeared in a Salt Lake newspapers, "'Vermont Party' Gathers on Birthday of Prophet," *Deseret News*, 25 December 1911, 1.
61. Ina Coolbrith (née Josephine Donna Smith) spent most of her life in the San Francisco Bay Area and kept her Latter-day Saint heritage hidden. Following the death of her older sister Agnes Charlotte Smith, Ina cared for her niece and nephew, taking work at the Oakland Free Library, where she later mentored prominent figures such as Isadora Duncan and Jack London. Following the devastating 1906 fire and earthquake, Ina found herself in financial difficulty.
62. Stamped with blue ink in the top left margin of page 1.

my dear beloved brother your favor containing the check for ten dolars came safly to hand yester day after noon ~~&~~ and a hankerchef & a poto of your self from Aunt Edna,[63] & cards from Rachel & Eadeth[64] & I thank you all very mutch I opreicate all more than words can express I was truly thankfull to you for the money it will help me thrue this cold weather after all you let me have while I was there the last time I did not expect any thing more I feal bad to think **[p. 2]** you have to do so mutch for me. Hyrum[65] sent me 50 dolars bless his dear good soal, but it took it all to pay for the pavement & for the taxes Franklin[66] wrote & told me he would try & send me enough to pay my taxes but I guess he has not been able to rais it yet I try & be as carefull as I can but there is a dream all the time for something I know I have to impose on you all the time. I am still very lame I have to limp round & do the best I can. my left hip pains me of nights so I can not **[p. 3]**[67] rest mutch.[68] ~~of nights~~ now I know you have troubls enough of your own with <out> me bothering you with mine. I red of Aunt Marys[69] mother[70] pasing away in the paper it is few people that has no pain like she was that is not our lot ours is to suffer pain. She must have been a wonderfull women I know she will miss her so beeing right there with her so long dear little Royel[71] will miss her to bless his sweet dear little heart pleas give my love to Aunt **[p. 4]** Mary & tell her I would liked to have went to the funerel but I was not able to come even if I could have come. I never hird of her death untill she was buried. the girls are none of them very well Arte Sarah nor Jessie[72] Sarahs baby[73] has been very poorly with gathering in her head caused I guess fom cutting her teeth the children are home from scholl with me this week & I am glad to have thir help I am so lame pleas give my love to your folks the children **[p. 5]**[74] joins me in love & thanks to you they think there is no one on irth like thir uncle Joseph. now my dear brother I sincerly thank you again, with all my heart, we had a little quiat dinner at home here yester day we ~~were~~ were invited out but I did not feel well enought to go your greatfull & affectionate sister Martha A Harris **[p. 6]**

63. Edna Lambson.
64. Joseph F. and Julina Lambson's daughters Rachel Smith and Edith Eleanor Smith.
65. Hyrum Smith Harris.
66. Franklin Hill Harris.
67. "[26 DEC 1911]" is written above "3" in an unknown hand.
68. Martha Ann suffered multiple accidents during her life, which may have added to her discomfort as she grew older. In addition to falling in 1892 (see Joseph F. to Martha Ann, 20 June 1892, herein), she fell and broke her right arm in 1898, an injury that, according to her granddaughter, caused her severe suffering "for many months, not only physically but emotionally." See Carole Call King, "History of Martha Ann Smith Harris, 1841–1923" (unpublished manuscript in editors' possession), 5. She had also previously fallen and shattered a bone in her knee (see Joseph F. to Martha Ann, 7 March 1894, herein), and she may have suffered from a hernia as well (see Joseph F. to Martha Ann, 1 February 1906, herein, note 109).
69. Mary Taylor Schwartz Smith, Joseph F.'s wife.
70. Agnes Taylor Rich Hoagland Schwartz died on 12 December and was buried on 15 December 1911. Joseph F. Smith, Francis M. Lyman, Charles W. Penrose, Frank Y. Taylor, and Hyrum M. Smith spoke at her funeral. See "Tributes to Worth of Mrs. Agnes Schwartz: President Smith and Others Speak Highly of Life of Noble Woman," *Deseret News*, 15 December 1911, 2.
71. Royal Grant Smith, son of Mary Schwartz and Joseph F., was five years old at this time.
72. Martha Artimissa Harris, Sarah Lovina Harris, and Jessie Lena Freckleton.
73. Verna Passey, born on 18 July 1910 to Sarah Lovina Harris Passey. See biographical register, "Passey, Verna."
74. "[26 DEC 1911]" is written above "5" in an unknown hand.

I got a letter fom little Franklin the other day <they are in mexico> they were all well & the children were going to school & doing nicly[75]

P.S I am so glad you can help our poor misguided cousin Ina[76] would that she could see the right way be fore it is to late pleas excuse all mistakes it is so hard for me to write at best

JOSEPH F. TO MARTHA ANN, 22 JUNE 1912

Salt Lake City, Utah, June 22.[d] 1912[77]

Martha Ann S. Harris
Provo—Utah Co.

My Dear Sister Martha:—I have just written to Sister Jerusha.[78] She is a very sick woman.[79] I called on and blessed and prayed for her several weeks ago, while in Brigham City.[80] Since then I have written to her and received letters from Eli,[81] about her. She is not able to write, herself. I rec'd a letter from Eli this morning, he thinks his mother is a little better than she was, but is very weak. She has jaundis,[82] or the in action of the liver—and is exceedingly yellow, or dark.

She is having a long seige of it, and I hope she will pull through. My folks are all usually well. Aunt Sarah[83] is visiting with her sisters at Fielding—in Box Elder Co.[84]

I send you $5[00] which will not come amiss—

I hope you and the children are well.

Give my love to them all—in which all here joine. With love your brother, Joseph F.——

75. Franklin Hill Harris was apparently working as a railroad contractor in New Mexico.
76. Ina Coolbrith (née Josephine Donna Smith). See Joseph F. to Martha Ann, 22 December 1911, herein.
77. Written on official letterhead of the Church from the Office of the First Presidency. Joseph F. was seventy-three, and Martha Ann was seventy-one.
78. Joseph F. noted in his diary, "Wrote to Jerusha, Martha Ann, & Sarah E." Joseph F., journal, 22 June 1912.
79. Jerusha Smith died five days later, on 27 June 1912. Joseph F. reported, "65 years today since the Martyrdom. At the Temple . . . Jerusha died today." Joseph F., journal, 27 June 1912.
80. Brigham City, Box Elder, Utah, is about sixty miles north of Salt Lake City.
81. Eli Thomas Pierce, son of Jerusha Smith and William Pierce. See biographical register, "Pierce, Eli Thomas."
82. Jaundice, a yellowing of the skin and whites of the eyes, is very often the result of liver disease such as hepatitis or liver cancer.
83. Sarah Ellen Richards.
84. Fielding is located about eighty-four miles north of Salt Lake City.

Joseph F. to Martha Ann, 20 August 1912 (envelope, front and back)

JOSEPH F. TO MARTHA ANN, 20 AUGUST 1912

Salt Lake City, Utah, Aug. 20th 1912[85]

Martha Ann Harris
214 South 3d West St. Provo—
My Dear Sister Martha.

I hope these few lines will find you well and will remind you that you still have a brother in the "land of the living".[86] I am pleased to say I am in usual health, and from day to day bent on the discharge of my duty to the best of my ability and understanding.[87]

I am delighted also to say that my family are enjoying their usual degrees of health and aptitude to make the most they can out of it. You know my family are workers. They spend no idle hours in gossip, and waste no precious moments in useless repining.[88] The Lord has been and is most merciful to me and mine.

We have with us Vonna Griffin, granddaughter of our deceased Sister Sarah.[89] She is earnest Griffin's[90] daughter. She has a faint resemblance to her lamented Grand-Mother both in features and personal characteristics. A nice, quiet, easy-going girl. She is under the Doctor's care for some kind [**p. 2**] of trouble with her eye-lids, and—of course—in the absence of her Uncle John,[91] and the non-existance of his home, she is staying with us.

Aunt Julina is overwhelmed with home—and Relief-Society duties and responsibilities.[92] She knows no rest except in the "wee-Smah"[93] hours of the night. But she is holding her own remarkably well. Aunt Alice K.[94] expects to start for Arazona tomorrow night on Y.L.M.I.A.[95] duties. She is the Treasurer of the General Board and also a member of it—and does her own house work, mending and making, cooking, washing and ironing. etc. etc. Aunt Edna is a Temple worker, and spends most of her time there. Our little Emma[96] keeps the home. Aunt Sarah not only has the watch-care of her home, but that of Darling Nonies[97] motherless

85. Written on official letterhead of the Church from the Office of the First Presidency.
86. Found in the Bible; see, for example, Job 28:13, Psalm 27:13, Isaiah 38:11, and Ezekiel 32:32. The phrase is also found in the Book of Mormon and Doctrine and Covenants; see Mosiah 14:8 and Doctrine and Covenants 81:3.
87. Joseph F. noted in his diary the day before, "Pres. Lund at Deseret. Prest. Penrose and I in the office, disposing of letters and other business." Joseph F., journal, 19 August 1912.
88. *Repining* means "to yearn for something; to be discontented, to complain or to fret."
89. Sarah Smith Griffin died on 6 November 1876. Her granddaughter Vaunie Griffin was sixteen at the time this letter was written. See biographical register, "Griffin, Vaunie."
90. Ernest Adelbert Griffin, the son of Sarah Smith Griffin and grandson of Hyrum (Joseph F. and Martha Ann's father) and Jerusha Smith.
91. John Smith.
92. Julina Lambson. See Joseph F. to Martha Ann, 14 May 1911, herein.
93. *Wee-Smah* refers to the "wee, small" (early) hours of the morning.
94. Alice Ann Kimball.
95. The Young Ladies' Mutual Improvement Association was originally organized by Brigham Young as a retrenchment society for his daughters. It eventually became a Churchwide organization for young women. See Joseph F. to Martha Ann, 3 May 1872, herein, note 224.
96. Emma Smith, daughter of Joseph F. and Edna, was unmarried at this time. See biographical register, "Smith, Emma."
97. Nonie is a nickname for Leonora Smith, Joseph F. and Sarah Ellen Richards's daughter, who passed away on 23 December 1907. She was survived by her four children.

children as well as Minervas[98] sweet little flock and Willards magnificent little Man.[99] Aunt Mary[100] and boys are running a 40 acre farm, at Taylorsville.[101] The home keeps itself just now. They have built a large Hay barn and stables; put up a hundred tons of hay—or less, and raised grain for their yearly keep. As for myself I continue at my daily grind in the Office.[102] I need say no more. I send you $10.00 with the love and best wish to yourself and all from your affectionate brother, Joseph F.——

JOSEPH F. TO MARTHA ANN, 22 NOVEMBER 1912

Salt Lake City, Utah, Nov. 22d 1912[103]

Martha Ann S. Harris—
214 South 3d West St. Provo—

My Dear Sister Martha:—

A few days ago I received a letter from Cousin Ina,[104] acknowledging receipt of a coppy of the last Conference report which I sent her.[105] She desired to be remembered to you. She is in chronic ill-health, but has better eye sight than for some time past. My last letter from you was written Aug. 26th and came to me Aug. 28th last.

Julina[106] and I have hard colds—she is improving. I am in the progressive stage, each day it seemes a little worse. some people in my condition would be "Sick-a-bed and worse up", but I have to "keep a digging". "no rest for the wicked"![107]

I would like to know if the boys[108] have paid your taxes, and provided you with winter fuel? Please let me know. Next Thursday will be Thanks-giving day. I send you $10.00 which you will no doubt put to the best use for yourself,

With love to you and all, in which my folks joine, I am your affectionate Brother
Joseph F.——

98. Minerva Smith, Joseph F. and Sarah Ellen Richards's daughter, had five children at this time.
99. Willard Grant Smith, son of Willard Richards Smith and Florence Grant, was born on 12 May 1911.
100. Mary Taylor Schwartz.
101. Taylorsville, Salt Lake County, Utah, is located about nine miles southwest from Salt Lake City.
102. Joseph F.'s diary for 1912 provides a remarkable number of responsibilities. For example, a few days after this letter was written, Joseph F. noted, "Long session of Council in Temple, and a long Session of Trustees of B.Y.U. held at Prests office." Joseph F., journal, 29 August 1912.
103. Written on official letterhead of the Church from the Office of the First Presidency.
104. Ina Coolbrith (née Josephine Donna Smith).
105. Joseph F. noted in his diary on 19 November 1912, a few days before he wrote this letter, "Busy in Office all day as usual. Recd letter from Ina D.C., S.S.U. Board meeting this evening. Lumbago!" Joseph F., journal, 19 November 1912. On the following day, Joseph F. wrote, "A.M. Cleared off letters from Table & at 11 a.m. went to Ogden & spoke at funeral of Aunt Jane S. Richards who died 17th buried today." Joseph F., journal, 20 November 1912.
106. Julina Lambson.
107. A common phrase based on three passages from Isaiah 48:22 and 57:20–21.
108. Martha Ann's living sons, William Jasper, Hyrum Smith, Franklin Hill, and John Fielding Harris.

JOSEPH F. TO MARTHA ANN, 23 DECEMBER 1912

Salt Lake City, Utah, December 23rd, 1912.[109]

My dear sister, Martha Ann Harris:
214 So. Third West St., Provo.

I have just written to Ina,[110] from whom I received a letter on the 11th inst., in which she spoke of you as being somewhat unwise in helping to bear the burdens of others, having reference, of course, to the care you are taking of Lucy's little children.[111] I have just been writing to her and have explained to her the situation. I have no idea that she would ever think of assuming such responsibilities as you willingly take upon yourself for the well-being of others. I am glad to say that the family are all usually well. I hope Willie[112] is better and that all the rest are in possession of good health. I sincerely wish you all the compliments of the season and take pleasure in enclosing herewith a small token of good feeling, which I hope will come in handy for your Christmas dinner. Give my love to the children, and try and take care of yourself.

Affectionately your brother,
Joseph F. Smith

P.S. I sent you a copy of the Christmas News[113]—which I hope you will look at. It is a big thing
Also $10.00[114]

JOSEPH F. TO MARTHA ANN, 28 FEBRUARY 1913

Salt Lake City, Utah, Feb—28th 1913[115]

Martha Ann Smith Harris
214 South 3d West St. Provo—

My Dear Sister Martha—

I hope this will find you all well, that William[116] is himself again, and that the rest of the children are happy and prosperous. We are all pretty well at present, for which we are most grateful.

109. Typewritten in blue ink on official letterhead of the Church from the Office of the First Presidency.
110. Ina Coolbrith (née Josephine Donna Smith).
111. Edna Mae Simmons, now thirteen years old, and John Arthur Simmons, twelve years old. See Joseph F. to Martha Ann, 2 April 1905 and 10 April 1907, herein.
112. William Jasper Harris Jr.
113. The Christmas edition of the *Deseret News* consisted of 114 pages and was published on 21 December 1912.
114. The postscript is handwritten with one bracket enclosing the whole of it.
115. Written on official letterhead of the Church from the Office of the First Presidency. Joseph F. was seventy-four, and Martha Ann was seventy-one.
116. William Jasper Harris Jr.

Some of the grand children are troubled with colds, but, so far as we know, none of them, are in serious condition.

Your Cousin <u>Ina</u> "Coolbrith"— sends her love and sympathy to you, and hopes the grand-children you are raising will always remember with gratitude your services and sacrifices for them. I saw a notice in the News[117] that you had met with a loss by fire, but have heard nothing more about it.[118] I send you herewith my cheque No. 19. for $19^{00/100.}$ (nineteen dollars.) as follows:—$\$9^{00/100}$ from Julina[119] to pay for some work you did, and $\$10^{00/100}$ from your brother as a gift. Ever true, Joseph F. Smith

MARTHA ANN TO JOSEPH F., 3 MARCH 1913

RECEIVED
MAR—6'13
PRESIDENT'S OFFICE[120]

Provo City March the 3^{ird} 1913

My dear brother Joseph F Smith your very kind & welcome letter of the 25th of Feburry came safly to hand Saturday afternoon & my dear brother I cirtenly do opricate your kindness to me poor old cripled up woman that I am I dont know what ever I would do if it was not for my dear good noble grand ~~dear~~ beloved generous harted even more than I could ever expect & I feel in my heart to say God bless you for ever. for you have helped me to bare my burdons helped to lighten the load that has rested on me if it had not have been for you I surly would hav sunk under the load I feel truly greatfull to you mor than I can express. I feel greatfull to all those who have been kind to me thrue the sore tryals I have had to pass ~~thrue~~.

you spoke of william[121] he is sill in a very bad condition yet after all he **[p. 2]** went thrue his piles[122] still bleeds & is very sore & he is not able to do hard work & I am afraid he will not be for some time Wilford[123] has sure <has> been a good boy to his parents this winter he has g<i>ven all ~~t~~his wages to them to help them william has not been able to irn any thing sence last June. the oldest girl Bessie[124] stayed home all winter to do the work for the family, untill a month ago then ~~she~~ she went out to work. there is another boy Ruel[125] 14 years old that will go to work as soon as he gets out of ~~work~~ <school> the others are, to lit[◊◊]le, to go out to

117. See Martha Ann to Joseph F., 3 March 1913, herein.
118. See Martha Ann to Joseph F., 3 March 1913, herein.
119. Julina Lambson.
120. Stamped in blue ink in the top left margin.
121. William Jasper Harris Jr.
122. Hemorrhoids.
123. Wilford Leroy Harris, son of William Jasper Harris Jr. and Jessie Lena Freckleton, was twenty years old at this time. See biographical register, "Harris, Wilford Leroy."
124. Bessie Irene Harris, daughter of William Jasper Harris Jr. and Jessie Lena Freckleton, was seventeen years old at this time. See biographical register, "Harris, Bessie Irene."
125. Reuel Smith Harris, son of William Jasper Harris Jr. and Jessie Lena Freckleton. See biographical register, "Harris, Reuel Smith."

work.[126] ~~he~~ <William>[127] has been suffering with the piles[128] of & on for 11 years working in the mines & shooing great big mules & horses has not helped it any. Atie has a very bad caugh her baby[129] has the ear ache. Sarahs babies has a fever coald & cough.[130] John F[131] has been down with lagripp[132] for nearly a week is some better can get round **[p. 3]**[133] as they are. I hope Aunt Julina[134] will have a nice pleasent trip & return home in safety when you wrte to her pleas thank her for me for the money she sent the work is done I will send it to the girls I would like very mutch to come to conference[135] & hope my poor feeble body can make the riffle[136] with love & gratitude & thanking you again for your kindness I am your affectionate sister
Martha Ann Smith Harris

PS I forgot to tell you about the house burning down.[137] they said it was a defective chimny but it was not that. the people that lived in the house hung thair close round the stove to dry & got up in the morning & made <by> a fire & went in the other room & shut the dore the close caught fire & soon the house was in flames it was quite a loss to me for the rent was a help to me[138] Frank[139] sais he will build another house there as soon as he can he is coming home for conferance if he posabley can get off

[p. 4] PS[140]

pleas give my love to cousin Ina[141] ~~&~~ I know she will not under stand how I can take care of these children[142] I can do it becaus I loved thir mother ~~mother~~ she was true & faithfull to me. & the Sunday before she died she said to me if <I> knew my childrin would be taken care of as good as little Sarah[143] is being taken care of. I could die contented I told her if any thing ever hapened too her I would take just as good care of them & I did of her that is Zinas little girl that I raised on a bottle. that is I said if I am alive I have tryed to do it the best I could. but I little thought that in one week ~~they~~ they would be in my care. & with the help of the Lord for he sure has given me strength & for the assistence of my dear ones I have willed them thrue

126. The other children of William Jasper Harris Jr. and Jessie Lena Freckleton were Ada Fern, Viola Myrtle, Alice Bernice, and Legrande Smith Harris.
127. William Jasper Harris Jr.
128. A nineteenth-century term for hemorrhoids.
129. Probably a misspelling of "Artie," a nickname for Martha Ann's daughter Martha Artimissa Harris. The baby she refers to is probably Elbert Harris Startup, who was eight months old at this time. See biographical register, "Startup, Elbert Harris."
130. Sarah Lovina Harris had three children at this time: Lee Roy (four years old), Verna (two), and Alene (nine months). See biographical register, "Passey, Lee Roy," "Passey, Verna," and "Passey, Alene."
131. John Fielding Harris, Martha Ann's son.
132. *La grippe* was a French term for influenza.
133. "[P. 3, 3 MAR 1913]" is written in the top margin in an unknown hand.
134. Julina Lambson.
135. The 83rd Annual General Conference was held on 4–6 April 1913.
136. *Riffle* has several meanings; none of them seem to fit Martha Ann's usage here.
137. See Joseph F. to Martha Ann, 28 February 1913, herein.
138. Renting the house had generated income for Martha Ann, so the fire was an unfortunate financial setback.
139. Franklin Hill Harris, son of William Jasper Harris and Martha Ann.
140. "[POSTSCRIPT, 3 MAR 1913]" is written in the top right margin in an unknown hand.
141. Ina Coolbrith (née Josephine Donna Smith).
142. See Joseph F. to Martha Ann, 23 December 1912, herein.
143. Possibly refers to Martha Ann's granddaughter Sarah Rachel Furner, daughter of Zina Christine Harris and George Thomas Furner. George Furner died on 3 June 1902, and it is likely that Martha Ann helped care for Sarah, who was a newborn baby at that time. See biographical register, "Furner, Sarah Rachel."

<this> far thrue I sincerly **[p. 5]** hope they will be greatfull <to> those who have imparted of thir substance & devided with us in our needs I know the Lord will reward them for all that that they have doun & I want them to aprciate thir goodness wheather they aprcate what I have done or not. I should have answerd sooner but some one coming in hinderd me all the time & I could not git it finnishe

JOSEPH F. TO MARTHA ANN, 18 JUNE 1913

Salt Lake City, Utah, June 18th 1913[144]

Martha Ann S. Harris
214 South 3d West St. Provo.

My Dear Sister Martha:—

I thought you would like to know that Julina[145] is 64 years old to day. She is in California[146] with Mamie and Donnie and their children,[147] and little Josephine, Joseph F., Junior's daughter.[148] We are all as well as usual at home. My Daughter Emma[149] has been quite poorly for about a week, but is feeling some better now. Our Cousin Maggie Smith Parry,[150] died last night. She has been an invallid almost all her life, and her death is like a release from mortal ills. I wrote Cousin Ina[151]—a short time ago, in answer to a letter from her. and sent her $10.00 There is verry little difference in your—and her ages, both 72. She on the 10th of march and you on the 14th of may. I send you $1000 as a birth day reminder. Hoping you are will—I am your affectionate brother
Joseph F. Smith

JOSEPH F. TO MARTHA ANN, 23 DECEMBER 1913

Salt Lake City, Utah, Dec. 23d 1913[152]

144. Written on official letterhead of the Church from the Office of the First Presidency. Joseph F. was seventy-four, and Martha Ann was seventy-two.
145. Julina Lambson.
146. In 1914 Joseph F. built a home in Santa Monica, Los Angeles County, California, as a retreat for his family, friends, and other Church leaders. The home became known as "Deseret."
147. Mamie is a nickname for Mary Sophronia Smith, and Donnie is Donnette Smith.
148. Josephine Smith, daughter of Emily Louie Shurtliff and Joseph Fielding Smith, was ten years old at this time. See biographical register, "Smith, Josephine."
149. Emma Smith, Joseph F. and Edna Lambson's daughter.
150. Margaret West Smith, daughter of George Albert Smith and Susan Elizabeth West, was second cousin to Joseph F. and Martha Ann. She died in her home on 18 June 1913. Funeral services were held in the Sixteenth Ward meetinghouse on 20 June. Her obituary was published in the *Deseret News* on 18 June 1913.
151. Ina Coolbrith (née Josephine Donna Smith).
152. Written on official letterhead of the Church from the Office of the First Presidency.

Martha Ann Harris
214 South 3d West St. Provo.

My Dear Sister Martha:

I wish you the compliments of the Season, and the same to all the children and their little ones. I need not remind you that this the 108 Anniversary of the birth of Uncle Joseph[153]—The Prophet.

I have just written the Ina "Coolbrith"—and reminded her of it, but you will remember it without reminding. Aunt Edna[154] has been sick with ptomaine poisening,[155] for ten days.

The rest of the folks are well—as usual.

I have had a cold for two weeks, which has troubled me some—but I am getting better. Julina[156] and family are all usually well and all send love and Christmas greetings. The children are all looking forward for Christmas.

I send you here with $10.00 which will help get you a good Christmas dinner.

Affectionately your brother Joseph F. Smith

JOSEPH F. TO MARTHA ANN, 24 JUNE 1914

Salt Lake City, Utah, June 24. 1914[157]

Martha Ann Harris—
Santa Monica, Cal.[158]

My Dear Sister Martha:—I sincerely hope you are enjoying your little visit down—from 4.300 feet[159] in the tops of the mountains, where you have so long existed, to the level of the great Pacific Ocean. The Ocean which I first saw in July 1854[160]—which is within a few days of 60 years ago. and across more than 2.000—miles of which I have sailed and steamed, back and forth 10 or 12 times—witnessing both its calms and its stormes, while you for the first time, now just gaze on its sunny shores, constantly washed by its restless waves. I want you to have a "good time"—while you are there—and hope you will stay as long as you desire. The folks are all well—and they also want you to have it as pleasant as possible. The weather is delightful here. All send love. Affectionately your brother
Joseph F. Smith

153. Joseph Smith Jr.
154. Edna Lambson.
155. Food poisoning. It was once believed that food poisoning was caused by chemicals called ptomaines, found in spoiled food. *Oxford English Dictionary*, s.v. "ptomaine."
156. Julina Lambson.
157. Written on official letterhead of the Church from the Office of the First Presidency. Joseph F. was seventy-five, and Martha Ann was seventy-three.
158. Smith home in Santa Monica.
159. The average elevation for Salt Lake City is 4,327 feet above sea level.
160. En route to Hawai'i for his first mission.

MARTHA ANN TO JOSEPH F., 7 JULY 1914

RECEIVED
JUL—9'14
PRESIDENT'S OFFICE[161]

Ans'd in person
July 23$^{\underline{d}}$ 1914[162]

Provo City July 7th
1914

Mr Joseph F Smith my dear beloved brother I will try & write you a few lines this after noon, hoping they may find your dear ones all well I should have writen you before now but I have ben very mutch under thee weather sence I came here. I am hear at my daughter Arties[163] yet have not been home sence I came but I am gaining sloly now & hope to be able to go home perhaps tomorrow she has been very [**p. 2**] kind to me & done all she could to make me comfortable while I have been here I have sufferd quite a bit with my knee & other ailments that I have to contend with.[164] but I am very thankfull that I am as well as I am, at the present & hope & pray I may <still> be improving I got a pare of crutches & have yoused them some but I have been very week I could not get round mutch, I have been able to sow some. & done all I could & I am very glad I am as well as I am [**p. 3**][165] & that I can do a little now my dear brother I want to thank you all once more for the nice time I had in Calaforna[166] & for the money you gave me the day you fetched me home, & for bringing me home. I would have been in a fix if I had come in the cars & no one to help me in my weak condition thos chills up set me they were caused by the shock of fooling & I think I caugght some [**p. 4**] while trav~~v~~ling on the train & I am very glad you did not get hurt when you got your fall brother & sister Hodson[167] who is on your place wished that I would ask you to have him prayd for in the temple for for his afflicted leg so I have done so hoping that you in your multiplicty of labors will have this attended to if you cannot get time perhaps Aunt Edna[168] can do it. or—I mean, have it attended to. Sarah[169] is not over her trouble yet but is expecting every minute now I am very anxious about her & will [**p. 5**][170] bee thankfull when it is over. I got a letter from Franklin in new Mexico,[171] & they

161. Stamped with blue ink in the top margin of page 1.
162. Written sideways in the top left margin of page 1.
163. Martha Artimissa Harris, Martha Ann's daughter. She and her husband, Harry W. Startup, lived at 345 South First West Street in Provo.
164. See Martha Ann to Joseph F., 26 December 1911, herein, note 62.
165. "[P.3, 7 JUL 1914]" is written in the top right margin in an unknown hand.
166. See Joseph F. to Martha Ann, 24 June 1914, herein.
167. Israel "Happy" and Melinda Lucretia "Lula" Hodson. They were living at 430 North 2nd West, Provo, in 1910. By 1915 they were living at 160 West 2nd North, Provo, a distance of about half a mile from Martha Ann's home.
168. Edna Lambson.
169. Likely refers to Sarah Lovina Harris, who gave birth to Richard Smith Passey on 14 July 1914.
170. "[P.5, 7 JUL 1914]" is written in the top right margin in an unknown hand.
171. Franklin Hill Harris was apparently working as a railroad contractor in New Mexico. See Martha Ann to Joseph F., 26 December 1911, herein.

ware all well out there they are working very hard. & They sent thir love to us all & to all of our loved ones they felt very greatfull to you for what you have done for me. I will close for this time with prayrs in my heart, for <the> well being & saf<e>ty of you all I was sorry I had to bother you for an [**p. 6**] other book & I thank you for that also. I will keep you posted in regard~~s~~ to Sarah. If you should see Andrew[172] pleas giv my love to him & tell him I should like very mutch to have seen him before I come home. your affectionate sister M. A. Harris Arte joins me in sending love to you all.

P.S. I also thank you for the dear letter[173] you wrote me while I was <away> I cannot begin <to> tell you how mutch I enjoyd it every minute of the time

MARTHA ANN TO JOSEPH F., 9 JULY 1914

RECEIVED
JUL 10'14
PRESIDENT'S OFFICE[174]

Ans'd in person
July 23^{d} 1914[175]

Provo City July the 9th
1914

Mr Joseph F Smith my dear <[*illegible strike-through*]> brother your letter of the 6th to hand was glad to hear you were all well but one I have not been able to make out who you sayd was not well I am not feeling as well as I would like but am thankfull I am no wors. the dolar came all right & thank you for sending it to me I did not want them to send it to me. but I can use it for something usefull to them when my poor lame, right arm gets [**p. 2**] so I can use it to work again. it is very lame in the sholder I must have strained it when I fell[176] we have had to work prtty lively with my kne. to<keep> it from blood poisening but I think we have got it over the worst of it now but my leg swells very bad yet. I have to yse the crutches to get round with for I cannot bare mutch waitt on it I got my money you sent all right & I thank you very mutch for the intres you took for me when I went away I told the post man to ~~sen~~ take my male to Artes[177] [**p. 3**][178] & that she would take care of it for me untill I came back I am still here at Arties she dont want me to go home untill I am able to get round & do my work Edna

172. Likely refers to Andrew Kimball Smith, son of Joseph F. and Alice Ann Kimball.
173. Joseph F. to Martha Ann, 24 June 1914, herein.
174. Stamped with blue ink in the top left margin of page 1.
175. Written sideways in the top left margin of page 1.
176. Martha Ann seems to have suffered from several falls at this time in her life. See Martha Ann to Joseph F., 26 December 1911, herein, note 62.
177. Martha Ann was staying with her daughter Martha Artimissa Harris. See Martha Ann to Joseph F., 7 July 1914, herein.
178. "[P.3 9 JUL 1914]" is written in the top right margin in an unknown hand.

May[179] is working for Sarah[180] untill she gets a girl to work for her thare is one coming Sunday if nothing hapens to prevent it, & then I can have my girl home with me. I will send a parsel to Aunt Julina[181] to day & I hope she [**p. 4**] get it all right we had a nice rain here last night it will do lots of good to the crops. I just made out that Mary~~s~~[182] is <is the one> who is sick I hope that it is nothng serious that ails her. Sarah is still very poorly & Aties children have colds Arte & the children all join me in sending love to you all your affectionate sister Martha A Harris

RECEIVED
JUL21'14
J. F. S.[183]
PRESIDENT'S OFFICE[184]

JOSEPH F. TO MARTHA ANN, 10 SEPTEMBER 1914

Salt Lake City, Utah, Sept. 10—1914[185]

My Dear Sister Martha:

Julina[186] sends you the enclosed Cheque for $\$10^{\underline{00}}$ for work done.[187]

I received a letter from Cousin Adele,[188] from Reno,[189] Nevada, soon after she arrived there. That is her home for the present. They do not seem to have a permanent home, some times they live in Tonopah,[190] Nevada, sometimes at Berekley,[191] California. She sends her love to you and regrets she did not have a longer visit. While she writes very conservitively, she appears to have enjoyed—to some-extent her visit here. [**p. 2**] No doubt everything was not entirely to her taste and liking. but she says she has many things to think about in her quiet moments at home.

179. Edna Mae Simmons. See Joseph F. to Martha Ann, 2 April 1905 and 10 April 1907, herein.
180. Likely refers to Sarah Lovina Harris, daughter of Martha Ann.
181. Julina Lambson.
182. Mary Taylor Schwartz.
183. The initials are handwritten and not part of the stamp.
184. Stamped sideways with blue ink in the bottom margin of page 4.
185. Written on official letterhead of the Church from the Office of the First Presidency.
186. Julina Lambson.
187. Martha Ann made temple clothing, including aprons, for individuals and for the Church's National Relief Society Burial Clothes Department. Julina was her connection for work in Salt Lake City, where Julina served as supervisor of the Wedding and Burial Clothes Department, overseeing the production and sale of temple and burial clothing to members of the Church.
188. Martha Ann and Joseph F.'s distant cousin Adele T. Jones. She was the great-granddaughter of Stephen Mack Jr., first cousin of Joseph Smith. See biographical register, "Terrill, Mary Adele." See Martha Ann to Joseph F., 17 July 1915, herein.
189. Reno, Washoe County, Nevada, is located in the high desert valley at the foot of the Sierra Nevada and officially came into existence when a railroad station was built there in 1868 while the transcontinental railway was being constructed.
190. Tonopah, Nye County, Nevada, is located midway between Reno and Las Vegas and was settled about 1910 after the discovery of gold and silver.
191. Berkeley, Alameda County, California, is the home of the University of California, established in 1868.

I have not the slightest idea that true religion—or the divinity of the mission of Joseph Smith, will make any lasting impression upon her mind. She is childless—duty-less—without human interest beyond herself and immediate relations—which are few—and with no great object in <this> life, or after it—and no zest for responsibility and an aim <only> only for social comforts—and temperal pleasures and enjoyments.

This is briefly my estimate of her—and yet I cannot but wish that ~~that~~ I have miss judged her.[192] We are all pretty well. Affectionately &c. Joseph F.

P.S. Wesley starts to night for Deseret,[193] and some time next week we may expect Emily and Marjorie will return home.[194] Love to the children
Affectionately your Brother.[195]

JOSEPH F. TO MARTHA ANN, 5 FEBRUARY 1915

Feb—5th 1915[196]

Martha A. Harris
214 South 3d West St—
Provo—Utah Co.

My Dear Sister Martha.

I have just written to Bro. Henry Stringham,[197] Manager of the Knight Woollen Mills Company,[198] to furnish you, Edna May and Arthur,[199] each a Mackinaw coat.[200] at my expense.

All you will need to do, will be to call at the Factory, with the children and this letter, and select just what you want—and I want you to choose the very best. David A.[201] will be in Provo to morrow—and if time will permit, he will call on you.

192. Joseph F. was aware of his past struggle in this regard. In 1905 he counseled his missionary son, "Your disposition is very much like my own. My greatest difficulty has been to guard my temper—to keep cool in the moment of excitement or trail. I have always been too quick to resent a wrong, too impatient, or hasty. I hope you will be very careful, my son, on these points. He who can govern himself is greater than he who ruleth a city." Joseph F. to Alvin F. Smith, 8 June 1905. See Smith and Kenney, *From Prophet to Son*, 84.

193. The Church built a large home, known as "Deseret," on Brentwood Terrace in Santa Monica, California, in 1913 to provide Joseph F. and other Church leaders a place to relax. Arriving by train, Joseph F. took advantage of his time away from Church Headquarters to golf, swim, and take long automobile drives. See Joseph F. to Martha Ann, 24 June 1914, herein.

194. Elias Wesley Smith, Emily Jane Smith, and Marjorie Virginia Smith are children of Joseph F. and Julina Lambson. See biographical register, "Smith, Marjorie Virginia."

195. Written upside down in the top margin of page 1.

196. Written on official letterhead of the Church from the Office of the Trustee-in-Trust. Joseph F. was seventy-six, and Martha Ann was seventy-three.

197. See biographical register, "Stringham, Henry."

198. Previously known as the Provo Woolen Mills Company, the mill changed names when Jesse Knight and associates purchased it in 1910.

199. Edna Mae Simmons and John Arthur Simmons. See Joseph F. to Martha Ann, 2 April 1905, herein, note 84.

200. A thick double-breasted plaid wool coat known in Canada as a "Mac."

201. David Asael Smith, son of Joseph F. and Julina. David was a counselor in the Presiding Bishopric at the time.

Aunt Sarah[202] has been very sick but I am thankful that she is getting some better—otherwise we are all well and improving. Zina[203] is in the Hospital, and Franklin has just got out.[204] Your brother,
Joseph F. Smith

JOSEPH F. TO MARTHA ANN, 17 FEBRUARY 1915

Salt Lake City, Utah, February 17th, 1915[205]

Mrs. Martha Ann Harris,[206]
214 So. Third West St.,
Provo.

My dear Sister:—

Your favor of the 10th inst. was duly received, and I have just received the bill for the coats, which seems evidence to me that you have duly received them. I hope you and the children will find them useful for all cold weather, and that the children's are made large enough to last them more than the present season. The mackinaw was not intended to be a fashionable article of dress, but one of durability and warmth and withal not overly expensive.

I feel grateful on being able to say that Aunt Sarah[207] is slowly, but I think surely, improving in strength, and we sincerely hope that she will soon be herself again. Zina[208] is stopping with her mother[209] and seems to be recovering her strength right along, I suppose you know that her husband[210] started on a mission to the Southern States on the day that we brought her from the hospital. I am also pleased to say that Franklin seems to be getting along as well as could be expected.[211] His was a very serious and severe operation. The rest of the family are enjoying usual health, and hoping this will find you enjoying similar blessings, I am,

Affectionately your brother,
Joseph F. Smith[212]

202. Sarah Ellen Richards.
203. Zina Smith was Joseph F. and Edna Lambson's daughter. She died eight months later on 25 October 1915.
204. Franklin Richards Smith, son of Joseph F. and Sarah Ellen Richards.
205. Written on official letterhead of the Church from the Office of the First Presidency.
206. Except for the signature, the entire letter is typewritten in blue ink.
207. Sarah Ellen Richards. See Joseph F. to Martha Ann, 5 February 1915, herein.
208. Zina Smith.
209. Edna Lambson.
210. Ambrose John Greenwell. See biographical register, "Greenwell, Ambrose John."
211. Franklin Richards Smith. See Joseph F. to Martha Ann, 5 February 1915, herein.
212. Signed by hand.

JOSEPH F. TO MARTHA ANN, 15 JULY 1915

Salt Lake City, Utah, July 15—1915[213]

Martha Ann Harris
214 South 3d West St—
Provo City, Utah County

My Dear Sister Martha,

It has been a long time since I either wrote to or heard from you.

I hope this will find you and all the children enjoying good health and other things you need.

I am writing a line or two to cousin "Ina D. Coolbrith" this morning, and am sending her ten dollars as a reminder of kinship: and I enclose herewith my Cheque No. 12—for $25^{00} as a small reminder to you, which I hope you will accept with my love and constant prayers for your well-being and happiness.

Julina[214] sends love, and says if you would like to make a few more aprons[215] she will pay you for them. She will send material

With love to all, affectionately your brother
Joseph F. Smith

MARTHA ANN TO JOSEPH F., 17 JULY 1915

Rec'd July 17—1915[216]

Provo City July the 17th
1915

My dearly beloved brother Joseph F your very welcome & kind letter of the 15th came safly to hand containing the check, you sent me for which I sincerly thank you [*illegible strike-through*] but that does not half express my gratitude for all your kindness to me. I was very sorry to hear that you had been suffering with your back again ~~all~~ all I could do was to pray for you. & that I never neglect to do I thank you for the [**p. 2**] kind rememberence of me in your prayrs, for I sorly need all the help I can get I am very lame can hardly get round some of the time but I try not give up I try to keep doing all I can I do hope & pray that I will

213. Written on official letterhead of the Church from the Office of the First Presidency.
214. Julina Lambson.
215. See Joseph F. to Martha Ann, 10 September 1914, herein. Edna Mae Headquest, Martha Ann's granddaughter, recalled, "Grandmother would sit in her chair and embroider temple aprons to send to Salt Lake for sale in the temple store. Some of the aprons had each green leaf embroidered and appliquéd on white satin. . . [she] made beautiful temple robes, too. She worked very hard pleating the robes in fine linen." Ruth Mae Harris, *Martha Ann*, 135–36.
216. Written sideways in the top left margin of page 1.

never get intierly helpless Edna May[217] is working at the candy factry[218] she got work yester day from her Uncle walter Startup we have a little garden stuff in, some potatoes & squash & Arthur[219] is tending to that. I got a letter from Frank[220] the other **[p. 3]**[221] day that they were all well or better than they had been his wife[222] is verry poorly she has been under the weather for a long time. her father[223] died week befor last & they buried him there Dealia[224] is home in Springvill[225] & Hyrum[226] will soon be coming home & I am very glad he is I think they are all anxious to come home, as soon as they can arange it that way. my family are all useualy well as far as I know at the **[p. 4]** at the present time. I have had severel bad spells with my heart it bothers me once in awhile. we had quite a shaking up here yesterday an irthquake.[227] Just a gentle reminder of what the Lord can do. I got out of the house with out being told. It stoped the clock opend the coubord doors & made the dishes rattle quite lively also the windos. we were very thankfull it was no wors, than it was. I will close with love to you all your loing sister M A Harris

thank you for the stamps[228] I have wrten to Aunt Julina[229] will be very glad to get some more work[230]

[p. 5][231] P S I got a letter from Cousin Adel Jones[232] she was well improoving in health all the time she wished me to give you her love & sympthy in the loss of dear Aunt Sarah[233] she said

217. Edna Mae Simmons.
218. The Startup Candy Factory was established by William B. Startup in Provo in 1875. Following William's death, the business was run by his wife and three sons. One of those sons was Harry Walter Startup, the "Uncle Walter Startup" mentioned in the letter. He was married to Martha Artimissa Harris, Martha Ann's daughter and Joseph F.'s niece.
219. John Arthur Simmons.
220. Franklin Hill Harris.
221. "[P.3, 17 JUL 1915]" is written in the top margin of page 3 in an unknown hand.
222. Josephine Parkes Robinson.
223. Joseph Robinson, died on 26 June 1915. See biographical register, "Robinson, Josephine Parkes" and "Robinson, Joseph."
224. Delia Sarah Rebekah Twede.
225. Springville, Utah County, Utah, is located five miles south of Provo.
226. Hyrum Smith Harris.
227. Provo experienced a minor earthquake on 29 May 1915; see "Earthquake Shock Felt," *Deseret Evening News*, 29 May 1915, 8. A month and a half later, Provo was hit with a 5.0 magnitude earthquake at 3:00 p.m. that was felt throughout Bear River, Utah, and Salt Lake Valleys, Tooele, Park City, and Parley's and Provo Canyons—an area measuring about five thousand square miles. In Provo, as Martha Ann mentioned, people ran out of doors. According to newspaper reports, Provo residents waited nearly an hour before returning to their activities after buildings swayed, clocks stopped, chimneys fell, dishes rattled, and walls cracked. The quake caused a rockslide that blocked the road in Provo Canyon. Some witnesses saw an upheaval of water, like a small tidal wave, at Utah Lake. See "Quake Sways Houses," *Salt Lake Herald-Republican*, 16 July 1915, 6.
228. Joseph F. often noted the purchase of stamps, envelopes, and stationery in his journals. See, for example, Joseph F., journal, 2 May, 30 July, 5 August, and 10 August 1912.
229. Julina Lambson.
230. Written upside down in the top margin of page 4.
231. "[P.S. 17 JUL 1915]" is written in the top right margin in an unknown hand.
232. Martha Ann and Joseph F.'s distant cousin, Adele T. Jones. See Joseph F. to Martha Ann, 10 September 1914, herein.
233. Sarah Ellen Richards died on 22 March 1915. See "Wife of President Joseph Smith Dies," *Salt Lake Telegram*, 22 March 1915, 9.

the first that she had hird of her death she read it in the paper[234] she said she sent my letter to Cousin Ina[235] & that she had beged her the privlige of keeping it she said she loved me & allways had & I am sure I have aw **[p. 6]** I have allways loved her I sure would like to se her once more in this life but I guess that is out of the question now. I am so glad you can do something for her. I do hope & prey that she will see her mistake befor it is all to geather to late. I pray for ~~her~~ her that her eyes may be opend that she may not be cast of in the day of her recking she youst to be so sweet any one could not help loing her.

JOSEPH F. TO MARTHA ANN, 20 NOVEMBER 1915

November[236]
Twentieth
Nineteen-fifteen

My Dear Sister,
Martha A. Smith Harris—
214 South 3d West St., Provo.

I suppose you have many things to be thankful for. It would be difficult for you to "count your many blessings"[237]—I suppose, and yet no one, so far as I know, has ever had so many blessings, that a little more, in addition to the stock already in hand, would be objectionable.

I cannot send you a Turkey for your Thanks-giving dinner, for I have none, besides if I could, some one would have to be cruel enough to kill the poor thing before it would be fit for use. So I am glad I have no Turkeys!! but if you have one, you can get something for the "Stuffing" with the enclosed $10.00

Affectionately your brother,
Joseph F. Smith

JOSEPH F. TO MARTHA ANN, 23 DECEMBER 1915

Salt Lake City, Utah, Dec. 23d 1915[238]

Martha Ann S. Harris
214 South 3d West—St. Provo.

234. Sarah Ellen Richards's death was widely reported in regional newspapers, including in Reno, Nevada, where Adele T. Jones lived at the time. See "Wife of President of Mormon Church Passes," *Nevada State Journal*, 23 March 1915, 1.
235. Ina Coolbrith (née Josephine Donna Smith).
236. From Joseph F.'s letterpress copybooks; original not extant.
237. Written by Johnson Oatman Jr., "Count Your Blessings" became a popular hymn when it was first published in 1897.
238. Written on official letterhead of the Church from the Office of the First Presidency.

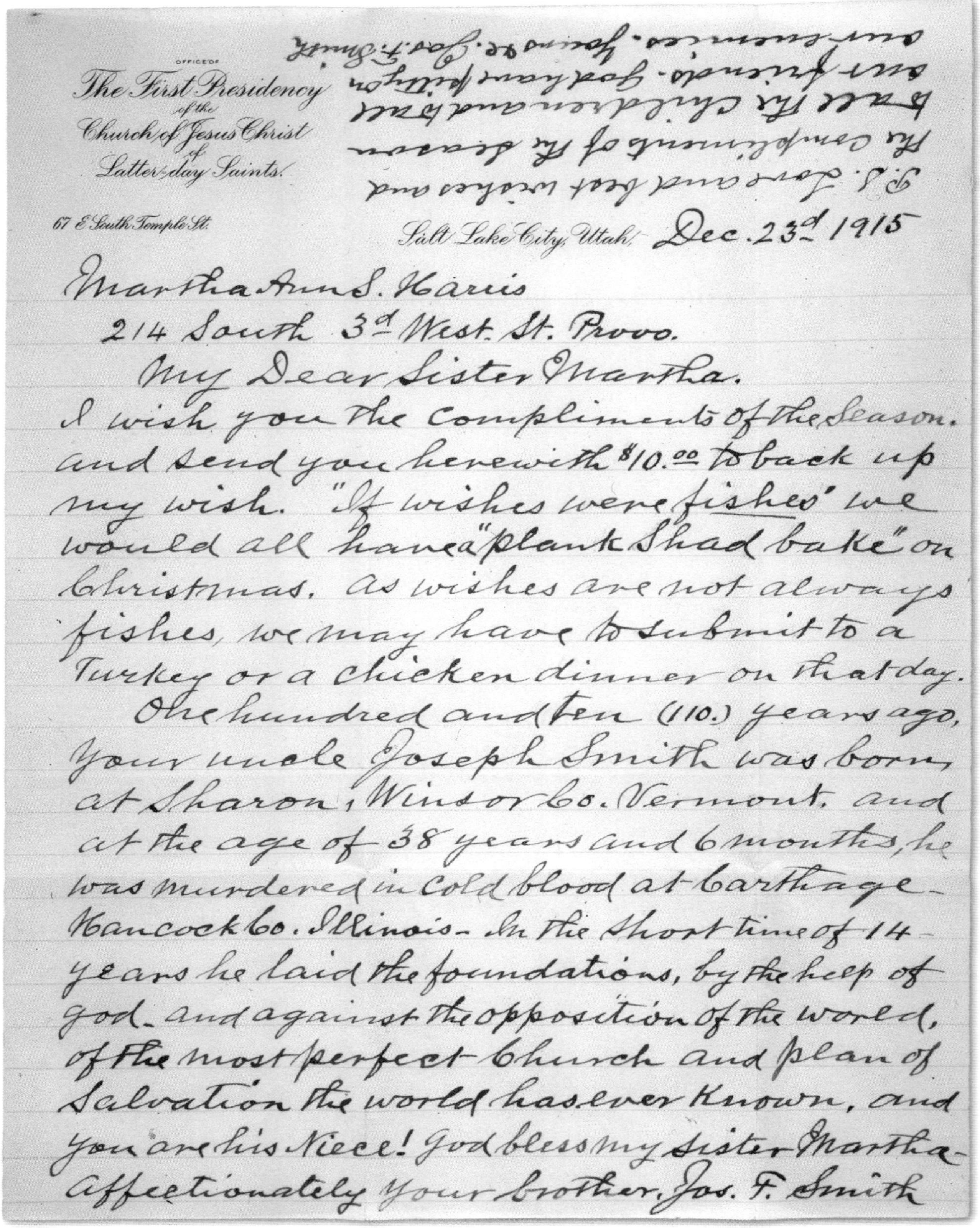

OFFICE OF
The First Presidency
of the
Church of Jesus Christ
of
Latter-day Saints.

67 E. South Temple St.

Salt Lake City, Utah, Dec. 23d 1915

Martha Ann S. Harris
214 South 3d West St. Provo.

My Dear Sister Martha.

I wish you the compliments of the Season. and send you herewith $10.00 to back up my wish. "If wishes were fishes" we would all have a "plank Shad bake" on Christmas. As wishes are not always fishes, we may have to submit to a Turkey or a chicken dinner on that day.

One hundred and ten (110.) years ago, your uncle Joseph Smith was born at Sharon, Winsor Co. Vermont. and at the age of 38 years and 6 months, he was murdered in cold blood at Carthage Hancock Co. Illinois. In the short time of 14 years he laid the foundations, by the help of God, and against the opposition of the world, of the most perfect Church and plan of Salvation the world has ever known, and you are his Niece! God bless my sister Martha.

Affectionately your brother, Jos. F. Smith

P.S. Love and best wishes and the compliments of the season to all the children and to all our friends. God have pity on our enemies. Yours &c. Jos. F. Smith

Joseph F. to Martha Ann, 23 December 1915 (p. 1)

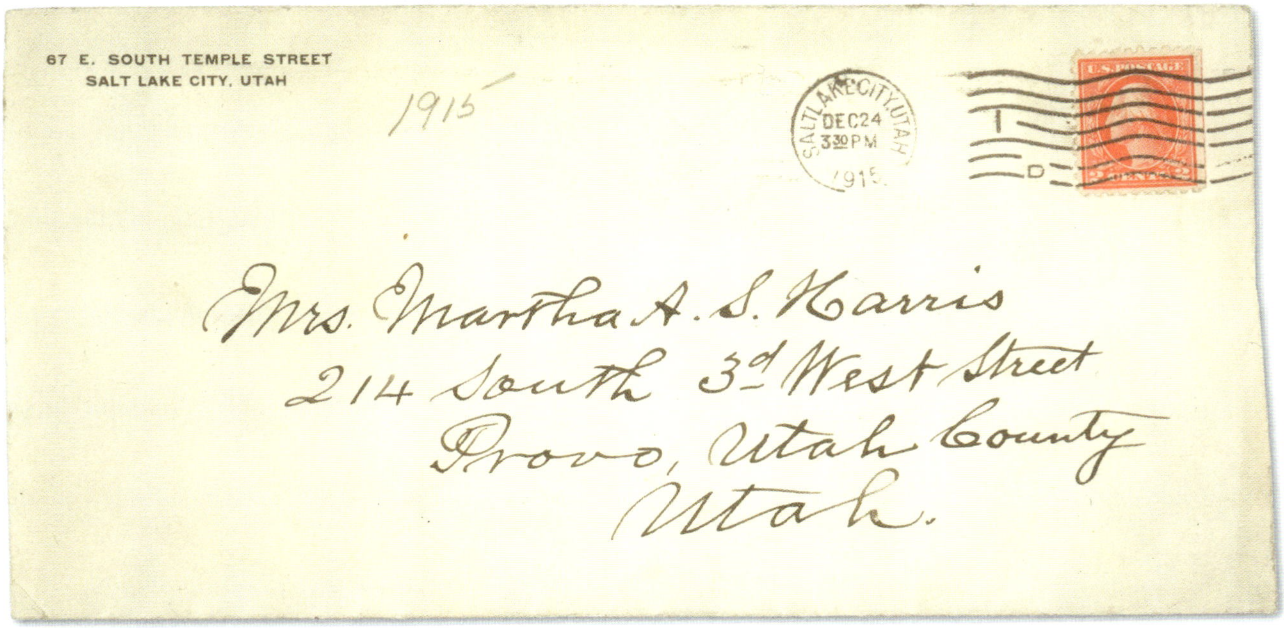

Joseph F. to Martha Ann, 23 December 1915 (envelope)

My Dear Sister Martha.

I wish you the compliments of the Season. and send you herewith $10.00 to back up my wish. "If wishes were <u>fishes</u>" we would all have a "plank Shad bake"[239] on Christmas, as wishes are not always fishes, we may have to submit to a Turkey or a chicken dinner on that day.

One hundred and ten (110.) years ago, Your uncle Joseph Smith was born, at Sharon, Winsor Co. Vermont, and at the age of 38 years and 6 months, he was murdered in cold blood at Carthage—Hancock Co. Illinois—In the short time of 14—years he laid the foundations, by the help of God—and against the opposition of the world, of the most perfect Church and Plan of Salvation the world has ever known, and you are his Niece! God bless my sister Martha—

Affectionately your brother, Jos. F. Smith

P.S. Love and best wishes and the compliments of the Season to all the children and to all our friends. God have pitty on our enemies—Yours &c. Jos. F. Smith[240]

239. Shad is a type of herring but is also a term often used for other fish. "Planked shad" refers to a method of preparing and baking fillets in which several fillets are nailed to an oak plank and smoked alongside an open fire. Sometimes many planks would be laid in a row next to several fires at a social gathering. *Oxford English Dictionary*, s.v. "planked," "shad."

240. Written upside down in the top margin of page 1.

JOSEPH F. TO MARTHA ANN, 17 FEBRUARY 1916

Salt Lake City, Utah, Feb—17—1916[241]

Martha Ann S. Harris.
214 South 3^d West St. Provo.

My Dear Sister Martha—

Please find herewith my Cheque No. 24—for $15^00 for your personal needs. I would gladly have made this double what it is—but I have been helping Jesse, Lucy, and Martha[242] to secure homes for themselves—and it has made "grass mighty short" with me, I am also writing Cousin Ina[243] to night and am sending her $15^00 to help her out a little.[244] She writes me very dolefully—about her physical and her financial condition.[245]

I have had a siege of La Grippe[246] but am much better. Julina[247] has been quite under the weather with cold and cough, but is improving. With love to you and all. I am sincerely your brother

Joseph F. Smith

JOSEPH F. TO MARTHA ANN, 20 MARCH 1916

SALT LAKE CITY, UTAH, Mar. 20—1916

Dear Martha:—

Aunt Julina[248] sends you the enclosed Cheque, No. 544, for $22.50—in payment for consignment of Aprons[249] just received. We hope this will find you well—and prosperous.

We got a glimpse or two of Frank[250] while he was here—but learned nothing about the object of his visit.

We are all just a little troubled with colds, but nothing serious and I hope we will soon be convellescent.

Give our love to the girls and children, Affectionately your brother. Joseph F.——[**p. 2**]

241. Written on official letterhead of the Church from the Office of the First Presidency. Joseph F. was seventy-seven, and Martha Ann was seventy-four.
242. Jesse Kimball Smith and Lucy Mack Smith, children of Joseph F. and Alice Ann Kimball, and Martha Smith, daughter of Joseph F. and Edna Lambson.
243. Ina Coolbrith (née Josephine Donna Smith).
244. See Joseph F. to Ina D. Coolbrith, 17 February 1916.
245. Ina D. Coolbrith to Joseph F., 20 January 1916.
246. *La grippe* was a French term for influenza.
247. Julina Lambson.
248. Julina Lambson.
249. Temple aprons; see Joseph F. to Martha Ann, 15 July 1915, herein, note 208.
250. Likely Franklin Hill Harris.

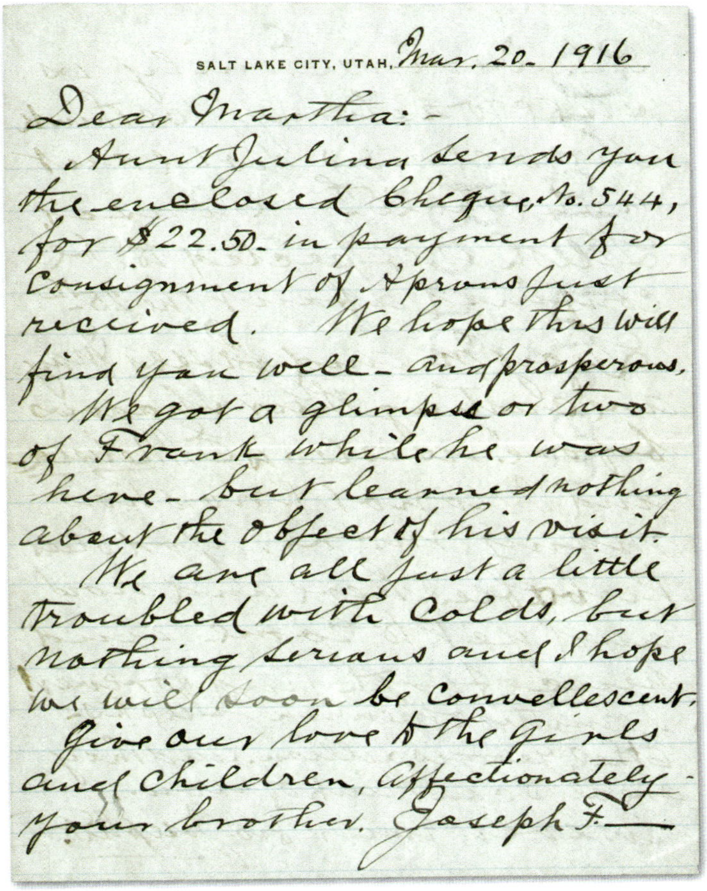

SALT LAKE CITY, UTAH, Mar. 20 - 1916

Dear Martha:-

Aunt Julina sends you the enclosed Cheque, No. 544, for $22.50 - in payment for Consignment of Aprons just received. We hope this will find you well - and prosperous.

We got a glimpse or two of Frank while he was here - but learned nothing about the object of his visit.

We are all just a little troubled with Colds, but nothing serious and I hope we will soon be convellescent.

Give our love to the girls and children, Affectionately - your brother. Joseph F.—

Joseph F. to Martha Ann, 20 March 1916 (p. 1)

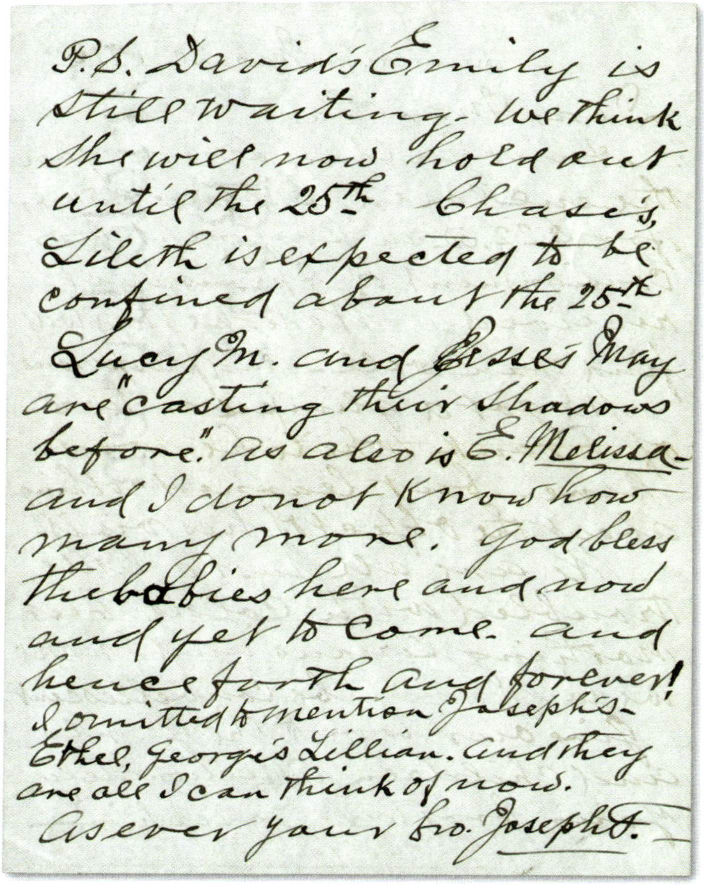

P.S. David's Emily is still waiting - we think she will now hold out until the 25th Chase's, Lileth is expected to be confined about the 25th

Lucy M. and Jesse's May are "casting their shadows before." As also is E. Melissa - and I donot know how many more. God bless the babies here and now and yet to come - and hence forth and forever! I omitted to mention Joseph's - Ethel, George's Lillian. And they are all I can think of now.

As ever your bro. Joseph F.—

Joseph F. to Martha Ann, 20 March 1916 (p. 2)

P.S. David's Emily[251] is still waiting—we think she will now hold out until the 25th Chase's, Lileth[252] is expected to be confined about the 25th

Lucy M. and Jesse's May are "casting their shadows before".[253] As also is E. Melissa[254]—and I donot know how many more. God bless the babies here and now and yet to come—and hence forth and forever! I omitted to mention Joseph's—Ethel,[255] George's Lillian[256]—and they are all I can think of now.

As ever your bro. Joseph F.——

251. Emily Jenkins, wife of David Asael Smith, gave birth to Louise Smith on 23 March 1916. See biographical register, "Jenkins, Emily."

252. Leileth Nelson, wife of Heber Chase Rich Smith, gave birth to Heber Chase Smith on 24 March 1916. See biographical register, "Nelson, Leileth."

253. "Casting their shadows before" is an idiom for pregnancy. Lucy Mack Smith gave birth to Helen Mar Carter on 21 April 1916; and Louise May Anderson, wife of Jesse Kimball Smith, gave birth to Jesse Kimball Smith Jr. on 3 October 1916. See biographical register, "Anderson, Louise May."

254. Edna Melissa Smith did not give birth to any more children after 1914. There may have been a stillbirth.

255. Joseph Fielding Smith's wife, Ethel Georgina Reynolds, gave birth to Amelia Smith on 21 June 1916. See biographical register, "Reynolds, Ethel Georgina."

256. George Carlos Smith's wife, Lillian Emery, gave birth to Wilford Emery Smith on 16 May 1916. See biographical register, "Emery, Lillian."

MARTHA ANN TO JOSEPH F., 27 MARCH 1916

RECEIVED
MAR 29'16
PRESIDENT'S OFFICE[257]

Provo City March 27 1916

Mr Joseph F Smith
My dear brother your short note of March the 20th came safely to hand with the check in it, for the aprons. I was glad to hear from you once more, that you had returned home from your journey[258] in safty & I thank you for the check pleas tell Aunt Julina[259] I thank her also. I have been very buisy sence recieveing it, making some temple clothes for a lady from Idiho I hope you will all [**p. 2**] be better of your colds by this time. & I thank you for the little bugit of news you sent me. I will give you a buget from our side of the house. I to have had quite a shour of home emigration Zina E had a fine, 11 pound <& a half> boy[260] & Ruby Williams daughter has her 4th son born[261] Stirling has a daughter born [*illegible strike-through*] in Feeb[262] Alva has

Martha Ann to Joseph F., 27 March 1916 (envelope)

257. Stamped with blue ink in the top left margin.
258. Joseph F. left Utah on 20 February to lay the cornerstones for the recently announced Hawaiian Temple in Lā'ie, O'ahu. However, heavy rains prevented this event, and Church leaders returned home on 20 March 1916. See "President Smith and Bishop Nibley to Go to Hawaii," *Deseret News*, 19 February 1916, 2; and "Hawaiian Temple Is Being Built," *Deseret Evening News*, 16 March 1916, 2.
259. Julina Smith.
260. Likely refers to Zina Christine Harris, who gave birth to William Henry Dennis on 4 February 1916. See biographical register, "Dennis, William Henry."
261. Unknown individuals.
262. Sterling Patten Harris's daughter Florence Ann Harris was born to Ann Lloyd on 29 February 1916. See biographical register, "Harris, Sterling Patten" and "Harris, Florence Ann."

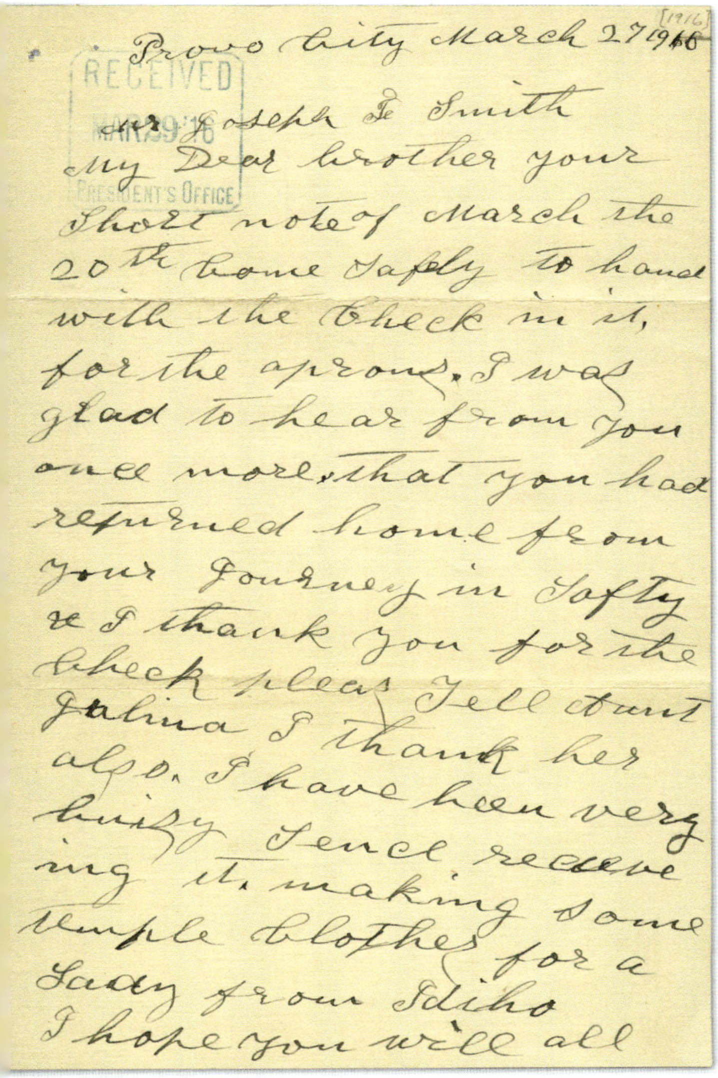
Provo City March 27 1916 [1916]
RECEIVED MAR 29 '16 PRESIDENT'S OFFICE
Mr Joseph F. Smith
My Dear brother your
short note of March the
20th come safely to hand
with the check in it,
for the aprons. I was
glad to hear from you
once more & that you had
returned home from
your journey in safty
& I thank you for the
check pleas tell aunt
Julina I thank her
also. I have been very
buisy sence receive
ing it, making some
temple clothes for a
Lady from Idiho
I hope you will all

Martha Ann to Joseph F., 27 March 1916 (p. 1)

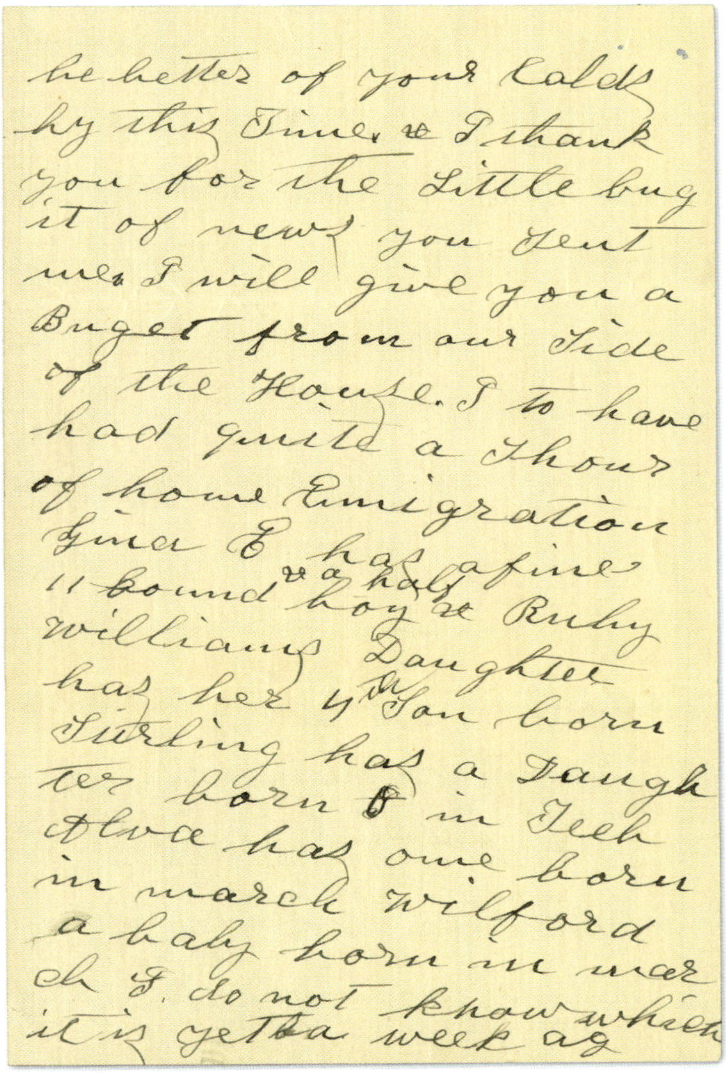
be better of your colds
by this time, & I thank
you for the little bug
it of news you sent
me. I will give you a
buget from our side
of the House. I to have
had quite a shour
of home emigration
Gina E has a fine
11 pound & a half boy & Ruby
Williams Daughter
has her 4th son born
Sterling has a Daugh
ter born [illegible] in Feeb
Alva has one born
in march Wilford
a baby born in mar
ch I do not know which
it is yet a week ag

Martha Ann to Joseph F., 27 March 1916 (p. 2)

one born in march[263] Wilford a baby born in march[264] I do not know which it is yet [*illegible strike-through*] a week ag [**p. 3**][265] so that makes 70 one gran children for me & thirty ~~3~~ 4 great grand children we have had a very heavy snow here but it is nearly all gon of now. I can join in with you in saying god bless the babyes for ever. I want to come up to conference[266] but do not know wheather I will bee able to come or not. I sirten do hope & pray that all may be well

263. Alva Robert Harris's daughter Virginia Louise was born to Anna Louise Herman on 10 March 1916. See biographical register, "Harris, Alva Robert" and "Harris, Virginia Louise."

264. Wilford Leroy Harris, Martha Ann's grandson, married Margery Ellen Sumner. Their daughter Ruth Harris was born on 20 March 1916. See biographical register, "Harris, Ruth."

265. "[3]" and "[27 MAR 1916]" are written in the top margin of page 3 in an unknown hand.

266. The 86th Annual General Conference was held on 6–7, 9 April 1916.

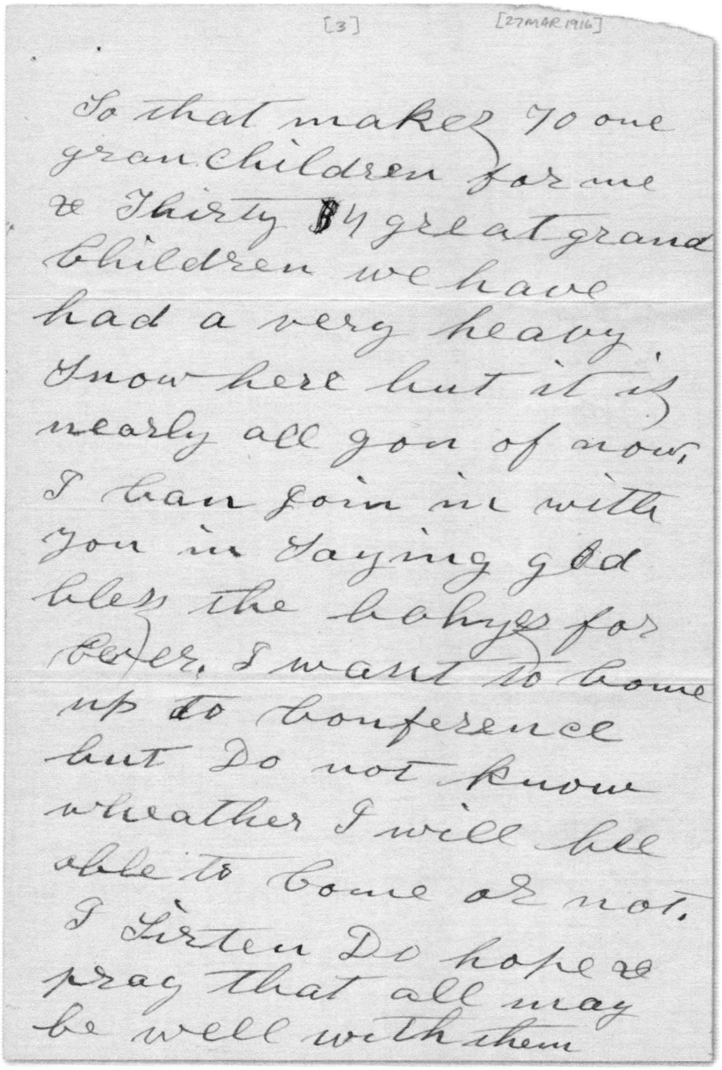

[3] [27MAR1916]
So that makes 70 one
granchildren for me
& Thirty 34 great grand
children we have
had a very heavy
snow here but it is
nearly all gon of now,
I can join in with
you in saying god
bless the babys for
ever. I want to come
up to conference
but Do not know
wheather I will be
able to come or not.
I sisten Do hope &
pray that all may
be well with them

Martha Ann to Joseph F., 27 March 1916 (p. 3)

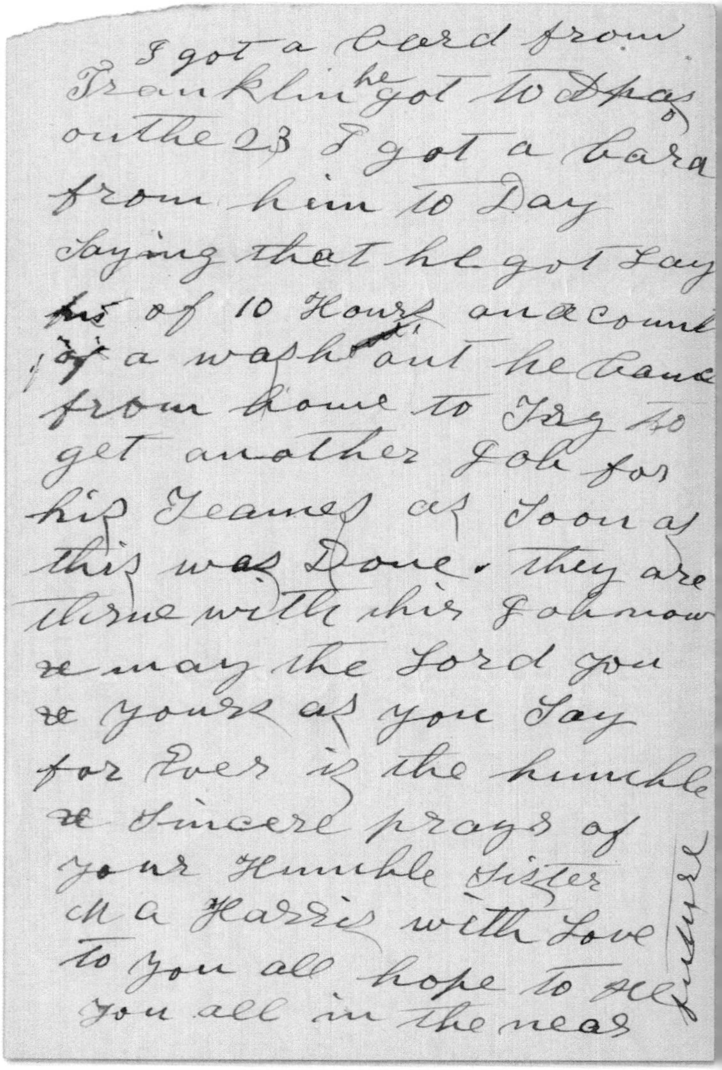

I got a card from
Franklin he got to Apaso
on the 23 I got a card
from him to Day
saying that he got lay
his of 10 Hours on acount
of a wash out he came
from home to try to
get another Job for
his Teames as soon as
this was Done. they are
thrue with thir Job now
& may the Lord you
& yours as you say
for ever is the humble
& sincere prays of
your humble sister
M a Harris with Love
to you all hope to see
you all in the near
future

Martha Ann to Joseph F., 27 March 1916 (p. 4)

with them [**p. 4**] I got a card from Franklin[267] <he> got to Apaso[268] on the 23 I got a card from him to day saying that he got lay [*illegible strike-through*] of 10 hours on acount of a wash <~~out~~> out he came from home to try to get another job for his teames as soon as this was done. they are thrue with thir job now & may the Lord you & yours as you say for ever is the humble & sincere prayr of your humble sister M A Harris with love to you all hope to see you all in the near future[269]

267. Franklin Hill Harris.
268. Likely El Paso.
269. The last word is written sideways in the right margin of page 4.

JOSEPH F. TO MARTHA ANN, 30 SEPTEMBER 1916

Sept. 30th–1916[270]

My Dear Sister:—

Martha Ann Smith Harris:
214 South 3^{d} West St. Provo.

We have not heard from you for a long time. nor you from us, perhapse. I hope you are all in good health, with something to eat, drink and wear. We are all usually well—but growing older at an excellerated pace, like the cart-wheel rolling down the hill, which gains speed as it nears the bottom!

Julina[271] says she has some more for you to do, if you want it, but she will ait until she sees you. She sends her love to you and the children. She expects her brother Alfred B. Lambson and family to come from the north[272] on a visit during Conference.[273]

There will always be room for you. I enclose herewith my cheque in your favor for $15.00 which hill help you to come to Conference.

Give my love to the Children in which Julina, Edna and Mary[274] join. Your brother Joseph F.——

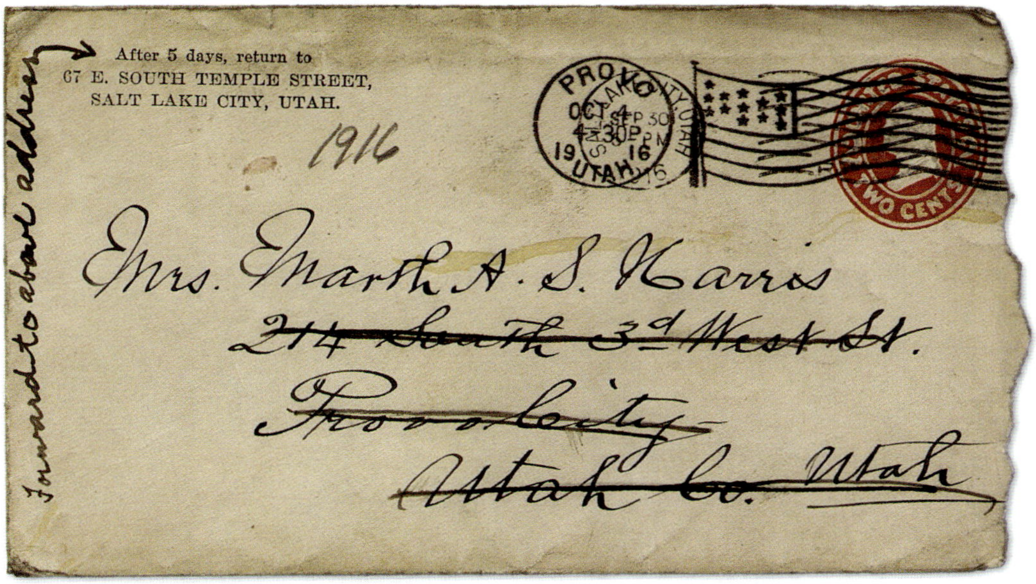

Joseph F. to Martha Ann, 30 September 1916 (envelope)

270. Written on official letterhead of the Church from the Office of the Trustee-in-Trust.
271. Julina Lambson.
272. Alfred Boaz Lambson Jr. and his family were living in Idaho at this time.
273. The 86th Semiannual General Conference was held on 6–8 October 1916 in Salt Lake City.
274. Living wives of Joseph F. at this time were Julina Lambson, Edna Lambson, and Mary Taylor Schwartz. Alice Ann Kimball was also living, though not included in this list.

JOSEPH F. TO MARTHA ANN, 14 NOVEMBER 1916

Beehive House[275]
Salt Lake City—
Nov.r 14th 1916

Martha A. S. Harris:—
214 South 3d West St. Provo,

Dear Aunt Martha:—

Your Card of gratulation in rememberance of myself and Nov. 13th[276] and that of Artie's,[277] reached me this morning. Thank you both, and all my kind friends and kinfolks for their kind wishes and rememberances!

There were 125 members of my family present at the Bishop's Building,[278] from 4—to 6 o'clock yesterday, including 65. Grand children out of a possible 79.

Some of the little ones were troubled with slight colds, and the weather was very cold, so it was thought best for them not to come out. Therefore 13 of the grand children remained at home—And One—Joseph S. Nelson[279]—is in England on a mission.

We are all pretty well. And hope you and children are also well—Julina[280] sends you a Cheque for $18.00

All send love to you and family, Your bro. Joseph F.

P.S. I also enclose for you a cheque for $10.00 to help you to get coal—or pay on tax a/c, as you wish.
Jos. F.——[281]

JOSEPH F. TO MARTHA ANN, 29 NOVEMBER 1916

Salt Lake City, Utah, Nov.r 29th 1916[282]

My Dear Sister Martha:—

Please accept the enclosed $10.00 bill as a trifeling remembrance for your Thanks-giving dinner. I should have sent it yesterday but was so much employed I could not get the time to do it. I hope it will reach you in time ~~in time~~ for an evening dinner, if too late for a mid-day meal.

275. The official residence of the President of the Church in 1916.
276. Joseph F. celebrated his seventy-eighth birthday on 13 November 1916.
277. Martha Artimissa Harris.
278. The Bishop's Building, located in Salt Lake City, was dedicated in 1910.
279. Joseph Smith Nelson, son of Joseph Nelson and Joseph F.'s daughter Leonora Smith. See biographical register, "Nelson, Joseph Smith."
280. Julina Lambson.
281. Written in the top left corner of the paper.
282. Written on official letterhead of the Church from the Office of the First Presidency.

I hope you are better in health. We all seem to be gaining a little

Some of the little ones are teathing and fretful, with the usual colds which come to babies when cutting teath. Julina is up at Inas,[283] and the girles[284] are out—and I want to get the first post-collection, so you will excuse haste. Ever your naughty brother
Joseph F.——

MARTHA ANN TO JOSEPH F., 13 DECEMBER 1916

RECEIVED
JAN—2'17
PRESIDENT'S OFFICE[285]

Provo City Dec the 13th
1916[286]

Mr Joseph F Smith my dearly beloved brother your dear letter came safly to hand with the check in it, for me & when I seen it it so over come <me> I had to have a good cry with gratitude to my Father in Heaven <for> giveing me such a dear brother. I do not know how to express my harts gratitude to you for your goodnes to me. I guess you think I am very on greatfull not to [**p. 2**] ~~in~~ answer before now I have been very buisy this is the ferst time I have been able to get at it & my dear brother I do thank you more than I can tell you but you will git tierd of this I am afraid. but it is a long lain that has no turn & I do hope it may turn some day in my way before it is to late I was so sorry to hear from Aunt Julinas[287] letter, that you had been troubled with that pain in your chest [**p. 3**][288] I do hope that it will soon be better. I have had a pain in my side for the last to days I guess it must be indigestion perhaps I have taken coald & it has settled there I hope Inas baby[289] will not take the meezles babys of that age re not so apt to take it. I went to my daughter Zinas[290] for Crsmass dinner John[291] sent for me to come to his house but I had promssed Zina so I had to put them [**p. 4**] for some other time Hyrum & Franklin are in new Mxico working the assesment on their mine thare.[292] I was pleased to hear

283. Julina Lambson was likely visiting her daughter Julina Clarissa Smith.
284. An affectionate nickname for Joseph F.'s wives.
285. Stamped with blue ink in the top left margin.
286. Joseph F. supplied Martha Ann with stamps and envelopes from time to time, beginning in the 1850s. In this case the envelope has a US two-cent George Washington preprinted stamp with the postal mark "PROVO UTAH DEC 30 3-30 p 1916." Additionally, Joseph F. preaddressed the envelope in his own hand, "Mr. Joseph F. Smith 67 East South Temple St. Salt Lake City Utah," and added the word *Personal* to the front cover.
287. Julina Lambson.
288. "[P.3, 13 DEC 1916]" is written in the top right margin in an unknown hand.
289. Likely refers to Luacine Peery, daughter of Julina Clarissa Smith. Julina had two children at this time; the youngest, Luacine, was four years old. See biographical register, "Peery, Luacine."
290. Zina Christine Harris.
291. Likely John Fielding Harris.
292. Hyrum Smith Harris and Franklin Hill Harris. See Martha Ann to Joseph F., 26 December 1911, herein.

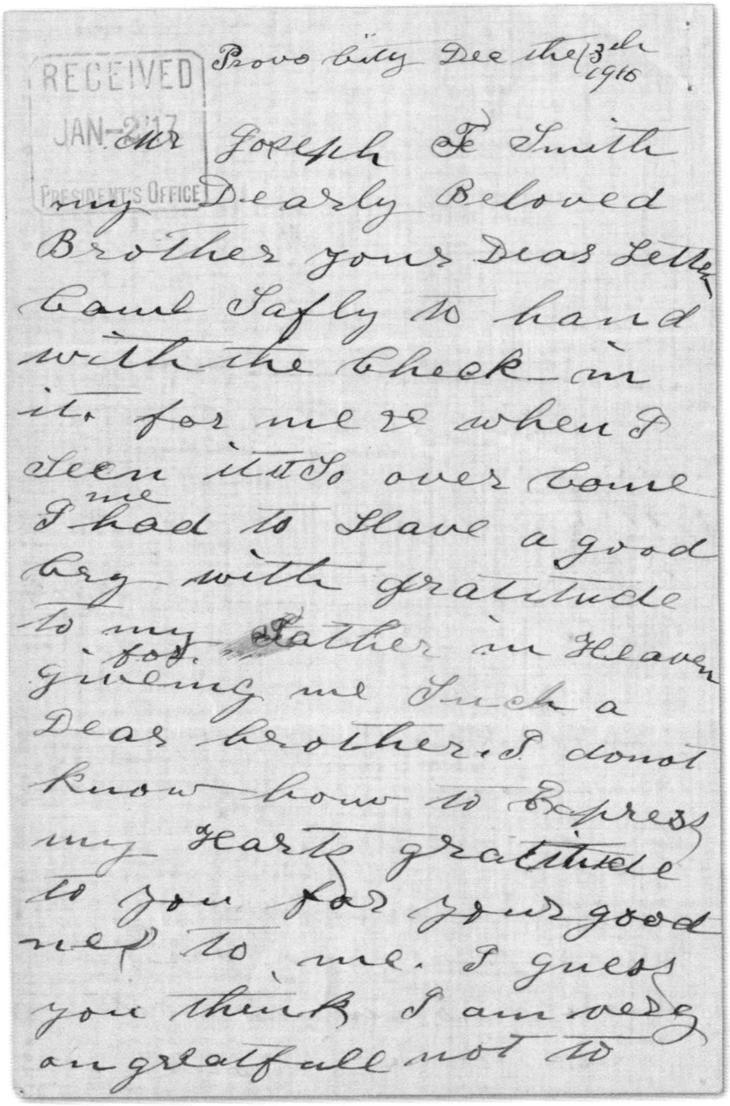

RECEIVED JAN-2 '17 PRESIDENT'S OFFICE

Provo City Dec the 13th 1916

Mr Joseph F Smith

my Dearly Beloved Brother your Dear Letter came Safly to hand with the check in it for me & when I seen it it So over come me I had to have a good cry with gratitude to my Father in Heaven for giving me such a Dear brother. I donot know how to Express my Harts grattitude to you for your goodness to me. I guess you think I am very ungreatfull not to

Martha Ann to Joseph F., 13 December 1916 (p. 1)

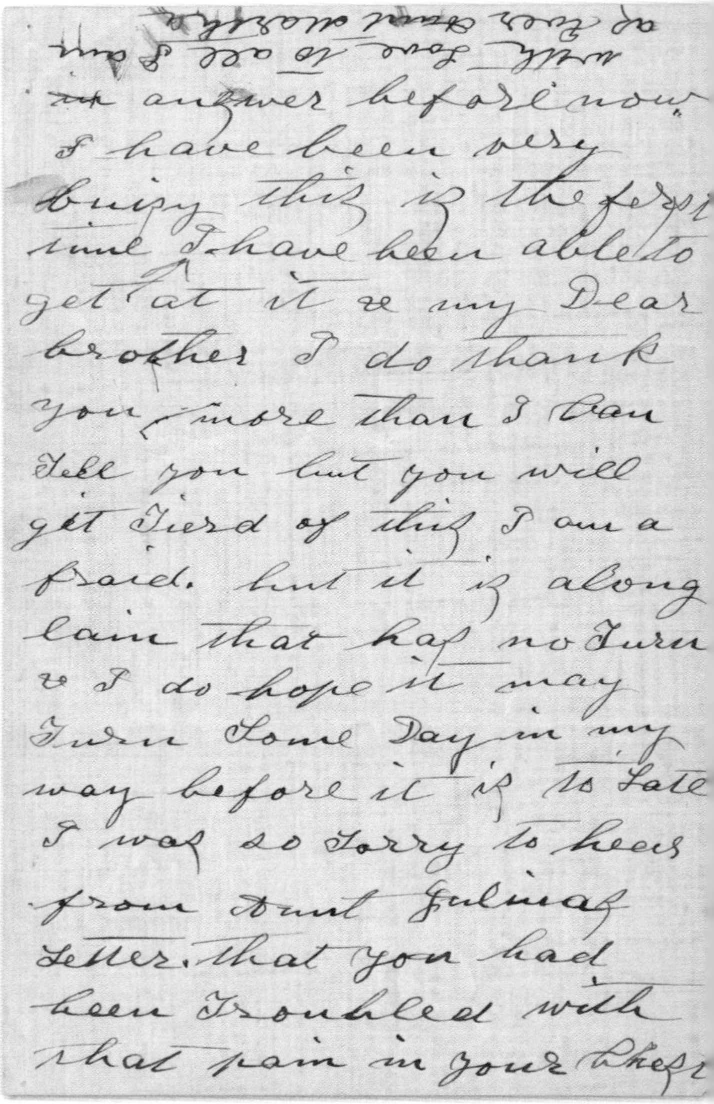

with love to all I am as ever Aunt Martha

answer before now I have been very buisy this is the first time I have been able to get at it & my Dear brother I do thank you more than I can tell you but you will get tired of this I am afraid. but it is a long lane that has no turn & I do hope it may turn some day in my way before it is to late I was so sorry to hear from Aunt Julinas letter that you had been troubled with that pain in your chest

Martha Ann to Joseph F., 13 December 1916 (p. 2)

you could help Ina[293] & our other cousin when you wrte pleas tell me whoo Athaia[294] is whos daughter she is. well I will close for the present for I have some more letters to wrte & my desire <is> that you may have [*illegible strike-through*] a hapy new year & a prosperous one & a whole lot of them

frrom your loing sisters M A. Harris[295]

with love to all I am as ever Aunt Martha[296]

293. Likely Ina Coolbrith (née Josephine Donna Smith).
294. Possibly refers to Joseph F. and Martha Ann's cousin Thalia Grant Smith. See Joseph F. to Martha Ann, 19 December 1916, herein. See also biographical register, "Smith, Thalia Grant."
295. Written sideways in the right margin of page 4.
296. Written upside down in the top margin of page 2.

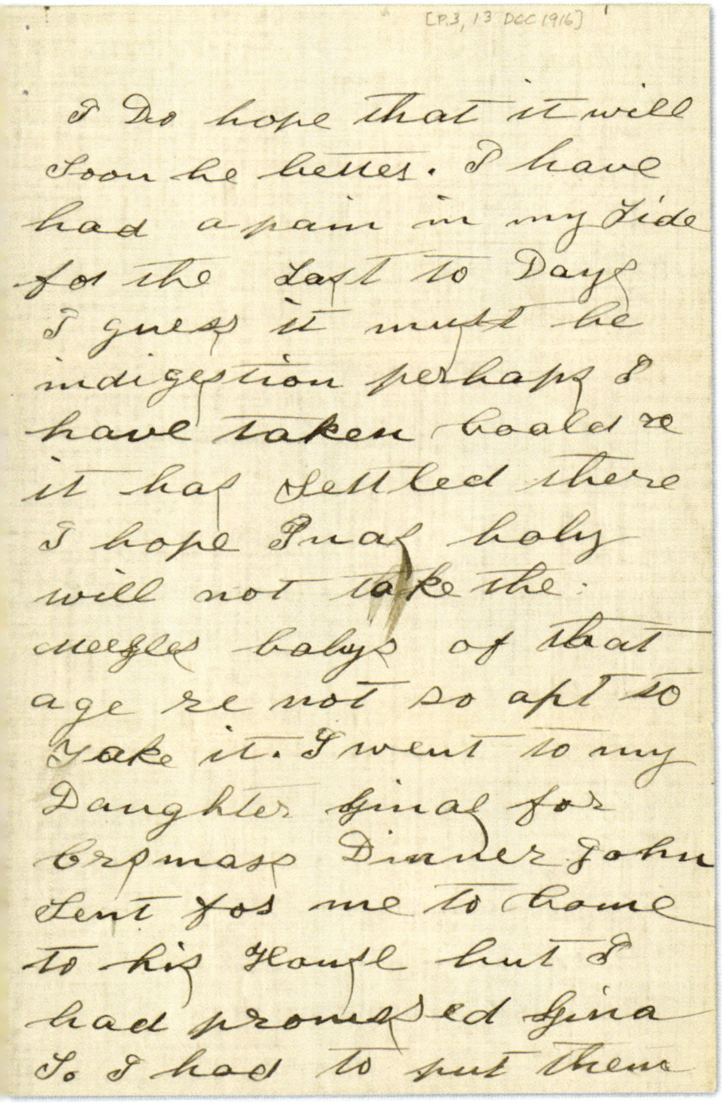
[P.3, 13 DEC 1916]

I Do hope that it will
Soon be better. I have
had a pain in my Side
for the Last to Days
I guess it must be
indigestion perhaps I
have taken Coald &
it has Settled there
I hope Inas baby
will not take the
measles babys of that
age are not so apt to
take it. I went to my
Daughter Gina for
Crismass Dinner John
Sent for me to come
to his House but I
had promised Gina
So I had to put them

Martha Ann to Joseph F., 13 December 1916 (p. 3)

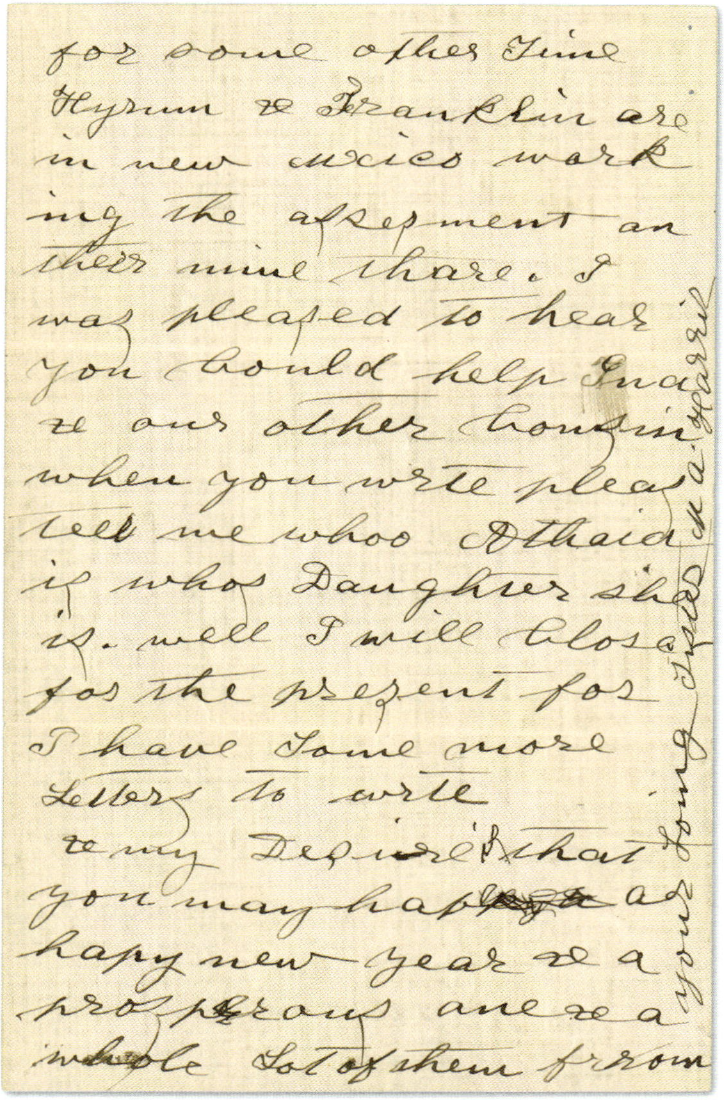
for some other time
Hyrum & Franklin are
in new mexico work
ing the assesment an
their mine thare. I
was pleased to hear
you could help Ina
& our other cousin
when you write pleas
tell me whoo Athaid
is whos Daughter she
is. well I will close
for the present for
I have Some more
Letters to write
& my Desire that
you may hap a
hapy new year & a
prosperous one & a
whole Lot of them from
your Loving Sister M. A. Harris

Martha Ann to Joseph F., 13 December 1916 (p. 4)

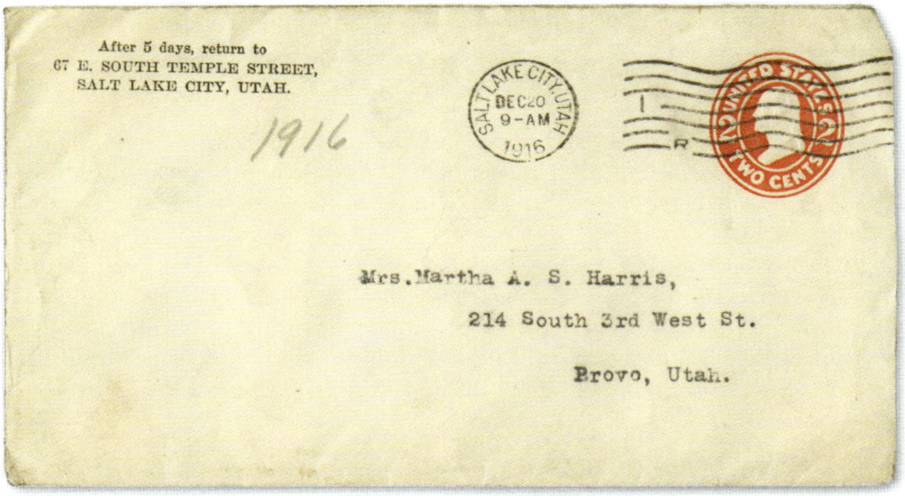
After 5 days, return to
67 E. SOUTH TEMPLE STREET,
SALT LAKE CITY, UTAH.

1916

SALT LAKE CITY, UTAH
DEC 20
9-AM
1916

UNITED STATES
TWO CENTS

Mrs. Martha A. S. Harris,
214 South 3rd West St.
Provo, Utah.

Joseph F. to Martha Ann, 19 December 1916 (envelope)

JOSEPH F. TO MARTHA ANN, 19 DECEMBER 1916

December 19, 1916.[297]

Martha A. S. Harris,
214 South 3rd West St.,
Provo, Utah

My Dear Sister:—

Thinking that you mught enjoy a turkey for your Christmas and a little cranberry sauce, I thought I would forward to you the enclosed check for $25.00, which I hope you will accept in the spirit in which it is offered, and will enjoy the use of it.

I am serving Cousin Ina[298] in the same way, but I do not expect from her the same sisterly appreciation that I usually receive from you. I am happy to say that we are all usually well, with the exception of some of the little ones who are suffering from teething and other little ailments incident to infancy. Our Ina[299] is in San Diego[300] with her three little children,[301] two of whom have the measles from the last account. One or two of Melissa's[302] also have the measles. You will be delighted to hear that Willard has another little son[303] added to his family. Wishing you and the children the compliments of the season, I am,

Affectionately your brother,
Joseph F. Smith[304]

P.S. I am also sending—a small remembrance to Cousin Thalia[305]—who is in Kansas[306]

297. Typewritten in black ink on official letterhead of the Church from the Office of the Trustee-in-Trust. Martha Ann was seventy-five, and Joseph F. was seventy-eight.
298. Ina Coolbrith (née Josephine Donna Smith).
299. Julina Clarissa Smith.
300. San Diego, San Diego County, California. Ina may have attended the San Diego 1916 Exposition, also known as the Panama-California International Exposition. Dedicated on 18 March 1916, the "New International Exposition" was held in Balboa Park in honor of the opening of the Panama Canal. See Richard W. Amero, *Balboa Park and the 1915 Exposition* (Charleston: History Press, 2013).
301. Julina Clarissa Smith, Ina, and her husband, Joseph Stras Peery, had three children at the time: Joseph Smith Perry (born on 6 February 1911), Luacine Perry (born on 2 December 1912), and Julina Perry (born on 19 February 1916).
302. Edna Melissa Smith.
303. Willard Richards Smith's son Briant Grant Smith was born to Florence Grant on 15 December 1916. See biographical register, "Smith, Briant Grant."
304. Signed by hand.
305. Thalia Grant Smith.
306. Written in the bottom left margin of the page.

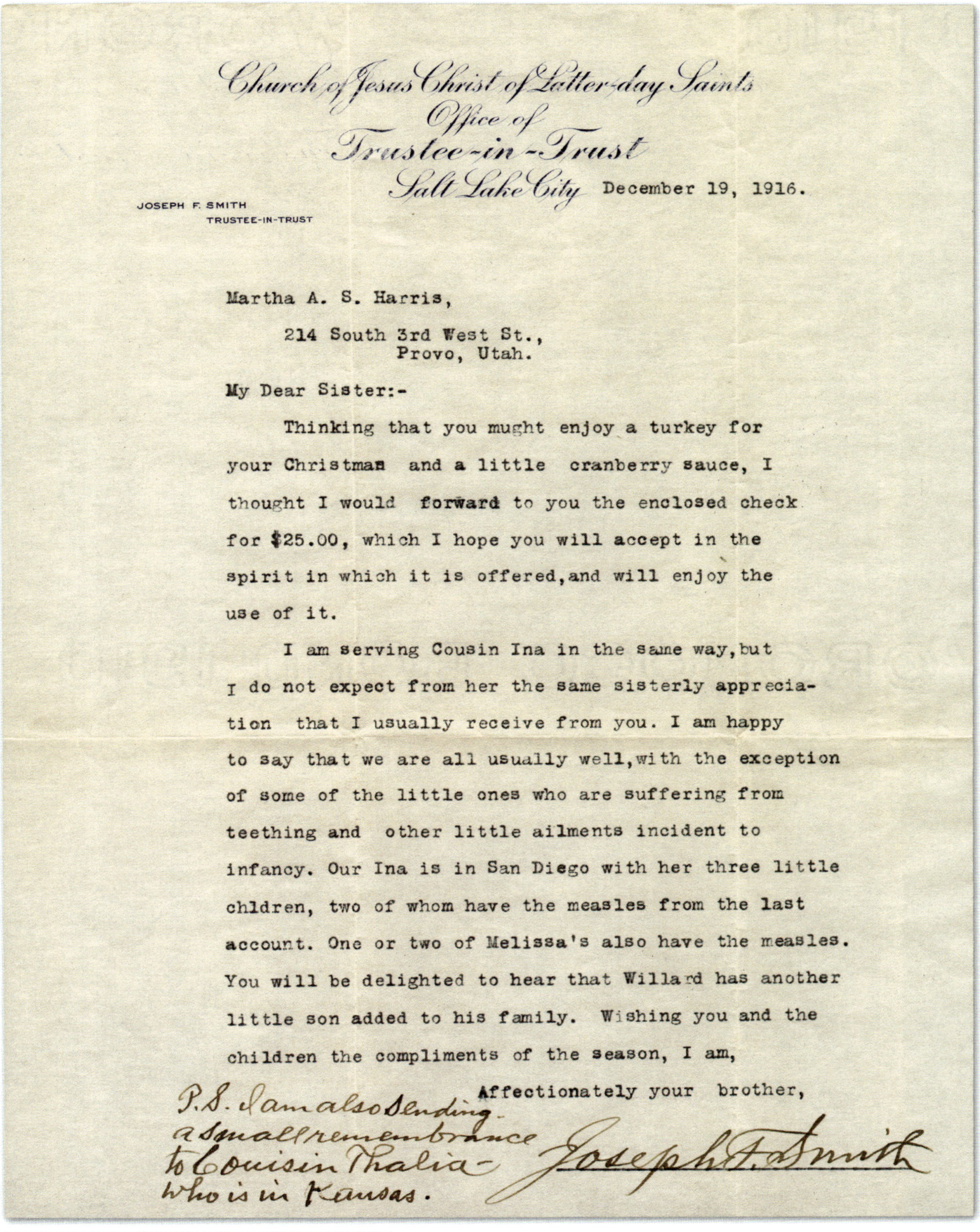

Church of Jesus Christ of Latter-day Saints
Office of
Trustee-in-Trust
Salt Lake City December 19, 1916.

JOSEPH F. SMITH
TRUSTEE-IN-TRUST

Martha A. S. Harris,

214 South 3rd West St.,
Provo, Utah.

My Dear Sister:-

Thinking that you mught enjoy a turkey for your Christmas and a little cranberry sauce, I thought I would forward to you the enclosed check for $25.00, which I hope you will accept in the spirit in which it is offered, and will enjoy the use of it.

I am serving Cousin Ina in the same way, but I do not expect from her the same sisterly apprecia-tion that I usually receive from you. I am happy to say that we are all usually well, with the exception of some of the little ones who are suffering from teething and other little ailments incident to infancy. Our Ina is in San Diego with her three little children, two of whom have the measles from the last account. One or two of Melissa's also have the measles. You will be delighted to hear that Willard has another little son added to his family. Wishing you and the children the compliments of the season, I am,

Affectionately your brother,

Joseph F. Smith

P.S. I am also sending a small remembrance to Cousin Thalia— who is in Kansas.

Joseph F. to Martha Ann, 19 December 1916 (p. 1)

Portrait of Joseph F. Smith, ca. 1916, by Albert J. F. Salzbrenner. Courtesy of CHM.

Conclusion

In 2018 the Joseph F. Smith family observed two centennial events, one celebrating the reception of the "Vision of the Redemption of the Dead" (3 October 1918) and the other marking the anniversary of Joseph F.'s death (19 November 1918). These events gave family members an opportunity to remember Joseph F.'s consecrated life and labors in behalf of the Church of Jesus Christ.

Joseph F. Smith's diaries, letters, sermons, and personal reminiscences from his first mission to Hawai'i reveal the beginnings of a lifelong process of steady self-improvement and accomplishment in building up the kingdom of God on earth. In 1861 during his mission to the British Isles, he acknowledged that this growth was going to take some time: "I have partly learned one thing, i.e. I am mighty small, and don't know much—if anything. [p. 3] and I see a great deal more to learn every day and still experience is such a slow-and-sure School Teacher that I do not seem to make scarcely any progress in my lessons, but I hope—'in patience to possess my soul' and struggle unceasingly t[*0.6 x 2.7 cm vertical tear along fold*] the end."[1]

In 1874, during another mission to England, Joseph F. reflected in his diary, "I pray God to give me the spirt of my mission & ability to performe every duty acceptably."[2] He had been struggling with an assignment to edit the Church's longest continuous publication, the *Millennial Star.* He recorded the day before, "[Tuesday, May 12, 1874] Busy most of the day trying to write for the Star, but did not get the Spirit."[3] What he noted in his journal the next day is indicative of the faith and persistence that characterized his life and so often bore fruit in projects both small and large: "Busy most of the day writing. Did not feel clear went and prayed & felt better."[4]

A source of Joseph F.'s motivation to dedicate his life's labors to the Church is evident in an 1883 letter to a member who had requested permission to be sealed to or adopted[5] into Hyrum Smith's family through Joseph F. "My father was a martyr for the truths sake," he averred, "and wears his crown as such, my prayer and earnest, live-long desire is to prove true and faithful to the end as he

1. Joseph F. to Martha Ann, 29 January 1861, herein.
2. Joseph F., journal, 13 May 1874.
3. Joseph F., journal, 12 May 1874.
4. Joseph F., journal, 13 May 1874.
5. The law of adoption was an ordinance generally performed in Latter-day Saint temples between 1846 and 1894 in which men who held the priesthood were sealed in a father-son relationship to other men who were not their biological offspring. It is generally assumed this practice occurred because many early adult converts did not have fathers who were members of the Church. See Gordon Irving, "The Law of Adoption: One Phase of the Development of the Mormon Concept of Salvation," *BYU Studies* 14, no. 3 (Spring 1974): 291–314.

did. . . . There is no doubt about the endurance or exaltation of those who die faithful but mortality is shrouded with uncertainty."[6]

Less than seven months before he became President of the Church in 1901, Joseph F. wrote a letter to President Lorenzo Snow (1814–1901) to seek forgiveness following meetings he had participated in with the First Presidency and Quorum of the Twelve Apostles. According to Elder Rudger J. Clawson, a member of the Twelve present at those two meetings, "a discussion was held on 26 February 1901 about a 'law now pending before the Utah legislature making it unlawful for anyone to bring a charge of adultery against a married man except the legal wife, she being the aggrieved party.'" Clawson noted that the purpose of the law was to "curtail the power of our enemies, who seek to bring trouble upon the Latter-day Saints by prosecuting polygamists for unlawful cohabitation."[7] Recalling that George Q. Cannon was concerned about "the wisdom of passing such a law at this time," Clawson reflected, "There is no question as to the advantages it would bring to our people, but it has been thought by some that it would bring trouble upon the church, as our enemies would claim that we were taking steps to revive the practice of polygamy, which is not true."[8]

As was common in these meetings, "the brethren were called upon to give an expression of their views, and all present expressed themselves in favor of the bill, except Pres. Cannon, who thought it an unwise measure. Pres. Snow said he was not quite clear in his mind as to the policy and wisdom of such a law at this time. A vote was taken and was unanimous in favor of the measure."[9]

Two days later, on Thursday, 28 February 1901, Church leaders met again at 11:00 a.m. The council opened with a hymn and a prayer. President Snow then raised concerns about the previous meeting (held on Tuesday, 26 February), indicating that "a difference of view existed among the brethren regarding the proposed law on adultery, and in the discussion that followed feelings of an improper character were manifested as between Pres. Cannon and Pres. J. F. Smith."[10] President Snow said "that the matter ought to be rectified and the perfect union of the Twelve restored. He took the view that Pres. Smith was at fault." Clawson further reported, "Pres. Smith made suitable acknowledgments and was freely forgiven. Pres. Geo. Q. Cannon also asked forgiveness, which was freely granted."[11] The meeting closed with a hymn, "School Thy Feelings, O My Brother," and a prayer.

Following this meeting, Joseph F. felt it necessary to send a personal letter of apology to President Snow:

> I was deeply moved and grieved and hurt that I had in the least wronged any of my brethren [including President George Q. Cannon] by thought, word, or deed without being, myself, conscious of it, thereby injuring myself, even more than any one else, and giving you occasion or necessity for administering such severe reproof. . . . This was very hard to bear. I deeply regret it. . . . I humbly bow to the chastisement I have received, accepting your reproof, and that of the other brethren and esteem it as a timely earning and a blessing to me which by the help of the Lord I will endeavor to profit by throughout the future. I sincerely ask the Lord, yourself, and the brethren to thoroughly forgive my past mistake

6. Joseph F. to Andrew Borgesen, 14 November 1883. In the end, Joseph F. advised the man to consider being sealed directly to Hyrum.
7. Rudger Clawson, journal, 26 February 1901, as quoted in Stan Larson, ed., *A Ministry of Meetings: The Apostolic Diaries of Rudger Clawson* (Salt Lake City, UT: Signature Books, 1993), 248.
8. Clawson, journal, 26 February 1901, as quoted in Larson, *Ministry of Meetings*, 249.
9. Clawson, journal, 26 February 1901, as quoted in Larson, *Ministry of Meetings*, 249.
10. Clawson, journal, 26 February 1901, as quoted in Larson, *Ministry of Meetings*, 250.
11. Clawson, journal, 26 February 1901; as quoted in Larson, *Ministry of Meetings*, 250.

> and follies, which I trust have been errors of the head more than of the heart, and I will try to do better.[12]

The refining process of a future President of the Church continued for another seventeen years. In 1907, after many years of being personally attacked and lampooned in the press, President Smith modestly reflected, "The Devil don't care much about me. I am insignificant, but he hates the Priesthood, which is after the order of the Son of God!"[13] Despite his realistic view of his personal weaknesses and his vulnerability as a public figure, he persevered and continually improved as a disciple of Jesus Christ.

In January 1907 President Smith gave a memorable discourse in Provo titled "At Rest in Christ."[14] In it he posited the question, "What does it mean to enter into the rest of the Lord?" His considered answer was emblematic of his own single-minded resolve to endure in faith and thereby win an eternal crown:

> Speaking for myself, it means that through the love of God I have been won over to Him, so I can feel rest in Christ, that I may no more be disturbed by every wind of doctrine, by the cunning and craftiness of men, whereby they lay in wait to deceive; and that I am established in the knowledge and testimony of Jesus Christ, so that no power can turn me aside from the straight and narrow path that leads back to the presence of God, to enjoy exaltation in His glorious kingdom; that from this time henceforth I shall enjoy that rest until I shall *rest* with Him in the heavens.[15]

Joseph F. had tasted that rest and lived accordingly until eventually, through a long refining process, he saw the fulfillment of the Patriarch's inspired declaration back in 1852: "Your name shall be had in honorable remembrance among the Saints for ever."[16]

Close associate and friend Charles W. Nibley reflected shortly after Joseph F.'s death in 1918 that "many of the older people now alive can recall that forty years ago, or even less, he [Joseph F.] was considered a radical, and many a one of that time shook his head and said, 'What will become of things if that fiery radical ever becomes president of the Church.' But from the time he was made president of the Church, and even before that time, he became one of the most tolerant of men; tolerant of others' opinions. . . . None more ready to forgive and forget."[17]

Another observer, Judge Charles C. Goodwin (1832–1917), the former editor of the anti-Church *Salt Lake Tribune* from 1883 to 1903, noted just two years before Joseph F. died that he had "mellowed as the years" went by and that he sees "the good in humanity and forgives men their trespasses." Goodwin added, "A more kindly and benevolent man has seldom held an exalted ecclesiastical position in these latter days than President Joseph F. Smith of the Church of Jesus Christ of Latter-day Saints." The former critic and enemy of Joseph F. observed, "To his people he

12. Joseph F. to Lorenzo Snow, 28 February 1901.
13. Joseph F. to Joseph E. Taylor, 16 November 1907.
14. Joseph F. Smith, "At Rest in Christ," *Latter-day Saints' Millennial Star* 69, no. 22 (30 May 1907): 337–49.
15. Smith, "At Rest in Christ," 338.
16. "Patriarchal Blessing of Joseph F. Smith, 1852."
17. Joseph F. Smith, *Gospel Doctrine: Selections from the Sermons and Writings of Joseph F. Smith*, comp. John A. Widtsoe, 5th ed. (Salt Lake City, UT: Deseret Book, 1939), 658.

is the great spiritual leader. To men at large he is a man of wide sympathies, great business acumen and a born leader of the great institution of which he is head."[18]

A biographer opined, "President Smith's accomplishments are remarkable. He husbanded five large families and steered Mormonism into a safe and uncontested position in American culture. He defined the nature of Mormonism *sans* theocracy, cooperatives, and polygamy. He is truly the father of modern Mormonism."[19]

All evidence suggests that Joseph F. the teenager returned to Utah from that very first mission to Hawai'i as a young adult having grown physically, intellectually, and spiritually. Moreover, through this three-year mission far away from home and his constant communication with his relatives, including Martha Ann, Joseph F. grounded himself with the same firmness of faith held by his honored father and mother and reflected in his very name, Joseph Fielding Smith.[20]

Joseph F.'s son and biographer, also named Joseph Fielding Smith, recounted his father's return home from this first mission. In this version of the story, Joseph F. came face-to-face with a drunken, gun-wielding ruffian who asked Joseph F. if he was a Latter-day Saint. Risking being shot on the spot if he responded positively, Joseph F. declared with conviction, "Yes, siree; dyed in the wool; true blue, through and through." The answer was given boldly and without any sign of fear, which completely disarmed the belligerent man, and in his bewilderment, he grasped the missionary by the hand and said: "Well, you are the —— pleasantest man I ever met! Shake, young fellow, I am glad to see a man that stands up for his convictions."[21]

As is so often seen in his letters to Martha Ann, Joseph F.'s commitment to the gospel cause was the central focus of his life. An 1885 letter is a prime example:

> I am well and as usual engaged in the duties of my calling as a messenger of the Gospel to the people of the Earth. I am as useful here at present as I could be any where. And when my labors will be more useful somewhere else I hope to be found there. With me it is the Kingdom

18. Charles C. Goodwin, "The Pioneers," *Goodwin's Weekly*, 8 April 1916, 1.
19. Kenney, "Before the Beard," 21.
20. See Ricks, *"My Candid Opinion,"* xi–xxii.
21. There is no contemporary account of this incident. Joseph F.'s 1850s Hawaiian missionary journals end on 20 October 1857, when he was sailing home, before the encounter took place on the mainland; and his next journal did not begin until 27 April 1860, when he started on a mission to England. Because of this gap in the record, this story is based on secondary sources by those who presumably heard Joseph F. recount it. A version of the incident appeared within two months of Joseph F.'s death (see Charles W. Nibley; "Reminiscences of President Joseph F. Smith," *Improvement Era*, January 1919, 192). Another version, used here with slight variations from Nibley's account, was published a few months later (see Smith, *Gospel Doctrine*, 657). Joseph Fielding Smith, who preserved another version in his book *Life of Joseph F. Smith*, repeated the story to his children and grandchildren so often that they could easily repeat it verbatim years later (Vivian McConkie Adams, Joseph Fielding McConkie, and Mary McConkie Donoh, interview, 6 July 2013). As New Testament scholars have often observed, in such stories inconsequential variations should be expected while the core remains consistent (see, for example, J. D. G. Dunn, *Jesus Remembered: Christianity in the Making, Volume 1* [Grand Rapids, MI: Eerdmans, 2003] 210–14).

    There are at least two letters in which Joseph F. used similar phrases found in the earliest versions of the story. The first reference—"I tell you martha they are going to flud the world with 'true blue' or with true borne 'Mormons' and I'm glad to here it"—appears in Joseph F. to Martha Ann, 15 February 1856, herein. The second reference—"I hope the boys will do well on their mission and will return 'true-blue' thoroughly 'died in the wool' Latter Day Saints, besides doing a good work"—appears in Joseph F. to Alma L. Smith, 29 March 1882. For a detailed analysis and discussion of the earliest versions, see Nathaniel R. Ricks, "True Blue, Depending on Who's Telling the Tale: The Redacted Story of Joseph F. Smith and the 'Ruffians,'" *The Juvenile Instructor: Organ for Young Latter-day Scholars*, 12 November 2013, https://juvenileinstructor.org/true-blue-depending-on-whos-telling-the-tale-the-redacted-story-of-joseph-f-smith-and-the-ruffians/.

of God or nothing. My only course is onward and, I trust, upward. I can yeald to nothing but the will and pleasure of the Almighty. It is my delight to serve the Lord and the people of God.[22]

His California cousin Ina Coolbrith, whom he continued to encourage and help financially throughout his life, recognized Joseph F.'s and Martha Ann's commitment to their faith, but not in the same way Joseph F. understood it. When a non–Latter-day Saint relative asked her to visit Salt Lake City after she herself had done so, Ina replied, "Joseph and his sister are good, I do not doubt that, but absolutely fanatic in their religion, and would not, I fear, know anything different from their belief for all the Universe. To me, in this age of reason, it seems almost impossible."[23]

Paralleling his lifelong commitment to The Church of Jesus Christ of Latter-day Saints, Joseph F. was his devotion to his family. Although his first marriage tragically ended in a divorce, Joseph F. was a loving and dedicated husband to five other wives and a devoted and much-beloved father to forty-eight children.[24]

Less than four months before his death, Joseph F. spoke at the dedication of a monument erected in honor of his father, Hyrum Smith (1800–1844), in the Salt Lake City Cemetery:

> I am rich; the Lord has given me great riches in children and in children's children; and in the fact that my children have, so far, honored me and their grandfather and their mothers and the Church of Jesus Christ of Latter-day Saints. . . . I trust and pray that all my children and my children's children to the latest generation will abide in the truth. I want you to just take a look here at a little flock of my grandchildren—right here, every one of them. I love them. I know them all I never meet them but what I kiss them just as I do my own children. I don't care how dirty their faces are, if I can only have the privilege of meeting with my grandchildren and kissing them and letting them know that I love them just as I love my own children. Then I shall be satisfied, and I expect to continue it as long as I can.[25]

Joseph F. Smith spoke his last words to his family from his deathbed in the Beehive House on Sunday, 10 November 1918. He compared the value of worldly riches and personal possessions with that of his family:

> I have a beautiful watch and chain and rings. I never spent a dollar for any of them in my life because I could not afford it, but I have had friends and they have, from time to time, given me rings. A beautiful watch chain and fob were given me on the day of the dedication of the monument to the honor of the Prophet Joseph Smith in Vermont [23 December 1905]. And I had left to me the gold watch that belonged to my Uncle Joseph Smith. . . . . But when I look around me and see my boys and girls, whom the Lord has given to me, and I have succeeded, with His help, to make them tolerably comfortable, and at least respectable in the world, I have reached the treasure of my life—the substance of life worth living—my family. I have a family I am proud of, every individual member of it I love.[26]

22. Joseph F. to Martha Ann, 18 March 1885, herein.
23. Ina Coobrith to Bio De Casseres, Adele T. De Casseres correspondence, 1910–1927.
24. Forty-three children were born to Joseph F. and his five wives. He also adopted two additional children and invited Alice Ann Kimball's three children from a previous marriage to become part of his family once he and Alice married in 1883. Some reminiscences from his children are found in Norman S. Bosworth, "Remembering Joseph F. Smith: Loving Father, Devoted Prophet," *Ensign*, June 1983, 20–24.
25. Joseph F. Smith, "Appreciation and Gratitude," *Improvement Era*, August 1918, 861–62.
26. See "Prest. Smith Is Called by Death," *Deseret Evening News*, 19 November 1918, 2.

Nine days later, on 19 November 1918, President Smith died. The primary sources are clear—he worked tirelessly to fulfil his duty in his family and his assignments in the Church. His unrelenting work schedule most likely contributed to his death. Even though he elevated his counselors as semi-equals, President Smith refused to delegate things that previous Church Presidents had been happy to unload. In particular, the diaries and letters reveal a grueling work ethic, often working until midnight or later. Family members, Church associates, and doctors warned him about the toll that such a regime would eventually have on his health. During the last decades of his life, he complained of severe back problems and a propensity to catching colds.[27] Joseph F.'s unrelenting dedication to minister to his family, his church, and those around him denied him the retirement that many Americans looked forward to and enjoyed.

MARTHA ANN'S DEVOTION TO FAMILY, COMMUNITY, AND CHURCH

Martha Ann lived a life centered on her family, community, and church. Despite the personal and family challenges she faced, she contributed to her community in various ways, including through Church service, good deeds for neighbors, and a willingness to help extended family members when they were sick or otherwise needed extra help. Joseph F. noted this characteristic in a closing salute to her in December 1912: "you willingly take upon yourself . . . the well-being of others."[28]

Martha Ann and William were also remembered as being generous, including paying tithes and offerings to the Church and helping others as they could. A grandson wrote, "Martha Ann Harris paid an honest tithing all her life," a lesson she learned from her widowed mother, Mary Fielding.[29]

One report said Martha Ann "possessed qualities that brought happiness in all the homes she visited. Her charitable nature, her kindness and her devotion to duty and responsibilities were proverbial."[30] Joseph F. gave his opinion, "The noblest, and therefore in the true sense, the highest ideas that men can entertain are those of 'faith, hope and charity', and in all these I award you credit of being superior to most women, else you would have succumbed to your misfortunes long ago. but your hope, your charity for others, and your faith in providence have sustained you."[31]

Joseph F. was a pillar of strength to his younger sister Martha Ann throughout her life. When he died in 1918, Martha Ann was undoubtedly overcome with grief. She had already lived nine years without her husband, William, who had passed away in 1909. She now faced the remaining days of her life without her devoted brother and substitute parent who had supported her and encouraged her since they had become orphans in 1852.[32]

27. We acknowledge Stephen C. Taysom's insights on this important point.
28. See, for example, Joseph F. to Martha Ann, 23 December 1912, herein.
29. Richard P. Harris, "Martha Ann Smith Harris," *Relief Society Magazine*, January 1924, 18.
30. "Daughter of Martyred Patriarch of Church Paid Final Tribute," *Deseret News*, 22 October 1923, 3.
31. Joseph F. to Martha Ann, 22 May 1890, herein.
32. Following Joseph F.'s death, Martha Ann was deprived of his financial help. It was fortuitous that Martha Ann had obtained a monthly pension of twelve dollars (based on William Jasper's service in the Utah Militia Cavalry during the 1865–1872 Black Hawk War) beginning on 4 March 1917. She had been assisted by Senator Reed Smoot in obtaining the pension. See "No. 10,561 Pension Certificate of Martha A. Harris Payable Monthly by the Disbursing Clerk, Bureau of Pensions. Group 3. United States of America Bureau of Pensions." Courtesy of Carole Call King. The pension was based on the Congressional Act of 4 March 1917 to help veterans of the "Indian Wars" during the nineteenth century. See "An Act to pension the survivors of certain Indian wars from January first, eighteen hundred and fifty-nine, to January, eighteen hundred and ninety-one, inclusive, and for other purposes," *Statutes of the United States of America Passed at the Second Session of the Sixty-Fourth Congress, 1916–1917* (Washington, DC: Government Printing Office, 1917), 2:1199.

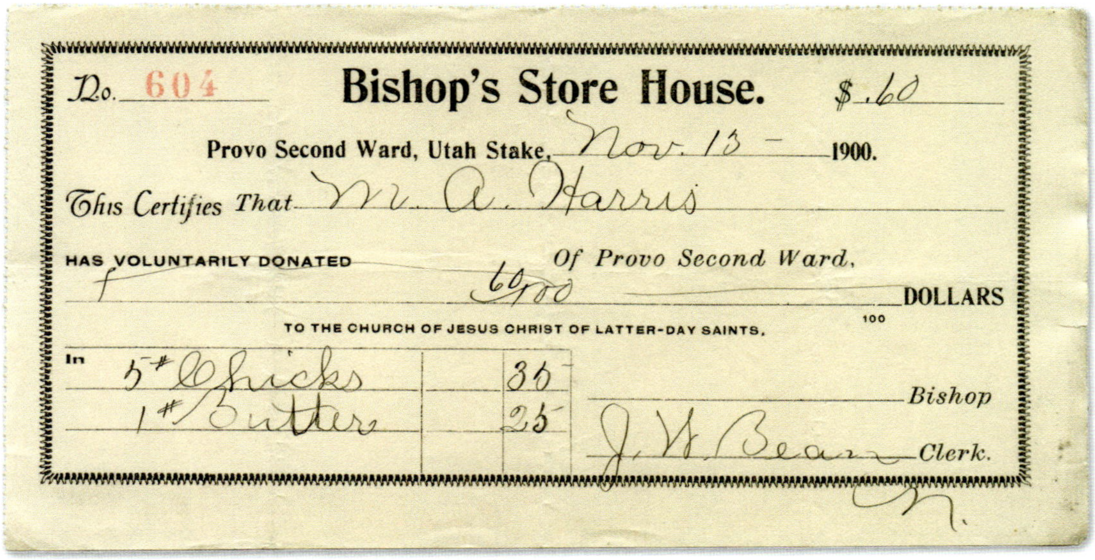

No. 604 **Bishop's Store House.** $.60

Provo Second Ward, Utah Stake, Nov. 13 — 1900.

This Certifies That M. A. Harris

HAS VOLUNTARILY DONATED Of Provo Second Ward,

60/100 DOLLARS

TO THE CHURCH OF JESUS CHRIST OF LATTER-DAY SAINTS.

In		
5# Chicks		35
1# Butter		25

Bishop

J. W. Bean Clerk.

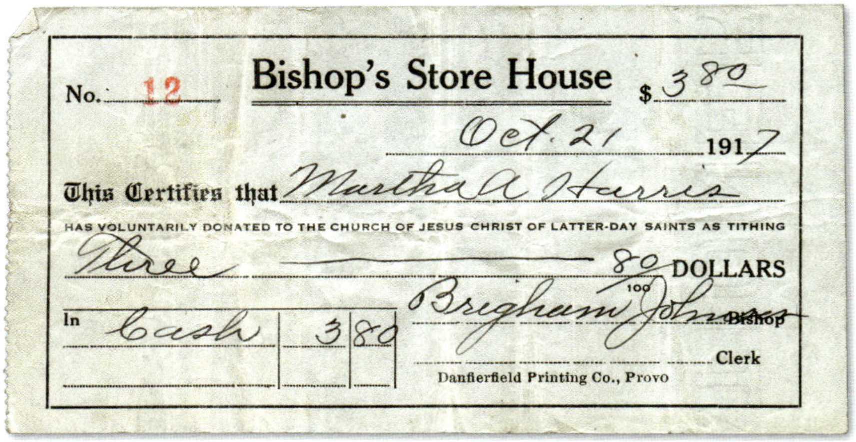

No. 12 **Bishop's Store House** $3.80

Oct. 21 1917

This Certifies that Martha A Harris

HAS VOLUNTARILY DONATED TO THE CHURCH OF JESUS CHRIST OF LATTER-DAY SAINTS AS TITHING

Three 80/100 DOLLARS

In		
Cash	3	80

Brigham Johnson Bishop

Clerk

Danfierfield Printing Co., Provo

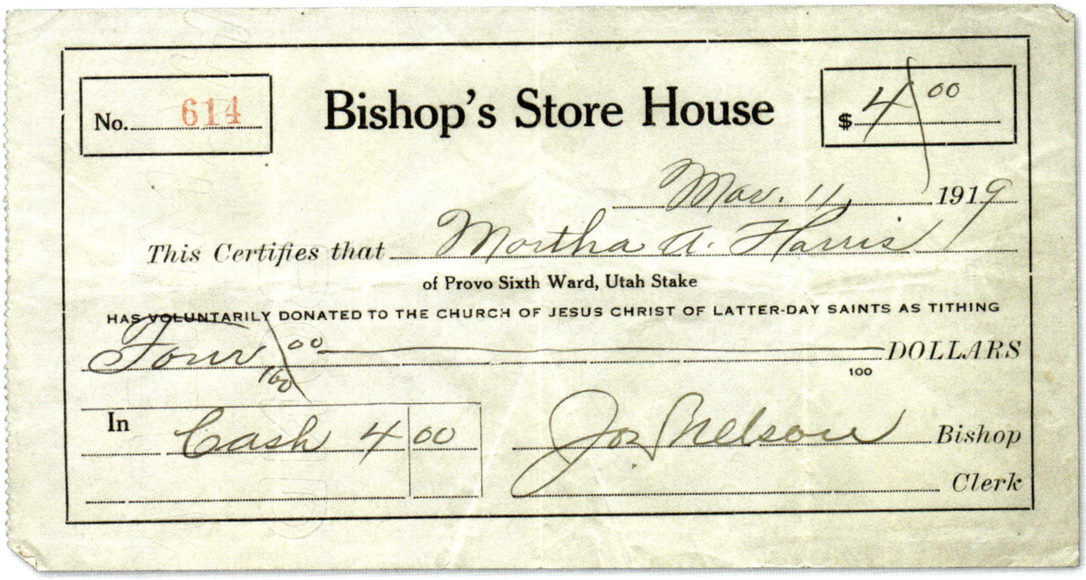

No. 614 **Bishop's Store House** $4.00

Mar. 11 1919

This Certifies that Martha A. Harris

of Provo Sixth Ward, Utah Stake

HAS VOLUNTARILY DONATED TO THE CHURCH OF JESUS CHRIST OF LATTER-DAY SAINTS AS TITHING

Four 00/100 DOLLARS

In		
Cash	4	00

Jos. Nelson Bishop

Clerk

Martha Ann's donation receipts from the "Bishop's Store House." Courtesy of Carole Call King.

Harris family reunion lunch, 11 April 1917, photograph by George Edward Anderson. Martha Ann Smith Harris is seated in the first seat on the left. Anderson took two photographs at the luncheon; see George Edward Anderson Collection, L. Tom Perry Special Collections, Harold B. Lee Library, Brigham Young University, Provo, Utah. The second image focuses on the family members seated at the long banquet tables seen to the right in this view.[33] Courtesy of Carole Call King.

Sometimes historians have not fully appreciated the role that women like Martha Ann played in establishing the pioneer settlements.[34] Martha Ann and her family were involved in the

33. The reunions were announced in the Provo newspaper, inviting all family members to attend. See, for example, "Harris Family Plans Annual Reunion," *Daily Herald*, 13 May 1930, 3 (held at the Provo Sixth Ward). In 1947 the general public was invited to an annual reunion where a special program took place at the Joseph Smith Building at Brigham Young University in honor of the pioneer centennial; see "Pageant to Depict Life History of Ancestors at Harris Reunion," *Daily Herald*, 5 June 1847, 7.
34. Wallace Stegner, one of the first to recognize Latter-day Saint women's contributions, observed, "That I do not accept the faith that possessed them does not mean I doubt their frequent devotion and heroism in its service. Especially their women. Their women were incredible." See Wallace Stegner, *The Gathering of Zion: The Story of the Mormon Trail* (New York: McGraw-Hill, 1964), 13.

transformation of Provo from a rough frontier settlement into a respectable, stable, and thriving long-term modern community. One scholar recently noted, "No one did more, for example, than Mormon women to provide stability and continuity in these communities." He further observed, "Most frontier women faced similar challenging circumstance, but Mormon women carried additional burdens. Church leadership responsibilities—particularly stints as overseas missionaries—often removed fathers, husbands, and brothers from farming and business operation, leaving these responsibilities in the hands of their women, who soon proved equal to managing the sometimes difficult tasks involved. . . . Although most Mormon women—as one might expect—claimed these burdens were light and their yokes easy, they were called to go with the church and their families an extra mile—or two or three." He concluded appropriately, "All the more extraordinary, then, that these hardy, hard-working, and dependable women viewed their roles as usual and commonplace, not in the least extraordinary."[35]

According to Martha Ann's son,

> All of her eleven children grew up and were married in the temple. . . . The death of one of her daughters left two little babies, a boy and a girl, whom she took and cared for as she had for her own children. Both of these grew up and were married. The girl's husband died leaving her to provide for herself and another little baby girl. This little girl she would often leave with her grandmother while she went out to work. Thus Martha Harris cared for three generations of babies, giving to each the same love, and care and attention that she had the others, and the first little girl brought her much cheer and happiness, and made her life seem less lonely."[36]

In May 1921 the Harris family gathered in Provo again—this time to celebrate Martha Ann's birthday. A Salt Lake City newspaper reported, "The eightieth birthday anniversary of Mrs. Martha A. Harris was celebrated Saturday afternoon at the home of her daughter, Mrs. Roy Passey. The affair was given by her four daughters, Mrs. Passey, Mrs. Walter Startup, Mrs. John Dennis and Mrs. Walter S. Corbett."[37]

More than 112 relatives and friends came together to honor Martha Ann, many of whom came from out of town to celebrate this happy occasion. Among those visiting were Martha Ann's two sisters-in-law, Edna Lambson Smith and Mary Schwartz Smith, both widows of Joseph F.[38] It was a milestone in many ways. For example, Martha Ann had lived longer than her parents (Hyrum was killed at age forty-four, and Mary Fielding died at fifty-one).

Family members continued to gather to celebrate special events, including Martha Ann's birthday in 1922. Two months later, according to a family tradition, Martha Ann went to Salt Lake City for the diamond anniversary of the arrival of the pioneers to Salt Lake Valley. On Saturday, 22 July 1922, a special banquet held in the Hotel Utah honored sixty-six of the original 1847 pioneers and 240 pioneers who came behind them, including Martha Ann, who had arrived in the valley

35. Richard W. Etulain, *Beyond the Missouri: The Story of the American West* (Albuquerque: University of New Mexico Press, 2006), 159.
36. Harris, "Martha Ann Smith Harris," 18.
37. "Provo," *Deseret News*, 21 May 1921, section 3, vii.
38. "Provo," *Deseret News*, 21 May 1921, section 3, vii.

Martha Ann Smith Harris family, including grandchildren and great-grandchildren, on her eightieth birthday, May 1921. The family gathered at Sarah Harris Passey's home, 618 East Center Street, Provo, Utah. Martha Ann raised eleven children and was loved by seventy-nine grandchildren and sixty-six great-grandchildren. Courtesy of Carole Call King.

in 1848.[39] A local newspaper described those honored as "a hale and hearty crowd for all their years and entered into the enjoyment of the affair with zest and displayed something of the great spirit which had carried them across the plains despite the greatest hardships befalling any band of pathmakers in history."[40]

Two days later, on Monday, 24 July 1922, the celebration continued at the Saltair Beach Resort on the shore of the Great Salt Lake. Organized by the Central Pioneer Day Committee and Daughters

39. According to one version of the story, Martha Ann "participated as a pioneer in the celebration in Salt Lake City in 1922 for the 75th anniversary of the pioneers' arrival, when This is the Place monument was dedicated" (in editors' possession). This memory cannot be completely relied on since the monument was dedicated by President George Albert Smith on 24 July 1947, more than twenty years after Martha Ann's death in 1923. See "50,000 Attend 'This Is the Place' Site Ceremony," *Deseret News*, July 24, 1947, 32.
40. "Glowing Tribute Is Paid Pioneers at Big Banquet," *Salt Lake Telegram*, 23 July 1922, 9.

of the Utah Pioneers, the activities included a pioneer banquet and concert from 5:00 pm until 7:00 p.m. The celebration ended with a "spectacular fireworks display in the evening at 9 p.m."[41]

In the fall of 1923, Martha Ann was at the end of her remarkable life. Silas Schwartz Smith (1900–1986), her nephew, wrote in September 1923:

> Dear Aunt Martha, Just a word to tell you how I appreciate that beautiful Temple Apron that you sent me. I wore it when I was married on the fifth of September, and assure you that I value it greatly, especially since I realize the many hours of labor that you placed upon it. It seems good to have something worked out by the hands of Father's only living Sister. Anella, my wife, and I leave in a few more days for Philadelphia where I will complete my medical training. Then after my hospital work, hope to return to Salt Lake City and take up a practice. It is my hope that Aunt Martha will still be enjoying good health, so that I may again see her. With much love for you, I remain your nephew. Silas S. Smith."[42]

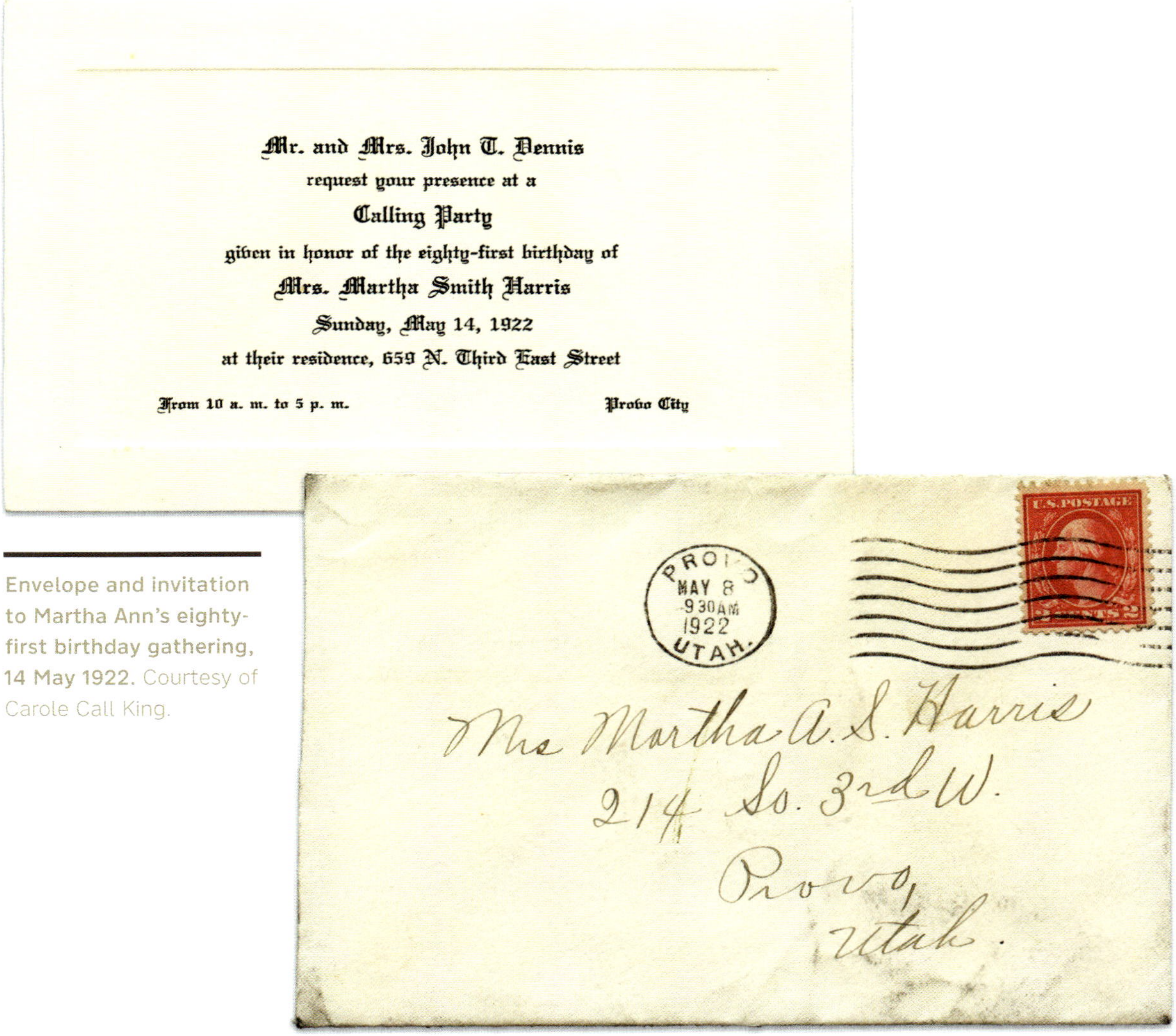

Envelope and invitation to Martha Ann's eighty-first birthday gathering, 14 May 1922. Courtesy of Carole Call King.

41. "Pioneer Program at Saltair Beach Monday," *Deseret News*, 22 July 1922, iv.
42. Silas S. Smith to Martha Ann, 9 September 1923.

Unfortunately, Silas did not see his beloved aunt again. Martha Ann died at 6:00 a.m. on Friday, 19 October 1923, while "sitting in her chair, making temple aprons, . . . alone with her thoughts."[43] She had lived to be eighty-two years, five months, and five days. Martha Ann's son John F. Harris (1872–1946) was the undertaker who took care of the funeral.[44] A local Provo newspaper announced her death in the Friday evening issue, identifying her as an "honored pioneer woman."[45]

Beyond her family and friends, Martha Ann was almost always identified as being the sister, daughter, or niece of an important leader in the Church. In death that did not change. When other newspapers in the state announced her death, it was always in relationship to her famous family.[46] Martha Ann had lived in the shadow of her well-known brother, Joseph F., and they both had lived in the shadows of their famous parents, Hyrum and Mary Fielding. Martha Ann was proud of her family and most likely would not have been surprised by the newspaper headlines announcing her death. She had lived most of her life away from the limelight and chose to focus her service on family, friends, neighbors, and the Church ward where she lived.

The funeral was held in the Provo Tabernacle on Monday afternoon, 22 October 1923. The Provo Sixth Ward bishop, Joseph Nelson, conducted the service, with members from the Provo Tabernacle Choir singing five beautiful compositions, including two Restoration hymns—"When First the Glorious Light Burst Forth in This Last Age" and "O My Father"—and a final hymn often sung at funerals, "I Know My Redeemer Lives."[47] A delegation from Church headquarters, including Apostles George Albert Smith and Joseph Fielding Smith, Church Patriarch Hyrum G. Smith, and Presiding Bishopric counselor David Smith, came to honor Martha Ann. In addition to representing the Church, they also represented Martha Ann's extended Smith family in Salt Lake City.

Local stake and ward leaders, family, friends, and neighbors also filled the Provo Tabernacle on Monday afternoon. George Albert Smith told those attending, "It will be strange to come to Provo and not find Aunt Martha here. She was one of the most remarkable women who has ever lived."[48] He added, "Without much help from the outside she has carried burdens that would have crushed one less courageous. She was always devoted to someone else."[49] Following the funeral, Martha Ann was buried next to her husband in the Provo City Cemetery.

In less than two months, a notice of Martha Ann's passing was published in the Church's monthly women's publication, the *Relief Society Magazine*, as an editorial titled "Martha Ann Smith Harris." The short announcement concluded, "Happily for us and happily for future generations, the sons and daughters of the great patriarch, Hyrum Smith, have given to the world a very large and honorable family of children and grandchildren, so that while we are no longer privileged to have among us the sons and daughters of one of the first founders of the Church of Jesus Christ of Latter-day Saints, we still have with us many of their descendants."[50]

43. Eva Maeser Crandall, "A Trip on Memory Ship," 7, BYU.
44. Martha Ann Harris's Death Certificate, 1 November 1923, Utah Department of Health. In a note to Joseph F., John F. Harris used his business letterhead, "Funeral Director and Licensed Embalmer, Depot Street, Burial Caskets Funeral Supplies." John F. Harris to Joseph F., 20 September 1916.
45. "Death Calls Aged Woman," *Daily Herald* (Provo), 19 October 1923, 1.
46. See, for example, "Niece of Prophet Jos. Smith Dies," *Ogden Standard-Examiner*, 20 October 1923, 1; and "Joseph Smith's Sister Claimed," *Salt Lake Telegram*, 20 October 1923, 5.
47. "Funeral for Aged Woman," *Daily Herald* (Provo), 22 October 1923, 1.
48. "Daughter of Martyred Patriarch of Church Is Paid Final Tribute," *Deseret News*, 22 October 1923, 3.
49. "Daughter of Martyred Patriarch," 3.
50. "Martha Ann Smith Harris," *Relief Society Magazine* 10, no, 12 (December 1923): 592.

Memorial marker for William Jasper Harris and Martha Ann Smith Harris, Provo City Cemetery, photograph by Brent R. Nordgren, July 2018. For many nineteenth-century Americans, their memorial markers were one of the few written records of their lives. Fortunately, Martha Ann wrote and saved letters and told stories handed down through her posterity, allowing her life to be reconstructed and preserved. Courtesy of Brent R. Nordgren.

A month later, in January 1924, a much longer article was published in the *Relief Society Magazine*[51] to help people beyond Provo, including Martha Ann's extended family, to become more acquainted with "one of the most remarkable women who has ever lived."[52]

Both Joseph F. and Martha Ann left large families and also a precious written record of their lives. It is apparent that the letter collections of Joseph F. and Martha Ann reveal more about his life and concerns than hers—a function of not only the greater quantity of extant Joseph F. letters but also the different content of his letters consistent with his different role in the sibling relationship. He was the elder brother who, as solicitous father figure and benefactor concerned about the welfare of his beloved Martha Ann, had wisdom, counsel, and encouragement to impart in an effort to lighten the burdens she carried. He also had missionary experiences and other adventures to report on that were largely foreign to Martha Ann's experience and station in life. It comes as no surprise, then, that the trove of letters between them can seem one-sided in key ways. First, Joseph F. is in the spotlight. Second, Martha Ann is often relegated to the roles of either grateful recipient of her brother's watchcare or primary source of family news. Because Martha Ann almost never provides her older brother counsel or direction for his life or the lives of his family, the reader may rashly assume that Joseph F. thought his life was nearly perfect and that only Martha Ann faced challenges requiring encouragement, advice, or admonition from concerned family members.

The Joseph F. and Martha Ann letter collection provides a view of their personal interaction. They were bound by blood, but also by their devotion to the restored gospel of Jesus Christ and to the Church their parents had supported until the end of their lives. From the martyrdom of their father, Hyrum, in 1844, and the death of their mother, Mary Fielding, in 1852, they continued to strengthen each other through visits and letters. To Martha Ann, her brother was "my truest most faithfull friend,"[53] and to Joseph F., she would always be "My Dear beloved Sister Martha Ann."[54]

51. See Richard P. Harris, "Martha Ann Smith Harris," *Relief Society Magazine* 11, no. 1 (January 1924), 11–18.
52. "Daughter of Martyred Patriarch," 3.
53. Martha Ann to Joseph F., 31 May 1874, herein.
54. Joseph F. to Martha Ann, 21 June 1869, herein.

Opposite: "Sketch Blank for L.D.S. Biographical Encyclopedia," Martha Ann Smith Harris life sketch, page 8 of 8 pages, ca. 1901. The publication *Latter-day Saint Biographical Encyclopedia: A Compilation of Biographical Sketches of Prominent Men and Women in the Church of Jesus Christ of Latter-day Saints* (Salt Lake City, UT: Andrew Jenson History Co., 1901–36), abbreviated *LDS Biographical Encyclopedia*, is a four-volume biographical dictionary collected and edited by Assistant Church Historian Andrew Jenson and published from 1901 to 1936. The volumes contain more than five thousand biographical sketches and two thousand photographs. By 1936 Jensen had more than fifteen thousand life sketches on hand, including one for Martha Ann. The sketch begins with her parents' trials and concludes with Martha Ann's move to Provo. The final page of Martha Ann's life sketch highlights some of her physical challenges and concludes, "As her mother stood her trials so has Sister Harris borne her burden with cheerfullness that is unequaled and continues to do charity and tend the sick whenever her help is needed." Courtesy of Church History Library.

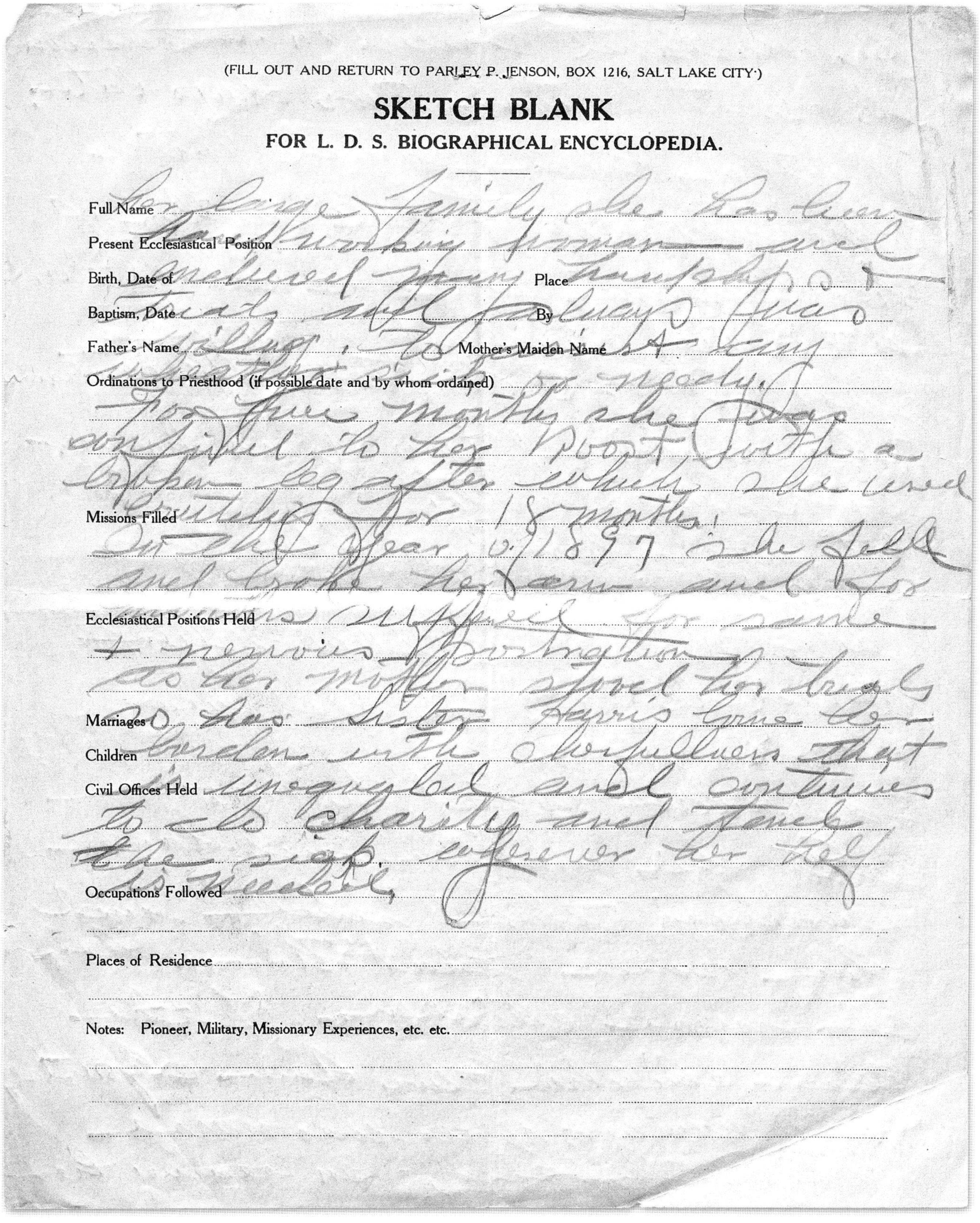
(FILL OUT AND RETURN TO PARLEY P. JENSON, BOX 1216, SALT LAKE CITY.)

SKETCH BLANK

FOR L. D. S. BIOGRAPHICAL ENCYCLOPEDIA.

Full Name her large family she has been
Present Ecclesiastical Position a hard working woman and
Birth, Date of endured many Place hardships &
Ready and always By was
Father's Name willing. to Mother's Maiden Name 54 very
successful with or needy.
Ordinations to Priesthood (if possible date and by whom ordained)
For three months she was
confined to her room with a
broken leg after which she used
Missions Filled crutches for 18 months.
In the year of 1897 she fell
and broke her arm and for
Ecclesiastical Positions Held months suffered for same
+ nervous prostration
As her mother spread her truly
Marriages as has Sister Harris borne her
Children burden with cheerfulness that
Civil Offices Held is unequaled and continues
to do charity and tend
the sick wherever her help
Occupations Followed is needed.

Places of Residence

Notes: Pioneer, Military, Missionary Experiences, etc. etc.

Taysom, Stephen C. "The Last Memory: Joseph F. Smith and *Lieux de Mémoire* in Late Nineteenth-Century Mormonism." *Dialogue: A Journal of Mormon Thought* 48, no. 3 (Fall 2015): 1–23.

Whitchurch, David M. "'My Dear Sister': Letters between Joseph F. Smith and His Sister, Martha Ann Smith Harris (1854–1916)." *Mormon Historical Studies* 5, no. 1 (Spring 2004): 195–202.

———. "The Pedagogy of a Church Leader: Lessons Learned from Joseph F. Smith's 1854–1916 Letters to His Sister, Martha Ann Smith Harris." *Religious Educator* 2, no. 2 (2001): 83–107.

Whitchurch, David M., and Mallory Hales Perry. "Friends and Enemies in Washington: Joseph F. Smith's Letter to Susa Young Gates, March 21, 1889." *Mormon Historical Studies* 13, nos. 1–2 (Spring/Fall 2012): 210–29.

Yorgason, Blaine M. *From Orphaned Boy to Prophet of God: The Story of Joseph F. Smith*. Ogden, UT: Living Scriptures, 2001.

Youngreen, Buddy. "Sons of the Martyrs' Nauvoo Reunion—1860." *BYU Studies* 20, no. 4 (Summer 1980): 351–70.

Appendix A: Joseph F. Smith's Family

* Adopted
~ Child from wife's previous marriage
† Died before Joseph F. Smith's death

Joseph F. Smith (13 November 1838–19 November 1918)

Levira Annette Clark Smith (29 April 1842–18 December 1888; married 5 April 1859)
No children
Julina Lambson Smith (15 June 1849–10 January 1936; married 5 May 1866)
*Edward Arthur (1 November 1858–17 July 1911)
†Mercy Josephine (14 August 1867–6 June 1870)
Mary Sophronia (7 October 1869–5 January 1948)
Donette (17 September 1872–15 September 1961)
Joseph Fielding (19 July 1876–2 July 1972)
David Asael (24 May 1879–6 April 1952)
George Carlos (14 October 1881–23 February 1931)
Julina Clarissa (10 February 1884–1 August 1923)
Elias Wesley (21 April 1886–28 December 1970)
Emily Jane (11 September 1888–12 December 1982)
Rachel (11 December 1890–14 December 1986)
Edith Eleanor (3 January 1894–21 May 1987)
*Marjorie Virginia (7 December 1906–17 November 1994)
Subtotal: 13 children, 2 adopted
Sarah Ellen Richards (25 August 1850–22 March 1915; married 1 March 1868)
†Sarah Ella (5 February 1869–11 February 1869)

†Leonora (30 January 1871–23 December 1907)
Joseph Richards (22 February 1873–2 October 1954)
†Heber John (3 July 1876–3 March 1877)
†Rhoda Ann (20 July 1878–6 July 1879)
Minerva (30 April 1880–24 January 1958)
†Alice (27 July 1882–29 April 1901)
Willard Richards (20 November 1884–11 September 1972)
Franklin Richards (12 May 1888–25 December 1967)
Jeanetta (25 August 1891–27 January 1932)
Asenath (28 December 1896–3 August 1982)
Subtotal: 11 children

Edna Lambson (3 March 1851–28 February 1928; married 1 January 1871)
†Hyrum Mack (21 March 1872–23 January 1918)
Alvin Fielding (7 August 1874–4 January 1948)
†Alfred Jason (13 December 1876–6 April 1878)
Edna Melissa (6 October 1879–26 October 1958)
†Albert Jesse (16 September 1881–25 August 1883)
†Robert (12 November 1883–4 February 1886)
Emma (21 August 1888–28 December 1969)
†Zina (11 October 1890–25 October 1915)
†Ruth (21 December 1893–17 March 1898)
Martha (12 May 1897–7 August 1977)
Subtotal: 10 children

Alice Ann Kimball (6 September 1858–19 December 1946; married 6 December 1883)
~Alice May (11 October 1877–20 October 1920)
~Heber Chase (19 November 1881–29 December 1971)
~Charles Coulson (19 November 1881–20 April 1933)
Lucy Mack (14 April 1890–24 November 1933)
Andrew Kimball (6 January 1893–23 August 1951)
Jesse Kimball (21 May 1896–9 June 1953)
Fielding Kimball (9 April 1900–20 October 1974)
Subtotal: 7 children, 3 from her previous marriage

Mary Taylor Schwartz (30 April 1865–5 December 1956; married 13 January 1884)
†John Schwartz (20 August 1888–3 August 1889)
Calvin Schwartz (29 May 1890–15 June 1966)
Samuel Schwartz (26 October 1892–10 May 1983)
James Schwartz (13 November 1894–6 November 1950)
Agnes (3 November 1897–9 March 1966)
Silas Schwartz (3 January 1900–23 April 1986)
Royal Grant (21 May 1906–30 May 1921)
Subtotal: 7 children

Total: 48 children (43 born to Joseph F. Smith and his wives, 2 adopted, 3 from Alice Ann Kimball's previous marriage)

Appendix B: Martha Ann Smith Harris's Family

† Died before Martha Ann Smith Harris's death

Martha Ann Smith Harris (14 May 1841–19 October 1923)

William Jasper Harris (25 October 1836–24 April 1909; married 21 April 1857)
- William Jasper Jr. (4 August 1859–23 August 1926)
- †Joseph Albert (19 August 1861–28 May 1911)
- Hyrum Smith (15 August 1863–24 February 1924)
- Mary Emily (23 October 1865–25 November 1947)
- Franklin Hill (11 September 1867–5 February 1947)
- †Lucy Smith (10 March 1870–26 July 1903)
- John Fielding (28 June 1872–28 November 1946)
- †Mercy Ann (30 March 1874–23 January 1905)
- Zina Christine (13 May 1876–16 March 1958)
- Martha Artimissa (27 June 1879–12 August 1965)
- Sarah Lovina (8 December 1882–21 April 1961)

Total: 11 children

Appendix C: Letter Summaries

Brief summaries of the 241 letters between Joseph F. and Martha Ann are listed chronologically by date of writing. The author and recipient of each letter are given, as well as corresponding letters when applicable.

DATE WRITTEN	AUTHOR & RECIPIENT	SUMMARY OF CONTENT
17 October 1854	**Joseph F. to Martha Ann**	Hopes Martha Ann will not be angry that Joseph F. has not written; encourages her to study and take care of ducks.
1 November 1854	**Joseph F. to Martha Ann**	Encourages Martha Ann to keep half sister Jerusha company; exhorts Jerusha to take care of Martha Ann.
28 January 1855	**Joseph F. to Martha Ann**	In good health, has grown taller; if Martha Ann is humble and prayerful she will become like their mother; Martha Ann should be kind to older siblings and never feel downhearted.
9 June 1855	**Joseph F. to Martha Ann**	Martha Ann had disagreement with sister-in-law Hellen; encourages Martha Ann to be patient; bad roads in Sandwich Islands; wants to see babies and animals at home; Martha Ann should be unlike cousins Agnes and Josephine.
18 October 1855	**Joseph F. to Martha Ann** *Corresponding letter: 31 January 1856*	Wishes Martha Ann would continue school; sent book to Martha Ann, hopes she receives it; education is a privilege; be steady.
23 November 1855	**Joseph F. to Martha Ann**	Advises Martha Ann to do and act right; has written to California cousins; Martha Ann should continue education.

DATE WRITTEN	AUTHOR & RECIPIENT	SUMMARY OF CONTENT
31 January 1856	**Martha Ann to Joseph F.** *Corresponding letter: 18 October 1855*	Is healthy, learning in finest schoolhouse with schoolmaster Bro. Eldredge; received book, learned pieces; thanks Joseph F. for advice; half sister Jerusha moved and had baby girl named Evalene.
18 February 1856	**Joseph F. to Martha Ann**	Hold fast to good, be mild and humble, listen to the Spirit; shares a parable of a swearing man; talks about the natives; signs of the times, Latter-day Saints will flood the earth.
2 March 1856	**Martha Ann to Joseph F.** *Corresponding letter: 25 May 1856*	Had chance to learn but didn't appreciate it; wrote last letter in a hurry; now stands five feet seven inches; Indians killed folks in Cedar Valley.
April 1856	**Martha Ann to Joseph F.** *Corresponding letter: 14 July 1856*	Learns from Joseph F.'s letters; mountains healthiest place in world; got poison ivy; half sister Sarah has baby girl; cousin Rachel Fielding married; their cow Rosey dies; Martha Ann to be fifteen, has grown a foot taller.
25 May 1856	**Joseph F. to Martha Ann** *Corresponding letter: March 1856*	Martha Ann should mind her dates; missionary work and integrity; missionaries imprisoned for preaching.
14 July 1856	**Joseph F. to Martha Ann** *Corresponding letters: April 1856 and 17 December 1856*	Grammar lesson; writes about marriage.
29 July 1856	**Martha Ann to Joseph F.** *Corresponding letter: 20 October 1856*	Not well in spirit; asks if Joseph F. is engaged; half brother John and his wife Hellen talk about Martha Ann behind her back.
2 October 1856	**Martha Ann to Joseph F.** *Corresponding letter: 20 October 1856*	Is downhearted; sister-in-law Hellen has toothache; ducks were caught; asks Joseph F. to excuse writing; hopes he is treated better than previous elders; handcart company came into valley.
20 October 1856	**Joseph F. to Martha Ann** *Corresponding letters: 29 July 1856, 2 October 1856, and 5 April 1857*	Advises Martha Ann to mind her own business; have moral courage; Joseph F. not engaged.
17 December 1856	**Martha Ann to Joseph F.** *Corresponding letters: 14 July 1856 and 17 April 1857*	Joseph F.'s letters do Martha Ann good; lives at half brother John's; Martha Ann couldn't attend school, no shoes; Joseph F. has patience; asks if his letters were burned; cousin Mary Jane getting married, Martha Ann not ready for marriage; description of children; snow is deep; mentions death of a faithful friend Jedediah M. Grant.

DATE WRITTEN	AUTHOR & RECIPIENT	SUMMARY OF CONTENT
3 February 1857	**Martha Ann to Joseph F.**	Going to school; is at Sister Harris's; folks send love; cousin Rachel has a girl; everyone getting married, Mary Smithies is married to Bro. Kimball; William Harris writes: forty couples married daily; Martha Ann rebaptized; Martha Ann loves William Harris.
5 April 1857	**Martha Ann to Joseph F.** *Corresponding letters: 20 October 1856 and 14 June 1857*	Trials for both Martha Ann and Joseph F.; discusses marriage, plenty of girls waiting for Joseph F. when he gets home; John Hyde apostatizes.
17 April 1857	**Joseph F. to Martha Ann** *Corresponding letter: 17 December 1856*	Relates story, 1/4-inch pine between Joseph F. and death; trust in Lord for deliverance; thirty-three dollars stolen; eternal progression; encourages Martha Ann, Christ once an infant; Joseph F. expects to return in two years.
3 May 1857	**Martha Ann to Joseph F.**	Has been thinking of Joseph F.'s struggles and discomfort; has guilty conscience, married to William Harris; events leading to marriage; married by Bro. Kimball; William Harris left on mission to England; thanks Joseph F. for kindness and love; never forgotten Joseph F.; mother-in-law Emily Harris will teach Martha Ann to weave; six nieces or nephews born since Joseph F. left; Martha Ann almost sixteen; cousin Hannah dies.
11 May 1857	**Martha Ann to Joseph F.**	Is in good health; perhaps going north with half sister Jerusha and Jerusha's husband, William Pierce.
14 June 1857	**Joseph F. to Martha Ann** *Corresponding letter: 5 April 1856*	A brother's love and sympathy; Martha Ann's humility is inspiring; implications of marriage, laws, and justice; talks about William Harris's letter.
3 July 1857	**Martha Ann to Joseph F.**	Troubled in mind, worried about Joseph F.; many changes since Joseph F. left; remembers Joseph F.'s departure; description of Martha Ann's appearance.
25 July 1857	**Joseph F. to Martha Ann** *Corresponding letter: 3 May 1857*	Rejoices in Martha Ann's marriage to William Harris; advises to stand fast and be true to William; never tattle; wear knowledge like a watch; loves the gospel, would die for it; encourages Martha Ann to improve writing; eating boiled pumpkins and squash.
19 August 1857	**Martha Ann to Joseph F.**	Ink made of gunpowder and vinegar; Joseph F. should not read too close to fire or it will blow up.
[1857?]	**Martha Ann to Joseph F.**	Writes a poem to Joseph F.; thanks him for his advice; expresses how much she misses him.

DATE WRITTEN	AUTHOR & RECIPIENT	SUMMARY OF CONTENT
20 May 1858	**Joseph F. to Martha Ann**	Is not cold and indifferent to Martha Ann, wishes she would have visited; niece Alice very sick; assigned to serve in the city; Martha Ann must not be down-hearted; she must write.
28 July 1860	**Joseph F. to Martha Ann**	England looks the same; glad to hear about sheep; encourages Martha Ann to watch over cows.
26 September 1860	**Martha Ann to Joseph F.**	Martha Ann's husband William contemplating going to California for business; half sister Jerusha gives birth at Martha Ann's house, names baby after Martha Ann.
15 December 1860	**Joseph F. to Martha Ann** *Corresponding letter: 26 September 1860*	Joseph F.'s wife Levira good at writing; good health a prize; family blessed; Fanny traded.
20 December 1860	**Martha Ann to Joseph F.** *Corresponding letter: 29 January 1861*	Martha Ann has been sick; son Willie is a crazy rascal; Joseph F.'s wife Levira is a sister and friend; Martha Ann visits family, prays for Joseph F.
29 January 1861	**Joseph F. to Martha Ann** *Corresponding letter: 20 December 1861*	Hard time in England for Saints; black clouds hang over England; discusses safety of animals in Provo; shares testimony of latter-day work; British are industrious.
12 March 1861	**Martha Ann to Joseph F.**	Martha Ann and family contemplating moving; husband William in police force; description of parties attended; shares a poem.
Spring 1861	**Joseph F. to Martha Ann**	Joseph F. talks about finding happiness, mentions not receiving many letters from other family members; gives his best wishes to several family members.
30 May 1861	**Martha Ann to Joseph F.**	Describes her weakness in writing; love for Joseph F. and the Lord; buys a home; describes family situation; discusses their mother's parenting.
8 December 1861	**Martha Ann to Joseph F.** *Corresponding letter: 1 March 1862*	Martha Ann has another baby; describes her weaving; family affairs.
12 January 1862	**Martha Ann to Joseph F.** *Corresponding letter: 1 March 1862*	Joseph F.'s wife Levira is sick; Martha Ann invites Levira to live with her; family affairs.
29 January 1862	**Martha Ann to Joseph F.**	Describes family affairs; worries about Joseph F. in England.
3 February 1862	**Martha Ann to Joseph F.**	Joseph F.'s wife Levira is sick, in care of Aunt Zina, wife of Brigham Young, at Lion House; escaping criminals are killed attempting to escape; grave robberies discovered.

DATE WRITTEN	AUTHOR & RECIPIENT	SUMMARY OF CONTENT
1 March 1862	**Joseph F. to Martha Ann** *Corresponding letters: 8 December 1861 and 12 January 1861*	Joseph F.'s wife Levira is ill, Joseph F. is torn; Joseph F. blesses Martha Ann's children; first ship of emigrant Saints to sail on 20 April; Martha Ann should take care of herself.
10 April 1862	**Joseph F. to Martha Ann**	Joseph F. recites his visit to many of the major sites in London.
30 September 1862	**Martha Ann to Joseph F.**	Gives dinner to a family Joseph F. knew; loves her children; was expecting a helper for the children but was disappointed.
Fall 1862	**Joseph F. to Martha Ann**	Joseph F. suggests that Martha Ann not send tin plate pictures; mentions that he might return home in the spring; we are sent to earth to do good.
22 February 1863	**Martha Ann to Joseph F.** *Corresponding letter: 3 April 1863*	Eager for Joseph F. to return home; man shot in courthouse; stops writing to fix children dinner; half sister Jerusha visits.
1863	**Martha Ann to Joseph F.** *Corresponding letter: 3 April 1863*	Family affairs; Martha Ann wants picture of Joseph F.
3 April 1863	**Joseph F. to Martha Ann** *Corresponding letter: 22 February 1863*	Time in England coming to a close; wishes blessings on relatives; children and their importance; never scold children, talk to them, do not box or slap.
12 June 1864	**Martha Ann to Joseph F.**	Has many burdens such as health, children; thanks Joseph F. for advice; Joseph F.'s wife Levira alone; shares family circumstances.
22 June 1864	**Joseph F. to Martha Ann**	Hopes Martha Ann's son Hyrum is better; loves the babies; hopes Martha Ann visits his wife Levira; remedy every wrong with a right; Walter Gibson is despised.
30 August 1864	**Joseph F. to Martha Ann**	Joseph F. recites part of a poem and then adds his own prose; poem is about a "one year old" and the innocence of children, referring to Martha Ann's son, Hyrum Smith Harris.
1864	**Martha Ann to Joseph F.**	Is in poor health, nursing big baby; husband William is on the plains; Indians are bad; tried to visit Bro. Brigham Young; Joseph F.'s trials; excited that Joseph F. is released from mission.
23 June 1868	**Joseph F. to Martha Ann**	Joseph F. and his wife Julina waiting for bed to arrive; Julina's nineteenth birthday; stepfather Heber C. Kimball's death and burial; sat with Bro. Kimball when he died.

DATE WRITTEN	AUTHOR & RECIPIENT	SUMMARY OF CONTENT
1 December 1868	**Joseph F. to Martha Ann**	Joseph F.'s wife Levira submits divorce papers.
21 June 1869	**Joseph F. to Martha Ann**	Prays for Martha Ann and family; cousins David and Alexander Smith come preaching against the "Brighamites."
13 July 1869	**Joseph F. to Martha Ann**	Joseph F.'s wife Sarah is in poor health and frets; niece Edwina Walker's knee is straightened; Joseph F. does endowments and baptisms; cousins David and Alexander Smith expected in town; Martha Ann's husband William avoids Joseph F.
17 August 1869	**Joseph F. to Martha Ann**	Cousins David and Alexander Smith are "Gurleyites"; God have mercy on the vile apostates.
24 December 1869	**Joseph F. to Martha Ann**	News of wives and children; anxious about Martha Ann's situation; encourages Martha Ann to cheer up.
3 January 1869 (1870)	**Joseph F. to Martha Ann**	Babies have chicken pox; cousin Mary Jane teaching school; killed "Old Cherry" for beef.
18 January 1870	**Joseph F. to Martha Ann**	Writing from legislative hall; Joseph F.'s adopted son Edward has mumps; Edward can't write as well as Martha Ann's son Willie; an account of Joseph F.'s trip to Ogden in *Deseret News*.
29 March 1870	**Joseph F. to Martha Ann**	Cousin Mary Jane has been ill; Pres. Brigham Young returns 17 April; mass meeting in Old Tabernacle about the Cullom Bill; Saints must deny religion or be subject to slavery; would rather die free than live bound; God and one good man is a majority.
3 (31) March 1870	**Joseph F. to Martha Ann**	Bishop Smoot, Martha Ann's stepfather-in-law, did not give Aunt Thompson (Mercy Rachel Fielding) a ride; cousin Mary Jane, her son Robert, and Joseph F.'s wife Sarah are unwell; broke two pens while writing.
25 June 1870	**Joseph F. to Martha Ann**	Martha Ann left items during visit; Joseph F.'s feelings after his daughter Mercy's death; God does not will children to die.
5 July 1870	**Joseph F. to Martha Ann**	Martha Ann's son Hyrum visiting Joseph F.; Fourth of July celebrations; grasshoppers damage vegetation.
6 August 1870	**Joseph F. to Martha Ann**	Weather is like day of their father's death; mourns his daughter Mercy's death.

DATE WRITTEN	AUTHOR & RECIPIENT	SUMMARY OF CONTENT
18 August 1870	**Joseph F. to Martha Ann**	Martha Ann having hardships and illness in family; sorry that horse of Martha Ann's husband William had accident; Lord tries his people; family is visiting Bear Lake.
27 October 1870	**Joseph F. to Martha Ann**	Joseph F.'s daughter Mary was very sick but saw Dr. Meeks; doesn't associate with sister-in-law Hellen or her mother.
7 December 1870	**Joseph F. to Martha Ann**	Martha Ann's letter advertised in newspaper by post office; baby is teething; Edna Lambson (future wife of Joseph F.) is visiting.
After 1870	**Joseph F. to Martha Ann**	Joseph F. desires to deed Martha Ann the property her house is on.
26 January 1871	**Joseph F. to Martha Ann**	Wishes wives would write Martha Ann more often; family affairs.
23 February 1871	**Joseph F. to Martha Ann**	Everyone sick with colds; daughter Mary got into sugar sack.
21 April 1871	**Joseph F. to Martha Ann**	Martha Ann ought to have bigger house; Joseph F.'s adopted son Edward is a good boy; Joseph F. admonishes Martha Ann's children to help their mother; buys more property.
26 May 1871	**Joseph F. to Martha Ann**	Pres. Brigham Young visits Martha Ann; advises Martha Ann to add on to her house; God bless the babies.
14 September 1871	**Joseph F. to Martha Ann**	Family illness; drying peaches; spread of typhoid fever.
21 November 1871	**Joseph F. to Martha Ann**	Asks about Martha Ann's shawl; Aunt Thompson (Mercy Rachel Fielding) goes to Canada; cousin Mary Jane renting out Aunt Thompson's room; district court deserves damnation.
12 December 1871	**Joseph F. to Martha Ann**	Martha Ann's husband William is ill; Joseph F. can't afford to keep team; Dr. Robinson murdered.
3 May 1872	**Joseph F. to Martha Ann**	Family news; Pres. Brigham Young and others no longer in prison; political demise of James B. McKean.
17 May 1872	**Joseph F. to Martha Ann**	Family news; struggle of Martha Ann's husband William with alcohol, Joseph F. advises him to quit wholly.
14 June 1872	**Joseph F. to Martha Ann**	Family rifts; Pres. Brigham Young helps family of their father, Hyrum Smith; birthdays; concern about Martha Ann's husband William.

DATE WRITTEN	AUTHOR & RECIPIENT	SUMMARY OF CONTENT
26 July 1872	**Joseph F. to Martha Ann**	Mentions the name of Brigham Young and that Joseph F. gave directions for David McKenzie to notify Brother Smoot about something. Most of the letter is missing.
18 January 1873	**Joseph F. to Martha Ann**	New schoolhouse in Salt Lake City; Martha Ann's husband William visits but doesn't stay; Joseph F. out of work, wives make income.
28 April 1873	**Joseph F. to Martha Ann**	Joseph F. serves on city council; infirmities help us appreciate good things of life.
1 July 1873	**Joseph F. to Martha Ann**	Still serves on city council; gave two blessings to Aunt Sarah Ann Whitney; cautioned Aunt Lucy (Walker) about keeping boarders.
10 November 1873	**Joseph F. to Martha Ann**	Birthday party invitation.
27 February 1874	**Joseph F. to Martha Ann**	Advises Martha Ann to be faithful, will gain same rewards as their mother; Bishop Smoot, Martha Ann's stepfather-in-law, and Pres. Brigham Young will help Martha Ann; traveling to the East.
31 May 1874	**Martha Ann to Joseph F.** *Corresponding letter: 15 July 1874*	Joseph F. is Martha Ann's best friend since death of their mother; talks about united orders; Joseph F. on the Lord's business; Martha Ann's sons Willie and Joseph run team; provisions come from tithing office; orchard and garden look good.
20 June 1874	**Martha Ann to Joseph F.** *Corresponding letter: 15 August 1874*	Martha Ann's son Johnny has scarlet fever; scarlet fever spreading around Provo; not earning much money; husband William not well, can't work much; children sick.
15 July 1874	**Joseph F. to Martha Ann** *Corresponding letter: 31 May 1874*	Helps a poor man and his family in England; gratitude for temporal blessings.
5 August 1874	**Joseph F. to Martha Ann** *Corresponding letter: 20 June 1874*	Missionaries arrive; Saints are near latter days; Martha Ann is patient like their mother.
15 August 1874	**Martha Ann to Joseph F.** *Corresponding letters: 15 July 1874 and 7 September 1874*	Grateful for Joseph F.'s letters; blessed not to have children die; traded cow; son Willie is running team; reports on Joseph F.'s new son; son John grows heavy.
7 September 1874 (first letter)	**Joseph F. to Martha Ann** *Corresponding letter: 15 August 1874*	553 Latter-day Saint immigrants sent off; members sending for undeserving relatives; hopes Martha Ann's boys will take care of her.

DATE WRITTEN	AUTHOR & RECIPIENT	SUMMARY OF CONTENT
7 September 1874 (second letter)	**Joseph F. to Martha Ann**	Writes to Bro. Samuel Jones; remembers "exile" in Provo and honors his friends there.
8 September 1874	**Martha Ann to Joseph F.**	Nicholas Muhlestein, Christian Schoeni, and John Liechty wish to be introduced to Joseph F.
5 October 1874	**Martha Ann to Joseph F.** *Corresponding letter: 8 December 1874*	Martha Ann went 180 miles to Ogden and back; stayed at Joseph F.'s house; gifts from Joseph F., dresses lost; husband William and son Willie working; dried fruit; several deaths in Provo.
6 November 1874	**Joseph F. to Martha Ann** *Corresponding letter: 8 September 1874*	Joseph F. disappointed by loss of gifts; half brother John says Martha Ann's husband William is doing better.
16 November 1874	**Martha Ann to Joseph F.**	Follows up on letter of recommendation (8 September 1874); gratitude for dress patterns.
24 November 1874	**Martha Ann to Joseph F.** *Corresponding letter: 9 February 1875*	Received Joseph F.'s photograph; dress patterns arrived; Martha Ann loves Joseph F.'s children; received other gifts; husband William works hard; apologizes for insufficient postage; Martha Ann has a "gathered" thumb.
8 December 1874	**Joseph F. to Martha Ann** *Corresponding letter: 5 October 1874*	England good for Joseph F.'s health; prays for his family's protection; sends Martha Ann a letter for Bro. Nicholas Muhlestein.
9 February 1875	**Joseph F. to Martha Ann** *Corresponding letter: 24 November 1874*	Death of half sister Sis. Griffin (Abigail Varney); advises Martha Ann's son Willie to learn a trade; sends materials to Martha Ann.
31 March 1875	**Joseph F. to Martha Ann**	Advises Martha Ann to teach her children good principles; discusses capital punishment of criminals.
15 May 1875	**Joseph F. to Martha Ann**	Martha Ann living in cramped quarters, her husband William and boys should add to house; remembers building their mother's house; will soon leave for London on another mission; mourns Gentile marriages.
7 September 1875	**Joseph F. to Martha Ann**	Joseph F. released from mission; Pres. George A. Smith dies.
26 November 1875	**Joseph F. to Martha Ann**	Martha Ann's son Hyrum injured in factory; attends a baby funeral; spread of terrible colds.
27 February 1876	**Joseph F. to Martha Ann**	Mentions a nonextant letter from 23 February; many children have terrible colds; addresses Martha Ann's apparent sadness from being separated from the family.
11 July 1876	**Joseph F. to Martha Ann**	Writes when convenient; son Heber John born, has large nose; will attend a meeting in Provo; blight on the trees; sends $1.25 for Martha Ann to use at Provo Factory.

DATE WRITTEN	AUTHOR & RECIPIENT	SUMMARY OF CONTENT
25 August 1877	**Joseph F. to Martha Ann**	Anti–Latter-day Saint sentiment in England; trusts the Lord; wives too busy to write; postage is five cents.
29 November 1877	**Joseph F. to Martha Ann**	Son Joseph is sick; Bro. Smoot, Martha Ann's stepfather-in-law, has deed to Martha Ann's house; Martha Ann's husband William building a barn; cousin Mary Lupton (Fielding) in poor circumstances.
6 April 1878	**Joseph F. to Martha Ann**	Telegraph stating the death of Enda's baby and scheduled funeral for the next day.
22 April 1878	**Joseph F. to Martha Ann**	Son Alfred dies, Joseph F. laments loss; lists children that have died; obtains deed for Martha Ann from Pres. Brigham Young; Pres. Smoot, Martha Ann's stepfather-in-law, will send it.
14 August 1878	**Joseph F. to Martha Ann**	In canyon with family getting berries and relaxing; grasshopper problem in Provo; temple work for the dead no longer in Endowment House.
23 October 1878	**Joseph F. to Martha Ann**	References nonextant letter from 20 October. Refers to the health of several family members including William, Aunt T, and M. J. Talks of the evils of interest; mentions being busy.
22 April 1879	**Joseph F. to Martha Ann**	Daughter Rhoda sick with pneumonia; pneumonia already killed three of Joseph F.'s children, Joseph F. worried; asks about Martha Ann's troubles.
7 July 1879	**Joseph F. to Martha Ann**	Daughter Rhoda dies; Joseph F. mourns.
21 May 1880	**Joseph F. to Martha Ann**	Joseph F. waiting to present Martha Ann's Tithing Office accounts to the Council; Sarah Ellen, Joseph F.'s wife, has given birth to a baby girl, Minerva Smith; Aunt Thompson (Mercy Rachel Fielding) is raising money to help a poor family from England.
4 June 1880	**Joseph F. to Martha Ann**	Nephew Willie Pierce dies; family affairs.
1 July 1881	**Joseph F. to Martha Ann**	Tours Davis and Weber counties with Presidents John Taylor and George Q. Cannon, along with Wilford Woodruff, half brother John, and others; Martha Ann takes care of sick children; offers to pay Bro. Peter Stubbs with tithing receipt on Martha Ann's behalf.
28 July 1881	**Joseph F. to Martha Ann**	Martha Ann's son Joseph ill; blessings by laying on of hands are powerful; Martha Ann has been blessed not to lose any children; niece Hellen is ill; money is low, wives need sewing machines; if M. Holt (Maria Mabey) gets divorced she can remarry.

DATE WRITTEN	AUTHOR & RECIPIENT	SUMMARY OF CONTENT
18 September 1881	**Joseph F. to Martha Ann**	Edna gives birth to a boy; reports on several other family members being sick; Mary Jane is still very feeble; Aunt Thompson is nearly worn out.
23 November 1881	**Joseph F. to Martha Ann**	Sends fifty dollars for Martha Ann to buy winter clothes, ten dollars for shoes; baby of wife Julina is fretful; wife Edna has best baby she ever had.
13 March 1883	**Joseph F. to Martha Ann**	Children have croup; Aunt Thompson (Mercy Rachel Fielding) and cousin Mary Jane have difficulty finding hired help; attends meetings, is a public servant; sees little of his family; compares Martha Ann's trials with their mother's.
27 March 1883	**Joseph F. to Martha Ann**	Children better; cousin Mary Jane and Aunt Thompson (Mercy Rachel Fielding) sick; Mary Lupton (Fielding) here until conference.
31 July 1883	**Joseph F. to Martha Ann**	Wife Edna is up the canyon; children Melissa and Albert have whooping cough; wife Sarah and children in Nephi.
26 August 1883	**Joseph F. to Martha Ann**	Son Albert Jesse dies.
12 November 1883	**Joseph F. to Martha Ann**	Encourages Martha Ann to take care in writing cousin Ina Coolbrith; Ina is well educated; sends Martha Ann twenty-five dollars for goods from the Deseret Co-op.
22 November 1883	**Joseph F. to Martha Ann**	Announces the birth of his nineteenth child and tenth son Robert; mother (Edna) and boy are well.
11 February 1884	**Joseph F. to Martha Ann**	Daughter Julina born, tenth daughter and twentieth child; wife Edna's baby keeps her busy.
1 August 1884	**Joseph F. to Martha Ann**	Presidents John Taylor and George Q. Cannon going north with Francis Lyman and Leonard Nuttall; beware of loose tongue; Leonard Hardy, William Taylor, and Orson Whitney die.
15 August 1884	**Joseph F. to Martha Ann**	Martha Ann suffers from rheumatism; warm and cool weather; sends ten dollars for expenses; Joseph F., Bro. Erastus Snow and others go to Colorado and San Juan County; two elders killed in Tennessee.
23 August 1884	**Joseph F. to Martha Ann**	Martha Ann not in good health; boys out of work; Aunt Thompson (Mercy Rachel Fielding) and cousin Mary Jane return from Logan, did temple work; sends list of names for Sis. Beesley (Mary Leese Miller).
26 January 1885	**Joseph F. to Martha Ann**	In exile; reminisces about ex-wife Levira; lists travels.

DATE WRITTEN	AUTHOR & RECIPIENT	SUMMARY OF CONTENT
18 March 1885	**Joseph F. to Martha Ann**	Martha Ann must keep contents of Joseph F.'s letter private; Ray Davis, son-in-law of half brother John, trying to indict Joseph F.; Joseph F. doesn't blame John; Martha Ann's daughter Mary called to court; Martha Ann's son Hyrum progressing in Hawaiian language; Joseph F.'s wives and children driven from home.
13 April 1885	**Joseph F. to Martha Ann**	Asks what Martha Ann's daughter Mary said in court; doesn't blame Mary.
22 May 1885	**Joseph F. to Martha Ann**	Wives driven from home; is angry, doesn't blame Martha Ann's daughter Mary.
30 November 1885	**Joseph F. to Martha Ann**	Martha Ann's son Hyrum progresses in Hawaiian language but lacks care in regard to his clothes and means.
11 February 1887	**Joseph F. to Martha Ann** *Corresponding letter:* *11 March 1887*	Pres. Smoot, stepfather-in-law to Martha Ann, helps Martha Ann's children; Joseph F. and family in exile; Martha Ann's husband William will be blessed if he stays true to family, God, and employers.
11 March 1887	**Martha Ann to Joseph F.** *Corresponding letters:* *11 February 1887 and* *May–June 1887*	Martha Ann worries about Joseph F., has bad dream about him; family affairs; baby of Martha Ann's daughter Mary dies.
May–June 1887	**Martha Ann to Joseph F.** *Corresponding letter:* *11 March 1887*	Martha Ann happy to hear from Joseph F.; husband William out of work; Martha Ann's daughter-in-law Jessie has healthy baby; wants to see baby of Joseph F.'s wife Julina; lists presents received for birthday.
17 April 1890	**Joseph F. to Martha Ann**	Invitation to wedding of Martha Ann's son Hyrum arrives one day too late; gives five dollars for reception expenses.
29 April 1890	**Martha Ann to Joseph F.** *Corresponding letter:* *2 May 1890*	Son Hyrum married, fiancé gets ready one week early.
2 May 1890	**Joseph F. to Martha Ann** *Corresponding letters:* *29 April 1890 and* *18 May 1890*	Martha Ann's son Hyrum married a tidy housekeeper; Martha Ann's son Franklin called as home missionary; children had scarlet fever.
18 May 1890	**Martha Ann to Joseph F.** *Corresponding letters:* *2 May 1890 and* *22 May 1890*	Martha Ann is sad that her boys are unable to serve missions; wants to attend temple to be baptized for her health and to perform ordinances for her relatives.

DATE WRITTEN	AUTHOR & RECIPIENT	SUMMARY OF CONTENT
22 May 1890	**Joseph F. to Martha Ann** *Corresponding letter: 18 May 1890*	Life is period of probation; rewards of doing good; has buried eight children; grown children should provide for parents; temple work for grandmother Lucy Mack Smith's family.
16 June 1890	**Martha Ann to Joseph F.**	Includes another letter from Sister Danelly, who has been a good friend to Martha Ann; hopes to see Joseph F. when she visits; was not feeling well but got a blessing.
18 June 1890	**Joseph F. to Martha Ann**	Praises his wives; Lizzie (Elizabeth) Hawkins sealed to their father, Hyrum Smith.
4 August 1890	**Martha Ann to Joseph F.** *Corresponding letter: 9 August 1890*	Son Willie turns thirty-one, in poor health; Bro. Edward Mecham near death; he expresses love for Joseph F.
9 August 1890	**Joseph F. to Martha Ann** *Corresponding letter: 4 August 1890*	Recommends possible treatment to help Martha Ann's son Willie; God bless Bro. Edward Mecham; expects to leave soon on mission.
15 January 1891	**Martha Ann to Joseph F.** *Corresponding letter: 16 January 1891*	Expresses love to Joseph F.; son Willie loses a baby.
16 January 1891	**Joseph F. to Martha Ann** *Corresponding letters: 15 January 1891 and 1 February 1891*	Sent photograph to Martha Ann; wishes Martha Ann understood his view and had not condemned his advice about union strikes to her sons; loves all Martha Ann's children.
1 February 1891	**Martha Ann to Joseph F.** *Corresponding letters: 16 January 1891 and 9 February 1891*	Sews burial clothes; thinks Joseph F. too severe to her sons; had dream of Uncle Joseph Smith.
9 February 1891	**Joseph F. to Martha Ann** *Corresponding letter: 1 February 1891*	Advises Martha Ann about being a nurse; hopes that son of Martha Ann's daughter Mary does not have croup.
11 February 1891	**Joseph F. to Martha Ann**	Encourages allegiance to God over wealth; cautions about trade unions and political affiliation.
7 June 1891	**Joseph F. to Martha Ann**	Family illness; cautions against Gentile boarders.
17 June 1891	**Joseph F. to Martha Ann**	Feels sorry that Martha Ann's daughter-in-law Delia is sick; steady work is important; continues to warn girls of keeping boarders; pray and trust in God.
13 August 1891	**Joseph F. to Martha Ann**	Remembers the martyrdom; baby of Martha Ann's son Hyrum dies; not good for Martha Ann's son Frank to work for railroad; sickness; wife Edna's house is robbed.

DATE WRITTEN	AUTHOR & RECIPIENT	SUMMARY OF CONTENT
20 June 1892	**Joseph F. to Martha Ann**	Baby Zina, daughter of Joseph F., recovers from sickness; John Liechty adopted and sealed to their father Hyrum Smith.
16 May 1893	**Joseph F. to Martha Ann**	Martha Ann's son John sends Martha Ann six dollars and Martha Ann's daughter Lucy four dollars.
7 March 1894	**Joseph F. to Martha Ann**	Martha Ann able to walk without crutches; hopes Martha Ann's sons will provide for her; Joseph F.'s burdens heavy, has thirty-five souls to feed.
24 December 1894	**Joseph F. to Martha Ann**	Joseph F. is supporting thirty-six; wishes he could provide for Martha Ann, sends ten dollars.
28 January 1895	**Joseph F. to Martha Ann**	Travels to Nephi; invites Martha Ann to family gathering at Julina's; Joseph F.'s daughter Ina (Julina) breaks her arm.
20 February 1895	**Joseph F. to Martha Ann**	Celebrates newborn baby of Martha Ann's daughter Zina.
6 August 1895	**Joseph F. to Martha Ann**	Talks of the death and funeral of their mutual friend and brother Edward Mecham.
27 September 1895	**Joseph F. to Martha Ann**	Talks of changing times with letter writing; speaks of how busy he has become and the impact it has had on many friendships and relationships; speaks of his trip to Alaska from the summer and the good it did him; talks of how good his kids are.
[1 November] 1895	**Joseph F. to Martha Ann**	Expresses sympathy for the death of Franklin Nephi Corbett; reflects on his own children's deaths and talks about the eternal joy of seeing them again.
23 March 1896	**Joseph F. to Martha Ann**	Joseph F.'s son Joseph Richards has appendix removed; afflictions are blessings in disguise.
28 March 1896	**Joseph F. to Martha Ann**	Joseph Richards continues to recover; Mamie and Donnie, nicknames for Mary Sophronia Smith and Donnette Smith, are sick while attending the Pratt Institute in Brooklyn; Hyrum Mack Smith is doing well on his mission.
21 April 1896	**Joseph F. to Martha Ann**	Explains that he does not know how contracts with dentists work; explains that having teeth that fit well is very important and worth any cost; he enclosed ten dollars to help with the cost of teeth; asks Martha Ann to acknowledge that it was received and includes a stamped envelope.
18 November 1896	**Joseph F. to Martha Ann**	Makes travel arrangements to Mammoth for Martha Ann and family.

DATE WRITTEN	AUTHOR & RECIPIENT	SUMMARY OF CONTENT
12 May 1897	**Joseph F. to Martha Ann**	Suffers with a boil; wife Edna gives birth; going to Ogden on business.
25 August 1897	**Joseph F. to Martha Ann**	Sealing of grandparents Joseph and Lucy Mack Smith and some of their family; other temple work.
19 March 1898	**Joseph F. to Martha Ann**	Sickness; daughter Ruth dies; yellow flag nailed to house; the Savior redeems little children; son Hyrum home from mission.
13 October 1898	**Joseph F. to Martha Ann**	Martha Ann leaves Joseph F.'s house upset; Joseph F. offers material to make a comforter.
25 October 1898	**Joseph F. to Martha Ann**	Something troubles Martha Ann, will converse with her in person; daughter Leonora has a baby boy.
23 December 1898	**Joseph F. to Martha Ann**	Ward gathers to celebrate ninety-third anniversary of Prophet Joseph Smith's birth; sends Martha Ann five dollars for Christmas turkey.
16 June 1899	**Joseph F. to Martha Ann**	Can Martha Ann come do temple work?
6 September 1899	**Joseph F. to Martha Ann**	Anxious to know how Martha Ann's daughter Sarah is doing.
4 October 1899	**Joseph F. to Martha Ann**	Joseph F. is having difficulties buying her a train ticket from Provo to Salt Lake; sends her five dollars so she can buy the fare and come.
5 October 1899	**Joseph F. to Martha Ann**	Hopes Martha Ann's daughter Sarah is well; asks when Martha Ann will arrive for conference.
16 October 1899	**Joseph F. to Martha Ann**	Girls leaving on 5:30 train; Martha Ann should meet them.
23 December 1899	**Joseph F. to Martha Ann**	Watch for letter.
23 December 1899	**Joseph F. to Martha Ann**	Ninety-fourth birthday of Uncle Joseph Smith; Merry Christmas; sends five dollars; Lord is merciful with Joseph F.'s family.
26 July 1900	**Joseph F. to Martha Ann**	Brother-in-law Charles E. Griffin dies; Joseph F. goes to Mexico on special mission.
26 January 1901	**Joseph F. to Martha Ann**	Has extra train ticket Martha Ann can use; attends a funeral.
7 February 1901	**Joseph F. to Martha Ann**	Children David and Donette ill; asks when Martha Ann wants ticket.
2 April 1901	**Joseph F. to Martha Ann**	Quarantine removed from wife Alice's home; Martha Ann's granddaughter Lucy dies by railroad tracks.

DATE WRITTEN	AUTHOR & RECIPIENT	SUMMARY OF CONTENT
23 December 1901	**Joseph F. to Martha Ann**	Joseph F. sends Martha Ann a check for ten dollars for Christmas dinner; reports that his family is healthy; Mamie is working at the Beehive House.
23 July 1902	**Joseph F. to Martha Ann**	Hyrum Mack was sent to check on Martha Ann and family; Martha Ann has family who are sick; teaches that God is not to blame.
26 July 1902	**Joseph F. to Martha Ann**	Martha Ann's granddaughter Mary dies; God tries his people even unto death; the Atonement redeems the innocent.
23 (24) December 1903	**Joseph F. to Martha Ann**	Joseph F. sends Martha Ann a check for ten dollars as a Christmas gift and expresses season's greetings; updates on family health, including Aunt Edna.
8 February 1904	**Joseph F. to Martha Ann**	Joseph F. shares his thoughts and scriptures on the death of children after commenting on the loss of Martha Corbett; mentions Hyrum Smith's Birthday and that cousins from Iowa are visiting; mentions that David has been sick; comments on the birth of his grandson born to his daughter Minerva.
25 July 1904	**Joseph F. to Martha Ann**	Joseph F. speaks of attending the cornerstone laying of the Richmond Tabernacle; speaks of health concerns in his own family and with Martha Ann's son John.
23 December 1904	**Joseph F. to Martha Ann**	Sends Martha Ann ten dollars for Christmas; wishes Martha Ann season's greetings and spends time remembering Joseph Smith's birthday.
23 January 1905	**Joseph F. to Martha Ann**	Joseph F. expresses sympathies on the death of Mercy Harris; explains that his words won't do much to comfort, but time and the blessings of the Lord will help; speaks of heaven and the joys with family there; mentions their mother.
2 April 1905	**Joseph F. to Martha Ann**	Many sick at home; Martha Ann's daughter Mercy and Joseph F.'s father-in-law Alfred Lambson die; four of Joseph F.'s sons about to start missions; Joseph F.'s daughters Alice May Rich Smith and Edna Melissa Smith have baby boys; receives invective and abusive slander from Franklin Cannon, apostate son of George Q. Cannon.
22 November 1905	**Joseph F. to Martha Ann**	Joseph F.'s grandson Alfred dies; much sickness at home; half brother John weighs over 200 pounds.
3 January 1906	**Joseph F. to Martha Ann**	Happy New Year and Christmas; sends fifteen dollars; discusses growing old.

DATE WRITTEN	AUTHOR & RECIPIENT	SUMMARY OF CONTENT
1 February 1906	**Joseph F. to Martha Ann**	Martha Ann broke her truss; sends five dollars; David Allen, second cousin twice removed, killed by horses.
8 March 1906	**Joseph F. to Martha Ann**	Cousin Ellen (Fielding) dies; Joseph F. very busy.
26 November 1906	**Joseph F. to Martha Ann**	Money is short, paid three-hundred-dollar fine for last baby; sends five dollars; wives have time only for work; Joseph F. arrested and risks jail for having child with polygamous wife.
24 December 1906	**Joseph F. to Martha Ann**	Son Charles Coulson Rich Smith had appendicitis; Merry Christmas; sends five dollars.
8 March 1907	**Joseph F. to Martha Ann**	Martha Ann's allowance raised; Joseph F. grows older each day; sends Martha Ann one dollar.
10 April 1907	**Joseph F. to Martha Ann**	Winding down from conference, Joseph F.'s voice hoarse from speaking; Martha Ann shouldn't take care of her daughter Lucy's children but should give them to her son Hyrum and his wife Delia.
16 July 1907	**Joseph F. to Martha Ann**	Discusses William's anger towards his bishop; encourages Martha Ann to have William read about Christ's example and warnings; encourages Martha Ann to warn William about the difficulties caused by not forgiving.
27 November 1907	**Joseph F. to Martha Ann**	Has indigestion; grandchildren have measles; sends five dollars; signs his name frequently even outside the office.
27 December 1908	**Joseph F. to Martha Ann**	Wishes Martha Ann a happy new year and encloses five dollars for a turkey; reports he has a lame back; reports that his family is doing well.
24 April 1909	**Joseph F. to Martha Ann**	Expresses sympathy at the loss of William; loss is difficult; the gospel provides comfort.
6 May 1909	**Joseph F. to Martha Ann**	Illness at home; wants to know how boys handled funeral expenses for funeral of Martha Ann's husband William; Joseph F. will help with undertaker; half sister Jerusha can come back with half brother John.
24 May 1909	**Joseph F. to Martha Ann**	Sends a check to pay for the burial of William; paying off the debts of Coulson and traveling to the Islands put him in a hard financial situation; several family members are sick.
22 December 1909	**Joseph F. to Martha Ann**	Season's greetings; children of Joseph F.'s daughter Donnie are sick; son Wesley left hospital in Honolulu; sends five dollars for turkey dinner.

DATE WRITTEN	AUTHOR & RECIPIENT	SUMMARY OF CONTENT
19 September 1910	**Joseph F. to Martha Ann**	Joseph F. tours eastern United States and Europe; accident at Startup candy factory.
7 November 1910	**Joseph F. to Martha Ann**	Martha Ann left quickly from Joseph F.'s home on her last visit; sends ten dollars; vote Republican against Thomas Kearns.
24 December 1910	**Joseph F. to Martha Ann**	Season's greetings; sends ten dollars; wives Julina and Alice suffer from rheumatism; celebrated Uncle Joseph Smith's birthday.
3 April 1911	**Joseph F. to Martha Ann**	Sends twenty dollars; has no time; Martha Ann's son Joseph sick; conference is near.
14 May 1911	**Joseph F. to Martha Ann**	Wishes Martha Ann a happy seventieth birthday; trials in Martha Ann's life; God is kind; sends twenty dollars; Seraph, daughter of cousin Josephine Fielding, dies; Abraham Cannon's son dies.
29 May 1911	**Joseph F. to Martha Ann**	Martha Ann's son Joseph Albert dies at age forty-nine after long-term illness; living death worse than death itself.
6 November 1911	**Joseph F. to Martha Ann**	Half brother John sick with pneumonia.
22 December 1911	**Joseph F. to Martha Ann** *Corresponding letter: 26 December 1911*	Sends twenty dollars for Christmas dinner; meeting in temple annex for Uncle Joseph Smith's birthday.
26 December 1911	**Martha Ann to Joseph F.** *Corresponding letter: 22 December 1911*	Son Hyrum sent Martha Ann fifty dollars to pay for pavement and taxes; mother of Joseph F.'s wife Mary dies; Martha Ann's children love Joseph F.
22 June 1912	**Joseph F. to Martha Ann**	Half sister Jerusha has jaundice; Joseph F. sends Martha Ann five dollars.
20 August 1912	**Joseph F. to Martha Ann**	Still in the "land of the living"; Lord has been merciful; family affairs; sends Martha Ann ten dollars.
22 November 1912	**Joseph F. to Martha Ann**	Gave cousin Ina Coolbrith a copy of conference sermons; Joseph F. and wife Julina have bad colds; wants to know if boys paid Martha Ann's taxes and fuel; sends ten dollars.
23 December 1912	**Joseph F. to Martha Ann**	Cousin Ina thinks Martha Ann unwise for taking her daughter Lucy's children; wishes compliments of the season; sends ten dollars for Christmas dinner along with a copy of the Christmas news.
28 February 1913	**Joseph F. to Martha Ann** *Corresponding letter: 3 March 1913*	Cousin Ina sends Martha Ann love and sympathy for raising her daughter Lucy's children; Martha Ann suffers loss from fire; Joseph F. sends nineteen dollars.

DATE WRITTEN	AUTHOR & RECIPIENT	SUMMARY OF CONTENT
3 March 1913	**Martha Ann to Joseph F.** *Corresponding letter: 28 February 1913*	Martha Ann grateful for Joseph F.'s kindness; William, Martha Ann's son, has hemorrhoids and cannot work; family affairs; describes fire of home Martha Ann rented out; explains decision to care for daughter Lucy's children.
18 June 1913	**Joseph F. to Martha Ann**	Wife Julina is sixty-four and in California; daughter Emma is ill; second cousin Margaret West Smith dies; sent letter and ten dollars to cousin Ina; sends Martha Ann ten dollars for her birthday.
23 December 1913	**Joseph F. to Martha Ann**	Wishes Martha Ann compliments of season; 108th anniversary of Uncle Joseph Smith's birth; wife Edna has food poisoning; Joseph F. has a cold; sends ten dollars for Christmas dinner.
24 June 1914	**Joseph F. to Martha Ann**	Martha Ann in California; Joseph F. remembers seeing and crossing the ocean for the first time in 1854; the weather in Salt Lake City is delightful.
7 July 1914	**Martha Ann to Joseph F.**	Staying with daughter Artimissa; suffers ailments; using crutches; thanks Joseph F. for time in California; Israel Hodson asks Joseph F. to pray for his leg in temple.
9 July 1914	**Martha Ann to Joseph F.**	Fell and hurt shoulder; leg still requires crutches; still staying with daughter Artimissa.
10 September 1914	**Joseph F. to Martha Ann**	Wife Julina sends ten dollars for work done; cousin Adele in Reno; Church will probably not make a lasting impression on Adele; son Wesley goes to Deseret.
5 February 1915	**Joseph F. to Martha Ann**	Bro. Henry Stringham will furnish Mackinaw coats at Joseph F.'s expense; wife Sarah is sick; Zina in hospital.
17 February 1915	**Joseph F. to Martha Ann**	Martha Ann got Mackinaw coats, not fashionable but durable; wife Sarah's health improving; daughter Zina recovering, her husband gone on a mission; son Franklin has serious operation.
15 July 1915	**Joseph F. to Martha Ann** *Corresponding letter: 17 July 1915*	Sends cousin Ina Coolbrith ten dollars and Martha Ann twenty-five dollars; wife Julina sends love and wants Martha Ann to make aprons.
17 July 1915	**Martha Ann to Joseph F.** *Corresponding letter: 15 July 1915*	Family affairs; small earthquake in Provo, a reminder of God's power; expresses love for cousin Ina.
20 November 1915	**Joseph F. to Martha Ann**	Martha Ann has much to be grateful for; sends ten dollars in place of turkey.

DATE WRITTEN	AUTHOR & RECIPIENT	SUMMARY OF CONTENT
23 December 1915	**Joseph F. to Martha Ann**	Sends ten dollars; reminisces about Uncle Joseph Smith's birth and life.
17 February 1916	**Joseph F. to Martha Ann**	Sends fifteen dollars; is helping his children financially, money is short; had the flu; wife Julina is ill.
20 March 1916	**Joseph F. to Martha Ann** *Corresponding letter: 27 March 1916*	Wife Julina sends money for aprons; sees Martha Ann's son Franklin; daughters Lucy and Melissa and daughters-in-law Louise May, Ethel, and Lillian all pregnant.
27 March 1916	**Martha Ann to Joseph F.** *Corresponding letter: 20 March 1916*	Busy making temple clothes; now has seventy-one grandchildren and thirty-four great-grandchildren.
30 September 1916	**Joseph F. to Martha Ann**	Quickly growing old, like a cartwheel rolling down a hill; wife Julina has more work for Martha Ann; Joseph F.'s brother-in-law Alfred Lambson and family coming to visit; invites Martha Ann to conference and sends her fifteen dollars.
14 November 1916	**Joseph F. to Martha Ann**	Thanks Martha Ann for birthday card; 125 family members present for party; grandson Joseph Nelson on mission; wife Julina sends eighteen dollars, Joseph F. sends ten dollars.
29 November 1916	**Joseph F. to Martha Ann**	Sends ten dollars for Thanksgiving dinner; some children teething and fretful; wife Julina is at home of daughter Ina (Julina Clarissa Smith); signed letter "Ever your naughty brother."
13 December 1916	**Martha Ann to Joseph F.**	Expresses gratitude to Joseph F. and sympathy for his chest pain; recounts her Christmas; sons Hyrum and Franklin working in New Mexico.
19 December 1916	**Joseph F. to Martha Ann**	Sends twenty-five dollars for turkey; little ones are teething; daughter Ina (Julina Clarissa Smith) in San Diego; some of daughter Melissa's children have measles; sends money to cousins Thalia Smith and Ina Coolbrith.

Appendix D: Biographical Register

In most cases, persons are listed alphabetically by last name given at birth. Bolded names designate people mentioned in the Joseph F. Smith and Martha Ann Smith Harris Letter Collection. All children of Joseph F. Smith and of Martha Ann Smith Harris are included in the biographical register, though not all are mentioned in the letters. Birth and death dates are given whenever possible. Marriage dates and family relationships pertinent to the letter collection are provided, including, in all cases, information for first marriages. Additional family and marriage information is summarized to include the number of additional husbands or wives and children. Research for the biographical register is based on a number of sources, including family records found in FamilySearch, Ancestry, MyHeritage, US census records, newspapers of the day, and family and personal histories. Expanded biographies are included for some family members, historically significant persons, and individuals mentioned frequently in the letter collection. At the end of each name entry is a list of letters in which that particular person is found.

A

Adkinson, William Cochran

- Born on 30 January 1828 in Roane County, TN, to Charles Adkinson and **Margaret Thompson**. Was adopted by and sealed to **Abraham Owen Smoot** as his son after **Abraham Owen Smoot** married his mother. Nickname was "Willie."
- Married (1) Martha Ann Sessions (1835–77) on 29 January 1852 in Salt Lake City. They were the parents of (1) William Cochran Adkinson Smoot Jr. (1853–1933), (2) Martha Ann Smoot (1854–68), (3) Abraham Owen Smoot (1857–1976), (4) Margaret Esther Smoot (1858–1909), (5) Julia Eliza Smoot (1860–1951), (6) Josephine Smoot (1862–1926), (7) **Lucina Smoot**, (8) Albert Carlos Smoot (1865–1946), (9) Linda Amanda Smoot (1869–85), (10) Louisa Smoot (1870–75), (11) Linnia Amanda Smoot (1869–85), (12) Sarah Emma

Smoot (1871–92), (13) Perregrine Smoot (1872–1916), (14) Wilson Parley Smoot (1875–1941), and (15) Philaprine Smoot (1876–1957).

- Married two other wives and had one more child.
- Cut stone for the Nauvoo Temple as a young man and was ordained a Seventy. Served a mission to the Indians in Las Vegas, Clark County, NV, in 1855. Later served as counselor to Bishop **Abraham Owen Smoot**, his adopted father, in the Sugar House Ward in 1856, and then as first counselor to Ira Eldredge, the next bishop of that ward. Served a mission to the southern states for two years.
- Died on 31 January 1920 in Salt Lake City.

Letter reference: 25 August 1877

ALLEN, DAVID ROBERT, JR.

- Born on 8 August 1884 in Salt Lake City to David Robert Allen and Leila Smith Merrill.
- His maternal grandmother, **Bathsheba Kate Smith**, was a second cousin to **Joseph F.** and **Martha Ann**. Was a second cousin twice removed to **Joseph F.** and **Martha Ann**.
- Died on 31 January 1906 in a wagon accident.

Letter reference: 1 February 1906

AMY, DUSTIN [ANEY, M. N.]

- Born on 24 October 1801 in Kingston, Addison County, VT, to Herman Amy and Lucy Patrina Dow.
- Married Lenora Scott (dates unknown). They were the parents of seven children, the first born in 1831. Dustin left Lenora in 1851 in Council Bluffs, IA, to go to Salt Lake City. There he married **Levira Clark**, widow of **Samuel Harrison Smith**, on 24 November 1851. They had one son, Oscar Amy; see "The Amy Case," *Park Record*, 11 February 1893, 1. Dustin lived just a few homes away from William Godbe and **Annie Thompson**. He married two additional wives in the 1850s: Christiana Collingwood on 25 February 1855 and Ester Mendenhall on 7 September 1856. **Joseph F.**'s wife **Levira Annette Clark Smith** lived in his home with her mother for a period of time while **Joseph F.** was on a mission to England. Leonora Scott divorced Dustin in 1856 but came to Salt Lake City in 1863, and eventually they were remarried and returned to Iowa.
- "M. N." is an unknown designation. It seems unlikely that it was an abbreviation for "minister," even though the 1860 US Census for Salt Lake City lists the occupation of a number of people as "Minister LDS." Bishop **A. O. Smoot** is referred to as "M N Smoot" in the same letter, but since Dustin did not hold any major ecclesiastical position, it seems unlikely that **Martha Ann** would identify him as such.
- Died on 13 June 1868 in Council Bluffs, IA.

Letter reference: 12 January 1862

ANDERSON, LOUISE MAY

- Born on 25 September 1897 in Salt Lake City to Robert Lawrence Anderson and Gertrude Elizabeth Willey.
- Married **Jesse Kimball Smith**, the son of **Joseph F.** and **Sarah Ann Kimball** and the nephew of **Martha Ann**, on 25 September 1915 in Salt Lake City. They were the parents of three children.
- Died in July 1986 in Salt Lake City.

Letter reference: 20 March 1916

Atwood, Mary

- Born about 1606 in England to John Atwood and Ann Lee Coleson.
- Married **Robert Lee** about 1625 in Barnstable County, MA. They were the parents of four children.
- Was the seventh great-grandmother to **Joseph F.** and **Martha Ann** through their grandmother **Lucy Mack**.
- Died in October 1681 in Barnstable, Barnstable County, MA.

Letter reference: 25 August 1897

B

Baptiste, Jean

- Born on 7 November 1814 in Venice, Italy.
- Married Dorothy Sarah Jennison (1827–1903) in 1861 in the Salt Lake City Cemetery. They were the parents of one child, Millecent Baptiste (1862–1952).
- Baptiste was converted in the Australian goldfields and came to Utah in 1857. By 1859 Baptiste had been hired to dig graves and bury the dead at the Salt Lake City Cemetery east of the city. He built a small home nearby and opened a millinery and tailor shop with his wife. Baptiste was arrested in 1862 for robbing more than three hundred Salt Lake City Cemetery graves and was sent to Fremont Island as punishment.
- Death unknown. He possibly escaped from Fremont Island and disappeared.

Letter reference: 3 February 1862

Barnes, Amanda Melissa

- Born on 22 February 1809 in Becket, Birkshire County, MA, to Ezekial Barnes and Fanny Johnson.
- Married Warren Smith (1794–1838) in 1826 in Nauvoo, Hancock County, IL. They were the parents of eleven children.
- Sealed to **Joseph Smith Jr.**, making her an aunt of **Joseph F.** and **Martha Ann**.
- Died on 30 June 1886 in Salt Lake City.

Letter reference: 1 August 1884

Barrows, Sophia

- Born in 1821 in Milton Bryant, Bedfordshire, England, to George Burrows and Mary Price.
- Married (1) William Osman (1794–1838) in Milton Bryant, Bedfordshire, England. No issue.
- Married (2) **Edward Mecham** on 29 October 1864 in Salt Lake City. They were the parents of two children.
- She and her husband Edward were neighbors of **Martha Ann** in Provo, Utah County, UT.
- Died in 1894.

Letter references: 27 October 1870, 23 February 1871, 20 June 1874, 5 August 1874, 15 August 1874, 7 September 1874 (first letter), 9 February 1875, 31 March 1875, 15 May 1875, 18 March 1885

Baskin, Robert N.

- Born in 1837.

- Served as an attorney, mayor, and associate justice in Salt Lake City. Openly opposed to Latter-day Saint involvement in Utah territorial government and used his influence in legal battles against the Church hierarchy. His *Reminiscences of Early Utah* is a classic in early Utah history.
- Died in 1918.

Letter reference: 31 March 1875

BEEBE, LAURA EMILY

- Born on 15 February 1838 in Hanover, Chautauqua County, NY, to William Albert Beebe and Louisa Newton.
- Married **Albert Bailey Griffin** on 13 November 1853 in Salt Lake City. They were the parents of seven children.
- Died on 17 January 1888 in Kanarra, Iron County, UT.

Letter references: 3 July 1857, 30 May 1861

BERRY, WILLIAM SHANKS

- Born on 3 February 1838 in Dresden, Weakly County, TN, to Jesse Woods Berry and Armelia Shanks.
- Married (1) Rebecca Rocena Beck (1843–1903) on 22 November 1860 in Spanish Fork, Utah County, UT. They were the parents of ten children.
- Married (2) Diantha Allen (1839–73) on 15 October 1864 in Salt Lake City. No issue.
- Married (3) Lovinia Nicholson Sylvester (1854–1955) on 22 June 1874 in Salt Lake City. They were the parents of five children.
- Was serving a mission in Tennessee when killed by a mob that attacked the home of James Conder.
- Died on 10 August 1884 in Cane Creek, Lewis County, TN.

Letter reference: 15 August 1884

BIGLER, BATHSHEBA WILSON

- Born on 3 May 1822 near Shinnston, Harrison County, WV, to Mark Bigler and Susannah Ogden.
- Married **George Albert Smith** on 25 July 1841 in Nauvoo, Hancock County, IL. They were the parents of (1) **George Albert Smith Jr.**, (2) **Bathsheba Kate Smith**, and (3) John Smith (born and died 1847).
- Her husband was a first cousin once removed to **Joseph F.** and **Martha Ann**. Was the aunt of **Joseph F.**'s wives **Julina** and **Edna Lambson**. Fulfilled many callings in the Church. Active on the Deseret Hospital board of directors. Counselor in the Retrenchment Organization, which held bimonthly meetings from 1869 to 1904; counselor to the general Relief Society president; and General President of the Relief Society from 1901 to 1910. Served as president of the Women Workers of the Salt Lake Temple. Experienced in needlework, spinning, weaving, and lacemaking. Had outstanding talents in art, music, poetry, and literature.
- Died on 20 September 1910 in Salt Lake City.

Letter reference: 3 May 1872

BIGLER, MELISSA JANE

- Born in March 1825 in Shinnston, Harrison County, WV, to Mark Bigler and Susannah Ogden.
- Married **Alfred Boaz Lambson** on 25 March 1845 in Nauvoo, Hancock County, IL. They were the parents of (1) **Melissa Jane Lambson**, (2) **Julina Lambson**, (3) **Edna Lambson**, and (4) **Alfred Boaz Lambson Jr.**

- She and her husband came to Utah in 1847. Theirs was the first house built by the pioneers in the valley. For a time, they relocated to Florence, NE, but in 1856 they returned to Utah, where they continued to live and raise their family.
- Died on 26 October 1899 in Salt Lake City.

Letter reference: 18 August 1870

Blyth, John Law

- Born on 27 June 1829 in Newmonkland, Lanark, Scotland, to John Blyth and Elizabeth Law.
- Married (1) Margaret Mitchell (1824–1911) on 17 December 1855 in Placer County, CA. They were the parents of seven children.
- Married (2) Margaret McKie (1831–95) on 16 August 1869. No issue.
- Emigrated from Scotland to the United States at age eighteen. Labored as a coal miner in Pennsylvania. When news of the California Gold Rush came, he sailed to California and used his mining skills to become very wealthy. Joined the Church in 1857 in California and then moved to Utah.
- Sustained a member of the high council of the Salt Lake Stake in 1861. Was a member of the Second Battalion of the First Division of the Nauvoo Legion. On 13 December 1871 accused and arrested for the murder of **Dr. John King Robinson** but later released. In 1873 called on a mission to help explore and settle Arizona. Appointed president and acting bishop of the Arizona Mission. **Brigham Young** asked him to take charge of a branch of the United Order in Salt Lake City. Served a mission to Scotland from 1878 to 1880. Spent the last three years of his life as a worker in the Logan Temple.
- Died on 27 April 1892 in Salt Lake City.

Letter reference: 12 December 1871

Bollwinkel, Sarah

- Born on 8 March 1840 in Liverpool, Lancashire, England, to John Bollwinkel and Sarah Williams. Also known as "Adelaide."
- Married (1) **William Nelson** on 13 March 1856 in Salt Lake City.
- Married (2) John L. Kramer (1836–death unknown) on 11 January 1860 in Salt Lake City. They were the parents of two children. They were later divorced on 22 February 1866.
- Married (3) James E. Dun (1841–death unknown) before 1885.
- She immigrated with her father and two brothers, John Murray and Frederick, to the United States after her mother's death in 1852. The family left Fort Leavenworth, KS, on 4 July 1852 in the Philip De La Mare Freight train when she was twelve years old. The family settled in the Sugar House Ward, where **Martha Ann** was living.
- Died on 29 December 1915 in Butte, Silver Bow County, MT.

Letter references: April 1856, 14 July 1856

Bowman, Richard Smith

- Born on 30 March 1905 in Salt Lake City to John Fife Bowman and **Edna Melissa Smith**.
- Was a grandson of **Joseph F.** and **Edna Lambson**.
- Died on 15 November 1908 in Salt Lake City.

Letter reference: 2 April 1905

Briggs, Eliza

- Born on 30 September 1836 in Middleton by Oldham, Lancashire, England, to John Briggs and Ruth Butterworth.
- Married **James Stratton** on 2 February 1857 in Salt Lake City. They were the parents of twelve children.
- Died on 8 January 1871 in Overton, Clark County, NV.

Letter reference: 5 April 1857

Brown, Lucy

- Born on 4 January 1821 in Biggleswade, Bedfordshire, England, to John Brown and Edith Atterton.
- Married **Elias Smith**, first cousin once removed to **Joseph F.** and **Martha Ann**, on 6 August 1845 in Nauvoo, Hancock County, IL. They were the parents of four children.
- Died on 4 April 1895 in Salt Lake City.

Letter references: 2 March 1856, 20 May 1858

Bullock, Isaac

- Born on 23 October 1825 in Grafton, Grafton County, NH, to Benjamin Bullock and Dorothy Kimball.
- Married (1) **Electa Wood** on 14 December 1856 in Salt Lake City. They were the parents of nine children.
- Married (2) Emma Stott (1840–1926) on 5 April 1857 in Salt Lake City. They were the parents of twelve children.
- Served in the Wyoming legislature, representing Green River County. Served as a missionary among the Shoshoni Indians and as an Indian interpreter in Fort Supply, WY. Served in the Forty-Fifth Quorum of the Seventy, which was a stake calling from 1883 to 1986. Served as mayor of Provo and was elected to the Utah Legislature. In 1867 appointed US Marshal.
- Died on 16 March 1891 in Provo, Utah County, UT.

Letter reference: 17 December 1856

Burdick, Horace

- Born on 7 November 1831 in Jamestown, Chautauqua County, NY, to Thomas Burdick and Ann Higley.
- Married Sarah Catherine Hodge (about 1834–1903) on 20 April 1851 in Kanesville, Pottawattamie County, IA. They were the parents of two children.
- Was a schoolteacher in the vicinity of Salt Lake City. Lived in Cedar Fort in the 1850s and in 1859 moved to the Los Angeles, CA, area.
- Died on 7 May 1877 in Los Angeles, Los Angeles County, CA.

Letter reference: 5 April 1857

Burrows, William Creeland

- Born on 6 November 1828 in Hillsborough, County Down, Ireland, to David Burrows and Sarah Creeland.
- Married **Catherine Lowder** on 1 January 1857 in Salt Lake City. They were the parents of eight children.
- He and his family served a colonizing mission to St. George, UT, in the 1860s.
- Died on 3 February 1910 in Salt Lake City.

Letter reference: 5 April 1857

Burton, Isabella

- Born on 26 December 1856 in Kaysville, Davis County, UT, to **William Walton Burton** and **Rachel Fielding**. Was a first cousin once removed to **Joseph F.** and **Martha Ann**.
- Married Frederick Foulger (1851–1936) on 21 December 1874 in Salt Lake City. They settled in Ogden and were the parents of eight children.
- Died on 26 October 1920 in Ogden, Weber County, UT.

Letter reference: 3 February 1857

Burton, Parley Parson

- Born on 10 July 1878 in Ogden, Weber County, UT, to **William Walton Burton** and Sarah Ann Fielding.
- Died on 8 March 1883 in Ogden, Weber County, UT.

Letter reference: 13 March 1883

Burton, William Walton

- Born on 23 March 1833 in Bradford, Yorkshire, England, to James Burton and Isabelle Walton. His three wives were sisters, the daughters of **Joseph Fielding** and first cousins to **Joseph F.** and **Martha Ann**.
- Married (1) **Rachel Fielding** on 28 March 1856 in Salt Lake City. They were the parents of thirteen children.
- Married (2) **Ellen Fielding** on 2 November 1862 in Salt Lake City. They were the parents of eight children.
- Married (3) Sarah Ann Fielding (1851–1938) on 23 May 1870 in Salt Lake City. They were the parents of nine children.
- Immigrated to Utah in the Job Smith Company, arriving on 23 September 1854. Served as a member of the Seventeenth Quorum of the Seventy. Served as a first counselor to Bishop Joseph Parry in Ogden and to George Ormond in the Star Valley stake presidency in Wyoming. Served as a high councilor in the Weber Stake. Was an Ogden city councilman for three terms.
- Died on 27 June 1918 in Ogden, Weber County, UT.

Letter references: April 1856, 18 January 1870, 6 August 1870, 13 March 1883, 27 March 1883, 8 March 1906

Buxton, Emma

- Born on 4 December 1847 in St. Louis, St. Louis County, MO, to George Joseph Buxton and Elizabeth Gladwin. The 1870 US Census lists her and her husband as neighbors of **Martha Ann** in Provo.
- Married **Joseph C. Jones** in 1868 in St. Louis, St. Louis County, MO. They were the parents of four children.
- Died on 22 February 1902.

Letter reference: 5 August 1874

C

Caine, John Thomas

- Born on 8 January 1829 in the Parish of Kirkpatrick near Peel, Isle of Man, Great Britain, to Thomas Caine and Elinor Cubbon. Served a mission to the Sandwich Islands.

- Married Margaret Nightingale (1833–1911) on 22 October 1850 in St. Louis, St. Louis County, MO. They were the parents of thirteen children.
- Was a schoolteacher in Utah. Served a mission to the Sandwich Islands from 1854 to 1856 in the company of **Joseph F.** Appointed counselor to mission president **Silas Smith**. Actively involved in government and served as Utah's fourth delegate to Congress. Did much to benefit the Saints by standing up for the Church's views in Washington, DC.
- Died on 20 September 1911 in Salt Lake City.

Letter reference: 20 October 1856

Cannon, Abraham Hoagland

- Born on 12 March 1859 in Salt Lake City to **George Quayle Cannon** and Elizabeth Hoagland. His father was a member of the Quorum of the Twelve Apostles and later of the First Presidency. Nickname was "Abram."
- Married (1) Sarah Ann Jenkins (1860–1940) on 16 October 1878 in Salt Lake City. They were the parents of four children.
- Married two other wives and had six more children.
- Was a carpenter and an architect. From 1879 to 1882 served a mission to Europe. Called as one of the seven Presidents of the Seventy in 1882. In October 1889 sustained as one of the Twelve Apostles. In charge of the *Deseret News* and connected with several railroad and banking businesses.
- Died on 19 July 1896 in Salt Lake City.

Letter reference: 14 May 1911

Cannon, Franklin Jenne

- Born on 25 January 1859 in Salt Lake City to **George Quayle Cannon** and Sarah Jane Jenne.
- Married Martha Anderson Brown (1858–1908) in April 1878 in Salt Lake City. They were the parents of five children.
- Publicly renounced his faith in the Church in January 1905 and was excommunicated in March 1905. As editor of the *Salt Lake Tribune* wrote scathing articles condemning **Joseph F.**, Elder Reed Smoot, and the Church hierarchy in general. In 1911 published a highly critical exposé titled "Under the Prophet in Utah."
- Died on 25 July 1933.

Letter reference: 2 April 1905

Cannon, George Quayle

- Born on 11 January 1827 in Liverpool, Lancashire, England, to George Cannon and Ann Quayle. Was a nephew of **Joseph Fielding**.
- Married (1) **Elizabeth Hoagland** on 11 December 1854 in Salt Lake City. They were the parents of (1) Rosina Matthews Cannon (1852–1939), who was adopted, (2) George Quayle Cannon Jr. (born and died 1856), (3) John Quayle Cannon (1857–1931), (4) **Abraham Hoagland Cannon**, (5) Georgianna Hoagland Cannon (1861–63), (6) George Hoagland Cannon (born and died 1863), (7) Elizabeth Hoagland Cannon (1865–67), (8) Mary Alice Hoagland Cannon (1867–1908), (9) Lillian Ann Hoagland Cannon (1869–70), (10) David Hoagland Cannon (1871–92), (11) Emily Hoagland Cannon (1874–1955), and (12) Sylvester Quayle Cannon (1877–1943).
- Married (2) Sarah Jane Jenne (1839–1928) on 11 April 1858 in Salt Lake City. They were the parents of (1) **Franklin Jenne Cannon**, (2) Angus Jenne Cannon (1867–1957), (3) Hugh Jenne Cannon (1870–1931), (4)

Rosannah Jenne Cannon (1872–1969), (5) Joseph Jenne Cannon (1877–1945), (6) Preston Jenne Cannon (1881–1941), and (7) Karl Quayle Cannon (1881–1934).

- Married five other wives and had twenty-three more children, two of whom were adopted.
- Held many important responsibilities in the Church. Worked in the *Times and Seasons* office in Nauvoo under **John Taylor**. Learned the printing business there. Ordained a Seventy in 1845 and served as secretary of the Nineteenth Quorum of the Seventy for many years. In 1850 embarked on a mission to the Sandwich Islands. Translated the Book of Mormon into the Hawaiian language and returned from his mission in 1854. Called as one of the presidents of the Thirtieth Quorum of the Seventy upon his arrival in Salt Lake City. Edited a Church newspaper titled *Western Standard* in San Francisco in 1856. Served as president of the California Mission from 1856 to 1858. Edited the *Millennial Star* while on a mission in Great Britain. Was director in the Union Pacific Railroad company. Founded the publishing firm George Q. Cannon and Sons Company, of which he was president. Was president of Utah Sugar Company, vice president and director of Zion's Savings Bank and Trust Company, director of the Co-op. Wagon and Machine Company, president of Brigham Young Trust Company, director of the Utah Light and Power Company, director of the Bullion-Beck and Champion Mining Company, and director of the Grand Central Mining Company. Established the *Juvenile Instructor* and became editor of the *Deseret News*. Called as a member of the Quorum of the Twelve Apostles and later as a counselor in the First Presidency under Presidents **John Taylor**, **Wilford Woodruff**, and Lorenzo Snow.
- Died on 12 April 1901 in Monterey, Monterey County, CA.

Letter references: 14 June 1872, 1 July 1881, 1 August 1884, 2 April 1905

Cannon, Lester Jenkins

- Born on 4 July 1888 in Salt Lake City to **Abraham Hoagland Cannon** and Sara Ann Jenkins.
- Married Hetty Smith Williams (1889–1907) sometime before 1907. No issue.
- Called to serve a mission in May 1909 and left Utah in July of that year to serve in the French-speaking section of the Netherlands Mission, which included Belgium and part of France. Suffered a painful illness on 8 May 1911 in Brussels, Belgium, which physicians diagnosed as appendicitis complicated with peritonitis. Died one day after what had appeared to be a successful surgery.
- Died on 16 May 1911 in Lille, France.

Letter reference: 14 May 1911

Carrington, Albert

- Born on 8 January 1813 in Springfield, Sangamon County, IL, to Daniel Van Carrington and Isabella Bownman.
- Married (1) Rhoda Maria Woods (1824–86) in about 1842 in Springfield. They were the parents of fifteen children.
- Married (2) Mary Ann Rock (1822–95) on 31 January 1846 in Nauvoo, Hancock County, IL. No issue.
- Graduated from Dartmouth College in 1833. Was a topographer and surveyor. Taught school and studied law for a few years in Pennsylvania. Engaged in lead mining in Wisconsin. Called as a member of the Quorum of the Twelve Apostles. Served as a member of Captain Howard Stansbury's party, which surveyed the Great Salt Lake. Was the second editor of the *Deseret News*. Was secretary to **Brigham Young** for twenty years. At times functioned as an assistant counselor to the President. Presided over the European Mission three different times. Excommunicated from the Church for sexual transgressions later in life but rebaptized prior to his death.

- Died on 19 September 1889 in Salt Lake City.

Letter reference: 7 September 1857

Clark, Levira

- Born on 30 July 1815 in Livonia, Livingston County, NY, to Gardner Clark and Delecta Farrer. Was the aunt of **Joseph F.** and **Martha Ann** and the mother-in-law of **Joseph F.**
- Married Samuel Harrison Smith (1808–44) on 29 April 1841 in Nauvoo, Hancock County, IL. They were the parents of (1) **Levira Annette Clark Smith**, (2) Lovisa C. Smith (born and died 1843), and (3) Lucy J. C. Smith (born and died 1844). She most likely came to Utah in the Harry Walton/Garden Grove Company in 1851 and married **Dustin Amy** on 24 November 1851 shortly after arriving.
- Died on 1 January 1883 in Salt Lake City.

Letter references: 8 December 1861, 12 January 1862

Clarkson, Elizabeth

- Born on 28 April 1836 in Hyson Green, Nottinghamshire, England, to Thomas Clarkson and Catharine McCoy.
- Married **Leonard John Nuttall** on 25 December 1856 in Provo, Utah County, UT. They were the parents of twelve children.
- A well-educated woman who fulfilled several leadership positions in the Church. Called to serve as president of the Relief Society of the Kanab Stake in Utah in June of 1878. In May of 1880 attended Mrs. Pratt's School of Obstetrics in Salt Lake City and passed the exam to be a midwife. Joined her husband in Washington, DC, in December 1890 while he was laboring as a missionary.
- Died on 18 July 1902 in Provo, Utah County, UT.

Letter reference: 24 November 1874

Clawson, Moroni, Sr.

- Born on 1 January 1837 in Far West, Caldwell County, MO, to Moses Clawson and Cornelia Brown.
- Married Eliza Manhardt (1841–1924) on 1 January 1859 in Draper, Salt Lake County, UT. They were the parents of two children.
- On 31 December 1861, he, **John P. Smith**, **Lot Elisha Huntington**, and others assaulted and robbed territorial governor John Dawson. The recently appointed governor was fleeing Utah after he made an indecent proposal to Albina Merrill Williams, a Latter-day Saint widow. Clawson, Huntington, and Smith were apprehended by Orrin Porter Rockwell. Huntington was shot and killed during the arrest, and Clawson and Smith were shot and killed on the following day while attempting to escape on 17 January 1862. He was initially buried in the Salt Lake City Cemetery. When the family came to claim his body, Clawson was found naked. This began an investigation that led to the arrest of **Jean Baptiste** for robbing as many as three hundred graves.
- Died on 17 January 1862 in Salt Lake City.

Letter reference: 3 February 1862

Cluff, William Wallace

- Born on 8 March 1832 in Willoughby, Lake County, OH, to David Cluff and Elizabeth Hall.

- Married **Ann Whipple** on 24 October 1863 in Pine Valley, Washington County, UT. They were the parents of eight children.
- Baptized in the Mississippi River in 1842 by Elder Peter Shurtz. Served in the Sandwich Islands Mission from 1854 to 1858. Served a mission to Denmark from 1858 to 1863. Returned to serve a second mission to the Sandwich Islands in March 1864 with Ezra Taft Benson, Alma Smith, Lorenzo Snow, and **Joseph F.** Was in a boat with Lorenzo Snow when it capsized.
- Appointed colonel of the Summit County Militia in the Black Hawk War of 1866 and elected to the Legislature of the Territory of Utah. Sat in the constitutional convention in 1872. Served as presiding bishop over the settlements of Morgan, Summit, and Wasatch Counties and served as president of Summit Stake from 1877 to 1901. Served as president of the Scandinavian Mission from 1870 to 1871. Again called to serve in the Hawaiian Islands Mission in 1887 and then again in 1900.
- Died on 21 August 1915 in Salt Lake City.

Letter references: 15 December 1860, 26 May 1871

Conder, William Martin

- Born on 3 March 1863 in Tennessee to William James Conder and Malinda Carroll.
- Killed along with three other members (including two missionaries) by a mob that attacked the home of his father in Tennessee.
- Died on 10 August 1884 in Cane Creek, Lewis County, TN.

Letter reference: 15 August 1884

Cook, James

- Born on 27 October 1728 in Yorkshire, Middlesbrough, England, to James Cook and Grace Pace.
- Married Elizabeth Batts (1742–1835) on 21 December 1762 in Barking, Essex, England. They were the parents of six children.
- Served as a member of the British Royal Navy and was an explorer and surveyor in southeast Canada. Became famous for his three voyages to the Pacific, where he mapped, for the first time, islands throughout the Pacific for Europeans. Killed in a skirmish with Native Hawaiians during his third voyage to the Pacific.
- Died on 14 February 1779 in Hawai‘i.

Letter references: 25 May 1856, 2 October 1856

Coolbrith, Agnes Moulton

- Born on 11 July 1811 in Scarboro, Cumberland County, ME, to Joseph Coolbrith and Mary Hasty Foss.
- Married (1) Don Carlos Smith (1816–41), uncle of **Joseph F.** and **Martha Ann**, on 30 July 1835 in Kirtland, Geauga County, OH. They were the parents of (1) **Agnes Charlotte Smith**, (2) Sophronia C. Smith (1838–43), and (3) **Josephine Donna Smith**. Sealed for eternity to Don Carlos Smith on 28 January 1846.
- Married (2) **Joseph Smith Jr.** on 6 January 1842. No issue.
- Married two other husbands and had two more children.
- Moved to Salt Lake City with her husband William Pickett in 1851. In 1852 moved to Marysville, CA, with her husband because of his legal difficulties. They later moved to San Francisco and Los Angeles.
- She and both of her daughters corresponded with **Joseph F.** by letter. He visited them multiple times in California, often while on his way to Hawaiian missions.

- Died on 26 December 1876 in Oakland, Alameda County, CA.

Letter reference: 25 July 1857

Corbett, Franklin Nephi

- Born on 17 February 1893, Provo, Utah County, UT, to **Walter Sutton Corbett** and **Mary Emily Harris**. Was a grandson of **William Jasper Harris** and **Martha Ann**.
- Died on 30 October 1895, Provo, Utah County, UT.

Letter reference: [1 November] 1895

Corbett, Joseph Smith

- Born on 29 January 1887 in Provo, Utah County, UT, to **Walter Sutton Corbett** and **Mary Emily Harris**. Was a grandson of **William Jasper Harris** and **Martha Ann**.
- Died on 31 January 1887 in Provo, Utah County, UT.

Letter reference: 11 February 1887

Corbett, Lucy Jane

- Born on 28 January 1899 in Provo, Utah County, UT, to **Walter Sutton Corbett** and **Mary Emily Harris**. Was a granddaughter of **William Jasper Harris** and **Martha Ann**.
- Died on 21 March 1901 in Provo, Utah County, UT, apparently as a result of a train accident.

Letter reference: 2 April 1901

Corbett, Mary Elizabeth

- Born on 15 February 1891 in Provo, Utah County, UT, to **Walter Sutton Corbett** and **Mary Emily Harris**. Was a granddaughter of **William Jasper Harris** and **Martha Ann**.
- Died on 26 July 1902 in Provo, Utah County, UT. **Martha Ann**'s daughter Lucy Smith Harris died on the same day. A discrepancy exists for the year they died. Joseph F. letter indicates 1902. Genealogical records state 1903.

Letter references: 23 July 1902, 26 July 1902

Corbett, Walter Harris

- Born on 28 October 1885 in Provo, Utah County, UT, to **Walter Sutton Corbett** and **Mary Emily Harris**. Was a grandson of **William Jasper Harris** and **Martha Ann** and a great-nephew of **Joseph F.**
- Married (1) Irene Colvin (1881–1912) on 13 December 1905 in Salt Lake City. They were the parents of three children.
- Married (2) Annie Dean (1884–1960) on 11 November 1914 in Salt Lake City. They were the parents of three children.
- Died on 4 February 1917 in Provo, Utah County, UT.

Letter references: 11 February 1887, 1 February 1891, 9 February 1891

Corbett, Walter Sutton

- Born on 15 September 1857 in Jacksonville, Morgan County, IL, to Walter Corbett and Elizabeth Sutton.

- Married **Mary Emily Harris**, the daughter of **William Jasper Harris** and **Martha Ann** and the niece of **Joseph F.**, on 12 November 1884 in Logan, Cache County, UT. They were the parents of (1) **Walter Harris Corbett**, (2) **Joseph Smith Corbett**, (3) William Moroni Corbett (1888–1928), (4) Hyrum Smith Corbett (born and died 1889), (5) Mary Elizabeth Corbett (1891–1902), (6) Franklin Nephi Corbett (1893–95), (7) Martha Corbett (1895–1904), (8) John Alvin Corbett (1897–1962), (9) **Lucy Jane Corbett**, (10) Pearson Harris Corbett (1900–1964), (11) Don Cecil Corbett (1903–71), and (12) George Leroy Corbett (1905–39).
- Died on 2 February 1912 in Provo, Utah County, UT.

Letter reference: 26 July 1902

D

Daniels, James Ephraim

- Born on 9 February 1825 in Manchester, Lancashire, England, to Joseph Ephraim Daniels and Elizabeth Salthouse.
- Married (1) Elizebeth Jane Jones (1836–84) on 28 April 1849 in Salt Lake City. They were the parents of six children.
- Married (2) **Marilla Lucretia Johnson** on 13 June 1878 in Manchester, Lancashire, England. No issue.
- Educated in the best schools of his day and was an expert penman. Became assessor and county collector for Utah County in 1870. In 1874 elected county recorder and was treasurer from 1874 to 1882. Served two terms in the Provo city council as an alderman. Elected lieutenant colonel of the first regiment of the Utah County militia under Colonel **Leonard J. Nuttall**. Was the president of the Utah Stake high priests quorum for many years. Ordained patriarch of the Utah Stake, which office he held until his death.
- Died on 16 June 1903 in Provo, Utah County, UT.

Letter reference: 18 June 1890

Davis, Albert Westley

- Born on 25 April 1841 in East Rochester, Columbiana County, OH, to Nathan Davis and Sarah Woolley.
- Married (1) **Melissa Jane Lambson**, the sister-in-law of **Joseph F.**, on 25 November 1865 in Salt Lake City. They were the parents of (1) Albert John Davis (1866–1939), (2) Melissa Elvira Davis (1868–1946), (3) **Edna May Davis**, (4) Nettie Maria Davis (1873–1956), (5) Westley Lambson Davis (1875–1957), (6) George A. Davis (1877–1939), (7) Sarah Woolley Davis (1880–1971), (8) Helen Davis (1883–1960), and (9) Ethel Davis (1888–1937).
- Married (2) Anne Lois Bacon (1862–1942) on 24 February 1884 in Salt Lake City. They were the parents of five children.
- Served as a counselor in the bishopric of the Salt Lake Seventeenth Ward. Served a mission to Hawai‘i, in the company of **Joseph F.**, from 1885 to 1887. Served as the first bishop of the Salt Lake Center Ward.
- Died on 3 December 1928 in Salt Lake City.

Letter reference: 26 January 1871

Davis, Edna May

- Born on 15 February 1871 in Salt Lake City to **Albert Westley Davis** and **Melissa Jane Lambson**.
- Was a niece of **Joseph F.** and his wives **Julina** and **Edna Lambson**.

- Sealed to **Joseph Fielding Smith**. No issue.
- Died on 14 November 1919 in Salt Lake City.

Letter reference: 23 February 1871

Davis, Ray Leroy

- Born on 8 November 1858 in Croydon, Wayne County, IA, to Morrill Lockwood Davis and Mary Thomas Kenner.
- Married **Lucy Smith** on 24 September 1879 in Salt Lake City. Lucy Smith was the daughter of **John Smith** and **Hellen Maria Fisher**. Ray Leroy and Lucy Smith Davis were the parents of three children.
- Was suspected by **Joseph F.** to have cooperated with government authorities in gathering evidence against him.
- Died on 2 February 1926 in Rigby, Jefferson County, ID.

Letter references: 18 March 1885, 13 April 1885, 6 November 1911

Dennis, William Henry

- Born on 4 February 1916 in Provo, Utah County, UT, to John Thomas Dennis and **Zina Christine Harris**. Was a grandson of **William Jasper Harris** and **Martha Ann**.
- Died on 16 December 1917 in Provo, Utah County, UT.

Letter reference: 27 March 1916

Dilworth, Mary Jane

- Born on 29 July 1831 in Uwchlan, Chester County, PA, to Caleb Dilworth and Eliza Wollerton.
- Married Francis Asbury Hammond (1822–1900) on 17 November 1848 in Salt Lake City. They were the parents of twelve children.
- Joined the Church with her family in 1854 and over the next years followed the Saints across the country. After reaching the Salt Lake Valley, became the first school teacher in Utah at the age of sixteen. Accompanied her husband in 1851 to the Sandwich Islands, where he served as a missionary. Worked there as a schoolteacher and raised their young, growing family. Also helped care for other missionaries, including young **Joseph F.** Was well beloved by the people there. After their return to Utah, served as the first Relief Society president in Huntsville, UT. Died shortly after the birth of her last child.
- Died on 6 June 1877 in Huntsville, Weber County, UT.

Letter reference: 28 January 1855

Doremus, Cora

- Born on 26 May 1870 in Salt Lake City to Abraham Fairbanks Doremus and **Pauline Richards**. Was a niece of **Joseph F.** and his wife **Sarah Ellen Richards**.
- Died on 24 February 1876 in Salt Lake City.

Letter reference: 23 February 1871

Dusenberry, Warren Newton

- Born on 1 November 1836 in Whitehaven, Luzerne County, PA, to Mahlon Dusenberry and Aurilla Coray.

- Married Adelaide Elizabeth Webb (1845–1940) on 18 June 1865 in Payson, Utah County, UT. They were the parents of one child.
- He and his brother, **Wilson Howard Dusenberry**, ran Dusenberry School, which later became Brigham Young Academy, in Provo. Was also president of the Timpanogos branch of the University of Deseret. Chosen as the first principal of Brigham Young Academy. After serving a few months as principal, furthered his studies of law. Served as mayor of Provo from 1892 to 1893.
- Died on 12 March 1915 in San Francisco, San Francisco County, CA.

Letter reference: 21 April 1871

Dusenberry, Wilson Howard

- Born on 7 April 1841 in Perry, Pike County, IL, to Mahlon Dusenberry and Aurilla Coray.
- Married (1) Harriet Virginia Knowlton Coray (1846–72) on 4 December 1864 in Provo, Utah County, UT. They were the parents of four children.
- Married (2) **Margaret Thompson Smoot**, daughter of **Abraham Owen Smoot** and **Almira Emily Hill**, on 25 November 1874 in Provo, Utah County, UT. They were the parents of eight children.
- Very active in religious, governmental, and educational affairs in Utah and was a high priest and a member of the high council. Was a schoolteacher in Utah County from 1863 to 1875 and Utah County superintendent of schools from 1874 to 1880. With his brother, **Warren Newton Dusenberry**, organized the Timpanogos branch of the University of Deseret in 1870. Was the first secretary and treasurer of Brigham Young Academy beginning in 1875. Was one of the original trustees chosen by **Brigham Young** to direct the affairs of Brigham Young Academy and was a member of the executive board. Was a member of Provo city council from 1872 to 1888. Was mayor of Provo for two terms and county clerk from 1875 to 1883. In 1880, 1882, and 1884, was a member of the state legislature and served as chairman of the House Committee on Education.
- Died on 20 March 1925 in Salt Lake City.

Letter references: 21 April 1871, 24 November 1874

E

Eldredge, Diana Tanner

- Born on 28 March 1837 in Warren Township, Marion County, IN, to Ira Eldredge and Nancy Black.
- Married **Abraham Owen Smoot** on 6 May 1855 in Salt Lake City. They were the parents of (1) **Abraham Owen Smoot Jr.**, (2) Nancy Diana Smoot (1858–1939), (3) Olive Smoot (1860–1943), (4) Elizabeth Smoot (1861–1932), (5) Ira Smoot (born and died 1863), (6) Lenora Ann Smoot (born and died 1864), (7) Joseph Edmund Smoot (1867–90), (8) Ella Deseret Smoot (1869–1916), (9) Arthur E. Smoot (1871–73), (10) Vilate Smoot (1873–1955), (11) Orson Parley Smoot (1876–1936), (12) Horace Alma Smoot (1880–1964), and (13) Wilford Smoot (1883–1953).
- Dedicated her life to taking care of her home and children. At the age of seventy-seven slipped on ice and broke her back; died a month later.
- Died on 29 January 1914 in Provo, Utah County, UT.

Letter references: 3 February 1857, 30 May 1861, 12 January 1862, 1 March 1862, 1864, 24 November 1874, 22 November 1905

Eldrege, Edmund or Edmond

- Born on 1 May 1835 in Warren Township, Marion County, IN, to Ira Eldrege and Nancy Black.
- Married Emma Staley (1839–63) in 1854 in Iowa. They were the parents of two children who died in Iowa in 1854.
- Went to Utah on 22 September 1847, but crossed the plains with the last mail before the Echo Canyon war in 1857. Most likely a schoolteacher in the Sugar House Ward in the late 1850s, although no occupation is provided in the 1860 census. He moved to Coalville in 1860. Served a mission to the British Isles in 1866.
- Died on 22 February 1924 in Coalville, Summit County, UT.
- Letter reference: 31 January 1856

Emery, Lillian

- Born on 4 August 1883 in Salt Lake City to George Rhodes Emery and Roselpha Wilding.
- Married **George Carlos Smith**, the son of **Joseph F.** and **Julina Lambson**, on 29 October 1902 in Salt Lake City. They were the parents of eleven children.
- Died on 18 February 1936 in Salt Lake City.

Letter reference: 20 March 1916

F

Farr, Sarah

- Born on 30 October 1849 in Salt Lake City to Lorin Farr and Nancy Bailey Chase. Was a second cousin to **Joseph F.** and **Martha Ann**.
- Married **John Henry Smith** on 20 October 1866 in Salt Lake City. They were the parents of (1) John Henry Smith Jr. (born and died 1868), (2) George Albert Smith (1870–1951), (3) **Lorin Farr Smith** (born and died 1872), (4) Don Carlos Smith (1874–1927), (5) Ezra Chase Smith (1876–1951), (6) Charles Warren Smith (born and died 1879), (7) Winslow Farr Smith (1881–1966), (8) Nathaniel Libby Smith (1883–1935), (9) Nancy Clarabell Smith (1886–1961), (10) Tirzah Priscille Smith (1888–1951), and (11) Elsie Louise Smith (1891–1926).
- Died on 4 February 1921 in Salt Lake City.

Letter reference: 3 May 1872

Ferguson, James

- Born on 23 February 1828 in Belfast, Antrim, Ireland, to Francis Ferguson and Mary Patrick.
- Married (1) Lucy Nutting (1825–95) on 12 March 1848 in San Francisco. They were the parents of six children.
- Married two other wives and had nine more children.
- Joined the Church in Ireland at the age of 14. Moved to Nauvoo in 1846 and there joined the Saints moving west. After joining the Mormon Battalion, was among the first to discover gold near San Francisco. Served as the first sheriff of Salt Lake County, as adjutant general in the Nauvoo Legion, and as bodyguard to Brigham Young. Served a mission to England and was well known as an actor and writer in Utah. Toward

the end of his life became an alcoholic and apparently died from excessive drinking. **Joseph F.** included him in a list of men whose lives stood as a warning against excessive drinking.

- Died on 30 August 1863 in Salt Lake City.

Letter reference: 14 June 1872

Fielding, Ann

- Born on 15 April 1799 in Honidon, Bedfordshire, England, to John Fielding and Rachel Ibbotson. Was the aunt of **Joseph F.** and **Martha Ann**.
- Married Rev. Timothy Richard Matthews (1795–1845) on 12 January 1821 in Colmworth, Bedfordshire, England. They were the parents of (1) Benjamin Fielding Matthews (1822–73), (2) Joseph Fielding Matthews (1824–1911), (3) Timothy Richard Matthews Jr. (1826–1910), (4) **Mercy Ann Matthews**, and (5) Hannah Rebecca Dolbeare Matthews (1835–1930).
- Died on 16 November 1884 in Beverley, Yorkshire, England.

Letter references: 7 September 1875, 18 May 1890

Fielding, Dorothy Rachel

- Born on 3 October 1857 in Sawtry, Huntingdonshire, England, to **John Osborn Fielding** and Elizabeth Ford. Was the cousin of **Joseph F.** and **Martha Ann**.
- Married George Smithers (1847–1926) on 19 November 1879 in Deptford, Kent, England. They were the parents of four children.
- In 1875 was living in London, where **Joseph F.** visited her during his mission there.
- Died on 8 August 1904 in Keston, Kent, England.

Letter reference: 7 September 1875

Fielding, Ellen

- Born on 9 February 1841 in Preston, Lancashire, England, to **Joseph Fielding** and **Hannah Greenwood**. Was a first cousin to **Joseph F.** and **Martha Ann**.
- Married **William Walton Burton** on 2 November 1862 in Salt Lake City. They were the parents of eight children.
- Came to the United States with her parents in 1843 and lived for four years in Nauvoo, IL, and one year at Winter Quarters, IA, before immigrating to Utah in 1848. Served as treasurer of the Relief Society in the Ogden Third Ward and as Relief Society visiting teacher. Encouraged the project of raising silkworms to produce silk, which she processed in a room in her home.
- Died on 8 March 1906 in Ogden, Weber County, UT.

Letter references: April 1856, 14 July 1856, 8 March 1906

Fielding, Hannah Alice

- Born on 20 May 1849 in Salt Lake City to **Joseph Fielding** and **Hannah Greenwood**. Was a first cousin to **Joseph F.** and **Martha Ann**.
- Died on 8 April 1857 in Salt Lake City.

Letter references: 31 January 1856, 3 May 1857

Fielding, Heber G.

- Born on 20 July 1843 in Nauvoo, Hancock, IL, to **Joseph Fielding** and **Hannah Greenwood**. Was a first cousin to **Joseph F.** and **Martha Ann**.
- Died on 15 April 1866, buried in Salt Lake City.

Letter reference: 22 June 1864

Fielding, James Ibbotson

- Born on 7 April 1793 in Halifax, Yorkshire, England, to John Fielding and Rachel Ibbotson. Was the uncle of **Joseph F.** and **Martha Ann**.
- Married Sarah Ann Fothergill (1792–death unknown) in 1818 in Halifax, Yorkshire, England. They were the parents of two children.
- Remained in the British Isles all his life. Was a religious reformer and minister.
- Died on 7 December 1877 in England.

Letter reference: 7 September 1875

Fielding, John

- Born on 4 July 1791 in Halifax, Yorkshire, England, to John Fielding and Rachel Ibbotson. Was the uncle of **Joseph F.** and **Martha Ann**.
- Married Ann Osborne (1795–1874) in 1815 in Halifax, Yorkshire, England. They were the parents of (1) Mary Ann Fielding (1814–16), (2) **Mary Fielding**, (3) Elizabeth Fielding (1820–49), (4) Sarah Ann Fielding (1823–death unknown), (5) **John Osborne Fielding**, (6) **James Ibbotson Fielding**, (7) Joseph Jabez Fielding (1836–66), (8) **Rachel Charlotte Fielding**, and (9) Frederick Benjamin Fielding (1839–40).
- Was a minister and preacher at a Wesleyan chapel in England.
- Died on 21 November 1839 in England.

Letter references: 7 September 1875, 29 November 1877

Fielding, John Osborne

- Born on 30 July 1825 in Gravely, Cambridge, England, to **John Fielding** and Ann Osborne. Was a cousin to **Joseph F.** and **Martha Ann**.
- Married Elizabeth Ford (1823–1920) in 1850 in Gravely, Cambridge, England. They were the parents of (1) Elizabeth Ann Fielding (1847–1920), (2) Mary Eliza Fielding (1849–death unknown), (3) John Josiah Fielding (1852–death unknown), (4) James Henry Fielding (1854–1926), (5) Frances Ford Fielding (1856–death unknown), (6) **Dorothy Rachel Fielding**, (7) George Fielding (1859–death unknown), and (8) Frederick Fielding (born and died 1862).
- Died on 28 February 1895.

Letter reference: 7 September 1875

Fielding, Joseph

- Born on 26 March 1797 in Honidon, Bedfordshire, England, to John Fielding and Rachel Ibbotson. Was the uncle of **Joseph F.** and **Martha Ann**.
- Married (1) **Hannah Greenwood** on 11 June 1838 in Preston, Lancashire, England. They were the parents of (1) **Rachel Fielding**, (2) **Ellen Fielding**, (3) Heber Fielding (1843–66), (4) Joseph Greenwood Fielding

(1846–66), (5) Hyrum Thomas Fielding (born and died 1847), (6) **Hannah Alice Fielding**, and (7) Sarah Ann Fielding (1851–1938).

- Married (2) **Mary Ann Peake** on 23 January 1846 in Nauvoo, Hancock County, IL. They were the parents of (1) Mary Ann Fielding (1846–1922), (2) John Hyrum Fielding (born and died 1847), and (3) **Josephine Fielding**.
- Served as mission president of the British Mission from 1838 to 1840. Was a farmer by occupation.
- Died on 19 December 1863 in Salt Lake City.

Letter references: 14 June 1857, 20 May 1858, 30 September 1862, Fall 1862, 22 June 1864

Fielding, Joseph Greenwood

- Born on 13 July 1845 in Nauvoo, Hancock, IL, to **Joseph Fielding** and **Hannah Greenwood**. Was a first cousin to **Joseph F.** and **Martha Ann**.
- Died on 6 March 1866 in Salt Lake City.

Letter reference: 22 June 1864

Fielding, Josephine

- Born on 4 January 1848 in Salt Lake City to **Joseph Fielding** and **Mary Ann Peake**. Was a first cousin to **Joseph F.** and **Martha Ann**.
- Married Orson Omer Heath (1846–1924) on 22 February 1868 in Salt Lake City. They were the parents of (1) Lyman Omer Heath (1862–73), (2) **Seraph Celestia Heath**, (3) Delos Robinson Heath (1876–1929), (4) Mary Ann Heath (1878–1958), (5) Emma Adella Heath (1880–82), (6) Pearl Josephine Heath (1883 or 1884–1965), (7) Luman Fielding Heath (1885–1931), (8) Donna Izora "Issoria" Heath (1887–1941), (9) Ethel Heath (born and died 1889), and (10) Jennie Rachel Heath (1890–91).
- Died on 13 December 1928 in Smithfield, Cache County, UT.

Letter reference: 14 May 1911

Fielding, Mary

- Born on 24 January 1817 in London, England, to **John Fielding** and Ann Osborne. Was a first cousin to **Joseph F.** and **Martha Ann**.
- Married William Lupton (1823–70) in 1843 in Liverpool, Lancashire, England. They were the parents of (1) **Ann Jane Lupton** and (2) William Lupton (1852–53).
- Immigrated to Utah with her daughter, Ann, aided by **Joseph F.**
- Died on 16 June 1886 in Draper, Salt Lake County, UT.

Letter references: 7 September 1875, 29 November 1877, 27 March 1883

Fielding, Mary

- Born on 21 July 1801 in Honidon, Bedfordshire, England, to John Fielding and Rachel Ibbotson. Was the mother of **Joseph F.** and **Martha Ann**.
- Married (1) **Hyrum Smith** on 24 December 1837 in Kirtland, Geauga County, OH. They were the parents of (1) **Joseph Fielding Smith** and (2) **Martha Ann Smith (Harris)**.
- Married (2) **Heber Chase Kimball** on 14 September 1844 in Nauvoo, Hancock County, IL. No issue.

- Received a good, liberal education as a young girl. Baptized by Elder Parley P. Pratt in 1836 in Upper Canada. Moved to Kirtland in 1837. Taught in both public and private schools, went through the terror of the mob threat in Far West and Nauvoo, helped establish the "Sister's Penny Subscription" for the purpose of buying nails and glass for the Nauvoo Temple. After the death of her husband, showed great faith in crossing the plains with her two small children and other members of her family. Arrived in the Great Salt Lake Valley in 1848 and settled on a farm in the Millcreek area, six miles south of Salt Lake City.
- Died on 21 September 1852 in Salt Lake City.

Letter references: 3 February 1857, 30 May 1861, 3 April 1863, 6 August 1870, 27 February 1874, 31 May 1874, 5 August 1874, 24 November 1874, 15 May 1875, 13 March 1883, 26 August 1883, 22 May 1890, 13 August 1891, 23 January 1905, 2 April 1905

Fielding, Mercy Rachel

- Born on 15 June 1807 in Honidon, Bedfordshire, England, to John Fielding and Rachel Ibbotson. Was a plural wife of **Hyrum Smith** and was a maternal aunt of **Joseph F.** and **Martha Ann**.
- Married (1) Robert Blashell Thompson (about 1807–41) on 4 June 1837 in Kirtland, Geauga County, OH. They were the parents of **Mary Jane Thompson**.
- Married, for time, (2) **Hyrum Smith** on 11 August 1843 in Nauvoo, Hancock County, IL. No issue.
- Served a mission to Canada in 1837 with her first husband, Robert. Helped establish and run a penny drive in which women gave one penny per week for the purpose of buying glass and nails for the Nauvoo Temple. Called as a temple worker in the Nauvoo Temple. Was a generous contributor to the Perpetual Emigrating Fund and gave liberally to assist missionaries and to build temples. Took care of **Martha Ann** for a short period of time following the death of her sister, **Martha Ann**'s mother, **Mary Fielding**. Was often referred to as "Aunt Thompson" by **Joseph F.** and **Martha Ann**.
- Died on 15 September 1893 in Salt Lake City.

Letter references: 1 November 1854, 9 June 1855, 14 July 1856, 3 February 1857, 14 June 1857, 25 July 1857, 20 December 1860, 12 March 1861, 29 January 1862, 22 June 1864, 1 December 1868, 21 June 1869, 24 December 1869, 3 January 1869 (1870), 18 January 1870, 29 March 1870, 3 (31) March 1870, 5 July 1870, 6 August 1870, 18 August 1870, 26 January 1871, 23 February 1871, 21 April 1871, 26 May 1871, 14 September 1871, 21 November 1871, 3 May 1872, 14 June 1872, 1 July 1873, 5 August 1874, 5 October 1874, 24 November 1874, 26 November 1875, 11 July 1876, 29 November 1877, 14 August 1878, 23 October 1878, 18 September 1881, 13 March 1883, 27 March 1883, 31 July 1883, 23 August 1884, May 1887, 22 May 1890

Fielding, Rachel

- Born on 27 June 1837 in Preston, Lincolnshire, England, to **Joseph Fielding** and **Hannah Greenwood**. Was a first cousin to **Joseph F.** and **Martha Ann**.
- Married **William Walton Burton** on 28 March 1856 in Salt Lake City. They were the parents of (1) **Isabella Burton**, (2) Hannah Burton (1859–1944), (3) Joseph Fielding Burton (1861–1924), (4) William Fielding Burton (1862–1923), (5) Rachel Burton (1865–1960), (6) Sarah Ellen Burton (1866–1965), (7) James Fielding Burton (1868–1924), (8) Mary Eliza Burton (1870–71), (9) Martha Burton (1872–1948), (10) Christopher Fielding Burton (1875–1965), (11) Robert Ibbotson Burton (1879–1967), (12) Vilate Pearl Burton (1881–1918), and (13) Julina May Burton (1884–88).
- Served as a Relief Society president for thirteen years and was a teacher in several organizations of the Church.
- Died on 20 July 1914 in Ogden, Weber County, UT.

Letter references: 31 January 1856, April 1856, 14 July 1856, 3 February 1857, 16 June 1899

Fisher, Elizabeth Jane

- Born on 9 February 1839 in Madison, Madison County, IL, to **Joseph Fisher** and Evaline McLean.
- Married Isaac Joseph Seely (1837–1902) on 17 May 1862 in Salt Lake City. They were the parents of eight children.
- Was a close childhood friend of both **Joseph F.** and **Martha Ann**. Wrote several letters to **Joseph F.** during his first mission to Hawai'i.
- Died on 12 December 1885 in East Millcreek, Salt Lake County, UT.

Letter references: 29 July 1856, 3 May 1857, 11 May 1857, 19 August 1857

Fisher, Hellen Maria

- Born on 20 September 1835 in Falston, Beaver County, PA, to **Joseph Fisher** and Evaline McLean.
- Married **John Smith**, half brother of **Joseph F.** and **Martha Ann**, on 25 December 1853 in Salt Lake City. They were the parents of (1) **Elizabeth Maria Smith**, (2) **Hyrum Fisher Smith**, (3) **Lucy Smith**, (4) Don Carlos Smith (1861–1937), (5) Alvin Fisher Smith (1867–1955), (6) Evaline Smith (1867–78), (7) John David Smith (1870–78), and (8) **Hellen Jerusha Smith**.
- Cared for **Martha Ann** for a time after the death of **Mary Fielding**.
- Died on 3 September 1907 in Salt Lake City.

Letter references: 9 June 1855, 31 January 1856, 18 February 1856, 29 July 1856, 2 October 1856, 17 December 1856, 5 April 1857, 3 May 1857, 14 June 1857, 12 June 1864, 27 October 1870, 18 March 1885, 13 April 1885, 16 January 1891

Fisher, James Madison

- Born on 22 July 1833 in Freedom, Beaver County, PA, to **Joseph Fisher** and Evaline McLean. Was the brother of **Hellen Maria Fisher**, wife of **John Smith** and sister-in-law to **Joseph F.** and **Martha Ann**.
- Married (1) **Edith Evelina Pierce** on 12 February 1857 in Brigham City, Box Elder County, UT. They were the parents of seven children.
- Married (2) Lydia Ann Ranck (1852–1934) on 31 May 1869 in Salt Lake City. They were the parents of seven children.
- Died on 1 January 1907 in East Millcreek, Salt Lake County, UT.

Letter references: 3 February 1857, 5 April 1857

Fisher, Joseph

- Born on 25 November 1801 in Ohio Township, Allegheny County, PA, to Jesse Fisher and Elizabeth Martin. Was the father-in-law of **John Smith**, who was a half brother of **Joseph F.** and **Martha Ann**.
- Married (1) **Evaline McLean** on 17 November 1831 in Freedom, Beaver County, PA. They were the parents of (1) **James Madison Fisher**, (2) **Hellen Maria Fisher**, (3) Curtis G. Fisher (1837–38), (4) **Elizabeth Jane Fisher**, (5) **Joseph Armstrong Fisher**, (6) Henry Charles Fisher (1844–1929), and (7) Rhuhamah Fisher (1847–75).
- Married (2) Catherine Field (1830–about 1877) on 19 November 1864 in Salt Lake City. They were the parents of one child.
- Was a high priest and a millwright and built several sawmills and gristmills in Utah.

- Died on 21 March 1867 in East Millcreek, Salt Lake County, UT.

Letter references: 17 December 1856, 25 July 1857

Fisher, Joseph Armstrong

- Born on 28 July 1841 in Nauvoo, Hancock, IL, to **Joseph Fisher** and Evaline McLean. His sister **Elizabeth Jane Fisher** was a childhood friend of **Joseph F.** and **Martha Ann**.
- Married (1) **Sarah Lovina Harris** in 1862 in Salt Lake City. They were the parents of eight children.
- Married (2) Mary Barr Carruth (1852–98) on 9 May 1870 in Salt Lake City. They were the parents of one child.
- Married (3) **Margaret May Merrill** in 1892 in Utah. They were the parents of four children.

Letter references: 17 December 1856, 25 July 1857, 27 February 1876

Freckleton, Jessie Lena

- Born on 22 September 1865 in Deseret, Millard County, UT, to John Orr Freckleton and Jessie Gardner.
- Married **William Jasper Harris Jr.**, the son of **William Jasper Harris** and **Martha Ann** and the nephew of **Joseph F.**, on 28 December 1882 in Salt Lake City. They were the parents of (1) William Ray Harris (1883–92), (2) Joseph Fielding Harris (1885–1936), (3) **John Ernest Harris**, (4) **Ruby Leona Harris**, (5) Delia Jessie Harris (born and died 1890), (6) baby girl Harris (born and died 1891), (7) **Wilford Leroy Harris**, (8) Emily Harris (born and died 1894), (9) **Bessie Irene Harris**, (10) **Reuel Smith Harris**, (11) Ada Fern Harris (1899–1963), (12) Viola Myrtle Harris (1901–21), (13) Alice Bernice Harris (1903–77), and (14) Legrande Smith Harris (1910–77).
- Died on 8 August 1945 in Provo, Utah County, UT.

Letter references: May 1887, 26 December 1911

Freeman, William Hamblin

- Born on 25 December 1833 in Wageburgh, Calloway County, KY, to John Freeman and Nancy Beal Smoot. Was a nephew of **Abraham Owen Smoot**.
- Married (1) Angeline Ameret Stocking (1834–1904) on 30 November 1854 in Salt Lake City. They were the parents of twelve children.
- Married (2) Sarah Butterfield (1849–1915) on 9 February 1867 in Salt Lake City. They were the parents of eleven children.
- Was a high priest. Served as counselor to James Crane in the Herriman Utah Branch. Served as senior president of the Quorum of the Seventy. Served a mission to southern Utah in 1855. Helped protect Echo Canyon against the Utah Expedition and was a member of the Utah militia. Also served as a constable, deputy sheriff, and justice of the peace.
- Died on 9 April 1912 in Herriman, Salt Lake County, UT.

Letter reference: 28 July 1860

Fuller, Sophina Alcesta

- Born on 5 May 1843 in Nashville, Lee County, IA, to Amos Botsford Fuller and Esther J. Smith. Was a second cousin to **Joseph F.** and **Martha Ann**.
- Married (1) James Byrd (1837–1902) on 25 March 1857 and later divorced. No issue.

- Married (2) **George Washington Gee II** on 4 May 1862 in Salt Lake City. They were the parents of ten children.
- Died on 26 December 1930 in Salt Lake City.

Letter reference: 5 August 1874

Furner, Merilla

- Born on 14 February 1895 in Provo, Utah County, UT, to George Thomas Furner and **Zina Christine Harris**. Was a granddaughter of **William Jasper Harris** and **Martha Ann**.
- Married Thomas Wilson Worthington (1879–1926) on 8 January 1919 in Salt Lake City. They were the parents of five children.
- Died on 12 October 1967 in Provo, Utah County, UT.

Letter reference: 20 February 1895

Furner, Sarah Rachel

- Born on 17 January 1902 in Mammoth, Juab, UT, to George Thomas Furner and **Zina Christine Harris**. Was a granddaughter of **Martha Ann**.
- Married Don Elmer Clark (1896–1975) on 22 June 1921 in Salt Lake City. They were the parents of two children.
- Was also the mother of Ivy Bruce Thompson (dates unknown), father unknown.
- Died on 10 February 1977 and was buried in Provo, Utah County, UT.

Letter reference: 3 March 1913

G

Gee, George Washington, II

- Born on 9 October 1841 in Ambrosia, Lee County, IA, to George Washington Gee and **Mary Jane Smith**. Was a second cousin to **Joseph F.** and **Martha Ann**.
- Married (1) **Sophina Alcesta Fuller** on 4 May 1862 in Salt Lake City. They were the parents of nine children.
- Married (2) Ursula Bandli (1858–1957) on 2 March 1877 in St. George, Washington County, UT. They were the parents of six children.
- Served a mission to the British Isles and Scandinavia from 1865 to 1867. Ordained a Seventy before departing on his mission. Served for fifty years as a member of the Forty-Fifth Quorum of the Seventy, which became a stake calling in 1883 and lasted at the stake level until 1986, acting as secretary, president, and senior president during his service. Served as director of the Provo Cooperative Store, deputy county assessor, member of the board of education, and city water master. Active in the development of the local irrigation system and helped build the Provo Woolen Mills.
- Died on 17 September 1919 in Provo, Utah County, UT.

Letter references: 25 July 1857, 29 January 1861, 5 August 1874, 7 September 1874 (first letter), 24 November 1874, 15 May 1875

Gibbs, John Henry

- Born on 28 July 1853 in St. Mary's Haverfordwest, Pembrook, Wales, to George Duggan Gibbs and Ellen Phillips.
- Married Loisa Shelton (1855–1927) on 2 November 1874 in Salt Lake City. They were the parents of three children.
- Was serving a mission in Tennessee when killed by a mob that attacked the home of James Conder.
- Died on 10 August 1884 in Cane Creek, Lewis County, TN.

Letter reference: 15 August 1884

Gibson, Walter Murray

- Born in 1822 (exact date unknown) to John Gibson and Lucy.
- Married Rachel Margaret Lewis (1824–44). They were the parents of three children.
- Was a sailor in the Caribbean before moving to New York. Traveled to Utah Territory in 1859 to learn more about the Church. After joining the Church, was sent on a mission to the eastern states. Received a second call to preach the gospel in the East Indies and the Malay Islands in 1861. En route, stopped in the Sandwich Islands and decided to establish a colony there. Used Church funds to buy property in his own name on the island of Lāna'i, and, at the same time, began using his authority as a missionary to usurp power from the island Saints. After a Church investigation regarding accusations of preaching false doctrine and embezzlement, was excommunicated from the Church. Continued to live in Hawai'i, where he ran for and won a seat in the House of Representatives in 1878. Published several newspapers in Hawai'i. In 1882 appointed Minister of Foreign Affairs. In 1886 King Kalakaua appointed him Prime Minister of the Kingdom of Hawai'i. After the government collapsed in 1887, escaped to California, where he died a pauper.
- Died on 21 January 1888 in San Francisco, San Francisco County, CA.

Letter reference: 22 June 1864

Grant, Jedediah Morgan

- Born on 21 February 1816 in Union, Madison County, NY, to Joshua Grant and Athalia Howard.
- Married seven wives and had thirteen children. Among these children was Heber J. Grant, who would become the seventh President of the Church.
- Joined the Church at age 17 in 1833 and was a member of Zion's Camp. Served as a missionary to the eastern states in the 1830s. Called as the President of the Seventy in 1845 and helped to organize the Saint's trek west. Was the first mayor of Salt Lake City, serving from 1851 to death. Served as second counselor in the First Presidency from 1854 to 1856.
- Was an influential speaker during the Reformation of 1855–56.
- Died on 1 December 1856 in Salt Lake City.

Letter reference: 17 December 1856

Gray, Jennie Isabell

- Born on 14 February 1871 near Toronto, Ontario, Canada, to Andrew Scott Gray and **Mary Elizabeth Russell**. **Joseph F.** mentions the birth of her and her twin sister, **Sarah Ellen Russell Gray**, in a letter to **Martha Ann**.
- Married Jacob Thomas Tanner (1871–1952) on 14 February 1895 in Salt Lake City. They were the parents of one child.

- Died on 21 November 1905 in Idaho Falls, Bingham County, ID.

Letter reference: 23 February 1871

Gray, Sarah Ellen Russell

- Born on 14 February 1871 near Toronto, Ontario, Canada, to Andrew Scott Gray and **Mary Elizabeth Russell**. **Joseph F.** mentions the birth of her and her twin sister, **Jennie Isabell Gray**, in a letter to **Martha Ann**.
- Died on 3 May 1885 in Salt Lake City.

Letter reference: 23 February 1871

Greenleaf, Silas C.

- Murdered by **Joseph Holladay** in the Salt Lake City courthouse while **William Jasper Harris** was on police duty in Salt Lake City in 1863. Was not a member of the Church. No other information known.

Letter reference: 22 February 1863

Greenwell, Ambrose John

- Born about 1890 in Salt Lake City.
- Married **Zina Smith**, the daughter of **Joseph F.** and **Edna Lambson**, on 12 December 1910 in Salt Lake City. They were the parents of one child.
- Died in 1915.

Letter reference: 17 February 1915

Greenwood, Hannah

- Born on 4 September 1818 in Bolton, Lancashire, England, to Thomas Greenwood and Ellen Haslam. Was the aunt of **Joseph F.** and **Martha Ann**.
- Married **Joseph Fielding** on 11 June 1838 in Preston, Lancashire, England. They were the parents of (1) **Rachel Fielding**, (2) **Ellen Fielding**, (3) **Heber G. Fielding**, (4) **Joseph Greenwood Fielding**, (5) Hyrum Thomas Fielding (born and died 1847), (6) **Hannah Alice Fielding**, and (7) Sarah Ann Fielding (1851–1938).
- Was a homemaker.
- Died on 9 September 1877 in Ogden, Weber County, UT.

Letter references: 14 July 1856, 3 May 1857, 14 June 1857, 20 December 1860, 18 January 1870, 21 April 1871, 18 January 1873

Griffin, Albert Bailey

- Born on 28 February 1809 in Essex, Chittenden County, VT, to Samuel Griffin and Sylvia Bradley. Was the father-in-law to **Sarah Smith**, the half sister of **Joseph F.** and **Martha Ann**.
- Married (1) **Abigail Varney** before 1830. They were the parents of (1) Sidney Griffin (1826–30), (2) Albert Bailey Griffin Jr. (born and died 1830), and (3) **Charles Emerson Griffin**.
- Married (2) Mary Olive Harris (about 1813–death unknown) in about 1834. No issue.
- Married (3) **Laura Emily Beebe** on 13 November 1853 in Salt Lake City. They were the parents of seven children.

- Participated in the Black Hawk War as a sergeant. Served as a member of the Quorum of the Seventy. Served as a counselor in a bishopric from 1865 to 1877.
- Died on 11 February 1896 in Kanarra, Iron County, UT.

Letter references: 18 February 1856, 30 May 1861

Griffin, Alice Lovina

- Born on 21 March 1856 in Sugar House, Salt Lake County, UT, to **Charles Emerson Griffin** and **Sarah Smith**. Was a niece of **Joseph F.** and **Martha Ann**.
- Married Jared Riley Porter (1848–1938) on 1 January 1872 in Coalville, Summit County, UT. They were the parents of (1) Charles Riley Porter (1872–73), (2) Sarah Inez Porter (1874–1953), (3) Earnest Porter (born and died 1876), (4) Joseph Jared Porter (1877–1951), (5) Emily Cornelia Porter (1880–1922), (6) Hyrum Adelbert Porter (1882–1946), (7) Edith Porter (1884–1914), (8) Alice Hannah Porter (1886–1966), (9) Adelia Porter (1888–1918), (10) Parley Pratt Porter (1890–1955), (11) Wilford Emerson Porter (1892–1977), (12) Leland Porter (1894–1965), and (13) Roland Porter (1896–1980).
- Died on 26 December 1936 in Escalante, Garfield County, UT.

Letter references: April 1856, 29 July 1856, 17 December 1856, 3 July 1857, 20 May 1858, 23 February 1871, 9 February 1875

Griffin, Charles Emerson

- Born on 10 May 1836 in Essex, Chittenden County, VT, to **Albert Bailey Griffin** and **Abigail Varney**. Was the brother-in-law of **Joseph F.** and **Martha Ann**. Nickname was "Charlie."
- Married (1) **Sarah Smith** on 16 January 1854 in Salt Lake City. They were the parents of (1) Charles Emerson Griffin Jr. (born and died 1855), (2) **Alice Lovina Griffin**, (3) Sarah Griffin (born and died 1858), (4) Joseph Emerson Griffin (1859–1929), (5) **Ernest Adelbert Griffin**, (6) **Hannah Griffin**, (7) John Marvin Griffin (1868–69), (8) Martha Ann Griffin (born and died 1870), (9) Hyrum Griffin (born and died 1871), (9) Abigail Griffin (born and died 1873), and (10) Helen Jerusha Griffin (1876–77).
- Married two other wives and had nine more children.
- Called to serve a mission to the British Isles in 1875.
- Died on 18 July 1900 in Coyote, Garfield County, UT.

Letter references: 9 June 1855, 18 February 1856, 14 July 1856, 29 July 1856, 17 December 1856, 14 June 1857, 20 December 1860, 30 May 1861, 29 January 1862, 30 September 1862, 12 June 1864, 22 June 1864, 23 February 1871, 6 November 1874, 9 February 1875, 26 July 1900

Griffin, Ernest Adelbert

- Born on 3 March 1863 in Salt Lake City to **Charles Emerson Griffin** and **Sarah Smith**. Was a nephew of **Joseph F.** and **Martha Ann**.
- Married (1) Christiana Adams (1868–87) on 28 October 1885 in St. George, Washington County, UT. No issue.
- Married (2) Amanda Ellen Riggs (1871–1936) on 21 March 1888 in St. George. They were the parents of (1) Sarah Rosalie Griffin (1889–1960), (2) Ella May Griffin (1891–1964), (3) **Vaunie Griffin**, (4) Ernest Dougal Griffin (born and died 1898), (5) Mildred Griffin (1900–1966), (6) Harold Griffin (1902–3), (7) Albern Smith Griffin (1904–73), (8) Eva Griffin (1907–77), (9) Nelly Flay Griffin (1909–94), and (10) Edith Griffin (1913–79).
- Served a mission to the southern states from 1892 to 1895 and was called to be president of the North Carolina Conference during a portion of that time. Was a farmer and stock grower.

- Died on 12 August 1944 in Escalante, Garfield County, UT.

Letter references: 26 July 1900, 20 August 1912

Griffin, Vaunie

- Born on 28 January 1896 in Escalante, Garfield County, UT, to **Ernest Adelbert Griffin** and **Amanda Ellen Riggs**. Was the great-niece of **Joseph F.** and **Martha Ann**.
- Married William Linford Jolley (1900–1979) on 7 January 1921 in Junction, Piute County, UT. No issue.
- Died on 18 November 1927.

Letter reference: 20 August 1912

Grinnels, Hannah

- Born about 1784 in Connecticut.
- Helped **Hyrum Smith** and his first wife, Jerusha Barden, as a housekeeper and caretaker. Took care of **Sarah**, their youngest, when Jerusha died. Stayed on to help with the family after **Hyrum Smith** married **Mary Fielding**. Known to the children as "Aunty." After the martyrdom of **Hyrum** and **Joseph Smith**, migrated west with the family and helped to care for the orphaned children after **Mary Fielding**'s death in 1852.
- Died in 1853 or 1854.

Letter reference: 14 July 1856

H

Hardy, Leonard Wilford

- Born on 31 December 1805 in Bradford, Essex County, MA, to Simon Hardy and Rhoda Hardy.
- Married (1) Elizabeth Harriman Nichols (1797–1872) on 22 October 1826 in Bradford. They were the parents of one child.
- Married four other wives and had sixteen other children.
- Was a merchant and stock raiser. Was a high priest and served a mission to England from 1844 to 1845 and to the eastern United States from 1869 to 1870. Presided over the Manchester Conference. Was bishop of the Salt Lake City Twelfth Ward from 1851 to 1876. Was a member of the Territorial legislature; in addition, was captain of police and a city councilman. Was captain of the Nauvoo Legion Company B.
- Died on 31 July 1884 in Salt Lake City.

Letter reference: 1 August 1884

Harris, Alva Robert

- Born on 28 December 1893 in Provo, Utah County, UT, to **Joseph Albert Harris** and **Johanna Patten**. Was a grandson of **William Jasper Harris** and **Martha Ann**.
- Married (1) Louisa A. Herman (1894–1924) on 11 October 1913 in Farmington, Davis County, UT. They were the parents of (1) Alton Robert Harris (1915–2000), (2) **Virginia Louise Harris**, (3) Betty Rose Harris (1917–98), and (4) Howard Herman Harris (1919–95).
- Married two other wives and had three more children.

- Died on 19 July 1967 in Salt Lake City.

Letter reference: 27 March 1916

Harris, Artimissa Ann

- Born on 3 January 1835 in Carrollton, Morgan County, IL, to Zachariah Harris and **Almira Emily Hill**. Was the sister-in-law of **Martha Ann**. Nickname was "Artie." After the death of Zachariah Harris, her mother married **Abraham Owen Smoot**.
- Married **Richard Dunwell Maxfield** on 31 October 1854 in Salt Lake City. They were the parents of eight children.
- Died on 3 June 1885 in Salt Lake City.

Letter reference: 20 December 1860

Harris, Bessie Irene

- Born on 27 May 1895 in Eureka, Juab County, UT, to **William Jasper Harris Jr.** and **Jessie Lena Freckleton**. Was a granddaughter of **Martha Ann**.
- Married Herbert Hans Thompson (1880–1967) on 12 February 1919 in Salt Lake City. They were the parents of two children.
- Died on 11 August 1981 in Blackfoot, Bingham County, ID.

Letter reference: 3 March 1913

Harris, Delia Jessie

- Born on 20 October 1890 in Provo, Utah County, UT, to **William Jasper Harris Jr.** and **Jessie Lena Freckleton**. Was a granddaughter of **Martha Ann**.
- Died on 26 December 1890 in Provo, Utah County, UT.

Letter reference: 15 January 1891

Harris, Florence Ann

- Born on 29 February 1916 in Salt Lake City to **Sterling Patten Harris** and Anne Lloyd. Was a great-granddaughter of **Martha Ann**.
- Married Jack Fowler Heath (1941–64) on 16 October 1936 in Salt Lake City. No issue.
- Died on 20 February 1975 in Douglas, Trinity County, CA.

Letter reference: 27 March 1916

Harris, Frank Ernest

- Born on 7 March 1883 in Provo, Utah County, UT, to **Joseph Albert Harris** and **Johanna Patten**. Was a grandson of **Martha Ann**. Also known as Ernest Franklin Harris.
- Married Maude MacBeth (1885–1975) on 13 January 1906 in Provo, Utah County, UT. They were the parents of three children.
- Died on 20 June 1951.

Letter reference: May 1887

Harris, Franklin Hill

- Born on 11 September 1867 in Salt Lake City to **William Jasper Harris** and **Martha Ann**. Was a nephew of **Joseph F.** Nicknames were "Frank" and "Frankie."
- Married **Josephine Parkes Robinson** on 26 January 1898 in Salt Lake City. They were the parents of five children.
- Worked as a machine miner in the mines at Mammoth. Was also a railroad worker and farmer.
- Died on 5 February 1947 in Provo, Utah County, UT.

Letter references: 31 May 1874, 7 September 1874 (first letter), 15 May 1875, 1 July 1881, 18 March 1885, 11 February 1887, May 1887, 2 May 1890, 4 August 1890, 16 January 1891, 1 February 1891, 11 February 1891, 17 June 1891, 13 August 1891, 18 November 1896, 6 May 1909, 26 December 1911, 3 March 1913, 7 July 1914, 17 July 1915, 20 March 1916, 27 March 1916, 13 December 1916

Harris, Hyrum Smith

- Born on 15 August 1863 in Salt Lake City to **William Jasper Harris** and **Martha Ann**.
- Married **Delia Sarah Rebekah Twede** on 9 April 1890 in Manti, Sanpete County, UT. They were the parents of (1) **Mercy Rachel Harris** and (2) Julina Harris (1909–91), an adopted daughter.
- Served a mission to Hawai'i from October 1884 to November 1887.
- Died on 24 February 1924.

Letter references: 12 June 1864, 22 June 1864, 1864, 5 July 1870, 21 April 1871, 31 May 1874, 7 September 1874 (first letter), 24 November 1874, 26 November 1875, 18 March 1885, 13 April 1885, 22 May 1885, 30 November 1885, 11 March 1887, May 1887, 17 April 1890, 29 April 1890, 2 May 1890, 16 January 1891, 1 February 1891, 11 February 1891, 17 June 1891, 13 August 1891, 10 April 1907, 26 December 1911, 17 July 1915, 13 December 1916

Harris, John Ernest

- Born on 19 April 1886 in Provo, Utah County, UT, to **William Jasper Harris Jr.** and **Jessie Lena Freckleton**. Was a grandson of **Martha Ann**. See note 9 of letter from **Martha Ann** to **Joseph F.**, ca. May–June 1887.
- Married (1) Ellen Pittman (1888–1982) on 5 September 1906 in Salt Lake City. They were the parents of four children.
- Married (2) Leah Moore (dates unknown). No issue.
- Died on 13 February 1964 in Provo, Utah County, UT.

Letter reference: May 1887

Harris, John Fielding

- Born on 28 June 1872 in Provo, Utah County, UT, to **William Jasper Harris** and **Martha Ann**. Was a nephew of **Joseph F.** Nickname was "Joney."
- Married (1) Lydia Ann Boyle (1876–1941) on 9 June 1897 in Salt Lake City. They were the parents of six children.
- Married (2) Evelyn Betsey Christensen (1875–1967) on 18 October 1941. No issue.
- Died on 28 November 1946 in Salt Lake City.

Letter references: 31 May 1874, 20 June 1874, 15 August 1874, 7 September 1874 (first letter), 5 October 1874, 18 March 1885, 2 May 1890, 1 February 1891, 11 February 1891, 17 June 1891, 16 May 1893, 3 March 1913, 13 December 1916

Harris, Joseph Albert

- Born on 19 August 1861 in Provo, Utah County, UT, to **William Jasper Harris** and **Martha Ann**. Nickname was "Jody" or "Jodie."
- Married Johanna Patten (1860–1948) on 13 September 1878 in Salt Lake City. They were the parents of (1) **Joseph Albert Harris Jr.**, (2) Joanna Harris (born and died 1880), (3) **Frank Ernest Harris**, (4) **Sterling Patten Harris**, (5) Maudie Harris (1886–88), (6) Zella Harris (1888–1973), (7) Emily Harris (1891–1979), and (8) **Alva Robert Harris**.
- Died on 28 May 1911 in Provo, Utah County, UT.

Letter references: 8 December 1861, 30 September 1862, Fall 1862, 22 February 1863, 22 June 1864, 1864, 21 June 1869, 21 April 1871, 15 August 1874, 7 September 1874 (first letter), 5 October 1874, 24 November 1874, 23 October 1878, 4 June 1880, 28 July 1881, 31 July 1883, 18 March 1885, 13 April 1885, 22 May 1885, 30 November 1885, May 1887, 1 February 1891, 11 February 1891, 17 June 1891, 3 January 1906, 24 December 1910, 3 April 1911, 29 May 1911

Harris, Joseph Albert, Jr.

- Born on 9 August 1879 in Provo, Utah County, UT, to **Joseph Albert Harris** and **Johanna Patten**. Was a grandson of **Martha Ann**.
- Married Mary Jane Simmons (1881–1967) on 24 January 1900 in Mammoth, Juab County, UT. They were the parents of eight children.
- Died on 10 September 1949 in Salt Lake City.

Letter references: 4 June 1880, May 1887

Harris, Lucy Smith

- Born on 10 March 1870 in Provo, Utah County, UT, to **William Jasper Harris** and **Martha Ann**. Was a niece of **Joseph F.**
- Married John or Jonathan Simmons (1867–1916) on 15 June 1898 in Salt Lake City. They were the parents of (1) **Edna Mae Simmons**, (2) **John Arthur Simmons**, and (3) Lucy Simmons (born and died 1902).
- Died on 26 July 1902 or 1903. Lucy apparently had a heart attack as she went into labor with her third child. Neither Lucy nor the baby survived. **Martha Ann**'s granddaughter **Mary Elizabeth Corbett** died on the same day. A discrepancy exists for the year they died: Joseph F. letter indicates 1902; genealogical records indicate 1903.

Letter references: 18 August 1870, 26 January 1871, 14 September 1871, 21 November 1871, 3 May 1872, 4 June 1880, 11 February 1887, 7 June 1891, 17 June 1891, 13 August 1891, 16 May 1893, 7 March 1894, 23 July 1902, 23 January 1905, 2 April 1905, 8 March 1907, 10 April 1907, 23 December 1912, 3 March 1913

Harris, Martha Ann

- See "**Smith, Martha Ann**."

Harris, Martha Artimissa

- Born on 27 June 1879 in Provo, Utah County, UT, to **William Jasper Harris** and **Martha Ann**. Was a niece of **Joseph F.** Middle name was also spelled "Artemissa" and "Artemesia."

- Married **Harry Walter Startup** on 16 September 1903 in Salt Lake City. They were the parents of (1) **Naomi Startup**, (2) LaRue Startup (1907–90), (3) Norell Startup (1909–97), (4) **Elbert Harris Startup**, (5) Harry Walter Startup Jr., (1918–2008) and (6) Maurine Startup (1920–90).
- Died on 12 August 1965 in Provo, Utah County, UT.

Letter references: 13 August 1891, 25 October 1898, 2 April 1901, 22 November 1905, 8 March 1907, 26 December 1911, 3 March 1913, 7 July 1914, 9 July 1914, 23 July 1914, 14 November 1916

Harris, Mary Emily

- Born on 23 October 1865 in Salt Lake City to **William Jasper Harris** and **Martha Ann**. Was a niece of **Joseph F.**
- Married **Walter Sutton Corbett** on 12 November 1884 in Logan, Cache County, UT. They were the parents of (1) **Walter Harris Corbett**, (2) **Joseph Smith Corbett**, (3) **William Moroni Corbett**, (4) **Hyrum Smith Corbett**, (5) **Mary Elizabeth Corbett**, (6) Franklin Nephi Corbett (1893–95), (7) Martha Corbett (1895–1904), (8) John Alvin Corbett (1897–1962), (9) **Lucy Jane Corbett**, (10) Pearson Harris Corbett (1900–1964), (11) Don Cecil Corbett (1903–71), and (12) George Leroy Corbett (1905–39).
- Died on 25 November 1947 in Provo, Utah County, UT.

Letter references: 31 May 1874, 15 July 1874, 31 March 1875, 1 July 1881, 26 January 1885, 18 March 1885, 13 April 1885, 22 May 1885, [1 November] 1895, 11 February 1887, 11 March 1887, May 1887, 1 February 1891, 9 February 1891, 2 April 1901, 26 July 1902, 8 March 1907

Harris, Mercy Ann

- Born on 30 March 1874 in Provo, Utah County, UT, to **William Jasper Harris** and **Martha Ann**. Was a niece of **Joseph F.**
- Married John Thomas Dennis (1866–1929) on 25 June 1903 in Salem, Utah County, UT. They were the parents of two children.
- Died on 23 January 1905 in Provo, Utah County, UT.

Letter references: 31 May 1874, 20 June 1874, 15 August 1874, 1 July 1881, 13 October 1898, 5 October 1899, 26 January 1901, 23 January 1905, 2 April 1905, 8 March 1907

Harris, Mercy Rachel

- Born on 14 March 1891 in Provo, Utah County, UT, to **Hyrum Smith Harris** and **Delia Sarah Rebekah Twede**. Was a granddaughter of **Martha Ann**.
- Died on 29 July 1891 in Provo, Utah County, UT.

Letter references: 17 June 1891, 13 August 1891

Harris, Reuel Smith

- Born on 29 October 1897 in Robinson, Juab County, UT, to **William Jasper Harris Jr.** and **Jessie Lena Freckleton**. Was a grandson of **Martha Ann**.
- Married **Alma Margaret Harker** on 3 September 1923 in Salt Lake City. They were the parents of five children.
- Died on 2 December 1979 in Salt Lake City.

Letter reference: 13 March 1913

Harris, Ruth

- Born on 20 March 1916 in Helper, Carbon County, UT, to **Wilford Leroy Harris** and Margery Ellen Sumner. Was a great-granddaughter of **Martha Ann**.
- Married Harold Wilbur Sowers (1915–45) on 25 April 1936. No issue.
- Died on 16 October 1981 in San Bernardino, San Bernardino County, CA.

Letter reference: 27 March 1916

Harris, Sarah Lovina

- Born on 8 December 1882 in Provo, Utah County, UT, to **William Jasper Harris** and **Martha Ann**.
- Married Roy Passey (1885–1968) on 26 March 1907 in Salt Lake City. They were the parents of (1) **Lee Roy Passey**, (2) **Verna Passey**, (3) **Alene Passey**, (4) Carlos Passey (born and died 1913), (4) Richard Smith Passey (1914–99), (5) Katherine Passey (1917–97), (6) Margaret June Passey (1920–83), (7) Dorothy Passey (1922–2002), and (8) Shirley Marilyn Passey (1924–97).
- Died on 21 April 1961 in Provo, Utah County, UT.

Letter references: 12 May 1897, 13 October 1898, 6 September 1899, 4 October 1899, 5 October 1899, 8 March 1907, 26 December 1911, 3 March 1913, 7 July 1914, 9 July 1914

Harris, Sterling Patten

- Born on 28 September 1884 in Provo, Utah County, UT, to **Joseph Albert Harris** and **Johanna Patten**. Was a grandson of **Martha Ann**.
- Married (1) Anna Lloyd (1885–1938) on 22 August 1903 in Spanish Fork, Utah County, UT. They were the parents of eight children.
- Married (2) Velma Gordon (1888–1986) on 19 January 1944 in Provo, Utah County, UT. No issue.
- Died on 7 April 1946 in Salt Lake City.

Letter reference: 27 March 1916

Harris, Virginia Louise

- Born on 10 March 1916 in Salt Lake City to Alva Robert Harris and Anna Louise Herman. Was a great-granddaughter of **Martha Ann**.
- Married (1) Hugh McClellan Clayson (1913–93) on 27 April 1938. No issue.
- Married (2) Owen Jensen Gumundson (1908–78) on 22 June 1946 in Ely, NV. No issue.
- Died on 15 October 1988 in Salt Lake City.

Letter reference: 27 March 1916

Harris, Wilford Leroy

- Born on 17 August 1892 in Provo, Utah County, UT, to **William Jasper Harris Jr.** and **Jessie Lena Freckleton**. Was a grandson of **Martha Ann**.
- Married Margery Ellen Sumner (1888–1963) on 18 May 1914 in Provo, Utah County, UT.
- Died on 15 March 1964 in Provo, Utah County, UT.

Letter references: 3 March 1913, 27 March 1916

Harris, William Jasper

- Born on 25 October 1836 in Geneva, Morgan County, IL, to Zachariah Harris and **Almira Emily Hill**. Was a brother-in-law of **Joseph F.** Youth nicknames were "Bill" and "Billy."
- Married **Martha Ann**, the daughter of **Hyrum Smith** and **Mary Fielding**, on 21 April 1857 in Salt Lake City. They were the parents of (1) **William Jasper Harris Jr.**, (2) **Joseph Albert Harris**, (3) **Hyrum Smith Harris**, (4) **Mary Emily Harris**, (5) **Franklin Hill Harris**, (6) **Lucy Smith Harris**, (7) **John Fielding Harris**, (8) **Mercy Ann Harris**, (9) **Zina Christine Harris**, (10) **Martha Artimissa Harris**, and (11) **Sarah Lovina Harris**.
- Walked across the plains at age ten. Served a mission to England from 1857 to 1858. Heber C. Kimball married him and **Martha Ann** two days before he left on his mission. After his mission, he and his wife lived for two years with his mother and stepfather, **Abraham Owen Smoot**. Moved with his family to Salt Lake City, where he was employed in freighting goods with team and wagon. Served as a policeman in Salt Lake City for eight years and was a first lieutenant during the Black Hawk War. In 1867, the Harris family moved to Provo, Utah County, UT. Called to serve as a personal bodyguard to **Brigham Young**. Remained in Provo for the duration of his life. Enjoyed prospecting and mining but was never prosperous at it.
- Died tragically on 24 April 1909 in Provo, Utah County, UT, when he was hit by a team of runaway horses.

Letter references: 3 February 1857, 3 May 1857, 14 June 1857, [1857?], 28 July 1860, 26 September 1860, 15 December 1860, 20 December 1860, 29 January 1861, 12 March 1861, Spring 1861, 30 May 1861, 8 December 1861, 12 January 1862, 29 January 1862, 1 March 1862, 30 September 1862, Fall 1862, 22 February 1863, 23 (24) February 1863, 3 April 1863, 12 June 1864, 22 June 1864, 1864, 1 December 1868, 21 June 1869, 13 July 1869, 3 January 1869 (1870), 6 August 1870, 18 August 1870, 26 January 1871, 21 April 1871, 21 November 1871, 12 December 1871, 3 May 1872, 17 May 1872, 14 June 1872, 18 January 1873, 28 April 1873, 1 July 1873, 10 November 1873, 31 May 1874, 20 June 1874, 15 July 1874, 5 August 1874, 15 August 1874, 7 September 1874 (first letter), 5 October 1874, 6 November 1874, 24 November 1874, 8 December 1874, 9 February 1875, 15 May 1875, 26 November 1875, 25 August 1877, 29 November 1877, 22 April 1878, 23 October 1878, 22 April 1879, 1 July 1881, 28 July 1881, 12 November 1883, 18 March 1885, 22 May 1885, 11 February 1887, 11 March 1887, May 1887, 17 April 1890, 2 May 1890, 18 May 1890, 16 January 1891, 1 February 1891, 28 January 1895, 23 March 1896, 18 November 1896, 12 May 1897, 25 October 1898, 26 January 1901, 23 December 1901, 23 December 1904, 2 April 1905, 3 January 1906, 10 April 1907, 24 April 1909, 6 May 1909, 24 May 1909

Harris, William Jasper, Jr.

- Born on 4 August 1859 in Salt Lake City to **William Jasper Harris** and **Martha Ann**. Was a nephew of **Joseph F.** Nickname was "Willie."
- Married **Jessie Lena Freckleton** on 28 December 1882 in Salt Lake City. They were the parents of (1) William Ray Harris (1883–92), (2) Joseph Fielding Harris (1885–1936), (3) John Ernest Harris (1886–1964), (4) **Ruby Leona Harris**, (5) Delia Jessie Harris (born and died 1890), (6) baby girl Harris (born and died 1891), (7) **Wilford Leroy Harris**, (8) Emily Harris (born and died 1894), (9) **Bessie Irene Harris**, (10) **Reuel Smith Harris**, (11) Ada Fern Harris (1899–1963), (12) Viola Myrtle Harris (1901–21), (13) Alice Bernice Harris (1903–77), and (14) Legrande Smith Harris (1910–77).
- Died on 23 August 1926 in Provo, Utah County, UT.

Letter references: 28 July 1860, 26 September 1860, 20 December 1860, 29 January 1861, 12 March 1861, Spring 1861, 30 May 1861, 8 December 1861, 30 September 1862, Fall 1862, 12 June 1864, 22 June 1864, 1864, 18 January 1870, 21 April 1871, 31 May 1874, 15 August 1874, 7 September 1874 (first letter), 5 October 1874, 24 November 1874, 9 February 1875, 15 May 1875, 14 August 1878, 22 April 1879, 18 March 1885, 22 May 1885, May 1887, 23 October 1878, 2 May 1890, 4 August 1890, 9 August 1890, 15 January 1891, 11 February 1891, 17 June 1891, 16 July 1907, 23 December 1912, 28 February 1913, 3 March 1913

Harris, Zina Christine

- Born on 13 May 1876 in Provo, Utah County, UT, to **William Jasper Harris** and **Martha Ann**. Was a niece of **Joseph F.**
- Married (1) George Thomas Furner (1868–1902) on 18 October 1893 in Salt Lake City. They were the parents of (1) **Merilla Furner**, (2) Zina May Furner (1897–1934), (3) Vera Furner (born and died 1899), (4) Pearl Irene Furner (1900–1987), and (5) **Sarah Rachel Furner**.
- Married two other husbands and had four more children.
- Died on 16 March 1958 in Provo, Utah County, UT.

Letter references: 29 November 1877, 1 July 1881, 17 June 1891, 28 January 1895, 20 February 1895, 8 March 1907, 3 March 1913, 27 March 1916, 13 December 1916

Harvey, Hannah

- Born on 4 June 1802 in Birmingham, Delaware County, PA, to Eli Harvey and Mary Painter. Was the mother-in-law of **Jerusha Smith**, the half sister of **Joseph F.** and **Martha Ann**. Two of her daughters married **Brigham Young**.
- Married Robert Pierce (1797–1884) on 23 January 1821 in Pennsylvania. They were the parents of (1) Mary Harvey Pierce (1821–47), (2) Margaret Pierce (1823–1907), (3) Anna Eliza Pierce (1826–29), (4) Eli Harvey Pierce (1827–58), (5) Thomas Pierce (1829–64), (6) Joseph Pierce (born and died 1831), (7) **William Pierce**, and (8) **Edith Evelina Pierce**.
- Died on 28 October 1872 in East Millcreek, UT.

Letter reference: 30 September 1862

Hawkins, Elizabeth

- Born on 3 January 1829 in Parish of St. Ann, London, Middlesex, England, to William Edward Hawkins and Elizabeth Spain. Nickname was "Lizzie."
- Married **Walter Eli Wilcox** on 4 September 1853 in Salt Lake City. They were the parents of five children. Was Walter's second of five wives.
- Died on 23 January 1901 in Midvale, Salt Lake County, UT.

Letter reference: 18 June 1890

Heath, Seraph Celestia

- Born on 9 June 1873 in Salt Lake City to Orson Omer Heath and **Josephine Fielding**. Was a granddaughter of **Joseph Fielding** and **Mary Ann Peake**. Was a first cousin once removed to **Joseph F.** and **Martha Ann**.
- Married John Alfred Ainscough (1873–1958) on 6 June 1894 in Logan, Cache County, UT. No issue.
- Died on 14 May 1911.

Letter reference: 14 May 1911

Heward, Harry

- Born on 26 August 1876 in London, England, to John Heward and **Ann Jane Lupton**. His mother was the first cousin once removed of **Joseph F.** and **Martha Ann**.
- Married Mary Isabelle Young (1866–1940) about 1886 in Salt Lake City. No issue.

- **Joseph F.** writes to **Martha Ann** that **Ann Jane Lupton**'s son is suffering from a sickness called the summer complaint. Was likely the son who was sick.
- Died on 10 March 1955 in Draper, Salt Lake County, UT.

Letter reference: 14 August 1878

Heward, Joseph Fielding

- Born on 15 July 1878 in Salt Lake City to John Heward and **Ann Jane Lupton**. Mother was the first cousin once removed of **Joseph F.** and **Martha Ann**.
- Married Hannah Precilda Day (1881–1941) in 1899 in Salt Lake City. They were the parents of two children.
- **Joseph F.** writes to **Martha Ann** that **Ann Jane Lupton**'s son is suffering from a sickness called the summer complaint. May have been the son who was sick.
- Died on 25 April 1961 in Provo, Utah County, UT.

Letter reference: 14 August 1878

Hill, Almira Emily

- Born on 25 November 1815 in Pendleton District, SC, to Jehu Hill and Martha Carlton. Was the mother-in-law of **Martha Ann**.
- Married (1) Zachariah Harris (1813–1839 or 1841) on 6 March 1834 in Carrollton, Greene County, IL. They were the parents of (1) **Artimissa Ann Harris**, (2) **William Jasper Harris**, (3) Martha Jane Harris (1838–40), and (4) Mary Elizabeth Harris (born and died 1840).
- Married (2) **Abraham Owen Smoot** on 9 January 1846 in Nauvoo, Hancock County, IL. They were the parents of (1) Abraham Albert Ether Smoot (1847–63), (2) Emily Ann Smoot (1851–55), (3) **Margaret Thompson Smoot**, and (4) **Zina Beal Smoot**.
- Made the exodus from Nauvoo to Utah. Retained first husband's surname after marriage to **Abraham Owen Smoot**. Soon after arriving to what is now Sugar House in Salt Lake City, she and the other wives of **Abraham O. Smoot** worked hard to sustain life on their meager supplies. Was given much of the responsibilities in tending the farm and raising the children while her husband was away on Church business. Also skilled in weaving and knitting.
- Died on 20 March 1882 in Provo, Utah County, UT.

Letter references: 3 February 1857, 3 May 1857, 14 June 1857, 3 July 1857, 25 July 1857, [1857?], 20 May 1858, 28 July 1860, 29 January 1861, 30 May 1861, 1 March 1862, 1864, 26 July 1872, 27 February 1874, 20 June 1874, 15 July 1874, 24 November 1874, 9 February 1875, 31 March 1875, 15 May 1875

Hoagland, Abraham Lucas

- Born on 24 March 1797 in Hillsborough, Somerset County, NJ, to Lucas Hoagland and Mary Bunn.
- Married (1) Margaret Quick (1802–71) on 24 November 1825. They were the parents of (1) Lucas Hoagland (1827–1906), (2) Mary Hoagland (1829–70), (3) Peter Hoagland (1831–73), (4) John Hoagland (1833–93), (5) **Elizabeth Hoagland**, (6) Emily Hoagland (1837–1906), and (7) Cornelia Hoagland (1842–43).
- Married (2) **Agnes Taylor** in 1847 in Salt Lake City. They were the parents of (1) Abraham Taylor Hoagland (1848–1939), (2) Agnes Taylor Hoagland (1850–1933), (3) Edward Taylor Hoagland (1852–1927), (4) Joseph Taylor Hoagland (born and died 1853), and (5) Sarah Taylor Hoagland (1855–96).
- Married two more wives and had no other children.
- Served as bishop of the Eleventh Ward in Winter Quarters, Nebraska. After arriving in Utah, served as the second bishop of the Salt Lake City Fourteenth Ward from 1851 to 1872.

- Died on 15 February 1872 in Salt Lake City.

Letter reference: 22 June 1864

Hoagland, Elizabeth

- Born on 3 November 1835 in Royal Oak, Oakland County, MI, to **Abraham Lucas Hoagland** and Margret Quick.
- Married **George Q. Cannon** on 11 December 1854 in Salt Lake City. They were the parents of (1) Rosina Matthews Cannon (1852–1939) (adopted), (2) George Quayle Cannon Jr. (born and died 1856), (3) John Quayle Cannon (1857–1931), (4) **Abraham Hoagland Cannon**, (5) Georgianna Hoagland Cannon (1861–63), (6) George Hoagland Cannon (born and died 1863), (7) Elizabeth Hoagland Cannon (1865–67), (8) Mary Alice Hoagland Cannon (1867–1908), (9) Lillian Ann Hoagland Cannon (1869–70), (10) David Hoagland Cannon (1871–92), (11) Emily Hoagland Cannon (1874–1955), and (12) Sylvester Quayle Cannon (1877–1943).
- Traveled across the plains with her family at age eleven. Was **George Q. Cannon**'s first wife and stood beside him through the persecutions against plural marriage. Was apparently a friend of **Joseph F.**, as he asks to be remembered to her in one letter.
- Died on 25 January 1882 in Salt Lake City.

Letter reference: 22 June 1864

Hodson, Israel William Roberts ("Happy")

- Born on 31 October 1872 in St. George, Washington County, UT, to William and Eliza Roberts Hodson.
- Married **Melinda Lucretia Singleton** on 9 September 1896 in Provo, Utah County, UT. They were the parents of seven children.
- Apparently rented a home in Provo that belonged to **Joseph F.** Worked as a delivery boy at a grocery store in 1910, was a helper at Knights Woolen Mills by 1915, and was a cook at BYU's Aspen Grove in Provo Canyon when he died in 1943.
- Died on 6 February 1943 in Provo, Utah County, UT.

Letter reference: 7 July 1914

Holbrook, Emmett Gordon

- Born on 23 March 1886 in Frisco, Beaver County, UT, to **Lafayette Holbrook** and Emily Angelina Hinckley.
- Died on 14 January 1891 in Provo, Utah County, UT.

Letter reference: 1 February 1891

Holbrook, Lafayette

- Born on 7 September 1850 in Salt Lake City to Chandler Holbrook and Eunice Dunning.
- Married Emily Angeline Hinckley (1856–1947) on 9 October 1876 in Salt Lake City. They were the parents of (1) Lafayette Hinckley Holbrook (1877–1969), (2) Jean Clara Holbrook (1878–1963), (3) Eunice Angeline Holbrook (1881–1967), (4) Ora Lavern Holbrook (1884–1969), (5) **Emmett Gordon Holbrook**, (6) Ava Lucille Holbrook (1889–91), (7) Florence Irene Holbrook (1891–1983), (8) Lillian Minerva Holbrook (born and died 1896), (9) Ruth Holbrook (1899–1972), and (10) Paul Lincoln Holbrook (1902–60).
- Served as mayor of Provo, Utah County, UT, from 1894 to 1897.
- Died on 1 January 1941 in Salt Lake City.

Letter reference: 1 February 1891

Holladay, Joseph

- Murdered **Silas C. Greenleaf** in the Salt Lake City courthouse while **William Jasper Harris** was on police duty in Salt Lake City in 1863. Was not a member of the Church. No other information known.

Letter reference: 22 February 1863

Hooper, William Henry

- Born on 25 December 1813 in Dorchester County, MD, to Henry Hooper and Mary N. Price. Nickname was "Captain Hooper."
- Married Mary Ann Knowlton (1829–87) on 24 December 1852 in Utah. They were the parents of nine children.
- Engaged in the mercantile business. Was a US congressional delegate from Utah Territory. Brought about many policies beneficial to the Saints.
- Died on 30 December 1882 in Salt Lake City.

Letter reference: 14 June 1872

Hopper, Mary

- Born about 1844 in Marion, Williamson County, IL.
- Married John M. Cunningham (1812–73) in 1866 or 1869 in Marion, Williamson County, IL.
- Mary, twenty-five years of age, is mentioned in the 1870 Census as living with John Cunningham, age fifty-six years of age, in Provo. She is mentioned in the 1879 Provo City Directory as "postmistress." Her husband John had been the "postmaster" before he died on 8 March 1873 in Provo. She is not listed in the 1880 Census or the 1884 Provo City Directory.
- Death unknown.

Letter reference: 14 August 1878

Houtz, Jacob

- Born on 12 October 1814 in Selinsgrove, Snyder County, PA, to Christian Houtz and Ann Elizabeth Zeller.
- Married (1) Lydia Mease (1818–88) on 22 February 1838 in Union County, PA. They were the parents of six children.
- Married (2) Bridget Daley (1828–1911) on 27 February 1854 in Salt Lake City. They were the parents of five children.
- Married (3) Anna Barr Bringhurst (1842–1912) on 15 February 1857 in Salt Lake City. They were the parents of seven children.
- Joined the Church in 1844 and ordained a Seventy in Nauvoo, IL, in 1846. Immigrated to the Salt Lake Valley in 1847. First settled in Salt Lake City and later moved to Springville, UT.
- Died on 11 December 1896 in Utah.

Letter references: 12 March 1861, 30 May 1861

Hudson, John Riley

- Born on 20 August 1856 in Tennessee to John Hudson and Malinda Carroll.
- Killed by a mob along with three other members (including two missionaries).

- Died on 10 August 1884 in Cane Creek, Lewis County, TN.

Letter reference: 15 August 1884

Huntington, Dimick Baker

- Born on 20 May 1808 in Watertown, Jefferson County, NY, to William and Zina Baker. His sister, **Zina Diantha Huntington**, married the Prophet **Joseph Smith**, uncle to **Joseph F.** and **Martha Ann**.
- Married (1) Fannie Maria Allen (1810–94) on 28 April 1830 in Watertown. They were the parents of (1) Clark Allen Huntington (1831–96), (2) **Lot Elisha Huntington**, (3) Margaret Huntington (1836–39), (4) Fannie Maria Huntington (1838–42), (5) Martha Zina Huntington (1844–83), (6) Betsy Prescindia Huntington (born and died 1846), (7) Julia Caroline Huntington (1848–1925), (8) Sarah Adaline Huntington (1851–56), and (9) Joseph Smith Huntington (1855–1907).
- Married four more wives. No issue.
- Was a high priest. Served a mission to the Indians for forty years. Was an Indian interpreter, a patriarch, and a drum major in the martial band. Was a farmer by occupation.
- Died on 1 February 1879 in Salt Lake City.

Letter reference: 13 August 1891

Huntington, Lot Elisha

- Born on 29 April 1834 in Watertown, Jefferson County, NY, to **Dimick Baker Huntington** and Fannie Maria Allen.
- Married Naomi Levina Gibson (1842–1940) in October 1861. No issue.
- Was a member of the Mormon Battalion. On 31 December 1861, he, **Moroni Clawson**, **John P. Smith**, and others assaulted and robbed territorial governor John Dawson. The recently appointed governor was fleeing Utah after he made an indecent proposal to Albina Merrill Williams, a Latter-day Saint widow. Clawson, Huntington, and Smith were apprehended by Orrin Porter Rockwell. Huntington was shot and killed during the arrest, and Clawson and Smith were shot and killed while attempting to escape on the following day, 17 January 1862.
- Died on 16 January 1862 in Salt Lake City.

Letter reference: 3 February 1862

Huntington, Zina Diantha

- Born on 31 January 1821 in Watertown, Jefferson County, NY, to William Huntington and Zina Baker. Was the aunt of **Joseph F.** and **Martha Ann**.
- Married (1) Henry Bailey Jacobs (1817–86) on 7 March 1841 in Nauvoo, Hancock County, IL. They were the parents of two children.
- Married (2) **Joseph Smith Jr.** on 27 October 1841 in Nauvoo, Hancock County, IL. No issue.
- Married (3) **Brigham Young** on 2 February 1846 in Nauvoo, Hancock County, IL. They were the parents of **Zina Presendia Young**.
- Called as the Church's third Relief Society General President. Was president of the Silk Association and made silk in the Salt Lake Valley. Was one of the first women to heed Brigham Young's call to study medicine.
- Died on 27 August 1901 in Salt Lake City.

Letter references: 3 February 1862, 22 June 1864, 1864, 29 March 1870, 4 June 1880

Hyde, John

- Born on 25 February 1833 in London, Middlesex, England, to John Hyde and Martha Marmoy.
- Married LaVinia Hawkins (1832–1910) on 10 November 1853 in Salt Lake City. They were the parents of one child.
- Converted to the Church with his family in England in 1848. Served a mission to France from 1851 to 1853. Ordained a Seventy during this time. Arrived in Salt Lake City in October 1853 and was employed as a schoolteacher. Became troubled by the practice of plural marriage and other Church teachings. Called on a mission to the Sandwich Islands in 1856 but publicly renounced the Church during this mission. Later wrote an exposé of the Church, an unpublished novel critical of the Church, and several articles, including a coauthored pamphlet in Native Hawaiian. Publicly cut off from the Church by Heber C. Kimball in January 1857. Returned to England in 1858, became a Swedenborgian minister, and published several more works.
- Died on 18 August 1876.

Letter reference: 5 April 1857

J

Jenkins, Emily

- Born on 17 November 1878 in Salt Lake City to Thomas Jenkins and Mahala Elmer. Was the daughter-in-law of **Joseph F.**
- Married **David Asael Smith** on 24 January 1901 in Salt Lake City. They were the parents of ten children.
- Died on 8 July 1959 in Salt Lake City.

Letter reference: 20 March 1916

Johnson, John Peter Rasmus

- Born on 10 April 1824 in Lindved, Vejle, Jutland, Denmark, to Johannes Christensen and Ane Dorthea Jonasdatter.
- Married (1) Karen Marie Nielsen Toft (1823–90) on 24 April 1847 in Lindved, Vejle, Denmark. They were the parents of ten children.
- Married (2) **Maren Poulsen** on 16 January 1857 in Salt Lake City. They were the parents of six children.
- Married two other wives and had eleven more children.
- Joined the Church in 1852. After serving a mission in Denmark, immigrated with his family to Salt Lake City. After moving to Provo, served as a bishop in 1874. Worked as a carpenter and a farmer. Served another mission to Scandinavia from 1860 to 1864. Also served several other missions in the northwestern states.
- Died on 9 July 1910 in Provo, Utah County, UT.

Letter reference: 5 October 1874

Johnson, Marilla Lucretia

- Born on 12 October 1830 in Haddam, Middlesex County, CT, to Aaron Johnson and Polly Zerviah Kelsey.
- Married (1) William Miller (1814–75) on 22 December 1845 in Nauvoo, Hancock County, IL. They were the parents of one child.

- Married (2) **James Ephraim Daniels** on 13 June 1878 in Manchester, Lancashire, England. No issue.
- Died on 22 January 1918 in Provo, Utah County, UT.

Letter reference: 18 June 1890

Jones, Joseph C.

- Born about 1843 in St. Louis, St. Louis County, MO, to Moses Jones and Eliza Case.
- Married **Emma Buxton** in 1868 in St. Louis, St. Louis County, MO. They were the parents of four children.
- According to the 1870 US Census, he and his family lived near **Martha Ann** in Provo.
- Died on 29 August 1906 in Provo, Utah County, UT.

Letter references: 1 December 1868, 5 August 1874

Jones, Mary Elizabeth

- Born on 15 April 1845 in Birkenhead, Cheshire, England, to John M. Jones and Elizabeth Hughes Jones.
- Married John Evans on 1 November 1862 in Salt Lake City. They were the parents of (1) John Evans (1869–72), (2) Cora Evans (born and died 1871), (3) Eva Evans (born and died 1871), (4) Ruth Evans (born and died 1871), (5) Mary Elizabeth Evans (1872–93), (6) Peter Evans (born and died 1874), (7) Ella Ann Evans (1875–1922), (8) Rhoda Evans (1879–1936), (9) Chloe Jane Evans (1880–1961), (10) Rebecca Pearl Evans (1882–1965), and (11) George Frederick Evans (1884–85). As mentioned by **Joseph F.**, the triplets died and were buried on the same day they were born. Only four of Mary Evans's eleven children lived to adulthood.
- Died on 5 July 1885 in Salt Lake City.

Letter reference: 23 February 1871

Jones, Samuel Stephen

- Born on 9 February 1837 in Brentford, Middlesex, England, to Samuel Jones and Sarah Ann Bradshaw.
- Married (1) Lydia Elizabeth Hooker (1837–74) on 9 February 1857 in Provo, Utah County, UT. They were the parents of one child.
- Had six other wives and thirteen other children.
- Was a well-known and successful businessman. Was also a farmer, railroad contractor, charcoal manufacturer, miner, and sawmill operator. Was a major adjutant in the Utah militia and participated in the Black Hawk War. Held the offices of high priest and Seventy. Promoted railway expansion into Salt Lake City and built the first charcoal kilns in Spanish Fork Canyon. Became vice president of the Sioux Mining Company and president of the Utah Consolidated Mining and Milling companies. Served as the mayor of Provo from 1898 to 1899.
- Died on 27 December 1923 in Provo, Utah County, UT.

Letter references: 5 August 1874, 15 August 1874, 7 September 1874 (second letter), 15 May 1875

K

Kearns, Thomas

- Born on 11 April 1862 in Woodstock, Ontario, Canada, to Thomas Kearns and Margaret Maher.

- Married Jennie Judge (1869–1943) on 14 September 1890. They were the parents of three children.
- Was a US Senator from Utah from 1901 to 1905 and owner of the *Salt Lake Tribune*. Instrumental in forming the American Party, which was antagonistic toward the Church.
- Died on 18 October 1918 in Salt Lake City.

Letter reference: 7 November 1910

Kesler, Donnette

- Born on 13 March 1902 in Salt Lake City to Alonzo Pratt Kesler and **Donnette Smith**. Was a granddaughter of **Joseph F.** Nickname was "Donnie."
- Married George Stanley McAllister (1900–1970) on 1 September 1926 in Salt Lake City. They were the parents of three children.
- Died on 18 March 1949 in Manhattan, New York County, NY.

Letter reference: 22 December 1909

Kesler, Henry Smith

- Born on 24 April 1907 in Salt Lake City to Alonzo Pratt Kesler and **Donnette Smith**. Was a grandson of **Joseph F.**
- Married Nancy Lee Hurt (1908–2003) on 11 March 1945 in Los Angeles, Los Angeles County, CA. They were the parents of two children.
- Died on 15 May 1997 in Los Angeles County, CA.

Letter reference: 22 December 1909

Kimball, Alice Ann

- Born on 6 September 1858 in Salt Lake City to **Heber Chase Kimball** and Ann Alice Gheen. Was a wife of **Joseph F.** and sister-in-law of **Martha Ann**.
- Married (1) David Patten Rich (1853–1930) on 5 December 1875 in Salt Lake City. They were the parents of (1) **Alice May Rich**, (2) **Heber Chase Rich**, and (3) **Charles Coulson Rich**. She and her husband later divorced. Children sealed to her second husband, **Joseph F.**, and carried the Smith surname.
- Married (2) **Joseph F.** on 6 December 1883 in Salt Lake City. They were the parents of (1) **Lucy Mack Smith**, (2) **Andrew Kimball Smith**, (3) **Jesse Kimball Smith**, and (4) **Fielding Kimball Smith**.
- Served as a Sunday School teacher, a counselor in the Salt Lake City Nineteenth Ward YLMIA (Young Ladies' Mutual Improvement Association, precursor to the Young Women organization), and ward primary president. Served for thirty years as a general board member and as general treasurer of the YLMIA. Was a delegate of the YLMIA and was sent to the International Council of Women in Rome, Italy, in 1914. Also wrote and published several articles in the *Young Woman's Journal* and the *Improvement Era*.
- Died on 19 December 1946 in Salt Lake City.

Letter references: 6 September 1899, 2 April 1901, 25 July 1904, 1 February 1906, 8 March 1907, 22 December 1909, 24 December 1910, 20 August 1912

Kimball, Heber Chase

- Born on 14 June 1801 in Sheldon, Franklin County, VT, to Solomon Farnham Kimball and Anna Spaulding. Was the stepfather of **Joseph F.** and **Martha Ann** and was later a father-in-law of **Joseph F.**
- Married (1) Vilate Murray (1806–67) on 7 November 1822 in Mendon, Monroe County, NY.

- Sealed to **Mary Fielding** on 14 September 1844.
- Had forty-two additional wives and sixty-five children.
- Took part in Zion's Camp. Was a potter by trade. Ordained an Apostle on 14 February 1835 under the hands of Oliver Cowdery, David Whitmer, and Martin Harris. Served a mission to the eastern states in the summer of 1835. Served a mission to New York and Vermont in the summer of 1836. Served as president of the British Mission from 1837 to 1838. Served a second mission to England from 1839 to 1841. Elected a member of the city council of Nauvoo in 1841. Served as first counselor to **Brigham Young** from 1847 to 1868. Was the first chief justice of the provisional government of Deseret and was also lieutenant governor. Was president of the senate of the State of Deseret legislature and also of the Territory of Utah in 1851.
- Died on 22 June 1868 in Salt Lake City.

Letter references: 3 February 1857, 3 May 1857, 12 March 1861, 22 June 1864, 23 June 1868, 15 May 1875

KIMBALL, LYDIA HOLMES

- Born on 18 January 1855 in Salt Lake City to **Heber Chase Kimball** and **Lucy Walker**.
- Married Frances Xavier Loughery (1844–1912) on 12 June 1875. Her husband was not a member of the Church.
- Died on 15 April 1928.

Letter reference: 15 May 1875

KING, AMY JANE

- Born on 3 October 1836 in Mantua, Portage County, OH, to Thomas Jefferson King and Rebecca Englesby Olin.
- Married **Elias Smith**, a first cousin once removed to **Joseph F.** and **Martha Ann**, on 15 April 1856 in Salt Lake City. They were the parents of (1) Silas Thomas Smith (1857–1931), (2) Jesse Moroni Smith (1858–1937), (3) Rebecca Jane Smith (1860–1923), (4) Albert William Smith (1862–66), (5) Mary Alzina Knapp Smith (1865–1953), (6) Martha Priscilla Smith (1865–1946), (7) Amy Esther Smith (1867–1910), (8) Angeline Adelia Smith (1869–1950), (9) Franklin Elias Smith (1871–1917), (10) Sarah Susannah Smith (1873–1952), (11) **Thomas King Smith**, (12) **Edward Hunter Smith**, and (13) Hiram Bennett Smith (1877–1951).
- Was a teacher in the Salt Lake City Seventeenth Ward Sunday School. Was an expert seamstress and quilter.
- Died on 8 November 1913 in Salt Lake City.

Letter reference: 20 May 1858

KNOWLTON, BENJAMIN FRANKLIN

- Born on 30 January 1838 in Bear Creek, Hancock County, IL, to Sidney Algernon Knowlton and Harriet Burnham. Nickname was "Frank."
- Married (1) **Rhoda Ann Jennetta Richards**, a sister-in-law of **Joseph F.**, on 31 October 1863 in Salt Lake City. They were the parents of (1) Willard Knowlton (born and died 1865), (2) Wilhelmina Knowlton (born and died 1865), (3) **Benjamin Franklin Knowlton Jr.**, (4) Jenetta Knowlton (1868–71), (5) **Harriet Knowlton**, (6) Sidney Richards Knowlton (1873–76), (7) William Hooper Knowlton (1874–76), (8) Ida Knowlton (1876–1961), (9) Heber John Knowlton (1878–1906), (10) George Quincy Knowlton (1880–1957), and (11) Willard Richards Knowlton (1882–84).
- Married two other wives and had fifteen more children.
- Was a farmer and stock raiser. Served as branch president in Skull Valley in the late 1870s and early 1880s.

- Died on 27 March 1901 in Farmington, Davis County, UT.

Letter reference: 26 January 1871

Knowlton, Benjamin Franklin, Jr.

- Born on 11 September 1866 in Salt Lake City to **Benjamin Franklin Knowlton** and **Rhoda Ann Jennetta Richards**. His mother was a sister-in-law of **Joseph F.** It appears **Sarah Ellen Richards**, wife of **Joseph F.**, sometimes took care of him in his youth.
- Married (1) Sarah Lavina Clark (1867–1955) on 14 April 1886 in Logan, Cache County, UT. They were the parents of nine children.
- Married (2) Louise Marie Buzzo (1855–1947). No issue.
- Died on 15 April 1933 in Salt Lake City.

Letter reference: 26 January 1871

Knowlton, Harriet

- Born on 23 November 1870 in Salt Lake City to **Benjamin Franklin Knowlton** and **Rhoda Ann Jennetta Richards**. Her mother was a sister-in-law of **Joseph F.**
- Married Daniel Thomas Miller (1870–1919) on 27 June 1897 in Salt Lake City. No issue.
- Died on 6 August 1898.

Letter reference: 23 February 1871

L

Lambson, Alfred Boaz, Jr.

- Born on 15 June 1855 in Huston, Custer County, ID, to **Alfred Boaz Lambson** and **Melissa Jane Bigler**. Was a brother-in-law of **Joseph F.**
- Married Amelia Eveline De Witt (1862–1937) on 20 July 1879 in Salt Lake City. They were the parents of nine children.
- Died on 3 February 1945 in Mackay, Custer County, ID.

Letter references: 2 April 1905, 30 September 1916

Lambson, Alfred Boaz, Sr.

- Born on 27 August 1820 in Royalton, Niagara County, NY, to Boaz Lambson and Polly Walworth. Was a father-in-law of **Joseph F.**
- Married (1) Melissa Jane Bigler (1825–99) on 25 March 1845 in Nauvoo, Hancock County, IL. They were the parents of (1) **Melissa Jane Lambson**, (2) **Julina Lambson**, (3) **Edna Lambson**, and (4) **Alfred Boaz Lambson Jr.**
- Married (2) Mary Jane Martin (1827–1909) on 24 October 1854 in Salt Lake City. They were the parents of four children.
- Was a blacksmith and an excellent mechanic. Served a mission to the West Indies from 1852 to 1854. Held the office of Seventy, which was a stake calling beginning in 1883 and remained at the local level until 1986.

- Died on 26 February 1905 in Salt Lake City.

Letter reference: 2 April 1905

Lambson, Edna

- Born on 3 March 1851 in Salt Lake City to **Alfred Boaz Lambson** and **Melissa Jane Bigler**.
- Married **Joseph F.** on 1 January 1871 in Salt Lake City. They were the parents of (1) **Hyrum Mack Smith**, (2) **Alvin Fielding Smith**, (3) **Alfred Jason Smith**, (4) **Edna Melissa Smith**, (5) **Albert Jesse Smith**, (6) **Robert Smith**, (7) **Emma Smith**, (8) **Zina Smith**, (9) **Ruth Smith**, and (10) **Martha Smith**.
- Contracted a severe, almost fatal, illness at age fifteen and was brought before **Joseph F.**, who was her sister **Julina**'s husband. **Joseph F.** prayed over her all night, and she lived. Married **Joseph F.** six years later. Served as president of the Women Workers of the Salt Lake Temple upon the death of **Bathsheba Wilson Bigler** in 1910. Was a member of the general board of the Primary Association for ten years. Chosen as historian of the Daughters of the Utah Pioneers.
- Died on 28 February 1926 in Salt Lake City.

Letter references: 7 December 1870, 26 January 1871, 23 February 1871, 21 April 1871, 14 September 1871, 3 May 1872, 17 May 1872, 28 April 1873, 31 May 1874, 8 September 1874, 5 October 1874, 26 November 1875, 11 July 1876, 6 April 1878, 22 April 1878, 18 September 1881, 23 November 1881, 22 November 1883, 31 July 1883, 1 August 1884, 11 February 1884, 18 March 1885, 13 August 1891, 20 June 1892, 12 May 1897, 24 December 1903, 1 February 1906, 8 March 1907, 27 November 1907, 24 April 1909, 26 December 1911, 20 August 1912, 23 December 1913, 7 July 1914, 17 February 1915, 30 September 1916

Lambson, Julina

- Born on 18 June 1849 in Salt Lake City to **Alfred Boaz Lambson Sr.** and **Melissa Jane Bigler**.
- Married **Joseph F.** on 5 May 1866 in Salt Lake City. They were the parents of (1) **Edward Arthur Smith** (adopted) (2) **Mercy Josephine Smith**, (3) **Mary Sophronia Smith**, (4) **Donnette Smith**, (5) **Joseph Fielding Smith**, (6) **David Asael Smith**, (7) **George Carlos Smith**, (8) **Julina Clarissa Smith**, (9) **Elias Wesley Smith**, (10) **Emily Jane Smith**, (11) **Rachael Smith**, (12) **Edith Eleanor Smith**, and (13) **Marjorie Virginia Smith**.
- Raised in the home of her uncle **George Albert Smith**. Met **Joseph F.** when he was working as a clerk in the Church Historian's Office and her uncle was serving as Church Historian. Studied obstetrics and brought nearly a thousand babies into the world. Served as a member of the general board of the Relief Society from 1892 to 1921 and as second counselor in the presidency of that organization from 1910 to 1921. After her husband's death, spent most of her time as a temple worker.
- Died on 10 January 1936 in Salt Lake City.

Letter references: 23 June 1968, 1 December 1868, 21 June 1869, 13 July 1869, 17 August 1869, 24 December 1869, 3 January 1869 (1870), 18 January 1870, 29 March 1870, 3 (31) March 1870, 5 July 1870, 18 August 1870, 7 December 1870, 26 January 1871, 23 February 1871, 14 September 1871, 3 May 1872, 14 June 1872, 18 January 1873, 31 May 1874, 5 August 1874, 5 October 1874, 16 November 1874, 26 November 1875, 11 July 1876, 18 September 1881, 23 November 1881, 31 July 1883, 11 February 1884, 18 March 1885, 30 November 1885, 11 February 1887, May 1887, 18 June 1890, 9 August 1890, 28 January 1895, 18 November 1896, 19 March 1898, 26 July 1900, 2 April 1905, 26 November 1906, 8 March 1907, 27 November 1907, 27 December 1908, 24 April 1909, 6 May 1909, 24 May 1909, 24 December 1910, 14 May 1911, 29 May 1911, 20 August 1912, 22 November 1912, 28 February 1913, 3 March 1913, 18 June 1913, 23 December 1913, 9 July 1914, 10 September 1914, 15 July 1915, 17 July 1915, 17 February 1916, 20 March 1916, 27 March 1916, 30 September 1916, 14 November 1916, 29 November 1916, 13 December 1916

Lambson, Melissa Jane

- Born on 13 November 1846 in Winter Quarters, Douglas County, NE, to **Alfred Boaz Lambson Sr.** and **Melissa Jane Bigler**. Was a sister-in-law of **Joseph F.**
- Married **Albert Westley Davis** on 25 November 1865 in Salt Lake City. They were the parents of (1) Albert John Davis (1866–1939), (2) Melissa Elvira Davis (1868–1946), (3) **Edna May Davis**, (4) Nettie Maria Davis (1873–1956), (5) Westley Lambson Davis (1875–1957), (6) George A. Davis (1877–1939), (7) Sarah Woolley Davis (1880–1971), (8) Helen Davis (1883–1960), and (9) Ethel Davis (1888–1937).
- Was an ardent Relief Society worker, a member of the Old Folks Committee, and a temple worker.
- Died on 23 August 1937 in Salt Lake City.

Letter references: 26 January 1871, 23 February 1871

Larsen, Christian Greis

- Born on 17 December 1828 in Moltum, Grejs, Vejle, Denmark, to Lauritz Johansen and Anna Margrethe Sorensen.
- Married (1) Caroline Marie Sorensen (1838–95) on 1 April 1857 in Denmark. They were the parents of ten children.
- Had four other wives and eight other children.
- Served in many capacities in the Church. Served a mission to the island of Bornholm from 1852 to 1857. Was bishop of the Spring City Ward and mayor of Spring City. Served as president of the Scandinavian Mission from 1873 to 1875.
- Died on 1 June 1911 in Castle Dale, Emery County, UT.

Letter reference: 15 July 1874

Lawson, James

- Born on 20 July 1820 in Kinross, Kinross-shire, Scotland, to David Lawson and Margaret Anderson.
- Married (1) Margaret Thomson (1820–42) on 28 April 1841 in Glasgow, Lanarkshire, Scotland. They were the parents of one child.
- Married two other wives and had ten more children.
- On the trek to Utah administered a blessing to a fallen ox at the request of **Mary Fielding Smith**, mother of **Joseph F.** and **Martha Ann**. The ox was healed. Served two missions to the Sandwich Islands from 1852 to 1853 and in 1856. Used his mechanical skills to establish shops and build houses during both missions. Became identified with the construction department of the Utah Central Railway and was highly skilled as an ironworker.
- Died on 14 September 1912 in Salt Lake City.

Letter references: 9 June 1855, 23 November 1855, 25 May 1856

Lee, Robert

- Born about 1602 in London, England, to Henry Lee and Elizabeth Fletcher.
- Married **Mary Atwood** about 1625 in Barnstable County, MA. They were the parents of four children.
- Was a seventh great-grandfather of **Joseph F.** and **Martha Ann** through their grandmother **Lucy Mack**.
- Died on 8 August 1663 in Barnstable, Barnstable County, MA.

Letter reference: 25 August 1897

Lemmon, Nancy Melissa

- Born on 6 September 1833 near Payson, Adams County, IL, to Washington Lemmon and Tamer Stephens.
- Married **John Smith**, a half brother of **Joseph F.** and **Martha Ann**, on 18 February 1857 in Salt Lake City. They were the parents of one child.
- Died on 29 March 1915 in Millcreek, Salt Lake County, UT.

Letter references: 5 April 1857, 14 June 1857, 18 March 1885

Liechty, John

- Born on 27 November 1827 in Biglen, Canton, Bern, Switzerland, to Johannes Liechty and Christina Guggisberg.
- Married Louisa Wintsh (1849–1908) on 24 August 1864 in Provo, Utah County, UT. They were the parents of ten children.
- Served a mission to Switzerland. Was a high priest and a ward teacher. Helped guard the Saints against Indian invasion and was a canal and road builder. Was a farmer by occupation. Wanted to be sealed to **Hyrum Smith**, the father of **Joseph F.** and **Martha Ann**.
- Died on 17 September 1910 in Provo, Utah County, UT.

Letter references: 8 September 1874, 6 November 1874, 8 December 1874, 20 June 1892

Long, John Varah

- Born on 28 September 1826 in Wath (also known as Wath-upon-Dearne) Wickersley, South Yorkshire, England, to John Long and Hannah Maria Scholey.
- Married (1) Elanor Oakes Betsy (1829–1905) on 9 July 1849. They were the parents of eleven children.
- Married (2) Sophia Badger (1832–1907) on 6 May 1855 in Salt Lake City. They were the parents of five children.
- Married (3) Lydia East (1826–92) on 6 May 1855 in Salt Lake City. They were the parents of three children.
- Married (4) Sarah Ann Burbage (1817–78) on 10 June 1856 in Salt Lake City. No issue.
- Married (5) Betsey Sanders (1834–92) on 27 March 1863 in Salt Lake City. They were the parents of two children.
- Immigrated to the United States through the Perpetual Emigrating Fund in 1854 and arrived in Utah by late December 1854. Was a member of the Nauvoo Legion, Salt Lake County representative to the Utah Territorial Legislature, Desert University regent, and stenographer in Brigham Young's office. Excommunicated in 1866.
- Died on 14 April 1869 in Salt Lake City.

Letter reference: 14 June 1872

Lowder, Catherine

- Born on 10 December 1830 in Grayson County, VA, to Jesse Lowder and Zilpha Bullard.
- Married (1) William Clements Sellwood (1831–56) on 1 August 1853 in Salt Lake City. No issue.
- Married (2) **William Creeland Burrows** on 1 January 1857 in Salt Lake City. They were the parents of eight children.
- Died on 31 October 1906 in Scofield, Carbon County, UT.

Letter reference: 5 April 1857

Lupton, Ann Jane

- Born on 23 September 1850 in Toxteth Park, Liverpool, Lancashire, England, to William Lupton and **Mary Fielding**, a cousin to **Joseph F.** and **Martha Ann**. Was a first cousin once removed to **Joseph F.** and **Martha Ann**. Nickname was "Annie."
- Married (1) John Coltman (1844–95) in 1874. They divorced. No issue.
- Married (2) John Heward (1813–90) on 25 July 1879 in Salt Lake City. They were the parents of (1) **Harry Heward**, (2) **Joseph Fielding Heward**, (3) William Alma Heward (1880–1941), and (4) Mary Lupton Heward (1884–1978).
- **Joseph F.** helped her and her mother emigrate from England to Utah Valley.
- Died on 23 June 1925 in Draper, Salt Lake County, UT.

Letter reference: 14 August 1878

Lyman, Amasa Mason

- Born on 30 March 1813 in Lyman, Grafton County, NH, to Roswell Lyman and Martha Mason. His fourth wife was a widow of **Joseph Smith Jr.**
- Married (1) Mary Louisa Tanner (1818–1906) on 10 June 1835 in Kirtland, Lake County, OH. They were the parents of (1) Matilda Lyman (1836–1903), (2) **Francis Marion Lyman**, (3) Ruth Adelia Deseret Lyman (1843–48), (4) Amasa Mason Lyman Jr. (1846–1937), (5) Mary Louisa Lyman (1849–77), (6) Lelia Deseret Lyman (1852–81), (7) Love Josephine Lyman (1854–1940), and (8) Agness Hilda Lyman (1857–81).
- Had seven other wives and twenty-nine other children.
- Served as a counselor to the Prophet **Joseph Smith**. Became a member of the Quorum of the Twelve Apostles following the Prophet's death. Served a mission to Great Britain. Also served missions to various parts of the United States. Participated in the Black Hawk War. Served as president of the California Mission from 1853 to 1854 and as president of the British Mission, assisted by **Charles C. Rich**, from 1860 to 1862. Was excommunicated from the Church in 1870 for teaching false doctrine.
- Died on 4 February 1877 in Fillmore, Millard County, UT.

Letter reference: 1 March 1862

Lyman, Francis Marion

- Born on 12 January 1840 in Good Hope, McDonough County, IL, to **Amasa Mason Lyman** and Maria Louisa Tanner.
- Married (1) Rhoda Ann Taylor (1840–1917) on 18 November 1857 in San Bernardino, San Bernardino County, CA. They were the parents of nine children.
- Married two more wives and had thirteen other children.
- Served a mission to England from 1860 to 1862. Served on the high council in the Millard Stake in Utah for about six years. Filled a second mission to Europe from 1873 to 1875. Was also district attorney, superintendent of common schools, county and probate clerk, and recorder, and presided over the Tooele Stake. In 1880 went on a mission with Elders **Erastus Snow** and **Brigham Young Jr.**, along with eight others, to San Juan County, UT; Colorado; New Mexico; and Arizona. Served as a member of the Quorum of the Twelve Apostles from 1880 to 1916.
- Served as a member of the YMMIA (Young Men's Mutual Improvement Association, precursor to the Young Men organization) General Board from 1898 to 1916. Also served as president of the British Mission from 1901 to 1904. At his death, he was serving as president of the Quorum of the Twelve Apostles.

- Died on 18 November 1916 in Salt Lake City.

Letter reference: 1 August 1884

M

MABEY, MARIA

- Born on 3 December 1838 in Kingcombe, Dorset, England, to Thomas Mabey and Esther Chalker.
- Married Albert Holt (1841–1907) on 12 October 1862 in Salt Lake City. They were the parents of thirteen children.
- Died on 2 December 1916 in Salt Lake City.

Letter reference: 28 July 1881

MACK, LOVINA

- Born in 1761 in Marlow, Cheshire County, NH, to Solomon Mack and Lydia Gates. Was a great-aunt of **Joseph F.** and **Martha Ann**.
- Died ca. 1794 in Gilsum, Cheshire County, NH, of consumption.

Letter reference: 18 May 1890

MACK, LOVISA

- Born in 1762 in Marlow, Cheshire County, NH, to Solomon Mack and Lydia Gates. Was a great-aunt of **Joseph F.** and **Martha Ann** and was called "Aunt Lovisa."
- Married Joseph Tuttle (1756–1816) on 31 January 1780 in Montague, Franklin County, MA. No issue.
- Died ca. 1794 while en route from South Hadley, Hampshire County, MA, to Gilsum, Cheshire County, NH.

Letter reference: 18 May 1890

MACK, LUCY

- Born on 8 July 1775 in Gilsum, Cheshire County, NH, to Solomon Mack and Lydia Gates. Was a paternal grandmother of **Joseph F.** and **Martha Ann**.
- Married **Joseph Smith Sr.** on 24 January 1796 in Tunbridge, Orange County, VT. They were the parents of (1) baby Smith (born and died 1797), (2) Alvin Smith (1798–1823), (3) **Hyrum Smith**, (4) Sophronia Smith (1803–96), (5) **Joseph Smith Jr.**, (6) Samuel Harrison Smith (1808–44), (7) Ephraim Smith (born and died 1810), (8) **William Smith**, (9) **Katherine Smith**, and (10) Don Carlos Smith (1816–41).
- Died on 14 May 1856 near Nauvoo, Hancock County, IL.

Letter references: 22 May 1890, 25 August 1897

MACK, SOLOMON

- Born on 28 January 1773 in Marlow, Cheshire County, NH, to Solomon Mack and Lydia Gates. Was a great-uncle of **Joseph F.** and **Martha Ann**.
- Married (1) Esther Hayward (1773–1844) on 29 August 1797 in Gilsum, Cheshire County, NH. They were the parents of nine children.

- Married two more wives and had no other children.
- Was a captain in the militia and served his town as selectman.
- Died on 28 October 1851 in Gilsum.

Letter reference: 22 May 1890

Madsen, Peter

- Born on 6 April 1824 in Studsdal, Taulov, Vejle, Denmark, to Mads Pedersen and Mette Marie Hansen.
- Married (1) Mariane Madsdatter (1815–81) on 12 November 1847 in Denmark. They were the parents of seven children.
- Married five other wives and had thirty-five more children.
- Immigrated in 1853 and settled in Sanpete County. Moved with his family to Provo sometime before 1870, where he lived until his death. Became a good friend to **Joseph F.** during the time **Joseph F.** lived in Provo.
- Died on 20 August 1911 in Provo, Utah County, UT.

Letter references: 7 September 1874 (second letter), 24 November 1874

Maeser, Karl Gottfried

- Born on 16 January 1828 in Meiszen, Saxony, Germany, to Johann Gottfried Maeser and Johanna Christina Friederika Zocher.
- Married (1) Anna Henrietta Therese Meith (1830–96) on 11 June 1854 in Neustadt, Dresden, Germany. They were the parents of eight children.
- Married (2) Emilie Caroline Damke (1829–1917) on 18 October 1875 in Salt Lake City. They were the parents of one child.
- He and his first wife joined the Church in Germany in 1855. After they immigrated to Salt Lake City, he served a mission to Virginia. Presided over the Swiss and German Mission and then over the California Mission from January August of 1894. In 1888 was appointed superintendent of the Church Educational System.
- Was an educator. His family moved to Provo when he was called to establish Brigham Young Academy, where he served as president and director from 1876 to 1892.
- Died on 15 February 1901 in Salt Lake City.

Letter reference: May 1887

Matthews, Mercy Ann

- Born on 30 January 1832 in Colmworth, Bedfordshire, England, to Timothy Richard Matthews and **Ann Fielding**. Was a first cousin to **Joseph F.** and **Martha Ann**.
- Married Graydon Harim Young (1826–72) on 3 August 1866 in Wetherden, Suffolk, England. No issue.
- Died on 16 July 1894.

Letter reference: 7 September 1875

Mauritzen, Anne Kirstine

- Born on 19 December 1833 in Brekke, Onso, Ostfold, Norway, to Mauritz Arvesen and Anne Malene Nielsen.
- Married **Abraham Owen Smoot** on 17 February 1856 in Salt Lake City. They were the parents of seven children.

- Worked to improve the economic base of Smoot's large family with the help of **Abraham Owen Smoot**'s other wives. Became Primary president of the Utah Stake and worked in that position until death.
- Died on 20 January 1894 in Provo, Utah County, UT.

Letter references: 20 May 1858, 30 May 1861, 12 January 1862, 1864

MAXFIELD, RICHARD DUNWELL

- Born on 5 May 1831 at Wilmont Creek, Bedeque, Prince Edward Island, Canada, to John Ellison Maxfield and Sarah Elizabeth Baker. Was a brother-in-law of **William Jasper Harris**.
- Married (1) **Artimissa Ann Harris** on 31 October 1854 in Salt Lake City. They were the parents of eight children.
- Married (2) Ellen Diadema Thompson (1837–1909) on 5 April 1862 in Salt Lake City. They were the parents of nine children.
- Died on 9 July 1916 in Salt Lake City.

Letter references: 20 December 1860, 21 June 1869, 22 April 1879

MAXWELL, GEORGE R.

- Born on 16 September 1842 in Little Swan Creek, Monroe County, MI, to Reuben Maxwell and Mary Elizabeth Heritage.
- Married (1) Emma Belle Turner (dates unknown) on 16 September 1865 in Monroe County, MI. No issue.
- Married (2) Mary Ann Sprague (1850–92) in 1872. They were the parents of three children.
- Fought in the American Civil War, serving as lieutenant colonel. Studied to be a lawyer and was appointed by US president Ulysses S. Grant as registrar of land in Utah Territory. Influential in the Liberal Party, which was established to oppose the power of Latter-day Saints in government of Utah Territory in the 1870s. Served as federal marshal for a time before being removed from office for embezzlement.
- Died on 2 July 1889 in Salt Lake City.

Letter reference: 31 March 1875

MCALLISTER, JOHN DANIEL THOMPSON

- Born on 19 February 1827 in Lewis, Sussex County, DE, to William James Frazier McAllister and Elizabeth Thompson.
- Married (1) Ellen Handley (1824–89) on 5 July 1847 in Philadelphia, Philadelphia County, PA. They were the parents of five children.
- Had eight other wives and twenty-eight more children.
- Was one of the presidents of the Sixteenth Quorum of the Seventy, which was a stake calling between 1883 and 1986. For many years was in charge of the Salt Lake Endowment House. Served as president of the St. George Temple and later the Manti Temple. Was a leading soloist in the Mormon Tabernacle Choir.
- Died on 18 January 1910 in St. George.

Letter reference: 14 August 1878

MCCOMB, ELEANOR JANE

- Born on 29 December 1817 in Wheeling, Ohio County, WV, to James Scott McComb and Anne Chidester.
- Married (1) Hector H. McLean (1813–67) in 1838 in Wheeling, WV. They were the parents of three children.

- Married (2) Parley P. Pratt (1807–57) on 14 November 1855 in Salt Lake City. No issue.
- Died on 24 October 1874 and was buried in Salt Lake City.

Letter reference: 18 January 1873

McKean, James B.

- Born on 5 August 1821 in Bennington, Bennington County, VT.
- Married Catherine Hay (1822–79) on 20 June 1850 in Hoosick, Rensselaer County, NY. They were the parents of one child.
- Republican politician and US federal Civil War officer. He was appointed chief justice of Utah Territory's Supreme Court from 1870 to 1875. Was dedicated to ending plural marriage in Utah. He arraigned **Brigham Young** before the Utah Supreme Court. However, this case was dismissed after the court ruled that Judge McKean had allowed juries to be drawn illegally. Eventually removed from office by President Ulysses S. Grant because of his abuse of civil rights in Utah.
- Died on 5 January 1879 in Salt Lake City.

Letter references: 3 May 1872, 31 March 1875

McKenzie, David

- Born on 27 December 1833 in Edinburgh, Midlothian, Scotland, to David McKenzie and Elizabeth White.
- Married Mary Ann Crowther (1840–1910) in 1858 in Salt Lake City. They were the parents of six children.
- Served a mission to Scotland, his home country. Immigrated to Utah in 1854 and later worked as a painter and engraver. In 1857 was ordained a Seventy and became a member of the Seventh Quorum of the Seventy. **Brigham Young** employed him as his private secretary. From 1874 to 1876 served a mission to Great Britain, where he labored in the Scottish conference. Later served as president of the Scotch mission and had charge of publishing the *Millennial Star*. From 1889 to 1891 acted as bookkeeper in the Presiding Bishop's office. Served as president of the high priests quorum in the Pioneer Stake.
- Died on 10 March 1912 in Salt Lake City.

Letter references: 26 July 1872, 5 August 1874

McLean, Albert

- Born about 1845 in New Orleans, Orleans County, LA, to Hector H. McLean and **Eleanor Jane McComb**.
- Worked as a schoolteacher in Salt Lake City for some time around 1873. No other information known.

Letter reference: 18 January 1873

McLean, Evaline

- Born on 25 December 1805 in Green Castle, Franklin County, PA, to John Steel McLean Sr. and Elizabeth Kirk.
- Married **Joseph Fisher** on 17 November 1831 in Freedom, Beaver County, PA. They were the parents of (1) **James Madison Fisher**, (2) **Hellen Maria Fisher**, (3) Curtis G. Fisher (1837–38), (4) **Elizabeth Jane Fisher**, (5) **Joseph Armstrong Fisher**, (6) Henry Charles Fisher (1844–1929), and (7) Rhuhamah Fisher (1847–75).
- Died on 19 July 1893 in Salt Lake City.

Letter reference: 27 October 1870

Mecham, Edward

- Born on 22 February 1802 in Canaan, Grafton County, NH, to Joshua Mecham and Permelia Chapman.
- Married (1) Irene Currier (1802–64) in 1826 in PA. They were the parents of three children.
- Married (6) **Sophia Barrows** on 29 October 1864 in Salt Lake City. They were the parents of two children.
- Married four more wives and had no other children.
- According to US census records, he and his wife **Sophia Barrows** lived in Provo next door to **Martha Ann** from at least the 1870s until their deaths.
- Died on 31 July 1895 in Provo, Utah County, UT.

Letter references: 27 October 1870, 23 February 1871, 20 June 1874, 5 August 1874, 15 August 1874, 7 September 1874 (second letter), 24 November 1874, 31 March 1875, 15 May 1875, 18 March 1885, 4 August 1890, 9 August 1890

Meeks, Priddy

- Born on 29 August 1795 in Greenville County, SC, to Athe Meeks and Mollie West.
- Married (1) Mary Bartlett (1792–1824) on 13 March 1815 in SC. They were the parents of four children.
- Married two other wives and had fifteen more children.
- Converted to the Church in 1840 and served as a bishop in Illinois. Joined the Saints in 1847 in Salt Lake City, where he founded the Society of Health. Helped settle several colonies in southern Utah and practiced medicine wherever he lived.
- Died on 7 October 1886 in Orderville, Kane County, UT.

Letter reference: 27 October 1870

Merrill, Margaret May

- Born on 5 February 1872 in Fillmore, Millard County, UT, to Clarence Merrill and Bathsheba Kate Smith.
- Married **Joseph Armstrong Fisher** on 30 November 1906 in Salt Lake City. They were the parents of four children.
- Died on 8 December 1946 in Salt Lake City.

Letter reference: 3 May 1872

Miller, Mary Leese

- Born about 1808 in Nelson, KY, to Aaron Miller and Sarah Thompson.
- Married (1) William Oxley (1804–death unknown) about 1829. No issue.
- Married (2) John Beesly (1797–1864) in 1836 in Ohio. They were the parents of nine children.
- Lived for a time in Provo, Utah County, UT, and apparently assisted **Joseph F.** with temple work.
- Died on 25 January 1888.

Letter reference: 23 August 1884

Molen, Simpson Montgomery

- Born on 14 September 1832 in Jacksonville, Morgan County, IL, to Jesse Molen and Laurany or Lieurany Huffaker.

- Married (1) Jane Elizabeth Hyde (1843–1934) on 7 August 1859 in Lehi, Utah County, UT. They were the parents of two children.
- Married (2) Elizabeth Collins (1837–1930) on 2 July 1863 in Salt Lake City. No issue.
- Left Salt Lake City in 1854 to serve a mission in the Sandwich Islands. Returned to Utah in 1858. Served as first counselor in the bishopric in Hyde Park, Cache Valley, UT. Was a lieutenant in the Nauvoo Legion. Called in the spring of 1876 to serve a second mission to the Sandwich Islands, on which his family accompanied him. Served a mission to the United States from 1874 to 1875. Presided over the Hawaiian Mission from 1876 to 1879, supervising the work on Church farms and sugar plantations. Returned to Utah in 1879. Elected assessor and collector of Cache County, UT. Served as bishop of the Hyrum Ward. Served as first counselor in the presidency of the Cache Stake of Zion.
- Died on 29 November 1900 in Hyrum, Cache County, UT.

Letter reference: 25 July 1857

Morgan, John Hamilton

- Born on 8 August 1842 in Greensburg, Decatur County, IN, to Gerrard Morgan III and Eliza Ann Hamilton.
- Married (1) Hellen Melvina Grosebeck (1852–1930) on 24 October 1868 in Salt Lake City. They were the parents of eleven children.
- Married two other wives and had eight more children.
- Fought in the Civil War in Illinois. Moved to Salt Lake City, where he founded the Morgan Commercial College in 1867. Taught there until it closed in 1874. Joined the Church in 1867 and then served in the Southern States Mission, first as a missionary and then as mission president. Served as president of a Quorum of the Seventy. Also served as a Republican representative on the Utah Territorial Legislature.
- Died on 14 August 1894 in Preston, Franklin County, ID.

Letter reference: 26 January 1885

Muhlestein, Nicholas

- Born on 7 October 1831 in Toffen, Canton Berne, Switzerland. Given name was also spelled "Nicholes."
- Married (1) Mary Howenstein (1835–92) on 6 May 1858 in Kolliken, Aagau, Switzerland. They were the parents of nine children.
- Married (2) Anna Caroline Wintsh (1851–1934) on 13 April 1868 in Salt Lake City. They were the parents of nine children.
- Was a high priest. Was one of the presidents of the Thirty-Fourth Quorum of the Seventy, which was a stake calling from 1883 to 1986. Was a musician, watchmaker, jeweler, farmer, and fruit grower. Participated in the Walker War.
- Died on 9 June 1916 in Provo, Utah County, UT.

Letter references: 8 September 1874, 6 November 1874, 16 November 1874, 8 December 1874

N

Nebeker, George

- Born on 22 January 1827 in Stantan, Newcastle County, DE, to George Nebeker and Susannah Meredith.
- Married (1) Maria Louisa Leonard (1834–1904) on 29 August 1863 in Salt Lake City. No issue.

- Married two other wives and had seventeen children.
- Served his first mission in 1854 among the Indians in the White and Elk Mountains. Served on the high council in the Salt Lake Stake of Zion from 1859 to 1864. Served as president of the Hawaiian Mission from 1865 to 1873. Served a mission to the United States in the fall and winter of 1879–80. Was also a colonizer in Utah and Nevada.
- Died on 1 December 1886 in Salt Lake City.

Letter reference: 26 May 1871

Nelson, George Smith

- Born on 20 October 1898 in Salt Lake City to Joseph Nelson and **Leonora Smith**. Was a grandson of **Joseph F.**
- Married Edna Virginia Cannon (1898–1990) on 15 August 1923. They were the parents of one child.
- Died on 7 March 1995 in Salt Lake City.

Letter reference: 25 October 1898

Nelson, Joseph Smith

- Born on 22 February 1897 in Salt Lake City to Joseph Nelson and **Leonora Smith**. Was a grandson of **Joseph F.** and a great-nephew of **Martha Ann**.
- Married (1) Nora Morris Cannon (1897–1964) on 17 August 1923 in Salt Lake City. They were the parents of four children.
- Married (2) Ethel Barbara Whitaker (1899–1994) on 9 April 1965 in Manti, Sanpete County, UT. No issue.
- Died on 13 May 1980 in Salt Lake City.

Letter reference: 14 November 1916

Nelson, Leileth

- Born on 9 February 1884 in Smithfield, Cache County, UT, to John Alexander Nelson and Ella Elizabeth Thomas. Was a daughter-in-law of **Joseph F.**
- Married **Heber Chase Rich** on 2 September 1902 in Magrath, Alberta, Canada. They were the parents of three children.
- Died on 17 January 1975 in Salt Lake City.

Letter reference: 20 March 1916

Nelson, William

- Born on 18 October 1812 in Morland, Westmoreland, England, to Thomas Nelson and Elizabeth Thompson.
- Married (1) Sarah Williams (1814–1901) on 17 February 1846 in Nauvoo, Hancock County, IL. They were the parents of four children.
- Married (2) **Sarah Bollwinkel** on 13 March 1856 in Salt Lake City. No issue.
- Married four other wives. No issue.
- Died on 31 March 1908 in Provo, Utah County, UT.

Letter reference: April 1856

Nibley, Charles Wilson

- Born on 5 February 1849 in Hunterfield, Midlothian, Scotland, to James Nibley and Jane Wilson Nibley.
- Married (1) Rebecca Neibaur (1851–1928) on 30 March 1869 in Logan, Cache County, UT. They were the parents of eight children.
- Married two other wives and had fourteen more children.
- Served in many capacities in the Church. Served a mission to New York in 1869. Served a mission to England and served as a counselor in a stake presidency. In 1907 chosen as Presiding Bishop of the Church. On several occasions accompanied **Joseph F.** on his travels around the world. Was also a successful businessman, lumberman, and merchant.
- Died on 11 December 1931 in Salt Lake City.

Letter reference: 19 September 1910

Nixon

- Unknown individual. In one letter to **Martha Ann**, **Joseph F.** used this man's life as an example of the dangers of drinking in excess.

Letter reference: 14 June 1872

Nuttall, Leonard John

- Born on 6 July 1834 in Liverpool, Lancashire, England, to William Nuttall and Mary Langhorn.
- Married (1) **Elizabeth Clarkson** on 25 December 1856 in Provo, Utah County, UT. They were the parents of twelve children.
- Married (2) Sophia Elizabeth Taylor (1849–1909) on 31 August 1875 in Salt Lake City. She was the daughter of **John Taylor** and Harriett Whitaker. They were the parents of six children.
- Was a colonel during the Black Hawk War. Served as a missionary to England from 1874 to 1875, bishop of the Kanab Ward from 1875 to 1877, president of the Kanab Stake from 1877 to 1884, and private secretary to **John Taylor** and **Wilford Woodruff**. Elected secretary of the Provo Co-operative Mercantile Institution. Served a mission to Washington, DC. Held several civic responsibilities in Provo, including probate judge, county recorder, and Utah County clerk.
- Died on 23 February 1905 in Salt Lake City.

Letter references: 20 June 1874, 5 August 1874, 6 November 1874, 24 November 1874, 15 May 1875, 7 September 1875, 29 November 1877, 1 August 1884

P

Passey, Alene

- Born on 7 June 1912 in Provo, Utah County, UT, to Roy Passey and **Sarah Lovina Harris**. Was a granddaughter of **Martha Ann**.
- Died on 10 December 1932 in Provo, Utah County, UT.

Letter reference: 3 March 1913

Passey, Lee Roy

- Born on 19 June 1908 in Provo, Utah County, UT, to Roy Passey and **Sarah Lovina Harris**. Was a grandson of **Martha Ann**.
- Died on 10 October 1928 in Provo, Utah County, UT.

Letter reference: 3 March 1913

Passey, Verna

- Born on 18 July 1910 in Provo, Utah County, UT, to Roy Passey and **Sarah Lovina Harris**. Was a grandson of **Martha Ann**.
- Married Anson Bowen Call Jr. (1900–1993) on 10 June 1931 in Salt Lake City. No issue.
- Died on 8 October 1986 in Logan, Cache County, UT.

Letter references: 26 December 1911, 3 March 1913

Patten, Johanna

- Born on 18 April 1860 in Provo, Utah County, UT, to Thomas Jefferson Patten and Johanna Hollister. Was a daughter-in-law of **Martha Ann**.
- Married **Joseph Albert Harris**, son of **William Jasper Harris** and **Martha Ann**, on 13 September 1878 in Salt Lake City. They were the parents of eight children.
- Died on 4 August 1948 in Salt Lake City.

Letter reference: 12 November 1883

Peake, Mary Ann

- Born on 29 October 1806 in Harwich, Lancashire, England, to Robert Peak and Dinah Walker. From various records it appears that at some point Mary Ann decided to add an *e* to the spelling of her last name. Of her eleven siblings, six spell their last name with an *e*. Was the aunt of **Joseph F.** and **Martha Ann**.
- Married (1) William Greenhalgh (1801–55) on 12 October 1823 in Deane, Lancashire, England. No issue.
- Married (2) **Joseph Fielding** on 23 January 1846 in Nauvoo, Hancock County, IL. They were the parents of (1) Mary Ann Fielding (1846–1922), (2) John Hyrum Fielding (born and died 1847), and (3) **Josephine Fielding**.
- Died on 12 January 1885 in Salt Lake City.

Letter reference: 20 May 1858

Peery, Luacine

- Born on 2 December 1912 in Salt Lake City to Joseph Strass Peery and **Julina Clarissa Smith**. Was a granddaughter of **Joseph F.**
- Married (1) Malcolm John Pingree (1908–70) on 19 September 1935 in Salt Lake City. They were the parents of five children.
- Married (2) Edward L. Bunnell (1928–2017) on 5 October 1987 in Utah. No issue.
- Died on 11 August 2011 in Roy, Weber County, UT.

Letter reference: 13 December 1916

Peterson, Alfred William, Jr.

- Born on 25 May 1905 in Salt Lake City to Alfred William Peterson and **Mary Sophronia Smith**. Was a grandson of **Joseph F.**
- Died on 21 November 1905 in Salt Lake City.

Letter reference: 22 November 1905

Phillips, Louisa Adelada

- Born on 29 December 1840 in Southampton, New Brunswick, Canada, to Matthew George Dow Phillips and Elizabeth Phillips.
- Married George W. Jacques (1836–1911) on 8 March 1856. Sealed in the Endowment House on 31 July 1857.
- Traveled with her family to Utah in 1855, when she was fourteen years old. The Phillips family started across the plains with the Seth M. Blair/Edward Stevenson Company, but family members soon died from cholera, so they stopped at the Big Nemaha River "to clean up the wagon and selves." They then continued on to Utah with the Richard Ballantyne Company, arriving on 25 September 1855.
- Died on 14 December 1915 in Provo, Utah County, UT.

Letter reference: 21 November 1871

Pierce, Edith Evelina

- Born on 18 November 1836 in Brandywine, Chester County, PA, to Robert Pierce and Hannah Harvey. Was the sister-in-law of **Jerusha Smith**, the half sister of **Joseph F.** and **Martha Ann**.
- Married **James Madison Fisher** on 12 February 1857 in Brigham City, Box Elder County, UT. They were the parents of seven children.
- Died on 19 May 1917 in East Millcreek, Salt Lake County, UT.

Letter references: 3 February 1857, 5 April 1857

Pierce, Eli Thomas

- Born on 27 January 1870 in North Ward, Box Elder County, UT, to **William Pierce** and **Jerusha Smith**. Was a nephew of **Joseph F.** and **Martha Ann**.
- Married (1) Annie Margrett Olsen (1871–1926) on 14 February 1890 in Logan, Cache County, UT. They were the parents of nine children.
- Married (2) Mary Augusta Atkinson (1877–1961) on 16 February 1927 in Salt Lake City. No issue.
- Was a farmer and stock raiser.
- Died on 22 July 1929 in Ogden, Weber County, UT.

Letter reference: 22 June 1912

Pierce, Hannah Eveline

- Born on 17 September 1855 in Brigham City, Box Elder County, UT, to **William Pierce** and **Jerusha Smith**. Was a niece of **Joseph F.** and **Martha Ann**.
- Married Aaron Beckstead (1858–1924) on 12 November 1876 in Brigham City. They were the parents of seven children.

- Died on 27 March 1916 in West Jordan, Salt Lake County, UT.

Letter references: 31 January 1856, 14 July 1856, 17 December 1856, 22 February 1863

Pierce, Hyrum Robert

- Born on 9 April 1857 in North Ward, Box Elder County, UT, to **William Pierce** and **Jerusha Smith**. Was a nephew of **Joseph F.** and **Martha Ann**.
- Married (1) Nellie Faith Hale (1871–1948) on 21 July 1891 in Ouray, Ouray County, CO. They were the parents of two children.
- Married (2) Lovina Rosalina Palmer (1866–1948) about 1882 in Salt Lake City. No issue.
- Died on 17 April 1917 in Brigham, Box Elder County, UT.

Letter references: 3 May 1857, 22 February 1863

Pierce, Lucy Lucinda

- Born on 22 January 1877 in North Ward, Box Elder County, UT, to **William Pierce** and **Jerusha Smith**. Was a niece of **Joseph F.** and **Martha Ann**.
- Died on 18 June 1880 in Calls Fort, Box Elder County, UT.

Letter reference: 4 June 1880

Pierce, Margaret Jerusha

- Born on 10 January 1863 in North Ward, Box Elder County, UT, to **William Pierce** and **Jerusha Smith**. Was a niece of **Joseph F.** and **Martha Ann**.
- Died on 12 October 1864, in Box Elder County, UT.

Letter reference: 22 February 1863

Pierce, Martha Lovina

- Born on 23 August 1860 in Brigham City, Box Elder County, UT, to **William Pierce** and **Jerusha Smith**. Was a niece of **Joseph F.** and **Martha Ann**.
- Married John Hyrum Green (1858–1944) on 30 November 1882 in Salt Lake City. They were the parents of eight children.
- Died on 1 March 1926 in Layton, Davis County, UT.

Letter references: 26 September 1860, 20 December 1860, 8 December 1861, 22 February 1863

Pierce, William

- Born on 2 April 1833 in Brandywine Township, Chester County, PA, to Robert Pierce and Hannah Harvey. Was a brother-in-law of **Joseph F.** and **Martha Ann**.
- Married (1) **Jerusha Smith** on 28 December 1854 in Salt Lake City. They were the parents of (1) **Hannah Eveline Pierce**, (2) **Hyrum Robert Pierce**, (3) **Martha Lovina Pierce**, (4) Margaret Jerusha Pierce (1863–64), (5) Sarah McKay Pierce (1865–1910), (6) **William Harvey Pierce**, (7) **Eli Thomas Pierce**, (8) Edith Irene Pierce (1872–1939), and (9) **Lucy Lucinda Pierce**.
- Married (2) Mary Electa Walker (1840–1904) on 21 November 1863 in Salt Lake City. They were the parents of five children. They later divorced.

- Died on 7 February 1908 in Harper Ward, Box Elder County, UT.

Letter references: 18 October 1855, 18 February 1856, 11 May 1857, 20 May 1858, 30 May 1861, 3 February 1862, Fall 1862, 22 June 1864, 7 December 1870

Pierce, William Harvey

- Born on 26 May 1868 in North Ward, Box Elder County, UT, to **William Pierce** and **Jerusha Smith**. Was a nephew of **Joseph F.** and **Martha Ann**. Nickname was "Willie."
- Died on 21 May 1880 in Box Elder County, UT.

Letter reference: 4 June 1880

Poulsen, Maren

- Born on 9 October 1835 in Lihmskov, Norup, Vejle, Denmark, to Mads Powelson and Dorthea Kirstine Mikkelson.
- Married **John Peter Rasmus Johnson** on 16 January 1857 in Salt Lake City. They were the parents of six children.
- Died on 5 October 1874 in Provo, Utah County, UT.

Letter reference: 5 October 1874

R

Raymond, Elizabeth C. "Libbie" Lattin

- Born about 1850 in Illinois.
- Married William Miner Raymond (dates unknown) on 22 July 1874 in Salt Lake City. They were the parents of two children.
- Died sometime after 1880.

Letter reference: 27 February 1876

Reynolds, Ethel Georgina

- Born on 23 October 1889 in Salt Lake City to George Reynolds and Amelia Jane Schofield. Was a daughter-in-law of **Joseph F.**
- Married **Joseph Fielding Smith** on 2 November 1908 in Salt Lake City. They were the parents of eight children.
- Served in various organizations of the Church from early girlhood and worked for a time in the Church Historian's Office. For several years served as chairman of the genealogical department of the Salt Lake Stake Relief Society and as assistant to Willard Young in the Salt Lake Genealogical Society. Also served as a member of the Relief Society General Board.
- Died on 26 August 1937 in Provo, Utah County, UT.

Letter reference: 20 March 1916

Rice, Leonard Gurley

- Born on 3 September 1829 in Northville, Wayne County, MI, to Ira Rice and Sarah Ann Harrington.
- Married (1) Elizabeth Almira Babbitt (1830–1907) on 18 March 1849 in Kanesville, Pottowattamie County, IA. They were the parents of twelve children.
- Leonard had two other wives and fourteen more children.
- Was an excellent horseman and ox team handler. Called on to help in the rescue of the Martin Handcart Company. Served a mission to England from 1865 to 1867.
- Died on 13 September 1886 in Farmington, Davis County, UT.

Letter reference: 14 June 1872

Rich, Alice May

- Born on 11 October 1877 in Salt Lake City to David Patten Rich and **Alice Ann Kimball**.
- Married Robert Roscoe Sant (1876–1942) on 16 June 1900 in Salt Lake City. They were the parents of (1) Sarah Kimball Sant (1901–79), (2) **Robert Smith Sant**, and (3) Kimball Smith Sant (1911–81).
- When her mother married **Joseph F.**, she was sealed into his family and her surname was changed from Rich to Smith.
- Died on 20 October 1920 in Long Beach, Los Angeles County, CA.

Letter references: 19 March 1898, 2 April 1905

Rich, Charles Coulson (1)

- Born on 21 August 1809 in Big Bone, Campbell County, KY, to Joseph Rich and Nancy O'Neal.
- Married (1) Sarah De Armon Pea (1814–93) on 11 February 1838 in Far West, Caldwell County, MO. They were the parents of nine children.
- Had five other wives and forty-two more children.
- Was a leader of Latter-day Saint defensive forces in Missouri, Illinois, and Utah. Led colonizing parties in Iowa, Idaho, and California. Served as a member of the Quorum of the Twelve Apostles from 1849 to 1883. Served a mission to California from 1849 to 1850 and to England from 1860 to 1862; in his second mission assisted mission president **Amasa Mason Lyman**. Served many years as a member of the Council and House Territorial Legislature.
- Died on 17 November 1883 in Paris, Bear Lake County, ID.

Letter reference: 1 March 1862

Rich, Charles Coulson (2)

- Born on 19 November 1881 in Salt Lake City to David Patten Rich and **Alice Ann Kimball**.
- Married Manon Lyman (1890–1964) on 16 April 1909 in Salt Lake City. They were the parents of seven children.
- After his mother married **Joseph F.**, he was sealed to **Joseph F.**'s family. Surname was changed from Rich to Smith.
- Died on 20 April 1933 in Salt Lake City.

Letter references: 24 December 1906, 24 May 1909

Rich, Heber Chase

- Born on 19 November 1881 in Salt Lake City to David Patten Rich and **Alice Ann Kimball**.
- Married **Leileth Nelson** on 2 September 1902 in Magrath, Alberta, Canada. They were the parents of three children.
- Sealed to the Smith family after his mother married **Joseph F.** Surname was changed from Rich to Smith.
- Died on 29 December 1971 in Salt Lake City.

Letter references: 2 April 1905, 20 March 1916

Richards, Joseph Smith

- Born on 4 October 1848 in Fort Bridger, Uinta County, WY, to Willard Richards and Sarah Longstroth. Was a brother-in-law of **Joseph F.**
- Married Louisa Marie Taylor (1857–1935) on 30 June 1876 in Salt Lake City. They were the parents of one child.
- Was a physician.
- Died on 30 October 1914 in Salt Lake City.

Letter references: 6 August 1870, 9 August 1890

Richards, Pauline

- Born on 11 May 1853 in Salt Lake City to Willard Richards and Sarah Longstroth. Was a sister-in-law of **Joseph F.**
- Married Abraham Fairbanks Doremus (1849–1933) on 15 November 1869 in Salt Lake City. They were the parents of (1) **Cora Doremus**, (2) Harriet Doremus (1872–76), (3) Abraham Fairbanks Doremus (born and died 1876), (4) Hattie Pauline Doremus Hagman (1878–1942), and (5) May Doremus (born and died 1887).
- Died on 21 September 1947 in Salt Lake City.

Letter reference: 23 February 1871

Richards, Rhoda Ann Jennetta

- Born on 15 September 1843 in Nauvoo, Hancock County, IL, to Willard Richards and Jennetta Richards. Was a sister-in-law of **Joseph F.**
- Married **Benjamin Franklin Knowlton** on 31 October 1863 in Salt Lake City. They were the parents of (1) Willard Knowlton (born and died 1865), (2) Wilhelmina Knowlton (born and died 1865), (3) Benjamin Franklin Knowlton (1866–1933), (4) Jenetta Knowlton (1868–71), (5) **Harriet Knowlton**, (6) Sidney Richards Knowlton (1873–76), (7) William Hooper Knowlton (1874–76), (8) Ida Knowlton (1876–1961), (9) Heber John Knowlton (1878–1906), (10) George Quincy Knowlton (1880–1957), and (11) Willard Richards Knowlton (1882–84).
- Educated her own children at home.
- Died on 3 May 1882 in Farmington, Davis County, UT.

Letter references: 6 August 1870, 26 January 1871, 23 February 1871

Richards, Sarah Ellen

- Born on 25 August 1850 in Salt Lake City to Willard Richards and Sarah Longstroth. Nickname was "Sary."

- Married **Joseph F.** on 1 March 1868 in Salt Lake City. They were the parents of (1) **Sarah Ellen Smith**, (2) **Leonora Smith**, (3) **Joseph Richards Smith**, (4) **Heber John Smith**, (5) **Rhoda Ann Smith**, (6) **Minerva Smith**, (7) **Alice Smith**, (8) **Willard Richards Smith**, (9) **Franklin Richards Smith**, (10) **Jeanetta Smith**, and (11) **Asenath Smith**.
- Was a very devoted and loving wife and mother. Enjoyed sewing. Served in the Relief Society and chosen as counselor in the Daughters of Utah Pioneers when the organization was created.
- Died on 22 March 1915 in Salt Lake City.

Letter references: 1 December 1868, 13 July 1869, 17 August 1869, 24 December 1869, 3 January 1869 (1870), 18 January 1870, 29 March 1870, 3 (31) March 1870, 5 July 1870, 6 August 1870, 18 August 1870, 7 December 1870, 26 January 1871, 23 February 1871, 26 May 1871, 14 September 1871, 3 May 1872, 18 January 1873, 20 June 1874, 15 August 1874, 5 October 1874, 24 November 1874, 26 November 1875, 11 July 1876, 25 August 1877, 14 August 1878, 22 April 1879, 18 September 1881, 13 March 1883, 31 July 1883, 15 August 1884, 18 March 1885, 2 May 1890, 9 August 1890, 12 May 1897, 19 March 1898, 13 October 1898, 2 April 1901, 8 March 1907, 22 June 1912, 20 August 1912, 5 February 1915, 17 February 1915, 17 July 1915

Richards, Willard Brigham

- Born on 25 January 1847 in Winter Quarters, Douglas County, NE, to Willard Richards and Sarah Longstroth. Was a brother-in-law of **Joseph F.**
- Married (1) Harriet Ann Fairbanks Doremus (1851–88) on 22 August 1877 in Salt Lake City. They were the parents of six children.
- Married (2) Mary Louisa Snelgrove (1856–1952) on 5 June 1889 in Salt Lake City. They were the parents of six children.
- Died on 30 May 1942 in Salt Lake City.

Letter reference: 12 December 1871

Robinson, John King

- Born on 12 July 1836 in St. Stephen, Charlotte, New Brunswick, Canada.
- Married Ellen Kay (1847–1929) in 1866 in Salt Lake City. No issue.
- Was the assistant surgeon at Fort Douglass in early 1866. After a time, he and other members of the fort established residence in Salt Lake City, where he became a prominent member of the non–Latter-day Saint community. Married the apostate daughter of a local doctor.
- Murdered in 1866 in Salt Lake City. Several well-known men in the Church were accused of committing the murder.
- Died on 22 October 1866 in Salt Lake City.

Letter reference: 12 December 1871

Robinson, Joseph

- Born on 4 September 1831 in Islip, Northamptonshire, England, to Samuel Robinson and Martha Barron. Was a father-in-law of **Franklin Hill Harris**, a son of **Martha Ann**.
- Married (1) Jemima Parkes (1831–1908) on 26 November 1853 in Derby, Derbyshire, England. They were the parents of (1) Elizabeth Annie Robinson (1857–1938), (2) Jemima Mary Robinson (1859–77), (3) Joseph William Robinson (1860–73), (4) Samuel John Robinson (1863–1948), (5) Jedde James Robinson (1865–1945), and (6) **Josephine Parkes Robinson**.
- Married (2) Anna (Addy) Maria Stephenson (1836–1900) on 5 February 1886. No issue. They later divorced.

- Operated a cooperative water-powered sawmill eight miles up Payson Canyon for years. Ordained a Seventy in Payson. In 1880 called to serve a mission to England. Was a cabinetmaker. In later years moved to Mexico in a colonizing group. Served in the temple whenever there was one nearby.
- Died on 26 June 1915 in Canutillo, El Paso County, TX.

Letter reference: 17 July 1915

Robinson, Josephine Parkes

- Born on 9 August 1868 in Payson, Utah County, UT, to **Joseph Robinson** and Jemima Parkes. Was a daughter-in-law of **Martha Ann**.
- Married **Franklin Hill Harris** on 26 January 1898 in Salt Lake City. They were the parents of five children.
- Died on 12 November 1965 in Provo, Utah County, UT.

Letter reference: 17 July 1915

Rogers, Washington Bolivar

- Born on 16 September 1826 in Mantua, Portage County, OH, to Noah Rogers and Eda Hollister.
- Married (1) Sarah Jane Thomas (1833–70) on 29 December 1859 in Salt Lake City. They were the parents of one child.
- Married two other wives and had twelve more children.
- Served a mission to Hawai'i beginning on 4 May 1854. Some of his fellow missionaries were **Joseph F.**, **Silas Smith**, **Silas S. Smith**, **Simpson M. Molen**, and **Orson K. Whitney**.
- Died on 14 January 1913 in Logan, Cache County, UT.

Letter reference: 20 October 1856

Russell, Mary Elizabeth

- Born on 11 February 1833 near Toronto, York, Canada, to Isaac Russell and Mary Walton.
- Married Andrew Scott Gray (1836–99) on 15 March 1862 in Salt Lake City. They were the parents of eight children.
- Died on 21 November 1905 in Salt Lake City.

Letter reference: 23 February 1871

S

Sansom, Charles

- Born on 16 April 1826 in Forest Green, Avening, Gloucester, England, to John Sansom and Sarah Lucas.
- Married (1) Mary Susannah Hartle (about 1830–51) on 31 October 1847. No issue.
- Married (2) Mary Ann Lewis (1835–1906) on 13 November 1853. They were the parents of eleven children.
- Married (3) Susannah Hartle in 1847, two years after his conversion. Immigrated to the United States from England, arriving in New Orleans in 1849 and settling in St. Louis, St. Louis County, MO. After his wife died, he moved to Salt Lake City in 1852. Lived in the Twentieth Ward in Salt Lake City and worked as a dry-goods clerk in a ward cooperative store. Ordained a Seventy and served a mission to England from 1873

to 1874. Also served as secretary in the Sunday School of the Salt Lake City Twentieth Ward from November 1888 to December 1899.

- Died on 28 March 1908 in Salt Lake City.

Letter reference: 7 September 1874 (first letter)

Sant, Robert Smith

- Born on 29 March 1905 in Salt Lake City to Robert Roscoe Sant and **Alice May Rich**. Was a grandson of **Joseph F.**
- Married Natalie Evelyn Willis (1901–92) on 2 June 1927 in Salt Lake City. They were the parents of one child.
- Died on 13 October 1988 in Logan, Cache County, UT.

Letter reference: 2 April 1905

Schoeni, Christian

- Born on 5 May 1831 in Otterback, Bern, Switzerland, to Christen Schoeni and Elisabeth Wenger.
- Married (1) Elisabeth Muhlestein (1834–66) in 1862 in Switzerland. They were the parents of three children.
- Married (2) Maria Burgener (1847–1922) in 1867 in Switzerland. They were the parents of ten children.
- Joined the Church in Switzerland and immigrated to Utah to be with the Saints. In several letters from **Martha Ann**, he requested to be sealed to **Joseph F.** It appears he was subsequently given permission.
- Died on 21 January 1900 in Midway, Wasatch County, UT.

Letter references: 8 September 1874, 6 November 1874, 8 December 1874

Schwartz, Mary Taylor

- Born on 30 April 1865 in Holladay, Salt Lake County, UT, to William Schwartz and **Agnes Taylor**.
- Married **Joseph F.** on 13 January 1884 in Salt Lake City. They were the parents of (1) John Schwartz Smith (1888–89), (2) **Calvin Schwartz Smith**, (3) Samuel Schwartz Smith (1892–1983), (4) James Schwartz Smith (1894–1950), (5) Agnes Smith (1897–1966), (6) Silas Schwartz Smith (1900–1983), and (7) **Royal Grant Smith**.
- Attended the public school in her ward and later attended Deseret University. While she was a teenager, her uncle **John Taylor** employed her as a housekeeper. During that time, she was introduced to **Joseph F.** While **Joseph F.** was away on a mission, she attended Brigham Young University. Completed courses in obstetrics and nursing. Later studied medicine and enjoyed playing the piano.
- Served in ward and stake Primaries, as president of the Fourteenth Ward Retrenchment Association, as an aide in the Salt Lake Stake Primary, as first Primary president of the Ensign Stake, and on the general board of the Relief Society. In 1910 accompanied **Joseph F.** on a trip to Europe. Following her husband's death, served almost daily as a temple worker in the Salt Lake Temple.
- Died on 5 December 1956 in Salt Lake City.

Letter references: 8 March 1907, 26 December 1911, 20 August 1912, 9 July 1914, 30 September 1916

Scott, Andrew Hunter

- Born on 21 August 1815 in Hulmeville, Middleton, Bucks County, PA, to Joshua Scott and Ann Keen.

- Married (1) Sarah Leeds Sleeper (1816–1900) on 18 February 1838 in Vincent Town, Burlington County, NJ. They were the parents of five children.
- Had two other wives and nineteen other children.
- Was a tailor by trade. Also farmed and imported sheep. Manufactured woolen cloth and engaged in bee raising and silk culture. Ordained a Seventy in 1854. Was the first director of the Deseret Agriculture and Manufacturing Society of Utah County. Built the first schoolhouse in the Provo Second Ward, the first courthouse in Utah County, the Provo meetinghouse, and the Provo Woolen Mills. Helped to construct canyon roads and bridges and dams on the Provo River. In 1861 ordained the second bishop of the Provo Second Ward. Served Provo City as recorder, assessor, collector, and watermaster. Served as mayor of Provo for six years.
- Died on 11 October 1874 in Provo, Utah County, UT.

Letter reference: 5 October 1874

SHARP, CECILIA

- Born on 27 November 1860 in Salt Lake City to **John Sharp** and Jane Patterson.
- Contracted spotted fever as a child and died soon after.
- Died on 16 May 1872 in Salt Lake City.

Letter reference: 17 May 1872

SHARP, JOHN

- Born on 9 November 1820 in Devonside, Tilliconltry, Clackmannan, Scotland, to John Sharp and Mary Hunter.
- Married (1) Jane Patterson (1818–82) in 1839 in Scotland. They were the parents of (1) John Sharp Jr. (1841–91), (2) James Sharp (1843–1903), (3) Margaret Sharp (1845–1906), (4) Adam Sharp (1849–50), (5) Jane Sharp (1849–53), (6) Catharine Sharp (1852–1901), (7) Adam Sharp (1855–90), (8) Agnes Sharp (1857–1921), (9) **Cecelia Sharp**, and (10) Elizabeth Alice Sharp (1864–1923).
- Married two other wives and had thirteen more children.
- Was bishop of the Salt Lake City Twentieth Ward and superintendent of the Utah Central Railroad.
- Died on 23 December 1891 in Salt Lake City.

Letter reference: 17 May 1872

SIMMONS, EDNA MAE

- Born on 1 April 1899 in Mammoth, Juab County, UT, to Jonothan Simmons and **Lucy Smith Harris**. Was a granddaughter of **Martha Ann**.
- Married (1) Vivian Clyde Safford (1896–1919) on 15 May 1918. They were the parents of Virginia Safford (1919–98).
- Married (2) Leon Albert Hedquist (1898–1991) on 28 June 1921. They were the parents of three children.
- Raised by **Martha Ann**, her maternal grandmother, following her mother's death in 1902 or 1903.
- Died on 14 May 1986 in Utah County, UT.

Letter references: 10 April 1907, 22 December 1911, 23 December 1912, 3 March 1913, 9 July 1914, 5 February 1915, 17 July 1915

Simmons, John Arthur

- Born on 17 December 1900 in Robinson, Juab County, UT, to Jonathan Simmons and **Lucy Smith Harris**. Was a grandson of **Martha Ann**.
- Married Blanche Dayton (1896–1980) on 6 March 1923 in Provo, Utah County, UT. They were the parents of two children.
- Died on 30 October 1961.

Letter references: 10 April 1907, 22 December 1911, 23 December 1912, 3 March 1913, 5 February 1915, 17 July 1915

Singleton, Melinda Lucretia ("Lula")

- Born on 15 August 1874 in Springville, Utah County, UT, to Hubert Singleton and Eliza Mower.
- Married **Israel William Roberts Hudson** on 9 September 1896 in Provo, Utah County, UT. They were the parents of seven children.
- Apparently rented a home in Provo that belonged to **Joseph F.**
- Died on 18 March 1955 in Provo, Utah County, UT.

Letter reference: 7 July 1914

Smith, Agnes Charlotte

- Born on 1 August 1836 in Kirtland, Geauga County, OH, to Don Carlos Smith and **Agnes Moulton Coolbrith**. Was a first cousin to **Joseph F.** and **Martha Ann**.
- Married William Henry Peterson (1826–68) on 3 March 1858 in Los Angeles, Los Angeles County, CA. They were the parents of seven children.
- Moved with her mother to Los Angeles, Los Angeles County, CA, in the 1850s.
- Died on 31 January 1873 in Los Angeles, Los Angeles County, CA.

Letter references: 9 June 1855, 23 November 1855, 25 July 1857

Smith, Albert Jesse

- Born on 16 September 1881 in Salt Lake City to **Joseph F.** and **Edna Lambson**.
- Died on 25 August 1883 in Salt Lake City.

Letter references: 18 September 1881, 23 November 1881, 13 March 1883, 27 March 1883, 31 July 1883, 26 August 1883, [1 November] 1895

Smith, Albert William

- Born on 4 August 1862 in Salt Lake City to **Elias Smith** and **Amy Jane King**. Was a second cousin to **Joseph F.** and **Martha Ann**.
- Died on 29 July 1866 in Salt Lake City.

Letter reference: 26 November 1875

Smith, Alexander Hale

- Born on 2 June 1838 in Far West, Caldwell County, MO, to **Joseph Smith Jr.** and Emma Hale. Was a first cousin to **Joseph F.** and **Martha Ann**.

- Married Elizabeth Agnes Kendall (1843–1919) on 23 May 1861 in Nauvoo, Hancock County, IL. They were the parents of nine children.
- Baptized a member of the Reorganized Church of Jesus Christ of Latter Day Saints (RLDS) on 25 May 1862 in Nauvoo by his brother Joseph Smith III. Served RLDS missions to Iowa, California, Utah, Missouri, Illinois, Kansas, Wisconsin, Minnesota, North and South Dakota, Hawai'i, and Australia. Ordained an RLDS Apostle on 10 April 1873 and served as counselor to RLDS Church President Joseph Smith III from 1897 to 1902. Also served as RLDS Church Patriarch from 1897 to 1909.
- Died on 12 August 1909 in Nauvoo, Hancock County, IL.

Letter references: 21 June 1869, 13 July 1869, 17 August 1869

Smith, Alfred Jason

- Born on 13 December 1876 in Salt Lake City to **Joseph F.** and **Edna Lambson**.
- Died on 6 April 1878 in Salt Lake City.

Letter references: 22 April 1878, 26 August 1883, [1 November] 1895

Smith, Alice

- Born on 27 July 1882 in Salt Lake City to **Joseph F.** and **Sarah Ellen Richards**.
- Died on 29 April 1901 in Salt Lake City.

Letter references: 13 March 1883, 27 March 1883, 31 July 1883, 2 April 1901

Smith, Alvin Fielding

- Born on 19 July 1874 in Salt Lake City to **Joseph F.** and **Edna Lambson**.
- Married Amelia Atkins (1875–1960) on 30 June 1903 in Salt Lake City. They were the parents of five children.
- Died on 4 January 1948 in Salt Lake City.

Letter references: 15 August 1874, 24 November 1874, 2 April 1905

Smith, Andrew Kimball

- Born on 6 January 1893 in Salt Lake City to **Joseph F.** and **Alice Ann Kimball**.
- Married (1) Gladys Nielsen (1898–1938) on 1 June 1921 in Logan, Cache County, UT. They were the parents of two children.
- Married two other wives. No issue.
- Died on 23 August 1951 in Salt Lake City.

Letter references: 19 March 1898, 25 July 1904, 7 July 1914

Smith, Andrew McLean

- Born on 16 May 1823 in Smith, Washington County, PA, to William Henderson Smith and Hannah McLean.
- Married **Serinna Thompson** on 14 August 1857 in Salt Lake City. No issue.
- No other information is known.

Letter reference: 5 April 1857

Smith, Asenath

- Born on 28 December 1896 in Salt Lake City to **Joseph F.** and **Sarah Ellen Richards**.
- Married Clifford Earl Conklin (1892–1992). They were the parents of three children.
- Died on 3 August 1982 in Salt Lake City.

Letter reference: 12 May 1897

Smith, Bathsheba Kate

- Born on 14 August 1844 in Nauvoo, Hancock County, IL, to **George Albert Smith** and **Bathsheba Wilson Bigler**. Was a second cousin to **Joseph F.** and **Martha Ann**. Nickname was "Kate."
- Married Clarence Merrill (1841–1918) on 3 January 1861 in Salt Lake City. They were the parents of fourteen children.
- Was a skilled artist. Could make shoes, hats, coats, and dresses. Active in drama and painted scenery for local theater productions following her family's move to Fillmore, Millard County, UT. Her husband, Clarence, was a good friend of her brother **George Albert Smith Jr.**
- Died on 22 December 1920 in Crescent, Salt Lake County, UT.

Letter references: 3 May 1872, 1 February 1906

Smith, Briant Grant

- Born on 15 December 1916 in Salt Lake City to **Willard Richards Smith** and Florence Grant.
- Married Cecile Eileen Jackson (1919–2004) on 16 March 1943 in Salt Lake City. They were the parents of one child.
- Died on 14 January 2006 and was buried in Salt Lake City.

Letter reference: 19 December 1916

Smith, Calvin Schwartz

- Born on 29 May 1890 in Salt Lake City to **Joseph F.** and **Mary Taylor Schwartz**.
- Married Ethel Lucille Dimond (1897–1986) on 28 September 1917 in Salt Lake City. They were the parents of thirteen children.
- Died on 15 June 1966 in Salt Lake City.

Letter reference: 22 November 1905

Smith, David Asael

- Born on 24 May 1879 in Salt Lake City to **Joseph F.** and **Julina Lambson**.
- Married **Emily Jenkins** on 24 January 1901 in Salt Lake City. They were the parents of ten children.
- Served as a member of the General Board of the Deseret Sunday School Union. Was a member of the Salt Lake Stake Sunday School Board, vice president of the Dr. W. H. Groves LDS Hospital, president of the Tabernacle Choir, and member of the Presiding Bishopric.
- Died on 6 April 1952 in Salt Lake City.

Letter references: 7 February 1901, 5 February 1915, 20 March 1916

Smith, David Hyrum

- Born on 17 November 1844 in Nauvoo, Hancock County, IL, to **Joseph Smith Jr.** and Emma Hale. Was a first cousin to **Joseph F.** and **Martha Ann**.
- Married Clara Charlotte Hartshom (1851–1926) on 10 May 1870 in Nauvoo, Hancock County, IL. They were the parents of one child.
- Baptized into the Reorganized Church of Jesus Christ of Latter Day Saints on 26 June 1861 in Nauvoo, Hancock County, IL. Served as a counselor in the RLDS Presidency from 1873 to 1885.
- Died on 29 August 1904 in Elgin, Kane County, IL.

Letter references: 21 June 1869, 13 July 1869, 17 August 1869

Smith, Donnette

- Born on 17 September 1872 in Salt Lake City to **Joseph F.** and **Julina Lambson**. Nickname was "Donnie."
- Married Alonzo Pratt Kesler (1868–1918) on 26 December 1900 in Salt Lake City. They were the parents of (1) **Donnette Kesler**, (2) Marion Kesler (1903–51), (3) Alonzo Pratt Kesler (1905–84), (4) **Henry Smith Kesler**, (5) Imogene Kesler (1909–93), and (6) Mack Smith Kesler (1911–99).
- Acted as superintendent of the LDS College from 1894 to 1896 and was a worker in the Red Cross social service in 1919. Presided over the YLMIA (Young Ladies' Mutual Improvement Association, precursor to the Young Women organization) of the Salt Lake City Sixteenth Ward and was a member of the Salt Lake Stake YLMIA board through 1904. Was a member of the Ensign Stake Sunday School board from 1924 to 1928 and of the Ensign Stake genealogical board from 1928 to 1936. Was president of the Utah State Kindergarten Association from 1902 to 1903 and vice president of the Daughters of Utah Pioneers in 1922. Also labored extensively as an ordinance worker in the Salt Lake Temple.
- Died on 15 September 1961 in Salt Lake City.

Letter references: 27 February 1874, 24 November 1874, 22 April 1878, 11 February 1887, 28 March 1896, 12 May 1897, 7 February 1901, 24 April 1909, 6 May 1909, 24 May 1909, 22 December 1909, 18 June 1913

Smith, Edith Eleanor

- Born on 3 January 1894 in Salt Lake City to **Joseph F.** and **Julina Lambson**.
- Married William Thorn Patrick (1890–1969) on 1 January 1918 in Salt Lake City. They were the parents of four children.
- Died on 21 May 1987 in Bountiful, Davis County, UT.

Letter references: 19 March 1898, 26 December 1911

Smith, Edna Melissa

- Born on 6 October 1879 in Salt Lake City to **Joseph F.** and **Edna Lambson**.
- Married John Fife Bowman (1880–1960) on 27 January 1903 in Salt Lake City. They were the parents of seven children.
- Died on 26 October 1958 in Salt Lake City.

Letter references: 13 March 1883, 31 July 1883, 6 September 1899, 16 October 1899, 2 April 1905, 27 November 1907, 20 March 1916, 19 December 1916

Smith, Edward Arthur

- Born on 1 November 1858 in Brampton, Chesterfield, Derbyshire, England. Was an adopted son of **Joseph F.**
- Married Cytha Ellen Smith (1863–1947) on 3 March 1881 in Salt Lake City. They were the parents of eleven children.
- Died on 17 July 1911 in Raymond, Alberta, Canada.

Letter references: 1 December 1868, 13 July 1869, 17 August 1869, 24 December 1869, 3 January 1869 (1870), 18 January 1870, 29 March 1870, 3 (31) March 1870, 5 July 1870, 7 December 1870, 26 January 1871, 23 February 1871, 21 April 1871, 12 December 1871, 18 January 1873

Smith, Edward Hunter

- Born on 5 August 1875 in Salt Lake City to **Elias Smith** and **Amy Jane King**. Was a second cousin to **Joseph F.** and **Martha Ann**.
- Died on 25 November 1875 in Salt Lake City.

Letter reference: 26 November 1875

Smith, Elias

- Born on 6 September 1804 in Royalton, Windsor County, VT, to Asael Smith and Elizabeth Schellenger. Was a first cousin once removed to **Joseph F.** and **Martha Ann**.
- Married (1) Charity Smith (1808–88) about 1829. No issue.
- Married (2) **Lucy Brown** on 6 August 1845 in Nauvoo, Hancock County, IL. They were the parents of (1) Emily Jane Smith (1850–78), (2) Lucy Elizabeth Smith (1855–1944), (3) Elias Asahel Smith (1857–1942), and (4) Edith Ann Smith (1861–1954).
- Married (3) **Amy Jane King** on 15 April 1856 in Salt Lake City. They were the parents of (1) Silas Thomas Smith (1857–1931), (2) Jesse Moroni Smith (1858–1937), (3) Rebecca Jane Smith (1860–1923), (4) Albert William Smith (1862–66), (5) Mary Alzina Knapp Smith (1865–1953), (6) Martha Priscilla Smith (1865–1946), (7) Amy Esther Smith (1867–1910), (8) Angeline Adelia Smith (1869–1950), (9) Franklin Elias Smith (1871–1917), (10) Sarah Susannah Smith (1873–1952), (11) **Thomas King Smith**, (12) **Edward Hunter Smith**, and (13) Hiram Bennett Smith (1877–1951).
- Was a schoolteacher. While living in Nauvoo was business manager of the *Times and Seasons* and the *Nauvoo Neighbor*. Elected probate judge of Salt Lake County. In 1862 was a member of the constitutional convention. Was business manager of the *Deseret News* and its third editor from 1859 to 1863, following **Albert Carrington**.
- Died on 24 June 1888 in Salt Lake City.

Letter references: 20 May 1858, 22 June 1864, 26 November 1875

Smith, Elias Wesley

- Born on 21 April 1886 in Lāʻie, Oʻahu, HI, to **Joseph F.** and **Julina Lambson**.
- Married Mary Huskinson Smith (1884–1973) on 15 December 1910 in Salt Lake City. They were the parents of five children.
- Served as a missionary to the Hawaiian Islands from 1907 to 1910. Later served as president of the Hawaiian Mission from 1919 to 1922.
- Died on 28 December 1970 in Salt Lake City.

Letter references: 11 February 1887, May 1887, 2 April 1905, 22 December 1909, 10 September 1914

SMITH, ELIZABETH MARIA

- Born on 8 October 1854 in Millcreek, Salt Lake County, UT, to **John Smith** and **Hellen Maria Fisher**. Was a niece of **Joseph F.** and **Martha Ann**.
- Married Charles Holding Evans (1852–1932) on 18 April 1873 in Salt Lake City. They were the parents of (1) Mary Elizabeth Smith Evans (1873–1943), (2) **Laura Smith Evans**, (3) Lillian Smith Evans (1877–1953), (4) Charles John Smith Evans (1879–1950), (5) Sidney Smith Evans (1881–83), (6) Florence Smith Evans (1883–1974), (7) Hyrum Smith Evans (1886–1982), (8) Helen J. Smith Evans (1889–death unknown), and (9) Eva Smith Evans (born and died 1891).
- Died on 8 April 1891.

Letter reference: 17 December 1856

SMITH, EMILY JANE

- Born on 11 September 1888 in Salt Lake City to **Joseph F.** and **Julina Lambson**.
- Married John William Walker (1872–1948) on 5 May 1918 in Salt Lake City. They were the parents of four children.
- Died on 12 December 1982 in Morgan, Morgan County, UT.

Letter references: 20 June 1892, 19 March 1898, 2 April 1905, 6 May 1909, 24 May 1909, 10 September 1914

SMITH, EMMA

- Born on 21 August 1888 in Salt Lake City to **Joseph F.** and **Edna Lambson**.
- Married Peter Joseph Jensen (1869–1957) on 9 October 1956 in Salt Lake City. No issue.
- Died on 28 December 1969 in Salt Lake City.

Letter references: 20 August 1912, 18 June 1913

SMITH, EMMA PEARL

- Born on 19 April 1871 in Salt Lake City to **George Albert Smith** and **Susan Elizabeth West**.
- Married William Nugent Williams (1851–1927). No issue.
- Died on 6 October 1905 in Salt Lake City.

Letter reference: 3 May 1872

SMITH, FIELDING KIMBALL

- Born on 9 April 1900 in Salt Lake City to **Joseph F.** and **Alice Ann Kimball**.
- Married (1) Norma Hughes (1893–1934) on 20 December 1933 in Salt Lake City. No issue.
- Married (2) Ruby Knowell (1893–death unknown) on 19 July 1956 in Jackson, Teton County, WY. No issue.
- Died on 20 October 1974 in Salt Lake City.

Letter reference: 25 July 1904

SMITH, FRANKLIN RICHARDS

- Born on 12 May 1888 in Salt Lake City to **Joseph F.** and **Sarah Ellen Richards**.

- Married (1) Ella Elise Olsen (1894–1965) on 18 August 1913 in Salt Lake City. They were the parents of three children.
- Married (2) Naomi Hollingsworth (1909–96) on 17 April 1929 in Farmington, Davis County, UT. They were the parents of two children.
- Died on 25 December 1967 in Salt Lake City.

Letter references: 7 June 1891, 5 February 1915, 17 February 1915

Smith, George Albert

- Born on 26 June 1817 in Potsdam, St. Lawrence County, NY, to John Smith and Clarissa Lyman. Was a first cousin once removed to **Joseph F.** and **Martha Ann**.
- Married (1) **Bathsheba Wilson Bigler** on 25 July 1841 in Nauvoo, Hancock County, IL. They were the parents of (1) **George Albert Smith Jr.** (1842–60), (2) **Bathsheba Kate Smith**, and (3) John Smith (born and died 1847).
- Married (2) **Susan Elizabeth West** on 28 October 1857 in Salt Lake City. They were the parents of (1) Clarissa West Smith (1859–1930), (2) **Margaret West Smith**, (3) Elizabeth Smith (1866–1921), (4) Priscilla Smith (1869–1907), and (5) Emma Pearl Smith (1871–1905).
- Married five other wives and had twelve more children.
- Served three missions in the 1830s to Ohio and the surrounding areas in the United States. Sent to Nauvoo for his fourth mission. Ordained an Apostle in 1839. Then served a mission to England. Headed the Iron Mission from 1850 to 1852, presided over Utah Valley from 1852 to 1853, and became Church Historian in 1854. The town of St. George, Washington County, UT, was named after him. Sent on a mission to Jerusalem in the early 1870s.
- Died on 1 September 1875 in Salt Lake City.

Letter references: 15 December 1860, 22 June 1864, 3 May 1872, 14 June 1872, 1 July 1873, 27 February 1874, 7 September 1875

Smith, George Albert, Jr.

- Born on 7 July 1842 in Nauvoo, Hancock County, IL, to **George Albert Smith** and **Bathsheba Wilson Bigler**. Was a second cousin to **Joseph F.** and **Martha Ann**.
- Killed by a Navajo Indian while serving a mission to the Indians.
- Died on 2 November 1860.

Letter reference: 20 December 1860

Smith, George Carlos

- Born on 14 October 1881 in Salt Lake City to **Joseph F.** and **Julina Lambson**.
- Married **Lillian Emery** on 29 October 1902 in Salt Lake City. They were the parents of eleven children.
- Died on 25 February 1931 in Salt Lake City.

Letter references: 23 November 1881, 13 March 1883, 31 July 1883, 2 April 1905, 20 March 1916

Smith, Heber John

- Born on 3 July 1876 in Salt Lake City to **Joseph F.** and **Sarah Ellen Richards**.

- Died on 3 March 1877 in Salt Lake City.

Letter references: 11 July 1876, 22 April 1878, 26 August 1883, [1 November] 1895

Smith, Hellen Jerusha

- Born on 26 October 1872 in Salt Lake City to **John Smith** and **Hellen Maria Fisher**.
- Died on 30 July 1881 in Salt Lake City.

Letter reference: 28 July 1881

Smith, Hyrum

- Born on 9 February 1800 in Tunbridge, Orange County, VT, to **Joseph Smith Sr.** and **Lucy Mack**. Was the father of **Joseph F.** and **Martha Ann**.
- Married (1) Jerusha Barden on 2 November 1826 in Manchester, Ontario County, NY. They were the parents of (1) **Lovina Smith**, (2) Mary Smith (1829–32), (3) **John Smith**, (4) Hyrum Smith (1834–41), (5) **Jerusha Smith**, and (6) **Sarah Smith**.
- Married (2) **Mary Fielding** on 24 December 1837 in Kirtland, Geauga County, OH. They were the parents of (1) **Joseph Fielding Smith** and (2) **Martha Ann Smith (Harris)**.
- Married (3) **Mercy Rachel Fielding** in August of 1843 in Nauvoo, Hancock County, IL. No issue.
- Married (4) Catharine Phillips (1819–1900) in August 1843 in Nauvoo, Hancock County, IL. No issue.
- Baptized by his brother **Joseph Smith Jr.** in June 1829. Appointed second counselor to the Prophet Joseph Smith in Far West, Caldwell County, MO, on 7 November 1837. Called by revelation to be Patriarch to the Church on 19 January 1841.
- Died on 27 June 1844 in Carthage Jail, Carthage, Hancock County, IL.

Letter references: 6 August 1870, 26 August 1883, 12 November 1883, 18 June 1890, 4 August 1890, 20 June 1892, 28 January 1895, 25 August 1897, 26 July 1902, 8 February 1904, 23 January 1905, 2 April 1905

Smith, Hyrum Fisher

- Born on 10 January 1856 in Sugar House, Salt Lake County, UT, to **John Smith** and **Hellen Maria Fisher**. Was a nephew of **Joseph F.** and **Martha Ann**.
- Married Hannah Marie Gibbs (1862–1924) on 12 December 1878 in Salt Lake City. They were the parents of nine children.
- Died on 9 March 1923 in Provo, Utah County, UT.

Letter references: 17 December 1856, 12 May 1897

Smith, Hyrum Mack

- Born on 21 March 1872 in Salt Lake City to **Joseph F.** and **Edna Lambson**.
- Married Ida Elizabeth Bowman (1872–1918) on 15 November 1895 in Salt Lake City. They were the parents of five children.
- Called to be an Apostle. Served as president of the European Mission from 1913 to 1916.
- Died on 23 January 1918 in Salt Lake City.

Letter references: 3 May 1872, 17 June 1872, 28 March 1896, 19 March 1898, 23 July 1902

Smith, Jeanetta

- Born on 25 August 1891 in Salt Lake City to **Joseph F.** and **Sarah Ellen Richards**. Nickname was "Nettie."
- Married Blanchard Pettit Ashton (1893–1922) on 9 June 1921 in Salt Lake City. No issue.
- Died on 27 January 1932 in Salt Lake City.

Letter reference: 19 March 1898

Smith, Jerusha

- Born on 13 January 1836 in Kirtland, Geauga County, OH, to **Hyrum Smith** and Jerusha Barden. Was a half sister of **Joseph F.** and **Martha Ann**.
- Married **William Pierce** on 28 December 1854 in Salt Lake City. They were the parents of (1) **Hannah Eveline Pierce**, (2) **Hyrum Robert Pierce**, (3) **Martha Lavinia Pierce**, (4) Margaret Jerusha Pierce (1863–64), (5) Sarah McGhie Pierce (1865–1910), (6) **William Harvey Pierce**, (7) **Eli Thomas Pierce**, (8) Edith Irene Pierce (1872–1939), and (9) **Lucy Lucinda Pierce**.
- Died on 27 June 1912 in Harper Ward, Box Elder County, UT.

Letter references: 1 November 1854, 28 January 1855, 18 October 1855, 31 January 1856, 18 February 1856, 14 July 1856, 2 October 1856, 17 December 1856, 3 May 1857, 11 May 1857, 14 June 1857, 25 July 1857, 20 May 1858, 26 September 1860, 15 December 1860, 20 December 1860, 8 December 1861, 12 January 1862, 3 February 1862, 1 March 1862, 30 September 1862, 22 February 1863, 22 June 1864, 1864, 21 June 1869, 27 October 1870, 23 February 1871, 14 June 1872, 27 February 1876, 18 June 1890, 16 January 1891, 27 September 1895, 25 August 1897, 26 July 1900, 22 November 1905, 6 May 1909, 19 September 1910, 7 November 1910, 24 December 1910, 22 June 1912

Smith, Jesse Kimball

- Born on 21 May 1896 in Salt Lake City to **Joseph F.** and **Alice Ann Kimball**.
- Married (1) **Louise May Anderson** on 25 September 1915 in Salt Lake City. They were the parents of three children.
- Married (2) Johanna Baty (1903–82) on 3 July 1944. No issue.
- Died on 9 June 1953.

Letter references: 19 March 1898, 25 July 1904, 17 February 1916, 20 March 1916

Smith, Jesse Nathaniel

- Born on 2 December 1834 in Stockholm, St. Lawrence County, NY, to Silas Smith and Mary Aikens. Was a first cousin to **Hyrum Smith** and a first cousin once removed to **Joseph F.** and **Martha Ann**.
- Married (1) Emma Saraphine West (1836–1910) on 13 May 1852 in Parowan, Iron County, UT. They were the parents of nine children.
- Had four other wives and thirty-five other children.
- Served in many civic and Church capacities. Participated in the Walker War of 1853–54. Ordained a Seventy on 12 March 1854 and became a member of the Ninth Quorum of the Seventy. Appointed a counselor in the Parowan Stake Presidency. Elected district attorney by the legislature and officiated as clerk of Iron County, UT. Taught school. Elected mayor of Parowan in 1859. Served a mission to Europe from 1861 to 1864 and presided over the Scandinavian Mission from 1862 to 1864. In 1866 elected as probate judge of Iron County. Served a second mission to Scandinavia from 1868 to 1870. In 1879 was called with his family to build up the settlement at Snowflake, Navajo County, Arizona. Served in the Utah legislature in 1880. Served as president of the Snowflake Stake.

- Died on 5 June 1906 in Snowflake, Navajo County, AZ.

Letter reference: 15 December 1860

Smith, John

- Born on 22 September 1832 in Kirtland, Geauga County, OH, to **Hyrum Smith** and Jerusha Barden. Was a half brother of **Joseph F.** and **Martha Ann**.
- Married (1) **Hellen Maria Fisher** on 25 December 1853 in Salt Lake City. They were the parents of (1) **Elizabeth Maria Smith**, (2) **Hyrum Fisher Smith**, (3) **Lucy Smith**, (4) Don Carlos Smith (1861–1937), (5) Joseph Smith (1865–1912), (6) Alvin Fisher Smith (1867–1955), (7) Evaline Smith (1867–78), (8) John David Smith (1870–78), and (9) **Hellen Jerusha Smith**.
- Married (2) **Nancy Melissa Lemmon** on 18 February 1857 in Salt Lake City. They were the parents of one child.
- Spent his childhood as a member of the Church. Moved west with the Saints from Nauvoo and traveled to the Salt Lake Valley with his siblings, driving one of his stepmother's wagons at age sixteen. Took over the family farm in East Millcreek after the death of his mother, Mary Fielding Smith. Called as the sixth presiding Patriarch to the Church in 1855, serving for fifty-six years. Known and recognized for his spiritual discernment and the simple and powerful patriarchal blessings that he gave. Served a mission to Scandinavia from 1862 to 1864.
- Died on 6 November 1911 in Salt Lake City.

Letter references: 28 January 1855, 9 June 1855, 23 November 1855, 31 January 1856, 18 February 1856, 14 July 1856, 29 July 1856, 2 October 1856, 20 October 1856, 17 December 1856, 3 February 1857, 5 April 1857, 17 April 1857, 3 May 1857, 14 June 1857, 25 July 1857, 20 May 1858, 28 July 1860, 12 March 1861, Spring 1861, 30 May 1861, 8 December 1861, 12 January 1862, 1 March 1862, 22 February 1863, 23 (24) February 1863, 12 June 1864, 21 June 1869, 17 August 1869, 3 January 1869 (1870), 18 August 1870, 27 October 1870, 7 December 1870, 23 February 1871, 5 October 1874, 6 November 1874, 14 August 1878, 4 June 1880, 1 July 1881, 28 July 1881, 18 March 1885, 13 April 1885, 22 May 1890, 18 June 1890, 16 January 1891, 27 September 1895, 26 July 1900, 22 November 1905, 24 April 1909, 6 May 1909, 19 September 1910, 24 December 1910, 6 November 1911, 20 August 1912

Smith, John Henry

- Born on 18 September 1848 in Carbunca, near Kanesville, Pottawattamie County, IA, to **George Albert Smith** and Sarah Ann Libby. Was a second cousin to **Joseph F.** and **Martha Ann**. Was also the father of George Albert Smith.
- Married (1) **Sarah Farr** on 20 October 1866 in Salt Lake City. They were the parents of (1) John Henry Smith Jr. (born and died 1868), (2) George Albert Smith (1870–1951), (3) **Lorin Farr Smith**, (4) Don Carlos Smith (1874–1927), (5) Ezra Chase Smith (1876–1951), (6) Charles Warren Smith (born and died 1879), (7) Winslow Farr Smith (1881–1966), (8) Nathaniel Libby Smith (1883–1935), (9) Nancy Clarabell Smith (1886–1961), (10) Tirzah Priscille Smith (1888–1951), and (11) Elsie Louise Smith (1891–1926).
- Married (2) Josephine Groesbeck (1857–1948) on 4 April 1877 in St. George, Washington County, UT. They were the parents of eight children.
- Worked on the railroad as a young man. Was assistant clerk of the House of Representatives of the territorial legislature of 1872. Served a mission to Europe from 1874 to 1875 and presided over the British Mission. Was an employee of the Utah Central Railway for several years. Ordained a high priest in 1875 and set apart to preside over the Salt Lake City Seventeenth Ward. Ordained an Apostle by **Wilford Woodruff** on 27 October 1880. Presided over the European Mission from 1882 to 1885. Chosen president of the constitutional convention during the term that Utah gained statehood in 1896. In 1910 set apart as second counselor in the First Presidency under **Joseph F.**

- Died on 13 October 1911 in Salt Lake City.

Letter references: 3 May 1872, 5 August 1874

Smith, John Lyman

- Born on 17 November 1823 in Potsdam, Lawrence County, NY, to John Smith and Clarissa Lyman. Was a first cousin once removed to **Joseph F.** and **Martha Ann**.
- Married (1) Augusta Bowen Cleveland (1828–1903) on 9 July 1845 in Nauvoo, Hancock County, IL. They were the parents of eight children.
- Married (2) Mary Adelia Haight (1830–90) on 2 March 1863 in Salt Lake City. They were the parents of two children.
- Served as president of the Swiss and Italian Mission from 1855 to 1858. Returned to Europe to serve a second mission to Switzerland from 1860 to 1864. Took part in the Walker Wars in Utah. Served as bishop over the Oakley Idaho Ward for thirteen years. Elected to the lower branch of the Utah territorial legislature.
- Died on 27 February 1893 in St. George, Washington County, UT.

Letter reference: 15 December 1860

Smith, John P.

- Born on 29 April 1834 in Jefferson, Schoharie County, NY.
- Assaulted and robbed territorial governor John Dawson on 31 December 1861 with **Moroni Clawson**, **Lot Elisha Huntington**, and others. The recently appointed governor was fleeing Utah after he made an indecent proposal to Albina Merrill Williams, a Latter-day Saint widow. Smith was apprehended, along with Clawson and Huntington, by Orrin Porter Rockwell. Was shot and killed with Clawson while attempting to escape on 17 January 1862. Huntington was shot and killed during the arrest the day before.
- Died on 17 January 1862 in Salt Lake City.

Letter reference: 3 February 1862

Smith, John Schwartz

- Born on 20 August 1880 in Salt Lake City to **Joseph F.** and **Mary Taylor Schwartz**.
- Died on 3 August 1889.

Letter reference: [1 November] 1895

Smith, Joseph Bailey

- Born on 9 August 1870 in Salt Lake City to **Samuel Harrison Bailey Smith** and Mary Catherine Smith. Was a first cousin once removed to **Joseph F.** and **Martha Ann**.
- Married (1) Effie Field Howell (1869–1941) on 25 May 1893 in Salt Lake City. They were the parents of nine children.
- Married (2) Martha Frieda Heidel (1889–1963) on 12 December 1925 in Salt Lake City. They were the parents of seven children.
- Died on 31 January 1944 in Salt Lake City.

Letter reference: 6 August 1870

Smith, Joseph F.

- Born on 13 November 1838 in Far West, Caldwell County, MO, to **Hyrum Smith** and **Mary Fielding**. Was the brother of **Martha Ann**.
- Married (1) **Levira Annette Clark Smith** on 4 April 1859 in Salt Lake City. They later divorced. No issue.
- Married (2) **Julina Lambson** on 5 May 1866 in Salt Lake City. They were the parents of (1) **Edward Arthur Smith** (adopted), (2) **Mercy Josephine Smith**, (3) **Mary Sophronia Smith**, (4) **Donnette Smith**, (5) **Joseph Fielding Smith**, (6) **David Asael Smith**, (7) **George Carlos Smith**, (8) **Julina Clarissa Smith**, (9) **Elias Wesley Smith**, (10) **Emily Jane Smith**, (11) **Rachael Smith**, (12) **Edith Eleanor Smith**, and (13) **Marjorie Virginia Smith**.
- Married (3) **Sarah Ellen Richards** on 1 March 1868 in Salt Lake City. They were the parents of (1) **Sarah Ellen Smith**, (2) **Leonora Smith**, (3) **Joseph Richards Smith**, (4) **Heber John Smith**, (5) **Rhoda Ann Smith**, (6) **Minerva Smith**, (7) **Alice Smith**, (8) **Willard Richards Smith**, (9) **Franklin Richards Smith**, (10) **Jeanetta Smith**, and (11) Asenath Smith (1896–1982).
- Married (4) **Edna Lambson** on 1 January 1871 in Salt Lake City. They were the parents of (1) **Hyrum Mack Smith**, (2) **Alvin Fielding Smith**, (3) **Alfred Jason Smith**, (4) **Edna Melissa Smith**, (5) **Albert Jesse Smith**, (6) **Robert Smith**, (7) **Emma Smith**, (8) **Zina Smith**, (9) **Ruth Smith**, and (10) **Martha Smith**.
- Married (5) **Alice Ann Kimball** on 6 December 1883 in Salt Lake City. They were the parents of (1) **Alice May Rich** (adopted by **Joseph F.**), (2) **Heber Chase Rich** (adopted by **Joseph F.**), (3) **Charles Coulson Rich** (adopted by **Joseph F.**), (4) **Lucy Mack Smith**, (5) **Andrew Kimball Smith**, (6) **Jesse Kimball Smith**, and (7) **Fielding Kimball Smith**.
- Married (6) **Mary Taylor Schwartz** on 13 January 1884 in Salt Lake City. They were the parents of (1) John Schwartz Smith (1888–89), (2) **Calvin Schwartz Smith**, (3) Samuel Schwartz Smith (1892–1983), (4) James Schwartz Smith (1894–1950), (5) Agnes Smith (1897–1966), (6) Silas Schwartz Smith (1900–1983), and (7) **Royal Grant Smith**.
- Served a mission to Hawai'i from 1854 to 1857. Served in the British Mission from 1860 to 1863. Served briefly as president over the Hawaiian Mission in 1864. Worked as a clerk in the Church Historian's Office. Served as president of the British Mission from 1874 to 1875 and from 1877 to 1878. Served a brief mission to the eastern United States in 1877. Served as a member of the Territorial House of Representatives seven consecutive terms, from 1865 to 1874. Ordained an Apostle in 1866 and filled a vacancy in the Quorum of the Twelve Apostles the following year. Performed another mission to the Sandwich Islands. Served as first assistant general superintendent of YMMIA from 1880 to 1901. Served as general superintendent of YMMIA from 1901 to 1918. Served as sixth President of the Church from 1901 to 1918.
- Died on 19 November 1918 in Salt Lake City.

Smith, Joseph Fielding

- Born on 19 July 1876 in Salt Lake City to **Joseph F.** and **Julina Lambson**.
- Married (1) Emily Louie Shurtliff (1876–1908) on 26 April 1898 in Salt Lake City. They were the parents of (1) **Josephine Smith** and (2) **Julina Smith**.
- Married (2) **Ethel Georgina Reynolds** on 2 November 1908 in Salt Lake City. They were the parents of eight children.
- Married (3) Jessie Ella Evans (1902–71) on 12 April 1938 in Salt Lake City. No issue.
- Served as Church Historian for forty-nine years. Published twenty-seven books on Church history and doctrine. Served a mission to Great Britain from 1899 to 1901. Ordained an Apostle in 1910. Served as a member of the general board of the YMMIA from 1903 to 1919. Served as secretary, treasurer, vice president, and president of the Genealogical Society of Utah. Served as president of the Quorum of the Twelve Apostles and a counselor in the First Presidency. Was President of the Church from 23 January 1970 to 2 July 1972.

- Died on 2 July 1972 in Salt Lake City.

Letter references: 29 November 1877, 22 December 1909, 18 June 1913, 20 March 1916

Smith, Joseph Richards

- Born on 22 February 1873 in Salt Lake City to **Joseph F.** and **Sarah Ellen Richards**.
- Married Florence Spencer Horne (1880–1961) on 20 May 1922 in Salt Lake City. They were the parents of one child.
- Died on 2 October 1954 in Salt Lake City.

Letter references: 1 July 1873, 23 March 1896, 28 March 1896

Smith, Joseph, Jr.

- Born on 23 December 1805 in Sharon, Windsor County, VT, to **Joseph Smith Sr.** and **Lucy Mack**. Was an uncle of **Joseph F.** and **Martha Ann**.
- Married (1) Emma Hale (1804–79) on 18 January 1827 in South Bainbridge, Chenango County, NY. They were the parents of (1) Alvin Smith (born and died 1828), (2) Thaddeus Smith (born and died 1831), (3) Louisa Smith (born and died 1831), (4) Joseph Smith III (1832–1914), (5) Frederick Granger Williams Smith (1836–62), (6) **Alexander Hale Smith**, (7) Don Carlos Smith (1840–41), (8) Infant male Smith (born and died 1842), (9) Infant male Smith (born and died 1842), and (10) **David Hyrum Smith**.
- Practiced plural marriage and had an unknown number of additional wives. No issue.
- Baptized on 15 May 1829 in the Susquehanna River by Oliver Cowdery and ordained to the Aaronic Priesthood that same day by John the Baptist. Translated the Book of Mormon and was essential to the organization of The Church of Jesus Christ of Latter-day Saints. The Church was officially organized on 6 April 1830 in Peter Whitmer's house in Fayette, Seneca County, NY. Served as President of the Church until his death.
- Died on 27 June 1844 in Carthage Jail, Carthage, Hancock County, IL.

Letter references: 25 June 1870, 4 August 1890, 1 February 1891, 27 September 1895, 23 December 1898, 23 December 1899, 26 July 1902, 23 December 1904, 24 December 1910, 22 December 1911, 23 December 1913, 10 September 1914, 23 December 1915

Smith, Joseph, Sr.

- Born on 12 July 1771 in Topsfield, Essex County, MA, to Asael Smith and Mary Duty. Was a grandfather of **Joseph F.** and **Martha Ann**.
- Married **Lucy Mack** on 24 January 1796 in Tunbridge, Orange County, VT. They were the parents of (1) Miss Smith (born and died 1797), (2) Alvin Smith (1798–1823), (3) **Hyrum Smith**, (4) Sophronia Smith (1803–96), (5) **Joseph Smith Jr.**, (6) Samuel Harrison Smith (1808–44), (7) Ephraim Smith (born and died 1810), (8) **William Smith**, (9) Katherine Smith (1813–1900), and (10) Don Carlos Smith (1816–41).
- Was the first Patriarch of the Church.
- Died on 14 September 1840 in Nauvoo, Hancock County, IL.

Letter reference: 25 August 1897

Smith, Josephine

- Born on 18 September 1902 in Salt Lake City to **Joseph Fielding Smith** and Emily Louie Shurtliff. Was a granddaughter of **Joseph F.**

- Married Henry Max Reinhardt (1901–46) on 28 May 1927 in Salt Lake City. They were the parents of one child.
- Died on 16 September 1995 in Bountiful, Davis County, UT.

Letter reference: 18 June 1913

Smith, Josephine Donna

- Born on 10 March 1841 in Nauvoo, Hancock County, IL, to Don Carlos Smith and **Agnes Moulton Coolbrith**. Was a first cousin to **Joseph F.** and **Martha Ann**.
- Married Robert Carsley (1836–1905) on 21 April 1858 in Los Angeles, Los Angeles County, CA. They were the parents of one child, who died in infancy.
- Moved to California in 1852 with her mother and siblings. As an adult changed her name to Ina Coolbrith but May have gone by "Pickett" at times. Was a writer, poet, and librarian. Published several books and became the first poet laureate of California. She and **Joseph F.** corresponded much of their lives. Though there seemed to be mutual respect and admiration of one another, there was also significant disagreement and disapproval from **Joseph F.** for her leaving the faith.
- Died on 29 February 1928 in California.

Letter references: 9 June 1855, 18 October 1855, 23 November 1855, 14 June 1857, 25 July 1857, 12 November 1883, 22 May 1885, 22 December 1911, 26 December 1911, 22 November 1912, 23 December 1912, 28 February 1913, 3 March 1913, 18 June 1913, 23 December 1913, 15 July 1915, 17 July 1915, 17 February 1916, 13 December 1916, 19 December 1916

Smith, Julina

- Born on 5 February 1906 in Salt Lake City to **Joseph Fielding Smith** and **Ethel Georgina Reynolds**. Was a granddaughter of **Joseph F.**
- Married Eldon Charles Hart (1914–84) in 1938 in Utah. They were the parents of four children.
- Died on 10 May 1997 in Rexburg, Madison County, ID.

Letter reference: 22 December 1909

Smith, Julina Clarissa

- Born on 10 February 1884 in Salt Lake City to **Joseph F.** and **Julina Lambson**. Nickname was "Ina."
- Married Joseph Strass Peery (1868–1946) on 23 December 1909 in Salt Lake City. They were the parents of five children.
- Died on 1 August 1923 in Ogden, Weber County, UT.

Letter references: 11 February 1884, 22 May 1885, 11 February 1887, 28 January 1895, 24 April 1909, 6 May 1909, 24 May 1909, 22 December 1909, 29 November 1916, 19 December 1916

Smith, Katherine

- Born on 28 July 1813 in Lebanon, Grafton County, NH, to **Joseph Smith Sr**. and **Lucy Mack**. Was an aunt of **Joseph F.** and **Martha Ann**. Name was also often spelled Catherine.
- Married (1) Wilkens Jenkins Salisbury (1809–53) on 8 January 1831. They were the parents of eleven children.
- Married (2) Joseph Younger (1805–1900) after 1853 in Fountain Green, IL. No issue.

- Supported her brother, Joseph Smith Jr., in the Restoration of the gospel in the early 1800s. Suffered much persecution after her husband apostatized from the Church. Did not move west with the Saints after the martyrdom of Joseph and Hyrum but stayed in Illinois with her family.
- Died on 1 February 1900 in Fountain Green, IL.

Letter reference: 14 June 1872

Smith, Leonora

- Born on 30 January 1871 in Salt Lake City to **Joseph F.** and **Sarah Ellen Richards**. Nickname was "Nonie."
- Married Joseph Nelson (1861–1955) on 14 June 1893 in Salt Lake City. They were the parents of (1) **Joseph Smith Nelson**, (2) **George Smith Nelson**, (3) Alvin Smith Nelson (1900–1975), (4) Alice Nelson (1901–96), (5) Amy Nelson (born and died 1904), (6) Franklin Smith Nelson (1906–41), and (7) Hope Nelson (born and died 1907).
- Died on 23 December 1907 in Salt Lake City.

Letter references: 23 February 1871, 26 May 1871, 14 September 1871, 21 November 1871, 3 May 1872, 17 May 1872, 14 June 1872, 24 December 1894, 25 October 1898, 20 August 1912

Smith, Levira Annette Clark

- Born on 29 April 1842 in Nauvoo, Hancock County, IL, to **Samuel Harrison Smith** and **Levira Clark**. Was a first cousin to **Joseph F.** and **Martha Ann** and was **Joseph F.**'s first wife.
- Married **Joseph F.** on 4 April 1859 in Salt Lake City. No issue.
- Lived with her mother and with relatives during much of her early married years as **Joseph F.** served missions in Hawai'i and England. Moved to California some time after **Joseph F.**'s marriage to his first plural wife. Divorced **Joseph F.** in 1868 and subsequently moved to St. Louis, St. Louis County, MO.
- Died on 18 December 1888 in St. Louis, St. Louis County, MO.

Letter references: 26 September 1860, 15 December 1860, 20 December 1860, 12 March 1861, 30 May 1861, 8 December 1861, 12 January 1862, 3 February 1862, 1 March 1862, 30 September 1862, Fall 1862, 22 February 1863, 23 (24) February 1863, 12 June 1864, 22 June 1864, 1864, 1 December 1868, 26 January 1885

Smith, Lorin Farr

- Born on 22 April 1872 in Salt Lake City to **John Henry Smith** and **Sarah Farr**. Her father was a distant cousin of **Joseph F.** and **Martha Ann**.
- Died on 9 July 1872 in Salt Lake City.

Letter reference: 3 May 1872

Smith, Lovina

- Born on 16 September 1827 in Manchester, Ontario County, NY, to **Hyrum Smith** and Jerusha Barden. Was a half sister of **Joseph F.** and **Martha Ann**.
- Married **Lorin Walker** on 23 June 1844 in Nauvoo, Hancock County, IL. They were the parents of (1) **Hyrum Smith Walker**, (2) Isabella Rosalie Walker (born and died 1847), (3) **Jerusha Celesta Walker**, (4) Edwina Mariah Walker (1851–1923), (5) **Emma Irene Walker**, (6) William Arthur Walker (1857–1930), (7) Sarah Ellen Walker (1859–1932), (8) Lucy Lovina Walker (1862–67), (9) John Lorin Walker (1864–1937), (10) Joseph Frederick Walker (1867–1939), (11) Don Carlos Walker (1870–1933), (12) Charles Henry Walker (1872–1900), and (13) David Henry Walker (1876–77).

- Died on 8 October 1876 in Farmington, Davis County, UT.

Letter references: 28 January 1855, 29 July 1856, 5 April 1857, 26 September 1860, 15 December 1860, Spring 1861, 30 May 1861, 22 February 1863, 22 June 1864, 27 October 1870, 7 December 1870, 14 June 1872, 26 August 1883

Smith, Lucy

- Born on 11 July 1858 in Provo, Utah County, UT, to **John Smith** and **Hellen Maria Fisher**.
- Married **Ray Leroy Davis** on 24 September 1879 in Salt Lake City. They were the parents of three children.
- Died on 10 September 1938 in Ogden, Weber County, UT.

Letter references: 18 March 1885, 16 January 1891

Smith, Lucy Mack

- Born on 14 April 1890 in Salt Lake City to **Joseph F.** and **Alice Ann Kimball**.
- Married Ralph Charles Carter (1888–1967) on 18 March 1915 in Salt Lake City. They were the parents of seven children.
- Died on 24 November 1933 in Salt Lake City.

Letter references: 7 March 1894, 25 July 1904, 17 February 1916, 20 March 1916

Smith, Lucy Meserve

- Born on 9 February 1817 in Newry, Oxford County, ME, to Josiah Smith and Lucy Meserve Bean.
- Married **George Albert Smith** on 29 November 1844 in Nauvoo, Hancock County, IL. They were the parents of two children.
- Died on 5 October 1892 in Salt Lake City.

Letter reference: 2 March 1856

Smith, Margaret West

- Born on 6 December 1862 in Salt Lake City to **George Albert Smith** and **Susan Elizabeth West**. Was a second cousin to **Joseph F.** and **Martha Ann**. Nickname was "Maggie."
- Married Edwin Francis Parry (1860–1935) on 22 December 1881 in Salt Lake City. They were the parents of six children.
- Was an invalid during much of her life, but managed to keep a good house and feed her children.
- Died on 18 June 1913 in Salt Lake City.

Letter references: 26 January 1871, 18 June 1913

Smith, Marjorie Virginia

- Born on 7 December 1906 in Salt Lake City to **Joseph F.** and **Julina Lambson**.
- Married Campbell McLeod Brown Jr. (1904–71) on 15 May 1929 in Salt Lake City. They were the parents of two children.
- Died on 17 November 1994 in Salt Lake City.

Letter reference: 10 September 1914

SMITH, MARTHA

- Born on 12 May 1897 in Salt Lake City to **Joseph F.** and **Edna Lambson**.
- Married Harold Howell Jenson (1895–1978) on 1 September 1914 in Salt Lake City. They were the parents of four children.
- Died on 7 August 1977 in Salt Lake City.

Letter references: 12 May 1897, 22 December 1909, 17 February 1916

SMITH, MARTHA ANN

- Born Martha Ann Smith on 14 May 1841 in Nauvoo, Hancock County, IL, to **Hyrum Smith** and **Mary Fielding**. Was the sister of **Joseph F.**
- Married **William Jasper Harris** on 21 April 1857 in Salt Lake City. They were the parents of (1) **William Jasper Harris Jr.**, (2) **Joseph Albert Harris**, (3) **Hyrum Smith Harris**, (4) **Mary Emily Harris**, (5) **Franklin Hill Harris**, (6) **Lucy Smith Harris**, (7) **John Fielding Harris**, (8) **Mercy Ann Harris**, (9) **Zina Christine Harris**, (10) **Martha Artimissa Harris**, and (11) **Sarah Lovina Harris**.
- Father, Hyrum Smith, died just before she turned three years old. Learned how to knit, spin, and weave as a young girl. Knew how to dye wool. After mother's death in 1852, was cared for by "Aunty" Hannah Grinnels, after whose death she lived for a time with her mother's sister, **Mercy Rachel Fielding**. Also lived in the family home in the Millcreek area of Salt Lake City with her half brother **John Smith** and his wife **Hellen Maria Fisher**. Attended school off and on until her marriage.
- Lived with her mother-in-law, **Almira Emily Hill**, the wife of **Abraham Owen Smoot**, while her husband was serving a mission to England. Learned the glove-making trade during her family's stay in Salt Lake City. Became a recognized authority in making temple aprons. When daughter Lucy Harris died at age thirty-three in 1902, took into her care her daughter's two young children **Edna Mae Simmons** and **Arthur Simmons**.
- Died on 19 October 1923 in Provo, Utah County, UT.

SMITH, MARY BAILEY

- Born on 27 March 1837 in Mentor, Lake County, OH, to **Samuel Harrison Smith** and **Mary Bailey**. Was a first cousin of **Joseph F.** and **Martha Ann**.
- Married John Joseph Norman (1833–1901) in 1858 in St. Louis, St. Louis County, MO.
- Lived with **Emma Hale Smith** following her father's death in 1844 and took care of **Lucy Mack Smith**, her grandmother, for eleven years until Lucy's death on 14 May 1856. Moved to St. Louis and married J. J. Norman. Moved to Utah in about 1896 with her husband. Was living in North Salt Lake when he died in 1902. Moved to Idaho Falls in about 1906. Was the last surviving child of **Samuel Harrison Smith**.
- Died on 14 October 1916 in Idaho Falls, Bonneville County, ID.

Letter reference: 26 January 1901

SMITH, MARY JANE

- Born on 29 April 1813 in Stockholm, St. Lawrence County, NY, to Asael Smith and Elizabeth Schellenger. Was a first cousin once removed to **Joseph F.** and **Martha Ann**.
- Married George Washington Gee (1815–42) on 5 February 1837 in Kirtland, Geauga County, OH. They were the parents of (1) Elias Smith Gee (1838–55) and (2) **George Washington Gee II**.

- Died on 1 March 1878 in Provo, Utah County, UT.

Letter references: 5 August 1874, 16 November 1874, 24 November 1874, 8 December 1874, 9 February 1875, 15 May 1875

Smith, Mary Sophronia

- Born on 7 October 1869 in Salt Lake City to **Joseph F.** and **Julina Lambson**. Nickname was "Mamie."
- Married Alfred William Peterson (1870–1956) on 17 December 1901 in Salt Lake City. They were the parents of (1) **Alfred William Peterson Jr.**, (2) Mary Peterson (1906–2003), (3) George Smith Peterson (1908–98), (4) Albert Wesley Peterson (1911–12), (5) Earl Albert Peterson (1911–92), and (6) Joseph Hyrum Peterson (1912–2001).
- Named after **Joseph F.**'s mother, **Mary Fielding**.
- Died on 5 January 1948 in Salt Lake City.

Letter references: 24 December 1869, 3 January 1869 (1870), 18 January 1870, 18 August 1870, 27 October 1870, 7 December 1870, 26 January 1871, 23 February 1871, 26 May 1871, 14 September 1871, 21 November 1871, 3 May 1872, 17 May 1872, 14 June 1872, 22 April 1878, 28 March 1896, 23 December 1901, 22 November 1905, 18 June 1913

Smith, Mercy Josephine

- Born on 14 August 1867 in Salt Lake City to **Joseph F.** and **Julina Lambson**.
- Died on 6 June 1870 in Salt Lake City.

Letter references: 23 June 1868, 1 December 1868, 21 June 1869, 13 July 1869, 17 August 1869, 24 December 1869, 3 January 1869 (1870), 18 January 1870, 25 June 1870, 6 August 1870, 3 May 1872, 14 June 1872, 22 April 1878, 26 August 1883, [1 November] 1895

Smith, Minerva

- Born on 30 April 1880 in Salt Lake City to **Joseph F.** and **Sarah Ellen Richards**.
- Married Matthew Alexander Miller (1870–1955) on 25 April 1903 in Salt Lake City. They were the parents of nine children.
- Died on 24 January 1958 in Salt Lake City.

Letter references: 13 March 1883, 8 February 1904, 20 August 1912

Smith, Rachel

- Born on 11 December 1890 in Salt Lake City to **Joseph F.** and **Julina Lambson**.
- Married Albert Leroy Taylor (1887–1963) on 2 June 1914 in Salt Lake City. They were the parents of five children.
- Died on 14 December 1986 in Salt Lake City.

Letter references: 19 March 1898, 13 October 1898, 25 October 1898, 26 December 1911

Smith, Rhoda Ann

- Born on 20 July 1878 in Salt Lake City to **Joseph F.** and **Sarah Ellen Richards**.
- Died on 6 July 1879 in Salt Lake City.

Letter references: 17 August 1878, 22 April 1879, 7 July 1879, 26 August 1883, [1 November] 1895

Smith, Robert

- Born on 12 November 1883 in Salt Lake City to **Joseph F.** and **Edna Lambson**.
- Died as a child on 4 February 1886 in Salt Lake City.

Letter references: 22 November 1883, 11 February 1884, [1 November] 1895

Smith, Royal Grant

- Born on 21 May 1906 in Salt Lake City to **Joseph F.** and **Mary Taylor Schwartz**.
- Married Gaynel Orthella Meik (1908–97) on 7 July 1933 in Salt Lake City. No issue.
- Died on 30 May 1971 in Bennion, Salt Lake County, UT.

Letter references: 26 November 1906, 26 December 1911

Smith, Ruth

- Born on 21 December 1893 in Salt Lake City to **Joseph F.** and **Edna Lambson**.
- Died on 17 March 1898 in Salt Lake City.

Letter reference: 19 March 1898

Smith, Samuel Harrison Bailey

- Born on 1 August 1838 in Shady Grove, Daviess County, MO, to Samuel Harrison Smith and Mary Bailey. Was a first cousin to **Joseph F.** and **Martha Ann**.
- Married (1) Mary Catherine Smith (1841–1916) on 17 April 1860 in Salt Lake City. They were the parents of nine children.
- Married three other wives and had fifteen more children.
- Served several missions, including two to Great Britain from 1860 to 1863 and one to California. In 1859 helped to open the lead mines at Minersville. Conducted a large dairy business for many years in Salt Lake City.
- Died on 12 June 1914 in Salt Lake City.

Letter references: 28 July 1860, 15 December 1860, 20 December 1860, 12 March 1861, 30 May 1861, 8 December 1861, 30 September 1862, 23 (24) February 1863, 22 June 1864, 6 August 1870, 14 June 1872, 11 July 1876

Smith, Sarah (1)

- Born on 21 March 1813 in Wheatley, Nottingham, England, to Robert Smith and Nancy Ann Appleby.
- Married William Markham Jackson on 10 December 1830 in Mattersey, Nottinghamshire, England.
- She and her husband were baptized in the Church. William Markham Jackson, her husband, died on 6 April 1855. Left England with her nine children on the *John J. Boyd* in April 1861. Arrived in Salt Lake City on 24 September 1862 with the Homer Duncan company. **Joseph F.** mentions Sarah Smith Jackson several times in his journal, including a specific reference to having a meal with her and receiving a "silk neck Tie" from a family member; see Joseph F., journal, 5 September 1861. Additional references to being in her home are found in Joseph F., journal, 17 December 1861, 24 December 1861, 30 January 1862, 3 February 1862, 24 March 1862, and 3 April 1862. In November 1861, **Joseph F.** confirmed Elizabeth Jackson, Sarah's daughter; see Joseph F., journal, 15 November 1861.

- Died on 10 July 1882 in Nephi, Juab County, UT.

Letter reference: 30 September 1862

Smith, Sarah (2)

- Born on 2 October 1837 in Kirtland, Lake County, OH, to **Hyrum Smith** and Jerusha Barden. Was a half sister of **Joseph F.** and **Martha Ann**.
- Married **Charles Emerson Griffin** on 16 January 1854 in Salt Lake City. They were the parents of (1) Charles Emerson Griffin Jr. (born and died 1855), (2) **Alice Lovina Griffin**, (3) Sarah Griffin (born and died 1858), (4) Joseph Emerson Griffin (1859–1929), (5) **Ernest Adelbert Griffin**, (6) Hannah Griffin (1865–1942), (7) John Marvin Griffin (1868–69), (8) Martha Ann Griffin (born and died 1870), (9) Hyrum Griffin (born and died 1871), (10) Abigail Griffin (born and died 1873), and (11) Helen Jerusha Griffin (1876–77).
- Died on 6 November 1876 in Ogden, Weber County, UT, while her husband was away serving a mission to the British Isles.

Letter references: 28 January 1855, 9 June 1855, 18 February 1856, April 1856, 14 July 1856, 29 July 1856, 2 October 1856, 17 December 1856, 14 June 1857, 3 July 1857, 25 July 1857, 20 May 1858, 15 December 1860, 20 December 1860, Spring 1861, 30 May 1861, 8 December 1861, 12 January 1862, 1 March 1862, 22 February 1863, 12 June 1846, 22 June 1864, 23 February 1871, 14 June 1872, 5 October 1874, 9 February 1875, 26 August 1883, 20 August 1912

Smith, Sarah Ellen

- Born on 5 February 1869 in Salt Lake City to **Joseph F.** and **Sarah Ellen Richards**. Nickname was "Ella."
- Died on 11 February 1869 in Salt Lake City.

Letter references: 13 July 1869, 6 August 1870, 23 February 1871, 26 August 1883, [1 November] 1895

Smith, Silas

- Born on 6 June 1822 in Stockholm, St. Lawrence County, NY, to Asael Smith and Elizabeth Schellenger. Was a first cousin once removed to **Joseph F.** and **Martha Ann**.
- Married Elizabeth Norton (1822–1909) on 9 February 1844 in Pennsylvania. They were the parents of eight children.
- Served a mission to the Sandwich Islands from 1854 to 1857, serving as president of the mission from 1855 to 1857. Served as a bishop in Provo. Was a farmer and lawyer.
- Died on 11 June 1892 in Meadow, Millard County, IL.

Letter reference: 20 October 1856

Smith, Silas Sanford

- Born on 26 October 1830 in Stockholm, St. Lawrence County, NY, to Silas Smith and Mary Aikens. Was a first cousin once removed to **Joseph F.** and **Martha Ann**.
- Married (1) Clarinda Ann Ricks (1835–64) on 9 July 1851 in Layton, Davis County, UT. They were the parents of five children.
- Married two other wives and had sixteen more children.
- Participated in the Walker War of 1853 and achieved the rank of major. In May of 1854 was called on a mission to the Sandwich Islands, serving along with **Joseph F.** While there, served as a counselor in the mission presidency. Returned home in November 1856. Served as bishop in the Paragonah Ward in Utah.

In 1859 first elected a member of the Utah legislature and served continually in this capacity over the next twenty years. Served as president of the San Luis Stake from 1883 to 1892. Was widely known throughout the Church as a missionary, explorer, pioneer, legislator, military officer, and civil officer.

- Died on 11 October 1910 in Layton, UT.

Letter references: 23 November 1855, 29 January 1861, 25 August 1897

Smith, Thalia Grant

- Born on 21 September 1848 in Altoona, Knox County, IL, to **William Smith** and Roxanna Grant. Was a first cousin to **Joseph F.** and **Martha Ann**.
- Died on 27 November 1924 in Independence, Jackson County, MO.

Letter references: 13 December 1916, 19 December 1916

Smith, Thomas King

- Born on 5 August 1875 in Salt Lake City to **Elias Smith** and **Amy Jane King**. Was a second cousin to **Joseph F.** and **Martha Ann**.
- Died on 12 August 1875.

Letter reference: 26 November 1875

Smith, Willard Grant

- Born on 12 May 1911 in Salt Lake City to **Willard Richards Smith** and Florence Grant. Was a grandson of **Joseph F.**
- Married (1) Virginia Buist (1912–62) on 4 September 1936 in Salt Lake City. No issue.
- Married (2) Lillian Anderson (1912–96) on 29 June 1963 in Salt Lake City. No issue.
- Died on 16 December 1996 in Provo, Utah County, UT.

Letter references: 18 March 1885, 20 August 1912

Smith, Willard Richards

- Born on 20 November 1884 in Salt Lake City to **Joseph F.** and **Sarah Ellen Richards**.
- Married Florence Grant (1883–1977) on 3 February 1910 in Salt Lake City. They were the parents of (1) **Willard Grant Smith**, (2) **Florence Smith**, (3) Richards Grant Smith (1915–2000), (4) Briant Grant Smith (1916–2006), (5) Heber Joseph Smith (1918–43), (6) Howard Grant Smith (1921–2010), (7) Sarah Ellen Smith (1923–80), and (8) Paul Grant Smith (1925–2000).
- Died on 11 September 1972 in Salt Lake City.

Letter references: 18 March 1885, 2 April 1905, 20 August 1912, 19 December 1916

Smith, William

- Born on 13 March 1811 in Royalton, Windsor County, VT, to **Joseph Smith Sr.** and **Lucy Mack**. Was an uncle of **Joseph F.** and **Martha Ann**.
- Married (1) Carolina Amanda Grant (1814–45) on 14 February 1833 in Kirtland, Lake County, OH. They were the parents of two children.
- Married three other wives and had five more children.

- Was excommunicated from the Church and later joined the RLDS Church in 1878.
- Died on 13 November 1894 in Osterdock, Clayton County, IA.

Letter reference: 11 July 1876

Smith, Zina

- Born on 11 October 1890 in Salt Lake City to **Joseph F.** and **Edna Lambson**.
- Married **Ambrose John Greenwell** on 12 December 1910 in Salt Lake City. They were the parents of one child.
- Died on 25 October 1915 in Salt Lake City.

Letter references: 20 June 1892, 19 March 1898, 5 February 1915, 17 February 1915

Smithies, Mary

- Born on 7 October 1837 in Barsh Lees, Lancashire, England, to James Smithies and Ann Knowles.
- Married **Heber Chase Kimball** of the Quorum of the Twelve Apostles on 25 January 1857 in Salt Lake City. They were the parents of five children.
- Was remembered as a good mother who taught her children to love and respect their parents and the Church.
- Died on 8 June 1880 in Salt Lake City.

Letter reference: 3 February 1857

Smoot, Abraham Owen

- Born on 17 February 1815 in Pleasant Home, Owen County, KY, to George Washington Smoot and Nancy Rowlett. He was the stepfather of **William Jasper Harris**, husband of **Martha Ann**.
- Married (1) **Margaret Thompson** on 11 November 1838 in Far West, Caldwell County, MO. Abraham adopted her son, **William Cochran Adkinson**.
- Married (2) **Almira Emily Hill** on 17 February 1846 in Nauvoo, Hancock County, IL. They were the parents of (1) Abraham Albert Ether Smoot (1847–63), (2) Emily Ann Smoot (1851–55), (3) **Margaret Thompson Smoot**, and (4) **Zina Beal Smoot**.
- Married (3) Sarah Gibbons (1800–1889) on 18 January 1846 in Nauvoo, Hancock County, IL. Did not go west with the Saints. They later divorced. No issue.
- Married (4) **Diana Tanner Eldredge** on 6 May 1855 in Salt Lake City. They were the parents of (1) **Abraham Owen Smoot Jr.**, (2) Nancy Diana Smoot (1858–1939), (3) Olive Smoot (1860–1943), (4) Elizabeth Smoot (1861–1932), (5) Ira Smoot (born and died 1863), (6) Lenora Ann Smoot (born and died 1864), (7) Joseph Edmund Smoot (1867–90), (8) Ella Deseret Smoot (1869–1916), (9) Arthur E. Smoot (1871–73), (10) Vilate Smoot (1873–1955), (11) Orson Parley Smoot (1876–1936), (12) Horace Alma Smoot (1880–1964), and (13) Wilford Smoot (1883–1953).
- Married (5) **Anne Kirstine Mauritzen** on 17 February 1856 in Salt Lake City. They were the parents of (1) Anna Christine Smoot (1858–1904), (2) Alice Smoot (1860–1950), (3) **Reed Smoot**, (4) George Morrison Smoot (1864–1915), (5) Agnes May Smoot (1866–1945), (6) Brigham Roland Smoot (1869–1946), and (7) Ida Maline Smoot (1873–1955).
- Married (6) Hannah Caroline Rogers (1827–1915) on 11 March 1886 in Logan, Cache County, UT. No issue. Four of Hannah's deceased children by a previous spouse were adopted by and sealed to Smoot.

- Was a high priest. Served missions to the United States and England. Called to serve as bishop of the Sugar House Ward in 1854. Was mayor of both Salt Lake City and Provo. Served as president of the Utah Stake. Following his family's 1858 relocation to Provo, he also served as bishop and stake president in Provo. Was president of the Provo Woolen Mills, First National Bank of Provo, Utah County Savings Bank, and Provo Cooperative Institution. Also served as president of the Board of Trustees of Brigham Young Academy and was instrumental in making that institution succeed.
- Died on 6 March 1895 in Provo, Utah County, UT.

Letter references: 20 May 1858, 28 July 1860, 12 January 1862, 1 March 1862, 30 September 1862, Fall 1862, 22 February 1863, 12 June 1864, 22 June 1864, 1864, 21 June 1869, 3 (31) March 1870, 7 December 1870, 26 January 1871, 26 July 1872, 27 February 1874, 5 August 1874, 7 September 1874 (first letter), 6 November 1874, 9 February 1875, 15 May 1875, 7 September 1875, 25 August 1877, 29 November 1877, 22 April 1878, 11 February 1887

Smoot, Abraham Owen, Jr.

- Born on 11 March 1856 in Salt Lake City to **Abraham Owen Smoot** and **Diana Tanner Eldredge**.
- Married (1) Electa Bullock (1859–87) on 30 October 1878 in Salt Lake City. They were the parents of six children.
- Married (2) Zina A. Huntington (1869–1922) on 6 June 1894 in Provo, Utah County, UT. They were the parents of one child.
- Was on the high council in Provo. Served a mission to England from 1875 to 1877. Was county assessor and collector, city councilman, state senator, secretary of the state insane asylum, and US commissioner. Was also the manager of a lumber company.
- Died on 22 May 1911 in Provo, Utah County, UT.

Letter reference: 25 August 1877

Smoot, Elizabeth

- Born on 7 December 1861 in Salt Lake City to **Abraham Owen Smoot** and **Diana Tanner Eldredge**.
- Married Milton Henry Hardy (1844–1905) on 16 October 1879 in Salt Lake City. They were the parents of seven children.
- Died on 13 December 1932 in Salt Lake City.

Letter reference: 12 January 1862

Smoot, Lucina

- Born on 7 February 1864 in Sugar House, Salt Lake County, UT, to **William Cochran Adkinson** and Martha Ann Sessions. Nickname May have been "Lucy."
- Married Alma Wilkinson Wagstaff (1874–1916) on 24 April 1884 in Salt Lake City. They were the parents of two children.
- Died on 24 October 1886.

Letter reference: 4 June 1880

Smoot, Margaret Thompson

- Born on 27 August 1854 in Salt Lake City to **Abraham Owen Smoot** and **Almira Emily Hill**. Was a half sister of **William Jasper Harris**, the husband of **Martha Ann**.

- Married **Wilson Howard Dusenberry** on 25 November 1874 in Provo, Utah County, UT. They were the parents of eight children.
- Died on 21 April 1932.

Letter reference: 24 November 1874

Smoot, Reed

- Born on 10 January 1862 in Salt Lake City to **Abraham Owen Smoot** and **Anne Kirstine Mauritzen**.
- Married Alpha May Eldredge (1863–1928) on 17 September 1884 in Logan, Cache County, UT. They were the parents of six children.
- Worked in the Provo Woolen Mills as a young man and was later promoted to manager of the company. Served a mission to Europe from 1890 to 1891. Was also involved in mining. Served in the stake presidency of the Utah Stake of Zion. Called to be a member of the Quorum of the Twelve Apostles in 1900. Served five terms in the US Senate from 1903 to 1933. Served as a member of the general board of YMMIA from 1900 to 1912. Served on the Board of Trustees and Executive Committee for Brigham Young Academy.
- Died on 9 February 1941 in St. Petersburg, Pinellas County, FL.

Letter reference: 12 January 1862

Snow, Erastus Fairbanks

- Born on 9 November 1818 in St. Johnsbury, Caledonia County, VT, to Levi Snow and Lucina Streeter.
- Married (1) Artimesia Beman (1819–82) on 13 December 1838 in Far West, Caldwell County, MO. They were the parents of twelve children.
- Had fifteen other wives and twenty-five other children.
- Served a mission to Pennsylvania, Ohio, and Maryland from 1836 to 1838. In 1839 served a brief mission to Illinois. Served a second mission to Pennsylvania from 1840 to 1843. Owned a mercantile business with Parley P. Pratt in Nauvoo, Hancock County, IL. Served a short mission to the eastern United States in 1844, returning home upon hearing of the martyrdom. Was also a member of the legislature. Became an Apostle in 1849 and served faithfully until his death. Opened up the Scandinavian Mission in Denmark. Served as president of the Scandinavian Mission from 1850 to 1852.
- Died on 27 May 1888 in Salt Lake City.

Letter references: 15 August 1884, 26 January 1885

Spencer, Catherine Curtis

- Born on 2 October 1836 in Middlefield, Hampshire County, MA, to Orson Spencer and Catherine Cannon Curtis.
- Married **Brigham Young Jr.** on 15 November 1855 in Salt Lake City. They were the parents of eleven children.
- Accompanied her husband on his mission to England.
- Died on 22 February 1922 at the home of her daughter Cora Young in Salt Lake City.

Letter reference: 18 February 1856

Staines, William Carter

- Born on 26 September 1818 in Higham Ferrers, Northampton, England, to Henry Staines and Blanche Freeman.

- Married (1) Lillias Thompson Lyon (1836–1919) in October 1854 in Salt Lake City.
- Had sixteen other wives and had one child.
- Converted to the Church in 1841 and in 1843 joined the Saints in Nauvoo, Hancock County, IL. Helped with the building of the Nauvoo temple. Was among the first companies of Saints to go west to Utah. Assisted in the Endowment House and served a mission to England from 1860 to 1863. According to the 1870 US Census, he was an "agent of [Brigham] Young."
- Died on 3 August 1881 in Salt Lake City.

Letter reference: 21 November 1871

Startup, Elbert Harris

- Born on 13 July 1912 in Provo, Utah County, UT, to **Harry Walter Startup** and **Martha Artimissa Harris**. Was a grandson of **Martha Ann**.
- Married (1) Maurine Brown (1913–83) on 30 August 1935 in Salt Lake City. They were the parents of two children.
- Married (2) Dorothy Elizabeth Mushett (1923–2007) on 17 August 1984 in Los Angeles, Los Angeles County, CA. No issue.
- Died on 17 December 1999 in Riverside, Riverside County, CA.

Letter reference: 3 March 1913

Startup, Harry Walter

- Born on 5 September 1874 in Salt Lake City to William Dawe Startup and Hagar Hick. Was a son-in-law of **Martha Ann**.
- Married **Martha Artimissa Harris** on 16 September 1903 in Salt Lake City. They were the parents of (1) **Naomi Startup**, (2) LaRue Startup (1907–90), (3) Norell Startup (1909–97), (4) **Elbert Harris Startup**, (5) Harry Walter Startup Jr. (1918–2008), and (6) Maurine Startup (1920–90).
- Died on 29 August 1957 in Provo, Utah County, UT.

Letter references: 8 March 1907, 17 July 1915

Startup, Naomi

- Born on 10 August 1905 in Provo, Utah County, UT, to **Harry Walter Startup** and **Martha Artimissa Harris**. Was a granddaughter of **Martha Ann**.
- Married Thomas Reginald Biggs (1905–2001) on 12 February 1937 in Salt Lake City. They were the parents of one child.
- Died on 19 February 2000 in Orem, Utah County, UT.

Letter references: 22 November 1905, 8 March 1907

Stratton, James

- Born on 22 December 1824 in Amwell, Parish Ware, Hertfordshire, England, to Barton Stratton and Susannah Vyse.
- Married (1) Frances Clark (1828–94) on 9 February 1851 on the Atlantic Ocean. They were the parents of ten children.
- Married (2) **Eliza Briggs** in 2 February 1857 in Salt Lake City. They were the parents of twelve children.

- Died on 23 March 1907 in Provo, Utah County, UT.

Letter reference: 5 April 1857

Stringham, Henry

- Born on 7 March 1865 in Salt Lake City to Briant Stringham and Harriet Maria Ashby.
- Married Fannie Janet Blair (1865–1944) on 22 September 1887 in Logan, Cache County, UT. They were the parents of nine children.
- Was the manager of Knight Woolen Mills in Salt Lake City. Served as bishop of the Liberty Ward in Salt Lake City in the late 1920s.
- Died on 13 April 1949 in Salt Lake City.

Letter reference: 5 February 1915

Stubbs, Peter

- Born on 13 December 1824, in Newton, Middlewich, Cheshire, England, to Peter Stubbs and Jane Steele.
- Married (1) Elizabeth Dunn (1840–1922) on 19 October 1856. They were the parents of nine children.
- Married (2) Ann Davis Wride (1839–86) on 4 October 1862. They were the parents of nine children.
- Left England on the ship *Elvira Owens*. Took a steamboat from St. Louis, St. Louis County, MO, to Keokuk, Lee County, IA, the Latter-day Saint staging ground that season. Peter made his way to Council Bluffs, Pottawattamie County, IA, with the Clawson Company. Traveled with the Moses Daley Freight Train in 1853 to Utah, arriving on 25 September 1853.
- Died on 1 June 1906 in Provo, Utah County, UT.

Letter references: 7 September 1874 (second letter), 5 October 1874, 24 November 1874, 15 May 1875, 1 July 1881

T

Taylor, Agnes

- Born on 2 October 1821 in Hale, Beetham Parish, Westmoreland, England, to James Taylor and Agnes Taylor. Was the mother-in-law of **Joseph F.** and the sister of **John Taylor**.
- Married (1) John Rich (1810–63) on 24 November 1838 in Carthage, Hancock County, IL. They were the parents of four children. They later divorced.
- Married (2) **Abraham Lucas Hoagland** in 1847 in Salt Lake City. They were the parents of five children. They later divorced in 1861.
- Married (3) William Schwartz (1837–1915) on 2 February 1862 in Salt Lake City. They were the parents of (1) Harriet Schwartz (born and died 1862) and (2) **Mary Taylor Schwartz**.
- Died on 12 December 1911 in Salt Lake City.

Letter reference: 26 December 1911

Taylor, David

- Born on 26 October 1833 in Clinton County, IL, to James Taylor and Leah Rinehart.

- Married (1) Mary Ann Ormiston (1837–1913) in 1854 in IL. They were the parents of ten children.
- Married (2) **Mary Jane Thompson**, first cousin to **Joseph F.** and **Martha Ann**, on 5 April 1859. They were the parents of (1) **Robert Blashel Thompson Taylor**.
- Married (3) Martha Thomas (1846–1909) on 16 November 1867 in Salt Lake City. They were the parents of one child.
- Died in August 1877 in Elnora, Daviess County, IN.

Letter references: 29 January 1862, Fall 1862, 22 June 1864, 6 August 1870, 18 August 1870

Taylor, John

- Born on 1 November 1808 in Milnthorpe, Westmoreland, England, to James Taylor and Agnes Taylor. His niece married **Joseph F.**
- Married (1) Leonora Cannon (1796–1868) on 28 January 1833 in Toronto, York, Ontario, Canada. They were the parents of four children.
- Married eight other women and had thirty-one other children.
- Was a Methodist minister when he was converted by the preaching of Elder Parley P. Pratt in Canada. In 1838 called to be an Apostle. Served a mission to Europe from 1839 to 1841. Edited the *Times and Seasons* and the *Nauvoo Neighbor*. Was also a city councilman, regent of the Nauvoo University, and Judge Advocate of the Nauvoo Legion during his time in Nauvoo. Imprisoned in Carthage Jail during the martyrdom of **Joseph** and **Hyrum Smith** and was shot there as well.
- Served a mission to Great Britain from 1846 to 1847. Built one of the first sawmills in Utah. Served a mission to France from 1849 to 1852. In 1854 elected a member of the territorial legislative council. Served a mission to New York and presided over the Church in the eastern states. Was many times a member of the Utah legislature and Speaker of the House. Served as probate judge of Utah County. Became President of the Quorum of the Twelve Apostles in 1877. In October 1880 sustained as President of the Church.
- Died on 25 July 1887 in Kaysville, Davis County, UT.

Letter references: 11 July 1876, 1 July 1881, 26 August 1883, 1 August 1884

Taylor, Robert Blashel Thompson

- Born on 17 September 1863 in Salt Lake City to **David Taylor** and **Mary Jane Thompson**.
- Married Elizabeth Ann White (1864–1949) on 7 April 1884 in Salt Lake City. They were the parents of one child.
- Died in 1946.

Letter references: 1 December 1868, 18 January 1870, 3 (31) March 1870, 5 July 1870, 6 August 1870, 18 August 1870, 21 April 1871, 26 May 1871, 14 September 1871, 28 April 1873, 14 August 1878, 18 March 1885

Taylor, William Whitaker

- Born on 11 September 1853 in Salt Lake City to **John Taylor** and Harriett Whitaker. Was a first cousin to **Mary Taylor Schwartz**, the wife of **Joseph F.**
- Married (1) Sarah Taylor Hoagland (1855–96) on 5 April 1875 in Salt Lake City. They were the parents of six children.
- Married (2) Selma Van Cott (1863–1935) on 29 March 1884 in Salt Lake City. They were the parents of two children.

- Served a mission to Great Britain from 1875 to 1877. Called as one of the Presidents of the Seventy from 1880 to 1884. In 1883 elected a member of the legislative assembly of Utah. In February 1884 elected assessor and collector of taxes for Salt Lake City.
- Died on 1 August 1884 in Salt Lake City.

Letter reference: 1 August 1884

Terrill, Mary Adele

- Born on 4 May 1876 in Mankato, Blue Earth, MN, to Isaac Terrill and Mary Mack.
- Married Harry C. Jones (1871–death unknown) about 1898.
- Originally known as Mary Adele Terrill, she was born on the Lake Crystal Reservation in Minnesota and was educated in a Catholic convent. Adele and Harry lived in the mining town of Tonopah, Nye County, NV, before taking a four-month business trip to New York City in about 1903, where Adele met Benjamin DeCasseres, a poet and journalist for the *New York Sun*. When Adele and Harry returned to Nevada, she began a sixteen-year correspondence with "Ben" DeCasseres. Adele left Harry and moved to New York. At this time she began to use the Native American name of Bio. According to the 1920 US Census, Bio and Ben lived together in New York City. Ben died in 1945. Adele was the great-granddaughter of Stephen Mack Jr. and Ho-no-ne-gah, the daughter of a Pottawattamie chief. Stephen Jr. was an adventurer and pioneer, American Fur Company employee, founder of Rockton, Winnebago County, IL, and a first cousin to **Joseph Smith Jr.**
- Died on 15 February 1964 in New York City, NY.

Letter references: 10 September 1914, 17 July 1915

Thompson, Anna or Annie [Anney Tomson]

- Born on 31 January 1840 in Alston, Cumberland, England. to Ralph Thompson and Ann Bentley.
- Married William Samuel Godbe on 15 November 1855 in Salt Lake City. They were the parents of (1) Samuel Thompson Godbe (1858–unknown), (2) Clara Godbe (1859–71), (3) William C. Godbe (1862–85), and (4) Alfred Thompson Godbe (1864–1916).
- Immigrated to Utah in the Heber C. Kimball Company in 1848. Lived with her husband next door to **Joseph F.**'s mother-in-law **Levira Clark Smith** and her husband **Dustin Amy**.
- Died on 6 January 1928 in Los Angeles, California.

Letter reference: 29 July 1856

Thompson, Margaret

- Born on 16 April 1809 in Chester District, Chester County, SC, to Anthony McMeans and Esther Hunter. Nickname was "Ma Smoot."
- Married (1) Charles Adkinson (1809–38) on 28 December 1826 in Roane County, TN. They were the parents of (1) **William Cochran Adkinson**. She and her husband later divorced. Their son, William, was sealed to her and her second husband.
- Married (2) **Abraham Owen Smoot** on 11 November 1838 in Far West, Caldwell County, MO. They were the parents of one child.
- Accompanied her second husband on several of his missions. Served for many years as the stake Relief Society president in Provo.

- Died on 1 September 1884 in Provo, Utah County, UT.

Letter references: 3 February 1857, 14 June 1857, 25 July 1857, 20 May 1858, 28 July 1860, 29 January 1861, 30 May 1861, 12 January 1862, 1 March 1862, 22 February 1863, 1864, 29 March 1870, 20 June 1874, 9 February 1875, 11 July 1876, 4 June 1880

Thompson, Mary Jane

- Born on 14 June 1838 in Far West, Caldwell County, MO, to Robert Blashell Thompson and **Mercy Rachel Fielding**.
- Married **David Taylor** on 5 April 1859. They were the parents of (1) **Robert Blashel Thompson Taylor**.
- Was both a first cousin to and the stepsister of **Joseph F.** and **Martha Ann**. Raised with **Joseph F.** and **Martha Ann**. Taught school in Salt Lake City.
- Died on 7 August 1901.

Letter references: 9 June 1855, 14 July 1856, 29 July 1856, 17 December 1856, 3 February 1857, 14 June 1857, 20 May 1858, 29 January 1862, 30 September 1862, Fall 1862, 22 June 1864, 1 December 1868, 3 January 1869 (1870), 18 January 1870, 29 March 1870, 3 (31) March 1870, 6 August 1870, 18 August 1870, 7 December 1870, 23 February 1871, 21 April 1871, 26 May 1871, 14 September 1871, 21 November 1871, 14 June 1872, 18 January 1873, 28 April 1873, 31 May 1874, 8 September 1874, 14 August 1878, 23 October 1878, 18 September 1881, 13 March 1883, 27 March 1883, 31 July 1883, 23 August 1884, May 1887, 26 July 1900, 7 February 1901

Thompson, Serinna

- Born on 1 May 1835 in Lemesco, Denmark.
- Married **Andrew McLean Smith** on 14 August 1857 in Salt Lake City. No issue.
- No other information found.

Letter reference: 5 April 1857

Twede, Delia Sarah Rebekah

- Born on 23 November 1870 in Provo, Utah County, UT, to Christian Frederick Nielsen and Christiane Christensdatter. Was a daughter-in-law of **Martha Ann**. Nicknamed "Adelia."
- Married **Hyrum Smith Harris** on 9 April 1890 in Manti, Sanpete County, UT. They were the parents of (1) **Mercy Rachel Harris** and (2) Julina Harris (1909–91).
- Died on 19 August 1959 in Salt Lake City.

Letter references: 17 April 1890, 29 April 1890, 2 May 1890, 17 June 1891, 13 August 1891, 10 April 1907, 17 July 1915

V

Vance, John

- Born on 8 November 1794 in Cocke County, TN, to James Vance and Margaret Reneau.
- Married (1) Sarah Lavinia Gant Perkins (1801–36) on 10 February 1817 in Jackson County, TN. They were the parents of ten children.
- Married two other wives and had three more children.

- Served as bishop in Winter Quarters, Nebraska. Was on the high council, served as a ward clerk, and helped settle St. George, UT. Served as counselor to the bishop in the Salt Lake City Seventh Ward. Was a school commissioner and justice of the peace. Was a farmer by trade.
- Died on 24 January 1882 in St. George, Washington County, UT.

Letter reference: 28 July 1860

Varney, Abigail

- Born on 6 February 1810 in Colchester, Chittenden County, VT, to Paul Varney and Anna Austin. Was the mother-in-law of **Sarah Smith**, a half sister of **Joseph F.** and **Martha Ann**.
- Married **Albert Bailey Griffin** before 1830. They were the parents of (1) Sidney Griffin (1826–30), (2) Albert Bailey Griffin Jr. (born and died 1830), and (3) **Charles Emerson Griffin**.
- Lived with her son Charles and his wife, Sarah, during the last years of her life.
- Died on 5 January 1875 in Ogden, Weber County, UT.

Letter references: 18 February 1856, 2 October 1856, 3 July 1857, 20 May 1858, 20 December 1860, 30 May 1861, 9 February 1875

W

Walker, Edwina Mariah

- Born on 26 November 1851 in Webster, Hancock County, IL, to **Lorin Walker** and **Lovina Smith**. Was a niece of **Joseph F.** and **Martha Ann**.
- Married George Henry Young (1847–1922) on 1 January 1872. They were the parents of four children.
- Died on 17 May 1923 in Clayton, Custer County, ID.

Letter references: 29 July 1856, 13 July 1869

Walker, Emma Irene

- Born on 28 July 1854 in Webster, Hancock County, IL, to **Lorin Walker** and **Lovina Smith**. Was a niece of **Joseph F.** and **Martha Ann**.
- Married Calvin Willard Richards (1851–1926) on 24 December 1872 in Salt Lake City. They were the parents of nine children.
- Died on 5 September 1893 in Fielding, Box Elder County, UT.

Letter reference: 29 July 1856

Walker, Hyrum Smith

- Born on 26 September 1845 in Nauvoo, Hancock County, IL, to **Lorin Walker** and **Lovina Smith**. Was a nephew of **Joseph F.** and **Martha Ann**.
- Married (1) Lucetta Ketura Clark (1848–1900) on 8 November 1869 in Salt Lake City. They were the parents of eight children.
- Married (2) Mary Ann Clark (1850–1936) on 8 November 1921. No issue.

- Died on 13 March 1923 in Rockland, Power County, ID.

Letter references: 29 July 1856, 16 January 1891

Walker, Jerusha Celeste

- Born on 6 July 1849 in Nauvoo, Hancock County, IL, to **Lorin Walker** and **Lovina Smith**. Was a niece of **Joseph F.** and **Martha Ann**.
- Married William Cook Blanchard (1848–1910) on 12 October 1867 in Salt Lake City. They were the parents of twelve children.
- Was a nurse. Successfully delivered hundreds of babies.
- Died on 28 July 1933 in Afton, Lincoln County, WY.

Letter reference: 29 July 1856

Walker, Lorin

- Born on 25 July 1822 in Peacham, Caledonia County, VT, to John Walker and Lydia Holmes. Was a brother-in-law of **Joseph F.** and **Martha Ann**.
- Married **Lovina Smith** on 23 June 1844 in Nauvoo, Hancock County, IL. They were the parents of (1) **Hyrum Smith Walker**, (2) Isabella Rosalie Walker (born and died 1847), (3) **Jerusha Celesta Walker**, (4) **Edwina Mariah Walker**, (5) **Emma Irene Walker**, (6) William Arthur Walker (1857–1930), (7) Sarah Ellen Walker (1859–1932), (8) Lucy Lovina Walker (1862–67), (9) John Lorin Walker (1864–1937), (10) Joseph Frederick Walker (1867–1939), (11) Don Carlos Walker (1870–1933), (12) Charles Henry Walker (1872–1900), and (13) David Henry Walker (1876–77).
- Was a carpenter and painter.
- Died on 26 September 1907 in Rockland, Power County, ID.

Letter references: 27 October 1870, 14 June 1872

Walker, Lucy

- Born on 30 April 1826 in Peacham, Caledonia County, VT, to John Walker and Lydia Holmes. Was an aunt to **Joseph F.** and **Martha Ann** through her marriage to **Joseph Smith Jr.** Was also the sister of **Lorin Walker**, who married **Lovina Smith**, the half sister of **Joseph F.** and **Martha Ann**.
- Married (1) **Joseph Smith Jr.** on 1 May 1843 in Nauvoo, Hancock County, IL. No issue.
- Married (2) **Heber Chase Kimball** on 8 February 1845 in Nauvoo, Hancock County, IL. They were the parents of (1) Rachel Sylvia Kimball (1846–47), (2) John Heber Kimball (1850–1918), (3) Willard H. Kimball (1853–54), (4) **Lydia Holmes Kimball**, (5) Anna Spaulding Kimball (1857–1932), (6) Eliza Kimball (1859–1906), (7) Washington Heber Kimball (1861–1914), (8) Joshua Heber Kimball (1862–63), and (9) Franklin Heber Kimball (1864–65).
- Was called by revelation to bear testimony of the truthfulness of plural marriage. Spent many hours ministering to those in need of assistance. Served as a temple worker starting in 1885 and officially called to serve in the Logan Temple from 1889 until her final illness.
- Died on 1 October 1910 in Salt Lake City.

Letter references: 1 July 1873, 5 August 1874, 6 November 1874, 15 May 1875

Wells, Daniel Hammer

- Born on 27 October 1814 in Trenton, Burlington County, NJ, to Daniel Welles and Honor Francis.

- Married (1) Eliza Rebecca Robinson in 1837 in IL. They were the parents of one child. They were later divorced.
- Married six other wives and had thirty-eight more children.
- Joined the Church after living among the Latter-day Saints in Nauvoo, Hancock County, IL. After moving to the Salt Lake Valley in 1848, served in many prominent positions, including lieutenant general of the territorial militia, mayor of Salt Lake City from 1866 to 1876, territorial legislator, Second Counselor to President Brigham Young in the First Presidency from 1857 to 1877, European Mission president from 1864 to 1865, counselor to the Twelve Apostles, and Manti Temple president.
- Died on 24 March 1891 in Salt Lake City.

Letter reference: 12 March 1861

West, Susan Elizabeth

- Born on 4 December 1833 in Chalk Level, Benton County, TN, to Samuel Walker West and Margaret Cooper.
- Married **George Albert Smith**, a first cousin once removed to **Joseph F.** and **Martha Ann**, on 28 October 1857 in Salt Lake City. They were the parents of (1) Clarissa West Smith (1859–1930), (2) **Margaret West Smith**, (3) Elizebeth Smith (1866–1921), (4) Priscilla Smith (1869–1907), and (5) **Emma Pearl Smith**.
- Attended school as a young girl in southern Utah. Learned at home how to cook, quilt, make soap, card wool, weave, knit, and perform other household tasks. At the dedication of the Salt Lake Temple, was called as an ordinance worker. Served as a temple worker for twenty years.
- Died on 14 October 1926 in Salt Lake City.

Letter reference: 3 May 1872

Whipple, Ann

- Born on 15 March 1842 in Bradford, McKean County, PA, to Eli Whipple and Patience Foster.
- Married **William Wallace Cluff** on 24 October 1863 in Pine Valley, Washington County, UT. They were the parents of eight children.
- Died on 31 January 1927 in Salt Lake City.

Letter reference: 21 April 1871

Whitney, Orson Kimball

- Born on 20 January 1830 in Kirtland, Geauga County, OH, to Newel K. Whitney and Elizabeth Anne Whitney.
- Married Joanna Hickey Robertson (1825–84) on 16 April 1854 in Salt Lake City. No issue.
- A member of vanguard pioneer company that entered Salt Lake Valley in July 1847. Called on mission to Hawaiʻi in 1854. Returned to Utah in 1857; participated in defense of territory during the 1857–58 Utah War.
- Died on 31 July 1884 in Salt Lake City.

Letter references: 20 October 1856, 14 June 1872, 1 August 1884

Whitney, Sarah Ann

- Born on 22 March 1825 in Kirtland, Geauga County, OH, to Newell Kimball Whitney and Elizabeth Ann Smith. Was an aunt of **Joseph F.** and **Martha Ann** through her marriage to **Joseph Smith Jr.**
- Married (1) **Joseph Smith Jr.** on 27 July 1842 in Nauvoo, Hancock County, IL. No issue.

- Married (2) **Heber Chase Kimball** on 17 March 1845 in Nauvoo, Hancock County, IL. They were the parents of seven children.
- Died on 4 September 1873 in Salt Lake City.

Letter reference: 1 July 1873

Wilcox, Walter Eli

- Born on 11 April 1821 in Dorchester, Suffolk County, MA, to William Wilcox and Huldah Lucas.
- Married (1) **Elizabeth Hawkins** on 4 September 1853 in Salt Lake City. They were the parents of five children.
- Married four other wives and had twenty-six more children.
- Died on 8 May 1919 in Salt Lake City.

Letter reference: 18 June 1890

Wood, Electa

- Born on 15 July 1834 in Florence, Huron County, OH, to Giden Durphy Wood and Nancy Maria Daley.
- Married **Isaac Bullock** on 14 December 1856 in Salt Lake City. They were the parents of nine children.
- Died on 15 August 1914 in Provo, Utah County, UT.

Letter reference: 17 December 1856

Woodruff, Wilford

- Born on 1 March 1807 in Farmington, Hartford County, CT, to Aphek Woodruff and Beulah Thompson.
- Married (1) Phoebe Whittemore Carter (1807–85) on 13 April 1837 in Kirtland, Geauga County, OH. They were the parents of nine children.
- Had four other wives and twenty-four other children.
- Participated in Zion's Camp. Served a mission to Arkansas and Tennessee from 1834 to 1836. Served a mission to the Fox Islands off the coast of Maine. Called as an Apostle in 1838. Served a mission to England from 1839 to 1841 and baptized hundreds of people. In 1842 became the business manager of the *Times and Seasons* and also served a mission to the eastern states to collect funds to construct the Nauvoo Temple. Served another mission to the eastern states in 1844. Served as president of the British Mission from 1845 to 1846. Served a mission to the eastern states from 1848 to 1850. Assisted in laying out Salt Lake City.
- Served several terms in the territorial legislature. Chosen as first president of the Horticultural Society of Salt Lake City in 1855. In 1883 sustained as Church Historian and general Church recorder. Had served as assistant Church historian since 1856. Called as president of the St. George Temple at the time of its dedication in 1877. Became President of the Twelve Apostles in 1880. Began to serve as President of the Church in 1889. Was very active in temple and family history work. Issued the Manifesto in 1890, which officially began the process to end new plural marriages.
- Died on 2 September 1898 in San Francisco, San Francisco County, CA.

Letter reference: 1 July 1881

Woodward, Emmeline Blanche

- Born on 29 February 1828 in Petersham, Worcester County, MA, to David Woodward and Deiadama Hare.
- Married (1) James Harris (1827–59), (2) Newel K. Whitney (1795–1850), and (3) **Daniel H. Wells**. She was the parent of seven children.

- Joined the Church in 1842 and migrated to Nauvoo, Hancock County, IL. Her first husband left to find work, but never returned. She married Newel K. Whitney as a plural wife. Following his death, she married Daniel H. Wells, becoming his seventh wife.
- Affectionately known as "Aunt Em." Was associated with the *Woman's Exponent*, an important voice for Latter-day Saint women from its founding in 1872. Became the editor in 1877 and continued in this role until 1914. Was an important advocate for women's rights, including suffrage and economic and educational opportunities, both in Utah and in the United States. In 1912, Brigham Young University bestowed upon her an honorary degree in literature, making her the first woman in Utah to receive this honor. Served as the General President of the Church's Relief Society from 1910 until her death.
- Died on 25 April 1921 in Salt Lake City.

Letter reference: 14 May 1911

Worley, Kleber

- Born on 11 November 1800 in Sturbridge, Worcester, Massachusetts to Aldrich Worley and Nancy Wight.
- Married Ann Eliza Nodine (1811–98) before 1836 in New York. They were the parents of (1) John Mansfield Worley (1836–1913), (2) Henry Louis Worley (1839–61), (3) Battiest Kleber Worley (1842–1912), (4) Caroline Worley (1844–death unknown), and (5) John Hyrum Worley (1847–1919). Immigrated with the John Hindley Company in 1855 to Salt Lake City. Worley was a leather dresser in Salt Lake City.
- Died on 4 December 1873 in Salt Lake City.

Letter reference: 26 January 1871

Y

Young, Brigham

- Born on 1 June 1801 in Whitingham, Windham County, VT, to John Young and Abigail Nabby Howe.
- Married (1) Miriam Angeline Works (1803–32) on 8 October 1824 in Cayuga County, NY. They had two children.
- Married thirty-six other wives and had fifty-four more children.
- Baptized and confirmed a member of the Church on 14 April 1832. Served a mission in and near West Laboro, Canada, from 1832 to 1833. Participated in Zion's Camp. Was ordained an Apostle on 14 February 1835. Served a mission with Willard Richards to the eastern states from 1836 to 1837. Served a mission to New York State in 1837. Became President of the Quorum of the Twelve Apostles on 19 January 1841. Served a mission to England from 1839 to 1841 and was president of the British Mission from 1840 to 1841. Served another mission to the eastern states from 1843 to 1844. Was the second President of the Church and led the Saints into the Salt Lake Valley.
- Died on 29 August 1877 in Salt Lake City.

Letter references: 3 May 1857, 25 July 1857, 12 March 1861, 3 February 1862, 1864, 29 March 1870, 27 October 1870, 26 May 1871, 3 May 1872, 14 June 1872, 26 July 1872, 7 September 1875, 22 April 1878

Young, Brigham, Jr.

- Born on 18 December 1836 in Kirtland, Geauga County, OH, to **Brigham Young** and Mary Ann Angell.

- Married (1) **Catherine Curtis Spencer** on 15 November 1855 in Salt Lake City. They were the parents of eleven children.
- Had five other wives and eight other children.
- Served a mission to Europe from 1862 to 1863. Served as president of the British Mission from 1865 to 1867 and from 1890 to 1893. Held prominent positions as a military man. Served several terms in the Utah legislature. Became a member of the Quorum of the Twelve Apostles in 1868. Served as President of the Council of the Twelve Apostles.
- Died on 11 April 1903 in Salt Lake City.

Letter reference: 18 February 1856

Young, Franklin Wheeler

- Born on 17 February 1839 in Winchester, Scott County, IL, to Lorenzo Dow Young and Persis Goodall. Was a nephew of **Brigham Young**.
- Married (1) Nancy Leonora Greene (1841–1901) on 5 March 1858 in Grantsville, Tooele County, UT. They were the parents of eight children.
- Married (2) Anna Maria Sabin (1846–95) on 6 July 1861 in Salt Lake City. They were the parents of eight children.
- Called on a mission to the Sandwich Islands in 1856. Assigned to Kohala District to labor under **Joseph F.** Left Hawai'i when the missionaries were called home due to the Johnston army troubles. Arrived back in the United States in San Francisco, California, on 20 January 1858.
- Died on 22 January 1911 in Provo, Utah County, UT.

Letter references: April 1856, 20 October 1856

Young, John Ray

- Born on 30 April 1837 in Kirtland, Lake County, OH, to Lorenzo Dow Young and Persis Goodall. Was a nephew of **Brigham Young**.
- Married (1) Albina Terry (1836–1913) in 1859 in Salt Lake City. They were the parents of eleven children.
- Married three other wives and had eleven other children.
- Called to serve in the Sandwich Islands in 1854. After serving for three years returned and began raising his family. Served on the high council in the St. George Stake and served further missions to the Sandwich Islands and Great Britain. Lived for a time in Mexico with his plural wives but finally returned to Utah.
- Died on 20 September 1931 in Provo, Utah County, UT, and buried in Blanding, San Juan County, UT.

Letter reference: April 1856

Young, Zina Presendia

- Born on 3 April 1830 in Salt Lake City to **Brigham Young** and **Zina Diantha Huntington**. Was a stepcousin to **Joseph F.** and **Martha Ann** through her mother's marriage to **Joseph Smith Jr.**
- Married (1) Thomas Williams (1828–74) on 12 October 1868 in Salt Lake City. They were the parents of two children.
- Married (2) Charles Ora Card (1839–1906) on 17 June 1884 in Logan, Cache County, UT. They were the parents of three children.
- Died on 31 January 1931 in Salt Lake City.

Letter reference: 1 August 1884

Appendix E: People and Places Gallery

This gallery is a photographic collection of various significant people and places in Joseph F. and Martha Ann's world during the decades of their correspondence captured in this book. Images courtesy of CHL except as noted.

Joseph Smith III, ca. 1855. Joseph F. and Martha Ann's cousin and president of the RLDS Church, 1860–1914.

Sarah Smith Griffin, ca. 1854, Maresena Cannon, Salt Lake City, Utah. Sarah was Joseph F. and Martha Ann's half sister. Martha Ann was very close to Sarah and her husband Charles while Joseph F. was on his first mission to the Sandwich Islands in the 1850s.

View of Church plantation in Hawai'i, ca. 1888. This photograph highlights a traditional grass house, or *hale*—the kind Joseph F. lived in during his first mission in the 1850s.

John Smith, 1866, photograph by Edward Martin, Salt Lake City, Utah. John was Joseph F. and Martha Ann's oldest half brother.

Endowment House, ca. 1885, photograph by F. I. Monson & Co., Salt Lake City, Utah. Joseph F. worked here as a recorder and was set apart as a member of the Quorum of Twelve Apostles by Brigham Young in one of the upper rooms of the Endowment House on 6 October 1867.

Historian's Office, 1866, photograph by Savage and Ottinger, Salt Lake City, Utah. Joseph F. worked here as a clerk and was ordained as an apostle by Brigham Young in one of the upper rooms following a prayer circle on 1 July 1866.

George Q. Cannon, ca. 1869, photograph by Charles R. Savage, Salt Lake City, Utah. Joseph F.'s association with Cannon began during his first mission to Hawai'i (1850s) and continued during his mission to England (early 1860s) and as they served together as counselors in three First Presidencies (1880s and 1890s).

Lovina Smith Walker, ca. 1870. Lovina was Joseph F. and Martha Ann's oldest half sister.

The First Presidency, 6 April 1893, photograph by Sainsbury and Johnson, Salt Lake City, Utah. From left: George Q. Cannon, Wilford Woodruff, and Joseph F. Smith. This photograph was taken on the day the Salt Lake Temple was dedicated.

Jerusha Smith and William Pierce, 30 December 1895, photographs by W. W. Compton, Brigham City, Utah. Jerusha was Joseph F. and Martha Ann's older half sister.

The First Presidency and the Apostles, 13 September 1898, photograph by Charles R. Savage, Salt Lake City, Utah.

The Joseph F. Smith family at Santa Monica (Ocean Park neighborhood), California, ca. 1912. Martha Ann stands behind Joseph F. in this photograph. She was often a guest of Joseph F. and his family on vacations to Southern California. Courtesy of UU.

Film frames featuring Joseph F. Smith removing his hat and glasses, ca. 1916, filmed by Shirley and Chester Clawson, Salt Lake City, Utah. President Joseph F. Smith authorized Shirley "Shirl" Young and Chester Clawson, two brothers, to film Church leaders beginning in 1916. Their work coincided with the rise of the motion picture industry that was making black-and-white films without sound. Church leaders believed that "the moving picture together with all the other modern inventions is to help us carry the Mission of Christ to all the world, and to bring humanity home to the true principles of salvation." Levi Edgar Young, "'Mormonism' in Picture," *Young Woman's Journal* 24 (February 1913): 80. Courtesy of Joseph Fielding and Brenda McConkie.

Index

A

B

C

D

E

F

G

H

I

J

K

L

M

N

P

R

S

T

U

V

W

Y

Z

About the Editors

Richard Neitzel Holzapfel was called as a member of the Seventy of The Church of Jesus Christ of Latter-day Saints in April 2018. He received a bachelor's degree from Brigham Young University and a master's degree and PhD in history from the University of California, Irvine. In 1993 he became a member of the Department of Church History and Doctrine at Brigham Young University. Currently, he is the senior manager of curriculum for the Missionary Department of the Church. Elder Holzapfel is the author of many articles and books, including *Joseph F. Smith: A Portrait of a Prophet*, published in 2000. He and his wife, Jeni, have five children and six grandchildren.

David M. Whitchurch is an associate professor in the Department of Ancient Scripture at Brigham Young University. He received a bachelor's degree from Utah State University and a master's degree and PhD in education from Brigham Young University. He has taught at BYU's Jerusalem Center for Near Eastern Studies on several occasions (1995–1996, 2000, and 2007). He recently returned to the BYU Provo campus after completing a three-year assignment as the associate director at the Jerusalem Center (2013–2016). In addition to extensive research on Joseph F. Smith, his research interests include biblical geography, history of the English Bible, Graeco-Roman Egypt, and the settlement and growth of downtown Salt Lake City. He and his wife, Tina, have three children and twelve grandchildren.

Salt Lake City December 19, 1916.

JOSEPH F. SMITH
TRUSTEE-IN-TRUST

Martha A. S. Harris,

214 South 3rd West St.,
Provo, Utah.

My Dear Sister:-

Thinking that you mught enjoy a turkey for your Christmas and a little cranberry sauce, I thought I would forward to you the enclosed check for $25.00, which I hope you will accept in the spirit in which it is offered, and will enjoy the use of it.

I am serving Cousin Ina in the same way, but I do not expect from her the same sisterly appreciation that I usually receive from you. I am happy to say that we are all usually well, with the exception of some of the little ones who are suffering from teething and other little ailments incident to infancy. Our Ina is in San Diego with her three little children, two of whom have the measles from the last account. One or two of Melissa's also have the measles. You will be delighted to hear that Willard has another little son added to his family. Wishing you and the children the compliments of the season, I am,

Affectionately your brother,

Joseph F. Smith

P.S. I am also sending a small remembrance to Cousin Thalia who is in Kansas.